W9-AWR-705

In this table, in which all amounts are in billions of dollars, we see historical data for the various components of nominal GDP. These are given in the first four columns. We then show the rest of the national income accounts going from GDP to NDP to NI to PI to DPI. The last column gives real GDP.

	The Sum of These Expenditures				Equals	Less	Equals	Plus	Less	Equals	Less			Plus	Equals	Less	Equals	
Year	Personal Consumption Expenditures	Gross Private Domestic Investment	Government Purchases of Goods and Services	Net Exports	Gross Domestic Product	Depreciation	Net Domestic Product	Net U.S. Income Earned Abroad	Indirect Business Taxes and Transfers and Other Adjustments	National Income	Undistributed Corporate Profits	Social Security Taxes	Corporate Income Taxes	Transfer Payments and Net Interest Earnings	Personal Income	Personal Income Taxes and Nontax Payments	Disposable Personal Income	Real GDP (2005 Dollars)
1988	3353.6	821.6	1039.0	−110.4	5103.8	611.0	4492.8	23.6	−33.0	4549.4	155.1	361.5	141.6	362.5	4253.7	505.0	3748.7	7607.4
1989	3598.5	874.9	1099.1	−88.2	5484.4	651.5	4832.9	26.2	32.5	4826.6	121.5	385.2	146.1	414.0	4587.8	566.1	4021.7	7879.2
1990	3839.9	861.0	1180.2	−78.0	5803.1	691.2	5111.9	34.8	57.6	5089.1	120.0	410.1	145.4	465.0	4878.6	592.8	4285.8	8027.1
1991	3986.1	802.9	1234.4	−27.5	5995.9	724.4	5271.5	30.4	74.0	5227.9	138.0	430.2	138.6	529.9	5051.0	586.7	4464.3	8008.3
1992	4235.3	864.8	1271.0	−33.2	6337.9	744.4	5593.5	29.7	110.4	5512.8	159.5	455.0	148.7	612.4	5362.0	610.6	4751.4	8280.0
1993	4477.9	953.4	1291.2	−65.0	6657.5	778.0	5879.5	31.9	138.0	5773.4	169.7	477.4	171.0	603.2	5558.5	646.6	4911.9	8516.2
1994	4743.3	1097.1	1325.5	−93.6	7072.3	819.2	6253.1	26.2	157.0	6122.3	199.4	508.2	193.1	620.9	5842.5	690.7	5151.8	8863.1
1995	4975.8	1144.0	1369.2	−91.4	7397.6	869.5	6528.1	35.8	110.0	6453.9	243.9	532.8	217.8	692.9	6152.3	744.1	5408.2	9086.0
1996	5256.8	1240.3	1416.0	−96.2	7816.9	912.5	6904.4	35.0	99.3	6840.1	272.3	555.1	231.5	739.4	6520.6	832.1	5688.5	9425.8
1997	5547.4	1389.8	1468.7	−101.6	8304.3	963.8	7340.5	33.0	81.3	7292.2	308.2	587.2	245.4	763.7	6915.1	926.3	5988.8	9845.9
1998	5879.5	1509.1	1518.3	−159.9	8747.0	1020.5	7726.5	21.3	−5.0	7752.8	212.6	624.7	248.4	755.9	7423.0	1027.1	6395.9	10274.7
1999	6342.8	1641.5	1631.3	−262.1	9353.5	1094.4	8259.1	33.8	−65.1	8358.0	260.1	661.4	258.8	733.1	7910.8	1107.5	6803.3	10770.7
2000	6830.4	1772.2	1731.0	−382.1	9951.5	1184.3	8767.2	39.0	−132.7	8938.9	176.3	705.8	265.1	767.7	8559.4	1232.2	7327.2	11216.4
2001	7148.8	1661.9	1846.4	−371.0	10286.1	1256.2	9029.9	43.6	−111.7	9185.2	210.0	733.2	203.3	844.6	8883.3	1234.8	7648.5	11337.5
2002	7439.2	1647.0	1983.3	−427.2	10642.3	1305.0	9337.3	30.7	−40.5	9408.5	280.6	751.5	192.3	876.0	9060.1	1050.4	8009.7	11543.1
2003	7804.0	1729.7	2112.6	−504.1	11142.2	1354.1	9788.1	68.1	16.0	9840.2	309.2	778.9	243.8	869.8	9378.1	1000.3	8377.8	11836.4
2004	8270.6	1968.6	2232.8	−618.7	11853.3	1432.8	10420.5	53.7	−59.8	10534.0	390.5	827.3	306.1	927.1	9937.2	1047.8	8889.4	12246.9
2005	8803.5	2172.3	2369.9	−722.7	12623.0	1541.4	11081.6	68.5	−123.7	11273.8	486.4	872.7	412.4	983.6	10485.9	1208.6	9277.3	12623.0
2006	9301.0	2327.1	2518.4	−769.3	13377.2	1660.7	11716.5	58.0	−256.7	12031.2	430.3	921.8	473.3	1062.3	11268.1	1352.4	9915.7	12958.5
2007	9772.3	2295.2	2674.2	−713.0	14028.7	1767.5	12261.2	64.4	−122.6	12448.2	270.7	959.5	445.5	1139.8	11912.3	1488.7	10423.6	13206.4
2008	10035.5	2087.6	2878.1	−709.7	14291.5	1854.1	12437.4	141.9	131.1	12448.2	152.5	987.3	309.0	1460.8	12460.2	1107.6	11024.5	13161.9
2009	9866.1	1546.8	2917.5	−391.4	13939.0	1866.2	12072.8	152.3	77.5	12147.6	469.6	964.1	272.4	1488.7	11930.2	1141.4	10788.8	12703.1
2010	10245.5	1795.1	3002.8	−516.9	14526.5	1874.9	12651.6	189.4	0.9	12840.1	651.7	986.8	411.1	1583.0	12373.5	1193.8	11179.7	13088.0
2011[a]	10726.0	1916.2	3030.6	−578.7	15094.1	1950.0	13144.1	192.3	−100.9	13437.3	677.2	920.1	453.2	1618.5	13005.3	1449.1	11556.2	13315.1
2012[a]	10915.3	1954.0	3439.8	−602.2	15706.9	2029.2	13677.7	198.3	−106.8	13982.8	704.7	957.5	471.6	1684.2	13533.3	1507.9	12025.4	13597.4
2013[a]	11211.5	2033.3	3726.6	−626.7	16344.7	2111.6	14233.1	205.6	−111.9	14550.6	733.3	996.3	490.7	1752.6	14082.8	1569.2	12513.6	13858.5

[a]Author's estimates.

*Note: Some rows may not add up due to rounding.

MACROECONOMIC PRINCIPLES

Nominal versus Real Interest Rate

$$i_n = i_r + \text{expected rate of inflation}$$

where i_n = nominal rate of interest
i_r = real rate of interest

Marginal versus Average Tax Rates

$$\text{Marginal tax rate} = \frac{\text{change in taxes due}}{\text{change in taxable income}}$$

$$\text{Average tax rate} = \frac{\text{total taxes due}}{\text{total taxable income}}$$

GDP—The Expenditure and Income Approaches

$$GDP = C + I + G + X$$

where C = consumption expenditures
I = investment expenditures
G = government expenditures
X = net exports

$$GDP = \text{wages} + \text{rent} + \text{interest} + \text{profits}$$

Say's Law

Supply creates its own demand, or *desired* aggregate expenditures will equal *actual* aggregate expenditures.

Saving, Consumption, and Investment

$$\text{Consumption} + \text{saving} = \text{disposable income}$$

$$\text{Saving} = \text{disposable income} - \text{consumption}$$

Average and Marginal Propensities

$$APC = \frac{\text{real consumption}}{\text{real disposable income}}$$

$$APS = \frac{\text{real saving}}{\text{real disposable income}}$$

$$MPC = \frac{\text{change in real consumption}}{\text{change in real disposable income}}$$

$$MPS = \frac{\text{change in real saving}}{\text{change in real disposable income}}$$

The Multiplier Formula

$$\text{Multiplier} = \frac{1}{MPS} = \frac{1}{1 - MPC}$$

$$\text{Multiplier} \times \begin{array}{c}\text{change in}\\\text{autonomous}\\\text{real spending}\end{array} = \begin{array}{c}\text{change in}\\\text{equilibrium}\\\text{real GDP}\end{array}$$

Relationship between Bond Prices and Interest Rates

The market price of existing (old) bonds is inversely related to "the" rate of interest prevailing in the economy.

Government Spending and Taxation Multipliers

$$M_g = \frac{1}{MPS}$$

$$M_t = -MPC \times \frac{1}{MPS}$$

Economics Today

Seventeenth Edition

Roger LeRoy Miller

Research Professor of Economics
University of Texas–Arlington

Boston   Columbus   Indianapolis   New York   San Francisco   Upper Saddle River
Amsterdam   Cape Town   Dubai   London   Madrid   Milan   Munich   Paris   Montréal   Toronto
Delhi   Mexico City   São Paulo   Sydney   Hong Kong   Seoul   Singapore   Taipei   Tokyo

MyEconLab® Provides the Power of Practice

Optimize your study time with **MyEconLab**, the online assessment and tutorial system. When you take a sample test online, **MyEconLab** gives you targeted feedback and a personalized Study Plan to identify the topics you need to review.

Study Plan

The Study Plan shows you the sections you should study next, gives easy access to practice problems, and provides you with an automatically generated quiz to prove mastery of the course material.

Unlimited Practice

As you work each exercise, instant feedback helps you understand and apply the concepts. Many Study Plan exercises contain algorithmically generated values to ensure that you get as much practice as you need.

Learning Resources

Study Plan problems link to learning resources that further reinforce concepts you need to master.

- **Help Me Solve This** learning aids help you break down a problem much the same way as an instructor would do during office hours. Help Me Solve This is available for select problems.

- **eText links** are specific to the problem at hand so that related concepts are easy to review just when they are needed.

- A **graphing tool** enables you to build and manipulate graphs to better understand how concepts, numbers, and graphs connect.

MyEconLab®

Find out more at www.myeconlab.com

Real-Time Data Analysis Exercises

Up-to-date macro data is a great way to engage in and understand the usefulness of macro variables and their impact on the economy. Real-Time Data Analysis exercises communicate directly with the Federal Reserve Bank of St. Louis's FRED site, so every time FRED posts new data, students see new data.

End-of-chapter exercises accompanied by the Real-Time Data Analysis icon 🔵 include Real-Time Data versions in **MyEconLab**.

Select in-text figures labeled **MyEconLab** Real-Time Data update in the electronic version of the text using FRED data.

Current News Exercises

Posted weekly, we find the latest microeconomic and macroeconomic news stories, post them, and write auto-graded multi-part exercises that illustrate the economic way of thinking about the news.

Interactive Homework Exercises

Participate in a fun and engaging activity that helps promote active learning and mastery of important economic concepts.

Pearson's experiments program is flexible and easy for instructors and students to use. For a complete list of available experiments, visit *www.myeconlab.com*.

Dedication

To Bonni and Peter,

There is at least one attribute that the three of us share: never standing still for long.

It continues to be a pleasure knowing you two.

—R.L.M.

Editor in Chief: Donna Battista
Executive Editor: David Alexander
Senior Editorial Project Manager: Carolyn Terbush
Editorial Assistant: Emily Brodeur
Director of Marketing: Maggie Moylan
Executive Marketing Manager: Lori DeShazo
Marketing Assistant: Kim Lovato
Managing Editor: Jeff Holcomb
Production Project Manager: Kathryn Dinovo
Senior Manufacturing Buyer: Carol Melville
Cover Designer: Jonathan Boylan
Manager, Visual Research: Rachel Youdelman

Photo Researcher: Jonathan Yonan
Manager, Rights and Permissions: Michael Joyce
Permissions Specialist/Project Manager: Jill C. Dougan
Digital Publisher, Economics: Denise Clinton
MyEconLab Content Media Leads: Noel Lotz, Courtney Kamauf
Executive Media Producer: Melissa Honig
Full-Service Project Management: Cenveo Publishing Services/
Nesbitt Graphics
Printer/Binder: Courier/Kendallville
Cover Printer: Lehigh-Phoenix Color/Hagerstown
Text Font: Janson Text LT Std.

Credits and acknowledgments borrowed from other sources and reproduced, with permission, in this textbook appear on page xxix.

Library of Congress Cataloging-in-Publication Data

Miller, Roger LeRoy.

  Economics today / Roger LeRoy Miller, Research Professor of Economics, University of Texas; Arlington. -- Seventeenth Edition.

    pages cm

  Includes bibliographical references and index.

  ISBN 978-0-13-294890-6 (comprehensive edition (hardcover) : alk. paper) -- ISBN 0-13-294890-7 (comprehensive edition (hardcover) : alk. paper) -- ISBN 978-0-13-294889-0 (the macro view (pbk.) : alk. paper) -- ISBN 0-13-294889-3 (the macro view (pbk.) : alk. paper) -- ISBN 978-0-13-294888-3 (the micro view (pbk.) : alk. paper) -- ISBN 0-13-294888-5 (the micro view (pbk.) : alk. paper)

  1. Economics. 2. Microeconomics. 3. Macroeconomics. I. Title.

  HB171.5.M642 2013

  330--dc23

                          2012046375

10 9 8 7 6 5 4 3 2

ISBN 10: 0-13-294890-7
ISBN 13: 978-0-13-294890-6

Brief Contents

Contents

3 Demand and Supply 48

4 Extensions of Demand and Supply Analysis 75

PART 5 Dimensions of Microeconomics

PART 6 Market Structure, Resource Allocation, and Regulation

27 Regulation and Antitrust Policy in a Globalized Economy 594

PART 7 Labor Resources and the Environment

28 The Labor Market: Demand, Supply, and Outsourcing 618

29 Unions and Labor Market Monopoly Power 642

One-Semester Course Outline

Economics Today—Bringing the Real World to Your Students

How do you compete for students' time and attention when their world is so fast paced? How do you get students to focus? How do you present the topics or principles of economics in a way that is both attention grabbing and meaningful? The best way to do so is through real-world examples. I believe in teaching by example. That is why *Economics Today* has always been a textbook filled with international, policy, and domestic examples. This edition is no exception—a total of 110 topics bring your students into the real world, including why it costs so much to go to college, why you should expect to pay more for what you buy on the Internet, why it will cost $700 million to be able to play 3D movies nationwide, and why e-books are upending the publishing business.

In keeping with this approach, I have changed almost every example as well as every Issues & Applications. This chapter-ending feature forms a "bookend" with the introduction presented on the first page of every chapter. Key Concepts are presented along with two Critical Thinking Questions and a Web Resources Project. The *You Are There* features remain student friendly and illustrate how people in the real world respond to changing economic conditions.

> "I believe in teaching by example. That is why *Economics Today* has always been a textbook filled with international, policy, and domestic examples."

An engaging new feature called *What If . . . ?* can be found in every chapter. Students new to economics sometimes believe that complex problems can be solved by simple government policies or solutions that require instantaneous changes in human behavior. In the new *What If . . . ?* features I attempt to dispel some of the current notions about how to solve economic issues facing the nation and also encourage students to think like economists. *What If . . . the government were to limit or even ban excessive advertising? What If . . . the government saved U.S. jobs from foreign competition by prohibiting all exports? What If . . . the government required U.S. firms to hire only workers who reside in the United States?* These are just a few examples of this new feature.

While this edition has been updated throughout, several topics have received special attention. For the macro policy chapters, issues relating to the growing U.S. federal deficit and public debt are covered in even more detail in Chapter 14. This chapter now discusses whether raising taxes on the highest earners can close

> "That is one of the underlying goals I have always set for myself when I revise *Economics Today*—to help students recognize the value of the concepts they are learning."

the deficit gap and whether official measures of the current public debt underestimate promised future benefits. Chapter 16 now provides an analysis of various instruments of credit policy that the Fed appears to have adopted for the foreseeable future as a supplement to traditional monetary policy tools. Along the microeconomic dimension, Chapter 26 extends the coverage of network effects by examining two-sided markets in which intermediary platforms link groups of end users. Finally, Chapter 27 includes discussions of real changes in concentration measures and thresholds used in enforcement of U.S. antitrust policy.

Timely and relevant learning continues with MyEconLab, Pearson's online tutorial and assessment system. You can assign homework, quizzes, and tests that are automatically graded. Students have access to a suite of learning aids that help them at the very moment they might be struggling with the concepts. There are weekly news articles, many experiments, and questions that update in real time with data from the Federal Reserve Bank of St. Louis.

The trained economist sees economics everywhere—we observe people responding to changes in incentives all of the time. We economists would all like to have our students not only understand how powerful economics is but also use their newly acquired skills in their daily and professional lives. That is one of the underlying goals I have always set for myself when I revise *Economics Today*—to help students recognize the value of the concepts they are learning.

—Roger LeRoy Miller

New to This Edition

This new edition of *Economics Today* covers leading-edge issues while lowering barriers to student learning. The text relentlessly pursues the fundamental objective of showing students how economics is front and center in *their* own lives while providing them with many ways to evaluate their understanding of key concepts covered in each chapter.

Modern topics in economic theory and policy are spotlighted throughout the text. These include:
- An appraisal of key questions raised by continuing growth of the **U.S. government deficit and the public debt:** Chapter 14 considers whether the federal government can rely on raising taxes to eliminate its budget deficit and whether official measures of *today's* public debt understate total promises of benefits to be paid in the *future*.
- An evaluation of a new aspect of **Federal Reserve policymaking:** Chapter 16 provides an analysis of various tools of *credit policy* adopted by the Federal Reserve in recent years to supplement its traditional monetary policy instruments.
- Coverage of **two-sided markets:** The discussion of network effects in Chapter 26 now includes consideration of oligopoly pricing complications that arise in markets in which intermediary *platforms* link groups of *end users*.
- An updated exposition of **antitrust guidelines:** Chapter 27 has been revised in light of recent changes in concentration measures and thresholds applied by authorities charged with enforcing U.S. *antitrust policy*.

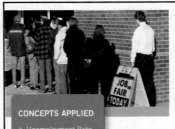

ISSUES & APPLICATIONS

Have Unemployment Benefits Boosted Unemployment?

CONCEPTS APPLIED
▶ Unemployment Rate
▶ Cyclical Unemployment
▶ Structural Unemployment

Between June 2008 and February 2009, the U.S. unemployment rate rose sharply, from 5.6 percent to more than 8 percent. Although the recession officially ended in June 2009, the unemployment rate ultimately reached a peak of 10.1 percent in October 2009. Since then, the unemployment rate has stayed near 8 percent. Thus, the unemployment rate remained above its prior level by at least 2 percentage points for more than three years. Many economists conclude that structural unemployment has risen. One element contributing to this rise, they suggest, was a substantial increase in the length of time the government paid benefits to unemployed workers.

Additional macro analyses include the following:
- Chapter 7 considers the extent to which lengthening the duration of **unemployment benefits** from 26 weeks to 99 weeks may have contributed to a higher U.S. unemployment rate.
- Chapter 11 explains why an index measure of **financial market fear** is often associated with short-term declines in total production of goods and services.
- Chapter 13 examines why most federal tax dollars recently transmitted to states to spend and thereby provide **stimulus to the U.S. economy** have failed to do so.
- Chapter 15 offers an explanation of why many banks no longer desire to expand **deposits** and indeed now actively discourage customers from depositing more funds.

The micro portion of the text now includes the following:
- Chapter 19 discusses how the concept of **price elasticity of demand** explains why many rock musicians have experienced declining revenues from sales of music recordings and concert tickets, even though the prices of recordings and tickets have increased.
- Chapter 24 examines the economic effects of a substantial expansion of **occupational licensing** requirements that many states impose on their citizens.
- Chapter 28 covers how groundbreaking new technology, such as **robotic apps,** might affect the labor market.
- Chapter 30 explains why the **income gap** between males and females has been shrinking and conceivably could eventually disappear.

Making the Connection— from the Classroom to the Real World

Economics Today provides current examples with critical analysis questions that show students how economic theory applies to their diverse interests and lives. For the Seventeenth Edition, **more than 90 percent** of the examples are new.

DOMESTIC TOPICS AND EVENTS are presented through thought-provoking discussions, such as:

- State University Tuition Rates Jump—Even at the Last Moment
- Price and Revenue Changes and Price Elasticity of Demand for Air Travel

EXAMPLE
Going Online for Credit When Bank Loans Dry Up

Today, a growing number of entrepreneurs who fail to receive loans from banks instead obtain credit from Internet-based companies such as Lending Club and Prosper Marketplace. These firms provide online forums for entrepreneurs to post detailed business plans along with the specific amounts of credit desired to try to achieve success. Individual savers can assess these plans and, if they wish, commit some of their own funds to help fund entrepreneurs' projects.

In exchange for service fees, the online firms pool these individual funding commitments into larger loan packages. For example, if an entrepreneur requests $15,000 in credit and 150 savers provide an average amount of $100 each, the online company collects the savers' funds and extends a loan to the entrepreneur. In this way, firms such as Lending Club and Prosper Marketplace act as financial intermediaries.

FOR CRITICAL THINKING
Why do you suppose that default rates on loans arranged by online firms tend to be substantially higher than default rates on bank loans?

IMPORTANT POLICY QUESTIONS help students understand public debates, such as:

- Federal Indebtedness Is Much Higher Than the Net Public Debt
- The Fed Becomes a Lender of Last Resort for Foreign Banks

POLICY EXAMPLE
A Proposed Wireless Merger Experiences a Dropped Connection

Recently, AT&T and T-Mobile sought to merge their wireless operations into a single firm providing cellular phone and broadband Internet services. The proposed merger would have increased the HHI value for the nationwide wireless market—which the Justice Department's Antitrust Division determined to be the relevant market—by nearly 600. The postmerger level of the HHI would have exceeded 2,800. These amounts were well above thresholds sufficient to raise U.S. antitrust authorities' concerns about potential monopoly capability generated by a horizontal merger. Thus, the Antitrust Division filed a lawsuit seeking to block the merger, based on a claim that if the merger occurred, consumers ultimately would face much higher prices for wireless services. A few weeks later, AT&T and T-Mobile abandoned their merger plans rather than combat the lawsuit in court.

FOR CRITICAL THINKING
By definition, any horizontal merger increases industry concentration. Why might some mergers lead to lower prices for consumers? (Hint: Recall that mergers might enable firms to experience economies of scale that reduce long-run average cost.)

INTERNATIONAL EXAMPLE
Why the Value of China's Consumer Price Index Is Rising

In China, food's weight in the CPI is slightly below 35 percent. Food prices have been rising so rapidly, though, that the overall rate of increase in food prices per year has been contributing to 75 percent of China's officially measured annual rate of CPI inflation. Consequently, during a recent 12-month period in which the nation's measured rate of CPI inflation was 6.4 percent, the rate of increase in food prices accounted for 4.8 percentage points

FOR CRITICAL THINKING
Food's weight in the U.S. CPI is about 16 percent. If U.S. food prices rose as rapidly as Chinese food prices, would the U.S. CPI increase as much as the CPI in China? Explain.

INTERNATIONAL POLICY EXAMPLE
African Nations Benefit from Lower U.S. Trade Barriers

In 2000, the U.S. Congress passed the African Growth and Opportunity Act, which reduced substantially the tariffs faced by African companies seeking to export goods and services to the United States. African-U.S. trade has risen considerably since. Earnings that African companies derive from exports are now 500 percent higher than in 2001. Furthermore, estimates indicate that export industries in African nations now employ 300,000 additional workers as a consequence of the increased volume of trade. Thus, slashing trade barriers has generated welfare gains for African residents.

FOR CRITICAL THINKING
How might U.S. residents have benefited from the fact that African countries granted reciprocal reductions in tariffs on imports into their nations from the United States?

GLOBAL AND INTERNATIONAL POLICY EXAMPLES emphasize the continued importance of international perspectives and policy, such as:

- Ireland Experiences Yet Another Big "Brain Drain"
- Utilizing Artificial Intelligence to Try to Beat the Market
- Iran Removes Four Zeroes from Each Unit of Its Currency
- In Greece, "Free" Care Now Includes Substantial Implicit Costs

Helping Students Focus and Think Critically

New and revised pedagogical tools engage students and help them focus on the central ideas in economics today.

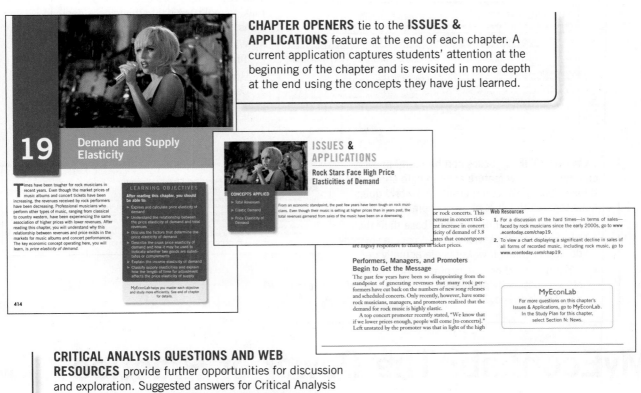

CHAPTER OPENERS tie to the **ISSUES & APPLICATIONS** feature at the end of each chapter. A current application captures students' attention at the beginning of the chapter and is revisited in more depth at the end using the concepts they have just learned.

CRITICAL ANALYSIS QUESTIONS AND WEB RESOURCES provide further opportunities for discussion and exploration. Suggested answers for Critical Analysis questions are in the **INSTRUCTOR'S MANUAL**. Visit MyEconLab for additional practice and assignable questions for each chapter topic.

The **END-OF-CHAPTER SUMMARY** shows students what they need to know and where to go in MyEconLab for more practice.

A VARIETY OF END-OF-CHAPTER PROBLEMS offer students opportunities to test their knowledge and review chapter concepts. Answers for odd-numbered questions are provided in the back of the text, and **ALL QUESTIONS** are assignable in MyEconLab.

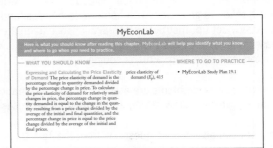

QUICK QUIZZES encourage student interaction and provide an opportunity for them to check their understanding before moving on. Answers are at the end of the chapter, and more practice questions can be found in MyEconLab.

YOU ARE THERE discusses real people making real personal and business decisions. Topics include:

- Why a Federal Stimulus Project Took Time to Provide Stimulus
- Using a Smartphone to Attain a Consumer Optimum

NEW! WHAT IF...? boxes can be found in every chapter. This new feature aims to help students think critically about important real-world questions through the eyes of an economist.

- What If... economists were to base their theories of human behavior on what people say they do, rather than on what people actually do?
- What if... a nation's government tries to head off a recession by pushing down the exchange value of the country's currency?

MyEconLab: The Power of Practice

MyEconLab is a powerful assessment and tutorial system that works hand-in-hand with *Economics Today*. MyEconLab includes comprehensive homework, quiz, test, and tutorial options, allowing instructors to manage all assessment needs in one program.

For the Instructor

- Instructors can now select a preloaded course option, which creates a ready-to-go course with homework, quizzes, and tests already set up. Instructors can also choose to create their own assignments and add them to the preloaded course. Or, instructors can start from a blank course.

- All end-of-chapter problems are assignable and automatically graded in MyEconLab, and for most chapters, additional algorithmic, draw-graph, and numerical exercises are available to choose among.

- Instructors can also choose questions from the Test Bank and use the Custom Exercise Builder to create their own problems for assignment.

- The powerful Gradebook records each student's performance and time spent on the Tests and Study Plan, and generates reports by student or by chapter.

MyEconLab *Real-Time Data Analysis*

We now offer new real-time data exercises that students can complete in MyEconLab.

- **Real-Time Data Analysis Exercises** are marked with and allow instructors to assign problems that use up-to-the-minute data. Each RTDA exercise loads the appropriate and most currently available data from FRED, a comprehensive and up-to-date data set maintained by the Federal Reserve Bank of St. Louis. Exercises are graded based on that instance of data, and feedback is provided.

- In the eText available in MyEconLab, select figures labeled MyEconLab Real-Time Data now include a popup graph updated with real-time data from FRED.

- Current News Exercises, new to this edition of the MyEconLab course, provide a turn-key way to assign gradable news-based exercises in MyEconLab. Every week, Pearson scours the news, finds a current article appropriate for the macroeconomics course, creates an exercise around this news article, and then automatically adds it to MyEconLab. Assigning and grading current news-based exercises that deal with the latest macro events and policy issues has never been more convenient.

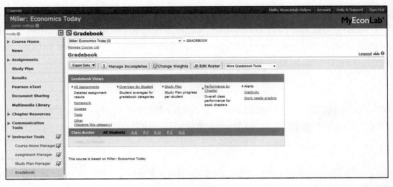

- Economics in the News is a turn-key solution to bringing current news into the classroom. Updated weekly during the academic year, this feature posts news articles with questions for further discussion.

- Experiments in MyEconLab are a fun and engaging way to promote active learning and mastery of important economic concepts. Pearson's experiments program is flexible and easy for instructors and students to use.
  - Single-player experiments allow your students to play an experiment against virtual players from anywhere at any time with an Internet connection.
  - Multiplayer experiments allow you to assign and manage a real-time experiment with your class.

  In both cases, pre- and post-questions for each experiment are available for assignment in MyEconLab.

For the Student

Students are in control of their own learning through a collection of tests, practice, and study tools. Highlights include:

- Two Sample Tests per chapter are preloaded in MyEconLab, enabling students to practice what they have learned, test their understanding, and identify areas for further work.

- Based on each student's performance on homework, quizzes, and tests, MyEconLab generates a Study Plan that shows where the student needs further study.

- Learning Aids, such as step-by-step guided solutions, a graphing tool, content-specific links to the eText, animated graphs, and glossary flashcards, help students master the material.

Please visit **www.myeconlab.com** for more information.

Supplemental Resources

Student and instructor materials provide tools for success.

Test Banks 1, 2, and 3 offer more than 10,000 multiple choice and short answer questions, all of which are available in computerized format in the TestGen software. The significant revision process by author Jim Lee of Texas A&M University–Corpus Christi and accuracy reviewers Ercument Aksoy of Los Angeles Valley College and Fatma Antar of Manchester Community College ensures the accuracy of problems and solutions in these revised and updated Test Banks. The Test Bank author has connected the questions to the general knowledge and skill guidelines found in the Association to Advance Collegiate Schools of Business (AACSB) assurance of learning standards.

The Instructor's Manual, prepared by Jim Lee of Texas A&M University–Corpus Christi, includes lecture-ready examples; chapter overviews, objectives, and outlines; points to emphasize; answers to all critical analysis questions; answers to even-numbered end-of-chapter problems; suggested answers to "You Are There" questions; and selected references.

PowerPoint lecture presentations for each chapter, revised by Debbie Evercloud of University of Colorado–Denver, include graphs from the text and outline key terms, concepts, and figures from the text.

Clicker PowerPoint slides, prepared by Rick Pretzsch of Lonestar College–CyFair, allow professors to instantly quiz students in class and receive immediate feedback through Clicker Response System technology.

The Instructor's Resource Disk offers all instructor supplements conveniently packaged on a disk.

The Instructor Resource Center puts supplements right at instructors' fingertips. Visit www.pearson highered.com/irc to register.

The Study Guide offers the practice and review that students need to excel. Written by Roger LeRoy Miller and updated by David Van Hoose of Baylor University, the Study Guide has been thoroughly revised to take into account changes to the Seventeenth Edition.

The CourseSmart eTextbook for the text is available through www.coursesmart.com. CourseSmart goes beyond traditional expectations by providing instant, online access to the textbooks and course materials you need at a lower cost to students. And, even as students save money, you can save time and hassle with a digital textbook that allows you to search the most relevant content at the very moment you need it. Whether you're evaluating textbooks or creating lecture notes to help students with difficult concepts, CourseSmart can make life a little easier. See how when you visit www.coursesmart.com/instructors.

Acknowledgments

I am the most fortunate of economics textbook writers, for I receive the benefit of literally hundreds of suggestions from those of you who use *Economics Today*. Some professors have been asked by my publisher to participate in a more detailed reviewing process of this edition. I list them below. I hope that each one of you so listed accepts my sincere appreciation for the fine work that you have done.

Hamilton Galloway, *College of Western Idaho*
Frank Garland, *TriCounty Technical College*
Reza G. Hamzaee, *Missouri Western State University*
Ricot Jean, *Valencia College*
Richard W. Kreissle, *Landmark College*
James M. Leaman, *Eastern Mennonite University*
Dr. Larry Olanrewaju, *John Tyler Community College*
Benny E. Overton, *Vance/Granville Community College*

Elizabeth Patch, *Broome Community College*
Van Thi Hong Pham, *Salem State University*
Leila Angelica Rodemann, *Trident Technical College*
Lewis Sage, *Baldwin-Wallace College*
Jonathan Silberman, *Oakland University*
Brian Sommer, *Lynn University*
Manjuri Talukdar, *Northern Illinois University*
Ethel C. Weeks, *Nassau Community College*

I also thank the reviewers of previous editions:

Rebecca Abraham
Cinda J. Adams
Esmond Adams
John Adams
Bill Adamson
Carlos Aguilar
John R. Aidem
Mohammed Akacem
Ercument Aksoy
M. C. Alderfer
John Allen
Ann Al-Yasiri
Charles Anderson
Leslie J. Anderson
Fatma W. Antar
Len Anyanwu
Rebecca Arnold
Mohammad Ashraf
Ali A. Ataiifar
Aliakbar Ataiifar
Leonard Atencio
John Atkins
Glen W. Atkinson
Thomas R. Atkinson
James Q. Aylesworth
John Baffoe-Bonnie
Kevin Baird
Maurice B. Ballabon
Charley Ballard
G. Jeffrey Barbour
Robin L. Barlett
Daniel Barszcz
Kari Battaglia
Robert Becker
Charles Beem
Glen Beeson
Bruce W. Bellner
Daniel K. Benjamin
Emil Berendt
Charles Berry
Abraham Bertisch
John Bethune
R. A. Blewett
Scott Bloom
John Bockino
M. L. Bodnar
Mary Bone
Karl Bonnhi

Thomas W. Bonsor
John M. Booth
Wesley F. Booth
Thomas Borcherding
Melvin Borland
Tom Boston
Barry Boyer
Maryanna Boynton
Ronald Brandolini
Fenton L. Broadhead
Elba Brown
William Brown
Michael Bull
Maureen Burton
Conrad P. Caligaris
Kevin Carey
James Carlson
Robert Carlsson
Dancy R. Carr
Scott Carson
Doris Cash
Thomas H. Cate
Richard J. Cebula
Catherine Chambers
K. Merry Chambers
Richard Chapman
Ronald Cherry
Young Back Choi
Marc Chopin
Carol Cies
Joy L. Clark
Curtis Clarke
Gary Clayton
Marsha Clayton
Dale O. Cloninger
Warren L. Coats
Ed Coen
Pat Conroy
James Cox
Stephen R. Cox

Eleanor D. Craig
Peggy Crane
Jerry Crawford
Patrick M. Crowley
Joanna Cruse
John P. Cullity
Will Cummings
Thomas Curtis
Margaret M. Dalton
Andrew J. Dane
Mahmoud Davoudi
Diana Denison
Edward Dennis
Julia G. Derrick
Sowjanya Dharmasankar
Carol Dimamro
William Dougherty
Barry Duman
Diane Dumont
Floyd Durham
G. B. Duwaji
James A. Dyal
Ishita Edwards
Robert P. Edwards
Alan E. Ellis
Miuke Ellis
Steffany Ellis
Frank Emerson
Carl Enomoto
Zaki Eusufzai
Sandy Evans
John L. Ewing-Smith
Frank Falero
Frank Fato
Abdollah Ferdowsi
Grant Ferguson
Victoria L. Figiel
Mitchell Fisher
David Fletcher
James Foley
John Foreman
Diana Fortier
Ralph G. Fowler
Arthur Friedberg
Peter Frost

Timothy S. Fuerst
Tom Fullerton
E. Gabriel
James Gale
Byron Gangnes
Peter C. Garlick
Steve Garner
Neil Garston
Alexander Garvin
Joe Garwood
Doug Gehrke
Robert Gentenaar
J. P. Gilbert
Otis Gilley
Frank Glesber
Jack Goddard
Michael G. Goode
Allen C. Goodman
Richard J. Gosselin
Paul Graf
Anthony J. Greco
Edward Greenberg
Gary Greene
Peter A. Groothuis
Philip J. Grossman
Nicholas Grunt
William Gunther
Kwabena Gyimah-Brempong
Demos Hadjiyanis
Martin D. Haney
Mehdi Haririan
Ray Harvey
Michael J. Haupert
E. L. Hazlett
Sanford B. Helman
William Henderson
Robert Herman
Gus W. Herring
Charles Hill
John M. Hill
Morton Hirsch

Benjamin Hitchner
Charles W. Hockert
R. Bradley Hoppes
James Horner
Grover Howard
Nancy Howe-Ford
Yu-Mong Hsiao
Yu Hsing
James Hubert
George Hughes
Joseph W. Hunt Jr.
Scott Hunt
John Ifediora
R. Jack Inch
Christopher Inya
Tomotaka Ishimine
E. E. Jarvis
Parvis Jenab
Allan Jenkins
John Jensel
Mark Jensen
S. D. Jevremovic
J. Paul Jewell
Nancy Jianakoplos
Frederick Johnson
David Jones
Lamar B. Jones
Paul A. Joray
Daniel A. Joseph
Craig Justice
M. James Kahiga
Septimus Kai Kai
Devajyoti Kataky
Timothy R. Keely
Ziad Keilany
Norman F. Keiser
Brian Kench
Randall G. Kesselring
Alan Kessler

E. D. Key
Saleem Khan
M. Barbara Killen
Bruce Kimzey
Terrence Kinal
Philip G. King
E. R. Kittrell
David Klingman
Charles Knapp
Jerry Knarr
Tori Knight
Faik Koray
Janet Koscianski
Dennis Lee Kovach
Marie Kratochvil
Peter Kressler
Paul J. Kubik
Michael Kupilik
Margaret Landman
Richard LaNear
Larry Landrum
Keith Langford
Theresa Laughlin
Anthony T. Lee
Jim Lee
Loren Lee
Bozena Leven
Donald Lien
George Lieu
Stephen E. Lile
Lawrence W. Lovick
Marty Ludlum
Laura Maghoney
G. Dirk Mateer
Robert McAuliffe
James C. McBrearty
Howard J. McBride
Bruce McClung
John McDowell
E. S. McKuskey
James J. McLain
Kevin McWoodson
John L. Madden
Mary Lou Madden
John Marangos
Dan Marburger
Glen Marston

John M. Martin
Paul J. Mascotti
James D. Mason
Paul M. Mason
Tom Mathew
Warren Matthews
Akbar Marvasti
Pete Mavrokordatos
Fred May
G. Hartley Mellish
Mike Melvin
Diego Mendez-Carbajo
Dan C. Messerschmidt
Michael Metzger
Herbert C. Milikien
Joel C. Millonzi
Glenn Milner
Daniel Mizak
Khan Mohabbat
Thomas Molloy
William H. Moon
Margaret D. Moore
William E. Morgan
Stephen Morrell
Irving Morrissett
James W. Moser
Thaddeaus Mounkurai
Martin F. Murray
Densel L. Myers
George L. Nagy

Solomon Namala
Ronald M. Nate
Jerome Neadly
James E. Needham
Claron Nelson
Douglas Nettleton
William Nook
Gerald T. O'Boyle
Greg Okoro
Richard E. O'Neill
Lucian T. Orlowski
Diane S. Osborne
Joan Osborne
Melissa A Osborne
James O'Toole
Jan Palmer
Zuohong Pan
Gerald Parker
Ginger Parker
Randall E. Parker
Mohammed Partapurwala
Kenneth Parzych
Norm Paul
Wesley Payne
Raymond A. Pepin
Martin M. Perline
Timothy Perri
Jerry Petr
Maurice Pfannesteil
James Phillips
Raymond J. Phillips
I. James Pickl
Bruce Pietrykowski
Dennis Placone

Mannie Poen
William L. Polvent
Robert Posatko
Greg Pratt
Leila J. Pratt
Steven Pressman
Rick Pretzsch
Reneé Prim
Robert E. Pulsinelli
Rod D. Raehsler
Kambriz Raffiee
Sandra Rahman
Jaishankar Raman
John Rapp
Richard Rawlins
Gautam Raychaudhuri
Ron Reddall
Mitchell Redlo
Charles Reichhelu
Robert S. Rippey
Charles Roberts
Ray C. Roberts
Richard Romano
Judy Roobian-Mohr
Duane Rosa
Richard Rosenberg
Larry Ross
Barbara Ross-Pfeiffer
Marina Rosser
Philip Rothman

John Roufagalas
Stephen Rubb
Henry Ryder
Basel Saleh
Patricia Sanderson
Thomas N. Schaap
William A. Schaeffer
William Schamoe
David Schauer
A. C. Schlenker
David Schlow
Scott J. Schroeder
William Scott
Dan Segebarth
Paul Seidenstat
Swapan Sen
Augustus Shackelford
Richard Sherman Jr.
Liang-rong Shiau
Gail Shields
David Shorow
Vishwa Shukla
R. J. Sidwell
David E. Sisk
Alden Smith
Garvin Smith
Howard F. Smith
Lynn A. Smith
Phil Smith
William Doyle Smith
Lee Spector

George Spiva
Richard L. Sprinkle
Alan Stafford
Amanda Stallings-Wood
Herbert F. Steeper
Diane L. Stehman
Columbus Stephens
William Stine
Allen D. Stone
Osman Suliman
J. M. Sullivan
Rebecca Summary
Terry Sutton
Joseph L. Swaffar
Thomas Swanke
Frank D. Taylor
Daniel Teferra
Lea Templer
Gary Theige
Dave Thiessen
Robert P. Thomas
Deborah Thorsen
Richard Trieff
George Troxler
William T. Trulove
William N. Trumbull
Arianne K. Turner
Kay Unger
Anthony Uremovic
John Vahaly
Jim Van Beek
David Van Hoose
Lee J. Van Scyoc
Roy Van Til
Sharmila Vishwasrao

Craig Walker
Robert F. Wallace
Henry C. Wallich
Milledge Weathers
Ethel Weeks
Roger E. Wehr
Robert G. Welch
Terence West
James Wetzel
Wylie Whalthall
James H. Wheeler
Everett E. White
Michael D. White
Mark A. Wilkening
Raburn M. Williams
James Willis
George Wilson
Travis Wilson
Mark Wohar
Ken Woodward
Tim Wulf
Peter R. Wyman
Whitney Yamamura
Donald Yankovic
Alex Yguado
Paul Young
Shik Young
Mohammed Zaheer
Ed Zajicek
Charles Zalonka
Sourushe Zandvakili
Paul Zarembka
George K. Zestos
William J. Zimmer Jr.

As always, a revision of *Economics Today* requires me to put in the latest data at the last minute. If I did not have such an incredible editorial and production team, I wouldn't be able to do so. I do have a fantastic team both at the publisher—Pearson—and at our production house—Nesbitt (Cenveo Publisher Services), working through them with my long-time Production Manager, John Orr of Orr Book Services. He again did a terrific job. I was fortunate to once more have Kathryn Dinovo, Senior Production Project Manager at Pearson, lead the production team to as perfect a textbook as possible. To be sure, I was pushed hard by my long-time Senior Acquisitions Editor, Noel Seibert, and I was helped greatly by Carolyn Terbush, the Senior Editorial Project Manager on this project. The "pushing" all makes sense now.

I am greatly pleased with the design revision created by Jerilyn Bockorick of Nesbitt Graphics. It is always a challenge to keep the traditional feel of this book, yet make it more exciting for today's students. I think that she succeeded. I am appreciative of the hard work my copy editor, Bonnie Boehme, did. And, of course, the proofreader *par excellence*, Pat Lewis, made sure that everything was perfect. As for the supplements for this edition, I wish to thank the team at Nesbitt for producing them for students and professors. On the marketing side, I appreciate the fine work performed by Lori DeShazo and Kim Lovato.

The online media materials, particularly great improvements in *MyEconLab*, were accomplished by Melissa Honig, Noel Lotz, and Courtney Kamauf.

Jim Lee of Texas A&M University–Corpus Christi, Ercument Aksoy of Los Angeles Valley College, and Fatma Antar of Manchester Community College undertook the vast job of revising and improving the three test banks. David Van Hoose of Baylor University continued to create an accurate *Study Guide*. The *Instructor's Manual* was masterfully revised by Jim Lee of Texas A&M University–Corpus Christi. PowerPoint presentations were updated and improved by Debbie Evercloud of the University of Colorado–Denver. Rick Pretzsch of Lonestar College–Cyfair provided the clicker PowerPoint slides.

As always, my "super reviewer," Professor Dan Benjamin of Clemson University, really kept me honest this time around. And, as always, my long-time assistant, Sue Jasin, did enough typing and retyping to fill a room with paper. I welcome comments and ideas from professors and students alike and hope that you enjoy this latest edition of *Economics Today*.

R. L. M.

Credits

Cover images: Solar power panel array, S.R. Lee Photo Traveller/Shutterstock; Woman riding a bicycle in Vietnam, MJ Prototype/Shutterstock; Eye chart test, Pinkcandy/Shutterstock; Plant sample, Chepko Danil Vitalevich/Shutterstock; Bags in warehouse in shop, Mikhail Zahranichny/Shutterstock; Apple on stack of books and laptop computer, Andreka Photography/Shutterstock; Crowd at a music concert, Alexey Lysenko/Shutterstock; Goalman on the stadium field, Andrey Yurlov/Shutterstock

FRED® is a registered trademark and the FRED® logo and ST. LOUIS FED are trademarks of the Federal Reserve Bank of St Louis, http://research.stlouisfed.org/fred2/

The Nature of Economics

1

Half of the babies delivered in 2011 in a typical Hong Kong hospital maternity ward were born to non–Hong Kong residents. This fact means that these babies were born to women classified as tourists visiting from the Chinese mainland. Why have nearly half of the babies born in Hong Kong hospitals had mothers who are not residents of Hong Kong? To formulate an answer, you must learn more about principles of economics. In particular, you must learn the key concepts discussed in this chapter, such as self-interest.

Incentives
Rewards or penalties for engaging in a particular activity.

the number of college students majoring in economics rose by more than 40 percent during the past decade? One reason that students opt for extensive study of economics is that they find the subject fascinating. Another reason, however, is self-interest. On average, students who major in economics earn 13 percent more than business management majors, 26 percent more than chemistry majors, and 50 percent more than psychology majors. Thus, students have a strong incentive to consider majoring in economics.

In this chapter, you will learn why contemplating the nature of self-interested responses to **incentives** is the starting point for analyzing choices people make in all walks of life. After all, how much time you devote to studying economics in this introductory course depends in part on the incentives established by your instructor's grading system. As you will see, self-interest and incentives are the underpinnings for all the decisions you and others around you make each day.

The Power of Economic Analysis

Simply knowing that self-interest and incentives are central to any decision-making process is not sufficient for predicting the choices that people will actually make. You also have to develop a framework that will allow you to analyze solutions to each economic problem—whether you are trying to decide how much to study, which courses to take, whether to finish school, or whether the U.S. government should provide more grants to universities or raise taxes. The framework that you will learn in this text is the *economic way of thinking*.

This framework gives you power—the power to reach informed judgments about what is happening in the world. You can, of course, live your life without the power of economic analysis as part of your analytical framework. Indeed, most people do. But economists believe that economic analysis can help you make better decisions concerning your career, your education, financing your home, and other important matters. In the business world, the power of economic analysis can help you increase your competitive edge as an employee or as the owner of a business. As a voter, for the rest of your life you will be asked to make judgments about policies that are advocated by political parties. Many of these policies will deal with questions related to international economics, such as whether the U.S. government should encourage or discourage immigration, prevent foreign residents and firms from investing in port facilities or domestic banks, or restrict other countries from selling their goods here.

Finally, just as taking an art, music, or literature appreciation class increases the pleasure you receive when you view paintings, listen to concerts, or read novels, taking an economics course will increase your understanding and pleasure when watching the news on TV or reading articles on your iPad.

Defining Economics

Economics
The study of how people allocate their limited resources to satisfy their unlimited wants.

Economics is part of the social sciences and, as such, seeks explanations of real events. All social sciences analyze human behavior, as opposed to the physical sciences, which generally analyze the behavior of electrons, atoms, and other nonhuman phenomena.

> *Economics is the study of how people allocate their limited resources in an attempt to satisfy their unlimited wants. As such, economics is the study of how people make choices.*

To understand this definition fully, two other words need explaining: *resources* and *wants*. **Resources** are things that have value and, more specifically, are used to produce goods and services that satisfy people's wants. **Wants** are all of the items that people would purchase if they had unlimited income.

Resources
Things used to produce goods and services to satisfy people's wants.

Wants
What people would buy if their incomes were unlimited.

Whenever an individual, a business, or a nation faces alternatives, a choice must be made, and economics helps us study how those choices are made. For example, you have to choose how to spend your limited income. You also have to choose how to spend your limited time. You may have to choose how many of your company's limited resources to allocate to advertising and how many to allocate to new-product research. In economics, we examine situations in which individuals choose how to do things, when to do things, and with whom to do them. Ultimately, the purpose of economics is to explain choices.

Microeconomics versus Macroeconomics

Economics is typically divided into two types of analysis: **microeconomics** and **macroeconomics.**

> *Microeconomics is the part of economic analysis that studies decision making undertaken by individuals (or households) and by firms. It is like looking through a microscope to focus on the small parts of our economy.*

> *Macroeconomics is the part of economic analysis that studies the behavior of the economy as a whole. It deals with economywide phenomena such as changes in unemployment, in the general price level, and in national income.*

Microeconomics
The study of decision making undertaken by individuals (or households) and by firms.

Macroeconomics
The study of the behavior of the economy as a whole, including such economywide phenomena as changes in unemployment, the general price level, and national income.

Microeconomic analysis, for example, is concerned with the effects of changes in the price of gasoline relative to that of other energy sources. It examines the effects of new taxes on a specific product or industry. If the government establishes new health care regulations, how individual firms and consumers would react to those regulations would be in the realm of microeconomics. The effects of higher wages brought about by an effective union strike would also be analyzed using the tools of microeconomics.

In contrast, issues such as the rate of inflation, the amount of economywide unemployment, and the yearly growth in the output of goods and services in the nation all fall into the realm of macroeconomic analysis. In other words, macroeconomics deals with **aggregates,** or totals—such as total output in an economy.

Aggregates
Total amounts or quantities. Aggregate demand, for example, is total planned expenditures throughout a nation.

Be aware, however, of the blending of microeconomics and macroeconomics in modern economic theory. Modern economists are increasingly using microeconomic analysis—the study of decision making by individuals and by firms—as the basis of macroeconomic analysis. They do this because even though macroeconomic analysis focuses on aggregates, those aggregates are the result of choices made by individuals and firms.

The Three Basic Economic Questions and Two Opposing Answers

In every nation, three fundamental questions must be addressed irrespective of the form of its government or who heads that government, how rich or how poor the nation may be, or what type of **economic system**—the institutional mechanism through which resources are utilized to satisfy human wants—has been chosen. The three questions concern the problem of how to allocate society's scarce resources:

Economic system
A society's institutional mechanism for determining the way in which scarce resources are used to satisfy human desires.

1. *What and how much will be produced?* Some mechanism must exist for determining which items will be produced while others remain inventors' pipe dreams or individuals' unfulfilled desires.

2. *How will items be produced?* There are many ways to produce a desired item. It is possible to use more labor and less capital, or vice versa. It is possible, for instance, to produce an item with an aim to maximize the number of people employed. Alternatively, an item may be produced with an aim to minimize the total expenses that members of society incur. Somehow, a decision must be made about the mix of resources used in production, the way in which they are organized, and how they are brought together at a particular location.

3. *For whom will items be produced?* Once an item is produced, who should be able to obtain it? People use scarce resources to produce any item, so typically people value access to that item. Thus, determining a mechanism for distributing produced items is a crucial issue for any society.

Now that you know the questions that an economic system must answer, how do current systems actually answer them?

Two Opposing Answers

At any point in time, every nation has its own economic system. How a nation goes about answering the three basic economic questions depends on that nation's economic system.

CENTRALIZED COMMAND AND CONTROL Throughout history, one common type of economic system has been *command and control* (also called *central planning*) by a centralized authority, such as a king or queen, a dictator, a central government, or some other type of authority that assumes responsibility for addressing fundamental economic issues. Under command and control, this authority decides what items to produce and how many, determines how the scarce resources will be organized in the items' production, and identifies who will be able to obtain the items.

For instance, in a command-and-control economic system, a government might decide that particular types of automobiles ought to be produced in certain numbers. The government might issue specific rules for how to marshal resources to produce these vehicles, or it might even establish ownership over those resources so that it can make all such resource allocation decisions directly. Finally, the government will then decide who will be authorized to purchase or otherwise utilize the vehicles.

How is centralized command and control affecting the net cost of constructing a high-speed rail project in California?

POLICY EXAMPLE

The Federal Government Directs New California Train Tracks

The U.S. Department of Transportation recently provided an initial $3 billion in federal tax funds for a 500-mile high-speed rail project stretching between the California cities of Anaheim and San Francisco. Local planners proposed construction of operating rail line segments in phases, starting at the highly populated ends of the route, at a projected total expense of about $18 billion. Planners suggested that opening operating segments at the more heavily populated ends of the line would generate revenues that could assist in financing the building of remaining segments of the multiyear rail construction project.

In reaction, Transportation Department officials mandated the rail line to start in California's less-populated Central Valley region. Of course, train passengers will be far fewer. Why did the U.S. government officials do this? They did so because they consider residents of the Central Valley to be "underserved" by rail transit services. The resulting completion delay will be at least two years and will add more than $1 billion to the project's ultimate net expense to taxpayers.

FOR CRITICAL THINKING

Would Transportation Department officials have made the same decision if they, rather than taxpayers, had to cover the added costs of starting construction in the Central Valley?

THE PRICE SYSTEM The alternative to command and control is the *price system* (also called a *market system*), which is a shorthand term describing an economic system that answers the three basic economic questions via decentralized decision making. Under a pure price system, individuals and families own all of the scarce resources used in production. Consequently, choices about what and how many items to produce are left to private parties to determine on their own initiative, as are decisions about how to go about producing those items. Furthermore, individuals and families choose how to allocate their own incomes to obtain the produced items at prices established via privately organized mechanisms.

In the price system, which you will learn about in considerable detail in Chapters 3 and 4, prices define the terms under which people agree to make exchanges. Prices signal to everyone within a price system which resources are relatively scarce and which resources are relatively abundant. This *signaling* aspect of the price system provides information to individual buyers and sellers about what and how many items should be produced, how production of items should be organized, and who will choose to buy the produced items.

Thus, in a price system, individuals and families own the facilities used to produce automobiles. They decide which types of automobiles to produce, how many of them to produce, and how to bring scarce resources together within their facilities to generate the desired production. Other individuals and families decide how much of their earnings they wish to spend on automobiles.

MIXED ECONOMIC SYSTEMS By and large, the economic systems of the world's nations are mixed economic systems that incorporate aspects of both centralized command and control and a decentralized price system. At any given time, some nations lean toward centralized mechanisms of command and control and allow relatively little scope for decentralized decision making. At the same time, other nations limit the extent to which a central authority dictates answers to the three basic economic questions, leaving people mostly free to utilize a decentralized price system to generate their own answers.

A given country may reach different decisions at different times about how much to rely on command and control versus a price system to answer its three basic economic questions. Until 2008, for instance, the people of the United States preferred to rely mainly on a decentralized price system to decide which and how many automobiles to produce, how to marshal scarce resources to produce those vehicles, and how to decide who should obtain them. Today, the U.S. government owns a substantial fraction of the facilities used to manufacture automobiles and hence has considerable command-and-control authority over U.S. vehicle production.

How has Cuba altered the extent to which it relies on command and control compared with the price system?

INTERNATIONAL POLICY EXAMPLE

Cuba Experiments with Mixing It Up

For more than half of a century, Cuba has been the Western Hemisphere's only Communist nation. The Cuban government sets the prices of most goods and services. For many years, the government also set the wages of about 85 percent of the country's 5.5 million workers who are government-employed. The government permitted the remaining 15 percent of employed individuals to work in 124 "authorized" private occupations, which include farming, teaching music, selling piñatas, and repairing existing items such as furniture and toys.

Today, the government is in the midst of letting go nearly 600,000 public employees, who will have to seek employment at privately determined wages. Although the nation will maintain its heavy reliance on command and control, a larger share of its workers will have their wages determined in the price system. Thus, Cuba's economy is becoming more mixed.

FOR CRITICAL THINKING

When there are fewer public workers and more private workers, will changes in wages be better or worse signals?

The Economic Approach: Systematic Decisions

Economists assume that individuals act *as if* they systematically pursue self-motivated interests and respond predictably to perceived opportunities to attain those interests. This central insight of economics was first clearly articulated by Adam Smith in 1776. Smith wrote in his most famous book, *An Inquiry into the Nature and Causes of the Wealth of Nations*, that "it is not from the benevolence of the butcher, the brewer, or the baker that we expect our dinner, but from their regard to their own interest." Thus, the typical person about whom economists make behavioral predictions is assumed to act *as though* he or she systematically pursues self-motivated interest.

The Rationality Assumption

The **rationality assumption** of economics, simply stated, is as follows:

We assume that individuals do not intentionally make decisions that would leave themselves worse off.

Rationality assumption
The assumption that people do not intentionally make decisions that would leave them worse off.

The distinction here is between what people may think—the realm of psychology and psychiatry and perhaps sociology—and what they do. Economics does *not* involve itself in analyzing individual or group thought processes. Economics looks at what people actually do in life with their limited resources. It does little good to criticize the rationality assumption by stating, "Nobody thinks that way" or "I never think that way" or "How unrealistic! That's as irrational as anyone can get!" In a world in which people can be atypical in countless ways, economists find it useful to concentrate on discovering the baseline. Knowing what happens on average is a good place to start. In this way, we avoid building our thinking on exceptions rather than on reality.

Take the example of driving. When you consider passing another car on a two-lane highway with oncoming traffic, you have to make very quick decisions: You must estimate the speed of the car that you are going to pass, the speed of the oncoming cars, the distance between your car and the oncoming cars, and your car's potential rate of acceleration. If we were to apply a model to your behavior, we would use the rules of calculus. In actual fact, you and most other drivers in such a situation do not actually think of using the rules of calculus, but to predict your behavior, we could make the prediction *as if* you understood those rules.

How are bankers reducing robbery rates by counting on the rationality of would-be thieves?

EXAMPLE

Hello, Bank Robber, I'll Remember You

Until recently, each year since 1979, on average 11 of every 100 U.S. bank branches experienced a robbery. Bankers have worked to bring down this robbery rate by treating prospective robbers as rational people. A would-be bank robber knows that the likelihood of being caught and sentenced to prison increases significantly when someone in the bank gets a good enough look at the robber's face to provide a positive identification.

Consequently, many banks now make a point of having a teller, guard, or branch manager greet each entering customer, look the customer directly in the eye, and say hello. Since banks around the nation have instituted a policy of greeting customers at the doors, the robbery rate has dropped to only 6 of every 100 bank branches.

FOR CRITICAL THINKING
What types of costs and benefits must a prospective criminal rationally weigh before deciding whether to attempt a bank robbery?

YOU ARE THERE

To contemplate how a higher corporate tax rate in the United States relative to other nations is affecting the incentive for U.S. firms to form corporate structures within U.S. borders, take a look at **Why So Many Firms Are Incorporating Outside the United States** on page 11.

Responding to Incentives

If it can be assumed that individuals never intentionally make decisions that would leave them worse off, then almost by definition they will respond to changes in incentives. Indeed, much of human behavior can be explained in terms of how individuals respond to changing incentives over time.

Schoolchildren are motivated to do better by a variety of incentive systems, ranging from gold stars and certificates of achievement when they are young, to better grades with accompanying promises of a "better life" as they get older. Of course, negative incentives affect our behavior, too. Penalties, punishments, and other forms of negative incentives can raise the cost of engaging in various activities.

Defining Self-Interest

Self-interest does not always mean increasing one's wealth measured in dollars and cents. We assume that individuals seek many goals, not just increased wealth measured in monetary terms. Thus, the self-interest part of our economic-person assumption includes goals relating to prestige, friendship, love, power, helping others, creating works of art, and many other matters. We can also think in terms of enlightened self-interest, whereby individuals, in the pursuit of what makes them better off, also achieve the betterment of others around them. In brief, individuals are assumed to want the ability to further their goals by making decisions about how things around them are used. The head of a charitable organization usually will not turn down an additional contribution, because accepting the funds yields control over how they are used, even though it is for other people's benefit.

Thus, self-interest does not rule out doing charitable acts. Giving gifts to relatives can be considered a form of charity that is nonetheless in the self-interest of the giver. But how efficient is such gift giving?

EXAMPLE

The Perceived Value of Gifts

Every holiday season, aunts, uncles, grandparents, mothers, and fathers give gifts to their college-aged loved ones. Joel Waldfogel, an economist at the University of Minnesota, has surveyed several thousand college students after Christmas to find out the value of holiday gifts. He finds that recorded music and outerwear (coats and jackets) have a perceived intrinsic value about equal to their actual cash equivalent. By the time he gets down the list to socks, underwear, and cosmetics, the students'

valuation is only about 82 percent of the cash value of the gift. He find that aunts, uncles, and grandparents give the "worst" gifts and friends, siblings, and parents give the "best."

FOR CRITICAL ANALYSIS
What argument could you use against the idea of substituting cash or gift cards for physical gifts?

QUICK QUIZ

See page 16 for the answers. Review concepts from this section in MyEconLab.

Economics is a social science that involves the study of how individuals choose among alternatives to satisfy their_____, which are what people would buy if their incomes were_____.

_____, the study of the decision-making processes of individuals (or households) and firms, and _____, the study of the performance of the economy as a whole, are the two main branches into which the study of economics is divided.

The three basic economic questions ask what and how much will be produced, how will items be produced, and for whom will items be produced. The two opposing answers are provided by the type of economic system: either_____ _____ _____ _____ or the_____ _____.

In economics, we assume that people do not intentionally make decisions that will leave them worse off. This is known as the _____ assumption.

Economics as a Science

Economics is a social science that employs the same kinds of methods used in other sciences, such as biology, physics, and chemistry. Like these other sciences, economics uses models, or theories. Economic **models,** or **theories,** are simplified representations of the real world that we use to help us understand, explain, and predict economic phenomena in the real world. There are, of course, differences between sciences. The social sciences—especially economics—make little use of laboratory experiments in which changes in variables are studied under controlled conditions. Rather, social scientists, and especially economists, usually have to test their models, or theories, by examining what has already happened in the real world.

Models, or theories
Simplified representations of the real world used as the basis for predictions or explanations.

Models and Realism

At the outset it must be emphasized that no model in *any* science, and therefore no economic model, is complete in the sense that it captures *every* detail or interrelationship that exists. Indeed, a model, by definition, is an abstraction from reality. It is conceptually impossible to construct a perfectly complete realistic model. For example, in physics we cannot account for every molecule and its position and certainly not for every atom and subatomic particle. Not only is such a model unreasonably expensive to build, but working with it would be impossibly complex.

The nature of scientific model building is that the model should capture only the *essential* relationships that are sufficient to analyze the particular problem or answer the particular question with which we are concerned. *An economic model cannot be faulted as unrealistic simply because it does not represent every detail of the real world.* A map of a city that shows only major streets is not faulty if, in fact, all you need to know is how to pass through the city using major streets. As long as a model is able to shed light on the *central* issue at hand or forces at work, it may be useful.

A map is the quintessential model. It is always a simplified representation. It is always unrealistic. But it is also useful in making predictions about the world. If the model—the map—predicts that when you take Campus Avenue to the north, you always run into the campus, that is a prediction. If a simple model can explain observed behavior in repeated settings just as well as a complex model, the simple model has some value and is probably easier to use.

Assumptions

Every model, or theory, must be based on a set of assumptions. Assumptions define the array of circumstances in which our model is most likely to be applicable. When some people predicted that sailing ships would fall off the edge of the earth, they used the *assumption* that the earth was flat. Columbus did not accept the implications of such a model because he did not accept its assumptions. He assumed that the world was round. The real-world test of his own model refuted the flat-earth model. Indirectly, then, it was a test of the assumption of the flat-earth model.

Is it possible to use our knowledge about assumptions to understand why driving directions sometimes contain very few details?

EXAMPLE

Getting Directions

Assumptions are a shorthand for reality. Imagine that you have decided to drive from your home in San Diego to downtown San Francisco. Because you have never driven this route, you decide to use a travel-planner device such as global-positioning-system equipment.

When you ask for directions, the electronic travel planner could give you a set of detailed maps that shows each city through which you will travel—Oceanside, San Clemente, Irvine, Anaheim, Los Angeles, Bakersfield, Modesto, and so on—with the individual maps showing you exactly how the freeway threads through each of these cities. You would get a nearly complete description of reality because the GPS travel planner will not have used many simplifying assumptions. It is more likely, however, that the travel planner will simply say, "Get on Interstate 5 going north. Stay on it for about 500 miles. Follow the signs for San Francisco. After crossing the toll bridge, take any exit marked 'Downtown.'" By omitting all of the trivial details, the travel planner has told you all that you really need and want to know. The models you will be using in this text are similar to the simplified directions on how to drive from San Diego to San Francisco—they focus on what is relevant to the problem at hand and omit what is not.

FOR CRITICAL ANALYSIS
In what way do small talk and gossip represent the use of simplifying assumptions?

THE *CETERIS PARIBUS* ASSUMPTION: ALL OTHER THINGS BEING EQUAL Everything in the world seems to relate in some way to everything else in the world. It would be impossible to isolate the effects of changes in one variable on another variable if we always had to worry about the many other variables that might also enter the analysis. Similar to other sciences, economics uses the **ceteris paribus assumption.** *Ceteris paribus* means "other things constant" or "other things equal."

Consider an example taken from economics. One of the most important determinants of how much of a particular product a family buys is how expensive that product is relative to other products. We know that in addition to relative prices, other factors influence decisions about making purchases. Some of them have to do with income, others with tastes, and yet others with custom and religious beliefs. Whatever these other factors are, we hold them constant when we look at the relationship between changes in prices and changes in how much of a given product people will purchase.

Ceteris paribus [KAY-ter-us PEAR-uh-bus] **assumption**
The assumption that nothing changes except the factor or factors being studied.

Deciding on the Usefulness of a Model

We generally do not attempt to determine the usefulness, or "goodness," of a model merely by evaluating how realistic its assumptions are. Rather, we consider a model "good" if it yields usable predictions that are supported by real-world observations. In other words, can we use the model to predict what will happen in the world around us? Does the model provide useful implications about how things happen in our world?

Once we have determined that the model may be useful in predicting real-world phenomena, the scientific approach to the analysis of the world around us requires that we consider evidence. Evidence is used to test the usefulness of a model. This is why we call economics an **empirical** science. *Empirical* means that evidence (data) is looked at to see whether we are right. Economists are often engaged in empirically testing their models.

Empirical
Relying on real-world data in evaluating the usefulness of a model.

Models of Behavior, Not Thought Processes

Take special note of the fact that economists' models do not relate to the way people *think*. Economic models relate to the way people *act*, to what they do in life with their limited resources. Normally, the economist does not attempt to predict how people will think about a particular topic, such as a higher price of oil products, accelerated inflation, or higher taxes. Rather, the task at hand is to predict how people will behave, which may be quite different from what they *say* they will do (much to the consternation of poll takers and market researchers). Thus, people's *declared* preferences are generally of little use in testing economic theories, which aim to explain and predict people's *revealed* preferences. The people involved in examining thought processes are psychologists and psychiatrists, not typically economists.

WHAT IF... economists were to base their theories of human behavior on what people *say* they do, rather than on what people *actually* do?

The task of economists is to try to predict decisions that people will make given the incentives that they face. Consider how people respond when asked by pollsters about whether they will cut back on charitable giving if the government eliminates tax breaks for such donations. Most people state that they will continue to give as much as before, because they suspect this answer will please those who have posed the question. In fact, studies of actual responses

to smaller tax breaks for charitable giving reveal that people pursue their own interest. Whether or not their true action might have pleased a pollster, they reduce donations. Thus, if economists were to rely on polls indicating how people claim that they respond to incentives such as diminished tax breaks, economists would persistently make erroneous predictions about the decisions that people actually make.

Behavioral Economics and Bounded Rationality

In recent years, some economists have proposed paying more attention to psychologists and psychiatrists. They have suggested an alternative approach to economic analysis. Their approach, which is known as **behavioral economics,** examines consumer behavior in the face of psychological limitations and complications that may interfere with rational decision making.

Behavioral economics
An approach to the study of consumer behavior that emphasizes psychological limitations and complications that potentially interfere with rational decision making.

BOUNDED RATIONALITY Proponents of behavioral economics suggest that traditional economic models assume that people exhibit three "unrealistic" characteristics:

1. *Unbounded selfishness.* People are interested only in their own satisfaction.

2. *Unbounded willpower.* Their choices are always consistent with their long-term goals.

3. *Unbounded rationality.* They are able to consider every relevant choice.

Bounded rationality
The hypothesis that people are *nearly*, but not fully, rational, so that they cannot examine every possible choice available to them but instead use simple rules of thumb to sort among the alternatives that happen to occur to them.

As an alternative, advocates of behavioral economics have proposed replacing the rationality assumption with the assumption of **bounded rationality,** which assumes that people cannot examine and think through every possible choice they confront. As a consequence, behavioral economists suggest, people cannot always pursue their best long-term personal interests. From time to time, they must also rely on other people and take into account other people's interests as well as their own.

RULES OF THUMB A key behavioral implication of the bounded rationality assumption is that people should use so-called *rules of thumb:* Because every possible choice cannot be considered, an individual will tend to fall back on methods of making decisions that are simpler than trying to sort through every possibility.

A problem confronting advocates of behavioral economics is that people who *appear* to use rules of thumb may in fact behave *as if* they are fully rational. For instance, if a person faces persistently predictable ranges of choices for a time, the individual may rationally settle into repetitive behaviors that an outside observer might conclude to be consistent with a rule of thumb. According to the bounded rationality assumption, the person should continue to rely on a rule of thumb even if there is a major change in the environment that the individual faces. Time and time again, however, economists find that people respond to altered circumstances by fundamentally changing their behaviors. Economists also generally observe that people make decisions that are consistent with their own self-interest and long-term objectives.

BEHAVIORAL ECONOMICS: A WORK IN PROGRESS It remains to be seen whether the application of the assumption of bounded rationality proposed by behavioral economists will truly alter the manner in which economists construct models intended to better predict human decision making. So far, proponents of behavioral economics have not conclusively demonstrated that paying closer attention to psychological thought processes can improve economic predictions.

As a consequence, the bulk of economic analysis continues to rely on the rationality assumption as the basis for constructing economic models. As you will learn in Chapter 20, advocates of behavioral economics continue to explore ways in which psychological elements might improve analysis of decision making by individual consumers.

Positive versus Normative Economics

Economics uses *positive analysis,* a value-free approach to inquiry. No subjective or moral judgments enter into the analysis. Positive analysis relates to statements such as "If A, then B." For example, "If the price of gasoline goes up relative to all other prices, then the amount of it that people buy will fall." That is a positive economic statement. It is a statement of *what is*. It is not a statement of anyone's value judgment or subjective feelings.

Distinguishing between Positive and Normative Economics

For many problems analyzed in the "hard" sciences such as physics and chemistry, the analyses are considered to be virtually value-free. After all, how can someone's values enter into a theory of molecular behavior? But economists face a different problem. They deal with the behavior of individuals, not molecules. That makes it more difficult to stick to what we consider to be value-free or **positive economics** without reference to our feelings.

Positive economics
Analysis that is *strictly* limited to making either purely descriptive statements or scientific predictions; for example, "If A, then B." A statement of *what is*.

Normative economics
Analysis involving value judgments about economic policies; relates to whether outcomes are good or bad. A statement of *what ought to be*.

When our values are interjected into the analysis, we enter the realm of **normative economics,** involving *normative analysis*. A positive economic statement is "If the price of gas rises, people will buy less." If we add to that analysis the statement "so we should not allow the price to go up," we have entered the realm of normative economics—we have expressed a value judgment. In fact, any time you see the word *should*, you will know that values are entering into the discussion. Just remember that positive statements are concerned with *what is*, whereas normative statements are concerned with *what ought to be*.

Each of us has a desire for different things. That means that we have different values. When we express a value judgment, we are simply saying what we prefer, like, or desire. Because individual values are diverse, we expect—and indeed observe—that people express widely varying value judgments about how the world ought to be.

A Warning: Recognize Normative Analysis

It is easy to define positive economics. It is quite another matter to catch all unlabeled normative statements in a textbook, even though an author goes over the manuscript many times before it is printed or electronically created. Therefore, do not get the impression that a textbook author will be able to keep all personal values out of the book. They will slip through. In fact, the very choice of which topics to include in an introductory textbook involves normative economics. There is no value-free way to decide which topics to use in a textbook. The author's values ultimately make a difference when choices have to be made. But from your own standpoint, you might want to be able to recognize when you are engaging in normative as opposed to positive economic analysis. Reading this text will help equip you for that task.

QUICK QUIZ See page 16 for the answers. Review concepts from this section in MyEconLab.

A _____, or _____, uses assumptions and is by nature a simplification of the real world. The usefulness of a _____ can be evaluated by bringing empirical evidence to bear on its predictions.

Most models use the _____ _____ assumption that all other things are held constant, or equal.

_____ economics emphasizes psychological constraints and complexities that potentially interfere with rational decision making. This approach utilizes the

_____ _____ hypothesis that people are not quite rational, because they cannot study every possible alternative but instead use simple rules of thumb to decide among choices.

_____ economics is value-free and relates to statements that can be refuted, such as "If A, then B." _____ economics involves people's values and typically uses the word *should*.

YOU ARE THERE
Why So Many Firms Are Incorporating Outside the United States

Willard Taylor, a tax attorney with Sullivan & Cromwell LLP, is contemplating the latest trend among U.S. firms that have been opting to become corporations. Until recently, it was unusual for U.S. family-owned companies or partnerships to "go public" by incorporating in another nation and selling shares of stock to residents of other nations. A decade ago, only about 1 percent of U.S. companies that became corporations did so outside the United States. During each of the past three years, however, more than 20 percent of U.S. firms choosing corporate structures have decided to incorporate abroad.

As a tax lawyer, Taylor pays close attention to tax rates assessed on corporations based abroad as well as those that apply to U.S. corporations. Most countries' governments, Taylor realizes, have slashed their corporate tax rates in recent years, whereas the U.S. corporate tax rate has remained unchanged at 35 percent. The result, Taylor notes, is that

the U.S. corporate tax rate is now second highest in the world, which provides a strong incentive to incorporate elsewhere. Taylor asks, "What are the pluses and minuses of being incorporated in the U.S. versus somewhere else?" He deduces that given the strong incentive provided by lower corporate tax rates abroad, "Very often, depending on what the business is, you'll conclude that there are no pluses to being in the United States."

Critical Thinking Questions

1. How have lower foreign tax rates affected the incentive to incorporate abroad?

2. What do you suppose has happened to federal collections of corporate taxes?

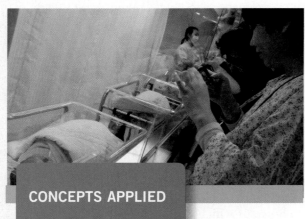

ISSUES & APPLICATIONS

Why So Many Tourists Have Been Giving Birth in Hong Kong

CONCEPTS APPLIED

▶ Rationality Assumption

▶ Incentives

▶ Self-Interest

There has been a significant upswing in the number of babies born in Hong Kong to mothers from China's mainland who officially are visiting Hong Kong as tourists. The number of births to this category of mothers rose from about 13,000 in 2004 to more than 40,000 in 2011—almost half of all Hong Kong births in the latter year. It turns out that this substantial increase in Hong Kong "tourist births" is consistent with the rationality assumption.

Incentives for a Mainland Resident to Desire a Hong Kong Birth

Why are so many more women who are officially in Hong Kong as tourists giving birth instead of visiting the city's sites? The answer is that mothers from mainland China are responding to incentives in a manner consistent with self-interested behavior.

Although the $5,000 price of hospital maternity care is several times higher in Hong Kong than in most hospitals on the mainland, the quality of care is considerably better in Hong Kong. In addition, the benefits for a child born in Hong Kong—and hence for the child's mother—are much greater than those available to a child born on the mainland. These benefits of a Hong Kong birth include twelve years of publicly provided education for the child at no explicit cost and close to zero out-of-pocket health care expenses. Furthermore, tourists who give birth in Hong Kong are exempt from China's "one-child policy," which limits women to bearing a single child. Such an exemption gives pregnant women desiring to raise a second child a strong incentive to "visit" Hong Kong.

Why the "Tourist" Fiction Has Been Rational for Hong Kong

Of course, nearly all tourist mothers who travel to Hong Kong to give birth actually plan to remain there. Why does the Hong Kong government permit these women to remain and to obtain publicly provided health care and education for their children? The answer to this second question also relates to the rationality assumption: The Hong Kong government is responding to incentives.

Since the 1990s, the birth rate among Hong Kong residents has declined by more than 33 percent. Early in the 2000s, government officials realized that unless more people immigrated to Hong Kong, its population would begin to shrink—perhaps eventually by about one-third. The city's leaders did not wish to open its borders to all who desired to immigrate, so they decided to permit more expectant mothers to enter under the tourist classification. Thus, it has been rational for the government of Hong Kong to allow numerous "tourist" births, just as it has been consistent with individual self-interest for "tourists" to give birth there.

For Critical Thinking

1. How have recent improvements in maternity care in mainland China likely affected the incentives to become a "tourist" mother in Hong Kong?

2. How are Hong Kong's incentives to allow "tourist" births affected by the fact that the city pays benefits to older residents from taxes paid by younger residents?

Web Resources

1. To contemplate the sources of pressures within Hong Kong to restrict tourist births, go to www.econtoday.com/chap01.

2. Read about the 2011 suspension of Hong Kong's tourist births at www.econtoday.com/chap01.

MyEconLab

For more questions on this chapter's Issues & Applications, go to MyEconLab. In the Study Plan for this chapter, select Section N: News.

MyEconLab

— WHAT YOU SHOULD KNOW ——————————————————— WHERE TO GO TO PRACTICE —

Answering the Three Basic Economic Questions Economics is the study of how individuals make choices to satisfy wants. Microeconomics is the study of decision making by individual households and firms, and macroeconomics is the study of nationwide phenomena such as inflation and unemployment. The three basic economic questions ask what and how much will be produced, how items will be produced, and for whom items will be produced. The two opposing answers to these questions are provided by the type of economic system: either centralized command and control or the price system.

incentives, 2
economics, 2
resources, 2
wants, 2
microeconomics, 3
macroeconomics, 3
aggregates, 3
economic system, 3

- MyEconLab Study Plans 1.1, 1.2, 1.3

Self-Interest in Economic Analysis Rational self-interest is the assumption that people never intentionally make decisions that would leave them worse off. Instead, they are motivated mainly by their self-interest, which can relate to monetary and nonmonetary goals, such as love, prestige, and helping others.

rationality
    assumption, 5

- MyEconLab Study Plan 1.3

Economics as a Science Economic models, or theories, are simplified representations of the real world. Economic models are never completely realistic because by definition they are simplifications using assumptions that are not directly testable. Nevertheless, economists can subject the predictions of economic theories to empirical tests in which real-world data are used to decide whether or not to reject the predictions.

models, or theories, 7
ceteris paribus
    assumption, 8
empirical, 9
behavioral
    economics, 9
bounded rationality, 10

- MyEconLab Study Plan 1.5

Positive and Normative Economics Positive economics deals with *what is*, whereas normative economics deals with *what ought to be*. Positive economic statements are of the "if . . . then" variety. They are descriptive and predictive. In contrast, statements embodying values are within the realm of normative economics, or how people think things ought to be.

positive economics, 10
normative
    economics, 10

- MyEconLab Study Plan 1.6

PROBLEMS

All problems are assignable in MyEconLab. Answers to odd-numbered problems appear at the back of the book.

1-1. Define economics. Explain briefly how the economic way of thinking—in terms of rational, self-interested people responding to incentives—relates to each of the following situations. (See pages 2, 5–6.)

  a. A student deciding whether to purchase a textbook for a particular class

  b. Government officials seeking more funding for mass transit through higher taxes

  c. A municipality taxing hotel guests to obtain funding for a new sports stadium

1-2. Some people claim that the "economic way of thinking" does not apply to issues such as health care. Explain how economics does apply to this issue by developing a "model" of an individual's choices. (See pages 7–8.)

1-3. Does the phrase "unlimited wants and limited resources" apply to both a low-income household and a middle-income household? Can the same phrase be applied to a very high-income household? (See page 2.)

1-4. In a single sentence, contrast microeconomics and macroeconomics. Next, categorize each of the following issues as a microeconomic issue, a macroeconomic issue, or not an economic issue. (See page 3.)

  a. The national unemployment rate

  b. The decision of a worker to work overtime or not

  c. A family's choice to have a baby

  d. The rate of growth of the money supply

  e. The national government's budget deficit

  f. A student's allocation of study time across two subjects

1-5. One of your classmates, Sally, is a hardworking student, serious about her classes, and conscientious about her grades. Sally is also involved, however, in volunteer activities and an extracurricular sport. Is Sally displaying rational behavior? Based on what you read in this chapter, construct an argument supporting the conclusion that she is. (See pages 5–7.)

1-6. Recently, a bank was trying to decide what fee to charge for "expedited payments"—payments that the bank would transmit extra-speedily to enable customers to avoid late fees on cable TV bills, electric bills, and the like. To try to determine what fee customers were willing to pay for expedited payments, the bank conducted a survey. It was able

to determine that many of the people surveyed already paid fees for expedited payment services that *exceeded* the maximum fees that they said they were willing to pay. How does the bank's finding relate to economists' traditional focus on what people do, rather than what they *say* they will do? (See page 9.)

1-7. Explain, in your own words, the rationality assumption, and contrast it with the assumption of bounded rationality proposed by adherents of behavioral economics. (See pages 5–6, 9–10.)

1-8. Why does the assumption of bounded rationality suggest that people might use rules of thumb to guide their decision making instead of considering every possible choice available to them? (See page 10.)

1-9. Under what circumstances might people appear to use rules of thumb, as suggested by the assumption of bounded rationality, even though they really are behaving in a manner suggested by the rationality assumption? (See page 10.)

1-10. For each of the following approaches that an economist might follow in examining a decision-making process, identify whether the approach relies on the rationality assumption or on the assumption of bounded rationality. (See page 10.)

  a. To make predictions about how many apps a person will download onto her tablet device, an economist presumes that the individual faces limitations that make it impossible for her to examine every possible choice among relevant apps.

  b. In evaluating the price that an individual will be willing to pay for a given quantity of a particular type of health care service, a researcher assumes that the person considers all relevant health care options in pursuit of his own long-term satisfaction with resulting health outcomes.

  c. To determine the amount of time that a person will decide to devote to watching online videos each week, an economist makes the assumption that the individual will feel overwhelmed by the sheer volume of videos available online and will respond by using a rule of thumb.

1-11. For each of the following approaches that an economist might follow in examining a decision-making process, identify whether the approach relies on the rationality assumption or on the assumption of bounded rationality. (See page 10.)

  a. An economic study of the number of online searches that individuals conduct before selecting a particular item to purchase online presumes that people are interested only in their own satisfaction, pursue their ultimate objectives, and consider every relevant option.

b. An economist seeking to predict the effect that an increase in a state's sales tax rate will have on consumers' purchases of goods and services presumes that people are limited in their ability to process information about how the tax-rate increase will influence the after-tax prices those consumers will pay.

c. To evaluate the impact of an increase in the range of choices that an individual confronts when deciding among devices for accessing the Internet, an economic researcher makes the assumption that the individual is unable to take into account every new Internet-access option available to her.

1-12. Which of the following predictions appear(s) to follow from a model based on the assumption that rational, self-interested individuals respond to incentives? (See pages 6–7.)

a. For every 10 exam points Myrna must earn in order to pass her economics course and meet her graduation requirements, she will study one additional hour for her economics test next week.

b. A coin toss will best predict Leonardo's decision about whether to purchase an expensive business suit or an inexpensive casual outfit to wear next week when he interviews for a high-paying job he is seeking.

c. Celeste, who uses earnings from her regularly scheduled hours of part-time work to pay for her room and board at college, will decide to purchase and download a newly released video this week only if she is able to work two additional hours.

1-13. Consider two models for estimating, in advance of an election, the shares of votes that will go to rival candidates. According to one model, pollsters' surveys of a randomly chosen set of registered voters before an election can be used to forecast the percentage of votes that each candidate will receive. This first model relies on the assumption that unpaid survey respondents will give truthful responses about how they will vote and that they will actually cast a ballot in the election. The other model uses prices of financial assets (legally binding

IOUs) issued by the Iowa Electronic Markets, operated by the University of Iowa, to predict electoral outcomes. The final payments received by owners of these assets, which can be bought or sold during the weeks and days preceding an election, depend on the shares of votes the candidates actually end up receiving. This second model assumes that owners of these assets wish to earn the highest possible returns, and it predicts that the market prices of these assets provide an indication of the percentage of votes that each candidate will actually receive on the day of the election. (See pages 8–9.)

a. Which of these two models for forecasting electoral results is more firmly based on the rationality assumption of economics?

b. How would an economist evaluate which is the better model for forecasting electoral outcomes?

1-14. Write a sentence contrasting positive and normative economic analysis. (See pages 10–11.)

1-15. Based on your answer to Problem 1–14, categorize each of the following conclusions as being the result of positive analysis or normative analysis.

a. A higher minimum wage will reduce employment opportunities for minimum wage workers.

b. Increasing the earnings of minimum wage employees is desirable, and raising the minimum wage is the best way to accomplish this.

c. Everyone should enjoy open access to health care at no explicit charge.

d. Heath care subsidies will increase the consumption of health care.

1-16. Consider the following statements, based on a positive economic analysis that assumes that all other things remain constant. For each, list one other thing that might change and thus offset the outcome stated. (See pages 8, 10.)

a. Increased demand for laptop computers will drive up their price.

b. Falling gasoline prices will result in additional vacation travel.

c. A reduction of income tax rates will result in more people working.

ECONOMICS ON THE NET

The Usefulness of Studying Economics This application helps you see how accomplished people benefited from their study of economics. It also explores ways in which these people feel others of all walks of life can gain from learning more about the economics field.

Title: How Taking an Economics Course Can Lead to Becoming an Economist

Navigation: Go to **www.econtoday.com/chap01** to visit the Federal Reserve Bank of Minneapolis publication, *The Region*. Select the last article of the issue, "Economists in *The Region* on Their Student Experiences and the Need for Economic Literacy."

Application Read the interviews of the six economists, and answer the following questions.

1. Based on your reading, which economists do you think other economists regard as influential? What educational institutions do you think are the most influential in economics?

2. Which economists do you think were attracted to microeconomics and which to macroeconomics?

For Group Study and Analysis Divide the class into three groups, and assign the groups the Blinder, Yellen, and Rivlin interviews. Have each group use the content of its assigned interview to develop a statement explaining why the study of economics is important, regardless of a student's chosen major.

ANSWERS TO QUICK QUIZZES

p. 7: (i) wants . . . unlimited; (ii) Microeconomics . . . macroeconomics; (iii) centralized command and control . . . price system; (iv) rationality

p. 11: (i) model . . . theory . . . model; (ii) *ceteris paribus*; (iii) Behavioral . . . bounded rationality; (iv) Positive . . . Normative

APPENDIX A

Reading and Working with Graphs

A graph is a visual representation of the relationship between variables. In this appendix, we'll deal with just two variables: an **independent variable,** which can change in value freely, and a **dependent variable,** which changes as a result of changes in the value of the independent variable. For example, even if nothing else is changing in your life, your weight depends on your intake of calories. The independent variable is caloric intake, and the dependent variable is weight.

A table is a list of numerical values showing the relationship between two (or more) variables. Any table can be converted into a graph, which is a visual representation of that list. Once you understand how a table can be converted to a graph, you will understand what graphs are and how to construct and use them.

Consider a practical example. A conservationist may try to convince you that driving at lower highway speeds will help you conserve gas. Table A-1 shows the relationship between speed—the independent variable—and the distance you can go on a gallon of gas at that speed—the dependent variable. This table does show a pattern. As the data in the first column get larger in value, the data in the second column get smaller.

Now let's take a look at the different ways in which variables can be related.

Direct and Inverse Relationships

Two variables can be related in different ways, some simple, others more complex. For example, a person's weight and height are often related. If we measured the height and weight of thousands of people, we would surely find that taller people tend to weigh more than shorter people. That is, we would discover that there is a **direct relationship** between height and weight. By this we simply mean that an *increase* in one variable is usually associated with an *increase* in the related variable. This can easily be seen in panel (a) of Figure A-1 below.

Let's look at another simple way in which two variables can be related. Much evidence indicates that as the price of a specific commodity rises, the amount purchased decreases—there is an **inverse relationship** between the variable's price per unit and quantity purchased. Such a relationship indicates that for higher and higher prices, smaller and smaller quantities will be purchased. We see this relationship in panel (b) of Figure A-1.

Independent variable
A variable whose value is determined independently of, or outside, the equation under study.

Dependent variable
A variable whose value changes according to changes in the value of one or more independent variables.

TABLE A-1

Gas Mileage as a Function of Driving Speed

Miles per Hour	Miles per Gallon
45	25
50	24
55	23
60	21
65	19
70	16
75	13

Direct relationship
A relationship between two variables that is positive, meaning that an increase in one variable is associated with an increase in the other and a decrease in one variable is associated with a decrease in the other.

Inverse relationship
A relationship between two variables that is negative, meaning that an increase in one variable is associated with a decrease in the other and a decrease in one variable is associated with an increase in the other.

FIGURE A-1

Direct and Inverse Relationships

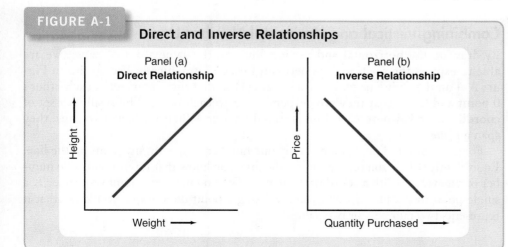

Panel (a)
Direct Relationship
Height / Weight →

Panel (b)
Inverse Relationship
Price / Quantity Purchased →

FIGURE A-2

Horizontal Number Line

Number line
A line that can be divided into segments of equal length, each associated with a number.

FIGURE A-3

Vertical Number Line

Constructing a Graph

Let us now examine how to construct a graph to illustrate a relationship between two variables.

A Number Line

The first step is to become familiar with what is called a **number line.** One is shown in Figure A-2 above. You should know two things about it:

1. The points on the line divide the line into equal segments.

2. The numbers associated with the points on the line increase in value from left to right. Saying it the other way around, the numbers decrease in value from right to left. However you say it, what you're describing is formally called an *ordered set of points.*

On the number line, we have shown the line segments—that is, the distance from 0 to 10 or the distance between 30 and 40. They all appear to be equal and, indeed, are each equal to $\frac{1}{2}$ inch. When we use a distance to represent a quantity, such as barrels of oil, graphically, we are *scaling* the number line. In the example shown, the distance between 0 and 10 might represent 10 barrels of oil, or the distance from 0 to 40 might represent 40 barrels. Of course, the scale may differ on different number lines. For example, a distance of 1 inch could represent 10 units on one number line but 5,000 units on another. Notice that on our number line, points to the left of 0 correspond to negative numbers and points to the right of 0 correspond to positive numbers.

Of course, we can also construct a vertical number line. Consider the one in Figure A-3 alongside. As we move up this vertical number line, the numbers increase in value; conversely, as we descend, they decrease in value. Below 0 the numbers are negative, and above 0 the numbers are positive. And as on the horizontal number line, all the line segments are equal. This line is divided into segments such that the distance between –2 and –1 is the same as the distance between 0 and 1.

Combining Vertical and Horizontal Number Lines

By drawing the horizontal and vertical lines on the same sheet of paper, we are able to express the relationships between variables graphically. We do this in Figure A-4 on the facing page. We draw them (1) so that they intersect at each other's 0 point and (2) so that they are perpendicular to each other. The result is a set of coordinate axes, where each line is called an *axis.* When we have two axes, they span a *plane.*

For one number line, you need only one number to specify any point on the line. Equivalently, when you see a point on the line, you know that it represents one number or one value. With a coordinate value system, you need two numbers to specify a single point in the plane; when you see a single point on a graph, you know that it represents two numbers or two values.

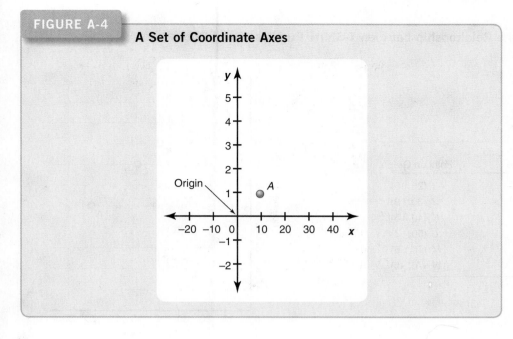

FIGURE A-4

A Set of Coordinate Axes

The basic things that you should know about a coordinate number system are that the vertical number line is referred to as the **y axis,** the horizontal number line is referred to as the **x axis,** and the point of intersection of the two lines is referred to as the **origin.**

Any point such as A in Figure A-4 above represents two numbers—a value of x and a value of y. But we know more than that: We also know that point A represents a positive value of y because it is above the x axis, and we know that it represents a positive value of x because it is to the right of the y axis.

Point A represents a "paired observation" of the variables x and y; in particular, in Figure A-4, A represents an observation of the pair of values $x = 10$ and $y = 1$. Every point in the coordinate system corresponds to a paired observation of x and y, which can be simply written (x, y)—the x value is always specified first and then the y value. When we give the values associated with the position of point A in the coordinate number system, we are in effect giving the coordinates of that point. A's coordinates are $x = 10$, $y = 1$, or $(10, 1)$.

y axis
The vertical axis in a graph.

x axis
The horizontal axis in a graph.

Origin
The intersection of the y axis and the x axis in a graph.

Graphing Numbers in a Table

Consider Table A-2 alongside. Column 1 shows different prices for T-shirts, and column 2 gives the number of T-shirts purchased per week at these prices. Notice the pattern of these numbers. As the price of T-shirts falls, the number of T-shirts purchased per week increases. Therefore, an inverse relationship exists between these two variables, and as soon as we represent it on a graph, you will be able to see the relationship. We can graph this relationship using a coordinate number system—a vertical and horizontal number line for each of these two variables. Such a graph is shown in panel (b) of Figure A-5 on the following page.

In economics, it is conventional to put dollar values on the y axis and quantities on the horizontal axis. We therefore construct a vertical number line for price and a horizontal number line, the x axis, for quantity of T-shirts purchased per week. The resulting coordinate system allows the plotting of each of the paired observation points. In panel (a), we repeat Table A-2, with a column added expressing these points in paired-data (x, y) form. For example, point J is the paired observation $(30, 9)$. It indicates that when the price of a T-shirt is $9, 30 will be purchased per week.

TABLE A-2

T-Shirts Purchased

(1) Price of T-Shirts	(2) Number of T-Shirts Purchased per Week
$10	20
9	30
8	40
7	50
6	60
5	70

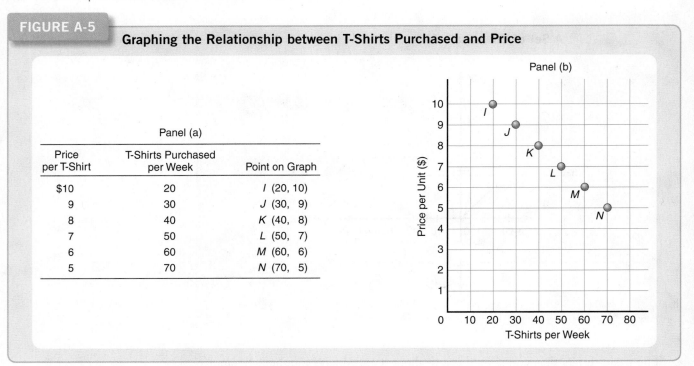

FIGURE A-5

Graphing the Relationship between T-Shirts Purchased and Price

Panel (a)

Price per T-Shirt	T-Shirts Purchased per Week	Point on Graph
$10	20	I (20, 10)
9	30	J (30, 9)
8	40	K (40, 8)
7	50	L (50, 7)
6	60	M (60, 6)
5	70	N (70, 5)

If it were possible to sell parts of a T-shirt ($\frac{1}{2}$ or $\frac{1}{20}$ of a shirt), we would have observations at every possible price. That is, we would be able to connect our paired observations, represented as lettered points. Let's assume that we can make T-shirts perfectly divisible so that the linear relationship shown in Figure A-5 also holds for fractions of dollars and T-shirts. We would then have a line that connects these points, as shown in the graph in Figure A-6 below.

In short, we have now represented the data from the table in the form of a graph. Note that an inverse relationship between two variables shows up on a graph as a line or curve that slopes *downward* from left to right. (You might as well get used to the idea that economists call a straight line a "curve" even though it may not curve at all. Economists' data frequently turn out to be curves, so they refer to everything represented graphically, even straight lines, as curves.)

FIGURE A-6

Connecting the Observation Points

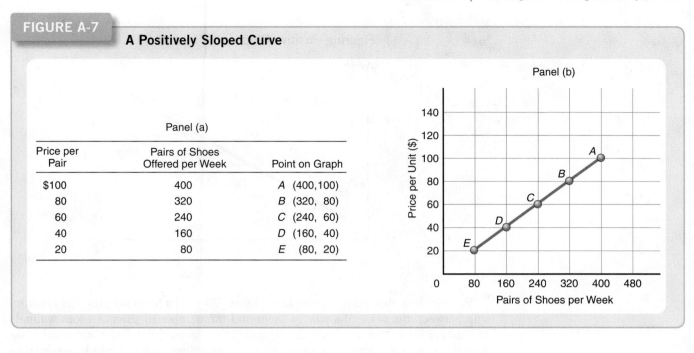

FIGURE A-7

A Positively Sloped Curve

Panel (a)

Price per Pair	Pairs of Shoes Offered per Week	Point on Graph
$100	400	A (400,100)
80	320	B (320, 80)
60	240	C (240, 60)
40	160	D (160, 40)
20	80	E (80, 20)

The Slope of a Line (A Linear Curve)

An important property of a curve represented on a graph is its *slope*. Consider Figure A-7 above, which represents the quantities of shoes per week that a seller is willing to offer at different prices. Note that in panel (a) of Figure A-7, as in Figure A-5 on page 20, we have expressed the coordinates of the points in parentheses in paired-data form.

The **slope** of a line is defined as the change in the y values divided by the corresponding change in the x values as we move along the line. Let's move from point E to point D in panel (b) of Figure A-7. As we move, we note that the change in the y values, which is the change in price, is $+20$, because we have moved from a price of $20 to a price of $40 per pair. As we move from E to D, the change in the x values is $+80$; the number of pairs of shoes willingly offered per week rises from 80 to 160 pairs. The slope, calculated as a change in the y values divided by the change in the x values, is therefore

Slope
The change in the y value divided by the corresponding change in the x value of a curve; the "incline" of the curve.

$$\frac{20}{80} = \frac{1}{4}$$

It may be helpful for you to think of slope as a "rise" (movement in the vertical direction) over a "run" (movement in the horizontal direction). We show this abstractly in Figure A-8 on the following page. The slope is the amount of rise divided by the amount of run. In the example in Figure A-8, and of course in Figure A-7 above, the amount of rise is positive and so is the amount of run. That's because it's a direct relationship. We show an inverse relationship in Figure A-9 on the next page. The slope is still equal to the rise divided by the run, but in this case the rise and the run have opposite signs because the curve slopes downward. That means that the slope is negative and that we are dealing with an inverse relationship.

Now let's calculate the slope for a different part of the curve in panel (b) of Figure A-7. We will find the slope as we move from point B to point A. Again, we note that the slope, or rise over run, from B to A equals

$$\frac{20}{80} = \frac{1}{4}$$

A specific property of a straight line is that its slope is the same between any two points. In other words, the slope is constant at all points on a straight line in a graph.

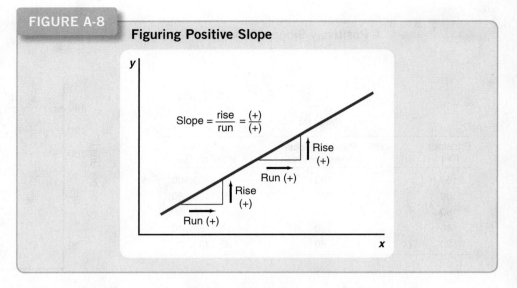

FIGURE A-8

Figuring Positive Slope

We conclude that for our example in Figure A-7 on the previous page, the relationship between the price of a pair of shoes and the number of pairs of shoes willingly offered per week is *linear*, which simply means "in a straight line," and our calculations indicate a constant slope. Moreover, we calculate a direct relationship between these two variables, which turns out to be an upward-sloping (from left to right) curve. Upward-sloping curves have positive slopes—in this case, the slope is $+\frac{1}{4}$.

We know that an inverse relationship between two variables is a downward-sloping curve—rise over run will be negative because the rise and run have opposite signs, as shown in Figure A-9 below. When we see a negative slope, we know that increases in one variable are associated with decreases in the other. Therefore, we say that downward-sloping curves have negative slopes. Can you verify that the slope of the graph representing the relationship between T-shirt prices and the quantity of T-shirts purchased per week in Figure A-6 on page 20 is $-\frac{1}{10}$?

Slopes of Nonlinear Curves

The graph presented in Figure A-10 on the facing page indicates a *nonlinear* relationship between two variables, total profits and output per unit of time. Inspection of this graph indicates that, at first, increases in output lead to increases in total profits; that is, total profits rise as output increases. But beyond some output level, further increases in output cause decreases in total profits.

FIGURE A-9

Figuring Negative Slope

FIGURE A-10

The Slope of a Nonlinear Curve

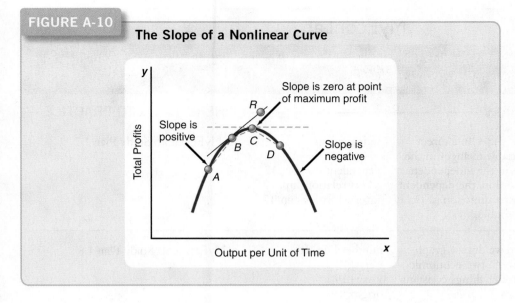

Can you see how this curve rises at first, reaches a peak at point *C*, and then falls? This curve relating total profits to output levels appears mountain-shaped.

Considering that this curve is nonlinear (it is obviously not a straight line), should we expect a constant slope when we compute changes in *y* divided by corresponding changes in *x* in moving from one point to another? A quick inspection, even without specific numbers, should lead us to conclude that the slopes of lines joining different points in this curve, such as between *A* and *B*, *B* and *C*, or *C* and *D*, will *not* be the same. The curve slopes upward (in a positive direction) for some values and downward (in a negative direction) for other values. In fact, the slope of the line between any two points on this curve will be different from the slope of the line between any two other points. Each slope will be different as we move along the curve.

Instead of using a line between two points to discuss slope, mathematicians and economists prefer to discuss the slope *at a particular point*. The slope at a point on the curve, such as point *B* in the graph in Figure A-10 above, is the slope of a line tangent to that point. A tangent line is a straight line that touches a curve at only one point. For example, it might be helpful to think of the tangent at *B* as the straight line that just "kisses" the curve at point *B*.

To calculate the slope of a tangent line, you need to have some additional information besides the two values of the point of tangency. For example, in Figure A-10, if we knew that the point *R* also lay on the tangent line and we knew the two values of that point, we could calculate the slope of the tangent line. We could calculate rise over run between points *B* and *R*, and the result would be the slope of the line tangent to the one point *B* on the curve.

MyEconLab

Here is what you should know after reading this appendix. MyEconLab will help you identify what you know, and where to go when you need to practice.

— WHAT YOU SHOULD KNOW —		— WHERE TO GO TO PRACTICE —
Direct and Inverse Relationships In a direct relationship, a dependent variable changes in the same direction as the change in the independent variable. In an inverse relationship, the dependent variable changes in the opposite direction of the change in the independent variable.	independent variable, 17 dependent variable, 17 direct relationship, 17 inverse relationship, 17	• MyEconLab Study Plan 1.7
Constructing a Graph When we draw a graph showing the relationship between two economic variables, we are holding all other things constant (the Latin term for which is *ceteris paribus*).	number line, 18 *y* axis, 19 *x* axis, 19 origin, 19	• MyEconLab Study Plan 1.8
Graphing Numbers We obtain a set of coordinates by putting vertical and horizontal number lines together. The vertical line is called the *y* axis; the horizontal line, the *x* axis.		• MyEconLab Study Plan 1.9
The Slope of a Linear Curve The slope of any linear (straight-line) curve is the change in the *y* values divided by the corresponding change in the *x* values as we move along the line. Otherwise stated, the slope is calculated as the amount of rise over the amount of run, where rise is movement in the vertical direction and run is movement in the horizontal direction.	slope, 21 **Key Figures** Figure A-8, 22 Figure A-9, 22	• MyEconLab Study Plan 1.10 • Animated Figures A-8, A-9
The Slope of a Nonlinear Curve The slope of a nonlinear curve changes; it is positive when the curve is rising and negative when the curve is falling. At a maximum or minimum point, the slope of the nonlinear curve is zero.	**Key Figure** Figure A-10, 23	• MyEconLab Study Plan 1.10 • Animated Figure A-10

Log in to MyEconLab, take an appendix test, and get a personalized Study Plan that tells you which concepts you understand and which ones you need to review. From there, MyEconLab will give you further practice, tutorials, animations, videos, and guided solutions. For more information, visit www.myeconlab.com

PROBLEMS

All problems are assignable in MyEconLab. *Answers to odd-numbered problems appear at the back of the book.*

A-1. Explain which is the independent variable and which is the dependent variable for each of the following examples. (See page 17.)

    a. Once you determine the price of a notebook at the college bookstore, you will decide how many notebooks to buy.

    b. You will decide how many credit hours to register for this semester once the university tells you how many work-study hours you will be assigned.

    c. You anticipate earning a higher grade on your next economics exam because you studied more hours in the weeks preceding the exam.

A-2. For each of the following items, state whether a direct or an inverse relationship is likely to exist. (See page 17.)

    a. The number of hours you study for an exam and your exam score

    b. The price of pizza and the quantity purchased

    c. The number of games the university basketball team won last year and the number of season tickets sold this year

A-3. Review Figure A-4 on page 19, and then state whether each of the following paired observations is on, above, or below the *x* axis and on, to the left of, or to the right of the *y* axis. (See page 19.)

    a. $(-10, 4)$

    b. $(20, -2)$

    c. $(10, 0)$

A-4. State whether each of the following functions specifies a direct or an inverse relationship. (See page 17.)

    a. $y = 5x$

    b. $y = 10 - 2x$

    c. $y = 3 + x$

    d. $y = -3x$

A-5. Given the function $y = 5x$, complete the following schedule and plot the curve. (See page 20.)

y	x
	−4
	−2
	0
	2
	4

A-6. Given the function $y = 8 - 2x$, complete the following schedule and plot the curve. (See page 21.)

y	x
	−4
	−2
	0
	2
	4

A-7. Calculate the slope of the function you graphed in Problem A-5. (See page 21.)

A-8. Calculate the slope of the function you graphed in Problem A-6. (See page 21.)

2

Scarcity and the World of Trade-Offs

The airliner in which you have been flying will land about an hour earlier than indicated by your formal travel itinerary. As the plane taxis to the gate, you contemplate how to use that extra hour. You might eat a more leisurely dinner at a nicer restaurant, grab an extra hour of sleep, or engage in additional income-generating work. Now you find out the bad news: No empty gates are available for your plane, and you will have to wait at least one hour to exit the plane. Nonetheless, the airline can now report your flight as "on time" because it touched down on the ground earlier than officially scheduled. The result is that you must remain on the plane for the hour you thought would be available for another, most-valued use off the plane. Thus, you will have to give up the alternative use of that hour after all. As you will learn in this chapter, you have incurred an *opportunity cost.*

the U.S. Department of Commerce recently published a report concluding that each year, U.S. consumers spend about $1.2 trillion, or more than 11 percent of total consumer expenditures, on "non-essential items"? Included among these items were candy, gambling, jewelry, liquor, and pleasure boats. During the weeks that followed, media commentators filled newspaper pages, TV airtime, and the blogosphere with laments about U.S. residents making "poor economic decisions" by paying prices that are "too high" to buy goods and services that "they don't really need."

You will discover in this chapter that economists do not rely on the particularly subjective concept of "needs" to explain people's decisions. What influences individuals' economic choices are their *wants*, which, you learned in the previous chapter, are all of the items that people would purchase if they had unlimited income. In reality, of course, people's incomes *are* limited. Irrespective of normative judgments by U.S. government officials to classify some items as "non-essential," *all* of the items among which consumers allocate their limited incomes are *scarce* goods available only at prices greater than zero.

Scarcity

Whenever individuals or communities cannot obtain everything they desire simultaneously, they must make choices. Choices occur because of *scarcity*. **Scarcity** is the most basic concept in all of economics. Scarcity means that we do not ever have enough of everything, including time, to satisfy our *every* desire. Scarcity exists because human wants always exceed what can be produced with the limited resources and time that nature makes available.

Scarcity
A situation in which the ingredients for producing the things that people desire are insufficient to satisfy all wants at a zero price.

What Scarcity Is Not

Scarcity is not a shortage. After a hurricane hits and cuts off supplies to a community, TV newscasts often show people standing in line to get minimum amounts of cooking fuel and food. A news commentator might say that the line is caused by the "scarcity" of these products. But cooking fuel and food are always scarce—we cannot obtain all that we want at a zero price. Therefore, do not confuse the concept of scarcity, which is general and all-encompassing, with the concept of shortages as evidenced by people waiting in line to obtain a particular product.

Scarcity is not the same thing as poverty. Scarcity occurs among the poor and among the rich. Even the richest person on earth faces scarcity. For instance, even the world's richest person has only limited time available. Low income levels do not create more scarcity. High income levels do not create less scarcity.

Scarcity is a fact of life, like gravity. And just as physicists did not invent gravity, economists did not invent scarcity—it existed well before the first economist ever lived. It has existed at all times in the past and will exist at all times in the future.

Scarcity and Resources

Scarcity exists because resources are insufficient to satisfy our every desire. Resources are the inputs used in the production of the things that we want. **Production** can be defined as virtually any activity that results in the conversion of resources into products that can be used in consumption. Production includes delivering items from one part of the country to another. It includes taking ice from an ice tray to put it in your soft-drink glass. The resources used in production are called *factors of production*, and some economists use the terms *resources* and *factors of production* interchangeably. The total quantity of all resources that an economy has at any one time determines what that economy can produce.

Factors of production can be classified in many ways. Here is one such classification:

1. *Land*. **Land** encompasses all the nonhuman gifts of nature, including timber, water, fish, minerals, and the original fertility of land. It is often called the *natural resource*.

2. *Labor*. **Labor** is the *human resource*, which includes productive contributions made by individuals who work, such as Web page designers, iPad applications creators, and professional football players.

Production
Any activity that results in the conversion of resources into products that can be used in consumption.

Land
The natural resources that are available from nature. Land as a resource includes location, original fertility and mineral deposits, topography, climate, water, and vegetation.

Labor
Productive contributions of humans who work.

How has Japan's energy policy reduced the productive contributions of many individuals who provide labor?

INTERNATIONAL POLICY EXAMPLE

A Lower Productive Contribution of Sweltering Japanese Labor

During the past few years, the Japanese government has established rules aimed at reducing the nation's emissions of carbon dioxide (CO_2) by nearly 3 million tons each summer. To attain this goal, Japan's government has effectively declared war on air conditioning. The government has mandated that thermostats in all government offices be set no lower than 82 degrees during the months spanning June to September. Private Japanese businesses have followed suit with a "Cool Biz" program establishing 82 degrees as the "new office norm" for indoor temperatures.

Of course, 82 degrees is above the temperature at which people in enclosed spaces are most effective at producing goods and services. Consequently, the productive contribution of Japanese labor now declines every summer.

FOR CRITICAL THINKING
What do you suppose happened to the productive contribution of labor when Japan's government temporarily raised the summer target office temperature to 86 degrees?

Physical capital
All manufactured resources, including buildings, equipment, machines, and improvements to land that are used for production.

Human capital
The accumulated training and education of workers.

Entrepreneurship
The component of human resources that performs the functions of raising capital; organizing, managing, and assembling other factors of production; making basic business policy decisions; and taking risks.

3. *Physical capital.* **Physical capital** consists of the factories and equipment used in production. It also includes improvements to natural resources, such as irrigation ditches.

4. *Human capital.* **Human capital** is the economic characterization of the education and training of workers. How much the nation produces depends not only on how many hours people work but also on how productive they are, and that in turn depends in part on education and training. To become more educated, individuals have to devote time and resources, just as a business has to devote resources if it wants to increase its physical capital. Whenever a worker's skills increase, human capital has been improved.

5. *Entrepreneurship.* **Entrepreneurship** (actually a subdivision of labor) is the component of human resources that performs the functions of organizing, managing, and assembling the other factors of production to create and operate business ventures. Entrepreneurship also encompasses taking risks that involve the possibility of losing large sums of wealth. It includes new methods of engaging in common activities and generally experimenting with any type of new thinking that could lead to making more income. Without entrepreneurship, hardly any business organizations could continue to operate.

Goods versus Economic Goods

Goods are defined as all things from which individuals derive satisfaction or happiness. Goods therefore include air to breathe and the beauty of a sunset as well as food, cars, and iPhones.

Economic goods are a subset of all goods—they are scarce goods, about which we must constantly make decisions regarding their best use. By definition, the desired quantity of an economic good exceeds the amount that is available at a zero price. Almost every example we use in economics concerns economic goods—cars, Blu-ray disc players, computers, socks, baseball bats, and corn. Weeds are a good example of *bads*—goods for which the desired quantity is much *less* than what nature provides at a zero price.

Sometimes you will see references to "goods and services." **Services** are tasks that are performed by individuals, often for someone else, such as laundry, Internet access, hospital care, restaurant meal preparation, car polishing, psychological counseling, and teaching. One way of looking at services is to think of them as *intangible goods*.

Goods
All things from which individuals derive satisfaction or happiness.

Economic goods
Goods that are scarce, for which the quantity demanded exceeds the quantity supplied at a zero price.

Services
Mental or physical labor or assistance purchased by consumers. Examples are the assistance of physicians, lawyers, dentists, repair personnel, housecleaners, educators, retailers, and wholesalers; items purchased or used by consumers that do not have physical characteristics.

Wants and Needs

Wants are not the same as needs. Indeed, from the economist's point of view, the term *needs* is objectively undefinable. When someone says, "I need some new clothes," there is no way to know whether that person is stating a vague wish, a want, or a lifesaving requirement. If the individual making the statement were dying of exposure in a northern country during the winter, we might conclude that indeed the person does need clothes—perhaps not new ones, but at least some articles of warm clothing. Typically, however, the term *need* is used very casually in conversation. What people mean, usually, is that they desire something that they do not currently have.

Humans have unlimited wants. Just imagine that every single material want that you might have was satisfied. You could have all of the clothes, cars, houses, downloadable movies, yachts, and other items that you want. Does that mean that nothing else could add to your total level of happiness? Undoubtedly, you might continue to think of new goods and services that you could obtain, particularly as they came to market. You would also still be lacking in fulfilling all of your wants for compassion, friendship, love, affection, prestige, musical abilities, sports abilities, and the like.

In reality, every individual has competing wants but cannot satisfy all of them, given limited resources. This is the reality of scarcity. Each person must therefore make choices. Whenever a choice is made to produce or buy something, something else that is also desired is not produced or not purchased. In other words, in a world of scarcity, every want that ends up being satisfied causes one or more other wants to remain unsatisfied or to be forfeited.

QUICK QUIZ See page 47 for the answers. Review concepts from this section in MyEconLab.

_____ is the situation in which human wants always exceed what can be produced with the limited resources and time that nature makes available.

We use scarce resources, such as_____, _____, _____ and _____ capital, and _____, to produce economic goods—goods that are desired but are not directly obtainable from nature to the extent demanded or desired at a zero price.

_____ are unlimited. They include all material desires and all nonmaterial desires, such as love, affection, power, and prestige.

The concept of _____ is difficult to define objectively for every person. Consequently, we simply consider every person's wants to be unlimited. In a world of **scarcity**, satisfaction of one want necessarily means nonsatisfaction of one or more other wants.

Scarcity, Choice, and Opportunity Cost

The natural fact of scarcity implies that we must make choices. One of the most important results of this fact is that every choice made means that some opportunity must be sacrificed. Every choice involves giving up an opportunity to produce or consume something else.

Valuing Forgone Alternatives

Consider a practical example. Every choice you make to study economics for one more hour requires that you give up the opportunity to choose to engage in any one of the following activities: study more of another subject, listen to music, sleep, browse at a local store, read a novel, or work out at the gym. The most highly valued of these opportunities is forgone if you choose to study economics an additional hour.

Because there were so many alternatives from which to choose, how could you determine the value of what you gave up to engage in that extra hour of studying economics? First of all, no one else can tell you the answer because only *you* can put a value on the alternatives forgone. Only you know the value of another hour of sleep or of an hour looking for the latest digital music downloads—whatever one activity *you* would have chosen if you had not opted to study economics for that hour. That means that only you can determine the highest-valued, next-best alternative that you had to sacrifice in order to study economics one more hour. Only you can determine the value of the next-best alternative.

Opportunity Cost

Opportunity cost
The highest-valued, next-best alternative that must be sacrificed to obtain something or to satisfy a want.

The value of the next-best alternative is called **opportunity cost.** The opportunity cost of any action is the value of what is given up—the next-highest-ranked alternative—because a choice was made. What is important is the choice that you would have made if you hadn't studied one more hour. Your opportunity cost is the *next-highest-ranked* alternative, not *all* alternatives.

> ### *In economics, cost is always a forgone opportunity.*

YOU ARE THERE

To consider why perceived opportunity costs induce residents of South Korea to work more hours each year than workers in many other countries and, hence, take fewer vacation days, read **The Opportunity Cost of Vacation Time in South Korea** on page 41.

One way to think about opportunity cost is to understand that when you choose to do something, you lose something else. What you lose is being able to engage in your next-highest-valued alternative. The cost of your chosen alternative is what you lose, which is by definition your next-highest-valued alternative. This is your opportunity cost.

What has a decrease in the daily amount of time spent working by a typical U.S. resident revealed about the opportunity cost of approximately a quarter hour of time?

EXAMPLE

The Opportunity Cost of 17 Minutes of Labor in the United States

In the aftermath of the significant economic downturn between 2007 and 2009, the average U.S. resident aged 15 years or older found herself working about 17 fewer minutes per day. The U.S. Labor Department has determined that there were no changes in the amounts of time that the typical resident devoted to engaging in pursuits such as education, volunteering, exercise, or religious activities. Instead, the amount of time per day that the average U.S. resident spent watching TV rose by nearly 12 minutes, and the amount of time she spent sleeping increased by more than

5 minutes. Hence, the implied opportunity cost of the 17 minutes per day that previously had been spent working is the value of passive leisure time that otherwise would have been devoted to TV viewing and sleeping.

FOR CRITICAL THINKING
For someone who could otherwise be working but decides to devote an extra hour per day to obtaining education, what is the opportunity cost of that hour of learning?

The World of Trade-Offs

Whenever you engage in any activity using any resource, even time, you are *trading off* the use of that resource for one or more alternative uses. The extent of the trade-off is represented by the opportunity cost. The opportunity cost of studying economics has already been mentioned—it is the value of the next-best alternative. When you think of *any* alternative, you are thinking of trade-offs.

Let's consider a hypothetical example of a trade-off between the results of spending time studying economics and mathematics. For the sake of this argument, we will assume that additional time studying either economics or mathematics will lead to a higher grade in the subject to which additional study time is allocated. One of the best ways to examine this trade-off is with a graph. (If you would like a refresher on graphical techniques, study Appendix A at the end of Chapter 1 before going on.)

Graphical Analysis

In Figure 2-1 on the facing page, the expected grade in mathematics is measured on the vertical axis of the graph, and the expected grade in economics is measured on the horizontal axis. We simplify the world and assume that you have a maximum of

FIGURE 2-1

Production Possibilities Curve for Grades in Mathematics and Economics (Trade-Offs)

We assume that only 12 hours can be spent per week on studying. If the student is at point x, equal time (6 hours a week) is spent on both courses, and equal grades of C will be received. If a higher grade in economics is desired, the student may go to point y, thereby receiving a B in economics but a D in mathematics. At point y, 3 hours are spent on mathematics and 9 hours on economics.

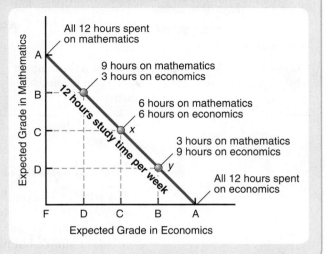

The Production Possibilities Curve (PPC)

The graph in Figure 2-1 above illustrates the relationship between the possible results that can be produced in each of two activities, depending on how much time you choose to devote to each activity. This graph shows a representation of a **production possibilities curve (PPC).**

Consider that you are producing a grade in economics when you study economics and a grade in mathematics when you study mathematics. Then the line that goes from A on one axis to A on the other axis therefore becomes a production possibilities curve. It is defined as the maximum quantity of one good or service that can be produced, given that a specific quantity of another is produced. It is a curve that shows the possibilities available for increasing the output of one good or service by reducing the amount of another. In the example in Figure 2-1, your time for studying was limited to 12 hours per week. The two possible outputs were your grade in mathematics and your grade in economics. The particular production possibilities curve presented in Figure 2-1 is a graphical representation of the opportunity cost of studying one more hour in one subject. It is a *straight-line production possibilities curve*, which is a special case. (The more general case will be discussed next.)

If you decide to be at point x in Figure 2-1, you will devote 6 hours of study time to mathematics and 6 hours to economics. The expected grade in each course will be a C. If you are more interested in getting a B in economics, you will go to point y on the production possibilities curve, spending only 3 hours on mathematics but 9 hours on economics. Your expected grade in mathematics will then drop from a C to a D.

Note that these trade-offs between expected grades in mathematics and economics are the result of *holding constant* total study time as well as all other factors that might influence your ability to learn, such as computerized study aids. Quite clearly, if you were able to spend more total time studying, it would be possible to have higher grades in both economics and mathematics. In that case, however, we would no longer be on the specific production possibilities curve illustrated in Figure 2-1. We would have to draw a new curve, farther to the right, to show the greater total study time and a different set of possible trade-offs.

Production possibilities curve (PPC)
A curve representing all possible combinations of maximum outputs that could be produced, assuming a fixed amount of productive resources of a given quality.

---

12 hours per week to spend studying these two subjects and that if you spend all 12 hours on economics, you will get an A in the course. You will, however, fail mathematics. Conversely, if you spend all of your 12 hours studying mathematics, you will get an A in that subject, but you will flunk economics. Here the trade-off is a special case: one to one. A one-to-one trade-off means that the opportunity cost of receiving one grade higher in economics (for example, improving from a C to a B) is one grade lower in mathematics (falling from a C to a D).

Scarcity requires us to choose. Whenever we choose, we lose the _____-_____-valued alternative.

Cost is always a forgone _____.

Another way to look at **opportunity cost** is the trade-off that occurs when one activity is undertaken rather than the _____-_____ alternative activity.

A _____ _____ curve graphically shows the trade-off that occurs when more of one output is obtained at the sacrifice of another. This curve is a graphical representation of, among other things, opportunity cost.

The Choices a Nation's Economy Faces

The straight-line production possibilities curve presented in Figure 2-1 on the previous page can be generalized to demonstrate the related concepts of scarcity, choice, and trade-offs that our entire nation faces. As you will see, the production possibilities curve is a simple but powerful economic model because it can demonstrate these related concepts.

A Two-Good Example

The example we will use is the choice between the production of smartphones and tablet devices. We assume for the moment that these are the only two goods that can be produced in the nation.

Panel (a) of Figure 2-2 below gives the various combinations of smartphones and tablet devices, or tablets, that are possible. If all resources are devoted to smartphone production, 50 million per year can be produced. If all resources are devoted to production of tablets, 60 million per year can be produced. In between are various possible combinations.

FIGURE 2-2

The Trade-Off between Smartphones and Tablet Devices

The production of smartphones and tablet devices is measured in millions of units per year. The various combinations are given in panel (a) and plotted in panel (b). Connecting the points *A–G* with a relatively smooth line gives society's production possibilities curve for smartphones and tablets. Point *R* lies outside the production possibilities curve and is therefore unattainable at the point in time for which the graph is drawn. Point *S* lies inside the production possibilities curve and therefore entails unemployed or underemployed resources.

Panel (a)

Combination	Smartphones (millions per year)	Tablets (millions per year)
A	50.0	0
B	48.0	10
C	45.0	20
D	40.0	30
E	33.0	40
F	22.5	50
G	0.0	60

Panel (b)

Production Trade-Offs

The nation's production combinations are plotted as points *A, B, C, D, E, F,* and *G* in panel (b) of Figure 2-2 on the previous page. If these points are connected with a smooth curve, the nation's production possibilities curve (PPC) is shown, demonstrating the trade-off between the production of smartphones and tablets. These trade-offs occur *on* the PPC.

Notice the major difference in the shape of the production possibilities curves in Figure 2-1 on page 31 and Figure 2-2. In Figure 2-1, there is a constant trade-off between grades in economics and in mathematics. In Figure 2-2, the trade-off between production of smartphones and tablet production is not constant, and therefore the PPC is a *bowed* curve. To understand why the production possibilities curve is typically bowed outward, you must understand the assumptions underlying the PPC.

How has a trade-off between roads and factories contributed to traffic problems in China?

Go to **www.econtoday.com/chap02** for one perspective, offered by the National Center for Policy Analysis, on whether society's production decisions should be publicly or privately coordinated.

INTERNATIONAL EXAMPLE

In China, More Factories Mean Fewer Roads—and More Traffic

Recently, a 62-mile section of highway between the Chinese cities of Beijing and Zhangjiakou became ensnarled in a massive traffic jam that took public safety officers nearly two weeks to break up. Traffic experts agree that this stretch of highway, which covers less than 0.7 square mile of area stretched thinly along the 62 miles, is often overburdened with much more traffic than it was designed to handle.

Most observers agree that this state of affairs has arisen because the people of China have allocated resources away from road construction in favor of building new manufacturing facilities. These facilities, though, churn out more products to be shipped by trucks that clog roads. Thus, in China the choice to build more factories to produce goods has entailed an opportunity cost: fewer roads for transporting those goods.

FOR CRITICAL THINKING

What is an example of an opportunity cost that a trucker may have incurred by spending a full day traversing the traffic jam between Beijing and Zhangjiakou?

Assumptions Underlying the Production Possibilities Curve

When we draw the curve that is shown in Figure 2-2, we make the following assumptions:

1. Resources are fully employed.

2. Production takes place over a specific time period—for example, one year.

3. The resource inputs, in both quantity and quality, used to produce smartphones or tablets are fixed over this time period.

4. Technology does not change over this time period.

Technology is defined as the total pool of applied knowledge concerning how goods and services can be produced by managers, workers, engineers, scientists, and artisans, using land, physical and human capital, and entrepreneurship. You can think of technology as the formula or recipe used to combine factors of production. (When better formulas are developed, more production can be obtained from the same amount of resources.) The level of technology sets the limit on the amount and types of goods and services that we can derive from any given amount of resources. The production possibilities curve is drawn under the assumption that we use the best technology that we currently have available and that this technology doesn't change over the time period under study.

Technology
The total pool of applied knowledge concerning how goods and services can be produced.

Being off the Production Possibilities Curve

Look again at panel (b) of Figure 2-2 on page 32. Point *R* lies *outside* the production possibilities curve and is *impossible* to achieve during the time period assumed. By definition, the PPC indicates the *maximum* quantity of one good, given the quantity produced of the other good.

It is possible, however, to be at point *S* in Figure 2-2. That point lies beneath the PPC. If the nation is at point *S*, it means that its resources are not being fully utilized. This occurs, for example, during periods of relatively high unemployment. Point *S* and all such points inside the PPC are always attainable but imply unemployed or underemployed resources.

Efficiency

The production possibilities curve can be used to define the notion of efficiency. Whenever the economy is operating on the PPC, at points such as *A*, *B*, *C*, or *D*, we say that its production is efficient. Points such as *S* in Figure 2-2, which lie beneath the PPC, are said to represent production situations that are not efficient.

Efficiency can mean many things to many people. Even in economics, there are different types of efficiency. Here we are discussing *productive efficiency*. An economy is productively efficient whenever it is producing the maximum output with given technology and resources.

A simple commonsense definition of efficiency is getting the most out of what we have. Clearly, we are not getting the most out of what we have if we are at point *S* in panel (b) of Figure 2-2. We can move from point *S* to, say, point *C*, thereby increasing the total quantity of smartphones produced without any decrease in the total quantity of tablets produced. Alternatively, we can move from point *S* to point *E*, for example, and have both more smartphones and more tablets. Point *S* is called an **inefficient point**, which is defined as any point below the production possibilities curve.

Efficiency
The case in which a given level of inputs is used to produce the maximum output possible. Alternatively, the situation in which a given output is produced at minimum cost.

Inefficient point
Any point below the production possibilities curve, at which the use of resources is not generating the maximum possible output.

The Law of Increasing Additional Cost

In the example in Figure 2-1 on page 31, the trade-off between a grade in mathematics and a grade in economics was one to one. The trade-off ratio was constant. That is, the production possibilities curve was a straight line. The curve in Figure 2-2 is a more general case. We have re-created the curve in Figure 2-2 as Figure 2-3 on the facing page. Each combination, *A* through *G*, of smartphones and tablets is represented on the PPC. Starting with the production of zero tablets, the nation can produce 50 million smartphones with its available resources and technology.

INCREASING ADDITIONAL COSTS When we increase production of tablet devices from zero to 10 million per year, the nation has to give up in smartphones an amount shown by that first vertical arrow, *Aa*. From panel (a) of Figure 2-2, you can see that this is 2 million per year (50 million minus 48 million). Again, if we increase production of tablets by another 10 million units per year, we go from *B* to *C*. In order to do so, the nation has to give up the vertical distance *Bb*, or 3 million smartphones per year. By the time we go from 50 million to 60 million tablets, to obtain that 10 million increase, we have to forgo the vertical distance *Ff*, or 22.5 million smartphones.

FIGURE 2-3

The Law of Increasing Additional Cost

Consider equal increments of production of tablets, as measured on the horizontal axis. All of the horizontal arrows—*aB, bC,* and so on—are of equal length (10 million). In contrast, the length of each vertical arrow—*Aa, Bb,* and so on—increases as we move down the production possibilities curve. Hence, the opportunity cost of going from 50 million tablets per year to 60 million (*Ff*) is much greater than going from zero units to 10 million (*Aa*). The opportunity cost of each additional equal increase in production of tablets rises.

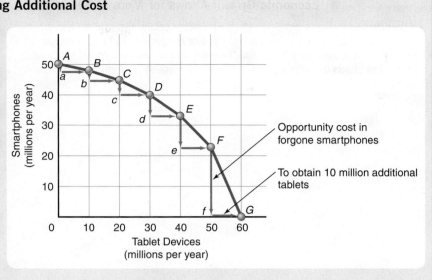

In other words, we see that the opportunity cost of the last 10 million tablets has increased to 22.5 million smartphones, compared to 2 million smartphones for the same increase in tablets when we started with none at all being produced.

What we are observing is called the **law of increasing additional cost.** When people take more resources and applies them to the production of any specific good, the opportunity cost increases for each additional unit produced.

EXPLAINING THE LAW OF INCREASING ADDITIONAL COST The reason that as a nation we face the law of increasing additional cost (shown as a production possibilities curve that is bowed outward) is that certain resources are better suited for producing some goods than they are for other goods. Generally, resources are not *perfectly* adaptable for alternative uses. When increasing the output of a particular good, producers must use less suitable resources than those already used in order to produce the additional output. Hence, the cost of producing the additional units increases.

With respect to our hypothetical example here, at first the computing specialists at smartphone firms would shift over to producing tablet devices. After a while, though, the workers who normally design and produce smartphones would be asked to help design and manufacture tablet components. Typically, they would be less effective at making tablets than the people who previously specialized in this task.

In general, *the more specialized the resources, the more bowed the production possibilities curve.* At the other extreme, if all resources are equally suitable for smartphone production or production of tablets, the curves in Figures 2-2 (p. 32) and 2-3 above would approach the straight line shown in our first example in Figure 2-1 on page 31.

Law of increasing additional cost
The fact that the opportunity cost of additional units of a good generally increases as people attempt to produce more of that good. This accounts for the bowed-out shape of the production possibilities curve.

QUICK QUIZ

See page 47 for the answers. Review concepts from this section in MyEconLab.

Trade-offs are represented graphically by a _____ _____ curve showing the maximum quantity of one good or service that can be produced, given a specific quantity of another, from a given set of resources over a specified period of time—for example, one year.

A **production possibilities curve** is drawn holding the quantity and quality of all resources _____ over the time period under study.

Points _____ the **production possibilities curve** are unattainable. Points _____ are attainable but represent an inefficient use or underuse of available resources.

Because many resources are better suited for certain productive tasks than for others, the production possibilities curve is bowed _____, reflecting the **law of increasing additional cost.**

Economic Growth Allows for More of Everything

If the nation experiences economic growth, the production possibilities curve between smartphones and tablets will move out as shown. This output increase takes time, however, and it does not occur automatically. This means, therefore, that we can have more of both smartphones and tablets only after a period of time during which we have experienced economic growth.

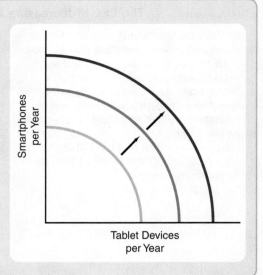

Economic Growth and the Production Possibilities Curve

At any particular point in time, a society cannot be outside the production possibilities curve. *Over time*, however, it is possible to have more of everything. This occurs through economic growth. (An important reason for economic growth, capital accumulation, is discussed next. A more complete discussion of why economic growth occurs appears in Chapter 9.) Figure 2-4 above shows the production possibilities curve for smartphones and tablet devices shifting outward. The two additional curves shown represent new choices open to an economy that has experienced economic growth. Such economic growth occurs for many reasons, including increases in the number of workers and productive investment in equipment.

Scarcity still exists, however, no matter how much economic growth there is. At any point in time, we will always be on some production possibilities curve. Thus, we will always face trade-offs. The more we have of one thing, the less we can have of others.

If economic growth occurs in the nation, the production possibilities curve between smartphones and tablets moves outward, as shown in Figure 2-4. This takes time and does not occur automatically. One reason it will occur involves the choice about how much to consume today.

The Trade-Off between the Present and the Future

Consumption
The use of goods and services for personal satisfaction.

The production possibilities curve and economic growth can be combined to examine the trade-off between present **consumption** and future consumption. When we consume today, we are using up what we call consumption or consumer goods—food and clothes, for example.

Why We Make Capital Goods

Why would we be willing to use productive resources to make things—capital goods—that we cannot consume directly? The reason is that capital goods enable us to produce larger quantities of consumer goods or to produce them less expensively than we otherwise could. Before fish are "produced" for the market, equipment such as fishing boats, nets, and poles is produced first. Imagine how expensive it would be to obtain fish for market without using these capital goods. Catching fish with one's hands is not an easy task. The cost per fish would be very high if capital goods weren't used.

Forgoing Current Consumption

Whenever we use productive resources to make capital goods, we are implicitly forgoing current consumption. We are waiting for some time in the future to consume the rewards that will be reaped from the use of capital goods. In effect, when we forgo current consumption to invest in capital goods, we are engaging in an economic activity that is forward-looking—we do not get instant utility or satisfaction from our activity.

The Trade-Off between Consumption Goods and Capital Goods

To have more consumer goods in the future, we must accept fewer consumer goods today, because resources must be used in producing capital goods instead of consumer goods. In other words, an opportunity cost is involved. Every time we make a choice of more goods today, we incur an opportunity cost of fewer goods tomorrow, and every time we make a choice of more goods in the future, we incur an opportunity cost of fewer goods today. With the resources that we don't use to produce consumer goods for today, we invest in capital goods that will produce more consumer goods for us later. The trade-off is shown in Figure 2-5 below. On the left in panel (a), you can see this trade-off depicted as a production possibilities curve between capital goods and consumption goods.

Assume that we are willing to give up $1 trillion worth of consumption today. We will be at point A in the left-hand diagram of panel (a). This will allow the economy to grow. We will have more future consumption because we invested in more capital goods today. In the right-hand diagram of panel (a), we see two consumer goods represented, food and entertainment. The production possibilities

---

FIGURE 2-5

Capital Goods and Growth

In panel (a), people choose not to consume $1 trillion, so they invest that amount in capital goods. As a result, more of all goods may be produced in the future, as shown in the right-hand diagram in panel (a). In panel (b), people choose even more capital goods (point C). The result is that the production possibilities curve (PPC) moves even more to the right on the right-hand diagram in panel (b).

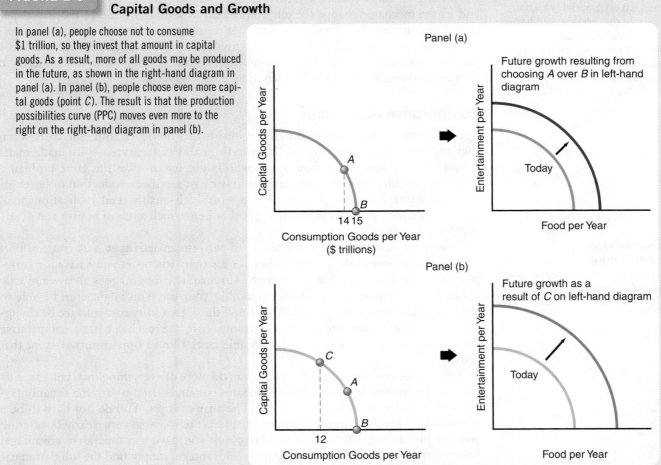

curve will move outward if individuals in the economy decide to restrict consumption now and invest in capital goods.

In panel (b) in Figure 2-5 on the previous page, we show the results of our willingness to forgo even more current consumption. We move from point *A* to point *C* in the left-hand side, where we have many fewer consumer goods today but produce many more capital goods. This leads to more future growth in this simplified model, and thus the production possibilities curve in the right-hand side of panel (b) shifts outward more than it did in the right-hand side of panel (a). In other words, the more we give up today, the more we can have tomorrow, provided, of course, that the capital goods are productive in future periods.

QUICK QUIZ   See page 47 for the answers. Review concepts from this section in MyEconLab.

_____ goods are goods that will later be used to produce consumer goods.

A trade-off is involved between current consumption and capital goods or, alternatively, between current consumption and future consumption. The _____ we invest in capital goods today, the greater the amount of consumer goods we can produce in the future and the _____ the amount of consumer goods we can produce today.

Specialization and Greater Productivity

Specialization

The organization of economic activity so that what each person (or region) consumes is not identical to what that person (or region) produces. An individual may specialize, for example, in law or medicine. A nation may specialize in the production of coffee, e-book readers, or digital cameras.

Specialization involves working at a relatively well-defined, limited endeavor, such as accounting or teaching. Most individuals do specialize. For example, you could change the oil in your car if you wanted to. Typically, though, you take your car to a garage and let the mechanic change the oil. You benefit by letting the garage mechanic specialize in changing the oil and in doing other repairs on your car.

The specialist normally will get the job finished sooner than you could and has the proper equipment to make the job go more smoothly. Specialization usually leads to greater productivity, not only for each individual but also for the nation.

Comparative Advantage

Specialization occurs because different individuals experience different costs when they engage in the same activities. Some individuals can accurately solve mathematical problems at lower cost than others who might try to solve the same problems. Thus, those who solve math problems at lower cost sacrifice production of fewer alternative items. Some people can develop more high-quality iPad applications than others while giving up less production of other items, such as clean houses and neatly manicured yards.

Comparative advantage

The ability to produce a good or service at a lower opportunity cost compared to other producers.

Comparative advantage is the ability to perform an activity *at a lower opportunity cost*. You have a comparative advantage in one activity whenever you have a lower opportunity cost of performing that activity. Comparative advantage is always a *relative* concept. You may be able to change the oil in your car. You might even be able to change it faster than the local mechanic. But if the opportunity cost you face by changing the oil exceeds the mechanic's opportunity cost, the mechanic has a comparative advantage in changing the oil. The mechanic faces a lower opportunity cost for that activity.

You may be convinced that everybody can do more of everything than you can during the same period of time and using the same resources. In this extreme situation, do you still have a comparative advantage? The answer is yes. You do not have to be a mathematical genius to figure this out. The market tells you so very clearly by offering you the highest income for the job for which you have a comparative advantage. Stated differently, to find your comparative advantage, simply find the job that maximizes your income.

When contemplating how to keep track of balances remaining on gift cards, some people find that doing their own tabulations entails a higher opportunity cost than others face. How has this increased opportunity cost given entrepreneurs an occasion to profit from providing gift-card tracking services?

EXAMPLE

A Comparative Advantage in Watching Gift-Card Balances

Each year, consumers juggle a total of $100 billion in balances on gift cards. Keeping track of these funds and making certain all funds are spent can require considerable time.

Increasingly, people are deciding that taking the time to keep tabs on their gift-card balances is a next-best alternative. These individuals pay others to make sure they are spending all available funds. For instance, a firm called Tango Card uses software to track gift-card balances and provide periodic reports to consumers. The company also sends e-mails warning consumers when unused cards are about to expire before all funds have been spent. The fact that owners of Tango Card have a comparative advantage in keeping tabs on gift-card balances enables its customers to devote extra time to other activities, such as earning additional income.

FOR CRITICAL THINKING
What is the comparative advantage of customers of Tango Cards who devote time to earning income instead of tracking their card balances?

Absolute Advantage

Suppose that you are the president of a firm and are convinced that you have the ability to do every job in that company faster than everyone else who works there. You might be able to enter data into a spreadsheet program faster than any of the other employees, file documents in order in a file cabinet faster than any of the file clerks, and wash windows faster than any of the window washers. Furthermore, you are able to manage the firm in less time more effectively than any other individual in the company.

If all of these self-perceptions were really true, then you would have an **absolute advantage** in all of these endeavors. In other words, if you were to spend a given amount of time in any one of them, you could produce more than anyone else in the company. Nonetheless, you would not spend your time doing these other activities. Why not? Because your time advantage in undertaking the president's managerial duties is even greater. Therefore, you would find yourself specializing in that particular task even though you have an *absolute* advantage in all these other tasks. Indeed, absolute advantage is irrelevant in predicting how you will allocate your time. Only *comparative advantage* matters in determining how you will allocate your time, because it is the relative cost that is important in making this choice.

The coaches of sports teams often have to determine the comparative advantage of an individual player who has an absolute advantage in every aspect of the sport in question. Babe Ruth, who could hit more home runs and pitch more strikeouts per game than other players on the Boston Red Sox, was a pitcher on that professional baseball team. After he was traded to the New York Yankees, the owner and the manager decided to make him an outfielder, even though he could also pitch more strikeouts per game than other Yankees. They wanted "The Babe" to concentrate on his hitting because a home-run king would bring in more paying fans than a good pitcher would. Babe Ruth had an absolute advantage in both aspects of the game of baseball, but his comparative advantage was clearly in hitting homers rather than in practicing and developing his pitching game.

Absolute advantage
The ability to produce more units of a good or service using a given quantity of labor or resource inputs. Equivalently, the ability to produce the same quantity of a good or service using fewer units of labor or resource inputs.

Scarcity, Self-Interest, and Specialization

In Chapter 1, you learned about the assumption of rational self-interest. To repeat, for the purposes of our analyses we assume that individuals are rational in that they will do what is in their own self-interest. They will not consciously carry out actions that will make them worse off. In this chapter, you learned that scarcity requires people to make choices. We *assume* that they make choices based on their self-interest. When people make choices, they attempt to maximize benefits net of opportunity cost. In so doing, individuals choose their comparative advantage and end up specializing.

The Division of Labor

Division of labor
The segregation of resources into different specific tasks. For instance, one automobile worker puts on bumpers, another doors, and so on.

In any firm that includes specialized human and nonhuman resources, there is a **division of labor** among those resources. The best-known example comes from Adam Smith (1723–1790), who in *The Wealth of Nations* illustrated the benefits of a division of labor in the making of pins, as depicted in the following example:

> One man draws out the wire, another straightens it, a third cuts it, a fourth points it, a fifth grinds it at the top for receiving the head; to make the head requires two or three distinct operations; to put it on is a peculiar business, to whiten the pins is another; it is even a trade by itself to put them into the paper.

Making pins this way allowed 10 workers without very much skill to make almost 48,000 pins "of a middling size" in a day. One worker, toiling alone, could have made perhaps 20 pins a day. Therefore, 10 workers could have produced 200. Division of labor allowed for an increase in the daily output of the pin factory from 200 to 48,000! (Smith did not attribute all of the gain to the division of labor but credited also the use of machinery and the fact that less time was spent shifting from task to task.)

What we are discussing here involves a division of the resource called labor into different uses of labor. The different uses of labor are organized in such a way as to increase the amount of output possible from the fixed resources available. We can therefore talk about an organized division of labor within a firm leading to increased output.

Comparative Advantage and Trade among Nations

Most of our analysis of absolute advantage, comparative advantage, and specialization has dealt with individuals. Nevertheless, it is equally applicable to groups of people.

Trade among Regions

Consider the United States. The Plains states have a comparative advantage in the production of grains and other agricultural goods. Relative to the Plains states, the states to the east tend to specialize in industrialized production, such as automobiles. Not surprisingly, grains are shipped from the Plains states to the eastern states, and automobiles are shipped in the reverse direction. Such specialization and trade allow for higher incomes and standards of living.

If both the Plains states and the eastern states were separate nations, the same analysis would still hold, but we would call it international trade. Indeed, the European Union (EU) is comparable to the United States in area and population, but instead of one nation, the EU has 27. What U.S. residents call *interstate* trade, Europeans call *international* trade. There is no difference, however, in the economic results—both yield greater economic efficiency and higher average incomes.

International Aspects of Trade

Political problems that normally do not occur within a particular nation often arise between nations. For example, if California avocado growers develop a cheaper method of producing avocados than growers in southern Florida use, the Florida growers will lose out. They cannot do much about the situation except try to lower their own costs of production or improve their product.

If avocado growers in Mexico, however, develop a cheaper method of producing avocados, both California and Florida growers can (and likely will) try to raise political barriers that will prevent Mexican avocado growers from freely selling their product in the United States. U.S. avocado growers will use such arguments as "unfair" competition and loss of U.S. jobs. Certainly, avocado-growing jobs may decline in the United States, but there is no reason to believe that U.S. jobs will decline overall. Instead, former U.S. avocado workers will move into alternative employment—something that 1 million people do every *week* in the United States. If the argument of U.S. avocado growers had any validity, every time a region in the United States developed a better way to produce a product manufactured somewhere else in the country, U.S. employment would decline. That has never happened and never will.

When nations specialize in an area of comparative advantage and then trade with the rest of the world, the average standard of living in the world rises. In effect, international trade allows the world to move from inside the global production possibilities curve toward the curve itself, thereby improving worldwide economic efficiency. Thus, all countries that engage in trade can benefit from comparative advantage, just as regions in the United States benefit from interregional trade.

Go to **www.econtoday.com/chap02** to find out from the World Trade Organization how much international trade takes place. Under "Resources," click on "Trade statistics" and then click on "International Trade Statistics" for the most recent year.

QUICK QUIZ

See page 47 for the answers. Review concepts from this section in MyEconLab.

With a given set of resources, specialization results in _____ output. In other words, there are gains to specialization in terms of greater material well-being.

Individuals and nations specialize in their areas of _____ advantage in order to reap the gains of specialization.

Comparative advantages are found by determining which activities have the _____ opportunity costs—that is,

which activities yield the highest return for the time and resources used.

A _____ of labor occurs when different workers are assigned different tasks. Together, the workers produce a desired product.

YOU ARE THERE
The Opportunity Cost of Vacation Time in South Korea

Lee Charm recently became head of the South Korean government's Korea Tourism Organization (KTO), which develops and promotes vacation tours for South Koreans. Shortly after assuming this position, Charm discovered that the agency's 550 employees were allocating only about five days to vacations each year, one fewer than for the average Korean.

Charm was rebuffed when he tried to convince KTO employees to take more vacation days each year voluntarily. A key reason for the unwillingness of KTO's employees to take off additional days for vacations was that KTO, like other government agencies and private firms in South Korea, rewards both workers and managers with extra pay for unused vacation days. Thus, if KTO employees had expanded their number of vacation days, they would have forgone income that could be

allocated to other purposes. They viewed the opportunity cost of any additional time spent on vacations as too high to justify taking more time off.

Critical Thinking Questions

1. Why do you suppose KTO employees were displeased when Charm required them to take more vacation days each year to "set a good example" for other workers?

2. During his first year as KTO's manager, what did Charm himself gain from taking one less day off than the average KTO employee's five vacation days?

ISSUES & APPLICATIONS

The Rising Opportunity Cost of Airlines' "Block Times"

CONCEPTS APPLIED

▶ Scarcity

▶ Opportunity Cost

▶ Trade-Offs

Average published durations of airline flights increased by about ten minutes between the late 1990s and early 2010s. Time is scarce for everyone, including air travelers, who are experiencing increases in opportunity costs equal to the values of alternative uses for which they could spend these extra minutes now allocated to air travel.

Why Published Flight Times Are Longer Than They Used to Be

For about fifteen years, airlines lengthened their *block times*—intervals of time for flight schedules. Block times include the sum of estimated times required to taxi out onto the runway, to travel in the air, to taxi to the destination terminal, and to pull into a gate. In addition, block times typically include a *buffer*, which is a period that can range from just a few minutes to more than an hour.

Airlines have long built buffer minutes into block times for flights, to allow for contrary winds and other weather-related factors that can lengthen time in the air. Figure 2-6 below displays buffer periods for a number of airlines' flights on a recent day and shows that airlines tend to set longer buffers for flights of greater duration.

Fewer than two of the ten extra minutes that airlines for a time added to the average per-flight block time reflected increased time spent taxiing at airports. What accounted for the additional eight minutes? Airlines lengthened buf-

FIGURE 2-6

Selected Block-Time Buffers during One Day of U.S. Commercial Air Flights

This chart displays the buffers that airlines included in block times for their flights departing during a typical 15-minute interval of an average day. Airlines tend to set longer buffers for lengthier flights.

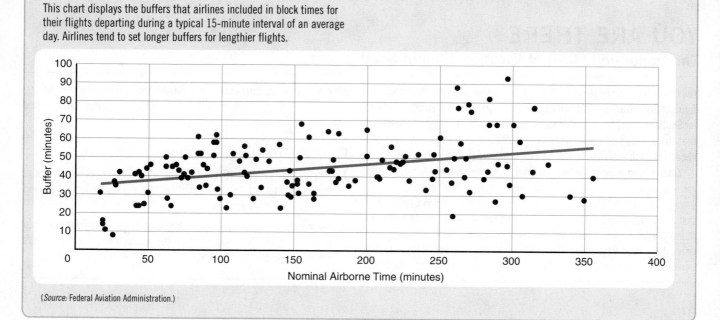

(*Source:* Federal Aviation Administration.)

fers to ensure that many flights that previously would have been marked a few minutes late instead would be listed as "on time." Being classified as consistently "on time" has considerable value to an airline company, because it helps the company sell more tickets.

A Higher Opportunity Cost of Air Travel Time

Traveling by air entails incurring both explicit and implicit costs. The explicit cost is the price of the plane ticket. A key implicit-cost component is the time that a person spends at and between airports instead of being able to allocate the time to the next-highest-valued activity—that is, the opportunity cost of the time.

For everyone who flies, the terms of the trade-off associated with flying worsened slightly between the late 1990s and early 2010s. Consider each individual who otherwise could have been earning the average U.S. hourly wage, for whom ten extra minutes devoted to a flight translates into approximately $3 of lost wages. Suppose that we use this figure to place a dollar value on each passenger's opportunity cost, and consider a "slow day" in which only 500,000 U.S. residents otherwise could have been earning hourly wages fly on airliners. Under these assumptions, the extra ten minutes of block time per passenger yielded an estimated additional $1.5 million total *daily* opportunity cost.

For Critical Thinking

1. Why might it prove difficult to measure the aggregate additional opportunity cost of ten extra minutes of airlines' block time across *all* individuals? (Hint: Not everyone works.)
2. Why did the extra ten minutes of block time constitute an opportunity cost even for an airline passenger who were on vacation from a job that pays hourly wages?

Web Resources

1. Learn about block time and other economic issues that airlines face in scheduling flights at www.econtoday.com /chap02.
2. To contemplate how adding block time can potentially boost airlines' own explicit labor costs, go to www .econtoday.com/chap02.

MyEconLab

For more questions on this chapter's
Issues & Applications, go to MyEconLab.
In the Study Plan for this chapter,
select Section N: News.

MyEconLab

Here is what you should know after reading this chapter. MyEconLab will help you identify what you know, and where to go when you need to practice.

— WHAT YOU SHOULD KNOW —		— WHERE TO GO TO PRACTICE —
The Problem of Scarcity, Even for the Affluent Even the richest people face scarcity because they have to make choices among alternatives. Despite their high levels of income or wealth, affluent people, like everyone else, want more than they can have (in terms of goods, power, prestige, and so on).	scarcity, 27 production, 27 land, 27 labor, 27 physical capital, 28 human capital, 28 entrepreneurship, 28 goods, 28 economic goods, 28 services, 28	• MyEconLab Study Plan 2.1
Why Economists Consider Individuals' Wants but Not Their "Needs" Goods are all things from which individuals derive satisfaction. Economic goods are those for which the desired quantity exceeds the amount that is available at a zero price. The term *need* is undefinable, whereas humans have unlimited *wants*, which are the items on which we place a positive value.		• MyEconLab Study Plan 2.2

MyEconLab *continued*

Why Scarcity Leads People to Evaluate Opportunity Costs Opportunity cost is the highest-valued alternative that one must give up to obtain an item. The trade-offs people face can be represented by a production possibilities curve (PPC). Moving along a PPC from one point to another entails incurring an opportunity cost of allocating scarce resources toward the production of one good instead of another good.

opportunity cost, 30
production possibilities curve (PPC), 31

Key Figure
Figure 2-1, 31

- MyEconLab Study Plans 2.3, 2.4

Why Obtaining Increasing Increments of a Good Requires Giving Up More and More Units of Other Goods When people allocate additional resources to producing more units of a good, it must increasingly employ resources that would be better suited for producing other goods. As a result, the law of increasing additional cost holds. Each additional unit of a good can be obtained only by giving up more and more of other goods. Hence, the production possibilities curve is bowed outward.

technology, 33
efficiency, 34
inefficient point, 34
law of increasing additional cost, 35

Key Figures
Figure 2-3, 35
Figure 2-4, 36

- MyEconLab Study Plan 2.5
- Animated Figures 2-3, 2-4

The Trade-Off between Consumption Goods and Capital Goods If we allocate more resources to producing capital goods today, then the production possibilities curve will shift outward by more in the future, which means that we can have additional future consumption goods. The trade-off is that producing more capital goods today entails giving up consumption goods today.

consumption, 36

- MyEconLab Study Plans 2.6, 2.7

Absolute Advantage versus Comparative Advantage A person has an absolute advantage if she can produce more of a good than someone else who uses the same amount of resources. An individual can gain from specializing in producing a good if she has a comparative advantage in producing that good, meaning that she can produce the good at a lower opportunity cost than someone else.

specialization, 38
comparative advantage, 38
absolute advantage, 39
division of labor, 40

- MyEconLab Study Plans 2.8, 2.9

Log in to MyEconLab, take a chapter test, and get a personalized Study Plan that tells you which concepts you understand and which ones you need to review. From there, MyEconLab will give you further practice, tutorials, animations, videos, and guided solutions. For more information, visit www.myeconlab.com

PROBLEMS

All problems are assignable in MyEconLab. *Answers to odd-numbered problems appear at the back of the book.*

2-1. Define opportunity cost. What is your opportunity cost of attending a class at 11:00 a.m.? How does it differ from your opportunity cost of attending a class at 8:00 a.m.? (See page 30.)

2-2. If you receive a ticket to a concert at no charge, what, if anything, is your opportunity cost of attending the concert? How does your opportunity cost change if miserable weather on the night of the concert requires you to leave much earlier for the concert hall and greatly extends the time it takes to get home afterward? (See page 30.)

2-3. You and a friend decide to spend $100 each on concert tickets. Each of you alternatively could have spent the $100 to purchase a textbook, a meal at a highly rated local restaurant, or several Internet movie downloads. As you are on the way to the concert, your friend tells you that if she had not bought the concert ticket, she would have opted for a restaurant meal, and you reply that you otherwise would have downloaded several movies. Identify the relevant opportunity costs for you and your friend of the concert tickets that you purchased. Explain briefly. (See page 30.)

2-4. After the concert discussed in Problem 2-3 is over and you and your friend are traveling home, you discuss how each of you might otherwise have used the four hours devoted to attending the concert. The four hours could have been used to study, to watch a sporting event on TV, or to get some extra sleep. Your friend decides that if she had not spent four hours attending the concert, she would have chosen to study, and you reply that you otherwise would have watched the televised sporting event. Identify the relevant opportunity costs for you and your friend for allocating your four hours to attending the concert. Explain briefly. (See page 30.)

2-5. Recently, a woman named Mary Krawiec attended an auction in Troy, New York. At the auction, a bank was seeking to sell a foreclosed property: a large Victorian house suffering from years of neglect in a neighborhood in which many properties had been on the market for years yet remained unsold. Her $10 offer was the highest bid in the auction, and she handed over a $10 bill for a title to ownership. Once she acquired the house, however, she became responsible for all taxes on the property and for an overdue water bill of $2,000. In addition, to make the house habitable, she and her husband devoted months of time and unpaid labor to renovating the property. In the process, they incurred explicit expenses totaling $65,000. Why do you suppose that the bank was willing to sell the house to Ms. Krawiec for only $10? (Hint: Contemplate the bank's expected gain, net of all explicit and opportunity costs, if it had attempted to make the house habitable. See page 30.)

2-6. The following table illustrates the points a student can earn on examinations in economics and biology if the student uses all available hours for study.

Economics	Biology
100	40
90	50
80	60
70	70
60	80
50	90
40	100

Plot this student's production possibilities curve. Does the PPC illustrate the law of increasing additional cost? (See page 31.)

2-7. Based on the information provided in Problem 2-6, what is the opportunity cost to this student of allocating enough additional study time on economics to move her grade up from a 90 to a 100?

2-8. Consider a change in the table in Problem 2-6. The student's set of opportunities is now as follows:

Economics	Biology
100	40
90	60
80	75
70	85
60	93
50	98
40	100

Does the PPC illustrate the law of increasing additional cost? What is the opportunity cost to this student for the additional amount of study time on economics required to move her grade from 60 to 70? From 90 to 100? (See page 35.)

2-9. Construct a production possibilities curve for a nation facing increasing opportunity costs for producing food and video games. Show how the PPC changes given the following events. (See page 37.)

   a. A new and better fertilizer is invented.

b. Immigration occurs, and immigrants' labor can be employed in both the agricultural sector and the video game sector.

c. People invent a new programming language that is much less costly to code and is more memory-efficient.

d. A heat wave and drought result in a 10 percent decrease in usable farmland.

Consider the following diagram when answering Problems 2-10, 2-11, and 2-12.

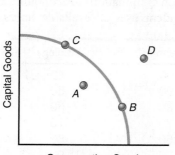

Consumption Goods

2-10. During a debate on the floor of the U.S. Senate, Senator Creighton states, "Our nation should not devote so many of its fully employed resources to producing capital goods because we already are not producing enough consumption goods for our citizens." Compared with the other labeled points on the diagram, which one could be consistent with the *current* production combination choice that Senator Creighton believes the nation has made? (See page 34.)

2-11. In response to Senator Creighton's statement reported in Problem 2-10, Senator Long replies, "We must remain at our current production combination if we want to be able to produce more consumption goods in the future." Of the labeled points on the diagram, which one could depict the *future* production combination Senator Long has in mind? (See page 34.)

2-12. Senator Borman interjects the following comment after the statements by Senators Creighton and Long reported in Problems 2-10 and 2-11: "In fact, both of my esteemed colleagues are wrong, because an unacceptably large portion of our nation's resources is currently unemployed." Of the labeled points on the diagram, which one is consistent with Senator Borman's position? (See page 34.)

2-13. A nation's residents can allocate their scarce resources either to producing consumption goods or to producing human capital—that is, providing themselves with training and education. (See page 35.) The table at the top of next column displays the production possibilities for this nation:

Production Combination	Units of Consumption Goods	Units of Human Capital
A	0	100
B	10	97
C	20	90
D	30	75
E	40	55
F	50	30
G	60	0

a. Suppose that the nation's residents currently produce combination A. What is the opportunity cost of increasing production of consumption goods by 10 units? By 60 units?

b. Does the law of increasing additional cost hold true for this nation? Why or why not?

2-14. Like physical capital, human capital produced in the present can be applied to the production of future goods and services. Consider the table in Problem 2-13, and suppose that the nation's residents are trying to choose between combination C and combination F. Other things being equal, will the future production possibilities curve for this nation be located farther outward if the nation chooses combination F instead of combination C? Explain. (See page 35.)

2-15. You can wash, fold, and iron a basket of laundry in two hours and prepare a meal in one hour. Your roommate can wash, fold, and iron a basket of laundry in three hours and prepare a meal in one hour. Who has the absolute advantage in laundry, and who has an absolute advantage in meal preparation? Who has the comparative advantage in laundry, and who has a comparative advantage in meal preparation? (See page 38.)

2-16. Based on the information in Problem 2-15, should you and your roommate specialize in a particular task? Why? And if so, who should specialize in which task? Show how much labor time you save if you choose to "trade" an appropriate task with your roommate as opposed to doing it yourself. (See page 38.)

2-17. Using only the concept of comparative advantage, evaluate this statement: "A professor with a Ph.D. in physics should never mow his or her own lawn, because this would fail to take into account the professor's comparative advantage." (See page 38.)

2-18. Country A and country B produce the same consumption goods and capital goods and currently have *identical* production possibilities curves. They also have the same resources at present, and they have access to the same technology. (See page 38.)

a. At present, does either country have a comparative advantage in producing capital goods? Consumption goods?

b. Currently, country A has chosen to produce more consumption goods, compared with country B. Other things being equal, which country will experience the larger outward shift of its PPC during the next year?

ECONOMICS ON THE NET

Opportunity Cost and Labor Force Participation Many students choose to forgo full-time employment to concentrate on their studies, thereby incurring a sizable opportunity cost. This application explores the nature of this opportunity cost.

Title: College Enrollment and Work Activity of High School Graduates

Navigation: Go to **www.econtoday.com/chap02** to visit the Bureau of Labor Statistics (BLS) home page. Select A–Z Index and then click on *Educational attainment (Statistics)*. Under "School Enrollment," click on *Recent High School Graduates and Labor Force Participation*.

Application Read the abbreviated report on college enrollment and work activity of high school graduates. Then answer the following questions.

1. Based on the article, explain who the BLS considers to be in the labor force and who it does not view as part of the labor force.

2. What is the difference in labor force participation rates between high school students entering four-year universities and those entering two-year universities? Using the concept of opportunity cost, explain the difference.

3. What is the difference in labor force participation rates between part-time college students and full-time college students? Using the concept of opportunity cost, explain the difference.

For Group Study and Analysis Read the last paragraph of the article. Then divide the class into two groups. The first group should explain, based on the concept of opportunity cost, the difference in labor force participation rates between youths not in school but with a high school diploma and youths not in school and without a high school diploma. The second group should explain, based on opportunity cost, the difference in labor force participation rates between men and women not in school but with a high school diploma and men and women not in school and without a high school diploma.

ANSWERS TO QUICK QUIZZES

p. 29: (i) Scarcity; (ii) land . . . labor . . . physical . . . human . . . entrepreneurship; (iii) Wants; (iv) need

p. 32: (i) next-highest; (ii) opportunity; (iii) next-best; (iv) production possibilities

p. 35: (i) production possibilities; (ii) fixed; (iii) outside . . . inside; (iv) outward

p. 38: (i) Capital; (ii) more . . . smaller

p. 41: (i) higher; (ii) comparative; (iii) lowest; (iv) division

3

Demand and Supply

A t the time that your parents might have attended college, average tuition and fees were more than 90 percent lower than their current levels. In addition, the prices of textbooks and supplies were more than 80 percent lower than current prices. For example, in comparison with a college student who pays $20,000 in annual tuition and fees today, a student in the 1980s would have paid not much over $1,600 in inflation-adjusted dollars. Compared with a student who spends $1,000 per year for textbooks and other supplies, a student in the 1980s would have spent about $110 in inflation-adjusted dollars. Why have these prices risen so much? In this chapter, you will learn the answer.

? **DID YOU KNOW THAT...** after truck freight-hauling prices jumped substantially in the early 2010s, rail shipments of freight containers rose by more than 10 percent? Higher truck-transportation prices induced many companies to substitute away from having their products moved by trucks in favor of rail transportation.

If we use the economist's primary set of tools, *demand* and *supply*, we can develop a better understanding of why we sometimes observe relatively large increases in the purchase, or consumption, of items such as rail freight services. We can also better understand why a persistent increase in the price of an item such as truck-hauling services ultimately induces an increase in consumption of rail freight services. Demand and supply are two ways of categorizing the influences on the prices of goods that you buy and the quantities available. Indeed, demand and supply characterize much economic analysis of the world around us.

As you will see throughout this text, the operation of the forces of demand and supply takes place in *markets*. A **market** is an abstract concept summarizing all of the arrangements individuals have for exchanging with one another. Goods and services are sold in markets, such as the automobile market, the health care market, and the market for high-speed Internet access. Workers offer their services in the labor market. Companies, or firms, buy workers' labor services in the labor market. Firms also buy other inputs to produce the goods and services that you buy as a consumer. Firms purchase machines, buildings, and land. These markets are in operation at all times. One of the most important activities in these markets is the determination of the prices of all of the inputs and outputs that are bought and sold in our complicated economy. To understand the determination of prices, you first need to look at the law of demand.

Market
All of the arrangements that individuals have for exchanging with one another. Thus, for example, we can speak of the labor market, the automobile market, and the credit market.

Demand

Demand has a special meaning in economics. It refers to the quantities of specific goods or services that individuals, taken singly or as a group, will purchase at various possible prices, other things being constant. We can therefore talk about the demand for microprocessor chips, french fries, multifunction digital devices, children, and criminal activities.

Demand
A schedule showing how much of a good or service people will purchase at any price during a specified time period, other things being constant.

The Law of Demand

Associated with the concept of demand is the **law of demand**, which can be stated as follows:

When the price of a good goes up, people buy less of it, other things being equal.
When the price of a good goes down, people buy more of it, other things being equal.

The law of demand tells us that the quantity demanded of any commodity is inversely related to its price, other things being equal. In an inverse relationship, one variable moves up in value when the other moves down. The law of demand states that a change in price causes a change in the quantity demanded in the *opposite* direction.

Notice that we tacked on to the end of the law of demand the statement "other things being equal." We referred to this in Chapter 1 as the *ceteris paribus* assumption. It means, for example, that when we predict that people will buy fewer digital devices if their price goes up, we are holding constant the price of all other goods in the economy as well as people's incomes. Implicitly, therefore, if we are assuming that no other prices change when we examine the price behavior of digital devices, we are looking at the *relative* price of digital devices.

The law of demand is supported by millions of observations of people's behavior in the marketplace. Theoretically, it can be derived from an economic model based on rational behavior, as was discussed in Chapter 1. Basically, if nothing else changes and the price of a good falls, the lower price induces us to buy more because we can enjoy additional net gains that were unavailable at the higher price. If you examine your own behavior, you will see that it generally follows the law of demand.

Law of demand
The observation that there is a negative, or inverse, relationship between the price of any good or service and the quantity demanded, holding other factors constant.

Relative Prices versus Money Prices

The **relative price** of any commodity is its price in terms of another commodity. The price that you pay in dollars and cents for any good or service at any point in time is called its **money price.** You might hear from your grandparents, "My first new car cost only

Relative price
The money price of one commodity divided by the money price of another commodity; the number of units of one commodity that must be sacrificed to purchase one unit of another commodity.

Money price
The price expressed in today's dollars; also called the *absolute* or *nominal price.*

Table 3-1

Money Price versus Relative Price

The money prices of both 350-gigabyte flash memory drives and 350-gigabyte external hard drives have fallen. But the relative price of external hard drives has risen (or conversely, the relative price of flash memory drives has fallen).

	Money Price		Relative Price	
	Price Last Year	Price This Year	Price Last Year	Price This Year
Flash memory drives	$300	$210	$\dfrac{\$300}{\$150} = 2.0$	$\dfrac{\$210}{\$140} = 1.50$
External hard drives	$150	$140	$\dfrac{\$150}{\$300} = 0.50$	$\dfrac{\$140}{\$210} = 0.67$

fifteen hundred dollars." The implication, of course, is that the price of cars today is outrageously high because the average new car may cost $32,000. But that is not an accurate comparison. What was the price of the average house during that same year? Perhaps it was only $12,000. By comparison, then, given that the average price of houses today is close to $180,000, the price of a new car today doesn't sound so far out of line, does it?

The point is that money prices during different time periods don't tell you much. You have to calculate relative prices. Consider an example of the price of 350-gigabyte flash memory drives versus the price of 350-gigabyte external hard drives from last year and this year. In Table 3-1 above, we show the money prices of flash memory drives and external hard drives for two years during which they have both gone down.

That means that in today's dollars we have to pay out less for both flash memory drives and external hard drives. If we look, though, at the relative prices of flash memory drives and external hard drives, we find that last year, flash memory drives were twice as expensive as external hard drives, whereas this year they are only one and a half times as expensive. Conversely, if we compare external hard drives to flash memory drives, last year the price of external hard drives was 50 percent of the price of external hard drives, but today the price of external hard drives is about 67 percent of the price of flash memory drives. In the one-year period, although both prices have declined in money terms, the relative price of external hard drives has risen in relation to that of flash memory drives.

Sometimes relative price changes occur because the quality of a product improves, thereby bringing about a decrease in the item's effective *price per constant-quality unit*. Or the price of an item may decrease simply because producers have reduced the item's quality. Thus, when evaluating the effects of price changes, we must always compare *price per constant-quality unit*.

Why is it that for most drivers, the quality-adjusted price of electric vehicles is higher than the posted price?

EXAMPLE

Why Sales of Electric Cars Are Stuck in Low Gear

Prices of solely battery-operated, "electric" autos exceed prices of hybrid (combined gasoline and battery-powered) versions of the same vehicles by at least 30 percent and of all-gasoline-powered versions by at least 50 percent. Nevertheless, the quality-adjusted prices of electric vehicles are even higher.

Not everyone uses an auto just for traveling short, local distances between home and schools, retail stores, and places of employment. Many people commonly desire to drive vehicles farther out than the roughly 250-mile range beyond which the batteries in electric autos

cease to function. The absence of networks of battery-charging or battery-swapping stations limits the usefulness of the vehicles, thereby increasing their quality-adjusted prices. This fact helps to explain why purchases of these vehicles have been trivial since the early 2010s.

FOR CRITICAL THINKING
As the prices of digital devices have declined over time—even as these devices have performed more functions—what has happened to their quality-adjusted prices?

The Demand Schedule

Let's take a hypothetical demand situation to see how the inverse relationship between the price and the quantity demanded looks (holding other things equal). We will consider the quantity of magneto optical (MO) disks—utilized for digital data storage—demanded *per year*. Without stating the *time dimension*, we could not make sense out of this demand relationship because the numbers would be different if we were talking about the quantity demanded per month or the quantity demanded per decade.

In addition to implicitly or explicitly stating a time dimension for a demand relationship, we are also implicitly referring to *constant-quality units* of the good or service in question. Prices are always expressed in constant-quality units in order to avoid the problem of comparing commodities that are in fact not truly comparable.

In panel (a) of Figure 3-1 below, we see that if the price is $1 apiece, 50 magneto optical (MO) disks will be bought each year by our representative individual, but if the price is $5 apiece, only 10 MO disks will be bought each year. This reflects the law of demand. Panel (a) is also called simply demand, or a *demand schedule*, because it gives a schedule of alternative quantities demanded per year at different possible prices.

FIGURE 3-1

The Individual Demand Schedule and the Individual Demand Curve

In panel (a), we show combinations *A* through *E* of the quantities of magneto optical disks demanded, measured in constant-quality units at prices ranging from $5 down to $1 apiece. These combinations are points on the demand schedule. In panel (b), we plot combinations *A* through *E* on a grid. The result is the individual demand curve for MO disks.

Panel (a)

Combination	Price per Constant-Quality Magneto Optical Disk	Quantity of Constant-Quality Titanium Batteries per Year
A	$5	10
B	4	20
C	3	30
D	2	40
E	1	50

The Demand Curve

Tables expressing relationships between two variables can be represented in graphical terms. To do this, we need only construct a graph that has the price per constant-quality magneto optical disk on the vertical axis and the quantity measured in constant-quality MO disks per year on the horizontal axis. All we have to do is take combinations *A* through *E* from panel (a) of Figure 3-1 on the previous page and plot those points in panel (b). Now we connect the points with a smooth line, and *voilà*, we have a **demand curve.** It is downward sloping (from left to right) to indicate the inverse relationship between the price of MO disks and the quantity demanded per year.

Our presentation of demand schedules and curves applies equally well to all commodities, including dental floss, bagels, textbooks, credit, and labor. Remember, the demand curve is simply a graphical representation of the law of demand.

Individual versus Market Demand Curves

The demand schedule shown in panel (a) of Figure 3-1 and the resulting demand curve shown in panel (b) are both given for an individual. As we shall see, the determination of price in the marketplace depends on, among other things, the **market demand** for a particular commodity. The way in which we measure a market demand schedule and derive a market demand curve for magneto optical disks or any other good or service is by summing (at each price) the individual quantities demanded by all buyers in the market. Suppose that the market demand for MO disks consists of only two buyers: buyer 1, for whom we've already shown the demand schedule, and buyer 2, whose demand schedule is displayed in column 3 of panel (a) of Figure 3-2 on the facing page. Column 1 shows the price, and column 2 shows the quantity demanded by buyer 1 at each price. These data are taken directly from Figure 3-1. In column 3, we show the quantity demanded by buyer 2. Column 4 shows the total quantity demanded at each price, which is obtained by simply adding columns 2 and 3. Graphically, in panel (d) of Figure 3-2, we add the demand curves of buyer 1 [panel (b)] and buyer 2 [panel (c)] to derive the market demand curve.

There are, of course, numerous potential consumers of MO disks. We'll simply assume that the summation of all of the consumers in the market results in a demand schedule, given in panel (a) of Figure 3-3 on page 54, and a demand curve, given in panel (b). The quantity demanded is now measured in millions of units per year. Remember, panel (b) in Figure 3-3 shows the market demand curve for the millions of buyers of MO disks. The "market" demand curve that we derived in Figure 3-2 on the facing page was undertaken assuming that there were only two buyers in the entire market. That's why we assume that the "market" demand curve for two buyers in panel (d) of Figure 3-2 is not a smooth line, whereas the true market demand curve in panel (b) of Figure 3-3 is a smooth line with no kinks.

Demand curve

A graphical representation of the demand schedule. It is a negatively sloped line showing the inverse relationship between the price and the quantity demanded (other things being equal).

Market demand

The demand of all consumers in the marketplace for a particular good or service. The summation at each price of the quantity demanded by each individual.

QUICK QUIZ See page 74 for the answers. Review concepts from this section in MyEconLab.

We measure the **demand schedule** in terms of a time dimension and in _____-quality units.

The _____ _____ curve is derived by summing the quantity demanded by individuals at each price.

Graphically, we add the individual demand curves horizontally to derive the total, or market, demand curve.

Shifts in Demand

Assume that the federal government gives every student registered in a college, university, or technical school in the United States a magneto optical disk drive. The demand curve presented in panel (b) of Figure 3-3 on page 54 would no longer

FIGURE 3-2

The Horizontal Summation of Two Demand Curves

Panel (a) shows how to sum the demand schedule for one buyer with that of another buyer. In column 2 is the quantity demanded by buyer 1, taken from panel (a) of Figure 3-1 on page 51. Column 4 is the sum of columns 2 and 3. We plot the demand curve for buyer 1 in panel (b) and the demand curve for buyer 2 in panel (c). When we add those two demand curves horizontally, we get the market demand curve for two buyers, shown in panel (d).

Panel (a)

(1) Price per Magneto Optical Disk	(2) Buyer 1's Quantity Demanded	(3) Buyer 2's Quantity Demanded	(4) = (2) + (3) Combined Quantity Demanded per Year
$5	10	10	20
4	20	20	40
3	30	40	70
2	40	50	90
1	50	60	110

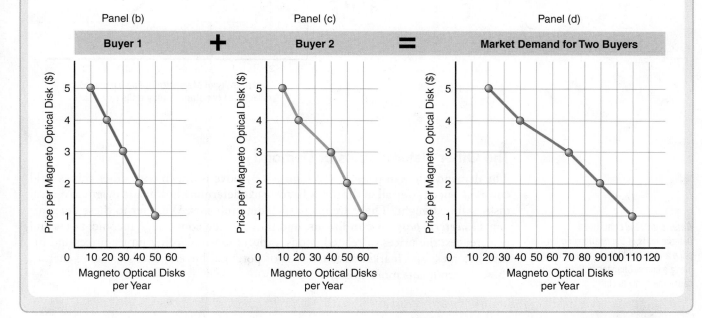

Panel (b) — Buyer 1 + Panel (c) — Buyer 2 = Panel (d) — Market Demand for Two Buyers

be an accurate representation of total market demand for MO disks. What we have to do is shift the curve outward, or to the right, to represent the rise in demand that would result from this program. There will now be an increase in the number of MO disks demanded at *each and every possible price*. The demand curve shown in Figure 3-4 on the following page will shift from D_1 to D_2. Take any price, say, $3 per MO disk. Originally, before the federal government giveaway of MO disk drives, the amount demanded at $3 was 6 million MO disks per year. After the government giveaway of MO disk drives, however, the new amount demanded at the $3 price is 10 million MO disks per year. What we have seen is a shift in the demand for MO disks.

Under different circumstances, the shift can also go in the opposite direction. What if colleges uniformly prohibited the use of magneto optical disk drives by any of their students? Such a regulation would cause a shift inward—to the left—of the demand curve for MO disks. In Figure 3-4 on the following page, the demand curve would shift to D_3. The quantity demanded would now be less at each and every possible price.

FIGURE 3-3

The Market Demand Schedule for Magneto Optical Disks

In panel (a), we add up the existing demand schedules for magneto optical disks. In panel (b), we plot the quantities from panel (a) on a grid. Connecting them produces the market demand curve for MO disks.

Panel (a)

Price per Constant-Quality Magneto Optical Disk	Total Quantity Demanded of Constant-Quality Magneto Optical Disks per Year (millions)
$5	2
4	4
3	6
2	8
1	10

The Other Determinants of Demand

The demand curve in panel (b) of Figure 3-3 above is drawn with other things held constant, specifically all of the other factors that determine how many magneto optical disks will be bought. There are many such determinants. We refer to these determinants as *ceteris paribus* **conditions,** and they include consumers' income; tastes and preferences; the prices of related goods; expectations regarding future prices and future incomes; and market size (number of potential buyers). Let's examine each of these determinants more closely.

Ceteris paribus **conditions**
Determinants of the relationship between price and quantity that are unchanged along a curve. Changes in these factors cause the curve to shift.

FIGURE 3-4

Shifts in the Demand Curve

If some factor other than price changes, we can show its effect by moving the entire demand curve, say, from D_1 to D_2. We have assumed in our example that this move was precipitated by the government's giving a magneto optical disk drive to every registered college student in the United States. Thus, at *all* prices, a larger number of MO disks would be demanded than before. Curve D_3 represents reduced demand compared to curve D_1, caused by a prohibition of MO disk drives on campus.

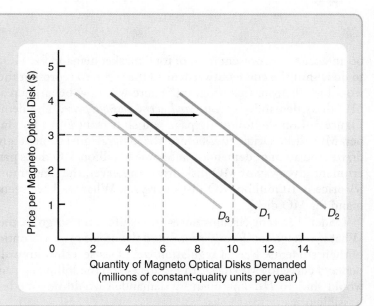

INCOME For most goods, an increase in income will lead to an increase in demand. That is, an increase in income will lead to a rightward shift in the position of the demand curve from, say, D_1 to D_2 in Figure 3-4 on the facing page. You can avoid confusion about shifts in curves by always relating a rise in demand to a rightward shift in the demand curve and a fall in demand to a leftward shift in the demand curve. Goods for which the demand rises when consumer income rises are called **normal goods.** Most goods, such as shoes, computers, and flash memory drives, are "normal goods." For some goods, however, demand *falls* as income rises. These are called **inferior goods.** Beans might be an example. As households get richer, they tend to purchase fewer and fewer beans and purchase more and more fish. (The terms *normal* and *inferior* are merely part of the economist's lexicon. No value judgments are associated with them.)

Remember, a shift to the left in the demand curve represents a decrease in demand, and a shift to the right represents an increase in demand.

How have recent declines in incomes for a large share of U.S. consumers affected the demand for used cell phones that specialty firms recondition and resell?

Normal goods
Goods for which demand rises as income rises. Most goods are normal goods.

Inferior goods
Goods for which demand falls as income rises.

EXAMPLE

Lower Incomes Boost the Demand for Reconditioned Cell Phones

The more than 15 percent of U.S. residents who either have been out of work or are classified by the government as discouraged workers who have given up looking for jobs. These people are earning much lower incomes than they did a few years ago. Many of these people are customers of companies such as ReCellular and Second Rotation, firms that obtain used cell phones from previous owners, recondition the devices, and resell them. Since the economy slipped into its dampened state, sales of reconditioned cell phones have increased by more than 150 percent. Thus, as incomes have fallen for a significant percentage of U.S. consumers, the amount of reconditioned cell phones demanded has increased, indicating that reconditioned cell phones are an inferior good.

FOR CRITICAL THINKING
What is your prediction about the likely effect on the amount of reconditioned cell phones demanded if the U.S. economy were to rebound?

TASTES AND PREFERENCES A change in consumer tastes in favor of a good can shift its demand curve outward to the right. When Pokémon trading cards became the rage, the demand curve for them shifted outward to the right. When the rage died out, the demand curve shifted inward to the left. Fashions depend to a large extent on people's tastes and preferences. Economists have little to say about the determination of tastes. That is, they don't have any "good" theories of taste determination or why people buy one brand of product rather than others. (Advertisers, however, have various theories that they use to try to make consumers prefer their products over those of competitors.)

PRICES OF RELATED GOODS: SUBSTITUTES AND COMPLEMENTS Demand schedules are always drawn with the prices of all other commodities held constant. That is to say, when deriving a given demand curve, we assume that only the price of the good under study changes. For example, when we draw the demand curve for laptop computers, we assume that the price of tablet devices is held constant. When we draw the demand curve for home cinema speakers, we assume that the price of surround-sound amplifiers is held constant. When we refer to *related goods*, we are talking about goods for which demand is interdependent. If a change in the price of one good shifts the demand for another good, those two goods have interdependent demands.

There are two types of demand interdependencies: those in which goods are *substitutes* and those in which goods are *complements*. We can define and distinguish between substitutes and complements in terms of how the change in price of one commodity affects the demand for its related commodity.

YOU ARE THERE

To contemplate how a widening spread between the price of an item and the price of another good that is a close substitute can affect the industry producing the item, take a look at **Why the Casket Industry Is on Life Support**, on page 69.

Substitutes

Two goods are substitutes when a change in the price of one causes a shift in demand for the other in the same direction as the price change.

Butter and margarine are **substitutes.** Either can be consumed to satisfy the same basic want. Let's assume that both products originally cost $2 per pound. If the price of butter remains the same and the price of margarine falls from $2 per pound to $1 per pound, people will buy more margarine and less butter. The demand curve for butter shifts inward to the left. If, conversely, the price of margarine rises from $2 per pound to $3 per pound, people will buy more butter and less margarine. The demand curve for butter shifts outward to the right. In other words, an increase in the price of margarine will lead to an increase in the demand for butter, and an increase in the price of butter will lead to an increase in the demand for margarine. For substitutes, a change in the price of a substitute will cause a change in demand *in the same direction*.

How has the availability of lower-priced plastic substitutes affected the market demand for natural cork stoppers for wine bottles?

EXAMPLE

Why Fewer Wine Bottles Have Natural Cork Stoppers

In the late 1600s, a French monk discovered that natural cork bottle stoppers seal wine into a bottle while allowing the wine to indirectly "breathe" air via the porous characteristics of natural cork's cell structure. Nevertheless, many of today's wine sellers utilize plastic stoppers. These plastic stoppers add to the overall price of a bottle of wine an amount ranging from $0.02 for screw-on stoppers to $0.20 for stoppers composed of extruded plastic that replicates the sponginess of natural cork.

Since the early 2000s, prices of natural cork stoppers have risen above those of plastic stoppers, to levels from about $0.03 for low-quality stoppers to as much as $2 for stoppers of the highest quality. Wine consumers have responded to higher prices of wines bottled with natural cork stoppers by substituting in favor of wines bottled with plastic stoppers. During the past decade, purchases of wine bottled with plastic stoppers have increased by more than 50 percent.

FOR CRITICAL THINKING

Natural cork producers advertise that plastic stoppers harm the environment. If such ads shift the preferences of wine producers and consumers back in favor of natural cork stoppers, what will happen to the market demand for plastic stoppers?

Complements

Two goods are complements when a change in the price of one causes an opposite shift in the demand for the other.

For **complements,** goods typically consumed together, the situation is reversed. Consider digital devices and online applications (apps). We draw the demand curve for apps with the price of digital devices held constant. If the price per constant-quality unit of digital devices decreases from, say, $500 to $300, that will encourage more people to purchase apps. They will now buy more apps, at any given app price, than before. The demand curve for apps will shift outward to the right. If, by contrast, the price of digital devices increases from $250 to $450, fewer people will purchase downloadable applications. The demand curve for apps will shift inward to the left.

To summarize, a decrease in the price of digital devices leads to an increase in the demand for apps. An increase in the price of digital devices leads to a decrease in the demand for apps. Thus, for complements, a change in the price of a product will cause a change in demand *in the opposite direction* for the other good.

EXPECTATIONS Consumers' expectations regarding future prices and future incomes will prompt them to buy more or less of a particular good without a change in its current money price. For example, consumers getting wind of a scheduled 100 percent increase in the price of magneto optical disks next month will buy more of them today at today's prices. Today's demand curve for MO disks will shift from D_1 to D_2 in Figure 3-4 on page 54. The opposite would occur if a decrease in the price of MO disks was scheduled for next month (from D_1 to D_3).

Expectations of a rise in income may cause consumers to want to purchase more of everything today at today's prices. Again, such a change in expectations of higher future income will cause a shift in the demand curve from D_1 to D_2 in Figure 3-4.

Finally, expectations that goods will not be available at any price will induce consumers to stock up now, increasing current demand.

In what ways did recent policy actions by several nations' governments regarding the use of nuclear power affect expectations of the future price of uranium and, as a result, the current market demand for uranium?

POLICY EXAMPLE

An Expected Uranium Price Implosion Cuts Current Uranium Demand

Following the meltdown of a Japanese nuclear reactor in the wake of that nation's disastrous earthquake and tsunami in 2011, governments of a number of countries announced that they planned to decrease their reliance on nuclear power as a source of energy. These policy actions led participants in the uranium market to anticipate a decrease in the future price of uranium. In turn, this expectation of a lower *future* uranium price induced consumers of the nuclear fuel to postpone *current* purchases to the future, when they expected lower prices to prevail. As a consequence, the expected drop in the future price of uranium generated a nearly 10 percent decrease in the contemporaneous market demand for uranium.

FOR CRITICAL THINKING

What would happen to the market demand for uranium if a different current event induced people to anticipate higher future uranium prices?

MARKET SIZE (NUMBER OF POTENTIAL BUYERS) An increase in the number of potential buyers (holding buyers' incomes constant) at any given price shifts the market demand curve outward. Conversely, a reduction in the number of potential buyers at any given price shifts the market demand curve inward.

Changes in Demand versus Changes in Quantity Demanded

We have made repeated references to demand and to quantity demanded. It is important to realize that there is a difference between a *change in demand* and a *change in quantity demanded*.

Demand refers to a schedule of planned rates of purchase and depends on a great many *ceteris paribus* conditions, such as incomes, expectations, and the prices of substitutes or complements. Whenever there is a change in a *ceteris paribus* condition, there will be a change in demand—a shift in the entire demand curve to the right or to the left.

A *quantity demanded* is a specific quantity at a specific price, represented by a single point on a demand curve. When price changes, quantity demanded changes according to the law of demand, and there will be a movement from one point to another along the same demand curve. Look at Figure 3-5 on the following page. At a price of $3 per magneto optical disk, 6 million MO disks per year are demanded. If the price falls to $1, quantity demanded increases to 10 million per year. This movement occurs because the current market price for the product changes. In Figure 3-5, you can see the arrow pointing down the given demand curve *D*.

When you think of demand, think of the entire curve. Quantity demanded, in contrast, is represented by a single point on the demand curve.

> *A change or shift in demand is a movement of the entire curve. The **only** thing that can cause the entire curve to move is a change in a determinant other than the good's own price.*

In economic analysis, we cannot emphasize too much the following distinction that must constantly be made:

> *A change in a good's own price leads to a change in quantity demanded for any given demand curve, other things held constant. This is a movement along the curve.*

> *A change in any of the ceteris paribus conditions for demand leads to a change in demand. This causes a shift of the curve.*

FIGURE 3-5

Movement along a Given Demand Curve

A change in price changes the quantity of a good demanded. This can be represented as movement along a given demand schedule. If, in our example, the price of magneto optical disks falls from $3 to $1 apiece, the quantity demanded will increase from 6 million to 10 million MO disks per year.

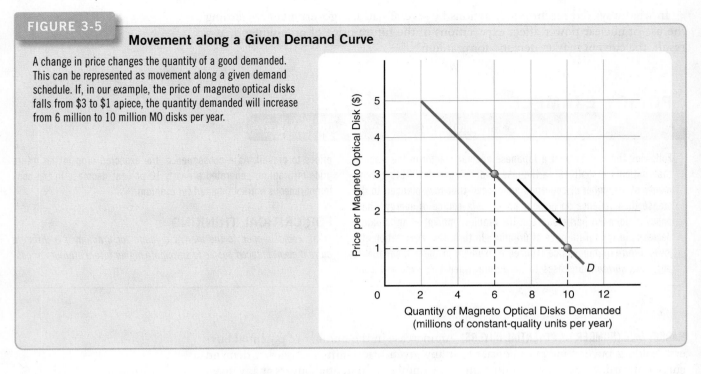

QUICK QUIZ

See page 74 for the answers. Review concepts from this section in MyEconLab.

Demand curves are drawn with determinants other than the price of the good held constant. These other determinants, called *ceteris paribus* conditions, are (1) _____, (2) _____, (3) _____, (4) _____, and (5) _____ at any given price. If any one of these determinants changes, the demand curve will shift to the right or to the left.

A change in demand comes about only because of a change in the _____ _____ conditions of

demand. This change in demand is a shift in the demand curve to the left or to the right.

A change in the quantity demanded comes about when there is a change in the price of the good (other things held constant). Such a change in quantity demanded involves a _____ _____ a given demand curve.

The Law of Supply

The other side of the basic model in economics involves the quantities of goods and services that firms will offer for sale to the market. The **supply** of any good or service is the amount that firms will produce and offer for sale under certain conditions during a specified time period. The relationship between price and quantity supplied, called the **law of supply,** can be summarized as follows:

> *At higher prices, a larger quantity will generally be supplied than at lower prices, all other things held constant. At lower prices, a smaller quantity will generally be supplied than at higher prices, all other things held constant.*

There is generally a direct relationship between price and quantity supplied. As the price rises, the quantity supplied rises. As the price falls, the quantity supplied also falls. Producers are normally willing to produce and sell more of their product at a higher price than at a lower price, other things being constant. At $5 per magneto optical disk, manufacturers would almost certainly be willing to supply a larger quantity than at $1 per MO disk, assuming, of course, that no other prices in the economy had changed.

As with the law of demand, millions of instances in the real world have given us confidence in the law of supply. On a theoretical level, the law of supply is based on a model in which producers and sellers seek to make the most gain possible from their activities. For example, as a manufacturer attempts to produce more and more MO disks over the same time period, it will eventually have to hire more workers,

Supply
A schedule showing the relationship between price and quantity supplied for a specified period of time, other things being equal.

Law of supply
The observation that the higher the price of a good, the more of that good sellers will make available over a specified time period, other things being equal.

pay overtime wages (which are higher), and overutilize its machines. Only if offered a higher price per MO disk will the manufacturer be willing to incur these higher costs. That is why the law of supply implies a direct relationship between price and quantity supplied.

Have steel manufacturers' responses to a decline in the price of steel been consistent with the law of supply?

EXAMPLE

Steel Producers Reduce Production When the Price of Steel Falls

Recently, the market price of steel declined from $660 per ton to below $625 per ton. Steel-producing firms responded by cutting back on their production of steel. Thus, as predicted by the law of supply, a decrease in the price of steel resulted in a decrease in the quantity of steel supplied. This direct relationship between price and quantity supplied is consistent with an upward-sloping supply curve for steel.

FOR CRITICAL THINKING
After the price of steel declined, which direction did each steel manufacturer move along its supply curve?

The Supply Schedule

Just as we were able to construct a demand schedule, we can construct a *supply schedule*, which is a table relating prices to the quantity supplied at each price. A supply schedule can also be referred to simply as *supply*. It is a set of planned production rates that depends on the price of the product. We show the individual supply schedule for a hypothetical producer in panel (a) of Figure 3-6 below. At a price of $1 per MO disk, for example, this producer will supply 20,000 MO disks per year. At a price of $5 per MO disk, this producer will supply 55,000 MO disks per year.

FIGURE 3-6

The Individual Producer's Supply Schedule and Supply Curve for Magneto Optical Disks

Panel (a) shows that at higher prices, a hypothetical supplier will be willing to provide a greater quantity of magneto optical disks. We plot the various price-quantity combinations in panel (a) on the grid in panel

(b). When we connect these points, we create the individual supply curve for MO disks. It is positively sloped.

Panel (a)

Combination	Price per Constant-Quality Magneto Optical Disk	Quantity of Magneto Optical Disks Supplied (thousands of constant-quality units per year)
F	$5	55
G	4	40
H	3	35
I	2	25
J	1	20

Panel (b)

The Supply Curve

We can convert the supply schedule from panel (a) of Figure 3-6 on the previous page into a **supply curve,** just as we earlier created a demand curve in Figure 3-1 on page 51. All we do is take the price-quantity combinations from panel (a) of Figure 3-6 and plot them in panel (b). We have labeled these combinations *F* through *J*. Connecting these points, we obtain an upward-sloping curve that shows the typically direct relationship between price and quantity supplied. Again, we have to remember that we are talking about quantity supplied *per year*, measured in constant-quality units.

The Market Supply Curve

Just as we summed the individual demand curves to obtain the market demand curve, we sum the individual producers' supply curves to obtain the market supply curve. Look at Figure 3-7 below, in which we horizontally sum two typical supply curves for manufacturers of magneto optical disks. Supplier 1's data are taken from Figure 3-6 on the previous page. Supplier 2 is added. The numbers are presented in panel (a). The graphical representation of supplier 1 is in panel (b), of supplier 2 in panel (c), and of the summation in panel (d). The result, then, is the supply curve for magneto optical

---

FIGURE 3-7

Horizontal Summation of Supply Curves

In panel (a), we show the data for two individual suppliers of magneto optical disks. Adding how much each is willing to supply at different prices, we come up with the combined quantities supplied in column 4. When we plot the values in columns 2 and 3 on grids from panels (b) and (c) and add them horizontally, we obtain the combined supply curve for the two suppliers in question, shown in panel (d).

Panel (a)

(1) Price per Magneto Optical Disk	(2) Supplier 1's Quantity Supplied (thousands)	(3) Supplier 2's Quantity Supplied (thousands)	(4) = (2) + (3) Combined Quantity Supplied per Year (thousands)
$5	55	35	90
4	40	30	70
3	35	20	55
2	25	15	40
1	20	10	30

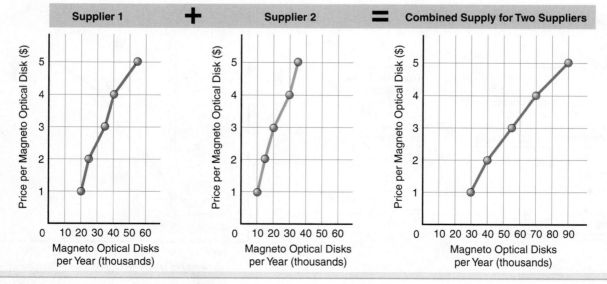

disks for suppliers 1 and 2. We assume that there are more suppliers of MO disks, however. The total market supply schedule and total market supply curve for MO disks are represented in Figure 3-8 below, with the curve in panel (b) obtained by adding all of the supply curves, such as those shown in panels (b) and (c) of Figure 3-7 on the facing page. Notice the difference between the market supply curve with only two suppliers in Figure 3-7 and the one with many suppliers—the entire true market—in panel (b) of Figure 3-8. (For simplicity, we assume that the true total market supply curve is a straight line.)

Note what happens at the market level when price changes. If the price is $3, the quantity supplied is 6 million. If the price goes up to $4, the quantity supplied increases to 8 million per year. If the price falls to $2, the quantity supplied decreases to 4 million per year. Changes in quantity supplied are represented by movements along the supply curve in panel (b) of Figure 3-8.

QUICK QUIZ See page 74 for the answers. Review concepts from this section in MyEconLab.

There is normally a _____ relationship between price and quantity of a good supplied, other things held constant.	The _____ curve normally shows a direct relationship between price and quantity supplied. The _____ _____ curve is obtained by horizontally adding individual supply curves in the market.

Shifts in Supply

When we looked at demand, we found out that any change in anything relevant besides the price of the good or service caused the demand curve to shift inward or outward. The same is true for the supply curve. If something besides price changes and alters the willingness of suppliers to produce a good or service, we will see the entire supply curve shift.

FIGURE 3-8

The Market Supply Schedule and the Market Supply Curve for Magneto Optical Disks

In panel (a), we show the summation of all the individual producers' supply schedules. In panel (b), we graph the resulting supply curve. It represents the market supply curve for MO disks and is upward sloping.

Panel (a)

Price per Constant-Quality Magneto Optical Disk	Quantity of Magneto Optical Disks Supplied (millions of constant-quality units per year)
$5	10
4	8
3	6
2	4
1	2

Panel (b)

FIGURE 3-9

Shifts in the Supply Curve

If the cost of producing magneto optical disks were to fall dramatically, the supply curve would shift rightward from S_1 to S_2 such that at all prices, a larger quantity would be forthcoming from suppliers. Conversely, if the cost of production rose, the supply curve would shift leftward to S_3.

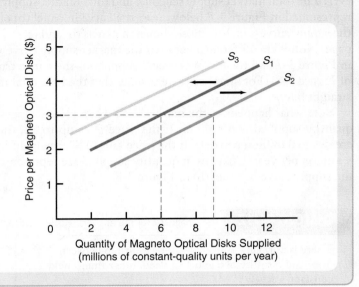

Consider an example. There is a new method of manufacturing magneto optical disks that significantly reduces the cost of production. In this situation, producers of MO disks will supply more product at *all* prices because their cost of so doing has fallen dramatically. Competition among manufacturers to produce more at each and every price will shift the supply curve outward to the right from S_1 to S_2 in Figure 3-9 above. At a price of $3, the number supplied was originally 6 million per year, but now the amount supplied (after the reduction in the costs of production) at $3 per MO disk will be 9 million a year. (This is similar to what has happened to the supply curve of digital devices in recent years as memory chip prices have fallen.)

Consider the opposite case. If the price of raw materials used in manufacturing magneto optical disks increases, the supply curve in Figure 3-9 will shift from S_1 to S_3. At each and every price, the quantity of MO disks supplied will fall due to the increase in the price of raw materials.

The Other Determinants of Supply

When supply curves are drawn, only the price of the good in question changes, and it is assumed that other things remain constant. The other things assumed constant are the *ceteris paribus* conditions of supply. They include the prices of resources (inputs) used to produce the product, technology and productivity, taxes and subsidies, producers' price expectations, and the number of firms in the industry. If *any* of these *ceteris paribus* conditions changes, there will be a shift in the supply curve.

COST OF INPUTS USED TO PRODUCE THE PRODUCT If one or more input prices fall, production costs fall, and the supply curve will shift outward to the right. That is, more will be supplied at each and every price. The opposite will be true if one or more inputs become more expensive. For example, when we draw the supply curve of new tablet devices, we are holding the price of microprocessors (and other inputs) constant. When we draw the supply curve of blue jeans, we are holding the cost of cotton fabric fixed.

Why have large swings in the price of cotton generated variations in the market supply of clothing?

EXAMPLE

Cotton Price Movements Squeeze and Stretch Clothing Supply

Between 2009 and 2010, the price of cotton, a key input cost in the production of many articles of clothing, increased by 55 percent. Clothing manufacturers responded by reducing the amount of clothing supplied at any given price of clothing, so the market supply of clothing decreased.

During 2011, the price of cotton decreased by 53 percent, to nearly its 2009 level. This cotton-price reversal induced clothing-producing firms

to increase the amount of clothing supplied at each possible clothing price. Thus, the market supply of clothing increased.

FOR CRITICAL THINKING
What do you think happened to the market supply of clothing when cotton prices rose somewhat again in 2012?

TECHNOLOGY AND PRODUCTIVITY Supply curves are drawn by assuming a given technology, or "state of the art." When the available production techniques change, the supply curve will shift. For example, when a better production technique for magneto optical disks becomes available, production costs decrease, and the supply curve will shift to the right. A larger quantity will be forthcoming at each and every price because the cost of production is lower.

TAXES AND SUBSIDIES Certain taxes, such as a per-unit tax, are effectively an addition to production costs and therefore reduce the supply. If the supply curve is S_1 in Figure 3-9 on the facing page, a per-unit tax increase would shift it to S_3. A per-unit **subsidy** would do the opposite. Every producer would get a "gift" from the government for each unit produced. This per-unit subsidy would shift the curve to S_2.

Subsidy
A negative tax; a payment to a producer from the government, usually in the form of a cash grant per unit.

WHAT IF... politicians simultaneously oppose a higher price for the current quantity of gasoline supplied yet favor higher taxes on the fuel?

A decrease in the market supply of gasoline implies that producers require a higher price to continue providing the same quantity of this fuel. When this occurs, media reports typically feature members of Congress complaining about gasoline sellers insisting on prices that are "too high." Voting records, though, often reveal that many of the politicians who make these complaints have voted to boost federal fuel taxes. Such

tax hikes generate decreases in the supply of gasoline and hence contribute to sellers' desires to receive a higher price for any given quantity. Thus, when politicians join congressional majorities to impose higher federal gasoline taxes, what results is the fuel supply reductions that these politicians criticize.

PRICE EXPECTATIONS A change in the expectation of a future relative price of a product can affect a producer's current willingness to supply, just as price expectations affect a consumer's current willingness to purchase. For example, suppliers of magneto optical disks may withhold from the market part of their current supply if they anticipate higher prices in the future. The current amount supplied at each and every price will decrease.

NUMBER OF FIRMS IN THE INDUSTRY In the short run, when firms can change only the number of employees they use, we hold the number of firms in the industry constant. In the long run, the number of firms may change. If the number of firms increases, supply will increase, and the supply curve will shift outward to the right. If the number of firms decreases, supply will decrease, and the supply curve will shift inward to the left.

How did a rash of tornadoes affect the supply curve in the U.S. poultry market?

EXAMPLE

How Deadly Southern Twisters Pummeled the U.S. Poultry Supply

During the course of the deadliest U.S. tornado season in decades, 278 tornadoes swept across the United States between April 26 and 28, 2011. Most of the twisters struck southern states. Particularly hard hit was Alabama, whose farmers typically contribute just over 1 billion chickens to the nation's production of poultry—about 12 percent of the total. Tornadoes damaged numerous feed mills and chicken-processing plants so severely that many poultry-producing companies were unable to supply poultry for a few months. This reduction in the number of chicken-producing firms in operation caused a decrease in the amount of poultry supplied at any given poultry price. That is, the U.S. market poultry supply decreased temporarily in 2011.

FOR CRITICAL THINKING
How did the outright destruction of millions of chickens by the April 2011 tornadoes affect the position of the market poultry supply curve?

Changes in Supply versus Changes in Quantity Supplied

We cannot overstress the importance of distinguishing between a movement along the supply curve—which occurs only when the price changes for a given supply curve—and a shift in the supply curve—which occurs only with changes in *ceteris paribus* conditions. A change in the price of the good in question always (and only) brings about a change in the quantity supplied along a given supply curve. We move to a different point on the existing supply curve. This is specifically called a *change in quantity supplied*. When price changes, quantity supplied changes—there is a movement from one point to another along the same supply curve.

When you think of *supply*, think of the entire curve. Quantity supplied is represented by a single point on the supply curve.

> *A change, or shift, in supply is a movement of the entire curve.* The **only** *thing that can cause the entire curve to move is a change in one of the* **ceteris paribus** *conditions.*

Consequently,

> *A change in price leads to a change in the quantity supplied, other things being constant. This is a movement* **along** *the curve.*

> *A change in any* **ceteris paribus** *condition for supply leads to a change in supply. This causes a* **shift** *of the curve.*

QUICK QUIZ See page 74 for the answers. Review concepts from this section in MyEconLab.

If the price changes, we _____ _____ a curve—there is a change in quantity demanded or supplied. If some other determinant changes, we _____ a curve—there is a change in demand or supply.

The **supply curve** is drawn with other things held constant. If these *ceteris paribus* conditions of supply change, the supply curve will shift. The major *ceteris paribus* conditions are (1) _____, (2) _____, (3) _____, (4) _____, and (5) _____.

Putting Demand and Supply Together

In the sections on demand and supply, we tried to confine each discussion to demand or supply only. But you have probably already realized that we can't view the world just from the demand side or just from the supply side. There is interaction between the two. In this section, we will discuss how they interact and how that interaction determines the prices that prevail in our economy and other economies in which the forces of demand and supply are allowed to work.

Let's first combine the demand and supply schedules and then combine the curves.

Go to www.econtoday.com/chap03 to see how the U.S. Department of Agriculture seeks to estimate demand and supply conditions for major agricultural products.

Demand and Supply Schedules Combined

Let's place panel (a) from Figure 3-3 (the market demand schedule) on page 54 and panel (a) from Figure 3-8 (the market supply schedule) on page 61 together in panel (a) of Figure 3-10 on the following page. Column 1 displays the price. Column 2 shows the quantity supplied per year at any given price. Column 3 displays the quantity demanded. Column 4 is the difference between columns 2 and 3, or the difference between the quantity supplied and the quantity demanded. In column 5, we label those differences as either excess quantity supplied (called a *surplus*, which we shall discuss shortly) or excess quantity demanded (commonly known as a *shortage*, also discussed shortly). For example, at a price of $1, only 2 million magneto optical disks would be supplied, but the quantity demanded would be 10 million. The difference would be −8 million, which we label excess quantity demanded (a shortage). At the other end, a price of $5 would elicit 10 million in quantity supplied. Quantity demanded would drop to 2 million, leaving a difference of +8 million units, which we call excess quantity supplied (a surplus).

Now, do you notice something special about the price of $3? At that price, both the quantity supplied and the quantity demanded per year are 6 million. The difference then is zero. There is neither excess quantity demanded (shortage) nor excess quantity supplied (surplus). Hence the price of $3 is very special. It is called the **market clearing price**—it clears the market of all excess quantities demanded or supplied. There are no willing consumers who want to pay $3 per MO disk but are turned away by sellers, and there are no willing suppliers who want to sell MO disks at $3 who cannot sell all they want at that price. Another term for the market clearing price is the **equilibrium price,** the price at which there is no tendency for change. Consumers are able to get all they want at that price, and suppliers are able to sell all they want at that price.

Market clearing, or equilibrium, price
The price that clears the market, at which quantity demanded equals quantity supplied; the price where the demand curve intersects the supply curve.

Equilibrium

We can define **equilibrium** in general as a point at which quantity demanded equals quantity supplied at a particular price. There tends to be no movement of the price or the quantity away from this point unless demand or supply changes. Any movement away from this point will set into motion forces that will cause movement back to it. Therefore, equilibrium is a stable point. Any point that is not an equilibrium is unstable and will not persist.

Equilibrium
The situation when quantity supplied equals quantity demanded at a particular price.

The equilibrium point occurs where the supply and demand curves intersect. The equilibrium price is given on the vertical axis directly to the left of where the supply and demand curves cross. The equilibrium quantity is given on the horizontal axis directly underneath the intersection of the demand and supply curves.

Panel (b) in Figure 3-3 (p. 54) and panel (b) in Figure 3-8 (p. 61) are combined as panel (b) in Figure 3-10 on the next page. The demand curve is labeled *D*, the supply curve *S*. We have labeled the intersection of the supply curve with the demand curve as point *E*, for equilibrium. That corresponds to a market clearing price of $3, at which both the quantity supplied and the quantity demanded are 6 million units per year. There is neither excess quantity supplied nor excess quantity demanded. Point *E*, the equilibrium point, always occurs at the intersection of the supply and demand curves. This is the price *toward which* the market price will automatically tend to gravitate, because there is no outcome more advantageous than this price for both consumers and producers.

FIGURE 3-10

Putting Demand and Supply Together

In panel (a), we see that at the price of $3, the quantity supplied and the quantity demanded are equal, resulting in neither an excess quantity demanded nor an excess quantity supplied. We call this price the equilibrium, or market clearing, price. In panel (b), the intersection of the supply and demand curves is at *E*, at a price of $3 and a quantity of 6 million per year. At point *E*, there is neither an excess quantity demanded nor an excess quantity supplied. At a price of $1, the quantity supplied will be only 2 million per year, but the quantity demanded will be 10 million. The difference is excess quantity demanded at a price of $1. The price will rise, so we will move from point *A* up the supply curve and from point *B* up the demand curve to point *E*. At the other extreme, a price of $5 elicits a quantity supplied of 10 million but a quantity demanded of only 2 million. The difference is excess quantity supplied at a price of $5. The price will fall, so we will move down the demand curve and the supply curve to the equilibrium price, $3 per magneto optical disk.

Panel (a)

(1) Price per Constant-Quality Magneto Optical Disk	(2) Quantity Supplied (magneto optical disks per year)	(3) Quantity Demanded (magneto optical disks per year)	(4) Difference (2) − (3) (magneto optical disks per year)	(5) Condition
$5	10 million	2 million	8 million	Excess quantity supplied (surplus)
4	8 million	4 million	4 million	Excess quantity supplied (surplus)
3	6 million	6 million	0	Market clearing price—equilibrium (no surplus, no shortage)
2	4 million	8 million	−4 million	Excess quantity demanded (shortage)
1	2 million	10 million	−8 million	Excess quantity demanded (shortage)

Panel (b)

Shortages

The price of $3 depicted in Figure 3-10 above represents a situation of equilibrium. If there were a non-market-clearing, or disequilibrium, price, this price would put into play forces that would cause the price to change toward the market clearing price, at which equilibrium would again be sustained. Look again at panel (b) in Figure 3-10. Suppose that instead of being at the equilibrium price of $3, for some reason the market price is $1. At this price, the quantity demanded of 10 million per year exceeds the quantity supplied of 2 million per year. We have a situation of excess quantity demanded at the price of $1. This is usually called a **shortage.** Consumers of magneto optical disks would find that they could not buy all that they wished at $1 apiece. But forces will cause the price to rise: Competing consumers will bid up the price, and suppliers will increase output in response. (Remember, some buyers would pay $5 or more rather than do without MO disks.) We would move from points A and B toward point E. The process would stop when the price again reached $3 per MO disk.

At this point, it is important to recall a distinction made in Chapter 2:

Shortages and scarcity are not the same thing.

A shortage is a situation in which the quantity demanded exceeds the quantity supplied at a price that is somehow kept *below* the market clearing price. Our definition of scarcity was much more general and all-encompassing: a situation in which the resources available for producing output are insufficient to satisfy all wants. Any choice necessarily costs an opportunity, and the opportunity is lost. Hence, we will always live in a world of scarcity because we must constantly make choices, but we do not necessarily have to live in a world of shortages.

What has caused a shortage of a key drug used to treat victims of a common form of leukemia?

Shortage
A situation in which quantity demanded is greater than quantity supplied at a price below the market clearing price.

EXAMPLE

Production Breakdowns Create a Shortage of a Life-Saving Drug

Each year, physicians diagnose more than 20,000 new cases of acute lymphoblastic leukemia. Recently, all of the companies that manufacture cytarabine, a drug commonly used in treatment regimens for this disease, experienced problems that slowed or halted production of the drug. As a consequence, the quantity of cytarabine supplied fell well below the quantity demanded for treatments at the prevailing price.

In response to the shortage, hospitals and clinics began limiting available cytarabine doses to children and to only a few adults judged most likely to benefit from treatment with that drug. Other adults had to switch to different drugs even if they were unlikely to be as effective. Physicians hope that eventually more adults will be able to undergo treatment with this drug, after resolution of production problems, albeit at a market clearing price that probably will be higher.

FOR CRITICAL THINKING
Why is the market clearing price of cytarabine likely to increase, and why might an increase in that price be required to eliminate the shortage of the drug?

Surpluses

Now let's repeat the experiment with the market price at $5 rather than at the market clearing price of $3. Clearly, the quantity supplied will exceed the quantity demanded at that price. The result will be an excess quantity supplied at $5 per unit. This excess quantity supplied is often called a **surplus.** Given the curves in panel (b) in Figure 3-10 on the facing page, however, there will be forces pushing the price back down toward $3 per magneto optical disk. Competing suppliers will cut prices and reduce output, and consumers will purchase more at these new lower prices. If the two forces of supply and demand are unrestricted, they will bring the price back to $3 per MO disk.

Shortages and surpluses are resolved in unfettered markets—markets in which price changes are free to occur. The forces that resolve them are those of competition: In the case of shortages, consumers competing for a limited quantity supplied drive up the price; in the case of surpluses, sellers compete for the limited quantity demanded, thus driving prices down to equilibrium. The equilibrium price is the only stable price, and the (unrestricted) market price tends to gravitate toward it.

What happens when the price is set below the equilibrium price? Here come the scalpers.

Surplus
A situation in which quantity supplied is greater than quantity demanded at a price above the market clearing price.

POLICY EXAMPLE

Should Shortages in the Ticket Market Be Solved by Scalpers?

If you have ever tried to get tickets to a playoff game in sports, a popular Broadway play, or a superstar's rap concert, you know about "shortages." The standard Super Bowl ticket situation is shown in Figure 3-11 below. At the face-value price of Super Bowl tickets ($800), the quantity demanded (175,000) greatly exceeds the quantity supplied (80,000). Because shortages last only as long as prices and quantities do not change, markets tend to exhibit a movement out of this disequilibrium toward equilibrium. Obviously, the quantity of Super Bowl tickets cannot change, but the price can go as high as $6,000.

Enter the scalper. This colorful term is used because when you purchase a ticket that is being resold at a price higher than face value, the seller is skimming profit off the top ("taking your scalp"). If an event sells out and people who wished to purchase tickets at current prices were unable to do so, ticket prices by definition were lower than market clearing prices. People without tickets may be willing to buy high-priced tickets because they place a greater value on the entertainment event than the face value of the ticket. Without scalpers, those individuals would not be able to attend the event. In the case of the Super Bowl, various forms of scalping occur nationwide. Tickets for a seat on the 50-yard line have been sold for as much as $6,000 apiece. In front of every Super Bowl arena, you can find ticket scalpers hawking their wares.

In most states, scalping is illegal. In Pennsylvania, convicted scalpers are either fined $5,000 or sentenced to two years behind bars. For an economist, such legislation seems strange. As one New York ticket broker said, "I look at scalping like working as a stockbroker, buying low and selling high. If people are willing to pay me the money, what kind of problem is that?"

FOR CRITICAL ANALYSIS

What happens to ticket scalpers who are still holding tickets after an event has started?

FIGURE 3-11

Shortages of Super Bowl Tickets

The quantity of tickets for a Super Bowl game is fixed at 80,000. At the price per ticket of $800, the quantity demanded is 175,000. Consequently, there is an excess quantity demanded at the below-market clearing price. In this example, prices can go as high as $6,000 in the scalpers' market.

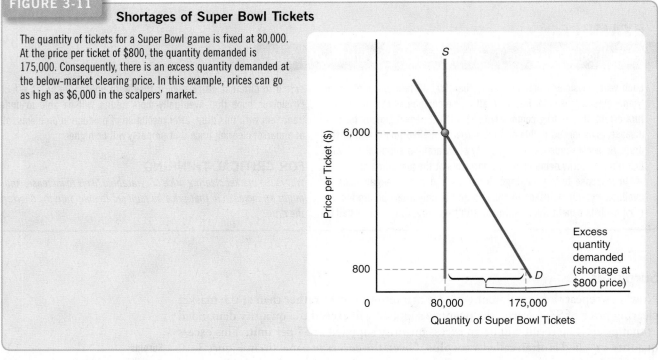

The market clearing price occurs at the _____ of the market demand curve and the market supply curve. It is also called the _____ price, the price from which there is no tendency to change unless there is a change in demand or supply.

Whenever the price is _____ than the equilibrium price, there is an excess quantity supplied (a **surplus**).

Whenever the price is _____ than the equilibrium price, there is an excess quantity demanded (a **shortage**).

YOU ARE THERE
Why the Casket Industry Is on Life Support

Ken Camp, the chief executive officer of Hillenbrand, Inc., has succinctly summed up his company's situation: "We are a very significant player in an industry that isn't growing." Hillenbrand is part of the casket industry, which is facing tough times as a consequence of the falling price of cremations, which are substitutes for casket burials of deceased individuals. The overall price of a traditional casket burial exceeds $7,200. In contrast, the price of a cremation service has recently fallen to about $1,300.

The widening differential between the price of traditional casket burials and the price of cremation services has induced many people to substitute away from purchasing caskets. Today, nearly 400,000 fewer caskets are purchased per year in the United States than were purchased

in 2008. Thus, the demand for caskets has declined in response to a decrease in the price of an already lower-priced substitute—cremation. This fact explains why Camp has concluded that the casket industry "isn't growing."

Critical Thinking Questions

1. What impact do you think that the decline in demand for caskets has had on sellers' total revenues, which equal price multiplied by quantity sold?

2. How have technological improvements in the cremation-services industry likely affected the supply curve for these services?

ISSUES & APPLICATIONS

Your Higher Education Bills Really Are Increasing

CONCEPTS APPLIED
▶ Money Price
▶ Relative Price
▶ Market Clearing Price

Undoubtedly, you have noticed that your college expenses have been rising. The reason is that the prices of goods and services that students must purchase to obtain higher education have been increasing persistently for more than three decades.

A Tale of Upward Trends in Two Sets of Money Prices

Figure 3-12 on the following page displays index measures of two sets of money prices that are important to current U.S. college students. One is an index measure of U.S. college tuition and fees. The other is an index measure of the prices of U.S. educational books and supplies.

Clearly, the figure indicates that both indexes of these money prices have increased substantially in recent years. The money value of tuition and fees that college students pay is about thirteen times greater today than in the late 1970s, and the money prices of educational books and supplies are more than nine times higher.

Relative Prices of Higher Education Are Also Rising

Have prices of higher education been rising faster than the average level of prices of all good and services? Figure 3-12 also shows an index measure of the level of prices of all goods and services purchased in the United States. Taking into account the significant increase in the prices of all goods and services during the past four decades indicates that *relative* prices of educational books and supplies have more than doubled. *Relative* tuition-and-fee prices have more than tripled.

Continuing increases in the relative prices of tuition and fees and of educational books and supplies reflect higher market clearing prices of college enrollment, books, and

FIGURE 3-12

Indexes of Prices for Higher-Education-Related Items and All Goods and Services since 1978

The rise in the index of U.S. tuition and fees from 100 in 1978 to the current level of just over 1,300 indicates that the money price of college enrollment is now thirteen times higher. Money prices of educational books and supplies are now more than nine times higher, and money prices of all goods and services are about four times higher.

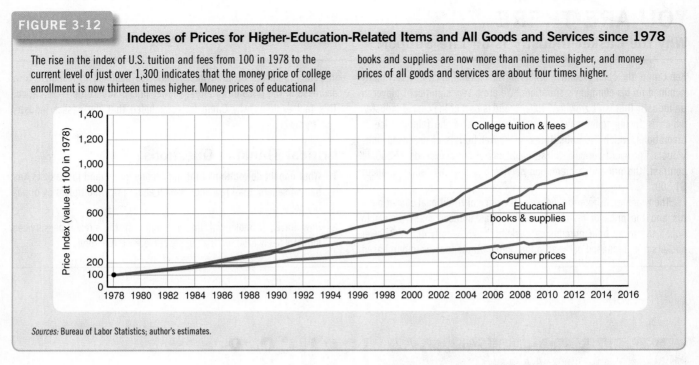

Sources: Bureau of Labor Statistics; author's estimates.

supplies. These are the prices at which the demand and supply curves for these items cross in the relevant markets—prices at intersections that have continued drifting upward over time.

For Critical Thinking

1. In relation to higher education, what has happened to the relative prices of other goods and services?

2. Given that market supply has increased steadily during the past four decades, what must account for rising money and relative prices of higher education?

Web Resources

1. Review a list of the highest-priced U.S. colleges at **www.econtoday.com/chap03**.

2. Compare the money prices of college enrollment in the United States to the lower money prices prevailing in the United Kingdom at **www.econtoday.com/chap03**.

> ### MyEconLab
> For more questions on this chapter's Issues & Applications, go to **MyEconLab**. In the Study Plan for this chapter, select Section N: News.

MyEconLab

Here is what you should know after reading this chapter. MyEconLab will help you identify what you know, and where to go when you need to practice.

— **WHAT YOU SHOULD KNOW** —

— **WHERE TO GO TO PRACTICE** —

The Law of Demand Other things being equal, individuals will purchase fewer units of a good at a higher price and will purchase more units at a lower price.

market, 49
demand, 49
law of demand, 49

• **MyEconLab** Study Plan 3.1

WHAT YOU SHOULD KNOW	MyEconLab *continued*	WHERE TO GO TO PRACTICE
Relative Prices versus Money Prices The relative price is the price of the good in terms of other goods. In a world of generally rising prices, people compare the price of one good with the general level of prices of other goods in order to decide whether the relative price of that one good has gone up, gone down, or stayed the same.	relative price, 49 money price, 49	• MyEconLab Study Plan 3.1
A Change in Quantity Demanded versus a Change in Demand The demand schedule shows quantities purchased per unit of time at various possible prices. Graphically, the demand schedule is a downward-sloping demand curve. A change in the price of the good generates a change in the quantity demanded, which is a movement along the demand curve. Factors other than the price of the good that affect the amount demanded are (1) income, (2) tastes and preferences, (3) the prices of related goods, (4) expectations, and (5) market size (the number of potential buyers). If any of these *ceteris paribus* conditions of demand changes, there is a change in demand, and the demand curve shifts to a new position.	demand curve, 52 market demand, 52 *ceteris paribus* conditions, 54 normal goods, 55 inferior goods, 55 substitutes, 56 complements, 56 **Key Figures** Figure 3-2, 53 Figure 3-4, 54 Figure 3-5, 58	• MyEconLab Study Plans 3.2, 3.3 • Animated Figures 3-2, 3-4, 3-5
The Law of Supply According to the law of supply, sellers will produce and offer for sale more units of a good at a higher price, and they will produce and offer for sale fewer units of the good at a lower price.	supply, 58 law of supply, 58	• MyEconLab Study Plan 3.4
A Change in Quantity Supplied versus a Change in Supply The supply schedule shows quantities produced and sold per unit of time at various possible prices. On a graph, the supply schedule is a supply curve that slopes upward. A change in the price of the good generates a change in the quantity supplied, which is a movement along the supply curve. Factors other than the price of the good that affect the amount supplied are (1) input prices, (2) technology and productivity, (3) taxes and subsidies, (4) price expectations, and (5) the number of sellers. If any of these *ceteris paribus* conditions changes, there is a change in supply, and the supply curve shifts to a new position.	supply curve, 60 subsidy, 63 **Key Figures** Figure 3-6, 59 Figure 3-7, 60 Figure 3-9, 62	• MyEconLab Study Plans 3.5, 3.6 • Animated Figures 3-6, 3-7, 3-9

MyEconLab *continued*

| WHAT YOU SHOULD KNOW | | WHERE TO GO TO PRACTICE |

Determining the Market Price and the Equilibrium Quantity The equilibrium price of a good and the equilibrium quantity of the good that is produced and sold are determined by the intersection of the demand and supply curves. At this intersection point, the quantity demanded by buyers of the good just equals the quantity supplied by sellers, so there is neither an excess quantity of the good supplied (surplus) nor an excess quantity of the good demanded (shortage).

market clearing, or equilibrium, price, 65
equilibrium, 65
shortage, 67
surplus, 67

Key Figure
Figure 3-11, 68

• MyEconLab Study Plan 3.7
• Animated Figure 3-11

Log in to MyEconLab, take a chapter test, and get a personalized Study Plan that tells you which concepts you understand and which ones you need to review. From there, MyEconLab will give you further practice, tutorials, animations, videos, and guided solutions. For more information, visit www.myeconlab.com

PROBLEMS

All problems are assignable in MyEconLab. Answers to odd-numbered problems appear at the back of the book.

3-1. Suppose that in a recent market period, the following relationship existed between the price of tablet devices and the quantity supplied and quantity demanded.

Price	Quantity Demanded	Quantity Supplied
$390	100 million	40 million
$400	90 million	60 million
$410	80 million	80 million
$420	70 million	100 million
$430	60 million	120 million

Graph the supply and demand curves for tablet devices using the information in the table. What are the equilibrium price and quantity? If the industry price is $400, is there a shortage or surplus of tablet devices? How much is the shortage or surplus? (See pages 66–67.)

3-2. Suppose that in a later market period, the quantities supplied in the table in Problem 3-1 are unchanged. The amount demanded, however, has increased by 30 million at each price. Construct the resulting demand curve in the illustration you made for Problem 3-1. Is this an increase or a decrease in demand? What are the new equilibrium quantity and the new market price? Give two

examples of changes in *ceteris paribus* conditions that might cause such a change. (See page 54.)

3-3. Consider the market for cable-based Internet access service, which is a normal good. Explain whether the following events would cause an increase or a decrease in demand or an increase or a decrease in the quantity demanded. (See page 57.)

a. Firms providing wireless (an alternative to cable) Internet access services reduce their prices.

b. Firms providing cable-based Internet access services reduce their prices.

c. There is a decrease in the incomes earned by consumers of cable-based Internet access services.

d. Consumers' tastes shift away from using wireless Internet access in favor of cable-based Internet access services.

3-4. In the market for flash memory drives (a normal good), explain whether the following events would cause an increase or a decrease in demand or an increase or a decrease in the quantity demanded. Also explain what happens to the equilibrium quantity and the market clearing price. (See page 54.)

a. There are increases in the prices of storage racks for flash memory drives.

b. There is a decrease in the price of computer drives that read the information contained on flash memory drives.

c. There is a dramatic increase in the price of secure digital cards that, like flash memory drives, can be used to store digital data.

d. A booming economy increases the income of the typical buyer of flash memory drives.

e. Consumers of flash memory drives anticipate that the price of this good will decline in the future.

3-5. Give an example of a complement and a substitute in consumption for each of the following items. (See pages 55–56.)

a. Bacon

b. Tennis racquets

c. Coffee

d. Automobiles

3-6. For each of the following shifts in the demand curve and associated price change of a complement or substitute item, explain whether the change in the price of the complement or substitute must have been an increase or a decrease. (See page 56.)

a. A rise in the demand for a dashboard global-positioning-system device follows a change in the price of automobiles, which are complements.

b. A fall in the demand for e-book readers follows a change in the price of e-books, which are complements.

c. A rise in the demand for tablet devices follows a change in the price of ultrathin laptop computers, which are substitutes.

d. A fall in the demand for physical books follows a change in the price of e-books, which are substitutes.

3-7. Identify which of the following would generate an increase in the market demand for tablet devices, which are a normal good. (See pages 54–57.)

a. A decrease in the incomes of consumers of tablet devices

b. An increase in the price of ultrathin computers, which are substitutes

c. An increase in the price of online apps, which are complements

d. An increase in the number of consumers in the market for tablet devices

3-8. Identify which of the following would generate a decrease in the market demand for e-book readers, which are a normal good. (See pages 54–57.)

a. An increase in the price of downloadable apps utilized to enhance the e-book reading experience, which are complements

b. An increase in the number of consumers in the market for e-book readers

c. A decrease in the price of tablet devices, which are substitutes

d. A reduction in the incomes of consumers of e-book readers

3-9. Consider the following diagram of a market for one-bedroom rental apartments in a college community. (See pages 66–67.)

a. At a rental rate of $1,000 per month, is there an excess quantity supplied, or is there an excess quantity demanded? What is the amount of the excess quantity supplied or demanded?

b. If the present rental rate of one-bedroom apartments is $1,000 per month, through what mechanism will the rental rate adjust to the equilibrium rental rate of $800?

c. At a rental rate of $600 per month, is there an excess quantity supplied, or is there an excess quantity demanded? What is the amount of the excess quantity supplied or demanded?

d. If the present rental rate of one-bedroom apartments is $600 per month, through what mechanism will the rental rate adjust to the equilibrium rental rate of $800?

3-10. Consider the market for paperbound economics textbooks. Explain whether the following events would cause an increase or a decrease in supply or an increase or a decrease in the quantity supplied. (See page 64.)

a. The market price of paper increases.

b. The market price of economics textbooks increases.

c. The number of publishers of economics textbooks increases.

d. Publishers expect that the market price of economics textbooks will increase next month.

3-11. Consider the market for smartphones. Explain whether the following events would cause an increase or a decrease in supply or an increase or a decrease in the quantity supplied. Illustrate each, and show what would happen to the equilibrium quantity and the market price. (See page 64.)

   a. The price of touch screens used in smartphones declines.

   b. The price of machinery used to produce smartphones increases.

   c. The number of manufacturers of smartphones increases.

   d. There is a decrease in the market demand for smartphones.

3-12. If the price of flash memory chips used in manufacturing smartphones decreases, what will happen in the market for smartphones? How will the equilibrium price and equilibrium quantity of smartphones change? (See page 56.)

3-13. Assume that the cost of aluminum used by soft-drink companies increases. Which of the following correctly describes the resulting effects in the market for soft drinks distributed in aluminum cans? (More than one statement may be correct. See page 56.)

   a. The demand for soft drinks decreases.

   b. The quantity of soft drinks demanded decreases.

   c. The supply of soft drinks decreases.

   d. The quantity of soft drinks supplied decreases.

ECONOMICS ON THE NET

The U.S. Nursing Shortage For some years media stories have discussed a shortage of qualified nurses in the United States. This application explores some of the factors that have caused the quantity of newly trained nurses demanded to tend to exceed the quantity of newly trained nurses supplied.

Title: Nursing Shortage Resource Web Link

Navigation: Go to the Nursing Shortage Resource Web Link at **www.econtoday.com/chap03**, and click on *Nursing Shortage Fact Sheet.*

Application Read the discussion, and answer the following questions.

  1. What has happened to the demand for new nurses in the United States? What has happened to the supply of new nurses? Why has the result been a shortage?

  2. If there is a free market for the skills of new nurses, what can you predict is likely to happen to the wage rate earned by individuals who have just completed their nursing training?

For Group Study and Analysis Discuss the pros and cons of high schools and colleges trying to factor predictions about future wages into student career counseling. How might this potentially benefit students? What problems might high schools and colleges face in trying to assist students in evaluating the future earnings prospects of various jobs?

ANSWERS TO QUICK QUIZZES

p. 51: (i) inverse; (ii) demand

p. 52: (i) constant; (ii) market demand

p. 58: (i) income . . . tastes and preferences . . . prices of related goods . . . expectations about future prices and incomes . . . market size (the number of potential buyers in the market); (ii) *ceteris paribus;* (iii) movement along

p. 61: (i) direct; (ii) supply; (iii) market supply

p. 64: (i) move along . . . shift; (ii) input prices . . . technology and productivity . . . taxes and subsidies . . . expectations of future relative prices . . . the number of firms in the industry

p. 68: (i) intersection . . . equilibrium; (ii) greater; (iii) less

Extensions of Demand and Supply Analysis

4

MyEconLab helps you master each objective and study more efficiently. See end of chapter for details.

LEARNING OBJECTIVES

After reading this chapter, you should be able to:

▶ Discuss the essential features of the price system

▶ Evaluate the effects of changes in demand and supply on the market price and equilibrium quantity

▶ Understand the rationing function of prices

▶ Explain the effects of price ceilings

▶ Explain the effects of price floors

▶ Describe various types of government-imposed quantity restrictions on markets

During the past couple of years, people shopping for cars have confronted an unusual type of "sticker shock": As the prices of new vehicles have increased, the prices of used models have risen even faster. Today, the prices of a number of used vehicles are only a few hundred dollars lower than those of newly produced versions of the same cars. To understand why this situation exists in the used-car market, you must learn more about the effects of changes in market demand and supply on equilibrium prices and quantities—one key topic of this chapter. Indeed, you must develop an ability to consider the effects of *simultaneous* changes in market demand and supply, because such variations have occurred in the market for used cars.

? DID YOU KNOW THAT... in Venezuela, in which substantial quantities of coffee once were produced and consumed year after year, so little coffee is now produced that persistent coffee *shortages* exist? As you learned in Chapter 3, normally we would anticipate that in the face of a shortage in which quantity supplied is less than the quantity demanded, the price of coffee would increase. A rise in the price to its market clearing level, you learned, would bring quantities demanded and supplied back into equality. Since 2003, however, Venezuela's government has maintained a *price ceiling* in the coffee market. This means that it is illegal in Venezuela for the price of coffee to increase in order to eliminate a shortage.

What effects can a price ceiling have on the availability and consumption of a good or service? As you will learn in this chapter, we can use the supply and demand analysis developed in Chapter 3 to answer this question. You will find that when a government sets a ceiling below the equilibrium price, the result will be a shortage. Similarly, you will learn how we can use supply and demand analysis to examine the "surplus" of various agricultural products, the "shortage" of apartments in certain cities, and many other phenomena. All of these examples are part of our economy, which we characterize as a *price system*.

The Price System and Markets

Price system
An economic system in which relative prices are constantly changing to reflect changes in supply and demand for different commodities. The prices of those commodities are signals to everyone within the system as to what is relatively scarce and what is relatively abundant.

In a **price system,** otherwise known as a *market system*, relative prices are constantly changing to reflect changes in supply and demand for different commodities. The prices of those commodities are the signals to everyone within the price system as to what is relatively scarce and what is relatively abundant. In this sense, prices provide information.

Indeed, it is the *signaling* aspect of the price system that provides the information to buyers and sellers about what should be bought and what should be produced. In a price system, there is a clear-cut chain of events in which any changes in demand and supply cause changes in prices that in turn affect the opportunities that businesses and individuals have for profit and personal gain. Such changes influence our use of resources.

Exchange and Markets

Voluntary exchange
An act of trading, done on an elective basis, in which both parties to the trade expect to be better off after the exchange.

The price system features **voluntary exchange,** acts of trading between individuals that make both parties to the trade subjectively better off. The prices we pay for the desired items are determined by the interaction of the forces underlying supply and demand. In our economy, exchanges take place voluntarily in markets. A market encompasses the exchange arrangements of both buyers and sellers that underlie the forces of supply and demand. Indeed, one definition of a market is that it is a low-cost institution for facilitating exchange. A market increases incomes by helping resources move to their highest-valued uses.

Transaction Costs

Transaction costs
All of the costs associated with exchange, including the informational costs of finding out the price and quality, service record, and durability of a product, plus the cost of contracting and enforcing that contract.

Individuals turn to markets because markets reduce the cost of exchanges. These costs are sometimes referred to as **transaction costs,** which are broadly defined as the costs associated with finding out exactly what is being transacted as well as the cost of enforcing contracts. If you were Robinson Crusoe and lived alone on an island, you would never incur a transaction cost. For everyone else, transaction costs are just as real as the costs of production. Today, high-speed computers have allowed us to reduce transaction costs by increasing our ability to process information and keep records.

Consider some simple examples of transaction costs. A club warehouse such as Sam's Club or Costco reduces the transaction costs of having to go to numerous specialty stores to obtain the items you desire. Financial institutions, such as commercial banks, have reduced the transaction costs of directing funds from savers to borrowers. In general, the more organized the market, the lower the transaction costs. Among those who constantly attempt to lower transaction costs are the much maligned middlemen.

The Role of Middlemen

As long as there are costs of bringing together buyers and sellers, there will be an incentive for intermediaries linking ultimate sellers and buyers, normally called middlemen, to lower those costs. This means that middlemen specialize in lowering transaction costs. Whenever producers do not sell their products directly to the final consumer, by definition, one or more middlemen are involved. Farmers typically sell their output to distributors, who are usually called wholesalers, who then sell those products to retailers such as supermarkets.

How have companies that offer downloadable apps altered the transaction costs of firms seeking to sell products to mobile consumers?

EXAMPLE

Linking Businesses to Customers on the Go via QR Apps

In recent years, firms seeking to simplify the process of selling their products to busy customers have been turning to online apps, or Web-based application programs. One increasingly useful type of app for many small businesses is the quick-response (QR) app. These apps are offered by middlemen companies, such as Kaywa AT and Scanbuy, Inc. The apps enable sellers to create codes that they can place on poster ads. Consumers can scan the ads with their smartphones to place orders for the firms' products.

For instance, an individual who is about to board a commuter train can use a smartphone to scan a code from the ad of a coffee shop near the train's destination. The code enables the smartphone to acquire the QR app, which in turn displays the coffee shop's menu, from which the individual can choose items to purchase remotely. The individual can then pick up those items at the coffee shop upon arrival—hence completing a mobile purchase made possible by a middlemen company that offers the QR app linking the individual to the coffee shop.

FOR CRITICAL THINKING
Why do you suppose that firms such as coffee shops are willing to pay fees to middlemen for ad codes to be used with QR apps?

Changes in Demand and Supply

A key function of middlemen is to reduce transaction costs of buyers and sellers in markets for goods and services, and it is in markets that we see the results of changes in demand and supply. Market equilibrium can change whenever there is a *shock* caused by a change in a *ceteris paribus* condition for demand or supply. A shock to the supply and demand system can be represented by a shift in the supply curve, a shift in the demand curve, or a shift in both curves. Any shock to the system will result in a new set of supply and demand relationships and a new equilibrium. Forces will come into play to move the system from the old price-quantity equilibrium (now a disequilibrium situation) to the new equilibrium, where the new demand and supply curves intersect.

Effects of Changes in Either Demand or Supply

In many situations, it is possible to predict what will happen to both equilibrium price and equilibrium quantity when demand or supply changes. Specifically, whenever one curve is stable while the other curve shifts, we can tell what will happen to both price and quantity. Consider the possibilities in Figure 4-1 on the following page. In panel (a), the supply curve remains unchanged, but demand increases from D_1 to D_2. Note that the results are an increase in the market clearing price from P_1 to P_2 and an increase in the equilibrium quantity from Q_1 to Q_2.

In panel (b) in Figure 4-1, there is a decrease in demand from D_1 to D_3. This results in a decrease in both the equilibrium price of the good and the equilibrium quantity. Panels (c) and (d) show the effects of a shift in the supply curve while the demand curve is unchanged. In panel (c), the supply curve has shifted rightward. The equilibrium price of the product falls, and the equilibrium quantity increases. In panel (d), supply has shifted leftward—there has been a supply decrease. The product's equilibrium price increases, and the equilibrium quantity decreases.

FIGURE 4-1

Shifts in Demand and in Supply: Determinate Results

In panel (a), the supply curve is unchanged at S. The demand curve shifts outward from D_1 to D_2. The equilibrium price and quantity rise from P_1, Q_1 to P_2, Q_2, respectively. In panel (b), again the supply curve is unchanged at S. The demand curve shifts inward to the left, showing a decrease in demand from D_1 to D_3. Both equilibrium price and equilibrium quantity fall. In panel (c), the demand curve now remains unchanged at D. The supply curve shifts from S_1 to S_2. The equilibrium price falls from P_1 to P_2. The equilibrium quantity increases, however, from Q_1 to Q_2. In panel (d), the demand curve is unchanged at D. Supply decreases as shown by a leftward shift of the supply curve from S_1 to S_3. The market clearing price increases from P_1 to P_3. The equilibrium quantity falls from Q_1 to Q_3.

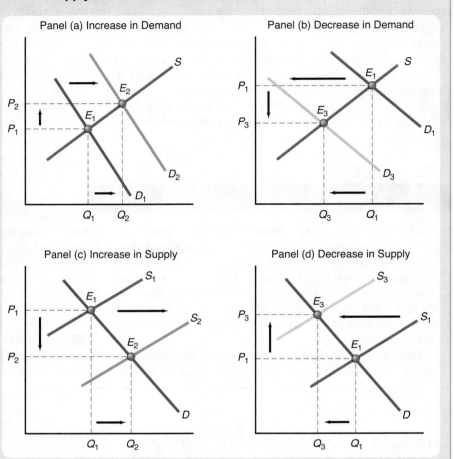

Situations in Which Both Demand and Supply Shift

The examples in Figure 4-1 above show a theoretically determinate outcome of a shift either in the demand curve, holding the supply curve constant, or in the supply curve, holding the demand curve constant. When both the supply and demand curves change, the outcome is indeterminate for either equilibrium price or equilibrium quantity.

When both demand and supply increase, the equilibrium quantity unambiguously rises, because the increase in demand and the increase in supply *both* tend to generate a rise in quantity. The change in the equilibrium price is uncertain without more information, because the increase in demand tends to increase the equilibrium price, whereas the increase in supply tends to decrease the equilibrium price.

Decreases in both demand and supply tend to generate a fall in quantity, so the equilibrium quantity falls. Again, the effect on the equilibrium price is uncertain without additional information, because a decrease in demand tends to reduce the equilibrium price, whereas a decrease in supply tends to increase the equilibrium price.

We can be certain that when demand decreases and supply increases at the same time, the equilibrium price will fall, because *both* the decrease in demand and the increase in supply tend to push down the equilibrium price. The change in the equilibrium quantity is uncertain without more information, because the decrease in demand tends to reduce the equilibrium quantity, whereas the increase in supply tends to increase the equilibrium quantity. If demand increases and supply decreases at the same time, both occurrences tend to push up the equilibrium price, so the equilibrium price definitely rises. The change in the equilibrium quantity cannot be determined without more information, because the increase in demand tends to raise the equilibrium quantity, whereas the decrease in supply tends to reduce the equilibrium quantity.

How have simultaneous shifts in demand and supply affected the equilibrium global price of shipping containers?

INTERNATIONAL EXAMPLE

What Accounts for the Rising Price of Shipping Containers?

Since 2011, shipping-container prices have surged. Several reasons account for the jump in the equilibrium price. One is that companies using the containers, which typically last no longer than 8 to 10 years, bought large quantities during a five-year period that began in 2001, and many of these containers now must be replaced to maintain shipping volumes. Hence, as shown in Figure 4-2 below, the demand curve for shipping containers has shifted rightward.

In addition, the massive tsunami that struck Japan in 2011 washed thousands of containers out to sea. Furthermore, the price of steel that serves as the primary input for the containers has increased by

7 percent. These events have contributed to a reduction in the supply of shipping containers. On net, the equilibrium quantity of shipping containers produced and purchased has risen, and the market clearing price of shipping containers has increased.

FOR CRITICAL THINKING
How do you suppose that a rise in the price of truck trailers that are substitutes for shipping containers has affected the market clearing price of shipping containers?

FIGURE 4-2

The Effects of a Simultaneous Decrease in Shipping-Container Supply and Increase in Shipping-Container Demand

Since 2011, various factors have contributed to a reduction in the supply of shipping containers, depicted by the leftward shift in the supply curve from S_1 to S_2. At the same time, there was an increase in the demand for shipping containers, as shown by the shift in the demand curve from D_1 to D_2. On net, the equilibrium quantity of shipping containers produced and purchased rose, from 750,000 containers per year at point E_1 to 900,000 containers per year at point E_2, and the equilibrium price of shipping containers increased from about \$3,000 per container to about \$3,500 per container.

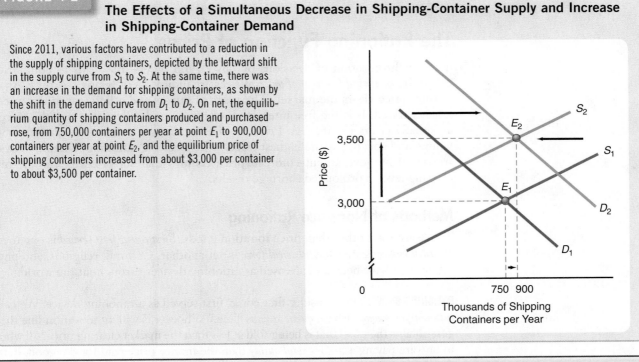

Price Flexibility and Adjustment Speed

We have used as an illustration for our analysis a market in which prices are quite flexible. Some markets are indeed like that. In others, however, price flexibility may take the form of subtle adjustments such as hidden payments or quality changes. For example, although the published price of bouquets of flowers may stay the same, the freshness of the flowers may change, meaning that the price per constant-quality unit changes. The published price of French bread might stay the same, but the quality could go up or down, perhaps through use of a different recipe, thereby changing the price per constant-quality unit. There are many ways to implicitly change prices without actually changing the published price for a *nominal* unit of a product or service.

We must also note that markets do not always return to equilibrium immediately. There may be a significant adjustment time. A shock to the economy in the form of an oil embargo, a drought, or a long strike will not be absorbed overnight. This means that even in unfettered market situations, in which there are no restrictions on changes in prices and quantities, temporary excess quantities supplied or excess quantities demanded may appear. Our analysis simply indicates what the market clearing price and equilibrium quantity ultimately will be, given a demand curve and a supply curve.

Nowhere in the analysis is there any indication of the speed with which a market will get to a new equilibrium after a shock. The price may even temporarily overshoot the new equilibrium level. Remember this warning when we examine changes in demand and in supply due to changes in their *ceteris paribus* conditions.

QUICK QUIZ   See page 95 for the answers. Review concepts from this section in MyEconLab.

When the _____ curve shifts outward or inward with an unchanged _____ curve, equilibrium price and quantity increase or decrease, respectively. When the _____ curve shifts outward or inward given an unchanged _____ curve, equilibrium

price moves in the direction opposite to equilibrium quantity.

When there is a shift in demand or supply, the new equilibrium price is not obtained _____. Adjustment takes _____.

The Rationing Function of Prices

The synchronization of decisions by buyers and sellers that leads to equilibrium is called the *rationing function of prices*. Prices are indicators of relative scarcity. An equilibrium price clears the market. The plans of buyers and sellers, given the price, are not frustrated. It is the free interaction of buyers and sellers that sets the price that eventually clears the market. Price, in effect, rations a good to demanders who are willing and able to pay the highest price. Whenever the rationing function of prices is frustrated by government-enforced price ceilings that set prices below the market clearing level, a prolonged shortage results.

Methods of Nonprice Rationing

There are ways other than price to ration goods. *First come, first served* is one method. *Political power* is another. *Physical force* is yet another. Cultural, religious, and physical differences have been and are used as rationing devices throughout the world.

RATIONING BY WAITING Consider first come, first served as a rationing device. We call this *rationing by queues*, where *queue* means "line." Whoever is willing to wait in line the longest obtains the good that is being sold at less than the market clearing price. All who wait in line are paying a higher *total outlay* than the money price paid for the good. Personal time has an opportunity cost. To calculate the total outlay expended on the good, we must add up the money price plus the opportunity cost of the time spent waiting.

Rationing by waiting may occur in situations in which entrepreneurs are free to change prices to equate quantity demanded with quantity supplied but choose not to do so. This results in queues of potential buyers. It may seem that the price in the market is being held below equilibrium by some noncompetitive force. That is not true, however. Such queuing may arise in a free market when the demand for a good is subject to large or unpredictable fluctuations, and the additional costs to firms (and ultimately to consumers) of constantly changing prices or of holding sufficient inventories or providing sufficient excess capacity to cover peak demands are greater than the costs to consumers of waiting for the good.

Common examples are waiting in line to purchase a fast-food lunch and queuing to purchase a movie ticket a few minutes before the next showing.

RATIONING BY RANDOM ASSIGNMENT OR COUPONS *Random assignment* is another way to ration goods. You may have been involved in a rationing-by-random-assignment scheme in college if you were assigned a housing unit. Sometimes rationing by random assignment is used to fill slots in popular classes.

Rationing by *coupons* has also been used, particularly during wartime. In the United States during World War II, families were allotted coupons that allowed them to purchase specified quantities of rationed goods, such as meat and gasoline. To purchase such goods, they had to pay a specified price *and* give up a coupon.

Why has American Airlines been randomly assigning its coach passengers to boarding groups?

EXAMPLE

An Airline Boarding Lottery

For several years now, U.S. airlines have charged coach passengers to transport bags as separate cargo. This practice has induced many passengers to pack more items into carry-on bags that they stuff under seats or into overhead compartments.

American Airlines has been assigning coach boarding-group numbers randomly, rather than by groups of rows starting with the rear of the plane and ending with the front coach rows. Under the latter boarding method, many people with seats at the rear of a plane tend to place their carry-on bags in compartments near the front of the plane. Then people arriving in the front at the end of the boarding process spend time scrambling to find places to stow their carry-ons. In contrast, under a randomized boarding process that ignores row locations, coach passengers are more likely to stow their bags near their seats. This mode of passenger behavior speeds the overall boarding process by several minutes, thereby ensuring that more flights depart on time.

FOR CRITICAL THINKING
Suppose the airline has established a system of boarding fees in which passengers wishing to be among the first to board a plane pay the highest fees. Would such a system likely reduce or lengthen boarding times? Why?

The Essential Role of Rationing

In a world of scarcity, there is, by definition, competition for what is scarce. After all, any resources that are not scarce can be obtained by everyone at a zero price in as large a quantity as everyone wants, such as air to burn in internal combustion engines. Once scarcity arises, there has to be some method to ration the available resources, goods, and services. The price system is one form of rationing. The others that we mentioned are alternatives. Economists cannot say which system of rationing is "best." They can, however, say that rationing via the price system leads to the most efficient use of available resources. As explained in Appendix B, this means that generally in a freely functioning price system, all of the gains from mutually beneficial trade will be captured.

QUICK QUIZ   See page 95 for the answers. Review concepts from this section in MyEconLab.

Prices in a market economy perform a rationing function because they reflect relative scarcity, allowing the market to clear. Other ways to ration goods include _____ _____, _____ _____, _____ _____, _____ _____, and _____.

Even when businesspeople can change prices, some rationing by waiting may occur. Such _____ arises when there are large changes in demand coupled with high costs of satisfying those changes immediately.

The Policy of Government-Imposed Price Controls

The rationing function of prices is prevented when governments impose price controls. **Price controls** often involve setting a **price ceiling**—the maximum price that may be allowed in an exchange. The world has had a long history of price ceilings

Price controls
Government-mandated minimum or maximum prices that may be charged for goods and services.

Price ceiling
A legal maximum price that may be charged for a particular good or service.

Price floor
A legal minimum price below which a good or service may not be sold. Legal minimum wages are an example.

YOU ARE THERE

To learn about how government controls of prices of life-saving medications are creating situations in which quantities demanded exceed quantities supplied year after year, read **Explaining the "Crisis" of Persistent Drug Shortages** on page 89.

Nonprice rationing devices
All methods used to ration scarce goods that are price-controlled. Whenever the price system is not allowed to work, nonprice rationing devices will evolve to ration the affected goods and services.

Black market
A market in which goods are traded at prices above their legal maximum prices or in which illegal goods are sold.

applied to product prices, wages, rents, and interest rates. Occasionally, a government will set a **price floor**—a minimum price below which a good or service may not be sold. Price floors have most often been applied to wages and agricultural products. Let's first consider price ceilings.

Price Ceilings and Black Markets

As long as a price ceiling is below the market clearing price, imposing a price ceiling creates a shortage, as can be seen in Figure 4-3 below. At any price below the market clearing, or equilibrium, price of $1,000, there will always be a larger quantity demanded than quantity supplied—a shortage, as you will recall from Chapter 3. Normally, whenever quantity demanded exceeds quantity supplied—that is, when a shortage exists—there is a tendency for the price to rise to its equilibrium level. But with a price ceiling, this tendency cannot be fully realized because everyone is forbidden to trade at the equilibrium price.

The result is fewer exchanges and **nonprice rationing devices.** Figure 4-3 shows the situation for portable electric generators after a natural disaster: The equilibrium quantity of portable generators demanded and supplied (or traded) would be 10,000 units, and the market clearing price would be $1,000 per generator. But, if the government essentially imposes a price ceiling by requiring the price of portable generators to remain at the predisaster level, which the government determines was a price of $600, the equilibrium quantity offered is only 5,000.

Because frustrated consumers will be able to purchase only 5,000 units, there is a shortage. The most obvious nonprice rationing device to help clear the market is queuing, or physical lines, which we have already discussed. To avoid physical lines, waiting lists may be established.

Typically, an effective price ceiling leads to a **black market.** A black market is a market in which the price-controlled good is sold at an illegally high price through various methods. For example, if the price of gasoline is controlled at lower than the market clearing price, drivers who wish to fill up their cars may offer the gas station attendant a cash payment on the side (as happened in the United States in the 1970s and in China and India in the mid-2000s during price controls on gasoline). If the price of beef is controlled at below its market clearing price, a customer who offers the butcher tickets for good seats to an upcoming football game may be allocated otherwise

---

FIGURE 4-3

Black Markets for Portable Electric Generators

The demand curve is *D*. The supply curve is *S*. The equilibrium price is $1,000. The government, however, steps in and imposes a maximum price of $600. At that lower price, the quantity demanded will be 15,000, but the quantity supplied will be only 5,000. There is a "shortage." The implicit price (including time costs) tends to increase to $1,400. If black markets arise, as they generally will, the equilibrium black market price will end up somewhere between $600 and $1,400. The actual quantity transacted will be between 5,000 and 10,000.

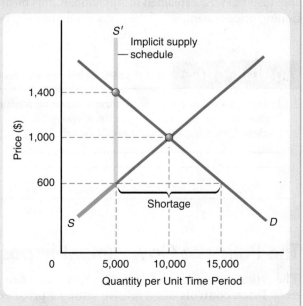

unavailable beef. Indeed, the true implicit price of a price-controlled good or service can be increased in an infinite number of ways, limited only by the imagination. (Black markets also occur when goods are made illegal.)

How have multiple price ceilings magnified electricity shortages in China?

INTERNATIONAL POLICY EXAMPLE

Multiple Price Ceilings Lead to Electricity Rationing in China

In China, two key sources of electricity are coal and diesel fuel that power generators. Sellers of both items, however, confront ceiling prices that are below market clearing levels. Hence, firms operating power generators often struggle to obtain enough coal and diesel fuel to provide as much electricity as they wish to produce. Power companies do not desire to sell as much electricity as many Chinese residents want to use, though, because China's government has also placed ceilings on electricity prices in a number of regional electricity markets.

These multiple price ceilings help to explain why most of the nation commonly faces electricity rationing in the form of "brownouts," or reductions in power flow. Shortages created by the ceiling prices also explain why businesses in more than one-third of China's provinces often have their power completely shut off for days at a time during the coldest weeks of winter and the warmest weeks of summer.

FOR CRITICAL THINKING
Given that China's electricity demand is growing at 13 percent per year, why do you suppose that electricity shortages likely will worsen in the future?

QUICK QUIZ

See page 95 for the answers. Review concepts from this section in MyEconLab.

Governments sometimes impose **price controls** in the form of price _____ and price _____.

An effective price _____ is one that sets the legal price below the market clearing price and is enforced.

Effective price _____ lead to nonprice rationing devices and black markets.

The Policy of Controlling Rents

More than 200 U.S. cities and towns, including Berkeley, California, and New York City, operate under some kind of rent control. **Rent control** is a system under which the local government tells building owners how much they can charge their tenants for rent. In the United States, rent controls date back to at least World War II. The objective of rent control is to keep rents below levels that would be observed in a freely competitive market.

Rent control
Price ceilings on rents.

The Functions of Rental Prices

In any housing market, rental prices serve three functions: (1) to promote the efficient maintenance of existing housing and to stimulate the construction of new housing, (2) to allocate existing scarce housing among competing claimants, and (3) to ration the use of existing housing by current demanders. Rent controls interfere with all of these functions.

RENT CONTROLS AND CONSTRUCTION Rent controls discourage the construction of new rental units. Rents are the most important long-term determinant of profitability, and rent controls artificially depress them. Consider some examples. In a recent year in Dallas, Texas, with a 16 percent rental vacancy rate but no rent control laws, 11,000 new rental housing units were built. In the same year in San Francisco, California, only 2,000 units were built, despite a mere 1.6 percent vacancy rate. The major difference? San Francisco has had stringent rent control laws. In New York City, most rental units being built are luxury units, which are exempt from controls.

EFFECTS ON THE EXISTING SUPPLY OF HOUSING When rental rates are held below equilibrium levels, property owners cannot recover the cost of maintenance, repairs, and capital improvements through higher rents. Hence, they curtail these activities. In the extreme situation, taxes, utilities, and the expenses of basic repairs exceed rental receipts. The result has been abandoned buildings from Santa Monica, California, to New York City. Some owners have resorted to arson, hoping to collect the insurance on their empty buildings before the city claims them to pay back taxes.

RATIONING THE CURRENT USE OF HOUSING Rent controls also affect the current use of housing because they restrict tenant mobility. Consider a family whose children have gone off to college. That family might want to live in a smaller apartment. But in a rent-controlled environment, giving up a rent-controlled unit can entail a substantial cost. In most rent-controlled cities, rents can be adjusted only when a tenant leaves. That means that a move from a long-occupied rent-controlled apartment to a smaller apartment can involve a hefty rent hike. In New York, this artificial preservation of the status quo came to be known as "housing gridlock."

Attempts to Evade Rent Controls

Go to www.econtoday.com/chap04 to learn more about New York City's rent controls from Tenant.net.

The distortions produced by rent controls lead to efforts by both property owners and tenants to evade the rules. These efforts lead to the growth of expensive government bureaucracies whose job it is to make sure that rent controls aren't evaded. In New York City, because rent on a rent-controlled apartment can be raised only if the tenant leaves, property owners have had an incentive to make life unpleasant for tenants in order to drive them out or to evict them on the slightest pretext. The city has responded by making evictions extremely costly for property owners. Eviction requires a tedious and expensive judicial proceeding.

Tenants, for their part, routinely try to sublet all or part of their rent-controlled apartments at fees substantially above the rent they pay to the owner. Both the city and the property owners try to prohibit subletting and often end up in the city's housing courts—an entire judicial system developed to deal with disputes involving rent-controlled apartments. The overflow and appeals from the city's housing courts sometimes clog the rest of New York's judicial system.

Who Gains and Who Loses from Rent Controls?

The big losers from rent controls are clearly property owners. But there is another group of losers—low-income individuals, especially single mothers, trying to find apartments. Some observers now believe that rent controls have worsened the problem of homelessness in cities such as New York.

Often, owners of rent-controlled apartments charge "key money" before allowing a new tenant to move in. This is a large up-front cash payment, usually illegal but demanded nonetheless—just one aspect of the black market in rent-controlled apartments. Poor individuals have insufficient income to pay the hefty key money payment, nor can they assure the owner that their rent will be on time or even paid each month.

Because controlled rents are usually below market clearing levels, apartment owners have little incentive to take any risk on low-income individuals as tenants. This is particularly true when a prospective tenant's chief source of income is a welfare check. Indeed, a large number of the litigants in the New York housing courts are welfare mothers who have missed their rent payments due to emergency expenses or delayed welfare checks. Their appeals often end in evictions and a new home in a temporary public shelter—or on the streets.

Who benefits from rent control? Ample evidence indicates that upper-income professionals benefit the most. These people can use their mastery of the bureaucracy and their large network of friends and connections to exploit the rent control system. Consider that in New York, actresses Mia Farrow and Cicely Tyson live in rent-controlled apartments, paying well below market rates. So do the former director of the Metropolitan Museum of Art and singer and children's book author Carly Simon.

_____ prices perform three functions: (1) allocating existing scarce housing among competing claimants, (2) promoting efficient maintenance of existing houses and stimulating new housing construction, and (3) rationing the use of existing houses by current demanders.

Effective rent _____ impede the functioning of rental prices. Construction of new rental units is discouraged.

Rent _____ decrease spending on maintenance of existing ones and also lead to "housing gridlock."

There are numerous ways to evade rent controls. _____ _____ is one.

Price Floors in Agriculture

Another way that government can affect markets is by imposing price floors or price supports. In the United States, price supports are most often associated with agricultural products.

Price Supports

During the Great Depression, the federal government swung into action to help farmers. In 1933, it established a system of price supports for many agricultural products. Since then, there have been price supports for wheat, feed grains, cotton, rice, soybeans, sorghum, and dairy products, among other foodstuffs. The nature of the supports is quite simple: The government simply chooses a *support price* for an agricultural product and then acts to ensure that the price of the product never falls below the support level. Figure 4-4 below shows the market demand for and supply of milk. Without a price-support program, competitive forces would yield an equilibrium price of $0.08 per pound and an equilibrium quantity of 15.4 billion pounds per year. Clearly, if the government were to set the support price at or below $0.08 per pound, the quantity of milk demanded would equal the quantity of milk supplied at point *E*, because farmers could sell all they wanted at the market clearing price of $0.08 per pound.

FIGURE 4-4

Agricultural Price Supports

Free market equilibrium occurs at *E*, with an equilibrium price of $0.08 per pound and an equilibrium quantity of 15.4 billion pounds. When the government sets a support price at $0.10 per pound, the quantity demanded is 15 billion pounds and the quantity supplied is 16 billion pounds. The difference is the surplus, which the government buys. Farmers' income from consumers equals $0.10 per pound × 1 billion pounds = $100 million.

But what happens when the government sets the support price *above* the market clearing price, at $0.10 per pound? At a support price of $0.10 per pound, the quantity demanded is only 15 billion pounds, but the quantity supplied is 16 billion pounds. The 1-billion-pound difference between them is called the *excess quantity supplied*, or *surplus*. As simple as this program seems, its existence creates a fundamental question: How can the government agency charged with administering the price-support program prevent market forces from pushing the actual price down to $0.08 per pound?

If production exceeds the amount that consumers want to buy at the support price, what happens to the surplus? Quite simply, if the price-support program is to work, the government has to buy the surplus—the 1-billion-pound difference. As a practical matter, the government acquires the 1-billion-pound surplus indirectly through a government agency. The government either stores the surplus or sells it to foreign countries at a greatly reduced price (or gives it away free of charge) under the Food for Peace program.

Who Benefits from Agricultural Price Supports?

Although agricultural price supports have traditionally been promoted as a way to guarantee "decent" earnings for low-income farmers, most of the benefits have in fact gone to the owners of very large farms. Price-support payments are made on a per-pound basis, not on a per-farm basis. Thus, traditionally, the larger the farm, the bigger the benefit from agricultural price supports. In addition, *all* of the benefits from price supports ultimately accrue to *landowners* on whose land price-supported crops grow.

KEEPING PRICE SUPPORTS ALIVE UNDER A NEW NAME Back in the early 1990s, Congress indicated an intention to phase out most agricultural subsidies by the early 2000s. What Congress actually *did* throughout the 1990s, however, was to pass a series of "emergency laws" keeping farm subsidies alive. Some of these laws aimed to replace agricultural price supports with payments to many farmers for growing no crops at all, thereby boosting the market prices of crops by reducing supply. Nevertheless, the federal government and several state governments have continued to support prices of a number of agricultural products, such as peanuts, through "marketing loan" programs. These programs advance funds to farmers to help them finance the storage of some or all of their crops. The farmers can then use the stored produce as collateral for borrowing or sell it to the government and use the proceeds to repay debts.

Marketing loan programs raise the effective price that farmers receive for their crops and commit federal and state governments to purchasing surplus production. Consequently, they lead to outcomes similar to those of traditional price-support programs.

THE MAIN BENEFICIARIES OF AGRICULTURAL SUBSIDIES In 2002, Congress enacted the Farm Security Act, which has perpetuated marketing loan programs and other subsidy and price-support arrangements for such farm products as wheat, corn, rice, peanuts, and soybeans. All told, the more than $9 billion in U.S. government payments for these and other products amounts to about 25 percent of the annual market value of all U.S. farm production.

The government seeks to cap the annual subsidy payment that an individual farmer can receive at $360,000 per year, but some farmers are able to garner higher annual amounts by exploiting regulatory loopholes. The greatest share of total agricultural subsidies goes to the owners of the largest farming operations. At present, 10 percent of U.S. farmers receive more than 70 percent of agricultural subsidies.

The 2008 Food, Conservation, and Energy Act expanded on the 2002 legislation by giving farmers raising any of a number of crops a choice between subsidy programs. On the one hand, farmers can opt to participate in traditional programs involving a mix of direct payments and marketing loan programs. On the other hand, farmers can choose a program offering guaranteed revenues. If market clearing crop prices end up higher than those associated with the government's revenue guarantee, farmers sell their crops at the higher prices instead of collecting government subsidies. But if equilibrium crop prices end up below a level consistent with the government guarantee, farmers receive direct subsidies to bring their total revenues up to the guaranteed level.

WHAT IF... the government decides to "help dairy farmers" by imposing a floor price in the market for milk that is above the equilibrium price?

The floor price above the equilibrium level would cause the quantity of milk supplied by dairy farmers to rise above the quantity demanded by consumers. The government would have to purchase the surplus milk, which would indeed "help" the dairy farmers from whom the milk would be purchased. As a result, consumers, such as parents of young children, would have to pay a higher price for each unit of the smaller quantity of milk that they will choose to buy. Thus, the government's price-support program would necessarily "help dairy farmers" at the expense of milk consumers.

Price Floors in the Labor Market

The **minimum wage** is the lowest hourly wage rate that firms may legally pay their workers. Proponents favor higher minimum wages to ensure low-income workers a "decent" standard of living. Opponents counter that higher minimum wages cause increased unemployment, particularly among unskilled minority teenagers.

Minimum wage
A wage floor, legislated by government, setting the lowest hourly rate that firms may legally pay workers.

Minimum Wages in the United States

The federal minimum wage started in 1938 at 25 cents an hour, about 40 percent of the average manufacturing wage at the time. Typically, its level has stayed at about 40 to 50 percent of average manufacturing wages. After holding the minimum wage at $5.15 per hour from 1997 to 2007, Congress enacted a series of phased increases in the hourly minimum wage, effective on July 24 of each year, to $5.85 in 2007, $6.55 in 2008, and $7.25 in 2009.

Many states and cities have their own minimum wage laws that exceed the federal minimum. A number of municipalities refer to their minimum wage rules as "living wage" laws. Governments of these municipalities seek to set minimum wages consistent with living standards they deem to be socially acceptable—that is, overall wage income judged to be sufficient to purchase basic items such as housing and food.

Go to www.econtoday.com/chap04 for information from the U.S. Department of Labor about recent developments concerning the federal minimum wage.

Economic Effects of a Minimum Wage

What happens when the government establishes a floor on wages? The effects can be seen in Figure 4-5 on the following page. We start off in equilibrium with the equilibrium wage rate of W_e and the equilibrium quantity of labor equal to Q_e. A minimum wage, W_m, higher than W_e, is imposed. At W_m, the quantity demanded for labor is reduced to Q_d, and some workers now become unemployed. Certain workers will become unemployed as a result of the minimum wage, but others will move to sectors where minimum wage laws do not apply. Wages will be pushed down in these uncovered sectors.

Note that the reduction in employment from Q_e to Q_d, or the distance from B to A, is less than the excess quantity of labor supplied at wage rate W_m. This excess quantity supplied is the distance between A and C, or the distance between Q_d and Q_s. The reason the reduction in employment is smaller than the excess quantity of

FIGURE 4-5

The Effect of Minimum Wages

The market clearing wage rate is W_e. The market clearing quantity of employment is Q_e, determined by the intersection of supply and demand at point E. A minimum wage equal to W_m is established. The quantity of labor demanded is reduced to Q_d. The reduction in employment from Q_e to Q_d is equal to the distance between B and A. That distance is smaller than the excess quantity of labor supplied at wage rate W_m. The distance between B and C is the increase in the quantity of labor supplied that results from the higher minimum wage rate.

labor supplied at the minimum wage is that the excess quantity of labor supplied also includes the *additional* workers who would like to work more hours at the new, higher minimum wage.

In the long run (a time period that is long enough to allow for full adjustment by workers and firms), some of the reduction in the quantity of labor demanded will result from a reduction in the number of firms, and some will result from changes in the number of workers employed by each firm. Economists estimate that a 10 percent increase in the inflation-adjusted minimum wage decreases total employment of those affected by 1 to 2 percent.

We can conclude from the application of demand and supply analysis that a minimum wage established above the equilibrium wage rate typically has two fundamental effects. On the one hand, it boosts the wage earnings of those people who obtain employment. On the other hand, the minimum wage results in unemployment for other individuals. Thus, demand and supply analysis implies that the minimum wage makes some people better off while making others worse off.

How have teenagers fared following successive increases in the minimum wage in 2007, 2008, and 2009?

POLICY EXAMPLE

A Higher Minimum Wage Translates into Fewer Employed Teens

In three steps between 2007 and 2009, the federal government boosted the minimum wage rate faced by all employers in the 50 states from $5.15 per hour to $7.25 per hour. The legislation had almost no effects in 18 states in which market wages were generally already higher than $7.25 per hour. In the other 32 states, though, the three-stage hike in the minimum wage reduced total employment of teens by an estimated 2.5 percentage points. The result for these states was an estimated reduction in the number of employed teens totaling more than 114,000 teens, who consequently joined the ranks of the nation's unemployed.

FOR CRITICAL THINKING

What do you suppose has happened to the teen unemployment rate as the demand for labor has fallen and remained dampened since the 2008–2009 economic downturn?

Quantity Restrictions

Governments can impose quantity restrictions on a market. The most obvious restriction is an outright ban on the ownership or trading of a good. It is currently illegal to buy and sell human organs. It is also currently illegal to buy and sell certain psychoactive drugs such as cocaine, heroin, and methamphetamine. In some states, it is illegal to start a new hospital without obtaining a license for a particular number of beds to be offered to patients. This licensing requirement effectively limits the quantity of hospital beds in some states. From 1933 to 1973, it was illegal for U.S. citizens to own gold except for manufacturing, medicinal, or jewelry purposes.

Some of the most common quantity restrictions exist in the area of international trade. The U.S. government, as well as many foreign governments, imposes import quotas on a variety of goods. An **import quota** is a supply restriction that prohibits the importation of more than a specified quantity of a particular good in a one-year period. The United States has had import quotas on tobacco, sugar, and immigrant labor. For many years, there were import quotas on oil coming into the United States. There are also "voluntary" import quotas on certain goods. For instance, since the mid-2000s, the Chinese government has agreed to "voluntarily" restrict the amount of textile products China sends to the United States and the European Union.

Import quota

A physical supply restriction on imports of a particular good, such as sugar. Foreign exporters are unable to sell in the United States more than the quantity specified in the import quota.

QUICK QUIZ   See page 95 for the answers. Review concepts from this section in MyEconLab.

With a price-_____ system, the government sets a minimum price at which, say, qualifying farm products can be sold. Any farmers who cannot sell at that price in the market can "sell" their surplus to the government. The only way a price-_____ system can survive is for the government or some other entity to buy up the excess quantity supplied at the support price.

When a _____ is placed on wages at a rate that is above market equilibrium, the result is an excess quantity of labor supplied at that minimum wage.

Quantity restrictions may take the form of _____ _____, which are limits on the quantity of specific foreign goods that can be brought into the United States for resale purposes.

YOU ARE THERE
Explaining the "Crisis" of Persistent Drug Shortages

According to Bona Benjamin of the American Society of Health-System Pharmacists, "We are in a crisis situation" in terms of shortages of many drugs used to treat a variety of diseases, including cancer. In 2006, the U.S. Food and Drug Administration (FDA) identified persistent shortages of 55 drugs. Today, there are shortages of about 300 drugs.

Benjamin and others involved in the markets for pharmaceuticals suggest that the persistent shortages of many drugs result from government price restrictions. The FDA can place limits on the percentage increase in a drug's price during a given year. Such a limitation often causes the allowed level of a drug's price in a given year to be lower than the market clearing price. Thus, the FDA's restraint on allowed price growth creates a shortage. If the FDA continues imposing limits on annual percentage increases in the price that are too low in relation to the rate of increase in the market clearing price, then the result is a persistent shortage.

Each year, the FDA has also broadened the list of medications for which limits on annual rates of allowed percentage price increases apply. This is why the number of drugs experiencing persistent shortages has increased.

Critical Thinking Questions

1. What would happen to the magnitudes of drug shortages if the FDA allowed higher annual price increases?

2. Would drug shortages be likely to persist if price controls were lifted? Explain.

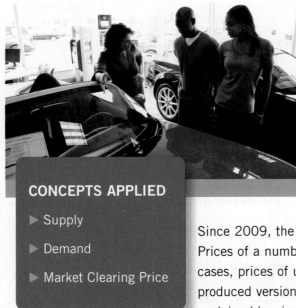

ISSUES & APPLICATIONS

Why Prices of Used Cars Are So High

CONCEPTS APPLIED

▶ Supply

▶ Demand

▶ Market Clearing Price

Since 2009, the average price of a used car has increased by nearly 10 percent. Prices of a number of used models have risen by more than 30 percent. In some cases, prices of used cars are within a few hundred dollars of the prices of newly produced versions of the same models. These significant price increases can be explained by simultaneous changes in the supply of and demand for used cars.

"Cash for Clunkers" and a Decreased Supply of Used Cars

During the summer of 2009, the federal government implemented a program that became widely known as "cash for clunkers." Under this program, the government provided owners of specific low-fuel-economy vehicles with vouchers that the owners could apply toward purchases of new, more fuel-efficient vehicles. Ultimately, the government expended nearly $3 billion to purchase and crush (or shred) almost 700,000 used vehicles.

In the years since 2009, many of the vehicles destroyed under the program would have been available for sale in the used-car market. Their absence reduced the market supply of used vehicles: Fewer used vehicles were offered for sale at any given used-car price. Consequently, as shown in Figure 4-6 below, the market supply curve for used cars shifted leftward.

FIGURE 4-6

The Effects of a Decrease in the Supply of Used Cars in Conjunction with an Increase in the Demand for Used Cars

The federal government's cash-for-clunkers program removed hundreds of thousands of used cars from the used-car market, resulting in a decrease in supply, depicted by the leftward shift in the supply curve from S_1 to S_2. In addition, higher new-car prices induced consumers to substitute in favor of used cars, resulting in an increase in demand, shown by the rightward shift in the demand curve from D_1 to D_2. The market clearing price of used cars increased, from P_1 to P_2, and the equilibrium quantity of used cars decreased, from Q_1 to Q_2.

Higher Prices of New Cars Boost the Demand for Used Cars

Then, in 2011, northeastern Japan was struck both by destructive earthquakes and by a massive tsunami. Manufacturers based in Japan supply one of every four newly produced autos sold in the United States. For months following the disaster, exports of vehicles produced in Japan and shipments of Japanese-produced vehicle parts to U.S.-based assembly facilities of Japanese automakers were halted or delayed. The result was a fall in the supply of *new* vehicles, which led to an increase in the market clearing price of *new* cars.

Because new cars are a substitute for used vehicles, the rise in the price of new cars generated an increase in the demand for *used* vehicles: People desired to purchase more used vehicles at any given used-car price. Thus, as shown in Figure 4-6, the demand curve for used cars shifted rightward.

Taken together, the reduction in the supply of used cars caused by the cash-for-clunkers program and the increase in demand caused by higher new-car prices generated an increase in the market clearing price of used cars. The observed equilibrium-quantity outcome in the used-car market has been a slight decrease, as displayed in the figure.

For Critical Thinking

1. If used cars are a normal good and consumers' incomes were to fall during the next few years, what would happen to the market clearing price of used cars?
2. If the price change discussed in Question 1 were to occur, would this cause a change in the supply of used cars or in the quantity supplied? Explain.

Web Resources

1. Learn more about the federal government's cash-for-clunkers program at www.econtoday.com/chap04.
2. For a discussion of the lengthy production delays faced by Japanese automakers for an extended period following the earthquake and tsunami disaster, go to www.econtoday.com/chap04.

MyEconLab

For more questions on this chapter's Issues & Applications, go to MyEconLab. In the Study Plan for this chapter, select Section N: News.

MyEconLab

Here is what you should know after reading this chapter. MyEconLab will help you identify what you know, and where to go when you need to practice.

WHAT YOU SHOULD KNOW		WHERE TO GO TO PRACTICE
Essential Features of the Price System In the price system, prices respond to changes in supply and demand. Decisions on resource use depend on what happens to prices. Middlemen reduce transaction costs by bringing buyers and sellers together.	price system, 76 voluntary exchange, 76 transaction costs, 76	• MyEconLab Study Plan 4.1
How Changes in Demand and Supply Affect the Market Price and Equilibrium Quantity With a given supply curve, an increase in demand causes increases in the market price and equilibrium quantity, and a decrease in demand induces decreases in the market price and equilibrium quantity. With a given demand curve, an increase in supply causes a fall in the market price and an increase in the equilibrium quantity, and a decrease in supply causes a rise in the market price and a decline in the equilibrium quantity. When both demand and supply shift at the same time, we must know the direction and amount of each shift in order to predict changes in the market price and the equilibrium quantity.	Key Figure Figure 4-1, 78	• MyEconLab Study Plan 4.2 • Animated Figure 4-1

MyEconLab continued

WHAT YOU SHOULD KNOW		WHERE TO GO TO PRACTICE
The Rationing Function of Prices In the price system, prices ration scarce goods and services. Other ways of rationing include first come, first served; political power; physical force; random assignment; and coupons.		• **MyEconLab** Study Plan 4.3

The Effects of Price Ceilings Government-imposed price controls that require prices to be no higher than a certain level are price ceilings. If a government sets a price ceiling below the market price, then at the ceiling price the quantity of the good demanded will exceed the quantity supplied. There will be a shortage at the ceiling price. Price ceilings can lead to nonprice rationing devices and black markets.	price controls, 81
	price ceiling, 81
	price floor, 82
	nonprice rationing
	  devices, 82
	black market, 82
	rent control, 83
	
	Key Figure
	Figure 4-3, 82
		• **MyEconLab** Study Plans 4.4,
		  4.5
		• Animated Figure 4-3

The Effects of Price Floors Government-mandated price controls that require prices to be no lower than a certain level are price floors. If a government sets a price floor above the market price, then at the floor price the quantity of the good supplied will exceed the quantity demanded. There will be a surplus at the floor price.	minimum wage, 87 **Key Figures** Figure 4-4, 85 Figure 4-5, 88	• **MyEconLab** Study Plans 4.6, 4.7 • Animated Figures 4-4, 4-5
Government-Imposed Restrictions on Market Quantities Quantity restrictions can take the form of outright government bans on the sale of certain goods. They can also arise from licensing and import restrictions that limit the number of sellers and thereby restrict the amount supplied.	import quota, 89	• **MyEconLab** Study Plan 4.8

Log in to MyEconLab, take a chapter test, and get a personalized Study Plan that tells you which concepts you understand and which ones you need to review. From there, MyEconLab will give you further practice, tutorials, animations, videos, and guided solutions. For more information, visit www.myeconlab.com

PROBLEMS

All problems are assignable in MyEconLab. Answers to odd-numbered problems appear at the back of the book.

4-1. In recent years, technological improvements have greatly reduced the costs of producing basic cell phones, and a number of new firms have entered the cell phone industry. At the same time, prices of substitutes for cell phones, such as smartphones and some tablet devices, have declined considerably. Construct a supply and demand diagram of the market for cell phones. Illustrate the impacts of these developments, and evaluate the effects on the market price and equilibrium quantity. (See page 78.)

4-2. Advances in research and development in the pharmaceutical industry have enabled manufacturers to identify potential cures more quickly and therefore at lower cost. At the same time, the aging of our society has increased the demand for new drugs. Construct a supply and demand diagram of the market for pharmaceutical drugs. Illustrate the impacts of these developments, and evaluate the effects on the market price and the equilibrium quantity. (See page 78.)

4-3. There are simultaneous changes in the demand for and supply of global-positioning-system (GPS) devices, with the consequences being an unambiguous increase in the market clearing price of these devices but no change in the equilibrium quantity. What changes in the demand for and supply of GPS devices could have generated these outcomes? Explain. (See pages 78–79.)

4-4. There are simultaneous changes in the demand for and supply of tablet devices, with the consequences being an unambiguous decrease in the equilibrium quantity of these devices but no change in the market clearing price. What changes in the demand for and supply of tablet devices could have generated these outcomes? Explain. (See pages 78–79.)

4-5. The following table depicts the quantity demanded and quantity supplied of studio apartments in a small college town.

Monthly Rent	Quantity Demanded	Quantity Supplied
$600	3,000	1,600
$650	2,500	1,800
$700	2,000	2,000
$750	1,500	2,200
$800	1,000	2,400

What are the market price and equilibrium quantity of apartments in this town? If this town imposes a rent control of $650 per month, how many studio apartments will be rented? (See pages 83–84.)

4-6. Suppose that the government places a ceiling on the price of a medical drug below the equilibrium price. (See page 82.)

   a. Show why there is a shortage of the medical drug at the new ceiling price.

   b. Suppose that a black market for the medical drug arises, with pharmaceutical firms secretly selling the drug at higher prices. Illustrate the black market for this medical drug, including the implicit supply schedule, the ceiling price, the black market supply and demand, and the highest feasible black market price.

4-7. The table below illustrates the demand and supply schedules for seats on air flights between two cities:

Price	Quantity Demanded	Quantity Supplied
$200	2,000	1,200
$300	1,800	1,400
$400	1,600	1,600
$500	1,400	1,800
$600	1,200	2,000

What are the market price and equilibrium quantity in this market? Now suppose that federal authorities limit the number of flights between the two cities to ensure that no more than 1,200 passengers can be flown. Evaluate the effects of this quota if price adjusts. (Hint: What price per flight are the 1,200 passengers willing to pay? See page 89.)

4-8. The consequences of decriminalizing illegal drugs have long been debated. Some claim that legalization will lower the price of these drugs and reduce related crime and that more people will use these drugs. Suppose that some of these drugs are legalized so that anyone may sell them and use them. Now consider the two claims—that price will fall and quantity demanded will increase. Based on positive economic analysis, are these claims sound? (See page 89.)

4-9. In recent years, the government of Pakistan has established a support price for wheat of about $0.20 per kilogram of wheat. At this price, consumers are willing to purchase 10 billion kilograms of wheat per year, while Pakistani farmers are willing to grow and harvest 18 billion kilograms of wheat per year. The government purchases and stores all surplus wheat. (See page 85.)

   a. What are annual consumer expenditures on the Pakistani wheat crop?

   b. What are annual government expenditures on the Pakistani wheat crop?

   c. How much, in total, do Pakistani wheat farmers receive for the wheat they produce?

4-10. Consider the information in Problem 4-9 and your answers to that question. Suppose that the market clearing price of Pakistani wheat in the absence of price supports is equal to $0.10 per kilogram. At this price, the quantity of wheat demanded is 12 billion kilograms. Under the government wheat price-support program, how much more is spent each year on wheat harvested in Pakistan than otherwise would have been spent in an unregulated market for Pakistani wheat? (See page 85.)

4-11. Consider the diagram below, which depicts the labor market in a city that has adopted a "living wage law" requiring employers to pay a minimum wage rate of $11 per hour. Answer the questions that follow. (See page 88.)

a. What condition exists in this city's labor market at the present minimum wage of $11 per hour? How many people are unemployed at this wage?

b. A city councilwoman has proposed amending the living wage law. She suggests reducing the minimum wage to $9 per hour. Assuming that the labor demand and supply curves were to remain in their present positions, how many people would be unemployed at a new $9 minimum wage?

c. A councilman has offered a counterproposal. In his view, the current minimum wage is too low and should be increased to $12 per hour. Assuming that the labor demand and supply curves remain in their present positions, how many people would be unemployed at a new $12 minimum wage?

4-12. A city has decided to impose rent controls, and it has established a rent ceiling below the previous equilibrium rental rate for offices throughout the city. How will the quantity of offices leased by building owners change? (See page 83.)

4-13. In 2011, the government of a nation established a price support for wheat. The government's support price has been above the equilibrium price each year since, and the government has purchased all wheat over and above the amounts that consumers have bought at the support price. Every year since 2011, there has been an increase in the number of wheat producers in the market. No other factors affecting the market for wheat have changed. Predict what has happened every year since 2011, to each of the following (see page 85):

a. Amount of wheat supplied by wheat producers

b. Amount of wheat demanded by all wheat consumers

c. Amount of wheat purchased by the government

4-14. In advance of the recent increase in the U.S. minimum wage rate, the government of the state of Arizona decided to boost its own minimum wage by an additional $1.60 per hour. This pushed the wage rate earned by Arizona teenagers above the equilibrium wage rate in the teen labor market. What is the predicted effect of this action by Arizona's government on each of the following? (See page 88.)

a. The quantity of labor supplied by Arizona teenagers

b. The quantity of labor demanded by employers of Arizona teenagers

c. The number of unemployed Arizona teenagers

ECONOMICS ON THE NET

The Floor on Milk Prices At various times, the U.S. government has established price floors for milk. This application gives you an opportunity to apply what you have learned in this chapter to this real-world issue.

Title: Northeast Dairy Compact Commission

Navigation: Go to **www.econtoday.com/chap04** to visit the Web site of the Northeast Dairy Compact Commission.

Application Read the contents and answer these questions.

1. Based on the government-set price control concepts discussed in Chapter 4, explain the Northeast Dairy Compact that was once in place in the northeastern United States.

2. Draw a diagram illustrating the supply of and demand for milk in the Northeast Dairy Compact and the supply of and demand for milk outside the Northeast

Dairy Compact. Illustrate how the compact affected the quantities demanded and supplied for participants in the compact. In addition, show how this affected the market for milk produced by those producers outside the dairy compact.

3. Economists have found that while the Northeast Dairy Compact functioned, midwestern dairy farmers lost their dominance of milk production and sales.

In light of your answer to Question 2, explain how this occurred.

For Group Discussion and Analysis Discuss the impact of congressional failure to reauthorize the compact based on your above answers. Identify which arguments in your debate are based on positive economic analysis and which are normative arguments.

ANSWERS TO QUICK QUIZZES

p. 80: (i) demand . . . supply . . . supply . . . demand; (ii) immediately . . . time

p. 81: (i) first come, first served . . . political power . . . physical force . . . random assignment . . . coupons; (ii) queuing

p. 83: (i) ceilings . . . floors; (ii) ceiling . . . controls

p. 85: (i) Rental; (ii) controls . . . controls; (iii) Key money

p. 89: (i) support . . . support; (ii) floor; (iii) import quotas

Consumer Surplus, Producer Surplus, and Gains from Trade within a Price System

A key principle of economics is that the price system enables people to benefit from the voluntary exchange of goods and services. Economists measure the benefits from trade by applying the concepts of *consumer surplus* and *producer surplus*, which are defined in the sections that follow.

Consumer Surplus

Let's first examine how economists measure the benefits that consumers gain from engaging in market transactions in the price system. Consider Figure B-1 below, which displays a market demand curve, D. We begin by assuming that consumers face a per-unit price of this item given by P_A. Thus, the quantity demanded of this particular product is equal to Q_A at point A on the demand curve.

FIGURE B-1

Consumer Surplus

If the per-unit price is P_A, then at point A on the demand curve D, consumers desire to purchase Q_A units. To purchase Q_1 units of this item, consumers would have been willing to pay the price P_1 for the last unit purchased, but they have to pay only the per-unit price P_A, so they gain a surplus equal to $P_1 - P_A$ for the last of the Q_1 units purchased. Likewise, to buy the last of the Q_2 units, consumers would have been willing to pay the price P_2, so they gain the surplus equal to $P_2 - P_A$ for the last of the Q_2 units purchased. Summing these and all other surpluses that consumers receive from purchasing each of the Q_A units at the price P_A yields the total consumer surplus at this price, shown by the blue-shaded area.

Typically, we visualize the market demand curve as indicating the quantities that all consumers are willing to purchase at each possible price. But the demand curve also tells us the price that consumers are willing to pay for a unit of output at various possible quantities. For instance, if consumers buy Q_1 units of this good, they will be willing to pay a price equal to P_1 for the last unit purchased. If they have to pay only the price P_A for each unit they buy, however, consumers gain an amount equal to $P_1 - P_A$ for the last of the Q_1 units purchased. This benefit to consumers equals the vertical distance between the demand curve and the level of the market clearing price. Economists call this vertical distance a *surplus* value to consumers from being able to consume the last of the Q_1 units at the lower, market clearing price.

Likewise, if consumers purchase Q_2 units of this good, they will be willing to pay a price equal to P_2 for the last unit. Nevertheless, because they have to pay only the price P_A for each unit purchased, consumers gain an amount equal to $P_2 - P_A$. Hence, this is the surplus associated with the last of the Q_2 units that consumers buy.

Of course, when consumers pay the same per-unit price P_A for every unit of this product that they purchase at point A, they obtain Q_A units. Thus, consumers gain surplus values—all of the vertical distances between the demand curve and the level of the market clearing price—for each unit consumed, up to the total of Q_A units. Graphically, this is equivalent to the blue-shaded *area under the demand curve but above the market clearing price* in Figure B-1 on the facing page. This entire area equals the total **consumer surplus,** which is the difference between the total amount that consumers *would have been willing to pay* for an item and the total amount that they actually pay.

Consumer surplus
The difference between the total amount that consumers would have been willing to pay for an item and the total amount that they actually pay.

Producer Surplus

Consumers are not the only ones who gain from exchange. Producers (suppliers) gain as well. To consider how economists measure the benefits to producers from supplying goods and services in exchange, look at Figure B-2 below, which displays a market supply curve, S. Let's begin by assuming that suppliers face a per-unit price of this item given by P_B. Thus, the quantity supplied of this particular product is equal to Q_B at point B on the supply curve.

FIGURE B-2

Producer Surplus

If the per-unit price is P_B, then at point B on the supply curve S, producers are willing to supply Q_B units. To sell Q_3 units of this item, producers would have been willing to receive the price P_3 for the last unit sold, but instead they accept the higher per-unit price P_B, so they gain a surplus equal to $P_B - P_3$ for the last of the Q_3 units sold. Similarly, producers would have been willing to accept P_4 to provide Q_4 units, so they gain the surplus equal to $P_B - P_4$ for the last of the Q_4 units sold. Summing these and all other surpluses that producers receive from supplying each of the Q_B units at the price P_B yields the total producer surplus at this price, shown by the red-shaded area.

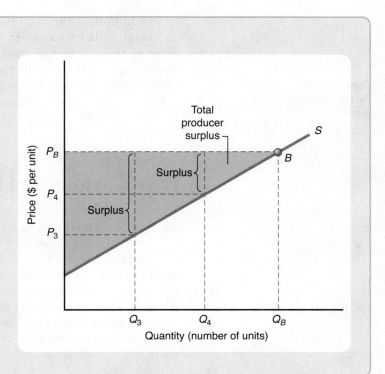

The market supply curve tells us the quantities that all producers are willing to to sell at each possible price. At the same time, the supply curve also indicates the price that producers are willing to accept to sell a unit of output at various possible quantities. For example, if producers sell Q_3 units of this good, they will be willing to accept a price equal to P_3 for the last unit sold. If they receive the price P_B for each unit that they supply, however, producers gain an amount equal to $P_B - P_3$ for the last of the Q_3 units sold. This benefit to producers equals the vertical distance between the supply curve and the market clearing price, which is a *surplus* value from being able to provide the last of the Q_3 units at the higher, market clearing price.

Similarly, if producers supply Q_4 units of this good, they will be willing to accept a price equal to P_4 for the last unit. Producers actually receive the price P_B for each unit supplied, however, so they gain an amount equal to $P_B - P_4$. Hence, this is the surplus gained from supplying the last of the Q_4 units.

Naturally, when producers receive the same per-unit price P_B for each unit supplied at point B, producers sell Q_B units. Consequently, producers gain surplus values—all of the vertical distances between the level of the market clearing price and the supply curve—for each unit supplied, up to the total of Q_B units. In Figure B-2 on the previous page, this is equivalent to the red-shaded *area above the supply curve but below the market clearing price*. This area is the total **producer surplus,** which is the difference between the total amount that producers actually receive for an item and the total amount that they *would have been willing to accept* for supplying that item.

Producer surplus

The difference between the total amount that producers actually receive for an item and the total amount that they would have been willing to accept for supplying that item.

Gains from Trade within a Price System

The concepts of consumer surplus and producer surplus can be combined to measure the gains realized by consumers and producers from engaging in voluntary exchange. To see how, take a look at Figure B-3 on the facing page. The market demand and supply curves intersect at point E, and as you have learned, at this point, the equilibrium quantity is Q_E. At the market clearing price P_E, this is both the quantity that consumers are willing to purchase and the quantity that producers are willing to supply.

In addition, at the market clearing price P_E and the equilibrium quantity Q_E, the blue-shaded area under the demand curve but above the market clearing price is the amount of consumer surplus. Furthermore, the red-shaded area under the market clearing price but above the supply curve is the amount of producer surplus. The sum of *both* areas is the total value of the **gains from trade**— the sum of consumer surplus and producer surplus—generated by the mutually beneficial voluntary exchange of the equilibrium quantity Q_E at the market clearing price P_E.

Gains from trade

The sum of consumer surplus and producer surplus.

Price Controls and Gains from Trade

How do price controls affect gains from trade? Consider first the effects of imposing a ceiling price that is lower than the market clearing price. As you learned in Chapter 4, the results are an increase in quantity demanded and a decrease in quantity supplied, so a shortage occurs. The smaller quantity supplied by firms is the amount actually produced and available in the market for the item in question. Thus, consumers are able to purchase fewer units, and this means that consumer surplus may be lower than it would have been without the government's price ceiling. Furthermore, because firms sell fewer units at the lower ceiling price, producer surplus definitely decreases. Thus, the government's imposition of the price ceiling tends to reduce gains from trade.

FIGURE B-3

Consumer Surplus, Producer Surplus, and Gains from Trade

At point E, the demand and supply curves intersect at the equilibrium quantity Q_E and the market clearing price P_E. Total consumer surplus at the market clearing price is the blue-shaded area under the demand curve but above the market clearing price. Total producer surplus is the red-shaded area below the market clearing price but above the supply curve. The sum of consumer surplus and producer surplus at the market clearing price constitutes the total gain to society from voluntary exchange of the quantity Q_E at the market clearing price P_E.

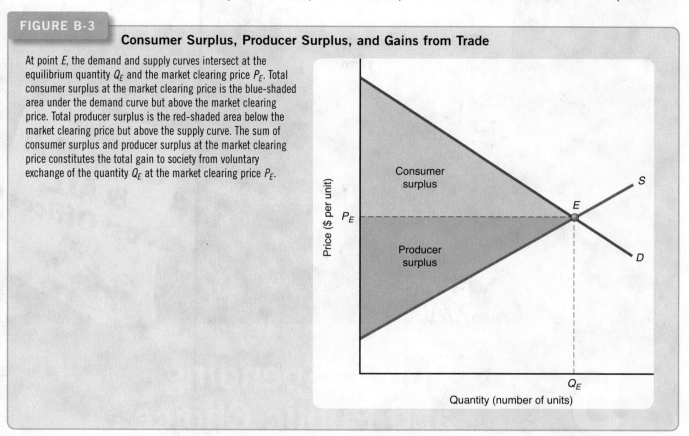

Now consider the effects of the establishment of a price floor above the market clearing price of a good. As discussed in Chapter 4, the effects of imposing such a floor price are an increase in the quantity supplied and a decrease in the quantity demanded. The smaller quantity demanded by consumers is the amount actually traded in the market. Thus, consumers purchase fewer units of the good, resulting in a reduction in consumer surplus. In addition, firms sell fewer units, so producer surplus may decrease. Thus, the establishment of a price floor also tends to reduce gains from trade.

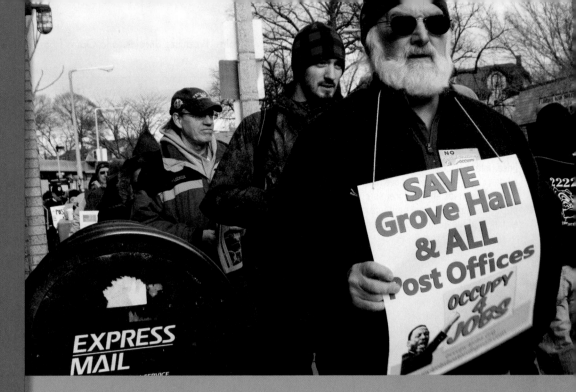

5

Public Spending and Public Choice

The U.S. Postal Service (USPS) delivers nearly 40 percent of the world's mail. Nevertheless, its annual volume of delivered mail has declined by more than 20 percent since 2006. Even though the USPS commonly refers to itself as a private enterprise, economists classify it as *government-sponsored*. Government sponsorship of the USPS is evidenced by the fact that the USPS now receives more than $15 billion in U.S. government loans. Without these funds, the USPS would have to shut down many of its operations. Why does the government sponsor the provision of certain items, such as mail delivery services, even though private firms otherwise could provide them? This is among the several questions relating to government's economic role that are addressed in the present chapter.

LEARNING OBJECTIVES

After reading this chapter, you should be able to:

▶ Explain how market failures such as externalities might justify economic functions of government

▶ Distinguish between private goods and public goods and explain the nature of the free-rider problem

▶ Describe political functions of government that entail its involvement in the economy

▶ Analyze how Medicare affects the incentives to consume medical services

▶ Explain why increases in government spending on public education have not been associated with improvements in measures of student performance

▶ Discuss the central elements of the theory of public choice

MyEconLab helps you master each objective and study more efficiently. See end of chapter for details.

a 75-year-old woman accidentally managed to halt all Internet traffic to the entire country of Armenia? The woman was shoveling for scrap metal in the Eastern European nation of Georgia, when she sliced through the single fiber optic cable routing all of Armenia's Web transmissions. In her defense, the woman stated that a jump in the market price of scrap metals had induced her to search beneath the ground for old, unused wires that might contain copper. She was only pursuing her own self-interest with an aim to profit from selling items in the scrap-metals market, she contended. She had not, she insisted, intended to cut off Internet access for thousands of people. This event was an example of how people interacting in markets, including the market for scrap metal, can create negative spillovers, such as interrupted Internet traffic, for people outside those markets. As you will learn in this chapter, economists classify such third-party spillovers, which they refer to as *externalities*, among flaws in the price system called *market failures*.

What a Price System Can and Cannot Do

Throughout the book so far, we have alluded to the advantages of a price system. High on the list is economic efficiency. In its ideal form, a price system allows all resources to move from lower-valued uses to higher-valued uses via voluntary exchange, by which mutually advantageous trades take place. In a price system, consumers are sovereign. That is to say, they have the individual freedom to decide what they wish to purchase. Politicians and even business managers do not ultimately decide what is produced. Consumers decide. Some proponents of the price system argue that this is its most important characteristic. Competition among sellers protects consumers from coercion by one seller, and sellers are protected from coercion by one consumer because other consumers are available.

Sometimes, though, the price system does not generate these results, and too few or too many resources go to specific economic activities. Such situations are **market failures.** Market failures prevent the price system from attaining economic efficiency and individual freedom. Market failures offer one of the strongest arguments in favor of certain economic functions of government, which we now examine.

Market failure
A situation in which the market economy leads to too few or too many resources going to a specific economic activity.

Correcting for Externalities

In a pure market system, competition generates economic efficiency only when individuals know and must bear the true opportunity cost of their actions. In some circumstances, the price that someone actually pays for a resource, good, or service is higher or lower than the opportunity cost that all of society pays for that same resource, good, or service.

Externalities

Consider a hypothetical world in which there is no government regulation against pollution. You are living in a town that until now has had clean air. A steel mill moves into town. It produces steel and has paid for the inputs—land, labor, capital, and entrepreneurship. The price the mill charges for the steel reflects, in this example, only the costs that it incurs. In the course of production, however, the mill utilizes one input—clean air—by simply using it. This is indeed an input because in making steel, the furnaces emit smoke. The steel mill doesn't have to pay the cost of dirtying the air. Rather, it is the people in the community who incur that cost in the form of dirtier clothes, dirtier cars and houses, and more respiratory illnesses.

The effect is similar to what would happen if the steel mill could take coal or oil or workers' services without paying for them. There is an **externality,** an external cost. Some of the costs associated with the production of the steel have "spilled over" to affect **third parties,** parties other than the buyer and the seller of the steel.

Externality
A consequence of an economic activity that spills over to affect third parties. Pollution is an externality.

Third parties
Parties who are not directly involved in a given activity or transaction.

Property rights
The rights of an owner to use and to exchange property.

A fundamental reason that air pollution creates external costs is that the air belongs to everyone and hence to no one in particular. Lack of clearly assigned **property rights,** or the rights of an owner to use and exchange property, prevents market prices from reflecting all the costs created by activities that generate spillovers onto third parties.

External Costs in Graphical Form

To consider how market prices fail to take into account external costs in situations in which third-party spillovers exist without a clear assignment of property rights, look at panel (a) in Figure 5-1 below. Here we show the demand curve for steel as D. The supply curve is S_1. The supply curve includes only the costs that the firms in the market have to pay. Equilibrium occurs at point E, with a price of $800 per ton and a quantity equal to 110 million tons per year.

But producing steel also involves externalities—the external costs that you and your neighbors pay in the form of dirtier clothes, cars, and houses and increased respiratory disease due to the air pollution emitted from the steel mill. In this case, the producers of steel use clean air without having to pay for it. Let's include these external costs in our graph to find out what the full cost of steel production would really be if property rights to the air around the steel mill could generate payments for "owners" of that air. We do this by imagining that steel producers have to pay the "owners" of the air for the input—clean air—that the producers previously used at a zero price.

Recall from Chapter 3 that an increase in input prices shifts the supply curve up and to the left. Thus, in panel (a) of the figure, the supply curve shifts from S_1 to S_2. External costs equal the vertical distance between A and E_1. In this example, if steel firms had to take into account these external costs, the equilibrium quantity would

---

FIGURE 5-1

External Costs and Benefits

Panel (a) shows a situation in which production of steel generates external costs. If the steel mills ignore pollution, at equilibrium the quantity of steel will be 110 million tons. If the steel mills had to pay external costs caused by the mills' production but currently borne by nearby residents, the supply curve would shift the vertical distance A–E_1, to S_2. If consumers of steel were forced to pay a price that reflected the spillover costs, the quantity demanded would fall to 100 million tons. Panel (b) shows a situation in which inoculations against communicable diseases generate

external benefits to those individuals who may not be inoculated but who will benefit because epidemics will not occur. If each individual ignores the external benefit of inoculations, the market clearing quantity will be 150 million. If external benefits were taken into account by purchasers of inoculations, however, the demand curve would shift to D_2. The new equilibrium quantity would be 200 million inoculations, and the price of an inoculation would rise from $10 to $15.

Panel (a)

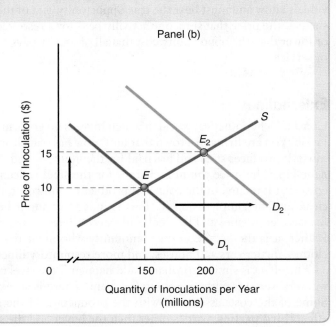

Panel (b)

fall to 100 million tons per year, and the price would rise to $900 per ton. Equilibrium would shift from E to E_1. In contrast, if the price of steel does not account for external costs, third parties bear those costs—represented by the distance between A and E_1—in the form of dirtier clothes, houses, and cars and increased respiratory illnesses.

External Benefits in Graphical Form

Externalities can also be positive. To demonstrate external benefits in graphical form, we will use the example of inoculations against communicable disease. In panel (b) of Figure 5-1 on the facing page, we show the demand curve as D_1 (without taking account of any external benefits) and the supply curve as S. The equilibrium price is $10 per inoculation, and the equilibrium quantity is 150 million inoculations.

We assume, however, that inoculations against communicable diseases generate external benefits to individuals who may not be inoculated but will benefit nevertheless because epidemics will not break out. If such external benefits were taken into account by those who purchase inoculations, the demand curve would shift from D_1 to D_2.

As a consequence of this shift in demand at point E_2, the new equilibrium quantity would be 200 million inoculations, and the new equilibrium price would be $15 per inoculation. If people who consider getting inoculations fail to take external benefits into account, individuals in society are not devoting enough resources to inoculations against communicable diseases.

Resource Misallocations of Externalities

When there are external costs, the market will tend to *overallocate* resources to the production of the good or service in question, for those goods or services are implicitly priced deceptively low. In the steel example, too many resources will be allocated to steel production, because the steel mill owners and managers are not required to take account of the external cost that steel production is imposing on other individuals. In essence, the full cost of production is not borne by the owners and managers, so the price they charge the public for steel is lower than it would otherwise be. And, of course, the lower price means that buyers are willing and able to buy more. More steel is produced and consumed than if the sellers and buyers were to bear external costs.

In contrast, when there are external benefits, the price is too low to induce suppliers to allocate resources to the production of that good or service (because the demand, which fails to reflect the external benefits, is relatively too low). Thus, the market *underallocates* resources to producing the good or service. Hence, in a market system, too many of the goods that generate external costs are produced, and too few of the goods that generate external benefits are produced.

How the Government Can Correct Negative Externalities

In theory, the government can take action to try to correct situations in which a lack of property rights allows third-party spillovers to create an externality. In the case of negative externalities, at least two avenues are open to the government: special taxes and legislative regulation or prohibition.

SPECIAL TAXES In our example of the steel mill, the externality problem arises because using the air for waste disposal is costless to the firm but not to society. The government could attempt to tax the steel mill commensurate with the cost to third parties from smoke in the air. This, in effect, would be a pollution tax or an **effluent fee**. The ultimate effect would be to reduce the supply of steel and raise the price to consumers, ideally making the price equal to the full cost of production to society.

Why has Hungary's government imposed taxes on foods that it has determined to be detrimental to the health of that nation's residents?

Effluent fee
A charge to a polluter that gives the right to discharge into the air or water a certain amount of pollution; also called a *pollution tax*.

INTERNATIONAL POLICY EXAMPLE

Hungary's Tax on Prepackaged Snacks

The government of Hungary has determined that the nation's health care system experiences external spillovers from the snack food market. People who consume too many chips, salted nuts, sweets, ice creams, instant soups, and energy drinks are, the government has concluded, experiencing worse health. As these people seek treatment for their health problems, they are clogging the nation's physicians' offices and hospitals. Thus, Hungary's government is seeking to induce producers of certain snack foods and beverages to cut back on an overallocation of resources that the government perceives to be creating a negative externality.

Toward this end, the government is placing special taxes on foodstuffs with high sugar, salt, and carbohydrate content and on fluid products containing more than 20 milligrams of caffeine per 100 milliliters. By imposing these taxes, it intends to reduce the supply of each of these items and thereby raise its price toward equality with the full cost of its production to society as a whole.

FOR CRITICAL THINKING

If untaxed bakery sweets and fast food are close substitutes for snack foods, could Hungary's tax on snack foods boost consumption of the untaxed items? Explain.

Go to www.econtoday.com/chap05 to learn more about how the Environmental Protection Agency uses regulations to try to protect the environment.

REGULATION Alternatively, to correct a negative externality arising from steel production, the government could specify a maximum allowable rate of pollution. This regulation would require that the steel mill install pollution abatement equipment at its facilities, reduce its rate of output, or some combination of the two. Note that the government's job would not be simple, for it would have to determine the appropriate level of pollution, which would require extensive knowledge of both the benefits and the costs of pollution control.

How the Government Can Correct Positive Externalities

What can the government do when the production of one good spills *benefits* over to third parties? It has several policy options: financing the production of the good or producing the good itself, subsidies (negative taxes), and regulation.

GOVERNMENT FINANCING AND PRODUCTION If the positive externalities seem extremely large, the government has the option of financing the desired additional production facilities so that the "right" amount of the good will be produced. Again consider inoculations against communicable diseases. The government could—and often does—finance campaigns to inoculate the population. It could (and does) even produce and operate inoculation centers where inoculations are given at no charge.

SUBSIDIES A subsidy is a negative tax. A subsidy is a per-unit payment made either to a business or to a consumer when the business produces or the consumer buys a good or a service. To generate more inoculations against communicable diseases, the government could subsidize everyone who obtains an inoculation by directly reimbursing those inoculated or by making per-unit payments to private firms that provide inoculations. Subsidies reduce the net price to consumers, thereby causing a larger quantity to be demanded.

How are some state governments seeking to help society capture external benefits that the governments suggest society derives from being kept informed?

POLICY EXAMPLE

Stop the Presses for Subsidies!

Since the late 2000s, total physical newspaper circulation to paid subscribers has declined by more than 5 percent per year. The cumulative reduction in readership of paper editions since 2000 has exceeded 50 percent.

Some state government officials suggest that local newspapers provide positive externalities. Making readers better informed, they argue, improves people's lives and in some cases saves lives. On the basis of this logic, several state governments are now providing subsidies to newspapers. For example, Minnesota's state government has provided hundreds of thousands of dollars to newspapers in Duluth and St. Paul. These newspapers have used the funds to train their staffs to post content and ads online instead of relying solely on physical print editions to generate revenues. In this way, the Minnesota state government seeks to help local newspapers keep operating.

FOR CRITICAL THINKING

How does the provision of subsidies to local newspapers likely affect the supply of news content at each possible price?

REGULATION In some cases involving positive externalities, the government can require by law that individuals in the society undertake a certain action. For example, regulations require that all school-age children be inoculated before entering public and private schools. Some people believe that a basic school education itself generates positive externalities. Perhaps as a result of this belief, we have regulations—laws—that require all school-age children to be enrolled in a public or private school.

QUICK QUIZ See page 121 for the answers. Review concepts from this section in MyEconLab.

External _____ lead to an overallocation of resources to the specific economic activity. Two possible ways of correcting these spillovers are _____ and _____.

External _____ result in an underallocation of resources to the specific activity. Three possible government

corrections are _____ the production of the activity, _____ private firms or consumers to engage in the activity, and _____.

The Other Economic Functions of Government

Besides correcting for externalities, the government performs many other economic functions that affect the way exchange is carried out. In contrast, the political functions of government have to do with deciding how income should be redistributed among households and selecting which goods and services have special merits and should therefore be treated differently. The economic and political functions of government can and do overlap.

Let's look at four more economic functions of government.

Providing a Legal System

The courts and the police may not at first seem like economic functions of government. Their activities nonetheless have important consequences for economic activities in any country. You and I enter into contracts constantly, whether they be oral or written, expressed or implied. When we believe that we have been wronged, we seek redress of our grievances through our legal institutions. Moreover, consider the legal system that is necessary for the smooth functioning of our economic system. Our system has defined quite explicitly the legal status of businesses, the rights of private ownership, and a method of enforcing contracts. All relationships among consumers and businesses are governed by the legal rules of the game.

In its judicial function, then, the government serves as the referee for settling disputes in the economic arena. In this role, the government often imposes penalties for violations of legal rules.

Much of our legal system is involved with defining and protecting property rights. One might say that property rights are really the rules of our economic game. When property rights are well defined, owners of property have an incentive to use that property efficiently. Any mistakes in their decisions about the use of property have negative consequences that the owners suffer. Furthermore, when property rights are well defined, owners of property have an incentive to maintain that property so that if they ever desire to sell it, it will fetch a better price.

What happens when the government fails to establish clear rights to private property and fails to enforce owners' rights fully? In such situations, individuals and firms are more likely to be willing to engage in activities that create spillover effects for other individuals. Thus, externalities will result. In such cases, however, these externalities result from ambiguously assigned and weakly enforced property rights. The government, rather than the market, is at fault.

Promoting Competition

Many economists argue that the only way to attain economic efficiency is through competition. One of the roles of government is to serve as the protector of a competitive economic system. Congress and the various state governments have passed **antitrust legislation.** Such legislation makes illegal certain (but not all) economic activities that might restrain trade—that is, that might prevent free competition among actual and potential rival firms in the marketplace. The avowed aim of antitrust legislation is to reduce the power of **monopolies**—firms that can determine the market price of the goods they sell. A large number of antitrust laws have been passed that prohibit specific anticompetitive actions. Both the Antitrust Division of the U.S. Department of Justice and the Federal Trade Commission attempt to enforce these antitrust laws. Various state judicial agencies also expend efforts at maintaining competition.

Antitrust legislation
Laws that restrict the formation of monopolies and regulate certain anticompetitive business practices.

Monopoly
A firm that can determine the market price of a good. In the extreme case, a monopoly is the only seller of a good or service.

Providing Public Goods

The goods used in our examples up to this point have been **private goods.** When I eat a cheeseburger, you cannot eat the same one. So you and I are rivals for that cheeseburger, just as much as contenders for the title of world champion are. When I use the services of an auto mechanic, that person cannot work at the same time for you. That is the distinguishing feature of private goods—their use is exclusive to the people who purchase them. The **principle of rival consumption** applies to most private goods. Rival consumption is easy to understand. Either you use such a private good or I use it.

Of course, private firms provide some goods and services that are not fully subject to the principle of rival consumption. For instance, you and a friend can both purchase tickets providing the two of you with the right to sit in a musical facility and listen to a concert during a specified period of time. Your friend's presence does not prohibit you from enjoying the music, nor does your presence prevent him from appreciating the concert. Nevertheless, the owner of the musical facility can prevent others who have not purchased tickets from entering the facility during the concert. Consequently, as long as nonpayers can be excluded from consuming an item, that item can also be produced and sold as a private good.

There is an entire class of goods that are not private goods. These are called **public goods.** Like musical concerts, public goods are items to which the principle of rival consumption does not apply. Hence, many individuals simultaneously can consume public goods *jointly.* What truly distinguishes public goods from all private goods is that the costs required to exclude nonpayers from consuming public goods are so high that doing so is infeasible. National defense and police protection are examples. Suppose that your next-door neighbor were to pay for protection from a terrorist effort to explode a large bomb. If so, your neighbor's life and property could not be defended from such a threat without your life and property also receiving the same defense, even if you had failed to provide any payment for protection. Finding a way to avoid protecting you while still protecting your neighbor would be so expensive that such exclusion of defense for you and your property would be difficult.

Private goods
Goods that can be consumed by only one individual at a time. Private goods are subject to the principle of rival consumption.

Principle of rival consumption
The recognition that individuals are rivals in consuming private goods because one person's consumption reduces the amount available for others to consume.

Public goods
Goods for which the principle of rival consumption does not apply and for which exclusion of nonpaying consumers is too costly to be feasible. They can be jointly consumed by many individuals simultaneously at no additional cost and with no reduction in quality or quantity. Furthermore, no one who fails to help pay for the good can be denied the benefit of the good.

CHARACTERISTICS OF PUBLIC GOODS Two fundamental characteristics of public goods set them apart from all other goods:

1. *Public goods can be used by more and more people at no additional opportunity cost and without depriving others of any of the services of the goods.* Once funds have been spent on national defense, the defense protection you receive does not reduce the amount of protection bestowed on anyone else. The opportunity cost of your receiving national defense once it is in place is zero because once national defense is in place to protect you, it also protects others.

2. *It is difficult to design a collection system for a public good on the basis of how much individuals use it.* Nonpayers can often utilize a public good without incurring any monetary cost, because the cost of excluding them from using the good is so high. Those

who provide the public good find that it is not cost-effective to prevent nonpayers from utilizing it. For instance, taxpayers who pay to provide national defense typically do not incur the costs that would be entailed in excluding nonpayers from benefiting from national defense.

The fundamental problem of public goods is that the private sector has a difficult, if not impossible, time providing them. Individuals in the private sector have little or no incentive to offer public goods. It is difficult for them to make a profit doing so, because it is too costly and, hence, infeasible to exclude nonpayers. Consequently, true public goods must necessarily be provided by government. (Note, though, that economists do not categorize something as a public good simply because the government provides it.)

Governments traditionally have operated facilities for space flight, so why are private firms now involved in placing humans beyond the earth's atmosphere?

EXAMPLE

Private Companies Look to Place Humans in Orbit—and Beyond

Would you like to live in earth orbit, or would you prefer landing on the moon? If you wish to go no farther than 228 miles above the earth, Bigelow Aerospace has developed, constructed, and tested low-cost inflatable space stations in which humans can reside. The company has already established a rental rate of $28,750,000 per astronaut per month. If your objective is to go to the moon—say, to mine platinum—then you could contact another firm called Moon Express. That company has developed a new technology for landing people on the moon at a cost 90 percent below that at which the U.S. government could manage to do it.

In both cases, the only catch is that you would have to find another company that could send you into orbit about the earth or take you to the moon. In fact, several private firms are working on developing rocket propulsion systems for transporting humans to and beyond earth orbit.

FOR CRITICAL THINKING
Do the services of transporting people to or beyond the earth's orbit or providing them with places to reside in space possess the characteristics of public or private goods?

FREE RIDERS The nature of public goods leads to the **free-rider problem,** a situation in which some individuals take advantage of the fact that others will assume the burden of paying for public goods such as national defense. Suppose that citizens were taxed directly in proportion to how much they tell an interviewer that they value national defense. Some people who actually value national defense will probably tell interviewers that it has no value to them—they don't want any of it. Such people are trying to be free riders. We may all want to be free riders if we believe that someone else will provide the commodity in question that we actually value.

The free-rider problem often arises in connection with sharing the burden of international defense. A country may choose to belong to a multilateral defense organization, such as the North Atlantic Treaty Organization (NATO), but then consistently attempt to avoid contributing funds to the organization. The nation knows it would be defended by others in NATO if it were attacked but would rather not pay for such defense. In short, it seeks a free ride.

Free-rider problem
A problem that arises when individuals presume that others will pay for public goods so that, individually, they can escape paying for their portion without causing a reduction in production.

Ensuring Economywide Stability

Our economy sometimes faces the problems of undesired unemployment and rising prices. The government, especially the federal government, has made an attempt to solve these problems by trying to stabilize the economy by smoothing out the ups and downs in overall business activity. The notion that the federal government should undertake actions to stabilize business activity is a relatively new idea in the United States, encouraged by high unemployment rates during the Great Depression of the 1930s and subsequent theories about possible ways that government could reduce unemployment. In 1946, Congress passed the Full-Employment Act, a landmark law concerning government responsibility for economic performance. It established three goals for government stabilization policy: full employment, price stability, and economic growth. These goals have provided the justification for many government economic programs during the post–World War II period.

The Political Functions of Government

At least two functions of government are political or normative functions rather than economic ones like those discussed in the first part of this chapter. These two areas are (1) the provision and regulation of government-sponsored and government-inhibited goods and (2) income redistribution.

Government-Sponsored and Government-Inhibited Goods

Government-sponsored good
A good that has been deemed socially desirable through the political process. Museums are an example.

Through political processes, governments often determine that certain goods possess special merit and seek to promote their production and consumption. A **government-sponsored good** is defined as any good that the political process has deemed socially desirable. (Note that nothing inherent in any particular good makes that item a government-sponsored good. The designation is entirely subjective.) Examples of government-sponsored goods in our society are sports stadiums, museums, ballets, plays, and concerts. In these areas, the government's role is the provision of these goods to the people in society who would not otherwise purchase them at market clearing prices or who would not purchase an amount of them judged to be sufficient. This provision may take the form of government production and distribution of the goods. It can also take the form of reimbursement for spending on government-sponsored goods or subsidies to producers or consumers for part of the goods' costs.

Governments do indeed subsidize such goods as professional sports, concerts, ballets, museums, and plays. In most cases, those goods would not be so numerous without subsidization.

Government-inhibited good
A good that has been deemed socially undesirable through the political process. Heroin is an example.

Government-inhibited goods are the opposite of government-sponsored goods. They are goods that, through the political process, have been deemed socially undesirable. Heroin, cigarettes, gambling, and cocaine are examples. The government exercises its role with respect to these goods by taxing, regulating, or prohibiting their manufacture, sale, and use. Governments justify the relatively high taxes on alcohol and tobacco by declaring that they are socially undesirable. The best-known example of governmental exercise of power in this area is the stance against certain psychoactive drugs. Most psychoactives (except nicotine, caffeine, and alcohol) are either expressly prohibited, as is the case for heroin, cocaine, and opium, or heavily regulated, as in the case of prescription psychoactives.

Income Redistribution

Transfer payments
Money payments made by governments to individuals for which no services or goods are rendered in return. Examples are Social Security old-age and disability benefits and unemployment insurance benefits.

Another relatively recent political function of government has been the explicit redistribution of income. This redistribution uses two systems: the progressive income tax (described in Chapter 6) and transfer payments. **Transfer payments** are payments made to individuals for which no services or goods are rendered in return. The two primary money transfer payments in our system are Social Security old-age and disability benefits and unemployment insurance benefits. Income redistribution also includes a large amount of income **transfers in kind,** rather than money transfers. Some income transfers in kind are food stamps, Medicare and Medicaid, government health care services, and subsidized public housing.

Transfers in kind
Payments that are in the form of actual goods and services, such as food stamps, subsidized public housing, and medical care, and for which no goods or services are rendered in return.

The government has also engaged in other activities as a form of redistribution of income. For example, the provision of public education is at least in part an attempt to redistribute income by making sure that the poor have access to education.

QUICK QUIZ See page 121 for the answers. Review concepts from this section in MyEconLab.

The economic activities of government include (1) correcting for _____, (2) providing a _____ _____, (3) promoting _____, (4) producing _____ goods, and (5) ensuring _____ _____.

The principle of _____ _____ does not apply to public goods as it does to private goods.

Public goods have two characteristics: (1) Once they are produced, there is no additional _____ _____

when additional consumers use them, because your use of a public good does not deprive others of its simultaneous use; and (2) consumers cannot conveniently be _____ on the basis of use.

Political, or normative, activities of the government include the provision and regulation of _____-_____ and _____-_____ goods and _____ redistribution.

Public Spending and Transfer Programs

The size of the public sector can be measured in many different ways. One way is to count the number of public employees. Another is to look at total government outlays. Government outlays include all government expenditures on employees, rent, electricity, and the like. In addition, total government outlays include transfer payments, such as welfare and Social Security. In Figure 5-2 below, you see that government outlays prior to World War I did not exceed 10 percent of annual national income. There was a spike during World War I, a general increase during the Great Depression, and then a huge spike during World War II. After World War II, government outlays as a percentage of total national income rose steadily before dropping in the 1990s, rising again in the early 2000s, and then jumping sharply beginning in 2008.

How do federal and state governments allocate their spending? A typical federal government budget is shown in panel (a) of Figure 5-3 on the following page. The three largest categories are Medicare and other health-related spending, Social Security and other income-security programs, and national defense, which together constitute 79.7 percent of the total federal budget.

The makeup of state and local expenditures is quite different. As panel (b) shows, education is the biggest category, accounting for 34.3 percent of all expenditures.

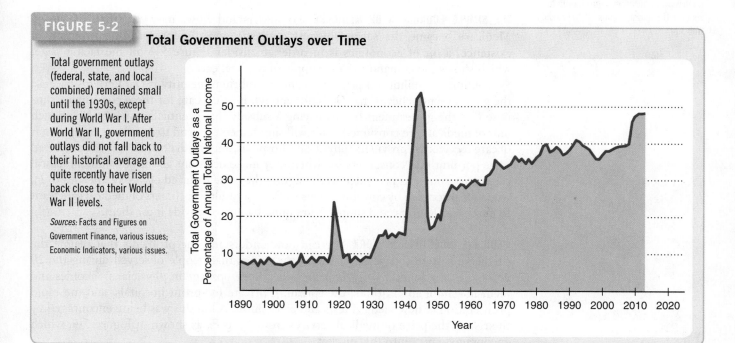

FIGURE 5-2

Total Government Outlays over Time

Total government outlays (federal, state, and local combined) remained small until the 1930s, except during World War I. After World War II, government outlays did not fall back to their historical average and quite recently have risen back close to their World War II levels.

Sources: Facts and Figures on Government Finance, various issues; Economic Indicators, various issues.

FIGURE 5-3

Federal Government Spending Compared to State and Local Spending

The federal government's spending habits are quite different from those of the states and cities. In panel (a), you can see that the most important categories in the federal budget are Medicare and other health-related spending, Social Security and other income-security programs, and national defense, which make up 79.7 percent. In panel (b), the most important category at the state and local level is education, which makes up 34.3 percent. "Other" includes expenditures in such areas as waste treatment, garbage collection, mosquito abatement, and the judicial system.

Sources: Economic Report of the President, Economic Indicators.

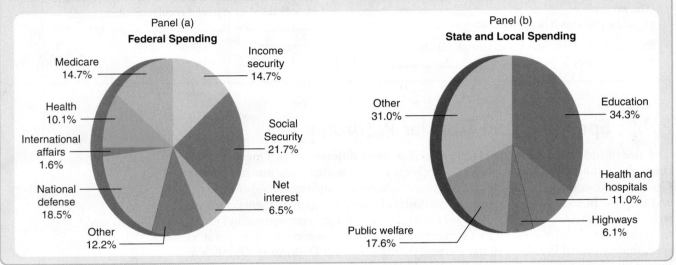

Publicly Subsidized Health Care: Medicare

Figure 5-3 above shows that health-related spending is a significant portion of total government expenditures. Certainly, medical expenses are a major concern for many elderly people. Since 1965, that concern has been reflected in the existence of the Medicare program, which pays hospital and physicians' bills for U.S. residents over the age of 65 (and for those younger than 65 in some instances). In return for paying a tax on their earnings while in the workforce (2.9 percent of wages and salaries, plus 3.8 percent on certain income for high-income households), retirees are assured that the majority of their hospital and physicians' bills will be paid for with public monies.

Go to www.econtoday.com/chap05 to visit the U.S. government's official Medicare Web site.

THE SIMPLE ECONOMICS OF MEDICARE To understand how, in fewer than 50 years, Medicare became the second-biggest domestic government spending program in existence, a bit of economics is in order. Consider Figure 5-4 on the facing page, which shows the demand for and supply of medical care.

The initial equilibrium price is P_0 and equilibrium quantity is Q_0. Perhaps because the government believes that Q_0 is not enough medical care for these consumers, suppose that the government begins paying a subsidy that eventually is set at M for each unit of medical care consumed. This will simultaneously tend to raise the price per unit of care received by providers (physicians, hospitals, and the like) and lower the perceived price per unit that consumers see when they make decisions about how much medical care to consume. As presented in the figure, the price received by providers rises to P_s, while the price paid by consumers falls to P_d. As a result, consumers of medical care want to purchase Q_m units, and suppliers are quite happy to provide it for them.

MEDICARE INCENTIVES AT WORK We can now understand the problems that plague the Medicare system today. First, one of the things that people observed during the 20 years after the founding of Medicare was a huge upsurge in physicians' incomes and medical school applications, the spread of private for-profit hospitals, and the rapid proliferation of new medical tests and procedures. All of this was being encouraged by the rise in the price of medical services from P_0 to P_s, as shown in Figure 5-4, which encouraged entry into this market.

FIGURE 5-4

The Economic Effects of Medicare Subsidies

When the government pays a per-unit subsidy M for medical care, consumers pay the price of services P_d for the quantity of services Q_m. Providers receive the price P_s for supplying this quantity. Originally, the federal government projected that its total spending on Medicare would equal an amount such as the area $Q_0 \times (P_0 - P_d)$. Because actual consumption equals Q_m, however, the government's total expenditures equal $Q_m \times M$.

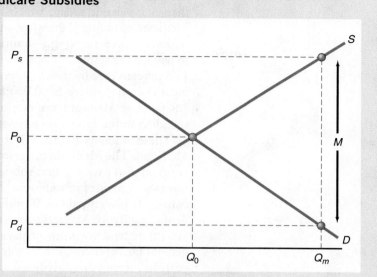

Second, government expenditures on Medicare have routinely turned out to be far in excess of the expenditures forecast at the time the program was put in place or was expanded. The reasons for this are easy to see. Bureaucratic planners often fail to recognize the incentive effects of government programs. On the demand side, they fail to account for the huge increase in consumption (from Q_0 to Q_m) that will result from a subsidy like Medicare. On the supply side, they fail to recognize that the larger number of services can only be extracted from suppliers at a higher price, P_s. Consequently, original projected spending on Medicare was an area like $Q_0 \times (P_0 - P_d)$, because original plans for the program only contemplated consumption of Q_0 and assumed that the subsidy would have to be only $P_0 - P_d$ per unit. In fact, consumption rises to Q_m, and the additional cost per unit of service rises to P_s, implying an increase in the per-unit subsidy to M. Hence, actual expenditures turn out to be the far larger number $Q_m \times M$. Every expansion of the program, including the 2004 broadening of Medicare to cover obesity as a new illness eligible for coverage and the extension of Medicare to cover patients' prescription drug expenses beginning in 2006, has followed the same pattern.

Third, total spending on medical services has soared, consuming far more income than initially expected. Originally, total spending on medical services was $P_0 \times Q_0$. In the presence of Medicare, spending rises to $P_s \times Q_m$.

In the past, why have government officials considerably underestimated taxpayers' actual expenses for health care programs such as Medicare?

POLICY EXAMPLE

The Great Underestimates of Government Health Care Expenses

When the federal government launched Medicare in 1965, officials estimated that its one-year inflation-adjusted cost in 1990 would turn out to be $12 billion, but the actual program cost in 1990 was $110 billion. When it initiated the Medicaid health-care-subsidy program for lower-income individuals in 1966, the government projected that its annual inflation-adjusted cost for 1990 would be about $7 billion, but that program's true expense in 1990 exceeded $45 billion. One reason for these underestimates was that as time passed, Congress expanded the number of people eligible for both programs. Another reason was that Congress assumed that creating the programs would not increase the quantity of health care demanded.

Of course, when the government offered per-unit subsidies that significantly pushed down the out-of-pocket price, people *did* raise their consumption. These increases in quantities of health care services consumed under Medicare and Medicaid dramatically raised the programs' actual expenses.

FOR CRITICAL THINKING

Why do you suppose that even though Medicare was supposed to be self-sustaining indefinitely, Medicare taxes will fail to cover program costs by 2024?

HEALTH CARE SUBSIDIES CONTINUE TO GROW Just how fast are Medicare subsidies growing? Medicare's cost has risen from 0.7 percent of U.S. national income in 1970 to more than 3.5 percent today, which amounts to nearly $550 billion per year. Because Medicare spending is growing much faster than total employer and employee contributions, future spending guarantees far outstrip the taxes to be collected in the future to pay for the system. (The current Medicare tax rate is 2.9 percent on all wages, with 1.45 percent paid by the employee and 1.45 percent paid by the employer. For certain income earned above $200,000 for individuals and $250,000 for married couples, a 3.8 percent Medicare tax rate applies.) Today, unfunded guarantees of Medicare spending in the future are estimated at more than $25 trillion (in today's dollars).

These amounts fail to reflect the costs of another federal health program called Medicaid. The Medicaid program is structured similarly to Medicare, in that the government also pays per-unit subsidies for health care to qualifying patients. Medicaid, however, provides subsidies only to people who qualify because they have lower incomes. At present, about 50 million people, or about one out of every six U.S. residents, qualify for Medicaid coverage. Medicaid is administered by state governments, but the federal government pays about 60 percent of the program's total cost from general tax revenues. The current cost of the program is more than $400 billion per year. In recent years, Medicaid spending has grown even faster than expenditures on Medicare, rising by more than 75 percent since 2000 alone.

Of course, in legislation enacted in 2010, the U.S. Congress further expanded by more than $100 billion per year the rate of growth of government health care spending, which already has been growing at an average pace of 8 percent per year.

WHAT IF... the federal government continues reducing the out-of-pocket prices that consumers must pay for health care services?

Persistent reductions in out-of-pocket prices of health care services would lead to higher quantities of services demanded by consumers. Providers of health care would be willing to supply these higher quantities only if they receive higher prices. Thus, to continue pushing downward the out-of-pocket price of health care services toward an explicit price of zero, the federal government would have to keep raising the per-unit subsidies that it pays health care providers. Multiplying the increased quantities of health care services consumed and provided times the higher per-unit subsidies would yield larger total subsidies that taxpayers would have to fund. Overall, the total expenses that society would incur for health care services would continue to climb.

Economic Issues of Public Education

In the United States, government involvement in health care is a relatively recent phenomenon. In contrast, state and local governments have assumed primary responsibility for public education for many years. Currently, these governments spend more than $900 billion on education—in excess of 6 percent of total U.S. national income. State and local sales, excise, property, and income taxes finance the bulk of these expenditures. In addition, each year the federal government provides tens of billions of dollars of support for public education through grants and other transfers to state and local governments.

THE NOW-FAMILIAR ECONOMICS OF PUBLIC EDUCATION State and local governments around the United States have developed a variety of complex mechanisms for funding public education. What all public education programs have in common, however, is the provision of educational services to primary, secondary, and college students at prices well below those that would otherwise prevail in the marketplace for these services.

So how do state and local governments accomplish this? The answer is that they operate public education programs that share some of the features of government-subsidized health care programs such as Medicare. Analogously to Figure 5-4 on page 111, public schools provide educational services at a price below the market price. They are willing to produce the quantity of educational services demanded at this below-market price as long as they receive a sufficiently high per-unit subsidy from state and local governments.

THE INCENTIVE PROBLEMS OF PUBLIC EDUCATION Since the 1960s, various measures of the performance of U.S. primary and secondary students have failed to increase even as public spending on education has risen. Some measures of student performance have even declined.

Many economists argue that the incentive effects that have naturally arisen with higher government subsidies for public education help to explain this lack of improvement in student performance. A higher per-pupil subsidy creates a difference between the relatively high per-unit costs of providing the number of educational services that parents and students are willing to purchase and lower valuations of those services. As a consequence, some schools have provided services, such as after-school babysitting and various social services, that have contributed relatively little to student learning.

A factor that complicates efforts to assess the effects of education subsidies is that the public schools often face little or no competition from unsubsidized providers of educational services. In addition, public schools rarely compete against each other. In most locales, therefore, parents who are unhappy with the quality of services provided at the subsidized price cannot transfer their child to a different public school.

Are higher school subsidies associated with improved learning outcomes?

YOU ARE THERE

To consider another setting in which government per-unit subsidies are important, read **The U.S. Government Ensures That an Airport Is "Convenient"** on page 116.

POLICY EXAMPLE

A Weak Relationship between Spending and Schooling Results

In a recent year, the five U.S. states with highest annual per-pupil spending were Alaska, New Jersey, New York, Vermont, and Washington, in which an average level of per-student expenditures was $16,106. This amount was more than twice as much as the average per-student expenditures of $7,409 in Arizona, Idaho, Oklahoma, Tennessee, and Utah, the five lowest-spending states. The differences in measurable outcomes were only minor, however.

For instance, in the five states with highest spending, an average of 25.2 percent of students failed to meet basic goals for math and reading. In the five states with lowest spending, this figure was only slightly higher at 30.6 percent. New York, the state with highest per-student

expenditures, spent nearly three times as much per pupil as lowest-spending Utah, yet both states had just over 26 percent of students who failed to satisfy basic math and reading objectives. By virtually every measure of schooling outcomes, studies consistently find at best a weak relationship—and often find no relationship—between per-pupil expenditures and educational results.

FOR CRITICAL THINKING
Could the fact that the valuation of the last unit of services falls as the per-student subsidy rises help to explain why higher spending is not closely related to learning outcomes?

QUICK QUIZ See page 121 for the answers. Review concepts from this section in MyEconLab.

Medicare subsidizes the consumption of medical care by the elderly, thus increasing the amount of such care consumed. People tend to purchase large amounts of _____-value, _____-cost services in publicly funded health care programs such as Medicare, because they do not directly bear the full cost of their decisions.

Basic economic analysis indicates that higher subsidies for public education have widened the differential between parents' and students' relatively _____ per-unit valuations of the educational services of public schools and the _____ costs that schools incur in providing those services.

Collective Decision Making: The Theory of Public Choice

Governments consist of individuals. No government actually thinks and acts. Instead, government actions are the result of decision making by individuals in their roles as elected representatives, appointed officials, and salaried bureaucrats. Therefore, to understand how government works, we must examine the incentives of the people in government as well as those who would like to be in government—avowed or would-be candidates for elective or appointed positions—and special-interest lobbyists attempting to get government to do something. At issue is the analysis of **collective decision making.**

Collective decision making involves the actions of voters, politicians, political parties, interest groups, and many other groups and individuals. The analysis of collective decision making is usually called the **theory of public choice.** It has been given this name because it involves hypotheses about how choices are made in the public sector, as opposed to the private sector. The foundation of public-choice theory is the assumption that individuals will act within the political process to maximize their *individual* (not collective) well-being. In that sense, the theory is similar to our analysis of the market economy, in which we also assume that individuals act as though they are motivated by self-interest.

To understand public-choice theory, it is necessary to point out other similarities between the private market sector and the public, or government, sector. Then we will look at the differences.

Similarities in Market and Public-Sector Decision Making

In addition to the assumption of self-interest being the motivating force in both sectors, there are other similarities.

OPPORTUNITY COST Everything that is spent by all levels of government plus everything that is spent by the private sector must add up to the total income available at any point in time. Hence, every government action has an opportunity cost, just as in the market sector.

COMPETITION Although we typically think of competition as a private market phenomenon, it is also present in collective action. Given the scarcity constraint government faces, bureaucrats, appointed officials, and elected representatives will always be in competition for available government funds. Furthermore, the individuals within any government agency or institution will act as individuals do in the private sector: They will try to obtain higher wages, better working conditions, and higher job-level classifications. We assume that they will compete and act in their own interest, not society's.

SIMILARITY OF INDIVIDUALS Contrary to popular belief, the types of individuals working in the private sector and working in the public sector are not inherently different. The difference, as we shall see, is that the individuals in government face a different **incentive structure** than those in the private sector. For example, the costs and benefits of being efficient or inefficient differ in the private and public sectors.

One approach to predicting government bureaucratic behavior is to ask what incentives bureaucrats face. Take the U.S. Postal Service (USPS) as an example. The bureaucrats running that government corporation are human beings with IQs not dissimilar to those possessed by workers in similar positions at Google or Apple. Yet the USPS does not function like either of these companies. The difference can be explained in terms of the incentives provided for managers in the two types of institutions. When the bureaucratic managers and workers at Google make incorrect decisions, work slowly, produce shoddy programs, and are generally "inefficient," the profitability of the company declines. The owners—millions of shareholders—express their displeasure by selling some of their shares of company stock. The market value, as tracked on the stock exchange, falls. This induces owners of shares of stock to pressure managers to pursue strategies more likely to boost revenues and reduce costs.

Collective decision making
How voters, politicians, and other interested parties act and how these actions influence nonmarket decisions.

Theory of public choice
The study of collective decision making.

Incentive structure
The system of rewards and punishments individuals face with respect to their own actions.

But what about the USPS? If a manager, a worker, or a bureaucrat in the USPS gives shoddy service, the organization's owners—the taxpayers—have no straightforward mechanism for expressing their dissatisfaction. Despite the postal service's status as a "government corporation," taxpayers as shareholders do not really own shares of stock in the organization that they can sell.

Thus, to understand purported inefficiency in the government bureaucracy, we need to examine incentives and institutional arrangements—not people and personalities.

Differences between Market and Collective Decision Making

There are probably more dissimilarities between the market sector and the public sector than there are similarities.

GOVERNMENT GOODS AND SERVICES AT ZERO PRICE The majority of goods that governments produce are furnished to the ultimate consumers without payment required. **Government, or political, goods** can be either private or public goods. The fact that they are furnished to the ultimate consumer free of charge does *not* mean that the cost to society of those goods is zero, however. It only means that the price *charged* is zero. The full opportunity cost to society is the value of the resources used in the production of goods produced and provided by the government.

> **Government, or political, goods**
> Goods (and services) provided by the public sector; they can be either private or public goods.

For example, none of us pays directly for each unit of consumption of defense or police protection. Rather, we pay for all these items indirectly through the taxes that support our governments—federal, state, and local. This special feature of government can be looked at in a different way. There is no longer a one-to-one relationship between consumption of government-provided goods and services and payment for these items. Indeed, most taxpayers will find that their tax bill is the same whether or not they consume government-provided goods.

USE OF FORCE All governments can resort to using force in their regulation of economic affairs. For example, governments can use *expropriation*, which means that if you refuse to pay your taxes, your bank account and other assets may be seized by the Internal Revenue Service. In fact, you have no choice in the matter of paying taxes to governments. Collectively, we decide the total size of government through the political process, but individually, we cannot determine how much service we pay for during any one year.

VOTING VERSUS SPENDING In the private market sector, a dollar voting system is in effect. This dollar voting system is not equivalent to the voting system in the public sector. There are at least three differences:

1. In a political system, one person gets one vote, whereas in the market system, each dollar a person spends counts separately.

2. The political system is run by **majority rule,** whereas the market system is run by **proportional rule.**

> **Majority rule**
> A collective decision-making system in which group decisions are made on the basis of more than 50 percent of the vote. In other words, whatever more than half of the electorate votes for, the entire electorate has to accept.

3. The spending of dollars can indicate intensity of want, whereas because of the all-or-nothing nature of political voting, a vote cannot.

Political outcomes often differ from economic outcomes. Remember that economic efficiency is a situation in which, given the prevailing distribution of income, consumers obtain the economic goods they want. There is no corresponding situation when political voting determines economic outcomes. Thus, a political voting process is unlikely to lead to the same decisions that a dollar voting process would yield in the marketplace.

> **Proportional rule**
> A decision-making system in which actions are based on the proportion of the "votes" cast and are in proportion to them. In a market system, if 10 percent of the "dollar votes" are cast for blue cars, 10 percent of automobile output will be blue cars.

Indeed, consider the dilemma every voter faces. Usually, a voter is not asked to decide on a single issue (although this happens). Rather, a voter is asked to choose among candidates who present a large number of issues and state a position on each of them. Just consider the average U.S. senator, who has to vote on several thousand different issues during a six-year term. When you vote for that senator, you are voting for a person who must make thousands of decisions during the next six years.

The theory of _____ _____ examines how voters, politicians, and other parties collectively reach decisions in the public sector of the economy.

As in private markets, _____ _____ and _____ have incentive effects that influence

public-sector decision making. In contrast to private market situations, however, there is not a one-to-one relationship between consumption of a publicly provided good and the payment for that good.

YOU ARE THERE
The U.S. Government Ensures That an Airport Is "Convenient"

Phil Ridenour, director of Hagerstown Regional Airport, in Hagerstown, Maryland, surveys the surroundings: free parking, short security lines for departing passengers, and plenty of space for passengers at the baggage carousel. "The convenience of it all is just phenomenal compared to going to any major airport," Ridenour remarks. Indeed, a flight to Baltimore takes only 40 minutes in the air, compared with an 80-minute automobile drive via highways, and each passenger's out-of-pocket ticket price is less than $60.

Nonetheless, all of this convenience comes at considerable expense to U.S. taxpayers. Each time a passenger boards a nine-seat plane providing the airline service connecting Hagerstown to Baltimore, the cost to taxpayers is $191. This is the additional per-passenger payment required to

induce Cape Air to provide its daily flights to and from Baltimore. Summing all of the subsidies that the federal government provides to keep the Hagerstown Regional Airport operating at its current pace requires an amount exceeding $1.2 million per year.

Critical Thinking Questions

1. What is the total subsidy paid by U.S. taxpayers each time a full Cape Air flight departs from Hagerstown for Baltimore?

2. Why do you suppose that 109 regional airports receiving federal support require about $175 million per year in total subsidies to provide current service flows?

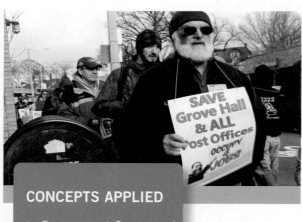

ISSUES & APPLICATIONS

The Government-Sponsored U.S. Postal Service

CONCEPTS APPLIED

▶ Government-Sponsored Goods

▶ Monopoly

▶ Subsidies

Since 1971, the legal classification of the U.S. Postal Service (USPS) has been as a private enterprise. That is, the USPS officially is a nongovernmental business. *Economic* functions of the USPS remain government-sponsored, however.

Implicit Government Sponsorship via Regulatory Controls

The USPS operates a network of more than 31,000 post offices. The majority of these post offices do not generate revenues sufficiently high in relation to costs to justify keeping them in operation. If the USPS were

truly a private firm, many of these post offices would be closed.

Until recently, what has enabled the USPS to keep these post offices operating in spite of their meager rates of profitability has been the receipt of an implicit subsidy in the form of protection from competition. The USPS is the only institution in the United States authorized to make regular deliveries of "non-urgent letters" to mailboxes of households, businesses, and government offices. Thus, the USPS faces no threat of being undersold by competitors in its primary business of delivering non-urgent mail.

Government Sponsorship Becomes Much More Explicit

In spite of these government protections of the USPS, the annual volume of mail handled by the USPS has fallen from 213 billion items per year in 2006 to about 165 billion items per year today. As a consequence, postage revenues at USPS have plummeted even as its labor expenses have remained nearly unchanged. Since 2007, the USPS has experienced average annual *losses* from its operations exceeding *$7 billion* per year.

What allows the USPS to continue operating without employee layoffs in spite of annual losses exceeding $120,000 per USPS worker per year? The answer is the sponsorship of U.S. taxpayers. The federal government continues lending funds to the USPS to enable it to keep providing the same level of services with an unchanged workforce. Few observers anticipate that the USPS will ever repay the loans, which likely will become explicit subsidies to this government-sponsored institution.

For Critical Thinking

1. Why would a non-government-sponsored firm have difficulty remaining in operation incurring $7 billion in losses per year?

2. Why might a government-sponsored firm such as the USPS be more willing than a non-government-sponsored firm to agree to non-layoff contracts for workers?

Web Resources

1. For a discussion of the deteriorating situation at the USPS, go to **www.econtoday.com/chap05**.

2. Take a look at a list of contemplated USPS post office closings—but no planned employee layoffs at **www.econtoday.com/chap05**.

MyEconLab

For more questions on this chapter's Issues & Applications, go to MyEconLab. In the Study Plan for this chapter, select Section N: News.

MyEconLab

Here is what you should know after reading this chapter. MyEconLab will help you identify what you know, and where to go when you need to practice.

— WHAT YOU SHOULD KNOW —

How Market Failures Such as Externalities Might Justify Economic Functions of Government A market failure occurs when too many or too few resources are directed to a specific form of economic activity. One type of market failure is an externality, which is a spillover effect on third parties not directly involved in producing or purchasing a good or service. In the case of a negative externality, firms do not pay for the costs arising from spillover effects that their production of a good imposes on others, so they produce too much of the good in question. In the case of a positive externality, buyers fail to take into account the benefits that their consumption of a good yields to others, so they purchase too little of the good.

market failure, 101
externality, 101
third parties, 101
property rights, 102
effluent fee, 103
antitrust legislation, 106
monopoly, 106

Key Figure
Figure 5-1, 102

— WHERE TO GO TO PRACTICE —

• MyEconLab Study Plans 5.1, 5.2
• Animated Figure 5-1

MyEconLab *continued*

— WHAT YOU SHOULD KNOW ——————————————— WHERE TO GO TO PRACTICE —

Private Goods versus Public Goods and the Free-Rider Problem Private goods are subject to the principle of rival consumption, meaning that one person's consumption of such a good reduces the amount available for another person to consume. In contrast, public goods can be consumed by many people simultaneously at no additional opportunity cost and with no reduction in quality or quantity. In addition, no individual can be excluded from the benefits of a public good even if that person fails to help pay for it.

private goods, 106
principle of rival
   consumption, 106
public goods, 106
free-rider problem, 107

- **MyEconLab** Study Plan 5.3

Political Functions of Government That Lead to Its Involvement in the Economy As a result of the political process, government may seek to promote the production and consumption of government-sponsored goods. The government may also seek to restrict the production and sale of goods that have been deemed socially undesirable, called government-inhibited goods. In addition, the political process may determine that income redistribution is socially desirable.

government-sponsored
   good, 108
government-inhibited
   good, 108
transfer payments, 108
transfers in kind, 108

- **MyEconLab** Study Plan 5.4

The Effect of Medicare on the Incentives to Consume Medical Services Medicare subsidizes the consumption of medical services. As a result, the quantity consumed is higher, as is the price sellers receive per unit of those services. Medicare also encourages people to consume medical services that are very low in per-unit value relative to the cost of providing them.

Key Figures
Figure 5-2, 109
Figure 5-4, 111

- **MyEconLab** Study Plan 5.5
- Animated Figures 5-2, 5-4

Why Bigger Subsidies for Public Schools Do Not Necessarily Translate into Improved Student Performance When governments subsidize public schools, the last unit of educational services provided by public schools costs more than its valuation by parents and students. Thus, public schools provide services in excess of those best suited to promoting student learning.

- **MyEconLab** Study Plan 5.5

Central Elements of the Theory of Public Choice The theory of public choice applies to collective decision making, or the process through which voters and politicians interact to influence nonmarket choices. Certain aspects of public-sector decision making, such as scarcity and competition, are similar to those that affect private-sector choices. Others, however, such as legal coercion and majority-rule decision making, differ from those involved in the market system.

collective decision
   making, 114
theory of public choice, 114
incentive structure, 114
government, or political,
   goods, 115
majority rule, 115
proportional rule, 115

- **MyEconLab** Study Plan 5.6

Log in to **MyEconLab**, take a chapter test, and get a personalized Study Plan that tells you which concepts you understand and which ones you need to review. From there, **MyEconLab** will give you further practice, tutorials, animations, videos, and guided solutions. For more information, visit www.myeconlab.com

PROBLEMS

All problems are assignable in MyEconLab. Answers to odd-numbered problems appear at the back of the book.

5-1. Many people who do not smoke cigars are bothered by the odor of cigar smoke. If private contracting is impossible, will too many or too few cigars be produced and consumed? Taking *all* costs into account, is the market price of cigars too high or too low? (See page 102.)

5-2. Suppose that repeated application of a pesticide used on orange trees causes harmful contamination of groundwater. The pesticide is applied annually in almost all of the orange groves throughout the world. Most orange growers regard the pesticide as a key input in their production of oranges. (See page 102.)

   a. Use a diagram of the market for the pesticide to illustrate the implications of a failure of orange producers' costs to reflect the social costs of groundwater contamination.

   b. Use your diagram from part (a) to explain a government policy that might be effective in achieving the amount of orange production that fully reflects all social costs.

5-3. Now draw a diagram of the market for oranges. Explain how the government policy you discussed in part (b) of Problem 5-2 is likely to affect the market price and equilibrium quantity in the orange market. In what sense do consumers of oranges now "pay" for dealing with the spillover costs of pesticide production? (See page 102.)

5-4. Suppose that the U.S. government determines that cigarette smoking creates social costs not reflected in the current market price and equilibrium quantity of cigarettes. A study has recommended that the government can correct for the externality effect of cigarette consumption by paying farmers *not* to plant tobacco used to manufacture cigarettes. It also recommends raising the funds to make these payments by increasing taxes on cigarettes. Assuming that the government is correct that cigarette smoking creates external costs, evaluate whether the study's recommended policies might help correct this negative externality. (See page 102.)

5-5. A nation's government has determined that mass transit, such as bus lines, helps alleviate traffic congestion, thereby benefiting both individual auto commuters and companies that desire to move products and factors of production speedily along streets and highways. Nevertheless, even though several private bus lines are in service, the country's commuters are failing to take into

account the social benefits of the use of mass transit. (See pages 102–103.)

   a. Discuss, in the context of demand-supply analysis, the essential implications of commuters' failure to take into account the social benefits associated with bus ridership.

   b. Explain a government policy that might be effective in achieving the socially efficient use of bus services.

5-6. Draw a diagram of this nation's market for automobiles, which are a substitute for buses. Explain how the government policy you discussed in part (b) of Problem 5-5 is likely to affect the market price and equilibrium quantity in the country's auto market. How are auto consumers affected by this policy to attain the spillover benefits of bus transit? (See pages 102–103.)

5-7. Consider a nation with a government that does not provide people with property rights for a number of items and that fails to enforce the property rights it does assign for remaining items. Would externalities be more or less common in this nation than in a country such as the United States? Explain. (See page 105.)

5-8. Many economists suggest that our nation's legal system is an example of a public good. Does the legal system satisfy the key properties of a public good? Explain your reasoning. (See page 106.)

5-9. Displayed in the diagram below are conditions in the market for residential Internet access in a U.S. state. The government of this state has determined that access to the Internet improves the learning skills of children, which it has concluded is an external benefit of Internet access. The government has also concluded that if these external benefits were to be taken into account, 3 million residences would have Internet access. Suppose that the state government's judgments about the

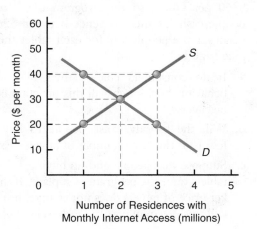

benefits of Internet access are correct and that it wishes to offer a per-unit subsidy just sufficient to increase total Internet access to 3 million residences. What per-unit subsidy should it offer? Use the diagram to explain how providing this subsidy would affect conditions in the state's market for residential Internet access. (See pages 102–103.)

5-10. The French government recently allocated the equivalent of more than $120 million in public funds to *Quaero* (Latin for "I search"), an Internet search engine analogous to Google or Yahoo. Does an Internet search engine satisfy the key characteristics of a public good? Why or why not? Based on your answer, is a publicly funded Internet search engine a public good or a government-sponsored good? (See page 106.)

5-11. A government offers to let a number of students at a public school transfer to a private school under two conditions: It will transmit to the private school the same per-pupil subsidy it provides the public school, and the private school will be required to admit the students at a below-market net tuition rate. Will the economic outcome be the same as the one that would have arisen if the government instead simply provided students with grants to cover the current market tuition rate at the private school? (Hint: Does it matter if schools receive payments directly from the government or from consumers? See pages 111–113.)

5-12. After a government implements a voucher program, granting funds that families can spend at schools of their choice, numerous students in public schools switch to private schools. Parents' and students' valuations of the services provided at both private and public schools adjust to equality with the true market price of educational services. Is anyone likely to lose out nonetheless? If so, who? (See page 113.)

5-13. Suppose that the current price of a tablet device is $300 and that people are buying 1 million drives per year. The government decides to begin subsidizing the purchase of new tablet devices. The government believes that the appropriate price is $260 per tablet, so the program offers to send people cash for the difference between $260 and whatever the people pay for each tablet they buy. (See page 111.)

a. If no consumers change their tablet-buying behavior, how much will this program cost the taxpayers?

b. Will the subsidy cause people to buy more, fewer, or the same number of tablets? Explain.

c. Suppose that people end up buying 1.5 million tablets once the program is in place. If the market price of tablets does not change, how much will this program cost the taxpayers?

d. Under the assumption that the program causes people to buy 1.5 million tablets and also causes the market price of tablets to rise to $320, how much will this program cost the taxpayers?

5-14. Scans of internal organs using magnetic resonance imaging (MRI) devices are often covered by subsidized health insurance programs such as Medicare. Consider the following table illustrating hypothetical quantities of individual MRI testing procedures demanded and supplied at various prices, and then answer the questions that follow. (See page 111.)

Price	Quantity Demanded	Quantity Supplied
$100	100,000	40,000
$300	90,000	60,000
$500	80,000	80,000
$700	70,000	100,000
$900	60,000	120,000

a. In the absence of a government-subsidized health plan, what is the equilibrium price of MRI tests? What is the amount of society's total spending on MRI tests?

b. Suppose that the government establishes a health plan guaranteeing that all qualified participants can purchase MRI tests at an effective price (that is, out-of-pocket cost) to the individual of $100 per test. How many MRI tests will people consume?

c. What is the per-unit price that induces producers to provide the number of MRI tests demanded at the government-guaranteed price of $100? What is society's total spending on MRI tests?

d. Under the government's coverage of MRI tests, what is the per-unit subsidy it provides? What is the total subsidy that the government pays to support MRI testing at its guaranteed price?

5-15. Suppose that, as part of an expansion of its State Care health system, a state government decides to offer a $50 subsidy to all people who, according to their physicians, should have their own blood pressure monitoring devices. Prior to this governmental decision, the market clearing price of blood pressure monitors in this state was $50, and the equilibrium quantity purchased was 20,000 per year. (See page 111.)

a. After the government expands its State Care plan, people in this state desire to purchase 40,000 devices each year. Manufacturers of blood pressure monitors are willing to provide 40,000 devices at a price of $60 per device. What out-of-pocket price does each consumer pay for a blood pressure monitor?

b. What is the dollar amount of the increase in total expenditures on blood pressure monitors in this state following the expansion in the State Care program?

c. Following the expansion of the State Care program, what *percentage* of total expenditures on blood pressure monitors is paid by the government? What percentage of total expenditures is paid by consumers of these devices?

5-16. A government agency is contemplating launching an effort to expand the scope of its activities. One rationale for doing so is that another government agency might make the same effort and, if successful, receive larger budget allocations in future years. Another rationale for expanding the agency's activities is that this will make the jobs of its workers more interesting, which may help the government agency attract better-qualified employees. Nevertheless, to broaden its legal mandate, the agency will have to convince more than half of the House of Representatives and the Senate to approve a formal proposal to expand its activities. In addition, to expand its activities, the agency must have the authority to force private companies it does not currently regulate to be officially licensed by agency personnel. Identify which aspects of this problem are similar to those faced by firms that operate in private markets and which aspects are specific to the public sector. (See pages 114–115.)

ECONOMICS ON THE NET

Putting Tax Dollars to Work In this application, you will learn about how the U.S. government allocates its expenditures. This will enable you to conduct an evaluation of the current functions of the federal government.

Title: Historical Tables: Budget of the United States Government

Navigation: Go to **www.econtoday.com/chap05** to visit the home page of the U.S. Government Printing Office. Click on "Browse the FY Budget" for the applicable year, and then click on "PDF" next to *Historical Tables*.

Application After the document downloads, examine Section 3, Federal Government Outlays by Function, and in particular Table 3.1, Outlays by Superfunction and Function. Then answer the following questions.

1. What government functions have been capturing growing shares of government spending in recent years? Which of these do you believe are related to the problem of addressing externalities, providing public goods, or dealing with other market failures? Which appear to be related to political functions instead of economic functions?

2. Which government functions are receiving declining shares of total spending? Are any of these related to the problem of addressing externalities, providing public goods, or dealing with other market failures? Are any related to political functions instead of economic functions?

For Group Study and Analysis Assign groups to the following overall categories of government functions: national defense, health, income security, and Social Security. Have each group prepare a brief report concerning long-term and recent trends in government spending on its category. Each group should take a stand on whether specific spending on items in its category is likely to relate to resolving market failures, public funding of government-sponsored goods, regulating the sale of government-inhibited goods, and so on.

ANSWERS TO QUICK QUIZZES

p. 105: (i) costs . . . taxation . . . regulation; (ii) benefits . . . financing . . . subsidizing . . . regulation

p. 109: (i) externalities . . . legal system . . . competition . . . public . . . economywide stability; (ii) rival consumption; (iii) opportunity cost . . . charged; (iv) government-sponsored . . . government-inhibited . . . income

p. 113: (i) low . . . high; (ii) low . . . higher

p. 116: (i) public choice; (ii) opportunity cost . . . competition

6 Funding the Public Sector

During the past few years, federal government spending as a percentage of total national income rose to about 25 percent before declining slightly. At the same time, total federal revenues from taxes and other sources fell to approximately 15 percent of national income before recovering somewhat. To cover expenditures out of national income not directly funded by revenues, the federal government resorted to borrowing. As you will learn in this chapter, however, the *government budget constraint* faced by the federal government dictates that ultimately spending and revenues must balance. As a consequence, eventually federal spending as a percentage of national income will have to equalize with federal revenues as a percentage of national income, which you will also learn is a measure of the nation's average federal tax rate.

governments of more than a dozen states have sold bonds promising annual payments based on more than $100 billion in projected shares of revenues from a legal settlement with the tobacco industry? The state governments have sold these "tobacco bonds" to raise funds for financing their operations now, rather than waiting for the streams of payments to arrive in future years. Of course, many state governments also have been selling more traditional bonds offering annual payments they plan to cover with future taxation. State and local governments assess sales taxes, property taxes, income taxes, hotel occupancy taxes, and electricity, gasoline, water, and sewage taxes. At the federal level, there are income taxes, Social Security taxes, Medicare taxes, and so-called excise taxes. When a person dies, state and federal governments also collect estate taxes. Clearly, governments give considerable attention to their roles as tax collectors.

Paying for the Public Sector

There are three sources of funding available to governments. One source is explicit fees, called user *charges*, for government services. The second and main source of government funding is taxes. Nevertheless, sometimes federal, state, and local governments spend more than they collect in taxes. To do this, they must rely on a third source of financing, which is borrowing. A government cannot borrow unlimited amounts, however. After all, a government, like an individual or a firm, can convince others to lend it funds only if it can provide evidence that it will repay its debts. A government must ultimately rely on taxation and user charges, the sources of its own current and future revenues, to repay its debts.

Over the long run, therefore, taxes and user charges are any government's *fundamental* sources of revenues. The **government budget constraint** states that each dollar of public spending on goods, services, transfer payments, and repayments of borrowed funds during a given period must be provided by tax revenues and user charges collected by the government. This long-term constraint indicates that the total amount a government plans to spend and transfer today and into the future cannot exceed the total taxes and user charges that it currently earns and can reasonably anticipate collecting in future years. Taxation dwarfs user charges as a source of government resources, so let's begin by looking at taxation from a government's perspective.

How has the fact that states must satisfy government budget constraints impinged directly on the personal budgets of students at a number of state universities?

YOU ARE THERE

To consider a real-world application regarding government budget constraints, take a look at **How to Keep Social Security in Business** on page 134.

Government budget constraint
The limit on government spending and transfers imposed by the fact that every dollar the government spends, transfers, or uses to repay borrowed funds must ultimately be provided by the user charges and taxes it collects.

EXAMPLE

State University Tuition Rates Jump—Even at the Last Moment

Spending on public education is one of the larger components of most states' budgets. Dampened economic activity since 2008 has led to lower tax revenues throughout the fifty states. To continue operating within their government budget constraints, more than half of the states have cut their spending on higher education. State universities face their own budget constraints, and in response to reduced funding from state governments, they have raised tuition rates charged to enrolled students.

At a number of state universities, tuition rates have jumped as late as the time of final course registration. In a few instances, state universities have even raised tuition after completion of the first semester of the academic year, before the start of the second semester. Students affected by such last-minute tuition increases have first-hand experience with government budget constraints.

FOR CRITICAL THINKING
How does the fact that government budget constraints must be satisfied help explain why many states have taken back scholarships that they initially offered to university enrollees?

Systems of Taxation

In light of the government budget constraint, a major concern of any government is how to collect taxes. Jean-Baptiste Colbert, the seventeenth-century French finance minister, said the art of taxation was in "plucking the goose so as to obtain the largest amount of feathers with the least possible amount of hissing." In the United States, governments have designed a variety of methods of plucking the private-sector goose.

The Tax Base and the Tax Rate

Tax base
The value of goods, services, wealth, or incomes subject to taxation.

Tax rate
The proportion of a tax base that must be paid to a government as taxes.

To collect a tax, a government typically establishes a **tax base,** which is the value of goods, services, wealth, or incomes subject to taxation. Then it assesses a **tax rate,** which is the proportion of the tax base that must be paid to the government as taxes.

As we discuss shortly, for the federal government and many state governments, incomes are key tax bases. Therefore, to discuss tax rates and the structure of taxation systems in more detail, let's focus for now on income taxation.

Marginal and Average Tax Rates

Marginal tax rate
The change in the tax payment divided by the change in income, or the percentage of *additional* dollars that must be paid in taxes. The marginal tax rate is applied to the highest tax bracket of taxable income reached.

Tax bracket
A specified interval of income to which a specific and unique marginal tax rate is applied.

Average tax rate
The total tax payment divided by total income. It is the proportion of total income paid in taxes.

If somebody says, "I pay 28 percent in taxes," you cannot really tell what that person means unless you know whether he or she is referring to average taxes paid or the tax rate on the last dollars earned. The latter concept refers to the **marginal tax rate,** with the word *marginal* meaning "incremental."

The marginal tax rate is expressed as follows:

$$\text{Marginal tax rate} = \frac{\text{change in taxes due}}{\text{change in taxable income}}$$

It is important to understand that the marginal tax rate applies only to the income in the highest **tax bracket** reached, with a tax bracket defined as a specified range of taxable income to which a specific and unique marginal tax rate is applied.

The marginal tax rate is not the same thing as the **average tax rate,** which is defined as follows:

$$\text{Average tax rate} = \frac{\text{total taxes due}}{\text{total taxable income}}$$

Why are governments contemplating a change in the tax base for the gasoline taxes that currently ring up at the pumps?

POLICY EXAMPLE

Is It Time to Replace Gasoline Taxes with Mileage Taxes?

A main source of revenues used by federal, state, and local governments to finance road construction and repair is taxation of gasoline purchases. As more vehicles that partly or fully rely on battery power have hit the road, gasoline purchases have been declining at any given price of gasoline. Thus, the gasoline tax base has been shrinking, so gasoline tax collections are dropping.

Battery-powered vehicles continue to subject roadways to wear and tear, so governments somehow must still obtain funds to finance road maintenance. Recently, the Congressional Budget Office has proposed a *mileage* tax base. Under a mileage-based taxation system, governments would require

vehicles to be equipped with special mileage meters. Government agencies would periodically tally the number of miles traveled by each vehicle, which would constitute a tax base. Then application of mileage tax rates to the new mileage tax base would determine the total mileage taxes owed by the vehicle's owner. In this way, governments could collect taxes on miles driven as well as on the gasoline that fuels the vehicle down the road.

FOR CRITICAL THINKING
Why would a mileage tax constitute "double taxation"?

Taxation Systems

No matter how governments raise revenues—from income taxes, sales taxes, or other taxes—all of those taxes fit into one of three types of taxation systems: proportional, progressive, or regressive, according to the relationship between the tax rate and income. To determine whether a tax system is proportional, progressive, or regressive, we simply ask, What is the relationship between the average tax rate and the marginal tax rate?

Proportional taxation
A tax system in which, regardless of an individual's income, the tax bill comprises exactly the same proportion.

PROPORTIONAL TAXATION **Proportional taxation** means that regardless of an individual's income, taxes comprise exactly the same proportion. In a proportional taxation system, the marginal tax rate is always equal to the average tax rate. If every dollar is taxed at 20 percent, then the average tax rate is 20 percent, and so is the marginal tax rate.

Under a proportional system of taxation, taxpayers at all income levels end up paying the same *percentage* of their income in taxes. With a proportional tax rate of 20 percent, an individual with an income of $10,000 pays $2,000 in taxes, while an individual making $100,000 pays $20,000. Thus, the identical 20 percent rate is levied on both taxpayers.

PROGRESSIVE TAXATION Under **progressive taxation,** as a person's taxable income increases, the percentage of income paid in taxes increases. In a progressive system, the marginal tax rate is above the average tax rate. If you are taxed 5 percent on the first $10,000 you earn, 10 percent on the next $10,000 you earn, and 30 percent on the last $10,000 you earn, you face a progressive income tax system. Your marginal tax rate is always above your average tax rate.

What is the marginal income tax rate faced by the highest U.S. income earners?

Go to www.econtoday.com/chap06 to learn from the National Center for Policy Analysis about what distinguishes recent flat tax proposals from a truly proportional income tax system. Click on "Flat Tax Proposals."

Progressive taxation

A tax system in which, as income increases, a higher percentage of the additional income is paid as taxes. The marginal tax rate exceeds the average tax rate as income rises.

POLICY EXAMPLE

Calculating the Top U.S. Marginal Tax Rate

Because the income tax systems of the federal government and of most state governments are progressive, the highest-income earners pay the highest overall income tax rates. The top federal income tax rate is at least 35 percent. In addition, the highest-income earners face the 2.9 percent Medicare payroll tax rate plus a "higher-earners surcharge" of 0.9 percent. Finally, the highest-income earners are hit with a 3.8 percent surcharge on investment and royalty earnings to fund the new national health care system. After taking into account allowed federal tax deductions based on state tax payments, the effective marginal state income tax rate for the average high earner is approximately 4 percent. Summing these rates yields a current top marginal income tax rate for U.S. high-income earners with investment and royalty earnings of about 46.2 percent. Thus, the highest-income earners can keep for their own use just over half of the last dollar they earn.

FOR CRITICAL THINKING

How does the fact that a number of cities and counties also have their own income taxes affect the top marginal tax rate for some high earners?

REGRESSIVE TAXATION With **regressive taxation,** a smaller percentage of taxable income is taken in taxes as taxable income increases. The marginal rate is *below* the average rate. As income increases, the marginal tax rate falls, and so does the average tax rate. The U.S. Social Security tax is regressive. Once the legislative maximum taxable wage base is reached, no further Social Security taxes are paid. Consider a simplified hypothetical example: Suppose that every dollar up to $100,000 is taxed at 10 percent. After $100,000 there is no Social Security tax. Someone making $200,000 still pays only $10,000 in Social Security taxes. That person's average Social Security tax is 5 percent. The person making $100,000, by contrast, effectively pays 10 percent. The person making $1 million faces an average Social Security tax rate of only 1 percent in our simplified example.

Regressive taxation

A tax system in which as more dollars are earned, the percentage of tax paid on them falls. The marginal tax rate is less than the average tax rate as income rises.

QUICK QUIZ   See page 138 for the answers. Review concepts from this section in MyEconLab.

Governments collect taxes by applying a tax _____ to a tax _____, which refers to the value of goods, services, wealth, or incomes. Income tax rates are applied to tax brackets, which are ranges of income over which the tax rate is constant.

The _____ tax rate is the total tax payment divided by total income, and the _____ tax rate is the change

in the tax payment divided by the change in income.

Tax systems can be _____, _____, or _____, depending on whether the marginal tax rate is the same as, greater than, or less than the average tax rate as income rises.

The Most Important Federal Taxes

What types of taxes do federal, state, and local governments collect? The two pie charts in Figure 6-1 on the following page show the percentages of receipts from various taxes obtained by the federal government and by state and local governments. For the federal government, key taxes are individual income taxes, corporate income taxes, Social

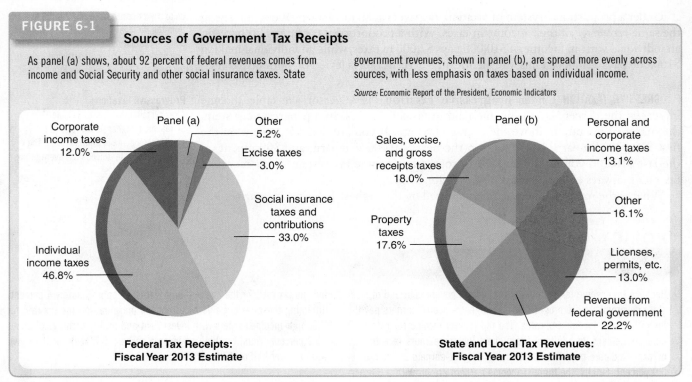

FIGURE 6-1

Sources of Government Tax Receipts

As panel (a) shows, about 92 percent of federal revenues comes from income and Social Security and other social insurance taxes. State government revenues, shown in panel (b), are spread more evenly across sources, with less emphasis on taxes based on individual income.

Source: Economic Report of the President, Economic Indicators

Panel (a)

Corporate income taxes 12.0%
Other 5.2%
Excise taxes 3.0%
Social insurance taxes and contributions 33.0%
Individual income taxes 46.8%

**Federal Tax Receipts:
Fiscal Year 2013 Estimate**

Panel (b)

Sales, excise, and gross receipts taxes 18.0%
Personal and corporate income taxes 13.1%
Other 16.1%
Property taxes 17.6%
Licenses, permits, etc. 13.0%
Revenue from federal government 22.2%

**State and Local Tax Revenues:
Fiscal Year 2013 Estimate**

Security taxes, and excise taxes on items such as gasoline and alcoholic beverages. For state and local governments, sales taxes, property taxes, and personal and corporate income taxes are the main types of taxes.

The Federal Personal Income Tax

The most important tax in the U.S. economy is the federal personal income tax, which, as Figure 6-1 above indicates, accounts for almost 47 percent of all federal revenues. All U.S. citizens, resident aliens, and most others who earn income in the United States are required to pay federal income taxes on all taxable income, including income earned abroad.

The rates that are paid rise as income increases, as can be seen in Table 6-1 below. Marginal income tax rates at the federal level have ranged from as low as 1 percent after the 1913 passage of the Sixteenth Amendment, which made the individual income tax constitutional, to as high as 94 percent (reached in 1944). There were 14 separate tax brackets prior to the Tax Reform Act of 1986, which reduced the number to three (now six, as shown in Table 6-1).

TABLE 6-1

Federal Marginal Income Tax Rates

These rates applied in 2012.

Single Persons		Married Couples	
Marginal Tax Bracket	Marginal Tax Rate	Marginal Tax Bracket	Marginal Tax Rate
$0–$8,700	10%	$0–$17,400	10%
$8,701–$35,350	15%	$17,401–$70,700	15%
$35,351–$85,650	25%	$70,701–$142,700	25%
$85,651–$178,650	28%	$142,701–$217,450	28%
$178,651–$388,350	33%	$217,451–$388,350	33%
$388,351 and up	35%	$388,351 and up	35%

Source: U.S. Department of the Treasury.

What is the annual cost to U.S. taxpayers of determining how much they owe in income taxes?

POLICY EXAMPLE

Figuring Out How Much to Pay in Income Taxes Is Not Cheap

The Internal Revenue Service's Taxpayer Advocate Service has estimated that U.S. taxpayers spend nearly $200 billion per year to determine how much they owe in income taxes. In the process, taxpayers also devote 7.6 billion hours, or the equivalent of time that otherwise could have been spent in 3.8 million full-time jobs. The average hourly wage earned by a U.S. resident exceeds $16 per hour, so the opportunity cost of calculating U.S. income taxes is about $125 billion. Thus, the combined explicit and opportunity costs of complying with the U.S. income tax code amount to roughly $325 billion per year, which is about 20 percent of all federal income taxes collected.

FOR CRITICAL THINKING
What professions benefit from the nearly $200 billion per year spent on preparing tax returns?

The Treatment of Capital Gains

The difference between the purchase price and sale price of an asset, such as a share of stock or a plot of land, is called a **capital gain** if it is a profit and a **capital loss** if it is not. The federal government taxes capital gains, and as of 2013, there were several capital gains tax rates.

What appear to be capital gains are not always real gains. If you pay $100,000 for a financial asset in one year and sell it for 50 percent more 10 years later, your nominal capital gain is $50,000. But what if during those 10 years inflation has driven average asset prices up by 50 percent? Your *real* capital gain would be zero, but you would still have to pay taxes on that $50,000. To counter this problem, many economists have argued that capital gains should be indexed to the rate of inflation. This is exactly what is done with the marginal tax brackets in the federal income tax code. Tax brackets for the purposes of calculating marginal tax rates each year are expanded at the rate of inflation, that is, the rate at which the average of all prices is rising. So, if the rate of inflation is 10 percent, each tax bracket is moved up by 10 percent. The same concept could be applied to capital gains and financial assets. So far, Congress has refused to enact such a measure.

Capital gain
A positive difference between the purchase price and the sale price of an asset. If a share of stock is bought for $5 and then sold for $15, the capital gain is $10.

Capital loss
A negative difference between the purchase price and the sale price of an asset.

The Corporate Income Tax

Figure 6-1 on the facing page shows that corporate income taxes account for 12 percent of all federal taxes collected. They also make up about 2 percent of all state and local taxes collected. Corporations are generally taxed on the difference between their total revenues and their expenses. The federal corporate income tax structure is given in Table 6-2 below.

TABLE 6-2

Federal Corporate Income Tax Schedule

These corporate tax rates were in effect through 2013.

Corporate Taxable Income	Corporate Tax Rate
$0–$50,000	15%
$50,001–$75,000	25%
$75,001–$100,000	34%
$100,001–$335,000	39%
$335,001–$10,000,000	34%
$10,000,001–$15,000,000	35%
$15,000,001–$18,333,333	38%
$18,333,334 and up	35%

Source: Internal Revenue Service.

DOUBLE TAXATION Because individual stockholders must pay taxes on the dividends they receive, and those dividends are paid out of *after-tax* profits by the corporation, corporate profits are taxed twice. If you receive $1,000 in dividends, you have to declare them as income, and you must normally pay taxes on them. Before the corporation was able to pay you those dividends, it had to pay taxes on all its profits, including any that it put back into the company or did not distribute in the form of dividends. Eventually, the new investment made possible by those **retained earnings**—profits not given out to stockholders—along with borrowed funds will be reflected in the value of the stock in that company. When you sell your stock in that company, you will have to pay taxes on the difference between what you paid for the stock and what you sold it for. In both cases, dividends and retained earnings (corporate profits) are taxed twice. In 2003, Congress reduced the double taxation effect somewhat by enacting legislation that allowed most dividends to be taxed at lower rates than are applied to regular income through 2012.

WHO REALLY PAYS THE CORPORATE INCOME TAX? Corporations can function only as long as consumers buy their products, employees make their goods, stockholders (owners) buy their shares, and bondholders buy their bonds. Corporations per se do not do anything. We must ask, then, who really pays the tax on corporate income? This is a question of **tax incidence.** (The question of tax incidence applies to all taxes, including sales taxes and Social Security taxes.) The incidence of corporate taxation is the subject of considerable debate. Some economists suggest that corporations pass their tax burdens on to consumers by charging higher prices.

Other economists argue that it is the stockholders who bear most of the tax. Still others contend that employees pay at least part of the tax by receiving lower wages than they would otherwise. Because the debate is not yet settled, we will not hazard a guess here as to what the correct conclusion may be. Suffice it to say that you should be cautious when you advocate increasing corporation income taxes. *People*, whether owners, consumers, or workers, end up paying all of the increase—just as they pay all of any tax.

Social Security and Unemployment Taxes

Each year, taxes levied on payrolls account for an increasing percentage of federal tax receipts. These taxes, which are distinct from personal income taxes, are for Social Security, retirement, survivors' disability, and old-age medical benefits (Medicare). The Social Security tax is imposed on earnings up to roughly $110,100 at a rate of 6.2 percent on employers and 6.2 percent on employees. That is, the employer matches your "contribution" to Social Security. (The employer's contribution is really paid by the employees, at least in part, in the form of a reduced wage rate.) As Chapter 5 explained, a Medicare tax is imposed on all wage earnings at a combined rate of 2.9 percent. The 2010 federal health care law also added a 3.8 percent Medicare tax on certain income above $200,000.

Social Security taxes came into existence when the Federal Insurance Contributions Act (FICA) was passed in 1935. At that time, many more people paid into the Social Security program than the number who received benefits. Currently, however, older people drawing benefits make up a much larger share of the population. Consequently, in recent years, outflows of Social Security benefit payments have sometimes exceeded inflows of Social Security taxes. Various economists have advanced proposals to raise Social Security tax rates on younger workers or to reduce benefit payouts to older retirees and disabled individuals receiving Social Security payments. So far, however, the federal government has failed to address Social Security's deteriorating funding situation.

There is also a federal unemployment tax, which helps pay for unemployment insurance. This tax rate is 0.6 percent on the first $7,000 of annual wages of each employee who earns more than $1,500. Only the employer makes this tax payment. This tax covers the costs of the unemployment insurance system. In addition to this federal tax, some states with an unemployment system impose their own tax of up to about

---

Retained earnings
Earnings that a corporation saves, or retains, for investment in other productive activities; earnings that are not distributed to stockholders.

Tax incidence
The distribution of tax burdens among various groups in society.

3 percent, depending on the past record of the particular employer. An employer who frequently lays off workers typically will have a slightly higher state unemployment tax rate than an employer who never lays off workers.

See page 138 for the answers. Review concepts from this section in MyEconLab.

QUICK QUIZ

The federal government raises most of its revenues through _____ taxes and social insurance taxes and contributions. State and local governments raise most of their tax revenues from _____ taxes, _____ taxes, and income taxes.

Because corporations must first pay an income tax on most earnings, the personal income tax shareholders pay on dividends received (or realized capital gains) constitutes _____ taxation.

Both employers and employees must pay _____ _____ taxes and contributions at rates of 6.2 percent on roughly the first $110,100 in wage earnings, and a 2.9 percent _____ tax rate is applied to all wage earnings. The federal government and some state governments also assess taxes to pay for _____ insurance systems.

Tax Rates and Tax Revenues

For most state and local governments, income taxes yield fewer revenues than taxes imposed on sales of goods and services. Figure 6-1 on page 126 shows that sales taxes, gross receipts taxes, and excise taxes generate almost one-fifth of the total funds available to state and local governments. Thus, from the perspective of many state and local governments, a fundamental issue is how to set tax rates on sales of goods and services to extract desired total tax payments.

Sales Taxes

Governments levy **sales taxes** on the prices that consumers pay to purchase each unit of a broad range of goods and services. Sellers collect sales taxes and transmit them to the government. Sales taxes are a form of **ad valorem taxation,** which means that the tax is applied "to the value" of the good. Thus, a government using a system of *ad valorem* taxation charges a tax rate equal to a fraction of the market price of each unit that a consumer buys. For instance, if the tax rate is 8 percent and the market price of an item is $100, then the amount of the tax on the item is $8.

A sales tax is therefore a proportional tax with respect to purchased items. The total amount of sales taxes a government collects equals the sales tax rate times the sales tax base, which is the market value of total purchases.

Sales taxes
Taxes assessed on the prices paid on most goods and services.

Ad valorem taxation
Assessing taxes by charging a tax rate equal to a fraction of the market price of each unit purchased.

Static Tax Analysis

There are two approaches to evaluating how changes in tax rates affect government tax collections. **Static tax analysis** assumes that changes in the tax rate have no effect on the tax base. Thus, this approach implies that if a state government desires to increase its sales tax collections, it can simply raise the tax rate. Multiplying the higher tax rate by the tax base thereby produces higher tax revenues.

Governments often rely on static tax analysis. Sometimes this yields unpleasant surprises. Consider, for instance, what happened in 1992 when Congress implemented a federal "luxury tax" on purchases of new pleasure boats priced at $100,000 or more. Applying the 10 percent luxury tax rate to the anticipated tax base—sales of new boats during previous years—produced a forecast of hundreds of millions of dollars in revenues from the luxury tax. What actually happened, however, was an 80 percent plunge in sales of new luxury boats. People postponed boat purchases or bought used boats instead. Consequently, the tax base all but disappeared, and the federal government collected only a few tens of millions of dollars in taxes on boat sales. Congress repealed the tax a year later.

Static tax analysis
Economic evaluation of the effects of tax rate changes under the assumption that there is no effect on the tax base, meaning that there is an unambiguous positive relationship between tax rates and tax revenues.

Have recent efforts by several state governments to include cyberspace-generated sales in their tax bases paid off?

POLICY EXAMPLE

States Seek to Apply Sales Taxes to Internet Retailers' Sales

In recent years, U.S. states have collected too few taxes to fund their expenditures. State governments have responded by seeking new sources of tax revenues. Several states, such as Arkansas, Hawaii, North Carolina, and Rhode Island, have cast their sights on sales programs operated by Internet retailers such as Amazon and Overstock. Under these programs, sellers—called "affiliates"—post links on their own Web sites. When the affiliates' customers click on those links and purchase items, the affiliates receive referral fees from the Internet retailers. The states listed above have declared such affiliate programs to constitute the "physical presences" of Internet retailers. This means that Internet retailers would have to collect sales taxes on *all* of their companies' sales.

Each time that state governments have passed such sales tax laws, Internet retailers have responded by eliminating affiliate programs within those states. Thus, these efforts to expand sales tax bases to include Internet retailers have failed thus far.

FOR CRITICAL THINKING

What do you suppose has happened to state income taxes collected from Internet retailers' former affiliates in Arkansas, Hawaii, North Carolina, and Rhode Island?

Dynamic Tax Analysis

Dynamic tax analysis
Economic evaluation of tax rate changes that recognizes that the tax base eventually declines with ever-higher tax rates, so that tax revenues may eventually decline if the tax rate is raised sufficiently.

The problem with static tax analysis is that it ignores incentive effects created by new taxes or hikes in existing tax rates. According to **dynamic tax analysis,** a likely response to an increase in a tax rate is a *decrease* in the tax base. When a government pushes up its sales tax rate, for example, consumers have an incentive to cut back on their purchases of goods and services subjected to the higher rate, perhaps by buying them in a locale where there is a lower sales tax rate or perhaps no tax rate at all. As shown in Figure 6-2 below, the maximum sales tax rate varies considerably from state to state.

Consider someone who lives in a state bordering Oregon. In such a border state, the sales tax rate can be as high as 8 percent, so a resident of that state has a strong incentive to buy higher-priced goods and services in Oregon, where there is no sales tax. Someone who lives in a high-tax county in Alabama has an incentive to buy an item online from an out-of-state firm to avoid paying sales taxes. Such shifts in expenditures in response to higher relative tax rates will reduce a state's sales tax base and thereby result in lower sales tax collections than the levels predicted by static tax analysis.

FIGURE 6-2

States with the Highest and Lowest Sales Tax Rates

A number of states allow counties and cities to collect their own sales taxes in addition to state sales taxes. This figure shows the maximum sales tax rates for selected states, including county and municipal taxes. Delaware, Montana, New Hampshire, and Oregon have no sales taxes.

Source: U.S. Department of Commerce.

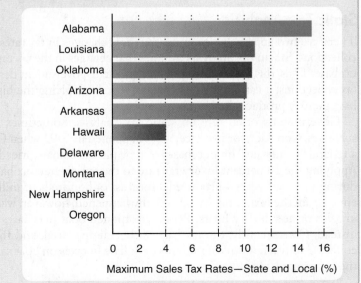

Maximum Sales Tax Rates—State and Local (%)

Dynamic tax analysis recognizes that increasing the tax rate could actually cause the government's total tax collections to *decline* if a sufficiently large number of consumers react to the higher sales tax rate by cutting back on purchases of goods and services included in the state's tax base. Some residents who live close to other states with lower sales tax rates might, for instance, drive across the state line to do more of their shopping. Other residents might place more orders with catalog companies or online firms located in other legal jurisdictions where their state's sales tax does not apply.

WHAT IF... the government seeks to collect higher taxes by increasing capital gains tax rates?

People who own assets the sale of which would generate capital gains subject to taxation have considerable discretion over when to sell assets and realize capital gains from such sales. When people learn about upcoming increases in tax rates that apply to capital gains, they can attempt to sell their assets immediately, before the higher tax rate goes into effect. Alternatively, they can indefinitely postpone sales of the assets in the hope that the tax rate will be cut in the future. Either response reduces capital gains subject to taxation when the higher tax rate becomes effective.

Indeed, the evidence for an inverse relationship between capital gains tax rates and realized capital gains is considerable. That is, when capital gains tax rates increase, taxable realized capital gains decline, and tax collections fail to rise as much as expected. Thus, as predicted by dynamic tax analysis, raising the tax rate causes an offsetting decline in the tax base, resulting in fewer tax collections than the government anticipates.

Maximizing Tax Revenues

Dynamic tax analysis indicates that whether a government's tax revenues ultimately rise or fall in response to a tax rate increase depends on exactly how much the tax base declines in response to the higher tax rate. On the one hand, the tax base may decline by a relatively small amount following an increase in the tax rate, or perhaps even imperceptibly, so that tax revenues rise. For instance, in the situation we imagine a government facing in Figure 6-3 below, a rise in the tax rate from 5 percent to 6 percent causes tax revenues to increase. Along this range, static tax analysis can provide a good approximation of the revenue effects of an increase in the tax rate. On the other hand, the tax base may decline so much that total tax revenues decrease. In Figure 6-3, for example, increasing the tax rate from 6 percent to 7 percent causes tax revenues to *decline*.

What is most likely is that when the tax rate is already relatively low, increasing the tax rate causes relatively small declines in the tax base. Within a range of relatively low sales tax rates, therefore, increasing the tax rate generates higher sales tax revenues, as illustrated along the upward-sloping portion of the curve depicted in Figure 6-3. If the government

FIGURE 6-3

Maximizing the Government's Sales Tax Revenues

Dynamic tax analysis predicts that ever-higher tax rates bring about declines in the tax base, so that at sufficiently high tax rates the government's tax revenues begin to fall off. This implies that there is a tax rate, 6 percent in this example, at which the government can collect the maximum possible revenues, T_{max}.

continues to push up the tax rate, however, people increasingly have an incentive to find ways to avoid purchasing taxable goods and services. Eventually, the tax base decreases sufficiently that the government's tax collections decline with ever-higher tax rates.

Consequently, governments that wish to maximize their tax revenues should not necessarily assess a high tax rate. In the situation illustrated in Figure 6-3, on the previous page, the government maximizes its tax revenues at T_{max} by establishing a sales tax rate of 6 percent. If the government were to raise the rate above 6 percent, it would induce a sufficient decline in the tax base that its tax collections would decline. If the government wishes to collect more than T_{max} in revenues to fund various government programs, it must somehow either expand its sales tax base or develop another tax.

QUICK QUIZ   See page 138 for the answers. Review concepts from this section in MyEconLab.

The _____ view of the relationship between tax rates and tax revenues implies that higher tax rates always generate increased government tax collections.

According to _____ tax analysis, higher tax rates cause the tax base to decrease. Tax collections will rise less than predicted by _____ tax analysis.

Dynamic tax analysis indicates that there is a tax rate that maximizes the government's tax collections. Setting the tax rate any higher would cause the tax base to _____ sufficiently that the government's tax revenues will _____.

Taxation from the Point of View of Producers and Consumers

Governments collect taxes on product sales at the source. They require producers to charge these taxes when they sell their output. This means that taxes on sales of goods and services affect market prices and quantities. Let's consider why this is so.

Taxes and the Market Supply Curve

Imposing taxes on final sales of a good or service affects the position of the market supply curve. To see why, consider panel (a) of Figure 6-4 on the facing page, which shows a gasoline market supply curve S_1 in the absence of taxation. At a price of $3.35 per gallon, gasoline producers are willing and able to supply 180,000 gallons of gasoline per week. If the price increases to $3.45 per gallon, firms increase production to 200,000 gallons of gasoline per week.

Both federal and state governments assess **excise taxes**—taxes on sales of particular commodities—on sales of gasoline. They levy gasoline excise taxes as a **unit tax**, or a constant tax per unit sold. On average, combined federal and state excise taxes on gasoline are about $0.40 per gallon.

Let's suppose, therefore, that a gasoline producer must transmit a total of $0.40 per gallon to federal and state governments for each gallon sold. Producers must continue to receive a net amount of $3.35 per gallon to induce them to supply 180,000 gallons each week, so they must now receive $3.75 per gallon to supply that weekly quantity. Likewise, gasoline producers now will be willing to supply 200,000 gallons each week only if they receive $0.40 more per gallon, or a total amount of $3.85 per gallon.

As you can see, imposing the combined $0.40 per gallon excise taxes on gasoline shifts the supply curve vertically by exactly that amount to S_2 in panel (a). Thus, the effect of levying excise taxes on gasoline is to shift the supply curve vertically by the total per-unit taxes levied on gasoline sales. Hence, there is a decrease in supply. (In the case of an *ad valorem* sales tax, the supply curve would shift vertically by a proportionate amount equal to the tax rate.)

Excise tax
A tax levied on purchases of a particular good or service.

Unit tax
A constant tax assessed on each unit of a good that consumers purchase.

FIGURE 6-4

The Effects of Excise Taxes on the Market Supply and Equilibrium Price and Quantity of Gasoline

Panel (a) shows what happens if the government requires gasoline sellers to collect and transmit a $0.40 unit excise tax on gasoline. To be willing to continue supplying a given quantity, sellers must receive a price that is $0.40 higher for each gallon they sell, so the market supply curve shifts vertically

by the amount of the tax. As illustrated in panel (b), this decrease in market supply causes a reduction in the equilibrium quantity of gasoline produced and purchased. It also causes a rise in the market clearing price, to $3.75, so that consumers pay part of the tax. Sellers pay the rest in lower profits.

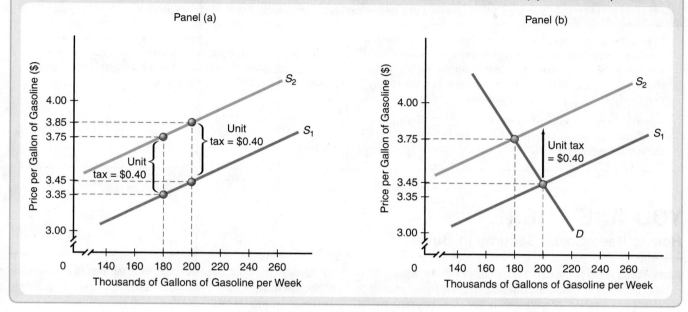

How Taxes Affect the Market Price and Equilibrium Quantity

Panel (b) of Figure 6-4 above shows how imposing $0.40 per gallon in excise taxes affects the market price of gasoline and the equilibrium quantity of gasoline produced and sold. In the absence of excise taxes, the market supply curve S_1 crosses the demand curve D at a market price of $3.45 per gallon. At this market price, the equilibrium quantity of gasoline is 200,000 gallons of gasoline per week.

The excise tax levy of $0.40 per gallon shifts the supply curve to S_2. At the original $3.45 per gallon price, there is now an excess quantity of gasoline demanded, so the market price of gasoline rises to $3.75 per gallon. At this market price, the equilibrium quantity of gasoline produced and consumed each week is 180,000 gallons.

What factors determine how much the equilibrium quantity of a good or service declines in response to taxation? The answer to this question depends on how responsive quantities demanded and supplied are to changes in price.

Who Pays the Tax?

In our example, imposing excise taxes of $0.40 per gallon of gasoline causes the market price to rise to $3.75 per gallon from $3.45 per gallon. Thus, the price that each consumer pays is $0.30 per gallon higher. Consumers pay three-fourths of the excise tax levied on each gallon of gasoline produced and sold in our example.

Gasoline producers must pay the rest of the tax. Their profits decline by $0.10 per gallon because costs have increased by $0.40 per gallon while consumers pay $0.30 more per gallon.

In the gasoline market, as in other markets for products subject to excise taxes and other taxes on sales, the shapes of the market demand and supply curves determine who pays most of a tax. The reason is that the shapes of these curves reflect the responsiveness to price changes of the quantity demanded by consumers and of the quantity supplied by producers.

In the example illustrated in Figure 6-4 on the previous page, the fact that consumers pay most of the excise taxes levied on gasoline reflects a relatively low responsiveness of quantity demanded by consumers to a change in the price of gasoline. Consumers pay most of the excise taxes on each gallon produced and sold because in this example the amount of gasoline they desire to purchase is relatively (but not completely) unresponsive to a change in the market price induced by excise taxes.

QUICK QUIZ See page 138 for the answers. Review concepts from this section in MyEconLab.

When the government levies a tax on sales of a particular product, firms must receive a higher price to continue supplying the same quantity as before, so the supply curve shifts _____. If the tax is a unit excise tax, the supply curve shifts _____ by the amount of the tax.

Imposing a tax on sales of an item _____ the equilibrium quantity produced and consumed and _____ the market price.

When a government assesses a unit excise tax, the market price of the good or service typically rises by an amount _____ than the per-unit tax. Hence, consumers pay a portion of the tax, and firms pay the remainder.

YOU ARE THERE
How to Keep Social Security in Business

Nancy Altman is the co-director of Social Security Works, a group dedicated to preserving the Social Security programs that provide benefits to the elderly and disabled. Altman's view is that these programs are "of crucial importance to every working American and his or her family." Nevertheless, the programs face eventual shortfalls of taxes in relation to promised benefits. Projections indicate that the government will be unable to fund promised benefits to the elderly sometime during the 2030s. The disability program will break down by the end of the 2010s.

Altman proposes two ways of preserving both Social Security programs. One is to combine the programs, so that tax dollars originally intended to fund only benefits for the elderly would begin covering disability benefits. Choosing this option would leave fewer tax funds to pay

for elderly benefits and cause that program to fail even sooner. The other option Altman suggests is to finance the disability program by increasing the Social Security tax rate.

One other approach could keep the disability program in operation. This option, which Altman opposes, would be to reduce disability benefits.

Critical Thinking Questions

1. Could borrowing help to finance Social Security benefits indefinitely? Explain.

2. What will be the effects of Social Security shortfalls on the overall U.S. government budget constraint, which sums all programs' constraints?

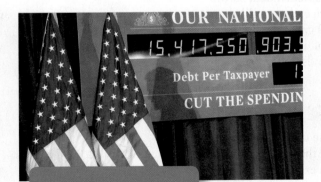

ISSUES & APPLICATIONS

What Determines the U.S. Long-Run Average Tax Rate?

CONCEPTS APPLIED

► Tax Rate

► Average Tax Rate

► Government Budget Constraint

If we view the overall tax base as the income earned by all residents during a given year, then the average tax rate equals all tax payments divided by income. This average tax rate is the proportion of total national income paid in taxes.

FIGURE 6-5

The Overall Average Federal Tax Rate and Its Components and Federal Spending as a Percentage of National Income

The overall average tax rate exhibits short-term volatility mainly because of changes in marginal tax rates and tax collections of individual income taxes. Ultimately, this overall tax rate must equal the ratio of federal spending to national income, but currently the government is making up the difference via borrowing.

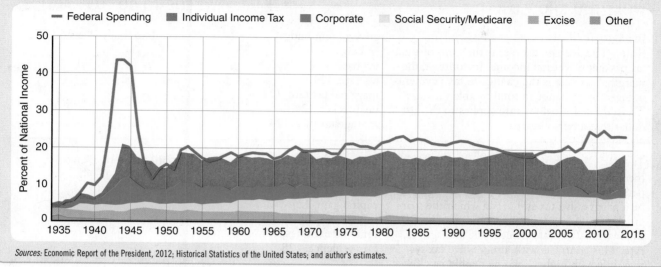

Sources: Economic Report of the President, 2012; Historical Statistics of the United States; and author's estimates.

The Overall Average U.S. Tax Rate and Its Components

Figure 6-5 above displays the average U.S. federal tax rate each year since 1934. Since the early 1950s, this overall average tax rate has ranged between 15 and 21 percent. The shaded regions show how this rate has been split among various forms of taxation.

The greater instability of the average individual income tax rate largely reflects two factors: changes in marginal income tax rates assessed by the federal government and variations in individual income subject to taxation. For instance, the gradual increase in the average individual income tax rate during the 1990s reflects higher marginal tax rates imposed in 1993. Drops in this average tax rate in the early 1980s and early 2000s help to account for declines in the average individual income rate during these intervals. Another key determinant, however, was declines in taxes collected during economic downturns. Since 2007, the significant dropoff in tax collections has been the primary reason for the fall in the average individual income tax rate.

The Role of the Government Budget Constraint

Recall that government spending ultimately must equal all revenues derived from taxes and fees. Thus, the average rate of federal spending out of national income eventually must be equalized with the overall average federal tax rate.

Plotted separately in the figure is federal spending as a percentage of national income. The current ratio of federal spending to national income of about 24 percent is well above the overall average tax rate of just over 15 percent. The federal government has had to make up the difference by borrowing, but it cannot do so indefinitely. If spending as a percentage of national income were to remain close to 24 percent, the overall average federal tax rate would have to rise to 24 percent as well. Ultimately, the average federal tax rate must adjust to equality with government spending's share of national income.

For Critical Thinking

1. If citizens were to decide that the overall average federal tax rate should not be greater than 18 percent, what must happen to the long-term rate of federal expenditures in relation to national income?

2. If citizens were to decide that in the long run, federal expenditures should be 28 percent of national income, what must be the required overall average federal tax rate?

Web Resources

1. Take a look at average federal tax rates for people in different income categories at **www.econtoday.com/chap06**.

2. Figure 6-5 displays only official "on-budget" federal spending as a percentage of national income. For a look at total—the sum of on-budget and unofficial "off-budget"—spending as a percentage of national income, go to **www.econtoday.com/chap06**.

MyEconLab

For more questions on this chapter's Issues & Applications, go to **MyEconLab**. In the Study Plan for this chapter, select Section N: News.

MyEconLab

Here is what you should know after reading this chapter. MyEconLab will help you identify what you know, and where to go when you need to practice.

WHAT YOU SHOULD KNOW		WHERE TO GO TO PRACTICE
Average Tax Rates versus Marginal Tax Rates The average tax rate is the ratio of total tax payments to total income. In contrast, the marginal tax rate is the change in tax payments induced by a change in total taxable income. Thus, the marginal tax rate applies to the last dollar that a person earns.	government budget constraint, 123 tax base, 124 tax rate, 124 marginal tax rate, 124 tax bracket, 124 average tax rate, 124	• MyEconLab Study Plans 6.1, 6.2
The U.S. Income Tax System The U.S. income tax system assesses taxes against both personal and business income. It is designed to be a progressive tax system, in which the marginal tax rate increases as income rises, so that the marginal tax rate exceeds the average tax rate. This contrasts with a regressive tax system, in which higher-income people pay lower marginal tax rates, resulting in a marginal tax rate that is less than the average tax rate. The marginal tax rate equals the average tax rate only under proportional taxation, in which the marginal tax rate does not vary with income.	proportional taxation, 124 progressive taxation, 125 regressive taxation, 125 capital gain, 127 capital loss, 127 retained earnings, 128 tax incidence, 128	• MyEconLab Study Plan 6.3
The Relationship between Tax Rates and Tax Revenues Static tax analysis assumes that the tax base does not respond significantly to an increase in the tax rate, so it seems to imply that a tax rate hike must always boost a government's total tax collections. Dynamic tax analysis reveals, however, that increases in tax rates cause the tax base to decline. Thus, there is a tax rate that maximizes the government's tax revenues. If the government pushes the tax rate higher, tax collections decline.	sales taxes, 129 *ad valorem* taxation, 129 static tax analysis, 129 dynamic tax analysis, 130 **Key Figure** Figure 6-3, 131	• MyEconLab Study Plan 6.4 • Animated Figure 6-3
How Taxes on Purchases of Goods and Services Affect Market Prices and Quantities When a government imposes a per-unit tax on a good or service, a seller is willing to supply any given quantity only if the seller receives a price that is higher by exactly the amount of the tax. Hence, the supply curve shifts vertically by the amount of the tax per unit. In a market with typically shaped demand and supply curves, this results in a fall in the equilibrium quantity and an increase in the market price. To the extent that the market price rises, consumers pay a portion of the tax on each unit they buy. Sellers pay the remainder in lower profits.	excise tax, 132 unit tax, 132 **Key Figure** Figure 6-4, 133	• MyEconLab Study Plan 6.5 • Animated Figure 6-4

Log in to MyEconLab, take a chapter test, and get a personalized Study Plan that tells you which concepts you understand and which ones you need to review. From there, MyEconLab will give you further practice, tutorials, animations, videos, and guided solutions. For more information, visit www.myeconlab.com

PROBLEMS

All problems are assignable in MyEconLab. Answers to odd-numbered problems appear at the back of the book.

6-1. A senior citizen gets a part-time job at a fast-food restaurant. She earns $8 per hour for each hour she works, and she works exactly 25 hours per week. Thus, her total pretax weekly income is $200. Her total income tax assessment each week is $40, but she has determined that she is assessed $3 in taxes for the final hour she works each week. (See page 124.)

  a. What is this person's average tax rate each week?

  b. What is the marginal tax rate for the last hour she works each week?

6-2. For purposes of assessing income taxes, there are three official income levels for workers in a small country: high, medium, and low. For the last hour on the job during a 40-hour workweek, a high-income worker pays a marginal income tax rate of 15 percent, a medium-income worker pays a marginal tax rate of 20 percent, and a low-income worker is assessed a 25 percent marginal income tax rate. Based only on this information, does this nation's income tax system appear to be progressive, proportional, or regressive? (See page 125.)

6-3. Consider the table below, in which each person's marginal tax rate is constant but differs from others' marginal tax rates, when answering the questions that follow. Show your work, and explain briefly. (See page 127.)

Christino		Jarius		Meg	
Income	Taxes Paid	Income	Taxes Paid	Income	Taxes Paid
$1,000	$200	$1,000	$200	$1,000	$200
$2,000	$300	$2,000	$400	$2,000	$500
$3,000	$400	$3,000	$600	$3,000	$800

  a. What is Christino's marginal tax rate?

  b. What is Jarius's marginal tax rate?

  c. What is Meg's marginal tax rate?

6-4. Refer to the table in Problem 6-3 when answering the following questions. Show your work, and explain briefly. (See pages 124–125.)

  a. Does Christino experience progressive, proportional, or regressive taxation?

  b. Does Jarius experience progressive, proportional, or regressive taxation?

  c. Does Meg experience progressive, proportional, or regressive taxation?

6-5. Suppose that a state has increased its sales tax rate every other year since 2005. Assume that the state collected all sales taxes that residents legally owed. The table below summarizes its experience. What were total taxable sales in this state during each year displayed in the table? (See page 129.)

Year	Sales Tax Rate	Sales Tax Collections
2005	0.03 (3 percent)	$9.0 million
2007	0.04 (4 percent)	$14.0 million
2009	0.05 (5 percent)	$20.0 million
2011	0.06 (6 percent)	$24.0 million
2013	0.07 (7 percent)	$29.4 million

6-6. The sales tax rate applied to all purchases within a state was 0.04 (4 percent) throughout 2012 but increased to 0.05 (5 percent) during all of 2013. The state government collected all taxes due, but its tax revenues were equal to $40 million each year. What happened to the sales tax base between 2012 and 2013? What could account for this result? (See pages 130–131.)

6-7. The British government recently imposed a unit excise tax of about $154 per ticket on airline tickets applying to flights to or from London airports. In answering the following questions, assume normally shaped demand and supply curves. (See page 133.)

  a. Use an appropriate diagram to predict effects of the ticket tax on the market clearing price of London airline tickets and on the equilibrium number of flights into and out of London.

  b. What do you predict is likely to happen to the equilibrium price of tickets for air flights into and out of cities that are in close proximity to London but are not subject to the new ticket tax? Explain your reasoning.

6-8. To raise funds aimed at providing more support for public schools, a state government has just imposed a unit excise tax equal to $4 for each monthly unit of wireless phone services sold by each company operating in the state. The following diagram depicts the positions of the demand and supply curves for wireless phone services *before* the unit excise tax was imposed. Use this diagram to determine the position of the new market supply curve now that the tax hike has gone into effect. (See pages 132–133.)

Quantity of Wireless Phone Services
(millions of units per month)

Price ($ per unit)	Quantity Supplied	Quantity Demanded
4	50	200
5	75	175
6	100	150
7	125	125
8	150	100
9	175	75

a. Does imposing the $4-per-month unit excise tax cause the market price of wireless phone services to rise by $4 per month? Why or why not?

b. What portion of the $4-per-month unit excise tax is paid by consumers? What portion is paid by providers of wireless phone services?

6-9. The following information applies to the market for a particular item in the *absence* of a unit excise tax (see pages 132–133):

a. According to the information in the table, in the *absence* of a unit excise tax, what is the market price? What is the equilibrium quantity?

b. Suppose that the government decides to subject producers of this item to a unit excise tax equal to $2 per unit sold. What is the new market price? What is the new equilibrium quantity?

c. What portion of the tax is paid by producers? What portion of the tax is paid by consumers?

ECONOMICS ON THE NET

Social Security Reform There are many proposals for reforming Social Security. The purpose of this exercise is to learn more about why changing Social Security is so often under discussion.

Title: Social Security Privatization

Navigation: Go to www.econtoday.com/chap06 to learn about Social Security privatization. Under "Recent Social Security Publications," click on "*Social Security, Ponzi Schemes, and the Need for Reform.*"

Application For each of the three entries noted here, read the entry and answer the question.

1. According to this article, when will the system begin to experience difficulties? Why?

2. Why does this article contend that Social Security is similar to a "Ponzi scheme"?

3. Why does this article argue that simply adding personal accounts will not solve Social Security's problems?

For Group Study and Analysis Go to www.econtoday.com/chap06 to read a proposal for Social Security reform. Accept or rebut the proposal, depending on the side to which you have been assigned. Be prepared to defend your reasons with more than just your feelings. At a minimum, be prepared to present arguments that are logical, if not entirely backed by facts.

ANSWERS TO QUICK QUIZZES

p. 125: (i) rate . . . base; (ii) average . . . marginal; (iii) proportional . . . progressive . . . regressive

p. 129: (i) income . . . sales . . . property; (ii) double; (iii) Social Security . . . Medicare . . . unemployment

p. 132: (i) static; (ii) dynamic . . . static; (iii) fall . . . decline

p. 134: (i) vertically . . . vertically; (ii) reduces . . . raises; (iii) less

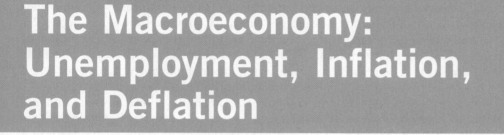

The Macroeconomy: Unemployment, Inflation, and Deflation

7

LEARNING OBJECTIVES

After reading this chapter, you should be able to:

▶ Explain how the U.S. government calculates the official unemployment rate

▶ Discuss the types of unemployment

▶ Describe how price indexes are calculated and define the key types of price indexes

▶ Distinguish between nominal and real interest rates

▶ Evaluate who loses and who gains from inflation

▶ Understand key features of business fluctuations

MyEconLab helps you master each objective and study more efficiently. See end of chapter for details.

At one time, a person who qualified for *unemployment benefits*—monthly payments that are coordinated by a U.S. government insurance program financed by taxes on employers—was eligible to receive benefits for no longer than 26 weeks. Since 2009, however, Congress has used general taxpayer funds to extend the duration of unemployment benefits. Thus, most people who qualify for such benefits are eligible to receive them for as long as 99 weeks. A number of economists have suggested that this policy change has resulted in at least 600,000 and perhaps even more than 4 million additional jobless people at any given time. In this chapter, you will learn how economists define unemployment. In addition, you will study concepts that will help you understand how extending unemployment benefits may have contributed to higher measured unemployment.

between 2008 and 2010, the number of people gainfully employed in the United States declined by nearly 9 million? Since then, more than 2 million of these people have found new jobs. Nevertheless, in excess of 6 million people who had jobs in 2008 were still not employed in 2013. Some of these people have given up looking for work, but most are classified by economists as *unemployed*—looking for positions, but so far unable to obtain jobs.

Trying to understand determinants of unemployment and of the overall performance of the national economy is a central objective of macroeconomics. This branch of economics seeks to explain and predict movements in the average level of prices, unemployment, and the total production of goods and services. This chapter introduces you to these key issues of macroeconomics.

Unemployment

Unemployment

The total number of adults (aged 16 years or older) who are willing and able to work and who are actively looking for work but have not found a job.

Unemployment is normally defined as the number of adults who are actively looking for work but do not have a job. Unemployment is costly in terms of lost output for the entire economy. One estimate indicates that at the end of the first decade of the twenty-first century, when the unemployment rate rose by more than 4 percentage points and firms were operating below 80 percent of their capacity, the amount of output that the economy lost due to idle resources was roughly 5 percent of the total production throughout the United States. (In other words, we were somewhere inside the production possibilities curve that we talked about in Chapter 2.)

That was the equivalent of more than an inflation-adjusted $700 billion of schools, houses, restaurant meals, cars, and movies that *could have been* produced. It is no wonder that policymakers closely watch the unemployment figures published by the Department of Labor's Bureau of Labor Statistics.

On a more personal level, the state of being unemployed often results in hardship and failed opportunities as well as a lack of self-respect. Psychological researchers believe that being fired creates at least as much stress as the death of a close friend. The numbers that we present about unemployment can never fully convey its true cost to the people of this or any other nation.

Historical Unemployment Rates

Labor force

Individuals aged 16 years or older who either have jobs or who are looking and available for jobs; the number of employed plus the number of unemployed.

The unemployment rate, defined as the proportion of the measured **labor force** that is unemployed, hit a low of 1.2 percent of the labor force at the end of World War II, after having reached 25 percent during the Great Depression in the 1930s. You can see in Figure 7-1 on the facing page what has happened to the unemployment rate in the United States since 1890. The highest level ever was reached in the Great Depression, but the unemployment rate was also high during the Panic of 1893.

Employment, Unemployment, and the Labor Force

Figure 7-2 on the facing page presents the population of individuals 16 years of age or older broken into three segments: (1) employed, (2) unemployed, and (3) not in the civilian labor force (a category that includes homemakers, full-time students, military personnel, persons in institutions, and retired persons). The employed and the unemployed, added together, make up the labor force. In 2013, the labor force amounted to 142.1 million + 12.4 million = 154.5 million people. To calculate the unemployment rate, we simply divide the number of unemployed by the number of people in the labor force and multiply by 100: 12.4 million/154.5 million × 100 = 8.0 percent.

FIGURE 7-1

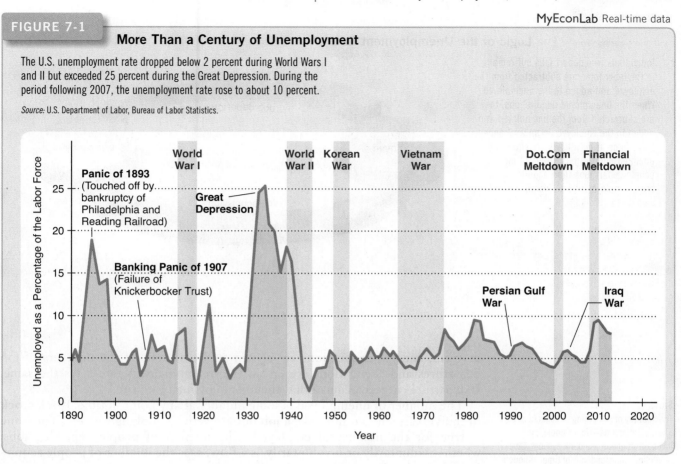

More Than a Century of Unemployment

The U.S. unemployment rate dropped below 2 percent during World Wars I and II but exceeded 25 percent during the Great Depression. During the period following 2007, the unemployment rate rose to about 10 percent.

Source: U.S. Department of Labor, Bureau of Labor Statistics.

The Arithmetic Determination of Unemployment

Because there is a transition between employment and unemployment at any point in time—people are leaving jobs and others are finding jobs—there is a simple relationship between the employed and the unemployed, as can be seen in Figure 7-3 on the following page. Job departures are shown at the top of the

FIGURE 7-2

Adult Population

The population aged 16 and older can be broken down into three groups: people who are employed, those who are unemployed, and those not in the labor force.

Source: U.S. Department of Labor, Bureau of Labor Statistics.

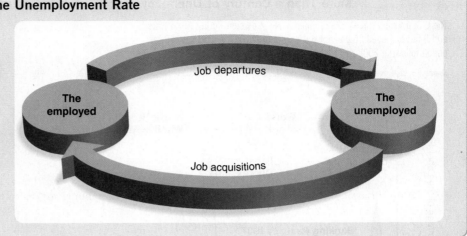

FIGURE 7-3

The Logic of the Unemployment Rate

Individuals who depart jobs but remain in the labor force are subtracted from the employed and added to the unemployed. When the unemployed acquire jobs, they are subtracted from the unemployed and added to the employed. In an unchanged labor force, if both flows are equal, the unemployment rate is stable. If more people depart jobs than acquire them, the unemployment rate increases, and vice versa.

Stock
The quantity of something, measured at a given point in time—for example, an inventory of goods or a bank account. Stocks are defined independently of time, although they are assessed at a point in time.

Flow
A quantity measured per unit of time; something that occurs over time, such as the income you make per week or per year or the number of individuals who are fired every month.

Job loser
An individual in the labor force whose employment was involuntarily terminated.

Reentrant
An individual who used to work full-time but left the labor force and has now reentered it looking for a job.

Job leaver
An individual in the labor force who quits voluntarily.

New entrant
An individual who has never held a full-time job lasting two weeks or longer but is now seeking employment.

diagram, and job acquisitions are shown at the bottom. If the numbers of job departures and acquisitions are equal, the unemployment rate stays the same. If departures exceed acquisitions, the unemployment rate rises.

The number of unemployed is some number at any point in time. It is a **stock** of individuals who do not have a job but are actively looking for one. The same is true for the number of employed. The number of people departing jobs, whether voluntarily or involuntarily, is a **flow,** as is the number of people acquiring jobs.

CATEGORIES OF INDIVIDUALS WHO ARE WITHOUT WORK According to the Bureau of Labor Statistics, an unemployed individual will fall into any of four categories:

1. A **job loser,** whose employment was involuntarily terminated or who was laid off (40 to 60 percent of the unemployed)

2. A **reentrant,** who worked a full-time job before but has been out of the labor force (20 to 30 percent of the unemployed)

3. A **job leaver,** who voluntarily ended employment (less than 10 to around 15 percent of the unemployed)

4. A **new entrant,** who has never worked a full-time job for two weeks or longer (10 to 15 percent of the unemployed)

DURATION OF UNEMPLOYMENT If you are out of a job for a week, your situation is typically much less serious than if you are out of a job for, say, 14 weeks. An increase in the duration of unemployment can increase the unemployment rate because workers stay unemployed longer, thereby creating a greater number of them at any given time.

The most recent information on duration of unemployment paints the following picture: More than a third of those who become unemployed acquire a new job by the end of one month, approximately one-third more acquire a job by the end of two months, and only about a sixth are still unemployed after six months. Since the mid-1960s, the average annual duration of unemployment for all the unemployed has varied between 10 and 20 weeks. The overall average duration for the past 25 years has been at least 16 weeks.

When overall business activity goes into a downturn, the duration of unemployment tends to rise, thereby accounting for much of the increase in the estimated unemployment rate. In a sense, then, it is the increase in the *duration* of unemployment during a downturn in national economic activity that generates the bad news that concerns policymakers in Washington, D.C. Furthermore, the individuals who stay unemployed longer than six months are the ones who create pressure on Congress to "do something." What Congress does, typically, is extend and supplement unemployment benefits.

THE DISCOURAGED WORKER PHENOMENON Critics of the published unemployment rate calculated by the federal government believe that it fails to reflect the true numbers of **discouraged workers** and "hidden unemployed." Though there is no agreed-on method to measure discouraged workers, the Department of Labor defines them as people who have dropped out of the labor force and are no longer looking for a job because they believe that the job market has little to offer them. To what extent do we want to include in the measured labor force individuals who voluntarily choose not to look for work or those who take only a few minutes a day to scan the want ads and then decide that there are no jobs?

Discouraged workers
Individuals who have stopped looking for a job because they are convinced that they will not find a suitable one.

Some economists argue that people who work part-time but are willing to work full-time should be classified as "semihidden" unemployed. Estimates range as high as 6 million workers at any one time. Offsetting this factor, though, is *overemployment*. An individual working 50 or 60 hours a week is still counted as only one full-time worker. Some people hold two or three jobs but still are counted as just one employed person.

LABOR FORCE PARTICIPATION The way in which we define unemployment and membership in the labor force will affect the **labor force participation rate.** It is defined as the proportion of noninstitutionalized (i.e., not in prisons, mental institutions, etc.) working-age individuals who are employed or seeking employment.

Labor force participation rate
The percentage of noninstitutionalized working-age individuals who are employed or seeking employment.

The U.S. labor force participation rate has risen somewhat over time, from 60 percent in 1950 to almost 64 percent today. The gender composition of the U.S. labor force has changed considerably during this time. In 1950, more than 83 percent of men and fewer than 35 percent of women participated in the U.S. labor force. Today, fewer than 70 percent of men and nearly 60 percent of women are U.S. labor force participants.

What do you suppose accounts for a recent decline in the U.S. labor force participation rate?

EXAMPLE

Fewer Men Are at Work—or Even Looking for It

Since the beginning of 2008, the overall U.S. labor force participation rate has decreased by nearly 3 percentage points, to less than 64 percent. Three percentage points may not sound like very much. Nevertheless, this reduction in labor force participation represents the steepest decline within a few years' time to have taken place over the past several decades. The nearly 3-percentage-point decrease translates into a labor force reduction of more than 7 million people.

Male workers who have dropped out of the labor force account for the bulk of this reduction. During the 2008–2009 recession, the unemployment rates of both men and women shot up, but occupations dominated by male workers, such as construction and manufacturing, experienced the largest job losses. Consequently, the differential between male and female unemployment rates rose by nearly 3 percentage points. Many of the men who lost jobs did not find new positions, became discouraged workers, and departed from the labor force. Thus, the primary element accounting for the recent drop in U.S. labor force participation is the transformation, since 2008, of millions of male employees into discouraged workers.

FOR CRITICAL THINKING

What would happen to the overall U.S. labor force participation rate if the construction and manufacturing industries were to experience significant upswings?

QUICK QUIZ   See page 160 for the answers. Review concepts from this section in MyEconLab.

_____ persons are adults who are willing and able to work and are actively looking for a job but have not found one. The unemployment rate is computed by dividing the number of unemployed by the total _____ _____, which is equal to those who are employed plus those who are unemployed.

The unemployed are classified as _____ _____, _____, _____ _____, and _____ _____ to the labor force. The flow of people departing jobs and people acquiring jobs

_____ determines the stock of the unemployed as well as the stock of the employed.

The duration of unemployment affects the unemployment rate. If the duration of unemployment increases, the measured unemployment rate will _____, even though the number of unemployed workers may remain the same.

Whereas overall labor force participation on net has risen only modestly since World War II, there has been a major increase in _____ labor force participation.

The Major Types of Unemployment

Unemployment has been categorized into four basic types: frictional, structural, cyclical, and seasonal.

Frictional Unemployment

Of the more than 154 million people in the labor force, more than 50 million will either change jobs or take new jobs during the year. In the process, in excess of 22 million persons will report themselves unemployed at one time or another each year. This continuous flow of individuals from job to job and in and out of employment is called **frictional unemployment.** There will always be some frictional unemployment as resources are redirected in the economy, because job-hunting costs are never zero, and workers never have full information about available jobs. To eliminate frictional unemployment, we would have to prevent workers from leaving their present jobs until they had already lined up other jobs at which they would start working immediately. And we would have to guarantee first-time job seekers a job *before* they started looking.

Frictional unemployment
Unemployment due to the fact that workers must search for appropriate job offers. This activity takes time, and so they remain temporarily unemployed.

Structural Unemployment

Structural changes in our economy cause some workers to become unemployed for very long periods of time because they cannot find jobs that use their particular skills. This is called **structural unemployment.** Structural unemployment is not caused by general business fluctuations, although business fluctuations may affect it. And unlike frictional unemployment, structural unemployment is not related to the movement of workers from low-paying to high-paying jobs.

At one time, economists thought about structural unemployment only from the perspective of workers. The concept applied to workers who did not have the ability, training, and skills necessary to obtain available jobs. Today, it still encompasses these workers. In addition, however, economists increasingly look at structural unemployment from the viewpoint of employers, many of whom face government mandates requiring them to take such steps as providing funds for social insurance programs for their employees and announcing plant closings months or even years in advance.

There is now considerable evidence that government labor market policies influence how many job positions businesses wish to create, thereby affecting structural unemployment. In the United States, many businesses appear to have adjusted to these policies by hiring more "temporary workers" or establishing short-term contracts with "private consultants." Such measures may have increased the extent of U.S. structural unemployment in recent years.

Structural unemployment
Unemployment of workers over lengthy intervals resulting from skill mismatches with position requirements of employers and from fewer jobs being offered by employers constrained by governmental business regulations and labor market policies.

How may a federal law be increasing structural unemployment?

Warning: WARN May Boost the Natural Unemployment Rate

In 1989, Congress passed the Worker Adjustment and Retraining Notification (WARN) Act. The law required firms to notify and provide special benefits to employees in advance of what the legislation defines as a "mass layoff" involving fifty or more full-time workers constituting at least one-third of a company's staff. The law rarely applied until the 2008–2009 recession. When their sales plummeted during that recession, a number of companies rapidly laid off large numbers of workers to cut costs in an attempt to remain in business. Job losers alleged violations of WARN and sought extra termination payments and benefits.

As economic activity recovered somewhat but remained dampened in the years following the recession, managers found out that WARN-related caseloads in the courts had tripled. Those managers worried that if they were to hire workers they might later have to lay off, WARN might apply. This concern discouraged managers from hiring back as many workers as they might have otherwise. As a consequence, unemployment remained high even as companies' prospects improved. Thus, the WARN law undoubtedly contributed to greater structural unemployment.

FOR CRITICAL THINKING

How has structural unemployment been affected by the actions of several state governments in requiring firms to grant longer paid "family leaves"?

Cyclical Unemployment

Cyclical unemployment is related to business fluctuations. It is defined as unemployment associated with changes in business conditions—primarily recessions and depressions. The way to lessen cyclical unemployment would be to reduce the intensity, duration, and frequency of downturns of business activity. Economic policymakers attempt, through their policies, to reduce cyclical unemployment by keeping business activity on an even keel.

Seasonal Unemployment

Seasonal unemployment comes and goes with seasons of the year in which the demand for particular jobs rises and falls. In northern states, construction workers can often work only during the warmer months. They are seasonally unemployed during the winter. Summer resort workers can usually get jobs in resorts only during the summer season. They, too, sometimes become seasonally unemployed during the winter. The opposite is sometimes true for ski resort workers.

The unemployment rate that the Bureau of Labor Statistics releases each month is "seasonally adjusted." This means that the reported unemployment rate has been adjusted to remove the effects of variations in seasonal unemployment. Thus, the unemployment rate that the media dutifully announce reflects only the sum of frictional unemployment, structural unemployment, and cyclical unemployment.

Cyclical unemployment
Unemployment resulting from business recessions that occur when aggregate (total) demand is insufficient to create full employment.

YOU ARE THERE

To consider how difficulties in finding workers with required skills might contribute to unemployment, take a look at **Struggling to Hire with the Unemployment Rate above 9 Percent** on page 155.

Seasonal unemployment
Unemployment resulting from the seasonal pattern of work in specific industries. It is usually due to seasonal fluctuations in demand or to changing weather conditions that render work difficult, if not impossible, as in the agriculture, construction, and tourist industries.

Full Employment and the Natural Rate of Unemployment

Does full employment mean that everybody has a job? Certainly not, for not everyone is looking for a job—full-time students and full-time homemakers, for example, are not. Is it always possible for everyone who is looking for a job to find one? No, because transaction costs (see Chapter 4) in the labor market are not zero. Transaction costs are those associated with any activity whose goal is to enter into, carry out, or terminate contracts. In the labor market, these costs involve time spent looking for a job, being interviewed, negotiating the terms of employment, and the like.

Full Employment

We will always have some frictional unemployment as individuals move in and out of the labor force, seek higher-paying jobs, and move to different parts of the country. **Full employment** is therefore a concept that implies some sort of balance or equilibrium in an ever-shifting labor market. Of course, this general notion of full employment must somehow be put into numbers so that economists and others can determine whether the economy has reached the full-employment point.

The Natural Rate of Unemployment

In trying to assess when a situation of balance has been attained in the labor market, economists estimate the **natural rate of unemployment,** the rate that is expected to prevail in the long run once all workers and employers have fully adjusted to any changes in the economy. If correctly estimated, the natural rate of unemployment should not include cyclical unemployment. When seasonally adjusted, the natural unemployment rate should include only frictional and structural unemployment.

A long-standing difficulty, however, has been a lack of agreement about how to estimate the natural unemployment rate. Until the late 2000s, most economists, including those with the president's Council of Economic Advisers and those at the Federal Reserve, had concluded that the natural unemployment rate was slightly above 5 percent.

Since the 2008–2009 recession, the actual unemployment rate has remained considerably above 5 percent. This fact suggests that perhaps the natural rate of unemployment has increased because of a rise in structural unemployment. Some economists propose that the collapse of the U.S. housing industry precipitated this rise. The housing meltdown, these economists suggest, left people possessing skills that were poorly matched to the requirements of jobs other than those in construction, housing finance, and real estate. In contrast, other economists contend that increases in the scope of government regulations and taxes have raised the costs confronted by firms when they contemplate hiring job applicants. Government policies, these economists argue, are to blame for a higher natural unemployment rate.

Of course, both explanations together could help to account for an upswing in structural unemployment. What has yet to be determined by economists is exactly how much higher than 5 percent the natural unemployment rate now may be. Some estimates indicate that it may be at least 7 percent.

Full employment
An arbitrary level of unemployment that corresponds to "normal" friction in the labor market. In 1986, a 6.5 percent rate of unemployment was considered full employment. Today it is somewhat higher.

Natural rate of unemployment
The rate of unemployment that is estimated to prevail in long-run macroeconomic equilibrium, when all workers and employers have fully adjusted to any changes in the economy.

WHAT IF... city governments passed more laws to benefit all employees?

Beginning in 2013, a new health care law went into effect that most businesses predict will raise their costs of providing health insurance coverage to employees. In addition, new federal laws and court interpretations of existing laws are increasing the number of days off that firms are obliged to grant employees who are parents of a new child. Many municipalities, such as Seattle, Washington, have even passed ordinances requiring companies to provide more paid "sick days" each year. These and many other laws reduce the incentive for companies to hire workers and thereby decrease employment. As a result, the proliferation of such laws drives up structural unemployment and boosts the natural rate of unemployment.

QUICK QUIZ See page 160 for the answers. Review concepts from this section in MyEconLab.

_____ **unemployment** occurs because of transaction costs in the labor market. For example, workers do not have full information about vacancies and must search for jobs.

_____ **unemployment** occurs when there is a poor match of workers' skills and abilities with available jobs,

perhaps because workers lack appropriate training or government labor rules reduce firms' willingness to hire.

The levels of frictional and structural unemployment are used in part to determine our (somewhat arbitrary) measurement of the _____ rate of unemployment.

Inflation and Deflation

During World War II, you could buy bread for 8 to 10 cents a loaf and have milk delivered fresh to your door for about 25 cents a half gallon. The average price of a new car was less than $700, and the average house cost less than $3,000. Today, bread, milk, cars, and houses all cost more—a lot more. Prices are about 15 times what they were in 1940. Clearly, this country has experienced quite a bit of *inflation* since then. We define **inflation** as an upward movement in the average level of prices. The opposite of inflation is **deflation,** defined as a downward movement in the average level of prices. Notice that these definitions depend on the *average* level of prices. This means that even during a period of inflation, some prices can be falling if other prices are rising at a faster rate. The prices of electronic equipment have dropped dramatically since the 1960s, even though there has been general inflation.

Inflation
A sustained increase in the average of all prices of goods and services in an economy.

Deflation
A sustained decrease in the average of all prices of goods and services in an economy.

Inflation and the Purchasing Power of Money

By definition, the value of a dollar does not stay constant when there is inflation. The value of money is usually talked about in terms of **purchasing power.** A dollar's purchasing power is the real goods and services that it can buy. Consequently, another way of defining inflation is as a decline in the purchasing power of money. The faster the rate of inflation, the greater the rate of decline in the purchasing power of money.

One way to think about inflation and the purchasing power of money is to discuss dollar values in terms of *nominal* versus *real* values. The nominal value of anything is simply its price expressed in today's dollars. In contrast, the real value of anything is its value expressed in purchasing power, which varies with the overall price level. Let's say that you received a $100 bill from your grandparents this year. One year from now, the nominal value of that bill will still be $100. The real value will depend on what the purchasing power of money is after one year's worth of inflation. Obviously, if there is inflation during the year, the real value of that $100 bill will have diminished. For example, if you keep the $100 bill in your pocket for a year during which the rate of inflation is 3 percent, at the end of the year you will have to come up with $3 more to buy the same amount of goods and services that the $100 bill can purchase today.

To discuss what has happened to prices here and in other countries, we have to know how to measure inflation.

Purchasing power
The value of money for buying goods and services. If your money income stays the same but the price of one good that you are buying goes up, your effective purchasing power falls.

Measuring the Rate of Inflation

How can we measure the rate of inflation? It is easy to determine how much the price of an individual commodity has risen: If last year a light bulb cost 50 cents, and this year it costs 75 cents, there has been a 50 percent rise in the price of that light bulb over a one-year period. We can express the change in the individual light bulb price in one of several ways: The price has gone up 25 cents. The price is one and a half (1.5) times as high. The price has risen by 50 percent. An *index number* of this price rise is simply the second way (1.5) multiplied by 100, meaning that the index today would stand at 150. We multiply by 100 to eliminate decimals because it is easier to think in terms of percentage changes using whole numbers. This is the standard convention adopted for convenience in dealing with index numbers or price levels.

Computing a Price Index

The measurement problem becomes more complicated when it involves a large number of goods, especially if some prices have risen faster than others and some have even fallen. What we have to do is pick a representative bundle, a so-called market basket, of goods and compare the cost of that market basket of goods over time. When we do this, we obtain a **price index,** which is defined as the cost of a market basket of goods today, expressed as a percentage of the cost of that identical market basket of goods in some starting year, known as the **base year.**

Price index
The cost of today's market basket of goods expressed as a percentage of the cost of the same market basket during a base year.

Base year
The year that is chosen as the point of reference for comparison of prices in other years.

$$\text{Price index} = \frac{\text{cost of market basket today}}{\text{cost of market basket in base year}} \times 100$$

Calculating a Price Index for a Two-Good Market Basket

In this simplified example, there are only two goods—corn and digital devices. The quantities and base-year prices are given in columns 2 and 3. The 2005 cost of the market basket, calculated in column 4, comes to $1,400. The 2015 prices are given in column 5. The cost of the market basket in 2015, calculated in column 6, is $1,650. The price index for 2015 compared with 2005 is 117.86.

(1) Commodity	(2) Market Basket Quantity	(3) 2005 Price per Unit	(4) Cost of Market Basket in 2005	(5) 2015 Price per Unit	(6) Cost of Market Basket in 2015
Corn	100 bushels	$ 4	$ 400	$ 8	$ 800
Digital devices	2	500	1,000	425	850
Totals			$1,400		$1,650

$$\text{Price index} = \frac{\text{cost of market basket in 2015}}{\text{cost of market basket in base year 2005}} \times 100 = \frac{\$1,650}{\$1,400} \times 100 = 117.86$$

In the base year, the price index will always be 100, because the year in the numerator and in the denominator of the fraction is the same. Therefore, the fraction equals 1, and when we multiply it by 100, we get 100. A simple numerical example is given in Table 7-1 above. In the table, there are only two goods in the market basket—corn and digital devices. The *quantities* in the basket are the same in the base year, 2005, and the current year, 2015. Only the *prices* change. Such a *fixed-quantity* price index is the easiest to compute because the statistician need only look at prices of goods and services sold every year rather than observing how much of these goods and services consumers actually purchase each year.

REAL-WORLD PRICE INDEXES Government statisticians calculate a number of price indexes. The most often quoted are the **Consumer Price Index (CPI)**, the **Producer Price Index (PPI)**, the **GDP deflator**, and the **Personal Consumption Expenditure (PCE) Index.** The CPI attempts to measure changes only in the level of prices of goods and services purchased by consumers. The PPI attempts to show what has happened to the average price of goods and services produced and sold by a typical firm. (There are also *wholesale price indexes* that track the price level for commodities that firms purchase from other firms.) The GDP deflator is the most general indicator of inflation because it measures changes in the level of prices of all new goods and services produced in the economy. The PCE Index measures average prices using weights from surveys of consumer spending.

THE CPI The Bureau of Labor Statistics (BLS) has the task of identifying a market basket of goods and services of the typical consumer. Today, the BLS uses the time period 1982–1984 as its base of market prices. The BLS has indicated an intention to change the base to 1993–1995 but has yet to do so. It has, though, updated the expenditure weights for its market basket of goods to reflect consumer spending patterns in 2001–2002. All CPI numbers since February 1998 reflect these expenditure weights.

Economists have known for years that there are possible problems in the CPI's market basket. Specifically, the BLS has been unable to account for the way consumers substitute less expensive items for higher-priced items. The reason is that the CPI is a fixed-quantity price index, meaning that the BLS implicitly ignores changes in consumption patterns that occur between years in which it revises the index. Until recently, the BLS has also been unable to take quality changes into account as they occur. Now, though, it is subtracting from certain list prices estimated effects of qualitative improvements and adding to other list prices to account for deteriorations in quality. An additional flaw is that the CPI usually ignores successful new products until long after they have been introduced. Despite these flaws, the CPI is widely followed because its level is calculated and published monthly.

Consumer Price Index (CPI)
A statistical measure of a weighted average of prices of a specified set of goods and services purchased by typical consumers in urban areas.

Producer Price Index (PPI)
A statistical measure of a weighted average of prices of goods and services that firms produce and sell.

GDP deflator
A price index measuring the changes in prices of all new goods and services produced in the economy.

Personal Consumption Expenditure (PCE) Index
A statistical measure of average prices that uses annually updated weights based on surveys of consumer spending.

Within which group of products are prices rising with sufficient speed to account for a significant portion of China's annual rate of consumer price inflation?

INTERNATIONAL EXAMPLE

Why the Value of China's Consumer Price Index Is Rising

In China, food's weight in the CPI is slightly below 35 percent. Food prices have been rising so rapidly, though, that the overall rate of increase in food prices per year has been contributing to 75 percent of China's officially measured annual rate of CPI inflation. Consequently, during a recent 12-month period in which the nation's measured rate of CPI inflation was 6.4 percent, the rate of increase in food prices accounted for 4.8 percentage points of that annual rate of inflation.

FOR CRITICAL THINKING
Food's weight in the U.S. CPI is about 16 percent. If U.S. food prices rose as rapidly as Chinese food prices, would the U.S. CPI increase as much as the CPI in China? Explain.

THE PPI There are a number of Producer Price Indexes, including one for foodstuffs, another for intermediate goods (goods used in the production of other goods), and one for finished goods. Most of the producer prices included are in mining, manufacturing, and agriculture. The PPIs can be considered general-purpose indexes for nonretail markets.

Although in the long run the various PPIs and the CPI generally show the same rate of inflation, that is not the case in the short run. Most often the PPIs increase before the CPI because it takes time for producer price increases to show up in the prices that consumers pay for final products. Changes in the PPIs are watched closely as a hint that CPI inflation is going to increase or decrease.

THE GDP DEFLATOR The broadest price index reported in the United States is the GDP deflator, where GDP stands for gross domestic product, or annual total national income. Unlike the CPI and the PPIs, the GDP deflator is *not* based on a fixed market basket of goods and services. The basket is allowed to change with people's consumption and investment patterns. In this sense, the changes in the GDP deflator reflect both price changes and the public's market responses to those price changes. Why? Because new expenditure patterns are allowed to show up in the GDP deflator as people respond to changing prices.

Go to www.econtoday.com/chap07 to obtain information about inflation and unemployment in other countries from the International Monetary Fund. Click on "World Economic Outlook Databases."

THE PCE INDEX Another price index that takes into account changing expenditure patterns is the Personal Consumption Expenditure (PCE) Index. The Bureau of Economic Analysis, an agency of the U.S. Department of Commerce, uses continuously updated annual surveys of consumer purchases to construct the weights for the PCE Index. Thus, an advantage of the PCE Index is that weights in the index are updated every year. The Federal Reserve has used the rate of change in the PCE Index as its primary inflation indicator because Fed officials believe that the updated weights in the PCE Index make it more accurate than the CPI as a measure of consumer price changes. Nevertheless, the CPI remains the most widely reported price index, and the U.S. government continues to use the CPI to adjust the value of Social Security benefits to account for inflation.

HISTORICAL CHANGES IN THE CPI Between World War II and the early 1980s, the Consumer Price Index showed a fairly dramatic trend upward. Figure 7-4 on the following page shows the annual rate of change in the CPI since 1860. Prior to World War II, there were numerous periods of deflation interspersed with periods of inflation. Persistent year-in and year-out inflation seems to be a post–World War II phenomenon, at least in this country. As far back as before the American Revolution, prices used to rise during war periods but then would fall back toward prewar levels afterward. This occurred after the Revolutionary War, the War of 1812, the Civil War, and to a lesser extent World War I. Consequently, the overall price level in 1940 wasn't much different from 150 years earlier.

MyEconLab Real-time data

FIGURE 7-4

Inflation and Deflation in U.S. History

For 80 years after the Civil War, the United States experienced alternating inflation and deflation. Here we show them as reflected by changes in the Consumer Price Index. Since World War II, the periods of inflation have not been followed by periods of deflation. Even during peacetime, the price index has continued to rise. The shaded areas represent wartime.
Source: U.S. Department of Labor, Bureau of Labor Statistics.

Why is Argentina's government imposing substantial fines on private firms that release their own independent estimates of the nation's inflation rate?

INTERNATIONAL POLICY EXAMPLE

Argentina Penalizes Inflation Estimates That Are "Too High"

Argentina's national statistics agency, Indec, releases official government measures of consumer price inflation. Many observers question the reliability of this agency's tabulations of price indexes and inflation rates. These observers give more credence to inflation estimates tabulated and released by private economic consulting firms in Argentina.

Recently, private firms such as Econviews, Finsoport, and GRA Consultoras have released estimates of annual inflation rates for Argentina that have been more than twice as high as Indec's. Argentina's government has accused these companies of engaging in activities that "lack scientific vigor" and that "undermine confidence in the nation's economy." The government has imposed fines exceeding $120,000 for publicly releasing inflation estimates that differ substantially from those of Indec. Today, most private companies in Argentina that independently tabulate price index and inflation data will provide them only to private customers at a price—and under the condition of confidentiality.

FOR CRITICAL THINKING

Argentina's government offers extra payments based on Indec's inflation tabulations to induce savers to buy its bonds. Could this explain its concern about competing private inflation estimates? Explain.

QUICK QUIZ See page 160 for the answers. Review concepts from this section in MyEconLab.

Once we pick a market basket of goods, we can construct a **price index** that compares the cost of that market basket today with the cost of the same market basket in a _____ year.

The _____ _____ Index is the most often used price index in the United States. The **Producer Price Index (PPI)** is also widely mentioned.

The _____ _____ measures what is happening to the average price level of *all* new, domestically produced final goods and services in our economy.

The _____ _____ _____ Index uses annually updated weights from consumer spending surveys to measure average prices faced by consumers.

Anticipated versus Unanticipated Inflation

To determine who is hurt by inflation and what the effects of inflation are in general, we have to distinguish between anticipated and unanticipated inflation. We will see that the effects on individuals and the economy are vastly different, depending on which type of inflation exists.

    Anticipated inflation is the rate of inflation that most individuals believe will occur. If the rate of inflation this year turns out to be 5 percent, and that's about what most people thought it was going to be, we are in a situation of fully anticipated inflation.

    Unanticipated inflation is inflation that comes as a surprise to individuals in the economy. For example, if the inflation rate in a particular year turns out to be 10 percent when, on average, people thought it was going to be 3 percent, there was unanticipated inflation—inflation greater than anticipated.

    Some of the problems caused by inflation arise when it is unanticipated, because then many people are unable to protect themselves from its ravages. Keeping the distinction between anticipated and unanticipated inflation in mind, we can easily see the relationship between inflation and interest rates.

Anticipated inflation
The inflation rate that we believe will occur. When it does occur, we are in a situation of fully anticipated inflation.

Unanticipated inflation
Inflation at a rate that comes as a surprise, either higher or lower than the rate anticipated.

Inflation and Interest Rates

Let's start in a hypothetical world in which there is no inflation and anticipated inflation is zero. In that world, you may be able to borrow funds—to buy a house or a car, for example—at a **nominal rate of interest** of, say, 6 percent. If you borrow the funds to purchase a house or a car and your anticipation of inflation turns out to be accurate, neither you nor the lender will have been fooled. Each dollar you pay back in the years to come will be just as valuable in terms of purchasing power as the dollar that you borrowed.

    What you ordinarily want to know when you borrow is the *real* rate of interest that you will have to pay. The **real rate of interest** is defined as the nominal rate of interest minus the anticipated rate of inflation. In effect, we can say that the nominal rate of interest is equal to the real rate of interest plus an *inflationary premium* to take account of anticipated inflation. That inflationary premium covers depreciation in the purchasing power of the dollars repaid by borrowers. (Whenever there are relatively high rates of anticipated inflation, we must add an additional factor to the inflationary premium—the product of the real rate of interest times the anticipated rate of inflation. Usually, this last term is omitted because the anticipated rate of inflation is not high enough to make much of a difference.)

Nominal rate of interest
The market rate of interest observed in contracts expressed in today's dollars.

Real rate of interest
The nominal rate of interest minus the anticipated rate of inflation.

Does Inflation Necessarily Hurt Everyone?

Most people think that inflation is bad. After all, inflation means higher prices, and when we have to pay higher prices, are we not necessarily worse off? The truth is that inflation affects different people differently. Its effects also depend on whether it is anticipated or unanticipated.

UNANTICIPATED INFLATION: CREDITORS LOSE AND DEBTORS GAIN In most situations, unanticipated inflation benefits borrowers because the nominal interest rate they are being charged does not fully compensate creditors for the inflation that actually occurred. In other words, the lender did not anticipate inflation correctly. Whenever inflation rates are underestimated for the life of a loan, creditors lose and debtors gain. Periods of considerable unanticipated (higher than anticipated) inflation occurred in the late 1960s and all of the 1970s. During those years, creditors lost and debtors gained.

PROTECTING AGAINST INFLATION Lenders attempt to protect themselves against inflation by raising nominal interest rates to reflect anticipated inflation. Adjustable-rate mortgages in fact do just that: The interest rate varies according to what happens to interest rates in the economy. Workers can protect themselves from inflation by obtaining **cost-of-living adjustments (COLAs),** which are automatic increases in wage rates to take account of increases in the price level.

To the extent that you hold non-interest-bearing cash, you will lose because of inflation. If you have put $100 in a mattress and the inflation rate is 5 percent for the year, you will have lost 5 percent of the purchasing power of that $100. If you have your funds in a non-interest-bearing checking account, you will suffer the same fate. Individuals attempt to reduce the cost of holding cash by putting it into interest-bearing accounts, some of which pay nominal rates of interest that reflect anticipated inflation.

THE RESOURCE COST OF INFLATION Some economists believe that the main cost of inflation is the opportunity cost of resources used to protect against distortions that inflation introduces as firms attempt to plan for the long run. Individuals have to spend time and resources to figure out ways to adjust their behavior in case inflation is different from what it has been in the past. That may mean spending a longer time working out more complicated contracts for employment, for purchases of goods in the future, and for purchases of raw materials to be delivered later.

Inflation requires that price lists be changed. This is called the **repricing,** or **menu, cost of inflation.** The higher the rate of inflation, the higher the repricing cost of inflation, because prices must be changed more often within a given period of time.

Cost-of-living adjustments (COLAs)
Clauses in contracts that allow for increases in specified nominal values to take account of changes in the cost of living.

Repricing, or menu, cost of inflation
The cost associated with recalculating prices and printing new price lists when there is inflation.

QUICK QUIZ   See page 160 for the answers. Review concepts from this section in MyEconLab.

Whenever inflation is _____ than anticipated, creditors lose and debtors gain. Whenever the rate of inflation is _____ than anticipated, creditors gain and debtors lose.

Holders of cash lose during periods of inflation because the _____ _____ of their cash depreciates at the rate of inflation.

Households and businesses spend resources in attempting to protect themselves against the prospect of inflation, thus imposing a _____ cost on the economy.

Changing Inflation and Unemployment: Business Fluctuations

Business fluctuations
The ups and downs in business activity throughout the economy.

Expansion
A business fluctuation in which the pace of national economic activity is speeding up.

Contraction
A business fluctuation during which the pace of national economic activity is slowing down.

Some years unemployment goes up, and some years it goes down. Some years there is a lot of inflation, and other years there isn't. We have fluctuations in all aspects of our macroeconomy. The ups and downs in economywide economic activity are sometimes called **business fluctuations.** When business fluctuations are positive, they are called **expansions**—speedups in the pace of national economic activity. The opposite of an expansion is a **contraction,** which is a slowdown in the pace of national economic activity. The top of an expansion is usually called its *peak,* and the bottom of a contraction is usually called its *trough.* Business fluctuations used to be called *business cycles,* but that term no longer seems appropriate because *cycle* implies regular or automatic recurrence, and we have never had automatic recurrent fluctuations in general business and

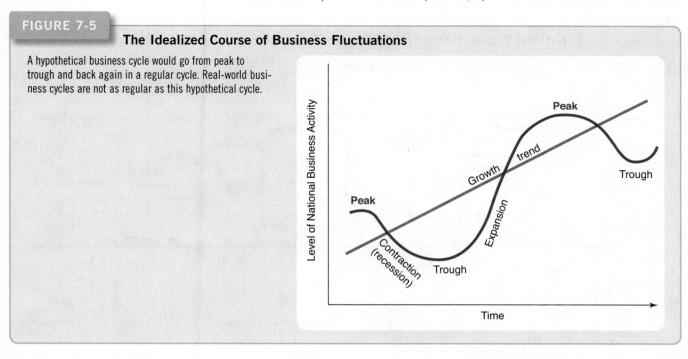

FIGURE 7-5

The Idealized Course of Business Fluctuations

A hypothetical business cycle would go from peak to trough and back again in a regular cycle. Real-world business cycles are not as regular as this hypothetical cycle.

economic activity. What we have had are contractions and expansions that vary greatly in length. For example, the 10 post–World War II expansions have averaged 57 months, but three of those exceeded 90 months, and two lasted less than 25 months.

If the contractionary phase of business fluctuations becomes severe enough, we call it a **recession.** An extremely severe recession is called a **depression.** Typically, at the beginning of a recession, there is a marked increase in the rate of unemployment, and the duration of unemployment increases. In addition, people's incomes start to decline. In times of expansion, the opposite occurs.

In Figure 7-5 above, you see that typical business fluctuations occur around a growth trend in overall national business activity shown as a straight upward-sloping line. Starting out at a peak, the economy goes into a contraction (recession). Then an expansion starts that moves up to its peak, higher than the last one, and the sequence starts over again.

Recession
A period of time during which the rate of growth of business activity is consistently less than its long-term trend or is negative.

Depression
An extremely severe recession.

A Historical Picture of Business Activity in the United States

Figure 7-6 on the following page traces changes in U.S. business activity from 1880 to the present. Note that the long-term trend line is shown as horizontal, so all changes in business activity focus around that trend line. Major changes in business activity in the United States occurred during the Great Depression, World War II, and, most recently, the sharp recession of the late 2000s. Note that none of the actual business fluctuations in Figure 7-6, exactly mirror the idealized course of a business fluctuation shown in Figure 7-5 above.

Go to **www.econtoday.com/chap07** to learn how economists at the National Bureau of Economic Research formally determine when a recession started.

Explaining Business Fluctuations: External Shocks

As you might imagine, because changes in national business activity affect everyone, economists for decades have attempted to understand and explain business fluctuations. For years, one of the most obvious explanations has been external events that tend to disrupt the economy. In many of the graphs in this chapter, you have seen that World War II was a critical point in this nation's economic history. A war is certainly an external shock—something that originates outside our economy.

In trying to help account for shocks to economic activity that may induce business fluctuations and thereby make fluctuations easier to predict, the U.S. Department of Commerce and private firms and organizations tabulate indexes (weighted averages) of

FIGURE 7-6

National Business Activity, 1880 to the Present

Variations around the trend of U.S. business activity have been frequent since 1880.

Sources: American Business Activity from 1790 to Today, 67th ed., AmeriTrust Co., January 1996, plus author's estimates.

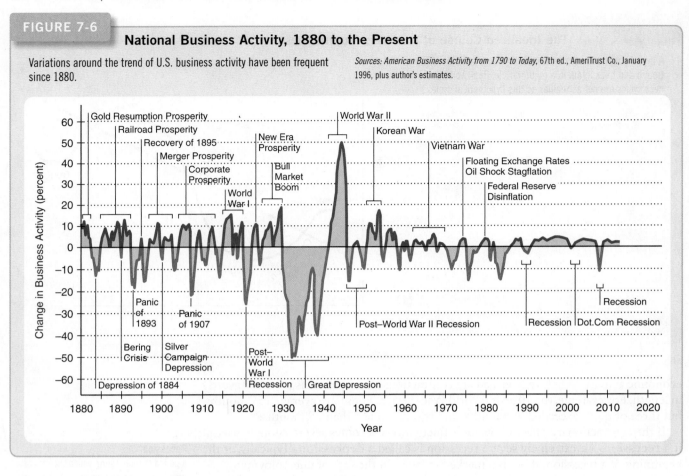

leading indicators. These are events that economists have noticed typically occur *before* changes in business activity. For example, economic downturns often follow such events as a reduction in the average workweek, an increase in unemployment insurance claims, a decrease in the prices of raw materials, or a drop in the quantity of money in circulation.

What new measure are economists at the Bank of England thinking of adding to their list of leading economic indicators?

Leading indicators
Events that have been found to occur before changes in business activity.`

INTERNATIONAL POLICY EXAMPLE

Internet Search Activity as a Leading Indicator

Economists at the Bank of England are studying the volume of Internet searches as a leading indicator of economic activity. The economists have found that Web search activity possesses appealing leading-indicator properties. First, Internet search data are readily available on a daily basis. Second, nearly 60 percent of the United Kingdom's adult population now regularly engages in Web searches every day. Third, evidence is increasing that the volume of online searches is related to key measures of economic activity, such as transactions in housing and labor markets. Thus, the Bank of

England is already employing data on Internet search volumes as leading indicators of activity in each of these sectors of the British economy. Its economists are experimenting with using these data as overall economic indicators.

FOR CRITICAL THINKING

Why are Bank of England economists seeking to determine whether the number of searches is closely related to purchases of goods and services from businesses?

To better understand the role of shocks in influencing business fluctuations, we need a theory of why national economic activity changes. The remainder of the macro chapters in this book develop the models that will help you understand the ups and downs of our business fluctuations.

QUICK QUIZ See page 160 for the answers. Review concepts from this section in MyEconLab.

The ups and downs in economywide business activity are called _____ _____, which consist of **expansions** and **contractions** in overall business activity.

The lowest point of a contraction is called the _____.
The highest point of an expansion is called the _____.

A _____ is a downturn in business activity for some length of time.

One possible explanation for business fluctuations relates to _____ _____, such as wars, dramatic increases in the prices of raw materials, and earthquakes, floods, and droughts.

YOU ARE THERE
Struggling to Hire with the Unemployment Rate above 8 Percent

Jack Kelly, chief executive officer of Hamill Manufacturing, is looking for people to hire, as the company seeks to replace older skilled workers who are choosing to retire. Even though millions of U.S. residents are unemployed and seeking work, Kelly is having trouble filling a handful of open positions. Kelly has received many applications. So far, however, none of the applicants possesses the skills required to operate and repair computer-controlled metal-shaping equipment.

Key skills sought by Kelly are not far beyond those that students can learn in high school courses in trigonometry and science. Kelly's problem is that most students who take such courses in high school go on to college and never consider a career as a skilled manufacturing laborer earning as much as $80,000 per year. Among the non-college-bound high school graduates who might consider such a position, it is rare to find one who has learned enough math and science even to begin to know how to set up and direct the firm's machinery. Thus, although thousands of people are unemployed in the area near Hamill's manufacturing facilities, Kelly finds it difficult to fill positions that have been open for several months. Amid a sea of unemployment, Kelly cannot find anyone to hire.

Critical Thinking Questions
1. What type of unemployment issue is Kelly confronting?
2. Is Kelly's failure to hire contributing to higher natural unemployment? Explain.

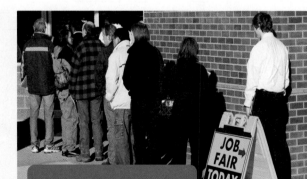

ISSUES & APPLICATIONS

Have Unemployment Benefits Boosted Unemployment?

CONCEPTS APPLIED
▶ Unemployment Rate
▶ Cyclical Unemployment
▶ Structural Unemployment

Between June 2008 and February 2009, the U.S. unemployment rate rose sharply, from 5.6 percent to more than 8 percent. Although the recession officially ended in June 2009, the unemployment rate ultimately reached a peak of 10.1 percent in October 2009. Since then, the unemployment rate has stayed near 8 percent. Thus, the unemployment rate remained above its prior level by at least 2 percentage points for more than three years. Many economists conclude that structural unemployment has risen. One element contributing to this rise, they suggest, was a substantial increase in the length of time the government paid benefits to unemployed workers.

The Significant Extension of Unemployment Benefits

People who lose jobs and are unable to find new positions are eligible for government unemployment benefits. Traditionally, these benefits constitute a form of insurance. Employers have long contributed to a government fund from which benefit payments to unemployed workers can be drawn for intervals up to 26 weeks. Nevertheless, during business contractions, Congress commonly has dipped into taxpayer funds to extend the duration of unemployment benefits. Such extensions typically have lasted for periods of about 15 weeks.

During 2008 and 2009, however, Congress nearly *quadrupled* the duration of unemployment benefits, to 99 weeks. This lengthened stream of government benefits reduced the incentive to find new jobs. As a consequence, many people spent more time searching for jobs that they hoped might be "better" instead of seeking out work that might have been more readily obtainable. So, the unemployment-benefits extension to 99 weeks tended to drive up structural unemployment and increase the measured unemployment rate.

The Benefits Extension's Impact on Structural Unemployment

Economists at the Federal Reserve Bank of San Francisco have estimated that the increase in unemployment benefits was sufficient to boost the U.S. unemployment rate by about 0.4 percentage point. Robert Barro of Harvard University has estimated a much larger effect—in excess of 2.7 percentage points.

Most other estimates of the benefits extension's impact on structural unemployment are about midway between these two extremes. If these "midpoint estimates" are correct, then the government's action to extend the duration of unemployment benefits by a factor of nearly four raised the U.S. unemployment rate by approximately 1.5 percentage points.

For Critical Thinking

1. What else might have accounted for an increase in structural unemployment in recent years? (Hint: Take a look back at the definition of structural unemployment on page 144.)
2. Given that the recession officially ended in June 2009, why might some economists contend that very little of the persistently high unemployment is cyclical unemployment?

Web Resources

1. Learn how economists at the Federal Reserve Bank of San Francisco obtained their estimate of the impact of extended unemployment benefits on structural unemployment at www.econtoday.com/chap07.
2. Read about how Robert Barro arrived at his much larger estimate of the effect of extended unemployment benefits on structural unemployment at www.econtoday.com/chap07.

MyEconLab

For more questions on this chapter's Issues & Applications, go to MyEconLab. In the Study Plan for this chapter, select Section N: News.

MyEconLab

Here is what you should know after reading this chapter. MyEconLab will help you identify what you know, and where to go when you need to practice.

WHAT YOU SHOULD KNOW

How the U.S. Government Calculates the Official Unemployment Rate The total number of workers who are officially unemployed consists of noninstitutionalized people aged 16 or older who are willing and able to work and who are actively looking for work but have not found a job. To calculate the unemployment rate, the government determines what percentage this quantity is of the labor force, which consists of all noninstitutionalized people aged 16 years or older who either have jobs or are available for and actively seeking employment.

unemployment, 140
labor force, 140
stock, 142
flow, 142
job loser, 142
reentrant, 142
job leaver, 142
new entrant, 142
discouraged workers, 143
labor force participation rate, 143

Key Figure
Figure 7-3, 142

WHERE TO GO TO PRACTICE

- MyEconLab Study Plan 7.1
- Animated Figure 7-3

MyEconLab continued

WHAT YOU SHOULD KNOW		WHERE TO GO TO PRACTICE
The Types of Unemployment Temporarily unemployed workers who are searching for appropriate job offers are frictionally unemployed. The structurally unemployed lack the skills currently required by prospective employers. People unemployed due to business contractions are cyclically unemployed. Seasonal patterns of occupations within specific industries generate seasonal unemployment.	frictional unemployment, 144 structural unemployment, 144 cyclical unemployment, 145 seasonal unemployment, 145 full employment, 146 natural rate of unemployment, 146	• **MyEconLab** Study Plans 7.2, 7.3
How Price Indexes Are Calculated and Key Price Indexes To calculate any price index, economists multiply 100 times the ratio of the cost of a market basket of goods and services in the current year to the cost of the same market basket in a base year. The Consumer Price Index (CPI) is computed using a weighted set of goods and services purchased by a typical consumer in urban areas. The Producer Price Index (PPI) is a weighted average of prices of goods sold by a typical firm. The GDP deflator measures changes in the overall level of prices of all goods produced during a given interval. The Personal Consumption Expenditure (PCE) Index is a measure of average prices using weights from surveys of consumer spending.	inflation, 146 deflation, 146 purchasing power, 147 price index, 147 base year, 147 Consumer Price Index (CPI), 148 Producer Price Index (PPI), 148 GDP deflator, 148 Personal Consumption Expenditure (PCE) Index, 148 **Key Figure** Figure 7-4, 150	• **MyEconLab** Study Plan 7.4 • Animated Figure 7-4
Nominal Interest Rate versus Real Interest Rate The nominal interest rate applies to contracts expressed in current dollars. The real interest rate is net of inflation anticipated to erode the value of nominal interest payments during the period that a loan is repaid. Hence, the real interest rate equals the nominal interest rate minus the expected inflation rate.	anticipated inflation, 151 unanticipated inflation, 151 nominal rate of interest, 151 real rate of interest, 151	• **MyEconLab** Study Plan 7.5
Losers and Gainers from Inflation Creditors lose as a result of unanticipated inflation, because the real value of the interest payments they receive will turn out to be lower than they had expected. Borrowers gain when unanticipated inflation occurs, because the real value of their interest and principal payments declines. Key costs of inflation include expenses of protecting against inflation, costs of altering business plans because of unexpected changes in prices, and menu costs of repricing goods and services.	cost-of-living adjustments (COLAs), 152 repricing, or menu, cost of inflation, 152	• **MyEconLab** Study Plan 7.5

MyEconLab *continued*

─── WHAT YOU SHOULD KNOW ───

─── WHERE TO GO TO PRACTICE ───

Key Features of Business Fluctuations
Business fluctuations are increases and decreases in business activity. A positive fluctuation is an expansion, which is an upward movement in business activity from a trough, or low point, to a peak, or high point. A negative fluctuation is a contraction, which is a drop in the pace of business activity from a previous peak to a new trough.

business fluctuations, 152
expansion, 152
contraction, 152
recession, 153
depression, 153
leading indicators, 154

Key Figure
Figure 7-6, 154

- MyEconLab Study Plan 7.6
- Animated Figure 7-6

Log in to MyEconLab, take a chapter test, and get a personalized Study Plan that tells you which concepts you understand and which ones you need to review. From there, MyEconLab will give you further practice, tutorials, animations, videos, and guided solutions. For more information, visit www.myeconlab.com

PROBLEMS

All problems are assignable in MyEconLab; *exercises that update with real-time data are marked with* 〰. *Answers to odd-numbered problems appear at the back of the book.*

7-1. Suppose that you are given the following information (see page 140):

Total population	300.0 million
Adult, noninstitutionalized, nonmilitary population	200.0 million
Unemployment	7.5 million

   a. If the labor force participation rate is 70 percent, what is the labor force?

   b. How many workers are employed?

   c. What is the unemployment rate?

7-2. Suppose that you are given the following information (see page 140):

Labor force	206.2 million
Adults in the military	1.5 million
Nonadult population	48.0 million
Employed adults	196.2 million
Institutionalized adults	3.5 million
Nonmilitary, noninstitutionalized adults not in labor force	40.8 million

   a. What is the total population?

   b. How many people are unemployed, and what is the unemployment rate?

   c. What is the labor force participation rate?

7-3. Suppose that the U.S. nonmilitary, noninstitutionalized adult population is 224 million, the number employed is 156 million, and the number unemployed is 8 million. (See page 140.)

   a. What is the unemployment rate?

   b. Suppose that there is a difference of 60 million between the adult population and the combined total of people who are employed and unemployed. How do we classify these 60 million people? Based on these figures, what is the U.S. labor force participation rate?

7-4. During the course of a year, the labor force consists of the same 1,000 people. Employers have chosen not to hire 20 of these people in the face of government regulations making it too costly to employ them. Hence, they remain unemployed throughout the year. At the same time, every month during the year, 30 different people become unemployed, and 30 other different people who were unemployed find jobs. There is no seasonal employment. (See pages 142–144.)

   a. What is the frictional unemployment rate?

   b. What is the unemployment rate?

   c. Suppose that a system of unemployment compensation is established. Each month, 30 new people (not including the 20 that employers have chosen not to employ) continue to become unemployed, but each monthly group of newly unemployed now takes two months to find a job. After this change, what is the frictional unemployment rate?

    d. After the change discussed in part (c), what is the unemployment rate?

7-5. Suppose that a nation has a labor force of 100 people. In January, Amy, Barbara, Carine, and Denise are unemployed. In February, those four find jobs, but Evan, Francesco, George, and Horatio become unemployed. Suppose further that every month, the previous four who were unemployed find jobs and four different people become unemployed. Throughout the year, however, three people—Ito, Jack, and Kelley—continually remain unemployed because firms facing government regulations view them as too costly to employ. (See page 144.)

    a. What is this nation's frictional unemployment rate?

    b. What is its structural unemployment rate?

    c. What is its unemployment rate?

7-6. In a country with a labor force of 200, a different group of 10 people becomes unemployed each month, but becomes employed once again a month later. No others outside these groups are unemployed. (See pages 142–144.)

    a. What is this country's unemployment rate?

    b. What is the average duration of unemployment?

    c. Suppose that establishment of a system of unemployment compensation increases to two months the interval that it takes each group of job losers to become employed each month. Nevertheless, a different group of 10 people still becomes unemployed each month. Now what is the average duration of unemployment?

    d. Following the change discussed in part (c), what is the country's unemployment rate?

7-7. A nation's frictional unemployment rate is 1 percent. Seasonal unemployment does not exist in this country. Its cyclical rate of unemployment is 3 percent, and its structural unemployment rate is 4 percent. What is this nation's overall rate of unemployment? (See pages 144–145.)

7-8. In 2012, the cost of a market basket of goods was $2,000. In 2014, the cost of the same market basket of goods was $2,100. Use the price index formula to calculate the price index for 2014 if 2012 is the base year. (See pages 147–148.)

7-9. Suppose that in 2013, a typical U.S. student attending a state-supported college bought 10 textbooks at a price of $100 per book and enrolled in 25 credit hours of coursework at a price of $360 per credit hour. In 2014, the typical student continued to purchase 10 textbooks and enroll in 25 credit hours, but the price of a textbook rose to $110 per book, and the tuition price increased to $400 per credit hour. The base year for computing a "student price index" using this information is 2013. What is the value of the student price index in 2013? In 2014? Show your work. (See pages 147–148.)

7-10. Between 2013 and 2014 in a particular nation, the value of the consumer price index—for which the base year is 2010—rose by 9.091 percent, to a value of 120 in 2014. What was the value of the price index in 2013? (See pages 147–148.)

7-11. Consider the following price indexes: 90 in 2013, 100 in 2014, 110 in 2015, 121 in 2016, and 150 in 2017. Answer the following questions. (See pages 147–148.)

    a. Which year is likely the base year?

    b. What is the inflation rate from 2014 to 2015?

    c. What is the inflation rate from 2015 to 2016?

    d. If the cost of a market basket in 2014 is $2,000, what is the cost of the same basket of goods and services in 2013? In 2017?

7-12. The real interest rate is 4 percent, and the nominal interest rate is 6 percent. What is the anticipated rate of inflation? (See page 151.)

7-13. Currently, the price index used to calculate the inflation rate is equal to 90. The general expectation throughout the economy is that next year its value will be 99. The current nominal interest rate is 12 percent. What is the real interest rate? (See page 151.)

7-14. At present, the nominal interest rate is 7 percent, and the expected inflation rate is 5 percent. The current year is the base year for the price index used to calculate inflation. (See page 151.)

    a. What is the real interest rate?

    b. What is the anticipated value of the price index next year?

7-15. Suppose that in 2017 there is a sudden, unanticipated burst of inflation. Consider the situations faced by the following individuals. Who gains and who loses? (See pages 151–152.)

    a. A homeowner whose wages will keep pace with inflation in 2017 but whose monthly mortgage payments to a savings bank will remain fixed

    b. An apartment landlord who has guaranteed to his tenants that their monthly rent payments during 2017 will be the same as they were during 2016

    c. A banker who made an auto loan that the auto buyer will repay at a fixed rate of interest during 2017

    d. A retired individual who earns a pension with fixed monthly payments from her past employer during 2017

7-16. Consider the diagram at the right. The line represents the economy's growth trend, and the curve represents the economy's actual course of business fluctuations. For each part below, provide the letter label from the portion of the curve that corresponds to the associated term. (See page 153.)

a. Contraction

b. Peak

c. Trough

d. Expansion

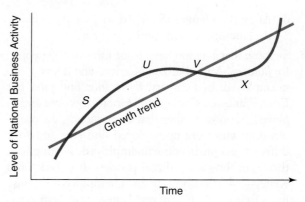

ECONOMICS ON THE NET

Looking at the Unemployment and Inflation Data This chapter reviewed key concepts relating to unemployment and inflation. In this application, you get a chance to examine U.S. unemployment and inflation data on your own.

Title: Bureau of Labor Statistics: Employment and Unemployment

Navigation: Use the link at **www.econtoday.com/chap07** to visit the "Employment" page of the Bureau of Labor Statistics (BLS). Click on "Top Picks" next to *Labor Force Statistics (Current Population Survey–CPS)*.

Application Perform the indicated operations, and answer the following questions.

1. Retrieve data for Civilian Labor Force Level, Employment Level, and Unemployment Level. Can you identify periods of sharp cyclical swings? Do they show up in data for the labor force, employment, or unemployment?

2. Are cyclical factors important?

For Group Study and Analysis Divide the class into groups, and assign a price index to each group. Ask each group to take a look at the index for All Years at the link to the BLS statistics on inflation at **www.econtoday.com /chap07**. Have each group identify periods during which their index accelerated or decelerated (or even fell). Do the indexes ever provide opposing implications about inflation and deflation?

ANSWERS TO QUICK QUIZZES

p. 143: (i) Unemployed . . . labor force; (ii) job losers . . . reentrants . . . job leavers . . . new entrants; (iii) increase; (iv) female

p. 146: (i) **Frictional;** (ii) **Structural;** (iii) natural

p. 151: (i) base; (ii) Consumer Price; (iii) GDP deflator; (iv) Personal Consumption Expenditure

p. 152: (i) greater . . . less; (ii) purchasing power; (iii) resource

p. 155: (i) business fluctuations; (ii) trough . . . peak; (iii) recession; (iv) external shocks

Measuring the Economy's Performance

8

LEARNING OBJECTIVES

After reading this chapter, you should be able to:

▶ Describe the circular flow of income and output

▶ Define gross domestic product (GDP)

▶ Understand the limitations of using GDP as a measure of national welfare

▶ Explain the expenditure approach to tabulating GDP

▶ Explain the income approach to computing GDP

▶ Distinguish between nominal GDP and real GDP

MyEconLab helps you master each objective and study more efficiently. See end of chapter for details.

Some commentators are already referring to the twenty-first century as the "Asian century." In contrast to the dampened economies of the United States and Europe, economic activity has been booming in China, Hong Kong, Singapore, South Korea, Taiwan, and other Asian countries. Some media reports are suggesting that China's economy will be "larger" than the U.S. economy by 2020. How might we go about trying to measure an economy's "size"? How could we then compare its "size" to the economy of another nation? The starting point for contemplating these questions is the market value of all final goods and services produced within a nation's borders during a given year. Economists refer to this quantity as *gross domestic product*, or *GDP*, which is a key concept covered in this chapter

National income accounting
A measurement system used to estimate national income and its components. One approach to measuring an economy's aggregate performance.

the flow of U.S. economic activity since June 2009, when the 2008–2009 recession officially ended, has been more dampened than during any other comparable postrecession period since the Great Depression of the 1930s? To measure the nation's overall economic performance over time, the government utilizes what has become known as **national income accounting**. How this measurement is done is the main focus of this chapter. But first we need to look at the flow of income within an economy, for it is the flow of goods and services from businesses to consumers and of payments from consumers to businesses, that constitutes economic activity.

The Simple Circular Flow

The concept of a circular flow of income (ignoring taxes) involves two principles:

1. In every economic exchange, the seller receives exactly the same amount that the buyer spends.

2. Goods and services flow in one direction and money payments flow in the other.

In the simple economy shown in Figure 8-1 below, there are only businesses and households. It is assumed that businesses sell their *entire* output in the current period to households and that households spend their *entire* income in the current period on consumer products. Households receive their income by selling the use of whatever factors of production they own, such as labor services.

FIGURE 8-1

The Circular Flow of Income and Product

Businesses provide final goods and services to households (upper clockwise loop), who in turn pay for them (upper counterclockwise loop). Payments flow in a counterclockwise direction and can be thought of as a circular flow. The dollar value of output is identical to total income because profits are defined as being equal to total business receipts minus business outlays for wages, rents, and interest. Households provide factor services to businesses and receive income (lower loops).

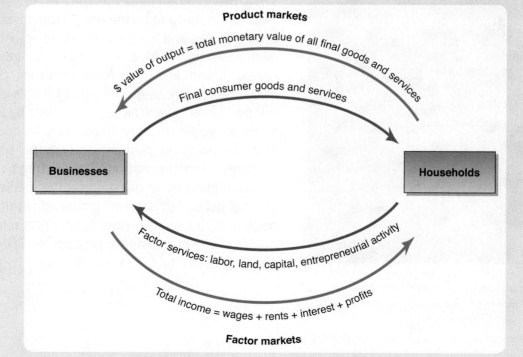

Profits Explained

We have indicated in Figure 8-1 on the facing page that profit is a cost of production. You might be under the impression that profits are not part of the cost of producing goods and services, but profits are indeed a part of this cost because entrepreneurs must be rewarded for providing their services or they won't provide them. Their reward, if any, is profit. The reward—the profit—is included in the cost of the factors of production. If there were no expectations of profit, entrepreneurs would not incur the risk associated with the organization of productive activities. That is why we consider profits a cost of doing business. Just as workers expect wages, entrepreneurs expect profits.

Total Income or Total Output

The arrow that goes from businesses to households at the bottom of Figure 8-1 is labeled "Total income." What would be a good definition of **total income?** If you answered "the total of all individuals' income," you would be right. But all income is actually a payment for something, whether it be wages paid for labor services, rent paid for the use of land, interest paid for the use of capital, or profits paid to entrepreneurs. It is the amount paid to the resource suppliers. Therefore, total income is also defined as the annual *cost* of producing the entire output of **final goods and services.**

The arrow going from households to businesses at the top of Figure 8-1 represents the dollar value of output in the economy. This is equal to the total monetary value of all final goods and services for this simple economy. In essence, it represents the total business receipts from the sale of all final goods and services produced by businesses and consumed by households. Business receipts are the opposite side of household expenditures. When households purchase goods and services, those payments become a *business receipt.* Every transaction, therefore, simultaneously involves an expenditure and a receipt.

PRODUCT MARKETS Transactions in which households buy goods take place in the product markets—that's where households are the buyers and businesses are the sellers of consumer goods. *Product market* transactions are represented in the upper loops in Figure 8-1 on the facing page. Note that consumer goods and services flow to household demanders, while money flows in the opposite direction to business suppliers.

FACTOR MARKETS *Factor market* transactions are represented by the lower loops in Figure 8-1. In the factor market, households are the sellers. They sell resources such as labor, land, capital, and entrepreneurial ability. Businesses are the buyers in factor markets. Business expenditures represent receipts or, more simply, income for households. Also, in the lower loops of Figure 8-1, factor services flow from households to businesses, while the payments for these services flow in the opposite direction from businesses to households. Observe also the flow of money (counterclockwise) from households to businesses and back again from businesses to households: It is an endless circular flow.

Why the Dollar Value of Total Output Must Equal Total Income

Total income represents the income received by households in payment for the production of goods and services. Why must total income be identical to the dollar value of total output? First, as Figure 8-1 shows, spending by one group is income to another. Second, it is a matter of simple accounting and the economic definition of profit as a cost of production. Profit is defined as what is *left over* from total business receipts after all other costs—wages, rents, interest—have been paid. If the dollar value of total output is $1,000 and the total of wages, rent, and interest for producing that output is $900, profit is $100. Profit is always the *residual* item that makes total income equal to the dollar value of total output.

Total income
The yearly amount earned by the nation's resources (factors of production). Total income therefore includes wages, rent, interest payments, and profits that are received by workers, landowners, capital owners, and entrepreneurs, respectively.

Final goods and services
Goods and services that are at their final stage of production and will not be transformed into yet other goods or services. For example, wheat ordinarily is not considered a final good because it is usually used to make a final good, bread.

QUICK QUIZ   See page 186 for the answers. Review concepts from this section in MyEconLab.

In the circular flow model of income and output, households sell _____ services to businesses that pay for those services. The receipt of payments is total _____. Businesses sell goods and services to households that pay for them.

The dollar value of total output is equal to the total monetary value of all _____ goods and services produced.

The dollar value of final output must always equal total income. The variable that adjusts to make this so is known as _____.

National Income Accounting

We have already mentioned that policymakers require information about the state of the national economy. Economists use historical statistical records on the performance of the national economy for testing their theories about how the economy really works. Thus, national income accounting is important. Let's start with the most commonly presented statistic on the national economy.

Gross Domestic Product (GDP)

Gross domestic product (GDP)
The total market value of all final goods and services produced during a year by factors of production located within a nation's borders.

Gross domestic product (GDP) represents the total market value of the nation's annual final product, or output, produced by factors of production located within national borders. We therefore formally define GDP as the total market value of all final goods and services produced in an economy during a year. We are referring here to the value of a *flow of production*. A nation produces at a certain rate, just as you receive income at a certain rate. Your income flow might be at a rate of $20,000 per year or $100,000 per year. Suppose you are told that someone earns $5,000. Would you consider this a good salary? There is no way to answer that question unless you know whether the person is earning $5,000 per month or per week or per day. Thus, you have to specify a time period for all flows. Income received is a flow. You must contrast this with, for example, your total accumulated savings, which are a stock measured at a point in time, not over time. Implicit in just about everything we deal with in this chapter is a time period—usually one year. All the measures of domestic product and income are specified as *rates* measured in dollars per year.

Stress on Final Output

Intermediate goods
Goods used up entirely in the production of final goods.

Value added
The dollar value of an industry's sales minus the value of intermediate goods (for example, raw materials and parts) used in production.

GDP does not count **intermediate goods** (goods used up entirely in the production of final goods) because to do so would be to count them twice. For example, even though grain that a farmer produces may be that farmer's final product, it is not the final product for the nation. It is sold to make bread. Bread is the final product.

We can use a numerical example to clarify this point further. Our example will involve determining the value added at each stage of production. **Value added** is the dollar value contributed to a product at each stage of its production. In Table 8-1 on the facing page, we see the difference between total value of all sales and value added in the production of a donut. We also see that the sum of the values added is equal to the sale price to the final consumer. It is the 45 cents that is used to measure GDP, not the 97 cents. If we used the 97 cents, we would be double counting from stages 2 through 5, for each intermediate good would be counted at least twice—once when it was produced and again when the good it was used in making was sold. Such double counting would greatly exaggerate GDP.

TABLE 8-1

Sales Value and Value Added at Each Stage of Donut Production

(1) Stage of Production	(2) Dollar Value of Sales	(3) Value Added
Stage 1: Fertilizer and seed	$.03	$.03
Stage 2: Growing	.07	.04
Stage 3: Milling	.12	.05
Stage 4: Baking	.30	.18
Stage 5: Retailing	.45	.15

Total dollar value of all sales $.97   Total value added $.45

Stage 1: A farmer purchases 3 cents worth of fertilizer and seed, which are used as factors of production in growing wheat.

Stage 2: The farmer grows the wheat, harvests it, and sells it to a miller for 7 cents. Thus, we see that the farmer has added 4 cents' worth of value. Those 4 cents represent income over and above expenses incurred by the farmer.

Stage 3: The miller purchases the wheat for 7 cents and adds 5 cents as the value added. That is, there is 5 cents for the miller as income. The miller sells the ground wheat flour to a donut-baking company.

Stage 4: The donut-baking company buys the flour for 12 cents and adds 18 cents as the value added. It then sells the donut to the final retailer.

Stage 5: The donut retailer sells donuts at 45 cents apiece, thus creating an additional value of 15 cents.

We see that the total value of the transactions involved in the production of one donut is 97 cents, but the total value added is 45 cents, which is exactly equal to the retail price. The total value added is equal to the sum of all income payments.

Exclusion of Financial Transactions, Transfer Payments, and Secondhand Goods

Remember that GDP is the measure of the dollar value of all final goods and services produced in one year. Many more transactions occur that have nothing to do with final goods and services produced. There are financial transactions, transfers of the ownership of preexisting goods, and other transactions that should not (and do not) get included in our measure of GDP.

Go to www.econtoday.com/chap08 for the most up-to-date U.S. economic data at the Web site of the Bureau of Economic Analysis.

FINANCIAL TRANSACTIONS There are three general categories of purely financial transactions: (1) the buying and selling of securities, (2) government transfer payments, and (3) private transfer payments.

Securities When you purchase shares of existing stock in Apple, Inc., someone else has sold it to you. In essence, there was merely a *transfer* of ownership rights. You paid $100 to obtain the stock. Someone else received the $100 and gave up the stock. No producing activity was consummated at that time, unless a broker received a fee for performing the transaction, in which case only the fee is part of GDP. The $100 transaction is not included when we measure GDP.

Government Transfer Payments Transfer payments are payments for which no productive services are concurrently provided in exchange. The most obvious government transfer payments are Social Security benefits and unemployment compensation. The recipients add nothing to current production in return for such transfer payments (although they may have contributed in the past to be eligible to receive them). Government transfer payments are not included in GDP.

Private Transfer Payments Are you receiving funds from your parents in order to attend school? Has a wealthy relative ever given you a gift of cash? If so, you have been the recipient of a private transfer payment. This payment is merely a transfer of funds from one individual to another. As such, it does not constitute productive activity and is not included in GDP.

TRANSFER OF SECONDHAND GOODS If I sell you my two-year-old laptop computer, no current production is involved. I transfer to you the ownership of a computer that was produced years ago. In exchange, you transfer to me $350. The original purchase price of the computer was included in GDP in the year I purchased it. To include the price again when I sell it to you would be counting the value of the computer a second time.

OTHER EXCLUDED TRANSACTIONS Many other transactions are not included in GDP for practical reasons:

- Household production—housecleaning, child care, and other tasks performed by people in their *own* households and for which they receive no payments through the marketplace

- Otherwise legal underground transactions—those that are legal but not reported and hence not taxed, such as paying housekeepers in cash that is not declared as income to the Internal Revenue Service

- Illegal underground activities—these include prostitution, illegal gambling, and the sale of illicit drugs

YOU ARE THERE

To consider how much difference it can make if economists broaden the measure of GDP in just a few ways, read on page 180 **Has the Economy Grown More Than Official GDP Data Suggest?**

WHAT IF... market prices of housecleaning, child care, and lawn care services were valued for inclusion in GDP?

Even if the prices of household services determined in markets were used to try to place a dollar value on nonmarket household production, national income accountants still would not know annual *volumes* of such nonmarket services. Thus, to attempt to include the total value of nonmarket household production in GDP, the accountants would have to *estimate* the volumes of production performed outside markets. Then they would multiply these volumes times the market prices. The resulting new measure of GDP would be subject to likely estimation mistakes, in addition to the measurement errors that already occur. This would make GDP a less reliable measure of the overall value of final production of goods and services within U.S. borders each year.

Recognizing the Limitations of GDP

Like any statistical measure, gross domestic product is a concept that can be both well used and misused. Economists find it especially valuable as an overall indicator of a nation's economic performance. But it is important to realize that GDP has significant weaknesses. Because it includes only the value of goods and services traded in markets, it excludes *nonmarket* production, such as the household services of homemakers discussed earlier. This can cause some problems in comparing the GDP of an industrialized country with the GDP of a highly agrarian nation in which nonmarket production is relatively more important.

It also causes problems if nations have different definitions of legal versus illegal activities. For instance, a nation with legalized gambling will count the value of gambling services, which has a reported market value as a legal activity. But in a country where gambling is illegal, individuals who provide such services will not report the market value of gambling activities, and so they will not be counted in that country's GDP. This can complicate comparing GDP in the nation where gambling is legal with GDP in the country that prohibits gambling.

Furthermore, although GDP is often used as a benchmark measure for standard-of-living calculations, it is not necessarily a good measure of the well-being of a nation. No measured figure of total national annual income can take account of changes in the degree of labor market discrimination, declines or improvements in personal safety, or the quantity or quality of leisure time. Measured GDP also says little about our environmental quality of life.

As the now-defunct Soviet Union illustrated to the world, the large-scale production of such items as minerals, electricity, and irrigation for farming can have negative effects on the environment: deforestation from strip mining, air and soil pollution from particulate emissions or nuclear accidents at power plants, and erosion of the natural balance between water and salt in bodies of water such as the Aral Sea. Other nations, such as China and India, have also experienced greater pollution problems as their levels of GDP have increased. Hence, it is important to recognize the following point:

GDP is a measure of the value of production in terms of market prices and an indicator of economic activity. It is not a measure of a nation's overall welfare.

Nonetheless, GDP is a relatively accurate and useful measure of the economy's domestic economic activity, measured in current dollars. Understanding GDP is thus an important first step for analyzing changes in economic activity over time.

What new index of a country's broad economic performance has been developed by a large group of developed nations?

POLICY EXAMPLE
Developed Nations Look for a "Happier" Alternative to GDP

The thirty-four member nations of the Organization for Economic Cooperation and Development (OECD) are aiming to supplement or even replace GDP with a new gauge of a country's standard of living and well-being called "Your Better Life Index." This index is geared to measure determinants of human happiness levels. Toward this end, it tabulates a nation's "quality scores" in eleven areas: community, education, environment, governance, health, housing, income, jobs, life satisfaction, safety, and work-life balance. A nation's scores in each of these areas are based on various economic indicators and public opinion polls.

To determine how these scores should be combined to calculate a single value for each nation's Your Better Life Index, the OECD is conducting surveys of large groups of residents in each member country. Each nation's weights for the eleven sets of quality scores will differ, but the OECD plans to rate nations on the basis of their overall index values. The OECD's initial values for the Your Better Life Index yielded rankings in which Denmark, Canada, and Norway rate highest among OECD nations, with Hungary, Portugal, and Estonia rating lowest.

FOR CRITICAL THINKING
How would you determine each person's level of life satisfaction?

QUICK QUIZ
See page 186 for the answers. Review concepts from this section in MyEconLab.

_____ _____ _____ is the total market value of final goods and services produced in an economy during a one-year period by factors of production within the nation's borders. It represents the dollar value of the flow of final production over a one-year period.

To avoid double counting, we look only at final goods and services produced or, equivalently, at _____ _____.

In measuring GDP, we must _____ (1) purely financial transactions, such as the buying and selling of securities; (2) government transfer payments and private transfer payments; and (3) the transfer of secondhand goods.

Many other transactions are excluded from measured _____, among them household services rendered by homemakers, underground economy transactions, and illegal economic activities, even though many of these result in the production of final goods and services.

GDP is a useful measure for tracking changes in the _____ _____ of overall economic activity over time, but it is not a measure of the well-being of a nation's residents because it fails to account for nonmarket transactions, the amount and quality of leisure time, environmental or safety issues, labor market discrimination, and other factors that influence general welfare.

Two Main Methods of Measuring GDP

The definition of GDP is the total dollar value of all final goods and services produced during a year. How, exactly, do we go about actually computing this number?

The circular flow diagram presented in Figure 8-1 on page 162 gave us a shortcut method for calculating GDP. We can look at the *flow of expenditures*, which consists of consumption, investment, government purchases of goods and services, and net expenditures in the foreign sector (net exports). In this **expenditure approach** to measuring GDP, we add the dollar value of all final goods and services. We could also use the *flow of income*, looking at the income received by everybody producing goods and services. In this **income approach,** we add the income received by all factors of production.

Deriving GDP by the Expenditure Approach

To derive GDP using the expenditure approach, we must look at each of the separate components of expenditures and then add them together. These components are consumption expenditures, investment, government expenditures, and net exports.

CONSUMPTION EXPENDITURES How do we spend our income? As households or as individuals, we spend our income through consumption expenditure (*C*), which falls into three categories: **durable consumer goods, nondurable consumer goods,** and **services.** Durable goods are *arbitrarily* defined as items that last more than three years. They include automobiles, furniture, and household appliances. Nondurable goods are all the rest, such as food and gasoline. Services are intangible commodities: medical care, education, and the like.

Housing expenditures constitute a major proportion of anybody's annual expenditures. Rental payments on apartments are automatically included in consumption expenditure estimates. People who own their homes, however, do not make rental payments. Consequently, government statisticians estimate what is called the *implicit rental value* of existing owner-occupied homes. It is roughly equal to the amount of rent you would have to pay if you did not own the home but were renting it from someone else.

GROSS PRIVATE DOMESTIC INVESTMENT We now turn our attention to **gross private domestic investment** (*I*) undertaken by businesses. When economists refer to investment, they are referring to additions to productive capacity. **Investment** may be thought of as an activity that uses resources today in such a way that they allow for greater production in the future and hence greater consumption in the future. When a business buys new equipment or puts up a new factory, it is investing. It is increasing its capacity to produce in the future.

In estimating gross private domestic investment, government statisticians also add consumer expenditures on *new* residential structures because new housing represents an addition to our future productive capacity in the sense that a new house can generate housing services in the future.

The layperson's notion of investment often relates to the purchase of stocks and bonds. For our purposes, such transactions simply represent the *transfer of ownership* of assets called stocks and bonds. Thus, you must keep in mind the fact that in economics, investment refers *only* to *additions* to productive capacity, not to transfers of assets.

FIXED VERSUS INVENTORY INVESTMENT In our analysis, we will consider the basic components of investment. We have already mentioned the first one, which involves a firm's purchase of equipment or construction of a new factory. These are called **producer durables,** or **capital goods.** A producer durable, or a capital good, is simply a good that is purchased not to be consumed in its current form but to be used to make other goods and services. The purchase of equipment and factories—capital goods—is called **fixed investment.**

Expenditure approach
Computing GDP by adding up the dollar value at current market prices of all final goods and services.

Income approach
Measuring GDP by adding up all components of national income, including wages, interest, rent, and profits.

Durable consumer goods
Consumer goods that have a life span of more than three years.

Nondurable consumer goods
Consumer goods that are used up within three years.

Services
Mental or physical labor or assistance purchased by consumers. Examples are the assistance of physicians, lawyers, dentists, repair personnel, housecleaners, educators, retailers, and wholesalers; items purchased or used by consumers that do not have physical characteristics.

Gross private domestic investment
The creation of capital goods, such as factories and machines, that can yield production and hence consumption in the future. Also included in this definition are changes in business inventories and repairs made to machines or buildings.

Investment
Any use of today's resources to expand tomorrow's production or consumption.

Producer durables, or **capital goods**
Durable goods having an expected service life of more than three years that are used by businesses to produce other goods and services.

Fixed investment
Purchases by businesses of newly produced producer durables, or capital goods, such as production machinery and office equipment.

The other type of investment has to do with the change in inventories of raw materials and finished goods. Firms do not immediately sell off all their products to consumers. Some of this final product is usually held in inventory waiting to be sold. Firms hold inventories to meet future expected orders for their products. When a firm increases its inventories of finished products, it is engaging in **inventory investment.** Inventories consist of all finished goods on hand, goods in process, and raw materials.

The reason that we can think of a change in inventories as being a type of investment is that an increase in such inventories provides for future increased consumption possibilities. When inventory investment is zero, the firm is neither adding to nor subtracting from the total stock of goods or raw materials on hand. Thus, if the firm keeps the same amount of inventories throughout the year, inventory *investment* has been zero.

Inventory investment
Changes in the stocks of finished goods and goods in process, as well as changes in the raw materials that businesses keep on hand. Whenever inventories are decreasing, inventory investment is negative. Whenever they are increasing, inventory investment is positive.

GOVERNMENT EXPENDITURES In addition to personal consumption expenditures, there are government purchases of goods and services (*G*). The government buys goods and services from private firms and pays wages and salaries to government employees. Generally, we value goods and services at the prices at which they are sold. But many government goods and services are not sold in the market. Therefore, we cannot use their market value when computing GDP. The value of these goods is considered equal to their *cost*. For example, the value of a newly built road is considered equal to its construction cost and is included in the GDP for the year it was built.

What portion of official U.S. GDP comprises transactions not directly valued in terms of actual market prices?

EXAMPLE

Imputing Part of the Government's Contribution to GDP

A number of items included in U.S. GDP are not explicitly priced in markets. This is particularly true of a significant portion of the government's provision of goods such as public education, fire protection, and national defense. National income accountants have decided that government expenditures on these activities understate the values they would have if private firms provided them in private markets. Thus, the accountants "impute" dollar amounts to these items by valuing them in terms of prices determined in markets for privately produced education, fire protection, and security services.

In recent years, imputed values of such government-provided activities have constituted as much as 15 percent of GDP. As the share of GDP involving activities by federal, state, and local governments continues to rise, this percentage likely will increase as well.

FOR CRITICAL THINKING

If governmental payments for educational services exceed families' valuations of those services, does the imputing process overstate or understate public education's contribution to GDP?

NET EXPORTS (FOREIGN EXPENDITURES) To obtain an accurate representation of GDP, we must include the foreign sector. As U.S. residents, we purchase foreign goods called *imports*. The goods that foreign residents purchase from us are our *exports*. To determine the *net* expenditures from the foreign sector, we subtract the value of imports from the value of exports to get net exports (*X*) for a year:

$$\text{Net exports } (X) = \text{total exports} - \text{total imports}$$

To understand why we subtract imports rather than ignoring them altogether, recall that we want to estimate *domestic* output, so we have to subtract U.S. expenditures on the goods produced in other nations.

Presenting the Expenditure Approach

We have just defined the components of GDP using the expenditure approach. When we add them all together, we get a definition for GDP, which is as follows:

$$GDP = C + I + G + X$$

MyEconLab Real-time data

FIGURE 8-2

GDP and Its Components

Here we see a display of gross domestic product, personal consumption expenditures, government purchases, and gross private domestic investment plus net exports for the years since 1929. (Note that the scale of the vertical axis changes as we move up the axis.) During the Great

Depression of the 1930s, gross private domestic investment *plus* net exports was negative because we were investing very little at that time. Since the late 1990s, the sum of gross private domestic investment and net exports has been highly variable.

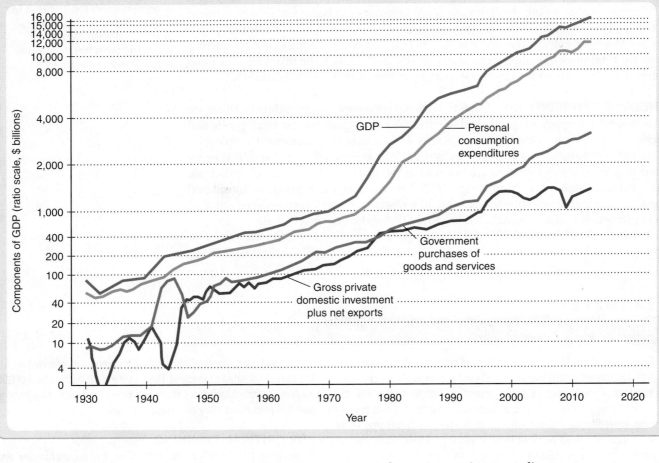

where

C = consumption expenditures
I = investment expenditures
G = government expenditures
X = net exports

THE HISTORICAL PICTURE To get an idea of the relationship among C, I, G, and X, look at Figure 8-2 above, which shows GDP, personal consumption expenditures, government purchases, and gross private domestic investment plus net exports since 1929. When we add up the expenditures of the household, business, government, and foreign sectors, we get GDP.

DEPRECIATION AND NET DOMESTIC PRODUCT We have used the terms *gross domestic product* and *gross private domestic investment* without really indicating what *gross* means. The dictionary defines it as "without deductions," the opposite of *net*. Deductions for what? you might ask. The deductions are for something we call **depreciation.** In the course of a year, machines and structures wear out or are used up in the production of domestic product. For example, houses deteriorate as they are occupied, and machines need repairs or they will fall apart and stop working. Most capital, or durable, goods depreciate.

An estimate of the amount that capital goods have depreciated during the year is subtracted from gross domestic product to arrive at a figure called **net domestic product (NDP),** which we define as follows:

$$\text{NDP} = \text{GDP} - \text{depreciation}$$

Depreciation
Reduction in the value of capital goods over a one-year period due to physical wear and tear and also to obsolescence; also called *capital consumption allowance.*

Net domestic product (NDP)
GDP minus depreciation.

Depreciation is also called **capital consumption allowance** because it is the amount of the capital stock that has been consumed over a one-year period. In essence, it equals the amount a business would have to put aside to repair and replace deteriorating machines. Because we know that

$$\text{GDP} = C + I + G + X$$

we know that the formula for NDP is

$$\text{NDP} = C + I + G + X - \text{depreciation}$$

Alternatively, because net $I = I -$ depreciation,

$$\text{NDP} = C + \text{net } I + G + X$$

Capital consumption allowance
Another name for depreciation, the amount that businesses would have to put aside in order to take care of deteriorating machines and other equipment.

Net investment measures *changes* in our capital stock over time and is positive nearly every year. Because depreciation does not vary greatly from year to year as a percentage of GDP, we get a similar picture of what is happening to our national economy by looking at either NDP or GDP data.

Net investment is an important variable to observe over time nonetheless. If everything else remains the same in an economy, changes in net investment can have dramatic consequences for future economic growth (a topic we cover in more detail in Chapter 9). Positive net investment by definition expands the productive capacity of our economy.

This capacity expansion means that there is increased capital, which will generate even more income in the future. When net investment is zero, we are investing just enough to take account of depreciation. Our economy's productive capacity remains unchanged. Finally, when net investment is negative, we can expect negative economic growth prospects in the future. Negative net investment means that our productive capacity is actually declining—we are disinvesting. This actually occurred during the Great Depression.

Net investment
Gross private domestic investment minus an estimate of the wear and tear on the existing capital stock. Net investment therefore measures the change in the capital stock over a one-year period.

QUICK QUIZ   See page 186 for the answers. Review concepts from this section in MyEconLab.

The _____ approach to measuring GDP requires that we add up consumption expenditures, gross private investment, government purchases, and net exports. Consumption expenditures include consumer _____, consumer _____, and _____.

Gross private domestic investment *excludes* transfers of asset ownership. It includes only additions to the productive _____ of a nation, repairs on existing capital goods, and changes in business _____.

We value most government expenditures at their cost because we usually do not have _____ prices at which to value government goods and services.

To obtain **net domestic product (NDP),** we subtract from GDP the year's _____ of the existing capital stock.

Deriving GDP by the Income Approach

If you go back to the circular flow diagram in Figure 8-1 on page 162, you see that product markets are at the top of the diagram and factor markets are at the bottom. We can calculate the value of the circular flow of income and product by looking at expenditures—which we just did—or by looking at total factor payments. Factor payments are called income. We calculate **gross domestic income (GDI),** which we will see is identical to gross domestic product (GDP). Using the income approach, we have four categories of payments to individuals: wages, interest, rent, and profits.

1. *Wages.* The most important category is, of course, wages, including salaries and other forms of labor income, such as income in kind and incentive payments.

Gross domestic income (GDI)
The sum of all income—wages, interest, rent, and profits—paid to the four factors of production.

We also count Social Security taxes (both the employees' and the employers' contributions).

2. *Interest.* Here interest payments do not equal the sum of all payments for the use of funds in a year. Instead, interest is expressed in *net* rather than in gross terms. The interest component of total income is only net interest received by households plus net interest paid to us by foreign residents. Net interest received by households is the difference between the interest they receive (from savings accounts, certificates of deposit, and the like) and the interest they pay (to banks for home mortgages, credit cards, and other loans).

3. *Rent.* Rent is all income earned by individuals for the use of their real (nonmonetary) assets, such as farms, houses, and stores. As stated previously, we have to include here the implicit rental value of owner-occupied houses. Also included in this category are royalties received from copyrights, patents, and assets such as oil wells.

4. *Profits.* Our last category includes total gross corporate profits plus *proprietors' income.* Proprietors' income is income earned from the operation of unincorporated businesses, which include sole proprietorships, partnerships, and producers' cooperatives. It is unincorporated business profit.

All of the payments listed are *actual* factor payments made to owners of the factors of production. When we add them together, though, we do not yet have gross domestic income. We have to take account of two other components: **indirect business taxes,** such as sales and business property taxes, and depreciation, which we have already discussed.

Go to www.econtoday.com/chap08 to examine recent trends in U.S. GDP and its components.

Indirect business taxes
All business taxes except the tax on corporate profits. Indirect business taxes include sales and business property taxes.

INDIRECT BUSINESS TAXES Indirect taxes are the (nonincome) taxes paid by consumers when they buy goods and services. When you buy a book, you pay the price of the book plus any state and local sales tax. The business is actually acting as the government's agent in collecting the sales tax, which it in turn passes on to the government. Such taxes therefore represent a business expense and are included in gross domestic income.

DEPRECIATION Just as we had to deduct depreciation to get from GDP to NDP, so we must *add* depreciation to go from net domestic income to gross domestic income. Depreciation can be thought of as the portion of the current year's GDP that is used to replace physical capital consumed in the process of production. Because somebody has paid for the replacement, depreciation must be added as a component of gross domestic income.

The last two components of GDP—indirect business taxes and depreciation—are called **nonincome expense items.**

Nonincome expense items
The total of indirect business taxes and depreciation.

Figure 8-3 on the facing page shows a comparison between estimated gross domestic product and gross domestic income for 2013. Whether you decide to use the expenditure approach or the income approach, you will come out with the same number. There are sometimes statistical discrepancies, but they are usually relatively small.

QUICK QUIZ See page 186 for the answers. Review concepts from this section in MyEconLab.

To derive GDP using the income approach, we add up all factor payments, including _____, _____, _____, and _____.

To get an accurate measure of GDP using the income approach, we must also add _____ _____ _____ and _____ to those total factor payments.

FIGURE 8-3

Gross Domestic Product and Gross Domestic Income, 2013 (in billions of 2005 dollars per year)

By using the two different methods of computing the output of the economy, we come up with gross domestic product and gross domestic income, which are by definition equal. One approach focuses on expenditures, or the flow of product. The other approach concentrates on income, or the flow of costs.

Sources: U.S. Department of Commerce and author's estimates.

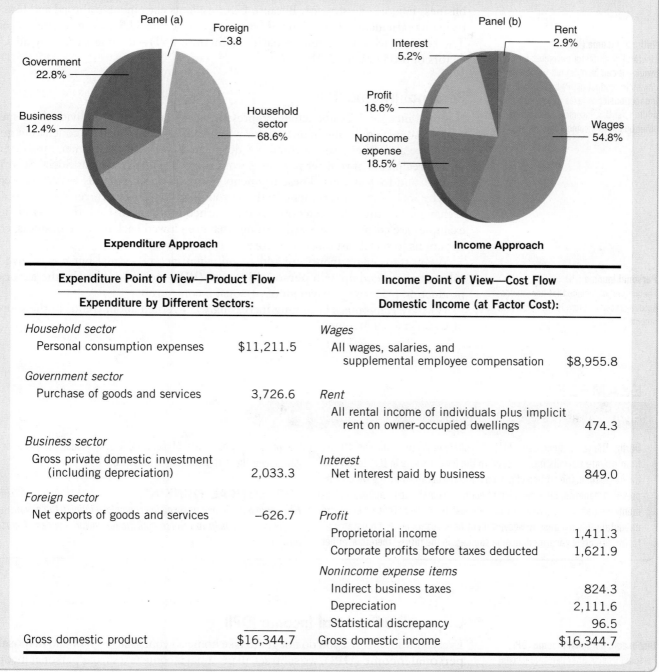

Expenditure Point of View—Product Flow		Income Point of View—Cost Flow	
Expenditure by Different Sectors:		**Domestic Income (at Factor Cost):**	
Household sector		*Wages*	
Personal consumption expenses	$11,211.5	All wages, salaries, and supplemental employee compensation	$8,955.8
Government sector		*Rent*	
Purchase of goods and services	3,726.6	All rental income of individuals plus implicit rent on owner-occupied dwellings	474.3
Business sector		*Interest*	
Gross private domestic investment (including depreciation)	2,033.3	Net interest paid by business	849.0
Foreign sector		*Profit*	
Net exports of goods and services	−626.7	Proprietorial income	1,411.3
		Corporate profits before taxes deducted	1,621.9
		Nonincome expense items	
		Indirect business taxes	824.3
		Depreciation	2,111.6
		Statistical discrepancy	96.5
Gross domestic product	$16,344.7	Gross domestic income	$16,344.7

Other Components of National Income Accounting

Gross domestic income or product does not really tell us how much income people have access to for spending purposes. To get to those kinds of data, we must make some adjustments, which we now do.

National Income (NI)

We know that net domestic product (NDP) is the total market value of goods and services available to consume and to add to the capital stock. NDP, however, includes indirect business taxes and transfers, which should not count as part of income earned by U.S. factors of production, but does not include various business incomes that should. We therefore subtract from NDP indirect taxes and transfers and add other business income adjustments. Because U.S. residents earn income abroad and foreign residents earn income in the United States, we also add *net* U.S. income earned abroad. The result is what we define as **national income (NI)**—income earned by all U.S. factors of production.

National income (NI)
The total of all factor payments to resource owners. It can be obtained from net domestic product (NDP) by subtracting indirect business taxes and transfers and adding net U.S. income earned abroad and other business income adjustments.

Personal Income (PI)

National income does not actually represent what is available to individuals to spend because some people obtain income for which they have provided no concurrent good or service and others earn income but do not receive it. In the former category are mainly recipients of transfer payments from the government, such as Social Security, welfare, and food stamps. These payments represent shifts of funds within the economy by way of the government, with no goods or services concurrently rendered in exchange. For the other category, income earned but not received, the most obvious examples are corporate retained earnings that are plowed back into the business, contributions to social insurance, and corporate income taxes.

When transfer payments are added and when income earned but not received is subtracted, we end up with **personal income (PI)**—income *received* by the factors of production prior to the payment of personal income taxes.

Why are economists becoming increasingly concerned about trends in the sources of U.S. personal income?

Personal income (PI)
The amount of income that households actually receive before they pay personal income taxes.

EXAMPLE

Sources of U.S. Personal Income Exhibit Unsustainable Trends

During the years since early 2010, the share of personal income derived from private payrolls has dropped to the lowest levels in U.S. history. At the same time, the portion of personal income obtained from government-provided benefits, such as Social Security, food stamps, and unemployment insurance, has risen to the highest level ever. These trends are unsustainable because the government finances its benefit programs by taxing privately generated income sources. In the future, therefore, either the private-payroll share of personal income must increase, or the government-benefit portion must decrease.

FOR CRITICAL THINKING
How could a sustained upswing in economic activity in the private sector of the economy help to reverse both trends in the sources of personal income?

Disposable Personal Income (DPI)

Everybody knows that you do not get to take home all your salary. To obtain **disposable personal income (DPI)**, we subtract all personal income taxes from personal income. This is the income that individuals have left for consumption and saving.

Disposable personal income (DPI)
Personal income after personal income taxes have been paid.

Deriving the Components of GDP

Table 8-2 on the facing page shows how to derive the various components of GDP. It explains how to go from gross domestic product to net domestic product to national income to personal income and then to disposable personal income. On the frontpapers of your book, you can see the historical record for GDP, NDP, NI, PI, and DPI for selected years since 1929.

TABLE 8-2

Going from GDP to Disposable Income, 2013

	Billions of Dollars
Gross domestic product (GDP)	16,344.7
Minus depreciation	−2,111.6
Net domestic product (NDP)	14,233.1
Minus indirect business taxes and transfers	−1,409.6
Plus other business income adjustments	1,521.5
Plus net U.S. income earned abroad	205.6
National income (NI)	14,550.6
Minus corporate taxes, Social Security contributions, corporate retained earnings	−2,220.3
Plus government transfer payments	1,752.5
Personal income (PI)	14,082.8
Minus personal income taxes	−1,569.2
Disposable personal income (DPI)	12,513.6

Sources: U.S. Department of Commerce and author's estimates.

We have completed our rundown of the different ways that GDP can be computed and of the different variants of national income and product. What we have not yet touched on is the difference between national income measured in this year's dollars and national income representing real goods and services.

QUICK QUIZ   See page 186 for the answers. Review concepts from this section in MyEconLab.

To obtain _____ _____, we subtract indirect business taxes and transfers from net domestic product and add other business income adjustments and net U.S. income earned abroad.

To obtain _____ _____, we must add government transfer payments, such as Social Security benefits and food stamps. We must subtract income earned but not received by factor owners, such as corporate retained earnings, Social Security contributions, and corporate income taxes.

To obtain disposable personal income, we subtract all personal _____ _____ from personal income. Disposable personal income is income that individuals actually have for consumption or saving.

Distinguishing between Nominal and Real Values

So far, we have shown how to measure *nominal* income and product. When we say "nominal," we are referring to income and product expressed in the current "face value" of today's dollar. Given the existence of inflation or deflation in the economy, we must also be able to distinguish between the **nominal values** that we will be looking at and the **real values** underlying them. Nominal values are expressed in current dollars. Real income involves our command over goods and services—purchasing power—and therefore depends on money income and a set of prices. Thus, real income refers to nominal income corrected for changes in the weighted average of all prices. In other words, we must make an adjustment for changes in the price level.

Consider an example. Nominal income *per person* in 1960 was only about $2,800 per year. In 2013, nominal income per person was about $50,000. Were people really that badly off in 1960? No, for nominal income in 1960 is expressed in 1960 prices, not in the prices of today. In today's dollars, the per-person income of 1960 would be

Nominal values

The values of variables such as GDP and investment expressed in current dollars, also called *money values;* measurement in terms of the actual market prices at which goods and services are sold.

Real values

Measurement of economic values after adjustments have been made for changes in the average of prices between years.

closer to $14,500, or about 30 percent of today's income per person. This is a meaningful comparison between income in 1960 and income today. Next we will show how we can translate nominal measures of income into real measures by using an appropriate price index, such as the Consumer Price Index or the GDP deflator discussed in Chapter 7.

Correcting GDP for Price Changes

If a tablet device costs $200 this year, 10 tablet devices will have a market value of $2,000. If next year they cost $250 each, the same 10 tablet devices will have a market value of $2,500. In this case, there is no increase in the total quantity of tablet devices, but the market value will have increased by one-fourth. Apply this to every single good and service produced and sold in the United States, and you realize that changes in GDP, measured in *current* dollars, may not be a very useful indication of economic activity.

If we are really interested in variations in the *real* output of the economy, we must correct GDP (and just about everything else we look at) for changes in the average of overall prices from year to year. Basically, we need to generate an index that approximates the average prices and then divide that estimate into the value of output in current dollars to adjust the value of output to what is called **constant dollars,** or dollars corrected for general price level changes. This price-corrected GDP is called *real GDP.*

How much has correcting for price changes caused real GDP to differ from nominal GDP during the past few years?

Constant dollars
Dollars expressed in terms of real purchasing power, using a particular year as the base or standard of comparison, in contrast to current dollars.

EXAMPLE

Correcting GDP for Price Index Changes, 2003–2013

Let's take a numerical example to see how we can adjust GDP for changes in the price index. We must pick an appropriate price index in order to adjust for these price level changes. We mentioned the Consumer Price Index, the Producer Price Index, and the GDP deflator in Chapter 7. Let's use the GDP deflator to adjust our figures. Table 8-3 on the facing page gives 11 years of GDP figures. Nominal GDP figures are shown in column 2. The price index (GDP deflator) is in column 3, with base year of 2005, when the GDP deflator equals 100. Column 4 shows real (inflation-adjusted) GDP in 2005 dollars.

The formula for real GDP is

$$\text{Real GDP} = \frac{\text{nominal GDP}}{\text{price index}} \times 100$$

The step-by-step derivation of real (constant-dollar) GDP is as follows: The base year is 2005, so the price index for that year must equal 100. In 2005, nominal GDP was $12,623.0 billion, and so was real GDP expressed in 2005 dollars. In 2006, the price index increased to 103.23108. Thus, to correct 2006's nominal GDP for inflation, we divide the price index, 103.23108, into the nominal GDP figure of $13,377.2 billion and then multiply it by 100. The rounded result is $12,958.5 billion, which is 2006 GDP expressed in terms of the purchasing power of dollars in 2005. What about a situation when the price index is lower than in 2005? Look at 2003. Here the price index shown in column 3 is only 94.13504. That means that in 2003, the average of all prices was just above 94 percent of prices in 2005. To obtain 2003 GDP expressed in terms of 2005 purchasing power, we divide nominal GDP, $11,142.2 billion, by 94.13504 and then multiply by 100. The rounded result is a larger number—$11,836.4 billion. Column 4 in Table 8-3 is a better measure of how the economy has performed than column 2, which shows nominal GDP changes.

FOR CRITICAL THINKING
Based on the information in Table 8-3, in what years was the economy in a recession? Explain briefly.

Plotting Nominal and Real GDP

Nominal GDP and real GDP since 1970 are plotted in Figure 8-4 on the facing page. There is quite a big gap between the two GDP figures, reflecting the amount of inflation that has occurred. Note that the choice of a base year is arbitrary. We have chosen 2005 as the base year in our example. This happens to be the base year that is currently used by the government for the GDP deflator.

TABLE 8-3

Correcting GDP for Price Index Changes

To correct GDP for price index changes, we first have to pick a price index (the GDP deflator) with a specific year as its base. In our example, the base year is 2005. The price index for that year is 100. To obtain 2005 constant-dollar GDP, we divide the price index into nominal GDP and multiply by 100. In other words, we divide column 3 into column 2 and multiply by 100. This gives us column 4, which (taking into account rounding of the deflator) is a measure of real GDP expressed in 2005 purchasing power.

(1) Year	(2) Nominal GDP (billions of dollars per year)	(3) Price Index (base year 2005 = 100)	(4) = [(2) ÷ (3)] × 100 Real GDP (billions of dollars per year, in constant 2005 dollars)
2003	11,142.2	94.13504	11,836.4
2004	11,853.3	96.78613	12,246.9
2005	12,623.0	100.00000	12,623.0
2006	13,377.2	103.23108	12,958.5
2007	14,028.7	106.22653	13,206.4
2008	14,291.5	108.58235	13,161.9
2009	13,939.0	109.72912	12,703.1
2010	14,526.5	110.99098	13,088.0
2011	15,094.0	113.36002	13,315.1
2012	15,706.9	115.51386	13,597.4
2013	16,344.7	117.93965	13,858.5

Sources: U.S. Department of Commerce, Bureau of Economic Analysis, and author's estimates.

Per Capita Real GDP

Looking at changes in real GDP as a measure of economic growth may be deceiving, particularly if the population size has changed significantly. If real GDP over a 10-year period went up 100 percent, you might jump to the conclusion that the real income of a typical person in the economy had increased by that amount. But what if during the

FIGURE 8-4

Nominal and Real GDP

Here we plot both nominal and real GDP. Real GDP is expressed in the purchasing power of 2005 dollars. The gap between the two represents price level changes.

Source: U.S. Department of Commerce.

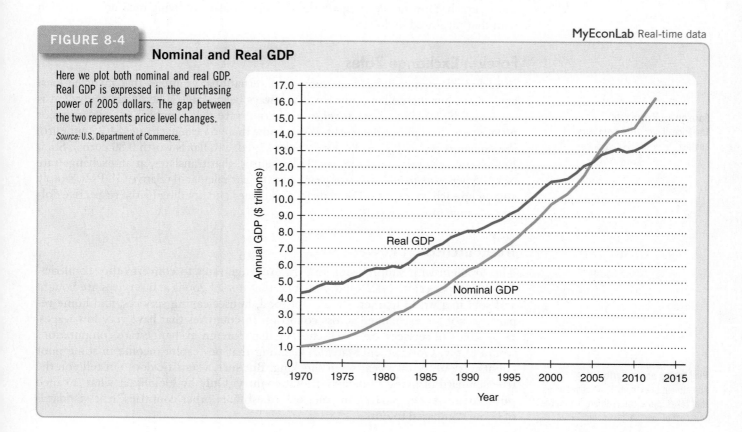

same period the population increased by 200 percent? Then what would you say? Certainly, the amount of real GDP per person, or *per capita real GDP*, would have fallen, even though *total* real GDP had risen. To account not only for price changes but also for population changes, we must first deflate GDP and then divide by the total population, doing this for each year. If we were to look at certain less developed countries, we would find that in many cases, even though real GDP has risen over the past several decades, per capita real GDP has remained constant or fallen because the population has grown just as rapidly or even more rapidly.

QUICK QUIZ   See page 186 for the answers. Review concepts from this section in MyEconLab.

To correct **nominal GDP** for price changes, we first select a base year for our price index and assign it the number _____. Then we construct an index based on how a weighted average of prices has changed relative to that base year. For example, if in the next year a weighted average of the prices indicates that prices have increased by 10

percent, we would assign it the number _____. We then divide each year's price index, so constructed, into its respective nominal GDP figure (and multiply by 100).

We can divide the _____ into real GDP to obtain per capita real GDP.

Comparing GDP throughout the World

It is relatively easy to compare the standard of living of a family in Los Angeles with that of one living in Boston. Both families get paid in dollars and can buy the same goods and services at Wal-Mart, McDonald's, and Costco. It is not so easy, however, to make a similar comparison between a family living in the United States and one in, say, Indonesia. The first problem concerns currency comparisons. Indonesian residents get paid in rupiah, their national currency, and buy goods and services with those rupiah. How do we compare the average standard of living measured in rupiah with that measured in dollars?

Foreign Exchange Rates

Foreign exchange rate
The price of one currency in terms of another.

In earlier chapters, you have encountered international examples that involved local currencies, but the dollar equivalent has always been given. The dollar equivalent is calculated by looking up the **foreign exchange rate** that is published daily in major newspapers throughout the world. If you know that you can exchange $1.25 per euro, the exchange rate is 1.25 to 1 (or otherwise stated, a dollar is worth 0.80 euros). So, if French incomes per capita are, say, 33,936 euros, that translates, at an exchange rate of $1.25 per euro, to $42,420. For years, statisticians calculated relative GDPs by simply adding up each country's GDP in its local currency and dividing by the respective dollar exchange rate.

True Purchasing Power

Purchasing power parity
Adjustment in exchange rate conversions that takes into account differences in the true cost of living across countries.

The problem with simply using foreign exchange rates to convert other countries' GDPs and per capita GDPs into dollars is that not all goods and services are bought and sold in a world market. Restaurant food, housecleaning services, and home repairs do not get exchanged across countries. In countries that have very low wages, those kinds of services are much cheaper than foreign exchange rate computations would imply. Government statistics claiming that per capita income in some poor country is only $300 a year seem shocking. But such a statistic does not tell you the true standard of living of people in that country. Only by looking at what is called **purchasing power parity** can you hope to estimate other countries' true standards of living compared to ours.

Given that nations use different currencies, how can we compare nations' levels of real GDP per capita?

INTERNATIONAL EXAMPLE

Purchasing Power Parity Comparisons of World Incomes

A few years ago, the International Monetary Fund accepted the purchasing power parity approach as the correct one. It started presenting international statistics on each country's GDP relative to every other's based on purchasing power parity relative to the U.S. dollar. The results were surprising. As you can see from Table 8-4 below, China's per capita GDP is higher based on purchasing power parity than when measured at market foreign exchange rates.

FOR CRITICAL THINKING

What is the percentage increase in China's per capita GDP when one switches from foreign exchange rates to purchasing power parity?

TABLE 8-4

Comparing GDP Internationally

Country	Annual GDP Based on Purchasing Power Parity (billions of U.S. dollars)	Per Capita GDP Based on Purchasing Power Parity (U.S. dollars)	Per Capita GDP Based on Foreign Exchange Rates (U.S. dollars)
United States	15,094	48,450	48,450
United Kingdom	2,287	36,511	37,780
Germany	3,221	39,414	43,980
France	2,303	35,194	42,420
Japan	4,381	34,278	45,180
Italy	1,979	32,569	35,330
Russia	3,031	21,358	10,400
Brazil	2,305	11,719	10,720
China	11,347	8,442	4,930
Indonesia	1,131	4,668	2,940

Source: World Bank.

QUICK QUIZ See page 186 for the answers. Review concepts from this section in MyEconLab.

The foreign _____ _____ is the price of one currency in terms of another.

Statisticians often calculate relative GDP by adding up each country's GDP in its local currency and dividing by the dollar _____ _____.

Because not all goods and services are bought and sold in the world market, we must correct exchange rate conversions of other countries' GDP figures to take into account differences in the true _____ of _____ across countries.

YOU ARE THERE

Has the Economy Grown More Than Official GDP Data Suggest?

Economists Bart Hobijn and Charles Steindel of the Federal Reserve Bank of New York are studying how to adjust GDP to take into account three items that the official measure ignores: (1)"intangible investment," including spending on research into new processes or products that currently is not counted within GDP as business fixed investment; (2) real investment in capital goods undertaken by the government but potentially undercounted in official GDP tabulations; and (3) the shift from nonmarket home production not counted as GDP to market production because more women are entering the U.S. labor force.

Hobijn and Steindel find that adding the first two items tends to push up fixed investment measures and consequently increases their broadened GDP measure. Taking into account the third item tends to reduce this broadened measure, because it subtracts an imputed value of

home production from the higher official market production of women who have joined the labor force. The net effect of taking all three items into account, Hobijn and Steindel conclude, is that the average official growth rate of inflation-adjusted (real) GDP is nearly 0.5 percentage point per year lower than the rate of growth of their altered GDP measure after adjusting for inflation. Consequently, they conclude that the official U.S. economic growth rate may be significantly understated.

Critical Thinking Questions

1. Why is intangible investment harder to measure than tangible investment?
2. What makes it difficult to assign a dollar value to nonmarket home production?

ISSUES & APPLICATIONS

Asia's "Economic Size" Depends on How It Is Measured

CONCEPTS APPLIED

▶ Real GDP

▶ Purchasing Power Parity

▶ Per Capita Real GDP

The media have reported on the growing economic clout of Asian nations. How large is the combined "economic size" of Asian nations in comparison with other nations, such as the United States? The answer depends on what measure we use when making comparisons between Asia and the world as a whole.

Asian Real GDP as a Percentage of Global Real GDP

Figure 8-5 on the facing page displays the combined real GDP of Asia as a percentage of the combined real GDP of the entire world. The figure displays this percentage according to two different measures. One measure uses prevailing exchange rates in currency markets to adjust all countries' real GDP levels to allow for comparisons. The other measure utilizes purchasing power parity adjustments.

Utilizing market exchange rates indicates that Asian real GDP's share of global real GDP generally rose steadily between 1980 and the mid-1990s from less than one-fifth to slightly more than one-fourth of global GDP. In contrast, purchasing power parity measures of real GDP indicate that Asia's measured share of the world economy has grown to more than 35 percent.

Asian versus Global Per Capita Real GDP

Another measure for comparing the relative "economic sizes" of Asia and the world is per capita real GDP. This measure also can be computed using either foreign exchange rates or purchasing power parities to allow for cross-country comparisons.

When per capita real GDP is computed using foreign exchange rates, Asian per capita real GDP is only 11 percent of global per capita real GDP. When the tabulation uses purchasing power parity adjustments, Asian per capita real GDP is 26 percent of global real GDP per capita. Thus, both measures indicate that although Asia's economic size has risen in relation to the world as a whole, Asia's per capita real GDP remains relatively low. Even though Asian real GDP is relatively high, so is Asia's population, which is why the region's per capita real GDP remains only a fraction of the global level.

FIGURE 8-5

Asia's Share of Global Real GDP

This figure displays two measures of real GDP in Asia as a percentage of worldwide real GDP. The measure that uses foreign exchange rates to adjust real GDP data to comparable amounts across countries indicates a rise in Asia's share until the mid-1990s and a leveling off since then. The measure based on purchasing power parity comparisons shows a larger and longer-lived rise in Asia's share of global real GDP.

Source: International Monetary Fund.

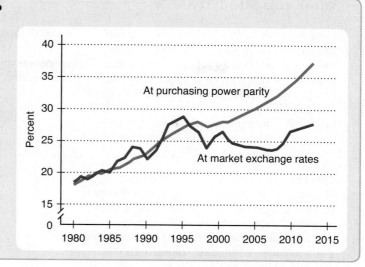

For Critical Thinking

1. Why is there such a difference in Asia's share of global real GDP, depending on whether the computation uses purchasing power parities or exchange rates?

2. Why is Asia's "economic size" so much smaller on a per capita basis than on an absolute basis?

Web Resources

1. For a recent analysis of the growth of Asia's share of global economic activity, go to www.econtoday.com/chap08.

2. To learn about a recent claim that China's economy is already "larger" than the U.S. economy, go to www.econtoday.com/chap08.

MyEconLab

For more questions on this chapter's Issues & Applications, go to MyEconLab. In the Study Plan for this chapter, select Section N: News.

MyEconLab

Here is what you should know after reading this chapter. MyEconLab will help you identify what you know, and where to go when you need to practice.

WHAT YOU SHOULD KNOW

The Circular Flow of Income and Output The circular flow of income and output captures two principles: (1) In every transaction, the seller receives the same amount that the buyer spends; and (2) goods and services flow in one direction, and money payments flow in the other direction. Households ultimately purchase the nation's total output of final goods and services. They make these purchases using income—wages, rents, interest, and profits—earned from selling labor, land, capital, and entrepreneurial services, respectively. Hence, income equals the value of output.

national income accounting, 162
total income, 163
final goods and services, 163

Key Figure
Figure 8-1, 162

WHERE TO GO TO PRACTICE

• MyEconLab Study Plan 8.1
• Animated Figure 8-1

MyEconLab *continued*

WHAT YOU SHOULD KNOW		WHERE TO GO TO PRACTICE
Gross Domestic Product (GDP) A nation's gross domestic product is the total market value of its final output of goods and services produced within a given year using factors of production located within the nation's borders. Because GDP measures the value of a flow of production during a year in terms of market prices, it is not a measure of a nation's wealth.	gross domestic product (GDP), 164 intermediate goods, 164 value added, 164	• MyEconLab Study Plan 8.2
The Limitations of Using GDP as a Measure of National Welfare Gross domestic product is a useful measure for tracking year-to-year changes in the value of a nation's over-all economic activity in terms of market prices. But it excludes nonmarket transactions that may add to or detract from general welfare. It also fails to account for factors such as environmental quality and the amount and quality of leisure time.		• MyEconLab Study Plan 8.2
The Expenditure Approach to Tabulating GDP To calculate GDP using the expenditure approach, we sum consumption spending, investment expenditures, government spending, and net export expenditures. Thus, we add up the total amount spent on newly produced goods and services to obtain the dollar value of the output produced and purchased during the year.	expenditure approach, 167 income approach, 167 durable consumer goods, 168 nondurable consumer goods, 168 services, 168 gross private domestic investment, 168 investment, 168 producer durables, or capital goods, 168 fixed investment, 168 inventory investment, 169 depreciation, 170 net domestic product (NDP), 170 capital consumption allowance, 171 net investment, 171 **Key Figure** Figure 8-2, 170	• MyEconLab Study Plan 8.3 • Animated Figure 8-2
The Income Approach to Computing GDP To tabulate GDP using the income approach, we add total wages and salaries, rental income, interest income, profits, and nonincome expense items—indirect business taxes and depreciation—to obtain gross domestic income, which is equivalent to gross domestic product. Thus, the total value of all income earnings (equivalent to total factor costs) equals GDP.	gross domestic income (GDI), 171 indirect business taxes, 172 nonincome expense items, 172 national income (NI), 174 personal income (PI), 174 disposable personal income (DPI), 174	• MyEconLab Study Plans 8.3, 8.4

─ WHAT YOU SHOULD KNOW ─────────

Distinguishing between Nominal GDP and Real GDP Nominal GDP is the value of newly produced output during the current year measured at current market prices. Real GDP adjusts the value of current output into constant dollars by correcting for changes in the overall level of prices from year to year. To calculate real GDP, we divide nominal GDP by the price index (the GDP deflator) and multiply by 100.

nominal values, 175
real values, 175
constant dollars, 176
foreign exchange rate, 178
purchasing power parity, 178

Key Figure
Figure 8-4, 177

── WHERE TO GO TO PRACTICE ──

• **MyEconLab** Study Plans 8.5, 8.6
• Animated Figure 8-4

Log in to MyEconLab, take a chapter test, and get a personalized Study Plan that tells you which concepts you understand and which ones you need to review. From there, MyEconLab will give you further practice, tutorials, animations, videos, and guided solutions. For more information, visit www.myeconlab.com

PROBLEMS

All problems are assignable in MyEconLab; exercises that update with real-time data are marked with 〽. *Answers to odd-numbered problems appear at the back of the book.*

8-1. Explain in your own words why the flow of gross domestic product during a given interval must always be equivalent to the flow of gross domestic income within that same period. (See page 162.)

8-2. In the first stage of manufacturing each final unit of a product, a firm purchases a key input at a price of $4 per unit. The firm then pays a wage rate of $3 for the time that labor is exerted, combining an additional $2 of inputs for each final unit of output produced. The firm sells every unit of the product for $10. What is the contribution of each unit of output to GDP in the current year? (See page 165.)

8-3. Each year after a regular spring cleaning, Maria spruces up her home a little by retexturing and repainting the walls of one room in her house. In a given year, she spends $25 on magazines to get ideas about wall textures and paint shades, $45 on newly produced texturing materials and tools, $35 on new paintbrushes and other painting equipment, and $175 on newly produced paint. Normally, she preps the walls, a service that a professional wall-texturing specialist would charge $200 to do, and applies two coats of paint, a service that a painter would charge $350 to do, on her own. (See pages 164–166.)

   a. When she purchases her usual set of materials and does all the work on her home by herself in a given spring, how much does Maria's annual spring texturing and painting activity contribute to GDP?

   b. Suppose that Maria hurt her back this year and is recovering from surgery. Her surgeon has

instructed her not to do any texturing work, but he has given her the go-ahead to paint a room as long as she is cautious. Thus, she buys all the equipment required to both texture and paint a room. She hires someone else to do the texturing work but does the painting herself. How much would her spring painting activity add to GDP?

   c. As a follow-up to part (b), suppose that as soon as Maria bends down to dip her brush into the paint, she realizes that painting will be too hard on her back after all. She decides to hire someone else to do all the work using the materials she has already purchased. In this case, how much will her spring painting activity contribute to GDP?

8-4. Each year, Johan typically does all his own landscaping and yard work. He spends $200 per year on mulch for his flower beds, $225 per year on flowers and plants, $50 on fertilizer for his lawn, and $245 on gasoline and lawn mower maintenance. The lawn and garden store where he obtains his mulch and fertilizer charges other customers $500 for the service of spreading that much mulch in flower beds and $50 for the service of distributing fertilizer over a yard the size of Johan's. Paying a professional yard care service to mow his lawn would require an expenditure of $1,200 per year, but in that case Johan would not have to buy gasoline or maintain his own lawn mower. (See pages 164–166.)

   a. In a normal year, how much does Johan's landscaping and yard work contribute to GDP?

   b. Suppose that Johan has developed allergy problems this year and will have to reduce the amount of his yard work. He can wear a mask while running his lawn mower, so he will keep mowing his yard, but he will pay the lawn and garden center to spread mulch and distribute fertilizer. How much will all the work on Johan's yard contribute to GDP this year?

c. As a follow-up to part (b), at the end of the year, Johan realizes that his allergies are growing worse and that he will have to arrange for all his landscaping and yard work to be done by someone else next year. How much will he contribute to GDP next year?

8-5. Consider the following hypothetical data for the U.S. economy in 2016 (all amounts are in trillions of dollars; see pages 168–171).

Consumption	11.0
Indirect business taxes	.8
Depreciation	1.3
Government spending	2.8
Imports	2.7
Gross private domestic investment	3.0
Exports	2.5

a. Based on the data, what is GDP? NDP? NI?

b. Suppose that in 2017, exports fall to $2.3 trillion, imports rise to $2.85 trillion, and gross private domestic investment falls to $2.25 trillion. What will GDP be in 2017, assuming that other values do not change between 2016 and 2017?

8-6. Look back at Table 8-3 on page 177, which explains how to calculate real GDP in terms of 2005 constant dollars. Change the base year to 2003. Recalculate the price index, and then recalculate real GDP—that is, express column 4 of Table 8-3 in terms of 2003 dollars instead of 2005 dollars. (See page 177.)

8-7. Consider the following hypothetical data for the U.S. economy in 2016 (in trillions of dollars), and assume that there are no statistical discrepancies or other adjustments. (See pages 169–175.)

Profit	2.8
Indirect business taxes and transfers	.8
Rent	.7
Interest	.8
Wages	8.2
Depreciation	1.3
Consumption	11.0
Exports	1.5
Government transfer payments	2.0
Personal income taxes and nontax payments	1.7
Imports	1.7
Corporate taxes and retained earnings	.5
Social Security contributions	2.0
Government spending	1.8

a. What is gross domestic income? GDP?

b. What is gross private domestic investment?

c. What is personal income? Personal disposable income?

8-8. Which of the following are production activities that are included in GDP? Which are not? (See pages 164–166.)

a. Mr. King performs the service of painting his own house instead of paying someone else to do it.

b. Mr. King paints houses for a living.

c. Mrs. King earns income from parents by taking baby photos in her digital photography studio.

d. Mrs. King takes photos of planets and stars as part of her astronomy hobby.

e. E*Trade charges fees to process Internet orders for stock trades.

f. Mr. Ho spends $10,000 on shares of stock via an Internet trade order and pays a $10 brokerage fee.

g. Mrs. Ho receives a Social Security payment.

h. Ms. Hernandez makes a $300 payment for an Internet-based course on stock trading.

i. Mr. Langham sells a used laptop computer to his neighbor.

8-9. Explain what happens to contributions to GDP in each of the following situations. (See page 165.)

a. A woman who makes a living charging for investment advice on her Internet Web site marries one of her clients, to whom she now provides advice at no charge.

b. A man who had washed the windows of his own house every year decides to pay a private company to wash those windows this year.

c. A company that had been selling used firearms illegally finally gets around to obtaining an operating license and performing background checks as specified by law prior to each gun sale.

8-10. Explain what happens to the official measure of GDP in each of the following situations. (See page 165.)

a. Air quality improves significantly throughout the United States, but there are no effects on aggregate production or on market prices of final goods and services.

b. The U.S. government spends considerably less on antipollution efforts this year than it did in recent years.

c. The quality of cancer treatments increases, so patients undergo fewer treatments, which hospitals continue to provide at the same price per treatment as before.

8-11. Which of the following activities of a computer manufacturer during the current year are included in this year's measure of GDP? (See page 165.)

a. The manufacturer produces a chip in June, uses it as a component in a computer in August, and sells the computer to a customer in November.

b. A retail outlet of the firm sells a computer completely built during the current year.

c. A marketing arm of the company receives fee income during the current year when a buyer of one of its computers elects to use the computer manufacturer as her Internet service provider.

8-12. A number of economists contend that official measures of U.S. gross private investment expenditures are understated. Answer parts (a) and (b) below to determine just how understated these economists believe that officially measured investment spending may be. (See page 168.)

a. Household spending on education, such as college tuition expenditures, is counted as consumption spending. Some economists suggest that these expenditures, which amount to 6 percent of GDP, should be counted as investment spending instead. Based on this 6 percent estimate and the GDP computations detailed in Figure 8-3 on page 173, how many billions of dollars would shift from consumption to investment if this suggestion was adopted?

b. Some economists argue that intangible forms of investment—business research spending, educational expenses for employees, and the like—should be included in the official measure of gross private domestic investment. These expenditures, which amount to about 9 percent of GDP, currently are treated as business input expenses and are not included in GDP. Based on this 9 percent estimate and the GDP computations detailed in Figure 8-3 on page 173, how much higher would gross private domestic investment be if intangible investment expenditures were counted as investment spending?

c. Based on your answers to parts (a) and (b), what is the total amount that gross private domestic investment may be understated, according to economists who argue that household education spending and business intangible investments should be added? How much may GDP be understated?

8-13. Consider the table at the top of the next column for the economy of a nation whose residents produce five final goods. (See pages 175–176.)

Good	2013 Price	2013 Quantity	2017 Price	2017 Quantity
Shampoo	$ 2	15	$ 4	20
External hard drives	200	10	250	10
Books	40	5	50	4
Milk	3	10	4	3
Candy	1	40	2	20

Assuming a 2013 base year:

a. What is nominal GDP for 2013 and 2017?

b. What is real GDP for 2013 and 2017?

8-14. Consider the following table for the economy of a nation whose residents produce four final goods. (See pages 175–176.)

Good	2015 Price	2015 Quantity	2016 Price	2016 Quantity
Computers	$1,000	10	$800	15
Bananas	6	3,000	11	1,000
Televisions	100	500	150	300
Cookies	1	10,000	2	10,000

Assuming a 2016 base year:

a. What is nominal GDP for 2015 and 2016?

b. What is real GDP for 2015 and 2016?

8-15. In the table for Problem 8-14, if 2016 is the base year, what is the price index for 2015? (Round decimal fractions to the nearest tenth.)

8-16. Suppose that early in a year, a hurricane hits a town in Florida and destroys a substantial number of homes. A portion of this stock of housing, which had a market value of $100 million (not including the market value of the land), was uninsured. The owners of the residences spent a total of $5 million during the rest of the year to pay salvage companies to help them save remaining belongings. A small percentage of uninsured owners had sufficient resources to spend a total of $15 million during the year to pay construction companies to rebuild their homes. Some were able to devote their own time, the opportunity cost of which was valued at $3 million, to work on rebuilding their homes. The remaining people, however, chose to sell their land at its market value and abandon the remains of their houses. What was the combined effect of these transactions on GDP for this year? (Hint: Which transactions took place in the markets for *final* goods and services?) In what ways, if any, does the effect on GDP reflect a loss in welfare for these individuals? (See page 165.)

8-17. Suppose that in 2015, geologists discover large reserves of oil under the tundra in Alaska. These new reserves have a market value estimated at $50 billion at current oil prices. Oil companies spend $1 billion to hire workers and move and position equipment to begin exploratory pumping during that same year. In the process of loading some of the oil onto tankers at a port, one company accidentally spills some of the oil into a bay and by the end of the year pays $1 billion to other companies to clean it up. The oil spill kills thousands of birds, seals, and other wildlife. What was the combined effect of these events on GDP for this year? (Hint: Which transactions took place in the markets for *final* goods and services?) In what ways, if any, does the effect on GDP reflect a loss in national welfare? (See page 165.)

8-18. Consider the diagram below, and answer the following questions. (See page 177.)

a. What is the base year? Explain.

b. Has this country experienced inflation or deflation since the base year? How can you tell?

ECONOMICS ON THE NET

Tracking the Components of Gross Domestic Product One way to keep tabs on the components of GDP is via the FRED database at the Web site of the Federal Reserve Bank of St. Louis.

Title: Gross Domestic Product and Components

Navigation: Use the link at www.econtoday.com/chap08 to visit the home page of the Federal Reserve Bank of St. Louis. Click on *Gross Domestic Product (GDP) and Components*.

Application

1. Click on *GDP/GNP*, and then click a checkmark next to *GDP (Gross Domestic Product)*. Write down nominal GDP data for the past 10 quarters.

2. Back up to *GDPCA (Real Gross Domestic Product) Dollars.* Write down the amounts for the past 10 quarters. Use the formula on page 176 to calculate the price level for each quarter. Has the price level decreased or increased in recent quarters?

For Group Study and Analysis Divide the class into "consumption," "investment," "government sector," and "foreign sector" groups. Have each group evaluate the contribution of each category of spending to GDP and to its quarter-to-quarter volatility. Reconvene the class, and discuss the factors that appear to create the most variability in GDP.

ANSWERS TO QUICK QUIZZES

p. 164: (i) factor . . . income; (ii) final; (iii) profit

p. 167: (i) Gross domestic product; (ii) value added; (iii) exclude; (iv) GDP; (v) market value

p. 171: (i) expenditure . . . durables . . . nondurables . . . services; (ii) capacity . . . inventories; (iii) market; (iv) depreciation

p. 172: (i) wages . . . interest . . . rent . . . profits; (ii) indirect business taxes . . . depreciation

p. 175: (i) national income; (ii) personal income; (iii) income taxes

p. 178: (i) 100 . . . 110; (ii) population

p. 179: (i) exchange rate; (ii) exchange rate; (iii) cost . . . living

Global Economic Growth and Development

LEARNING OBJECTIVES

After reading this chapter, you should be able to:

▶ Define economic growth

▶ Recognize the importance of economic growth rates

▶ Explain why productivity increases are crucial for maintaining economic growth

▶ Describe the fundamental determinants of economic growth

▶ Understand the basis of new growth theory

▶ Discuss the fundamental factors that contribute to a nation's economic development

MyEconLab helps you master each objective and study more efficiently. See end of chapter for details.

From the late 1990s through most of the first decade of the 2000s, media reports bemoaned the sorry state of the U.S. private *saving rate,* or the annual flow of saving per year as a percentage of households' personal disposable income per year. U.S. residents were saving only a little over 2 percent of their annual personal disposable income, so few resources were available to finance the purchase of capital goods. This fact, observers worried, would tend to drag down U.S. economic growth. Since 2007, the average private saving rate has increased significantly, which has led some observers to become more optimistic about U.S. growth prospects. Nevertheless, others point to a sharp drop in the *overall* national saving rate, inclusive of *government* saving, as reason for even greater concern about the prospects for future U.S. economic growth. By the time you have completed this chapter, you will be able to evaluate these alternative perspectives about the U.S. saving rate and economic growth.

?DID YOU KNOW THAT... since 2009, the U.S. birthrate has been at its lowest level in a century? This development is a striking turnabout from 2007, when more babies were born in the United States than in any prior year in the nation's history. In this chapter, you will learn why this lower U.S. birthrate would tend to boost the near-term measured rate of U.S. *economic growth,* other things being equal. You will also discover why a prolonged drop in the country's birthrate would have a theoretically ambiguous effect on the long-term economic growth rate.

How Do We Define Economic Growth?

Recall from Chapter 2 that we can show economic growth graphically as an outward shift of a production possibilities curve, as is seen in Figure 9-1 below. If there is economic growth between 2015 and 2037, the production possibilities curve will shift outward toward the red curve. The distance that it shifts represents the amount of economic growth, defined as the increase in the productive capacity of a nation. Although it is possible to come up with a measure of a nation's increased productive capacity, it would not be easy. Therefore, we turn to a more readily obtainable definition of economic growth.

Most people have a general idea of what economic growth means. When a nation grows economically, its citizens must be better off in at least some ways, usually in terms of their material well-being. Typically, though, we do not measure the well-being of any nation solely in terms of its total output of real goods and services or in terms of real GDP without making some adjustments. After all, India has a real GDP more than 15 times as large as that of Denmark. The population in India, though, is about 200 times greater than that of Denmark. Consequently, we view India as a relatively poor country and Denmark as a relatively rich country. Thus, when we measure economic growth, we must adjust for population growth. Our formal definition becomes this: **Economic growth** occurs when there are increases in *per capita* real GDP, measured by the rate of change in per capita real GDP per year. Figure 9-2 on page 190 presents the historical record of real GDP per person in the United States.

Economic growth
Increases in per capita real GDP measured by its rate of change per year.

Problems in Definition

Our definition of economic growth says nothing about the *distribution* of output and income. A nation might grow very rapidly in terms of increases in per capita real GDP, while its poor people remain poor or become even poorer. Therefore, in assessing the economic growth record of any nation, we must be careful to pinpoint which income groups have benefited the most from such growth. How much does economic growth differ across countries?

FIGURE 9-1

Economic Growth

If there is growth between 2015 and 2037, the production possibilities curve for the entire economy will shift outward from the blue line labeled 2015 to the red line labeled 2037. The distance that it shifts represents an increase in the productive capacity of the nation.

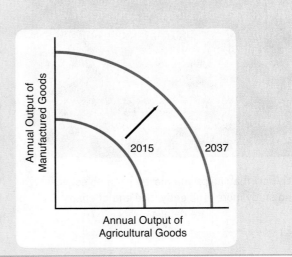

INTERNATIONAL EXAMPLE

Growth Rates around the World

Table 9-1 shows the average annual rate of growth of real GDP per person in selected countries since 1970. During this time period, the United States has been positioned about midway in the pack. Thus, even though we are one of the world's richest countries, our rate of economic growth has been in the middle range. The reason that U.S. per capita real GDP has remained higher than per capita real GDP in most other nations is that, despite the late-2000s downturn, U.S. growth has been sustained over many decades. This is something that most other countries have so far been unable to accomplish.

FOR CRITICAL THINKING

"The largest change is from zero to one." Does this statement have anything to do with relative growth rates in poorer versus richer countries?

TABLE 9-1

Per Capita Real GDP Growth Rates in Various Countries

Country	Average Annual Rate of Growth of Real GDP Per Capita, 1970–2013 (%)
Sweden	1.6
France	1.7
Germany	1.7
United States	1.8
Canada	1.9
Japan	2.0
Turkey	2.0
Brazil	2.3
India	3.3
Indonesia	4.3
Malaysia	4.8
China	7.1

Sources: World Bank, International Monetary Fund, and author's estimates.

Real standards of living can go up without any positive economic growth. This can occur if individuals are, on average, enjoying more leisure by working fewer hours but producing as much as they did before. For example, if per capita real GDP in the United States remained at $55,000 a year for a decade, we could not automatically jump to the conclusion that U.S. residents were, on average, no better off. What if, during that same 10-year period, average hours worked fell from 37 per week to 33 per week? That would mean that during the 10 years under study, individuals in the labor force were "earning" 4 more hours of leisure a week.

Nothing so extreme as this example has occurred in this country, but something similar has. Average hours worked per week fell steadily until the 1960s, when they leveled off. That means that during much of the history of this country, the increase in per capita real GDP *understated* the growth in living standards that we were experiencing because we were enjoying more and more leisure as time passed.

Go to www.econtoday.com/chap09 to get the latest figures and estimates on economic growth throughout the world.

Is Economic Growth Bad?

Some commentators on our current economic situation believe that the definition of economic growth ignores its negative effects. Some psychologists even contend that economic growth makes us worse off. They say that the more the economy grows, the more "needs" are created so that we feel worse off as we become richer. Our expectations are rising faster than reality, so we presumably always suffer from a sense of disappointment. Also, economists' measurement of economic growth does not take into account the spiritual and cultural aspects of the good life. As with all activities, both costs and benefits are associated with growth. You can see some of those listed in Table 9-2 on the bottom of the next page.

FIGURE 9-2

The Historical Record of U.S. Economic Growth

The graph traces per capita real GDP in the United States since 1900. Data are given in 2005 dollars.

Source: U.S. Department of Commerce.

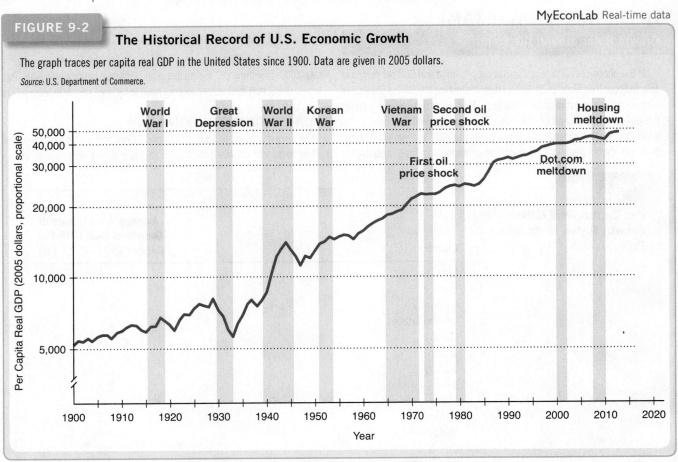

Any measure of economic growth that we use will be imperfect. Nonetheless, the measures that we do have allow us to make comparisons across countries and over time and, if used judiciously, can enable us to gain important insights. Per capita real GDP, used so often, is not always an accurate measure of economic well-being, but it is a serviceable measure of productive activity.

The Importance of Growth Rates

Notice in Table 9-1 on the previous page that the growth rates in real per capita income for most countries differ very little—generally by only a few percentage points. You might want to know why such small differences in growth rates are important. What does it matter if we grow at 3 percent rather than at 4 percent per year? The answer is that in the long run, it matters a lot.

A small difference in the rate of economic growth does not matter very much for next year or the year after. For the more distant future, however, it makes considerable difference. The power of *compounding* is impressive. Let's see what happens with three different annual rates of growth: 3 percent, 4 percent, and 5 percent. We start with

TABLE 9-2

Costs and Benefits of Economic Growth

Benefits	Costs
Reduction in illiteracy	Environmental pollution
Reduction in poverty	Breakdown of the family
Improved health	Isolation and alienation
Longer lives	Urban congestion
Political stability	

TABLE 9-3							

One Dollar Compounded Annually at Different Interest Rates

Here we show the value of a dollar at the end of a specified period during which it has been compounded annually at a specified interest rate. For example, if you took $1 today and invested it at 5 percent per year, it would yield $1.05 at the end of one year. At the end of 10 years, it would equal $1.63, and at the end of 50 years, it would equal $11.50.

| Number of Years | Interest Rate | | | | | | |
	3%	4%	5%	6%	8%	10%	20%
1	1.03	1.04	1.05	1.06	1.08	1.10	1.20
2	1.06	1.08	1.10	1.12	1.17	1.21	1.44
3	1.09	1.12	1.16	1.19	1.26	1.33	1.73
4	1.13	1.17	1.22	1.26	1.36	1.46	2.07
5	1.16	1.22	1.28	1.34	1.47	1.61	2.49
6	1.19	1.27	1.34	1.41	1.59	1.77	2.99
7	1.23	1.32	1.41	1.50	1.71	1.94	3.58
8	1.27	1.37	1.48	1.59	1.85	2.14	4.30
9	1.30	1.42	1.55	1.68	2.00	2.35	5.16
10	1.34	1.48	1.63	1.79	2.16	2.59	6.19
20	1.81	2.19	2.65	3.20	4.66	6.72	38.30
30	2.43	3.24	4.32	5.74	10.00	17.40	237.00
40	3.26	4.80	7.04	10.30	21.70	45.30	1,470.00
50	4.38	7.11	11.50	18.40	46.90	117.00	9,100.00

$1 trillion per year of U.S. GDP at some time in the past. We then compound this $1 trillion, or allow it to grow at these three different growth rates. The difference is huge. In 50 years, $1 trillion per year becomes $4.38 trillion per year if compounded at 3 percent per year. Just one percentage point more in the growth rate, 4 percent, results in a real GDP of $7.11 trillion per year in 50 years, almost double the previous amount. Two percentage points' difference in the growth rate—5 percent per year—results in a real GDP of $11.5 trillion per year in 50 years, or nearly three times as much. Obviously, very small differences in annual growth rates result in great differences in cumulative economic growth. That is why nations are concerned if the growth rate falls even a little in absolute percentage terms.

Thus, when we talk about growth rates, we are talking about compounding. In Table 9-3 above, we show how $1 compounded annually grows at different interest rates. We see in the 3 percent column that $1 in 50 years grows to $4.38. We merely multiplied $1 trillion times 4.38 to get the growth figure in our earlier example. In the 5 percent column, $1 grows to $11.50 after 50 years. Again, we multiplied $1 trillion times 11.50 to get the growth figure for 5 percent in the preceding example.

How much of a difference in your future income would result from a 1-percentage-point drop in the long-term U.S. growth rate?

EXAMPLE

Gauging the Future Impact of a 1-Percentage-Point Growth Drop

Over nearly four decades, the rate of growth in U.S. per capita real GDP has averaged close to 2 percent. Since 2008, however, the average growth rate of the nation's per capita real GDP has remained below 1 percent. If this were to become the new long-term average rate of economic growth in a dampened U.S. economy, how much lower would per capita real GDP be in future years?

Gross domestic product represents both the value of production of goods and services per year and the income generated during that year. Thus, U.S. per capita real GDP is equal to the annual inflation-adjusted income earned by an average resident during a year. This means that a permanent drop in the rate of economic growth from 2 percent to 1 percent would translate into an 18 percent dampening in that resident's income after 20 years. After 50 years, the 1-percentage-point reduction in the growth rate would cause the resident's real income to be more than 60 percent less than it would have been at the higher growth rate.

FOR CRITICAL THINKING

Why does just a 1-percentage-point reduction in the rate of economic growth make such a significant difference if it persists for many years?

Rule of 70
A rule stating that the approximate number of years required for per capita real GDP to double is equal to 70 divided by the average rate of economic growth.

THE RULE OF 70 Table 9-3 on the preceding page indicates that how quickly the level of a nation's per capita real GDP increases depends on the rate of economic growth. A formula called the **rule of 70** provides a shorthand way to calculate approximately how long it will take a country to experience a significant increase in per capita real GDP. According to the rule of 70, the approximate number of years necessary for a nation's per capita real GDP to increase by 100 percent—that is, to *double*—is equal to 70 divided by the average rate of economic growth. Thus, at an annual growth rate of 10 percent, per capita real GDP should double in about 7 years.

As you can see in Table 9-3, at a 10 percent growth rate, in 7 years per capita real GDP would rise by a factor of 1.94, which is very close to 2, or very nearly the doubling predicted by the rule of 70. At an annual growth rate of 8 percent, the rule of 70 predicts that nearly 9 years will be required for a nation's per capita real GDP to double. Table 9-3 verifies that this prediction is correct. Indeed, the table shows that after 9 years an exact doubling will occur at a growth rate of 8 percent.

The rule of 70 implies that at lower rates of economic growth, much more time must pass before per capita real GDP will double. At a 3 percent growth rate, just over 23 (70 ÷ 3) years must pass before per capita real income doubles. At a rate of growth of only 1 percent per year, 70 (70 ÷ 1) years must pass. This means that if a nation's average rate of economic growth is 1 percent instead of 3 percent, 47 more years—about two generations—must pass for per capita real GDP to double. Clearly, the rule of 70 verifies that even very slight differences in economic growth rates are important.

QUICK QUIZ See page 209 for the answers. Review concepts from this section in MyEconLab.

Economic growth can be defined as the increase in _____ _____ real GDP, measured by its rate of change per year.

The _____ of economic growth are reductions in illiteracy, poverty, and illness and increases in life spans and political stability. The _____ of economic growth may include environmental pollution, alienation, and urban congestion.

Small percentage-point differences in growth rates lead to _____ differences in per capita real GDP over time. These differences can be seen by examining a compound interest table such as the one in Table 9-3 on page 191.

Productivity Increases: The Heart of Economic Growth

Let's say that you are required to type 10 term papers and homework assignments a year. You have a digital device, but you do not know how to touch-type. You end up spending an average of two hours per typing job. The next summer, you buy a touch-typing tutorial to use on your digital device and spend a few minutes a day improving your speed. The following term, you spend only one hour per typing assignment, thereby saving 10 hours a semester. You have become more productive. This concept of productivity summarizes your ability (and everyone else's) to produce the same output with fewer inputs. Thus, **labor productivity** is normally measured by dividing total real domestic output (real GDP) by the number of workers or the number of labor hours. By definition, labor productivity increases whenever average output produced per worker (or per hour worked) during a specified time period increases.

Labor productivity
Total real domestic output (real GDP) divided by the number of workers (output per worker).

Clearly, there is a relationship between economic growth and increases in labor productivity. If you divide all resources into just capital and labor, economic growth can be defined simply as the cumulative contribution to per capita GDP growth of three components: the rate of growth of capital, the rate of growth of labor, and the rate of growth of capital and labor productivity. If everything else remains constant, improvements in labor productivity ultimately lead to economic growth and higher living standards.

Go to www.econtoday.com/chap09 for information about the latest trends in U.S. labor productivity.

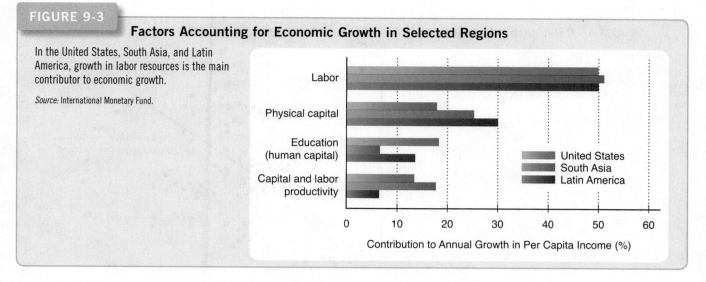

FIGURE 9-3

Factors Accounting for Economic Growth in Selected Regions

In the United States, South Asia, and Latin America, growth in labor resources is the main contributor to economic growth.

Source: International Monetary Fund.

Figure 9-3 above displays estimates of the relative contributions of the growth of labor and capital and the growth of labor and capital productivity to economic growth in the United States, nations in South Asia, and Latin American countries. The growth of labor resources, through associated increases in labor force participation, has contributed to the expansion of output that has accounted for at least half of economic growth in all three regions. Total capital is the sum of physical capital, such as tools and machines, and human capital, which is the amount of knowledge acquired from research and education.

Figure 9-3 shows the separate contributions of the growth of these forms of capital, which together have accounted for roughly a third of the growth rate of per capita incomes in the United States, South Asia, and Latin America. In these three parts of the world, growth in overall capital and labor productivity has contributed the remaining 7 to 18 percent.

Saving: A Fundamental Determinant of Economic Growth

Economic growth does not occur in a vacuum. It is not some predetermined fate of a nation. Rather, economic growth depends on certain fundamental factors. One of the most important factors that affect the rate of economic growth and hence long-term living standards is the rate of saving.

A basic proposition in economics is that if you want more tomorrow, you have to consume less today.

To have more consumption in the future, you have to consume less today and save the difference between your income and your consumption.

On a national basis, this implies that higher saving rates eventually mean higher living standards in the long run, all other things held constant. Although the U.S. saving rate has recently increased, concern has been growing that we still are not saving enough. Saving is important for economic growth because without saving, we cannot have investment. If there is no investment in our capital stock, there would be much less economic growth.

The relationship between the rate of saving and per capita real GDP is shown in Figure 9-4 on the next page. Among the nations with the highest rates of saving are China, Germany, Japan, and Saudi Arabia.

FIGURE 9-4

Relationship between Rate of Saving and Per Capita Real GDP

This diagram shows the relationship between per capita real GDP and the rate of saving expressed as the average share of annual real GDP saved.

Source: World Bank.

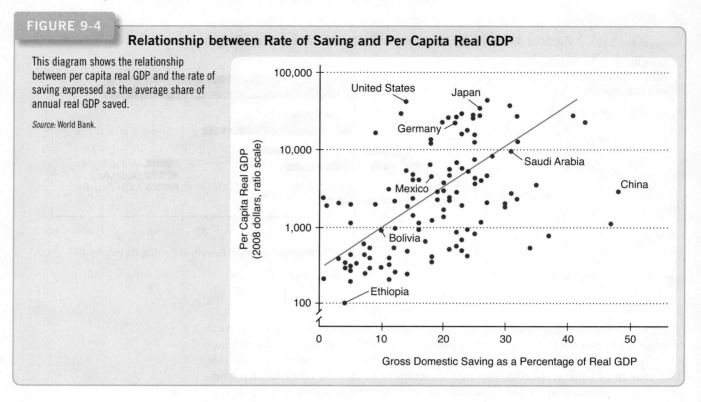

QUICK QUIZ   See page 209 for the answers. Review concepts from this section in MyEconLab.

Economic growth is numerically equal to the rate of growth of _____ plus the rate of growth of _____ plus the rate of growth in the productivity of _____ and of _____. Improvements in labor productivity, all other things being equal, lead to greater economic growth and higher living standards.

One fundamental determinant of the rate of growth is the rate of _____. To have more consumption in the future, we have to _____ rather than consume. In general, countries that have had higher rates of _____ have had higher rates of growth in per capita real GDP.

New Growth Theory and the Determinants of Growth

A simple arithmetic definition of economic growth has already been given. The per capita growth rates of capital and labor plus the per capita growth rate of their productivity constitute the rate of economic growth. Economists have had good data on the growth of the physical capital stock in the United States as well as on the labor force. But when you add those two growth rates together, you still do not get the total economic growth rate in the United States. The difference has to be due to improvements in productivity. Economists typically labeled this "improvements in technology," and that was that. More recently, proponents of what is now called **new growth theory** argue that technology cannot simply be viewed as an outside factor without explanation. Technology must be understood in terms of what drives it. What are the forces that make productivity grow in the United States and elsewhere?

New growth theory

A theory of economic growth that examines the factors that determine why technology, research, innovation, and the like are undertaken and how they interact.

Growth in Technology

Consider some startling statistics about the growth in technology. Microprocessor speeds may increase from 4,000 megahertz to 10,000 megahertz by the year 2025. By that same year, the size of the thinnest circuit line within a transistor may decrease by 90 percent. The typical memory capacity (RAM) of digital devices will jump from 8 gigabytes, or more than 100 times the equivalent text in the Internal Revenue Code, to more than 400 gigabytes. Recent developments in phase-change memory technologies and in new techniques for storing bits of data on molecules and even individual atoms promise even greater expansions of digital memory capacities. Predictions are that computers may become as powerful as the human brain by 2030.

Technology: A Separate Factor of Production

We now recognize that technology must be viewed as a separate factor of production that is sensitive to rewards. Indeed, one of the major foundations of new growth theory is this:

When the rewards are greater, more technological advances will occur.

Let's consider several aspects of technology here, the first one being research and development.

Research and Development

A certain amount of technological advance results from research and development (R&D) activities that have as their goal the development of specific new materials, new products, and new machines. How much spending a nation devotes to R&D can have an impact on its long-term economic growth. Part of how much a nation spends depends on what businesses decide is worth spending. That in turn depends on their expected rewards from successful R&D. If your company develops a new way to produce computer memory chips, how much will it be rewarded? The answer depends on what you can charge others to use the new technique.

PATENTS To protect new techniques developed through R&D, we have a system of **patents,** in which the federal government gives the patent holder the exclusive right to make, use, and sell an invention for a period of 20 years. One can argue that this special protection given to owners of patents increases expenditures on R&D and therefore adds to long-term economic growth. Figure 9-5 below shows

YOU ARE THERE

To learn about the economic implications of a change in how the U.S. legal system handles patents, take a look at **Implementing a New Patent Framework to Promote Innovation** on page 204.

Patent

A government protection that gives an inventor the exclusive right to make, use, or sell an invention for a limited period of time (currently, 20 years).

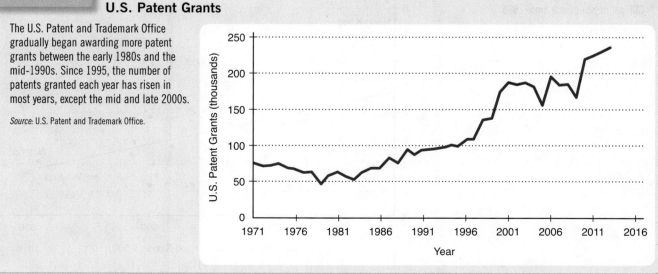

FIGURE 9-5

U.S. Patent Grants

The U.S. Patent and Trademark Office gradually began awarding more patent grants between the early 1980s and the mid-1990s. Since 1995, the number of patents granted each year has risen in most years, except the mid and late 2000s.

Source: U.S. Patent and Trademark Office.

that U.S. patent grants fell during the 1970s, increased steadily after 1982, surged following 1995, dropped in 2004 and 2005, and increased again after 2007.

POSITIVE EXTERNALITIES AND R&D As we discussed in Chapter 5, positive externalities are benefits from an activity that are enjoyed by someone besides the instigator of the activity. In the case of R&D spending, a certain amount of the benefits go to other companies that do not have to pay for them. In particular, according to economists David Coe of the International Monetary Fund and Elhanan Helpman of Harvard University, about a quarter of the global productivity gains of R&D investment in the top seven industrialized countries goes to other nations. For every 1 percent rise in the stock of R&D in the United States alone, for example, productivity in the rest of the world increases by about 0.25 percent.

One country's R&D expenditures benefit other countries because they are able to import capital goods—say, computers and telecommunications networks—from technologically advanced countries and then use them as inputs in making their own industries more efficient. In addition, countries that import high-tech goods are able to imitate the technology.

The Open Economy and Economic Growth

People who study economic growth today emphasize the importance of the openness of the economy. Free trade encourages a more rapid spread of technology and industrial ideas. Moreover, open economies may experience higher rates of economic growth because their own industries have access to a bigger market. When trade barriers are erected in the form of tariffs and the like, domestic industries become isolated from global technological progress. This occurred for many years in Communist countries and in most developing countries in Africa, Latin America, and elsewhere. Figure 9-6 below shows the relationship between economic growth and openness as measured by the level of tariff barriers.

Is China's rapid pace of economic growth threatened by a reduction in the nation's international openness?

FIGURE 9-6

The Relationship between Economic Growth and Tariff Barriers to International Trade

Nations with low tariff barriers are relatively open to international trade and have tended to have higher average annual rates of real GDP per capita growth since 1965.

Source: World Bank.

INTERNATIONAL POLICY EXAMPLE

China Rethinks Its Openness to Merchandise Trade

During the latter 1990s and 2000s, China's annual rate of economic growth often exceeded 8 percent. In recent years, however, its average growth rate has dropped slightly. Some observers suggest that this growth dip has resulted from an "indigenous (home-developed) innovation" policy implemented by the nation's government. This policy gives advantages to domestic sellers of a variety of goods, including computing and telecommunications devices and office equipment. The policy thus effectively discourages imports of these items.

China's government has extended special protections to financial services, such as property-casualty and life insurance, from foreign competition. The indigenous innovation policy therefore now includes imports of services as well as physical goods. Consequently, China has a less open economy, one not so likely to grow quite as rapidly as before.

FOR CRITICAL THINKING

Why might restrictions on imports of the latest digital devices particularly threaten China's rapid pace of economic growth?

Innovation and Knowledge

We tend to think of technological progress as, say, the invention of the transistor. But invention means little by itself. **Innovation** is required. Innovation involves the transformation of something new, such as an invention, into something that benefits the economy either by lowering production costs or by providing new goods and services. Indeed, the new growth theorists believe that real wealth creation comes from innovation and that invention is but a facet of innovation.

Historically, technologies have moved relatively slowly from invention to innovation to widespread use. The dispersion of new technology remains for the most part slow and uncertain. The inventor of the transistor thought it might be used to make better hearing aids. At the time it was invented, the *New York Times*'s sole reference to it was in a small weekly column called "News of Radio." When the laser was invented, no one really knew what it could be used for. It was initially used to help in navigation, measurement, and chemical research. Today, it is used in the reproduction of music, printing, surgery, telecommunications, and optical data transmittal and storage. Tomorrow, who knows?

Typically, thousands of raw ideas emerge each year at a large firm's R&D laboratories. Only a few hundred of these ideas develop into formal proposals for new processes or products. Of these proposals, the business selects perhaps a few dozen that it deems suitable for further study to explore their feasibility. After careful scrutiny, the firm concludes that only a handful of these ideas are inventions worthy of being integrated into actual production processes or launched as novel products. The firm is fortunate if one or two ultimately become successful marketplace innovations.

How have efforts by physicists to hide objects from sight set off a search for innovations applying to a variety of markets?

Innovation
Transforming an invention into something that is useful to humans.

EXAMPLE

The Quest for Invisibility Promises Waves of Innovation

Physicists have developed ways to make objects disappear by using fabrics called *metamaterials* to deflect electromagnetic—for instance, light and magnetic—waves and thereby create artificial blind spots. Originally, the idea behind such inventive activities was to make items invisible to the human eye, thereby rendering magicians' tricks using mirrors and sleight of hand obsolete. Once physicists realized that metamaterials could effectively cancel out electromagnetic waves, however, they began to concentrate on developing potentially marketable innovations.

One possible innovation is elimination of cell phone static by making buildings disappear to wireless signals. Another is the potential for dramatic improvements in magnetic resonance images (MRIs) used to diagnose physical ailments. Finally, deflection of electromagnetic waves offers promise in canceling out waves of water, such as tsunamis that otherwise might damage offshore oil platforms. Thus, the pursuit of invisibility may produce several innovations.

FOR CRITICAL THINKING

So far, does invisibility research appear to have yielded inventions or innovations? Explain.

The Importance of Ideas and Knowledge

Economist Paul Romer has added at least one other important factor that determines the rate of economic growth. He contends that production and manufacturing knowledge is just as important as the other determinants and perhaps even more so. He considers knowledge a factor of production that, like capital, has to be paid for by forgoing current consumption. Economies must therefore invest in knowledge just as they invest in machines. Because past investment in capital may make it more profitable to acquire more knowledge, there may be an investment-knowledge cycle in which investment spurs knowledge and knowledge spurs investment.

A once-and-for-all increase in a country's rate of investment may permanently raise that country's growth rate. (According to traditional theory, a once-and-for-all increase in the rate of saving and therefore in the rate of investment simply leads to a new steady-state standard of living, not one that continues to increase.)

Another way of looking at knowledge is that it is a store of ideas. According to Romer, ideas are what drive economic growth. In fact, we have become an idea economy. Consider Apple, Inc. A relatively small percentage of that company's labor force is involved in actually building products. Rather, a majority of Apple's employees are attempting to discover new ideas that can be translated into computer code that can then be turned into products. The major conclusion that Romer and other new growth theorists draw is this:

Economic growth can continue as long as we keep coming up with new ideas.

The Importance of Human Capital

Knowledge, ideas, and productivity are all tied together. One of the threads is the quality of the labor force. Increases in the productivity of the labor force are a function of increases in human capital, the fourth factor of production discussed in Chapter 2. Recall that human capital consists of the knowledge and skills that people in the workforce acquire through education, on-the-job training, and self-teaching. To increase your own human capital, you have to invest by forgoing income-earning activities while you attend school. Society also has to invest in the form of teachers and education.

According to the new growth theorists, human capital is becoming nearly as important as physical capital, particularly when trying to explain international differences in living standards. It is therefore not surprising that one of the most effective ways that developing countries can become developed is by investing in secondary schooling.

One can argue that policy changes that increase human capital will lead to more technological improvements. One of the reasons that concerned citizens, policymakers, and politicians are looking for a change in the U.S. schooling system is that our educational system seems to be falling behind those of other countries. This lag is greatest in science and mathematics—precisely the areas required for developing better technology.

How have periodic drains of human capital affected economic growth in Ireland?

INTERNATIONAL EXAMPLE

Ireland Experiences Yet Another Big "Brain Drain"

It is common to refer to an emigration of many of a nation's most skilled residents to other countries as a "brain drain." During the past two centuries, Ireland has experienced several brain drains. Most well known was the departure of about a million Irish residents in response to the great potato famine of the mid-nineteenth century. About a century later, an economic meltdown induced tens of thousands of Irish residents to move to Britain. A similar population shift took place in the late 1980s, when about 120,000 Irish residents left for England.

Following a major business downturn in Ireland in 2008, yet another emigration wave began. During the past couple of years, about 1,000 people per week have departed from Ireland's shores. Current forecasts suggest that this latest population shift away from Ireland eventually will total at least 150,000 people, including many of that nation's best-educated professionals. In response to this latest Irish brain drain, many economists have reduced substantially their estimates for Ireland's long-term rate of economic growth.

FOR CRITICAL THINKING

Can you think of any policy actions, short of explicit limits on emigration, that a nation's government might implement in an effort to slow or even halt a brain drain?

QUICK QUIZ   See page 209 for the answers. Review concepts from this section in MyEconLab.

_____ _____ theory argues that the greater the rewards, the more rapid the pace of technology. And greater rewards spur research and development.

The openness of a nation's economy to international _____ seems to correlate with its rate of economic growth.

Invention and innovation are not the same thing. _____ are useless until _____ transforms them into goods and services that people find valuable.

According to _____ _____ theory, economic growth can continue as long as we keep coming up with new ideas.

Increases in _____ capital can lead to greater rates of economic growth. These come about by increased education, on-the-job training, and self-teaching.

Immigration, Property Rights, and Growth

New theories of economic growth have also shed light on two additional factors that play important roles in influencing a nation's rate of growth of per capita real GDP: immigration and property rights.

Population and Immigration as They Affect Economic Growth

There are several ways to view population growth as it affects economic growth. On the one hand, population growth can result in a larger labor force and increases in human capital, which contribute to economic growth. On the other hand, population growth can be seen as a drain on the economy because for any given amount of GDP, more population means lower per capita GDP. According to Harvard economist Michael Kremer, the first of these effects is historically more important. His conclusion is that population growth drives technological progress, which then increases economic growth. The theory is simple: If there are 50 percent more people in the United States, there will be 50 percent more geniuses. And with 50 percent more people, the rewards for creativity are commensurately greater. Otherwise stated, the larger the potential market, the greater the incentive to become ingenious.

A larger market also provides an incentive for well-trained people to immigrate, which undoubtedly helps explain why the United States attracts a disproportionate number of top scientists from around the globe.

Does immigration help spur economic growth? Yes, according to the late economist Julian Simon, who pointed out that "every time our system allows in one more immigrant, on average, the economic welfare of American citizens goes up. . . . Additional immigrants, both the legal and the illegal, raise the standard of living of U.S. natives and have little or no negative impact on any occupational or income class." He further argued that immigrants do not displace natives from jobs but rather create jobs through their purchases and by starting new businesses. Immigrants' earning and spending simply expand the economy.

Not all researchers agree with Simon, and few studies have tested the theories he and Kremer have advanced. This area is currently the focus of much research.

WHAT IF...   **the government halted inflows of immigrants possessing scientific training?**

Economists have found that the influx of scientifically trained immigrants contributes to about one-third of the annual flow of new inventions that obtain U.S. patents. This means that if the already-constrained inflow of immigrants with academic backgrounds in math and science were halted, the number of inventions per year likely would drop to about two-thirds of its current number. Thus, further limits on immigration of foreign scientists would substantially reduce innovative activity in the United States.

Property Rights and Entrepreneurship

If you were in a country where bank accounts and businesses were periodically expro-priated by the government, how willing would you be to leave your financial assets in a savings account or to invest in a business? Certainly, you would be less willing than if such actions never occurred. In general, the more securely private property rights (see page 102) are assigned, the more capital accumulation there will be. People will be willing to invest their savings in endeavors that will increase their wealth in future years. This requires that property rights in their wealth be sanctioned and enforced by the government. In fact, some economic historians have attempted to show that it was the development of well-defined private property rights and legal structures that allowed Western Europe to increase its growth rate after many centuries of stagna-tion. The ability and certainty with which they can reap the gains from investing also determine the extent to which business owners in other countries will invest capital in developing countries. The threat of loss of property rights that hangs over some developing nations undoubtedly stands in the way of foreign investments that would allow these nations to develop more rapidly.

The legal structure of a nation is closely tied to the degree with which its citizens use their own entrepreneurial skills. In Chapter 2, we identified entrepreneurship as the fifth factor of production. Entrepreneurs are the risk takers who seek out new ways to do things and create new products. To the extent that entrepreneurs are allowed to capture the rewards from their entrepreneurial activities, they will seek to engage in those activities. In countries where such rewards cannot be captured because of a lack of property rights, there will be less entrepreneurship. Typically, this results in fewer investments and a lower rate of growth. We shall examine the implications this has for policymakers in Chapter 18.

QUICK QUIZ See page 209 for the answers. Review concepts from this section in MyEconLab.

While some economists argue that population growth reduces _____ growth, others contend that the opposite is true. The latter economists consequently believe that immigration should be encouraged rather than discouraged.

Well-defined and protected _____ rights are important for fostering entrepreneurship. In the absence of well-defined _____ rights, individuals have less incentive to take risks, and economic growth rates suffer.

Economic Development

Development economics
The study of factors that contribute to the economic growth of a country.

How did developed countries travel paths of growth from extreme poverty to relative riches? That is the essential issue of **development economics,** which is the study of why some countries grow and develop and others do not and of policies that might help developing economies get richer. It is not enough simply to say that people in different countries are different and that is why some countries are rich and some countries are poor. Economists do not deny that different cultures have different work ethics, but they are unwilling to accept such a pat and fatalistic answer.

Look at any world map. About four-fifths of the countries you will see on the map are considered relatively poor. The goal of economists who study development is to help the more than 4 billion people today with low living standards join the more than 2 billion people who have at least moderately high living standards.

Putting World Poverty into Perspective

Most U.S. residents cannot even begin to understand the reality of poverty in the world today. At least one-half, if not two-thirds, of the world's population lives at subsistence level, with just enough to eat for survival. Indeed, the World Bank esti-mates that nearly 20 percent of the world's people live on less than $1.50 per day. The official poverty line in the United States is above the annual income of at least half the human beings on the planet. This is not to say that we should ignore domestic problems with the poor and homeless simply because they are living better than many people elsewhere in the world. Rather, it is necessary for us to maintain an appropriate perspective on what are considered problems for this country relative to what are considered problems elsewhere.

The Relationship between Population Growth and Economic Development

The world's population is growing at the rate of about 2 people a second. That amounts to 172,800 a day or 63.1 million a year. Today, there are more than 6.8 billion people on earth. By 2050, according to the United Nations, the world's population will be close to leveling off at around 9 billion. Panel (a) of Figure 9-7 on the following page shows population growth. Panel (b) emphasizes an implication of panel (a), which is that almost all the growth in population is occurring in developing nations. Many developed countries are expected to lose population over the next several decades.

Ever since the Reverend Thomas Robert Malthus wrote *An Essay on the Principle of Population* in 1798, excessive population growth has been a concern. Modern-day Malthusians are able to generate great enthusiasm for the concept that population growth is bad. Over and over, media pundits and a number of scientists tell us that rapid population growth threatens economic development and the quality of life.

MALTHUS WAS PROVED WRONG Malthus predicted that population would outstrip food supplies. This prediction has never been supported by the facts, according to economist Nicholas Eberstadt of the American Enterprise Institute for Public Policy Research. As the world's population has grown, so has the world's food stock, measured by calories per person. Furthermore, the price of food, corrected for inflation, has generally been falling for more than a century. That means that the amount of food has been expanding faster than the increase in demand caused by increased population.

GROWTH LEADS TO SMALLER FAMILIES Furthermore, economists have found that as nations become richer, average family size declines. Otherwise stated, the more economic development occurs, the slower the population growth rate becomes. This has certainly been true in Western Europe and in the former Soviet Union, where populations in some countries are actually declining. Predictions of birthrates in developing countries have often turned out to be overstated if those countries experience rapid economic growth. This was the case in Chile, Hong Kong, Mexico, and Taiwan.

Recent research on population and economic development has revealed that social and economic modernization has been accompanied by a decline in childbearing significant enough that it might be called a fertility revolution. Modernization reduces infant mortality, which in turn reduces the incentive for couples to have many children to make sure that a certain number survive to adulthood. Modernization also lowers the demand for children for a variety of reasons, not the least being that couples in more developed countries do not need to rely on their children to take care of them in old age.

The Stages of Development: Agriculture to Industry to Services

If we analyze the development of modern rich nations, we find that they went through three stages. First is the agricultural stage, when most of the population is involved in agriculture. Then comes the manufacturing stage, when much of the population becomes involved in the industrialized sector of the economy. And finally there is a shift toward services. That is exactly what happened in the United States: The so-called tertiary, or service, sector of the economy continues to grow, whereas the manufacturing sector (and its share of employment) is declining in relative importance.

FIGURE 9-7

Expected Growth in World Population by 2050

Panel (a) displays the percentages of the world's population residing in the various continents by 2050 and shows projected population growth for these continents and for selected nations. It indicates that Asia and Africa are expected to gain the most in population by the year 2050.

Panel (b) indicates that population will increase in developing countries before beginning to level off around 2050, whereas industrially advanced nations will grow very little in population in the first half of this century.

Source: United Nations.

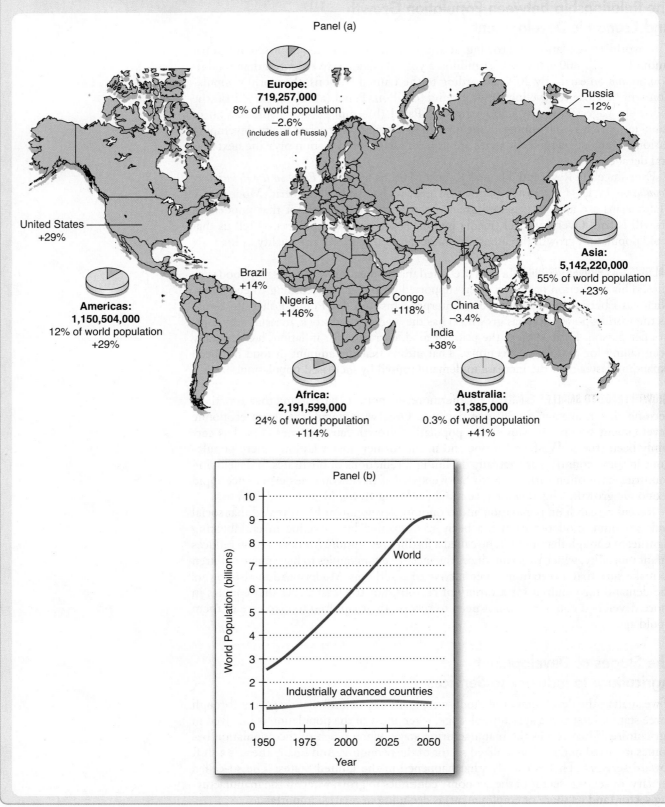

Panel (a)

Europe:
719,257,000
8% of world population
−2.6%
(includes all of Russia)

Russia
−12%

United States
+29%

Brazil
+14%

Nigeria
+146%

Congo
+118%

China
−3.4%

India
+38%

Asia:
5,142,220,000
55% of world population
+23%

Americas:
1,150,504,000
12% of world population
+29%

Africa:
2,191,599,000
24% of world population
+114%

Australia:
31,385,000
0.3% of world population
+41%

Panel (b)

World

Industrially advanced countries

World Population (billions)

Year

Of particular significance, however, is the requirement for early specialization in a nation's comparative advantage (see Chapter 2). The doctrine of comparative advantage is particularly appropriate for the developing countries of the world. If trading is allowed among nations, a country is best off if it produces what it has a comparative advantage in producing and imports the rest (for more details, see Chapter 32). This means that many developing countries should continue to specialize in agricultural production or in labor-intensive manufactured goods.

Keys to Economic Development

According to one theory of development, a country must have a large natural resource base in order to develop. This theory goes on to assert that much of the world is running out of natural resources, thereby limiting economic growth and development. Only the narrowest definition of a natural resource, however, could lead to such an opinion. In broader terms, a natural resource is something occurring in nature that we can use for our own purposes. As emphasized by new growth theory, natural resources therefore include human capital—education and experience. Also, natural resources change over time. Several hundred years ago, for example, they did not include hydroelectric power—no one knew that such a natural resource existed or how to bring it into existence.

Natural resources by themselves are not a prerequisite for or a guarantee of economic development, as demonstrated by Japan's extensive development despite a lack of domestic oil resources and by Brazil's slow pace of development in spite of a vast array of natural resources. Resources must be transformed into something usable for either investment or consumption.

Economists have found that four factors seem to be highly related to the pace of economic development:

1. *Establishing a system of property rights.* As noted earlier, if you were in a country where bank accounts and businesses were periodically expropriated by the government, you would be reluctant to leave some of your wealth in a savings account or to invest in a business. Expropriation of private property rarely takes place in developed countries. It has occurred in numerous developing countries, however. For example, private property has been nationalized in Venezuela and in Cuba. Economists have found that other things being equal, the more secure private property rights are, the more private capital accumulation and economic growth there will be.

2. *Developing an educated population.* Both theoretically and empirically, we know that a more educated workforce aids economic development because it allows individuals to build on the ideas of others. Thus, developing countries can advance more rapidly if they increase investments in education. Or, stated in the negative, economic development is difficult to sustain if a nation allows a sizable portion of its population to remain uneducated. Education allows impoverished young people to acquire skills that enable them to avoid poverty as adults.

3. *Letting "creative destruction" run its course.* The twentieth-century Harvard economist Joseph Schumpeter championed the concept of "creative destruction," through which new businesses ultimately create new jobs and economic growth after first destroying old jobs, old companies, and old industries. Such change is painful and costly, but it is necessary for economic advancement. Nowhere is this more important than in developing countries, where the principle is often ignored. Many governments in developing nations have had a history of supporting current companies and industries by discouraging new technologies and new companies from entering the marketplace. The process of creative destruction has not been allowed to work its magic in these countries.

4. *Limiting protectionism.* Open economies experience faster economic development than economies closed to international trade. Trade encourages people and businesses to discover ways to specialize so that they can become more productive and earn higher incomes. Increased productivity and subsequent increases in economic growth are the results. Thus, having fewer trade barriers promotes faster economic development.

Go to www.econtoday.com/chap09 to contemplate whether there may be a relationship between inequality and a nation's growth and to visit the home page of the World Bank's Thematic Group on Inequality, Poverty, and Socioeconomic Performance.

Go to www.econtoday.com/chap09 to link to a World Trade Organization explanation of how free trade promotes greater economic growth and higher employment.

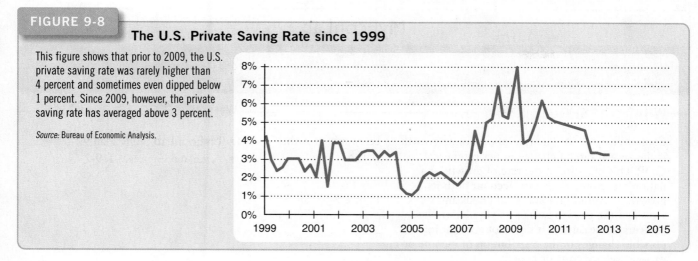

QUICK QUIZ See page 209 for the answers. Review concepts from this section in MyEconLab.

Although many people believe that population growth hinders economic development, there is little evidence to support that notion. What is clear is that economic development tends to lead to a reduction in the rate of _________ growth.

Historically, there are three stages of economic development: the _________ stage, the _________ stage, and the _________-_________ stage, when a large part of the workforce is employed in providing services.

Although one theory of economic development holds that a sizable natural resource base is the key to a nation's development, this fails to account for the importance of the human element: The _________ _________ must be capable of using a country's natural resources.

Fundamental factors contributing to the pace of economic development are a well-defined system of _________ _________, training and _________, allowing new generations of companies and industries to _________ older generations, and promoting an open economy by allowing _________ _________.

YOU ARE THERE

Implementing a New Patent Framework to Promote Innovation

Senator Patrick Leahy looks on as President Barack Obama signs into law the America Invents Act, a law Leahy had authored with the aim of boosting the rate of U.S. innovation via an overhaul of the nation's patent system. Under the prior law governing patents, property rights to the returns from invention were determined on a "first-to-invent" basis. This meant that if two individuals or companies happened to invent similar products or processes at about the same time, they had to prove in court whose invention was first. Over the years, this requirement had touched off thousands of court fights among patent holders.

The legislation drawn up by Leahy and approved by Congress and the president has established a "first-to-file" rule for patents. Now the property rights associated with any invention are automatically assigned to the first individual or firm to apply for a patent for that invention. Leahy's expectation is that patent holders who once directed financial resources toward funding court battles now will use them to transform more inventions into market innovations. Speeding along the innovation process, Leahy anticipates, will help to fuel economic growth.

Critical Thinking Questions

1. Why are inventions alone insufficient to help boost economic growth?
2. What role do you think that markets perform in determining whether inventions of new products or processes translate into longer-lasting innovations?

ISSUES & APPLICATIONS

Does a Household Shift to Thrift Signal a Growth Recovery?

CONCEPTS APPLIED

- Saving Rate
- Economic Growth
- Investment

A nation's saving rate is fundamental to its economic growth. Higher saving today can be channeled to current investment in capital goods, which people can use to produce more goods and services for future consumption.

FIGURE 9-8

The U.S. Private Saving Rate since 1999

This figure shows that prior to 2009, the U.S. private saving rate was rarely higher than 4 percent and sometimes even dipped below 1 percent. Since 2009, however, the private saving rate has averaged above 3 percent.

Source: Bureau of Economic Analysis.

A Higher Private Saving Rate in the United States

Figure 9-8 above indicates that during the 2000s, the U.S. *private* saving rate—annual saving as a percentage of disposable personal income—averaged only about 2.5 percent per year. This low private saving rate helped to explain the dampened growth rate of about 1 percent during subsequent years.

Figure 9-8 shows that the private saving rate has averaged above 3 percent since 2009. This fact has generated greater optimism for some economists that U.S. economic growth might begin to recover.

A Still Low—Actually, Negative—*Overall* National Saving Rate

Bringing government actions into the story complicates the picture. Between 2000 and 2008, the government borrowed an average of $264 billion per year, so flows of public saving were *negative*. This implied an average public saving rate, relative to disposable personal income, of about −2.4 percent. Adding the private saving rate for 2000–2008 of +2.5 percent suggests that over this interval the national saving rate was about 0.1 percent. Overall, therefore, the national saving rate between 2000 and 2008 was nearly zero.

Since 2009, government borrowing has ballooned to about $1,300 billion per year, yielding a public saving rate, in relation to disposable personal income, equal to approx-

imately −11 percent. Adding this negative public saving rate to the private saving rate of about 3 percent yields an overall national saving rate of −8 percent. The fact that the national saving rate in the United States has become highly *negative* since 2009 implies that U.S. economic growth prospects actually have diminished.

For Critical Thinking

1. Why does borrowing constitute negative saving?
2. Given that a negative flow of annual national saving implies that residents of the United States are net borrowers, who must be funding this borrowing each year?

Web Resources

1. For the latest data on U.S. private saving, go to **www.econtoday.com/chap09**.
2. To see when the overall U.S. national saving rate first became negative, go to **www.econtoday.com/chap09**.

MyEconLab

For more questions on this chapter's Issues & Applications, go to MyEconLab. In the Study Plan for this chapter, select Section N: News.

MyEconLab

Here is what you should know after reading this chapter. MyEconLab will help you identify what you know, and where to go when you need to practice.

WHAT YOU SHOULD KNOW		WHERE TO GO TO PRACTICE
Economic Growth The rate of economic growth is the annual rate of change in per capita real GDP. This measure of the rate of growth of a nation's economy takes into account both its growth in overall production of goods and services and the growth rate of its population. It is an average measure that does not account for possible changes in the distribution of income or various welfare costs or benefits.	economic growth, 188 **Key Figures** Figure 9-1, 188 Figure 9-2, 190	• MyEconLab Study Plan 9.1 • Animated Figures 9-1, 9-2
Why Economic Growth Rates Are Important Economic growth compounds over time. Thus, over long intervals, relatively small differences in the rate of economic growth can accumulate to produce large disparities in per capita incomes.	rule of 70, 192	• MyEconLab Study Plan 9.1
Why Productivity Increases Are Crucial for Maintaining Economic Growth Productivity growth is a fundamental factor influencing near-term changes in economic growth. Higher productivity growth unambiguously contributes to greater annual increases in a nation's per capita real GDP.	labor productivity, 192	• MyEconLab Study Plan 9.2
The Key Determinants of Economic Growth The fundamental factors contributing to economic growth are growth in a nation's pool of labor, growth of its capital stock, and growth in the productivity of its capital and labor. A key determinant of capital accumulation is a nation's saving rate. Higher saving rates contribute to greater investment and hence increased capital accumulation and economic growth.		• MyEconLab Study Plan 9.3
New Growth Theory This theory examines why individuals and businesses conduct research into inventing and developing new technologies and how this innovation process interacts with the rate of economic growth. A key implication of the theory is that ideas and knowledge are crucial elements of the growth process.	new growth theory, 194 patent, 195 innovation, 197 **Key Figures** Figure 9-5, 195 Figure 9-6, 196	• MyEconLab Study Plan 9.4 • Animated Figures 9-5, 9-6

MyEconLab *continued*

Log in to MyEconLab, take a chapter test, and get a personalized Study Plan that tells you which concepts you understand and which ones you need to review. From there, MyEconLab will give you further practice, tutorials, animations, videos, and guided solutions. For more information, visit www.myeconlab.com

PROBLEMS

All problems are assignable in MyEconLab; *exercises that update with real-time data are marked with* 🌐. *Answers to odd-numbered problems appear at the back of the book.*

9-1. The graph below shows a production possibilities curve for 2016 and two potential production possibilities curves for 2017, denoted 2017$_A$ and 2017$_B$. (See page 188.)

    a. Which of the labeled points corresponds to maximum feasible 2016 production that is more likely to be associated with the curve denoted 2017$_A$?

    b. Which of the labeled points corresponds to maximum feasible 2016 production that is more likely to be associated with the curve denoted 2017$_B$?

9-2. A nation's capital goods wear out over time, so a portion of its capital goods become unusable every year. Last year, its residents decided to produce no capital goods. It has experienced no growth in its population or in the amounts of other productive resources during the past year. In addition, the nation's technology and resource productivity have remained unchanged during the past year. Will the nation's economic growth rate for the current year be negative, zero, or positive? (See page 192.)

9-3. In the situation described in Problem 9-2, suppose that vocational training during the past year enable the people of this nation to repair all capital goods so that they continue to function as well as new. All other factors are unchanged, however. In light of this single change to the conditions faced in this nation, will the nation's economic growth rate for the current year be negative, zero, or positive? (See page 192.)

9-4. Consider the following data. What is the per capita real GDP in each of these countries? (See page 189.)

Country	Population (millions)	Real GDP ($ billions)
A	10	55
B	20	60
C	5	70

9-5. Suppose that during the next 10 years, real GDP triples and population doubles in each of the nations in Problem 9-4. What will per capita real GDP be in each country after 10 years have passed? (See pages 188–190.)

9-6. Consider the following table displaying annual growth rates for nations X, Y, and Z, each of which entered 2013 with real per capita GDP equal to $20,000 (see pages 188–190.)

	Annual Growth Rate (%)			
Country	2013	2014	2015	2016
X	7	1	3	4
Y	4	5	7	9
Z	5	5	3	2

a. Which nation most likely experienced a sizable earthquake in late 2013 that destroyed a significant portion of its stock of capital goods, but was followed by speedy investments in rebuilding the nation's capital stock? What is this nation's per capita real GDP at the end of 2016, rounded to the nearest dollar?

b. Which nation most likely adopted policies in 2013 that encouraged a gradual shift in production from capital goods to consumption goods? What is this nation's per capita real GDP at the end of 2016, rounded to the nearest dollar?

c. Which nation most likely adopted policies in 2013 that encouraged a quick shift in production from consumption goods to capital goods? What is this nation's per capita real GDP at the end of 2016, rounded to the nearest dollar?

9-7. Per capita real GDP grows at a rate of 3 percent in country F and at a rate of 6 percent in country G. Both begin with equal levels of per capita real GDP. Use Table 9-3 on page 191 to determine how much higher per capita real GDP will be in country G after 20 years. How much higher will real GDP be in country G after 40 years? (See page 191.)

9-8. Per capita real GDP in country L is three times as high as in country M. The economic growth rate in country M, however, is 8 percent, while country L's economy grows at a rate of 5 percent. Use Table 9-3 on page 191 to determine approximately how many years will pass before per capita real GDP in country M surpasses per capita real GDP in country L. (See page 191.)

9-9. Per capita real GDP in country S is only half as great as per capita real GDP in country T. Country T's rate of economic growth is 4 percent. The government of country S, however, enacts policies that achieve a growth rate of 20 percent. Use Table 9-3 on page 191 to determine how long country S must maintain this growth rate before its per capita real GDP surpasses that of country T. (See page 191.)

9-10. Since the early 1990s, the average rate of growth of per capita real GDP in Mozambique has been 3 percent per year, as compared with a growth rate of 8 percent in China. Refer to Table 9-3 on page 191. If a typical resident of each of these nations begins this year with a per capita real GDP of $3,000 per year, about how many more dollars' worth of real GDP per capita would the person in China be earning 10 years from now than the individual in Mozambique? (See page 191.)

9-11. On the basis of the information in Problem 9-10 and reference to Table 9-3 on page 191, about how many more dollars' worth of real GDP per capita would the person in China be earning 50 years from now than the individual in Mozambique? (See page 191.)

9-12. In 2014, a nation's population was 10 million. Its nominal GDP was $40 billion, and its price index was 100. In 2015, its population had increased to 12 million, its nominal GDP had risen to $57.6 billion, and its price index had increased to 120. What was this nation's economic growth rate during the year? (See page 191.)

9-13. Between the start of 2014 and the start of 2015, a country's economic growth rate was 4 percent. Its population did not change during the year, nor did its price level. What was the rate of increase of the country's nominal GDP during this one-year interval? (See page 191.)

9-14. In 2014, a nation's population was 10 million, its real GDP was $1.21 billion, and its GDP deflator had a value of 121. By 2015, its population had increased to 12 million, its real GDP had risen to $1.5 billion, and its GDP deflator had a value of 125. What was the percentage change in per capita real GDP between 2014 and 2015? (See page 191.)

9-15. A nation's per capita real GDP was $2,000 in 2013, and the nation's population was 5 million in that year. Between 2013 and 2014, the inflation rate in this country was 5 percent, and the nation's annual rate of economic growth was 10 percent. Its population remained unchanged. What was per capita real GDP in 2014? What was the *level* of real GDP in 2014? (See page 191.)

9-16. Brazil has a population of about 200 million, with about 145 million over the age of 15. Of these, an estimated 25 percent, or 35 million people, are functionally illiterate. The typical literate individual reads only about two nonacademic books per year, which is less than half the number read by the typical literate U.S. or European resident. Answer the following questions solely from the perspective of new growth theory (see page 194):

a. Discuss the implications of Brazil's literacy and reading rates for its growth prospects in light of the key tenets of new growth theory.

b. What types of policies might Brazil implement to improve its growth prospects? Explain.

ECONOMICS ON THE NET

Multifactor Productivity and Its Growth Growth in productivity is a key factor determining a nation's overall economic growth.

Title: Bureau of Labor Statistics: Multifactor Productivity Trends

Navigation: Use the link at www.econtoday.com/chap09 to visit the multifactor productivity home page of the Bureau of Labor Statistics.

Application Read the summary, and answer the following questions.

1. What does multifactor productivity measure? Based on your reading of this chapter, how does multifactor productivity relate to the determination of economic growth?

2. Click on *Multifactor Productivity Trends in Manufacturing*. According to these data, which industries have exhibited the greatest productivity growth in recent years?

For Group Study and Analysis Divide the class into three groups to examine multifactor productivity data for the private business sector, the private nonfarm business sector, and the manufacturing sector. Have each group identify periods when multifactor productivity growth was particularly fast or slow. Then compare notes. Does it appear to make a big difference which sector one looks at when evaluating periods of greatest and least growth in multifactor productivity?

ANSWERS TO QUICK QUIZZES

p. 192: (i) per capita; (ii) benefits . . . costs; (iii) large

p. 194: (i) capital . . . labor . . . capital . . . labor; (ii) saving . . . save . . . saving

p. 199: (i) New growth; (ii) trade; (iii) Inventions . . . innovation; (iv) new growth; (v) human

p. 200: (i) economic; (ii) property . . . property

p. 204: (i) population; (ii) agricultural . . . manufacturing . . . service-sector; (iii) working population; (iv) property rights . . . education . . . replace . . . international trade

10

Real GDP and the Price Level in the Long Run

conomic growth has trended steadily downward during the past four decades in nations with northern borders that lie within the Arctic Circle, such as Canada, Russia, and the United States. Nevertheless, estimates indicate that if underutilized and untapped Arctic and near-Arctic resources were fully exploited, substantial long-term improvements in these nations' economic growth rates would occur. How could increased use of resources within Arctic regions, as well as in other areas, contribute to the aggregate production of goods and services? What would be additional economywide effects of increased resource exploitation, such as impacts on the average level of prices? In this chapter, you will contemplate the answers to these questions.

the Venezuelan president has used powers granted him by the nation's parliament to decree legislation, called the Fair Prices and Costs Law, that prevents increases in the prices of all goods and services? In this way, the Venezuelan government essentially sought to make illegal an increase in the overall level of prices, or *inflation.* In most nations, of course, governments rarely resort to such dramatic efforts to contain inflation. What causes inflation? In this chapter, you will find out the answer.

Output Growth and the Long-Run Aggregate Supply Curve

In Chapter 2, we showed the derivation of the production possibilities curve (PPC). At any point in time, the economy can be inside or on the PPC but never outside it. Along the PPC, a country's resources are fully employed in the production of goods and services, and the sum total of the inflation-adjusted value of all final goods and services produced is the nation's real GDP. Economists refer to the total of all planned production for the entire economy as the **aggregate supply** of real output.

Aggregate supply
The total of all planned production for the economy.

The Long-Run Aggregate Supply Curve

Put yourself in a world in which nothing has been changing, year in and year out. The price level has not changed. Technology has not changed. The prices of inputs that firms must purchase have not changed. Labor productivity has not changed. All resources are fully employed, so the economy operates on its production possibilities curve, such as the one depicted in panel (a) of Figure 10-1 below. This is a world that is fully adjusted and in which people have all the information they are ever going to have about that world. The **long-run aggregate supply curve** (*LRAS*) in this world is some amount of real GDP—say, $15 trillion of real GDP—which is the value of the flow of production of final goods and services measured in **base-year dollars.**

We can represent long-run aggregate supply by a vertical line at $15 trillion of real GDP. This is what you see in panel (b) of the figure below. That curve, labeled *LRAS*, is a vertical line determined by technology and **endowments,** or resources that exist in our economy. It is the full-information and full-adjustment level of real output of goods and services. It is the level of real GDP that will continue being produced year after year, forever, if nothing changes.

Long-run aggregate supply curve
A vertical line representing the real output of goods and services after full adjustment has occurred. It can also be viewed as representing the real GDP of the economy under conditions of full employment—the full-employment level of real GDP.

Base-year dollars
The value of a current sum expressed in terms of prices in a base year.

Endowments
The various resources in an economy, including both physical resources and such human resources as ingenuity and management skills.

FIGURE 10-1

The Production Possibilities Curve and the Economy's Long-Run Aggregate Supply Curve

At a point in time, a nation's base of resources and its technological capabilities define the position of its production possibilities curve (PPC), as shown in panel (a). This defines the real GDP that the nation can produce when resources are fully employed, which determines the position of the long-run aggregate supply curve (*LRAS*) displayed in panel (b). Because people have complete information and input prices adjust fully in the long run, the *LRAS* is vertical.

THE *LRAS* CURVE AND FULL-EMPLOYMENT REAL GDP Another way of viewing the *LRAS* is to think of it as the full-employment level of real GDP. When the economy reaches full employment along its production possibilities curve, no further adjustments will occur unless a change occurs in the other variables that we are assuming to be stable.

Some economists suggest that the *LRAS* occurs at the level of real GDP consistent with the natural rate of unemployment, the unemployment rate that occurs in an economy with full adjustment in the long run. As we discussed in Chapter 7, many economists like to think of the natural rate of unemployment as consisting of frictional and structural unemployment.

WHY THE *LRAS* CURVE IS VERTICAL To understand why the *LRAS* is vertical, think about the long run. To an economist examining the economy as a whole, the long run is a sufficiently long period that all factors of production and prices, including wages and other input prices, can change.

A change in the level of prices of goods and services has no effect on real GDP per year in the long run, because higher prices will be accompanied by comparable changes in input prices. Suppliers will therefore have no incentive to increase or decrease their production of goods and services. Remember that in the long run, everybody has full information, and there is full adjustment to price level changes. (Of course, this is not necessarily true in the short run, as we shall discuss in Chapter 11.)

Go to www.econtoday.com/chap10 to find out how fast wages are adjusting. Under "Latest Numbers," click on "Employment Cost Index."

Economic Growth and Long-Run Aggregate Supply

In Chapter 9, you learned about the determinants of growth in per capita real GDP: the annual growth rate of labor, the rate of year-to-year capital accumulation, and the rate of growth of the productivity of labor and capital. As time goes by, population gradually increases, and labor force participation rates may even rise. The capital stock typically grows as businesses add such capital equipment as new information-technology hardware. Furthermore, technology improves. Thus, the economy's production possibilities increase, and as a consequence, the production possibilities curve shifts outward, as shown in panel (a) of Figure 10-2 below.

The result is economic growth: Aggregate real GDP and per capita real GDP increase. This means that in a growing economy such as ours, the *LRAS* will shift outward to the right, as in panel (b) below. We have drawn the *LRAS* for the year 2015 to the right of our original *LRAS* of $14.3 trillion of real GDP. We assume that between

FIGURE 10-2

The Long-Run Aggregate Supply Curve and Shifts in It

In panel (a), we repeat a diagram that we used in Chapter 2, on page 37, to show the meaning of economic growth. Over time, the production possibilities curve shifts outward. In panel (b), we demonstrate the same principle by showing the long-run aggregate supply curve initially as a vertical line at $14.3 trillion of real GDP per year. As our productive abilities increase, the *LRAS* moves outward to *LRAS*₂₀₁₅ at $15 trillion.

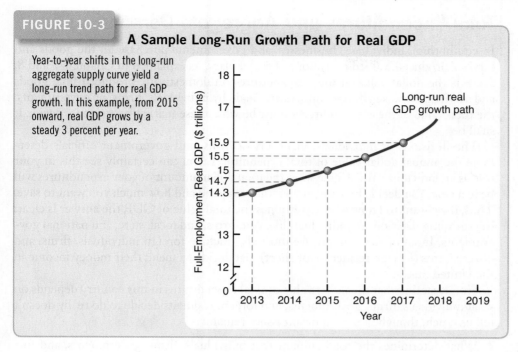

FIGURE 10-3

A Sample Long-Run Growth Path for Real GDP

Year-to-year shifts in the long-run aggregate supply curve yield a long-run trend path for real GDP growth. In this example, from 2015 onward, real GDP grows by a steady 3 percent per year.

now and 2015, real GDP increases to $15 trillion, to give us the position of the $LRAS_{2015}$ curve. Thus, it is to the right of today's *LRAS* curve.

We may conclude that in a growing economy, the *LRAS* shifts ever farther to the right over time. If the *LRAS* happened to shift rightward at a constant pace, real GDP would increase at a steady annual rate. As shown in Figure 10-3, this means that real GDP would increase along a long-run, or *trend*, path that is an upward-sloping line. Thus, if the *LRAS* shifts rightward from $14.3 trillion to $15 trillion between now and 2015 and then increases at a steady 3 percent annual rate every year thereafter, in 2016 long-run real GDP will equal $15.5 trillion, in 2017 it will equal $15.9 trillion, and so on.

How much less is the U.S. long-run aggregate supply shifting to the right each year as a consequence of dampened economic growth?

YOU ARE THERE

To contemplate how a country's long-run trend path for real GDP could slope *downward*, take a look at **A Nation Confronts a Leftward-Shifting *LRAS* Curve** on page 223.

POLICY EXAMPLE

Shrinking Rightward Shifts in the U.S. *LRAS* Curve

Between 2000 and 2007, U.S. real GDP grew at an average annual rate of 2.6 percent. As a consequence, U.S. long-run aggregate supply increased by an average of nearly $300 billion per year. Since 2007, U.S. real GDP grew on average at a much slower pace of about 0.5 percent per year. During this interval, the nation's long-run aggregate supply rose by an average of less than $70 billion per year. Thus, the average annual

amount by which the U.S. long-run aggregate supply curve is shifting rightward is now considerably reduced.

FOR CRITICAL THINKING

Is the U.S. production possibilities curve shifting outward more or less rapidly today than it was a decade ago? Explain your answer.

QUICK QUIZ   See page 228 for the answers. Review concepts from this section in MyEconLab.

The **long-run aggregate supply curve,** *LRAS*, is a _____ line determined by amounts of available resources such as labor and capital and by technology and resource productivity. The position of the *LRAS* gives the full-information and full-adjustment level of real GDP per year.

The _____ rate of unemployment occurs at the long-run level of real GDP per year given by the position of the *LRAS*.

If labor or capital increases from year to year or if the productivity of either of these resources rises from one year to the next, the *LRAS* shifts _____. In a growing economy, therefore, real GDP per year gradually _____ over time.

Total Expenditures and Aggregate Demand

In equilibrium, individuals, businesses, and governments purchase all the goods and services produced, valued in trillions of real dollars. As explained in Chapters 7 and 8, GDP is the dollar value of total expenditures on domestically produced final goods and services. Because all expenditures are made by individuals, firms, or governments, the total value of these expenditures must be what these market participants decide it shall be.

The decisions of individuals, managers of firms, and government officials determine the annual dollar value of total expenditures. You can certainly see this in your role as an individual. You decide what the total dollar amount of your expenditures will be in a year. You decide how much you want to spend and how much you want to save. Thus, if we want to know what determines the total value of GDP, the answer is clear: the spending decisions of individuals like you, firms, and local, state, and national governments. In an open economy, we must also include foreign individuals, firms, and governments (foreign residents, for short) that decide to spend their money income in the United States.

Simply stating that the dollar value of total expenditures in this country depends on what individuals, firms, governments, and foreign residents decide to do really doesn't tell us much, though. Two important issues remain:

1. What determines the total amount that individuals, firms, governments, and foreign residents want to spend?

2. What determines the equilibrium price level and the rate of inflation (or deflation)?

The *LRAS* tells us only about the economy's long-run real GDP. To answer these additional questions, we must consider another important concept. This is **aggregate demand**, which is the total of all *planned* real expenditures in the economy.

Aggregate demand
The total of all planned expenditures in the entire economy.

The Aggregate Demand Curve

Aggregate demand curve
A curve showing planned purchase rates for all final goods and services in the economy at various price levels, all other things held constant.

The **aggregate demand curve,** *AD*, gives the various quantities of all final commodities demanded at various price levels, all other things held constant. Recall the components of GDP that you studied in Chapter 8: consumption spending, investment expenditures, government purchases, and net foreign demand for domestic production. They are all components of aggregate demand. Throughout this chapter and the next, whenever you see the aggregate demand curve, realize that it is a shorthand way of talking about the components of GDP that are measured by government statisticians when they calculate total economic activity each year. In Chapter 12, you will look more closely at the relationship between these components and, in particular, at how consumption spending depends on income.

The aggregate demand curve gives the total amount, measured in base-year dollars, of *real* domestic final goods and services that will be purchased at each price level—everything produced for final use by households, businesses, the government, and foreign (non-U.S.) residents. It includes iPads, socks, shoes, medical and legal services, digital devices, and millions of other goods and services that people buy each year.

A graphical representation of the aggregate demand curve is seen in Figure 10-4 on the facing page. On the horizontal axis, real GDP is measured. For our measure of the price level, we use the GDP price deflator on the vertical axis. The aggregate demand curve is labeled *AD*. If the GDP deflator is 110, aggregate quantity demanded is $15 trillion per year (point *A*). At the price level 115, it is $14 trillion per year (point *B*). At the price level 120, it is $13 trillion per year (point *C*). The higher the price level, the lower the total real amount of final goods and services demanded in the economy, everything else remaining constant, as shown by the arrow along *AD* in Figure 10-4. Conversely, the lower the price level, the higher the total real GDP demanded by the economy, everything else staying constant.

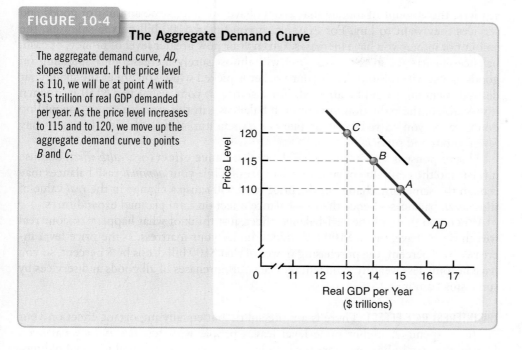

FIGURE 10-4

The Aggregate Demand Curve

The aggregate demand curve, *AD*, slopes downward. If the price level is 110, we will be at point *A* with $15 trillion of real GDP demanded per year. As the price level increases to 115 and to 120, we move up the aggregate demand curve to points *B* and *C.*

Let's take the year 2013. Estimates based on U.S. Department of Commerce preliminary statistics reveal the following information:

- Nominal GDP was estimated to be $16,344.7 billion.
- The price level as measured by the GDP deflator was about 117.9 (base year is 2005, for which the index equals 100).
- Real GDP was approximately $13,858.5 billion in 2005 dollars.

What can we say about 2013? Given the dollar cost of buying goods and services and all of the other factors that go into spending decisions by individuals, firms, governments, and foreign residents, the total amount of planned spending on final goods and services by firms, individuals, governments, and foreign residents was $13,858.5 billion in 2013 (in terms of 2005 dollars).

What Happens When the Price Level Rises?

What if the price level in the economy rose to 160 tomorrow? What would happen to the amount of real goods and services that individuals, firms, governments, and foreigners wish to purchase in the United States? We know from Chapter 3 that when the price of one good or service rises, the quantity of it demanded will fall. But here we are talking about the *price level*—the average price of *all* goods and services in the economy.

The answer is still that the total quantities of real goods and services demanded would fall, but the reasons are different. When the price of one good or service goes up, the consumer substitutes other goods and services. For the entire economy, when the price level goes up, the consumer doesn't simply substitute one good for another, for now we are dealing with the demand for *all* goods and services in the nation. There are *economywide* reasons that cause the aggregate demand curve to slope downward. They involve at least three distinct forces: the *real-balance effect*, the *interest rate effect*, and the *open economy effect*.

THE REAL-BALANCE EFFECT A rise in the price level will have an effect on spending. Individuals, firms, governments, and foreign residents carry out transactions using money, a portion of which consists of currency and coins that you have in your pocket (or stashed away) right now. Because people use money to purchase goods and services, the amount of money that people have influences the amount of goods and services they want to buy. For example, if you find a $100 bill on the sidewalk, the amount of money you have increases. Given your now greater level of money, or cash, balances—currency in this case—you will almost surely increase your spending on goods and services. Similarly, if your pocket is picked while you are at the mall, your desired spending would be affected. For instance, if your wallet had $150 in it when it was stolen, the reduction in your cash balances—in this case, currency—would no doubt cause you to reduce your planned expenditures. You would ultimately buy fewer goods and services.

This response is sometimes called the **real-balance effect** (or *wealth effect*) because it relates to the real value of your cash balances. While your *nominal* cash balances may remain the same, any change in the price level will cause a change in the *real* value of those cash balances—hence the real-balance effect on total planned expenditures.

When you think of the real-balance effect, just think of what happens to your real wealth if you have, say, a $100 bill hidden under your mattress. If the price level increases by 5 percent, the purchasing power of that $100 bill drops by 5 percent, so you have become less wealthy. You will reduce your purchases of all goods and services by some small amount.

THE INTEREST RATE EFFECT There is a more subtle but equally important effect on your desire to spend. A higher price level leaves people with too few money balances. Hence, they try to borrow more (or lend less) to replenish their real money holdings. This drives up interest rates. Higher interest rates raise borrowing costs for consumers and businesses. They will borrow less and consequently spend less. The fact that a higher price level pushes up interest rates and thereby reduces borrowing and spending is known as the **interest rate effect.**

Higher interest rates make it more costly for people to finance purchases of houses and cars. Higher interest rates also make it less profitable for firms to install new equipment and to erect new office buildings. Whether we are talking about individuals or firms, a rise in the price level will cause higher interest rates, which in turn reduce the amount of goods and services that people are willing to purchase. Therefore, an increase in the price level will tend to reduce total planned expenditures. (The opposite occurs if the price level declines.)

THE OPEN ECONOMY EFFECT: THE SUBSTITUTION OF FOREIGN GOODS Recall from Chapter 8 that GDP includes net exports—the difference between exports and imports. In an open economy, we buy imports from other countries and ultimately pay for them through the foreign exchange market. The same is true for foreign residents who purchase our goods (exports). Given any set of exchange rates between the U.S. dollar and other currencies, an increase in the price level in the United States makes U.S. goods more expensive relative to foreign goods. Foreign residents have downward-sloping demand curves for U.S. goods. When the relative price of U.S. goods goes up, foreign residents buy fewer U.S. goods and more of their own. At home, relatively cheaper prices for foreign goods cause U.S. residents to want to buy more foreign goods instead of domestically produced goods. Thus, when the domestic price level rises, the result is a fall in exports and a rise in imports. That means that a price level increase tends to reduce net exports, thereby reducing the amount of real goods and services purchased in the United States. This is known as the **open economy effect.**

What Happens When the Price Level Falls?

What about the reverse? Suppose now that the GDP deflator falls to 100 from an initial level of 120. You should be able to trace the three effects on desired purchases of goods and services. Specifically, how do the real-balance, interest rate, and open economy effects cause people to want to buy more? You should come to the conclusion that the lower the price level, the greater the total planned spending on goods and services.

Real-balance effect
The change in expenditures resulting from a change in the real value of money balances when the price level changes, all other things held constant; also called the *wealth effect.*

Interest rate effect
One of the reasons that the aggregate demand curve slopes downward: Higher price levels increase the interest rate, which in turn causes businesses and consumers to reduce desired spending due to the higher cost of borrowing.

Open economy effect
One of the reasons that the aggregate demand curve slopes downward: Higher price levels result in foreign residents desiring to buy fewer U.S.-made goods, while U.S. residents now desire more foreign-made goods, thereby reducing net exports. This is equivalent to a reduction in the amount of real goods and services purchased in the United States.

The aggregate demand curve, *AD*, shows the quantity of aggregate output that will be demanded at alternative price levels. It is downward sloping, just like the demand curve for individual goods. The higher the price level, the lower the real amount of total planned expenditures, and vice versa.

Demand for All Goods and Services versus Demand for a Single Good or Service

Even though the aggregate demand curve, *AD*, in Figure 10-4 on page 215 looks similar to the one for individual demand, *D*, for a single good or service that you encountered in Chapters 3 and 4, the two are not the same. When we derive the aggregate demand curve, we are looking at the entire economic system. The aggregate demand curve, *AD*, differs from an individual demand curve, *D*, because we are looking at total planned expenditures on *all* goods and services when we construct *AD*.

Shifts in the Aggregate Demand Curve

In Chapter 3, you learned that any time a nonprice determinant of demand changes, the demand curve will shift inward to the left or outward to the right. The same analysis holds for the aggregate demand curve, except we are now talking about the non-price-level determinants of aggregate demand. So, when we ask the question, "What determines the position of the aggregate demand curve?" the fundamental proposition is as follows:

> *Any non-price-level change that increases aggregate spending (on domestic goods) shifts* **AD** *to the right. Any non-price-level change that decreases aggregate spending (on domestic goods) shifts* **AD** *to the left.*

The list of potential determinants of the position of the aggregate demand curve is long. Some of the most important "curve shifters" for aggregate demand are presented in Table 10-1 below.

TABLE 10-1

Determinants of Aggregate Demand

Aggregate demand consists of the demand for domestically produced consumption goods, investment goods, government purchases, and net exports. Consequently, any change in total planned spending on any one of these components of real GDP will cause a change in aggregate demand. Some possibilities are listed here.

Changes That Cause an Increase in Aggregate Demand	Changes That Cause a Decrease in Aggregate Demand
An increase in the amount of money in circulation	A decrease in the amount of money in circulation
Increased security about jobs and future income	Decreased security about jobs and future income
Improvements in economic conditions in other countries	Declines in economic conditions in other countries
A reduction in real interest rates (nominal interest rates corrected for inflation) not due to price level changes	A rise in real interest rates (nominal interest rates corrected for inflation) not due to price level changes
Tax decreases	Tax increases
A drop in the foreign exchange value of the dollar	A rise in the foreign exchange value of the dollar

How can economists track the extent to which changes in security about jobs and future incomes affect aggregate demand?

POLICY EXAMPLE

The Consumer Confidence Index and Aggregate Demand

An independent economic research organization called The Conference Board tracks an indicator of U.S. consumer sentiment called the Consumer Confidence Index (CCI). The CCI is intended to measure the degree of security that U.S. households have about their future employment and income status, as revealed by a range of data on their spending and saving activities.

Because consumer spending typically accounts for at least two-thirds of total U.S. planned expenditures, variations in the CCI normally indicate changes in U.S. aggregate demand. For instance, during a 6-month interval between late 2007 and early 2008, the CCI lost nearly half of its value. Then U.S. aggregate demand, which had been rising at about $300 billion per year during the 5 years preceding 2008, suddenly *decreased* by more than $300 billion between 2008 and 2009. Thus, a significant reduction in household security about the future, as revealed by the CCI, is associated with a leftward shift in the aggregate demand curve.

FOR CRITICAL THINKING

What would be the predicted effect on the position of the aggregate demand curve of a substantial increase in the Consumer Confidence Index?

QUICK QUIZ See page 228 for the answers. Review concepts from this section in MyEconLab.

Aggregate demand is the total of all planned _____ in the economy, and **aggregate supply** is the total of all planned _____ in the economy. The aggregate demand curve shows the various quantities of total planned _____ on final goods and services at various price levels; it is downward sloping.

There are three reasons why the aggregate demand curve is downward sloping. They are the _____-_____ effect, the _____ _____ effect, and the _____ _____ effect.

The _____-_____ effect occurs because price level changes alter the real value of cash balances, thereby causing people to desire to spend more or less, depending on whether the price level decreases or increases.

The _____ _____ effect is caused by interest rate changes that mimic price level changes. At higher interest rates, people seek to buy _____ houses and cars, and at lower interest rates, they seek to buy _____.

The **open economy effect** occurs because of a shift away from expenditures on _____ goods and a shift toward expenditures on _____ goods when the domestic price level increases.

Long-Run Equilibrium and the Price Level

As noted in Chapter 3, equilibrium occurs where the demand and supply curves intersect. The same is true for the economy as a whole, as shown in Figure 10-5 on the facing page: The equilibrium price level occurs at the point where the aggregate demand curve *(AD)* crosses the long-run aggregate supply curve *(LRAS)*. At this equilibrium price level of 120, the total of all planned real expenditures for the entire economy is equal to actual real GDP produced by firms after all adjustments have taken place. Thus, the equilibrium depicted in Figure 10-5 is the economy's *long-run equilibrium*.

The Long-Run Equilibrium Price Level

Note in Figure 10-5 that if the price level were to increase to 140, actual real GDP would exceed total planned real expenditures. Inventories of unsold goods would begin to accumulate, and firms would stand ready to offer more services than people wish to purchase. As a result, the price level would tend to fall.

In contrast, if the price level were 100, then total planned real expenditures by individuals, businesses, and the government would exceed actual real GDP. Inventories of unsold goods would begin to be depleted. The price level would rise toward 120, and higher prices would encourage firms to expand production and replenish inventories of goods available for sale.

FIGURE 10-5

Long-Run Economywide Equilibrium

For the economy as a whole, long-run equilibrium occurs at the price level where the aggregate demand curve crosses the long-run aggregate supply curve. At this long-run equilibrium price level, which is 120 in the diagram, total planned real expenditures equal real GDP at full employment, which in our example is a real GDP of $15 trillion.

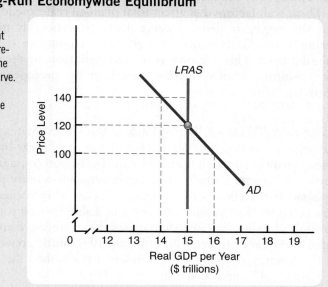

The Effects of Economic Growth on the Price Level

We now have a basic theory of how real GDP and the price level are determined in the long run when all of a nation's resources can change over time and all input prices can adjust fully to changes in the overall level of prices of goods and services that firms produce. Let's begin by evaluating the effects of economic growth on the nation's price level.

ECONOMIC GROWTH AND SECULAR DEFLATION Take a look at panel (a) of Figure 10-6 below, which shows what happens, other things being equal, when the *LRAS* shifts rightward over time. If the economy were to grow steadily during, say, a 10-year interval, the long-run aggregate supply schedule would shift to the right, from $LRAS_1$ to $LRAS_2$.

FIGURE 10-6

Secular Deflation versus Long-Run Price Stability in a Growing Economy

Panel (a) illustrates what happens when economic growth occurs without a corresponding increase in aggregate demand. The result is a decline in the price level over time, known as *secular deflation*. Panel (b) shows that, in principle, secular deflation can be eliminated if the aggregate demand curve shifts rightward at the same pace that the long-run aggregate supply curve shifts to the right.

In panel (a), this results in a downward movement along the aggregate demand schedule. The equilibrium price level falls, from 120 to 80.

Thus, if all factors that affect total planned real expenditures are unchanged, so that the aggregate demand curve does not noticeably move during the 10-year period of real GDP growth, the growing economy in the example would experience deflation. This is known as **secular deflation,** or a persistently declining price level resulting from economic growth in the presence of relatively unchanged aggregate demand.

Secular deflation
A persistent decline in prices resulting from economic growth in the presence of stable aggregate demand.

SECULAR DEFLATION IN THE UNITED STATES In the United States, between 1872 and 1894, the price of bricks fell by 50 percent, the price of sugar by 67 percent, the price of wheat by 69 percent, the price of nails by 70 percent, and the price of copper by nearly 75 percent. Founders of a late-nineteenth-century political movement called *populism* offered a proposal for ending deflation: They wanted the government to issue new money backed by silver. As noted in Table 10-1 on page 217, an increase in the quantity of money in circulation causes the aggregate demand curve to shift to the right. It is clear from panel (b) of Figure 10-6 on the previous page that the increase in the quantity of money would indeed have pushed the price level back upward, because the *AD* curve would shift from AD_1 to AD_2.

Go to www.econtoday.com/chap10 to learn about how the price level has changed during recent years. Then click on "Gross Domestic Product and Components" (for GDP deflators) or "Consumer Price Indexes."

Nevertheless, money growth remained low for several more years. Not until the early twentieth century would the United States put an end to secular deflation, namely, by creating a new monetary system.

Causes of Inflation

Of course, so far during your lifetime, deflation has not been a problem in the United States. Instead, what you have experienced is inflation. Figure 10-7 below shows annual U.S. inflation rates for the past few decades. Clearly, inflation rates have been variable. The other obvious fact, however, is that inflation rates have been consistently *positive*. The price level in the United States has *risen* almost every year. For today's United States, secular deflation has not been a big political issue. If anything, it is secular *inflation* that has plagued the nation.

MyEconLab Real-time data

FIGURE 10-7

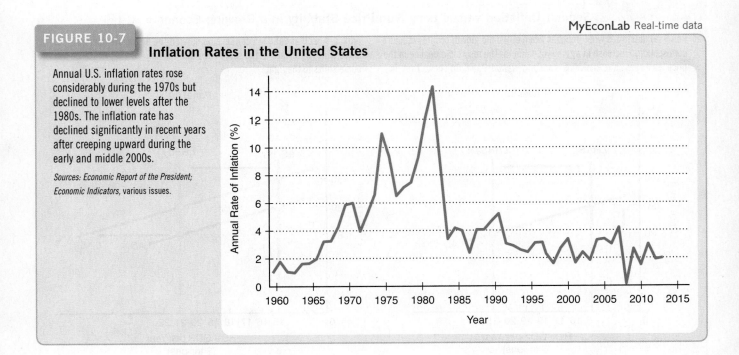

Inflation Rates in the United States

Annual U.S. inflation rates rose considerably during the 1970s but declined to lower levels after the 1980s. The inflation rate has declined significantly in recent years after creeping upward during the early and middle 2000s.

Sources: Economic Report of the President; Economic Indicators, various issues.

FIGURE 10-8

Explaining Persistent Inflation

As shown in panel (a), it is possible for a decline in long-run aggregate supply to cause a rise in the price level. Long-run aggregate supply *increases* in a growing economy, however, so this cannot explain the observation of persistent U.S. inflation. Panel (b) provides the actual explanation of persistent inflation in the United States and most other nations today, which is that increases in aggregate demand push up the long-run equilibrium price level. Thus, it is possible to explain persistent inflation if the aggregate demand curve shifts rightward at a faster pace than the long-run aggregate supply curve.

Supply-Side Inflation?

What causes such persistent inflation? The model of aggregate demand and long-run aggregate supply provides two possible explanations for inflation. One potential rationale is depicted in panel (a) of Figure 10-8 above. This panel shows a rise in the price level caused by a *decline in long-run aggregate supply*. Hence, one possible reason for persistent inflation would be continual reductions in economywide production.

A leftward shift in the aggregate supply schedule could be caused by several factors, such as reductions in labor force participation, higher marginal tax rates on wages, or the provision of government benefits that give households incentives *not* to supply labor services to firms. Tax rates and government benefits have increased during recent decades, but so has the U.S. population. The significant overall rise in real GDP that has taken place during the past few decades tells us that population growth and productivity gains undoubtedly have dominated other factors. In fact, the aggregate supply schedule has actually shifted *rightward*, not leftward, over time. Consequently, this supply-side explanation for persistent inflation *cannot* be the correct explanation.

Demand-Side Inflation

This leaves only one other explanation for the persistent inflation that the United States has experienced in recent decades. This explanation is depicted in panel (b) of Figure 10-8 above. If aggregate demand increases for a given level of long-run aggregate supply, the price level must increase. The reason is that at an initial price level such as 120, people desire to purchase more goods and services than firms are willing and able to produce, given currently available resources and technology. As a result, the rise in aggregate demand leads only to a general rise in the price level, such as the increase to a value of 140, depicted in the figure.

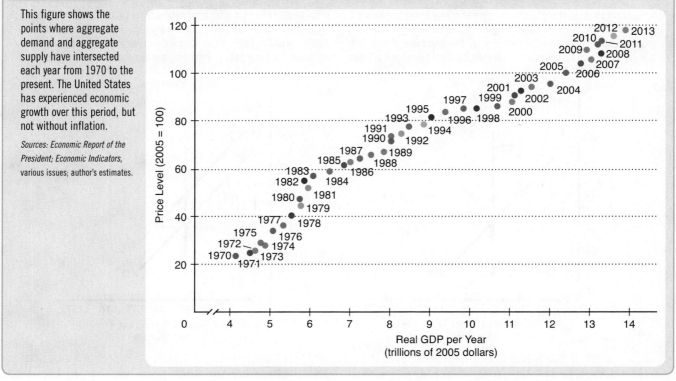

FIGURE 10-9

Real GDP and the Price Level in the United States, 1970 to the Present

This figure shows the points where aggregate demand and aggregate supply have intersected each year from 1970 to the present. The United States has experienced economic growth over this period, but not without inflation.

Sources: Economic Report of the President; Economic Indicators, various issues; author's estimates.

WHAT IF... there was a sustained increase in the amount of money in circulation intended to generate a rise in the nation's real GDP per year?

A sustained increase in the quantity of money in circulation would cause persistent rightward shifts in the aggregate demand curve. Because the long-run aggregate supply curve is vertical at the annual real output level after full adjustment has taken place, increases in aggregate demand cannot influence the equilibrium level of *real* GDP per year. What a sustained increase in the amount of money in circulation *can* do is bring about persistently higher values of the equilibrium price level. Thus, this monetary policy action would generate only sustained inflation and would fail in its objective to raise long-run annual real GDP.

From a long-run perspective, we are left with only one possibility: Persistent inflation in a growing economy is possible only if the aggregate demand curve shifts rightward over time at a faster pace than the rightward progression of the long-run aggregate supply curve. Thus, in contrast to the experience of people who lived in the latter portion of the nineteenth century, when aggregate demand grew too slowly relative to aggregate supply to maintain price stability, your grandparents, parents, and you have lived in times when aggregate demand has grown too *speedily*. The result has been a continual upward drift in the price level, or long-term inflation.

Figure 10-9 above shows that U.S. real GDP has grown in most years since 1970. Nevertheless, this growth has been accompanied by a higher price level every single year. Has aggregate supply growth dropped below growth in aggregate demand?

EXAMPLE

Will Slowed Growth of Potential U.S. Real GDP Fuel Inflation?

To measure the pace of growth of long-run aggregate supply, economists estimate the rate of growth of *potential real GDP*, which is a measure of how fast the long-run aggregate supply curve shifts outward. Most economists conclude that U.S. potential real GDP growth rose from about 3.5 percent in the 1940s to above 4 percent in the 1960s.

Between the 1970s and 1990s, however, this growth rate dropped to nearly 3 percent. During the 2000s, it fell even further, to between 2 and 2.5 percent. By the early 2010s, potential real GDP growth was between 1 and 1.5 percent. Thus, the position of the U.S. long-run aggregate supply curve now is shifting rightward at the slowest pace in more than 80 years. If aggregate demand continues growing at the same average pace as in years past, the U.S. inflation rate necessarily will tend to rise.

FOR CRITICAL THINKING

Could the lower growth of long-run aggregate supply in the 2000s help account for why the average inflation rate was higher in the 2000s than in the 1990s? Explain.

QUICK QUIZ See page 228 for the answers. Review concepts from this section in MyEconLab.

When the economy is in long-run equilibrium, the price level adjusts to equate total planned real _____ by individuals, businesses, the government, and foreign (non-U.S.) residents with total planned _____ by firms.

Economic growth causes the long-run aggregate supply schedule to shift _____ over time. If the position of the aggregate demand curve does not change, the long-run

equilibrium price level tends to _____, and there is **secular deflation.**

Because the U.S. economy has grown in recent decades, the persistent inflation during those years has been caused by the aggregate demand curve shifting _____ at a faster pace than the long-run aggregate supply curve.

YOU ARE THERE
A Nation Confronts a Leftward-Shifting *LRAS* Curve

Goncalo Pascoal, chief economist at Millennium BCP, the largest bank in Portugal, sees little to cheer about when he examines the nation's economic performance. In the years since 2007, Portugal's real GDP has been *shrinking* at an average pace of 1 percent per year. Thus, the nation's long-run aggregate supply curve has been exhibiting a sustained leftward shift.

Pascoal does not have to look far for the causes of this shrinkage. In cities such as Felgueiras, once a thriving center of shoe production, empty factories with mostly broken windows line the streets. Throughout the nation, many textile and clothing facilities lie vacant. Over the years, these and other Portuguese manufacturing resources began wearing out. Instead of preventing obsolescence from reducing the nation's stock of productive capital goods, the countries' residents directed many available

resources to consumption goods. Eventually, the country's overall capital stock began to shrink. Now, Pascoal realizes, so much of the nation's capital stock is depleted and unusable that the flow of production of goods and services has declined with each passing year. This is why real GDP is steadily dropping, yielding leftward shifts in Portugal's long-run aggregate supply curve.

Critical Thinking Questions

1. In what direction is Portugal's production possibilities curve shifting over time?

2. What type of inflation might Portugal experience during the coming years?

ISSUES & APPLICATIONS

Will Arctic Assets Unfreeze Long-Run Aggregate Supply?

CONCEPTS APPLIED

▶ Aggregate Supply

▶ Long-Run Aggregate Supply Curve

▶ Endowments

Some economists have begun factoring into their long-run aggregate supply evaluations the underutilized and untapped resource endowments near and within the Arctic Circle. Bringing those resources into broader use, these economists suggest, could do much to generate speedier rightward shifts of the long-run aggregate supply curves of the United States and other northern nations.

Lands with Unexploited Resource Endowments

The Arctic, the global region north of 66.33 degrees latitude, contains only slightly more than 4 percent of the earth's surface area. Nevertheless, nearby regions stretching southward to 45 degrees latitude encompass another 11 percent of the earth's surface and an additional 25 percent of its land mass. Wide swaths of these lands contain significant endowments of as-yet unexploited resources, including minerals, oil, and natural gas.

Three key explanations can be offered for the meager utilization of Arctic and near-Arctic resources. First, the region is not particularly hospitable to people, who must adapt to long summer days and winter nights and to lengthy periods of extreme cold. Second, large tracts of land are covered with thick permafrost and with heavy sheets of ice, or glaciers. Third, much of the land near and within the Arctic is publicly owned. Governments have fewer incentives than private individuals and businesses to extract productive resources from these lands. Indeed, failure to place Arctic and near-Arctic resources in private hands has done more to consign them to an economic deep freeze than the cold air above them.

Could Unfreezing Arctic Endowments Heat Up Aggregate Supply Growth?

The volume of untapped Arctic oil is thought to be sufficiently large to provide the *entire world's* requirements for about half a year, and today's technology could fuel *global* natural gas requirements for an estimated 2 years. If all estimated Arctic oil could be extracted, it would last the world at least 3 years, and all of the region's likely natural gas reserves would be enough for about 25 years. Mineral endowments are less certain, but most geologists suspect that unexploited Arctic and near-Arctic lands contain vast amounts of metal ores.

Of course, making most Arctic resources accessible to private producers would *gradually* add to annual flows of resources that residents of northern nations such as the United States could use to produce goods and services. Estimates indicate that drawing on these endowments would boost annual U.S. real GDP growth by an appreciable fraction of a percentage point. Thus, reducing government ownership of these underutilized and untapped endowments would contribute to higher economic growth.

For Critical Thinking

1. Why do you suppose that firms in Arctic nations are already developing specialized tanker ships and platforms for use in privately accessible Arctic areas?

2. What are possible opportunity costs of opening Arctic lands to private extraction of as-yet unavailable resource endowments?

Web Resources

1. For a summary of current data about likely Arctic oil and natural gas endowments, go to www.econtoday.com/chap10.

2. To learn about economic issues faced in extracting metal ores in the Arctic, go to www.econtoday.com/chap10.

MyEconLab

For more questions on this chapter's Issues & Applications, go to MyEconLab. In the Study Plan for this chapter, select Section N: News.

MyEconLab

Here is what you should know after reading this chapter. MyEconLab will help you identify what you know, and where to go when you need to practice.

—— WHAT YOU SHOULD KNOW ——

Long-Run Aggregate Supply The long-run aggregate supply curve is vertical at the amount of real GDP that firms plan to produce when they have full information and when complete adjustment of input prices to any changes in output prices has taken place.

aggregate supply, 211
long-run aggregate
 supply curve, 211
base-year dollars, 211
endowments, 211

Key Figure
Figure 10-1, 211

—— WHERE TO GO TO PRACTICE ——

- MyEconLab Study Plan 10.1
- Animated Figure 10-1

MyEconLab *continued*

WHAT YOU SHOULD KNOW		WHERE TO GO TO PRACTICE
Economic Growth and the Long-Run Aggregate Supply Curve The production possibilities curve shifts rightward when the economy grows, and so does the nation's long-run aggregate supply curve. In a growing economy, the changes in full-employment real GDP defined by the shifting long-run aggregate supply curve define the nation's long-run, or trend, growth path.	**Key Figures** Figure 10-2, 212 Figure 10-3, 213	• **MyEconLab** Study Plan 10.1 • Animated Figures 10-2, 10-3
Why the Aggregate Demand Curve Slopes Downward and Factors That Cause It to Shift The real-balance effect occurs when a rise in the price level reduces the real value of cash balances, which induces people to cut back on planned spending. Higher interest rates typically accompany increases in the price level, and this interest rate effect induces people to cut back on borrowing and spending. Finally, a rise in the price level at home causes domestic goods to be more expensive relative to foreign goods, so there is a fall in exports and a rise in imports, both of which cause domestic planned expenditures to fall. These three factors together account for the downward slope of the aggregate demand curve, which shifts if there is any other change in total planned real expenditures at any given price level.	aggregate demand, 214 aggregate demand curve, 214 real-balance effect, 216 interest rate effect, 216 open economy effect, 216 **Key Figure** Figure 10-4, 215	• **MyEconLab** Study Plans 10.2, 10.3 • Animated Figure 10-4
Long-Run Equilibrium for the Economy In a long-run economywide equilibrium, the price level adjusts until total planned real expenditures equal actual real GDP. Thus, the long-run equilibrium price level is determined at the point where the aggregate demand curve intersects the long-run aggregate supply curve.	**Key Figure** Figure 10-5, 219	• **MyEconLab** Study Plan 10.4 • Animated Figure 10-5
Why Economic Growth Can Cause Deflation If the aggregate demand curve is stationary during a period of economic growth, the long-run aggregate supply curve shifts rightward along the aggregate demand curve. The long-run equilibrium price level falls, so there is secular deflation.	secular deflation, 220 **Key Figure** Figure 10-6, 219	• **MyEconLab** Study Plan 10.4 • Animated Figure 10-6
Likely Reasons for Recent Persistent Inflation Inflation can result from a fall in long-run aggregate supply, but in a growing economy, long-run aggregate supply generally rises. Thus, a much more likely cause of persistent inflation is a pace of aggregate demand growth that exceeds the pace at which long-run aggregate supply increases.	**Key Figures** Figure 10-7, 220 Figure 10-8, 221	• **MyEconLab** Study Plan 10.5 • Animated Figures 10-7, 10-8

Log in to **MyEconLab**, take a chapter test, and get a personalized Study Plan that tells you which concepts you understand and which ones you need to review. From there, **MyEconLab** will give you further practice, tutorials, animations, videos, and guided solutions. For more information, visit www.myeconlab.com

PROBLEMS

All problems are assignable in MyEconLab. Answers to odd-numbered problems appear at the back of the book.

10-1. Many economists view the natural rate of unemployment as the level observed when real GDP is given by the position of the long-run aggregate supply curve. How can there be positive unemployment in this situation? (See page 211.)

10-2. Suppose that the long-run aggregate supply curve is positioned at a real GDP level of $15 trillion in base-year dollars, and the long-run equilibrium price level (in index number form) is 115. What is the full-employment level of *nominal* GDP? (See page 219.)

10-3. Continuing from Problem 10-2, suppose that the full-employment level of *nominal* GDP in the following year rises to $17.7 trillion. The long-run equilibrium price level, however, remains unchanged. By how much (in real dollars) has the long-run aggregate supply curve shifted to the right in the following year? By how much, if any, has the aggregate demand curve shifted to the right? (Hint: The equilibrium price level can stay the same only if *LRAS* and *AD* shift rightward by the same amount (See page 219.)

10-4. Suppose that the position of a nation's long-run aggregate supply curve has not changed, but its long-run equilibrium price level has increased. Which of the following factors might account for this event? (See page 219.)

a. A rise in the value of the domestic currency relative to other world currencies

b. An increase in the quantity of money in circulation

c. An increase in the labor force participation rate

d. A decrease in taxes

e. A rise in real incomes of countries that are key trading partners of this nation

f. Increased long-run economic growth

10-5. Identify the combined shifts in long-run aggregate supply and aggregate demand that could explain the following simultaneous occurrences. (See page 219).

a. An increase in equilibrium real GDP and an increase in the equilibrium price level

b. A decrease in equilibrium real GDP with no change in the equilibrium price level

c. An increase in equilibrium real GDP with no change in the equilibrium price level

d. A decrease in equilibrium real GDP and a decrease in the equilibrium price level

10-6. Suppose that during the past 3 years, equilibrium real GDP in a country rose steadily, from $450 billion to $500 billion, but even though the position of its aggregate demand curve remained unchanged, its equilibrium price level steadily declined, from 110 to 103. What could have accounted for these outcomes, and what is the term for the change in the price level experienced by this country? (See page 219.)

10-7. Suppose that during a given year, the quantity of U.S. real GDP that can be produced in the long run rises from $14.9 trillion to $15.0 trillion, measured in base-year dollars. During the year, no change occurs in the various factors that influence aggregate demand. What will happen to the U.S. long-run equilibrium price level during this particular year? (See page 219.)

10-8. Assume that the position of a nation's aggregate demand curve has not changed, but the long-run equilibrium price level has declined. Other things being equal, which of the following factors might account for this event? (See page 219.)

a. An increase in labor productivity

b. A decrease in the capital stock

c. A decrease in the quantity of money in circulation

d. The discovery of new mineral resources used to produce various goods

e. A technological improvement

10-9. Suppose that there is a sudden rise in the price level. What will happen to economywide planned spending on purchases of goods and services? Why? (See page 215.)

10-10. Assume that the economy is in long-run equilibrium with complete information and that input prices adjust rapidly to changes in the prices of goods and services. If there is a rise in the price level induced by an increase in aggregate demand, what happens to real GDP? (See page 219.)

10-11. Consider the diagram below when answering the questions that follow. (See page 219.)

Real GDP per Year (base-year dollars)

a. Suppose that the current price level is P_2. Explain why the price level will decline toward P_1.

b. Suppose that the current price level is P_3. Explain why the price level will rise toward P_1.

10-12. Explain whether each of the following events would cause a movement along or a shift in the position of the *LRAS* curve, other things being equal. In each case, explain the direction of the movement along the curve or shift in its position. (See page 212.)

a. Last year, businesses invested in new capital equipment, so this year the nation's capital stock is higher than it was last year.

b. There has been an 8 percent increase in the quantity of money in circulation that has shifted the *AD* curve.

c. A hurricane of unprecedented strength has damaged oil rigs, factories, and ports all along the nation's coast.

d. Inflation has occurred during the past year as a result of rightward shifts of the *AD* curve.

10-13. Explain whether each of the following events would cause a movement along or a shift in the position of the *AD* curve, other things being equal. In each case, explain the direction of the movement along the curve or shift in its position. (See page 217.)

a. Deflation has occurred during the past year.

b. Real GDP levels of all the nation's major trading partners have declined.

c. There has been a decline in the foreign exchange value of the nation's currency.

d. The price level has increased this year.

10-14. This year, a nation's long-run equilibrium real GDP and price level both increased. Which of the following combinations of factors might simultaneously account for *both* occurrences? (See page 219.)

a. An isolated earthquake at the beginning of the year destroyed part of the nation's capital stock, and the nation's government significantly reduced its purchases of goods and services.

b. There was a technological improvement at the end of the previous year, and the quantity of money in circulation rose significantly during the year.

c. Labor productivity increased throughout the year, and consumers significantly increased their total planned purchases of goods and services.

d. The capital stock increased somewhat during the year, and the quantity of money in circulation declined considerably.

10-15. Explain how, if at all, each of the following events would affect equilibrium real GDP and the long-run equilibrium price level. (See page 219.)

a. A reduction in the quantity of money in circulation

b. An income tax rebate (the return of previously paid taxes) from the government to households, which they can apply only to purchases of goods and services

c. A technological improvement

d. A decrease in the value of the home currency in terms of the currencies of other nations

10-16. For each question, suppose that the economy *begins* at the long-run equilibrium point *A* in the diagram below. Identify which of the other points on the diagram—points *B*, *C*, *D*, or *E*—could represent a *new* long-run equilibrium after the described events take place and move the economy away from point *A*. (See page 219.)

a. Significant productivity improvements occur, and the quantity of money in circulation increases.

b. No new capital investment takes place, and a fraction of the existing capital stock depreciates and becomes unusable. At the same time, the government imposes a large tax increase on the nation's households.

c. More efficient techniques for producing goods and services are adopted throughout the economy at the same time that the government reduces its spending on goods and services.

10-17. In Ciudad Barrios, El Salvador, the latest payments from relatives working in the United States have finally arrived. When the credit unions open for business, up to 150 people are already waiting in line. After receiving the funds their relatives have transmitted to these institutions, customers go off to outdoor markets to stock up on food or clothing or to appliance stores to purchase new stereos or televisions. Similar scenes occur throughout the developing world, as each year migrants working in higher-income, developed nations send around $200 billion of their earnings back to their relatives in less developed nations.

Evidence indicates that the relatives, such as those in Ciudad Barrios, typically spend nearly all of the funds on current consumption. (See page 219.)

a. Based on the information supplied, are developing countries' income inflows transmitted by migrant workers primarily affecting their economies' long-run aggregate supply curves or aggregate demand curves?

b. How are equilibrium price levels in nations that are recipients of large inflows of funds from migrants likely to be affected? Explain your reasoning.

ECONOMICS ON THE NET

Wages, Productivity, and Aggregate Supply How much firms pay their employees and the productivity of those employees influence firms' total planned production, so changes in these factors affect the position of the aggregate supply curve. This application gives you the opportunity to examine recent trends in measures of the overall wages and productivity of workers.

Title: Bureau of Labor Statistics: Economy at a Glance

Navigation: Use the link at www.econtoday.com/chap10 to visit the Bureau of Labor Statistics (BLS) Web site.

Application Perform the indicated operations, and answer the following questions.

1. In the "Pay and Benefits" popup menu, click on *Employment Costs*. Choose *Employment Cost Index*. What are the recent trends in wages and salaries and in benefits? In the long run, how should these trends be related to movements in the overall price level?

2. Back up to the home page, and in the "Productivity" popup menu, click on *Labor Productivity and Costs* and then on *PDF* next to "LPC News Releases: Productivity and Costs." How has labor productivity behaved recently? What does this imply for the long-run aggregate supply curve?

3. Back up to the home page, and now in the "Employment" popup menu, click on *National Employment* and then on *PDF* next to "Current CES Economic News Release: Employment Situation Summary." Does it appear that the U.S. economy is currently in a long-run growth equilibrium?

For Group Study and Analysis

1. Divide the class into aggregate demand and long-run aggregate supply groups. Have each group search the Internet for data on factors that influence its assigned curve. For which factors do data appear to be most readily available? For which factors are data more sparse or more subject to measurement problems?

2. The BLS home page displays a map of the United States. Assign regions of the nation to different groups, and have each group develop a short report about current and future prospects for economic growth within its assigned region. What similarities exist across regions? What regional differences are there?

ANSWERS TO QUICK QUIZZES

p. 213: (i) vertical; (ii) natural; (iii) rightward . . . increases

p. 218: (i) expenditures . . . production . . . spending; (ii) real-balance . . . interest rate . . . open economy; (iii) real-balance; (iv) interest rate . . . fewer . . . more; (v) domestic . . . foreign

p. 223: (i) expenditures . . . production; (ii) rightward . . . decline; (iii) rightward

Classical and Keynesian Macro Analyses

11

LEARNING OBJECTIVES

After reading this chapter, you should be able to:

▶ Discuss the central assumptions of the classical model

▶ Describe the short-run determination of equilibrium real GDP and the price level in the classical model

▶ Explain circumstances under which the short-run aggregate supply curve may be either horizontal or upward sloping

▶ Understand what factors cause shifts in the short-run and long-run aggregate supply curves

▶ Evaluate the effects of aggregate demand and supply shocks on equilibrium real GDP in the short run

▶ Determine the causes of short-run variations in the inflation rate

MyEconLab helps you master each objective and study more efficiently. See end of chapter for details.

Many Wall Street observers refer to it as the "fear index." Its true name is the *VIX index*, and it has become the most commonly used gauge of volatility in U.S. financial markets. Prior to and during the severe 2008–2009 recession, the VIX index increased substantially, reflecting significant variability of the value of financial claims traded in financial markets as well as volatility in real interest rates. How can major disturbances in financial markets sometimes translate into reductions in real GDP and even decreases in the price level? To understand the answer, you must learn about determination of the equilibrium price level in the short run, which is a fundamental topic of this chapter.

? DID YOU KNOW THAT... the price of a bottle containing 6.5 ounces of Coca-Cola remained unchanged at 5 cents from 1886 to 1959? The prices of many other goods and services changed at least slightly during that 73-year period, and since then the prices of most items, including Coca-Cola, have generally moved in an upward direction. Nevertheless, prices of final goods and services have not always adjusted immediately in response to changes in aggregate demand. Consequently, one approach to understanding the determination of real GDP and the price level emphasizes *incomplete* adjustment in the prices of many goods and services. The simplest version of this approach was first developed by a twentieth-century economist named John Maynard Keynes (pronounced like *canes*). It assumes that in the short run, prices of most goods and services are nearly as rigid as the price of Coca-Cola from 1886 to 1959. Although the modern version of the Keynesian approach allows for greater flexibility of prices in the short run, incomplete price adjustment still remains a key feature of the modern Keynesian approach.

The Keynesian approach does not retain the long-run assumption, which you encountered in Chapter 10, of fully adjusting prices. Economists who preceded Keynes employed this assumption in creating an approach to understanding variations in real GDP and the price level that Keynes called the *classical model*. Like Keynes, we shall begin our study of variations in real GDP and the price level by considering the earlier, classical approach.

The Classical Model

The classical model, which traces its origins to the 1770s, was the first systematic attempt to explain the determinants of the price level and the national levels of real GDP, employment, consumption, saving, and investment. Classical economists—Adam Smith, J. B. Say, David Ricardo, John Stuart Mill, Thomas Malthus, A. C. Pigou, and others—wrote from the 1770s to the 1930s. They assumed, among other things, that all wages and prices were flexible and that competitive markets existed throughout the economy.

Say's Law

Every time you produce something for which you receive income, you generate the income necessary to make expenditures on other goods and services. That means that an economy producing $15 trillion of real GDP, measured in base-year dollars (the value of current goods and services expressed in terms of prices in a base year), simultaneously produces the income with which these goods and services can be purchased. As an accounting identity, *actual* aggregate output always equals *actual* aggregate income. Classical economists took this accounting identity one step further by arguing that total national supply creates its own national demand. They asserted what has become known as **Say's law:**

Say's law
A dictum of economist J. B. Say that supply creates its own demand. Producing goods and services generates the means and the willingness to purchase other goods and services.

> *Supply creates its own demand. Hence, it follows that* desired *expenditures will equal* actual *expenditures.*

THE IMPLICATION OF SAY'S LAW What does Say's law really mean? It states that the very process of producing specific goods (supply) is proof that other goods are desired (demand). People produce more goods than they want for their own use only if they seek to trade them for other goods. Someone offers to supply something only because he or she has a demand for something else.

The implication of this, according to Say, is that no general glut, or overproduction, is possible in a market economy. From this reasoning, it seems to follow that full employment of labor and other resources would be the normal state of affairs in such an economy.

Say acknowledged that an oversupply of some goods might occur in particular markets. He argued that such surpluses would simply cause prices to fall, thereby decreasing production as the economy adjusted. The opposite would occur in markets in which shortages temporarily appeared.

FIGURE 11-1

Say's Law and the Circular Flow

Here we show the circular flow of income and output. The very act of supplying a certain level of goods and services necessarily equals the level of goods and services demanded, in Say's simplified world.

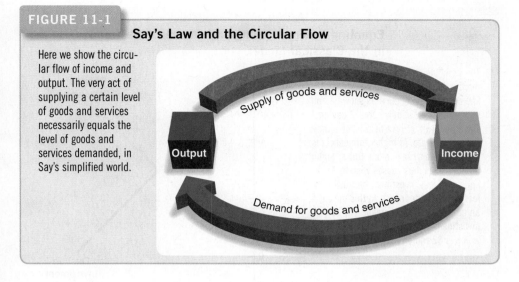

SAY'S LAW IN A MODERN ECONOMY All this seems reasonable enough in a simple barter economy in which households produce most of the goods they want and trade for the rest. This is shown in Figure 11-1 above, where there is a simple circular flow. But what about a more sophisticated economy in which people work for others and money is used instead of barter? Can these complications create the possibility of unemployment? And does the fact that laborers receive money income, some of which can be saved, lead to unemployment? No, said the classical economists to these last two questions. They based their reasoning on a number of key assumptions.

Assumptions of the Classical Model

The classical model makes four major assumptions:

1. *Pure competition exists.* No single buyer or seller of a commodity or an input can affect its price.

2. *Wages and prices are flexible.* The assumption of pure competition leads to the notion that prices, wages and interest rates are free to move to whatever level supply and demand dictate (as the economy adjusts). Although no *individual* buyer can set a price, the community of buyers or sellers can cause prices to rise or to fall to an equilibrium level.

3. *People are motivated by self-interest.* Businesses want to maximize their profits, and households want to maximize their economic well-being.

4. *People cannot be fooled by money illusion.* Buyers and sellers react to changes in relative prices. That is to say, they do not suffer from **money illusion.** For example, workers will not be fooled into thinking that doubling their wages makes them better off if the price level has also doubled during the same time period.

Money illusion
Reacting to changes in money prices rather than relative prices. If a worker whose wages double when the price level also doubles thinks he or she is better off, that worker is suffering from money illusion.

The classical economists concluded, after taking account of the four major assumptions, that the role of government in the economy should be minimal. They assumed that pure competition prevails, all prices and wages are flexible, and people are self-interested and do not experience money illusion. If so, they argued, then any problems in the macroeconomy will be temporary. The market will correct itself.

Equilibrium in the Credit Market

When income is saved, it is not reflected in product demand. It is a type of *leakage* from the circular flow of income and output because saving withdraws funds from the income stream. Therefore, total planned consumption spending *can* fall short of total current real GDP. In such a situation, it appears that supply does not necessarily create its own demand.

FIGURE 11-2

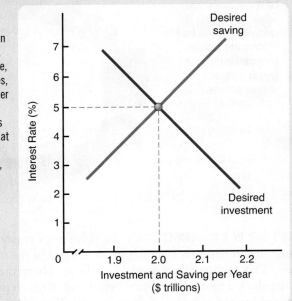

Equating Desired Saving and Desired Investment in the Classical Model

The schedule showing planned investment is labeled "Desired investment." The desired saving curve is shown as an upward-sloping supply curve of saving. The equilibrating force here is, of course, the interest rate. At higher interest rates, people desire to save more. But at higher interest rates, businesses wish to engage in less investment because it is less profitable to invest. In this model, at an interest rate of 5 percent, planned investment just equals planned saving, which is $2 trillion per year.

Go to www.econtoday.com/chap11 to link to Federal Reserve data on U.S. interest rates.

THE RELATIONSHIP BETWEEN SAVING AND INVESTMENT The classical economists did not believe that the complicating factor of saving in the circular flow model of income and output was a problem. They contended that each dollar saved would be invested by businesses so that the leakage of saving would be matched by the injection of business investment. *Investment* here refers only to additions to the nation's capital stock. The classical economists believed that businesses as a group would intend to invest as much as households wanted to save.

THE EQUILIBRIUM INTEREST RATE Equilibrium between the saving plans of consumers and the investment plans of businesses comes about, in the classical model, through the working of the credit market. In the credit market, the *price* of credit is the interest rate. At equilibrium, the price of credit—the interest rate—ensures that the amount of credit demanded equals the amount of credit supplied. Planned investment just equals planned saving, so there is no reason to be concerned about the leakage of saving. This fact is illustrated graphically in Figure 11-2 above.

In the figure, the vertical axis measures the rate of interest in percentage terms, and the horizontal axis measures flows of desired saving and desired investment per unit time period. The desired saving curve is really a supply curve of saving. It shows that people wish to save more at higher interest rates than at lower interest rates.

In contrast, the higher the rate of interest, the less profitable it is to invest and the lower is the level of desired investment. Thus, the desired investment curve slopes downward. In this simplified model, the equilibrium rate of interest is 5 percent, and the equilibrium quantity of saving and investment is $2 trillion per year.

Equilibrium in the Labor Market

Go to www.econtoday.com/chap11 to find out the latest U.S. saving rate from the Bureau of Economic Analysis. Select "Personal saving as a percentage of disposable personal income."

Now consider the labor market. If an excess quantity of labor is supplied at a particular wage level, the wage level must be above equilibrium. By accepting lower wages, unemployed workers will quickly be put back to work. We show equilibrium in the labor market in Figure 11-3 on the facing page.

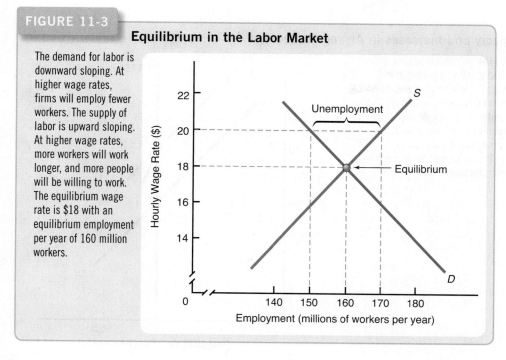

FIGURE 11-3

Equilibrium in the Labor Market

The demand for labor is downward sloping. At higher wage rates, firms will employ fewer workers. The supply of labor is upward sloping. At higher wage rates, more workers will work longer, and more people will be willing to work. The equilibrium wage rate is $18 with an equilibrium employment per year of 160 million workers.

Assume that equilibrium exists at $18 per hour and 160 million workers employed. If the wage rate were $20 per hour, there would be unemployment—170 million workers would want to work, but businesses would want to hire only 150 million. In the classical model, this unemployment is eliminated rather rapidly by wage rates dropping back to $18 per hour, as seen in Figure 11-3 above.

THE RELATIONSHIP BETWEEN EMPLOYMENT AND REAL GDP Employment is not to be regarded simply as some isolated figure that government statisticians estimate. Rather, the level of employment in an economy determines its real GDP (output), other things held constant. A hypothetical relationship between input (number of employees) and the value of output (real GDP per year) is shown in Table 11-1 below. The row that has 160 million workers per year as the labor input is highlighted. That might be considered a hypothetical level of full employment, and it is related to a rate of real GDP, in base-year dollars, of $15 trillion per year.

Classical Theory, Vertical Aggregate Supply, and the Price Level

In the classical model, unemployment greater than the natural unemployment rate is impossible. Say's law, coupled with flexible interest rates, prices, and wages, would always tend to keep workers fully employed so that the aggregate supply curve, as

TABLE 11-1

The Relationship between Employment and Real GDP

Other things being equal, an increase in the quantity of labor input increases real GDP. In this example, if 160 million workers are employed, real GDP is $15 trillion in base-year dollars.

Labor Input per Year (millions of workers)	Real GDP per Year ($ trillions)
150	12
154	13
158	14
160	15
164	16
166	17

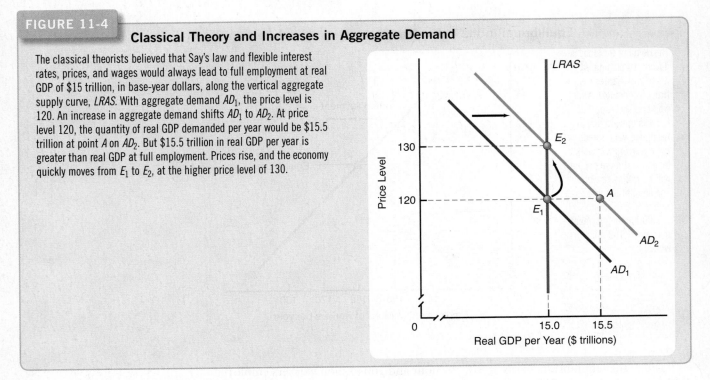

FIGURE 11-4

Classical Theory and Increases in Aggregate Demand

The classical theorists believed that Say's law and flexible interest rates, prices, and wages would always lead to full employment at real GDP of $15 trillion, in base-year dollars, along the vertical aggregate supply curve, *LRAS*. With aggregate demand AD_1, the price level is 120. An increase in aggregate demand shifts AD_1 to AD_2. At price level 120, the quantity of real GDP demanded per year would be $15.5 trillion at point *A* on AD_2. But $15.5 trillion in real GDP per year is greater than real GDP at full employment. Prices rise, and the economy quickly moves from E_1 to E_2, at the higher price level of 130.

shown in Figure 11-4 above, is vertical at the real GDP of $15 trillion, in base-year dollars. We have labeled the supply curve *LRAS*, which is the long-run aggregate supply curve introduced in Chapter 10. It was defined there as the real GDP that would be produced in an economy with full information and full adjustment of wages and prices year in and year out. *LRAS* therefore corresponds to the long-run rate of unemployment.

In the classical model, this happens to be the *only* aggregate supply curve. The classical economists made little distinction between the long run and the short run. Prices adjust so fast that the economy is essentially always on or quickly moving toward *LRAS*. Furthermore, because the labor market adjusts rapidly, real GDP is always at, or soon to be at, full employment. Full employment does not mean zero unemployment because there is always some frictional and structural unemployment (discussed in Chapter 7), which yields the natural rate of unemployment.

EFFECT OF AN INCREASE IN AGGREGATE DEMAND IN THE CLASSICAL MODEL In this model, any change in aggregate demand will quickly cause a change in the price level. Consider starting at E_1, at price level 120, in Figure 11-4. If aggregate demand shifts to AD_2, the economy will tend toward point *A*, but because this is beyond full-employment real GDP, prices will rise, and the economy will find itself back on the vertical *LRAS* at point E_2 at a higher price level, 130. The price level will increase as a result of the increase in *AD* because employers will end up bidding up wages for workers, as well as bidding up the prices of other inputs.

The level of real GDP per year clearly does not depend on the level of aggregate demand. Hence, we say that in the classical model, the equilibrium level of real GDP per year is completely *supply determined*. Changes in aggregate demand affect only the price level, not real GDP.

EFFECT OF A DECREASE IN AGGREGATE DEMAND IN THE CLASSICAL MODEL The effect of a decrease in aggregate demand in the classical model is the converse of the analysis just presented for an increase in aggregate demand. You can simply reverse AD_2 and AD_1 in Figure 11-4 above. To help you see how this analysis works, consider the flowchart in Figure 11-5 on the facing page.

FIGURE 11-5

Effect of a Decrease in Aggregate Demand in the Classical Model

Starting with the economy at full employment, aggregate demand decreases. → Real GDP falls below its long-run level as represented by the position of *LRAS*. → Unemployment increases. → Competition among workers pushes down wage rates. The same occurs for other input prices. → The economy again finds itself on the vertical *LRAS*.

QUICK QUIZ See page 249 for the answers. Review concepts from this section in MyEconLab.

Say's law states that _____ creates its own _____ and therefore *desired* expenditures will equal *actual* expenditures.

The classical model assumes that (1) _____ _____ exists, (2) _____ and _____ are completely flexible, (3) individuals are motivated by _____-_____, and (4) they cannot be fooled by _____ _____.

When saving is introduced into the model, equilibrium occurs in the credit market through changes in the interest rate such that desired _____ equals desired _____ at the equilibrium rate of interest.

In the labor market, full employment occurs at a _____ _____ at which quantity demanded equals quantity supplied. That particular level of employment is associated with the full-employment level of real GDP per year.

In the classical model, because *LRAS* is _____, the equilibrium level of real GDP is supply determined. Any changes in aggregate demand simply change the _____ _____.

Keynesian Economics and the Keynesian Short-Run Aggregate Supply Curve

The classical economists' world was one of fully utilized resources. There would be no unused capacity and no unemployment. But then in the 1930s, Europe and the United States entered a period of economic decline that seemingly could not be explained by the classical model. John Maynard Keynes developed an explanation that has since become known as the Keynesian model. Keynes and his followers argued that prices, especially the price of labor (wages), were inflexible downward due to the existence of unions and long-term contracts between businesses and workers. That meant that prices were "sticky." Keynes contended that in such a world, which has large amounts of excess capacity and unemployment, an increase in aggregate demand will not raise the price level, and a decrease in aggregate demand will not cause firms to lower prices.

Demand-Determined Real GDP

This situation is depicted in Figure 11-6 on the next page. For simplicity, Figure 11-6 does not show the point where the economy reaches capacity, and that is why the *short-run aggregate supply curve* (to be discussed later) never starts to slope upward and is simply the horizontal line labeled *SRAS*. Moreover, we don't show *LRAS* in Figure 11-6 either. It would be a vertical line at the level of real GDP per year that is consistent with full employment. If we start out in equilibrium with aggregate demand at AD_1, the equilibrium level of real GDP per year, measured in base-year dollars, is $15 trillion at point E_1, and the equilibrium price level is 120. If there is a rise in aggregate demand, so that the aggregate demand curve shifts outward to the right to AD_2, the equilibrium price level at point E_2 will not change. Only the equilibrium level of real GDP per year will increase, to $15.5 trillion. Conversely, if there is a fall in aggregate demand that shifts the aggregate demand curve to AD_3, the equilibrium price level will again remain at 120 at point E_3, but the equilibrium level of real GDP per year will fall to $14.5 trillion.

FIGURE 11-6

Demand-Determined Equilibrium Real GDP at Less Than Full Employment

Keynes assumed that prices will not fall when aggregate demand falls and that there is excess capacity, so prices will not rise when aggregate demand increases. Thus, the short-run aggregate supply curve is simply a horizontal line at the given price level, 120, represented by *SRAS*. An aggregate demand shock that increases aggregate demand to AD_2 will increase the equilibrium level of real GDP per year to $15.5 trillion. An aggregate demand shock that decreases aggregate demand to AD_3 will decrease the equilibrium level of real GDP to $14.5 trillion. The equilibrium price level will not change.

Under such circumstances, the equilibrium level of real GDP per year is completely *demand determined*.

The Keynesian Short-Run Aggregate Supply Curve

Keynesian short-run aggregate supply curve

The horizontal portion of the aggregate supply curve in which there is excessive unemployment and unused capacity in the economy.

The horizontal short-run aggregate supply curve represented in Figure 11-6 above is often called the **Keynesian short-run aggregate supply curve.** According to Keynes, unions and long-term contracts are real-world factors that explain the inflexibility of *nominal* wage rates. Such stickiness of wages makes *involuntary* unemployment of labor a distinct possibility, because leftward movements along the Keynesian short-run aggregate supply curve reduce real production and, hence, employment. The classical assumption of everlasting full employment no longer holds.

Have U.S. nominal wages remained too high to reduce unemployment?

EXAMPLE

Have Inflation-Adjusted U.S. Wages Been "Too High"?

Unemployment occurs when a surplus exists in the labor market—that is, when the quantity of labor supplied by workers at the current inflation-adjusted, or *real*, wage rate exceeds the quantity of labor that firms demand at that real wage rate. Other things being equal, a labor surplus will begin to disappear only if the inflation-adjusted wage rate drops toward that market clearing wage rate.

Since 2008, inflation-adjusted wages in the United States have declined by about 0.2 percent per year. Many economists contend that this low rate of decrease explains why unemployment has declined only from 14.3 million at the end of 2008 to just about 12.5 million today. Because

the U.S. inflation rate has remained very low, they argue, nominal wages would have to drop at a faster pace to push down the labor market surplus more rapidly and thereby bring about a quicker decline in U.S. unemployment. Thus, they conclude that nominal wages have been too inflexible to reduce the nation's unemployment level significantly.

FOR CRITICAL THINKING
In principle, if nominal wages were to remain "too high," could a sustained increase in the inflation rate significantly reduce labor unemployment? Explain.

Data from the 1930s offer evidence of a nearly horizontal aggregate supply curve. Between 1934 and 1940, the GDP deflator stayed in a range from about 8.3 to less than 9.0, implying that the price level changed by no more than 8 percent. Yet the level of real GDP measured in 2005 dollars varied between nearly $0.7 trillion and close to $1.1 trillion, or by more than 50 percent. Thus, between 1934 and 1940, the U.S. short-run aggregate supply curve was almost flat.

FIGURE 11-7

Real GDP Determination with Fixed versus Flexible Prices

In panel (a), the price level index is fixed at 120. An increase in aggregate demand from AD_1 to AD_2 moves the equilibrium level of real GDP from $15 trillion per year to $16 trillion per year in base-year dollars. In panel

(b), $SRAS$ is upward sloping. The same shift in aggregate demand yields an equilibrium level of real GDP of only $15.5 trillion per year and a higher price level index at 130.

Output Determination Using Aggregate Demand and Aggregate Supply: Fixed versus Changing Price Levels in the Short Run

The underlying assumption of the simplified Keynesian model is that the relevant range of the short-run aggregate supply schedule ($SRAS$) is horizontal, as depicted in panel (a) of Figure 11-7 above. There you see that short-run aggregate supply is fixed at price level 120. If aggregate demand is AD_1, then the equilibrium level of real GDP, in base-year dollars, is $15 trillion per year. If aggregate demand increases to AD_2, then the equilibrium level of real GDP increases to $16 trillion per year.

As discussed in Chapter 10, the price level has drifted upward during recent decades. Hence, prices are not totally sticky. Modern Keynesian analysis recognizes that *some*—but not complete—price adjustment takes place in the short run. Panel (b) of Figure 11-7 above displays a more general **short-run aggregate supply curve** ($SRAS$). This curve represents the relationship between the price level and real GDP with incomplete price adjustment and in the absence of complete information in the short run. Allowing for partial price adjustment implies that $SRAS$ slopes upward, and its slope is steeper after it crosses long-run aggregate supply, $LRAS$. This is because higher and higher prices are required to induce firms to raise their production of goods and services to levels that temporarily exceed full-employment real GDP.

With partial price adjustment in the short run, if aggregate demand is AD_1, then the equilibrium level of real GDP in panel (b) is also $15 trillion per year, at a price level of 120, too. An increase in aggregate demand to AD_2 such as occurred in panel (a) produces a different short-run equilibrium, however. Equilibrium real GDP increases to $15.5 trillion per year, which is less than in panel (a) because an increase in the price level to 130 causes planned purchases of goods and services to decline.

In the modern Keynesian short run, when the price level rises partially, real GDP can be expanded beyond the level consistent with its long-run growth path, discussed in Chapter 10, for a variety of reasons:

Short-run aggregate supply curve
The relationship between total planned economywide production and the price level in the short run, all other things held constant. If prices adjust incompletely in the short run, the curve is positively sloped.

1. In the short run, most labor contracts implicitly or explicitly call for flexibility in hours of work at the given wage rate. Therefore, firms can use existing workers more intensively in a variety of ways: They can get workers to work harder, to work more hours per day, and to work more days per week. Workers can also be switched from *uncounted* production, such as maintenance, to *counted* production, which generates counted production of goods and services. The distinction between counted and uncounted is what is measured in the marketplace, particularly by government statisticians and accountants. If a worker cleans a machine, there is no measured output. But if that worker is put on the production line and helps increase the number of units produced each day, measured output will go up. That worker's production has then been counted.

2. Existing capital equipment can be used more intensively. Machines can be worked more hours per day. Some can be made to operate faster. Maintenance can be delayed.

3. Finally, if wage rates are held constant, a higher price level leads to increased profits from additional production, which induces firms to hire more workers. The duration of unemployment falls, and thus the unemployment rate falls. And people who were previously not in the labor force (homemakers and younger or older workers) can be induced to enter it.

All these adjustments cause real GDP to rise as the price level increases.

Shifts in the Aggregate Supply Curve

Just as non-price-level factors can cause a shift in the aggregate demand curve, there are non-price-level factors that can cause a shift in the aggregate supply curve. The analysis here is more complicated than the analysis for the non-price-level determinants for aggregate demand, for here we are dealing with both the short run and the long run—*SRAS* and *LRAS*. Still, anything other than the price level that affects the production of final goods and services will shift aggregate supply curves.

Shifts in Both Short- and Long-Run Aggregate Supply

There is a core class of events that cause a shift in both the short-run aggregate supply curve and the long-run aggregate supply curve. These include any change in our endowments of the factors of production. Any change in factors of production—labor, capital, or technology—that influence economic growth will shift *SRAS* and *LRAS*. Look at Figure 11-8 on the facing page. Initially, the two curves are $SRAS_1$ and $LRAS_1$. Now consider a situation in which large amounts of irreplaceable resources are lost *permanently* in a major oil spill and fire. This shifts $LRAS_1$ to $LRAS_2$ at \$14.5 trillion of real GDP, measured in base-year dollars. $SRAS_1$ also shifts leftward horizontally to $SRAS_2$.

Shifts in SRAS Only

Some events, particularly those that are short-lived, will temporarily shift *SRAS* but not *LRAS*. One of the most obvious is a change in production input prices, particularly those caused by external events that are not expected to last forever. Consider a major hurricane that temporarily shuts down a significant portion of U.S. oil production. Oil is an important input in many production activities. The resulting drop in oil production would cause at least a temporary increase in the price of this input. In this case, the long-run aggregate supply curve would remain at $LRAS_1$ in Figure 11-8.

The short-run aggregate supply curve *alone* would shift from $SRAS_1$ to $SRAS_2$, reflecting the increase in input prices—the higher price of oil. This is because the rise in the costs of production at each level of real GDP per year would require a higher price level to cover those increased costs.

FIGURE 11-8

Shifts in Long-Run and Short-Run Aggregate Supply

Initially, the two aggregate supply curves are $SRAS_1$ and $LRAS_1$. An event that permanently reduces reserves of a key productive resource such as oil shifts $LRAS_1$ to $LRAS_2$ at $14.5 trillion of real GDP, in base-year dollars, and also shifts $SRAS_1$ horizontally leftward to $SRAS_2$. If, instead, a temporary increase in an input price occurred, $LRAS_1$ would remain unchanged, and only the short-run aggregate supply curve would shift, from $SRAS_1$ to $SRAS_2$.

How can a single insect species generate an aggregate supply shock?

INTERNATIONAL EXAMPLE

Australia's Short-Run Aggregate Supply Hit by a Locust Plague

Recently, Australia has experienced its worst plague of locusts in half of a century. The 3-inch-long insects, ferocious eaters that forage in massive swarms, have ravaged large portions of the nation's crops. Included among the damaged crops are cereal grains, such as rice, wheat, and barley, which are important inputs for many food products. Also heavily damaged by the insects are feed crops that are key inputs in livestock production. The resulting decreases in market supplies of these fundamental inputs have pushed up a wide array of input prices. The result has been a decrease in short-run aggregate supply. Thus, the plague of locusts has shifted Australia's short-run aggregate supply curve leftward.

FOR CRITICAL THINKING

Why would a plague of locusts, which rarely lasts more than two or three crop seasons, fail to generate a leftward shift of the long-run aggregate supply curve?

We summarize the possible determinants of aggregate supply in Table 11-2 on the next page. These determinants will cause a shift in the short-run or the long-run aggregate supply curve or both, depending on whether they are temporary or permanent.

QUICK QUIZ   See page 249 for the answers. Review concepts from this section in MyEconLab.

If we assume that the economy is operating on a horizontal short-run aggregate supply curve, the equilibrium level of real GDP per year is completely _____ determined.

The horizontal short-run aggregate supply curve has been called the **Keynesian short-run aggregate supply curve** because Keynes believed that many prices, especially wages, would not be _____ even when aggregate demand decreased.

In modern Keynesian theory, the **short-run aggregate supply curve, SRAS,** shows the relationship between the price level and real GDP without full adjustment or full information. It is upward sloping because it allows for only _____ price adjustment in the short run.

Real GDP can be expanded in the short run because firms can use existing workers and capital equipment more _____. Also, in the short run, when input prices are fixed, a higher price level means _____ profits, which induce firms to hire more workers.

Any change in factors influencing long-run output, such as labor, capital, or technology, will shift both *SRAS* and *LRAS*. A temporary change in input prices, however, will shift only _____.

Table 11-2

Determinants of Aggregate Supply

The determinants listed here can affect short-run or long-run aggregate supply (or both), depending on whether they are temporary or permanent.

Changes That Cause an Increase in Aggregate Supply	Changes That Cause a Decrease in Aggregate Supply
Discoveries of new raw materials	Depletion of raw materials
Increased competition	Decreased competition
A reduction in international trade barriers	An increase in international trade barriers
Fewer regulatory impediments to business	More regulatory impediments to business
An increase in the supply of labor	A decrease in labor supplied
Increased training and education	Decreased training and education
A decrease in marginal tax rates	An increase in marginal tax rates
A reduction in input prices	An increase in input prices

Consequences of Changes in Aggregate Demand

We now have a basic model to apply when evaluating short-run adjustments of the equilibrium price level and equilibrium real GDP when there are shocks to the economy. Whenever there is a shift in the aggregate demand or short-run aggregate supply curves, the short-run equilibrium price level or real GDP level (or both) may change. These shifts are called **aggregate demand shocks** on the demand side and **aggregate supply shocks** on the supply side.

Aggregate demand shock

Any event that causes the aggregate demand curve to shift inward or outward.

Aggregate supply shock

Any event that causes the aggregate supply curve to shift inward or outward.

When Aggregate Demand Falls While Aggregate Supply Is Stable

Now we can show what happens in the short run when aggregate supply remains stable but aggregate demand falls. The short-run outcome will be a rise in the unemployment rate. In Figure 11-9 below, you see that with AD_1, both long-run and short-run

FIGURE 11-9

The Short-Run Effects of Stable Aggregate Supply and a Decrease in Aggregate Demand: The Recessionary Gap

If the economy is at equilibrium at E_1, with price level 120 and real GDP per year of $15 trillion, a shift inward of the aggregate demand curve to AD_2 will lead to a new short-run equilibrium at E_2. The equilibrium price level will fall to 115, and the short-run equilibrium level of real GDP per year will fall to $14.8 trillion. There will be a recessionary gap of $200 billion.

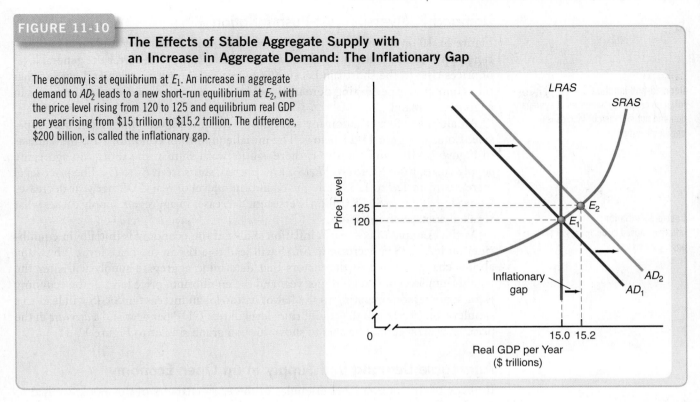

FIGURE 11-10

The Effects of Stable Aggregate Supply with an Increase in Aggregate Demand: The Inflationary Gap

The economy is at equilibrium at E_1. An increase in aggregate demand to AD_2 leads to a new short-run equilibrium at E_2, with the price level rising from 120 to 125 and equilibrium real GDP per year rising from $15 trillion to $15.2 trillion. The difference, $200 billion, is called the inflationary gap.

equilibrium are at $15 trillion (in base-year dollars) of real GDP per year (because *SRAS* and *LRAS* also intersect AD_1 at that level of real GDP). The long-run equilibrium price level is 120. A reduction in aggregate demand shifts the aggregate demand curve to AD_2. The new intersection with *SRAS* is at $14.8 trillion per year, which is less than the long-run equilibrium level of real GDP. The difference between $15 trillion and $14.8 trillion is called a **recessionary gap,** defined as the difference between the short-run equilibrium level of real GDP and real GDP if the economy were operating at full employment on its *LRAS*.

In effect, at E_2, the economy is in short-run equilibrium at less than full employment. With too many unemployed inputs, input prices will begin to fall. Eventually, *SRAS* will have to shift vertically downward.

Recessionary gap
The gap that exists whenever equilibrium real GDP per year is less than full-employment real GDP as shown by the position of the long-run aggregate supply curve.

Short-Run Effects When Aggregate Demand Increases

We can reverse the situation and have aggregate demand increase to AD_2, as is shown in Figure 11-10 above. The initial equilibrium conditions are exactly the same as in Figure 11-9 on the facing page. The move to AD_2 increases the short-run equilibrium from E_1 to E_2 such that the economy is operating at $15.2 trillion of real GDP per year, which exceeds *LRAS*. This is a condition of an overheated economy, typically called an **inflationary gap.**

At E_2 in Figure 11-10, the economy is at a short-run equilibrium that is beyond full employment. In the short run, more can be squeezed out of the economy than occurs in the long-run, full-information, full-adjustment situation. Firms will be operating beyond long-run capacity. Inputs will be working too hard. Input prices will begin to rise. That will eventually cause *SRAS* to shift vertically upward.

Inflationary gap
The gap that exists whenever equilibrium real GDP per year is greater than full-employment real GDP as shown by the position of the long-run aggregate supply curve.

YOU ARE THERE

To contemplate cost-push and demand-pull inflation from the perspective of a business manager, take a look at **Worried about Shocks to Aggregate Supply—and Demand** on page 244.

Explaining Short-Run Variations in Inflation

In Chapter 10, we noted that in a growing economy, the explanation for persistent inflation is that aggregate demand increases over time at a faster pace than the full-employment level of real GDP. Short-run variations in inflation, however, can arise as a result of both demand *and* supply factors.

Demand-Pull versus Cost-Push Inflation

Demand-pull inflation

Inflation caused by increases in aggregate demand not matched by increases in aggregate supply.

Figure 11-10 on the previous page presents a demand-side theory explaining a short-run jump in prices, sometimes called *demand-pull inflation*. Whenever the general level of prices rises in the short run because of increases in aggregate demand, we say that the economy is experiencing **demand-pull inflation**—inflation caused by increases in aggregate demand.

An alternative explanation for increases in the price level comes from the supply side. Look at Figure 11-11 below. The initial equilibrium conditions are the same as in Figure 11-10. Now, however, there is a leftward shift in the short-run aggregate supply curve, from $SRAS_1$ to $SRAS_2$. Equilibrium shifts from E_1 to E_2. The price level increases from 120 to 125, while the equilibrium level of real GDP per year decreases from $15 trillion to $14.8 trillion. Persistent decreases in aggregate supply causes what is called **cost-push inflation**.

Cost-push inflation

Inflation caused by decreases in short-run aggregate supply.

As the example of cost-push inflation shows, if the economy is initially in equilibrium on its *LRAS*, a decrease in *SRAS* will lead to a rise in the price level. Thus, any abrupt change in one of the factors that determine aggregate supply will alter the equilibrium level of real GDP per year and the equilibrium price level. If the economy is for some reason operating to the left of its *LRAS*, an increase in *SRAS* will lead to a simultaneous *increase* in the equilibrium level of real GDP per year and a *decrease* in the price level. You should be able to show this in a graph similar to Figure 11-11.

Aggregate Demand and Supply in an Open Economy

In many of the international examples in the early chapters of this book, we had to translate foreign currencies into dollars when the open economy was discussed. We used the exchange rate, or the dollar price of other currencies. In Chapter 10, you also learned that the open economy effect was one of the reasons why the aggregate demand curve slopes downward. When the domestic price level rises, U.S. residents want to buy cheaper-priced foreign goods. The opposite occurs when the U.S. domestic price level falls. Currently, the foreign sector of the U.S. economy constitutes more than 15 percent of all economic activities.

FIGURE 11-11

Cost-Push Inflation

If aggregate demand remains stable but $SRAS_1$ shifts to $SRAS_2$, equilibrium changes from E_1 to E_2. The price level rises from 120 to 125. If there are continual decreases in aggregate supply of this nature, the situation is called cost-push inflation.

HOW A STRONGER DOLLAR AFFECTS AGGREGATE SUPPLY Assume that the dollar becomes stronger in international foreign exchange markets. If last year the dollar could buy 50 *rupees*, the Indian currency, but this year it buys 60 rupees, the dollar has become stronger. To the extent that U.S. companies import physical inputs and labor services from India, a stronger dollar can lead to lower input prices.

For instance, if a U.S. firm purchases 5 million rupees' worth of labor services per year from an Indian company, then before the strengthening of the dollar, that company paid $100,000 per year for those labor services. After the dollar's strengthening, however, the U.S. firm's Indian-labor-input expense drops to $83,333. This U.S. firm's cost reduction generated by the dollar's strengthening, as well as similar reductions in foreign-input expenses at other U.S. firms, will induce those firms to produce more final goods and services per year at any given price level.

Thus, a general strengthening of the dollar against the rupee and other world currencies will lead the short-run aggregate supply curve to shift outward to the right, as shown in panel (a) of Figure 11-12 below. In that simplified model, equilibrium real GDP would rise, and the price level would decline. Employment would also tend to increase.

HOW A STRONGER DOLLAR AFFECTS AGGREGATE DEMAND A stronger dollar has another effect that we must consider. Foreign residents will find that U.S.-made goods are now more expensive, expressed in their own currency. Suppose that as a result of the dollar's strengthening, the dollar, which previously could buy 0.80 euro, can now buy 0.85 euro. Before the dollar strengthened, a U.S.-produced $10 downloadable music album cost a French resident 8.00 euros at the exchange rate of 0.80 euro per $1. After the dollar strengthens and the exchange rate changes to 0.85 euro per $1, that same $10 digital album will cost 8.50 euros. Conversely, U.S. residents will find that the stronger dollar makes imported goods less expensive. The result for U.S. residents is fewer exports and more imports, or lower net exports (exports minus imports). If net exports fall,

Go to www.econtoday.com/chap11 for Federal Reserve Bank of New York data showing how the dollar's value is changing relative to other currencies.

FIGURE 11-12

The Two Effects of a Stronger Dollar

When the dollar increases in value in the international currency market, there are two effects. The first is lower prices for imported inputs, causing a shift in the short-run aggregate supply schedule outward and to the right, from $SRAS_1$ to $SRAS_2$ in panel (a). Equilibrium tends to move from E_1 to E_2 at a lower price level and a higher equilibrium real GDP per year. Second, a stronger dollar can also affect the aggregate demand curve because it will lead to lower net exports and cause AD_1 to shift inward to AD_2 in panel (b). Due to this effect, equilibrium will move from E_1 to E_2 at a lower price level and a lower equilibrium real GDP per year. On balance, the combined effects of the decrease in aggregate demand and increase in aggregate supply will be to push down the price level, but real GDP may rise or fall.

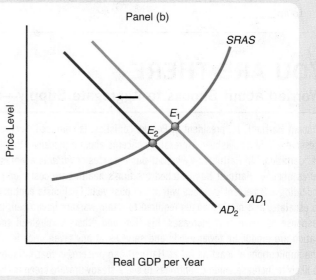

employment in export industries will fall: This is represented in panel (b) of Figure 11-12 on the previous page. After the dollar becomes stronger, the aggregate demand curve shifts inward from AD_1 to AD_2. The result is a tendency for equilibrium real GDP and the price level to fall and for unemployment to increase.

THE NET EFFECTS ON INFLATION AND REAL GDP We have learned, then, that a stronger dollar *simultaneously* leads to an increase in *SRAS* and a decrease in *AD*. In such situations, the equilibrium price level definitely falls. A stronger dollar contributes to deflation.

The effect of a stronger dollar on real GDP depends on which curve—*AD* or *SRAS*—shifts more. If the aggregate demand curve shifts more than the short-run aggregate supply curve, equilibrium real GDP will decline. Conversely, if the aggregate supply curve shifts more than the aggregate demand curve, equilibrium real GDP will rise.

You should be able to redo this entire analysis for a weaker dollar.

WHAT IF... a nation's government tries to head off a recession by pushing down the exchange value of the country's currency?

On the one hand, reducing the exchange value of the currency would make the nation's export goods less expensive in foreign currencies, thereby boosting foreign spending on home exports and, hence, domestic aggregate demand. On the other hand, the fall in the foreign value of the nation's currency would cause home-currency prices of inputs that home firms import from abroad to increase. This would induce the country's firms to cut back on production of final goods and services at any given price level. The result would be a reduction in aggregate supply, which would reinforce any economic downturn already under way. On net, therefore, pushing down the exchange value of the home currency might not necessarily help to head off an economic downturn.

QUICK QUIZ See page 249 for the answers. Review concepts from this section in MyEconLab.

_____-run equilibrium occurs at the intersection of the aggregate demand curve, *AD*, and the short-run aggregate supply curve, *SRAS*. _____-run equilibrium occurs at the intersection of *AD* and the long-run aggregate supply curve, *LRAS*. Any unanticipated shifts in aggregate demand or supply are called aggregate demand _____ or aggregate supply _____.

When aggregate demand decreases while aggregate supply is stable, a _____ gap can occur, defined as the difference between how much the economy could be producing if it were operating on its *LRAS* and the equilibrium level of real GDP. An increase in aggregate demand leads to an _____ gap.

With stable aggregate supply, an abrupt outward shift in *AD* may lead to what is called _____-_____ inflation. With stable aggregate demand, an abrupt shift inward in *SRAS* may lead to what is called _____-_____ inflation.

A _____ dollar will reduce the cost of imported inputs, thereby causing *SRAS* to shift outward to the right. At the same time, a _____ dollar will also lead to lower net exports, causing the aggregate demand curve to shift inward. The equilibrium price level definitely falls, but the net effect on equilibrium real GDP depends on which shift is larger.

YOU ARE THERE
Worried about Shocks to Aggregate Supply—and Demand

Vincent Hartnett, Jr., president of Penske Logistics, is confused. Federal Reserve officials have been expressing concerns about a perceived threat of "deflation." In Hartnett's view, cost-push sources of *inflationary* pressures abound. Hartnett has watched his firm's health care costs jump, including a 9 percent increase within the past year. Fuel costs continue to escalate, and market wages required to retain workers have risen. In response to these cost increases, his firm and others throughout the nation are producing fewer goods and services at any given price level. The implication, at least as far as Hartnett can discern, is that inflation is likely to increase, and he continues to see a steady upward creep in the annual U.S. inflation rate in monthly government reports.

The fact that Fed officials keep fretting about a potential decline in the price level has made Hartnett concerned that the Fed may unexpectedly increase the quantity of money in circulation to try to raise aggregate demand. Such an action, Hartnett worries, would essentially produce an aggregate demand shock that would lead to a higher rate of inflation.

Critical Thinking Questions

1. How would "cost-push pressures" that Hartnett perceives raise the price level?

2. Why would an unexpected increase in the quantity of money generate inflation?

ISSUES & APPLICATIONS

Gauging Financial Sources of Aggregate Demand Shocks

CONCEPTS APPLIED

▶ Aggregate Demand Shock

▶ Short-Run Aggregate Supply Curve

▶ Recessionary Gap

During a period spanning about 2 weeks in the summer of 2011, the average value of shares of corporate ownership traded in the U.S. stock market dropped by more than 15 percent. About $2 trillion of household wealth effectively ceased to exist. In response, total planned expenditures began to decline at any given price level. Financial-market shocks generated a negative aggregate demand shock.

Tracking Financial Shocks: The VIX Index

To gauge the size of financial shocks, many observers use a measure of financial-market volatility called the *VIX index*. This measure, displayed in Figure 11-13 below for the period since 1990, is intended to indicate variability that people interacting in financial markets anticipate in the near future.

As you can see, significant jumps in the VIX index can occur because of unusual events, such as the Persian Gulf War, the September 11, 2001 ("9/11") terrorist attacks, and the Iraq War. Usually, however, large changes in the VIX index result from shocks that occur solely within financial markets.

FIGURE 11-13

The VIX Index of Financial-Market Volatility since 1990

The VIX index measure of anticipated financial volatility has exhibited substantial jumps during wars and in response to major events affecting U.S. financial markets.

Source: U.S. Department of Commerce.

Examples include a default by a major financial firm called Long-Term Capital Management in 1998, substantial accounting scandals in 2002, and the massive credit crisis and associated financial panic in 2008. In addition, jumps in the VIX index in 2010 and 2011 were caused by worries about the inability of the Greek government to honor its debts and then broader concerns about debts of other European governments as well as the U.S. government. During this latter situation in the summer of 2011, U.S. residents briefly lost almost $2 trillion of financial wealth, and real interest rates began to rise, resulting in a temporary decrease in aggregate demand.

From Financial Shocks to Aggregate Demand Shocks

Also shown in Figure 11-13 on the previous page are shaded intervals of U.S. recessions. The most recent recession is clearly related to a substantial increase in the VIX index. Indeed, the VIX index began rising prior to the onset of the 2008–2009 recession and reached its highest peak in the midst of the business downturn.

In the case of this recent recession, financial shocks were so great that a significant, prolonged reduction in aggregate demand occurred. This decrease in aggregate demand generated a upward movement along the short-run aggregate supply curve, a recessionary gap, and a significant decline in U.S. real GDP.

For Critical Thinking

1. Why do you suppose that the U.S. price level decreased over a 12-month interval during the 2008–2009 recession?

2. On the basis of Figure 11-13, are jumps in the VIX index always associated with reductions in aggregate demand that induce recessions?

Web Resources

1. Learn about the VIX index at www.econtoday.com/chap11.

2. For a discussion of the rise in the VIX index as stock share prices declined and real interest rates rose in the summer of 2011, go to www.econtoday.com/chap11.

MyEconLab

For more questions on this chapter's
Issues & Applications, go to MyEconLab.
In the Study Plan for this chapter,
select Section N: News.

MyEconLab

Here is what you should know after reading this chapter. MyEconLab will help you identify what you know, and where to go when you need to practice.

WHAT YOU SHOULD KNOW		WHERE TO GO TO PRACTICE
Central Assumptions of the Classical Model The classical model makes four key assumptions: (1) pure competition prevails, so no individual buyer or seller of a good or service or of a factor of production can affect its price, (2) wages and prices are completely flexible, (3) people are motivated by self-interest, and (4) buyers and sellers do not experience money illusion, meaning that they respond only to changes in relative prices.	Say's law, 230 money illusion, 231	• MyEconLab Study Plan 11.1
Short-Run Determination of Equilibrium Real GDP and the Price Level in the Classical Model Under the four assumptions of the classical model, the short-run aggregate supply curve is vertical at full-employment real GDP and thus corresponds to the long-run aggregate supply curve. Variations in the position of the aggregate demand curve along the classical aggregate supply curve generate changes in the equilibrium price level.	Key Figures Figure 11-2, 232 Figure 11-3, 233 Figure 11-4, 234 Figure 11-5, 235	• MyEconLab Study Plan 11.1 • Animated Figures 11-2, 11-3, 11-4, 11-5

MyEconLab *continued*

WHAT YOU SHOULD KNOW		WHERE TO GO TO PRACTICE
Circumstances under Which the Short-Run Aggregate Supply Curve May Be Horizontal or Upward Sloping If product prices and wages and other input prices are "sticky," the short-run aggregate supply schedule can be horizontal over much of its range. This is the Keynesian short-run aggregate supply curve. More generally, however, to the extent that there is incomplete adjustment of prices in the short run, the short-run aggregate supply curve slopes upward.	Keynesian short-run aggregate supply curve, 236 short-run aggregate supply curve, 237 **Key Figures** Figure 11-6, 236 Figure 11-7, 237	• **MyEconLab** Study Plans 11.2, 11.3 • Animated Figures 11-6, 11-7
Factors That Induce Shifts in the Short-Run and Long-Run Aggregate Supply Curves Both the long-run aggregate supply curve and the short-run aggregate supply curve shift in response to changes in the availability of labor or capital or to changes in technology and productivity. A wide-spread temporary change in the prices of factors of production, however, can cause a shift in the short-run aggregate supply curve without affecting the long-run aggregate supply curve.	**Key Table** Table 11-2, 240 **Key Figure** Figure 11-8, 239	• **MyEconLab** Study Plan 11.4 • Animated Figure 11-8
Effects of Aggregate Demand and Supply Shocks on Equilibrium Real GDP in the Short Run An aggregate demand shock that causes the aggregate demand curve to shift leftward pushes equilibrium real GDP below the level of full-employment real GDP in the short run, so there is a recessionary gap. An aggregate demand shock that induces a rightward shift in the aggregate demand curve results in an inflationary gap, in which short-run equilibrium real GDP exceeds full-employment real GDP.	aggregate demand shock, 240 aggregate supply shock, 240 recessionary gap, 241 inflationary gap, 241 **Key Figures** Figure 11-9, 240 Figure 11-10, 241	• **MyEconLab** Study Plan 11.5 • Animated Figures 11-9, 11-10
Causes of Short-Run Variations in the Inflation Rate Demand-pull inflation occurs when the aggregate demand curve shifts rightward along an upward-sloping short-run aggregate supply curve. Cost-push inflation occurs when the short-run aggregate supply curve shifts leftward along the aggregate demand curve. A strengthening of the dollar shifts the short-run aggregate supply curve rightward and the aggregate demand curve leftward, which causes inflation but has uncertain effects on real GDP.	demand-pull inflation, 242 cost-push inflation, 242 **Key Figure** Figure 11-11, 242	• **MyEconLab** Study Plan 11.6 • Animated Figure 11-11

Log in to MyEconLab, take a chapter test, and get a personalized Study Plan that tells you which concepts you understand and which ones you need to review. From there, MyEconLab will give you further practice, tutorials, animations, videos, and guided solutions. For more information, visit www.myeconlab.com

PROBLEMS

All problems are assignable in MyEconLab. *Answers to odd-numbered problems appear at the back of the book.*

11-1. Consider a country whose economic structure matches the assumptions of the classical model. After reading a recent best-seller documenting a growing population of low-income elderly people who were ill prepared for retirement, most residents of this country decide to increase their saving at any given interest rate. Explain whether or how this could affect the following (see page 232):

   a. The current equilibrium interest rate

   b. Current equilibrium real GDP

   c. Current equilibrium employment

   d. Current equilibrium investment

   e. Future equilibrium real GDP (see Chapter 9)

11-2. Consider a country with an economic structure consistent with the assumptions of the classical model. Suppose that businesses in this nation suddenly anticipate higher future profitability from investments they undertake today. Explain whether or how this could affect the following (see page 232):

   a. The current equilibrium interest rate

   b. Current equilibrium real GDP

   c. Current equilibrium employment

   d. Current equilibrium saving

   e. Future equilibrium real GDP (see Chapter 9)

11-3. "There is *absolutely no distinction* between the classical model and the model of long-run equilibrium discussed in Chapter 10." Is this statement true or false? Support your answer. (See page 234.)

11-4. Suppose that the Keynesian short-run aggregate supply curve is applicable for a nation's economy. Use appropriate diagrams to assist in answering the following questions (see page 236):

   a. What are two factors that can cause the nation's real GDP to increase in the short run?

   b. What are two factors that can cause the nation's real GDP to increase in the long run?

11-5. What determines how much real GDP responds to changes in the price level along the short-run aggregate supply curve? (See page 236.)

11-6. Suppose that there is a temporary, but significant, increase in oil prices in an economy with an upward-sloping *SRAS* curve. If policymakers wish to prevent the equilibrium price level from changing in response to the oil price increase, should they increase or decrease the quantity of money in circulation? Why? (See page 242.)

11-7. As in Problem 11-6, suppose that there is a temporary, but significant, increase in oil prices in an economy with an upward-sloping *SRAS* curve. In this case, however, suppose that policymakers wish to prevent equilibrium real GDP from changing in response to the oil price increase. Should they increase or decrease the quantity of money in circulation? Why? (See page 240.)

11-8. Based on your answers to Problems 11-6 and 11-7, can policymakers stabilize *both* the price level *and* real GDP simultaneously in response to a short-lived but sudden rise in oil prices? Explain briefly. (See pages 240–242.)

11-9. Between early 2005 and late 2007, total planned expenditures by U.S. households substantially increased in response to an increase in the quantity of money in circulation. Explain, from a short-run Keynesian perspective, the predicted effects of this event on the equilibrium U.S. price level and equilibrium U.S. real GDP. Be sure to discuss the spending gap that the Keynesian model indicates would result in the short run. (See page 241.)

11-10. Between early 2008 and the beginning of 2009, a gradual stock-market downturn and plummeting home prices generated a substantial reduction in U.S. household wealth that induced most U.S. residents to reduce their planned real spending at any given price level. Explain, from a short-run Keynesian perspective, the predicted effects of this event on the equilibrium U.S. price level and equilibrium U.S. real GDP. Be sure to discuss the spending gap that the Keynesian model indicates would result in the short run. (See page 240.)

11-11. For each question that follows, suppose that the economy *begins* at point A. Identify which of the other points on the diagram—point B, C, D, or E—could represent a *new* short-run equilibrium after the described events take place and move the economy away from point A. Briefly explain your answers. (See pages 240–242.)

reducing real GDP and disposable income in other nations of the world.

  b. A major hurricane has caused short-term halts in production at many firms and created major bottlenecks in the distribution of goods and services that had been produced prior to the storm. At the same time, the nation's central bank has significantly pushed up the rate of growth of the nation's money supply.

  c. A strengthening of the value of this nation's currency in terms of other countries' currencies affects both the *SRAS* curve and the *AD* curve.

11-12. Consider an open economy in which the aggregate supply curve slopes upward in the short run. Firms in this nation do not import raw materials or any other productive inputs from abroad, but foreign residents purchase many of the nation's goods and services. What is the most likely short-run effect on this nation's economy if there is a significant downturn in economic activity in other nations around the world? (See page 243.)

  a. Most workers in this nation's economy are union members, and unions have successfully negotiated large wage boosts. At the same time, economic conditions suddenly worsen abroad,

ECONOMICS ON THE NET

Money, the Price Level, and Real GDP The classical and Keynesian theories have differing predictions about how changes in the money supply should affect the price level and real GDP. Here you get to look at data on growth in the money supply, the price level, and real GDP.

Title: Federal Reserve Bank of St. Louis Monetary Trends

Navigation: Use the link at **www.econtoday.com/chap11** to visit the Federal Reserve Bank of St. Louis. Click on *Gross Domestic Product and M2*.

Application Read the article; then answer these questions.

  1. Classical theory indicates that, *ceteris paribus*, changes in the price level should be closely related to changes in aggregate demand induced by variations in the quantity of money. Click on *Gross Domestic Product and M2*, and take a look at the charts labeled "Gross Domestic Product Price Index" and "M2." (M2 is a

measure of the quantity of money in circulation.) Are annual percentage changes in these variables closely related?

  2. Keynesian theory predicts that, *ceteris paribus*, changes in GDP and the quantity of money should be directly related. Take a look at the charts labeled "Real Gross Domestic Product" and "M2." Are annual percentage changes in these variables closely related?

For Group Study and Analysis Both classical and Keynesian theories of relationships among real GDP, the price level, and the quantity of money hinge on specific assumptions. Have class groups search through the FRED database (accessible at **www.econtoday.com/chap11**) to evaluate factors that provide support for either theory's predictions. Which approach appears to receive greater support from recent data? Does this necessarily imply that this is the "true theory"? Why or why not?

ANSWERS TO QUICK QUIZZES

p. 235: (i) supply . . . demand; (ii) pure competition . . . wages . . . prices . . . self-interest . . . money illusion; (iii) saving . . . investment; (iv) wage rate; (v) vertical . . . price level

p. 239: (i) demand; (ii) reduced; (iii) partial; (iv) intensively . . . higher; (v) *SRAS*

p. 244: (i) Short . . . Long . . . shocks . . . shocks; (ii) recessionary . . . inflationary; (iii) demand-pull . . . cost-push; (iv) stronger . . . stronger

12 Consumption, Real GDP, and the Multiplier

Since the early 2000s, *planned real investment spending*—intended inflation-adjusted expenditures on new buildings and equipment and changes in business inventories—has increased in most of the world's nations. As a percentage of global real GDP, however, planned real investment spending in the world's developed countries, including the United States, has declined. In contrast, planned real investment spending as a percentage of global real GDP has been rising in *emerging-economy nations*—that is, countries with economies that are transitioning from a less developed to a developed status. How do changes in planned real investment spending affect a country's equilibrium annual flow of real GDP? In this chapter, you will learn the answer.

the share of real GDP allocated to real consumption spending by households is about 60 percent in Germany, 66 percent in the United Kingdom, and 70 percent in the United States, but less than 41 percent in China? In all of the world's nations, inflation-adjusted consumption spending on domestically produced final goods and services is a significant component of real GDP. In this chapter, you will learn how an understanding of households' real consumption spending can assist in evaluating fluctuations in any country's real GDP.

Some Simplifying Assumptions in a Keynesian Model

Continuing in the Keynesian tradition, we will assume that the short-run aggregate supply curve within the current range of real GDP is horizontal. That is, we assume that it is similar to Figure 11-6 on page 236. Thus, the equilibrium level of real GDP is demand determined. This is why Keynes wished to examine the elements of desired aggregate expenditures. Because of the Keynesian assumption of inflexible prices, inflation is not a concern in this analysis. Hence, real values are identical to nominal values.

To simplify the income determination model that follows, a number of assumptions are made:

1. Businesses pay no indirect taxes (for example, sales taxes).

2. Businesses distribute all of their profits to shareholders.

3. There is no depreciation (capital consumption allowance), so gross private domestic investment equals net investment.

4. The economy is closed—that is, there is no foreign trade.

Given all these simplifying assumptions, **real disposable income,** or after-tax real income, will be equal to real GDP minus net taxes—taxes paid less transfer payments received.

Real disposable income
Real GDP minus net taxes, or after-tax real income.

Another Look at Definitions and Relationships

You can do only two things with a dollar of disposable income: Consume it or save it. If you consume it, it is gone forever. If you save the entire dollar, however, you will be able to consume it (and perhaps more if it earns interest) at some future time. That is the distinction between **consumption** and **saving.** Consumption is the act of using income for the purchase of consumption goods. **Consumption goods** are goods purchased by households for immediate satisfaction. (These also include services.) Consumption goods are such things as food and movies. By definition, whatever you do not consume you save and can consume at some time in the future.

STOCKS AND FLOWS: THE DIFFERENCE BETWEEN SAVING AND SAVINGS It is important to distinguish between *saving* and *savings*. *Saving* is an action that occurs at a particular rate—for example, $40 per week or $2,080 per year. This rate is a flow. It is expressed per unit of time, usually a year. Implicitly, then, when we talk about saving, we talk about a *flow*, or rate, of saving. *Savings*, by contrast, are a *stock* concept, measured at a certain point or instant in time. Your current *savings* are the result of past *saving*. You may currently have *savings* of $8,000 that are the result of four years' *saving* at a rate of $2,000 per year. Consumption is also a flow concept. You consume from after-tax income at a certain rate per week, per month, or per year.

RELATING INCOME TO SAVING AND CONSUMPTION A dollar of take-home income can be allocated either to consumption or to saving. Realizing this, we can see the

Consumption
Spending on new goods and services to be used up out of a household's current income. Whatever is not consumed is saved. Consumption includes such things as buying food and going to a concert.

Saving
The act of not consuming all of one's current income. Whatever is not consumed out of spendable income is, by definition, saved. *Saving* is an action measured over time (a flow), whereas *savings* are a stock, an accumulation resulting from the act of saving in the past.

Consumption goods
Goods bought by households to use up, such as food and movies.

relationship among saving, consumption, and disposable income from the following expression:

$$\text{Consumption} + \text{saving} \equiv \text{disposable income}$$

This is called an *accounting identity*, meaning that it has to hold true at every moment in time. (To indicate that the relationship is always true, we use the $\equiv$ symbol.)

From this relationship, we can derive the following definition of saving:

$$\text{Saving} \equiv \text{disposable income} - \text{consumption}$$

Hence, saving is the amount of disposable income that is not spent to purchase consumption goods.

Investment

Investment is also a flow concept. As noted in Chapter 8, *investment* as used in economics differs from the common use of the term. In common speech, it is often used to describe putting funds into the stock market or real estate. In economic analysis, investment is defined to include expenditures on new machines and buildings—**capital goods**—that are expected to yield a future stream of income. This is called *fixed investment*. We also include changes in business inventories in our definition. This we call *inventory investment*.

Investment
Spending on items such as machines and buildings, which can be used to produce goods and services in the future. (It also includes changes in business inventories.) The investment part of real GDP is the portion that will be used in the process of producing goods *in the future*.

Capital goods
Producer durables; nonconsumable goods that firms use to make other goods.

QUICK QUIZ See page 277 for the answers. Review concepts from this section in MyEconLab.

If we assume that we are operating on a _____ short-run aggregate supply curve, the equilibrium level of real GDP per year is completely demand determined.

_____ is a flow, something that occurs over time. It equals disposable income minus consumption.

_____ are a stock. They are the accumulation resulting from saving.

_____ is also a flow. It includes expenditures on new machines, buildings, and equipment and changes in business inventories.

Determinants of Planned Consumption and Planned Saving

In the classical model discussed in Chapter 11 on pages 230–235, the supply of saving was determined by the rate of interest. Specifically, the higher the rate of interest, the more people wanted to save and consequently the less people wanted to consume.

In contrast, according to Keynes, the interest rate is *not* the most important determinant of an individual's real saving and consumption decisions. In his view, the flow of income, not the interest rate, is the main determinant of consumption and saving.

How Income Flows Can Influence Consumption and Saving

When a person decides how much to consume and save today, Keynes reasoned, that individual must take into account both current and anticipated future incomes. After all, a higher income this year enables an individual *both* to purchase more final goods and services *and* to increase the flow of saving during the current year. Furthermore, a person's anticipation about the *future* flow of income likely influences how much of *current* income is allocated to consumption and how much to saving.

The Life-Cycle Theory of Consumption

The most realistic and detailed theory of consumption, often called the **life-cycle theory of consumption,** considers how a person varies consumption and saving as income ebbs and flows during the course of an entire life span. This theory predicts that when an individual anticipates a higher income in the future, the individual will tend to consume more and save less in the current period than would have been the case otherwise. In contrast, when a person expects the flow of income to drop in the future, the individual responds in the present by allocating less of current income to consumption and more to saving.

Life-cycle theory of consumption
A theory in which a person bases decisions about current consumption and saving on both current income and anticipated future income.

The Permanent Income Hypothesis

In a related theory, called the **permanent income hypothesis,** the income level that matters for a person's decision about current consumption and saving is *permanent income*, or expected average lifetime income. The permanent income hypothesis suggests that people increase their flow of consumption only if their anticipated average lifetime income rises. Thus, if a person's flow of income temporarily rises without an increase in average lifetime income, the individual responds by saving the extra income and leaving consumption unchanged.

Permanent income hypothesis
A theory of consumption in which an individual determines current consumption based on anticipated average lifetime income.

The Keynesian Theory of Consumption and Saving

Keynes recognized that expectations about future income could affect current consumption and saving decisions. For purposes of developing a basic theory of consumption and saving, however, Keynes focused solely on the relationship between current income and current consumption and saving. Thus:

> *Keynes argued that real consumption and saving decisions depend primarily on a household's current real disposable income.*

YOU ARE THERE

To consider a real-world application of the basic consumption and saving functions, read **Evaluating the Effects of Declining Real Disposable Income** on page 271.

The relationship between planned real consumption expenditures of households and their current level of real disposable income has been called the **consumption function.** It shows how much all households plan to consume per year at each level of real disposable income per year. Columns (1) and (2) of Table 12-1 on the following page illustrate a consumption function for a hypothetical household.

We see from Table 12-1 that as real disposable income rises, planned consumption also rises, but by a smaller amount, as Keynes suggested. Planned saving also increases with disposable income. Notice, however, that below an income of $60,000, the planned saving of this hypothetical household is actually negative. The further that income drops below that level, the more the household engages in **dissaving,** either by going into debt or by using up some of its existing wealth.

Consumption function
The relationship between amount consumed and disposable income. A consumption function tells us how much people plan to consume at various levels of disposable income.

Dissaving
Negative saving; a situation in which spending exceeds income. Dissaving can occur when a household is able to borrow or use up existing assets.

Graphing the Numbers

We now graph the consumption and saving relationships presented in Table 12-1. In the upper part of Figure 12-1 on page 255, the vertical axis measures the level of planned real consumption per year, and the horizontal axis measures the level of real disposable income per year. In the lower part of the figure, the horizontal axis is again real disposable income per year, but now the vertical axis is planned real saving per year. All of these are on a dollars-per-year basis, which emphasizes the point that we are measuring flows, not stocks.

CONSUMPTION AND SAVING FUNCTIONS As you can see, we have taken income-consumption and income-saving combinations *A* through *K* and plotted them. In the upper part of

TABLE 12-1

Real Consumption and Saving Schedules: A Hypothetical Case

Column 1 presents real disposable income from zero up to $120,000 per year. Column 2 indicates planned real consumption per year. Column 3 presents planned real saving per year. At levels of real disposable income below $60,000, planned real saving is negative. In column 4, we see the average propensity to consume, which is merely planned consumption divided by disposable income. Column 5 lists average propensity to save, which is planned saving divided by disposable income. Column 6 is the marginal propensity to consume, which shows the proportion of *additional* income that will be consumed. Finally, column 7 shows the proportion of *additional* income that will be saved, or the marginal propensity to save. (Δ represents "change in.")

Combination	(1) Real Disposable Income per Year (Y_d)	(2) Planned Real Consumption per Year (C)	(3) Planned Real Saving per Year $(S \equiv Y_d - C)$ (1) − (2)	(4) Average Propensity to Consume $(APC \equiv C/Y_d)$ (2) ÷ (1)	(5) Average Propensity to Save $(APS \equiv S/Y_d)$ (3) ÷ (1)	(6) Marginal Propensity to Consume $(MPC \equiv \Delta C/\Delta Y_d)$	(7) Marginal Propensity to Save $(MPS \equiv \Delta S/\Delta Y_d)$
A	$ 0	$ 12,000	$−12,000	–	–	–	–
B	12,000	21,600	−9,600	1.8	−0.8	0.8	0.2
C	24,000	31,200	−7,200	1.3	−0.3	0.8	0.2
D	36,000	40,800	−4,800	1.133	−0.133	0.8	0.2
E	48,000	50,400	−2,400	1.05	−0.05	0.8	0.2
F	60,000	60,000	0	1.0	0.0	0.8	0.2
G	72,000	69,600	2,400	0.967	0.033	0.8	0.2
H	84,000	79,200	4,800	0.943	0.057	0.8	0.2
I	96,000	88,800	7,200	0.925	0.075	0.8	0.2
J	108,000	98,400	9,600	0.911	0.089	0.8	0.2
K	120,000	108,000	12,000	0.9	0.1	0.8	0.2

Figure 12-1 on the facing page, the result is called the *consumption function*. In the lower part, the result is called the *saving function*.

Mathematically, the saving function is the *complement* of the consumption function because consumption plus saving always equals disposable income. What is not consumed is, by definition, saved. The difference between actual disposable income and the planned rate of consumption per year *must* be the planned rate of saving per year.

THE 45-DEGREE REFERENCE LINE How can we find the rate of saving or dissaving in the upper part of Figure 12-1? We begin by drawing a line that is equidistant from both the horizontal and the vertical axes. This line is 45 degrees from either axis and is often called the **45-degree reference line.** At every point on the 45-degree reference line, a vertical line drawn to the income axis is the same distance from the origin as a horizontal line drawn to the consumption axis. Thus, at point *F*, where the consumption function intersects the 45-degree line, real disposable income equals planned real consumption.

Point *F* is sometimes called the *break-even income point* because there is neither positive nor negative real saving. This can be seen in the lower part of Figure 12-1 as well. The planned annual rate of real saving at a real disposable income level of $60,000 is indeed zero.

45-degree reference line
The line along which planned real expenditures equal real GDP per year.

Dissaving and Autonomous Consumption

To the left of point *F* in either part of Figure 12-1, this hypothetical family engages in dissaving, either by going into debt or by consuming existing assets. The rate of real saving or dissaving in the upper part of the figure can be found by measuring the

The Consumption and Saving Functions

If we plot the combinations of real disposable income and planned real consumption from columns 1 and 2 in Table 12-1 on the facing page, we get the consumption function.

At every point on the 45-degree line, a vertical line drawn to the income axis is the same distance from the origin as a horizontal line drawn to the consumption axis. Where the consumption function crosses the 45-degree line at *F*, we know that planned real consumption equals real disposable income and there is zero saving. The vertical distance between the 45-degree line and the consumption function measures the rate of real saving or dissaving at any given income level.

If we plot the relationship between column 1 (real disposable income) and column 3 (planned real saving) from Table 12-1 on the facing page, we arrive at the saving function shown in the lower part of this diagram. It is the complement of the consumption function presented above it.

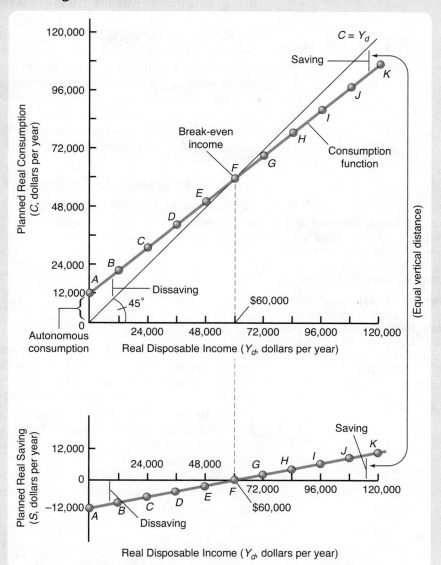

vertical distance between the 45-degree line and the consumption function. This simply tells us that if our hypothetical household sees its real disposable income fall to less than $60,000, it will not limit its consumption to this amount. It will instead go into debt or consume existing assets in some way to compensate for part of the lost income.

AUTONOMOUS CONSUMPTION Now look at the point on the diagram where real disposable income is zero but planned consumption is $12,000. This amount of real planned consumption, which does not depend at all on actual real disposable income, is called **autonomous consumption.** The autonomous consumption of $12,000 is *independent* of disposable income. That means that no matter how low the level of real income of our hypothetical household falls, the household will always attempt to consume at least $12,000 per year. (We are, of course, assuming here that the household's real disposable income does not equal zero year in and year out. There is certainly a limit to how long our hypothetical household could finance autonomous consumption without any income.)

Autonomous consumption
The part of consumption that is independent of (does not depend on) the level of disposable income. Changes in autonomous consumption shift the consumption function.

The $12,000 of yearly consumption is determined by things other than the level of income. We don't need to specify what determines autonomous consumption. We merely state that it exists and that in our example it is $12,000 per year.

THE MEANING OF AUTONOMOUS SPENDING Just remember that the word *autonomous* means "existing independently." In our model, autonomous consumption exists independently of the hypothetical household's level of real disposable income. (Later we will review some of the determinants of consumption other than real disposable income.)

There are many possible types of autonomous expenditures. Hypothetically, we can assume that investment is autonomous—independent of income. We can assume that government expenditures are autonomous. We will do just that at various times in our discussions to simplify our analysis of income determination.

Average Propensity to Consume and to Save

> **Average propensity to consume (APC)**
> Real consumption divided by real disposable income. For any given level of real income, the proportion of total real disposable income that is consumed.

> **Average propensity to save (APS)**
> Real saving divided by real disposable income. For any given level of real income, the proportion of total real disposable income that is saved.

Let's now go back to Table 12-1 on page 254, and this time let's look at columns 4 and 5: **average propensity to consume (APC)** and **average propensity to save (APS)**. They are defined as follows:

$$APC \equiv \frac{\text{real consumption}}{\text{real disposable income}}$$

$$APS \equiv \frac{\text{real saving}}{\text{real disposable income}}$$

Notice from column 4 in Table 12-1 that for this hypothetical household, the average propensity to consume decreases as real disposable income increases. This decrease simply means that the fraction of the household's real disposable income going to consumption falls as income rises. Column 5 shows that the average propensity to save, which at first is negative, finally hits zero at an income level of $60,000 and then becomes positive. In this example, the APS reaches a value of 0.1 at income level $120,000. This means that the household saves 10 percent of a $120,000 income.

It's quite easy for you to figure out your own average propensity to consume or to save. Just divide the value of what you consumed by your total real disposable income for the year, and the result will be your personal APC at your current level of income. Also, divide your real saving during the year by your real disposable income to calculate your own APS.

Marginal Propensity to Consume and to Save

> **Marginal propensity to consume (MPC)**
> The ratio of the change in consumption to the change in disposable income. A marginal propensity to consume of 0.8 tells us that an additional $100 in take-home pay will lead to an additional $80 consumed.

> **Marginal propensity to save (MPS)**
> The ratio of the change in saving to the change in disposable income. A marginal propensity to save of 0.2 indicates that out of an additional $100 in take-home pay, $20 will be saved. Whatever is not saved is consumed. The marginal propensity to save plus the marginal propensity to consume must always equal 1, by definition.

Now we go to the last two columns in Table 12-1 on page 254: **marginal propensity to consume (MPC)** and **marginal propensity to save (MPS)**. The term *marginal* refers to a small incremental or decremental change (represented by the Greek letter delta, Δ, in Table 12-1). The marginal propensity to consume, then, is defined as

$$MPC \equiv \frac{\text{change in real consumption}}{\text{change in real disposable income}}$$

The marginal propensity to save is defined similarly as

$$MPS \equiv \frac{\text{change in real saving}}{\text{change in real disposable income}}$$

MARGINAL VERSUS AVERAGE PROPENSITIES What do MPC and MPS tell you? They tell you what percentage of a given increase or decrease in real income will go toward consumption and saving, respectively. The emphasis here is on the word *change*.

The marginal propensity to consume indicates how much you will change your planned real consumption if there is a change in your actual real disposable income.

If your marginal propensity to consume is 0.8, that does *not* mean that you consume 80 percent of *all* disposable income. The percentage of your total real disposable income that you consume is given by the average propensity to consume, or APC. As Table 12-1 on page 254 indicates, the APC is not equal to 0.8 anywhere in its column. Instead, an MPC of 0.8 means that you will consume 80 percent of any *increase* in your disposable income. Hence, the MPC cannot be less than zero or greater than one. It follows that households increase their planned real consumption by between 0 and 100 percent of any increase in real disposable income that they receive.

DISTINGUISHING THE MPC FROM THE APC Consider a simple example in which we show the difference between the average propensity to consume and the marginal propensity to consume. Assume that your consumption behavior is exactly the same as our hypothetical household's behavior depicted in Table 12-1. You have an annual real disposable income of $108,000. Your planned consumption rate, then, from column 2 of Table 12-1 is $98,400. So your average propensity to consume is $98,400/$108,000 = 0.911. Now suppose that at the end of the year, your boss gives you an after-tax bonus of $12,000.

What would you do with that additional $12,000 in real disposable income? According to the table, you would consume $9,600 of it and save $2,400. In that case, your *marginal* propensity to consume would be $9,600/$12,000 = 0.8 and your marginal propensity to save would be $2,400/$12,000 = 0.2. What would happen to your *average* propensity to consume? To find out, we add $9,600 to $98,400 of planned consumption, which gives us a new consumption rate of $108,000. The average propensity to consume is then $108,000 divided by the new higher salary of $120,000. Your APC drops from 0.911 to 0.9.

In contrast, your MPC remains, in our simplified example, 0.8 all the time. Look at column 6 in Table 12-1. The MPC is 0.8 at every level of income. (Therefore, the MPS is always equal to 0.2 at every level of income.) The constancy of MPC reflects the assumption that the amount that you are willing to consume out of additional income will remain the same in percentage terms no matter what level of real disposable income is your starting point.

Some Relationships

Consumption plus saving must equal income. Both your total real disposable income and the change in total real disposable income are either consumed or saved. The sums of the proportions of either measure that are consumed and saved must equal 1, or 100 percent. This allows us to make the following statements:

$$APC + APS \equiv 1 \; (= 100 \text{ percent of total income})$$

$$MPC + MPS \equiv 1 \; (= 100 \text{ percent of the } \textit{change} \text{ in income})$$

The average propensities as well as the marginal propensities to consume and save must total 1, or 100 percent. Check the two statements by adding the figures in columns 4 and 5 for each level of real disposable income in Table 12-1 on page 254. Do the same for columns 6 and 7.

Causes of Shifts in the Consumption Function

A change in any other relevant economic variable besides real disposable income will cause the consumption function to shift. The number of such nonincome determinants of the position of the consumption function is almost unlimited. Real household **net wealth** is one determinant of the position of the consumption function. An increase in the real net wealth of the average household will cause the consumption function to shift upward. A decrease in real net wealth will cause it to shift downward. So far we have been talking about the consumption function of an individual or a household. Now let's move on to the national economy.

Net wealth
The stock of assets owned by a person, household, firm, or nation (net of any debts owed). For a household, net wealth can consist of a house, cars, personal belongings, stocks, bonds, bank accounts, and cash (minus any debts owed).

Why did real consumption expenditures of U.S. households decline between 2008 and 2009 and then fail to bounce back quickly in subsequent years?

EXAMPLE

Lower Household Wealth and Subdued Growth in Consumption

Between 2007 and 2009, two key components of real household wealth—inflation-adjusted wealth in housing and in corporate stocks—declined substantially. During that interval, aggregate real wealth in housing dropped by about 25 percent, and at one point real household wealth held in stocks fell by more than 50 percent. These wealth reductions shifted the U.S. consumption function downward. Real disposable income also fell. Consequently, there was also a leftward movement along the now lower consumption function that contributed to a further drop in real household consumption between 2008 and 2009.

Inflation-adjusted household disposable income has increased each year since 2009. Nevertheless, real housing wealth held by households

has declined by another 10 percentage points. Inflation-adjusted household wealth in corporate stocks has recovered considerably but has remained between 10 percent and 20 percent lower than the peak it had reached in 2008. As a result, the U.S. consumption function has remained at a lower position than in 2007, which has dampened growth in real consumption spending during the following years.

FOR CRITICAL THINKING
Why do both *movements along and any shifts in the consumption function ultimately* jointly *determine observed changes in desired total real consumption spending?*

QUICK QUIZ See page 277 for the answers. Review concepts from this section in MyEconLab.

The **consumption function** shows the relationship between planned rates of real consumption and real _____ _____ per year. The saving function is the complement of the consumption function because real saving plus real _____ must equal real disposable income.

The _____ propensity to consume is equal to real consumption divided by real disposable income. The _____ propensity to save is equal to real saving divided by real disposable income.

The _____ propensity to consume is equal to the change in planned real consumption divided by the change

in real disposable income. The _____ propensity to save is equal to the change in planned real saving divided by the change in real disposable income.

Any change in real disposable income will cause the planned rate of consumption to change. This is represented by a _____ _____ the consumption function. Any change in a nonincome determinant of consumption will cause a _____ _____ the consumption function.

Determinants of Investment

Investment, you will remember, consists of expenditures on new buildings and equipment and changes in business inventories. Historically, real gross private domestic investment in the United States has been extremely volatile over the years, relative to real consumption. If we were to look at net private domestic investment (investment after depreciation has been deducted), we would see that in the depths of the Great Depression and at the peak of the World War II effort, the figure was negative. In other words, we were eating away at our capital stock—we weren't even maintaining it by fully replacing depreciated equipment.

If we compare real investment expenditures historically with real consumption expenditures, we find that the latter are less variable over time than the former. Why is this so? One possible reason is that the real investment decisions of businesses are based on highly variable, subjective estimates of how the economic future looks.

The Planned Investment Function

Consider that at all times, businesses perceive an array of investment opportunities. These investment opportunities have rates of return ranging from zero to very high, with the number (or dollar value) of all such projects increasing if the rate of return rises.

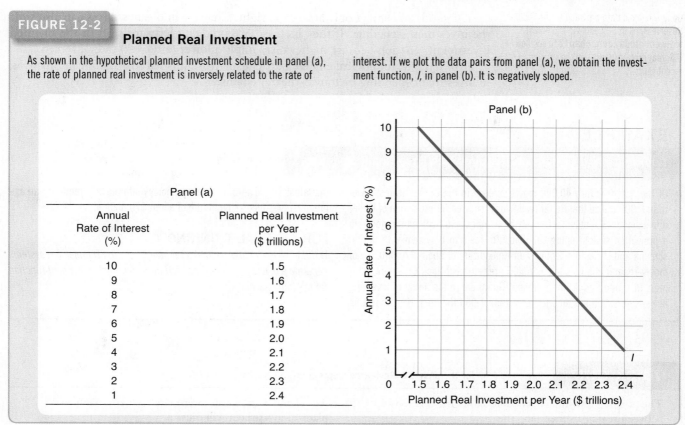

FIGURE 12-2

Planned Real Investment

As shown in the hypothetical planned investment schedule in panel (a), the rate of planned real investment is inversely related to the rate of interest. If we plot the data pairs from panel (a), we obtain the investment function, *I*, in panel (b). It is negatively sloped.

Panel (a)

Annual Rate of Interest (%)	Planned Real Investment per Year ($ trillions)
10	1.5
9	1.6
8	1.7
7	1.8
6	1.9
5	2.0
4	2.1
3	2.2
2	2.3
1	2.4

Because a project is profitable only if its rate of return exceeds the opportunity cost of the investment—the rate of interest—it follows that as the interest rate falls, planned investment spending increases, and vice versa. Even if firms use retained earnings (internal financing) to fund an investment, the lower the market rate of interest, the smaller the *opportunity cost* of using those retained earnings.

Thus, it does not matter in our analysis whether the firm must seek financing from external sources or can obtain such financing by using retained earnings. Whatever the method of financing, as the interest rate falls, more investment opportunities will be profitable, and planned investment will be higher.

It should be no surprise, therefore, that the investment function is represented as an inverse relationship between the rate of interest and the value of planned real investment. In Figure 12-2 above, a hypothetical investment schedule is given in panel (a) and plotted in panel (b). We see from this schedule that if, for example, the rate of interest is 5 percent, the dollar value of planned investment will be $2 trillion per year. Notice that planned investment is also given on a per-year basis, showing that it represents a flow, not a stock. (The stock counterpart of investment is the stock of capital in the economy measured in inflation-adjusted dollars at a point in time.)

What Causes the Investment Function to Shift?

Because planned real investment is assumed to be a function of the rate of interest, any non-interest-rate variable that changes can have the potential of shifting the investment function. One of those variables is the expectations of businesses. If higher profits are expected, more machines and bigger plants will be planned for the future. More investment will be undertaken because of the expectation of higher profits. In this case, the investment function, *I*, in panel (b) of Figure 12-2, would shift outward to the right, meaning that more investment would be desired at all rates of interest.

Any change in productive technology can potentially shift the investment function. A positive change in productive technology would stimulate demand for additional

Go to economic data provided by the Federal Reserve Bank of St. Louis via the link at www.econtoday.com/chap12 to see how U.S. real private investment has varied in recent years.

capital goods and shift *I* outward to the right. Changes in business taxes can also shift the investment schedule. If they increase, we predict a leftward shift in the planned investment function because higher taxes imply a lower (after-tax) rate of return.

How has a technological change in the display of films led to a significant upswing in investment spending by movie-theater chains?

EXAMPLE

Adding a Third Dimension Requires New Investment Spending

Of the approximately 40,000 movie screens in the United States, fewer than 8,000 utilize the digital technology required for projection of three-dimensional (3D) movies. Converting a typical multiscreen theater from a projection system using celluloid film reels to a system with digital screens and projectors requires an expenditure of about $70,000. Major movie-theater chains such as AMC Entertainment, Inc., Cinemark Holdings, Inc., and Regal Entertainment Group are in the midst of investing in new projection systems for more than 1,000 theaters. Hence, putting the latest 3D movie-projection technology into place is requiring an aggregate investment expenditure of about $70 million.

FOR CRITICAL THINKING
Will the movie-theater chains' total investment in 3D projection systems generate a movement along or a shift in the planned investment function for the United States?

QUICK QUIZ   See page 277 for the answers. Review concepts from this section in MyEconLab.

The planned investment schedule shows the relationship between real investment and the _____ _____; it slopes _____.

The non-interest-rate determinants of planned investment are _____, innovation and technological changes, and _____ _____.

Any change in the non-interest-rate determinants of planned investment will cause a _____ _____ the planned investment function so that at each and every rate of interest a different amount of planned investment will be made.

Determining Equilibrium Real GDP

We are interested in determining the equilibrium level of real GDP per year. But when we examined the consumption function earlier in this chapter, it related planned real consumption expenditures to the level of real disposable income per year. We have already shown where adjustments must be made to GDP in order to get real disposable income (see Table 8-2 on page 175). Real disposable income turns out to be less than real GDP because real net taxes (real taxes minus real government transfer payments) are usually about 14 to 21 percent of GDP. A representative average is about 18 percent, so disposable income, on average, has in recent years been around 82 percent of GDP.

Consumption as a Function of Real GDP

To simplify our model, assume that real disposable income, Y_d, differs from real GDP by the same absolute amount every year. Therefore, we can relatively easily substitute real GDP for real disposable income in the consumption function.

We can now plot any consumption function on a diagram in which the horizontal axis is no longer real disposable income but rather real GDP, as in Figure 12-3 on the facing page. Notice that there is an autonomous part of real consumption that is so labeled. The difference between this graph and the graphs presented earlier in this chapter is the change in the horizontal axis from real disposable income to real GDP per year. For the rest of this chapter, assume that the MPC out of real GDP equals 0.8, so that 20 percent of changes in real disposable income is saved. Of an additional after-tax $100 earned, an additional $80 will be consumed.

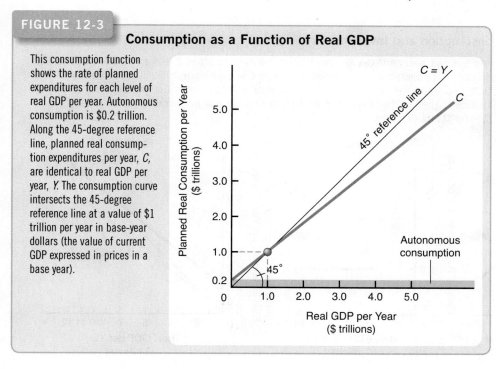

FIGURE 12-3

Consumption as a Function of Real GDP

This consumption function shows the rate of planned expenditures for each level of real GDP per year. Autonomous consumption is $0.2 trillion. Along the 45-degree reference line, planned real consumption expenditures per year, C, are identical to real GDP per year, Y. The consumption curve intersects the 45-degree reference line at a value of $1 trillion per year in base-year dollars (the value of current GDP expressed in prices in a base year).

The 45-Degree Reference Line

As in the earlier graphs, Figure 12-3 above shows a 45-degree reference line. The 45-degree line bisects the quadrant into two equal spaces. Thus, along the 45-degree reference line, planned real consumption expenditures, C, equal real GDP per year, Y. One can see, then, that at any point where the consumption function intersects the 45-degree reference line, planned real consumption expenditures will be exactly equal to real GDP per year, or $C = Y$. Note that in this graph, because we are looking only at planned real consumption on the vertical axis, the 45-degree reference line is where planned real consumption, C, is always equal to real GDP per year, Y. Later, when we add real investment, government spending, and net exports to the graph, *all* planned real expenditures will be labeled along the vertical axis. In any event, real consumption and real GDP are equal at $1 trillion per year. That is where the consumption curve, C, intersects the 45-degree reference line. At that GDP level, all real GDP is consumed.

Adding the Investment Function

Another component of private aggregate demand is, of course, real investment spending, *I*. We have already looked at the planned investment function, which related real investment, which includes changes in inventories of final products, to the rate of interest.

PLANNED INVESTMENT AND THE INTEREST RATE In panel (a) of Figure 12-4 on the following page, you see that at an interest rate of 5 percent, the rate of real investment is $2 trillion per year. The $2 trillion of real investment per year is *autonomous* with respect to real GDP—that is, it is independent of real GDP.

In other words, given that we have a determinant investment level of $2 trillion at a 5 percent rate of interest, we can treat this level of real investment as constant, regardless of the level of GDP. This is shown in panel (b) of Figure 12-4. The vertical distance of real investment spending is $2 trillion. Businesses plan on investing a particular amount—$2 trillion per year—and will do so no matter what the level of real GDP.

COMBINING PLANNED INVESTMENT AND CONSUMPTION How do we add this amount of real investment spending to our consumption function? We simply add a line above the C

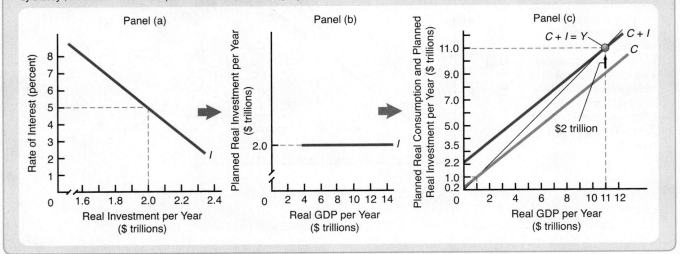

FIGURE 12-4

Combining Consumption and Investment

In panel (a), we show that at an interest rate of 5 percent, real investment is equal to $2 trillion per year. In panel (b), investment is a constant $2 trillion per year. When we add this amount to the consumption line, we obtain in panel (c) the $C + I$ line, which is vertically higher than the C line by exactly $2 trillion. Real GDP is equal to $C + I$ at $11 trillion per year

where total planned real expenditures, $C + I$, are equal to actual real GDP, for this is where the $C + I$ line intersects the 45-degree reference line, on which $C + I$ is equal to Y at every point. (For simplicity, we ignore the fact that the dependence of saving on income can influence investment.)

line that we drew in Figure 12-3 on the previous page that is higher by the vertical distance equal to $2 trillion of autonomous real investment spending. This is shown by the arrow in panel (c) of Figure 12-4 above.

Our new line, now labeled $C + I$, is called the *consumption plus investment line*. In our simple economy without real government expenditures and net exports, the $C + I$ curve represents total planned real expenditures as they relate to different levels of real GDP per year. Because the 45-degree reference line shows all the points where planned real expenditures (now $C + I$) equal real GDP, we label it $C + I = Y$. Thus, in equilibrium, the sum of consumption spending (C) and investment spending (I) equals real GDP (Y), which is $11 trillion per year. Equilibrium occurs when total planned real expenditures equal real GDP (given that any amount of production of goods and services in this model in the short run can occur without a change in the price level).

Saving and Investment: Planned versus Actual

Figure 12-5 on the facing page shows the planned investment curve as a horizontal line at $2 trillion per year in base-year dollars. Real investment is completely autonomous in this simplified model—it does not depend on real GDP.

The planned saving curve is represented by S. Because in our model whatever is not consumed is, by definition, saved, the planned saving schedule is the complement of the planned consumption schedule, represented by the C line in Figure 12-3 on the previous page. For better exposition, we look at only a part of the saving and investment schedules—annual levels of real GDP between $9 trillion and $13 trillion.

Why does equilibrium have to occur at the intersection of the planned saving and planned investment schedules? If we are at E in Figure 12-5, planned saving equals planned investment. All anticipations are validated by reality. There is no tendency for businesses to alter the rate of production or the level of employment because they are neither increasing nor decreasing their inventories in an unplanned way.

UNPLANNED CHANGES IN BUSINESS INVENTORIES If real GDP is $13 trillion instead of $11 trillion, planned investment, as usual, is $2 trillion per year. It is exceeded, however, by planned saving, which is $2.4 trillion per year. The additional $0.4 trillion

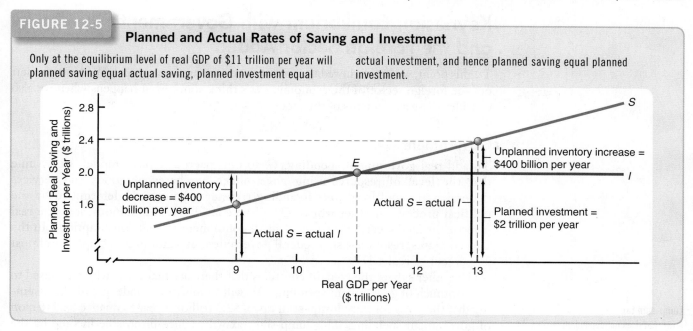

FIGURE 12-5

Planned and Actual Rates of Saving and Investment

Only at the equilibrium level of real GDP of $11 trillion per year will planned saving equal actual saving, planned investment equal actual investment, and hence planned saving equal planned investment.

($400 billion) in saving by households over and above planned investment represents less consumption spending and will translate into unsold goods that accumulate as unplanned business inventory investment. Thus, consumers will *actually* purchase fewer goods and services than businesses had *anticipated*. This will leave firms with unsold products, and their inventories will begin to rise above the levels they had planned.

Unplanned business inventories will now rise at the rate of $400 billion per year, or $2.4 trillion in actual investment (including inventories) minus $2 trillion in planned investment by firms that had not anticipated an inventory buildup. But this situation cannot continue for long. Businesses will respond to the unplanned increase in inventories by cutting back production of goods and services and reducing employment, and we will move toward a lower level of real GDP.

Naturally, the adjustment process works in reverse if real GDP is less than the equilibrium level. For instance, if real GDP is $9 trillion per year, an unintended inventory decrease of $0.4 trillion ultimately brings about an increase in real GDP toward the equilibrium level of $11 trillion.

Every time the saving rate planned by households differs from the investment rate planned by businesses, there will be a shrinkage or an expansion in the circular flow of income and output (introduced in Chapter 8) in the form of unplanned inventory changes. Real GDP and employment will change until unplanned inventory changes are again zero—that is, until we have attained the equilibrium level of real GDP.

QUICK QUIZ   See page 277 for the answers. Review concepts from this section in MyEconLab.

We assume that the consumption function has an _____ part that is independent of the level of real GDP per year. It is labeled "_____ consumption."

For simplicity, we assume that real investment is _____ with respect to real GDP and therefore unaffected by the level of real GDP per year.

The _____ level of real GDP can be found where planned saving equals planned investment.

Whenever planned saving exceeds planned investment, there will be unplanned inventory _____, and real GDP will fall as producers cut production of goods and services. Whenever planned saving is less than planned investment, there will be unplanned inventory _____, and real GDP will rise as producers increase production of goods and services.

Keynesian Equilibrium with Government and the Foreign Sector Added

To this point, we have ignored the role of government in our model. We have also left out the foreign sector of the economy. Let's think about what happens when we also consider these as elements of the model.

Government

To add real government spending, *G*, to our macroeconomic model, we assume that the level of resource-using government purchases of goods and services (federal, state, and local), *not* including transfer payments, is determined by the political process. In other words, *G* will be considered autonomous, just like real investment (and a certain relatively small component of real consumption). In the United States, resource-using federal government expenditures account for almost 25 percent of real GDP.

The other side of the coin, of course, is that there are real taxes, which are used to pay for much of government spending. We will simplify our model greatly by assuming that there is a constant **lump-sum tax** of $2.3 trillion a year to finance $2.3 trillion of government spending. This lump-sum tax will reduce disposable income by the same amount. We show this below in Table 12-2 (column 2) below, where we give the numbers for a complete model.

Lump-sum tax
A tax that does not depend on income. An example is a $1,000 tax that every household must pay, irrespective of its economic situation.

The Foreign Sector

For years, the media have focused attention on the nation's foreign trade deficit. We have been buying merchandise and services from foreign residents—real imports—the value of which exceeds the value of the real exports we have been selling to them. The difference between real exports and real imports is *real net exports*, which we will label *X* in our graphs. The level of real exports depends on

---

TABLE 12-2

The Determination of Equilibrium Real GDP with Government and Net Exports Added
Figures are trillions of dollars.

(1) Real GDP	(2) Real Taxes	(3) Real Disposable Income	(4) Planned Real Consumption	(5) Planned Real Saving	(6) Planned Real Investment	(7) Real Government Spending	(8) Real Net Exports (exports minus imports)	(9) Total Planned Real Expenditures (4)+(6)+(7)+(8)	(10) Unplanned Inventory Changes	(11) Direction of Change in Real GDP
9.0	2.3	6.7	6.7	0.0	2.0	2.3	−0.8	10.2	−1.2	Increase
10.0	2.3	7.7	7.5	0.2	2.0	2.3	−0.8	11.0	−1.0	Increase
11.0	2.3	8.7	8.3	0.4	2.0	2.3	−0.8	11.8	−0.8	Increase
12.0	2.3	9.7	9.1	0.6	2.0	2.3	−0.8	12.6	−0.6	Increase
13.0	2.3	10.7	9.9	0.8	2.0	2.3	−0.8	13.4	−0.4	Increase
14.0	2.3	11.7	10.7	1.0	2.0	2.3	−0.8	14.2	−0.2	Increase
15.0	2.3	12.7	11.5	1.2	2.0	2.3	−0.8	15.0	0	Neither (equilibrium)
16.0	2.3	13.7	12.3	1.4	2.0	2.3	−0.8	15.8	+0.2	Decrease
17.0	2.3	14.7	13.1	1.6	2.0	2.3	−0.8	16.6	+0.4	Decrease

international economic conditions, especially in the countries that buy our products. Real imports depend on economic conditions here at home. For simplicity, assume that real imports exceed real exports (real net exports, X, is negative) and furthermore that the level of real net exports is autonomous—independent of real national income. Assume a level of X of –$0.8 trillion per year, as shown in column 8 of Table 12-2 on the facing page.

Determining the Equilibrium Level of GDP per Year

We are now in a position to determine the equilibrium level of real GDP per year under the continuing assumptions that the price level is unchanging; that investment, government, and the foreign sector are autonomous; and that planned consumption expenditures are determined by the level of real GDP. As can be seen in Table 12-2, total planned real expenditures of $15 trillion per year equal real GDP of $15 trillion per year, and this is where we reach equilibrium.

Remember that equilibrium *always* occurs when total planned real expenditures equal real GDP. Now look at Figure 12-6 below, which shows the equilibrium level of real GDP. There are two curves, one showing the consumption function, which is the exact duplicate of the one shown in Figure 12-3 on page 261, and the other being the C + I + G + X curve, which intersects the 45-degree reference line (representing equilibrium) at $15 trillion per year.

Whenever total planned real expenditures differ from real GDP, there are unplanned inventory changes. When total planned real expenditures are greater than real GDP, inventory levels drop in an unplanned manner. To get inventories back up, firms seek to expand their production of goods and services, which increases real GDP. Real GDP rises toward its equilibrium level. Whenever total planned real expenditures are less than real GDP, the opposite occurs. There are unplanned inventory increases, causing firms to cut back on their production of goods and services in an effort to push inventories back down to planned levels. The result is a drop in real GDP toward the equilibrium level.

FIGURE 12-6

The Equilibrium Level of Real GDP

The consumption function, with no government and thus no taxes, is shown as C. When we add autonomous investment, government spending, and net exports, we obtain C + I + G + X. We move from E₁ to E₂. Equilibrium real GDP is $15 trillion per year.

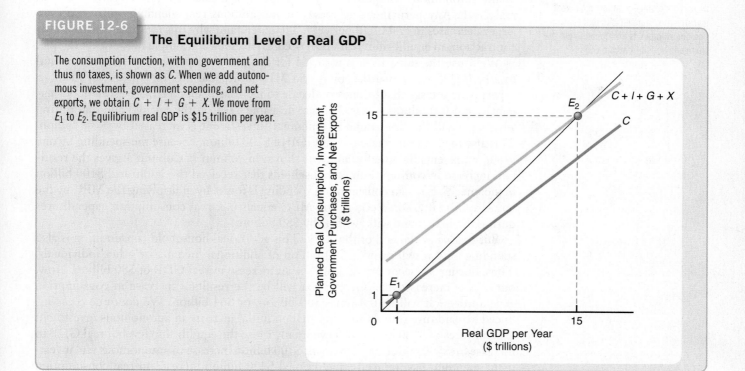

When we add autonomous investment, I, and autonomous government spending, G, to the consumption function, we obtain the $C + I + G$ curve, which represents total _____ _____ for a closed economy. In an open economy, we add the foreign sector, which consists of exports minus imports, or net exports, X. Total planned expenditures are thus represented by the $C + I + G + X$ curve.

Equilibrium real GDP can be found by locating the intersection of the total planned real expenditures curve with the _____-_____ reference line. At that level of real GDP per year, planned real consumption plus

planned real investment plus real government expenditures plus real net exports will equal real GDP.

Whenever total planned real expenditures exceed real GDP, there will be unplanned _____ in inventories. Production of goods and services will increase, and a higher level of equilibrium real GDP will prevail. Whenever total planned real expenditures are less than real GDP, there will be unplanned _____ in inventories. Production of goods and services will decrease, and equilibrium real GDP will decrease.

The Multiplier

Look again at panel (c) of Figure 12-4 on page 262. Assume for the moment that the only real expenditures included in real GDP are real consumption expenditures. Where would the equilibrium level of real GDP be in this case? It would be where the consumption function (C) intersects the 45-degree reference line, which is at $1 trillion per year. Now we add the autonomous amount of planned real investment, $2 trillion, and then determine what the new equilibrium level of real GDP will be. It turns out to be $11 trillion per year. Adding $2 trillion per year of investment spending increased equilibrium real GDP by *five* times that amount, or by $10 trillion per year.

The Multiplier Effect

What is operating here is the multiplier effect of changes in autonomous spending. The **multiplier** is the number by which a permanent change in autonomous real investment or autonomous real consumption is multiplied to get the change in the equilibrium level of real GDP. Any permanent increases in autonomous real investment or in any autonomous component of consumption will cause an even larger increase in real GDP. Any permanent decreases in autonomous real spending will cause even larger decreases in real GDP per year. To understand why this multiple expansion (or contraction) in equilibrium real GDP occurs, let's look at a simple numerical example.

We'll use the same figures we used for the marginal propensity to consume and to save. MPC will equal 0.8, or $\frac{4}{5}$, and MPS will equal 0.2, or $\frac{1}{5}$. Now let's run an experiment and say that businesses decide to increase planned real investment permanently by $100 billion a year. We see in Table 12-3 on the facing page that during what we'll call the first round in column 1, investment is increased by $100 billion. This also means an increase in real GDP of $100 billion, because the spending by one group represents income for another, shown in column 2. Column 3 gives the resultant increase in consumption by households that received this additional $100 billion in income. This rise in consumption spending is found by multiplying the MPC by the increase in real GDP. Because the MPC equals 0.8, real consumption expenditures during the first round will increase by $80 billion.

But that's not the end of the story. This additional household consumption is also spending, and it will provide $80 billion of additional income for other individuals. Thus, during the second round, we see an increase in real GDP of $80 billion. Now, out of this increased real GDP, what will be the resultant increase in consumption expenditures? It will be 0.8 times $80 billion, or $64 billion. We continue these induced expenditure rounds and find that an initial increase in autonomous investment expenditures of $100 billion will eventually cause the equilibrium level of real GDP to increase by $500 billion. A permanent $100 billion increase in autonomous real investment spending has induced an additional $400 billion increase in real consumption

Multiplier
The ratio of the change in the equilibrium level of real GDP to the change in autonomous real expenditures. The number by which a change in autonomous real investment or autonomous real consumption, for example, is multiplied to get the change in equilibrium real GDP.

TABLE 12-3

The Multiplier Process

We trace the effects of a *permanent* $100 billion increase in autonomous real investment spending on real GDP per year. If we assume a marginal propensity to consume of 0.8, such an increase will eventually elicit a $500 billion increase in equilibrium real GDP per year.

(1) Round	(2) Annual Increase in Real GDP ($ billions)	(3) Annual Increase in Planned Real Consumption ($ billions)	(4) Annual Increase in Planned Real Saving ($ billions)
Assumption: MPC = 0.8, or $\frac{4}{5}$			
1 ($100 billion per year increase in I)	100.00 →	80.000	20.000
2	80.00 ← →	64.000	16.000
3	64.00 ← →	51.200	12.800
4	51.20 ← →	40.960	10.240
5	40.96 ← →	32.768	8.192
.	.	.	.
.	.	.	.
.	.	.	.
All later rounds	163.84	131.072	32.768
Totals (C + I + X)	500.00	400.000	100.000

spending, for a total increase in real GDP of $500 billion. In other words, equilibrium real GDP will change by an amount equal to five times the change in real investment.

The Multiplier Formula

It turns out that the autonomous spending multiplier is equal to 1 divided by the marginal propensity to save. In our example, the MPC was 0.8, or $\frac{4}{5}$. Therefore, because MPC + MPS = 1, the MPS was equal to 0.2, or $\frac{1}{5}$. When we divide 1 by $\frac{1}{5}$, we get 5. That was our multiplier. A $100 billion increase in real planned investment led to a $500 billion increase in the equilibrium level of real GDP. Our multiplier will always be the following:

$$\text{Multiplier} \equiv \frac{1}{1 - \text{MPC}} \equiv \frac{1}{\text{MPS}}$$

You can always figure out the multiplier if you know either the MPC or the MPS. Let's consider an example. If MPS = 0.25 or $\frac{1}{4}$,

$$\text{Multiplier} = \frac{1}{\frac{1}{4}} = 4$$

Because MPC + MPS = 1, it follows that MPS = 1 − MPC. Hence, we can always figure out the multiplier if we are given the marginal propensity to consume. In this example, if the marginal propensity to consume is given as 0.75 or $\frac{3}{4}$,

$$\text{Multiplier} = \frac{1}{1 - \frac{3}{4}} = \frac{1}{\frac{1}{4}} = 4$$

By taking a few numerical examples, you can demonstrate to yourself an important property of the multiplier:

The smaller the marginal propensity to save, the larger the multiplier.

Otherwise stated:

The larger the marginal propensity to consume, the larger the multiplier.

Demonstrate this to yourself by computing the multiplier when the marginal propensity to save equals $\frac{3}{4}$, $\frac{1}{2}$, and $\frac{1}{4}$. What happens to the multiplier as the MPS gets smaller?

When you have the multiplier, the following formula will then give you the change in equilibrium real GDP due to a permanent change in autonomous spending:

$$\text{Change in equilibrium real GDP} = \text{multiplier} \times \text{change in autonomous spending}$$

The multiplier, as noted earlier, works for a permanent increase or a permanent decrease in autonomous spending per year. In our earlier example, if the autonomous component of real consumption had fallen permanently by $100 billion, the reduction in equilibrium real GDP would have been $500 billion per year.

Significance of the Multiplier

Depending on the size of the multiplier, it is possible that a relatively small change in planned investment or in autonomous consumption can trigger a much larger change in equilibrium real GDP per year. In essence, the multiplier magnifies the fluctuations in yearly equilibrium real GDP initiated by changes in autonomous spending.

As was just noted, the larger the marginal propensity to consume, the larger the multiplier. If the marginal propensity to consume is $\frac{1}{2}$, the multiplier is 2. In that case, a $1 billion decrease in (autonomous) real investment will elicit a $2 billion decrease in equilibrium real GDP per year. Conversely, if the marginal propensity to consume is $\frac{9}{10}$, the multiplier will be 10. That same $1 billion decrease in planned real investment expenditures with a multiplier of 10 will lead to a $10 billion decrease in equilibrium real GDP per year.

WHAT IF... the government seeks a larger multiplier effect by funding private spending on certain items rather than buying those items directly?

Whether the government gives private firms or households funds to purchase particular goods or purchases those same goods itself, the resulting increase in total autonomous expenditures is the same. The overall theoretical multiplier effect on equilibrium real GDP would be the same as well. Hence, providing a grant of public funds for private purchase of the same items the government alternatively would have bought with the same funds will not enlarge the overall theoretical multiplier effect.

How a Change in Real Autonomous Spending Affects Real GDP When the Price Level Can Change

So far, our examination of how changes in real autonomous spending affect equilibrium real GDP has considered a situation in which the price level remains unchanged. Thus, our analysis has only indicated how much the aggregate demand curve shifts in response to a change in investment, government spending, net exports, or lump-sum taxes.

Of course, when we take into account the aggregate supply curve, we must also consider responses of the equilibrium price level to a multiplier-induced change in aggregate demand. We do so in Figure 12-7 on the facing page. The intersection of AD_1 and $SRAS$ is at a price level of 120 with equilibrium real GDP of $15 trillion per year. An increase in autonomous spending shifts the aggregate demand curve outward to the right to AD_2. If the price level remained at 120, the short-run equilibrium level of real GDP would increase to $15.5 trillion per year because, for the $100 billion increase in autonomous spending, the multiplier would be 5, as it was in Table 12-3 on the previous page.

FIGURE 12-7

Effect of a Rise in Autonomous Spending on Equilibrium Real GDP

A $100 billion increase in autonomous spending (investment, government, or net exports) moves AD_1 to AD_2. If the price index increases from 120 to 125, equilibrium real GDP goes up only to, say, $15.3 trillion per year instead of $15.5 trillion per year.

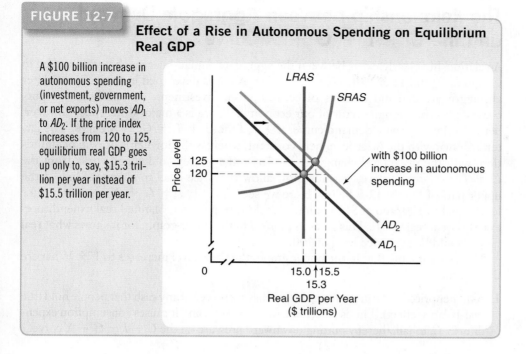

The price level does not stay fixed, however, because ordinarily the *SRAS* curve is positively sloped. In this diagram, the new short-run equilibrium level of real GDP is hypothetically $15.3 trillion. The ultimate effect on real GDP is smaller than the multiplier effect on nominal income because part of the additional income is used to pay higher prices. Not all is spent on additional goods and services, as is the case when the price level is fixed.

If the economy is at an equilibrium level of real GDP that is greater than *LRAS*, the implications for the eventual effect on real GDP are even more severe. Look again at Figure 12-7 above. The *SRAS* curve starts to slope upward more dramatically after $15 trillion of real GDP per year. Therefore, any increase in aggregate demand will lead to a proportionally greater increase in the price level and a smaller increase in equilibrium real GDP per year. The ultimate effect on real GDP of any increase in autonomous spending will be relatively small because most of the changes will be in the price level. Moreover, any increase in the short-run equilibrium level of real GDP will tend to be temporary because the economy is temporarily above *LRAS*—the strain on its productive capacity will raise the price level.

How much is the initial multiplier effect of a rise in real autonomous spending on real GDP in China offset by the resulting short-run adjustment in China's price level?

INTERNATIONAL EXAMPLE

The Effect of Higher Autonomous Spending on China's Real GDP

Most estimates indicate that the marginal propensity to consume in China is approximately 0.50. If we ignore a rise in the price level generated by a boost in aggregate demand that results from an increase in real autonomous spending, the value of the multiplier would be about 2. [This is so because $1/(1 - MPC) = 1/(1 - 0.5) = 1/0.5 = 2$.] Economists at the Hong Kong Monetary Authority have estimated, though, that the short-run effect of an initial rise in real autonomous spending on China's real GDP is actually much smaller—about 1.1. Therefore, once the effect on real GDP

of an upward price level adjustment is taken into account, the estimated result from a one-unit increase in real autonomous expenditures is only a 1.1-unit increase in China's annual real GDP.

FOR CRITICAL THINKING

By about how much would China's equilibrium real GDP change if the nation's net export spending declined by 1 trillion yuan (the Chinese currency unit)?

The Relationship between Aggregate Demand and the C + I + G + X Curve

A relationship clearly exists between the aggregate demand curves that you studied in Chapters 10 and 11 and the $C + I + G + X$ curve developed in this chapter. After all, aggregate demand consists of consumption, investment, and government purchases, plus the foreign sector of our economy. There is a major difference, however, between the aggregate demand curve, AD, and the $C + I + G + X$ curve: The latter is drawn with the price level held constant, whereas the former is drawn, by definition, with the price level changing. To derive the aggregate demand curve from the $C + I + G + X$ curve, we must now allow the price level to change. Look at the upper part of Figure 12-8 below. Here we see the $C + I + G + X$ curve at a price level equal to 100, and at $15 trillion of real GDP per year, planned real expenditures exactly equal real GDP. This gives us point A in the lower graph, for it shows what real GDP would be at a price level of 100.

Now let's assume that in the upper graph, the price level increases to 125. What are the effects?

1. A higher price level can decrease the purchasing power of any cash that people hold (the real-balance effect). This is a decrease in real wealth, and it causes consumption expenditures, C, to fall, thereby putting downward pressure on the $C + I + G + X$ curve.

FIGURE 12-8

The Relationship between *AD* and the *C + I + G + X* Curve

In the upper graph, the $C + I + G + X$ curve at a price level equal to 100 intersects the 45-degree reference line at E_1, or $15 trillion of real GDP per year. That gives us point A (price level = 100; real GDP = $15 trillion) in the lower graph. When the price level increases to 125, the $C + I + G + X$ curve shifts downward, and the new level of real GDP at which planned real expenditures equal real GDP is at E_2 at $13 trillion per year. This gives us point B in the lower graph. Connecting points A and B, we obtain the aggregate demand curve.

2. Because individuals attempt to borrow more to replenish their real cash balances, interest rates will rise, which will make it more costly for people to buy houses and cars (the interest rate effect). Higher interest rates also make it less profitable to install new equipment and to erect new buildings. Therefore, the rise in the price level indirectly causes a reduction in total planned spending on goods and services.

3. In an open economy, our higher price level causes foreign spending on our goods to fall (the open economy effect). Simultaneously, it increases our demand for others' goods. If the foreign exchange price of the dollar stays constant for a while, there will be an increase in imports and a decrease in exports, thereby reducing the size of X, again putting downward pressure on the $C + I + G + X$ curve.

The result is that a new $C + I + G + X$ curve at a price level equal to 125 generates an equilibrium at E_2 at \$13 trillion of real GDP per year. This gives us point B in the lower part of Figure 12-8 on the facing page. When we connect points A and B, we obtain the aggregate demand curve, AD.

QUICK QUIZ See page 277 for the answers. Review concepts from this section in MyEconLab.

Any change in autonomous spending shifts the expenditure curve and causes a _____ effect on equilibrium real GDP per year.

The **multiplier** is equal to 1 divided by the _____ propensity to _____.

The smaller the marginal propensity to _____, the larger the **multiplier.** Otherwise stated, the larger the

marginal propensity to _____, the larger the **multiplier.**

The $C + I + G + X$ curve is drawn with the price level held constant, whereas the AD curve allows the price level to _____. Each different price level generates a new $C + I + G + X$ curve.

YOU ARE THERE
Evaluating the Effects of Declining Real Disposable Income

Mark Vitner, an economist with Wells Fargo Bank, examines the latest monthly economic data. U.S. real disposable personal income fell by 0.3 percent during the month, the first such decline since the 2008–2009 economic downturn. Vitner notes that other data display patterns consistent with the theory of consumption and saving. Because households consume and save out of real disposable income, real consumption spending and real saving both dipped during the month.

Vitner returns a call to a financial news reporter seeking his comments on the implications of these declines. "Everything that we see in these numbers tells us that household budgets are extremely tight and getting tighter," he states. "Consumers are having to pull out all the stops in order to try to maintain their standard of living." This dreary

assessment is the best that Vitner can offer. After all, a key measure of households' living standards is real consumption spending, which in turn derives from real disposable income. If real disposable income continues to fall, persistent downward pressure will be exerted on real consumption spending—and, hence, on estimated standards of living—of U.S. households.

Critical Thinking Questions

1. Is Vitner contemplating a shift of or movement along the consumption function?

2. Did a shift of or movement along the *saving* function occur?

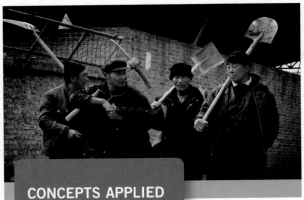

ISSUES & APPLICATIONS

A Global Reversal in Planned Investment Spending

CONCEPTS APPLIED

▶ Planned Investment Spending

▶ Multiplier

▶ Planned Investment Function

In years past, countries that experienced the largest upward shifts in their planned investment functions over time were developed countries, including European nations, Japan, and the United States. Recently, however, relatively larger upward shifts in planned investment functions have occurred among *emerging-economy nations*, such as China, India, South Korea, and Singapore.

Groups of Nations Trading Places in Planned Investment

Figure 12-9 below displays real investment spending as a percentage of global real GDP since the mid-1990s for developed versus emerging nations. The figure shows that in recent years, *decreases* in planned investment expenditures as a percentage of global real GDP have occurred in highly developed countries. In contrast, planned investment spending as a percentage of global real GDP has been *rising* for nations with emerging economies.

Global real GDP has increased every year except for a brief dip during 2009. Consequently, planned real investment has risen in all nations in most years. What Figure 12-9

depicts, therefore, is a shift toward relatively greater increases in planned investment in emerging nations compared with developed countries.

Higher Real Investment Yields Faster-Growing Real GDP

Within any nation's economy, variations in planned real investment spending operate through the multiplier to bring about changes in equilibrium real GDP. Thus, a country that experiences a larger upward shift in its planned investment function than another nation will, if both countries' multipliers have close to the same values, observe a greater increase in its equilibrium real GDP.

FIGURE 12-9

Real Investment Spending as a Percentage of Global Real GDP in Two Groups of Nations since 1995

Since the early 2000s, developed countries have experienced a decrease in planned investment expenditures as a percentage of global real GDP, whereas nations with emerging economies have observed an increase in planned investment spending as a percentage of global real GDP.

Sources: International Monetary Fund; author's estimates.

This relatively larger increase in investment spending helps to explain why countries such as China, India, South Korea, and Singapore are *emerging* from a status of less developed toward eventual classification among developed nations. Relatively higher planned real investment expenditures in these nations are, through multiplier effects, boosting real GDP per year. Thus, flows of real GDP are expanding faster in these emerging-economy countries than in developed ones.

For Critical Thinking

1. If interest rates, or opportunity costs of investment, happened to be the same in both developed countries and emerging-economy nations, what could account for faster upward shifts in the latter group's planned investment functions?
2. Are stocks of productive capital currently growing at a faster pace in developed countries or in emerging-economy nations? Explain.

Web Resources

1. To track real investment spending as a percentage of real GDP in recent years for individual nations, go to **www.econtoday.com/chap12**.
2. For links to economic data for both developed countries and emerging-economy nations, go to **www.econtoday.com/chap12**.

MyEconLab

For more questions on this chapter's Issues & Applications, go to **MyEconLab**. In the Study Plan for this chapter, select Section N: News.

MyEconLab

Here is what you should know after reading this chapter. MyEconLab will help you identify what you know, and where to go when you need to practice.

— **WHAT YOU SHOULD KNOW** —

The Difference between Saving and Savings and the Relationship between Saving and Consumption Saving is a flow over time, whereas savings are a stock of resources at a point in time. Thus, the portion of your disposable income that you do not consume during a week, a month, or a year is an addition to your stock of savings. By definition, saving during a year plus consumption during that year must equal total disposable (after-tax) income earned that year.

real disposable income, 251
consumption, 251
saving, 251
consumption goods, 251
investment, 252
capital goods, 252

— **WHERE TO GO TO PRACTICE** —

- **MyEconLab** Study Plan 12.1

Key Determinants of Consumption and Saving in the Keynesian Model In the Keynesian model, as real disposable income increases, so do real consumption expenditures. The portion of consumption unrelated to disposable income is autonomous consumption. The ratio of saving to disposable income is the average propensity to save (APS), and the ratio of consumption to disposable income is the average propensity to consume (APC). A change in saving divided by the corresponding change in disposable income is the marginal propensity to save (MPS), and a change in consumption divided by the corresponding change in disposable income is the marginal propensity to consume (MPC).

life-cycle theory of consumption, 253
permanent income hypothesis, 253
consumption function, 253
dissaving, 253
45-degree reference line, 254
autonomous consumption, 255
average propensity to consume (APC), 256
average propensity to save (APS), 256
marginal propensity to consume (MPC), 256
marginal propensity to save (MPS), 256
net wealth, 257

- **MyEconLab** Study Plan 12.2
- Animated Figure 12-1

— WHAT YOU SHOULD KNOW —		— WHERE TO GO TO PRACTICE —
	Key Figure Figure 12-1, 255	
Key Determinants of Planned Investment Planned investment varies inversely with the interest rate, so the investment schedule slopes downward. Changes in business expectations, productive technology, or business taxes cause the investment schedule to shift.		• MyEconLab Study Plan 12.3
How Equilibrium Real GDP Is Established in the Keynesian Model In equilibrium, total planned real consumption, investment, government, and net export expenditures equal real GDP, so $C + I + G + X = Y$. This occurs at the point where the $C + I + G + X$ curve crosses the 45-degree reference line. In a world without government spending and taxes, equilibrium also occurs when planned saving is equal to planned investment, and there is no tendency for business inventories to expand or contract.	lump-sum tax, 264 **Key Figures** Figure 12-5, 263 Figure 12-6, 265	• MyEconLab Study Plans 12.4, 12.5 • Animated Figures 12-5, 12-6
Why Autonomous Changes in Total Planned Real Expenditures Have a Multiplier Effect on Equilibrium Real GDP Any increase in autonomous expenditures causes a direct rise in real GDP. The resulting increase in disposable income in turn stimulates increased consumption by an amount equal to the marginal propensity to consume multiplied by the rise in disposable income that results. As consumption increases, so does real GDP, which induces a further increase in consumption spending. The ultimate expansion of real GDP is equal to the multiplier, $1/(1 - MPC)$, or $1/MPS$, times the increase in autonomous expenditures.	multiplier, 266 **Key Table** Table 12-3, 267	• MyEconLab Study Plans 12.6, 12.7 • Animated Table 12-3
The Relationship between Total Planned Expenditures and the Aggregate Demand Curve An increase in the price level induces households and businesses to cut back on spending. Thus, the $C + I + G + X$ curve shifts downward following a rise in the price level, so that equilibrium real GDP falls. This yields the downward-sloping aggregate demand curve.	**Key Figures** Figure 12-7, 269 Figure 12-8, 270	• MyEconLab Study Plan 12.8 • Animated Figures 12-7, 12-8

Log in to MyEconLab, take a chapter test, and get a personalized Study Plan that tells you which concepts you understand and which ones you need to review. From there, MyEconLab will give you further practice, tutorials, animations, videos, and guided solutions. For more information, visit www.myeconlab.com

PROBLEMS

All problems are assignable in MyEconLab. *Answers to odd-numbered problems appear at the back of the book.*

12-1. Classify each of the following as either a stock or a flow. (See page 251.)

   a. Myung Park earns $850 per week.

   b. Time Warner purchases $100 million in new telecomunications equipment this month.

   c. Sally Schmidt has $1,000 in a savings account at a credit union.

   d. XYZ, Inc., produces 200 units of output per week.

   e. Giorgio Giannelli owns three private jets.

   f. Apple's production declines by 750 digital devices per month.

   g. Russia owes $25 billion to the International Monetary Fund.

12-2. Consider the table below when answering the following questions. For this hypothetical economy, the marginal propensity to save is constant at all levels of real GDP, and investment spending is autonomous. There is no government. (See pages 253–263.)

Real GDP	Consumption	Saving	Investment
$ 2,000	$2,200	$_____	$400
4,000	4,000	_____	_____
6,000	_____	_____	_____
8,000	_____	_____	_____
10,000	_____	_____	_____
12,000	_____	_____	_____

   a. Complete the table. What is the marginal propensity to save? What is the marginal propensity to consume?

   b. Draw a graph of the consumption function. Then add the investment function to obtain $C + I$.

   c. Under the graph of $C + I$, draw another graph showing the saving and investment curves. Note that the $C + I$ curve crosses the 45-degree reference line in the upper graph at the same level of real GDP where the saving and investment curves cross in the lower graph. (If not, redraw your graphs.) What is this level of real GDP?

   d. What is the numerical value of the multiplier?

   e. What is equilibrium real GDP without investment? What is the multiplier effect from the inclusion of investment?

   f. What is the average propensity to consume at equilibrium real GDP?

   g. If autonomous investment declines from $400 to $200, what happens to equilibrium real GDP?

12-3. Consider the table below when answering the following questions. For this economy, the marginal propensity to consume is constant at all levels of real GDP, and investment spending is autonomous. Equilibrium real GDP is equal to $8,000. There is no government. (See pages 253–263.)

Real GDP	Consumption	Saving	Investment
$ 2,000	$ 2,000	_____	_____
4,000	3,600	_____	_____
6,000	5,200	_____	_____
8,000	6,800	_____	_____
10,000	8,400	_____	_____
12,000	10,000	_____	_____

   a. Complete the table. What is the marginal propensity to consume? What is the marginal propensity to save?

   b. Draw a graph of the consumption function. Then add the investment function to obtain $C + I$.

   c. Under the graph of $C + I$, draw another graph showing the saving and investment curves. Does the $C + I$ curve cross the 45-degree reference line in the upper graph at the same level of real GDP where the saving and investment curves cross in the lower graph, at the equilibrium real GDP of $8,000? (If not, redraw your graphs.)

   d. What is the average propensity to save at equilibrium real GDP?

   e. If autonomous consumption were to rise by $100, what would happen to equilibrium real GDP?

12-4. Calculate the multiplier for the following cases. (See page 267.)

   a. MPS = 0.25

   b. MPC = $\frac{5}{6}$

   c. MPS = 0.125

   d. MPC = $\frac{6}{7}$

12-5. Given each of the following values for the multiplier, calculate both the MPC and the MPS. (See page 267.)

   a. 20

   b. 10

   c. 8

   d. 5

12-6. The marginal propensity to consume is equal to 0.80. An increase in household wealth causes autonomous consumption to rise by $10 billion. By how much will equilibrium real GDP increase at the current price level, other things being equal? (See page 267.)

12-7. Assume that the multiplier in a country is equal to 4 and that autonomous real consumption spending is $1 trillion. If current real GDP is $15 trillion, what is the current value of real consumption spending? (See page 267.)

12-8. The multiplier in a country is equal to 5, and households pay no taxes. At the current equilibrium real GDP of $14 trillion, total real consumption spending by households is $12 trillion. What is real autonomous consumption in this country? (See page 267.)

12-9. At an initial point on the aggregate demand curve, the price level is 125, and real GDP is $15 trillion. When the price level falls to a value of 120, total autonomous expenditures increase by $250 billion. The marginal propensity to consume is 0.75. What is the level of real GDP at the new point on the aggregate demand curve? (See pages 270–271.)

12-10. At an initial point on the aggregate demand curve, the price level is 100, and real GDP is $15 trillion. After the price level rises to 110, however, there is an upward movement along the aggregate demand curve, and real GDP declines to $14 trillion. If total planned spending declined by $200 billion in response to the increase in the price level, what is the marginal propensity to consume in this economy? (See pages 270–271.)

12-11. In an economy in which the multiplier has a value of 3, the price level has decreased from 115 to 110. As a consequence, there has been a movement along the aggregate demand curve from $15 trillion in real GDP to $15.9 trillion in real GDP. (See pages 270–271.)

a. What is the marginal propensity to save?

b. What was the amount of the change in planned expenditures generated by the decline in the price level?

12-12. Consider the diagram below, which applies to a nation with no government spending, taxes, and net exports. Use the information in the diagram to answer the following questions, and explain your answers. (See pages 253–263.)

a. What is the marginal propensity to save?

b. What is the present level of planned investment spending for the present period?

c. What is the equilibrium level of real GDP for the present period?

d. What is the equilibrium level of saving for the present period?

e. If planned investment spending for the present period increases by $25 billion, what will be the resulting *change* in equilibrium real GDP? What will be the new equilibrium level of real GDP if other things, including the price level, remain unchanged?

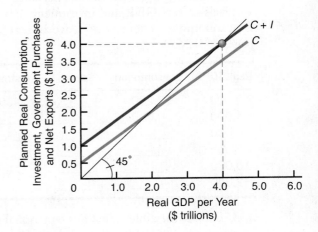

ECONOMICS ON THE NET

The Relationship between Consumption and Real GDP?
According to the basic consumption function we considered in this chapter, consumption rises at a fixed rate when both disposable income and real GDP increase. Your task here is to evaluate how reasonable this assumption is and to determine the relative extent to which variations in consumption appear to be related to variations in real GDP.

Title: Gross Domestic Product and Components

Navigation: Use the link at **www.econtoday.com/chap12** to visit the Federal Reserve Bank of St. Louis's Web page on *National Income and Product Accounts*. Then click on *Personal Income and Outlays*.

Application

1. Scan down the list, and click on *Real Personal Consumption Expenditures*. Then click on "Download Data." Write down consumption expenditures for the past eight quarters. Now back up to *National Income and Product*

Accounts, click on *Gross GDP/GNP* and then *Real Gross Domestic Product, 1 Decimal,* click on "Download Data," and write down GDP for the past eight quarters. Use these data to calculate implied values for the marginal propensity to consume, assuming that taxes do not vary with income. Is there any problem with this assumption?

2. Back up to *National Income and Product Accounts.* Select "Price Indexes & Deflators." Now click on *Gross Domestic Product: Implicit Price Deflator.* Scan

through the data since the mid-1960s. In what years did the largest variations in GDP take place? What component or components of GDP appear to have accounted for these large movements?

For Group Study and Analysis Assign groups to use the FRED database to try to determine the best measure of aggregate U.S. disposable income for the past eight quarters. Reconvene as a class, and discuss each group's approach to this issue.

ANSWERS TO QUICK QUIZZES

p. 252: (i) horizontal; (ii) Saving . . . Savings; (iii) Investment

p. 258: (i) disposable income . . . consumption; (ii) average . . . average; (iii) marginal . . . marginal; (iv) movement along . . . shift in

p. 260: (i) interest rate . . . downward; (ii) expectations . . . business taxes; (iii) shift in

p. 263: (i) autonomous . . . autonomous; (ii) autonomous; (iii) equilibrium; (iv) increases . . . decreases

p. 266: (i) planned expenditures; (ii) 45-degree; (iii) decreases . . . increases

p. 271: (i) multiplier; (ii) marginal . . . save; (iii) save . . . consume; (iv) change

The Keynesian Model and the Multiplier

We can see the multiplier effect more clearly if we look at Figure C-1 below, in which we see only a small section of the graphs that we used in Chapter 12. We start with equilibrium real GDP of $14.5 trillion per year. This equilibrium occurs with total planned real expenditures represented by $C + I + G + X$. The $C + I + G + X$ curve intersects the 45-degree reference line at $14.5 trillion per year. Now we increase real investment, I, by $100 billion. This increase in investment shifts the entire $C + I + G + X$ curve vertically to $C + I' + G + X$. The vertical shift represents that $100 billion increase in autonomous investment. With the higher level of planned expenditures per year, we are no longer in equilibrium at E. Inventories are falling. Production of goods and services will increase as firms try to replenish their inventories.

Eventually, real GDP will catch up with total planned expenditures. The new equilibrium level of real GDP is established at E' at the intersection of the new $C + I' + G + X$ curve and the 45-degree reference line, along which $C + I + G + X = Y$ (total planned expenditures equal real GDP). The new equilibrium level of real GDP is $15 trillion per year. Thus, the increase in equilibrium real GDP is equal to five times the permanent increase in planned investment spending.

FIGURE C-1

Graphing the Multiplier

We can translate Table 12-3 on page 267 into graphic form by looking at each successive round of additional spending induced by an autonomous increase in planned investment of $100 billion. The total planned expenditures curve shifts from $C + I + G + X$, with its associated equilibrium level of real GDP of $14.5 trillion, to a new curve labeled $C + I' + G + X$. The new equilibrium level of real GDP is $15 trillion. Equilibrium is again established.

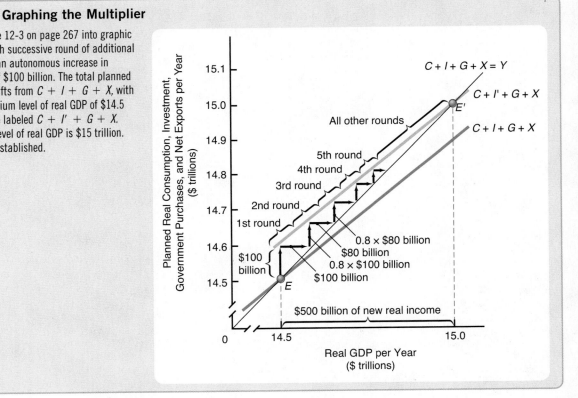

Fiscal Policy

13

LEARNING OBJECTIVES

After reading this chapter, you should be able to:

▶ Use traditional Keynesian analysis to evaluate the effects of discretionary fiscal policies

▶ Discuss ways in which indirect crowding out and direct expenditure offsets can reduce the effectiveness of fiscal policy actions

▶ Explain why the Ricardian equivalence theorem calls into question the usefulness of tax changes

▶ List and define fiscal policy time lags and explain why they complicate efforts to engage in fiscal "fine-tuning"

▶ Describe how certain aspects of fiscal policy function as automatic stabilizers for the economy

MyEconLab helps you master each objective and study more efficiently. See end of chapter for details.

In the midst of the sharp economic downturn of 2008–2009, Congress passed the American Recovery and Reinvestment Act (ARRA). The ARRA was meant to stimulate total planned expenditures via hundreds of billions of dollars of additional government spending. Hence, the media have tended to refer to the law as the "Stimulus Act." A large portion of the federal funds authorized by the ARRA went to state governments for spending at local levels. In fact, however, most estimates indicate that states used no more than 5 percent of the total ARRA funds they received to purchase final goods and services. What did the U.S. government hope to accomplish by adding hundreds of billions in additional spending to its budget? Why were so few of the funds distributed to state governments actually spent on goods and services? You will find out in this chapter.

the U.S. government's American Recovery and Reinvestment Act of 2009 entailed a greater overall expenditure of funds than the eight-year-long Iraqi conflict? Military and other U.S. government spending related to the war effort in Iraq totaled $709 billion, or about 4.7 percent of the value of a typical year's output of goods and services. The 2009 "Stimulus Act," which was intended to boost economic activity and reduce the unemployment rate, authorized $862 billion in spending, or about 5.7 percent of the value of annual U.S. production. In this chapter, you will learn how variations in government spending and taxation affect both real GDP and the price level.

Discretionary Fiscal Policy

Fiscal policy
The discretionary changing of government expenditures or taxes to achieve national economic goals, such as high employment with price stability.

The making of deliberate, discretionary changes in federal government expenditures or taxes (or both) to achieve certain national economic goals is the realm of **fiscal policy**. Some national goals are high employment (low unemployment), price stability, and economic growth. Fiscal policy can be thought of as a deliberate attempt to cause the economy to move to full employment and price stability more quickly than it otherwise might.

Fiscal policy has typically been associated with the economic theories of John Maynard Keynes and what is now called *traditional* Keynesian analysis. Recall from Chapter 11 that Keynes's explanation of the Great Depression was that there was insufficient aggregate demand. Because he believed that wages and prices were "sticky downward," he argued that the classical economists' picture of an economy moving automatically and quickly toward full employment was inaccurate. To Keynes and his followers, government had to step in to increase aggregate demand. Expansionary fiscal policy initiated by the federal government was the preferred way to ward off recessions and depressions.

Changes in Government Spending

In Chapter 11, we looked at the recessionary gap and the inflationary gap (see Figures 11-9 and 11-10 on pages 242 and 243). The recessionary gap was defined as the amount by which the current level of real GDP falls short of the economy's *potential* production if it were operating on its *LRAS* curve. The inflationary gap was defined as the amount by which the short-run equilibrium level of real GDP exceeds the long-run equilibrium level as given by *LRAS*. Let us examine fiscal policy first in the context of a recessionary gap.

WHEN THERE IS A RECESSIONARY GAP The government, along with firms, individuals, and foreign residents, is one of the spending entities in the economy. When the government spends more, all other things held constant, the dollar value of total spending initially must rise. Look at panel (a) of Figure 13-1 on the facing page. We begin by assuming that some negative shock in the near past has left the economy at point E_1, which is a short-run equilibrium in which AD_1 intersects $SRAS$ at $14.5 trillion of real GDP per year. There is a recessionary gap of $500 billion of real GDP per year—the difference between *LRAS* (the economy's long-run potential) and the short-run equilibrium level of real GDP per year.

When the government decides to spend more (expansionary fiscal policy), the aggregate demand curve shifts to the right to AD_2. Here we assume that the government knows exactly how much more to spend so that AD_2 intersects $SRAS$ at $15 trillion, or at *LRAS*. Because of the upward-sloping *SRAS*, the price level rises from 120 to 130 as real GDP goes to $15 trillion per year.

Did U.S. government purchases of old cars induce enough private spending on new vehicles to contribute to higher real GDP?

FIGURE 13-1

Expansionary and Contractionary Fiscal Policy: Changes in Government Spending

If there is a recessionary gap and short-run equilibrium is at E_1, in panel (a), fiscal policy can presumably increase aggregate demand to AD_2. The new equilibrium is at E_2 at higher real GDP per year and a higher price level. In panel (b), the economy is at short-run equilibrium at E_1, which is at a higher real GDP than the *LRAS*. To reduce this inflationary gap, fiscal policy can be used to decrease aggregate demand from AD_1 to AD_2. Eventually, equilibrium will fall to E_2, which is on the *LRAS*.

POLICY EXAMPLE

Net Real GDP Effect of "Cash-for-Clunkers" Spending: Zero

In 2009, the U.S. government offered $3,500 to $4,500 to people who surrendered used cars and bought new vehicles. Policymakers who promoted this "Cash-for-Clunkers" program at a $2.8 billion expense for taxpayers argued that it had two desirable effects. One was the removal of high-pollution vehicles from roads. The other was that consumers bought 450,000 new vehicles, which generated $12.6 billion in private expenditures that otherwise would not have taken place.

Adam Copeland and James Kahn, economists at the Federal Reserve Bank of Kansas City, have determined that many people delayed buying new vehicles until the Cash-for-Clunkers subsidies were available. Even more people bought vehicles earlier than originally planned. This meant that consumers responded to the program by shifting the *timing* of purchases of new vehicles they *already* intended to buy. Copeland and Kahn concluded that the real GDP impact of the program was zero. Hence, it was not a particularly effective fiscal policy program.

FOR CRITICAL THINKING

Why might any temporary government subsidy program mainly end up affecting the timing of spending instead of actually boosting overall planned expenditures?

WHEN THERE IS AN INFLATIONARY GAP The entire process shown above in panel (a) of Figure 13-1 can be reversed, as shown in panel (b). There, we assume that a recent shock has left the economy at point E_1, at which an inflationary gap exists at the intersection of *SRAS* and AD_1. Real GDP cannot be sustained at $15.5 trillion indefinitely, because this exceeds long-run aggregate supply, which in real terms is $15 trillion. If the government recognizes this and reduces its spending (pursues a contractionary fiscal policy), this action reduces aggregate demand from AD_1 to AD_2. Equilibrium will fall to E_2 on the *LRAS*, where real GDP per year is $15 trillion. The price level will fall from 140 to 130.

Changes in Taxes

The spending decisions of firms, individuals, and other countries' residents depend on the taxes levied on them. Individuals in their role as consumers look to their disposable (after-tax) income when determining their desired rates of consumption. Firms look at their after-tax

FIGURE 13-2

Expansionary and Contractionary Fiscal Policy: Changes in Taxes

In panel (a), the economy is initially at E_1, where real GDP is less than long-run equilibrium real GDP. Expansionary fiscal policy via a tax reduction can move aggregate demand to AD_2 so that the new equilibrium is at E_2 at a higher price level. Real GDP is now consistent with *LRAS*, which eliminates the recessionary gap. In panel (b), with an inflationary gap (in this case of $500 billion), taxes are increased. AD_1 moves to AD_2. The economy moves from E_1 to E_2, and real GDP is now at $15 trillion per year, the long-run equilibrium level.

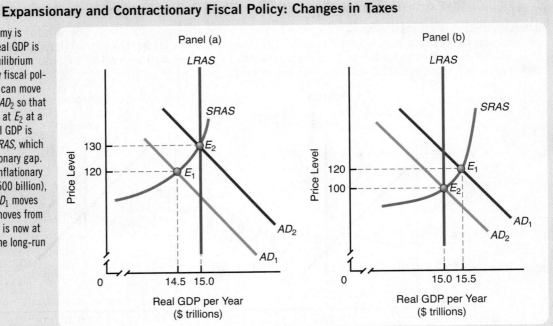

profits when deciding on the levels of investment per year to undertake. Foreign residents look at the tax-inclusive cost of goods when deciding whether to buy in the United States or elsewhere. Therefore, holding all other things constant, an increase in taxes causes a reduction in aggregate demand because it reduces consumption, investment, or net exports.

WHEN THE CURRENT SHORT-RUN EQUILIBRIUM IS TO THE LEFT OF *LRAS* Look at panel (a) in Figure 13-2. AD_1 intersects *SRAS* at E_1, with real GDP at $14.5 trillion, less than the *LRAS* of $15 trillion. In this situation, a decrease in taxes shifts the aggregate demand curve outward to the right. At AD_2, equilibrium is established at E_2, with the price level at 130 and equilibrium real GDP at $15 trillion per year.

WHEN THE CURRENT SHORT-RUN EQUILIBRIUM IS TO THE RIGHT OF *LRAS* Assume that aggregate demand is AD_1 in panel (b) of Figure 13-2 above. It intersects *SRAS* at E_1, which yields real GDP greater than *LRAS*. In this situation, an increase in taxes shifts the aggregate demand curve inward to the left. For argument's sake, assume that it intersects *SRAS* at E_2, or exactly where *LRAS* intersects AD_2. In this situation, the level of real GDP falls from $15.5 trillion per year to $15 trillion per year. The price level falls from 120 to 100.

QUICK QUIZ See page 296 for the answers. Review concepts from this section in MyEconLab.

Fiscal policy is defined as making discretionary changes in government _____ or _____ to achieve such national goals as high employment or reduced inflation.

To address a situation in which there is a _____ gap and the economy is operating at less than long-run aggregate supply (*LRAS*), the government can _____ its spending. This policy action shifts the aggregate demand curve to the right, causing the equilibrium level of real GDP per year to increase.

To address a situation in which there is an _____ gap, the government can _____ its spending and

cause the aggregate demand curve to shift to the left, which reduces the equilibrium level of real GDP per year.

Changes in taxes can have similar effects on the equilibrium rate of real GDP and the price level. If there is an inflationary gap, an _____ in taxes can lead to a decrease in the equilibrium level of real GDP per year. In contrast, if there is a recessionary gap, a _____ in taxes can increase equilibrium real GDP per year.

Possible Offsets to Fiscal Policy

Fiscal policy does not operate in a vacuum. Important questions must be answered: If government spending rises by, say, $300 billion, how is the spending financed, and by whom? If taxes are increased, what does the government do with the taxes? What will happen if individuals anticipate higher *future* taxes because the government is spending more today without raising current taxes? These questions involve *offsets* to the effects of current fiscal policy. We consider them in detail here.

Indirect Crowding Out

Let's take the first example of fiscal policy in this chapter—an increase in government expenditures. If government expenditures rise and taxes are held constant, something has to give. Our government does not simply take goods and services when it wants them. It has to pay for them. When it pays for them and does not simultaneously collect the same amount in taxes, it must borrow. That means that an increase in government spending without raising taxes creates additional government borrowing from the private sector (or from other countries' residents).

INDUCED INTEREST RATE CHANGES If the government attempts to borrow in excess of $1 trillion more per year from the private sector, as it has since 2009, it will have to offer a higher interest rate to lure the additional funds from savers. This is the interest rate effect of expansionary fiscal policy financed by borrowing from the public. Consequently, when the federal government finances increased spending by additional borrowing, it will push interest rates up. When interest rates go up, firms' borrowing costs rise, which induces them to cut back on planned investment spending. Borrowing costs also increase for households, who reduce planned expenditures on cars and homes.

Thus, a rise in government spending, holding taxes constant (that is, deficit spending), tends to crowd out private spending, dampening the positive effect of increased government spending on aggregate demand. This is called the **crowding-out effect.** In the extreme case, the crowding out may be complete, with the increased government spending having no net effect on aggregate demand. The final result is simply more government spending and less private investment and consumption. Figure 13-3 below shows how the crowding-out effect occurs.

THE FIRM'S INVESTMENT DECISION To understand the crowding-out effect better, consider a firm that is contemplating borrowing $100,000 to expand its business. Suppose that the interest rate is 5 percent. The interest payments on the debt will be 5 percent times $100,000, or $5,000 per year ($417 per month). A rise in the interest rate to 8 percent will push the payments to 8 percent of $100,000, or $8,000 per year ($667 per month). The extra $250 per month in interest expenses will discourage some firms from making the investment. Consumers face similar decisions when they purchase

Crowding-out effect
The tendency of expansionary fiscal policy to cause a decrease in planned investment or planned consumption in the private sector. This decrease normally results from the rise in interest rates.

FIGURE 13-3

The Crowding-Out Effect, Step by Step

The Crowding-Out Effect

Expansionary fiscal policy that causes deficit financing initially shifts AD_1 to AD_2. Equilibrium initially moves toward E_2. But expansionary fiscal policy pushes up interest rates, thereby reducing interest-sensitive spending. This effect causes the aggregate demand curve to shift inward to AD_3, and the new short-run equilibrium is at E_3.

houses and cars. An increase in the interest rate causes their monthly payments to go up, thereby discouraging some of them from purchasing cars and houses.

GRAPHICAL ANALYSIS You see in Figure 13-4 above that the economy is in a situation in which, at point E_1, equilibrium real GDP is below the long-run level consistent with the position of the *LRAS* curve. But suppose that government expansionary fiscal policy in the form of increased government spending (without increasing current taxes) attempts to shift aggregate demand from AD_1 to AD_2. In the absence of the crowding-out effect, real GDP would increase to $15 trillion per year, and the price level would rise to 140 (point E_2). With the (partial) crowding-out effect, however, as investment and consumption decline, partly offsetting the rise in government spending, the aggregate demand curve shifts inward to the left to AD_3.

The new short-run equilibrium is now at E_3, with real GDP of $14.75 trillion per year at a price level of 135. In other words, crowding out dilutes the effect of expansionary fiscal policy, and a recessionary gap remains.

Planning for the Future: The Ricardian Equivalence Theorem

Economists have often implicitly assumed that people look at changes in taxes or changes in government spending only in the present. What if people actually think about the size of *future* tax payments? Does this have an effect on how they react to an increase in government spending with no current tax increases? Some economists believe that the answer is yes. What if people's horizons extend beyond this year? Don't we then have to take into account the effects of today's government policies on the future?

Consider an example. The government wants to reduce taxes by $200 billion today, as it did in 2008 and 2009 via tax "rebate" programs. Assume that government spending remains constant. Assume further that the government initially has a balanced budget. Thus, the only way for the government to pay for this $200 billion tax cut is to borrow $200 billion today. The public will owe $200 billion plus interest later. Realizing that a $200 billion tax cut today is mathematically equivalent to $200 billion plus interest later, people may wish to save the proceeds from the tax cut to meet future tax liabilities—payment of interest and repayment of debt.

Consequently, a tax cut may not affect total planned expenditures. A reduction in taxes without a reduction in government spending may therefore have no impact on aggregate demand. Similarly, an increase in taxes without an increase in government spending may not have a large (negative) impact on aggregate demand.

Suppose that a decrease in taxes shifts the aggregate demand curve from AD_1 to AD_2 in Figure 13-4 on the facing page. If consumers partly compensate for a higher future tax liability by saving more, the aggregate demand curve shifts leftward, to a position such as AD_3. In the extreme case in which individuals fully take into account their increased tax liabilities, the aggregate demand curve shifts all the way back to AD_1, so that there is no effect on the economy. This is known as the **Ricardian equivalence theorem,** after the nineteenth-century economist David Ricardo, who first developed the argument publicly.

According to the Ricardian equivalence theorem, it does not matter how government expenditures are financed—by taxes or by borrowing. Is the theorem correct? Research indicates that Ricardian equivalence effects likely exist but has not provided much compelling evidence about their magnitudes.

Ricardian equivalence theorem
The proposition that an increase in the government budget deficit has no effect on aggregate demand.

Restrained Consumption Effects of Temporary Tax Changes

Recall from Chapter 12 (page 253) that a person's consumption and saving decisions realistically depend on *both* current income *and* anticipated future income. On the basis of this fact, the theory of consumption known as the *permanent income hypothesis* proposes that an individual's current flow of consumption depends on the individual's permanent, or anticipated lifetime, income.

Sometimes, the government seeks to provide a short-term "stimulus" to economic activity through temporary tax cuts that last no longer than a year or two or by rebating lump-sum amounts back to taxpayers. According to the permanent income hypothesis, such short-term tax policies at best have minimal effects on total consumption spending. The reason is that *temporary* tax cuts or one-time tax rebates fail to raise the recipients' *permanent* incomes. Even after receiving such a temporary tax cut or rebate, therefore, people usually do not respond with significant changes in their consumption. Instead of spending the tax cut or rebate, they typically save most of the funds or use the funds to make payments on outstanding debts.

Thus, temporary tax cuts or rebates tend to have restrained effects on aggregate consumption, as the U.S. government has discovered when it has provided temporary tax rebates. For instance, one-time federal tax rebates totaling at least $200 billion in 2008 and again in 2009 boosted real disposable income temporarily in each year but had no perceptible effects on flows of real consumption spending.

Direct Expenditure Offsets

Government has a distinct comparative advantage over the private sector in certain activities such as diplomacy and national defense. Otherwise stated, certain resource-using activities in which the government engages do not compete with the private sector. In contrast, some of what government does, such as public education, competes directly with the private sector. When government competes with the private sector, **direct expenditure offsets** to fiscal policy may occur. For example, if the government starts providing milk at no charge to students who are already purchasing milk, there is a direct expenditure offset. Direct household spending on milk decreases, but government spending on milk increases.

Normally, the impact of an increase in government spending on aggregate demand is analyzed by implicitly assuming that government spending is *not* a substitute for private spending. This is clearly the case for a cruise missile. Whenever government spending is a substitute for private spending, however, a rise in government spending causes a direct reduction in private spending to offset it.

Direct expenditure offsets
Actions on the part of the private sector in spending income that offset government fiscal policy actions. Any increase in government spending in an area that competes with the private sector will have some direct expenditure offset.

THE EXTREME CASE In the extreme case, the direct expenditure offset is dollar for dollar, so we merely end up with a relabeling of spending from private to public. Assume that you have decided to spend $100 on groceries. Upon your arrival at the checkout counter, you find a U.S. Department of Agriculture official. She announces that she will pay for your groceries—but only the ones in the cart. Here increased government spending is $100. You leave the store in bliss. But just as you are deciding how to spend the $100, an Internal Revenue Service agent appears. He announces that as a result of the current budgetary crisis, your taxes are going to rise by $100. You have to pay on the spot. Increases in taxes have now been $100. We have a balanced-budget increase in government spending. In this scenario, *total* spending does not change. We simply end up with higher government spending, which directly offsets exactly an equal reduction in consumption. Aggregate demand and GDP are unchanged. Otherwise stated, if there is a full direct expenditure offset, the government spending multiplier is zero.

THE LESS EXTREME CASE Much government spending has a private-sector substitute. When government expenditures increase, private spending tends to decline somewhat (but generally not dollar for dollar), thereby mitigating the upward impact on total aggregate demand. To the extent that there are some direct expenditure offsets to expansionary fiscal policy, predicted changes in aggregate demand will be lessened. Consequently, real GDP and the price level will be less affected.

WHAT IF... the federal government seeks to boost real GDP by funding health care expenditures that people had already planned to undertake on their own?

In recent years, the U.S. government has shifted a larger share of discretionary expenditures toward construction of more public hospitals and clinics. A number of politicians have suggested that such federal health care spending adds to total planned expenditures in today's dampened economy. In many instances, however, private health care companies had originally planned to expand their facilities in response to an increasing demand for health care by an aging U.S. population. When the federal government funded construction of competing hospitals and clinics, the private firms' intended capital investments were no longer economically viable. Thus, public health care facilities were built, and private facilities were not constructed after all. Direct fiscal offsets occurred, and, on net, total planned expenditures did not change.

The Supply-Side Effects of Changes in Taxes

We have talked about changing taxes and changing government spending, the traditional tools of fiscal policy. Let's now consider the possibility of changing *marginal* tax rates.

ALTERING MARGINAL TAX RATES Recall from Chapter 6 that the marginal tax rate is the rate applied to the last, or highest, bracket of taxable income. In our federal tax system, higher marginal tax rates are applied as income rises. In that sense, the United States has a progressive federal individual income tax system. Expansionary fiscal policy could involve reducing marginal tax rates. Advocates of such changes argue that lower tax rates will lead to an increase in productivity. They contend that individuals will work harder and longer, save more, and invest more and that increased productivity will lead to more economic growth, which will lead to higher real GDP. The government, by applying lower marginal tax rates, will not necessarily lose tax revenues, for the lower marginal tax rates will be applied to a growing tax base because of economic growth—after all, tax revenues are the product of a tax rate times a tax base.

The relationship between tax rates and tax revenues, which you may recall from the discussion of sales taxes in Chapter 6, is sometimes called the *Laffer curve*, named after economist Arthur Laffer, who explained the relationship to some journalists and politicians in 1974. It is reproduced in Figure 13-5 on the facing page. On the vertical axis are tax revenues, and on the horizontal axis is the marginal tax rate. As you can see, total tax revenues initially rise but then eventually fall as the tax rate continues to increase after reaching some unspecified tax-revenue-maximizing rate at the top of the curve.

SUPPLY-SIDE ECONOMICS People who support the notion that reducing tax rates does not necessarily lead to reduced tax revenues are called supply-side economists. **Supply-side economics** involves changing the tax structure to create incentives to increase productivity. Due to a shift in the aggregate supply curve to the right, there can be greater real GDP without upward pressure on the price level.

Consider the supply-side effects of changes in marginal tax rates on labor. An increase in tax rates reduces the opportunity cost of leisure, thereby inducing individuals to reduce their work effort and to consume more leisure. But an increase in tax rates

Supply-side economics
The suggestion that creating incentives for individuals and firms to increase productivity will cause the aggregate supply curve to shift outward.

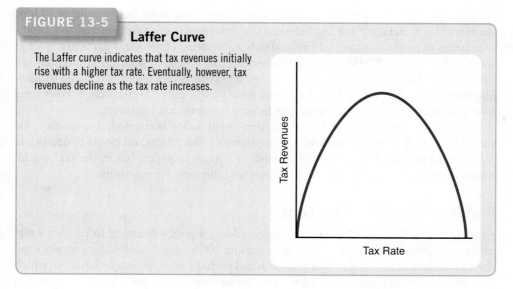

FIGURE 13-5

Laffer Curve

The Laffer curve indicates that tax revenues initially rise with a higher tax rate. Eventually, however, tax revenues decline as the tax rate increases.

will also reduce spendable income, thereby shifting the demand curve for leisure inward to the left, which tends to increase work effort. The outcome of these two effects on the choice of leisure (and thus work) depends on which of them is stronger. Supply-side economists argue that the first effect often dominates: Increases in marginal tax rates cause people to work less, and decreases in marginal tax rates induce workers to work more.

QUICK QUIZ See page 296 for the answers. Review concepts from this section in MyEconLab.

Indirect crowding out occurs because of an interest rate effect in which the government's efforts to finance its deficit spending cause interest rates to _____, thereby crowding out private investment and spending, particularly on cars and houses. This is called the **crowding-out effect.**

_____ _____ _____ occur when government spending competes with the private sector and is increased. A direct crowding-out effect may occur.

The _____ _____ theorem holds that an increase in the government budget deficit has no effect on aggregate demand because individuals anticipate that their future taxes will increase and therefore save more today to pay for them.

Changes in marginal tax rates may cause _____-_____ effects if a reduction in marginal tax rates induces enough additional work, saving, and investing. Government tax receipts can actually increase. This is called _____-_____ economics.

Discretionary Fiscal Policy in Practice: Coping with Time Lags

We can discuss fiscal policy in a relatively precise way. We draw graphs with aggregate demand and supply curves to show what we are doing. We could in principle estimate the offsets that we just discussed. Even if we were able to measure all of these offsets exactly, however, would-be fiscal policymakers still face a problem: The conduct of fiscal policy involves a variety of time lags.

Policy Time Lags

Policymakers must take time lags into account. Not only is it difficult to measure economic variables, but it also takes time to collect and assimilate such data. Consequently, policymakers must contend with the **recognition time lag,** the months that may elapse before national economic problems can be identified.

Recognition time lag
The time required to gather information about the current state of the economy.

Action time lag
The time between recognizing an economic problem and implementing policy to solve it. The action time lag is quite long for fiscal policy, which requires congressional approval.

Effect time lag
The time that elapses between the implementation of a policy and the results of that policy.

After an economic problem is recognized, a solution must be formulated. Thus, there will be an **action time lag** between the recognition of a problem and the implementation of policy to solve it. For fiscal policy, the action time lag is particularly long. Such policy must be approved by Congress and is subject to political wrangling and infighting. The action time lag can easily last a year or two. Then it takes time to actually implement the policy. After Congress enacts fiscal policy legislation, it takes time to decide such matters as who gets new federal construction contracts.

Finally, there is the **effect time lag:** After fiscal policy is enacted, it takes time for the policy to affect the economy. To demonstrate the effects, economists need only shift curves on a chalkboard, a whiteboard, or a piece of paper, but in the real world, such effects take quite a while to work their way through the economy.

Problems Posed by Time Lags

Because the various fiscal policy time lags are long, a policy designed to combat a significant recession such as the recession of the late 2000s might not produce results until the economy is already out of that recession and perhaps experiencing inflation, in which case the fiscal policy action would worsen the situation. Or a fiscal policy designed to eliminate inflation might not produce effects until the economy is in a recession. In that case, too, fiscal policy would make the economic problem worse rather than better.

Furthermore, because fiscal policy time lags tend to be *variable* (each lasting anywhere from one to three years), policymakers have a difficult time fine-tuning the economy. Clearly, fiscal policy is more guesswork than science.

YOU ARE THERE

To consider a specific example of how time lags can slow the economic effects of fiscal policy, take a look at **Why a Federal Stimulus Project Took Time to Provide Stimulus** on page 291.

Automatic Stabilizers

Not all changes in taxes (or in tax rates) or in government spending (including government transfers) constitute discretionary fiscal policy. There are several types of automatic (or nondiscretionary) fiscal policies. Such policies do not require new legislation on the part of Congress. Specific automatic fiscal policies—called **automatic,** or **built-in, stabilizers**—include the tax system itself, unemployment compensation, and income transfer payments.

Automatic, or built-in, stabilizers
Special provisions of certain federal programs that cause changes in desired aggregate expenditures without the action of Congress and the president. Examples are the federal progressive tax system and unemployment compensation.

The Tax System as an Automatic Stabilizer

You know that if you work less, you are paid less, and therefore you pay fewer taxes. The amount of taxes that our government collects falls automatically during a recession. Basically, as observed in the U.S. economy during the severe recession of the late 2000s, incomes and profits fall when business activity slows down, and the government's tax revenues drop, too. Some economists consider this an automatic tax cut, which therefore may stimulate aggregate demand. It thereby may reduce the extent of any negative economic fluctuation.

The progressive nature of the federal personal and corporate income tax systems magnifies any automatic stabilization effect that might exist. If your hours of work are reduced because of a recession, you still pay some federal personal income taxes. But because of our progressive system, you may drop into a lower tax bracket, thereby paying a lower marginal tax rate. As a result, your disposable income falls by a smaller percentage than your before-tax income falls.

Unemployment Compensation and Income Transfer Payments

Like our tax system, unemployment compensation payments stabilize aggregate demand. Throughout the course of business fluctuations, unemployment compensation reduces *changes* in people's disposable income. When business activity drops, most laid-off workers automatically become eligible for unemployment compensation from their state governments. Their disposable income therefore remains positive, although at a lower level than when they were employed. During boom periods, there is less

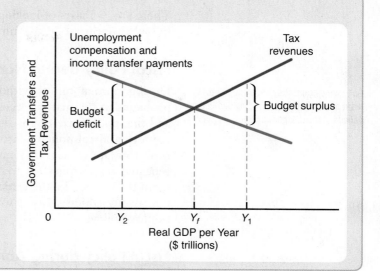

FIGURE 13-6

Automatic Stabilizers

Here we assume that as real GDP rises, tax revenues rise and government transfers fall, other things remaining constant. Thus, as the economy expands from Y_f to Y_1, a budget surplus automatically arises. As the economy contracts from Y_f to Y_2, a budget deficit automatically arises. Such automatic changes tend to drive the economy back toward its full-employment real GDP.

unemployment, and consequently fewer unemployment payments are made to the labor force. Less purchasing power is being added to the economy because fewer unemployment checks are paid out. In contrast, during recessions the opposite is true.

Income transfer payments act similarly as an automatic stabilizer. When a recession occurs, more people become eligible for income transfer payments, such as Supplemental Security Income and Temporary Assistance to Needy Families. Therefore, those people do not experience as dramatic a drop in disposable income as they otherwise would have.

Stabilizing Impact

The key stabilizing impact of our tax system, unemployment compensation, and income transfer payments is their ability to mitigate changes in disposable income, consumption, and the equilibrium level of real GDP. If disposable income is prevented from falling as much as it otherwise would during a recession, the downturn will be moderated. In contrast, if disposable income is prevented from rising as rapidly as it otherwise would during a boom, the boom is less likely to get out of hand. The progressive income tax and unemployment compensation thus provide automatic stabilization to the economy. We present the argument graphically in Figure 13-6 above.

Does the current state of the business cycle influence the effects of fiscal policy actions on real GDP?

POLICY EXAMPLE

Do Fiscal Policy Effects Vary as Real GDP Rises or Falls?

Alan Auerbach and Yuriy Gorodnichenko of the University of California at Berkeley have recently estimated the impacts of discretionary fiscal policy actions on U.S. real GDP. They found that increases in government *non*-defense spending have similar effects on real GDP during either business contractions or expansions. The effects are relatively small, with each $1 increase in *non*-defense expenditures estimated to boost real GDP by not much more than $1.10.

In contrast, Auerbach and Gorodnichenko's estimates indicate that changes in government *defense* spending consistently have larger ultimate real GDP effects during recessions than during business expansions. During a recession, each $1 increase in defense spending boosts

real GDP by more than $3.50, whereas during an expansion, the resulting increase in real GDP is less than $1.20. Thus, if the effect lag associated with a rise in defense spending is the same during either a recession or an expansion, the "bang for the buck" from an increase in defense spending per unit of time is much greater during a recession.

FOR CRITICAL THINKING

Why might boosting defense spending have a larger impact on real GDP than increasing non-defense spending? (Hint: Which form of spending is least likely to be subject to direct fiscal offsets?)

What Do We Really Know about Fiscal Policy?

There are two ways of looking at fiscal policy. One prevails during normal times and the other during abnormal times.

Go to www.econtoday.com/chap13 to learn about expanding spending and budget deficits of the U.S. government.

Fiscal Policy during Normal Times

During normal times (without "excessive" unemployment, inflation, or unusual problems in the national economy), we know that due to the recognition time lag and the modest size of any fiscal policy action that Congress will actually take, discretionary fiscal policy is probably not very effective. Congress ends up doing too little too late to help in a minor recession. Moreover, fiscal policy that generates repeated tax changes (as has happened) creates uncertainty, which may do more harm than good. To the extent that fiscal policy has any effect during normal times, it probably achieves this by way of automatic stabilizers rather than by way of discretionary policy.

Fiscal Policy during Abnormal Times

During abnormal times, fiscal policy may be effective. Consider some classic examples: the Great Depression and war periods.

THE GREAT DEPRESSION When there is a catastrophic drop in real GDP, as there was during the Great Depression, fiscal policy may be able to stimulate aggregate demand. Because so many people have few assets left and thus are income-constrained during such periods, government spending is a way to get income into their hands—income that they are likely to spend immediately.

WARTIME Wars are in fact reserved for governments. War expenditures are not good substitutes for private expenditures—they have little or no direct expenditure offsets. Consequently, war spending as part of expansionary fiscal policy usually has noteworthy effects, such as occurred while we were waging World War II, when real GDP increased dramatically (though much of the output of new goods and services was expended for military uses).

The "Soothing" Effect of Keynesian Fiscal Policy

One view of traditional Keynesian fiscal policy does not call for it to be used on a regular basis but nevertheless sees it as potentially useful. As you have learned in this chapter, many problems are associated with attempting to use fiscal policy. But if we should encounter a severe downturn, fiscal policy is available. Knowing this may reassure consumers and investors. Thus, the availability of fiscal policy may induce more buoyant and stable expectations of the future, thereby smoothing investment spending.

QUICK QUIZ See page 296 for the answers. Review concepts from this section in MyEconLab.

Time lags of various sorts reduce the effectiveness of fiscal policy. These include the _____ time lag, the _____ time lag, and the _____ time lag.

Two _____, or built-in, stabilizers are the progressive income tax and unemployment compensation.

Built-in stabilizers automatically tend to _____ changes in disposable income resulting from changes in overall business activity.

Although discretionary fiscal policy may not necessarily be a useful policy tool in normal times because of time lags, it may work well during _____ times, such as depressions and wartimes. In addition, the existence of fiscal policy may have a soothing effect on consumers and investors.

YOU ARE THERE
Why a Federal Stimulus Project Took Time to Provide Stimulus

Shenetta Coleman directs the Detroit agency charged with spending the city's share of $5 billion that the American Recovery and Reinvestment Act (ARRA) authorized to fund insulation of private homes. Hoping to help stimulate the struggling local economy, Coleman immediately placed a want ad for contractors to install insulation in drafty Detroit homes. Soon, 46 firms responded. When Coleman wanted to start home weatherizing projects, however, she learned that she had not met the federal government's requirements for placing her ad. The ad failed to specify wages that firms would have to pay their employees, rules governing other labor standards, legally permissible forms for contract bids, and special rules for preserving historic homes.

Thus, Coleman had to start the process all over again. Two years after her initial efforts to speed government spending on weatherizing Detroit homes, only about half of the houses she had targeted had new insulation. Thus, her efforts "stimulated" the Detroit economy at a much slower pace than she had anticipated when the ARRA funds first became available.

Critical Thinking Questions

1. What policy time lag did Detroit experience in implementing the ARRA?
2. Did another policy time lag likely follow the above lag? Explain.

ISSUES & APPLICATIONS

How Federal "Stimulus" Was Swallowed Up by States

CONCEPTS APPLIED

▶ Fiscal Policy

▶ Direct Expenditure Offsets

▶ Effect Time Lag

Although the federal government directly spent some funds authorized by the American Recovery and Reinvestment Act (ARRA) of 2009, it turned many of those funds over to state governments to spend locally. The bulk of these funds contributed very little to raising the flow of total expenditures, however.

Paying Off State Debts Instead of Boosting Expenditures

Figure 13-7 on the following page displays two sets of data. One is the cumulative quantity of grants of discretionary funds transmitted from the federal government to state governments since late 2008. The other is the net amount of borrowing by state governments.

As grants of federal funds to state governments accumulated after 2008, the net borrowing of state governments declined. Many state governments were heavily in debt at the end of 2008, with borrowings in excess of $160 billion. For these states, the receipt of discretionary federal grants beginning in 2009 was a godsend, because it allowed them to start paying off a number of existing debts.

Debt Repayments Are Not Immediate Flows of Spending

The funds intended by the federal government to enter the nation's flow of income and expenditures did not reach that flow. States sent them to creditors.

Rather than direct the federal funds to *additional* spending, therefore, the state governments used the bulk of ARRA federal grants to pay off part of debts generated by spending projects completed in prior years. Most estimates indicate that of the federal "stimulus" funds given to state governments, less than 5 percent were directed toward *new* spending within the nation's flow of income and expenditures. Thus, a 95 percent direct fiscal offset resulted. Instead of providing an immediate boost in state infrastructure spending on roads, bridges, and the like, nearly all of the federal funds transmitted to state governments for spending instead were saved.

FIGURE 13-7

Federal Funds Transmittals to State Governments and Net Borrowings of State Governments since 2008

As discretionary funds transfers from the federal government to state governments increased from 2008 onward, the net amount of state government borrowing declined.

Source: U.S. Department of Commerce.

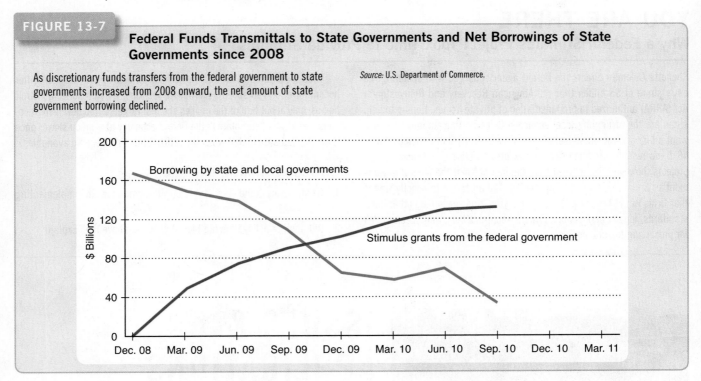

For Critical Thinking

1. Why might federal spending on roads, waterways, or national security be less subject to direct expenditure offsets than spending on health care or education?
2. What might account for the fact that estimates of effect time lags for fiscal policy often differ considerably across different types of government expenditures?

Web Resources

1. Take a look at the U.S. government's official Web site for tracking the use of ARRA funds at **www.econtoday.com/chap13**.

2. For further discussion of why directing so many federal ARRA funds to the states failed to produce very much fiscal stimulus to the U.S. economy, go to **www.econtoday.com/chap13**.

MyEconLab

For more questions on this chapter's Issues & Applications, go to **MyEconLab**. In the Study Plan for this chapter, select Section N: News.

MyEconLab

Here is what you should know after reading this chapter. MyEconLab will help you identify what you know, and where to go when you need to practice.

─ WHAT YOU SHOULD KNOW ─

The Effects of Discretionary Fiscal Policies Using Traditional Keynesian Analysis In short-run Keynesian analysis, an increase in government spending or tax decrease shifts the aggregate demand curve outward and thereby closes a recessionary gap in which current real GDP is less than the long-run level of real GDP. Likewise, a reduction in government spending or a tax increase shifts the aggregate demand curve inward and closes an inflationary gap in which current real GDP exceeds the long-run level of real GDP.

fiscal policy, 280

Key Figures
Figure 13-1, 281
Figure 13-2, 282

─ WHERE TO GO TO PRACTICE ─

- **MyEconLab** Study Plan 13.1
- Animated Figures 13-1, 13-2

MyEconLab *continued*

How Indirect Crowding Out and Direct Expenditure Offsets Can Reduce the Effectiveness of Fiscal Policy Actions Indirect crowding out occurs when the government must borrow from the private sector because government spending exceeds tax revenues. To obtain the necessary funds, the government must offer a higher interest rate, thereby driving up market interest rates. This reduces, or crowds out, interest-sensitive private spending. Increased government spending may also substitute directly for private expenditures and thereby offset the increase in total planned expenditures that the government had intended to bring about.	crowding-out effect, 283 direct expenditure offsets, 285 supply-side economics, 286 **Key Figures** Figure 13-3, 283 Figure 13-4, 284 Figure 13-5, 287	• **MyEconLab** Study Plan 13.2 • Animated Figures 13-3, 13-4, 13-5
The Ricardian Equivalence Theorem This proposition states that when the government cuts taxes and borrows to finance the tax reduction, people realize that in the future the government will have to raise taxes to repay the loan. This induces them to save the proceeds of the tax cut to meet their future tax liabilities. Thus, a tax cut fails to induce an increase in aggregate consumption spending and consequently has no effect on total planned expenditures and aggregate demand.	Ricardian equivalence theorem, 285 **Key Figure** Figure 13-4, 284	• **MyEconLab** Study Plan 13.2 • Animated Figure 13-4
Fiscal Policy Time Lags and the Effectiveness of Fiscal "Fine-Tuning" Efforts to use fiscal policy to bring about changes in aggregate demand are complicated by policy time lags. One of these is the recognition time lag, which is the time required to collect information about the economy's current situation. Another is the action time lag, the period between recognition of a problem and implementation of a policy intended to address it. Finally, there is the effect time lag, which is the interval between the implementation of a policy and its having an effect on the economy.	recognition time lag, 287 action time lag, 288 effect time lag, 288	• **MyEconLab** Study Plan 13.3
Automatic Stabilizers Income taxes diminish automatically when economic activity drops, and unemployment compensation and income transfer payments increase. Thus, when there is a decline in real GDP, the automatic reduction in income tax collections and increases in unemployment compensation and income transfer payments tend to minimize the reduction in total planned expenditures that would otherwise have resulted.	automatic, or built-in, stabilizers, 288 **Key Figure** Figure 13-6, 289	• **MyEconLab** Study Plans 13.4, 13.5 • Animated Figure 13-6

Log in to MyEconLab, take a chapter test, and get a personalized Study Plan that tells you which concepts you understand and which ones you need to review. From there, MyEconLab will give you further practice, tutorials, animations, videos, and guided solutions. For more information, visit www.myeconlab.com

PROBLEMS

All problems are assignable in MyEconLab. *Answers to odd-numbered problems appear at the back of the book.*

13-1. Suppose that Congress and the president decide that the nation's economic performance is weakening and that the government should "do something" about the situation. They make no tax changes but do enact new laws increasing government spending on a variety of programs. (See page 281.)

  a. Prior to the congressional and presidential action, careful studies by government economists indicated that the direct multiplier effect of a rise in government expenditures on equilibrium real GDP per year is equal to 3. In the 12 months since the increase in government spending, however, it has become clear that the actual ultimate effect on real GDP will be less than half of that amount. What factors might account for this?

  b. Another year and a half elapses following passage of the government spending boost. The government has undertaken no additional policy actions, nor have there been any other events of significance. Nevertheless, by the end of the second year, real GDP has returned to its original level, and the price level has increased sharply. Provide a possible explanation for this outcome.

13-2. Suppose that Congress enacts a significant tax cut with the expectation that this action will stimulate aggregate demand and push up real GDP in the short run. In fact, however, neither real GDP nor the price level changes significantly as a result of the tax cut. What might account for this outcome? (See pages 284–285)

13-3. Explain how time lags in discretionary fiscal policy making could thwart the efforts of Congress and the president to stabilize real GDP in the face of an economic downturn. Is it possible that these time lags could actually cause discretionary fiscal policy to *destabilize* real GDP?

13-4. Determine whether each of the following is an example of a situation in which a direct expenditure offset to fiscal policy occurs. (See page 285.)

  a. In an effort to help rejuvenate the nation's railroad system, a new government agency buys unused track, locomotives, and passenger and freight cars, many of which private companies would otherwise have purchased and put into regular use.

  b. The government increases its expenditures without raising taxes. To cover the resulting budget deficit, it borrows more funds from the private sector, thereby pushing up the market interest rate and discouraging private planned investment spending.

  c. The government finances the construction of a classical music museum that otherwise would never have received private funding.

13-5. Determine whether each of the following is an example of a situation in which there is indirect crowding out resulting from an expansionary fiscal policy action. (See pages 283–284.)

  a. The government provides a subsidy to help keep an existing firm operating, even though a group of investors otherwise would have provided a cash infusion that would have kept the company in business.

  b. The government reduces its taxes without decreasing its expenditures. To cover the resulting budget deficit, it borrows more funds from the private sector, thereby pushing up the market interest rate and discouraging private planned investment spending.

  c. Government expenditures fund construction of a high-rise office building on a plot of land where a private company otherwise would have constructed an essentially identical building.

13-6. The U.S. government is in the midst of spending more than $1 billion on seven buildings containing more than 100,000 square feet of space to be used for study of infectious diseases. Prior to the government's decision to construct these buildings, a few universities had been planning to build essentially the same facilities using privately obtained funds. After construction on the government buildings began, however, the universities dropped their plans. Evaluate whether the government's $1 billion expenditure is actually likely to push U.S. real GDP above the level it would have reached in the absence of the government's construction spree. (See page 285.)

13-7. Determine whether each of the following is an example of a discretionary fiscal policy action. (See page 285.)

  a. A recession occurs, and government-funded unemployment compensation is paid to laid-off workers.

  b. Congress votes to fund a new jobs program designed to put unemployed workers to work.

  c. The Federal Reserve decides to reduce the quantity of money in circulation in an effort to slow inflation.

d. Under powers authorized by an act of Congress, the president decides to authorize an emergency release of funds for spending programs intended to head off economic crises.

13-8. Determine whether each of the following is an example of an automatic fiscal stabilizer. (See pages 288–289.)

    a. A federal agency must extend loans to businesses whenever an economic downturn begins.

    b. As the economy heats up, the resulting increase in equilibrium real GDP per year immediately results in higher income tax payments, which dampen consumption spending somewhat.

    c. As the economy starts to recover from a severe recession and more people go back to work, government-funded unemployment compensation payments begin to decline.

    d. To stem an overheated economy, the president, using special powers granted by Congress, authorizes emergency impoundment of funds that Congress had previously authorized for spending on government programs.

13-9. Consider the diagram below, in which the current short-run equilibrium is at point A, and answer the questions that follow. (See pages 281–282.)

    a. What type of gap exists at point A?

    b. If the marginal propensity to save equals 0.20, what change in government spending financed by borrowing from the private sector could eliminate the gap identified in part (a)? Explain.

13-10. Consider the diagram in the next column, in which the current short-run equilibrium is at point A, and answer the questions that follow. (See pages 281–282.)

    a. What type of gap exists at point A?

    b. If the marginal propensity to consume equals 0.75, what change in government spending financed by borrowing from the private sector could eliminate the gap identified in part (a)? Explain.

13-11. Currently, a government's budget is balanced. The marginal propensity to consume is 0.80. The government has determined that each additional $10 billion it borrows to finance a budget deficit pushes up the market interest rate by 0.1 percentage point. It has also determined that every 0.1-percentage-point change in the market interest rate generates a change in planned investment expenditures equal to $2 billion. Finally, the government knows that to close a recessionary gap and take into account the resulting change in the price level, it must generate a net rightward shift in the aggregate demand curve equal to $200 billion. Assuming that there are no direct expenditure offsets to fiscal policy, how much should the government increase its expenditures? (See pages 283–284. Hint: How much private investment spending will each $10 billion increase in government spending crowd out?)

13-12. A government is currently operating with an annual budget deficit of $40 billion. The government has determined that every $10 billion reduction in the amount it borrows each year would reduce the market interest rate by 0.1 percentage point. Furthermore, it has determined that every 0.1-percentage-point change in the market interest rate generates a change in planned investment expenditures in the opposite direction equal to $5 billion. The marginal propensity to consume is 0.75. Finally, the government knows that to eliminate an inflationary gap and take into account the resulting change in the price level, it must generate a net leftward shift in the aggregate demand curve equal to $40 billion. Assuming that there are no direct expenditure offsets to fiscal policy, how much should the government increase taxes? (See pages 283–284. Hint: How much new private investment spending is induced by each $10 billion decrease in government spending?)

13-13. Assume that the Ricardian equivalence theorem is not relevant. Explain why an income-tax-rate cut should affect short-run equilibrium real GDP. (See pages 286–287.)

13-14. Suppose that Congress enacts a lump-sum tax cut of $750 billion. The marginal propensity to consume is equal to 0.75. Assuming that Ricardian equivalence holds true, what is the effect on equilibrium real GDP? On saving? (See page XXX.)

13-15. In May and June of 2008, the federal government issued one-time tax rebates—checks returning a small portion of taxes previously paid—to millions of U.S residents, and U.S. real disposable income temporarily jumped by nearly $500 billion. Household real consumption spending did not increase in response to the short-lived increase in real disposable income. Explain how the logic of the permanent income hypothesis might help to account for this apparent non-relationship between real consumption and real disposable income in the late spring of 2008. (See page 285.)

13-16. It is late 2017, and the U.S. economy is showing signs of slipping into a potentially deep recession. Government policymakers are searching for income-tax-policy changes that will bring about a significant and lasting boost to real consumption spending. According to the logic of the permanent income hypothesis, should the proposed income-tax-policy changes involve tax increases or tax reductions, and should the policy changes be short-lived or long-lasting? (See page 285.)

ECONOMICS ON THE NET

Federal Government Spending and Taxation A quick way to keep up with the federal government's spending and taxation is by examining federal budget data at the White House Internet address.

Title: Historical Tables: Budget of the United States Government

Navigation: Use the link at **www.econtoday.com/chap13** to visit the Office of Management and Budget. Select the most recent budget. Then click on *Historical Tables.*

Application After the document downloads, perform the indicated operations and answer the questions.

1. Go to section 2, "Composition of Federal Government Receipts." Take a look at Table 2.2, "Percentage Composition of Receipts by Source." Before World War II, what was the key source of revenues of the federal government? What has been the key revenue source since World War II?

2. Now scan down the document to Table 2.3, "Receipts by Source as Percentages of GDP." Have any government revenue sources declined as a percentage of GDP? Which ones have noticeably risen in recent years?

For Group Study and Analysis Split into four groups, and have each group examine section 3, "Federal Government Outlays by Function," and in particular Table 3-1, "Outlays by Superfunction and Function." Assign groups to the following functions: national defense, health, income security, and Social Security. Have each group prepare a brief report concerning recent and long-term trends in government spending on each function. Which functions have been capturing growing shares of government spending in recent years? Which have been receiving declining shares of total spending?

ANSWERS TO QUICK QUIZZES

p. 282: (i) expenditures . . . taxes; (ii) recessionary . . . increase; (iii) inflationary . . . decrease; (iv) increase . . . decrease

p. 287: (i) increase; (ii) Direct expenditure offsets; (iii) Ricardian equivalence; (iv) supply-side . . . supply-side

p. 290: (i) recognition . . . action . . . effect; (ii) automatic; (iii) moderate; (iv) abnormal

APPENDIX D

Fiscal Policy: A Keynesian Perspective

The traditional Keynesian approach to fiscal policy differs in three ways from that presented in Chapter 13. First, it emphasizes the underpinnings of the components of aggregate demand. Second, it assumes that government expenditures are not substitutes for private expenditures and that current taxes are the only taxes taken into account by consumers and firms. Third, the traditional Keynesian approach focuses on the short run and so assumes that as a first approximation, the price level is constant.

Changes in Government Spending

Figure D-1 below measures real GDP along the horizontal axis and total planned real expenditures (aggregate demand) along the vertical axis. The components of aggregate demand are real consumption (C), investment (I), government spending (G), and net exports (X). The height of the schedule labeled $C + I + G + X$ shows total planned real expenditures (aggregate demand) as a function of real GDP. This schedule slopes upward because consumption depends positively on real GDP. Everywhere along the 45-degree reference line, planned real spending equals real GDP.

At the point Y^*, where the $C + I + G + X$ line intersects the 45-degree line, planned real spending is consistent with real GDP per year. At any income less than Y^*, spending exceeds real GDP, and so real GDP and thus real spending will tend to rise. At any level of real GDP greater than Y^*, planned spending is less than real GDP, and so real GDP and thus spending will tend to decline. Given the determinants of C, I, G, and X, total real spending (aggregate demand) will be Y^*.

FIGURE D-1

The Impact of Higher Government Spending on Aggregate Demand

Government spending increases, causing $C + I + G + X$ to move to $C + I + G' + X$. Equilibrium real GDP per year increases to Y^{**}.

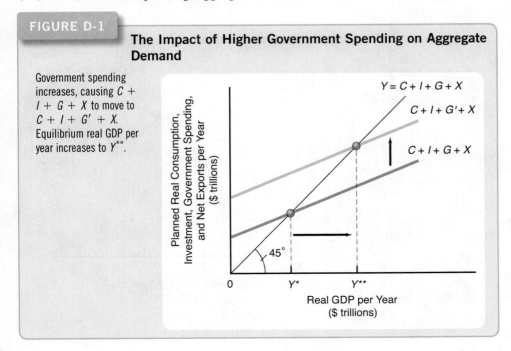

The Keynesian approach assumes that changes in government spending cause no direct offsets in either consumption or investment spending because G is not a substitute for C, I, or X. Hence, a rise in government spending from G to G' causes the $C + I + G + X$ line to shift upward by the full amount of the rise in government spending, yielding the line $C + I + G' + X$. The rise in real government spending causes real GDP to rise, which in turn causes consumption spending to rise, which further increases real GDP. Ultimately, aggregate demand rises to the level Y^{**}, where spending again equals real GDP. A key conclusion of the traditional Keynesian analysis is that total spending rises by *more* than the original rise in government spending because consumption spending depends positively on real GDP.

Changes in Taxes

According to the Keynesian approach, changes in current taxes affect aggregate demand by changing the amount of real disposable (after-tax) income available to consumers. A rise in taxes reduces disposable income and thus reduces real consumption; conversely, a tax cut raises disposable income and thus causes a rise in consumption spending. The effects of a tax increase are shown in Figure D-2 below. Higher taxes cause consumption spending to decline from C to C', causing total spending to shift downward to $C' + I + G + X$. In general, the decline in consumption will be less than the increase in taxes because people will also reduce their saving to help pay the higher taxes.

The Balanced-Budget Multiplier

One interesting implication of the Keynesian approach concerns the impact of a balanced-budget change in government real spending. Suppose that the government increases spending by $1 billion and pays for it by raising current taxes by $1 billion. Such a policy is called a *balanced-budget increase in real spending*. Because the higher spending tends to push aggregate demand *up* by *more* than $1 billion while the higher taxes tend to push aggregate demand *down* by *less* than $1 billion, a most remarkable thing happens: A balanced-budget increase in G causes total spending to rise by *exactly* the amount of the rise in G—in this case, $1 billion. We say that the *balanced-budget multiplier* is equal to 1. Similarly, a balanced-budget reduction in government spending will cause total spending to fall by exactly the amount of the government spending cut.

FIGURE D-2

The Impact of Higher Taxes on Aggregate Demand

Higher taxes cause consumption to fall to C'. Equilibrium real GDP per year decreases to Y''.

The Fixed Price Level Assumption

The final key feature of the traditional Keynesian approach is that it typically assumes that as a first approximation, the price level is fixed. Recall that nominal GDP equals the price level multiplied by real GDP. If the price level is fixed, an increase in government spending that causes nominal GDP to rise will show up exclusively as a rise in *real* GDP. This will in turn be accompanied by a decline in the unemployment rate because the additional real GDP can be produced only if additional factors of production, such as labor, are utilized.

PROBLEMS

All problems are assignable in MyEconLab. *Answers to odd-numbered problems appear at the back of the book.*

D-1. Assume that equilibrium real GDP is $15.2 trillion and full-employment equilibrium (*FE*) is $15.55 trillion. The marginal propensity to save is $\frac{1}{7}$. Answer the questions using the data in the following graph. (See pages 297–298.)

a. What is the marginal propensity to consume?

b. By how much must new investment or government spending increase to bring the economy up to full employment?

c. By how much must government cut personal taxes to stimulate the economy to the full-employment equilibrium?

D-2. Assume that MPC $= \frac{4}{5}$ when answering the following questions. (See pages 297–298.)

a. If government expenditures rise by $2 billion, by how much will the aggregate expenditure curve shift upward? By how much will equilibrium real GDP per year change?

b. If taxes increase by $2 billion, by how much will the aggregate expenditure curve shift downward? By how much will equilibrium real GDP per year change?

D-3. Assume that MPC $= \frac{4}{5}$ when answering the following questions (See pages 297–298.)

a. If government expenditures rise by $1 billion, by how much will the aggregate expenditure curve shift upward?

b. If taxes rise by $1 billion, by how much will the aggregate expenditure curve shift downward?

c. If both taxes and government expenditures rise by $1 billion, by how much will the aggregate expenditure curve shift? What will happen to the equilibrium level of real GDP?

d. How does your response to the second question in part (c) change if MPC $= \frac{3}{4}$? If MPC $= \frac{1}{2}$?

Rising deficit threatens U.S. credit rating

Standard & Poor's warned that it could downgrade the United State(s) sterling debt rating if the White House and Congress fail to reach a deal to control the massive federal deficit, which is feeding the nation's debt. Here is a look at growth of the debt in recent decade(s)

Annual gross national debt in trillions of dollars

201(
$20.8 trilli(

Estimated

2010
$13.5 trillion

1940
$50.7 billion

14

Deficit Spending and the Public Debt

In recent years, the federal government's total expenditures—the sum of discretionary spending and nondiscretionary expenditures on programs such as Social Security and Medicare—have been considerably greater than receipts. Indeed, total federal spending is now so high that discretionary spending eats up nearly all of the borrowed funds. Every discretionary federal spending program, including those for developing green technologies or finding cures for cancer and other diseases, has been financed almost fully with borrowed funds. Because its nondiscretionary discretionary spending has exceeded its tax revenues, the federal government has had to borrow more than $1 trillion per year to pay for its discretionary expenditures. In this chapter, you will contemplate the economic implications of this federal borrowing.

even though the government projected for two decades that 2020 would be the year in which tax collections to fund the Social Security program would fall below beneficiary payments, the actual year was 2011? The federal government is making up the difference by allocating a portion of regular government spending to payments to Social Security beneficiaries. Nevertheless, the federal government's tax revenues are already insufficient to cover all of its other expenditures—that is, the rest of the government's budget also is in deficit. Consequently, the federal government is borrowing from domestic and foreign residents, firms, and governments to finance a portion of the Social Security program's payments. Some elderly and disabled U.S. residents are receiving Social Security benefits from funds that the federal government has borrowed and must repay in future years.

Every year since 2001, the U.S. government has spent more than it collected in taxes. The government anticipates that it will continue to spend more than it receives indefinitely. Should you be worried about this? The answer, as you will see in this chapter, is both yes and no. First, let's examine what the government does when it spends more than it receives.

Public Deficits and Debts: Flows versus Stocks

A **government budget deficit** exists if the government spends more than it receives in taxes during a given period of time. The government has to finance this shortfall somehow. Barring any resort to money creation (the subject matter of Chapters 15 and 16), the U.S. Treasury sells IOUs on behalf of the U.S. government, in the form of securities that are normally called bonds. In effect, the federal government asks U.S. and foreign households, businesses, and governments to lend funds to the government to cover its deficit. For example, if the federal government spends $1 trillion more than it receives in revenues, the Treasury will obtain that $1 trillion by selling $1 trillion of new Treasury bonds. Those who buy the Treasury bonds (lend funds to the U.S. government) will receive interest payments over the life of the bond plus eventual repayment of the entire amount lent. In return, the U.S. Treasury receives immediate purchasing power. In the process, it also adds to its indebtedness to bondholders.

Government budget deficit
An excess of government spending over government revenues during a given period of time.

Distinguishing between Deficits and Debts

You have already learned about flows. GDP, for instance, is a flow because it is a dollar measure of the total amount of final goods and services produced within a given period of time, such as a year.

The federal deficit is also a flow. Suppose that the current federal deficit is $1.5 trillion. Consequently, the federal government is currently spending at a rate of $1.5 trillion *per year* more than it is collecting in taxes and other revenues.

Of course, governments do not always spend more each year than the revenues they receive. If a government spends an amount exactly equal to the revenues it collects during a given period, then during this interval the government operates with a **balanced budget.** If a government spends less than the revenues it receives during a given period, then during this interval it experiences a **government budget surplus**.

Balanced budget
A situation in which the government's spending is exactly equal to the total taxes and other revenues it collects during a given period of time.

Government budget surplus
An excess of government revenues over government spending during a given period of time.

The Public Debt

You have also learned about stocks, which are measured at a point in time. Stocks change between points in time as a result of flows. The amount of unemployment, for example, is a stock. It is the total number of people looking for work but unable to find it at a given point in time. Suppose that the stock of unemployed workers at the beginning of the month is 12.8 million and that at the end of the month the stock of unemployed workers has increased to 13.0 million. This means that during the month, assuming an unchanged labor force, there was a net flow of 0.2 million individuals away from the state of being employed into the state of being out of work but seeking employment.

Public debt
The total value of all outstanding federal government securities.

Likewise, the total accumulated **public debt** is a stock measured at a given point in time, and it changes from one time to another as a result of government budget deficits or surpluses. For instance, on December 31, 2011, one measure of the public debt was about $10.1 trillion. During 2012, the federal government operated at a deficit of about $1.3 trillion. As a consequence, on December 31, 2012, this measure of the public debt had increased to about $11.4 trillion.

Government Finance: Spending More Than Tax Collections

Go to www.econtoday.com/chap14 to learn more about the activities of the Congressional Budget Office, which reports to the legislative branch of the U.S. government about the current state of the federal government's spending and receipts.

Following four consecutive years—1998 through 2001—of official budget surpluses, the federal government began to experience budget deficits once more beginning in 2002. Since then, government spending has increased considerably, and tax revenues have failed to keep pace. Consequently, the federal government has operated with a deficit. Indeed, since 2009 the federal budget deficit has widened dramatically—to inflation-adjusted levels not seen since World War II.

The Historical Record of Federal Budget Deficits

Figure 14-1 below charts inflation-adjusted expenditures and revenues of the federal government since 1940. The *real* annual budget deficit is the arithmetic difference between real expenditures and real revenues during years in which the government's spending has exceeded its revenues. As you can see, this nation has experienced numerous years of federal budget deficits. Indeed, the annual budget surpluses of 1998 through 2001 were somewhat out of the ordinary. The 1998 budget surplus was the first since 1968, when the government briefly operated with a surplus. Before the 1998–2001 budget surpluses, the U.S. government had not experienced back-to-back annual surpluses since the 1950s.

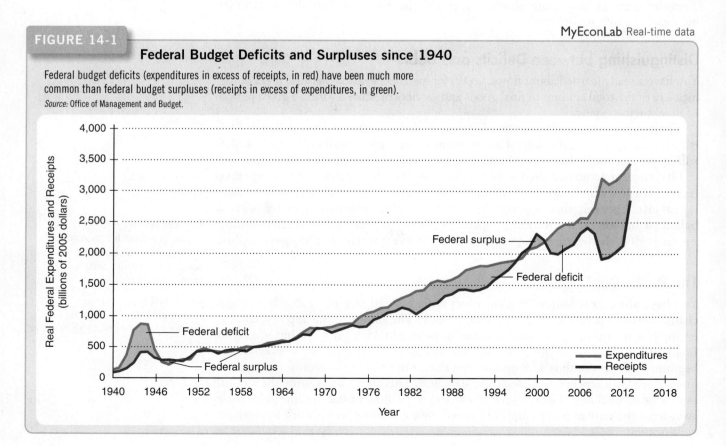

FIGURE 14-1

MyEconLab Real-time data

Federal Budget Deficits and Surpluses since 1940

Federal budget deficits (expenditures in excess of receipts, in red) have been much more common than federal budget surpluses (receipts in excess of expenditures, in green).

Source: Office of Management and Budget.

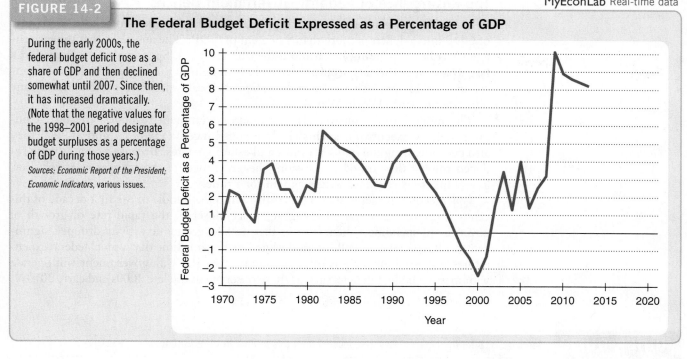

MyEconLab Real-time data

FIGURE 14-2

The Federal Budget Deficit Expressed as a Percentage of GDP

During the early 2000s, the federal budget deficit rose as a share of GDP and then declined somewhat until 2007. Since then, it has increased dramatically. (Note that the negative values for the 1998–2001 period designate budget surpluses as a percentage of GDP during those years.)

Sources: Economic Report of the President; Economic Indicators, various issues.

Indeed, since 1940 the U.S. government has operated with an annual budget surplus for a total of only 13 years. In all other years, it has collected insufficient taxes and other revenues to fund its spending. Every year this has occurred, the federal government has borrowed to finance its additional expenditures.

Even though Figure 14-1 on the facing page accounts for inflation, it does not give a clear picture of the size of the federal government's deficits or surpluses in relation to overall economic activity in the United States. Figure 14-2 above provides a clearer view of the size of government deficits or surpluses relative to the size of the U.S. economy by expressing them as percentages of GDP. As you can see, the federal budget deficit rose to nearly 6 percent of GDP in the early 1980s. It then fell back, increased once again during the late 1980s and early 1990s, and then declined steadily into the budget surplus years of 1998–2001. Since 2001, the government budget deficit has increased to nearly 4 percent of GDP, dropped back below 3 percent of GDP, and then risen rapidly, to more than 8 percent of GDP.

Why do you suppose some nations complain that the U.S. government performs "cosmetic surgery" on its reports about public deficits and debts?

INTERNATIONAL EXAMPLE

Cosmetic Enhancement of the U.S. Deficits and Debts?

The official U.S. government deficit and net public debt may be huge, but the reality is even worse. Most other countries' reports combine figures for *all* governments—that is, national, state or provincial, and municipal governments. U.S. reports, in contrast, typically provide only data on the *federal* government's annual budget deficit and net public debt. The U.S. federal government's budget deficit per year as a percentage of the nation's annual GDP is close to 8.2 percent.

If U.S. statistical reports were altered to include state and municipal budget deficits, about 2 more percentage points would be added. Thus, the resulting *aggregate* national government budget deficit,

inclusive of *all* government entities in the United States, would rise as a percentage of U.S. annual GDP to more than 10.2 percent. In addition, if the net public indebtedness of U.S. states and municipalities were included, the aggregate net debt of all U.S. government entities would rise from more than 77 percent of GDP per year to about 80 percent of GDP per year.

FOR CRITICAL THINKING

Why might differences in the reporting of national debt and deficit levels complicate governments' abilities to finance these debts and deficits?

The Resurgence of Federal Government Deficits

Why has the government's budget slipped from a surplus equal to nearly 2.5 percent of GDP into a deficit of more than 8 percent of GDP? The answer is that the government has been spending much more than its revenues. Spending has increased at a faster pace since the early 2000s—particularly in light of the ongoing bailout of financial institutions and a sharp rise in discretionary fiscal expenditures—than during any other decade since World War II.

The more complex answer also considers government revenues. In 2001, Congress and the executive branch slightly reduced income tax rates, and in 2003 they also cut federal capital gains tax rates and estate tax tates. Because tax rates were reduced toward the end of a recession when real income growth was relatively low, government tax revenues were stagnant for a time.

When economic activity began to expand into the middle of the first decade of this century, tax revenues started rising at a pace closer to the rapid rate of growth of government spending. Then, later in that decade, economic activity dropped significantly. Thus, annual tax collections declined at the same time that annual federal expenditures increased. As long as this situation persists, the U.S. government will operate with massive budget deficits such as those observed in the late 2000s and early 2010s.

QUICK QUIZ See page 318 for the answers. Review concepts from this section in MyEconLab.

Whenever the federal government spends more than it receives during a given year, it operates with a _____ _____. If federal government spending exactly equals government revenues, then the government experiences a _____ _____. If the federal government collects more revenues than it spends, then it operates with a _____ _____.

The federal budget deficit is a flow, whereas accumulated budget deficits represent a _____, called the **public debt**.

The federal budget deficit expressed as a percentage of GDP rose to around 6 percent in the early 1980s. Between 1998 and 2001, the federal government experienced a budget _____, but since then its budget has once more been in _____. Currently, the budget _____ is more than 8 of GDP.

Evaluating the Rising Public Debt

Gross public debt
All federal government debt irrespective of who owns it.

Net public debt
Gross public debt minus all government interagency borrowing.

All federal public debt, taken together, is called the **gross public debt.** We arrive at the **net public debt** when we subtract from the gross public debt the portion that is held by government agencies (in essence, what the federal government owes to itself). For instance, if the Social Security Administration holds U.S. Treasury bonds, the U.S. Treasury makes debt payments to another agency of the government. On net, therefore, the U.S. government owes these payments to itself.

The net public debt increases whenever the federal government experiences a budget deficit. That is, the net public debt increases when government outlays are greater than total government receipts.

Accumulation of the Net Public Debt

Table 14-1 on the facing page displays, for various years since 1940, real values, in base-year 2005 dollars, of the federal budget deficit, the total and per capita net public debt (the amount owed on the net public debt by a typical individual), and the net interest cost of the public debt in total and as a percentage of GDP. It shows that the level of the real net public debt and the real net public debt per capita grew following the early 1980s and rose again very dramatically after 2007. Thus, the real, inflation-adjusted amount that a typical individual owes to holders of the net public debt has varied considerably over time.

TABLE 14-1

The Federal Deficit, Our Public Debt, and the Interest We Pay on It

The inflation-adjusted net public debt in column 3 is defined as total federal debt *excluding* all loans between federal government agencies. Per capita net public debt shown in column 4 is obtained by dividing the net public debt by the population.

(1) Year	(2) Federal Budget Deficit (billions of 2005 dollars)	(3) Net Public Debt (billions of 2005 dollars)	(4) Per Capita Net Public Debt (2005 dollars)	(5) Net Interest Costs (billions of 2005 dollars)	(6) Net Interest as a Percentage of GDP
1940	8.9	97.3	736.2	2.1	0.9
1945	492.9	2,150.7	15,372.8	28.3	1.45
1950	21.1	1,490.7	9,788.0	32.7	1.68
1955	18.0	1,360.8	8,202.8	29.4	1.23
1960	1.6	1,253.5	6,937.0	36.5	1.37
1965	7.9	1,287.7	6,627.5	42.3	1.26
1970	11.5	1,169.1	5,700.1	59.1	1.47
1975	134.1	1,180.0	5,463.1	69.3	1.52
1980	154.3	1,482.6	6,564.3	109.7	1.92
1985	344.1	2,430.0	10,247.4	209.7	3.22
1990	306.5	3,337.4	13,349.4	243.1	3.23
1995	201.2	4,421.6	16,585.2	284.7	3.24
2000	−267.1	3,853.1	13,644.1	252.0	2.34
2005	318.3	4,592.2	15,480.8	184.0	1.38
2010	1,165.3	8,125.1	29,814.3	176.8	1.35
2011	1,146.4	8,934.5	29,902.1	202.9	1.52
2012	1,189.5	10,379.5	33,309.6	201.5	1.63
2013	1,194.2	11,304.0	36,026.6	221.6	1.52

Sources: U.S. Department of the Treasury; Office of Management and Budget. *Note:* Data for 2013 are estimates.

The net public debt levels reported in Table 14-1 do not provide a basis of comparison with the overall size of the U.S. economy. Figure 14-3 below does this by displaying the net public debt as a percentage of GDP. We see that after World War II, this ratio fell steadily until the early 1970s (except for a small rise in the late 1950s)

MyEconLab Real-time data

FIGURE 14-3

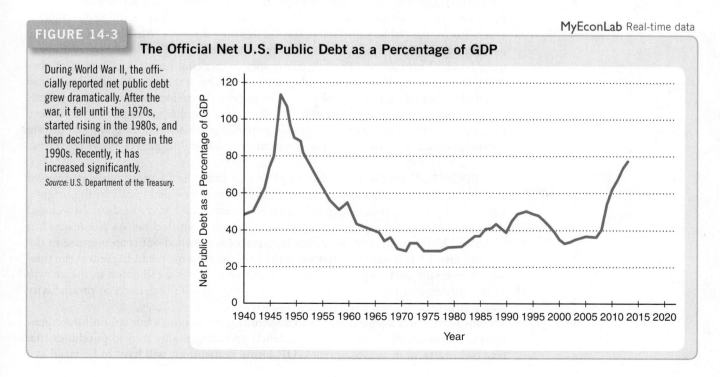

The Official Net U.S. Public Debt as a Percentage of GDP

During World War II, the officially reported net public debt grew dramatically. After the war, it fell until the 1970s, started rising in the 1980s, and then declined once more in the 1990s. Recently, it has increased significantly.

Source: U.S. Department of the Treasury.

and then leveled off until the 1980s. After that, the ratio of the net public debt to GDP more or less continued to rise to around 50 percent of GDP, before dropping slightly in the late 1990s. The ratio has been rising once again since 2001 and has jumped dramatically since 2007.

Annual Interest Payments on the Public Debt

Columns 5 and 6 of Table 14-1 show an important consequence of the net public debt. This is the interest that the government must pay to those who hold the bonds it has issued to finance past budget deficits. Those interest payments started rising dramatically around 1975 and then declined into the middle of the first decade of this century. Deficits have recently been higher. Interest payments expressed as a percentage of GDP will rise in the years to come.

If U.S. residents were the sole owners of the government's debts, the interest payments on the net public debt would go only to U.S. residents. In this situation, we would owe the debt to ourselves, with most people being taxed so that the government could pay interest to others (or to ourselves). During the 1970s, however, the share of the net public debt owned by foreign individuals, businesses, and governments started to rise, reaching 20 percent in 1978. From there it declined until the late 1980s, when it began to rise rapidly. Today, foreign residents, businesses, and governments hold more than 50 percent of the net public debt. Thus, we do not owe the debt just to ourselves.

Burdens of the Public Debt

Do current budget deficits and the accumulating public debt create social burdens? One perspective on this question considers possible burdens on future generations. Another focuses on transfers from U.S. residents to residents of other nations.

HOW TODAY'S BUDGET DEFICITS MIGHT BURDEN FUTURE GENERATIONS If the federal government wishes to purchase goods and services valued at $300 billion, it can finance this expenditure either by raising taxes by $300 billion or by selling $300 billion in bonds. Many economists maintain that the second option, deficit spending, would lead to a higher level of national consumption and a lower level of national saving than the first option.

The reason, say these economists, is that if people are taxed, they will have to forgo private consumption now as society substitutes government goods for private goods. If the government does not raise taxes but instead sells bonds to finance the $300 billion in expenditures, the public's disposable income remains the same. Members of the public have merely shifted their allocations of assets to include $300 billion in additional government bonds. There are two possible circumstances that could cause people to treat government borrowing differently than they treat taxes. One is that people will fail to realize that their liabilities (in the form of higher future taxes due to increased interest payments on the public debt) have *also* increased by $300 billion. Another is that people will believe that they can consume the governmentally provided goods without forgoing any private consumption because the bill for the government goods will be paid by *future* taxpayers.

THE CROWDING-OUT EFFECT But if full employment exists, and society raises its present consumption by adding consumption of government-provided goods to the original quantity of privately provided goods, then something must be *crowded out*. In a closed economy, investment expenditures on capital goods must decline. As you learned in Chapter 13, the mechanism by which investment is crowded out is an increase in the interest rate. Deficit spending increases the total demand for credit but leaves the total supply of credit unaltered. The rise in interest rates causes a reduction in the growth of investment and capital formation, which in turn slows the growth of productivity and improvement in society's living standard.

This perspective suggests that deficit spending can impose a burden on future generations in two ways. First, unless the deficit spending is allocated to purchases that lead to long-term increases in real GDP, future generations will have to be taxed at a higher rate. That is, only by imposing higher taxes on future generations will the government be able to retire the higher public debt resulting from the present generation's consumption of governmentally provided goods. Second, the increased level of spending by the present generation crowds out investment and reduces the growth of capital goods, leaving future generations with a smaller capital stock and thereby reducing their wealth.

PAYING OFF THE PUBLIC DEBT IN THE FUTURE Suppose that after several more years of running substantial deficits financed by selling bonds to U.S. residents, the public debt becomes so large that each adult person's implicit share of the net public debt liability is $60,000. Suppose further that the government chooses (or is forced) to pay off the debt at that time. Will that generation be burdened with our government's overspending? Assume that all of the debt is owed to ourselves.

It is true that every adult will have to come up with $60,000 in taxes to pay off the debt, but then the government will use these funds to pay off the bondholders. Sometimes the bondholders and taxpayers will be the same people. Thus, *some* people will be burdened because they owe $60,000 and own less than $60,000 in government bonds. Others, however, will receive more than $60,000 for the bonds they own. Nevertheless, as a generation within society, they could—if all government debt were issued within the nation's borders—pay and receive about the same amount of funds.

Of course, there could be a burden on some low-income adults who will find it difficult or impossible to obtain $60,000 to pay off the tax liability. Still, nothing says that taxes to pay off the debt must be assessed equally. Indeed, it seems likely that a special tax would be levied, based on the ability to pay.

OUR DEBT TO FOREIGN RESIDENTS So far we have been assuming that we owe all of the public debt to ourselves. But, as we saw earlier, that is not the case. What about the more than 50 percent owned by foreign residents?

It is true that if foreign residents buy U.S. government bonds, we do not owe that debt to ourselves. Thus, when debts held by foreign residents come due, future U.S. residents will be taxed to repay these debts plus accumulated interest. Portions of the incomes of future U.S. residents will then be transferred abroad. In this way, a potential burden on future generations may result.

But this transfer of income from U.S. residents to residents of other nations will not necessarily be a burden. It is important to realize that if the rate of return on projects that the government funds by operating with deficits exceeds the interest rate paid to foreign residents, both foreign residents and future U.S. residents will be better off. If funds obtained by selling bonds to foreign residents are expended on wasteful projects, however, a burden will be placed on future generations.

We can apply the same reasoning to the problem of current investment and capital creation being crowded out by current deficits. If deficits lead to slower growth rates, future generations will be poorer. But if the government expenditures are really investments, and if the rate of return on such public investments exceeds the interest rate paid on the bonds, both present and future generations will be economically better off.

To learn about the agency that manages the public debt, go to www.econtoday.com/chap14.

QUICK QUIZ See page 318 for the answers. Review concepts from this section in MyEconLab.

When we subtract the funds that government agencies borrow from each other from the _____ public debt, we obtain the _____ public debt.

The public debt may impose a burden on _____ generations if they have to be taxed at higher rates to pay for the _____ generation's increased consumption of governmentally provided goods. In addition, there may be a burden if the debt leads to crowding out of current investment, resulting in _____ capital formation and hence a _____ economic growth rate.

If foreign residents hold a significant part of our public debt, then we no longer "owe it to ourselves." If the rate of return on the borrowed funds is _____ than the interest to be paid to foreign residents, future generations can be made better off by government borrowing. Future generations will be worse off, however, if the opposite is true.

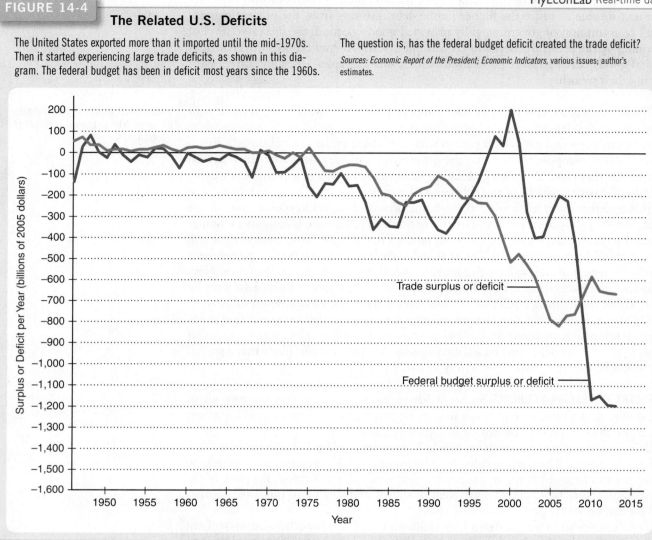

MyEconLab Real-time data

FIGURE 14-4

The Related U.S. Deficits

The United States exported more than it imported until the mid-1970s. Then it started experiencing large trade deficits, as shown in this diagram. The federal budget has been in deficit most years since the 1960s.

The question is, has the federal budget deficit created the trade deficit?

Sources: *Economic Report of the President; Economic Indicators,* various issues; author's estimates.

Federal Budget Deficits in an Open Economy

Many economists believe that it is no accident that foreign residents hold such a large portion of the U.S. public debt. Their reasoning suggests that a U.S. trade deficit—a situation in which the value of U.S. imports of goods and services exceeds the value of its exports—will often accompany a government budget deficit.

Trade Deficits and Government Budget Deficits

Figure 14-4 above shows U.S. trade deficits and surpluses compared with federal budget deficits and surpluses. In the mid-1970s, imports of goods and services began to consistently exceed exports of those items on an annual basis in the United States. At the same time, the federal budget deficit rose dramatically. Both deficits increased once again in the early 2000s. Then, during the economic turmoil of the late 2000s, the budget deficit exploded while the trade deficit shrank somewhat.

Overall, however, it appears that larger trade deficits tend to accompany larger government budget deficits.

Why the Two Deficits Tend to Be Related

Intuitively, there is a reason why we would expect federal budget deficits to be associated with trade deficits. You might call this the unpleasant arithmetic of trade and budget deficits.

Suppose that, initially, the government's budget is balanced; government expenditures are matched by an equal amount of tax collections and other government revenues. Now assume that the federal government begins to operate with a budget deficit. It increases its spending, collects fewer taxes, or both. Assume further that domestic consumption and domestic investment do not decrease relative to GDP. Where, then, do the funds come from to finance the government's budget deficit? A portion of these funds must come from abroad. That is to say, dollar holders abroad ultimately will purchase newly created government bonds.

Of course, foreign dollar holders will choose to hold the new U.S. government bonds only if there is an economic inducement to do so, such as an increase in U.S. interest rates. Given that private domestic spending and other factors are unchanged, interest rates will indeed rise whenever there is an increase in deficits financed by increased borrowing.

When foreign dollar holders purchase the new U.S. government bonds, they will have fewer dollars to spend on U.S. items, including U.S. export goods. Hence, when our nation's government operates with a budget deficit, we should expect to see foreign dollar holders spending more on U.S. government bonds and less on U.S.-produced goods and services. As a consequence of the U.S. government deficit, therefore, we should generally anticipate a decline in U.S. exports relative to U.S. imports, or a higher U.S. trade deficit.

Growing U.S. Government Deficits: Implications for U.S. Economic Performance

We have seen that one consequence of higher U.S. government budget deficits tends to be higher international trade deficits. Higher budget deficits, such as the much higher deficits of recent years (especially during the recession of the late 2000s), are also likely to have broader consequences for the economy.

For more information about the role of the Office of Management and Budget in the government's budgeting process, go to www.econtoday.com/chap14.

The Macroeconomic Consequences of Budget Deficits

When evaluating additional macroeconomic effects of government deficits, two important points must be kept well in mind. First, given the level of government expenditures, the main alternative to the deficit is higher taxes. Therefore, the effects of a deficit should be compared to the effects of higher taxes, not to zero. Second, it is important to distinguish between the effects of deficits when full employment exists and the effects when substantial unemployment exists.

SHORT-RUN MACROECONOMIC EFFECTS OF HIGHER BUDGET DEFICITS How do increased government budget deficits affect the economy in the short run? The answer depends on the initial state of the economy. Recall from Chapter 13 that higher government spending and lower taxes that generate budget deficits typically add to total planned expenditures, even after taking into account direct and indirect expenditure offsets. When there is a recessionary gap, the increase in aggregate demand can eliminate the recessionary gap and push the economy toward its full-employment real GDP level. In the presence of a short-run recessionary gap, therefore, government deficit spending can influence both real GDP and employment.

If the economy is at the full-employment level of real GDP, however, increased total planned expenditures and higher aggregate demand generated by a larger government budget deficit create an inflationary gap. Although greater deficit spending temporarily raises equilibrium real GDP above the full-employment level, the price level also increases.

LONG-RUN MACROECONOMIC EFFECTS OF HIGHER BUDGET DEFICITS In a long-run macroeconomic equilibrium, the economy has fully adjusted to changes in all factors. These factors include changes in government spending and taxes and, consequently, the government budget deficit. Although increasing the government budget deficit raises aggregate demand, in the long run equilibrium real GDP remains at its full-employment level. Further increases in the government deficit via higher government expenditures or tax cuts can only be inflationary. They have no effect on equilibrium real GDP, which remains at the full-employment level in the long run.

The fact that long-run equilibrium real GDP is unaffected in the face of increased government deficits has an important implication:

> *In the long run, higher government budget deficits have no effect on equilibrium real GDP per year. Ultimately, therefore, government spending in excess of government receipts simply redistributes a larger share of real GDP per year to government-provided goods and services.*

Thus, if the government operates with higher deficits over an extended period, the ultimate result is a shrinkage in the share of privately provided goods and services. By continually spending more than it collects in taxes and other revenue sources, the government takes up a larger portion of economic activity.

QUICK QUIZ See page 318 for the answers. Review concepts from this section in MyEconLab.

To obtain the dollars required to purchase newly issued U.S. government bonds, foreign residents must sell _____ goods and services in the United States than U.S. residents sell abroad. Thus, U.S. imports must _____ U.S. exports. For this reason, the federal budget deficit and the international trade _____ tend to be related.

Higher government deficits arise from increased government spending or tax cuts, which raise aggregate demand. Thus, larger government budget deficits can raise real GDP in a _____ gap situation. If the economy is

already at the full-employment level of real GDP, however, higher government deficits can only temporarily push equilibrium real GDP _____ the full-employment level.

In the long run, higher government budget deficits cause the equilibrium price level to rise but fail to raise equilibrium real GDP above the full-employment level. Thus, the long-run effect of increased government deficits is simply a redistribution of real GDP per year from _____ provided goods and services to _____-provided goods and services.

How Could the Government Reduce All of Its Red Ink?

There have been many suggestions about how to reduce the government deficit. One way to reduce the deficit is to increase tax collections.

INCREASING TAXES FOR EVERYONE From an arithmetic point of view, a federal budget deficit can be wiped out by simply increasing the amount of taxes collected. Let's see what this would require. Projections for 2013 are instructive. The Office of Management and Budget estimated the 2013 federal budget deficit at about $1 trillion. To have prevented this deficit from occurring by raising taxes, in 2013 the government would have had to collect more than $8,000 in additional taxes from *every worker* in the United States. Needless to say, reality is such that we will never see annual federal budget deficits wiped out by simple tax increases.

YOU ARE THERE

To consider some "easy" cuts that the government could make to its budget deficit, read **A Long List of Ways to Cut the Federal Budget Deficit** on page 313.

WHAT IF... the government imposed a one-time tax to pay off all of the net public debt?

The net public debt is nearly $13 trillion and rising, while nominal GDP exceeds $15 trillion. If the government confiscated about three-fourths of all income generated by production in a single year, it could repay the outstanding net public debt. To avoid creating more debt during that year, however, the government also would have to

seize almost $3 trillion to fund its continued spending. Thus, to eliminate the net public debt within a single year, the government would have to confiscate at least 100 percent of all income generated during that year. In theory, this could be done, but only at the expense of impoverishing the nation's residents for 12 months.

TAXING THE RICH Some people suggest that the way to eliminate the deficit is to raise taxes on the rich. What does it mean to tax the rich more? If you talk about taxing "millionaires," you are referring to those who pay taxes on more than $1 million in income per year. There are fewer than 100,000 of them. Even if you were to double the taxes they now pay, the reduction in the deficit would be relatively trivial. Changing marginal tax rates at the upper end will produce similarly unimpressive results. The Internal Revenue Service (IRS) has determined that an increase in the top marginal tax rate from 35 percent to 45 percent would raise, at best, only about $35 billion in additional taxes. (This assumes that people do not figure out a way to avoid the higher tax rate.) Extra revenues of $35 billion per year represent only about 3 percent of the estimated 2013 federal budget deficit.

The reality is that the data do not support the notion that tax increases can completely *eliminate* deficits. Although eliminating a deficit in this way is possible arithmetically, politically just the opposite has occurred. When more tax revenues have been collected, Congress has usually responded by increasing government spending.

Could taxing more of the incomes of people earning in excess of $1 million per year eliminate the federal government's current annual deficit?

POLICY EXAMPLE

Could a 100 Percent Tax on "Millionaires" Eliminate the Deficit?

Some have claimed that raising income tax rates for "millionaires and billionaires" could eliminate the federal deficit. To contemplate this suggestion, consider Figure 14-5 below, and imagine a 100 percent income tax rate on all people earning more than $1 million per year.

The last bar displayed in the figure indicates that in a typical year, the sum of *all* incomes earned by these high-income individuals is less than $1 trillion. Since 2008, however, the average federal deficit has exceeded $1 trillion per year. Thus, even if the federal government were

to *confiscate* each year *all* of the earnings of people with incomes exceeding $1 million per year—thereby ending their incentives to earn incomes—this action could not cover the government's annual deficit.

FOR CRITICAL THINKING
Why do you think that most economists suggest that ending deficits without cutting spending would require the government to raise tax rates on middle-income earners?

FIGURE 14-5

Distribution of Total Taxable Income Based on Annual Taxpayer Earnings

This figure shows that the largest amount of total annual taxable income—more than $1.3 trillion per year—goes to people who earn between $100,000 and $200,000 per year. The total income received by individuals who earn more than $1 million per year—indicated by the last bar on the right-hand side of the figure—typically is less than $1 trillion.

Source: Internal Revenue Service.

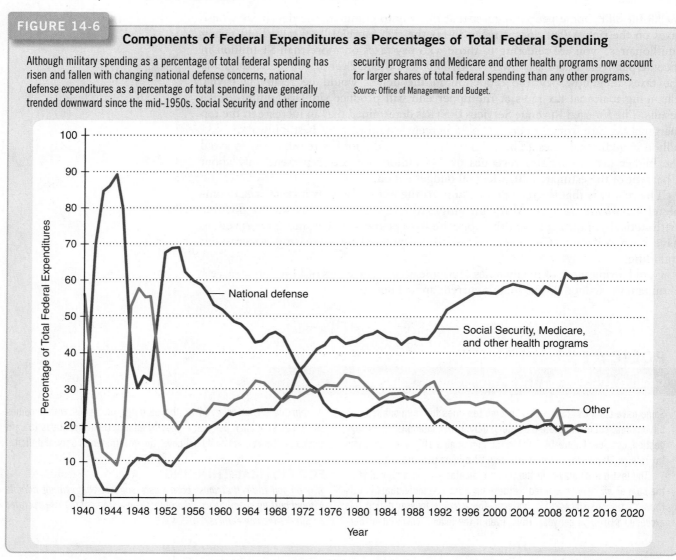

FIGURE 14-6

Components of Federal Expenditures as Percentages of Total Federal Spending

Although military spending as a percentage of total federal spending has risen and fallen with changing national defense concerns, national defense expenditures as a percentage of total spending have generally trended downward since the mid-1950s. Social Security and other income security programs and Medicare and other health programs now account for larger shares of total federal spending than any other programs.

Source: Office of Management and Budget.

REDUCING EXPENDITURES Reducing expenditures is another way to decrease the federal budget deficit. Figure 14-6 above shows various components of government spending as a percentage of total expenditures. There you see that military spending (national defense) as a share of total federal expenditures has risen slightly in some recent years, though it remains much lower than in most previous years.

During the period from the conclusion of World War II until 1972, military spending was the most important aspect of the federal budget. Figure 14-6 shows that it no longer is, even taking into account the war on terrorism that began in late 2001. **Entitlements,** which are legislated federal government payments that anyone who qualifies is entitled to receive, are now the most important component of the federal budget. These include payments for Social Security and other income security programs and for Medicare and other health programs such as Medicaid. Entitlements are consequently often called **noncontrollable expenditures,** or nondiscretionary expenditures unrelated to national defense that automatically change without any direct action by Congress.

Entitlements
Guaranteed benefits under a government program such as Social Security, Medicare, or Medicaid.

Noncontrollable expenditures
Government spending that changes automatically without action by Congress.

IS IT TIME TO BEGIN WHITTLING AWAY AT ENTITLEMENTS? In 1960, spending on entitlements represented about 20 percent of the total federal budget. Today, entitlement expenditures make up more than 60 percent of total federal spending. Consider Social Security, Medicare, and Medicaid. In constant 2005 dollars, in 2013 Social Security, Medicare, and Medicaid represented about $2,200 billion of estimated federal expenditures. (This calculation excludes military and international payments and interest on the government debt.)

Entitlement payments for Social Security, Medicare, and Medicaid now exceed all other domestic spending. Entitlements are growing faster than any other part of the federal government budget. During the past two decades, real spending on entitlements (adjusted for inflation) grew between 7 and 8 percent per year, while the economy grew less than 3 percent per year. Social Security payments are growing in real terms at about 6 percent per year, but Medicare and Medicaid are growing at double-digit rates. The passage of Medicare prescription drug benefits in 2003 and the new federal health care legislation in 2010 simply added to the already rapid growth of these health care entitlements.

Many people believe that entitlement programs are "necessary" federal expenditures. Interest on the public debt must be paid, but Congress can change just about every other federal expenditure labeled "necessary." The federal budget deficit is not expected to drop in the near future because entitlement programs are not likely to be reduced. Governments have trouble cutting government benefit programs once they are established. One must conclude that containing federal budget deficits is likely to prove a difficult task.

By how much does an accurate accounting of entitlement promises by the U.S. government increase its measured indebtedness?

POLICY EXAMPLE

Federal Indebtedness Is *Much* Higher Than the Net Public Debt

The U.S. government's *official* net public debt has been ballooning in recent years, but its *actual* indebtedness has increased even more rapidly. Every year, Congress borrows and spends more than contributions to Social Security payments made to these beneficiaries. Thus, instead of saving these funds to finance payments to future Social Security beneficiaries, every year Congress uses the funds for other purposes. Congress likewise has promised Medicare and Medicaid benefits to future beneficiaries but has not set aside funds to pay for those benefits.

Laurence Kotlikoff of Boston University has calculated the current dollar value of all amounts the U.S. government has promised to

provide to future Social Security, Medicare, and Medicaid recipients. Kotlikoff estimates that the total value of these currently *unfunded* promises amounts to more than $200 trillion. This amount, which is twelve times greater than a typical year's entire flow of national income, is almost *sixteen times* larger than the official value of today's net public debt.

FOR CRITICAL THINKING

How could the federal government try to reduce its entitlement indebtedness?

QUICK QUIZ See page 318 for the answers. Review concepts from this section in MyEconLab.

One way to reduce federal budget _____ is to increase taxes. Proposals to reduce deficits by raising taxes on the highest-income individuals will not appreciably reduce budget deficits, however.

Another way to decrease federal budget _____ is to cut back on government spending, particularly on _____, defined as benefits guaranteed under government programs such as Social Security and Medicare.

YOU ARE THERE
A Long List of Ways to Cut the Federal Budget Deficit

Gene Dodaro, head of the Government Accountability Office (GAO), issues a report listing separately funded programs with "duplicative" objectives. Among these are:

- 100 programs related to highway and rail transportation
- 82 programs to improve teacher quality
- 80 programs to help low-income people with transportation
- 80 programs to promote economic development
- 57 programs to help U.S. residents become more financially literate
- 52 programs to promote entrepreneurship
- 47 programs to assist with job training

Eliminating the duplicative programs, Dodaro and the GAO report, would permit the federal government to cut about $200 billion per year from its annual deficit.

After reporting to Congress, Dodaro returns to his office. He and others at the GAO have accomplished their task. But only Congress can make budget cuts.

Critical Thinking Questions

1. By what percentage could a $1 trillion annual deficit be reduced if Congress were to enact the spending cuts identified by Dodaro and the GAO?

2. How much less would be added to the net public debt every year if duplicative programs were eliminated?

Rising deficit threatens U.S. credit rating
Standard & Poor's warned that it could downgrade the United States' sterling debt rating if the White House and Congress fail to reach a deal to control the massive federal deficit, which is feeding the nation's debt. Here is a look at growth of the debt in recent decades.

Annual gross national debt in trillions of dollars

ISSUES & APPLICATIONS

Borrowing Total Discretionary Spending—And More

CONCEPTS APPLIED

▶ Government Budget Deficit

▶ Entitlements

▶ Noncontrollable Expenditures

Since 2008, higher federal budget deficits have had three causes: lower tax revenues, higher discretionary spending, and greater entitlement expenditures. Tax revenues have dropped so much that in some recent years, the government has borrowed to fund *all* discretionary spending.

The Share of Tax Revenues Going to Discretionary Spending

Figure 14-6 on page 312 shows that the share of total federal spending on entitlements has increased during the past 20 years. How has this trend affected the government's ability to fund its *discretionary* spending? Figure 14-7 below displays the percentage of tax revenues available to apply toward discretionary spending—that is, after paying for

entitlement expenditures—since the early 1990s. During the late 1990s, this percentage rose above 100 percent, meaning that the federal government officially operated with surpluses and paid down some of its outstanding debts.

After the late 1990s, however, the percentage of tax revenues available to cover discretionary spending after paying entitlements steadily declined. Since the late 2000s, this percentage has dropped substantially.

FIGURE 14-7

The Percentage of Federal Tax Receipts Available for Federal Discretionary Spending

The share of federal tax revenues available for discretionary spending after paying for entitlement expenditures declined after the late 1990s and has fallen considerably since the mid-2000s. Indeed, during some recent years the percentage of federal tax receipts allocated to discretionary spending has even dropped to or below zero. Within these intervals, the federal government has had to borrow funds to finance all of its discretionary spending plus part of its noncontrollable expenditures on entitlements.

Source: Congressional Budget Office.

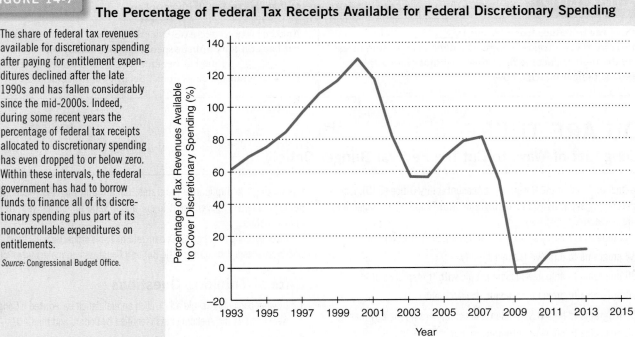

Indeed, during periods in which the percentage of tax revenues available to allocate to discretionary spending has been zero or negative, the federal government's tax revenues have been insufficient to pay for *any* of its discretionary spending. During these intervals, *all* discretionary spending has been financed with borrowed funds.

Borrowing in Part to Cover Entitlement Spending

When the share of federal tax revenues allocated to discretionary spending is below zero, the government borrows *more* than the amount of its discretionary spending. During these intervals, the government borrows funds to help pay some of its noncontrollable expenditures on entitlements as well as to cover its discretionary spending.

For Critical Thinking

1. What would be true of entitlement spending if the percentage of taxes allocated to discretionary spending rose to 100 percent and the federal budget was balanced? (Hint: Under a balanced budget, tax revenues equal the sum of discretionary and nondiscretionary expenditures.)
2. How would entitlement spending be funded if tax revenues just covered discretionary spending and there was a government budget deficit?

Web Resources

1. To review recent trends in federal discretionary and entitlement expenditures, go to www.econtoday.com/chap14.
2. For projections of federal entitlement expenditures for the first half of this century, go to www.econtoday.com/chap14.

> ## MyEconLab
> For more questions on this chapter's Issues & Applications, go to MyEconLab. In the Study Plan for this chapter, select Section N: News.

MyEconLab

Here is what you should know after reading this chapter. MyEconLab will help you identify what you know, and where to go when you need to practice.

WHAT YOU SHOULD KNOW		WHERE TO GO TO PRACTICE
Federal Government Budget Deficits A budget deficit occurs whenever the flow of government expenditures exceeds the flow of government revenues during a period of time. If government expenditures are less than government revenues during a given interval, a budget surplus occurs. The government operates with a balanced budget during a specific period if its expenditures equal its revenues. The deficit recently has risen to more than 8 percent of GDP.	government budget deficit, 301 balanced budget, 301 government budget surplus, 301 public debt, 302 **Key Figures** Figure 14-1, 302 Figure 14-2, 303	• MyEconLab Study Plans 14.1, 14.2 • Animated Figures 14-1, 14-2
The Public Debt The federal budget deficit is a flow, whereas accumulated budget deficits are a stock, called the public debt. The gross public debt is the stock of total government bonds, and the net public debt is the difference between the gross public debt and the amount of government agencies' holdings of government bonds. In recent years, the net public debt as a share of GDP has exceeded 70 percent of GDP.	gross public debt, 304 net public debt, 304 **Key Figure** Figure 14-3, 305	• MyEconLab Study Plan 14.3 • Figure 14-3

MyEconLab *continued*

How the Public Debt Might Prove a Burden to Future Generations People taxed at a higher rate must forgo private consumption as society substitutes government goods for private goods. Any current crowding out of investment as a consequence of additional debt accumulation can reduce capital formation and future economic growth. Furthermore, if capital invested by foreign residents who purchase some of the U.S. public debt has not been productively used, future generations will be worse off.

Key Figure
Figure 14-4, 308

- **MyEconLab** Study Plans 14.3, 14.4
- Animated Figure 14-4

The Macroeconomic Effects of Government Budget Deficits Higher government deficits contribute to a rise in total planned expenditures and aggregate demand. If there is a short-run recessionary gap, higher government deficits can thereby push equilibrium real GDP toward the full-employment level. If the economy is already at the full-employment level of real GDP, however, then a higher deficit creates a short-run inflationary gap.

- **MyEconLab** Study Plan 14.5

Possible Ways to Reduce the Government Budget Deficit Suggested ways to reduce the deficit are to increase taxes, particularly on the rich, and to reduce expenditures, particularly on entitlements, defined as guaranteed benefits under government programs such as Social Security and Medicare.

entitlements, 312
noncontrollable
  expenditures, 312

Key Figure
Figure 14-6, 312

- **MyEconLab** Study Plan 14.5
- Animated Figure 14-6

Log in to **MyEconLab**, take a chapter test, and get a personalized Study Plan that tells you which concepts you understand and which ones you need to review. From there, **MyEconLab** will give you further practice, tutorials, animations, videos, and guided solutions. For more information, visit www.myeconlab.com

PROBLEMS

All problems are assignable in MyEconLab; exercises that update with real-time data are marked with 🌐. *Answers to odd-numbered problems appear at the back of the book.*

14-1. In 2015, government spending is $4.3 trillion, and 🌐 taxes collected are $3.9 trillion. What is the federal government deficit in that year? (See page 302.)

14-2. Suppose that the Office of Management and Budget 🌐 provides the estimates of federal budget receipts, federal budget spending, and GDP at the right, all expressed in billions of dollars. Calculate the implied

estimates of the federal budget deficit as a percentage of GDP for each year. (See pages 302–303.)

Year	Federal Budget Receipts	Federal Budget Spending	GDP
2015	3,829.8	4,382.6	15,573.2
2016	3,892.4	4,441.6	16,316.0
2017	3,964.2	4,529.3	16,852.1
2018	4,013.5	4,600.1	17,454.4

14-3. It may be argued that the effects of a higher public debt are the same as the effects of a higher deficit. Why? (See pages 302–304.)

14-4. What happens to the net public debt if the federal government operates next year with the following (see page 302):

a. A budget deficit?

b. A balanced budget?

c. A budget surplus?

14-5. What is the relationship between the gross public debt and the net public debt? (See page 304.)

14-6. Explain how each of the following will affect the net public debt, other things being equal. (See page 302.)

a. Previously, the government operated with a balanced budget, but recently there has been a sudden increase in federal tax collections.

b. The government had been operating with a very small annual budget deficit until three hurricanes hit the Atlantic Coast, and now government spending has risen substantially.

c. The Government National Mortgage Association, a federal government agency that purchases certain types of home mortgages, buys U.S. Treasury bonds from another government agency.

14-7. Explain in your own words why there is likely to be a relationship between federal budget deficits and U.S. international trade deficits. (See page 308.)

14-8. Suppose that the share of U.S. GDP going to domestic consumption remains constant. Initially, the federal government was operating with a balanced budget, but this year it has increased its spending well above its collections of taxes and other sources of revenues. To fund its deficit spending, the government has issued bonds. So far, very few foreign residents have shown any interest in purchasing the bonds. (See page 306.)

a. What must happen to induce foreign residents to buy the bonds?

b. If foreign residents desire to purchase the bonds, what is the most important source of dollars to buy them?

14-9. Suppose that the economy is experiencing the short-run equilibrium position depicted at point *A* in the diagram near the top of the next column. Then the government raises its spending and thereby runs a budget deficit in an effort to boost equilibrium real GDP to its long-run equilibrium level of $15 trillion (in base-year dollars). Explain the effects of an increase in the government deficit on equilibrium real GDP and the equilibrium price level. In addition, given that many taxes and

government benefits vary with real GDP, discuss what change we might expect to see in the budget deficit as a result of the effects on equilibrium real GDP. (See pages 309–310.)

Real GDP per Year
($ trillions)

14-10. Suppose that the economy is experiencing the short-run equilibrium position depicted at point *B* in the diagram below. Explain the short-run effects of an increase in the government deficit on equilibrium real GDP and the equilibrium price level. What will be the long-run effects? (See pages 309–310.)

Real GDP per Year
($ trillions)

14-11. To eliminate the deficit (and halt the growth of the net public debt), a politician suggests that "we should tax the rich." The politician makes a simple arithmetic calculation in which he applies a higher tax rate to the total income reported by "the rich" in a previous year. He says that the government could thereby solve the deficit problem by taxing "the rich." What is the major fallacy in such a claim? (See page 311.)

14-12. Refer back to Problem 14-11. If the politician defines "the rich" as people with annual taxable incomes exceeding $1 million per year, what is another difficulty with the politician's reasoning, given that "the rich" rarely earn a combined taxable income exceeding $1 trillion, yet the federal deficit has regularly exceeded $1 trillion in recent years? (See page 311.)

14-13. In each of the past few years, the federal government has regularly borrowed funds to pay for at least one-third of expenditures that tax revenues were insufficient to cover. More than 60 percent of all federal expenditures now go for entitlement spending. What does this fact imply about how the government is paying for most of its discretionary expenditures? (See page 314.)

ECONOMICS ON THE NET

The Public Debt By examining the federal government's budget data, its current estimates of the public debt can be determined.

Title: Historical Tables: Budget of the United States Government

Navigation: Use the link at **www.econtoday.com/chap14** to visit the Office of Management and Budget. Select the most recent budget. Then select *Historical Tables*.

Application After the document downloads, perform each of the indicated operations and answer the following questions.

1. In the Table of Contents in the left-hand margin of the Historical Tables, click on Table 7.1, "Federal Debt at the End of the Year, 1940–2015." In light of the discussion in this chapter, which column shows the net public debt? What is the conceptual difference between the gross public debt and the net public debt? Last year, what was the dollar difference between these two amounts?

2. Table 7.1 includes estimates of the gross and net public debt over the next several years. Suppose that these estimates turn out to be accurate. Calculate how much the net public debt would increase on average each year. What are possible ways that the government could prevent these predicted increases from occurring?

For Group Study and Analysis Divide into two groups, and have each group take one side in answering the question, "Is the public debt a burden or a blessing?" Have each group develop rationales for supporting its position. Then reconvene the entire class, and discuss the relative merits of the alternative positions and rationales.

ANSWERS TO QUICK QUIZZES

p. 304: (i) budget deficit . . . balanced budget . . . budget surplus; (ii) stock; (iii) surplus . . . deficit . . . deficit

p. 307: (i) gross . . . net; (ii) future . . . current . . . less . . . lower; (iii) higher

p. 310: (i) more . . . exceed . . . deficit; (ii) recessionary . . . above; (iii) privately . . . government

p. 313: (i) deficits; (ii) deficits . . . entitlements

Money, Banking, and Central Banking

15

LEARNING OBJECTIVES

After reading this chapter, you should be able to:

▶ Define the fundamental functions of money and identify key properties that any good that functions as money must possess

▶ Explain official definitions of the quantity of money in circulation

▶ Understand why financial intermediaries such as banks exist

▶ Describe the basic structure and functions of the Federal Reserve System

▶ Determine the maximum potential extent that the money supply will change following a Federal Reserve monetary policy action

▶ Explain the essential features of federal deposit insurance

MyEconLab helps you master each objective and study more efficiently. See end of chapter for details.

During the early 2000s, bank managers across the United States sought to boost total deposits at their institutions, both by inducing existing customers to increase their deposits and by attracting new depositors. In the early 2010s, their efforts paid off: Total deposits at U.S. banks had increased by about 10 percent. Since then, however, banks generally have reversed course. Most banks have halted their efforts to gain more deposits, and a few even have begun actively discouraging increases in funds held on deposit with their institutions. What accounts for this abrupt change in course on the part of U.S. banks? In this chapter, you will find out.

? DID YOU KNOW THAT... since 2009, U.S. consumers' use of currency and coins to make payments has, for the first time since the 1970s, increased relative to other means of making payments? In other words, consumers now are buying more items with cash. As a consequence, the public's desired holdings of currency and coins have risen even as they have boosted their holdings of funds on deposit with banks. The Federal Reserve includes currency and coins and deposits in its measure of the quantity of money in circulation. Thus, this increase in the public's holdings of cash and deposits has translated into substantial recent growth in these measures of the quantity of money.

Traditionally, the primary task of the Federal Reserve System has been to regulate the quantity of money in circulation in the U.S. economy—that is, to conduct *monetary policy*. Money has been important to society for thousands of years. In the fourth century BC, Aristotle claimed that everything had to "be accessed in money, for this enables men always to exchange their services, and so makes society possible." Money is indeed a part of our everyday existence. Nevertheless, we have to be careful when we talk about money. Often we hear a person say, "I wish I had more money," instead of "I wish I had more wealth," thereby confusing the concepts of money and wealth. Economists use the term **money** to mean anything that people generally accept in exchange for goods and services. Table 15-1 below provides a list of some items that various civilizations have used as money. The best way to understand how these items served this purpose is to examine the functions of money.

Money
Any medium that is universally accepted in an economy both by sellers of goods and services as payment for those goods and services and by creditors as payment for debts.

The Functions of Money

Money traditionally has four functions. The one that most people are familiar with is money's function as a *medium of exchange*. Money also serves as a *unit of accounting*, a *store of value* or *purchasing power*, and a *standard of deferred payment*. Anything that serves these four functions is money. Anything that could serve these four functions could be considered money.

Money as a Medium of Exchange

Medium of exchange
Any item that sellers will accept as payment.

Barter
The direct exchange of goods and services for other goods and services without the use of money.

When we say that money serves as a **medium of exchange,** we mean that sellers will accept it as payment in market transactions. Without some generally accepted medium of exchange, we would have to resort to *barter*. In fact, before money was used, transactions took place by means of barter. **Barter** is simply a direct exchange of goods for goods. In a barter economy, the shoemaker who wants to obtain a dozen water glasses must seek out a glassmaker who at exactly the same time is interested in obtaining a pair of shoes. For this to occur, there has to be a high likelihood of a *double coincidence of wants* for each specific item to be exchanged. If there isn't, the shoemaker

---

TABLE 15-1

Types of Money

This is a partial list of items that have been used as money. Native Americans used *wampum*, beads made from shells. Fijians used whale teeth. The early colonists in North America used tobacco. And cigarettes were used in post–World War II Germany and in Poland during the breakdown of Communist rule in the late 1980s.

Boar tusk	Goats	Rice
Boats	Gold	Round stones with centers removed
Cigarettes	Horses	Rum
Copper	Iron	Salt
Corn	Molasses	Silver
Cows	Polished beads (wampum)	Tobacco
Feathers	Pots	Tortoise shells
Glass	Red woodpecker scalps	Whale teeth

Source: Adapted from MONEY, BANKING, and FINANCIAL MARKETS, Third Edition, by Roger Miller and David VanHoose. Copyright © 2007 by Cengage Learning, Inc..

must go through several trades in order to obtain the desired dozen glasses—perhaps first trading shoes for jewelry, then jewelry for some pots and pans, and then the pots and pans for the desired glasses.

Money facilitates exchange by reducing the transaction costs associated with means-of-payment uncertainty. That is, the existence of money means that individuals no longer have to hold a diverse collection of goods as an exchange inventory. As a medium of exchange, money allows individuals to specialize in producing those goods for which they have a comparative advantage and to receive money payments for their labor. Money payments can then be exchanged for the fruits of other people's labor. The use of money as a medium of exchange permits more specialization and the inherent economic efficiencies that come with it (and hence greater economic growth).

Money as a Unit of Accounting

A **unit of accounting** is a way of placing a specific price on economic goods and services. It is the common denominator, the commonly recognized measure of value. The dollar is the unit of accounting in the United States. It is the yardstick that allows individuals easily to compare the relative value of goods and services. Accountants at the U.S. Department of Commerce use dollar prices to measure national income and domestic product, a business uses dollar prices to calculate profits and losses, and a typical household budgets regularly anticipated expenses using dollar prices as its unit of accounting.

Another way of describing money as a unit of accounting is to say that it serves as a *standard of value* that allows people to compare the relative worth of various goods and services. This allows for comparison shopping, for example.

Unit of accounting
A measure by which prices are expressed; the common denominator of the price system; a central property of money.

Money as a Store of Value

One of the most important functions of money is that it serves as a **store of value** or purchasing power. The money you have today can be set aside to purchase things later on. If you have $1,000 in your checking account, you can choose to spend it today on goods and services, spend it tomorrow, or spend it a month from now. In this way, money provides a way to transfer value (wealth) into the future.

Store of value
The ability to hold value over time; a necessary property of money.

Money as a Standard of Deferred Payment

The fourth function of the monetary unit is as a **standard of deferred payment.** This function involves the use of money both as a medium of exchange and as a unit of accounting. Debts are typically stated in terms of a unit of accounting, and they are paid with a monetary medium of exchange. That is to say, a debt is specified in a dollar amount and paid in currency (or by debit card or check). A corporate bond, for example, has a face value—the dollar value stated on it, which is to be paid upon maturity. The periodic interest payments on that corporate bond are specified and paid in dollars, and when the bond comes due (at maturity), the corporation pays the face value in dollars to the holder of the bond.

Standard of deferred payment
A property of an item that makes it desirable for use as a means of settling debts maturing in the future; an essential property of money.

Properties of Money

Money is an asset—something of value—that accounts for part of personal wealth. Wealth in the form of money can be exchanged for other assets, goods, or services. Although money is not the only form of wealth that can be exchanged for goods and services, it is the most widely and readily accepted one.

Money—The Most Liquid Asset

Money's attribute as the most readily tradable asset is called **liquidity.** We say that an asset is *liquid* when it can easily be acquired or disposed of without high transaction costs and with relative certainty as to its value. Money is by definition the most

Liquidity
The degree to which an asset can be acquired or disposed of without much danger of any intervening loss in *nominal* value and with small transaction costs. Money is the most liquid asset.

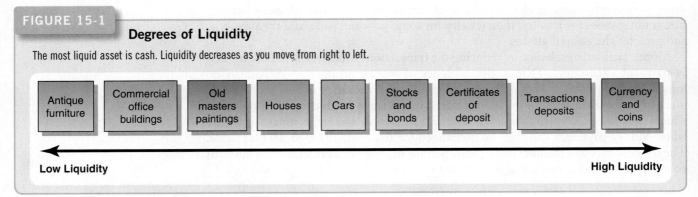

FIGURE 15-1

Degrees of Liquidity

The most liquid asset is cash. Liquidity decreases as you move from right to left.

| Antique furniture | Commercial office buildings | Old masters paintings | Houses | Cars | Stocks and bonds | Certificates of deposit | Transactions deposits | Currency and coins |

Low Liquidity ←——————————————————————————————→ **High Liquidity**

liquid asset. People can easily convert money to other asset forms. Therefore, most individuals hold at least a part of their wealth in the form of the most liquid of assets, money. You can see how assets rank in liquidity relative to one another in Figure 15-1 above.

When we hold money, however, we incur a cost for this advantage of liquidity. Because cash in your pocket and many checking or debit account balances do not earn interest, that cost is the interest yield that could have been obtained had the asset been held in another form—for example, in the form of stocks and bonds.

> *The cost of holding money (its opportunity cost) is measured by the alternative interest yield obtainable by holding some other asset.*

Monetary Standards, or What Backs Money

In the past, many different monetary standards have existed. For example, commodity money, which is a physical good that may be valued for other uses it provides, has been used (see Table 15-1 on page 320). The main forms of commodity money were gold and silver. Today, though, most people throughout the world accept coins, paper currency, and balances held on deposit as **transactions deposits** (debitable and checkable accounts with banks and other financial institutions) in exchange for items sold, including labor services.

But these forms of money raise a question: Why are we willing to accept as payment something that has no intrinsic value? After all, you could not sell checks or debit cards to very many producers for use as a raw material in manufacturing. The reason is that payments in the modern world arise from a **fiduciary monetary system.** This concept refers to the fact that the value of the payments rests on the public's confidence that such payments can be exchanged for goods and services. *Fiduciary* comes from the Latin *fiducia*, which means "trust" or "confidence." In our fiduciary monetary system, there is no legal requirement for money, in the form of currency or transactions deposits, to be convertible to a fixed quantity of gold, silver, or some other precious commodity. The bills are just pieces of paper. Coins have a value stamped on them that today is usually greater than the market value of the metal in them. Nevertheless, currency and transactions deposits are money because of their acceptability and predictability of value.

ACCEPTABILITY Transactions deposits and currency are money because they are accepted in exchange for goods and services. They are accepted because people have confidence that these items can later be exchanged for other goods and services. This confidence is based on the knowledge that such exchanges have occurred in the past without problems.

PREDICTABILITY OF VALUE Money retains its usefulness even if its purchasing power is declining year in and year out, as during periods of inflation, if it still retains the characteristic of predictability of value. If you anticipate that the inflation rate is

Transactions deposits

Checkable and debitable account balances in commercial banks and other types of financial institutions, such as credit unions and savings banks. Any accounts in financial institutions from which you can easily transmit debit-card and check payments without many restrictions.

Fiduciary monetary system

A system in which money is issued by the government and its value is based uniquely on the public's faith that the currency represents command over goods and services and will be accepted in payment for debts.

going to be around 3 percent during the next year, you know that any dollar you receive a year from now will have a purchasing power equal to 3 percent less than that same dollar today. Thus, you will not necessarily refuse to accept money in exchange simply because you know that its value will decline by the rate of inflation during the next year.

YOU ARE THERE

To learn about how private currencies are circulating widely in Brazil, read **Why a Currency Displaying a Giant Rodent Circulates in Brazil** on page 340.

QUICK QUIZ See page 345 for the. Review concepts from this section in MyEconLab.

Money is defined by its functions, which are as a _____ of _____, _____ of _____, _____ of _____, and _____ of _____.

Money is a highly _____ asset because it can be disposed of with low transaction costs and with relative certainty as to its value.

Modern nations have _____ monetary systems—national currencies are not convertible into a fixed quantity of a commodity such as gold or silver.

Money is accepted in exchange for goods and services because people have confidence that it can later be exchanged for other goods and services. In addition, money has _____ value.

Defining Money

Money is important. Changes in the total **money supply**—the amount of money in circulation—and changes in the rate at which the money supply increases or decreases affect important economic variables, such as the rate of inflation, interest rates, and (at least in the short run) employment and the level of real GDP. Economists have struggled to reach agreement about how to define and measure money, however. There are two basic approaches: the **transactions approach,** which stresses the role of money as a medium of exchange, and the **liquidity approach,** which stresses the role of money as a temporary store of value.

The Transactions Approach to Measuring Money: M1

Using the transactions approach to measuring money, the money supply consists of currency, transactions deposits, and traveler's checks not issued by banks. One key designation of the money supply, including currency, transactions deposits, and traveler's checks not issued by banks, is **M1.** The various elements of M1 for a typical year are presented in panel (a) of Figure 15-2 on the following page.

CURRENCY The largest component of U.S. currency is paper bills called Federal Reserve notes, which are designed and printed by the U.S. Bureau of Engraving and Printing. U.S. currency also consists of coins minted by the U.S. Treasury. Federal Reserve banks (to be discussed shortly) issue paper notes and coins throughout the U.S. banking system.

TRANSACTIONS DEPOSITS Individuals transfer ownership of deposits in financial institutions by using debit cards and checks. Hence, debitable and checkable transactions deposits are normally acceptable as a medium of exchange. The **depository institutions** that offer transactions deposits are numerous and include commercial banks and almost all **thrift institutions**—savings banks, savings and loan associations (S&Ls), and credit unions.

TRAVELER'S CHECKS Traveler's checks are paid for by the purchaser at the time of transfer. The total quantity of traveler's checks outstanding issued by institutions other than banks is part of the M1 money supply. American Express and other institutions issue traveler's checks.

Money supply
The amount of money in circulation.

Transactions approach
A method of measuring the money supply by looking at money as a medium of exchange.

Liquidity approach
A method of measuring the money supply by looking at money as a temporary store of value.

M1
The money supply, measured as the total value of currency plus transactions deposits plus traveler's checks not issued by banks.

Depository institutions
Financial institutions that accept deposits from savers and lend funds from those deposits out at interest.

Thrift institutions
Financial institutions that receive most of their funds from the savings of the public. They include savings banks, savings and loan associations, and credit unions.

Traveler's checks
Financial instruments obtained from a bank or a nonbanking organization and signed during purchase that can be used in payment upon a second signature by the purchaser.

FIGURE 15-2

Composition of the U.S. M1 and M2 Money Supply, 2013

Panel (a) shows estimates of the M1 money supply, of which the largest component (over 52 percent) is transactions deposits. M2 consists of M1 plus three other components, the most important of which is savings deposits at all depository institutions.

Sources: Federal Reserve Bulletin; Economic Indicators, various issues; author's estimates.

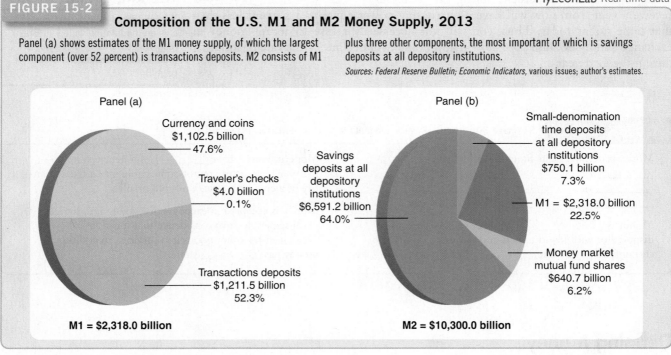

Panel (a)

Currency and coins
$1,102.5 billion
47.6%

Traveler's checks
$4.0 billion
0.1%

Transactions deposits
$1,211.5 billion
52.3%

M1 = $2,318.0 billion

Panel (b)

Savings deposits at all depository institutions
$6,591.2 billion
64.0%

Small-denomination time deposits at all depository institutions
$750.1 billion
7.3%

M1 = $2,318.0 billion
22.5%

Money market mutual fund shares
$640.7 billion
6.2%

M2 = $10,300.0 billion

The Liquidity Approach to Measuring Money: M2

The liquidity approach to defining and measuring the U.S. money supply views money as a temporary store of value and so includes all of M1 *plus* several other highly liquid assets. Panel (b) of Figure 15-2 above shows the components of **M2**—money as a temporary store of value. These components include the following:

M2

M1 plus (1) savings deposits at all depository institutions, (2) small-denomination time deposits, and (3) balances in retail money market mutual funds.

1. *Savings deposits.* Total *savings deposits*—deposits with no set maturities—are the largest component of the M2 money supply.

2. *Small-denomination time deposits.* With a *time deposit*, the funds must be left in a financial institution for a given period before they can be withdrawn without penalty. To be included in the M2 definition of the money supply, time deposits must be less than $100,000—hence, the designation *small-denomination time deposits*.

3. *Money market mutual fund balances.* Many individuals keep part of their assets in the form of shares in *money market mutual funds*—highly liquid funds that investment companies obtain from the public. All money market mutual fund balances except those held by large institutions (which typically use them more like large time deposits) are included in M2 because they are very liquid.

When all of these assets are added together, the result is M2, as shown in panel (b) of Figure 15-2.

For Federal Reserve data concerning the latest trends in the monetary aggregates, go to **www.econtoday.com/chap15** and click on "Money Stock Measures—H.6" under Money Stock and Reserve Balances.

OTHER MONEY SUPPLY DEFINITIONS Economists and other researchers have come up with additional definitions of money. Some businesspeople and policymakers prefer a monetary aggregate known as *MZM*. The MZM aggregate is the so-called money-at-zero-maturity money stock. Obtaining MZM entails adding to M1 those deposits without set maturities, such as savings deposits, that are included in M2. MZM includes *all* money market funds but excludes all deposits with fixed maturities, such as small-denomination time deposits.

The **money supply** can be defined in a variety of ways, depending on whether we use the transactions approach or the liquidity approach. Using the _____ approach, the money supply consists of currency, **transactions deposits,** and traveler's checks. This is called _____.

_____ deposits are any deposits in financial institutions from which the deposit owner can transfer funds using a debit card or checks.

When we add savings deposits, small-denomination time deposits, and retail money market mutual fund balances to _____, we obtain the measure known as _____.

Financial Intermediation and Banks

Most nations, including the United States, have a banking system that encompasses two types of institutions. One type consists of privately owned profit-seeking institutions, such as commercial banks and thrift institutions. The other type of institution is a **central bank,** which typically serves as a banker's bank and as a bank for the national treasury or finance ministry.

Direct versus Indirect Financing

When individuals choose to hold some of their savings in new bonds issued by a corporation, their purchases of the bonds are in effect direct loans to the business. This is an example of *direct finance*, in which people lend funds directly to a business. Business financing is not always direct. Individuals might choose instead to hold a time deposit at a bank. The bank may then lend to the same company. In this way, the same people can provide *indirect finance* to a business. The bank makes this possible by *intermediating* the financing of the company.

Financial Intermediation

Banks and other financial institutions are all in the same business—transferring funds from savers to investors. This process is known as **financial intermediation,** and its participants, such as banks and savings institutions, are **financial intermediaries.** The process of financial intermediation is illustrated in Figure 15-3 on the following page.

ASYMMETRIC INFORMATION, ADVERSE SELECTION, AND MORAL HAZARD Why might people wish to direct their funds through a bank instead of lending them directly to a business? One important reason is **asymmetric information**—the fact that the business may have better knowledge of its own current and future prospects than potential lenders do. For instance, the business may know that it intends to use borrowed funds for projects with a high risk of failure that would make repaying the loan difficult.

This potential for borrowers to use the borrowed funds in high-risk projects is known as **adverse selection.** Alternatively, a business that had intended to undertake low-risk projects may change management after receiving a loan, and the new managers may use the borrowed funds in riskier ways. The possibility that a borrower might engage in behavior that increases risk after borrowing funds is called **moral hazard.**

To minimize the possibility that a business might fail to repay a loan, people thinking about lending funds directly to the business must study the business carefully before making the loan, and they must continue to monitor its performance afterward. Alternatively, they can choose to avoid the trouble by holding deposits with financial intermediaries, which then specialize in evaluating the creditworthiness of business borrowers and in keeping tabs on their progress until loans are repaid. Thus, adverse selection and moral hazard both help explain why people use financial intermediaries.

Central bank
A banker's bank, usually an official institution that also serves as a bank for a nation's government treasury. Central banks normally regulate commercial banks.

Financial intermediation
The process by which financial institutions accept savings from businesses, households, and governments and lend the savings to other businesses, households, and governments.

Financial intermediaries
Institutions that transfer funds between ultimate lenders (savers) and ultimate borrowers.

Asymmetric information
Information possessed by one party in a financial transaction but not by the other party.

Adverse selection
The tendency for high-risk projects and clients to be overrepresented among borrowers.

Moral hazard
The possibility that a borrower might engage in riskier behavior after a loan has been obtained.

The Process of Financial Intermediation

The process of financial intermediation is depicted here. Note that ultimate lenders and ultimate borrowers are the same economic units—households, businesses, and governments—but not necessarily the same individuals. Whereas individual households can be net lenders or borrowers, households as an economic unit typically are net lenders. Specific businesses or governments similarly can be net lenders or borrowers. As economic units, both are net borrowers.

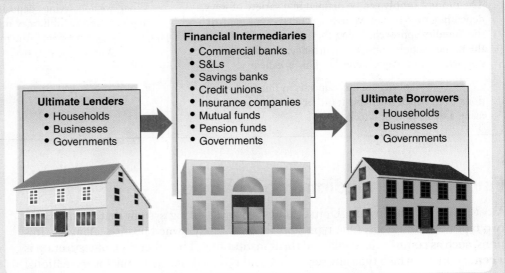

LARGER SCALE AND LOWER MANAGEMENT COSTS Another important reason that financial intermediaries exist is that they make it possible for many people to pool their funds, thereby increasing the size, or *scale*, of the total amount of savings managed by an intermediary. This centralization of management reduces costs and risks below the levels savers would incur if all were to manage their savings alone.

Pension fund companies, which are institutions that specialize in managing funds that individuals save for retirement, owe their existence largely to their abilities to provide such cost savings to individual savers. Likewise, *investment companies*, which are institutions that manage portfolios of financial instruments called mutual funds on behalf of shareholders, also exist largely because of cost savings from their greater scale of operations. In addition, *government-sponsored financial institutions*, such as the Federal National Mortgage Association, seek to reduce overall lending costs by pooling large volumes of funds from investors in order to buy groups of mortgage loans.

Liabilities
Amounts owed; the legal claims against a business or household by nonowners.

FINANCIAL INSTITUTION LIABILITIES AND ASSETS Every financial intermediary has its own sources of funds, which are **liabilities** of that institution. When you place $100 in your

Financial Intermediaries and Their Assets and Liabilities

Financial Intermediary	Assets	Liabilities
Commercial banks, savings and loan associations, savings banks, and credit unions	Car loans and other consumer debt, business loans, government securities, home mortgages	Transactions deposits, savings deposits, various other time deposits
Insurance companies	Mortgages, stocks, bonds, real estate	Insurance contracts, annuities, pension plans
Pension and retirement funds	Stocks, bonds, mortgages, time deposits	Pension plans
Money market mutual funds	Short-term credit instruments such as large-denomination certificates of deposit, Treasury bills, and high-grade commercial paper	Fund shares with limited checking privileges
Government-sponsored financial institutions	Home mortgages	Mortgage-backed securities issued to investors

transactions deposit at a bank, the bank creates a liability—it owes you $100—in exchange for the funds deposited. A commercial bank gets its funds from transactions and savings accounts, and an insurance company gets its funds from insurance policy premiums.

Each financial intermediary has a different primary use of its **assets**. For example, a credit union usually makes small consumer loans, whereas a savings bank makes mainly mortgage loans. Table 15-2 on the bottom of the facing page lists the assets and liabilities of typical financial intermediaries. Be aware, though, that the distinctions between different types of financial institutions are becoming more and more blurred. As laws and regulations change, there will be less need to make any distinction. All may ultimately be treated simply as financial intermediaries.

Assets
Amounts owned; all items to which a business or household holds legal claim.

How are online firms pooling funds to assist small-business entrepreneurs in obtaining loans when banks have rejected their requests?

EXAMPLE

Going Online for Credit When Bank Loans Dry Up

Today, a growing number of entrepreneurs who fail to receive loans from banks instead obtain credit from Internet-based companies such as Lending Club and Prosper Marketplace. These firms provide online forums for entrepreneurs to post detailed business plans along with the specific amounts of credit desired to try to achieve success. Individual savers can assess these plans and, if they wish, commit some of their own funds to help fund entrepreneurs' projects.

In exchange for service fees, the online firms pool these individual funding commitments into larger loan packages. For example, if an entrepreneur requests $15,000 in credit and 150 savers provide an average amount of $100 each, the online company collects the savers' funds and extends a loan to the entrepreneur. In this way, firms such as Lending Club and Prosper Marketplace act as financial intermediaries.

FOR CRITICAL THINKING
Why do you suppose that default rates on loans arranged by online firms tend to be substantially higher than default rates on bank loans?

Transmitting Payments via Debit-Card Transactions

Since 2006, the dollar volume of payments transmitted using debit cards has exceeded the value of checking transactions. To see how a debit-card transaction clears, take a look at Figure 15-4 on the next page. Suppose that Bank of America has provided a debit card to a college student named Jill Jones, who in turn uses the card to purchase $200 worth of clothing from Macy's, which has an account at Citibank. The debit-card transaction generates an electronic record, which the debit-card system transmits to Citibank.

The debit-card system also automatically uses the electronic record to determine the bank that issued the debit card used to purchase the clothing. It transmits this information to Bank of America. Then Bank of America verifies that Jill Jones is an account holder, deducts $200 from her transactions deposit account, and transmits these funds electronically, via the debit-card system, to Citibank. Finally, Citibank credits $200 to Macy's transactions deposit account, and payment for the clothing purchase is complete.

How can food-cart and farmers' market vendors accept debit cards today?

EXAMPLE

Vendors Use Smartphones to Process Debit-Card Purchases

A company called Square makes it possible for small retailers on the move, such as mobile food-cart and farmers' market vendors, to accept card payments. Square distributes plastic card-reading devices at no charge to owners of such businesses. The retailers can attach them to smartphones and thereby transform the devices into payment terminals. After a payment card is swiped through the device, the smartphone transmits payment information for Square to process, at a fee, to complete a purchase. In this way, Square enables sellers to move wherever buyers are located while broadening the means of payment that sellers can accept.

FOR CRITICAL THINKING
In what sense is a payment order sent using a smartphone economically indistinguishable from a payment order made via a check?

FIGURE 15-4

How a Debit-Card Transaction Clears

A college student named Jill Jones uses a debit card issued by Bank of America to purchase clothing valued at $200 from Macy's, which has an account with Citibank. The debit-card transaction creates an electronic record that is transmitted to Citibank. The debit-card system forwards this record to Bank of America, which deducts $200 from Jill Jones's transactions deposit account. Then the debit-card system transmits the $200 payment to Citibank, which credits the $200 to Macy's account.

QUICK QUIZ See page 345 for the answers. Review concepts from this section in MyEconLab.

_____ intermediaries, including depository institutions such as commercial banks and savings institutions, insurance companies, mutual funds, and pension funds, transfer funds from ultimate lenders (savers) to ultimate borrowers.

Financial intermediaries specialize in tackling problems of _____ information. They address the _____ _____ problem by carefully reviewing the creditworthiness of loan applicants, and they deal with the _____ _____ problem by monitoring borrowers after they receive loans. Many financial intermediaries also take advantage of cost reductions arising from the centralized management of funds pooled from the savings of many individuals.

The Federal Reserve System: The U.S. Central Bank

The Federal Reserve System, which serves as the nation's central bank, is one of the key banking institutions in the United States. It is partly a creature of government and partly privately directed.

The Federal Reserve System

The Fed
The Federal Reserve System; the central bank of the United States.

The Federal Reserve System, also known simply as **the Fed,** is the most important regulatory agency in the U.S. monetary system and is usually considered the monetary authority. The Fed was established by the Federal Reserve Act, signed on December 13, 1913, by President Woodrow Wilson.

FIGURE 15-5

Organization of the Federal Reserve System

The 12 Federal Reserve district banks are headed by 12 separate presidents. The main authority of the Fed resides with the Board of Governors of the Federal Reserve System, whose seven members are appointed for 14-year terms by the president of the United States and confirmed by the Senate. Open market operations are carried out through the Federal Open

Market Committee (FOMC), consisting of the seven members of the Board of Governors plus five presidents of the district banks (always including the president of the New York bank, with the others rotating).

Source: Board of Governors of the Federal Reserve System, *The Federal Reserve System: Purposes and Functions*, 7th ed. (Washington, D.C., 1984), p. 5.

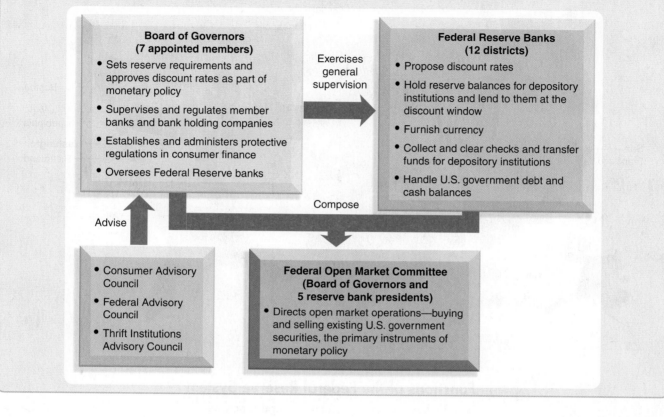

ORGANIZATION OF THE FEDERAL RESERVE SYSTEM Figure 15-5 above shows how the Federal Reserve System is organized. It is managed by the Board of Governors, composed of seven full-time members appointed by the U.S. president with the approval of the Senate. The chair of the Board of Governors is the leading official of the Board of Governors and of the Federal Reserve System. Since 2006, Ben Bernanke has held this position.

The 12 Federal Reserve district banks have a total of 25 branches. The boundaries of the 12 Federal Reserve districts and the cities in which Federal Reserve banks are located are shown in Figure 15-6 on the following page. The Federal Open Market Committee (FOMC) determines the future growth of the money supply and other important variables. This committee is composed of the members of the Board of Governors, the president of the New York Federal Reserve Bank, and presidents of four other Federal Reserve banks, rotated periodically. The chair of the Board of Governors also chairs the FOMC.

DEPOSITORY INSTITUTIONS Depository institutions—all financial institutions that accept deposits—comprise our monetary system consisting of nearly 6,500 commercial banks, 1,100 savings and loan associations and savings banks, and about 8,000 credit unions. All depository institutions may purchase services from the Federal Reserve System on an equal basis. Also, almost all depository institutions are required to keep a certain percentage of their deposits in reserve at the Federal Reserve district banks or as vault cash. This percentage depends on the bank's volume of business.

FIGURE 15-6

The Federal Reserve System

The Federal Reserve System is divided into 12 districts, each served by one of the Federal Reserve district banks, located in the cities indicated. The Board of Governors meets in Washington, D.C.

Source: Board of Governors of the Federal Reserve System.

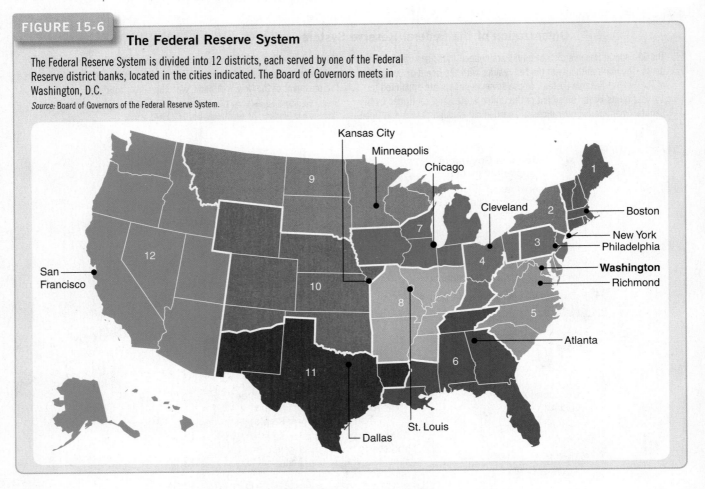

Functions of the Federal Reserve System

The Federal Reserve performs several functions:

1. ***The Fed supplies the economy with fiduciary currency.*** The Federal Reserve banks supply the economy with paper currency called Federal Reserve notes. Even though all Federal Reserve notes are printed at the Bureau of Engraving and Printing in Washington, D.C., each note is assigned a code indicating which of the 12 Federal Reserve banks first introduced the note into circulation. Moreover, each of these notes is an obligation (liability) of the Federal Reserve System, *not* the U.S. Treasury.

2. ***The Fed holds depository institutions' reserves and provides payment-clearing systems.*** The 12 Federal Reserve district banks hold the reserves (other than vault cash) of depository institutions. Depository institutions are required by law to keep a certain percentage of their transactions deposits as reserves. Even if they weren't required to do so by law, they would still wish to keep some reserves on which they can draw funds as needed for expected and unexpected transactions. The Federal Reserve System also operates systems for transmitting and clearing payments among depository institutions' reserve accounts. Federal Reserve banks all offer check-clearing services and electronic payments transfer services to commercial banks, savings institutions, and credit unions.

3. ***The Fed acts as the government's fiscal agent.*** The Federal Reserve is the primary banker and fiscal agent for the federal government. Consequently, the U.S. Treasury has a transactions account with the Federal Reserve, which helps the government collect certain tax revenues and aids in the purchase and sale of government securities.

4. ***The Fed supervises depository institutions.*** The Fed (along with the Comptroller of the Currency, the Federal Deposit Insurance Corporation, the Office of Thrift

Supervision in the Treasury Department, and the National Credit Union Administration) is a supervisor and regulator of depository institutions.

5. ***The Fed conducts monetary policy.*** Perhaps the Fed's most important task is to regulate the nation's money supply. To understand how the Fed manages the money supply, we must examine more closely its reserve-holding function and the way in which depository institutions aid in expansion and contraction of the money supply. We will do this later in this chapter.

6. ***The Fed intervenes in foreign currency markets.*** Sometimes the Fed attempts to keep the value of the dollar from changing. It does this by buying and selling U.S. dollars in foreign exchange markets. You will read more about this important topic in Chapter 33.

7. ***The Fed acts as the "lender of last resort."*** From time to time, an individual bank that is otherwise in good financial condition may be temporarily low on cash and other liquid assets. Such an institution is said to be illiquid. A key justification for the formation of the Federal Reserve System was that the Fed would stand ready to prevent temporarily illiquid banks from failing by serving as the financial system's **lender of last resort.** In this capacity, the Fed stands ready to lend to any temporarily illiquid but otherwise financially healthy banking institution. In this way, the Fed seeks to prevent illiquidity at a few banks from leading to a general loss of depositors' confidence in the overall soundness of the banking system.

Lender of last resort
The Federal Reserve's role as an institution that is willing and able to lend to a temporarily illiquid bank that is otherwise in good financial condition to prevent the bank's illiquid position from leading to a general loss of confidence in that bank or in others.

What institutions, to the surprise of many U.S. residents, were among the largest recipients of Fed lender-of-last-resort loans at the height of the financial panic of the late 2000s?

POLICY EXAMPLE

The Fed Becomes a Lender of Last Resort for Foreign Banks

During the financial meltdown that stretched across several months in the late 2000s, the Federal Reserve extended more than $3 trillion in emergency loans to financial institutions that it judged to be illiquid but otherwise financially healthy. What the Fed did not reveal until years later, however, was that emergency loans totaling hundreds of billions of dollars went to private financial institutions based outside the United States. The Fed also extended more than $600 billion in additional credit to a number of central banks around the globe. Thus,

in the midst of the financial panic of 2008 and 2009, the Fed became a key lender of last resort for many financial institutions located outside the United States.

FOR CRITICAL THINKING

How do you suppose the fact that foreign banks owed substantial funds to U.S. banks influenced the Federal Reserve's decision to lend to these institutions?

QUICK QUIZ   See page 345 for the answers. Review concepts from this section in MyEconLab.

The central bank in the United States is the _____ _____ _____, which was established on December 13, 1913.

There are 12 Federal Reserve district banks, with 25 branches. The Federal Reserve System is managed by the _____ of _____ in Washington, D.C. The Fed interacts with almost all depository institutions in the United States, most of which must keep a certain percentage of their transactions deposits on reserve with the Fed. The Fed serves as the chief regulatory agency for all

depository institutions that have Federal Reserve System membership.

The functions of the Federal Reserve System are to supply fiduciary _____, provide payment-clearing services, hold depository institution _____, act as the government's fiscal agent, supervise depository institutions, regulate the supply of money, intervene in foreign currency markets, and act as the _____ of _____ _____.

Fractional Reserve Banking, the Federal Reserve, and the Money Supply

As early as 1000 B.C., uncoined gold and silver were being used as money in Mesopotamia. Goldsmiths weighed and assessed the purity of those metals. Later they started issuing paper notes indicating that the bearers held gold or silver of given weights and purity on deposit with the goldsmith. These notes could be transferred in exchange for goods and became the first paper currency. The gold and silver on deposit with the goldsmiths were the first bank deposits. Eventually, goldsmiths realized that inflows of gold and silver for deposit always exceeded the average amount of gold and silver withdrawn at any given time—often by a predictable ratio.

These goldsmiths started making loans by issuing to borrowers paper notes that exceeded in value the amount of gold and silver the goldsmiths actually kept on hand. They charged interest on these loans. This constituted the earliest form of what is now called **fractional reserve banking.** We know that goldsmiths operated this way in Delphi, Didyma, and Olympia in Greece as early as the seventh century B.C. In Athens, fractional reserve banking was well developed by the sixth century B.C.

Depository Institution Reserves

In a fractional reserve banking system, banks do not keep sufficient funds on hand to cover 100 percent of their depositors' accounts. And the funds held by depository institutions in the United States are not kept in gold and silver, as they were with the early goldsmiths. Instead, the funds are held as **reserves** in the form of cash in banks' vaults and deposits that banks hold on deposit with Federal Reserve district banks.

The fraction of deposits that banks hold as reserves is called the **reserve ratio.** There are two determinants of the size of this ratio. One is the quantity of reserves that the Federal Reserve requires banks to hold, which are called *required reserves.* The other determinant of the reserve ratio is whatever additional amount of reserves that banks voluntarily hold, known as *excess reserves*.

To show the relationship between reserves and deposits at an individual bank, let's examine the **balance sheet,** or statement of assets owned and liabilities (amounts owed to others), for a particular depository institution. Balance Sheet 15-1 below displays a balance sheet for a depository institution called Typical Bank. Liabilities for this institution consist solely of $1 million in transactions deposits. Assets consist of $100,000 in reserves and $900,000 in loans to customers. Total assets of $1 million equal total liabilities of $1 million. Because Typical Bank has $100,000 of reserves and $1 million of transactions deposits, its reserve ratio is 10 percent. Thus, Typical Bank is part of a system of fractional reserve banking, in which it holds only 10 percent of its deposits as reserves.

Fractional reserve banking
A system in which depository institutions hold reserves that are less than the amount of total deposits.

Reserves
In the U.S. Federal Reserve System, deposits held by Federal Reserve district banks for depository institutions, plus depository institutions' vault cash.

Reserve ratio
The fraction of transactions deposits that banks hold as reserves.

Balance sheet
A statement of the assets and liabilities of any business entity, including financial institutions and the Federal Reserve System. Assets are what is owned; liabilities are what is owed.

BALANCE SHEET 15-1

Typical Bank

Assets		Liabilities	
Reserves	$100,000	Transactions deposits	$1,000,000
Loans	$900,000		
Total	$1,000,000	Total	$1,000,000

Fractional Reserve Banking and Money Expansion

Under fractional reserve banking, the Federal Reserve can add to the quantity of money in circulation by bringing about an expansion of deposits within the banking system. To understand how the Fed can create money within the banking system, we must look at how depository institutions respond to Fed actions that increase reserves in the entire system.

Let's consider the effect of a Fed **open market operation,** which is a Fed purchase or sale of existing U.S. government securities in the open market—the private secondary market in which people exchange securities that have not yet matured. Assume that the Fed engaged in an *open market purchase* by buying a $100,000 U.S. government security from a bond dealer. The Fed does this by electronically transferring $100,000 to the bond dealer's transactions deposit account at Bank 1. Thus, as shown in Balance Sheet 15-2 below, Bank 1's transactions deposit liabilities increase by $100,000.

Let's suppose that the reserve ratio for Bank 1 and all other depository institutions is 10 percent. As shown in Balance Sheet 15-2, therefore, Bank 1 responds to this $100,000 increase in transactions deposits by adding 10 percent of this amount, or $10,000, to its reserves. The bank allocates the remaining $90,000 of additional deposits to new loans, so its loans increase by $90,000.

Open market operations
The purchase and sale of existing U.S. government securities (such as bonds) in the open private market by the Federal Reserve System.

BALANCE SHEET 15-2

Bank 1

Assets		Liabilities	
Reserves	+$10,000	Transactions deposits	+$100,000
Loans	+$90,000		
Total	+$100,000	Total	+$100,000

EFFECT ON THE MONEY SUPPLY At this point, the Fed's purchase of a $100,000 U.S. government security from a bond dealer has increased the money supply immediately by $100,000. This occurs because transactions deposits held by the public—bond dealers are part of the public—are part of the money supply. Hence, the addition of $100,000 to deposits with Bank 1, with no corresponding deposit reduction elsewhere in the banking system, raises the money supply by $100,000. (If another member of the public, instead of the Fed, had purchased the bond, that person's transactions deposit would have been reduced by $100,000, so there would have been no change in the money supply.)

The process of money creation does not stop here. The borrower who receives the $90,000 loan from Bank 1 will spend these funds, which will then be deposited in other banks. In this instance, suppose that the $90,000 spent by Bank 1's borrower is deposited in a transactions deposit account at Bank 2. At this bank, as shown in Balance Sheet 15-3 below, transactions deposits and hence the money supply increase by $90,000. Bank 2 adds 10 percent of these deposits, or $9,000, to its reserves. It uses the remaining $81,000 of new deposits to add $81,000 to its loans.

BALANCE SHEET 15-3

Bank 2

Assets		Liabilities	
Reserves	+$9,000	Transactions deposits	+$90,000
Loans	+$81,000		
Total	+$90,000	Total	+$90,000

CONTINUATION OF THE DEPOSIT CREATION PROCESS Look at Bank 3's account in Balance Sheet 15-4 on the following page. Assume that the borrower receiving the $81,000 loan from Bank 2 spends these funds, which then are deposited in an account at Bank 3.

Transactions deposits and the money supply increase by $81,000. Reserves of Bank 3 rise by 10 percent of this amount, or $8,100. Bank 3 uses the rest of the newly deposited funds, or $72,900, to increase its loans.

BALANCE SHEET 15-4

Bank 3

Assets		Liabilities	
Reserves	+$8,100	Transactions deposits	+$81,000
Loans	+$72,900		
Total	+$81,000	Total	+$81,000

This process continues to Banks 4, 5, 6, and so forth. Each bank obtains smaller and smaller increases in deposits because banks hold 10 percent of new deposits as reserves. Thus, each succeeding depository institution makes correspondingly smaller loans. Table 15-3 below shows new deposits, reserves, and loans for the remaining depository institutions.

EFFECT ON TOTAL DEPOSITS AND THE MONEY SUPPLY In this example, deposits and the money supply increased initially by the $100,000 that the Fed paid the bond dealer in exchange for a U.S. government security. Deposits and the money supply were further increased by a $90,000 deposit in Bank 2, and they were again increased by an $81,000 deposit in Bank 3. Eventually, total deposits and the money supply increase by $1 million, as shown in Table 15-3. This $1 million expansion of deposits and the money supply consists of the original $100,000 created by the Fed, plus an extra $900,000 generated by deposit-creating bank loans. The deposit creation process is portrayed graphically in Figure 15-7 on the facing page.

You should be able to work through the foregoing example to show the reverse process when there is a *decrease* in reserves because the Fed engages in an *open market sale* by selling a $100,000 U.S. government security. The result is a multiple contraction of deposits and, therefore, of the total money supply in circulation.

The Money Multiplier

In the example just given, a $100,000 increase in reserves generated by the Fed's purchase of a security yielded a $1 million increase in transactions deposits and, hence, the money supply. Thus, deposits and the money supply increased by a multiple of

TABLE 15-3

Maximum Money Creation with 10 Percent Reserve Ratio

This table shows the maximum new loans that banks can make, given the Fed's electronic transfer of $100,000 to a transactions deposit account at Bank 1. The reserve ratio is 10 percent.

Bank	New Deposits	New Reserves	Maximum New Loans
1	$100,000 (from Fed)	$10,000	$90,000
2	90,000	9,000	81,000
3	81,000	8,100	72,900
4	72,900	7,290	65,610
.	.	.	.
.	.	.	.
.	.	.	.
All other banks	656,100	65,610	590,490
Totals	$1,000,000	$100,000	$900,000

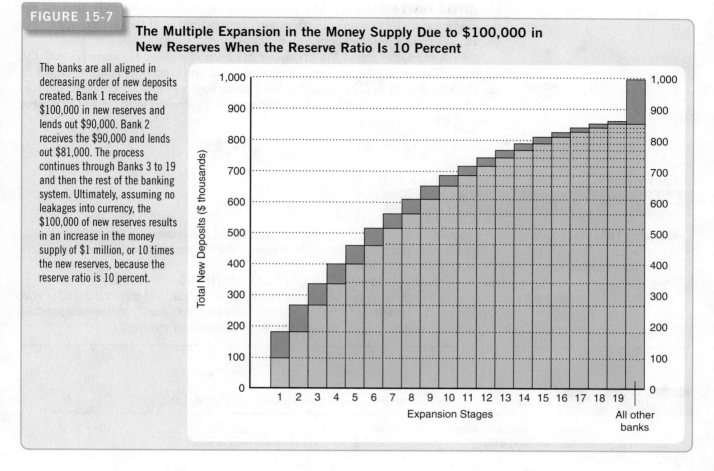

FIGURE 15-7

The Multiple Expansion in the Money Supply Due to $100,000 in New Reserves When the Reserve Ratio Is 10 Percent

The banks are all aligned in decreasing order of new deposits created. Bank 1 receives the $100,000 in new reserves and lends out $90,000. Bank 2 receives the $90,000 and lends out $81,000. The process continues through Banks 3 to 19 and then the rest of the banking system. Ultimately, assuming no leakages into currency, the $100,000 of new reserves results in an increase in the money supply of $1 million, or 10 times the new reserves, because the reserve ratio is 10 percent.

10 times the initial $100,000 increase in overall reserves. Conversely, a $100,000 decrease in reserves generated by a Fed sale of a security will yield a decrease in total deposits of $1 million—that is, a multiple of 10 times the initial $100,000 decrease in overall reserves.

We can now make a generalization about the extent to which the total money supply will change when the banking system's reserves are increased or decreased. The **money multiplier** gives the change in the money supply due to a change in reserves. In our example, the value of the money multiplier is 10.

POTENTIAL VERSUS ACTUAL MONEY MULTIPLIERS If we assume, as in our example, that all loan proceeds are deposited with banks, we obtain the **potential money multiplier**— the *maximum* possible value of the money multiplier:

$$\text{Potential money multiplier} = \frac{1}{\text{reserve ratio}}$$

That is, the potential money multiplier is equal to 1 divided by the fraction of transactions deposits that banks hold as reserves. In our example, the reserve ratio was 10 percent, or 0.10 expressed as a decimal fraction. Thus, in the example the value of the potential money multiplier was equal to 1 divided by 0.10, which equals 10.

What happens if the entire amount of a loan from a depository institution is not redeposited? When borrowers want to hold a portion of their loans as currency outside the banking system, these funds cannot be held by banks as reserves from which to make loans. The greater the amount of cash leakage, the smaller the *actual* money multiplier. Typically, borrowers do hold a portion of loan proceeds as currency, so the actual money multiplier usually is smaller than the potential money multiplier.

Money multiplier
A number that, when multiplied by a change in reserves in the banking system, yields the resulting change in the money supply.

Potential money multiplier
The reciprocal of the reserve ratio, assuming no leakages into currency. It is equal to 1 divided by the reserve ratio.

REAL-WORLD MONEY MULTIPLIERS The potential money multiplier is rarely attained for the banking system as a whole. Furthermore, each definition of the money supply, M1 or M2, will yield a different actual money multiplier.

In most years, the actual M1 multiplier has been in a range between 1.5 and 2.0. The actual M2 multiplier showed an upward trend until recently, rising from 6.5 in the 1960s to over 12 in the mid-2000s. Since then, however, it has dropped to about 6.

What was the ultimate effect of a steady stream of increases in the required reserve ratio for China's banking system?

INTERNATIONAL POLICY EXAMPLE

Seeking to Slash the Money Multiplier in China

Most central banks only rarely change required reserve ratios for bank deposits. The Federal Reserve, for instance, last changed the required reserve ratio in 1990. Nevertheless, China's central bank, the People's Bank of China, raised its required reserve ratio a number of times during the early 2010s, including more than a dozen increases during a single two-year interval. The cumulative effect of these increases was that the average required reserve ratio exceeded 20 percent—nearly twice its initial value.

As a result, the potential and actual money multipliers for China's banking system fell to approximately 50 percent of their original levels.

FOR CRITICAL THINKING
If the People's Bank of China increases bank reserves by 100 billion yuan, by how many fewer yuan will China's quantity of money now potentially expand? (Hint: What is the new money multiplier?)

QUICK QUIZ See page 345 for the answers. Review concepts from this section in MyEconLab.

_____ of depository institutions consist of their vault cash and deposits that they hold with _____ _____ district banks.

The fraction of transactions deposit liabilities that depository institutions hold as reserves is the _____ _____.

The _____ _____ _____ is equal to 1 divided by the reserve ratio.

Federal Deposit Insurance

As you have seen, fractional reserve banking enables the Federal Reserve to use an open market purchase (or sale) of U.S. government bonds to generate an expansion (or contraction) of deposits. The change in the money supply is a multiple of the open market purchase (or sale). Another effect of fractional reserve banking is to make depository institutions somewhat fragile. After all, the institutions have only a fraction of reserves on hand to honor their depositors' requests for withdrawals.

If many depositors simultaneously rush to their bank to withdraw all of their transactions and time deposits—a phenomenon called a **bank run**—the bank would be unable to satisfy their requests. The result would be the failure of that depository institution. Widespread bank runs could lead to the failure of many institutions.

Bank run
Attempt by many of a bank's depositors to convert transactions and time deposits into currency out of fear that the bank's liabilities may exceed its assets.

Seeking to Limit Bank Failures with Deposit Insurance

When businesses fail, they create hardships for creditors, owners, and customers. But when a depository institution fails, an even greater hardship results, because many individuals and businesses depend on the safety and security of banks. As Figure 15-8 on the facing page shows, during the 1920s an average of about 600 banks failed each year. In the early 1930s, during the Great Depression, that average soared to nearly 3,000 failures each year.

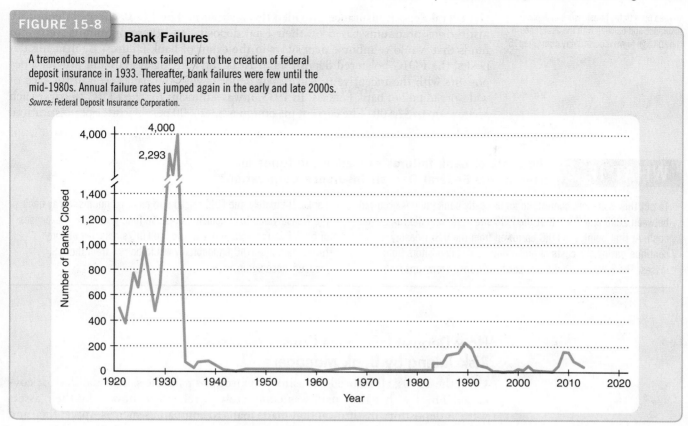

FIGURE 15-8

Bank Failures

A tremendous number of banks failed prior to the creation of federal deposit insurance in 1933. Thereafter, bank failures were few until the mid-1980s. Annual failure rates jumped again in the early and late 2000s.

Source: Federal Deposit Insurance Corporation.

In 1933, at the height of these bank failures, the **Federal Deposit Insurance Corporation (FDIC)** was founded to insure the funds of depositors and remove the reason for ruinous runs on banks. In 1934, federal deposit insurance was extended to deposits in savings and loan associations and mutual savings banks, and in 1971 it was offered for deposits in credit unions.

As can be seen in Figure 15-8 above, bank failure rates dropped dramatically after passage of the early federal legislation. The long period from 1935 until the 1980s was relatively quiet. From World War II to 1984, fewer than nine banks failed per year. From 1995 until 2008, failures again averaged about nine per year. Since 2009, however, more than 400 banks have failed, and hundreds more are still in danger of failing. We will examine the reasons for this shortly. But first we need to understand how deposit insurance works.

Federal Deposit Insurance Corporation (FDIC)
A government agency that insures the deposits held in banks and most other depository institutions. All U.S. banks are insured this way.

The Rationale for Deposit Insurance

Consider the following scenario. A bank begins to look shaky. Its assets do not seem sufficient to cover its liabilities. If the bank has no deposit insurance, depositors in this bank (and any banks associated with it) will all want to withdraw their funds from the bank at the same time. Their concern is that this shaky bank will not have enough assets to return their deposits to them in the form of currency.

Indeed, this is what happens in a bank failure when insurance doesn't exist. Just as when a regular business fails, the creditors of the bank may not all get paid, or if they do, they will get paid less than 100 percent of what they are owed. Depositors are creditors of a bank because their funds are on loan to the bank. As explained earlier, however, banks do not hold 100 percent of their depositors' funds as cash. Instead, banks lend out most of their deposit funds to borrowers. Consequently, all depositors cannot withdraw all their funds simultaneously. Hence, the intent of the legislation enacted in the 1930s was to assure depositors that they could have their deposits converted into cash when they wished, no matter how serious the financial situation of the bank.

To keep up with the latest issues in deposit insurance and banking with the assistance of the FDIC, go to www.econtoday.com/chap15.

Federal deposit insurance provided this assurance. The FDIC charged depository institutions premiums based on their total deposits, and these premiums went into funds that would reimburse depositors in the event of bank failures. By insuring deposits, the FDIC bolstered depositors' trust in the banking system and provided depositors with the incentive to leave their deposits with the bank, even in the face of widespread talk of bank failures. In 1933, it was sufficient for the FDIC to cover each account up to $2,500. The current maximum is $250,000 per depositor per institution.

WHAT IF... the costs of bank failures exceeded the funds on hand at the Federal Deposit Insurance Corporation?

To put this issue into context, so many costly bank failures occurred between 2008 and 2010 that the FDIC's reserve fund did run out of cash. At that point, the FDIC borrowed from the U.S. Treasury to continue paying the costs of protecting banks' depositors from losses. The FDIC raised more deposit insurance premiums from banks. Ultimately, the FDIC raised sufficient premiums to pay back the Treasury and to replenish its reserve fund gradually. If expenses of bank failures were to rise above the FDIC's reserves at some future date, the FDIC undoubtedly would borrow from the U.S. Treasury once again.

How Deposit Insurance Causes Increased Risk Taking by Bank Managers

Until the 1990s, all insured depository institutions paid the same small fee for coverage. The fee that they paid was completely unrelated to how risky their assets were. A depository institution that made loans to companies such as Apple, Inc., and Google, Inc. paid the same deposit insurance premium as another depository institution that made loans (at higher interest rates) to the governments of developing countries that were teetering on the brink of financial collapse.

Although deposit insurance premiums for a while were adjusted somewhat in response to the riskiness of a depository institution's assets, they never reflected all of the relative risk. Indeed, between the late 1990s and the late 2000s, very few depository institutions paid *any* deposit insurance premiums. This lack of correlation between risk and premiums can be considered a fundamental flaw in the deposit insurance scheme. Because bank managers do not have to pay higher insurance premiums when they make riskier loans, they have an incentive to invest in more assets of higher yield, and therefore necessarily higher risk, than they would if there were no deposit insurance.

ARTIFICIALLY LOW INSURANCE PREMIUMS The problem with the insurance scheme is that the premium rate is artificially low. Depository institution managers are able to obtain deposits at less than full cost (because depositors will accept a lower interest payment on insured deposits). Consequently, managers can increase their profits by using insured deposits to purchase higher-yield, higher-risk assets. The gains to risk taking accrue to the managers and stockholders of the depository institutions. The losses go to the deposit insurer (and, as we will see, ultimately to taxpayers).

A REGULATORY SOLUTION To combat these flaws in the financial industry and in the deposit insurance system, a vast regulatory apparatus oversees depository institutions. The FDIC and other federal deposit insurance agencies possess regulatory powers to offset the risk-taking temptations to depository institution managers.

These regulatory powers include the ability to require higher capital investment, to regulate, examine, and supervise bank affairs, and to enforce regulatory decisions. Higher capital requirements were imposed in the early 1990s and then adjusted somewhat beginning in 2000, but the recent jump in bank failures reveals that basic flaws remain.

Deposit Insurance, Adverse Selection, and Moral Hazard

As a deposit insurer, the FDIC effectively acts as a government-run insurance company. This means that the FDIC's operations expose the federal government to the same kinds of asymmetric information problems that other financial intermediaries face.

ADVERSE SELECTION IN DEPOSIT INSURANCE One of these problems is *adverse selection*, which is often a problem when insurance is involved because people or firms that are relatively poor risks are sometimes able to disguise that fact from insurers. It is instructive to examine the way this works with the deposit insurance provided by the FDIC. Deposit insurance shields depositors from the potential adverse effects of risky decisions and so makes depositors willing to accept riskier investment strategies by their banks. Clearly, protection of depositors from risks encourages more high-flying, risk-loving entrepreneurs to become managers of banks.

Moreover, because depositors have so little incentive to monitor the activities of insured banks, it is also likely that the insurance actually encourages outright crooks—embezzlers and con artists—to enter the industry. The consequences for the FDIC—and for taxpayers—are larger losses.

MORAL HAZARD IN DEPOSIT INSURANCE Moral hazard is also an important phenomenon in the presence of insurance contracts, such as the deposit insurance provided by the FDIC. Insured depositors know that they will not suffer losses if their bank fails. Hence, they have little incentive to monitor their bank's investment activities or to punish their bank by withdrawing their funds if the bank assumes too much risk. This means that insured banks have incentives to take on more risks than they otherwise would.

Can Deposit Insurance Be Reformed?

Since 2005, Congress has sought to reform federal deposit insurance. These efforts are still under way.

A REFORM EFFORT THAT CAME TOO LATE The Federal Deposit Insurance Reform Act of 2005 aimed to reform federal deposit insurance. On the one hand, this legislation expanded deposit insurance coverage and potentially added to the system's moral hazard problems. It increased deposit insurance coverage for Individual Retirement Accounts (IRAs) offered by depository institutions from $100,000 to $250,000 and authorized the FDIC to periodically adjust the insurance limit on all deposits to reflect inflation.

On the other hand, the act provided the FDIC with improved tools for addressing moral hazard risks. The law changed a rule that had prevented the FDIC from charging deposit insurance premiums if total insurance funds exceeded 1.25 percent of all insured deposits. This limit had enabled practically all U.S. depository institutions to avoid paying deposit insurance premiums for about a decade. Now the FDIC can adjust deposit insurance premiums at any time.

A NEW STRUCTURAL REFORM IN PROGRESS During the banking troubles of the late 2000s, Congress sought to increase the public's confidence in depository institutions by extending coverage to virtually all liabilities in the banking system. Although this move succeeded in boosting trust in banks, it also expanded the scope of deposit insurance. To reflect this fact, in late 2010 the FDIC altered the structure for deposit insurance premiums. The FDIC now assesses premium rates on banks' total liabilities—that is, the banks' deposits plus their borrowings from other sources.

The FDIC also raised its premium rates. Because the base for assessing premiums and the premium rates are both higher, the FDIC is now collecting premiums and adding to its reserve fund at a faster pace. Nevertheless, most economists agree that, on net, the FDIC's exposure to moral hazard risks has increased considerably in recent years.

To limit the fallout from systemwide failures and bank runs, Congress created the _____ _____ _____ _____ in 1933. Since the advent of federal deposit insurance, there have been no true bank runs at federally insured banks.

Federal insurance of bank deposits insulates depositors from risks, so depositors are _____ concerned about riskier investment strategies by depository institutions. Thus, bank managers have an incentive to invest in _____ assets to make _____ rates of return.

On the one hand, the Federal Deposit Insurance Reform Act of 2005 expanded the _____ hazard risks associated with deposit insurance by increasing limits for insured retirement deposits and indexing limits for other deposits to inflation. On the other hand, the law granted the FDIC greater discretion to assess risk-based deposit insurance _____ intended to restrain _____ hazard risks.

YOU ARE THERE

Why a Currency Displaying a Giant Rodent Circulates in Brazil

What induces firms in Silva Jardim, Brazil, to accept a private regional money called the *capivari*—named for the capybara, a pig-sized rodent common in a local river—in payment for goods and services? Roseanne Augusto, the manager of a hardware store, offers a simple answer: "It brings customers through the door."

The *capivari* that Augusto accepts at her store is one of 63 circulating private currencies in Brazil. Each currency's value is based on Brazil's official currency, the *real* (with multiple units called *reais*). In Silva Jardim, a local bank holds, on deposit, an amount of *reais* equal to the number of *capivaris* placed into circulation. Merchants such as Augusto's retail establishment offer price discounts to customers who pay with the private *capivaris* instead of the official *reais*. Consequently, people who use the *capivari* add "discount coupon" to the currency's function as a

medium of exchange. Indeed, for Silva Jardim consumers, this discount is the only advantage of the *capivari* over the government's *real*. For sellers, Augusto's statement above sums up the key advantage: Consumers are willing to use the currency to buy enough items to raise sales by more than the discounts offered by the sellers when they accept the currency.

Critical Thinking Questions

1. If price tags in Augusto's retail store display prices in terms of *capivaris,* what function does the currency fulfill?

2. When Silva Jardim residents set *capivari* notes aside today for possible use a few weeks from now, what function does the currency fulfill?

CONCEPTS APPLIED

▶ Balance Sheet

▶ Net Worth

▶ Fractional Reserve Banking

ISSUES & APPLICATIONS

Bankers Are Not Sure That They Want More Deposits

Between the early 1960s and late 2000s, bankers sought to raise and lend out more deposit funds. Today, however, a number of banks have stopped trying to attract more deposits. A few are even actively discouraging deposits by charging customers fees if they deposit "too many" funds. Why have bankers' views about the desirability of increased deposits shifted so dramatically in recent years?

Low Returns on Lending

One key reason that banks have soured on deposits is that earnings they can anticipate from lending deposit funds are now very low. In today's dampened U.S. economy, many fewer households and firms are seeking credit than in years past. As a consequence, banks have been competing with one another for a dwindling set of borrowers, and they have bid market interest rates on bank loans downward.

Thus, existing deposits are now yielding lower returns for banks. This fact gives them less incentive to seek out more deposits from current or new customers.

Higher Deposit Insurance Premiums

Even as banks' returns from lending deposit funds have dropped, the costs they must pay for deposits have increased. Since 2006, the premium rate that banks must pay the Federal Deposit Insurance Corporation has jumped from close to zero to more than $0.30 per $100 of insured deposits—the highest rate since the FDIC's establishment in 1933.

The net result? Some banks have begun actively discouraging customers from substantially increasing their deposits. Recently, for instance, the Bank of New York Mellon began *charging* large depositors for the privilege of holding federally insured deposits. The bank now charges an annual interest fee of 0.13 percent to customers with deposit accounts of $50 million or more. Unless market loan rates rise and deposit insurance premiums fall, it appears likely that other banks will follow suit. Some banking experts speculate that eventually banks might begin charging interest fees to customers with small deposits.

For Critical Thinking

1. Why do you suppose that the market clearing interest rates on bank savings and time deposits have fallen as the interest rates on bank loans have dropped?
2. If interest rates earned by banks on their assets fell close to zero, why might all bank customers have to pay interest fees on deposits they hold with banks?

Web Resources

1. To take a look at the latest statistics on the status and performance of U.S. commercial banks, go to www .econtoday.com/chap15.
2. For a look at historical U.S. commercial banking data, go to www.econtoday.com/chap15.

MyEconLab

For more questions on this chapter's Issues & Applications, go to MyEconLab. In the Study Plan for this chapter, select Section N: News.

MyEconLab

Here is what you should know after reading this chapter. MyEconLab will help you identify what you know, and where to go when you need to practice.

— WHAT YOU SHOULD KNOW —

The Key Functions and Properties of Money
Money is a medium of exchange that people use to make payments for goods, services, and financial assets. It is also a unit of accounting for quoting prices in terms of money values. In addition, money is a store of value, so people can hold money for future use in exchange. Finally, money is a standard of deferred payment, enabling lenders to make loans and buyers to repay those loans with money. A good will function as money only if people are widely willing to accept the good in exchange for other goods and services. People will use money only if its value is relatively predictable.

money, 320
medium of exchange, 320
barter, 320
unit of accounting, 321
store of value, 321
standard of deferred payment, 321
liquidity, 321
transactions deposits, 322
fiduciary monetary system, 322

Key Figure
Figure 15-1, 322

— WHERE TO GO TO PRACTICE —

- MyEconLab Study Plans 15.1, 15.2
- Animated Figure 15-1

MyEconLab *continued*

WHAT YOU SHOULD KNOW ———————————————————————— WHERE TO GO TO PRACTICE ——

Official Definitions of the Quantity of Money in Circulation The narrow definition of the quantity of money in circulation, called M1, includes only currency, transactions deposits, and traveler's checks. A broader definition, called M2, is equal to M1 plus savings deposits, small-denomination time deposits, and noninstitutional holdings of money market mutual fund balances.

money supply, 323
transactions approach, 323
liquidity approach, 323
M1, 323
depository institutions, 323
thrift institutions, 323
traveler's checks, 323
M2, 324

- MyEconLab Study Plan 15.3

Why Financial Intermediaries Such as Banks Exist Financial intermediaries help reduce problems stemming from the existence of asymmetric information. Adverse selection arises when uncreditworthy individuals and firms seek loans, Moral hazard problems exist when an individual or business that has been granted credit begins to engage in riskier practices. Financial intermediaries may also permit savers to benefit from economies of scale, which is the ability to reduce the costs and risks of managing funds by pooling funds and spreading costs and risks across many savers.

central bank, 325
financial intermediation, 325
financial intermediaries, 325
asymmetric information, 325
adverse selection, 325
moral hazard, 325
liabilities, 326
assets, 327

Key Figures
Figure 15-3, 326
Figure 15-4, 328

- MyEconLab Study Plan 15.4
- Animated Figures 15.3, 15.4

The Basic Structure and Functions of the Federal Reserve System The Federal Reserve System consists of 12 district banks overseen by the Board of Governors. The Fed's main functions are supplying fiduciary currency, holding banks' reserves and clearing payments, acting as the goverment's fiscal agent, supervising banks, regulating the money supply, intervening in foreign exchange markets, and acting as a lender of last resort.

The Fed, 328
lender of last resort, 331

Key Figure
Figure 15-6, 330

- MyEconLab Study Plan 15.5
- Animated Figure 15-6

The Maximum Potential Change in the Money Supply Following a Federal Reserve Monetary Policy Action When a bond dealer deposits funds received from the Fed in payment for a security following a Fed open market purchase, there is an increase in the total deposits in the banking system. The money supply increases by the amount of the initial deposit. The bank receiving this deposit can lend out funds in excess of those it holds as reserves, which will generate a rise in deposits at another bank. The maximum potential change in deposits throughout the banking system equals the amount of reserves injected (or withdrawn) by the Fed times the potential money multiplier, which is 1 divided by the reserve ratio.

fractional reserve banking, 332
reserves, 332
reserve ratio, 332
balance sheet, 332
open market operations, 333
money multiplier, 335
potential money multiplier, 335

Key Table
Table 15-3, 334

Key Figure
Figure 15-7, 335

- MyEconLab Study Plan 15.6
- Animated Table 15-3
- Animated Figure 15-7

MyEconLab

Log in to MyEconLab, take a chapter test, and get a personalized Study Plan that tells you which concepts you understand and which ones you need to review. From there, MyEconLab will give you further practice, tutorials, animations, videos, and guided solutions. For more information, visit www.myeconlab.com

PROBLEMS

All problems are assignable in MyEconLab; exercises that update with real-time data are marked with (W). *Answers to odd-numbered problems appear at the back of the book.*

15-1. Until 1946, residents of the island of Yap used large doughnut-shaped stones as financial assets. Although prices of goods and services were not quoted in terms of the stones, the stones were often used in exchange for particularly large purchases, such as livestock. To make the transaction, several individuals would insert a large stick through a stone's center and carry it to its new owner. A stone was difficult for any one person to steal, so an owner typically would lean it against the side of his or her home as a sign to others of accumulated purchasing power that would hold value for later use in exchange. Loans would often be repaid using the stones. In what ways did these stones function as money? (See pages 320–322.)

15-2. During the late 1970s, prices quoted in terms of the Israeli currency, the shekel, rose so fast that grocery stores listed their prices in terms of the U.S. dollar and provided customers with dollar-shekel conversion tables that they updated daily. Although people continued to buy goods and services and make loans using shekels, many Israeli citizens converted shekels to dollars to avoid a reduction in their wealth due to inflation. In what way did the U.S. dollar function as money in Israel during this period? (See pages 320–322.)

15-3. During the 1945–1946 Hungarian hyperinflation, when the rate of inflation reached 41.9 *quadrillion* percent per month, the Hungarian government discovered that the real value of its tax receipts was falling dramatically. To keep real tax revenues more stable, it created a good called a "tax pengö,"

in which all bank deposits were denominated for purposes of taxation. Nevertheless, payments for goods and services were made only in terms of the regular Hungarian currency, whose value tended to fall rapidly even though the value of a tax pengö remained stable. Prices were also quoted only in terms of the regular currency. Lenders, however, began denominating loan payments in terms of tax pengös. In what ways did the tax pengö function as money in Hungary in 1945 and 1946? (See pages 320–322.)

15-4. Considering the following data (expressed in billions of U.S. dollars), calculate M1 and M2. (See pages 323–324.)

Currency	1,050
Savings deposits	5,500
Small-denomination time deposits	1,000
Traveler's checks outside banks and thrifts	10
Total money market mutual funds	800
Institution-only money market mutual funds	1,800
Transactions deposits	1,140

15-5. Considering the following data (expressed in billions of U.S. dollars), calculate M1 and M2. (See pages 323–324.)

Transactions deposits	1,025
Savings deposits	3,300
Small-denomination time deposits	1,450
Money market deposit accounts	1,950
Noninstitution money market mutual funds	1,900
Traveler's checks outside banks and thrifts	25
Currency	1,050
Institution-only money market mutual funds	1,250

15-6. Identify whether each of the following amounts is counted in M1 only, M2 only, both M1 and M2, or neither. (See pages 323–324.)

    a. $50 billion in U.S. Treasury bills

    b. $15 billion in small-denomination time deposits

    c. $5 billion in traveler's checks not issued by a bank

    d. $20 billion in money market deposit accounts

15-7. Identify whether each of the following items is counted in M1 only, M2 only, both M1 and M2, or neither. (See pages 323–324.)

    a. A $1,000 balance in a transactions deposit at a mutual savings bank

    b. A $100,000 time deposit in a New York bank

    c. A $10,000 time deposit an elderly widow holds at her credit union

    d. A $50 traveler's check not issued by a bank

    e. A $50,000 savings deposit

15-8. Match each of the rationales for financial intermediation listed below with at least one of the following financial intermediaries: insurance company, pension fund, savings bank. Explain your choices. (See pages 325–326.)

    a. Adverse selection

    b. Moral hazard

    c. Lower management costs generated by larger scale

15-9. Identify whether each of the following events poses an adverse selection problem or a moral hazard problem in financial markets. (See pages 325–326.)

    a. A manager of a savings and loan association responds to reports of a likely increase in federal deposit insurance coverage. She directs loan officers to extend mortgage loans to less creditworthy borrowers.

    b. A loan applicant does not mention that a legal judgment in his divorce case will require him to make alimony payments to his ex-wife.

    c. An individual who was recently approved for a loan to start a new business decides to use some of the funds to take a Hawaiian vacation.

15-10. In what sense is currency a liability of the Federal Reserve System? (See page 330.)

15-11. In what respects is the Fed like a private banking institution? In what respects is it more like a government agency? (See pages 328–331.)

15-12. Take a look at the map of the locations of the Federal Reserve districts and their headquarters in Figure 15-6 on page 330. Today, the U.S. population is centered just west of the Mississippi River—that is, about half of the population is either to the west or the east of a line running roughly just west of this river. Can you reconcile the current locations of Fed districts and banks with this fact? Why do you suppose the Fed has its current geographic structure? (See page 330.)

15-13. Draw an empty bank balance sheet, with the heading "Assets" on the left and the heading "Liabilities" on the right. Then place the following items on the proper side of the balance sheet (see page 332):

    a. Loans to a private company

    b. Borrowings from a Federal Reserve district bank

    c. Deposits with a Federal Reserve district bank

    d. U.S. Treasury bills

    e. Vault cash

    f. Transactions deposits

15-14. Draw an empty bank balance sheet, with the heading "Assets" on the left and the heading "Liabilities" on the right. Then place the following items on the proper side of the balance sheet. (see page 332.)

    a. Borrowings from another bank in the interbank loans market

    b. Deposits this bank holds in an account with another private bank

    c. U.S. Treasury bonds

    d. Small-denomination time deposits

    e. Mortgage loans to household customers

    f. Money market deposit accounts

15-15. The reserve ratio is 11 percent. What is the value of the potential money multiplier? (See page 335.)

15-16. The Federal Reserve purchases $1 million in U.S. Treasury bonds from a bond dealer, and the dealer's bank credits the dealer's account. The reserve ratio is 15 percent. Assuming that no currency leakage occurs, how much will the bank lend to its customers following the Fed's purchase? (See pages 333–334.)

15-17. Suppose that the value of the potential money multiplier is equal to 4. What is the reserve ratio? (See page 335.)

15-18. Consider a world in which there is no currency and depository institutions issue only transactions deposits. The reserve ratio is 20 percent. The central bank sells $1 billion in government securities. What ultimately happens to the money supply? (See page 335.)

15-19. Assume a 1 percent reserve ratio and no currency leakages. What is the potential money multiplier? How will total deposits in the banking system ultimately change if the Federal Reserve purchases $5 million in U.S. government securities? (See page 335.)

ECONOMICS ON THE NET

What's Happened to the Money Supply? Deposits at banks and other financial institutions make up a portion of the U.S. money supply. This exercise gives you the chance to see how changes in these deposits influence the Fed's measures of money.

Title: FRED (Federal Reserve Economic Data)

Navigation: Go to www.econtoday.com/chap15 to visit the Web page of the Federal Reserve Bank of St. Louis.

Application

1. Select the data series for *Demand Deposits at Commercial Banks (Bil. of $; M)*, either seasonally adjusted or not. Scan through the data. Do you notice any recent trend? (Hint: Compare the growth in the figures before 1993 with their growth after 1993.) In addition, take a look at the data series for currency and for other transactions deposits. Do you observe similar recent trends in these series?

2. Back up, and click on *M1 Money Stock (Bil. of $; M)*, again either seasonally adjusted or not. Does it show any change in pattern beginning around 1993?

For Group Study and Analysis FRED contains considerable financial data series. Assign individual members or groups of the class the task of examining data on assets included in M1, M2, and MZM. Have each student or group look for big swings in the data. Then ask the groups to report to the class as a whole. When did clear changes occur in various categories of the monetary aggregates? Were there times when people appeared to shift funds from one aggregate to another? Are there any other noticeable patterns that may have had something to do with economic events during various periods?

ANSWERS TO QUICK QUIZZES

p. 323: (i) medium of exchange . . . unit of accounting . . . store of value . . . standard of deferred payment; (ii) liquid; (iii) fiduciary; (iv) predictable

p. 325: (i) transactions . . . M1; (ii) Transactions; (iii) M1 . . . M2

p. 328: (i) Financial; (ii) asymmetric . . . adverse selection . . . moral hazard

p. 331: (i) Federal Reserve System; (ii) Board . . . Governors; (iii) currency . . . reserves . . . lender of last resort

p. 336: (i) Reserves . . . Federal Reserve; (ii) reserve ratio; (iii) potential money multiplier

p. 340: (i) Federal Deposit Insurance Corporation; (ii) less . . . riskier . . . higher; (iii) moral . . . premiums . . . moral

16

Domestic and International Dimensions of Monetary Policy

Since 2008, the Fed has provided a number of "credit programs" through which it transmitted funds directly to individual financial institutions. In addition, the Fed bought bad debts from selected institutions, and it even purchased securities issued by nonfinancial firms, such as General Electric and McDonald's. The fundamental aims of this new Fed *credit policy* included making banks and firms more liquid and preventing insolvencies of selected institutions. Another objective was to keep borrowing costs low for all households and firms in order to stimulate borrowing that would fuel increases in total planned expenditures and aggregate demand. At various times between 2008 and 2010, though, the Fed failed to make sure that its monetary policy actions supported this latter credit policy goal. To understand how this policy breakdown occurred, you first must learn about the implementation of monetary policy, a key topic of this chapter.

during a couple of brief intervals within the past few years, Apple had more cash on hand than did the U.S. Treasury? For instance, at one point, the U.S. Treasury held just over $73 billion in accounts from which federal government checks could be written, whereas Apple's accounts contained more than $76 billion. Of course, one reason for this situation has been that the federal government's tax collections have been lower than in prior years, leading to reduced Treasury cash balances. In addition, Apple has maintained unusually large stockpiles of funds in checkable accounts. Indeed, total cash balances across all U.S. nonfinancial companies have recently totaled in excess of $1.8 trillion, or about 7 percent of all businesses' assets, which is the highest percentage since the early 1960s.

Most economists agree that a major reason U.S. companies are holding so much cash is that the rate of interest—the opportunity cost of holding money instead of an interest-bearing asset—has been very low. In this chapter, you will learn about determinants of how much money people desire to hold—that is, about their *demand for money.*

The Demand for Money

In the previous chapter, we saw how the Federal Reserve's open market operations can increase or decrease the money supply. Our focus was on the effects of the Fed's actions on the banking system. In this chapter, we widen our discussion to see how Fed monetary policy actions have an impact on the broader economy by influencing market interest rates. First, though, you must understand the factors that determine how much money people desire to hold—in other words, you must understand the demand for money.

All of us engage in a flow of transactions. We buy and sell things all of our lives. But because we use money—dollars—as our medium of exchange, all *flows* of nonbarter transactions involve a *stock* of money. We can restate this as follows:

To use money, one must hold money.

Given that everybody must hold money, we can now talk about the *demand* to hold it. People do not demand to hold money just to look at pictures of past leaders. They hold it to be able to use it to buy goods and services.

The Demand for Money: What People Wish to Hold

People have certain motivations that cause them to want to hold **money balances.** Individuals and firms could try to do without non-interest-bearing money balances. But life is inconvenient without a ready supply of money balances. Thus, the public has a demand for money, motivated by several factors.

Money balances
Synonymous with money, money stock, money holdings.

THE TRANSACTIONS DEMAND The main reason people hold money is that money can be used to purchase goods and services. People are paid at specific intervals (once a week, once a month, and the like), but they wish to make purchases more or less continuously. To free themselves from having to buy goods and services only on payday, people find it beneficial to hold money. The benefit they receive is convenience: They willingly forgo interest earnings in order to avoid the inconvenience of cashing in nonmoney assets such as bonds every time they wish to make a purchase. Thus, people hold money to make regular, *expected* expenditures under the **transactions demand.** As nominal GDP (see page 176 in Chapter 8) rises, people will want to hold more money because they will be making more transactions.

Transactions demand
Holding money as a medium of exchange to make payments. The level varies directly with nominal GDP.

THE PRECAUTIONARY DEMAND The transactions demand involves money held to make *expected* expenditures. People also hold money for the **precautionary demand** to make *unexpected* purchases or to meet emergencies. When people hold money for the precautionary demand, they incur a cost in forgone interest earnings that they balance against the benefit of having cash on hand. The higher the rate of interest, the lower the precautionary money balances people wish to hold.

Precautionary demand
Holding money to meet unplanned expenditures and emergencies.

Asset demand
Holding money as a store of value instead of other assets such as corporate bonds and stocks.

THE ASSET DEMAND Remember that one of the functions of money is to serve as a store of value. People can hold money balances as a store of value, or they can hold bonds or stocks or other interest-earning assets. The desire to hold money as a store of value leads to the **asset demand** for money. People choose to hold money rather than other assets for two reasons: its liquidity and the lack of risk.

The disadvantage of holding money balances as an asset, of course, is the interest earnings forgone. Each individual or business decides how much money to hold as an asset by looking at the opportunity cost of holding money. The higher the interest rate—which is the opportunity cost of holding money—the lower the money balances people will want to hold as assets. Conversely, the lower the interest rate offered on alternative assets, the higher the money balances people will want to hold as assets.

The Demand for Money Curve

Assume for simplicity's sake that the amount of money demanded for transactions purposes is proportionate to income. That leaves the precautionary and asset demands for money, both determined by the opportunity cost of holding money. If we assume that the interest rate represents the cost of holding money balances, we can graph the relationship between the interest rate and the quantity of money demanded.

In Figure 16-1 below, the demand for money curve shows a familiar downward slope. The horizontal axis measures the quantity of money demanded, and the vertical axis is the interest rate. The rate of interest is the cost of holding money. At a higher interest rate, a lower quantity of money is demanded, and vice versa.

To see this, imagine two scenarios. In the first one, you can earn 20 percent a year if you put your funds into purchases of U.S. government securities. In the other scenario, you can earn 1 percent if you put your funds into purchases of U.S. government securities. If you have $1,000 average cash balances in a non-interest-bearing checking account, in the first scenario over a one-year period, your opportunity cost would be 20 percent of $1,000, or $200. In the second scenario, the opportunity cost that you would incur would be 1 percent of $1,000, or $10. Under which scenario would you hold more funds in your checking account instead of securities?

QUICK QUIZ See page 369 for the answers. Review concepts from this section in MyEconLab.

To use money, people must hold money. Therefore, they have a _____ for money balances.

The determinants of the demand for money balances are the _____ demand, the _____ demand, and the _____ demand.

Holding money carries an _____ cost—the interest income forgone. Hence, the demand for money curve showing the relationship between the quantity of money balances demanded and the interest rate slopes _____.

FIGURE 16-1

The Demand for Money Curve

If we use the interest rate as a proxy for the opportunity cost of holding money balances, the demand for money curve, M_d, is downward sloping, similar to other demand curves

How the Fed Influences Interest Rates

When the Fed takes actions that alter the rate of growth of the money supply, it is seeking to influence investment, consumption, and total aggregate expenditures. In taking these monetary policy actions, the Fed in principle has four tools at its disposal: open market operations, changes in the reserve ratio, changes in the interest rates paid on reserves, and discount rate changes. The first two tools were introduced in Chapter 15. The discount rate and interest rates paid on reserves will be discussed later in this chapter. Let's consider the effects of open market operations, the tool that the Fed regularly employs on a day-to-day basis.

Open Market Operations

As we saw in the previous chapter, the Fed changes the amount of reserves in the banking system by its purchases and sales of government bonds issued by the U.S. Treasury. To understand how these actions by the Fed influence the market interest rate, we start out in an equilibrium in which all individuals, including the holders of bonds, are satisfied with the current situation. There is some equilibrium level of interest rate (and bond prices). Now, if the Fed wants to conduct open market operations, it must somehow induce individuals, businesses, and foreign residents to hold more or fewer U.S. Treasury bonds. The inducement must take the form of making people better off. So, if the Fed wants to buy bonds, it will have to offer to buy them at a higher price than exists in the marketplace. If the Fed wants to sell bonds, it will have to offer them at a lower price than exists in the marketplace. Thus, an open market operation must cause a change in the price of bonds.

GRAPHING THE SALE OF BONDS The Fed sells some of the bonds it has on hand. This is shown in panel (a) of Figure 16-2 below. Notice that the supply of bonds in the private market is shown here as a vertical line with respect to price. The demand for bonds is downward sloping. If the Fed offers more bonds it owns for sale, the supply curve shifts from S_1 to S_2. People will not be willing to buy the extra bonds at the initial equilibrium bond price, P_1. They will be satisfied holding the additional bonds at the new equilibrium price, P_2.

THE FED'S PURCHASE OF BONDS The opposite occurs when the Fed purchases bonds. You can view this purchase of bonds as a reduction in the stock of bonds available for

Go to www.econtoday.com/chap16 to learn about the Federal Reserve's current policy regarding open market operations. Scan down the page, and select the "Minutes" for the most recent date.

FIGURE 16-2

Determining the Price of Bonds

In panel (a), the Fed offers more bonds for sale. The price drops from P_1 to P_2. In panel (b), the Fed purchases bonds. This is the equivalent of a reduction in the supply of bonds available for private investors to hold. The price of bonds must rise from P_1 to P_3 to clear the market.

private investors to hold. In panel (b) of Figure 16-2 on the previous page, the original supply curve is S_1. The new supply curve of outstanding bonds will end up being S_3 because of the Fed's purchases of bonds. To get people to give up these bonds, the Fed must offer them a more attractive price. The price will rise from to P_1 to P_3.

Relationship between the Price of Existing Bonds and the Rate of Interest

The price of existing bonds and the rate of interest are inversely related. Assume that the average yield on bonds is 5 percent. You decide to purchase a bond. A local corporation agrees to sell you a bond that will pay you $50 a year forever. What is the price you are willing to pay for the bond? It is $1,000. Why? Because $50 divided by $1,000 equals 5 percent, which is as good as the best return you can earn elsewhere. You purchase the bond. The next year something happens in the economy, and you can now obtain bonds that have effective yields of 10 percent. (In other words, the prevailing interest rate in the economy is now 10 percent.) What will happen to the market price of the existing bond that you own, the one you purchased the year before? It will fall.

If you try to sell the bond for $1,000, you will discover that no investors will buy it from you. Why should they when they can obtain the same $50-a-year yield from someone else by paying only $500? Indeed, unless you offer your bond for sale at a price that is no higher than $500, no buyers will be forthcoming. Hence, an increase in the prevailing interest rate in the economy has caused the market value of your existing bond to fall.

The important point to be understood is this:

> ***The market price of existing bonds (and all fixed-income assets) is inversely related to the rate of interest prevailing in the economy.***

As a consequence of the inverse relationship between the price of existing bonds and the interest rate, the Fed is able to influence the interest rate by engaging in open market operations. A Fed open market sale that reduces the equilibrium price of bonds brings about an increase in the interest rate. A Fed open market purchase that boosts the equilibrium price of bonds generates a decrease in the interest rate.

QUICK QUIZ See page 369 for the answers. Review concepts from this section in MyEconLab.

When the Fed sells bonds, it must offer them at a _____ price. When the Fed buys bonds, it must pay a _____ price.

There is an _____ relationship between the prevailing rate of interest in the economy and the market price of *existing* bonds (and all fixed-income assets).

A Federal Reserve open market sale generates a _____ in the price of *existing* bonds and an _____ in the market interest rate. An open market purchase brings about an _____ in the price of *existing* bonds and a _____ in the market rate of interest.

Effects of an Increase in the Money Supply

Now that we've seen how the Fed's monetary policy actions influence the market interest rate, we can ask a broader question: How does monetary policy influence real GDP and the price level? To understand how monetary policy works in its simplest form, we are going to run an experiment in which you increase the money supply in a very direct way. Assume that the government has given you hundreds of millions of dollars in just-printed bills. You then fly around the country in a helicopter, dropping the money out of the window. People pick it up and put it in their pockets. Some deposit the money in their transactions deposit accounts. As a result, they now have too much money—not in the sense that they want to throw it away but rather in relation to other assets that they own. There are a variety of ways to dispose of this "new" money.

Direct Effect

The simplest thing that people can do when they have excess money balances is to go out and spend them on goods and services. Here they have a direct impact on aggregate demand. Aggregate demand rises because with an increase in the money supply, at any given price level people now want to purchase more output of real goods and services.

Indirect Effect

Not everybody will necessarily spend the newfound money on goods and services. Some people may wish to deposit a portion or all of those excess money balances in banks. The recipient banks now discover that they have higher reserves than they wish to hold. As you learned in Chapter 15, one thing that banks can do to get higher-interest-earning assets is to lend out the excess reserves. But banks cannot induce people to borrow more funds than they were borrowing before unless the banks lower the interest rate that they charge on loans. This lower interest rate encourages people to take out those loans. Businesses will therefore engage in new investment with the funds loaned. Individuals will engage in more consumption of durable goods such as housing, autos, and home entertainment centers. Either way, the increased loans generate a rise in aggregate demand. More people will be involved in more spending—even those who did not pick up any of the money that was originally dropped out of your helicopter.

What happens if the market interest rate on bonds falls close to zero, as has occurred in recent years? In that case, monetary policy traditionally must rely on the direct effect of a change in bank reserves and, through the money multiplier effect, the quantity of money in circulation. Monetary policy cannot depend on the indirect effect of an interest rate that is already at zero. A policy action in which the Federal Reserve conducts open market purchases to increase bank reserves without seeking to alter the interest rate, which is already zero, is called **quantitative easing.**

Quantitative easing
Federal Reserve open market purchases intended to generate an increase in bank reserves at a nearly zero interest rate.

Graphing the Effects of an Expansionary Monetary Policy

To consider the effects of an expansionary monetary policy on real GDP and the price level, look at Figure 16-3 below. We start out in a situation in which the economy is operating at less than full employment. You see a recessionary gap in the figure, which is

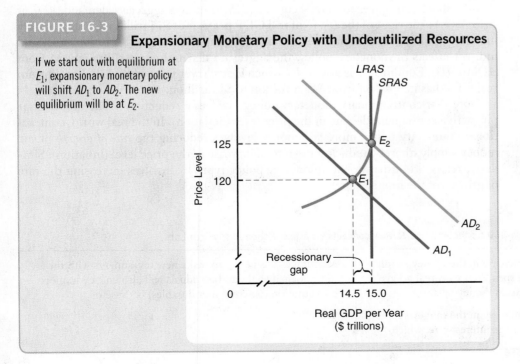

FIGURE 16-3

Expansionary Monetary Policy with Underutilized Resources

If we start out with equilibrium at E_1, expansionary monetary policy will shift AD_1 to AD_2. The new equilibrium will be at E_2.

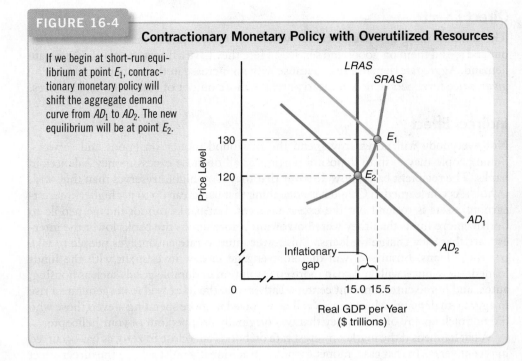

FIGURE 16-4

Contractionary Monetary Policy with Overutilized Resources

If we begin at short-run equilibrium at point E_1, contractionary monetary policy will shift the aggregate demand curve from AD_1 to AD_2. The new equilibrium will be at point E_2.

measured as the horizontal difference between the long-run aggregate supply curve, *LRAS*, and the current equilibrium. Short-run equilibrium is at E_1, with a price level of 120 and real GDP of $14.5 trillion. The *LRAS* curve is at $15 trillion. Assume now that the Fed increases the money supply. Because of the direct and indirect effects of this increase in the money supply, aggregate demand shifts outward to the right to AD_2. The new equilibrium is at an output rate of $15 trillion of real GDP per year and a price level of 125. Here expansionary monetary policy can move the economy toward its *LRAS* curve sooner than otherwise.

Graphing the Effects of Contractionary Monetary Policy

Assume that there is an inflationary gap as shown in Figure 16-4 above. There you see that the short-run aggregate supply curve, *SRAS*, intersects aggregate demand, AD_1, at E_1. This is to the right of the *LRAS* of real GDP per year of $15 trillion. Contractionary monetary policy can eliminate this inflationary gap. Because of both the direct and indirect effects of monetary policy, the aggregate demand curve shifts inward from AD_1 to AD_2. Equilibrium is now at E_2, which is at a lower price level, 120. Equilibrium real GDP has now fallen from $15.5 trillion to $15 trillion.

Note that contractionary monetary policy involves a reduction in the money supply, with a consequent decline in the price level (deflation). In the real world, contractionary monetary policy more commonly involves reducing the *rate of growth* of the money supply, thereby reducing the rate of increase in the price level (inflation). Similarly, real-world expansionary monetary policy typically involves increasing the rate of growth of the money supply.

QUICK QUIZ See page 369 for the answers. Review concepts from this section in MyEconLab.

The _____ effect of an increase in the money supply arises because people desire to spend more on real goods and services when they have excess money balances.

The _____ effect of an increase in the money supply works through a _____ in the interest rate, which

encourages businesses to make new investments with the funds loaned to them. Individuals will also engage in more consumption (on consumer durables) because of _____ interest rates.

Open Economy Transmission of Monetary Policy

So far we have discussed monetary policy in a closed economy. When we move to an open economy, with international trade and the international purchases and sales of all assets including dollars and other currencies, monetary policy becomes more complex. Consider first the effect of monetary policy on exports.

Go to www.econtoday.com/chap16 for links to central banks around the globe, provided by the Bank for International Settlements.

The Net Export Effect of Contractionary Monetary Policy

To see how a change in monetary policy can affect net exports, suppose that the Federal Reserve implements a contractionary policy that boosts the market interest rate. The higher U.S. interest rate, in turn, tends to attract foreign investment in U.S. financial assets, such as U.S. government securities.

If more residents of foreign countries decide that they want to purchase U.S. government securities or other U.S. assets, they first have to obtain U.S. dollars. As a consequence, the demand for dollars goes up in foreign exchange markets. The international price of the dollar therefore rises. This is called an *appreciation* of the dollar, and it tends to reduce net exports because it makes our exports more expensive in terms of foreign currency and imports cheaper in terms of dollars. Foreign residents demand fewer of our goods and services, and we demand more of theirs.

This reasoning implies that when contractionary monetary policy increases the U.S. interest rate at the current price level, there will be a negative net export effect because foreign residents will want more U.S. financial instruments. Hence, they will demand additional dollars, thereby causing the international price of the dollar to rise. This makes our exports more expensive for the rest of the world, which then demands a smaller quantity of our exports. It also means that foreign goods and services are less expensive in the United States, so we therefore demand more imports. We come up with this conclusion:

> *Contractionary monetary policy causes interest rates to rise. Such a rise will induce international inflows of funds, thereby raising the international value of the dollar and making U.S. goods less attractive abroad. The net export effect of contractionary monetary policy will be in the same direction as the monetary policy effect, thereby amplifying the effect of such policy.*

The Net Export Effect of Expansionary Monetary Policy

Now assume that the economy is experiencing a recession and the Federal Reserve wants to pursue an expansionary monetary policy. In so doing, it will cause interest rates to fall in the short run, as discussed earlier. Declining interest rates will cause funds to flow out of the United States. The demand for dollars will decrease, and their international price will go down. Foreign goods will now look more expensive to U.S. residents, and imports will fall. Foreign residents will desire more of our exports, and exports will rise. The result will be an increase in net exports. Again, the international consequences reinforce the domestic consequences of monetary policy, in this case by stimulating the economy.

On a broader level, the Fed's ability to control the rate of growth of the money supply may be hampered as U.S. money markets become less isolated. With the push of a computer button, billions of dollars can change hands halfway around the world. If the Fed reduces the growth of the money supply, individuals and firms in the United States can obtain dollars from other sources. People in the United States who want more liquidity can obtain their dollars from foreign residents. Indeed, as world markets become increasingly integrated, U.S. residents, who can already hold U.S. bank accounts denominated in foreign currencies, more regularly conduct transactions using other nations' currencies.

QUICK QUIZ See page 369 for the answers. Review concepts from this section in MyEconLab.

Monetary policy in an open economy has repercussions for net _____.

If contractionary monetary policy raises U.S. interest rates, there is a _____ net export effect because foreign residents will demand _____ U.S. financial instruments, thereby demanding _____ dollars and hence causing the international price of the dollar to rise.

This makes our exports more expensive for the rest of the world.

When expansionary monetary policy causes interest rates to fall, foreign residents will want _____ U.S. financial instruments. The resulting _____ in the demand for dollars will reduce the dollar's value in foreign exchange markets, leading to an _____ in net exports.

Monetary Policy and Inflation

Most media discussions of inflation focus on the short run. The price index can fluctuate in the short run because of events such as oil price shocks, labor union strikes, or discoveries of large amounts of new natural resources. In the long run, however, empirical studies show that excessive growth in the money supply results in inflation.

If the supply of money rises relative to the demand for money, people have more money balances than desired. They adjust their mix of assets to reduce money balances in favor of other items. This ultimately causes their spending on goods and services to increase. The result is a rise in the price level, or inflation.

The Equation of Exchange and the Quantity Theory

A simple way to show the relationship between changes in the quantity of money in circulation and the price level is through the **equation of exchange,** developed by Irving Fisher (note that ≡ refers to an identity or truism):

$$M_s V \equiv PY$$

where M_s = actual money balances held by the nonbanking public

V = **income velocity of money,** which is the number of times, on average per year, each monetary unit is spent on final goods and services

P = price level or price index

Y = real GDP per year

Consider a numerical example involving the entire economy. Assume that in this economy, the total money supply, Ms, is $10 trillion; real GDP, Y, is $15 trillion (in base-year dollars); and the price level, P, is 1.3333 (133.33 in index number terms). Using the equation of exchange,

$$M_s V \equiv PY$$
$$\$10 \text{ trillion} \times V \equiv 1.3333 \times \$15 \text{ trillion}$$
$$\$10 \text{ trillion} \times V \equiv \$20 \text{ trillion}$$
$$V \equiv 2.0$$

Thus, each dollar is spent an average of 2 times per year.

THE EQUATION OF EXCHANGE AS AN IDENTITY The equation of exchange must always be true—it is an *accounting identity*. The equation of exchange states that the total amount of funds spent on final output, $M_s V$, is equal to the total amount of funds *received* for final output, PY. Thus, a given flow of funds can be viewed from either the buyers' side or the producers' side. The value of goods purchased is equal to the value of goods sold.

If Y represents real GDP and P is the price level, PY equals the dollar value of national output of goods and services or *nominal* GDP. Thus,

$$M_s V \equiv PY \equiv \text{nominal GDP}$$

THE QUANTITY THEORY OF MONEY AND PRICES If we now make some assumptions about different variables in the equation of exchange, we come up with the simplified theory of

Equation of exchange
The formula indicating that the number of monetary units (M_s) times the number of times each unit is spent on final goods and services (V) is identical to the price level (P) times real GDP (Y).

Income velocity of money (V)
The number of times per year a dollar is spent on final goods and services; identically equal to nominal GDP divided by the money supply.

FIGURE 16-5

The Relationship between Money Supply Growth Rates and Rates of Inflation

If we plot rates of inflation and rates of monetary growth for different countries, we come up with a scatter diagram that reveals an obvious direct relationship. If you were to draw a line through the "average" of the points in this figure, it would be upward sloping, showing that an increase in the rate of growth of the money supply leads to an increase in the rate of inflation.

Sources: International Monetary Fund and national central banks. Data are for latest available periods.

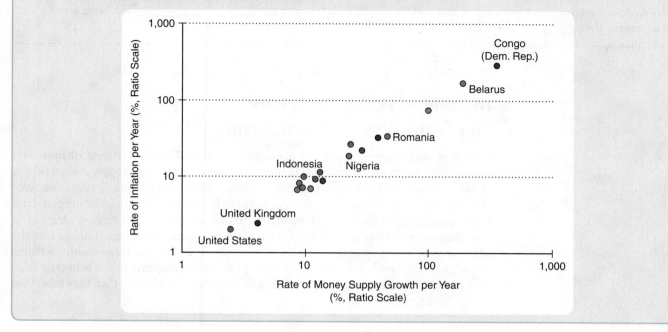

why the price level changes, called the **quantity theory of money and prices.** If we assume that the velocity of money, V, is constant and that real GDP, Y, is also constant, the simple equation of exchange tells us that a change in the money supply can lead only to an equiproportional change in the price level. Continue with our numerical example. Y is $15 trillion. V equals 2.0. If the money supply increases by 20 percent, to $12 trillion, the only thing that can happen is that the price level, P, has to go up from 1.3333 to 1.6. In other words, the price level must also increase by 20 percent. Otherwise the equation is no longer in balance. An increase in the money supply of 20 percent results in a rise in the price level (inflation) of 20 percent.

EMPIRICAL VERIFICATION There is considerable evidence of the empirical validity of the relationship between monetary growth and high rates of inflation. Figure 16-5 above tracks the correspondence between money supply growth and the rates of inflation in various countries around the world.

Why did Iran recently decide to make each unit of its money 10,000 times smaller?

Quantity theory of money and prices
The hypothesis that changes in the money supply lead to equiproportional changes in the price level.

YOU ARE THERE

To contemplate how the quantity theory of money and prices operates in a multiplayer online game, take a look at **Applying the Quantity Theory of Money and Prices to a Universe of Star Systems** on page 363.

INTERNATIONAL POLICY EXAMPLE

Iran Removes Four Zeros from Each Unit of Its Currency

In recent years, the annual inflation rate reported by Iran's government has ranged from about 15 percent to just over 20 percent. These high inflation rates followed on the heels of double-digit-percentage rates of growth in the quantity of *rials*—Iran's currency—in circulation. So many rials circulated and the average price level rose so high that the currency note most widely used in trade was the 100,000-rial note (worth less than $10).

To save Iranian residents the complication of keeping careful track of the extra zeros in their currency notes and posted prices, the Central Bank of the Iranian Republic took the step of dividing the value of every unit of its currency by 10,000. To implement this change, the central bank announced the formal removal of four zeros from every currency note. It also gradually introduced into circulation a new currency, called the *parsi*, defined as equal to 10,000 rials, and began gradually removing rials from circulation.

FOR CRITICAL THINKING

Even after the new parsi notes replace the old rial notes, will the inflation rate change if the rate of growth of Iran's money supply stays the same?

Monetary Policy in Action: The Transmission Mechanism

Earlier in this chapter, we talked about the direct and indirect effects of monetary policy. The direct effect is simply that an increase in the money supply causes people to have excess money balances. To get rid of these excess money balances, people increase their expenditures. The indirect effect, depicted in Figure 16-6 below, as the interest-rate-based money transmission mechanism, occurs because some people have decided to purchase interest-bearing assets with their excess money balances. This causes the price of such assets—bonds—to go up. Because of the inverse relationship between the price of existing bonds and the interest rate, the interest rate in the economy falls. This lower interest rate induces people and businesses to spend more than they otherwise would have spent.

An Interest-Rate-Based Transmission Mechanism

The indirect, interest-rate-based transmission mechanism can be seen explicitly in Figure 16-7 on the facing page. In panel (a), you see that an increase in the money supply reduces the interest rate. The economywide demand curve for money is labeled M_d in panel (a). At first, the money supply is at M_s, a vertical line determined by the Federal Reserve. The equilibrium interest rate is r_1. This occurs where the money supply curve intersects the money demand curve.

Now assume that the Fed increases the money supply, say, via open market operations. This will shift the money supply curve outward to the right to M_s'. People find themselves with too much cash (liquidity). They buy bonds. When they buy bonds, they bid up the prices of bonds, thereby lowering the interest rate. The interest rate falls to r_2, where the new money supply curve M_s' intersects the money demand curve M_d. This reduction in the interest rate from r_1 to r_2 has an effect on planned investment, as can be seen in panel (b). Planned investment per year increases from I_1 to I_2. An increase in investment will increase aggregate demand, as shown in panel (c). Aggregate demand increases from AD_1 to AD_2. Equilibrium in the economy increases from real GDP per year of $14.5 trillion, which is not on the $LRAS$, to equilibrium real GDP per year of $15 trillion, which is on the $LRAS$.

FIGURE 16-6

The Interest-Rate-Based Money Transmission Mechanism

FIGURE 16-7

Adding Monetary Policy to the Aggregate Demand–Aggregate Supply Model

In panel (a), we show a demand for money function, M_d. It slopes downward to show that at lower rates of interest, a larger quantity of money will be demanded. The money supply is given initially as M_s, so the equilibrium rate of interest will be r_1. At this rate of interest, we see from the planned investment schedule given in panel (b) that the quantity of

planned investment demanded per year will be I_1. After the shift in the money supply to M'_s, the resulting increase in investment from I_1 to I_2 shifts the aggregate demand curve in panel (c) outward from AD_1 to AD_2. Equilibrium moves from E_1 to E_2, at real GDP of \$15 trillion per year.

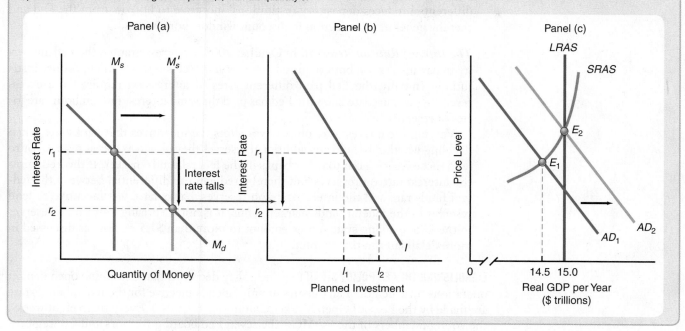

Targeting the Federal Funds Rate

As we have seen, the Fed can influence interest rates only by actively entering the market for federal government securities (usually Treasury bills). So, if the Fed wants to raise "the" interest rate, it essentially must engage in contractionary open market operations. That is to say, it must sell more Treasury securities than it buys, thereby reducing total reserves in the banking system and, hence, the money supply. This tends to boost the rate of interest. Conversely, when the Fed wants to decrease "the" rate of interest, it engages in expansionary open market operations, thereby increasing reserves and the money supply. But what interest rate is the Fed attempting to change?

In reality, more than one interest rate matters for Fed policymaking. Three interest rates are particularly relevant.

1. **The Federal Funds Rate.** In normal times, depository institutions wishing to borrow funds rarely seek to borrow directly from the Fed. In years past, this was because the Fed would not lend them all they wanted to borrow. Instead, the Fed encouraged banks to obtain funds in the **federal funds market** when they wanted to expand their reserves. The federal funds market is an interbank market in reserves where one bank borrows the excess reserves—resources held voluntarily over and above required reserves—of another. The generic term *federal funds market* refers to the borrowing or lending of reserve funds that are usually repaid within the same 24-hour period.

    Depository institutions that borrow in the federal funds market pay an interest rate called the **federal funds rate.** Because the federal funds rate is a ready measure of the cost that banks must incur to raise funds, the Federal Reserve often uses it as a yardstick by which to measure the effects of its policies. Consequently, the federal funds rate is closely watched as an indicator of the Fed's intentions.

Federal funds market
A private market (made up mostly of banks) in which banks can borrow reserves from other banks that want to lend them. Federal funds are usually lent for overnight use.

Federal funds rate
The interest rate that depository institutions pay to borrow reserves in the interbank federal funds market.

2. *The Discount Rate.* When the Fed does lend reserves directly to depository institutions, the rate of interest that it charges is called the **discount rate.** When depository institutions borrow reserves from the Fed at this rate, they are said to be borrowing through the Fed's "discount window." Borrowing from the Fed increases reserves and thereby expands the money supply, other things being equal.

Since 2003, the differential between the discount rate and the federal funds rate has ranged from 0.25 percentage point to 1.0 percentage point. An increase in this differential reduces depository institutions' incentive to borrow from the Fed and thereby generates a reduction in discount window borrowings.

3. *The Interest Rate on Reserves.* In October 2008, Congress granted the Fed authority to pay interest on both required reserves and excess reserves of depository institutions. Initially, the Fed paid different rates of interest on required and excess reserves, but since late 2008 the Fed has paid the same interest rate on both categories of reserves.

Varying the interest rate on reserves alters the incentives that banks face when deciding whether to hold any additional reserves they obtain as excess reserves or to lend those reserves out to other banks in the federal funds market. If the Fed raises the interest rate on reserves and thereby reduces the differential between the federal funds rate and the interest rate on reserves, banks have less incentive to lend reserves in the federal funds market. Thus, it is not surprising that excess reserves in the U.S. banking system now amount to more than $1.5 trillion, as discussed in more detail later in this chapter.

ESTABLISHING THE FED POLICY STRATEGY The policy decisions that determine open market operations by which the Fed pursues its announced objective for the federal funds rate are made by the Federal Open Market Committee (FOMC). Every six to eight weeks, the voting members of the FOMC—the seven Fed board governors and five regional bank presidents—determine the Fed's general strategy of open market operations.

The FOMC outlines its strategy in a document called the **FOMC Directive.** This document lays out the FOMC's general economic objectives, establishes short-term federal funds rate objectives, and specifies target ranges for money supply growth. After each meeting, the FOMC issues a brief statement to the media, which then publish stories about the Fed's action or inaction and what it is likely to mean for the economy. Typically, these stories have headlines such as "Fed Cuts Key Interest Rate," "Fed Acts to Push Up Interest Rates," or "Fed Decides to Leave Interest Rates Alone."

THE TRADING DESK The FOMC leaves the task of implementing the Directive to officials who manage an office at the Federal Reserve Bank of New York known as the **Trading Desk.** The media spend little time considering how the Fed's Trading Desk conducts its activities, taking for granted that the Fed can implement the policy action that it has announced to the public. The Trading Desk's open market operations typically are confined within a one-hour interval each weekday morning.

The Taylor Rule

In 1990, John Taylor of Stanford University suggested a relatively simple equation that the Fed might use for the purpose of selecting a federal funds rate target. This equation would direct the Fed to set the federal funds rate target based on an estimated long-run real interest rate (see page 151 in Chapter 7), the current deviation of the actual inflation rate from the Fed's inflation objective, and the proportionate gap between actual real GDP per year and a measure of potential real GDP per year. Taylor and other economists have applied his equation, which has become known as the **Taylor rule,** to actual Fed policy choices. They have concluded that the Taylor rule's recommendations for federal funds rate target values come close to the actual targets the Fed has selected over time.

MyEconLab Real-time data

FIGURE 16-8

Actual Federal Funds Rates and Values Predicted by a Taylor Rule

This figure displays both the actual path of the federal funds rate since
2002 and the target paths specified by a Taylor-rule equation for a
Federal Reserve annual inflation objective of 0 percent.

Source: Federal Reserve Bank of St. Louis; *Monetary Trends,* various issues.

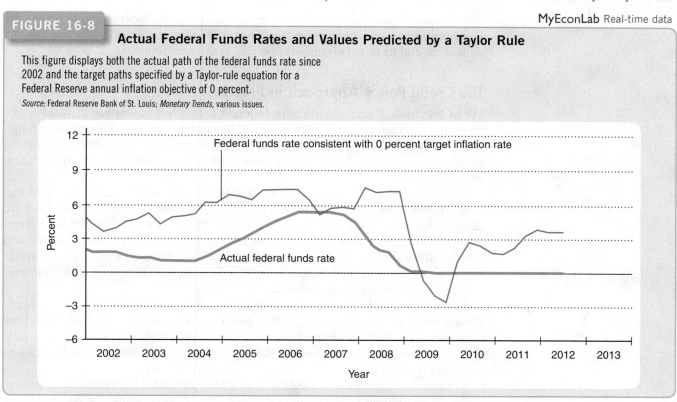

PLOTTING THE TAYLOR RULE ON A GRAPH The Federal Reserve Bank of St. Louis now regularly tracks target levels for the federal funds rate predicted by a basic Taylor-rule equation. Figure 16-8 above displays paths of both the actual federal funds rate (the orange line) and the Taylor-rule recommendation if the Fed's inflation objective (the green line) is 0 percent inflation.

ASSESSING THE STANCE OF FED POLICY WITH THE TAYLOR RULE Suppose that the actual federal funds rate is *below* the rate implied by a 0 percent inflation goal. In this situation, the Taylor rule implies that the Fed's policymaking is expansionary. As a consequence, the actual inflation rate will rise above 0 percent. Thus, during the 2003–2005 interval, the actual federal funds rate was well below the level consistent with a 0 percent inflation rate. This implies that Fed policymaking was very expansionary during this period, sufficiently so as to be expected to yield a long-run inflation rate substantially in excess of 0 percent per year. The Taylor-rule graph implies that in late 2006, the Fed's policy stance became much more contractionary, with the actual federal funds rate above the level consistent with 0 percent inflation. Then, the graph suggests, Fed policymaking became expansionary once more beginning in late 2007.

Until the early 2000s, the actual federal funds rate remained relatively close to the Taylor-rule predictions over time. Since 2003, the Fed has failed to set its federal funds rate target in a manner consistent with the Taylor rule.

Credit Policy at Today's Fed

Federal Reserve policymakers continue to announce and to try to achieve a target value for the federal funds rate. Since the financial meltdown of the late 2000s, however, the Fed has pursued a new approach to policymaking, called **credit policy,** under which it directly extends credit to specific banks, other financial intermediaries, and even nonfinancial companies. When Fed officials initiated this new policy approach in

Credit policy
Federal Reserve policymaking involving direct lending to financial and nonfinancial firms.

2008, they indicated their intention to make it a temporary undertaking. In reality, the Fed continues to use credit policy alongside traditional monetary policy and appears unlikely to end its direct extensions of credit in the near future.

The Credit Policy Approach in Practice

When hundreds of banking institutions found themselves struggling to avoid severe illiquidity and bankruptcy in 2008, the Fed introduced a number of programs through which it provided credit directly to these institutions. The Fed auctioned funds to banking institutions and also bought many debt securities held by a number of these institutions.

In addition, the Fed purchased some of the debts of auto finance companies and then later allowed the companies to obtain bank charters so that they could receive direct loans from the Fed's discount window. The Fed even provided short-term emergency financing arrangements for nonfinancial firms such as Caterpillar, Inc. and Toyota. Even though the Fed had engaged in none of these varied forms of credit policy activities prior to 2008, *today more than $1 trillion, or 40 percent, of the Fed's asset holdings relate to its conduct of credit policy.*

In recent years, the Fed has slowed its extension of credit to institutions and firms. Nevertheless, many of the debts that it purchased from banks and other firms have long *maturities*—periods of time before full repayments are due. This situation is quite different from the situation prior to 2008, when only a small portion of the Fed's assets had lengthy maturities.

Furthermore, a number of the debts the Fed has purchased from private institutions are based on mortgage obligations of dubious value. Consequently, the Fed faces considerable risk that at least some of the debts will never be fully repaid. This state of affairs is also quite different from the situation in preceding years, when the bulk of the Fed's assets, about 80 percent of which were U.S. government securities, offered very low risks of loss.

How the Fed Finances the Credit It Extends

In an important sense, the Fed's credit policy results in its activities more closely resembling those of a private bank than a central bank. Like a private banking institution, the Fed extends credit by lending out funds that it obtains from depositors. Unlike private banks, however, the Fed collects the bulk of its deposits from banking institutions instead of from households and firms. These deposits consist of the reserve deposits that banks hold with Federal Reserve banks.

To engage in its active and substantial credit policy, the Fed must induce private banks to maintain substantial reserve deposits with the Federal Reserve banks. A key inducement is the interest rate the Fed pays on reserves. Even though the Fed has paid a very low interest rate of about 0.25 percent on reserve deposits since 2008, throughout most this period, the market clearing federal funds rate has been even lower. Thus, banks have earned more by setting funds aside in reserve deposit accounts at Federal Reserve banks than by lending to other banks in the federal funds market. This means that the Fed essentially has paid banks a per-unit *subsidy* to keep hundreds of billions of dollars on deposit with the Fed.

All such funds held at Federal Reserve banks do not remain idle, though. Just as private banks can use the deposits of households and firms to fund loans and purchases of securities, the Fed can use the reserve deposits of private banks to fund its own lending and securities-buying activities. Since 2008, reserve deposits at Federal Reserve banks have risen from less than $50 billion to more than $1.5 *trillion*. These funds have financed the Fed's credit policy—lending to domestic and foreign banks, nonfinancial companies, and central banks and buying risky, longer-term mortgage obligations.

How has payment of interest on banks' *excess* reserves constituted a subsidy?

POLICY EXAMPLE

Interest on Excess Reserves as a Subsidy

To induce banks to hold the more than $1.5 trillion in funds desired by the Fed to finance its credit policy, in 2008 the Fed began paying interest on excess as well as required reserves. Receipt of these interest payments gave banks an incentive to borrow funds from other sources (at a lower interest rate) to hold on reserve at the Fed. These sources of funds were the government-sponsored housing finance institutions—the Federal National Mortgage Association (FNMA) and the Federal Home Loan Mortgage Corporation (FHLMC).

Banks thereby borrow from FNMA and FHLMC to add to their excess reserves holdings with the Fed at a slightly higher interest rate. In this way, the Fed effectively pays interest on reserves that banks split with FNMA and FHLMC. As a result, the Fed's policy of paying interest on excess reserves effectively grants an estimated $1 billion per year in subsidies to banks and to these two government-sponsored housing finance institutions.

FOR CRITICAL THINKING

How does interest on excess reserves reduce bank lending to households and firms?

Arguments in Favor of the Fed's Credit Policy

Three arguments support the Federal Reserve's credit policy:

1. *Giving Banks Time to Recover from the Financial Meltdown.* The original rationale for initiating the credit policy was to address the deteriorating condition of the U.S. banking industry that began in 2007. As more and more banks weakened during 2008 and 2009, the Fed created an array of lending programs aimed at countering the fact that institutions were less willing to lend to one another in private markets. These new Fed lending programs made banks much more liquid than they would have been otherwise, which ensured their ability to withstand bank runs. The Fed's lending programs also succeeded in keeping many otherwise insolvent banks—those for which the value of assets dropped below the value of liabilities—afloat until they could become more economically viable. A few large institutions ultimately could not continue as stand-alone banks, and hundreds of smaller community banks failed. Nevertheless, the programs provided "breathing space" until other financial institutions could acquire those banks and their lower-valued assets.

2. *Making Financial Markets and Institutions More Liquid and Solvent.* The Fed's purchases of debt securities also helped make financial markets and institutions more liquid and solvent. At the height of the financial crisis, the Fed's purchases of debt securities from companies such as Ford Motor Company and Harley & Davidson, Inc. ensured that these otherwise profitable and solvent firms remained liquid. The Fed's later purchases of mortgage-obligation debt securities removed many high-risk assets from banks' balance sheets and thereby improved the banks' longer-term solvency prospects.

3. *Contributing to International Financial Liquidity.* Finally, the credit extended by the Fed to foreign private banks and central banks enabled these institutions to maintain holdings of U.S. dollars. This credit policy action helped ensure liquidity in international financial markets.

Thus, the Fed's credit policy activities did much to help prevent banks, firms, and financial markets from becoming illiquid, which undoubtedly forestalled possible bank runs in 2008 and 2009. Its credit policy actions also prevented a number of bank failures.

Arguments Against the Fed's Credit Policy

Critics of the Fed's credit policy have offered three arguments against it.

1. *Providing an Incentive for Institutions to Operate Less Efficiently.* Critics point out that the Fed is capable of creating as much liquidity as desired via open market purchases. These critics worry that the Fed encourages institutions to which it directs credit to operate with less attention to minimizing operating costs than they would otherwise.

2. *Reducing Incentives to Screen and Monitor in Order to Limit Asymmetric Information Problems.* Critics of the Fed argue that preventing insolvencies via this credit policy interferes with the functions of private institutions and markets in identifying and addressing asymmetric information problems (see Chapter 15). If banks know the Fed will bail them out, critics suggest, banks will do poorer jobs of screening and monitoring borrowers. Hence, in the longer term, the Fed's credit policy could broaden the scope of asymmetric information problems.

3. *Making Monetary Policy Less Effective.* Critics suggest that the Fed has pursued its credit policy so vigorously that its performance in the realm of monetary policy has worsened. They point out that while the Fed was providing credit to many individual institutions and firms, difficulties in predicting how these actions would affect the money supply contributed to substantial swings in monetary aggregates. In fact, although quantitative-easing policies when the interest rate was near zero raised bank reserves by more than $1.5 trillion, the Fed's credit policies induced banks to hold those reserves idle at Federal Reserve banks. Thus, the reserve ratio increased, and the money multiplier fell. On net, therefore, the money supply failed to grow very much in response to the Fed's quantitative easing. Indeed, over some intervals the money supply even declined.

WHAT IF... the Fed responded to a future financial meltdown by buying up *all* bad debts?

In principle, the Fed possesses authority to buy IOUs from anyone in the event of an emergency. If the Fed were to respond to a future financial meltdown by buying up *all* bad debts, its actions technically would prevent *any* failures from occurring and effectively "bail out" the entire U.S. financial system. Purchasing all bad debts would increase the Fed's assets considerably. Because the Fed's total assets equal its total liabilities, the Fed's liabilities, including reserves of banks, would also increase by a significant amount. The result would be a multiplier effect on the money supply. Consequently, the quantity of money in circulation would rise substantially, which likely would contribute to higher annual inflation rates.

QUICK QUIZ See page 369 for the answers. Review concepts from this section in MyEconLab.

At present, the policy strategy of the Federal Open Market Committee (FOMC) focuses on aiming for a target value of the _____ _____ rate, which the FOMC seeks to achieve via _____ _____ _____ that alter the supply of reserves to the banking system.

The FOMC outlines the Fed's general monetary policy strategy in the FOMC _____, which it transmits to the Trading Desk of the Federal Reserve Bank of _____ _____ for implementation.

Since 2008, the Fed has implemented _____ policy, under which it has extended _____ directly to selected financial institutions and has purchased debt securities that have lost much of their market value.

Advantages of the Fed's _____ policy are that it has provided institutions with more liquidity, has helped to limit the number of bank _____, and has provided more dollars for use in international markets. Disadvantages include reduced incentives for banks to minimize operating costs and to screen and to _____ borrowers and potential conflicts of _____ policy with the Fed's monetary policy responsibilities.

YOU ARE THERE

Applying the Quantity Theory of Money and Prices to a Universe of Star Systems

Eyjolfur Gudmundsson is the central banker for a universe of 7,000 star systems traversed by more than 300,000 starship pilots. The stars and pilots are located in cyberspace, scattered among hundreds of thousands of computers worldwide.

Gudmundsson determines the supply of money used in exchange by players ("starship pilots") who participate in a multiplayer Internet-based game called Eve Online. Gudmundsson has learned that when Eve Online's general level of prices—tabulated from a consumer price index based on game items such as asteroid-mining gear and laser guns—begins to tick upward, a policy response is required. In Eve Online's economy, Gudmundsson has determined, reducing the inflation rate requires decreasing the rate of growth of the quantity of money in circulation. He brings about a lower money growth

rate by reducing the amount of new game currency transmitted to players whenever they succeed in certain tasks required to move to different levels within the game. In this way, Gudmundsson conducts monetary policy based on the quantity theory of money and prices.

Critical Thinking Questions

1. How would Gudmundsson respond if Eve Online's economy experiences deflation?

2. If Eve Online's real GDP and income velocity of money remain unchanged, what determines the rate of inflation experienced by its "starship pilots"?

ISSUES & APPLICATIONS

While Credit Policy Gives, Monetary Policy Takes Away

CONCEPTS APPLIED

▶ Credit Policy

▶ Federal Funds Rate

▶ Money Balances

Since the Fed began implementing credit policy alongside traditional monetary policy in 2008, it has struggled to coordinate these two forms of policymaking. A consequence has been greater variability in the money supply and in the real interest rate.

Increased Money Supply Variability during the Recession

Panel (a) of Figure 16-9 on the following page shows the M2 measure of the money supply since 2001. As you can see, aside from some intermittent and very brief dips, the money supply generally rose at a steady pace until 2008.

When the Fed first began its credit policy programs in 2008, the M2 measure of aggregate money balances dipped and did not grow for several months. Throughout the rest of 2008, M2 grew rapidly. Then M2 steadily *decreased* during the middle part of 2009 before very slightly increasing during 2010.

Thus, just as the economic downturn began in 2008, the Fed allowed money supply growth to drop. Moreover, just as a recovery began in 2009 and 2010, the Fed again allowed the money supply to decline. Both actions reduced aggregate demand.

A "Low" Nominal Federal Funds Rate but a Volatile Real Rate

Panel (b) displays the nominal federal funds rate and the estimated real federal funds rate—the nominal rate minus the estimated expected inflation rate. Until 2008, the nominal and estimated real values of the federal funds rate moved in tandem.

During 2008, the Fed acted to keep the nominal federal funds rate very close to zero. Through its credit policy programs, the Fed extended loans to selected institutions at very low nominal rates of interest. After the Fed allowed money growth to falter in 2008, a significant decrease in inflation occurred. (Indeed, there was a short period of deflation.) As a consequence, although the nominal federal funds rate remained close to zero after 2008, the estimated real federal funds rate rose in 2008, and again during 2009 and 2010 following the second dip in money growth during 2009.

FIGURE 16-9

M2 and Nominal and Estimated Real Federal Funds Rates since 2001

Panel (a) shows that M2 generally increased until 2008. Its level dropped early that year and again during 2009. As indicated in panel (b), even though the nominal federal funds rate has been very low since 2008, the real federal funds rate increased in 2008 and again during 2009 and 2010 following the declines in M2.

Source: Board of Governors of the Federal Reserve System.

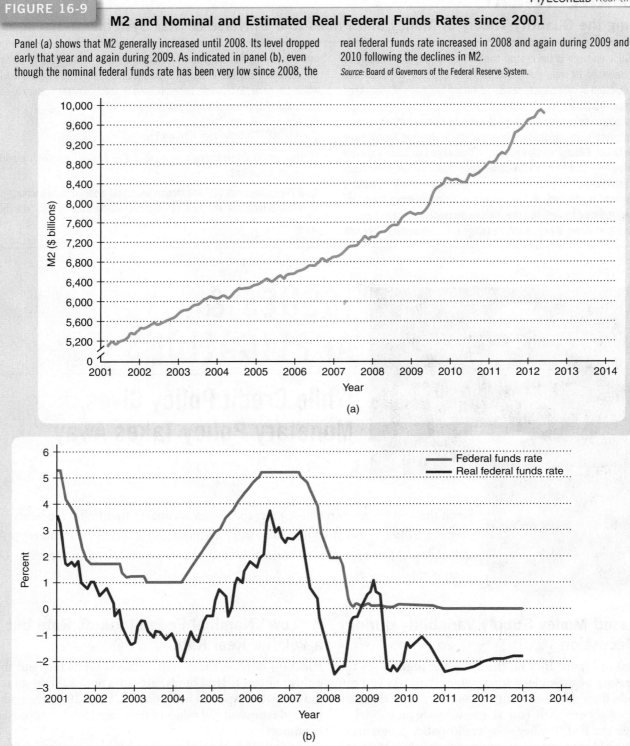

(a)

(b)

The Fed sought to support its credit policy with a near-zero nominal interest rate after 2008, but volatility in aggregate money balances contributed to variable real interest rates. Higher real interest rates raised real borrowing costs in 2009 and again in 2010 even as the Fed perceived that its credit policy was helping to keep borrowing costs low. Thus, the Fed failed to implement a consistently counter-recessionary monetary policy in conjunction with its credit policy.

For Critical Thinking

1. Why did decreases in inflation follow the drops in the money supply?

2. How does deflation raise real interest expenses for borrowers?

Web Resources

1. Take a look at recent values of M2 at www.econtoday.com /chap16.

2. Track the nominal federal funds rate at www.econtoday .com/chap16.

MyEconLab

For more questions on this chapter's Issues & Applications, go to MyEconLab. In the Study Plan for this chapter, select Section N: News.

MyEconLab

Here is what you should know after reading this chapter. MyEconLab will help you identify what you know, and where to go when you need to practice.

WHAT YOU SHOULD KNOW

Key Factors That Influence the Quantity of Money That People Desire to Hold People desire to hold more money to make transactions when nominal GDP increases. In addition, money is a store of value that people may hold alongside bonds, stocks, and other interest-earning assets. The opportunity cost of holding money as an asset is the interest rate, so the quantity of money demanded declines as the market interest rate increases.

money balances, 347
transactions demand, 347
precautionary demand, 347
asset demand, 348

Key Figure
Figure 16-1, 348

WHERE TO GO TO PRACTICE

- **MyEconLab** Study Plan 16.1

How the Federal Reserve's Open Market Operations Influence Market Interest Rates When the Fed sells U.S. government bonds, it must offer them for sale at a lower price to induce buyers to purchase the bonds. The market price of existing bonds and the prevailing interest rate in the economy are inversely related, so the market interest rate rises when the Fed sells bonds.

Key Figure
Figure 16-2, 349

- **MyEconLab** Study Plan 16.2
- Animated Figure 16-2

How Expansionary and Contractionary Monetary Policies Affect Equilibrium Real GDP and the Price Level in the Short Run An expansionary monetary policy action increases the money supply and causes a decrease in market interest rates. The aggregate demand curve shifts rightward, which can eliminate a short-run recessionary gap in real GDP. In contrast, a contractionary monetary policy action reduces the money supply and causes an increase in market interest rates. This results in a leftward shift in the aggregate demand curve, which can eliminate a short-run inflationary gap.

quantitative easing 351

Key Figures
Figure 16-3, 351
Figure 16-4, 352

- **MyEconLab** Study Plan 16.3
- Animated Figures 16-3, 16-4

MyEconLab *continued*

The Equation of Exchange and the Quantity Theory of Money and Prices The equation of exchange states that the quantity of money times the average number of times a unit of money is used in exchange—the income velocity of money—must equal the price level times real GDP. The quantity theory of money and prices assumes that the income velocity of money is constant and real GDP is relatively stable. Thus, a rise in the quantity of money leads to an equiproportional increase in the price level.

equation of exchange, 354
income velocity of money (V), 354
quantity theory of money and prices, 355

- MyEconLab Study Plan 16.3

The Interest-Rate-Based Transmission Mechanism of Monetary Policy The interest-rate-based approach to the monetary policy transmission mechanism operates through effects of monetary policy actions on market interest rates, which bring about changes in desired investment and thereby affect equilibrium real GDP via the multiplier effect. At present, the Fed uses an interest rate target, which is the federal funds rate. Some economists favor selecting the federal funds rate target using a Taylor rule, which specifies an equation for the federal funds rate target based on an estimated long-run real interest rate, the current deviation of actual inflation from the Fed's inflation goal, and the gap between actual real GDP and a measure of potential real GDP.

federal funds market, 357
federal funds rate, 357
discount rate, 358
FOMC Directive, 358
Trading Desk, 358
Taylor rule, 358

Key Figures
Figure 16-6, 356
Figure 16-7, 357
Figure 16-8, 359

- MyEconLab Study Plans 16.3, 16.4, 16.5
- Animated Figures 16-6, 16-7, 16-8

The Use of Credit Policy by Today's Fed Since the late 2000s, the Federal Reserve has used credit policy, which involves direct lending to financial and nonfinancial firms. Today, more than $1.5 trillion, or 40 percent, of the Fed's asset holdings are related to the conduct of credit policy. The Fed's payment of an interest subsidy on reserves provides banks with an incentive to hold the reserves the Fed requires to obtain the funds that it lends. Arguments favoring the Fed credit policy are that it has helped banks recover from the financial meltdown, has contributed to liquidity and solvency of financial markets and institutions, and has made global financial markets more liquid. Arguments against the policy are that it contributes to lower efficiency of the banking system, has reduced bank incentives to screen and monitor in order to reduce asymmetric information problems, and has reduced the effectiveness of monetary policy.

credit policy, 359

- MyEconLab Study Plans 16.5, 16.6, 16.7

Log in to MyEconLab, take a chapter test, and get a personalized Study Plan that tells you which concepts you understand and which ones you need to review. From there, MyEconLab will give you further practice, tutorials, animations, videos, and guided solutions. For more information, visit www.myeconlab.com

PROBLEMS

All problems are assignable in MyEconLab; exercises that update with real-time data are marked with 🌐. Answers to odd-numbered problems appear at the back of the book.

16-1. Let's denote the price of a nonmaturing bond (called a *consol*) as P_b. The equation that indicates this price is $P_b = I/r$, where I is the annual net income the bond generates and r is the nominal market interest rate. (See pages 349–350.)

   a. Suppose that a bond promises the holder $500 per year forever. If the nominal market interest rate is 5 percent, what is the bond's current price?

   b. What happens to the bond's price if the market interest rate rises to 10 percent?

16-2. On the basis of Problem 16-1, imagine that initially the market interest rate is 5 percent and at this interest rate you have decided to hold half of your financial wealth as bonds and half as holdings of non-interest-bearing money. You notice that the market interest rate is starting to rise, however, and you become convinced that it will ultimately rise to 10 percent. (See pages 347–350.)

   a. In what direction do you expect the value of your bond holdings to go when the interest rate rises?

   b. If you wish to prevent the value of your financial wealth from declining in the future, how should you adjust the way you split your wealth between bonds and money? What does this imply about the demand for money?

16-3. You learned in Chapter 11 that if there is an inflationary gap in the short run, then in the long run a new equilibrium arises when input prices and expectations adjust upward, causing the short-run aggregate supply curve to shift upward and to the left and pushing equilibrium real GDP per year back to its long-run value. In this chapter, however, you learned that the Federal Reserve can eliminate an inflationary gap in the short run by undertaking a policy action that reduces aggregate demand. (See page 352.)

   a. Propose one monetary policy action that could eliminate an inflationary gap in the short run.

   b. In what way might society gain if the Fed implements the policy you have proposed instead of simply permitting long-run adjustments to take place?

16-4. You learned in Chapter 11 that if a recessionary gap occurs in the short run, then in the long run a new equilibrium arises when input prices and expectations adjust downward, causing the short-run aggregate supply curve to shift downward and to the right and pushing equilibrium real GDP per year back to its long-run value. In this chapter, you learned that the Federal Reserve can eliminate a recessionary gap in the short run by undertaking a policy action that increases aggregate demand. (See page 352.)

   a. Propose one monetary policy action that could eliminate the recessionary gap in the short run.

   b. In what way might society gain if the Fed implements the policy you have proposed instead of simply permitting long-run adjustments to take place?

16-5. Suppose that the economy currently is in long-run equilibrium. Explain the short- and long-run adjustments that will take place in an aggregate demand–aggregate supply diagram if the Fed expands the quantity of money in circulation. (See page 352.)

16-6. Explain why the net export effect of a contractionary monetary policy reinforces the usual impact that monetary policy has on equilibrium real GDP per year in the short run. (See page 353.)

16-7. Suppose that, initially, the U.S. economy was in an aggregate demand–aggregate supply equilibrium at point A along the aggregate demand curve AD in the diagram below. Now, however, the value of the U.S. dollar suddenly appreciates relative to foreign currencies. This appreciation happens to have no measurable effects on either the short-run or the long-run aggregate supply curve in the United States. It does, however, influence U.S. aggregate demand. (See page 353.)

a. Explain in your own words how the dollar appreciation will affect net export expenditures in the United States.

b. Of the alternative aggregate demand curves depicted in the figure—AD_1 versus AD_2—which could represent the aggregate demand effect of the U.S. dollar's appreciation? What effects does the appreciation have on real GDP and the price level?

c. What policy action might the Federal Reserve take to prevent the dollar's appreciation from affecting equilibrium real GDP in the short run?

16-8. Suppose that the quantity of money in circulation is fixed but the income velocity of money doubles. If real GDP remains at its long-run potential level, what happens to the equilibrium price level? (See page 354.)

16-9. Suppose that following adjustment to the events in Problem 16-8, the Fed cuts the money supply in half. How does the price level now compare with its value before the income velocity and the money supply changed? (See page 354.)

16-10. Consider the following data: The money supply is $1 trillion, the price level equals 2, and real GDP is $5 trillion in base-year dollars. What is the income velocity of money? (See page 354.)

16-11. Consider the data in Problem 16-10. Suppose that the money supply increases by $100 billion and real GDP and the income velocity remain unchanged. (See pages 354–355.)

a. According to the quantity theory of money and prices, what is the new equilibrium price level after full adjustment to the increase in the money supply?

b. What is the percentage increase in the money supply?

c. What is the percentage change in the price level?

d. How do the percentage changes in the money supply and price level compare?

16-12. Assuming that the Fed judges inflation to be the most significant problem in the economy and that it wishes to employ all of its policy instruments except interest on reserves, what should the Fed do with its three policy tools? (See page 357.)

16-13. Suppose that the Fed implements each of the policy changes you discussed in Problem 16-12.

Now explain how the net export effect resulting from these monetary policy actions will reinforce their effects that operate through interest rate changes. (See page 353.)

16-14. Imagine working at the Trading Desk at the New York Fed. Explain whether you would conduct open market purchases or sales in response to each of the following events. Justify your recommendation. (See page 353.)

a. The latest FOMC Directive calls for an increase in the target value of the federal funds rate.

b. For a reason unrelated to monetary policy, the Fed's Board of Governors has decided to raise the differential between the discount rate and the federal funds rate. Nevertheless, the FOMC Directive calls for maintaining the present federal funds rate target.

16-15. To implement a credit policy intended to expand liquidity of the banking system, the Fed desires to increase its assets by lending to a substantial number of banks. How might the Fed adjust the interest rate that it pays banks on reserves in order to induce them to hold the reserves required for funding this credit policy action? What will happen to the Fed's liabilities if it implements this policy action? (See pages 359–362.)

16-16. Suppose that to finance its credit policy, the Fed pays an annual interest rate of 0.25 percent on bank reserves. During the course of the current year, banks hold $1 trillion in reserves. What is the total amount of interest the Fed pays banks during the year? (See pages 359–362.)

16-17. During an interval between mid-2010 and early 2011, the Federal Reserve embarked on a policy it termed "quantitative easing." Total reserves in the banking system increased. Hence, the Federal Reserve's liabilities to banks increased, and at the same time its assets rose as it purchased more assets—many of which were securities with private market values that had dropped considerably. The money multiplier declined, so the net increase in the money supply was negligible. Indeed, during a portion of the period, the money supply actually declined before rising near its previous value. Evaluate whether the Fed's "quantitative easing" was a monetary policy or credit policy action. (See pages 351 and 359–362.)

ECONOMICS ON THE NET

The Fed's Policy Report to Congress Congress requires the Fed to make periodic reports on its recent activities. In this application, you will study recent reports to learn about what factors affect Fed decisions.

Title: Monetary Policy Report to the Congress

Navigation: Go to www.econtoday.com/chap16 to view the Federal Reserve's Monetary Policy Report to the Congress (formerly called the Humphrey-Hawkins Report).

Application Read the report; then answer the following questions.

1. According to the report, what economic events were most important in shaping recent monetary policy?
2. Based on the report, what are the Fed's current monetary policy goals?

For Group Study and Analysis Divide the class into "domestic" and "foreign" groups. Have each group read the past four monetary policy reports and then explain to the class how domestic and foreign factors, respectively, appear to have influenced recent Fed monetary policy decisions. Which of the two types of factors seems to have mattered most during the past year?

ANSWERS TO QUICK QUIZZES

p. 348: (i) demand; (ii) transactions . . . precautionary . . . asset; (iii) opportunity . . . downward

p. 350: (i) lower . . . higher; (ii) inverse; (iii) decrease . . . increase . . . increase . . . decrease

p. 352: (i) direct; (ii) indirect . . . reduction . . . lower

p. 354: (i) exports; (ii) negative . . . more . . . more; (iii) fewer . . . decrease . . . increase

p. 356: (i) equation . . . exchange; (ii) true . . . spent . . . received; (iii) money supply . . . price level

p. 362: (i) federal funds . . . open market operations; (ii) Directive . . . New York; (iii) credit . . . loans; (iv) credit . . . failures . . . monitor . . . credit

APPENDIX E

Monetary Policy: A Keynesian Perspective

According to the traditional Keynesian approach to monetary policy, changes in the money supply can affect the level of aggregate demand only through their effect on interest rates. Moreover, interest rate changes act on aggregate demand solely by changing the level of real planned investment spending. Finally, the traditional Keynesian approach argues that there are plausible circumstances under which monetary policy may have little or no effect on interest rates and thus on aggregate demand.

Figure E-1 below measures real GDP per year along the horizontal axis and total planned expenditures (aggregate demand) along the vertical axis. The components of aggregate demand are real consumption (C), investment (I), government spending (G), and net exports (X). The height of the schedule labeled $C + I + G + X$ shows total real planned expenditures (aggregate demand) as a function of real GDP per year. This schedule slopes upward because consumption depends positively on real GDP. All along the line labeled $Y = C + I + G + X$, real planned spending equals real GDP per year. At point Y^*, where the $C + I + G + X$ line intersects this 45-degree reference line, real planned spending is consistent with real GDP.

At any real GDP level less than Y^*, spending exceeds real GDP, so real GDP and thus spending will tend to rise. At any level of real GDP greater than Y^*, real planned spending is less than real GDP, so real GDP and thus spending will tend to decline. Given the determinants of $C, I, G,$ and X, total spending (aggregate demand) will be Y^*.

FIGURE E-1

An Increase in the Money Supply

An increase in the money supply increases real GDP by lowering interest rates and thus increasing investment from I to I'.

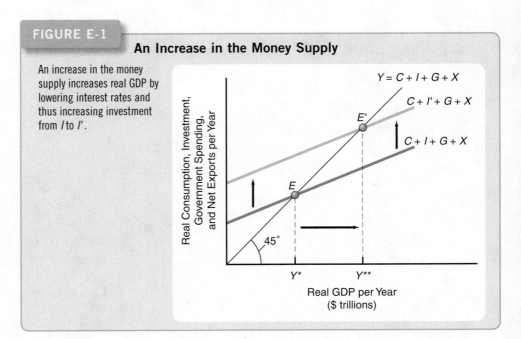

Increasing the Money Supply

According to the Keynesian approach, an increase in the money supply pushes interest rates down. This induces firms to increase the level of investment spending from I to I'. As a result, the $C + I + G + X$ line shifts upward in Figure E-1 on the facing page by the full amount of the rise in investment spending, thus yielding the line $C + I' + G + X$. The rise in investment spending causes real GDP to rise, which in turn causes real consumption spending to rise, further increasing real GDP. Ultimately, aggregate demand rises to Y^{**}, where spending again equals real GDP. A key conclusion of the Keynesian analysis is that total spending rises by *more* than the original rise in investment spending because consumption spending depends positively on real GDP.

Decreasing the Money Supply

Not surprisingly, contractionary monetary policy works in exactly the reverse manner. A reduction in the money supply pushes interest rates up. Firms respond by reducing their investment spending, and this pushes real GDP downward. Consumers react to the lower real GDP by scaling back on their real consumption spending, which further depresses real GDP. Thus, the ultimate decline in real GDP is larger than the initial drop in investment spending. Indeed, because the change in real GDP is a multiple of the change in investment, Keynesians note that changes in investment spending (similar to changes in government spending) have a *multiplier* effect on the economy.

Arguments Against Monetary Policy

It might be thought that this multiplier effect would make monetary policy a potent tool in the Keynesian arsenal, particularly when it comes to getting the economy out of a recession. In fact, however, many traditional Keynesians argue that monetary policy is likely to be relatively ineffective as a recession fighter.

According to their line of reasoning, although monetary policy has the potential to reduce interest rates, changes in the money supply have little *actual* impact on interest rates. Instead, during recessions, people try to build up as much as they can in liquid assets to protect themselves from risks of unemployment and other losses of income. When the monetary authorities increase the money supply, individuals are willing to allow most of it to accumulate in their bank accounts. This desire for increased liquidity thus prevents interest rates from falling very much, which in turn means that there will be almost no change in investment spending and thus little change in aggregate demand.

PROBLEMS

All problems are assignable in MyEconLab. Answers to odd-numbered problems appear at the back of the book.

E-1. Suppose that each 0.1-percentage-point decrease in the equilibrium interest rate induces a $10 billion increase in real planned investment spending by businesses. In addition, the investment multiplier is equal to 5, and the money multiplier is equal to 4. Furthermore, every $20 billion increase in the money supply brings about a 0.1-percentage-point reduction in the equilibrium interest rate. Use this information to answer the following questions under the assumption that all other things are equal. (See page 370–371.)

a. How much must real planned investment increase if the Federal Reserve desires to bring about a $100 billion increase in equilibrium real GDP?

b. How much must the money supply change for the Fed to induce the change in real planned investment calculated in part (a)?

c. What dollar amount of open market operations must the Fed undertake to bring about the money supply change calculated in part (b)?

E-2. Suppose that each 0.1-percentage-point increase in the equilibrium interest rate induces a $5 billion decrease in real planned investment spending by businesses. In addition, the investment multiplier is equal to 4, and the money multiplier is equal to 3. Furthermore, every $9 billion decrease in the money supply brings about a 0.1-percentage-point increase in the equilibrium interest rate. Use this information to answer the following questions under the assumption that all other things are equal. (See pages 370–371.)

   a. How much must real planned investment decrease if the Federal Reserve desires to bring about an $80 billion decrease in equilibrium real GDP?

   b. How much must the money supply change for the Fed to induce the change in real planned investment calculated in part (a)?

   c. What dollar amount of open market operations must the Fed undertake to bring about the money supply change calculated in part (b)?

E-3. Assume that the following conditions exist (see pages 370–371):

   a. All banks are fully loaned up—there are no excess reserves, and desired excess reserves are always zero.

   b. The money multiplier is 3.

   c. The planned investment schedule is such that at a 6 percent rate of interest, investment is $1,200 billion; at 5 percent, investment is $1,225 billion.

   d. The investment multiplier is 3.

   e. The initial equilibrium level of real GDP is $12 trillion.

   f. The equilibrium rate of interest is 6 percent.

Now the Fed engages in expansionary monetary policy. It buys $1 billion worth of bonds, which increases the money supply, which in turn lowers the market rate of interest by 1 percentage point. Determine how much the money supply must have increased, and then trace out the numerical consequences of the associated reduction in interest rates on all the other variables mentioned.

E-4. Assume that the following conditions exist (see pages 370–371):

   a. All banks are fully loaned up—there are no excess reserves, and desired excess reserves are always zero.

   b. The money multiplier is 4.

   c. The planned investment schedule is such that at a 4 percent rate of interest, investment is $1,400 billion. At 5 percent, investment is $1,380 billion.

   d. The investment multiplier is 5.

   e. The initial equilibrium level of real GDP is $13 trillion.

   f. The equilibrium rate of interest is 4 percent.

Now the Fed engages in contractionary monetary policy. It sells $2 billion worth of bonds, which reduces the money supply, which in turn raises the market rate of interest by 1 percentage point. Determine how much the money supply must have decreased, and then trace out the numerical consequences of the associated increase in interest rates on all the other variables mentioned.

Stabilization in an Integrated World Economy

17

For more than 50 years, many economists have used an inverse relationship between the unemployment rate and real GDP as a guide to macroeconomic policymaking. Since 2009, however, this relationship appears to have broken down. Now some economists are suggesting that the inverse relationship may not return for a long time—or perhaps never. If these economists are correct, the case for discretionary policymaking is weaker than it was prior to 2009. Studying this chapter will help you understand why such a policy implication follows if the inverse relationship between the unemployment rate and real GDP has indeed broken down.

LEARNING OBJECTIVES

After reading this chapter, you should be able to:

▶ Explain why the actual unemployment rate might depart from the natural rate of unemployment

▶ Describe why there may be an inverse relationship between the inflation rate and the unemployment rate, reflected by the Phillips curve

▶ Evaluate how expectations affect the actual relationship between the inflation rate and the unemployment rate

▶ Understand the rational expectations hypothesis and its implications for economic policymaking

▶ Distinguish among alternative modern approaches to strengthening the case for active policymaking

MyEconLab helps you master each objective and study more efficiently. See end of chapter for details.

analysis of prices posted on Internet Web sites and processed by automatic scanners in brick-and-mortar stores verifies that by far the most common ending number in a price for an item priced as high as $11 is "9"? In addition, prices ending in the number "9" change less often than prices ending in other numbers. When prices ending in the number "9" *do* change, though, the price changes typically are larger than those from prices ending in numbers other than "9." Some economists who study these and other data relating to how firms price their goods and services suggest that these facts contribute to "price stickiness"—that is, a generalized tendency for prices to adjust sluggishly over time.

In this chapter, you will learn about possible consequences of widespread price stickiness. Among these is that sticky prices may help to make macroeconomic policies aimed at stabilizing the economy more potent.

Active versus Passive Policymaking

If it is true that monetary and fiscal policy actions aimed at exerting significant stabilizing effects on overall economic activity are likely to succeed, then this would be a strong argument for **active (discretionary) policymaking.** This is the term for actions that monetary and fiscal policymakers undertake in reaction to or in anticipation of a change in economic performance. On the other side of the debate is the view that the best way to achieve economic stability is through **passive (nondiscretionary) policymaking,** in which there is no deliberate stabilization policy at all. Policymakers follow a rule and do not attempt to respond in a discretionary manner to actual or potential changes in economic activity.

Recall from Chapter 13 that there are lags between the time when the national economy enters a recession or a boom and the time when that fact becomes known and acted on by policymakers. Proponents of passive policy argue that such time lags often render short-term stabilization policy ineffective or, worse, procyclical.

To take a stand on this debate concerning active versus passive policymaking, you first need to know the potential trade-offs that policymakers believe they face. Then you need to see what the data actually show. The most important policy trade-off appears to be between price stability and unemployment. Before exploring that, however, we need to look at the economy's natural, or long-run, rate of unemployment.

The Natural Rate of Unemployment

Recall from Chapter 7 that there are different types of unemployment: frictional, cyclical, structural, and seasonal. *Frictional unemployment* arises because individuals take the time to search for the best job opportunities. Much unemployment is of this type, except when the economy is in a recession or a depression, when cyclical unemployment rises.

Note that we did not say that frictional unemployment was the *sole* form of unemployment during normal times. *Structural unemployment* is caused by a variety of "rigidities" throughout the economy. Structural unemployment results from factors such as these:

1. Government-imposed minimum wage laws, laws restricting entry into occupations, and welfare and unemployment insurance benefits that reduce incentives to work

2. Union activity that sets wages above the equilibrium level and also restricts the mobility of labor

All of these factors reduce individuals' abilities or incentives to choose employment rather than unemployment.

Consider the effect of unemployment insurance benefits on the probability of an unemployed person's finding a job. When unemployment benefits run out, according to economists Lawrence Katz and Bruce Meyer, the probability of an unemployed person's finding a job doubles. The conclusion is that unemployed workers are more serious about finding a job when they are no longer receiving such benefits.

Active (discretionary) policymaking
All actions on the part of monetary and fiscal policymakers that are undertaken in response to or in anticipation of some change in the overall economy.

Passive (nondiscretionary) policymaking
Policymaking that is carried out in response to a rule. It is therefore not in response to an actual or potential change in overall economic activity.

Frictional unemployment and structural unemployment both exist even when the economy is in long-run equilibrium—they are a natural consequence of costly information (the need to conduct a job search) and the existence of rigidities such as those noted above. Because these two types of unemployment are a natural consequence of imperfect and costly information and rigidities, they are components of what economists call the **natural rate of unemployment.** As we discussed in Chapter 7, this is defined as the rate of unemployment that would exist in the long run after everyone in the economy fully adjusted to any changes that have occurred. Recall that real GDP per year tends to return to the level implied by the long-run aggregate supply curve (*LRAS*). Thus, whatever rate of unemployment the economy tends to return to in long-run equilibrium can be called the natural rate of unemployment.

How has the natural rate of unemployment changed over the years?

Natural rate of unemployment
The rate of unemployment that is estimated to prevail in long-run macroeconomic equilibrium, when all workers and employers have fully adjusted to any changes in the economy.

EXAMPLE

The U.S. Natural Rate of Unemployment

In 1982, the unemployment rate was nearly 10 percent. By the late 2000s and early 2010s, it was at this level once again. These two nearly matching unemployment rates prove nothing by themselves. But look at Figure 17-1 below. There you see not only what has happened to the unemployment rate since 1950 but an estimate of the natural rate of unemployment. The line labeled "Natural rate of unemployment" is produced by averaging unemployment rates from five years earlier to five years later at each point in time (except for the end period, which is

estimated). This computation reveals that until the late 1980s, the natural rate of unemployment was rising. Then it trended downward until the late 2000s, when it began to rise once more, to nearly 8 percent by 2013.

FOR CRITICAL THINKING
Why does the natural rate of unemployment differ from the actual rate of unemployment?

MyEconLab Real-time data

FIGURE 17-1

Estimated Natural Rate of Unemployment in the United States

As you can see, the actual rate of unemployment has varied widely in the United States in recent decades. If we generate the natural rate of unemployment by averaging unemployment rates from five years earlier to five years later at each point in time, we get the line so labeled. It rose from the 1950s until the late 1980s and then declined until the late 2000s, when it began to rise again.

Sources: Economic Report of the President; Economic Indicators, various issues; author's estimates.

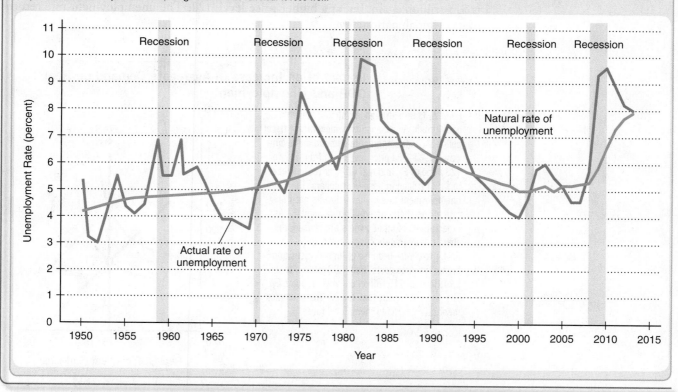

Departures from the Natural Rate of Unemployment

Even though the unemployment rate has a strong tendency to stay at and return to the natural rate, it is possible for other factors, such as changes in private spending or fiscal and monetary policy actions, to move the actual unemployment rate away from the natural rate, at least in the short run. Deviations of the actual unemployment rate from the natural rate are called *cyclical unemployment* because they are observed over the course of nationwide business fluctuations. During recessions, the overall unemployment rate exceeds the natural rate, so cyclical unemployment is positive. During periods of economic booms, the overall unemployment rate can go below the natural rate. At such times, cyclical unemployment is negative.

To see how departures from the natural rate of unemployment can occur, let's consider two examples. In Figure 17-2 below, we begin in equilibrium at point E_1 with the associated price level 117 and real GDP per year of $15 trillion.

THE IMPACT OF EXPANSIONARY POLICY Now imagine that the government decides to use fiscal or monetary policy to stimulate the economy. Further suppose, for reasons that will soon become clear, that this policy surprises decision makers throughout the economy in the sense that they did not anticipate that the policy would occur.

As shown in Figure 17-2, the expansionary policy action causes the aggregate demand curve to shift from AD_1 to AD_2. The price level rises from 117 to 120. Real GDP, measured in base-year dollars, increases from $15 trillion to $15.4 trillion.

In the labor market, individuals find that conditions have improved markedly relative to what they expected. Firms seeking to expand output want to hire more workers. To accomplish this, they recruit more actively and possibly ask workers to work overtime, so individuals in the labor market find more job openings and more possible hours they can work. Consequently, as you learned in Chapter 7, the average duration of unemployment falls, and so does the unemployment rate.

The *SRAS* curve does not stay at $SRAS_1$ indefinitely, however. Input owners, such as workers and owners of capital and raw materials, revise their expectations. The short-run aggregate supply curve shifts to $SRAS_2$ as input prices rise. We find ourselves at a new equilibrium at E_3, which is on the *LRAS*. Long-run real GDP per year is $15 trillion again, but at a higher price level, 122. The unemployment rate returns to its original, natural level.

YOU ARE THERE

To learn more about the extent to which active fiscal policy stabilizes employment in the dampened economy, take a look at **Active Policies Can Raise Employment—At a Substantial Cost** on page 390.

FIGURE 17-2

Impact of an Increase in Aggregate Demand on Real GDP and Unemployment

Point E_1 is an initial short-run and long-run equilibrium. An expansionary monetary or fiscal policy shifts the aggregate demand curve outward to AD_2. The price level rises from 117 to 120 at point E_2, and real GDP per year increases to $15.4 trillion in base-year dollars. The unemployment rate is now below its natural rate at the short-run equilibrium point E_2. As expectations of input owners are revised, the short-run aggregate supply curve shifts from $SRAS_1$ to $SRAS_2$ because of higher prices and higher resource costs. Real GDP returns to the *LRAS* level of $15 trillion per year, at point E_3. The price level increases to 122. The unemployment rate returns to the natural rate.

WHAT IF... the government were to boost economic expansion by offering people more food stamps?

In recent years, some U.S. government officials have claimed that surging use of the Supplemental Nutrition Assistance (food stamp) Program and various other transfer programs has helped contribute to increases in total planned expenditures. Indeed, Agriculture Secretary Tom Vilsack has referred to the food stamp program as an "economic stimulus." According to the secretary, "every dollar of food stamp benefits generates $1.84 in the economy in terms of economic activity." By definition, however, the food stamp program is a transfer program. That is, the program *transfers* a portion of income earned by some people during a given year to other people without influencing the *aggregate* income flow. Hence, higher food stamp benefits—as well as increases in any other forms of transfer payments—have virtually no effects on total planned expenditures, aggregate demand, or equilibrium real GDP.

THE CONSEQUENCES OF CONTRACTIONARY POLICY Instead of expansionary policy, the government could have decided to engage in contractionary (or deflationary) policy. As shown in Figure 17-3 below, the sequence of events would have been in the opposite direction of those in Figure 17-2 on the facing page.

Beginning from an initial equilibrium E_1, an unanticipated reduction in aggregate demand puts downward pressure on both prices and real GDP. The price level falls from 120 to 118, and real GDP declines from $15 trillion to $14.7 trillion. Fewer firms are hiring, and those that are hiring offer fewer overtime possibilities. Individuals looking for jobs find that it takes longer than predicted. As a result, unemployed individuals remain unemployed longer. The average duration of unemployment rises, and so does the rate of unemployment.

The equilibrium at E_2 is only a short-run situation, however. As input owners change their expectations about future prices, $SRAS_1$ shifts to $SRAS_2$, and input prices fall. The new long-run equilibrium is at E_3, which is on the long-run aggregate supply curve, $LRAS$. In the long run, the price level declines farther, to 116, as real GDP returns to $15 trillion. Thus, in the long run the unemployment rate returns to its natural level.

The Phillips Curve: A Rationale for Active Policymaking?

Let's recap what we have just observed. In the short run, an *unexpected increase* in aggregate demand causes the price level to rise and the unemployment rate to fall. Conversely, in the short run, an *unexpected decrease* in aggregate demand causes the

FIGURE 17-3

Impact of a Decline in Aggregate Demand on Real GDP and Unemployment

Starting from equilibrium at E_1, a decline in aggregate demand to AD_2 leads to a lower price level, 118, and real GDP declines to $14.7 trillion. The unemployment rate will rise above the natural rate of unemployment. Equilibrium at E_2 is temporary, however. At the lower price level, the expectations of input owners are revised. $SRAS_1$ shifts to $SRAS_2$. The new long-run equilibrium is at E_3, with real GDP equal to $15 trillion and a price level of 116. The actual unemployment rate is once again equal to the natural rate of unemployment.

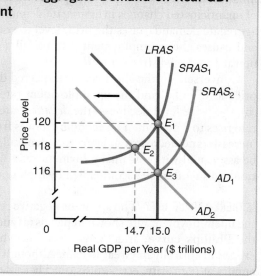

FIGURE 17-4

The Phillips Curve

Unanticipated changes in aggregate demand produce a negative relationship between the inflation rate and unemployment. U^* is the natural rate of unemployment.

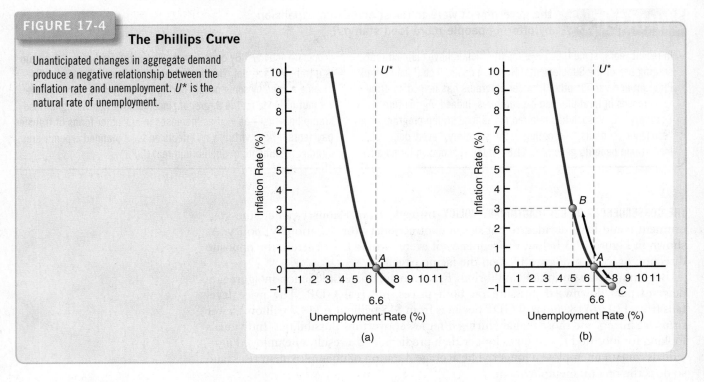

(a)   (b)

price level to fall and the unemployment rate to rise. Moreover, although not shown explicitly in either diagram, two additional points are true:

1. The greater the unexpected increase in aggregate demand, the greater the amount of inflation that results in the short run, and the lower the unemployment rate.

2. The greater the unexpected decrease in aggregate demand, the greater the deflation that results in the short run, and the higher the unemployment rate.

THE NEGATIVE SHORT-RUN RELATIONSHIP BETWEEN INFLATION AND UNEMPLOYMENT Figure 17-4 above summarizes these findings. The inflation rate (*not* the price level) is measured along the vertical axis, and the unemployment rate is measured along the horizontal axis. Panel (a) shows the unemployment rate at a sample natural rate, U^*, that is assumed to be 6.6 percent at point A. At this point, the actual inflation rate and anticipated inflation rate are both equal to 0 percent. Panel (b) of Figure 17-4 depicts the effects of unanticipated changes in aggregate demand. In panel (b), an unexpected increase in aggregate demand causes the price level to rise—the inflation rate rises to 3 percent— and causes the unemployment rate to fall to 5 percent. Thus, the economy moves upward to the left from A to B.

Conversely, in the short run, unexpected decreases in aggregate demand cause the price level to fall and the unemployment rate to rise above the natural rate. In panel (b), the price level declines—the *deflation* rate is –1 percent—and the unemployment rate rises to 8 percent. The economy moves from point A to point C. If we look at both increases and decreases in aggregate demand, we see that high inflation rates tend to be associated with low unemployment rates (as at B) and that low (or negative) inflation rates tend to be accompanied by high unemployment rates (as at C).

IS THERE A TRADE-OFF? The apparent negative relationship between the inflation rate and the unemployment rate shown in panels (a) and (b) of Figure 17-4 has come to be called the **Phillips curve**, after A. W. Phillips, who discovered that a similar relationship existed historically in Great Britain. Although Phillips presented his findings only as an empirical regularity, economists quickly came to view the relationship as representing

Phillips curve
A curve showing the relationship between unemployment and changes in wages or prices. It was long thought to reflect a trade-off between unemployment and inflation.

a *trade-off* between inflation and unemployment. In particular, policymakers who favored active policymaking believed that they could *choose* alternative combinations of unemployment and inflation. Thus, it seemed that a government that disliked unemployment could select a point like B in panel (b) of Figure 17-4 on the facing page, with a positive inflation rate but a relatively low unemployment rate. Conversely, a government that feared inflation could choose a stable price level at A, but only at the expense of a higher associated unemployment rate. Indeed, the Phillips curve seemed to suggest that it was possible for discretionary policymakers to fine-tune the economy by selecting the policies that would produce the exact mix of unemployment and inflation that suited current government objectives. As it turned out, matters are not so simple.

The Importance of Expectations

The reduction in unemployment that takes place as the economy moves from A to B in Figure 17-4 occurs because the wage offers encountered by unemployed workers are unexpectedly high. As far as the workers are concerned, these higher *nominal* wages appear, at least initially, to be increases in *real* wages. It is this perception that induces them to reduce the duration of their job search. This is a sensible way for the workers to view the world if aggregate demand fluctuates up and down at random, with no systematic or predictable variation one way or another. But if activist policymakers attempt to exploit the apparent trade-off in the Phillips curve, according to economists who support passive policymaking, aggregate demand will no longer move up and down in an *unpredictable* way.

THE EFFECTS OF AN UNANTICIPATED POLICY Consider, for example, Figure 17-5 below. If the Federal Reserve attempts to reduce the unemployment rate to 5 percent, it must increase the rate of growth of the money supply enough to produce an inflation rate of 3 percent. If this is an unexpected one-shot action in which the rate of growth of the money supply is first increased and then returned to its previous level, the inflation rate will temporarily rise to 3 percent, and the unemployment rate will temporarily fall to 5 percent. Proponents of passive policymaking contend that past experience with active policies indicates that after the money supply stops growing, the inflation

---

A Shift in the Phillips Curve

When there is a change in the expected inflation rate, the Phillips curve (*PC*) shifts to incorporate the new expectations. PC_0 shows expectations of zero inflation. PC_3 reflects a higher expected inflation rate, such as 3 percent.

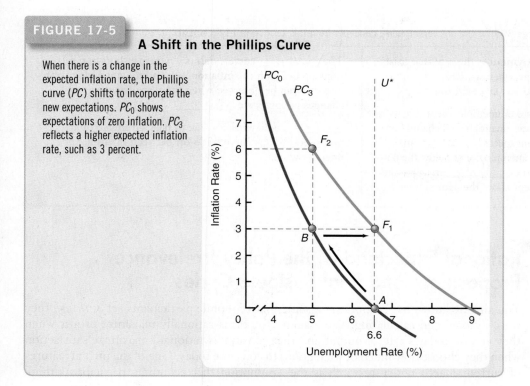

rate will soon return to zero and unemployment will return to 6.6 percent, its natural rate. Thus, an unexpected temporary increase in money supply growth will cause a movement from point A to point B, and the economy will move on its own back to A.

ADJUSTING EXPECTATIONS AND A SHIFTING PHILLIPS CURVE Why do those advocating passive policymaking argue that variations in the unemployment rate from its natural rate typically are temporary? If activist authorities wish to prevent the unemployment rate from returning to $U^* = 6.6$ percent in Figure 17-5 on the previous page, they will conclude that the money supply must grow fast enough to keep the inflation rate up at 3 percent. But if the Fed does this, argue those who favor passive policymaking, all of the economic participants in the economy—workers and job seekers included—will come to *expect* that inflation rate to continue. This, in turn, will change their expectations about wages.

For example, when the expected inflation rate was zero, a 3 percent rise in nominal wages meant a 3 percent expected rise in real wages, and this was sufficient to induce some individuals to take jobs rather than remain unemployed. It was this expectation of a rise in real wages that reduced search duration and caused the unemployment rate to drop from $U^* = 6.6$ percent to 5 percent. But if the expected inflation rate becomes 3 percent, a 3 percent rise in nominal wages means *no* rise in *real* wages. Once workers come to expect the higher inflation rate, rising nominal wages will no longer be sufficient to entice them out of unemployment. As a result, as the *expected* inflation rate moves up from 0 percent to 3 percent, the unemployment rate will move up also.

In terms of Figure 17-5, as authorities initially increase aggregate demand, the economy moves from point A to point B. If the authorities continue the stimulus in an effort to keep the unemployment rate down, workers' expectations will adjust, causing the unemployment rate to rise. In this second stage, the economy moves from B to point F_1. The unemployment rate returns to the natural rate, $U^* = 6.6$ percent, but the inflation rate is now 3 percent instead of zero. Once the adjustment of expectations has taken place, any further changes in policy will have to take place along a curve such as PC_3, say, a movement from F_1 to F_2. This new schedule is also a Phillips curve, differing from the first, PC_0, in that the actual inflation rate consistent with a 5 percent unemployment rate is higher, at 6 percent, because the expected inflation rate is higher.

To try out the "biz/ed" Web site's virtual economy and use the Phillips curve as a guide for policymaking in the United Kingdom, go to www.econtoday.com/chap17.

QUICK QUIZ See page 395 for the answers. Review concepts from this section in MyEconLab.

The **natural rate of unemployment** is the rate that exists in _____-run equilibrium, when workers' _____ are consistent with actual conditions.

Departures from the natural rate of unemployment can occur when individuals encounter unanticipated changes in fiscal or monetary policy. An unexpected _____ in aggregate demand will reduce unemployment below the natural rate, whereas an unanticipated _____ in aggregate demand will push unemployment above the natural rate.

The _____ curve exhibits a negative short-run relationship between the inflation rate and the unemployment rate that can be observed when there are *unanticipated* changes in aggregate _____.

_____ policymakers seek to take advantage of a proposed Phillips curve trade-off between inflation and unemployment.

Rational Expectations, the Policy Irrelevance Proposition, and Real Business Cycles

You already know that economists assume that economic participants act *as though* they were rational and calculating. We assume that firms rationally maximize profits when they choose today's rate of output and that consumers rationally maximize satisfaction when they choose how much of what goods to consume today. One of the pivotal features of current macro policy research is the assumption that economic participants think rationally about the future as well as the present. This relationship was developed by Robert Lucas, who won the Nobel Prize in 1995 for his work. In particular, there is widespread agreement among many macroeconomics researchers that the **rational expectations hypothesis** extends our understanding of the behavior of the macro-economy. This hypothesis has two key elements:

Rational expectations hypothesis
A theory stating that people combine the effects of past policy changes on important economic variables with their own judgment about the future effects of current and future policy changes.

1. Individuals base their forecasts (expectations) about the future values of economic variables on all readily available past and current information.

2. These expectations incorporate individuals' understanding about how the economy operates, including the operation of monetary and fiscal policy.

In essence, the rational expectations hypothesis holds that Abraham Lincoln was correct when he said, "You can fool all the people some of the time. You can even fool some of the people all of the time. But you can't fool *all* of the people *all* the time."

If we further assume that there is pure competition in all markets and that all prices and wages are flexible, we obtain what many call the *new classical* approach to evaluating the effects of macroeconomic policies. To see how rational expectations operate in the new classical perspective, let's take a simple example of the economy's response to a change in monetary policy.

Flexible Wages and Prices, Rational Expectations, and Policy Irrelevance

Consider Figure 17-6 below, which shows the long-run aggregate supply curve (*LRAS*) for the economy, as well as the initial aggregate demand curve (*AD*₁) and the short-run aggregate supply curve (*SRAS*₁). The money supply is initially given by $M_1 = \$10$ trillion, and the price level and real GDP are equal to 110 and $15 trillion, respectively. Consequently, point *A* represents the initial long-run equilibrium.

Suppose now that the money supply is unexpectedly increased to $M_2 = \$11$ trillion, thereby causing the aggregate demand curve to shift outward to AD_2. Given the location of the short-run aggregate supply curve, this increase in aggregate demand

---

FIGURE 17-6

Responses to Anticipated and Unanticipated Increases in Aggregate Demand

A $1 trillion increase in the money supply causes the aggregate demand curve to shift rightward. If people anticipate the increase in the money supply, then workers will insist on higher nominal wages, which causes the short-run aggregate supply curve to shift leftward immediately, from $SRAS_1$ to $SRAS_2$. Hence, there is a direct movement, indicated by the green arrow, from point *A* to point *C*. In contrast, an unanticipated increase in the money supply causes an initial upward movement along $SRAS_1$ from point *A* to point *B*, indicated by the black arrow. Thus, in the short run, real GDP rises from $15 trillion to $15.3 trillion. In the long run, workers recognize that the price level has increased and demand higher wages, causing the *SRAS* curve to shift leftward, resulting in a movement from point *B* to point *C*.

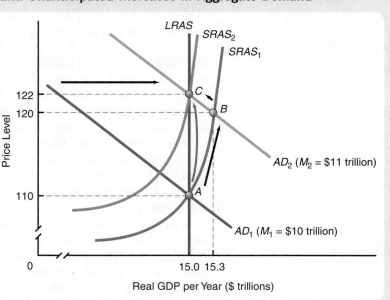

will cause the price level and real GDP to rise to 120 and $15.3 trillion, respectively. The new short-run equilibrium is at *B*. Because real GDP is *above* the long-run equilibrium level of $15 trillion, unemployment must be below long-run levels (the natural rate), and so workers will soon respond to the higher price level by demanding higher nominal wages. This will cause the short-run aggregate supply curve to shift upward vertically. As indicated by the black arrow, the economy moves from point *B* to a new long-run equilibrium at *C*.

The price level thus continues its rise to 122, even as real GDP declines back down to $15 trillion (and unemployment returns to the natural rate). So, as we have seen before, even though an increase in the money supply can raise real GDP and lower unemployment in the short run, it has no effect on either variable in the long run.

ANTICIPATED POLICY AND THE POLICY IRRELEVANCE PROPOSITION What if people *anticipate* the policy action discussed above? Let's look again at Figure 17-6 on the previous page to consider the answer to this question. In the initial equilibrium at point *A* of the figure, the short-run aggregate supply curve $SRAS_1$ corresponds to a situation in which the expected money supply and the actual money supply are equal. When the money supply changes in a way that is anticipated by economic participants, the aggregate supply curve will shift to reflect this expected change in the money supply. The new short-run aggregate supply curve $SRAS_2$ reflects this. According to the rational expectations hypothesis, the short-run aggregate supply curve will shift upward *simultaneously* with the rise in aggregate demand. As a result, the economy will move directly from point *A* to point *C*, without passing through *B*, as depicted by the green arrow in Figure 17-6.

The *only* response to the rise in the money supply is a rise in the price level from 110 to 122. Neither output nor unemployment changes at all. This conclusion—that fully anticipated monetary policy is irrelevant in determining the levels of real variables—is called the **policy irrelevance proposition:**

> *Under the assumption of rational expectations on the part of decision makers in the economy,* anticipated *monetary policy cannot alter either the rate of unemployment or the level of real GDP. Regardless of the nature of the anticipated policy, the unemployment rate will equal the natural rate, and real GDP will be determined solely by the economy's long-run aggregate supply curve.*

Policy irrelevance proposition
The conclusion that policy actions have no real effects in the short run if the policy actions are anticipated and none in the long run even if the policy actions are unanticipated.

Another Challenge to Policy Activism: Real Business Cycles

When confronted with the policy irrelevance proposition, many economists began to reexamine the first principles of macroeconomics with fully flexible wages and prices.

THE DISTINCTION BETWEEN REAL AND MONETARY SHOCKS Some economists argue that real, as opposed to purely monetary, forces might help explain aggregate economic fluctuations. These shocks may take various forms such as technological advances that improve productivity, changes in the composition of the labor force, or changes in availability of a key resource. Consider Figure 17-7 on the facing page, which illustrates the concept of *real business cycles*. We begin at point E_1 with the economy in both short- and long-run equilibrium, with the associated supply curves, $SRAS_1$ and $LRAS_1$. Initially, the level of real GDP is $15 trillion, and the price level is 118. Because the economy is in long-run equilibrium, the unemployment rate must be at the natural rate.

A permanent reduction in the supply of a key productive resource, such as oil, causes both the *SRAS* and *LRAS* curves to shift to the left, to $SRAS_2$ and $LRAS_2$, because fewer goods will be available for sale due to the reduced supplies. In the short run, two adjustments begin to occur simultaneously. First, the prices of oil and petroleum-based products begin to rise, so the overall price level rises to 121. Second, the higher costs

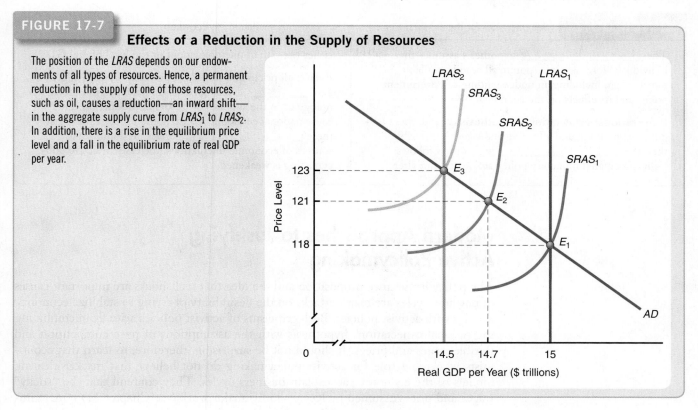

FIGURE 17-7

Effects of a Reduction in the Supply of Resources

The position of the *LRAS* depends on our endowments of all types of resources. Hence, a permanent reduction in the supply of one of those resources, such as oil, causes a reduction—an inward shift— in the aggregate supply curve from *LRAS₁* to *LRAS₂*. In addition, there is a rise in the equilibrium price level and a fall in the equilibrium rate of real GDP per year.

of production occasioned by the rise in oil prices induce firms to cut back production, so real GDP falls to $14.7 trillion in the short run. The new temporary short-run equilibrium occurs at E_2, with a higher price level (121) and a lower level of real GDP ($14.7 trillion).

This is not the full story, however. Owners of nonoil inputs, such as labor, are also affected by the reduction in oil supplies. For instance, as the real wage falls as a result of the higher price level, some workers who were willing to continue on the job at lower real wages in the short run will eventually decide to switch from full-time to part-time employment or to drop out of the labor force altogether. Thus, there will be a fall in the supply of nonoil inputs, reflected in an upward shift in the *SRAS* curve from $SRAS_2$ to $SRAS_3$. This puts additional upward pressure on the price level and exerts a downward force on real GDP. Thus, the final long-run equilibrium occurs at point E_3, with the price level at 123 and real GDP at $14.5 trillion.

STAGFLATION Notice that in the example depicted in Figure 17-7 above, real GDP declines over the same interval that the price level increases. This decline in real GDP is associated with lower employment and a higher unemployment rate. At the same time, there is higher inflation. Such a situation involving lower real GDP and increased inflation is called **stagflation.**

The most recent prolonged periods of stagflation in the United States occurred during the 1970s and early 1980s. One factor contributing to stagflation episodes during those years was sharp reductions in the supply of oil, as in the example illustrated in Figure 17-7. In addition, Congress enacted steep increases in marginal tax rates and implemented a host of new federal regulations on firms in the early 1970s. All these factors together acted to reduce long-run aggregate supply and hence contributed to stagflation. Increases in oil supplies, cuts in marginal tax rates, and deregulation during the 1980s and 1990s helped to prevent stagflation episodes from occurring after the early 1980s.

Stagflation

A situation characterized by lower real GDP, lower employment, and a higher unemployment rate during the same period that the rate of inflation increases.

The _____ _____ hypothesis assumes that individuals' forecasts incorporate all readily available information, including an understanding of government policy and its effects on the economy.

If the **rational expectations hypothesis** is valid, there is pure competition, and all prices and wages are flexible, then the _____ _____ proposition follows: Fully anticipated monetary policy actions cannot alter either the rate of unemployment or the level of real GDP.

Even if all prices and wages are perfectly flexible, aggregate _____ shocks such as sudden changes in technology or in the supplies of factors of production can cause national economic fluctuations. To the extent that these _____ _____ cycles predominate as sources of economic fluctuations, the case for active policymaking is weakened.

Modern Approaches to Justifying Active Policymaking

The policy irrelevance proposition and the idea that real shocks are important causes of business cycles are major attacks on the desirability of trying to stabilize economic activity with activist policies. Both criticisms of activist policies arise from combining the rational expectations hypothesis with the assumptions of pure competition and flexible wages and prices. It should not be surprising, therefore, to learn that economists who see a role for activist policymaking do not believe that market clearing models of the economy can explain business cycles. They contend that the "sticky" wages and prices assumed by Keynes in his major work (see Chapter 11) remain important in today's economy. To explain how aggregate demand shocks and policies can influence a nation's real GDP and unemployment rate, these economists, who are sometimes called *new Keynesians*, have tried to refine the theory of aggregate supply.

Small Menu Costs and Sticky Prices

One approach to explaining why many prices might be sticky in the short run supposes that much of the economy is characterized by imperfect competition and that it is costly for firms to change their prices in response to changes in demand. The costs associated with changing prices are called *menu costs*. These include the costs of renegotiating contracts, printing price lists (such as menus), and informing customers of price changes.

Many such costs may not be very large, so economists call them **small menu costs.** Some of the costs of changing prices, however, such as those incurred in bringing together business managers from points around the nation or the world for meetings on price changes or renegotiating deals with customers, may be significant.

What are the estimated magnitudes of small menu costs?

Small menu costs
Costs that deter firms from changing prices in response to demand changes—for example, the costs of renegotiating contracts or printing new price lists.

EXAMPLE

Just How "Small" Are Small Menu Costs?

Economists have developed two ways of gauging small menu costs experienced by sellers. One method is to try to measure the average dollar amount of menu cost per change in each item's price. Such a cost includes the average expense that a firm incurs in expending managerial resources to decide on a price change, as well as costs of printing new menus or attaching updated price tags. Estimates of per-unit menu costs across a number of industries and types of products range from as low as about 50 cents to as high as several dollars.

Another approach to estimating menu costs is to try measuring them in relation to firms' revenues. According to this approach, most estimates indicate that menu costs range between about 0.2 percent and 1 percent of the total revenues of firms. Thus, with menu costs as high as 1 percent of revenues, it does not pay for firms to change prices unless they anticipate the resulting increase in total revenues to be at least 1 percent.

FOR CRITICAL THINKING
If the average menu cost of changing the per-unit price of an item is $1, how much must revenues per item increase for the price change to be profitable?

Real GDP and the Price Level in a Sticky-Price Economy

According to the new Keynesians, sticky prices strengthen the argument favoring active policymaking as a means of preventing substantial short-run swings in real GDP and, as a consequence, employment.

NEW KEYNESIAN INFLATION DYNAMICS To see why the idea of price stickiness strengthens the case for active policymaking, consider panel (a) of Figure 17-8 below. If a significant portion of all prices do not adjust rapidly, then in the short run the aggregate supply curve effectively is horizontal, as assumed in the traditional Keynesian theory discussed in Chapter 11. This means that a decline in aggregate demand, such as the shift from AD_1 to AD_2 shown in panel (a), will induce the largest possible decline in equilibrium real GDP, from $15 trillion to $14.7 trillion at E_2. When prices are sticky, economic contractions induced by aggregate demand shocks are as severe as they can be.

As panel (a) shows, in contrast to the traditional Keynesian theory, the new Keynesian sticky-price theory indicates that the economy will find its own way back to a long-run equilibrium. The theory presumes that small menu costs induce firms not to change their prices in the short run. In the long run, however, the profit gains to firms from reducing their prices to induce purchases of more goods and services cause them to cut their prices. Thus, in the long run, the price level declines in response to the decrease in aggregate demand. As firms reduce their prices, the horizontal aggregate supply curve shifts downward, from $SRAS_1$ to $SRAS_2$, and equilibrium real GDP returns to its former level at E_3, other things being equal.

Of course, an increase in aggregate demand would have effects opposite to those depicted in panel (a) of Figure 17-8. A rise in aggregate demand would cause real GDP to rise in the short run. In the long run, firms would gain sufficient profits from raising

---

FIGURE 17-8

Short- and Long-Run Adjustments in the New Keynesian Sticky-Price Theory

Panel (a) shows that when prices are sticky, the short-run aggregate supply curve is horizontal, here at a price level of 118. As a consequence, the short-run effect of a fall in aggregate demand from AD_1 to AD_2 generates the largest possible decline in real GDP, from $15 trillion at point E_1 to $14.7 trillion at point E_2. In the long run, producers perceive that they can increase their profits sufficiently by cutting prices and incurring the menu costs of doing so. The resulting decline in the price level implies a downward shift of the $SRAS$ curve, so that the price level falls to 116 and real GDP returns to $15 trillion at point E_3. Panel (b) illustrates the argument for active policymaking based on the new Keynesian theory. Instead of waiting for long-run adjustments to occur, policymakers can engage in expansionary policies that shift the aggregate demand curve back to its original position, thereby shortening or even eliminating a recession.

New Keynesian inflation dynamics
In new Keynesian theory, the pattern of
inflation exhibited by an economy with
growing aggregate demand—initial
sluggish adjustment of the price level in
response to increased aggregate demand
followed by higher inflation later.

their prices to compensate for incurring menu costs, and the short-run aggregate supply curve would shift upward. Consequently, an economy with growing aggregate demand should exhibit so-called **new Keynesian inflation dynamics:** initial sluggish adjustment of the price level in response to aggregate demand increases followed by higher inflation later on.

WHY ACTIVE POLICYMAKING CAN PAY OFF WHEN PRICES ARE STICKY To think about why the new Keynesian sticky-price theory supports the argument for active policymaking, let's return to the case of a decline in aggregate demand illustrated in panel (a) of Figure 17-8 on the previous page. Panel (b) shows the same decline in aggregate demand as in panel (a) and the resulting maximum contractionary effect on real GDP.

Monetary and fiscal policy actions that influence aggregate demand are as potent as possible when prices are sticky and short-run aggregate supply is horizontal. In principle, therefore, all that a policymaker confronted by the leftward shift in aggregate demand depicted in panel (b) must do is to conduct the appropriate policy to induce a rightward shift in the *AD* curve back to its previous position. Indeed, if the policymaker acts rapidly enough, the period of contraction experienced by the economy may be very brief. Active policymaking can thereby moderate or even eliminate recessions.

Is There a New Keynesian Phillips Curve?

A fundamental thrust of the new Keynesian theory is that activist policymaking can promote economic stability. Assessing this implication requires evaluating whether policymakers face an *exploitable* relationship between the inflation rate and the unemployment rate and between inflation and real GDP. By "exploitable," economists mean a relationship that is sufficiently predictable (for policymakers only) and long-lived to allow enough time for policymakers to reduce unemployment or to push up real GDP when economic activity falls below its long-run level.

According to the new Keynesian theory, how much active policymaking speeds up the stabilization process relative to a longer-term self-adjustment by natural economic forces depends on how quickly firms adjust prices. What is the evidence on the speed of overall U.S. price adjustment?

POLICY EXAMPLE

How Fast Do U.S. Firms Change Their Prices?

During the late 1990s and early 2000s, a number of studies by new Keynesian economists estimated that it took U.S. companies an average of two years to alter the prices of their products. These estimates suggested considerable time was available for active policymaking to reduce unemployment and boost real GDP whenever the pace of economic activity fell below its long-run trend.

Critics of these early studies argued that they were biased by reliance on studying changes in the GDP deflator, which tends to exhibit smooth changes over time, instead of examining changes in prices of individual items sold by U.S. firms. The critics also maintained that the initial studies' use of aggregate measures of U.S. firms' costs was inappropriate and that data on firms' *actual* costs should be used instead. Making these measurement changes reduces estimates of the average time it takes U.S. firms to adjust their prices to as low as four months. If the latter estimate is correct, active policymaking must be employed very rapidly if it is to provide clear-cut stabilization benefits for the U.S. economy.

FOR CRITICAL THINKING
How does the fact that estimated average price-adjustment intervals for Europe almost always exceed 1½ years affect the case for active policymaking in that region?

The U.S. Experience with the Phillips Curve

For more than fifty years, economists have debated the existence of a policy-exploitable Phillips curve relationship between the inflation rate and the rate of unemployment. In separate articles in 1968, the late Milton Friedman and Edmond Phelps published pioneering studies suggesting that the apparent trade-off suggested by the Phillips curve could *not* be exploited by activist policymakers. Friedman and Phelps both argued that any attempt to reduce unemployment by boosting inflation would soon be thwarted by the incorporation of the new higher inflation rate into the public's expectations. The Friedman-Phelps research thus implies that for any given unemployment rate, *any* inflation rate is possible, depending on the actions of policymakers.

Figure 17-9 below appears to provide support for the propositions of Friedman and Phelps. It clearly shows that in the past, a number of inflation rates have proved feasible at the same rates of unemployment.

The New Keynesian Phillips Curve

Today's new Keynesian theorists are not concerned about the lack of an apparent long-lived relationship between inflation and unemployment revealed by Figure 17-9. From their point of view, the issue is not whether a relationship between inflation and unemployment or between inflation and real GDP breaks down over a period of years. All that matters for policymakers, the new Keynesians suggest, is whether such a relationship is exploitable in the near term. If so, policymakers can intervene in the economy as soon as actual unemployment and real GDP vary from their long-run levels. Appropriate activist policies, new Keynesians conclude, can dampen cyclical fluctuations and make them shorter-lived.

EVALUATING NEW KEYNESIAN INFLATION DYNAMICS To assess the predictions of new Keynesian inflation dynamics, economists seek to evaluate whether inflation is closely related to two key factors that theory indicates should determine the inflation rate. The first of these factors is anticipated future inflation. The new Keynesian theory implies that menu costs reduce firms' incentive to adjust their prices. When some

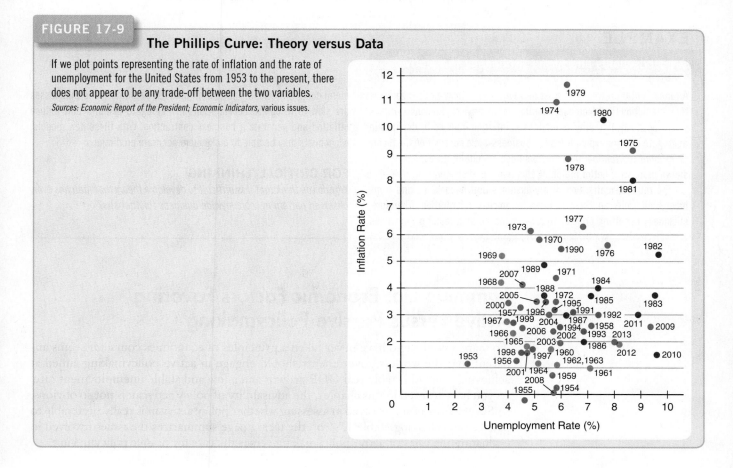

FIGURE 17-9

The Phillips Curve: Theory versus Data

If we plot points representing the rate of inflation and the rate of unemployment for the United States from 1953 to the present, there does not appear to be any trade-off between the two variables.

Sources: Economic Report of the President; Economic Indicators, various issues.

firms *do* adjust their prices, however, they will seek to set prices at levels based on expected future positions of demand curves for their products. The expected future inflation rate signals to firms how much equilibrium prices are likely to increase during future months, so firms will take into account the expected future inflation rate when setting prices at the present time.

The second key factor that new Keynesian theory indicates should affect current inflation is the average inflation-adjusted (real) per-unit costs that firms incur in producing goods and services. Thus, new Keynesians propose a positive relationship between inflation and an aggregate measure of real per-unit costs faced by firms throughout the economy. If firms' average inflation-adjusted per-unit costs increase, the prediction is that there will be higher prices charged by that portion of firms that do adjust their prices in the current period and, hence, greater current inflation.

Empirical evidence does indicate that increases in expected future inflation and greater real per-unit production costs are indeed associated with higher observed rates of inflation. In light of this support for these key predictions of the new Keynesian theory, the theory is exerting increasing influence on U.S. policymakers. For instance, media reports commonly refer to Fed officials' careful attention to changes in inflation expectations and firms' production costs that they interpret as signals of altered inflationary pressures.

JUST HOW EXPLOITABLE IS THE NEW KEYNESIAN PHILLIPS CURVE? Not all economists are persuaded that the new Keynesian theory is correct. They point out that new classical theory already indicates that when prices are *flexible*, higher inflation expectations should reduce short-run aggregate supply. Such a decline in aggregate supply should, in turn, contribute to increased inflation.

Even if one were convinced that new Keynesian theory is correct, a fundamental issue is whether the new Keynesian theory has truly identified *exploitable* relationships. At the heart of this issue is just how often firms adjust their prices.

How might difficulties that people experience in processing large volumes of information help to explain real-world macroeconomic phenomena?

EXAMPLE

Are Households and Firms "Rationally Inattentive"?

A fundamental drawback of most new Keynesian sticky-price theories is their prediction that decreases in inflation will have expansionary effects on the economy. In reality, reductions in inflation induced by declines in aggregate demand typically lead to business-cycle contractions. A theory of *rational inattention* based on bounded rationality (see page 9) has shown promise of better matching this real-world observation.

The rational-inattention theory assumes that households and firms have limitations on their abilities to process information. Therefore, stickiness in setting prices naturally increases as a result of presumed menu costs. In rational-inattention models, consumers and businesses are slow to recognize decelerations in aggregate demand that reduce inflation and generate a business contraction. With these new models, economists may be able to make more accurate predictions.

FOR CRITICAL THINKING
Why do you think that it is difficult to develop a theory that matches every observed pattern in economywide business fluctuations?

Summing Up: Economic Factors Favoring Active versus Passive Policymaking

To many people who have never taken a principles of economics course, it seems apparent that the world's governments should engage in active policymaking aimed at achieving high and stable real GDP growth and a low and stable unemployment rate. As you have learned in this chapter, the advisability of policy activism is not so obvious.

Several factors are involved in assessing whether policy activism is really preferable to passive policymaking. Table 17-1 on the facing page summarizes the issues involved in evaluating the case for active policymaking versus the case for passive policymaking.

TABLE 17-1

Issues That Must Be Assessed in Determining the Desirability of Active versus Passive Policymaking

Economists who contend that active policymaking is justified argue that for each issue listed in the first column, there is evidence supporting the conclusions listed in the second column. In contrast, economists who suggest that passive policymaking is appropriate argue that for each issue in the first column, there is evidence leading to the conclusions in the third column.

Issue	Support for Active Policymaking	Support for Passive Policymaking
Phillips curve inflation–unemployment trade-off	Stable in the short run; perhaps predictable in the long run	Varies with inflation expectations; at best fleeting in the short run and nonexistent in the long run
Aggregate demand shocks	Induce short-run and perhaps long-run effects on real GDP and unemployment	Have little or no short-run effects and certainly no long-run effects on real GDP and unemployment
Aggregate supply shocks	Can, along with aggregate demand shocks, influence real GDP and unemployment	Cause movements in real GDP and unemployment and hence explain most business cycles
Pure competition	Is not typical in most markets, where imperfect competition predominates	Is widespread in markets throughout the economy
Price flexibility	Is uncommon because factors such as small menu costs induce firms to change prices infrequently	Is common because firms adjust prices immediately when demand changes
Wage flexibility	Is uncommon because labor market adjustments occur relatively slowly	Is common because nominal wages adjust speedily to price changes, making real wages flexible

The current state of thinking on the relative desirability of active or passive policymaking may leave you somewhat frustrated. On the one hand, most economists agree that active policymaking is unlikely to exert sizable long-run effects on any nation's economy. Most also agree that aggregate supply shocks contribute to business cycles. Consequently, it is generally agreed that there are limits on the effectiveness of monetary and fiscal policies. On the other hand, a number of economists continue to argue that there is evidence indicating stickiness of prices and wages. They argue, therefore, that monetary and fiscal policy actions can offset, at least in the short run and perhaps even in the long run, the effects that aggregate demand shocks would otherwise have on real GDP and unemployment.

These diverging perspectives help explain why economists reach differing conclusions about the advisability of pursuing active or passive approaches to macroeconomic policymaking. Different interpretations of evidence on the issues summarized in Table 17-1 above will likely continue to divide economists for years to come.

QUICK QUIZ See page 395 for the answers. Review concepts from this section in MyEconLab.

Some new Keynesian economists suggest that _____ _____ costs inhibit many firms from making speedy changes in their prices and that this price stickiness can make the short-run aggregate supply curve _____. Variations in aggregate demand have the largest possible effects on real GDP in the short run, so policies that influence aggregate demand also have the greatest capability to stabilize real GDP in the face of aggregate demand shocks.

Even though there is little evidence supporting a long-run trade-off between inflation and unemployment, new Keynesian theory suggests that activist policymaking may be able to stabilize real GDP and employment in the _____ run. This is possible, according to the theory, if stickiness of _____ adjustment is sufficiently great that policymakers can exploit a _____-run trade-off between inflation and real GDP.

YOU ARE THERE
Active Policies Can Raise Employment—At a Substantial Cost

James Feyrer and Bruce Sacerdote of Dartmouth College have just completed a study of the effects on U.S. employment exerted by active fiscal policy actions implemented under the American Recovery and Reinvestment Act (ARRA) of 2009. One conclusion that Feyrer and Sacerdote have reached is that the number of new jobs attributable to ARRA varied considerably across different forms of discretionary fiscal expenditures. Federal spending directed to states for infrastructure projects, such as road construction and bridge repair, definitely led to new positions. In contrast, no jobs resulted from government grants for education.

Feyrer and Sacerdote conclude that ARRA made a significant contribution to the number of jobs available to about 2 million U.S. residents who were able to find new positions after losing jobs in 2008 and 2009. They

have trouble reaching firm conclusions regarding the net effect of ARRA on aggregate employment, given that about 6 million people have not yet found positions to replace lost jobs. They are, however, certain that the jobs "created" by ARRA had a substantial cost to taxpayers. They estimate this cost as somewhere between $170,000 and $400,000 per position.

Critical Thinking Questions

1. Why might one argue that ARRA's policy activism helped stabilize employment?

2. How could someone argue that ARRA failed to help stabilize employment?

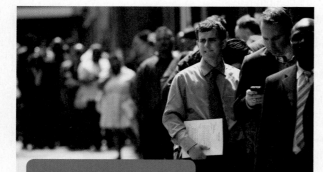

ISSUES & APPLICATIONS

A "Law" for Guiding Active Policymaking Breaks Down

CONCEPTS APPLIED

▶ Active (Discretionary) Policymaking

▶ Passive (Nondiscretionary) Policymaking

▶ Phillips Curve

Ever since an economist named Arthur Okun proposed in 1962 the existence of a stable relationship, known as "Okun's law," economists have suggested that it can help guide active policymaking. Okun's law describes an inverse empirical relationship between deviations of the unemployment rate from its long-run trend value and the gap between actual real GDP and potential real GDP. Keeping the unemployment rate close to its long-run trend level, active-policy proponents suggest, requires policies to reduce the gap between actual real GDP and potential real GDP.

Okun's Law Breaks Down

Figure 17-10 on the facing page displays observed pairings between unemployment rate deviations and output gaps for the United States. Consistent with Okun's law, most of these observations cluster along a downward-sloping line.

Dots predate late 2009; and square points follow that date with 2009i denoting the first three-month interval in 2009, and so on. Clearly, since the end of 2009, Okun's

law appears to have broken down. The unemployment rate has remained high even though the output gap has declined.

Alternative Views of Implications of the Breakdown

Proponents of active policymaking argue that the breakdown of Okun's law is temporary. The unemployment rate

FIGURE 17-10

An Altered Relationship between Unemployment Deviations from Trend and the Percentage "Output Gap"

Traditionally, a stable relationship existed between deviations of the unemployment rate from its long-term trend value and the percentage gap between actual real GDP and potential real GDP. The succession of square points for the most recent three-month intervals indicates that this relationship has not been stable since early 2009, however.

Sources: Bureau of Labor Statistics; Congressional Budget Office: author's estimates.

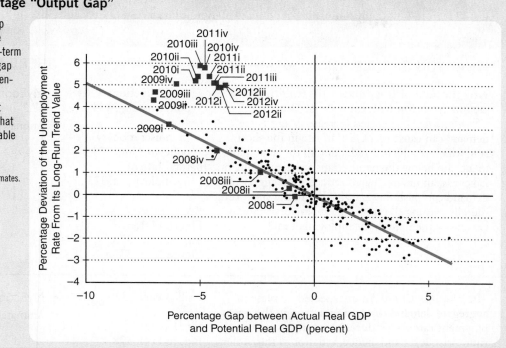

eventually will drop toward its long-run trend value, they contend, as the output gap shrinks in response to discretionary policies.

Those who support passive policymaking argue that the breakdown in Okun's law likely will be much more persistent, just as breakdowns in the theory of a downward-sloping Phillips curve (see page 387) often have lasted for lengthy periods. Proponents of passive policymaking contend that extended unemployment benefits have given people incentives not to look as intensively for new jobs and that new government regulations have reduced labor demand by firms. According to this perspective, active policies aimed at reducing the gap between actual real GDP and potential real GDP will not necessarily generate a lower unemployment rate.

For Critical Thinking

1. Would a breakdown in the Okun's law relationship strengthen or weaken the case for active policymaking?

2. Do Okun's law and the short-run Phillips curve appear to be related concepts?

Web Resources

1. Learn more about Okun's law at **www.econtoday.com/chap17**.

2. For a discussion of the applicability of Okun's law around the globe during the recent economic downturn, go to **www.econtoday.com/ch17**.

MyEconLab

For more questions on this chapter's Issues & Applications, go to MyEconLab. In the Study Plan for this chapter, select Section N: News.

MyEconLab

Here is what you should know after reading this chapter. MyEconLab will help you identify what you know, and where to go when you need to practice.

WHAT YOU SHOULD KNOW		WHERE TO GO TO PRACTICE
Why the Actual Unemployment Rate Might Depart from the Natural Rate of Unemployment An unexpected increase in aggregate demand can cause real GDP to rise in the short run, which results in a reduction in the unemployment rate below the natural rate of unemployment. Likewise, an unanticipated reduction in aggregate demand can push down real GDP in the short run, thereby causing the actual unemployment rate to rise above the natural unemployment rate.	active (discretionary) policymaking, 374 passive (nondiscretionary) policymaking, 374 natural rate of unemployment, 375 **Key Figures** Figure 17-1, 375 Figure 17-2, 376 Figure 17-3, 377	• MyEconLab Study Plans 17.1, 17.2 • Animated Figures 17-1, 17-2, 17-3
The Phillips Curve An unexpected increase in aggregate demand that causes a drop in the unemployment rate also induces a rise in the equilibrium price level and, hence, inflation. Thus, other things being equal, there should be an inverse relationship between the inflation rate and the unemployment rate. This downward-sloping relationship is called the Phillips curve.	Phillips curve, 378 **Key Figures** Figure 17-4, 378 Figure 17-5, 379	• MyEconLab Study Plan 17.2 • Animated Figures 17-4, 17-5
How Expectations Affect the Actual Relationship between the Inflation Rate and the Unemployment Rate A Phillips curve relationship will exist only when expectations are unchanged. If people anticipate policymakers' efforts to exploit the Phillips curve trade-off via inflationary policies aimed at pushing down the unemployment rate, then input prices such as nominal wages will adjust more rapidly to an increase in the price level. As a result, the Phillips curve will shift outward, and the economy will adjust more speedily toward the natural rate of unemployment.		• MyEconLab Study Plan 17.2
Rational Expectations, Policy Ineffectiveness, and Real-Business-Cycle Theory The rational expectations hypothesis suggests that people form expectations of inflation using all available past and current information and an understanding of how the economy functions. If pure competition prevails, wages and prices are flexible, and people completely anticipate the actions of policymakers, so real GDP remains unaffected by anticipated policy actions. Technological changes and labor market shocks such as variations in the composition of the labor force can induce business fluctuations, called real business cycles, which weaken the case for active policymaking.	rational expectations hypothesis, 381 policy irrelevance proposition, 382 stagflation, 383 **Key Figures** Figure 17-6, 381 Figure 17-7, 383	• MyEconLab Study Plan 17.3 • Animated Figures 17-6, 17-7

— WHAT YOU SHOULD KNOW ————————————— WHERE TO GO TO PRACTICE —

Modern Approaches to Bolstering the Case for Active Policymaking New Keynesian approaches suggest that firms may be slow to change prices in the face of variations in demand. Thus, the short-run aggregate supply curve is horizontal, and changes in aggregate demand have the largest possible effects on real GDP in the short run. If prices and wages are sufficiently inflexible in the short run that there is an exploitable trade-off between inflation and real GDP, discretionary policy actions can stabilize real GDP.

small menu costs, 384
new Keynesian inflation
 dynamics, 386

- MyEconLab Study Plans 17.4, 17.5, 17.6

Log in to **MyEconLab**, take a chapter test, and get a personalized Study Plan that tells you which concepts you understand and which ones you need to review. From there, **MyEconLab** will give you further practice, tutorials, animations, videos, and guided solutions. For more information, visit www.myeconlab.com

PROBLEMS

*All problems are assignable in **MyEconLab**. Answers to odd-numbered problems appear at the back of the book.*

17-1. Suppose that the government altered the computation of the unemployment rate by including people in the military as part of the labor force. (See page 374.)

　a. How would this affect the actual unemployment rate?

　b. How would such a change affect estimates of the natural rate of unemployment?

　c. If this computational change were made, would it in any way affect the logic of the short-run and long-run Phillips curve analysis and its implications for policymaking? Why might the government wish to make such a change?

17-2. The natural rate of unemployment depends on factors that affect the behavior of both workers and firms. Make lists of possible factors affecting workers and firms that you believe are likely to influence the natural rate of unemployment. (See pages 374–375.)

17-3. Suppose that more unemployed people who are classified as part of frictional unemployment decide to stop looking for work and start their own businesses instead. What is likely to happen to each of the following, other things being equal? (See pages 375–379.)

　a. The natural unemployment rate

　b. The economy's Phillips curve

17-4. Suppose that people who previously had held jobs become cyclically unemployed at the same time the inflation rate declines. Would the result be a movement along or a shift of the short-run Phillips curve? Explain your reasoning. (See pages 376–379.)

17-5. Suppose that people who previously had held jobs become structurally unemployed due to establishment of new government regulations during a period in which the inflation rate remains unchanged. Would the result be a movement along or a shift of the short-run Phillips curve? Explain your reasoning. (See pages 376–379.)

17-6. Suppose that the greater availability of online job placement services generates a reduction in frictional unemployment during an interval in which the inflation rate remains unchanged. Would the result be a movement along or a shift of the short-run Phillips curve? Explain your reasoning. (See pages 376–379.)

17-7. Consider a situation in which a future president has appointed Federal Reserve leaders who conduct monetary policy much more erratically than in past years. The consequence is that the quantity of money in circulation varies in a much more unsystematic and, hence, hard-to-predict manner. According to the policy irrelevance proposition, is it more or less likely that the Fed's policy actions will cause real GDP to change in the short run? Explain. (See pages 379–380.)

17-8. People called "Fed watchers" earn their living by trying to forecast what policies the Federal Reserve will implement within the next few weeks and months. Suppose that Fed watchers discover that the current group of Fed officials is following very systematic and predictable policies intended to reduce the unemployment rate. The Fed watchers then sell this information to firms, unions, and others in the private sector. If pure competition prevails, prices and wages are flexible, and people form rational expectations, are the Fed's policies enacted after the information sale likely to have their intended effects on the unemployment rate? (See pages 379–381.)

17-9. Suppose that economists were able to use U.S. economic data to demonstrate that the rational expectations hypothesis is true. Would this be sufficient to demonstrate the validity of the policy irrelevance proposition? (See page 381.)

17-10. Evaluate the following statement: "In an important sense, the term *policy irrelevance proposition* is misleading because even if the rational expectations hypothesis is valid, economic policy actions can have significant effects on real GDP and the unemployment rate." (See page 381.)

17-11. Consider the diagram below, which is drawn under the assumption that the new Keynesian sticky-price theory of aggregate supply applies. Assume that at present, the economy is in long-run equilibrium at point *A*. Answer the following questions. (See page 385.)

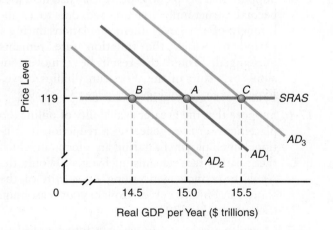

a. Suppose that there is a sudden increase in desired investment expenditures. Which of the alternative aggregate demand curves—AD_2 or AD_3—will apply after this event occurs? Other things being equal, what will happen to the

equilibrium price level and to equilibrium real GDP in the *short run*? Explain.

b. Other things being equal, after the event and adjustments discussed in part (a) have taken place, what will happen to the equilibrium price level and to equilibrium real GDP in the *long run*? Explain.

17-12. Both the traditional Keynesian theory discussed in Chapter 11 and the new Keynesian theory considered in this chapter indicate that the short-run aggregate supply curve is horizontal. (See page 385.)

a. In terms of their *short-run* implications for the price level and real GDP, is there any difference between the two approaches?

b. In terms of their *long-run* implications for the price level and real GDP, is there any difference between the two approaches?

17-13. The real-business-cycle approach attributes even short-run increases in real GDP largely to aggregate supply shocks. Rightward shifts in aggregate supply tend to push down the equilibrium price level. How could the real-business-cycle perspective explain the low but persistent inflation that the United States experienced until 2007? (See pages 382–383.)

17-14. Normally, when aggregate demand increases, firms find it more profitable to raise prices than to leave prices unchanged. The idea behind the small-menu-cost explanation for price stickiness is that firms will leave their prices unchanged if their profit gain from adjusting prices is less than the menu costs they would incur if they change prices. If firms anticipate that a rise in demand is likely to last for a long time, does this make them more or less likely to adjust their prices when they face small menu costs? (See page 384. Hint: Profits are a flow that firms earn from week to week and month to month, but small menu costs are a one-time expense.)

17-15. The policy relevance of new Keynesian inflation dynamics based on the theory of small menu costs and sticky prices depends on the exploitability of the implied relationship between inflation and real GDP. Explain in your own words why the average time between price adjustments by firms is a crucial determinant of whether policymakers can actively exploit this relationship to try to stabilize real GDP. (See page 386.)

ECONOMICS ON THE NET

The Inflation–Unemployment Relationship According to the basic aggregate demand and aggregate supply model, the unemployment rate should be inversely related to changes in the inflation rate, other things being equal. This application allows you to take a direct look at unemployment and inflation data to judge for yourself whether the two variables appear to be related.

Title: Bureau of Labor Statistics: Economy at a Glance

Navigation: Go to **www.econtoday.com/ch17** to visit the Bureau of Labor Statistics Economy at a Glance home page.

Application Perform the indicated operations, and then answer the following questions.

1. Click on the "back data" box next to *Consumer Price Index*. Has the U.S. economy consistently experienced inflation since 2008? Was there consistently inflation prior to 2008?

2. Back up to *Economy at a Glance*, and now click on the "back data" box next to *Unemployment Rate*. Was the unemployment rate lower or higher before 2008? Do you note any appearance of an inverse relationship between the unemployment rate and the inflation rate?

For Group Study and Analysis Divide the class into groups, and have each group search through the *Economy at a Glance* site to develop an explanation for the key factors accounting for the recent behavior of the unemployment rate. Have each group report on its explanation. Is there any one factor that best explains the recent behavior of the unemployment rate?

ANSWERS TO QUICK QUIZZES

p. 380: (i) long . . . expectations; (ii) increase . . . decrease; (iii) Phillips . . . demand; (iv) Activist

p. 384: (i) rational expectations; (ii) policy irrelevance; (iii) supply . . . real business

p. 389: (i) small menu . . . horizontal; (ii) short . . . price . . . short

18

Policies and Prospects for Global Economic Growth

For years, a large portion of Mongolia's capital equipment, including drills and excavating machines, has lain idle, and operations of key industries such as mining have ebbed about as often as they have flowed. Brief intervals of meager economic growth have been followed by lengthy periods during which the nation's per capita real GDP has remained stagnant. Suddenly, however, Mongolia's longer-term economic situation appears brighter. The catalyst for change has been a government plan to issue shares of ownership in future returns derived from the mining of newly discovered coal and copper deposits. Mongolian capital investment has exploded, and the nation's economic growth rate has more than doubled. After reading this chapter, you will understand why the granting of private ownership shares in mining operations has had such a significant impact on economic growth in Mongolia.

LEARNING OBJECTIVES

After reading this chapter, you should be able to:

▶ Explain why population growth can have uncertain effects on economic growth

▶ Understand why the existence of dead capital retards investment and economic growth in much of the developing world

▶ Describe how government inefficiencies have contributed to the creation of relatively large quantities of dead capital in the world's developing nations

▶ Discuss the sources of international investment funds for developing nations and identify obstacles to international investment in these nations

▶ Identify the key functions of the World Bank and the International Monetary Fund

▶ Explain the problems faced by policymakers at the World Bank and the International Monetary Fund and discuss some proposals for dealing with these problems

92 percent of Egypt's residents do not hold official legal title to the properties in which they reside and conduct their business affairs? The estimated value of all of these not-legally-owned capital assets is more than 30 times the value of private assets that people formally own. Furthermore, about 43 percent of Egyptian residents are employed by businesses that have no official legal standing on which to operate.

Economists' understanding of the determinants of economic growth suggests that in light of the above figures it is not surprising that the long-run average rate of economic growth is much lower in Egypt than in most of the rest of the world. After reading this chapter, you will be equipped to undertake your own evaluation of the prospects for global economic growth.

Labor Resources and Economic Growth

You learned in Chapter 9 that the main determinants of economic growth are the growth of labor and capital resources and the rate of increase of labor and capital productivity. Human resources are abundant around the globe. Currently, the world's population increases by more than 70 million people each year. This population growth is not spread evenly over the earth's surface. Among the relatively wealthy nations of Europe, women bear an average of just over one child during their lifetimes. In the United States, a typical woman bears about 1.5 children. But in the generally poorer nations of Africa, women bear an average of six children.

Population growth does not necessarily translate into an increase in labor resources in the poorest regions of the world. Many people in poor nations do not join the labor force. Many who do so have trouble obtaining employment.

A common assumption is that high population growth in a less developed nation hinders the growth of its per capita GDP. Certainly, this is the presumption in China, where the government has imposed an absolute limit of one child per female resident. In fact, however, the relationship between population growth and economic growth is not really so clear-cut.

Basic Arithmetic of Population Growth and Economic Growth

Does a larger population raise or lower per capita real GDP? If a country has fixed borders and an unchanged level of aggregate real GDP, a higher population directly reduces per capita real GDP. After all, if there are more people, then dividing a constant amount of real GDP by a larger number of people reduces real GDP per capita.

This basic arithmetic works for growth rates too. We can express the growth rate of per capita real GDP in a nation as

$$\text{Rate of growth of per capita real GDP} = \text{rate of growth in real GDP} - \text{rate of growth of population}$$

Hence, if real GDP grows at a constant rate of 4 percent per year and the annual rate of population growth increases from 2 percent to 3 percent, the annual rate of growth of per capita real GDP will decline, from 2 percent to 1 percent.

HOW POPULATION GROWTH CAN CONTRIBUTE TO ECONOMIC GROWTH The arithmetic of the relationship between economic growth and population growth can be misleading. Certainly, it is a mathematical fact that the rate of growth of per capita real GDP equals the difference between the rate of growth in real GDP and the rate of growth of the population. Economic analysis, however, indicates that population growth can affect the rate of growth of real GDP. Thus, these two growth rates generally are not independent.

Recall from Chapter 9 that a higher rate of labor force participation by a nation's population contributes to increased growth of real GDP. If population growth is also accompanied by growth in the rate of labor force participation, then population growth can positively contribute to *per capita* real GDP growth. Even though population growth by itself tends to reduce the growth of per capita real GDP, greater labor force participation by an expanded population can boost real GDP growth sufficiently to more than compensate for the increase in population. On balance, the rate of growth of per capita real GDP can thereby increase.

WHETHER POPULATION GROWTH HINDERS OR CONTRIBUTES TO ECONOMIC GROWTH DEPENDS ON WHERE YOU LIVE On net, does an increased rate of population growth detract from or add to the rate of economic growth? Table 18-1 below indicates that the answer depends on which nation one considers. In some nations that have experienced relatively high rates of population growth, such as Egypt, Indonesia, and Malaysia, and, to a lesser extent, Chile and China, economic growth has accompanied population growth. In contrast, in nations such as the Congo Democratic Republic, Liberia, and Togo, there has been a negative relationship between population growth and per capita real GDP growth. Other factors apparently must affect how population growth and economic growth ultimately interrelate.

The Role of Economic Freedom

A crucial factor influencing economic growth is the relative freedom of a nation's residents. Particularly important is the degree of **economic freedom**—the rights to own private property and to exchange goods, services, and financial assets with minimal government interference—available to the residents of a nation.

Approximately two-thirds of the world's people reside in about three dozen nations with governments unwilling to grant residents significant economic freedom. The economies of these nations, even though they have the majority of the world's population, produce less than 20 percent of the world's total output. Some of these countries have experienced rates of economic growth at or above the 1.2 percent annual average for the world's nations during the past 30 years, but many are growing much more slowly. More than 30 of these countries have experienced negative rates of per capita income growth.

Only 17 nations, with 17 percent of the world's people, grant their residents high degrees of economic freedom. These nations together account for 81 percent of total world output. All of the countries that grant considerable economic freedom have experienced positive rates of economic growth, and most are close to or above the world's average rate of economic growth.

Economic freedom
The rights to own private property and to exchange goods, services, and financial assets with minimal government interference.

Go to www.econtoday.com/chap18 to review the Heritage Foundation's evaluations of the degree of economic freedom in different nations.

TABLE 18-1

Population Growth and Growth in Per Capita Real GDP in Selected Nations since 1970

Country	Average Annual Population Growth Rate (%)	Average Annual Rate of Growth of Per Capita Real GDP (%)
Central African Republic	2.5	−1.2
Chile	1.5	2.8
China	1.2	7.1
Congo Democratic Republic	3.1	−3.3
Egypt	2.3	3.4
Haiti	1.8	0.0
Indonesia	1.8	4.1
Liberia	2.4	−1.3
Madagascar	2.9	−0.4
Malaysia	2.3	4.7
Togo	3.0	−1.0
United States	1.0	1.8

Source: Penn World Tables, International Monetary Fund.

Why is per capita real GDP growth lower in Jamaica than in Singapore?

INTERNATIONAL POLICY EXAMPLE

A Tale of Diverging Economic Growth Rates in Two Island Nations

During the first half of the 1960s, two island countries with nearly identical levels of per capita real GDP—about $2,700—and the same populations—just over 1,700,000 at that time—became independent nations. One was Jamaica, and the other was Singapore. Since that time, Jamaica's population has grown to 2,700,000 people. Singapore's population has grown to 3,500,000. Today, Jamaica's per capita real GDP is about $4,800. In contrast, Singapore's per capita real GDP exceeds $31,000.

Why has Jamaica's per capita real GDP grown so much less than Singapore's, even though Singapore's population has increased at a faster pace? The fundamental answer is that people in Jamaica have considerably less economic freedom. In contrast to Singapore, which has business taxation and regulations rated among the least burdensome in the world, tax rates and regulatory rules in Jamaica rank among the most oppressive. As a consequence, rates of growth of saving, investment, and productivity—and, hence, per capita real GDP—in Jamaica have been far below corresponding growth rates in Singapore.

FOR CRITICAL THINKING

In Jamaica, the cost of registering a business is 13 percent of the value of a firm's capital, as compared with less than 0.2 percent in Singapore. In which country would you guess that more new companies are started each year?

The Role of Political Freedom

Interestingly, *political freedom*—the right to openly support and democratically select national leaders—appears to be less important than economic freedom in determining economic growth. Some countries that grant considerable economic freedom to their citizens have relatively strong restrictions on their residents' freedoms of speech and the press.

When nondemocratic countries have achieved high standards of living through consistent economic growth, they tend to become more democratic over time. This suggests that economic freedom tends to stimulate economic growth, which then leads to more political freedom.

QUICK QUIZ   See page 413 for the answers. Review concepts from this section in MyEconLab.

For a given rate of growth of aggregate real GDP, higher population growth tends to _____ the growth of per capita real GDP.

To the extent that increased population growth also leads to greater _____ _____ participation that raises the growth of total real GDP, a higher population growth

rate can potentially _____ the rate of growth in per capita real GDP.

In general, the extent of _____ freedom does not necessarily increase the rate of economic growth. A greater degree of _____ freedom, however, does have a positive effect on a nation's growth prospects.

Capital Goods and Economic Growth

A fundamental problem developing countries face is that a significant portion of their capital goods, or manufactured resources that may be used to produce other items in the future, is what economists call **dead capital,** a term coined by economist Hernando de Soto. This term describes a capital resource lacking clear title of ownership. Dead capital may actually be put to some productive purpose, but individuals and firms face difficulties in exchanging, insuring, and legally protecting their rights to this resource. Thus, dead capital is a resource that people cannot readily allocate to its *most efficient* use. As economists have dug deeper into the difficulties confronting residents of the world's poorest nations, they have found that dead capital is among the most significant impediments to growth of per capita incomes in these countries.

Dead capital
Any capital resource that lacks clear title of ownership.

Dead Capital and Inefficient Production

Physical structures used to house both business operations and labor resources are forms of capital goods. Current estimates indicate that unofficial, nontransferable physical structures valued at more than $10 trillion are found in developing nations around the world. Because people in developing countries do not officially own this huge volume of capital goods, they cannot easily trade these resources. Thus, it is hard for many of the world's people to use capital goods in ways that will yield the largest feasible output of goods and services.

Consider, for instance, a hypothetical situation faced by an individual in Cairo, Egypt, a city in which an estimated 95 percent of all physical structures are unofficially owned. Suppose this person unofficially owns a run-down apartment building but has no official title of ownership for this structure. Also suppose that the building is better suited for use as a distribution center for a new import-export firm. The individual would like to sell or lease the structure to the new firm, but because he does not formally own the building, he is unable to do so. If the costs of obtaining formal title to the property are sufficiently high relative to the potential benefit—as they apparently are at present for more than 9 out of every 10 Cairo businesses and households—this individual's capital resource will likely not be allocated to its highest-valued use.

This example illustrates a basic problem of dead capital. People who unofficially own capital goods are commonly constrained in their ability to employ them in their most productive uses. As a result, large quantities of capital goods throughout the developing world are inefficiently employed.

Dead Capital and Economic Growth

Recall from Chapter 2 that when we take into account production choices over time, any society faces a trade-off between consumption goods and capital goods. Whenever we make a choice to produce more consumption goods today, we incur an opportunity cost of fewer goods in the future. This means that when we make a choice to aim for more future economic growth to permit consumption of more goods in the future, we must allocate more resources to producing capital goods today. This entails incurring an opportunity cost today because society must allocate fewer resources to the current production of consumption goods.

This growth trade-off applies to any society, whether in a highly industrialized nation or a developing country. In a developing country, however, the inefficiencies of dead capital greatly reduce the rate of return on investment by individuals and firms. The resulting disincentives to invest in new capital goods can greatly hinder economic growth.

GOVERNMENT INEFFICIENCIES, INVESTMENT, AND GROWTH A major factor contributing to the problem of dead capital in many developing nations is significant and often highly inefficient government regulation. Governments in many of the world's poorest nations place tremendous obstacles in the way of entrepreneurs interested in owning capital goods and directing them to profitable opportunities.

In addition to creating dead capital, overzealously administered government regulations that impede private resource allocation tend to reduce investment in new capital goods. If newly produced capital goods cannot be easily devoted to their most efficient uses, there is less incentive to invest. In a nation with a stifling government bureaucracy regulating the uses of capital goods, newly created capital will all too likely become dead capital.

Thus, government inefficiency can be a major barrier to economic growth. Figure 18-1 on the facing page depicts the relationship between average growth of per capita incomes and index measures of governmental inefficiency for various nations. As you can see, the economies of countries with less efficient governments tend to grow at relatively slower rates. The reason is that bureaucratic inefficiencies complicate private individuals' efforts to direct capital goods to their most efficient uses.

FIGURE 18-1

Bureaucratic Inefficiency and Economic Growth

Inefficiencies in government bureaucracies reduce the incentive to invest and thereby detract from economic growth.

Sources: International Monetary Fund; World Bank.

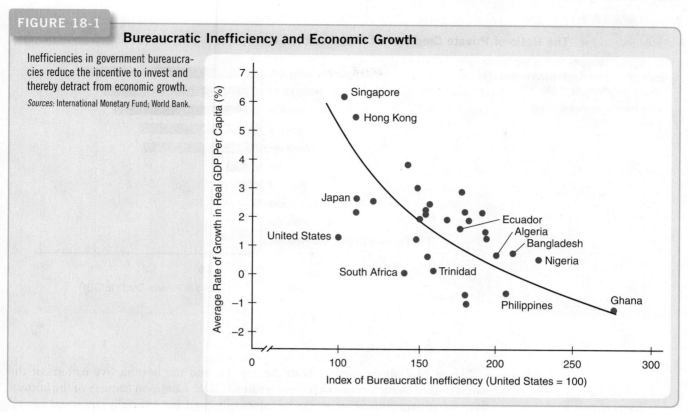

ACCESS TO CREDIT MATTERS The 2006 Nobel Peace Prize went to Muhammad Yunus of Bangladesh. Yunus contends that access to private credit is vital for promoting economic growth in poverty-stricken countries, where, in his view, present credit arrangements are inadequate. Yunus received the Nobel Peace Prize for his efforts to operate a *microlender*—a banking institution that specializes in making very small loans to entrepreneurs seeking to lift themselves up from the lowest rungs of poverty.

How are microlenders attracting deposit funds to lend to entrepreneurs in developing nations?

YOU ARE THERE

To contemplate some of the complications entailed in providing banking services in developing areas of the world, take a look at **Generating New Saving on a Floating Amazon River Bank Branch** on page 408.

INTERNATIONAL EXAMPLE

Mobile Microsaving Enables Microlending in Africa

To be able to extend small loans to entrepreneurs in developing nations, microlenders must obtain funds from savers. In sub-Saharan Africa, people who have accounts with microlenders can transmit securely encrypted funds as attachments to cell phone messages. In this way, individuals can submit small deposits to microlenders as they receive income payments—often via cell phones. Cell phone–to–cell phone deposits are one of the fastest-growing sources of saving in sub-Saharan Africa, and

the resulting growth of deposits is creating increased microlending in that part of the world.

FOR CRITICAL THINKING

Why are rates of interest that microlenders pay to their depositors related to rates of interest that microlenders earn on the credit that they extend to borrowers?

Private lenders such as microlenders, Yunus suggests, are more likely to grant loans if borrowers can provide marketable collateral in the form of capital assets that lenders can obtain if a borrower defaults. Loan applicants cannot offer as collateral capital assets that they do not officially own, however. Even if an applicant has legal title to capital assets, a lender is unlikely to accept them as collateral if government rules and inefficiencies inhibit the marketability of those assets in the event that the borrower defaults.

FIGURE 18-2

The Ratio of Private Credit to GDP in Selected Nations

This figure displays the top five and bottom five nations of the world ranked according to ratios of private credit to GDP.

Source: Federal Reserve Bank of St. Louis.

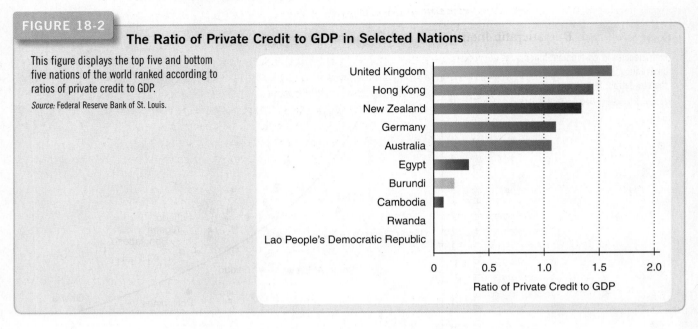

Figure 18-2 above displays both the top five and the bottom five nations of the world ranked by their ratios of private credit to GDP. Common features of the bottom five nations are significant stocks of informally used but officially unowned capital goods and very inefficient government bureaucracies. Access to credit in these nations is very limited, so ratios of private credit to GDP are low.

In some of the poorest nations in which microlending activities are beginning to flourish, tens of millions of people are obtaining access to credit for the first time in their lives. As a consequence, ratios of private credit to GDP are climbing.

WHAT IF... **governments force more saving to be channeled to microfinance, with the goal of enhancing economic growth?**

Successful microfinance institutions typically arise to fill niches in private markets and thereby lead to higher rates of saving and investment by lower-income people, more capital formation, and greater economic growth. When a nation's government requires a portion of the existing flow of saving to be shifted from its current use in financing investment to microfinance, the result is primarily a redistribution of resources. To be sure, lower-income people often are made better off when they receive the shifted saving as loans that help finance new entrepreneurial activities. Nevertheless, saving shifted away from previous uses generates lower capital investment in other sectors of a nation's economy. Overall capital accumulation remains virtually unaffected, so that the economic growth effects of the forced redistribution of national saving are negligible.

QUICK QUIZ See page 413 for the answers. Review concepts from this section in MyEconLab.

Dead capital is a capital resource without clear title of _____. It is difficult for a buyer to trade, insure, or maintain a right to use dead capital.

The inability to put dead capital to its most efficient use contributes to _____ economic growth, particularly in _____ nations, where dead capital can be a relatively large portion of total capital goods.

Inefficient government _____ contribute to the dead capital problem, which reduces the incentive to invest in additional capital goods.

Private International Financial Flows as a Source of Global Growth

Given the large volume of inefficiently employed capital goods in developing nations, what can be done to promote greater global growth? One approach is to rely on private markets to find ways to direct capital goods toward their best uses in most nations. Another is to entrust the world's governments with the task of developing and implementing policies that enhance economic growth in developing nations. Let's begin by considering the market-based approach to promoting global growth.

Private Investment in Developing Nations

Between 1995 and 2007, at least $150 billion per year in private funds flowed to developing nations in the form of loans or purchases of bonds or stock. Of course, in some years, international investors stop lending to developing countries or sell off government-issued bonds and private-company stocks of those countries. When these international outflows of funds are taken into account, the *net* flows of funds to developing countries have averaged just over $80 billion per year since 1995. This is nearly 5 percent of the annual net investment within the United States.

Nearly all the funds that flow into developing countries do so to finance investment projects in those nations. Economists group these international flows of investment funds into three categories. One is loans from banks and other sources. The second is **portfolio investment,** or purchases of less than 10 percent of the shares of ownership in a company. The third is **foreign direct investment,** or the acquisition stocks to obtain more than a 10 percent share of a firm's ownership.

Figure 18-3 below displays percentages of each type of international investment financing provided to developing nations since 1981. As you can see, three decades ago, bank loans accounted for the bulk of international funding of investment in the world's less developed nations. Today, direct ownership shares in the form of portfolio investment and foreign direct investment together account for most international investment financing.

Obstacles to International Investment

There is an important difficulty with depending on international flows of funds to finance capital investment in developing nations. The markets for loans, bonds, and stocks in developing countries are particularly susceptible to problems relating to

Portfolio investment
The purchase of less than 10 percent of the shares of ownership in a company in another nation.

Foreign direct investment
The acquisition of more than 10 percent of the shares of ownership in a company in another nation.

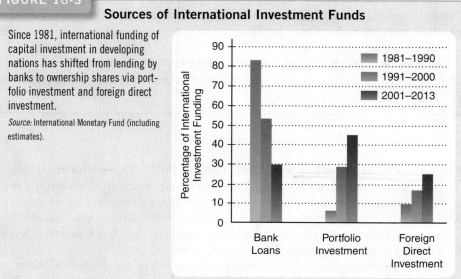

FIGURE 18-3

Sources of International Investment Funds

Since 1981, international funding of capital investment in developing nations has shifted from lending by banks to ownership shares via portfolio investment and foreign direct investment.

Source: International Monetary Fund (including estimates).

For a link to an Asian Development Bank analysis of the effects of foreign direct investment on developing nations, go to www.econtoday.com/chap18.

asymmetric information (see Chapter 15). International investors are well aware of the informational problems to which they are exposed in developing nations, so many stand ready to withdraw their financial support at a moment's notice.

ASYMMETRIC INFORMATION AS A BARRIER TO FINANCING GLOBAL GROWTH Recall from Chapter 15 that asymmetric information in financial markets exists when institutions that make loans or investors who hold bonds or stocks have less information than those who seek to use the funds. *Adverse selection* problems arise when those who wish to obtain funds for the least worthy projects are among those who attempt to borrow or issue bonds or stocks. If banks and investors have trouble identifying these higher-risk individuals and firms, they may be less willing to channel funds to even creditworthy borrowers. Another asymmetric information problem is *moral hazard*. This is the potential for recipients of funds to engage in riskier behavior after receiving financing.

In light of the adverse selection problem, anyone thinking about funding a business endeavor in any locale must study the firm carefully before extending financial support. The potential for moral hazard requires a lender to a firm or someone who has purchased the firm's bonds or stock to continue to monitor the company's performance after providing financial support.

By definition, financial intermediation is still relatively undeveloped in less advanced regions of the world. Consequently, individuals interested in financing potentially profitable investments in developing nations typically cannot rely on financial intermediaries based in these countries. Asymmetric information problems may be so great in some developing nations that very few private lenders or investors will wish to direct their funds to worthy capital investment projects. In some countries, therefore, concerns about adverse selection and moral hazard can be a significant obstacle to economic growth.

How are farmers in Kenya using cell phones to overcome asymmetric information problems, obtain insurance, and produce and sell larger grain harvests?

INTERNATIONAL EXAMPLE

Insuring Crops and Increased Harvests in Kenya

In years past, Kenyan farmers, who have always feared destruction of their crops by periodic droughts, cut their costs by using substandard seeds. This practice reduced harvests and lowered their quality.

Today, firms that sell high-quality crop seeds use insurance contracts to reduce Kenyan farmers' risks of drought losses and thereby boost sales of "good" seeds. When farmers buy these seeds, the retailer scans a barcode on each farmer's cell phone. The phone sends a message to the seed seller, which pays a premium for an insurance policy to cover the farmer's seed costs in the event of a drought. Purchase of the seeds also automatically connects the farmer's cell phone with a system

of 30 weather stations. If this system determines that the farmer's crop will not be viable because of insufficient moisture, the farmer is entitled to an insurance payment covering the initial seed expense.

The seed-insurance system has benefited everyone involved. Seed companies sell more of their products, insurance companies earn more revenues, and insured farmers produce more bountiful, higher-quality harvests.

FOR CRITICAL THINKING
How does increased agricultural productivity contribute to higher economic growth?

INCOMPLETE INFORMATION AND INTERNATIONAL FINANCIAL CRISES Those who are willing to contemplate making loans or buying bonds or stocks issued in developing nations must either do their own careful homework or follow the example of other lenders or investors whom they regard as better informed. Many relatively unsophisticated lenders and investors, such as relatively small banks and individual savers, rely on larger lenders and investors to evaluate risks in developing nations.

This has led some economists to suggest that a follow-the-leader mentality can influence international flows of funds. In extreme cases, they contend, the result can be an **international financial crisis.** This is a situation in which lenders rapidly

International financial crisis
The rapid withdrawal of foreign investments and loans from a nation.

withdraw loans made to residents of developing nations and investors sell off bonds and stocks issued by firms and governments in those countries.

An international financial crisis began in 2008. Unlike the crisis that started in 1997 and radiated outward from Southeast Asia, Central Asia, and Latin America, the more recent crisis began in the United States. It then spread to Europe before adversely affecting most developing nations. Although economies of several Asian nations have weathered the crisis relatively well so far, the world economy shrank for the first time in decades. Undoubtedly, this has contributed to a decline in flows of private funds to developing nations.

QUICK QUIZ   See page 413 for the answers. Review concepts from this section in MyEconLab.

The three main categories of international flows of investment funds are loans by _____, _____ investment that involves purchasing less than 10 percent of the shares of ownership in a company, and _____ _____ investment that involves purchasing more than 10 percent of a company's ownership shares.

On net, an average of about $_____ billion in international investment funds flows to developing nations each year. In years past, bank loans were the source of most foreign funding of investment in developing countries, but recently _____ investment and _____ _____ investment have increased.

Obstacles to private financing of capital accumulation and growth in developing nations include _____ _____ and _____ _____ problems caused by asymmetric information, which can restrain and sometimes destabilize private flows of funds.

International Institutions and Policies for Global Growth

There has long been a recognition that adverse selection and moral hazard problems can both reduce international flows of private funds to developing nations and make these flows relatively variable. Since 1945, the world's governments have taken an active role in supplementing private markets. Two international institutions, the World Bank and the International Monetary Fund, have been at the center of government-directed efforts to attain higher rates of global economic growth.

The World Bank

The **World Bank** specializes in extending relatively long-term loans for capital investment projects that otherwise might not receive private financial support. When the World Bank was first formed in 1945, it provided assistance in the post–World War II rebuilding period. In the 1960s, the World Bank broadened its mission by widening its scope to encompass global antipoverty efforts.

Today, the World Bank makes loans solely to about 100 developing nations containing roughly half the world's population. Governments and firms in these countries typically seek loans from the World Bank to finance specific projects, such as better irrigation systems, road improvements, and better hospitals.

The World Bank is actually composed of five separate institutions: the International Development Association, the International Bank for Reconstruction and Development, the International Finance Corporation, the Multinational Investment Guarantee Agency, and the International Center for Settlement of Investment Disputes. These World Bank organizations each have between 144 and 186 member nations, and on their behalf, the approximately 10,000 people employed by World Bank institutions coordinate the funding of investment activities undertaken by various governments and private firms in developing nations. Figure 18-4 on the following page displays the current regional distribution of about $20 billion yearly in World Bank lending. Governments of the world's wealthiest countries provide most of the funds that the World Bank lends each year, although the World Bank also raises some of its funds in private financial markets.

World Bank
A multinational agency that specializes in making loans to about 100 developing nations in an effort to promote their long-term development and growth.

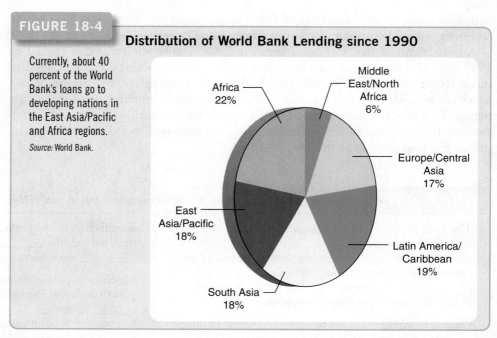

FIGURE 18-4

Distribution of World Bank Lending since 1990

Currently, about 40 percent of the World Bank's loans go to developing nations in the East Asia/Pacific and Africa regions.

Source: World Bank.

- Africa 22%
- Middle East/North Africa 6%
- Europe/Central Asia 17%
- Latin America/Caribbean 19%
- South Asia 18%
- East Asia/Pacific 18%

The International Monetary Fund

International Monetary Fund (IMF)
A multinational organization that aims to promote world economic growth through more financial stability.

Quota subscription
A nation's account with the International Monetary Fund, denominated in special drawing rights.

The **International Monetary Fund (IMF)** is an international organization that aims to promote global economic growth by fostering financial stability. Currently, the IMF has more than 180 member nations.

When a country joins the IMF, it deposits funds to an account called its **quota subscription.** These funds are measured in terms of an international unit of accounting called *special drawing rights* (*SDRs*), which have a value based on a weighted average of a basket of four key currencies: the euro, the pound sterling, the yen, and the dollar. At present, one SDR is equivalent to just over $1.50.

The IMF assists developing nations primarily by making loans to their governments. Originally, the IMF's primary function was to provide short-term loans, and it continues to offer these forms of assistance.

After the 1970s, however, nations' demands for short-term credit declined, and the IMF adapted by expanding its other lending programs. It now provides certain types of credit directly to poor and heavily indebted countries, either as long-term loans intended to support growth-promoting projects or as short- or long-term assistance aimed at helping countries experiencing problems in repaying existing debts. Under these funding programs, the IMF seeks to assist any qualifying member experiencing an unusual fluctuation in exports or imports, a loss of confidence in its own financial system, or spillover effects from financial problems originating elsewhere.

The World Bank and the IMF: Problems and Proposals

Among the World Bank's client nations, meager economic growth in recent decades shows up in numerous ways. The average resident in a nation receiving World Bank assistance lives on less than $2 per day. Hundreds of millions of people in nations receiving its financial support will never attend school, and tens of thousands of people in these countries die of preventable diseases every day. Thus, there is an enormous range of areas where World Bank funds might be put to use.

The International Monetary Fund also continues to deal with an ongoing string of major international financial crisis situations. Countries most notably involved in such crises have included Mexico in 1995; Thailand, Indonesia, Malaysia, and South Korea in 1997; Russia in 1998; Brazil in 1999 and 2000; Turkey in 2001; Argentina in 2001 and 2002; and Greece, Spain, and other European nations since 2008.

ASYMMETRIC INFORMATION AND THE WORLD BANK AND IMF Like any other lenders, the World Bank and IMF encounter adverse selection and moral hazard problems. In an effort to address these problems, both institutions impose conditions that borrowers must meet to receive funds.

Officials of these organizations do not publicly announce all terms of lending agreements, however, so it is largely up to the organizations to monitor whether borrower nations are wisely using funds donated by other countries. In addition, the World Bank and IMF tend to place very imprecise initial conditions on the loans they extend. They typically toughen conditions only after a borrowing nation has violated the original arrangement. By giving nations that are most likely to try to take advantage of vague conditions a greater incentive to seek funding, this policy worsens the adverse selection problem the World Bank and IMF face.

RETHINKING LONG-TERM DEVELOPMENT LENDING Since the early 1990s, one of the main themes of development economics has been the reform of market processes in developing nations. Markets work better at promoting growth when a developing nation has more effective institutions, such as basic property rights, well-run legal systems, and uncorrupt government agencies.

Hence, there is considerable agreement that a top priority of the World Bank and the IMF should be to identify ways to put basic market foundations into place by guaranteeing property and contract rights. Doing so would require constructing legal systems that can credibly enforce laws protecting these rights. Another key requirement is simplifying the processes for putting capital goods to work most efficiently in developing countries.

ALTERNATIVE INSTITUTIONAL STRUCTURES FOR LIMITING FINANCIAL CRISES In recent years, economists have advanced a wide variety of proposals on the appropriate role for the International Monetary Fund in anticipating and reacting to international financial crises. Many of these proposals share common features, such as more frequent and in-depth releases of information both by the IMF and by countries that borrow from this institution. Nearly all economists also recommend improved financial and accounting standards for those receiving funds from the World Bank and the IMF, as well as other changes that might help reduce moral hazard problems in such lending.

To learn about the International Monetary Fund's view on its role in international financial crises, go to www.econtoday.com/chap18.

Nevertheless, proposals for change diverge sharply. The IMF and its supporters have suggested maintaining its current structure but working harder to develop so-called early warning systems of financial crises so that aid can be provided to head off crises before they develop. Some economists have proposed establishing an international system of rules restricting capital outflows that might threaten international financial stability.

Other economists call for more dramatic changes. For instance, one proposal suggests creating a board composed of finance ministers of member nations to be directly in charge of day-to-day management of the IMF. Another recommends providing government incentives, in the form of tax breaks and subsidies, for increased private-sector lending that would supplement or even replace loans now made by the IMF.

QUICK QUIZ See page 413 for the answers. Review concepts from this section in MyEconLab.

The **World Bank** is an umbrella institution for _____ international organizations, each of which has more than 140 member nations, which coordinate _____-term loans to governments and private firms in developing nations.

The **International Monetary Fund** is an organization with more than 180 member nations. It coordinates mainly _____-term and some longer-term financial assistance to developing nations in an effort to _____ international flows of funds.

Like other lenders, the World Bank and the IMF confront _____ _____ and _____ _____ problems. Recently, there have been suggestions for restructuring the operations of both institutions, but so far there is little agreement about how to do so.

YOU ARE THERE
Generating New Saving on a Floating Amazon River Bank Branch

Luzia Moraes faces different problems than most bank branch managers confront—she must watch out for rainstorms and leaks in her bank branch's hull. Moraes takes in saving and extends loans from a boat along Brazil's Amazon River. Every two weeks, her "branch" begins a nine-day trip on a 125-foot boat called the *Voyager III*. Her bank branch offers financial services to hundreds of customers who live along the river. While *Voyager III* is moored, Moraes continues to provide services on canoes and rafts to customers along smaller Amazon tributaries. Most of Moraes's customers seek access to her bank branch's interest-bearing deposit accounts. Other customers desire loans to buy capital goods, such as structures suitable for small businesses.

Several Brazilian banks now have floating branches such as the one operated by Moraes. Bank branches established in some of Brazil's poorest regions since the 1990s have generated a tripling of that nation's savings accounts and a substantial increase in the national saving rate. There has been a corresponding growth in lending to finance capital investment throughout the Brazilian countryside. The upsurge in saving and investment helps to explain how Brazil's real GDP per capita has risen by more than 60 percent since the late 1990s.

Critical Thinking Questions

1. Why is saving an important contributor to Brazil's economic growth?
2. How does an increase in the rate of capital investment boost economic growth?

ISSUES & APPLICATIONS

A New Mongol Hoard Raises Investment and Growth

CONCEPTS APPLIED
▶ Economic Freedom
▶ Foreign Direct Investment
▶ Dead Capital

Most rankings of all the world's nations based on their levels of economic freedom place Mongolia near the middle. Recently, however, the country took a major step toward improving its economic freedom rating, increasing capital investment, and raising its rate of economic growth.

Stock Shares of a Mining Boom

Geologists have found substantial new deposits of coal and copper in Mongolia. The government has arranged for foreign companies to assist in constructing mines to extract these minerals. The companies' capital investments in these mining operations constitute foreign direct investment.

Foreign firms provide the Mongolian government with guaranteed rights to future returns on their mining operations. The government, in turn, transferred these rights to each Mongolian resident in the form of shares of stock. The initial dollar value of each resident's shares was equal to nearly $360—about 10 percent of the nation's per capita real GDP at the time of the rights transferal.

Previously Dead Capital Livens Up

The mining industry had already been an important part of Mongolia's economy prior to the discovery of even more mineral deposits. In past years, however, the government's partial share of the ownership in mining equipment created uncertainty about managing the capital equipment, thereby rendering a large portion of the equipment dead capital. The government's transferal of rights to future returns from mining to the nation's residents immediately shifted most existing equipment out of this category. The action also moved Mongolia up a number of places on the economic freedom list.

Other consequences of the government's rights transferal have been significant upswings in capital investment and in the rate of economic growth. The year that the

Mongolian government announced its plans to transfer the rights to mining returns to its residents, the nation's economic growth rate rose from below 5 percent per year to about 10 percent. During the first two years following the transferal, Mongolia's annual economic growth rate jumped to above 20 percent per year.

For Critical Thinking

1. How might freeing up dead capital have helped to increase Mongolia's rate of economic growth?
2. What type of investment would foreign residents undertake if they were to purchase a small fraction of the shares of stocks owned by Mongolia's residents?

Web Resources

1. View a video discussing the Mongolian government's mining rights transferal at www.econtoday.com/chap18.
2. Learn about how the government transmitted shares to future returns from mineral mines to the country's residents at www.econtoday.com/chap18.

MyEconLab

For more questions on this chapter's Issues & Applications, go to MyEconLab. In the Study Plan for this chapter, select Section N: News.

MyEconLab

Here is what you should know after reading this chapter. MyEconLab will help you identify what you know, and where to go when you need to practice.

WHAT YOU SHOULD KNOW		WHERE TO GO TO PRACTICE
Effects of Population Growth on Economic Growth Increased population growth has contradictory effects on economic growth. On the one hand, for a given growth rate of real GDP, increased population growth tends to reduce growth of per capita real GDP. On the other hand, if increased population growth is accompanied by higher labor productivity and participation, the growth rate of real GDP can increase.	economic freedom, 398	• MyEconLab Study Plan 18.1
Why Dead Capital Deters Investment and Slows Economic Growth Relatively few people in less developed countries establish legal ownership of capital goods. Unofficially owned resources are known as dead capital. Inability to trade, insure, and enforce rights to dead capital makes it difficult to employ these resources most efficiently, and this tends to limit economic growth.	dead capital, 399	• MyEconLab Study Plan 18.2
Government Inefficiencies and Dead Capital in Developing Nations In many developing nations, government regulations and red tape impose very high costs on those who officially register capital ownership. The dead capital problem that these government inefficiencies create reduces investment and growth.	Key Figure Figure 18-1, 401	• MyEconLab Study Plan 18.2 • Animated Figure 18-1

MyEconLab *continued*

WHAT YOU SHOULD KNOW — WHERE TO GO TO PRACTICE

Sources of International Investment Funds and Obstacles to Investing in Developing Nations International flows of funds to developing nations promote global economic growth. Asymmetric information problems, such as adverse selection and moral hazard problems, hinder international flows of funds and thereby slow economic growth in developing nations.

portfolio investment, 403
foreign direct investment, 403
international financial crisis, 404

Key Figure
Figure 18-3, 403

• MyEconLab Study Plan 18.3
• Animated Figure 18-3

The Functions of the World Bank and the International Monetary Fund Adverse selection and moral hazard problems faced by private investors can both limit and destabilize international flows of funds to developing countries. The World Bank finances capital investment in countries that have trouble attracting funds from private sources. The International Monetary Fund attempts to stabilize international financial flows by extending loans to countries caught up in international financial crises.

World Bank, 405
International Monetary Fund (IMF), 406
quota subscription, 406

• MyEconLab Study Plan 18.4

Problems Faced by Policymakers at the World Bank and IMF Both the World Bank and the IMF face adverse selection and moral hazard problems that may be worsened by the imprecise initial conditions they impose on the loans they extend. Development economists generally agree that both institutions should emphasize reforms such as basic property rights that give domestic residents more incentive to invest.

• MyEconLab Study Plan 18.4

Log in to MyEconLab, take a chapter test, and get a personalized Study Plan that tells you which concepts you understand and which ones you need to review. From there, MyEconLab will give you further practice, tutorials, animations, videos, and guided solutions. For more information, visit www.myeconlab.com

PROBLEMS

All problems are assignable in MyEconLab; exercises that update with real-time data are marked with ⬢. Answers to odd-numbered problems appear at the back of the book.

18-1. A country's real GDP is growing at an annual rate of 3.1 percent, and the current rate of growth of per capita real GDP is 0.3 percent per year. What is the population growth rate in this nation? (See page 397.)

18-2. A nation's current annual rate of growth of per capita real GDP is 3.0 percent, and its annual rate of population growth is 3.4 percent. What is the nation's annual rate of growth of real GDP? (See page 397.)

18-3. Currently, the rate of growth of real GDP in a nation is 1.3 percent per year. Its population growth rate is 2.7 percent per year. What is the nation's annual rate of growth of per capita real GDP? (See page 397.)

18-4. The annual rate of growth of real GDP in a developing nation is 0.3 percent. Initially, the country's population was stable from year to year. Recently, however, a significant increase in the nation's birthrate has raised the annual rate of population growth to 0.5 percent. (See page 397.)

a. What was the rate of growth of per capita real GDP before the increase in population growth?

b. If the rate of growth of real GDP remains unchanged, what is the new rate of growth of per capita real GDP following the increase in the birthrate?

18-5. A developing country has determined that each additional $1 billion of net investment in capital goods adds 0.01 percentage point to its long-run average annual rate of growth of per capita real GDP. (See pages 399–400.)

a. Domestic entrepreneurs recently began to seek official approval to open a range of businesses employing capital resources valued at $20 billion. If the entrepreneurs undertake these investments, by what fraction of a percentage point will the nation's long-run average annual rate of growth of per capita real GDP increase, other things being equal?

b. After weeks of effort trying to complete the first of 15 stages of bureaucratic red tape necessary to obtain authorization to start their businesses, a number of entrepreneurs decide to drop their investment plans completely, and the amount of official investment that actually takes place turns out to be $10 billion. Other things being equal, by what fraction of a percentage point will this decision reduce the nation's long-run average annual rate of growth of per capita real GDP from what it would have been if investment had been $20 billion?

18-6. Consider the estimates that the World Bank has assembled for the following nations:

Country	Legal Steps Required to Start a Business	Days Required to Start a Business	Cost of Starting a Business as a Percentage of Per Capita GDP
Angola	14	146	838%
Bosnia-Herzegovina	12	59	52%
Morocco	11	36	19%
Togo	14	63	281%
Uruguay	10	27	47%

Rank the nations in order starting with the one you would expect to have the highest rate of economic growth, other things being equal. Explain your reasoning. (See pages 399–400.)

18-7. Suppose that every $500 billion of dead capital reduces the average rate of growth in worldwide per capita real GDP by 0.1 percentage point. If there is $10 trillion in dead capital in the world, by how many percentage points does the existence of dead capital reduce average worldwide growth of per capita real GDP? (See page 400.)

18-8. Assume that each $1 billion in net capital investment generates 0.3 percentage point of the average percentage rate of growth of per capita real GDP, given the nation's labor resources. Firms have been investing exactly $6 billion in capital goods each year, so the annual average rate of growth of per capita real GDP has been 1.8 percent. Now a government that fails to consistently adhere to the rule of law has come to power, and firms must pay $100 million in bribes to gain official approval for every $1 billion in investment in capital goods. In response, companies cut back their total investment spending to $4 billion per year. If other things are equal and companies maintain this rate of investment, what will be the nation's new average annual rate of growth of per capita real GDP? (See page 400.)

18-9. During the past year, several large banks extended $200 million in loans to the government and several firms in a developing nation. International investors also purchased $150 million in bonds and $350 million in stocks issued by domestic firms. Of the stocks that foreign investors purchased, $100 million were shares that amounted to less than a 10 percent interest in domestic firms. This was the first year this nation had ever permitted inflows of funds from abroad. (See page 403.)

a. Based on the investment category definitions discussed in this chapter, what was the amount of portfolio investment in this nation during the past year?

b. What was the amount of foreign direct investment in this nation during the past year?

18-10. Last year, $100 million in outstanding bank loans to a developing nation's government were not renewed, and the developing nation's government paid off $50 million in maturing government bonds that had been held by foreign residents. During that year, however, a new group of banks participated in a $125 million loan to help finance a major government construction project in the capital city. Domestic firms also issued $50 million in bonds and $75 million in stocks to foreign investors. All of the stocks issued gave the foreign investors more than 10 percent shares of the domestic firms. (See page 403.)

a. What was gross foreign investment in this nation last year?

b. What was net foreign investment in this nation last year?

18-11. Identify which of the following situations currently faced by international investors are examples of adverse selection and which are examples of moral hazard. (See pages 404–405.)

a. Among the governments of several developing countries that are attempting to issue new bonds this year, it is certain that a few will fail to collect taxes to repay the bonds when they mature. It is difficult, however, for investors considering buying government bonds to predict which governments will experience this problem.

b. Foreign investors are contemplating purchasing stock in a company that, unknown to them, may have failed to properly establish legal ownership over a crucial capital resource.

c. Companies in a less developed nation have already issued bonds to finance the purchase of new capital goods. After receiving the funds from the bond issue, however, the company's managers pay themselves large bonuses instead.

d. When the government of a developing nation received a bank loan three years ago, it ultimately repaid the loan but had to reschedule its payments after officials misused the funds for unworthy projects. Now the government, which still has many of the same officials, is trying to raise funds by issuing bonds to foreign investors, who must decide whether or not to purchase them.

18-12. Identify which of the following situations currently faced by the World Bank or the International Monetary Fund are examples of adverse selection and which are examples of moral hazard. (See pages 404–405.)

a. The World Bank has extended loans to the government of a developing country to finance construction of a canal with a certain future flow of earnings. Now, however, the government has decided to redirect those funds to build a casino that may or may not generate sufficient profits to allow the government to repay the loan.

b. The IMF is considering extending loans to several nations that failed to fully repay loans they received from the IMF during the past decade but now claim to be better credit risks. Now the IMF is not sure in advance which of these nations are unlikely to fully repay new loans.

c. The IMF recently extended a loan to a government directed by democratically elected officials that would permit the nation to adjust to an abrupt reduction in private flows of funds from abroad. A coup has just occurred, however,

in response to newly discovered corruption within the government's elected leadership. The new military dictator has announced tentative plans to disburse some of the funds in equal shares to all citizens.

18-13. For each of the following situations, explain which of the policy issues discussed in this chapter is associated with the stance the institution has taken. (See pages 405–407.)

a. The World Bank offers to make a loan to a company in an impoverished nation at a lower interest rate than the company had been about to agree to pay to borrow the same amount from a group of private banks.

b. The World Bank makes a loan to a company in a developing nation that has not yet received formal approval to operate there, even though the government approval process typically takes 15 months.

c. The IMF extends a loan to a developing nation's government, with no preconditions, to enable the government to make already overdue payments on a loan it had previously received from the World Bank.

18-14. For each of the following situations, explain which of the policy issues discussed in this chapter is associated with the stance the institution has taken. (See pages 405–407.)

a. The IMF extends a long-term loan to a nation's government to help it maintain publicly supported production of goods and services that the government otherwise would have turned over to private companies.

b. The World Bank makes a loan to companies in an impoverished nation in which government officials typically demand bribes equal to 50 percent of companies' profits before allowing them to engage in any new investment projects.

c. The IMF offers to make a loan to banks in a country in which the government's rulers commonly require banks to extend credit to finance high-risk investment projects headed by the rulers' friends and relatives.

18-15. Answer the following questions concerning proposals to reform long-term development lending programs currently offered by the IMF and World Bank. (See pages 406–407.)

a. Why might the World Bank face moral hazard problems if it were to offer to provide funds to governments that promise to allocate the funds to major institutional reforms aimed at enhancing economic growth?

b. How does the IMF face an adverse selection problem if it is considering making loans to governments in which the ruling parties have already shown predispositions to try to "buy" votes by creating expensive public programs in advance of elections? How might following an announced rule in which the IMF cuts off future loans to governments that engage in such activities reduce this problem and promote increased economic growth in nations that do receive IMF loans?

ECONOMICS ON THE NET

The International Monetary Fund The purpose of this exercise is to evaluate the IMF's role in promoting global economic growth.

Title: International Monetary Fund

Navigation: Go to the home page of the IMF on the Web at **www.econtoday.com/chap18**.

Application Read each entry, and then answer the question.

1. Click on the link on the Web page titled *Our Work*. Which of the IMF's purposes are most directly related to promoting a higher rate of global economic growth? Are any related more indirectly to this goal?

2. Click on *Surveillance*. Based on this discussion, what type of asymmetric information problem does IMF surveillance attempt to address?

3. Click on *Lending*, and then click on *Main Lending Facilities*. Which IMF lending "facilities" appear to be aimed at maintaining stability of international flows of funds? Which appear to be longer-term loans similar to those extended by the World Bank?

For Group Study and Analysis The full reading at the *Lending* link, titled "Lending by the IMF," discusses terms of lending that the IMF imposes on different groups of nations. What are the likely rationales for charging some nations lower interest rates than others? Are there any potential problems with this policy? (Hint: Consider the adverse selection and moral hazard problems faced by the IMF.)

ANSWERS TO QUICK QUIZZES

p. 399: (i) reduce; (ii) labor force . . . increase; (iii) political . . . economic

p. 402: (i) ownership; (ii) lower . . . developing; (iii) bureaucracies

p. 405: (i) banks . . . portfolio . . . foreign direct; (ii) 80 . . . portfolio . . . foreign direct; (iii) adverse selection . . . moral hazard

p. 407: (i) five . . . long; (ii) short . . . stabilize; (iii) adverse selection . . . moral hazard

19

Demand and Supply Elasticity

Times have been tougher for rock musicians in recent years. Even though the market prices of music albums and concert tickets have been increasing, the revenues received by rock performers have been decreasing. Professional musicians who perform other types of music, ranging from classical to country western, have been experiencing the same association of higher prices with lower revenues. After reading this chapter, you will understand why this relationship between revenues and price exists in the markets for music albums and concert performances. The key economic concept operating here, you will learn, is *price elasticity of demand*.

Federal Reserve economists have estimated that when bank debit-card transaction fees increase by 10 percent, the number of debit-card transactions that people wish to utilize declines by nearly 67 percent? Thus, an increase as small as 1 percent in the price of debit-card usage generates a significant proportionate reduction in the quantity of transactions demanded by debit-card users.

Businesses must constantly take into account consumers' response to changing fees and prices. If Apple reduces its prices by 10 percent, will consumers respond by buying so many more digital devices that the company's revenues rise? At the other end of the spectrum, can Ferrari dealers "get away" with a 2 percent increase in prices? That is, will Ferrari purchasers respond so little to the relatively small increase in price that the total revenues received for Ferrari sales will not fall and may actually rise? The only way to answer these questions is to know how responsive consumers in the real world will be to changes in prices. Economists have a special name for quantity responsiveness—*elasticity*, which is the subject of this chapter.

Price Elasticity

To begin to understand what elasticity is all about, just keep in mind that it means "responsiveness." Here we are concerned with the price elasticity of demand. We wish to know the extent to which a change in the price of, say, petroleum products will cause the quantity demanded to change, other things held constant. We want to determine the percentage change in quantity demanded in response to a percentage change in price.

Price Elasticity of Demand

We will formally define the **price elasticity of demand,** which we will label E_p, as follows:

$$E_p = \frac{\text{percentage change in quantity demanded}}{\text{percentage change in price}}$$

What will price elasticity of demand tell us? It will tell us the *relative* amount by which the quantity demanded will change in response to a change in the price of a particular good.

Consider an example in which a 10 percent rise in the price of oil leads to a reduction in quantity demanded of only 1 percent. Putting these numbers into the formula, we find that the price elasticity of demand for oil in this case equals the percentage change in quantity demanded divided by the percentage change in price, or

$$E_p = \frac{-1\%}{+10\%} = -0.1$$

An elasticity of −0.1 means that a 1 percent *increase* in the price would lead to a mere 0.1 percent *decrease* in the quantity demanded. If you were now told, in contrast, that the price elasticity of demand for oil was −1, you would know that a 10 percent increase in the price of oil would lead to a 10 percent decrease in the quantity demanded.

RELATIVE QUANTITIES ONLY Notice that in our elasticity formula, we talk about *percentage* changes in quantity demanded divided by *percentage* changes in price. We focus on relative amounts of price changes, because percentage changes are independent of the units chosen. This means that it doesn't matter if we measure price changes in terms of cents, dollars, or hundreds of dollars. It also doesn't matter whether we measure quantity changes in ounces, grams, or pounds.

Price elasticity of demand (E_p)
The responsiveness of the quantity demanded of a commodity to changes in its price; defined as the percentage change in quantity demanded divided by the percentage change in price.

Go to www.econtoday.com/chap19 for additional review of the price elasticity of demand.

ALWAYS NEGATIVE The law of demand states that quantity demanded is *inversely* related to the relative price. An *increase* in the price of a good leads to a *decrease* in the quantity demanded. If a *decrease* in the relative price of a good should occur, the quantity demanded would *increase* by some percentage. The point is that price elasticity of demand will always be negative. By convention, however, *we will ignore the minus sign in our discussion from this point on.*

Basically, the greater the *absolute* price elasticity of demand (disregarding the sign), the greater the demand responsiveness to relative price changes—a small change in price has a great impact on quantity demanded. Conversely, the smaller the absolute price elasticity of demand, the smaller the demand responsiveness to relative price changes—a large change in price has little effect on quantity demanded.

Calculating Elasticity

To calculate the price elasticity of demand, we must compute percentage changes in quantity demanded and in price. To calculate the percentage change in quantity demanded, we might divide the absolute change in the quantity demanded by the original quantity demanded:

$$\frac{\text{change in quantity demanded}}{\text{original quantity demanded}}$$

To find the percentage change in price, we might divide the change in price by the original price:

$$\frac{\text{change in price}}{\text{original price}}$$

There is an arithmetic problem, though, when we calculate percentage changes in this manner. The percentage change, say, from 2 to 3—50 percent—is not the same as the percentage change from 3 to 2—$33\frac{1}{3}$ percent. In other words, it makes a difference where you start. One way out of this dilemma is simply to use average values.

To compute the price elasticity of demand, we take the *average* of the two prices and the two quantities over the range we are considering and compare the change with these averages. Thus, the formula for computing the price elasticity of demand is as follows:

$$E_p = \frac{\text{change in quantity}}{\text{sum of quantities/2}} \div \frac{\text{change in price}}{\text{sum of prices /2}}$$

We can rewrite this more simply if we do two things: (1) We can let Q_1 and Q_2 equal the two different quantities demanded before and after the price change and let P_1 and P_2 equal the two different prices. (2) Because we will be dividing a percentage by a percentage, we simply use the ratio, or the decimal form, of the percentages. Therefore,

$$E_p = \frac{\Delta Q}{(Q_1 + Q_2)/2} \div \frac{\Delta P}{(P_1 + P_2)/2}$$

where the Greek letter Δ (delta) stands for "change in."

How can we use actual changes in the price of a particular brand of tablet device and associated changes in the quantity of tablet devices demanded to calculate the price elasticity of demand with this formula?

EXAMPLE

The Price Elasticity of Demand for a Tablet Device

During a two-month period, the price of Hewlett-Packard's TouchPad tablet device decreased from $499.99 to $99.99. As a consequence, during this two-month period the total quantity of tablet devices demanded increased from 25,000 per month to 425,000 per month.

Assuming other things were equal, we can calculate the price elasticity of demand for TouchPad tablets during this period:

$$E_p = \frac{\text{change in } Q}{\text{sum of quantities}/2} \div \frac{\text{change in } P}{\text{sum of prices}/2}$$

$$= \frac{425,000 - 25,000}{(425,000 + 25,000)/2} \div \frac{\$499.99 - \$99.99}{(\$499.99 + \$99.99)/2}$$

$$= \frac{400,000}{450,000/2} \div \frac{\$400.00}{\$599.98/2} = 1.33$$

The price elasticity of 1.33 means that each 1 percent decrease in price generated a 1.33 percent increase in the quantity of TouchPad tablet devices demanded. Thus, the quantity of tablets demanded was relatively responsive to a reduction in the price of the devices.

FOR CRITICAL THINKING
Would the estimated price elasticity of demand for TouchPad tablets have been different if we had not used the average-values formula? How?

Price Elasticity Ranges

We have names for the varying ranges of price elasticities, depending on whether a 1 percent change in price elicits more or less than a 1 percent change in the quantity demanded.

- We say that a good has an **elastic demand** whenever the price elasticity of demand is greater than 1. A change in price of 1 percent causes a greater than 1 percent change in the quantity demanded.

- In a situation of **unit elasticity of demand,** a change in price of 1 percent causes exactly a 1 percent change in the quantity demanded.

- In a situation of **inelastic demand,** a change in price of 1 percent causes a change of less than 1 percent in the quantity demanded.

When we say that a commodity's demand is elastic, we are indicating that consumers are relatively responsive to changes in price. When we say that a commodity's demand is inelastic, we are indicating that its consumers are relatively unresponsive to price changes. When economists say that demand is inelastic, it does not necessarily mean that quantity demanded is *totally* unresponsive to price changes. Remember, the law of demand implies that there will almost always be some responsiveness in quantity demanded to a price change. The question is how much. That's what elasticity attempts to determine.

Extreme Elasticities

There are two extremes in price elasticities of demand. One extreme represents total unresponsiveness of quantity demanded to price changes, which is referred to as **perfectly inelastic demand,** or zero elasticity. The other represents total responsiveness, which is referred to as infinitely or **perfectly elastic demand.**

We show perfect inelasticity in panel (a) of Figure 19-1 on the following page. Notice that the quantity demanded per year is 8 million units, no matter what the price. Hence, for any price change, the quantity demanded will remain the same, and thus the change in the quantity demanded will be zero. Look back at our formula for computing elasticity. If the change in the quantity demanded is zero, the numerator is also zero, and a nonzero number divided into zero results in a value of zero too. This is true at any point along the demand curve. Hence, there is perfect inelasticity.

Elastic demand

A demand relationship in which a given percentage change in price will result in a larger percentage change in quantity demanded.

Unit elasticity of demand

A demand relationship in which the quantity demanded changes exactly in proportion to the change in price.

Inelastic demand

A demand relationship in which a given percentage change in price will result in a less-than-proportionate percentage change in the quantity demanded.

Perfectly inelastic demand

A demand that exhibits zero responsiveness to price changes. No matter what the price is, the quantity demanded remains the same.

Perfectly elastic demand

A demand that has the characteristic that even the slightest increase in price will lead to zero quantity demanded.

FIGURE 19-1

Extreme Price Elasticities

In panel (a), we show complete price unresponsiveness. The demand curve is vertical at the quantity of 8 million units per year. This means that the price elasticity of demand is zero. In panel (b), we show complete price responsiveness. At a price of 30 cents, in this example, consumers will demand an unlimited quantity of the particular good in question, over the relevant range of quantities. This is a case of infinite price elasticity of demand.

At the opposite extreme is the situation depicted in panel (b) of Figure 19-1 above. Here we show that at a price of 30 cents, an unlimited quantity will be demanded over the relevant range of quantities. At a price that is only slightly above 30 cents, no quantity will be demanded. There is perfect, or infinite, responsiveness at each point along this curve, and hence we call the demand schedule in panel (b) perfectly elastic.

The **price elasticity of demand** is equal to the percentage change in _____ _____ divided by the percentage change in _____.

Price elasticity of demand is calculated in terms of _____ changes in quantity demanded and in price. Thus, it is expressed as a unitless, dimensionless number that is _____ of units of measurement.

The price elasticity of demand is always _____, because an increase in price will lead to a _____ in quantity demanded and a decrease in price will lead to an _____ in quantity demanded. By convention, we ignore the negative sign in discussions of the price elasticity of demand.

One extreme elasticity occurs when a demand curve is vertical. It has _____ price elasticity of demand. It is completely _____. Another extreme elasticity occurs when a demand curve is horizontal. It has completely _____ demand. Its price elasticity of demand is _____.

Elasticity and Total Revenues

Suppose that you are an employee of a firm in the cellular phone service industry. How would you know when a rise in the market clearing price of cellular phone services will result in an increase in the total revenues, or the total receipts, of firms in the industry? It is commonly thought that the way for total receipts to rise is for the price per unit to increase. But is it possible that a rise in price per unit could lead to a decrease in total revenues? The answer to this question depends on the price elasticity of demand.

Let's look at Figure 19-2 on the facing page. In panel (a), column 1 shows the price of cellular phone service in cents per minute, and column 2 represents billions of minutes per year. In column 3, we multiply column 1 times column 2 to derive total revenue because total revenue is always equal to the number of units (quantity) sold times

FIGURE 19-2

The Relationship between Price Elasticity of Demand and Total Revenues for Cellular Phone Service

In panel (a), we show the elastic, unit-elastic, and inelastic sections of a straight-line demand schedule according to whether a reduction in price increases total revenues, causes them to remain constant, or causes them to decrease, respectively. In panel (b), we show these regions graphically on the demand curve. In panel (c), we show them on the total revenue curve.

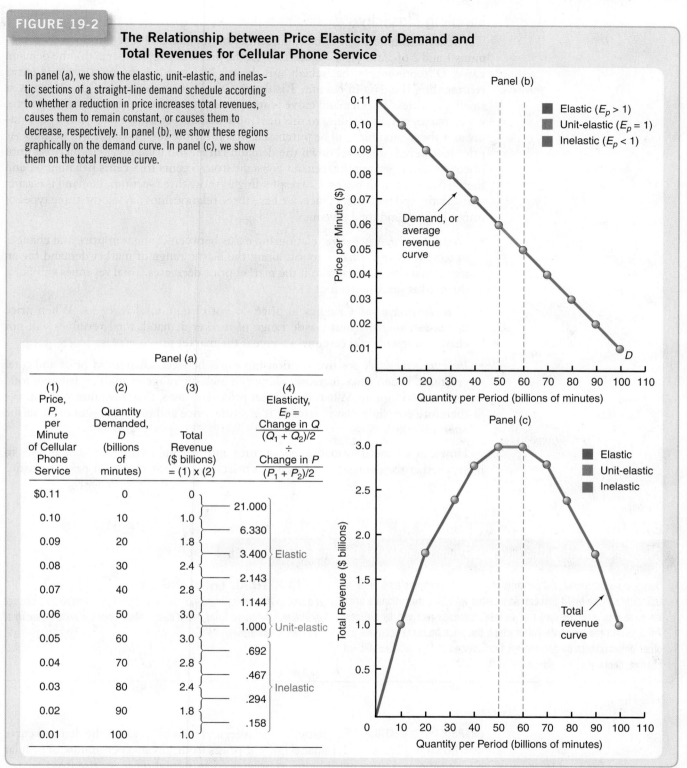

Panel (a)

(1) Price, P, per Minute of Cellular Phone Service	(2) Quantity Demanded, D (billions of minutes)	(3) Total Revenue ($ billions) = (1) x (2)	(4) Elasticity, $E_p = \dfrac{\text{Change in } Q}{(Q_1 + Q_2)/2} \div \dfrac{\text{Change in } P}{(P_1 + P_2)/2}$	
$0.11	0	0		
0.10	10	1.0	21.000	
0.09	20	1.8	6.330	
0.08	30	2.4	3.400	Elastic
0.07	40	2.8	2.143	
0.06	50	3.0	1.144	
0.05	60	3.0	1.000	Unit-elastic
0.04	70	2.8	.692	
0.03	80	2.4	.467	Inelastic
0.02	90	1.8	.294	
0.01	100	1.0	.158	

the price per unit. In column 4, we calculate values of elasticity. Notice what happens to total revenues throughout the schedule. They rise steadily as the price rises from 1 cent to 5 cents per minute. When the price rises further to 6 cents per minute, total revenues remain constant at $3 billion. At prices per minute higher than 6 cents, total revenues fall as price increases. Indeed, if prices are above 6 cents per minute, total revenues will increase only if the price *declines*, not if the price rises.

Labeling Elasticity

The relationship between price and quantity on the demand schedule is given in columns 1 and 2 of panel (a) in Figure 19-2 on the previous page. In panel (b), the demand curve, D, representing that schedule is drawn. In panel (c), the total revenue curve representing the data in column 3 is drawn. Notice first the level of these curves at small quantities. The demand curve is at a maximum height, but total revenue is zero, which makes sense according to this demand schedule—at a price of 11 cents per minute and above, no units will be purchased, and therefore total revenue will be zero. As price is lowered, we travel down the demand curve, and total revenues increase until price is 6 cents per minute, remain constant from 6 cents to 5 cents per minute, and then fall at lower unit prices. Corresponding to those three sections, demand is elastic, unit-elastic, and inelastic. Hence, we have three relationships among the three types of price elasticity and total revenues.

- *Elastic demand.* A negative relationship exists between changes in price and changes in total revenues. That is to say, along the elastic range of market demand for an item, total revenues will rise if the market price decreases. Total revenues will fall if the market price increases.

- *Unit-elastic demand.* Changes in price do not change total revenues. When price increases along the unit-elastic range of market demand, total revenues will not change, nor will total revenues change if the market price decreases.

- *Inelastic demand.* A positive relationship exists between changes in price and total revenues. When price increases along the inelastic range of market demand, total revenues will go up. When the market price decreases, total revenues will fall. We therefore conclude that if demand is inelastic, price and total revenues move in the *same* direction.

How can we use information about price and revenue changes at U.S. airlines to infer whether the demand for air travel is price-elastic, unit-elastic, or price-inelastic?

EXAMPLE

Price and Revenue Changes and Price Elasticity of Demand for Air Travel

During a recent period, the per-mile price that passengers paid to fly on U.S. airlines rose by 14 percent. Associated with this proportionate price increase was a 17 percent rise in total revenues received by airlines. Thus, within the time interval in which the price increase occurred but other determinants of demand for the services of U.S. airlines did not change, demand was inelastic.

FOR CRITICAL THINKING
If a rise in the per-mile price of flying instead had generated no change in airlines' revenues, what would have been true of the price elasticity of demand for air travel?

GRAPHIC PRESENTATION   The elastic, unit-elastic, and inelastic areas of the demand curve are shown in Figure 19-2, in panel (a). For prices from 11 cents per minute of cellular phone time to 6 cents per minute, as price decreases, total revenues rise from zero to $3 billion. Demand is elastic. When price changes from 6 cents to 5 cents, however, total revenues remain constant at $3 billion. Demand is unit-elastic. Finally, when price falls from 5 cents to 1 cent, total revenues decrease from $3 billion to $1 billion. Demand is inelastic. In panels (b) and (c) of Figure 19-2, we have labeled the sections of the demand curve accordingly, and we have also shown how total revenues first rise, then remain constant, and finally fall.

THE ELASTICITY-REVENUE RELATIONSHIP   The relationship between price elasticity of demand and total revenues brings together some important microeconomic concepts.

TABLE 19-1

Relationship between Price Elasticity of Demand and Total Revenues	Price Elasticity of Demand (E_p)		Effect of Price Change on Total Revenues (TR)	
			Price Decrease	Price Increase
	Inelastic	($E_p < 1$)	TR ↓	TR ↑
	Unit-elastic	($E_p = 1$)	No change in TR	No change in TR
	Elastic	($E_p > 1$)	TR ↑	TR ↓

Total revenues, as we have noted, are the product of price per unit times number of units purchased. The law of demand states that along a given demand curve, price and quantity changes will move in opposite directions: One increases as the other decreases. Consequently, what happens to the product of price times quantity depends on which of the opposing changes exerts a greater force on total revenues. But this is just what price elasticity of demand is designed to measure—responsiveness of quantity demanded to a change in price. The relationship between price elasticity of demand and total revenues is summarized in Table 19-1 above.

WHAT IF... the government offers to pay for higher-priced health care to try to reduce society's overall health care expenditures?

Estimates of the price elasticity of demand for most health care services vary between 0.2 and 0.6. These low elasticity values indicate that the demand for health care is inelastic. Thus, whenever health care prices increase, total revenues of health care providers will rise, which means that total expenditures by health care consumers must also increase. Suppose that the government were to step into the market to pay for health care in response to an observed increase in prices. The government's expenditures on health care would increase. Taken together, the private sector and the government together constitute "society." Thus, total health care expenditures for society as a whole would be higher—not lower—after the government's interventions.

QUICK QUIZ See page 433 for the answers. Review concepts from this section in MyEconLab.

Price elasticity of demand is related to total _____.

When demand is *elastic*, the change in price elicits a change in total revenues in the _____ direction from the price change.

When demand is *unit-elastic*, a change in price elicits _____ change in total revenues (or in total consumer expenditures).

When demand is *inelastic*, a change in price elicits a change in total revenues in the _____ direction as the price change.

Determinants of the Price Elasticity of Demand

We have learned how to calculate the price elasticity of demand. We know that theoretically it ranges numerically from zero (completely inelastic) to infinity (completely elastic). What we would like to do now is to come up with a list of the determinants of the price elasticity of demand. The price elasticity of demand for a particular commodity at any price depends, at a minimum, on the following factors:

- The existence, number, and quality of substitutes
- The share of a consumer's total budget devoted to purchases of that commodity
- The length of time allowed for adjustment to changes in the price of the commodity

Existence of Substitutes

The closer the substitutes for a particular commodity and the more substitutes there are, the greater will be its price elasticity of demand. At the limit, if there is a perfect substitute, the elasticity of demand for the commodity will be infinity. Thus, even the slightest increase in the commodity's price will cause a dramatic reduction in the quantity demanded: Quantity demanded will fall to zero.

Keep in mind that in this extreme example, we are really talking about two goods that the consumer believes are exactly alike and equally desirable, like dollar bills whose only difference is their serial numbers. When we talk about less extreme examples, we can speak only in terms of the number and the similarity of substitutes that are available.

Thus, we will find that the more narrowly we define a good, the closer and greater will be the number of substitutes available. For example, the demand for diet soft drinks may be relatively elastic because consumers can switch to other low-calorie liquid refreshments. The demand for diet drinks (as a single group), however, is relatively less elastic because there are fewer substitutes.

Share of Budget

We know that the greater the share of a person's total budget that is spent on a commodity, the greater that person's price elasticity of demand is for that commodity. A key reason that the demand for pepper is very inelastic is because individuals spend so little on it relative to their total budgets. In contrast, the demand for items such as transportation and housing is far more elastic because they occupy a large part of people's budgets—changes in their prices cannot easily be ignored without sacrificing a lot of other alternative goods that could be purchased.

Consider a numerical example. A household spends $40,000 a year. It purchases $4 of pepper per year and $4,000 of transportation services. Now consider the spending power of this family when the price of pepper and the price of transportation both double. If the household buys the same amount of pepper, it will now spend $8. It will thus have to reduce other expenditures by $4. This $4 represents only 0.01 percent of the entire household budget. By contrast, if transportation costs double, the family will have to spend $8,000, or $4,000 more on transportation, if it is to purchase the same quantity. That increased expenditure on transportation of $4,000 represents 10 percent of total expenditures that must be switched from other purchases.

We would therefore predict that the household will react differently if the price of pepper doubles than it will if transportation prices double. It will reduce its transportation purchases by a proportionately greater amount.

Time for Adjustment

When the price of a commodity changes and that price change persists, more people will learn about it. Further, consumers will be better able to revise their consumption patterns the longer the time period they have to do so. And in fact, the longer the time they do take, the less costly it will be for them to engage in this revision of consumption patterns. Consider a price decrease. The longer the price decrease persists, the greater will be the number of new uses that consumers will discover for the particular commodity, and the greater will be the number of new users of that particular commodity.

It is possible to make a very strong statement about the relationship between the price elasticity of demand and the time allowed for adjustment:

> *The longer any price change persists, the greater the elasticity of demand, other things held constant. Elasticity of demand is greater in the long run than in the short run.*

SHORT-RUN VERSUS LONG-RUN ADJUSTMENTS Let's consider an example. Suppose that the price of electricity goes up 50 percent. How do you adjust in the short run? You can turn the lights off more often, you can stop using your personal computer as much as you usually do, and similar measures. Otherwise it's very difficult to cut back on your consumption of electricity.

In the long run, though, you can devise other methods to reduce your consumption. Instead of using only electric heaters, the next time you have a house built you will install solar panels. You will purchase fluorescent bulbs because they use less electricity. The more time you have to think about it, the more ways you will find to cut your electricity consumption.

DEMAND ELASTICITY IN THE SHORT RUN AND IN THE LONG RUN We would expect, therefore, that the short-run demand curve for electricity would be relatively less elastic (in the price range around P_e), as demonstrated by D_1 in Figure 19-3 below. The long-run demand curve, however, will exhibit more elasticity (in the neighborhood of P_e), as demonstrated by D_3. Indeed, we can think of an entire family of demand curves such as those depicted in the figure. The short-run demand curve is for the period when there is little time for adjustment. As more time is allowed, the demand curve goes first to D_2 and then all the way to D_3. Thus, in the neighborhood of P_e, elasticity differs for each of these curves. It is greater for the less steep curves (but slope alone does not measure elasticity for the entire curve). What are short- and long-run price elasticities of demand for actual goods?

FIGURE 19-3

Short-Run and Long-Run Price Elasticity of Demand

Consider a situation in which the market price is P_e and the quantity demanded is Q_e. Then there is a price increase to P_1. In the short run, as evidenced by the demand curve D_1, we move from equilibrium quantity demanded, Q_e, to Q_1. After more time is allowed for adjustment, the demand curve rotates at original price P_e to D_2. Quantity demanded falls again, now to Q_2. After even more time is allowed for adjustment, the demand curve rotates at price P_e to D_3. At the higher price P_1 in the long run, the quantity demanded falls all the way to Q_3.

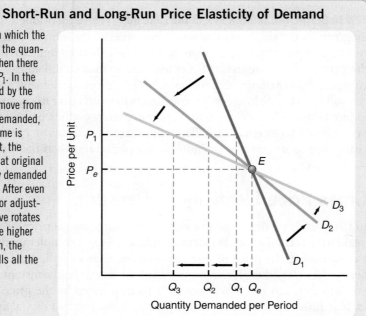

EXAMPLE

What Do Real-World Price Elasticities of Demand Look Like?

In Table 19-2 A below, we present demand elasticities for selected goods. None of them is zero, and the largest is 4.6. Remember that even though we are omitting the negative sign, there is an inverse relationship between price and quantity demanded. Also remember that these elasticities are measured over given price ranges. Recall from the example of the demand curve in Figure 19-2 on page 419 that choosing different price ranges could yield different elasticity estimates for these goods.

Economists have consistently found that estimated price elasticities of demand are greater in the long run than in the short run, as seen in

Table 19-2. There you see that all available estimates indicate that the long-run price elasticity of demand for vacation air travel is 2.7, whereas the estimate for the short run is 1.1. Throughout the table, you see that all estimates of long-run price elasticities of demand exceed their short-run counterparts.

FOR CRITICAL THINKING

Explain the intuitive reasoning behind the difference between long-run and short-run price elasticity of demand.

TABLE 19-2

Price Elasticities of Demand for Selected Goods

Here are estimated demand elasticities for selected goods. All of them are negative, although we omit the minus sign. We have given some estimates of the long-run price elasticities of demand. The long run is associated with the time necessary for consumers to adjust fully to any given price change. (Note: "N.A." indicates that no estimate is available.)

Category	Estimated Elasticity	
	Short Run	Long Run
Air travel (business)	0.4	1.2
Air travel (vacation)	1.1	2.7
Beef	0.6	N.A.
Cheese	0.3	N.A.
Electricity	0.1	1.7
Fresh tomatoes	4.6	N.A.
Gasoline	0.2	0.5
Hospital services	0.1	0.7
Intercity bus service	0.6	2.2
Physician services	0.1	0.6
Private education	1.1	1.9
Restaurant meals	2.3	N.A.
Tires	0.9	1.2

HOW TO DEFINE THE SHORT RUN AND THE LONG RUN We've mentioned the short run and the long run. Is the short run one week, two weeks, one month, two months? Is the long run three years, four years, five years? There is no single answer. The long run is the period of time necessary for consumers to make a full adjustment to a given price change, all other things held constant. In the case of the demand for electricity, the long run will be however long it takes consumers to switch over to cheaper sources of heating, to buy houses and appliances that are more energy-efficient, and so on. The long-run price elasticity of demand for electricity therefore relates to a period of at least several years. The short run—by default—is any period less than the long run.

Cross Price Elasticity of Demand

In Chapter 3, we discussed the effect of a change in the price of one good on the demand for a related good. We defined substitutes and complements in terms of whether a reduction in the price of one caused a decrease or an increase, respectively, in the demand for the other. If the price of Blu-ray discs is held constant, the number of discs purchased (at any price) will certainly be influenced by the price of a close substitute such as Internet digital movie downloads. If the price of digital apps is held constant, the amount of apps demanded (at any price) will certainly be affected by changes in the price of digital devices. (These goods are complements.)

Measuring the Cross Price Elasticity of Demand

What we now need to do is come up with a numerical measure of the responsiveness of the amount of an item demanded to the prices of related goods. This is called the **cross price elasticity of demand (E_{xy})**, which is defined as the percentage change in the amount of a particular item demanded at the item's current price (a shift in the demand curve) divided by the percentage change in the price of the related good. In equation form, the cross price elasticity of demand between good X and good Y is

$$E_{xy} = \frac{\text{percentage change in the amount of good X demanded}}{\text{percentage change in price of good Y}}$$

Cross price elasticity of demand (E_{xy})
The percentage change in the amount of an item demanded (holding its price constant) divided by the percentage change in the price of a related good.

Alternatively, the cross price elasticity of demand between good Y and good X would use the percentage change in the amount of good Y demanded as the numerator and the percentage change in the price of good X as the denominator.

Substitutes and Complements

When two goods are substitutes, the cross price elasticity of demand will be positive. For example, when the price of portable hard drives goes up, the amount of flash memory drives demanded at their current price will rise—the demand curve for flash drives will shift horizontally rightward—in response as consumers shift away from the now relatively more expensive portable hard drives to flash memory drives. A producer of flash memory drives could benefit from a numerical estimate of the cross price elasticity of demand between portable hard drives and flash memory drives. For example, if the price of portable hard drives goes up by 10 percent and the producer of flash memory drives knows that the cross price elasticity of demand is 1, the flash drive producer can estimate that the amount of flash memory drives demanded will also go up by 10 percent at any given price of flash memory drives. Plans for increasing production of flash memory drives can then be made.

When two related goods are complements, the cross price elasticity of demand will be negative (and we will *not* disregard the minus sign). For example, when the price of personal computers declines while all other determinants of demand are unchanged, the amount of computer printers demanded will rise. This is because as prices of computers decrease, the number of printers purchased at any given price of printers will naturally increase, because computers and printers are often used together. Any manufacturer of computer printers must take this into account in making production plans.

If goods are completely unrelated, their cross price elasticity of demand will, by definition, be zero.

Income Elasticity of Demand

In Chapter 3, we discussed the determinants of demand. One of those determinants was income. We can apply our understanding of elasticity to the relationship between changes in income and changes in the amount of a good demanded at that good's current price.

Measuring the Income Elasticity of Demand

We measure the responsiveness of the amount of an item demanded at that item's current price to a change in income by the **income elasticity of demand (E_i)**:

$$E_i = \frac{\text{percentage change in amount of a good demanded}}{\text{percentage change in income}}$$

Income elasticity of demand (E_i)
The percentage change in the amount of a good demanded, holding its price constant, divided by the percentage change in income. The responsiveness of the amount of a good demanded to a change in income, holding the good's relative price constant.

holding relative price constant.

Income elasticity of demand refers to a *horizontal shift* in the demand curve in response to changes in income, whereas price elasticity of demand refers to a *movement along* the curve in response to price changes. Thus, income elasticity of demand is calculated at a given price, and price elasticity of demand is calculated at a given income.

TABLE 19-3

How Income Affects Quantity of Digital Apps Demanded

Period	Number of Digital Apps Demanded per Month	Income per Month
1	6	$4,000
2	8	6,000

Calculating the Income Elasticity of Demand

To get the same income elasticity of demand over the same range of values regardless of the direction of change (increase or decrease), we can use the same formula that we used in computing the price elasticity of demand. When doing so, we have

$$E_i = \frac{\text{change in quantity}}{\text{sum of quantities}/2} \div \frac{\text{change in income}}{\text{sum of incomes}/2}$$

YOU ARE THERE

To contemplate how to apply the concepts of income elasticity of demand and price elasticity of demand in a real-world market, take a look at **Implications of Housing Demand Elasticities in China** on page 429.

A simple example will demonstrate how income elasticity of demand can be computed. Table 19-3 above gives the relevant data. The product in question is digital apps. We assume that the price of digital apps remains constant relative to other prices. In period 1, six apps per month are purchased. Income per month is $4,000. In period 2, monthly income increases to $6,000, and the number of apps demanded per month increases to eight. We can apply the following calculation:

$$E_i = \frac{2/[(6 + 8)/2]}{\$2,000/[(\$4,000 + \$6,000)/2]} = \frac{2/7}{2/5} = 0.71$$

Hence, measured income elasticity of demand for digital apps for the individual represented in this example is 0.71.

What retailer sells a line of products that taken together constitute an inferior good (see page 55 in Chapter 3)?

EXAMPLE

Are Walmart's Products Inferior Goods?

Since the economic downturn of 2008–2009, Walmart's sales have outpaced those of other retailers. Retailing experts have suggested the reason is that consumers buy a larger amount of items at Walmart when their incomes decline. To evaluate this hypothesis, Emek Basker of the University of Missouri at Columbia has estimated the income elasticity of demand for products sold by Walmart. He estimated that this income elasticity of demand is equal to −0.7, which indicates that when consumers' incomes fall by 1 percent, purchases from Walmart increase by 0.7 percent. Thus, an inverse relationship exists between income and the amount of Walmart products demanded, indicating that Walmart's retail product line constitutes an inferior good.

FOR CRITICAL THINKING
Would you guess that the income elasticity of demand for high-quality jewelry is positive or negative? Based on your guess, is jewelry an inferior or normal good?

You have just been introduced to three types of elasticities. All three elasticities are important in influencing the consumption of most goods. Reasonably accurate estimates of these elasticities can go a long way toward making accurate forecasts of demand for goods or services.

QUICK QUIZ See page 433 for the answers. Review concepts from this section in MyEconLab.

Some determinants of price elasticity of demand are (1) the existence, number, and quality of _____, (2) the _____ of the total budget spent on the good in question, and (3) the length of time allowed for _____ to a change in prices.

_____ price elasticity of demand measures the responsiveness of the amount of one good demanded to another's price changes. For substitutes, the cross price elasticity of demand is _____. For complements, it is _____.

Income elasticity of demand tells you by what percentage the amount of a good _____ will change for a particular percentage change in _____.

Price Elasticity of Supply

The **price elasticity of supply** (**E_s**) is defined similarly to the price elasticity of demand. Supply elasticities are generally positive. The reason is that at higher prices, larger quantities will generally be forthcoming from suppliers. The definition of the price elasticity of supply is as follows:

$$E_s = \frac{\text{percentage change in quantity supplied}}{\text{percentage change in price}}$$

Price elasticity of supply (E_s)
The responsiveness of the quantity supplied of a commodity to a change in its price—the percentage change in quantity supplied divided by the percentage change in price.

Classifying Supply Elasticities

Just as with demand, there are different ranges of supply elasticities. They are similar in definition to the ranges of demand elasticities.

If a 1 percent increase in price elicits a greater than 1 percent increase in the quantity supplied, we say that at the particular price in question on the supply schedule, *supply is elastic*. The most extreme elastic supply is called **perfectly elastic supply**—the slightest reduction in price will cause quantity supplied to fall to zero.

If, conversely, a 1 percent increase in price elicits a less than 1 percent increase in the quantity supplied, we refer to that as an *inelastic supply*. The most extreme inelastic supply is called **perfectly inelastic supply**—no matter what the price, the quantity supplied remains the same.

If the percentage change in the quantity supplied is just equal to the percentage change in the price, we call this *unit-elastic supply*.

Figure 19-4 on the next page shows two supply schedules, S and S'. You can tell at a glance, even without reading the labels, which one is perfectly elastic and which one is perfectly inelastic. As you might expect, most supply schedules exhibit elasticities that are somewhere between zero and infinity.

Perfectly elastic supply
A supply characterized by a reduction in quantity supplied to zero when there is the slightest decrease in price.

Perfectly inelastic supply
A supply for which quantity supplied remains constant, no matter what happens to price.

Price Elasticity of Supply and Length of Time for Adjustment

We pointed out earlier that the longer the time period allowed for adjustment, the greater the price elasticity of demand. It turns out that the same proposition applies to supply. The longer the time for adjustment, the more elastic the supply curve. Consider why this is true:

1. The longer the time allowed for adjustment, the more resources can flow into (or out of) an industry through expansion (or contraction) of existing firms. As an example, suppose that there is a long-lasting, significant increase in the demand for gasoline. The result is a sustained rise in the market price of gasoline. Initially, gasoline refiners will be hampered in expanding their production with the operating refining equipment available to them. Over time, however, some refining companies might be able to recondition old equipment that had fallen into disuse. They can

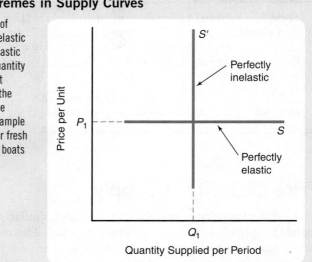

FIGURE 19-4

The Extremes in Supply Curves

Here we have drawn two extremes of supply schedules: S is a perfectly elastic supply curve; S' is a perfectly inelastic one. In the former, an unlimited quantity will be supplied within the relevant range of quantities at price P_1. In the latter, no matter what the price, the quantity supplied will be Q_1. An example of S' might be the supply curve for fresh (unfrozen) fish on the morning the boats come in.

also place orders for construction of new gasoline-refining equipment, and once the equipment arrives, they can also put it into place to expand their gasoline production. Given sufficient time, therefore, existing gasoline refiners can eventually respond to higher gasoline prices by adding new refining operations.

2. The longer the time allowed for adjustment, the entry (or exit) of firms increases (or decreases) production in an industry. Consider what happens if the price of gasoline remains higher than before as a result of a sustained rise in gasoline demand. Even as existing refiners add to their capability to produce gasoline by retooling old equipment, purchasing new equipment, and adding new refining facilities, additional businesses may seek to earn profits at the now-higher gasoline prices. Over time, the entry of new gasoline-refining companies adds to the productive capabilities of the entire refining industry, and the quantity of gasoline supplied increases.

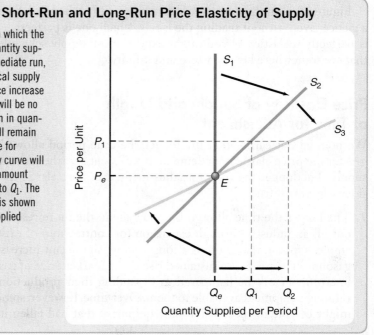

FIGURE 19-5

Short-Run and Long-Run Price Elasticity of Supply

Consider a situation in which the price is P_e and the quantity supplied is Q_e. In the immediate run, we hypothesize a vertical supply curve, S_1. With the price increase to P_1, therefore, there will be no change in the short run in quantity supplied, which will remain at Q_e. Given some time for adjustment, the supply curve will rotate to S_2. The new amount supplied will increase to Q_1. The long-run supply curve is shown by S_3. The amount supplied again increases to Q_2.

We therefore talk about short-run and long-run price elasticities of supply. The short run is defined as the time period during which full adjustment has not yet taken place. The long run is the time period during which firms have been able to adjust fully to the change in price.

A GRAPHIC PRESENTATION We can show a whole set of supply curves similar to the ones we generated for demand. As Figure 19-5 on the facing page shows, when nothing can be done in the immediate run, the supply curve is vertical, S_1. As more time is allowed for adjustment, the supply curve rotates to S_2 and then to S_3, becoming more elastic as it rotates.

QUICK QUIZ　See page 433 for the answers. Review concepts from this section in MyEconLab.

Price elasticity of supply is calculated by dividing the percentage change in the _____ _____ by the percentage change in _____.

Usually, price elasticities of supply are _____—higher prices yield _____ quantities supplied.

Long-run supply curves are _____ elastic than short-run supply curves because the _____ the time allowed, the more resources can flow into or out of an industry when price changes.

YOU ARE THERE
Implications of Housing Demand Elasticities in China

During the past few years, housing prices in China have been rising at a rate of about 10 percent per year. To assess how responsive China's housing demand and supply are to changes in housing prices, Gregory Chow of Princeton University and Linlin Niu of Xiamen University have estimated housing demand and supply elasticities. Chow and Niu estimate that the income elasticity of housing demand is about 0.7. Average Chinese household income has been increasing at an annual pace of close to 10 percent, which implies that, with other things (including housing prices) being equal, the amount of housing demanded rises by almost 7 percent per year. This steady increase in the demand for housing helps to explain the persistent rise in the price of housing.

Chow and Niu's estimate for the price elasticity of demand is about 0.3. Consequently, each 10 percent annual increase in the price of housing

in China results in only a 3 percent reduction in the quantity of housing demanded. Thus, Chow and Niu conclude that higher incomes in China have generated increases in the demand for housing that have pushed up the market price of housing substantially. This increase in the price of housing has then generated a less-than-proportionate decrease in desired housing purchases.

Critical Thinking Questions

1. Is housing a normal good in China? Explain. (See page 55 in Chapter 3.)
2. As the market price of housing has been rising each year, what has happened to the revenues received by suppliers of housing?

CONCEPTS APPLIED
▶ Total Revenues
▶ Elastic Demand
▶ Price Elasticity of Demand

ISSUES & APPLICATIONS

Rock Stars Face High Price Elasticities of Demand

From an economic standpoint, the past few years have been tough on rock musicians. Even though their music is selling at higher prices than in years past, the total revenues garnered from sales of the music have been on a downswing.

Price Increases for Digital Music Translate into Revenue Dips

Most rock musicians earn revenues from sales of recorded music and from concerts. When prices of digital albums increased by 5 percent during a recent 12-month period, revenues derived from sales of digital albums declined by 13 percent. This inverse relationship between the price change and total digital-music revenues suggests that the demand for recorded music is elastic.

During the same interval, prices of tickets to live performances by top rock acts increased by 3.9 percent, and concert revenues fell by 12 percent. This negative relationship between the price change and total concert revenues is consistent with an elastic demand for rock concerts. This fact is borne out by the 15 percent decrease in concert tickets sold in response to the 3.9 percent increase in concert ticket prices. The implied price elasticity of demand of 3.8 (15 percent/3.9 percent = 3.8) indicates that concertgoers are highly responsive to changes in ticket prices.

Performers, Managers, and Promoters Begin to Get the Message

The past few years have been so disappointing from the standpoint of generating revenues that many rock performers have cut back on the numbers of new song releases and scheduled concerts. Only recently, however, have some rock musicians, managers, and promoters realized that the demand for rock music is highly elastic.

A top concert promoter recently stated, "We know that if we lower prices enough, people will come [to concerts]." Left unstated by the promoter was that in light of the high price elasticities of demand that rock musicians confront, lower prices of recorded music and live performances should also generate higher revenues.

For Critical Thinking

1. If the position of the demand curve for digital rock music albums has remained unchanged, what can account for a continuing rise in the market clearing price? (See page 78 in Chapter 4.)

2. If your answer to Question 1 explains why album prices have been rising, what can you predict is likely to happen to revenues from albums in the near future?

Web Resources

1. For a discussion of the hard times—in terms of sales—faced by rock musicians since the early 2000s, go to **www.econtoday.com/chap19**.

2. To view a chart displaying a significant decline in sales of all forms of recorded music, including rock music, go to **www.econtoday.com/chap19**.

MyEconLab

For more questions on this chapter's Issues & Applications, go to MyEconLab. In the Study Plan for this chapter, select Section N: News.

MyEconLab

Here is what you should know after reading this chapter. MyEconLab will help you identify what you know, and where to go when you need to practice.

--- WHAT YOU SHOULD KNOW ---

Expressing and Calculating the Price Elasticity of Demand The price elasticity of demand is the percentage change in quantity demanded divided by the percentage change in price. To calculate the price elasticity of demand for relatively small changes in price, the percentage change in quantity demanded is equal to the change in the quantity resulting from a price change divided by the average of the initial and final quantities, and the percentage change in price is equal to the price change divided by the average of the initial and final prices.

price elasticity of demand (E_p), 415

--- WHERE TO GO TO PRACTICE ---

• MyEconLab Study Plan 19.1

MyEconLab *continued*

WHAT YOU SHOULD KNOW ——————————————————— WHERE TO GO TO PRACTICE ——

The Relationship between the Price Elasticity of Demand and Total Revenues Demand is elastic when the price elasticity of demand exceeds 1, and over the elastic range of a demand curve, an increase in price reduces total revenues. Demand is inelastic when the price elasticity of demand is less than 1, and over this range of a demand curve, an increase in price raises total revenues. Finally, demand is unit-elastic when the price elasticity of demand equals 1, and over this range of a demand curve, an increase in price does not affect total revenues.

elastic demand, 417
unit elasticity of demand, 417
inelastic demand, 417
perfectly inelastic demand, 417
perfectly elastic demand, 417

Key Figures
Figure 19-1, 418
Figure 19-2, 419

• **MyEconLab** Study Plans 19.2, 19.3
• Animated Figures 19-1, 19-2

Factors That Determine the Price Elasticity of Demand If there are more close substitutes, the price elasticity of demand increases. The price elasticity of demand also tends to be higher when a larger portion of a person's budget is spent on the good. In addition, if people have a longer period of time to adjust to a price change, the price elasticity of demand tends to be higher.

Key Figure
Figure 19-3, 423

• **MyEconLab** Study Plan 19.4
• Animated Figure 19-3

The Cross Price Elasticity of Demand and Using It to Determine Whether Two Goods Are Substitutes or Complements The cross price elasticity of demand for a good is the percentage change in the amount of that good demanded divided by the percentage change in the price of a related good. If two goods are substitutes, the cross price elasticity of demand is positive. In contrast, if two goods are complements, the cross price elasticity of demand is negative.

cross price elasticity of demand (E_{xy}), 425

• **MyEconLab** Study Plan 19.5

The Income Elasticity of Demand The income elasticity of demand is equal to the percentage change in the amount of a good demanded divided by the percentage change in income, holding the good's relative price unchanged.

income elasticity of demand (E_i), 425

• **MyEconLab** Study Plan 19.6

Classifying Supply Elasticities and How the Length of Time for Adjustment Affects the Price Elasticity of Supply The price elasticity of supply equals the percentage change in quantity supplied divided by the percentage change in price. If the price elasticity of supply exceeds 1, supply is elastic, and if the price elasticity of supply is less than 1, supply is inelastic. Supply is unit-elastic if the price elasticity of supply equals 1. Supply is more likely to be elastic when sellers have more time to adjust to price changes.

price elasticity of supply (E_s), 427
perfectly elastic supply, 427
perfectly inelastic supply, 427

Key Figure
Figure 19-5, 428

• **MyEconLab** Study Plan 19.7
• Animated Figure 19-5

Log in to MyEconLab, take a chapter test, and get a personalized Study Plan that tells you which concepts you understand and which ones you need to review. From there, MyEconLab will give you further practice, tutorials, animations, videos, and guided solutions. For more information, visit www.myeconlab.com

PROBLEMS

All problems are assignable in MyEconLab. *Answers to odd–numbered problems appear at the back of the book.*

19-1. When the price of shirts emblazoned with a college logo is $20, consumers buy 150 per week. When the price declines to $19, consumers purchase 200 per week. Based on this information, calculate the price elasticity of demand for logo-emblazoned shirts. (See page 416.)

19-2. Table 19-2 on page 424 indicates that the short-run price elasticity of demand for tires is 0.9. If an increase in the price of petroleum (used in producing tires) causes the market prices of tires to rise from $50 to $60, by what percentage would you expect the quantity of tires demanded to change? (See page 416.)

19-3. The diagram below depicts the demand curve for "miniburgers" in a nationwide fast-food market. Use the information in this diagram to answer the questions that follow. (See pages 416–418.)

a. What is the price elasticity of demand along the range of the demand curve between a price of $0.20 per miniburger and a price of $0.40 per miniburger? Is demand elastic or inelastic over this range?

b. What is the price elasticity of demand along the range of the demand curve between a price of $0.80 per miniburger and a price of $1.20 per miniburger? Is demand elastic or inelastic over this range?

c. What is the price elasticity of demand along the range of the demand curve between a price of $1.60 per miniburger and a price of $1.80 per miniburger? Is demand elastic or inelastic over this range?

19-4. In a local market, the monthly price of Internet access service decreases from $20 to $10, and the total quantity of monthly accounts across all Internet access providers increases from 100,000 to 200,000. What is the price elasticity of demand? Is demand elastic, unit-elastic, or inelastic? (See page 417.)

19-5. At a price of $57.50 to play 18 holes on local golf courses, 1,200 consumers pay to play a game of golf each day. A rise in the price to $62.50 causes the number of consumers to decline to 800. What is the price elasticity of demand? Is demand elastic, unit-elastic, or inelastic? (See page 417.)

19-6. It is very difficult to find goods with perfectly elastic or perfectly inelastic demand. We can, however, find goods that lie near these extremes. Characterize demands for the following goods as being near perfectly elastic or near perfectly inelastic. (See pages 417–418.)

   a. Corn grown and harvested by a small farmer in Iowa

   b. Heroin for a drug addict

   c. Water for a desert hiker

   d. One of several optional textbooks in a pass-fail course

19-7. In the market for hand-made guitars, when the price of guitars is $800, annual revenues are $640,000. When the price falls to $700, annual revenues decline to $630,000. Over this range of guitar prices, is the demand for hand-made guitars elastic, unit-elastic, or inelastic? (See page 419.)

19-8. Suppose that over a range of prices, the price elasticity of demand varies from 15.0 to 2.5. Over another range of prices, the price elasticity of demand varies from 1.5 to 0.75. What can you say about total revenues and the total revenue curve over these two ranges of the demand curve as price falls? (See page 419.)

19-9. Based solely on the information provided below, characterize the demands for the following goods as being more elastic or more inelastic. (See page 422.)

   a. A 45-cent box of salt that you buy once a year

   b. A type of high-powered ski boat that you can rent from any one of a number of rental agencies

   c. A specific brand of bottled water

   d. Automobile insurance in a state that requires autos to be insured but has only a few insurance companies

   e. A 75-cent guitar pick for the lead guitarist of a major rock band

19-10. The value of cross price elasticity of demand between goods X and Y is 1.25, while the cross price elasticity of demand between goods X and Z is −2.0. Characterize X and Y and X and Z as substitutes or complements. (See page 425.)

19-11. Suppose that the cross price elasticity of demand between eggs and bacon is -0.5. What would you expect to happen to purchases of bacon if the price of eggs rises by 10 percent? (See page 425.)

19-12. A 5 percent increase in the price of digital apps reduces the amount of tablet devices demanded by 3 percent. What is the cross price elasticity of demand? Are tablet devices and digital apps complements or substitutes? (See page 425.)

19-13. An individual's income rises from $80,000 per year to $84,000 per year, and as a consequence the person's purchases of movie downloads rise from four per month to six per month. What is this individual's income elasticity of demand? Are movie downloads a normal or inferior good? (See page 426. Hint: You may want to refer to the discussion of normal and inferior goods on page 55 in Chapter 3.)

19-14. Assume that the income elasticity of demand for hot dogs is −1.25 and that the income elasticity

of demand for lobster is 1.25. Based on the fact that the measure for hot dogs is negative while that for lobster is positive, are these normal or inferior goods? (See page 426.)

19-15. At a price of $25,000, producers of midsized automobiles are willing to manufacture and sell 75,000 cars per month. At a price of $35,000, they are willing to produce and sell 125,000 a month. Using the same type of calculation method used to compute the price elasticity of demand, what is the price elasticity of supply? Is supply elastic, unit-elastic, or inelastic? (See page 427.)

19-16. An increase in the market price of men's haircuts, from $15 per haircut to $25 per haircut, initially causes a local barbershop to have its employees work overtime to increase the number of daily haircuts provided from 35 to 45. When the $25 market price remains unchanged for several weeks and all other things remain equal as well, the barbershop hires additional employees and provides 65 haircuts per day. What is the short-run price elasticity of supply? What is the long-run price elasticity of supply? (See pages 427–428.)

ECONOMICS ON THE NET

Price Elasticity and Consumption of Illegal Drugs Making the use of certain drugs illegal drives up their market prices, so the price elasticity of demand is a key factor affecting the use of illegal drugs. This application applies concepts from this chapter to analyze how price elasticity of demand affects drug consumption.

Title: The Demand for Illicit Drugs

Navigation: Go to **www.econtoday.com/chap19**, and follow the link to the summary of this paper published by the National Bureau of Economic Research.

Application Read the summary of the results of this study of price elasticities of participation in use of illegal drugs, and answer the following questions.

1. Based on the results of the study, is the demand for cocaine more or less price elastic than the demand for heroin? For which drug, therefore, will quantity

demanded fall by a greater percentage in response to a proportionate increase in price?

2. The study finds that decriminalizing currently illegal drugs would bring about sizable increases both in overall consumption of heroin and cocaine and in the price elasticity of demand for both drugs. Why do you suppose that the price elasticity of demand would rise? (Hint: At present, users of cocaine and heroin are restricted to only a few illegal sources of the drugs, but if the drugs could legally be produced and sold, there would be many more suppliers providing a variety of different types of both drugs.)

For Group Study and Analysis Discuss ways that government officials might use information about the price elasticities of demand for illicit drugs to assist in developing policies intended to reduce the use of these drugs. Which of these proposed policies might prove most effective? Why?

ANSWERS TO QUICK QUIZZES

p. 418: (i) quantity demanded . . . price; (ii) percentage . . . independent; (iii) negative . . . decrease . . . increase; (iv) zero . . . inelastic . . . elastic . . . infinite

p. 421: (i) revenues; (ii) opposite; (iii) zero; (iv) same

p. 427: (i) substitutes . . . share . . . adjustment;

(ii) Cross . . . positive . . . negative; (iii) demanded . . . income

p. 429: (i) quantity supplied . . . price; (ii) positive . . . greater; (iii) more . . . longer

20

Consumer Choice

For years, a number of U.S. households have allocated significant portions of expenditures out of their money incomes to purchases of unhealthful items, such as alcohol, high-fat meals at restaurants, and tobacco products. Many households also have consumed relatively small amounts of more healthful items, such as vegetables. Recently, spending on alcoholic beverages, restaurant meals, and tobacco products has decreased considerably, and expenditures on vegetables have increased. Some public officials attribute this shift to governmental efforts to provide consumers with product information, but economists suggest that other determinants of consumers' choices likely have proved more important. Before you can understand why households' spending allocations among healthful and unhealthful products have changed, you must first learn how people make choices intended to maximize their levels of satisfaction. That is the main topic of this chapter.

a consumer who shops at a typical U.S. supermarket chooses among 48,750 different items, more than five times as many as in 1975? The largest among these supermarkets commonly stock more than 80 brands of shampoo, about 90 varieties of toothpaste, and at least 100 types of household cleaning products. Of course, the vast array of goods and services among which individuals make consumption decisions from week to week and from month to month extends far beyond supermarket aisles.

In Chapter 3, you learned that a determinant of the quantity demanded of any particular item is the price of that item. The law of demand implies that at a lower overall price, there will be a higher quantity demanded. Understanding the derivation of the law of demand is useful because it allows us to examine the relevant variables, such as price, income, and tastes, in such a way as to make better sense of the world and even perhaps generate predictions about it. One way of deriving the law of demand involves an analysis of the logic of consumer choice in a world of limited resources. In this chapter, therefore, we discuss what is called *utility analysis*.

Utility Theory

When you buy something, you do so because of the satisfaction you expect to receive from having and using that good. For everything that you like to have, the more you have of it, the higher the level of total satisfaction you receive. Another term that can be used for satisfaction is **utility,** or want-satisfying power. This property is common to all goods that are desired. The concept of utility is purely subjective, however. There is no way that you or I can measure the amount of utility that a consumer might be able to obtain from a particular good, for utility does not imply "useful" or "utilitarian" or "practical." Thus, there can be no accurate scientific assessment of the utility that someone might receive by consuming a fast-food dinner or a movie relative to the utility that another person might receive from that same good or service.

The utility that individuals receive from consuming a good depends on their tastes and preferences. These tastes and preferences are normally assumed to be given and stable for a particular individual. An individual's tastes determine how much utility that individual derives from consuming a good, and this in turn determines how that individual allocates his or her income to purchases of that good. But we cannot explain why tastes are different between individuals. For example, we cannot explain why some people like yogurt but others do not.

We can analyze in terms of utility the way consumers decide what to buy, just as physicists have analyzed some of their problems in terms of what they call force. No physicist has ever seen a unit of force, and no economist has ever seen a unit of utility. In both cases, however, these concepts have proved useful for analysis.

Throughout this chapter, we will be discussing **utility analysis,** which is the analysis of consumer decision making based on utility maximization—that is, making choices with the aim of attaining the highest feasible satisfaction.

Utility and Utils

Economists once believed that utility could be measured. In fact, there is a philosophical school of thought based on utility theory called *utilitarianism*, developed by the English philosopher Jeremy Bentham (1748–1832). Bentham held that society should seek the greatest happiness for the greatest number. He sought to apply an arithmetic formula for measuring happiness. He and his followers developed the notion of measurable utility and invented the **util** to measure it. For the moment, we will also assume that we can measure satisfaction using this representative unit. Our assumption will allow us to quantify the way we examine consumer behavior.

Thus, the first chocolate bar that you eat might yield you 4 utils of satisfaction. The first peanut cluster, might yield 6 utils, and so on. Today, no one really believes that we can actually measure utils, but the ideas forthcoming from such analysis will prove useful in understanding how consumers choose among alternatives.

Utility
The want-satisfying power of a good or service.

Utility analysis
The analysis of consumer decision making based on utility maximization.

Util
A representative unit by which utility is measured.

Total and Marginal Utility

Consider the satisfaction, or utility, that you receive each time that you download and utilize digital apps. To make the example straightforward, let's say that there are thousands of apps to choose from each year and that each of them is of the same quality. Let's say that you normally download and utilize one app per week. You could, of course, download two, or three, or four per week. Presumably, each time you download and utilize another app per week, you will get additional satisfaction, or utility. The question that we must ask, though, is, given that you are already downloading and using one app per week, will the next one downloaded and utilized during that week give you the same amount of additional utility?

That additional, or incremental, utility is called **marginal utility,** where *marginal* means "incremental" or "additional." (Marginal changes also refer to decreases, in which cases we talk about *decremental* changes.) The concept of marginality is important in economics because we can think of people comparing additional (marginal) benefits with additional (marginal) costs.

Applying Marginal Analysis to Utility

The example in Figure 20-1 on the facing page will clarify the distinction between total utility and marginal utility. The table in panel (a) shows the total utility and the marginal utility of downloading and using digital apps each week. Marginal utility is the difference between total utility derived from one level of consumption and total utility derived from another level of consumption within a given time interval. A simple formula for marginal utility is this:

$$\text{Marginal utility} = \frac{\text{change in total utility}}{\text{change in number of units consumed}}$$

In our example, when a person has already downloaded and utilized two digital apps in one week and then downloads and uses another, total utility increases from 16 utils to 19 utils. Therefore, the marginal utility (of downloading and utilizing one more app after already having downloaded and used two in one week) is equal to 3 utils.

Graphical Analysis

We can transfer the information in panel (a) onto a graph, as we do in panels (b) and (c) of Figure 20-1 on the next page. Total utility, which is represented in column 2 of panel (a), is transferred to panel (b).

Total utility continues to rise until four digital apps are downloaded and utilized per week. This measure of utility remains at 20 utils through the fifth app, and at the sixth app per week it falls to 18 utils. We assume that at some quantity consumed per unit time period, boredom with consuming more digital apps begins to set in. Thus, at some quantity consumed, the additional utility from consuming an additional app begins to fall, so total utility first rises and then declines in panel (b).

Marginal Utility

If you look carefully at panels (b) and (c) of Figure 20-1, the notion of marginal utility becomes clear. In economics, the term *marginal* always refers to a *change* in the total. The marginal utility of consuming three downloaded digital apps per week instead of two apps per week is the increment in total utility and is equal to 3 utils per week. All of the points in panel (c) are taken from column 3 of the table in panel (a). Notice that marginal utility falls throughout the graph. A special point occurs after four apps are downloaded and used per week because the total utility curve in panel (b) is unchanged after the consumption of the fourth app. That means that the consumer receives no additional (marginal) utility from downloading and using five apps rather than four.

Marginal utility
The change in total utility due to a one-unit change in the quantity of a good or service consumed.

FIGURE 20-1

Total and Marginal Utility of Downloading and Utilizing Digital Apps

If we were able to assign specific values to the utility derived from downloading and utilizing digital apps each week, we could obtain a marginal utility schedule similar in pattern to the one shown in panel (a). In column 1 is the number of apps downloaded and used per week. Column 2 is the total utility derived from each quantity. Column 3 shows the marginal utility derived from each additional quantity, which is defined as the change in total utility due to a change of one unit of using downloaded apps per week. Total utility from panel (a) is plotted in panel (b). Marginal utility is plotted in panel (c), where you see that it reaches zero where total utility hits its maximum at between 4 and 5 units.

Panel (a)

(1) Number of Digital Apps Downloaded and Utilized per Week	(2) Total Utility (utils per week)	(3) Marginal Utility (utils per week)
0	0	
		10 (10 − 0)
1	10	
		6 (16 − 10)
2	16	
		3 (19 − 16)
3	19	
		1 (20 − 19)
4	20	
		0 (20 − 20)
5	20	
		−2 (18 − 20)
6	18	

This is shown in panel (c) as *zero* marginal utility. After that point, marginal utility becomes negative.

In our example, when marginal utility becomes negative, it means that the consumer is tired of consuming digital apps and would require some form of compensation to consume any more. When marginal utility is negative, an additional unit consumed actually lowers total utility by becoming a nuisance. Rarely does a consumer face a situation of negative marginal utility. Whenever this point is reached, goods in effect become "bads." Consuming more units actually causes total utility to *fall* so that marginal utility is negative. A rational consumer will stop consuming at the point at which marginal utility becomes negative, even if the good is available at a price of zero.

QUICK QUIZ   See page 451 for the answers. Review concepts from this section in MyEconLab.

_____ is defined as want-satisfying power. It is a characteristic common to all desired goods and services.

We arbitrarily measure **utility** in units called _____.

It is important to distinguish between **total utility** and **marginal utility**. _____ utility is the total satisfaction derived from the consumption of a given quantity of a good or service. _____ utility is the *change* in total utility due to a one-unit change in the consumption of the good or service.

Diminishing Marginal Utility

Diminishing marginal utility
The principle that as more of any good or service is consumed, its *extra* benefit declines. Otherwise stated, increases in total utility from the consumption of a good or service become smaller and smaller as more is consumed during a given time period.

Notice that in panel (c) of Figure 20-1 on the previous page, marginal utility is continuously declining. This property has been named the principle of **diminishing marginal utility.** There is no way that we can prove diminishing marginal utility. Nevertheless, diminishing marginal utility has even been called a law. This supposed law concerns a psychological, or subjective, utility that you receive as you consume more and more of a particular good.

The Law of Diminishing Marginal Utility

Stated formally, the law of diminishing marginal utility is as follows:

> *As an individual consumes more of a particular commodity, the total level of util-ity, or satisfaction, derived from that consumption usually increases. Eventually, however, the rate at which it increases diminishes as more is consumed.*

Take a hungry individual at a dinner table. The first serving is greatly appreciated, and the individual derives a substantial amount of utility from it. Consumption of the second serving does not have quite as much pleasurable impact as the first one, and consumption of the third serving is likely to be even less satisfying. This individual experiences diminishing marginal utility of food until he or she stops eating, and this is true for most people. All-you-can-eat restaurants count on this fact. A second helping of ribs may provide some marginal utility, but the third helping would have only a little or even negative marginal utility.

Marginal Utility Cannot Persistently Increase

Consider for a moment the opposite possibility—increasing marginal utility. Under such a situation, the marginal utility after consuming, say, one hamburger would increase. Consuming the second hamburger would yield more utility to you, and consuming the third would yield even more.

Thus, if increasing marginal utility existed, each of us would consume only one good or service! Rather than observing that "variety is the spice of life," we would see that monotony in consumption was preferred. We do not observe such single-item consumption, and therefore we have great confidence in the concept of diminishing marginal utility.

Can diminishing marginal utility explain why newspaper vending machines rarely prevent people from taking more than the one current issue they have paid to purchase?

EXAMPLE

Newspaper Vending Machines versus Candy Vending Machines

Have you ever noticed that newspaper vending machines nearly everywhere in the United States allow you to put in the correct change, lift up the door, and—if you were willing to violate the law—take as many newspapers as you want? Contrast this type of vending machine with candy machines. They are securely locked at all times. You must designate the candy that you wish, normally by using some type of keypad. The candy then drops down so that you can retrieve it, but you cannot grab any other candy.

The difference between these two types of vending machines is explained by diminishing marginal utility. Newspaper companies dispense newspapers from coin-operated boxes that allow dishonest people to take more copies than they pay for. What would a dishonest person do with more than one copy of a newspaper, however? The marginal utility of reading a second newspaper is normally zero. The benefit of storing excessive newspapers is usually nil because yesterday's news has no value. But the same analysis does not hold for candy. The marginal utility of consuming a second candy bar is certainly less than the marginal utility of consuming the first, but it is normally not zero. Moreover, one can store candy for relatively long periods of time at relatively low cost. Consequently, food vending machine companies have to worry about dishonest users of their equipment and must make that equipment more theft-proof than newspaper vending machines.

FOR CRITICAL THINKING
Can you think of a circumstance under which a substantial number of newspaper purchasers might be inclined to take more than one newspaper out of a vending machine?

Optimizing Consumption Choices

Every consumer has a limited income, so choices must be made. When a consumer has made all of his or her choices about what to buy and in what quantities, and when the total level of satisfaction, or utility, from that set of choices is as great as it can be, we say that the consumer has *optimized*. When the consumer has attained an optimum consumption set of goods and services, we say that he or she has reached **consumer optimum.**

Consumer optimum
A choice of a set of goods and services that maximizes the level of satisfaction for each consumer, subject to limited income.

A Two-Good Example

Consider a simple two-good example. During a given period, the consumer has to choose between spending income on downloads of digital apps at $5 per app and on purchasing cappuccinos at $3 each. Let's say that when the consumer has spent all income on digital apps and cappuccinos, the last dollar spent on a cappuccino yields 3 utils of utility but the last dollar spent on apps yields 10 utils. Wouldn't this consumer increase total utility if some dollars were taken away from consumption of cappuccinos and allocated to apps? The answer is yes. More dollars spent downloading apps will reduce marginal utility per last dollar spent, whereas fewer dollars spent on consumption of cappuccinos will increase marginal utility per last dollar spent. The loss in utility from spending fewer dollars purchasing fewer cappuccinos is more than made up by spending additional dollars on more digital apps. As a consequence, total utility increases.

The consumer optimum—where total utility is maximized—occurs when the satisfaction per last dollar spent on both cappuccinos and digital apps per week is equal for the two goods. Thus, the amount of goods consumed depends on the prices of the goods, the income of the consumer, and the marginal utility derived from the amounts of each good consumed.

Table 20-1 below presents information on utility derived from consuming various quantities of digital apps and cappuccinos. Columns 4 and 8 show the marginal utility per dollar spent on apps and cappuccinos, respectively. If the prices of both goods are

TABLE 20-1

Total and Marginal Utility from Consuming Digital Apps and Cappuccinos on an Income of $26

(1) Digital Apps per Period	(2) Total Utility of Digital Apps per Period (utils)	(3) Marginal Utility (utils) MU_d	(4) Marginal Utility Per Dollars Spent (MU_d/P_d) (price = $5)	(5) Cappuccinos per Period	(6) Total Utility of Cappuccinos per Period (utils)	(7) Marginal Utility (utils) MU_c	(8) Marginal Utility per Dollar Spent (MU_c/P_c) (price = $3)
0	0	–	–	0	0	–	–
1	50.0	50.0	10.0	1	25	25	8.3
2	95.0	45.0	9.0	2	47	22	7.3
3	135.0	40.0	8.0	3	65	18	6.0
4	171.5	36.5	7.3	4	80	15	5.0
5	200.0	28.5	5.7	5	89	9	3.0

zero, individuals will consume each as long as their respective marginal utility is positive (at least five units of each and probably much more). It is also true that a consumer with unlimited income will continue consuming goods until the marginal utility of each is equal to zero. When the price is zero or the consumer's income is unlimited, there is no effective constraint on consumption.

Why do some people pay a price as high as $665 for a pair of blue jeans?

EXAMPLE

High-Priced Blue Jeans as Part of a Consumer Optimum

Only about 1 percent of the nearly $14 billion in annual U.S. expenditures on blue jeans goes toward pairs of jeans priced above $50. Among jeans with prices exceeding $200 per pair are J Brand's Maria jeans, Seven for All Mankind's Men's Aidan jeans, and True Religion's Phantom jeans. Certain styles of Gucci jeans have prices as high as $665 per pair.

The theory of the consumer optimum explains why some people are willing to pay such high prices for jeans. For these individuals, it must be the case that the last dollar spent on the pair of, say, Gucci jeans generates the same amount of marginal utility as a dollar spent on any other item. Because these consumers allocate so many dollars of their money income to a pair of Gucci jeans, the marginal utility they derive from buying and wearing the jeans must be substantial. Thus, consuming Gucci jeans must add considerably to these individuals' levels of satisfaction.

FOR CRITICAL THINKING

What condition must be satisfied for the last dollar of money income that a consumer of Gucci jeans spends on chewing gum?

YOU ARE THERE

To contemplate a real-world example of an individual reaching a consumer optimum, take a look at **Using a Smartphone to Attain a Consumer Optimum** on page 446.

A Two-Good Consumer Optimum

Consumer optimum is attained when the marginal utility of the last dollar spent on each good yields the same utility and income is completely exhausted. In the situation in Table 20-1 on the previous page, the individual's income is $26. From columns 4 and 8 of Table 20-1, equal marginal utilities per dollar spent occur at the consumption level of four digital apps and two cappuccinos (the marginal utility per dollar spent equals 7.3). Notice that the marginal utility per dollar spent for both goods is also (approximately) equal at the consumption level of three apps and one cappuccino, but here total income is not completely exhausted. Likewise, the marginal utility per dollar spent is (approximately) equal at five apps and three cappuccinos, but the expenditures necessary for that level of consumption ($34) exceed the individual's income.

Table 20-2 on the facing page shows the steps taken to arrive at consumer optimum. Using the first digital app would yield a marginal utility per dollar of 10 (50 units of utility divided by $5 per digital app), while consuming the first cappuccino would yield a marginal utility of only 8.3 per dollar (25 units of utility divided by $3 per cappuccino). Because it yields the higher marginal utility per dollar, the app is purchased. This leaves $21 of income. Consuming the second digital app yields a higher marginal utility per dollar (9, versus 8.3 for a cappuccino), so this app is also purchased, leaving an unspent income of $16. Purchasing and consuming the first cappuccino now yield a higher marginal utility per dollar than the next digital app (8.3 versus 8), so the first cappuccino is purchased. This leaves income of $13 to spend. The process continues until all income is exhausted and the marginal utility per dollar spent is equal for both goods.

To restate, consumer optimum requires the following:

> *A consumer's money income should be allocated so that the last dollar spent on each good purchased yields the same amount of marginal utility (when all income is spent), because this rule yields the largest possible total utility.*

A Little Math

We can state the rule of consumer optimum in algebraic terms by examining the ratio of marginal utilities and prices of individual products. The rule simply states that a consumer maximizes personal satisfaction when allocating money income in such a

TABLE 20-2

Steps to Consumer Optimum

In each purchase situation described here, the consumer always purchases the good with the higher marginal utility per dollar spent (*MU/P*). For example, at the time of the third purchase, the marginal utility per last dollar spent on digital apps is 8, but it is 8.3 for cappuccinos, and $16 of income remains, so the next purchase will be a cappuccino. Here the price of digital apps is $P_d = \$5$, the price of cappuccinos is $P_c = \$3$, MU_d is the marginal utility of consumption of digital apps, and MU_c is the marginal utility of consumption of cappuccinos.

	Choices					
	Digital Apps		Cappuccinos			
Purchase	Unit	MU_d/P_d	Unit	MU_c/P_c	Buying Decision	Remaining Income
1	First	10.0	First	8.3	First digital app	$26 - \$5 = \$21$
2	Second	9.0	First	8.3	Second digital app	$21 - \$5 = \$16$
3	Third	8.0	First	8.3	First cappuccino	$16 - \$3 = \$13$
4	Third	8.0	Second	7.3	Third digital app	$13 - \$5 = \$8$
5	Fourth	7.3	Second	7.3	Fourth digital app and second cappuccino	$8 - \$5 = \$3$ $\$3 - \$3 = \$0$

way that the last dollars spent on good A, good B, good C, and so on, yield equal amounts of marginal utility. Marginal utility (*MU*) from good A is indicated by "*MU* of good A." For good B, it is "*MU* of good B." Our algebraic formulation of this rule, therefore, becomes

$$\frac{MU \text{ of good A}}{\text{Price of good A}} = \frac{MU \text{ of good B}}{\text{price of good B}} = \cdots = \frac{MU \text{ of good Z}}{\text{price of good Z}}$$

The letters A, B, . . . , Z indicate the various goods and services that the consumer might purchase.

We know, then, that in order for the consumer to maximize utility, the marginal utility of good A divided by the price of good A must equal the marginal utility of any other good divided by its price. Note, though, that the application of the rule of equal marginal utility per dollar spent does not necessarily describe an explicit or conscious act on the part of consumers. Rather, this is a *model* of consumer optimum.

What does a consumer's willingness to pay a relatively high price for an item indicate about the marginal utility that the consumer derives from the good or service?

INTERNATIONAL EXAMPLE

Inferring Substantial Marginal Utility from an Oil Change

Recently, a resident of Qatar decided to purchase an oil change for the Lamborghini Murciélago LP640 sports car that he had bought at an earlier date at a price of $376,000. He decided to have the lubrication work done in London, which required airlifting the auto to London's Heathrow Airport. Inclusive of transportation costs, the price of obtaining the vehicle's oil change exceeded $45,000.

According to the rule for a consumer optimum, this Qatar resident viewed the marginal utility per dollar spent on the oil change as equal to the marginal utility per dollar spent on other goods and services. This amount would have been his marginal utility from the oil change divided by more than $45,000, which suggests that he derived substantial marginal utility from the work that London mechanics performed on his sports car.

FOR CRITICAL THINKING

What must have been true about the Qatar consumer's marginal utility per dollar spent on fuel for his vehicle compared with the marginal utility per dollar spent on the London oil change?

The principle of **diminishing marginal utility** tells us that each successive marginal unit of a good consumed adds _____ extra utility.

The consumer maximizes total utility by _____ the marginal utility of the last dollar spent on one good with

the marginal utility per last dollar spent on all other goods. That is the state of consumer _____.

When a consumer optimum has been reached, _____ additional income is available to spend, and total utility is _____.

How a Price Change Affects Consumer Optimum

Consumption decisions are summarized in the law of demand, which states that the amount purchased is inversely related to price. We can now see why by using utility analysis.

A Consumer's Response to a Price Change

When a consumer has optimally allocated all her income to purchases, the marginal utility per dollar spent at current prices of goods and services is the same for each good or service she buys. No consumer will, when optimizing, buy 10 units of a good per unit of time when the marginal utility per dollar spent on the tenth unit of that good is less than the marginal utility per dollar spent on a unit of some other item.

A PRICE CHANGE AND THE CONSUMER OPTIMUM If we start out at a consumer optimum and then observe a good's price decrease, we can predict that consumers will respond to the price decrease by consuming more of that good. This is because before the price change, the marginal utility per dollar spent on each good or service consumed was the same. Now, when a specific good's price is lower, it is possible to consume more of that good while continuing to equalize the marginal utility per dollar spent on that good with the marginal utility per dollar spent on other goods and services.

The purchase and consumption of additional units of the lower-priced good will cause the marginal utility from consuming the good to fall. Eventually, it will fall to the point at which the marginal utility per dollar spent on the good is once again equal to the marginal utility per dollar spent on other goods and services. At this point, the consumer will stop buying additional units of the lower-priced good.

A hypothetical demand curve for digital apps for a typical consumer during a specific time interval is presented in Figure 20-2 on the facing page. Suppose that at point A, at which the price per digital app is $5, the marginal utility of the last app consumed during the period is MU_A. At point B, at which the price is $4 per app, the marginal utility is represented by MU_B. With the consumption of more digital apps, the marginal utility of the last unit of these additional digital apps is lower—MU_B must be less than MU_A. What has happened is that at a lower price, the number of digital app downloads per week increased from four to five. Marginal utility must have fallen. At a higher consumption rate, the marginal utility falls in response to the rise in digital app consumption so that the marginal utility per dollar spent is equalized across all purchases.

The Substitution Effect

Substitution effect
The tendency of people to substitute cheaper commodities for more expensive commodities.

What is happening as the price of digital app downloads falls is that consumers are substituting the now relatively cheaper digital apps for other goods and services, such as restaurant meals and live concerts. We call this the **substitution effect** of a change in the price of a good because it occurs when consumers substitute relatively cheaper goods for relatively more expensive ones.

FIGURE 20-2

Digital App Prices and Marginal Utility

When consumers respond to a reduction in the price of digital app from $5 per app to $4 per app by increasing consumption, marginal utility falls. The movement is from point A, at which marginal utility is MU_A, to point B, at which marginal utility is MU_B, which is less than MU_A. This brings about the equalization of the marginal utility per dollar spent across all purchases.

We assume that people desire a variety of goods and pursue a variety of goals. That means that few, if any, goods are irreplaceable in meeting demand. We are generally able to substitute one product for another to satisfy demand. This is commonly referred to as the **principle of substitution.**

AN EXAMPLE Let's assume now that there are several goods, not exactly the same, and perhaps even very different from one another, but all contributing to consumers' total utility. If the relative price of one particular good falls, individuals will substitute in favor of the now lower-priced good and against the other goods that they might have been purchasing. Conversely, if the price of that good rises relative to the price of the other goods, people will substitute in favor of them and not buy as much of the now higher-priced good. An example is the growth in purchases of tablet devices, or digital tablets, since the early 2010s. As the relative price of tablets has plummeted, people have substituted away from other, now relatively more expensive goods in favor of purchasing additional digital tablets.

PURCHASING POWER AND REAL INCOME If the price of some item that you purchase goes down while your money income and all other prices stay the same, your ability to purchase goods goes up. That is to say, your effective **purchasing power** has increased, even though your money income has stayed the same. If you purchase 20 gallons of gas a week at $5 per gallon, your total outlay for gas is $100. If the price goes down by 50 percent, to $2.50 per gallon, you would have to spend only $50 a week to purchase the same number of gallons of gas. If your money income and the prices of other goods remain the same, it would be possible for you to continue purchasing 20 gallons of gas a week *and* to purchase more of other goods. You will feel richer and will indeed probably purchase more of a number of goods, including perhaps even more gasoline.

The converse will also be true. When the price of one good you are purchasing goes up, without any other change in prices or income, the purchasing power of your income drops. You will have to reduce your purchases of either the now higher-priced good or other goods (or a combination).

In general, this **real-income effect** is usually quite small. After all, unless we consider broad categories, such as housing or food, a change in the price of one particular item that we purchase will have a relatively small effect on our total purchasing power. Thus, we anticipate that the substitution effect will be more important than the real-income effect in causing us to purchase more of goods that have become cheaper and less of goods that have become more expensive.

Principle of substitution
The principle that consumers shift away from goods and services that become priced relatively higher in favor of goods and services that are now priced relatively lower.

Purchasing power
The value of money for buying goods and services. If your money income stays the same but the price of one good that you are buying goes up, your effective purchasing power falls, and vice versa.

Real-income effect
The change in people's purchasing power that occurs when, other things being constant, the price of one good that they purchase changes. When that price goes up, real income, or purchasing power, falls, and when that price goes down, real income increases.

The Demand Curve Revisited

Linking the law of diminishing marginal utility and the rule of equal marginal utilities per dollar gives us a negative relationship between the quantity demanded of a good or service and its price. As the relative price of digital apps goes up, for example, the quantity demanded will fall, and as the relative price of digital apps goes down, the quantity demanded will rise. Figure 20-2 on the previous page showed this demand curve for digital apps. As the price of digital apps falls, the consumer can maximize total utility only by purchasing more apps, and vice versa.

In other words, the relationship between price and quantity desired is simply a downward-sloping demand curve. Note, though, that this downward-sloping demand curve (the law of demand) is derived under the assumption of constant tastes and incomes. You must remember that we are keeping these important determining variables constant when we look at the relationship between price and quantity demanded.

Marginal Utility, Total Utility, and the Diamond-Water Paradox

Even though water is essential to life and diamonds are not, water is relatively cheap and diamonds are relatively expensive. The economist Adam Smith in 1776 called this the "diamond-water paradox."

UNDERSTANDING THE PARADOX The diamond-water paradox is easily understood when we make the distinction between total utility and marginal utility. The total utility of water greatly exceeds the total utility derived from diamonds. What determines the price, though, is what happens on the margin. We have relatively few diamonds, so the marginal utility of the last diamond consumed is relatively high. The opposite is true for water. Total utility does not determine what people are willing to pay for a unit of a particular commodity—marginal utility does.

Look at the situation graphically in Figure 20-3 below. We show the demand curve for diamonds, labeled $D_{diamonds}$. The demand curve for water is labeled D_{water}. We plot quantity in terms of kilograms per unit time period on the horizontal axis. On the vertical axis, we plot price in dollars per kilogram. We use kilograms as our common unit of measurement for water and for diamonds. We could just as well have used pounds or liters.

FIGURE 20-3

The Diamond-Water Paradox

We pick kilograms as a common unit of measurement for both water and diamonds. To demonstrate that the demand for and supply of water are immense, we have put a break in the horizontal quantity axis. Although the demand for water is much greater than the demand for diamonds, the marginal valuation of water is given by the marginal value placed on the *last* unit of water consumed. To find that, we must know the supply of water, which is given as S_1. At that supply, the price of water is P_{water}. But the supply for diamonds is given by S_2. At that supply, the price of diamonds is $P_{diamonds}$. The total valuation that consumers place on water is tremendous relative to the total valuation consumers place on diamonds. What is important for price determination, however, is the marginal valuation, or the marginal utility received.

WHY THE PRICE OF DIAMONDS EXCEEDS THE PRICE OF WATER Notice in Figure 20-3 on the facing page that the demand for water is many, many times the demand for diamonds (even though we really can't show this in the diagram). We draw the supply curve of water as S_1 at a quantity of Q_{water}. The supply curve for diamonds is given as S_2 at quantity $Q_{diamonds}$.

At the intersection of the supply curve of water with the demand curve of water, the price per kilogram is P_{water}. The intersection of the supply curve of diamonds with the demand curve of diamonds is at $P_{diamonds}$. Notice that $P_{diamonds}$ exceeds P_{water}. Diamonds sell at a higher price than water.

Behavioral Economics and Consumer Choice Theory

Utility analysis has long been appealing to economists because it makes clear predictions about how individuals will adjust their consumption of different goods and services based on the prices of those items and their incomes. Traditionally, another attraction of utility analysis to many economists has been its reliance on the assumption that consumers behave *rationally*, or that they do not intentionally make decisions that would leave them worse off. As we discussed in Chapter 1, proponents of behavioral economics have doubts about the rationality assumption, which causes them to question the utility-based theory of consumer choice.

Does Behavioral Economics Better Predict Consumer Choices?

Advocates of behavioral economics question whether utility theory is supported by the facts, which they argue are better explained by applying the assumption of *bounded rationality*. Recall from Chapter 1 that this assumption states that human limitations prevent people from examining every possible choice available to them and thereby thwart their efforts to effectively pursue long-term personal interests.

As evidence favoring the bounded rationality assumption, proponents of behavioral economics point to real-world examples that they claim violate rationality-based utility theory. For instance, economists have found that when purchasing electric appliances such as refrigerators, people sometimes buy the lowest-priced, energy-inefficient models even though the initial purchase-price savings often fail to compensate for higher future energy costs. There is also evidence that people who live in earthquake- or flood-prone regions commonly fail to purchase sufficient insurance against these events. In addition, experiments have shown that when people are placed in situations in which strong emotions come into play, they may be willing to pay different amounts for items than they would pay in calmer settings.

These and other observed behaviors, behavioral economists suggest, indicate that consumers do not behave as if they are rational. If the rationality assumption does not apply to actual behavior, they argue, it follows that utility-based consumer choice theory cannot, either.

Consumer Choice Theory Remains Alive and Well

In spite of the doubts expressed by proponents of behavioral economics, most economists continue to apply the assumption that people behave *as if* they act rationally with an aim to maximize utility. These economists continue to utilize utility theory because of a fundamental strength of this approach: It yields clear-cut predictions regarding consumer choices that receive support from real-world evidence.

In contrast, if the rationality assumption is rejected, any number of possible human behaviors might be considered. To proponents of behavioral economics, ambiguities about actual outcomes make the bounded rationality approach to consumer choice more realistic than utility-based consumer choice theory. Nevertheless, a major drawback is that no clearly testable predictions emerge from the many alternative behaviors that people might exhibit if they fail to behave *as if* they are rational.

Certainly, arguments among economists about the "reasonableness" of rational consumers maximizing utility are likely to continue. So far, however, the use of utility-based consumer choice theory has allowed economists to make a wide array of predictions about how consumers respond to changes in prices, incomes, and other factors. In general, these key predictions continue to be supported by the actual choices that consumers make.

WHAT IF... the government bans certain products to try to prevent poor decisions?

The U.S. government limits choices for certain products. Often, government officials say that such limitations aim to prevent ill-informed consumers from making bad decisions. U.S. Secretary of Energy Steven Chu offered such a rationale for banning the sale of incandescent light bulbs. "We are taking away a choice that lets you waste your own money," Chu suggested. The market price of the alternative fluorescent bulb is about six times higher, but the government determined that the fluorescent bulb lasts about six times longer and requires less energy. Hence, the government judged the quality-adjusted price of fluorescent bulbs to be lower. This determination was based on the assumption that consumers leave bulbs lighted for lengthy intervals. In fact, though, consumers who turn lights off and on many times each day would achieve greater energy savings from using incandescent bulbs. Thus, outlawing incandescent bulbs undoubtedly makes many of these consumers worse off than they would have been without the ban. Government limits on the range of choices of other products likewise reduce utility for at least some consumers.

QUICK QUIZ   See page 451 for the answers. Review concepts from this section in MyEconLab.

To remain in consumer optimum, a price decrease requires an _____ in consumption. A price increase requires a _____ in consumption.

Each change in price has a **substitution effect.** When the price of a good _____, the consumer _____ in favor of that relatively cheaper good.

Each change in price also has a **real-income effect.** When price _____, the consumer's real purchasing power increases, causing the consumer to purchase _____ of most goods. Assuming that the principle of diminishing marginal utility holds, the demand curve must slope downward.

The price of water is lower than the price of diamonds because people consume _____ water than diamonds, which results in a _____ marginal utility of water compared with the marginal utility of diamonds.

YOU ARE THERE
Using a Smartphone to Attain a Consumer Optimum

Tri Tang walks into a Sunnyvale, California, Best Buy store and spots what he regards as a perfect gift for his girlfriend: a GPS device with exactly the features he is certain she will desire to use. The Best Buy price for the item is $200 inclusive of sales taxes, which is a higher price than Tang wishes to pay. At that price, his marginal utility per dollar spent would be too low in relation to other items that he consumes to justify purchasing the GPS device. Tang's desired quantity is zero.

Tang pulls out his smartphone and types the model number of the GPS device into a price-comparison app he recently downloaded onto the phone. The app informs him that the item is available for online purchase from Amazon at a no-tax, no-shipping-fee price of about $100. Tang orders the GPS device on the spot. At that price, his marginal utility per dollar spent is sufficiently high in relation to other goods and services he buys to justify purchasing the device. Using his smartphone has enabled Tang to attain a consumer optimum that includes the GPS device for his girlfriend.

Critical Thinking Questions

1. By about what percentage did Tang's anticipated marginal utility per dollar spent increase after he consulted his smartphone app?

2. If Tang decided to buy a second GPS device at the lower price, did his marginal utility per dollar spent on the second unit rise or fall? Explain.

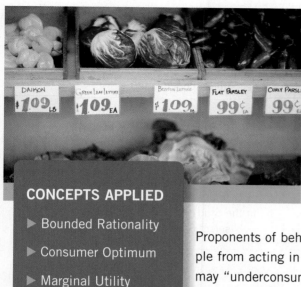

ISSUES & APPLICATIONS

Why Are Consumers Making More Healthful Choices?

CONCEPTS APPLIED

▶ Bounded Rationality

▶ Consumer Optimum

▶ Marginal Utility

Proponents of behavioral economics argue that *bounded rationality* prevents people from acting in their own best interests. For instance, they suggest that people may "underconsume" healthful foods and "overconsume" unhealthful items.

The Tide Turns in Favor of "Eating Your Vegetables"

For years, a number of government agencies have advertised the unhealthful properties of alcohol, tobacco, and fatty foods, in contrast to the healthful characteristics of vegetables.

Recently, government officials have taken heart from the changes in consumer expenditures depicted in Figure 20-4 below. The figure shows substantial decreases in a typical U.S. consumer's inflation-adjusted purchases of alcoholic beverages, restaurant meals, and tobacco products since 2008. During the same period, a significant rise in spending on vegetables has occurred. According to officials at government agencies that have sought to better educate

consumers, the data in Figure 20-4 provide evidence of success in easing informational limits that have "bound" consumers in the past.

Another Key Element: Altered Relative Prices

Further consideration of the data indicates that an additional element has played a key role in explaining the consumption shift depicted in Figure 20-4—significant changes in relative prices. Since 2008, average relative prices of vegetables have decreased by 1 percent. During the same period, average relative prices have risen by 4 percent for restaurant food, by more than 6 percent for alcoholic beverages, and by nearly 40 percent for tobacco products.

FIGURE 20-4

Changes in Spending on Selected Items by the Typical U.S. Consumer since 2008

Examination of changes in U.S. consumer spending on healthful vegetables versus less healthful items such as alcoholic beverages, restaurant food, and tobacco products appears to indicate a shift in consumer preferences. Key elements influencing the spending shift were changes in relative prices, which fell for vegetables but rose for the other items.

Source: Bureau of Labor Statistics.

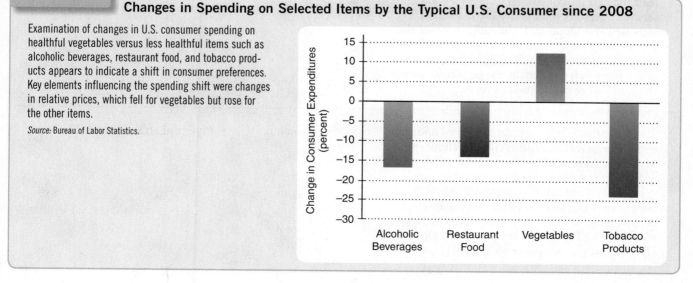

A rational consumer evaluating the marginal utility per dollar spent on vegetables, compared with less healthful items, following changes in relative prices has responded by buying more vegetables. The consumer also has purchased fewer of the less healthful items. Thus, rational consumer responses to relative price changes surely help to explain the spending shift displayed in Figure 20-4.

For Critical Thinking

1. How could the receipt of new information about health implications of foods, alcohol, and tobacco affect a consumer optimum?

2. Other things being equal, would a consumer optimum change if the prices of all items consumed rise at an identical rate? Explain.

Web Resources

1. Track changes in the prices of food items in relation to the overall price level at www.econtoday.com/chap20.

2. For detailed information on consumer food expenditures, go to www.econtoday.com/chap20.

MyEconLab

For more questions on this chapter's Issues & Applications, go to MyEconLab. In the Study Plan for this chapter, select Section N: News.

MyEconLab

Here is what you should know after reading this chapter. MyEconLab will help you identify what you know, and where to go when you need to practice.

— WHAT YOU SHOULD KNOW —		— WHERE TO GO TO PRACTICE —
Total Utility versus Marginal Utility Total utility is the total satisfaction that an individual derives from consuming a given amount of a good or service during a given period. Marginal utility is the additional satisfaction that a person gains by consuming an additional unit of the good or service.	utility, 435 utility analysis, 435 util, 435 marginal utility, 436 **Key Figure** Figure 20-1, 437	• MyEconLab Study Plans 20.1, 20.2 • Animated Figure 20-1
The Law of Diminishing Marginal Utility For at least the first unit of consumption of a good or service, a person's total utility increases with increased consumption. Eventually, however, the rate at which an individual's utility rises with greater consumption tends to fall. Thus, marginal utility ultimately declines as the person consumes more and more of the good or service.	diminishing marginal utility, 438	• MyEconLab Study Plan 20.3
The Consumer Optimum An individual optimally allocates available income to consumption of all goods and services when the marginal utility per dollar spent on the last unit consumed of each good is equalized. Thus, a consumer optimum occurs when (1) the ratio of the marginal utility derived from an item to the price of that item is equal across all items that the person consumes and (2) when the person spends all available income.	consumer optimum, 439	• MyEconLab Study Plan 20.4

MyEconLab *continued*

WHAT YOU SHOULD KNOW		WHERE TO GO TO PRACTICE
The Substitution Effect of a Price Change One effect of a change in the price of a good or service is that the price change induces people to substitute among goods. For example, if the price of a good rises, the individual will tend to consume some other good that has become relatively less expensive as a result. In addition, the individual will tend to reduce consumption of the good whose price increased.	substitution effect, 442 principle of substitution, 443 **Key Figure** Figure 20-2, 443	• **MyEconLab** Study Plan 20.5 • Animated Figure 20-2
The Real-Income Effect of a Price Change If the price of a good increases, a person responds to the loss of purchasing power of available income by reducing purchases of either the now higher-priced good or other goods (or a combination of both of these responses). Normally, we anticipate that the real-income effect is smaller than the substitution effect, so that when the price of a good or service increases, people will purchase more of goods or services that have lower relative prices as a result.	purchasing power, 443 real-income effect, 443 **Key Figures** Figure 20-2, 443 Figure 20-3, 444	• **MyEconLab** Study Plan 20.5 • Animated Figures 20-2, 20-3

Log in to MyEconLab, take a chapter test, and get a personalized Study Plan that tells you which concepts you understand and which ones you need to review. From there, MyEconLab will give you further practice, tutorials, animations, videos, and guided solutions. For more information, visit www.myeconlab.com

PROBLEMS

All problems are assignable in MyEconLab. Answers to odd-numbered problems appear at the back of the book.

20-1. The campus pizzeria sells a single pizza for $12. If you order a second pizza, however, the pizzeria charges a price of only $5 for the additional pizza. Explain how an understanding of marginal utility helps to explain the pizzeria's pricing strategy. (See pages 437–438.)

20-2. As an individual consumes more units of an item, the person eventually experiences diminishing marginal utility. This means that to increase marginal utility, the person must consume less of an item. Explain the logic of this behavior using the example in Problem 20-1. (See pages 437–438.)

20-3. Where possible, complete the missing cells in the table in the next column. (See page 439.)

Number of Cheeseburgers	Total Utility of Cheeseburgers	Marginal Utility of Cheeseburgers	Bags of French Fries	Total Utility of French Fries	Marginal Utility of French Fries
0	0	—	0	0	—
1	20	—	1	—	10
2	36	—	2	—	8
3	—	12	3	—	2
4	—	8	4	21	—
5	—	4	5	21	—

20-4. From the data in Problem 20-3, if the price of a cheeseburger is $2, the price of a bag of french fries is $1, and you have $6 to spend (and you spend all of it), what is the utility-maximizing combination of cheeseburgers and french fries? (See page 441.)

20-5. Return to Problem 20-4 on page 449. Suppose that the price of cheeseburgers falls to $1. Determine the new utility-maximizing combination of cheeseburgers and french fries. (See pages 439–441.)

20-6. Suppose that you observe that total utility rises as more of an item is consumed. What can you say for certain about marginal utility? Can you say for sure that it is rising or falling or that it is positive or negative? (See page 437.)

20-7. You determine that your daily consumption of soft drinks is 3 and your daily consumption of tacos is 4 when the prices per unit are 50 cents and $1, respectively. Explain what happens to your consumption bundle, and, after your consumption choices adjust, to the marginal utility of soft drinks and the marginal utility of tacos, when the price of soft drinks rises to 75 cents. (See page 442.)

20-8. At a consumer optimum, for all goods purchased, marginal utility per dollar spent is equalized. A high school student is deciding between attending Western State University and Eastern State University. The student cannot attend both universities simultaneously. Both are fine universities, but the reputation of Western is slightly higher, as is the tuition. Use the rule of consumer optimum to explain how the student will go about deciding which university to attend. (See page 441.)

20-9. Consider the movements that take place from one point to the next (*A* to *B* to *C* and so on) along the total utility curve below as the individual successively increases consumption by one more unit, and answer the questions that follow. (See page 437.)

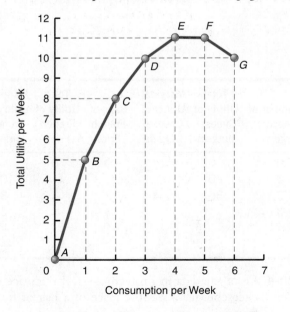

a. Which one-unit increase in consumption from one point to the next along the total utility curve generates the highest marginal utility?

b. Which one-unit increase in consumption from one point to the next along the total utility curve generates zero marginal utility?

c. Which one-unit increase in consumption from one point to the next along the total utility curve generates negative marginal utility?

20-10. Draw a marginal utility curve corresponding to the total utility curve depicted in Problem 20-9. (See page 437.)

20-11. Refer to the table below. If the price of a fudge bar is $2, the price of a Popsicle is $1, and a student has $9 to spend, what quantities will she purchase at a consumer optimum? (See pages 439–441.)

Quantity of Fudge Bars per Week	Marginal Utility (utils)	Quantity of Popsicles per Week	Marginal Utility (utils)
1	1,200	1	1,700
2	1,000	2	1,400
3	800	3	1,100
4	600	4	800
5	400	5	500
6	100	6	200

20-12. Refer to the following table for a different consumer, and assume that each week this consumer buys only hot dogs and tickets to baseball games. The price of a hot dog is $2, and the price of a baseball game is $60. If the consumer's income is $128 per week, what quantity of each item will he purchase each week at a consumer optimum? (See pages 439–441.)

Quantity of Hot Dogs per Week	Total Uility (utils)	Quantity of Baseball Games per Week	Total Utility (utils)
1	40	1	400
2	60	2	700
3	76	3	850
4	86	4	950
5	91	5	1,000
6	93	6	1,025

20-13. In Problem 20–12, if the consumer's income rises to $190 per week, what new quantities characterize the new consumer optimum? (See page 442.)

20-14. At a consumer optimum involving goods A and B, the marginal utility of good A is twice the marginal utility of good B. The price of good B is $3.50. What is the price of good A? (See page 441.)

20-15. At a consumer optimum involving goods X and Y, the marginal utility of good X equals 3 utils. The price of good Y is three times the price of good X. What is the marginal utility of good Y? (See page 441.)

20-16. At a consumer optimum involving goods A and B, the marginal utility of good A is 2 utils, and the marginal utility of good B is 8 utils. How much greater or smaller is the price of good B compared with the price of good A? (See page 441.)

20-17. At a consumer optimum involving goods X and Y, the price of good X is $3 per unit, and the price of good Y is $9 per unit. How much greater or smaller is the marginal utility of good Y than the marginal utility of good X? (See page 441.)

ECONOMICS ON THE NET

Book Prices and Consumer Optimum This application helps you see how a consumer optimum can be attained when one engages in Internet shopping.

Title: Amazon.com Web site

Navigation: Go to **www.econtoday.com/chap20** to start at Amazon.com's home page. In the pull-down menu, click on *Books*.

Application

1. Type "top sellers" in the search box, and then search for "Hardbacks." Record the price of the number one book. Then locate the Search window. Type in *Economics Today*. Scroll down until you find your class text listed. Record the price.

2. Suppose you are an individual who has purchased both the number one book and *Economics Today*

through Amazon.com. Describe how economic analysis would explain this choice.

3. Using the prices you recorded for the two books, write an equation that relates the prices and your marginal utilities of the two books. Use this equation to explain verbally how you might quantify the magnitude of your marginal utility for the number one book relative to your marginal utility for your class text.

For Group Study and Analysis Discuss what changes might occur if the price of the number one book were lowered but the student remains enrolled in this course. Discuss what changes might take place regarding the consumer optimum if the student were not enrolled in this course.

ANSWERS TO QUICK QUIZZES

p. 438: (i) Utility; (ii) utils; (iii) Total . . . Marginal

p. 442: (i) less; (ii) equating . . . optimum; (iii) no . . . maximized

p. 446: (i) increase . . . decrease; (ii) falls . . . substitutes; (iii) falls . . . more; (iv) more . . . lower

More Advanced Consumer Choice Theory

It is possible to analyze consumer choice verbally, as we did for the most part in Chapter 20. The theory of diminishing marginal utility can be fairly well accepted on intuitive grounds and by introspection. If we want to be more formal and perhaps more elegant in our theorizing, however, we can translate our discussion into a graphical analysis with what we call *indifference curves* and the *budget constraint*. Here we discuss these terms and their relationship and demonstrate consumer equilibrium in geometric form.

On Being Indifferent

What does it mean to be indifferent? It usually means that you don't care one way or the other about something—you are equally disposed to either of two alternatives. With this interpretation in mind, we will turn to two choices, viewing films at theaters and consuming fast-food meals. In panel (a) of Figure F-1 below, we show several combinations of fast food and movie tickets per week that a representative consumer considers equally satisfactory. That is to say, for each combination, *A*, *B*, *C*, and *D*, this consumer will have exactly the same level of total utility.

The simple numerical example that we have used happens to concern the consumption of fast-food meals and visits to movie theaters (both of which we assume this consumer enjoys) per week. This example is used to illustrate general features of

FIGURE F-1

Combinations That Yield Equal Levels of Satisfaction

A, *B*, *C*, and *D* represent combinations of fast-food meals and movie tickets per week that give an equal level of satisfaction to this consumer. In other words, the consumer is indifferent among these four combinations.

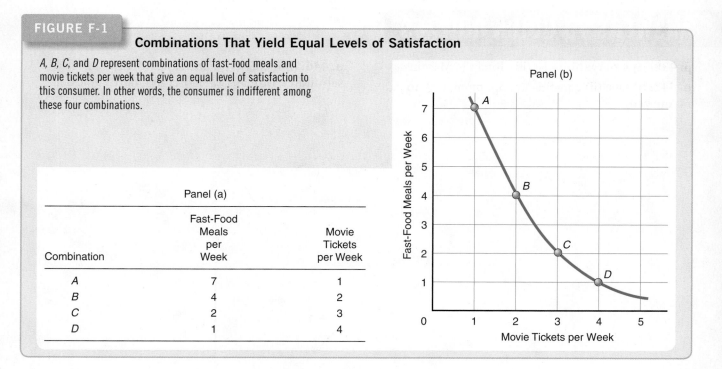

Panel (a)

Combination	Fast-Food Meals per Week	Movie Tickets per Week
A	7	1
B	4	2
C	2	3
D	1	4

indifference curves and related analytical tools that are necessary for deriving the demand curve. Obviously, we could have used any two commodities. Just remember that we are using a *specific* example to illustrate a *general* analysis.

We plot these combinations graphically in panel (b) of Figure F-1 on the facing page, with movie tickets per week on the horizontal axis and fast-food meals per week on the vertical axis. These are our consumer's indifference combinations—the consumer finds each combination as acceptable as the others. These combinations lie along a smooth curve that is known as the consumer's **indifference curve.** Along the indifference curve, every combination of the two goods in question yields the same level of satisfaction. Every point along the indifference curve is equally desirable to the consumer. For example, one fast-food meal per week and four movie tickets per week will give our representative consumer exactly the same total satisfaction as consuming four fast-food meals per week and viewing two movies per week.

Indifference curve
A curve composed of a set of consumption alternatives, each of which yields the same total amount of satisfaction.

Properties of Indifference Curves

Indifference curves have special properties relating to their slope and shape.

Downward Slope

The indifference curve shown in panel (b) of Figure F-1 on the preceding page slopes downward. That is, the indifference curve has a negative slope. Now consider Figure F-2 below. Here we show two points, A and B. Point A represents four fast-food meals per week and two movie tickets per week. Point B represents five fast-food meals per week and six movie viewings per week. Clearly, B is always preferred to A for a consumer who enjoys both fast-food meals and movies, because B represents more of everything. If B is always preferred to A, it is impossible for points A and B to be on the same indifference curve because the definition of the indifference curve is a set of combinations of two goods that are preferred equally.

FIGURE F-2

Indifference Curves: Impossibility of an Upward Slope

Point B represents a consumption of more movie tickets per week and more fast-food meals per week than point A. B is always preferred to A. Therefore, A and B cannot be on the same *positively* sloped indifference curve. An indifference curve shows *equally preferred* combinations of the two goods.

FIGURE F-3

Implications of a Straight-Line Indifference Curve

This straight-line indifference curve indicates that the consumer will always be willing to give up the same number of fast-food meals to get one more movie ticket per week. For example, the consumer at point A consumes five fast-food meals and views no movies at theaters per week. She is willing to give up one fast-food meal in order to get one movie ticket per week. At point C, however, the consumer has only one fast-food meal and views four movies per week. Because of the straight-line indifference curve, this consumer is willing to give up the last fast-food meal in order to get one more movie ticket per week, even though she already has four.

Curvature

The indifference curve that we have drawn in panel (b) of Figure F-1 on page 452 is special. Notice that it is curved. Why didn't we just draw a straight line, as we have usually done for a demand curve?

IMAGINING A STRAIGHT-LINE INDIFFERENCE CURVE To find out why we don't posit straight-line indifference curves, consider the implications. We show such a straight-line indifference curve in Figure F-3 above. Start at point *A*. The consumer has no movie tickets and five fast-food meals per week. Now the consumer wishes to go to point *B*. She is willing to give up only one fast-food meal in order to get one ticket to a movie. Now let's assume that the consumer is at point *C*, consuming one fast-food meal per week and viewing four movies at a theater per week. If the consumer wants to go to point *D*, she is again willing to give up one fast-food meal in order to get one more movie ticket per week.

In other words, no matter how many times the consumer consumes a fast-food meal, she is willing to give up one fast-food meal to get one movie viewing per week—which does not seem plausible. Doesn't it make sense to hypothesize that the more times the consumer consumes fast-food meals per week, the less she will value an *additional* fast-food meal that week? Presumably, when the consumer has five fast-food meals and no movie tickets per week, she should be willing to give up *more than* one fast-food meal in order to get one movie ticket. Therefore, a straight-line indifference curve as shown in Figure F-3 above no longer seems plausible.

CONVEXITY OF THE INDIFFERENCE CURVE In mathematical jargon, an indifference curve is convex with respect to the origin. Let's look at this in panel (a) of Figure F-1 on page 452. Starting with combination *A*, the consumer has one movie ticket but seven fast-food meals per week. To remain indifferent, the consumer would have to be willing to give up three fast-food meals to obtain one more ticket to a movie (as shown in combination *B*). To go from combination *C* to combination *D*, however, notice that the consumer would have to be willing to give up only one fast-food meal for an additional movie ticket per week. The quantity of the substitute considered acceptable changes as the rate of consumption of the original item changes.

	TABLE F-1			
	(1)	**(2)**	**(3)**	**(4)**

TABLE F-1

Calculating the Marginal Rate of Substitution

As we move from combination *A* to combination *B*, we are still on the same indifference curve. To stay on that curve, the number of fast-food meals decreases by three and the number of movie tickets increases by one. The marginal rate of substitution is 3:1. A three-unit decrease in fast-food meals requires an increase in one movie ticket to leave the consumer's total utility unaltered.

	(1) Combination	(2) Fast-Food Meals per Week	(3) Movie Tickets per Week	(4) Marginal Rate of Substitution of Fast-Food Meals for Movie Tickets
	A	7	1	
	B	4	2	3:1
	C	2	3	2:1
	D	1	4	1:1

Consequently, the indifference curve in panel (b) of Figure F-1 on page 452 will be convex when viewed from the origin.

The Marginal Rate of Substitution

Instead of using marginal utility, we can talk in terms of the *marginal rate of substitution* between fast-food meals and movie tickets per week. We can formally define the consumer's marginal rate of substitution as follows:

> *The marginal rate of substitution is equal to the change in the quantity of one good that just offsets a one-unit change in the consumption of another good, such that total satisfaction remains constant.*

We can see numerically what happens to the marginal rate of substitution in our example if we rearrange panel (a) of Figure F-1 on page 452 into Table F-1 above. Here we show fast-food meals in the second column and movie tickets in the third. Now we ask the question, what change in the number of movie tickets per week will just compensate for a three-unit change in the consumption of fast-food meals per week and leave the consumer's total utility constant? The movement from *A* to *B* increases the number of weekly movie tickets by one. Here the marginal rate of substitution is 3:1—a three-unit decrease in fast-food meals requires an increase of one movie ticket to leave the consumer's total utility unaltered. Thus, the consumer values the three fast-food meals as the equivalent of one movie ticket.

We do this for the rest of the table and find that as fast-food meals decrease, the marginal rate of substitution goes from 3:1 to 2:1 to 1:1. The marginal rate of substitution of fast-food meals for movie tickets per week falls as the consumer views more films at theaters. That is, the consumer values successive movie viewings less and less in terms of fast-food meals. The first movie ticket is valued at three fast-food meals. The last (fourth) movie ticket is valued at only one fast-food meal. The fact that the marginal rate of substitution falls is sometimes called the *law of substitution*.

In geometric language, the slope of the consumer's indifference curve (actually, the negative of the slope of the indifference curve) measures the consumer's marginal rate of substitution.

The Indifference Map

Let's now consider the possibility of having both more movie tickets *and* more fast-food meals per week. When we do this, we can no longer stay on the same indifference curve that we drew in Figure F-1. That indifference curve was drawn for

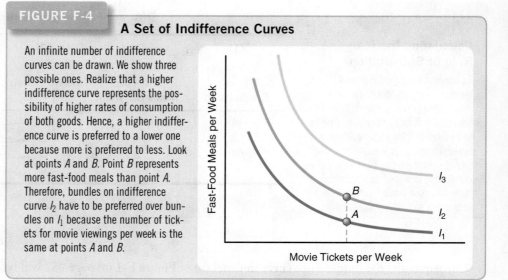

FIGURE F-4

A Set of Indifference Curves

An infinite number of indifference curves can be drawn. We show three possible ones. Realize that a higher indifference curve represents the possibility of higher rates of consumption of both goods. Hence, a higher indifference curve is preferred to a lower one because more is preferred to less. Look at points A and B. Point B represents more fast-food meals than point A. Therefore, bundles on indifference curve I_2 have to be preferred over bundles on I_1 because the number of tickets for movie viewings per week is the same at points A and B.

equally satisfying combinations of movie tickets and fast-food meals per week. If the individual can now obtain more of both, a new indifference curve will have to be drawn, above and to the right of the one shown in panel (b) of Figure F-1 on page 452. Alternatively, if the individual faces the possibility of having less of both movie tickets and fast-food meals per week, an indifference curve will have to be drawn below and to the left of the one in panel (b) of Figure F-1. We can map out a whole set of indifference curves corresponding to these possibilities.

Figure F-4 above shows three possible indifference curves. Indifference curves that are higher than others necessarily imply that for every given quantity of one good, more of the other good can be obtained on a higher indifference curve. Looked at one way, if one goes from curve I_1 to I_2, it is possible to view the same number of movies *and* be able to consume more fast-food meals each week. This is shown as a movement from point A to point B in Figure F-4. We could do it the other way. When we move from a lower to a higher indifference curve, it is possible to consume the same number of fast-food meals *and* to view more movies each week. Thus, the higher an indifference curve is for a consumer, the greater that consumer's total level of satisfaction.

The Budget Constraint

Our problem here is to find out how to maximize consumer satisfaction. To do so, we must consult not only our *preferences*—given by indifference curves—but also our *market opportunities*, which are given by our available income and prices, called our **budget constraint**. We might want more of everything, but for any given budget constraint, we have to make choices, or trade-offs, among possible goods. Everyone has a budget constraint. That is, everyone faces a limited consumption potential. How do we show this graphically? We must find the prices of the goods in question and determine the maximum consumption of each allowed by our budget.

For example, let's assume that there is a $5 price for each fast-food meal and that a ticket to a movie costs $10. Let's also assume that our representative consumer has a total budget of $30 per week. What is the maximum number of fast-food meals this individual can consume? Six. And the maximum number of films per week she can view? Three. So now, as shown in Figure F-5 on the facing page, we have two points on our budget line, which is sometimes called the *consumption possibilities curve*. These anchor points of the budget line are obtained by dividing money income by the price of each product. The first point is at *b* on the vertical axis.

Budget constraint
All of the possible combinations of goods that can be purchased (at fixed prices) with a specific budget.

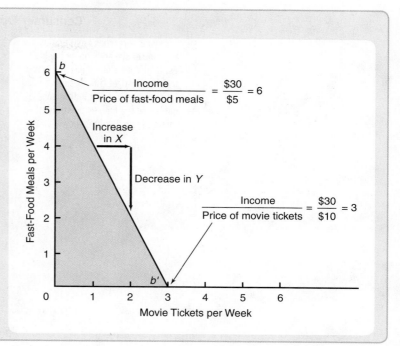

FIGURE F-5

The Budget Constraint

The line *bb'* represents this individual's budget constraint. Assuming that meals at fast-food restaurants cost $5 each, movie tickets cost $10 each, and the individual has a budget of $30 per week, a maximum of six fast-food meals or three movie tickets can be bought each week. These two extreme points are connected to form the budget constraint. All combinations within the colored area and on the budget constraint line are feasible.

$$\frac{\text{Income}}{\text{Price of fast-food meals}} = \frac{\$30}{\$5} = 6$$

$$\frac{\text{Income}}{\text{Price of movie tickets}} = \frac{\$30}{\$10} = 3$$

The second point is at *b'* on the horizontal axis. The budget line is linear because prices are constant.

Any combination along line *bb'* is possible; in fact, any combination in the colored area is possible. We will assume, however, that there are sufficient goods available that the individual consumer completely uses up the available budget, and we will consider as possible only those points along *bb'*.

Slope of the Budget Constraint

The budget constraint is a line that slopes downward from left to right. The slope of that line has a special meaning. Look carefully at the budget line in Figure F-5 above. Remember from our discussion of graphs in Appendix A on page 21 that we measure a negative slope by the ratio of the decrease in *Y* over the run in *X*. In this case, *Y* is fast-food meals per week and *X* is movie tickets per week. In Figure F-5, the decrease in *Y* is −2 fast-food meals per week (a drop from 4 to 2) for an increase in *X* of one movie ticket per week (an increase from 1 to 2). Therefore, the slope of the budget constraint is −2/1 or −2. This slope of the budget constraint represents the *rate of exchange* between meals at fast-food restaurants and tickets to movies.

Now we are ready to determine how the consumer achieves the optimum consumption rate.

Consumer Optimum Revisited

Consumers will try to attain the highest level of total utility possible, given their budget constraints. How can this be shown graphically? We draw a set of indifference curves similar to those in Figure F-4 on the facing page, and we bring in reality—the budget constraint *bb'*. Both are drawn in Figure F-6 on the following page. Because a higher level of total satisfaction is represented by a higher indifference curve, we know that the consumer will strive to be on the highest indifference curve possible.

FIGURE F-6

Consumer Optimum

A consumer reaches an optimum when he or she ends up on the highest indifference curve possible, given a limited budget. This occurs at the tangency between an indifference curve and the budget constraint. In this diagram, the tangency is at *E*.

Go to **www.econtoday.com/chap20** for a numerical example illustrating the consumer optimum.

The consumer cannot get to indifference curve I_3, however, because the budget will be exhausted before any combination of fast-food meals and movie tickets represented on indifference curve I_3 is attained. This consumer can maximize total utility, subject to the budget constraint, only by being at point *E* on indifference curve I_2 because here the consumer's income is just being exhausted. Mathematically, point *E* is called the *tangency point* of the curve I_2 to the straight line *bb′*.

Consumer optimum is achieved when the marginal rate of substitution (which is subjective) is just equal to the feasible rate of exchange between meals at fast-food restaurants and tickets to movies. This rate is the ratio of the two prices of the goods involved. It is represented by the absolute value of the slope of the budget constraint (i.e., ignoring the negative signs). At point *E*, the point of tangency between indifference curve I_2 and budget constraint *bb′*, the rate at which the consumer wishes to substitute fast-food meals for movie tickets (the numerical value of the slope of the indifference curve) is just equal to the rate at which the consumer *can* substitute fast-food meals for tickets to movies (the slope of the budget line).

Deriving the Demand Curve

We are now in a position to derive the demand curve using indifference curve analysis. In panel (a) of Figure F-7 on the facing page, we show what happens when the price of tickets to movies decreases, holding both the price of meals at fast-food restaurants and income constant. If the price of movie tickets decreases, the budget line rotates from *bb′* to *bb″*.

The two optimum points are given by the tangency at the highest indifference curve that just touches those two budget lines. This is at *E* and *E′*. But those two points give us two price-quantity pairs. At point *E*, the price of movie tickets is $10; the quantity demanded is 2. Thus, we have one point that we can transfer to panel (b) of Figure F-7. At point *E′*, we have another price-quantity pair. The price has fallen to $5, and the quantity demanded has increased to 5. We therefore transfer this other point to panel (b). When we connect these two points (and all the others in between), we derive the demand curve for tickets to movies, which slopes downward.

FIGURE F-7

Deriving the Demand Curve

In panel (a), we show the effects of a decrease in the price of movie tickets from $10 to $5. At $10, the highest indifference curve touches the budget line *bb'* at point *E*. The number of movies viewed is two. We transfer this combination—price, $10; quantity demanded, 2—down to panel (b). Next we decrease the price of movie tickets to $5. This generates a new budget line, or constraint, which is *bb''*. Consumer optimum is now at *E'*. The optimum quantity of movie tickets demanded at a price of $5 is five. We transfer this point—price, $5; quantity demanded, 5—down to panel (b). When we connect these two points, we have a demand curve, *D*, for tickets to movies.

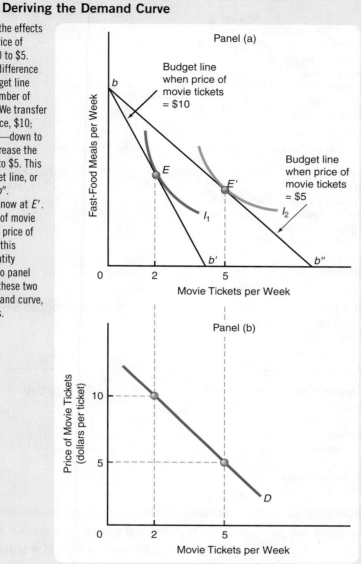

MyEconLab

Here is what you should know after reading this appendix. MyEconLab will help you identify what you know, and where to go when you need to practice.

— WHAT YOU SHOULD KNOW —		— WHERE TO GO TO PRACTICE —
On Being Indifferent Along an indifference curve, the consumer experiences equal levels of satisfaction. That is to say, along any indifference curve, every combination of the two goods in question yields exactly the same level of satisfaction.	indifference curve, 453	• MyEconLab Study Plan 20.8
Properties of Indifferent Curves Indifference curves typically slope downward and are usually convex to the origin.		• MyEconLab Study Plan 20.9

MyEconLab *continued*

WHAT YOU SHOULD KNOW		WHERE TO GO TO PRACTICE
The Marginal Rate of Substitution To measure the marginal rate of substitution, we find out how much of one good has to be given up in order to allow the consumer to consume one more unit of the other good while still remaining on the same indifference curve. The marginal rate of substitution falls as one moves down an indifference curve.	Key Figure Figure F-1, 452	• MyEconLab Study Plan 20.10
The Budget Constraint Indifference curves represent preferences. A budget constraint represents opportunities—how much can be purchased with a given level of income. Consumer optimum is obtained when the highest feasible indifference curve is just tangent to the budget constraint line. At that point, the consumer reaches the highest feasible indifference curve.	budget constraint, 456 Key Figure Figure F-5, 457	• MyEconLab Study Plans 20.9, 20.10, 20.11, 20.12
Slope of the Budget Constraint The slope of the budget constraint is the rate of exchange between two goods, which is the ratio of their dollar prices.	Key Figure Figure F-5, 457	• MyEconLab Study Plan 20.10
Deriving the Demand Curve A decrease in the price of an item causes the budget line to rotate outward. This generates a new consumer optimum, at which the individual chooses to consume more units of the item. Hence, a decrease in price generates an increase in quantity demanded, or a movement down along a derived demand curve.	Key Figure Figure F-7, 459	• MyEconLab Study Plan 20.13

Log in to MyEconLab, take an appendix test, and get a personalized Study Plan that tells you which concepts you understand and which ones you need to review. From there, MyEconLab will give you further practice, tutorials, animations, videos, and guided solutions. For more information, visit www.myeconlab.com

PROBLEMS

All problems are assignable in MyEconLab. Answers to odd-numbered problems appear at the back of the book.

F-1. Consider the indifference curve illustrated in Figure F-1 on page 452. Explain, in economic terms, why the curve is convex to the origin. (See page 454.)

F-2. Your classmate tells you that he is indifferent between three soft drinks and two hamburgers or two soft drinks and three hamburgers. (See page 454.)

   a. Draw a rough diagram of an indifference curve containing your classmate's consumption choices.

   b. Suppose that your classmate states that he is also indifferent between two soft drinks and three hamburgers or one soft drink and four hamburgers, but that he prefers three soft drinks and two hamburgers to one soft drink and four hamburgers. Use your diagram from part (a) to reason out whether he can have these preferences.

F-3. The table at the top of the facing page represents Sue's preferences for bottled water and soft drinks, the combination of which yields the same level of utility.

Combination of Bottled Water and Soft Drinks	Bottled Water per Month	Soft Drinks per Month
A	5	11
B	10	7
C	15	4
D	20	2
E	25	1

Calculate Sue's marginal rate of substitution of soft drinks for bottled water at each rate of consumption of water (or soft drinks). Relate the marginal rate of substitution to marginal utility. (See pages 455–456.)

F-4. Using the information provided in Problem F-3, illustrate Sue's indifference curve, with water on the horizontal axis and soft drinks on the vertical axis. (See pages 455–456.)

F-5. Sue's monthly budget for bottled water and soft drinks is $23. The price of bottled water is $1 per bottle, and the price of soft drinks is $2 per bottle. Calculate the slope of Sue's budget constraint. Given this information and the information provided in Problem F-3, find the combination of goods that satisfies Sue's utility maximization problem in light of her budget constraint. (See page 458.)

F-6. Using the indifference curve diagram you constructed in Problem F-4, add in Sue's budget constraint using the information in Problem F-5. Illustrate the utility-maximizing combination of bottled water and soft drinks. (See page 458.)

F-7. Suppose that at a higher satisfaction level than in Problem F-3, Sue's constant-utility preferences are as shown in the table below. Calculate the slope of Sue's new budget constraint using the information provided in Problem F-5. Supposing now that the price of a soft drink falls to $1, find the combination of goods that satisfies Sue's utility maximization problem in light of her budget constraint. (See page 458.)

Combination of Bottled Water and Soft Drinks	Bottled Water per Month	Soft Drinks per Month
A	5	22
B	10	14
C	15	8
D	20	4
E	25	2

F-8. Illustrate Sue's new budget constraint and indifference curve in a diagram from the data in Problem F-3. Illustrate also the utility-maximizing combination of goods. (See page 458.)

F-9. Given your answers to Problems F-5 and F-7, are Sue's preferences for soft drinks consistent with the law of demand? (See pages 458–459.)

F-10. Using your answer to Problem F-8, draw Sue's demand curve for soft drinks. (See page 459.)

21

Rents, Profits, and the Financial Environment of Business

Since the mid-2000s, in the United States fewer individually owned or co-owned business establishments have opened each year than in prior years. In addition, since the early 2000s, fewer new firms have been formed as U.S. corporations. How can economists explain these recent declines in new business formation in the United States? Why do some firms choose to conduct business with individual owners or a few co-owners while others operate as corporations? In this chapter, you will learn the answers.

DID YOU KNOW THAT...

U.S. residents have borrowed more funds to finance their educations than the total amount of debt that all residents owe on their credit cards? The student loan debt in the United States now totals more than $1 trillion, which exceeds by $200 billion the amount that U.S. households currently owe on all of their credit cards.

A typical individual with student loans owes about $25,000 in outstanding debts. In addition to amounts borrowed, however, a person with these loans also must eventually pay interest. The interest payments on a student loan depend on the interest rate—the annual amount of interest to be paid as a percentage of the amount borrowed—specified by the student loan contracts.

What is the economic role of interest? What are alternative ways of measuring interest rates? In this chapter, you will learn the answers. First, however, you must learn about the important function of *economic rent*.

Economic Rent

When you hear the term *rent*, you are accustomed to having it mean the payment made to property owners for the use of land or dwellings. The term *rent* has a different meaning in economics. **Economic rent** is payment to the owner of a resource in excess of its *opportunity cost*—that is, the minimum payment that would be necessary to call forth production of that amount (and quality) of the resource.

Economic rent
A payment for the use of any resource over and above its opportunity cost.

Determining Land Rent

Economists originally used the term *rent* to designate payment for the use of land. What was thought to be important about land was that its supply was completely inelastic. That is, the supply curve for land was thought to be a vertical line, so that no matter what the prevailing market price for land, the quantity supplied would remain the same.

The concept of economic rent is associated with the British economist David Ricardo (1772–1823). Here is how Ricardo analyzed economic rent for land. He first simplified his model by assuming that all land is equally productive. Then Ricardo assumed that the quantity of land in a country is *fixed* so that land's opportunity cost is equal to zero. Graphically, then, in terms of supply and demand, we draw the supply curve for land vertically (zero price elasticity). In Figure 21-1 below, the supply curve of land is represented by S. If the demand curve is D_1, it intersects the supply curve, S, at price P_1. The entire

---

FIGURE 21-1

Economic Rent

If indeed the supply curve of land were completely price-inelastic in the long run, it would be depicted by S. The opportunity cost of land is zero, so the same quantity of land is forthcoming at any constant-quality price. Thus, at the quantity in existence, Q_1, any and all revenues are economic rent. If demand is D_1, the price will be P_1. If demand is D_2, price will rise to P_2. Economic rent would be $P_1 \times Q_1$ and $P_2 \times Q_1$, respectively.

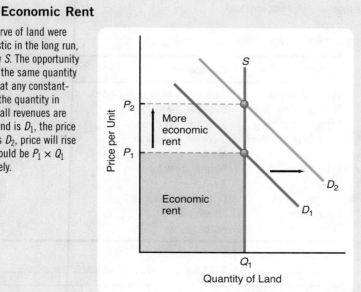

amount of revenues obtained, $P_1 \times Q_1$, is labeled "Economic rent." If the demand for land increases to D_2, the equilibrium price will rise to P_2. Additions to economic rent are labeled "More economic rent." Notice that the quantity of land remains insensitive to the change in price. Another way of stating this is that the supply curve is perfectly inelastic.

Economic Rent to Labor

Land and natural resources are not the only factors of production to which the analysis of economic rent can be applied. In fact, the analysis is probably more often applicable to labor. Here is a list of people who provide different labor services, some of whom probably receive large amounts of economic rent:

- Professional sports superstars
- Hip-hop stars
- Movie stars
- World-class models
- Successful inventors and innovators
- World-famous opera stars

Just apply the definition of economic rent to the phenomenal earnings that these people make. They would undoubtedly work for considerably less than they earn. Therefore, much of their earnings constitutes economic rent (but not all, as we shall see). Economic rent occurs because specific resources cannot be replicated exactly. No one can duplicate today's most highly paid entertainment figures, and therefore they receive economic rent. How much do top performers earn?

EXAMPLE

Do Entertainment Superstars Make Super Economic Rents?

Superstars certainly do well financially. Table 21-1 below shows the one-year earnings of selected individuals in the entertainment industry as estimated by *Forbes* magazine. How much of these earnings can be called economic rent? The question is not easy to answer, because an entertainment newcomer would almost certainly work for much less than she or he earns, implying that the newcomer is making high economic rent. The same cannot necessarily be said for entertainers who have been raking in millions for years. They probably have very high accumulated wealth and also a more jaded outlook about their work. It is therefore not clear how much they would work if they were not offered those huge sums of income.

FOR CRITICAL THINKING

Even if some superstar entertainers would work for less, what forces cause them to earn so much income anyway?

TABLE 21-1

Superstar Earnings

Name	Occupation	One-Year Earnings
Oprah Winfrey	Talk show host and owner, author	$165,000,000
Michael Bay	Director, producer	160,000,000
Steven Spielberg	Director, producer	130,000,000
Jerry Bruckheimer	Director, producer	115,000,000
Dr. Dre	Musician, producer	110,000,000
Tyler Perry	Writer, director, producer	105,000,000
Howard Stern	Talk show host	95,000,000
George Lucas	Director, producer	90,000,000
Elton John	Musician	80,000,000
Tom Cruise	Actor	75,000,000

Source: Forbes, 2012.

Economic Rent and the Allocation of Resources

Suppose that a highly paid movie star would make the same number of movies at half his or her current annual earnings. Why, then, does the superstar receive a higher income? Look again at Figure 21-1 on page 463, but substitute *entertainment activities of the superstars* for the word *land*. The high "price" received by the superstar is due to the demand for his or her services. If Anne Hathaway announces that she will work for a million dollars per movie and do two movies a year, how is she going to know which production company values her services the most highly? Hathaway and other movie stars let the market decide where their resources should be used. In this sense, we can say the following:

Economic rent allocates resources to their highest-valued use.

Otherwise stated, economic rent directs resources to the people who can use them most efficiently.

QUICK QUIZ   See page 482 for the answers. Review concepts from this section in MyEconLab.

Economic rent is defined as payment for a factor of production that is completely _____ in supply.	Economic rent _____ resources to their _____-valued use.

Firms and Profits

Firms or businesses, like individuals, seek to earn the highest possible returns. We define a **firm** as follows:

A firm is an organization that brings together factors of production—labor, land, physical capital, human capital, and entrepreneurial skill—to produce a product or service that it hopes to sell at a profit.

Firm
A business organization that employs resources to produce goods or services for profit. A firm normally owns and operates at least one "plant" or facility in order to produce.

A typical firm will have an organizational structure consisting of an entrepreneur, managers, and workers. The entrepreneur is the person who takes the risks, mainly of losing his or her personal wealth. In compensation, the entrepreneur will get any profits that are made. Recall from Chapter 2 that entrepreneurs take the initiative in combining land, labor, and capital to produce a good or a service. Entrepreneurs are the ones who innovate in the form of new production and new products. The entrepreneur also decides whom to hire to manage the firm. Some economists maintain that the true quality of an entrepreneur becomes evident with his or her selection of managers.

Managers, in turn, decide who else should be hired and fired and how the business should be operated on a day-to-day basis. The workers ultimately use the other inputs to produce the products or services that are being sold by the firm. Workers and managers are paid contractual wages. They receive a specified amount of income for a specified time period. Entrepreneurs are not paid contractual wages. They receive no reward specified in advance. The entrepreneurs make profits if there are any, for profits accrue to those who are willing to take risks. (Because the entrepreneur gets only what is left over after all expenses are paid, she or he is often referred to as a *residual claimant*. The entrepreneur lays claim to the residual—whatever is left.)

The Legal Organization of Firms

We all know that firms differ from one another. Some sell frozen yogurt, others make automobiles. Some advertise. Some do not. Some have annual sales of a few thousand dollars. Others have sales in the billions of dollars. The list of differences is probably endless. Yet for all this diversity, the basic organization of *all* firms can be thought of

TABLE 21-2

Forms of Business Organization

Type of Firm	Percentage of U.S. Firms	Average Size (annual sales in dollars)	Percentage of Total Business Revenues
Proprietorship	71.3	57,000	4.0
Partnership	9.7	1,389,000	13.0
Corporation	19.0	4,501,000	83.0

Sources: U.S. Bureau of the Census. *Statistical Abstract.*

in terms of a few simple structures, the most important of which are the proprietorship, the partnership, and the corporation.

PROPRIETORSHIP The most common form of business organization is the **proprietorship.** As shown in Table 21-2 above, about 71 percent of all firms in the United States are proprietorships. Each is owned by a single individual who makes the business decisions, receives all the profits, and is legally responsible for all the debts of the firm. Although proprietorships are numerous, they are generally rather small businesses, with annual sales averaging about $57,000. For this reason, even though there are more than 22 million proprietorships in the United States, they account for only 4 percent of all business revenues.

Advantages of Proprietorships. Proprietorships offer several advantages as a form of business organization. First, they are *easy to form and to dissolve*. In the simplest case, all one must do to start a business is to start working. To dissolve the firm, one simply stops working. Second, *all decision-making power resides with the sole proprietor*. No partners, shareholders, or board of directors need be consulted. The third advantage is that its *profit is taxed only once*. All profit is treated by law as the net income of the proprietor and as such is subject only to personal income taxation.

Disadvantages of Proprietorships. The most important disadvantage of a proprietorship is that the proprietor faces **unlimited liability** *for the debts of the firm*. This means that the owner is personally responsible for all of the firm's debts. The second disadvantage is that many lenders are reluctant to lend large (or any) sums to a proprietorship. Consequently, a proprietorship may have a *limited ability to raise funds*, to expand the business or even simply to help it survive bad times. The third disadvantage of proprietorships is that they normally *end with the death of the proprietor*, which creates added uncertainty for prospective lenders or employees.

PARTNERSHIP The second important form of business organization is the **partnership.** As shown in Table 21-2 above, partnerships are far less numerous than proprietorships but tend to be larger businesses—about 24 times greater on average. A partnership differs from a proprietorship chiefly in that there are two or more co-owners, called partners. They share the responsibilities of operating the firm and its profits, and they are *each* legally responsible for *all* of the debts incurred by the firm. In this sense, a partnership may be viewed as a proprietorship with more than one owner.

Advantages of Partnerships. The first advantage of a partnership is that it is *easy to form*. In fact, it is almost as easy to form as a proprietorship. Second, partnerships, like proprietorships, often help *reduce the costs of monitoring job performance*. This is particularly true when interpersonal skills are important for successful performance and in lines of business in which, even after the fact, it is difficult to measure performance objectively. Thus, attorneys and physicians often organize themselves as partnerships. A third advantage of the partnership is that it *permits more effective specialization* in

Proprietorship

A business owned by one individual who makes the business decisions, receives all the profits, and is legally responsible for the debts of the firm.

Unlimited liability

A legal concept whereby the personal assets of the owner of a firm can be seized to pay off the firm's debts.

Partnership

A business owned by two or more joint owners, or partners, who share the responsibilities and the profits of the firm and are individually liable for all the debts of the partnership.

occupations in which, for legal or other reasons, the multiple talents required for success are unlikely to be uniform across individuals. Finally, the income of the partnership is treated as personal income and thus is *subject only to personal taxation*.

Disadvantages of Partnerships. Partnerships also have their disadvantages. First, the *partners each have unlimited liability*. Thus, the personal assets of *each* partner are at risk due to debts incurred on behalf of the partnership by *any* of the partners. Second, *decision making is generally more costly* in a partnership than in a proprietorship. More people are involved in making decisions, and they may have differences of opinion that must be resolved before action is possible. Finally, *dissolution of the partnership* often occurs when a partner dies or voluntarily withdraws or when one or more partners wish to remove someone from the partnership. This creates potential uncertainty for creditors and employees.

CORPORATION A **corporation** is a legal entity that may conduct business in its own name just as an individual does. The owners of a corporation are called *shareholders* because they own shares of the profits earned by the firm. By law, shareholders have **limited liability,** meaning that if the corporation incurs debts that it cannot pay, the shareholders' personal property is shielded from claims by the firm's creditors. As shown in Table 21-2 on the facing page, corporations are far less numerous than proprietorships, but because of their large size, they are responsible for 83 percent of all business revenues in the United States.

Advantages of Corporations. Perhaps the greatest advantage of corporations is that their owners (the shareholders) have *limited liability*. The liability of shareholders is limited to the value of their shares. The second advantage is that, legally, the corporation *continues to exist* even if one or more owners cease to be owners. A third advantage of the corporation stems from the first two: Corporations are well positioned to *raise large sums of financial capital*. People are able to buy ownership shares or lend funds to the corporation knowing that their liability is limited to the amount of funds they invest and confident that the corporation's existence does not depend on the life of any one of the firm's owners.

Disadvantages of Corporations. The chief disadvantage of the corporation is that corporate income is subject to *double taxation*. The profits of the corporation are subject first to corporate taxation. Then, if any of the after-tax profits are distributed to shareholders as **dividends,** such payments are treated as personal income to the shareholders and subject to personal taxation. Because the corporate income is also taxed at the corporate level, owners of corporations generally pay higher taxes on corporate income than on other forms of income.

A second disadvantage of the corporation is that corporations are potentially subject to problems associated with the *separation of ownership and control*. The owners and managers of a corporation are typically different persons and may have different incentives. The problems that can result are discussed later in the chapter.

Could a policy decision to permit "crowd funding" of businesses reduce the incentive for partnerships to become corporations?

Corporation
A legal entity that may conduct business in its own name just as an individual does. The owners of a corporation, called shareholders, own shares of the firm's profits and have the protection of limited liability.

Limited liability
A legal concept in which the responsibility, or liability, of the owners of a corporation is limited to the value of the shares in the firm that they own.

YOU ARE THERE

To consider the partnership-versus-corporation advantages and disadvantages faced by two former college students who established a junk-hauling business, take a look at **College Hunks Hauling Junk Weighs Partnership Pros and Cons,** on page 477.

Dividends
Portion of a corporation's profits paid to its owners (shareholders).

POLICY EXAMPLE

The Government Considers Allowing "Crowd Funding" of Firms

Under past federal rules administered by the Securities and Exchange Commission (SEC), a firm could have no more than 499 investing partners before it had to subject itself to regulation as a corporation. The Jumpstart Our Business Startups Act, however, instructs the SEC to develop rules to permit firms organized as private partnerships to raise financial capital on social networks such as Facebook and Twitter. Under this proposal, noncorporate enterprises would be allowed to engage in so-called crowd funding by inviting numerous investors to buy partnership shares valued at no more than $100 per investor. Furthermore, the total amount of partnership shares that a small firm could sell would be capped at $100,000. If the SEC approves this proposal, an advantage of corporations over partnerships would be reduced, which could result in fewer partnerships opting for corporate structures.

FOR CRITICAL THINKING

Even if the SEC approves the crowd-funding proposal, why might a number of partnerships nonetheless decide eventually to become publicly held corporations?

The Profits of a Firm

Most people think of a firm's profit as the difference between the amount of revenues the firm takes in and the amount it spends for wages, materials, and so on. In a bookkeeping sense, the following formula could be used:

$$\text{Accounting profit} = \text{total revenues} - \text{explicit costs}$$

where **explicit costs** are expenses that must actually be paid out by the firm. This definition of profit is known as **accounting profit.** It is appropriate when used by accountants to determine a firm's taxable income. Economists are more interested in how firm managers react not just to changes in explicit costs but also to changes in **implicit costs,** defined as expenses that business managers do not have to pay out of pocket but are costs to the firm nonetheless because they represent an opportunity cost. They do not involve any direct cash outlay by the firm and must therefore be measured by the *opportunity cost principle.* That is to say, they are measured by what the resources (land, capital) currently used in producing a particular good or service could earn in other uses. Consequently, a better definition of implicit cost is the opportunity cost of using factors that a producer does not buy or hire but already owns.

Economists use the full opportunity cost of all resources (including both explicit and implicit costs) as the figure to subtract from revenues to obtain a definition of profit.

Opportunity Cost of Capital

Firms enter or remain in an industry if they earn, at minimum, a **normal rate of return.** People will not invest their wealth in a business unless they obtain a positive normal (competitive) rate of return—that is, unless their invested wealth pays off. Any business wishing to attract capital must expect to pay at least the same rate of return on that capital as all other businesses (of similar risk) are willing to pay. Put another way, when a firm requires the use of a resource in producing a particular product, it must bid against alternative users of that resource. Thus, the firm must offer a price that is at least as much as other potential users are offering to pay.

For example, if individuals can invest their wealth in almost any publishing firm and get a rate of return of 10 percent per year, each firm in the publishing industry must *expect* to pay 10 percent as the normal rate of return to present and future investors. This 10 percent is a *cost to the firm,* the **opportunity cost of capital.** The opportunity cost of capital is the amount of income, or yield, that could have been earned by investing in the next-best alternative. Capital will not stay in firms or industries in which the expected rate of return falls below its opportunity cost—that is, what could be earned elsewhere. If a firm owns some capital equipment, it can either use it or lease it out and earn a return. If the firm uses the equipment for production, part of the cost of using that equipment is the forgone revenue that the firm could have earned had it leased out that equipment.

Opportunity Cost of Owner-Provided Labor and Capital

Single-owner proprietorships often grossly exaggerate their profit rates because they understate the opportunity cost of the labor that the proprietor provides to the business. Here we are referring to the opportunity cost of labor. For example, you may know people who run a small grocery store. These people will sit down at the end of the year and figure out what their "profits" are. They will add up all their sales and subtract what they had to pay to other workers, what they had to pay to their suppliers, what they had to pay in taxes, and so on. The end result they will call "profit." They normally will not, however, have figured into their costs the salary that they could have made if they had worked for somebody else in a similar type of job.

By working for themselves, they become residual claimants—they receive what is left after all explicit costs have been accounted for. Part of the costs, however, should include the salary the owner-operator could have received working for someone else.

Explicit costs
Costs that business managers must take account of because they must be paid. Examples are wages, taxes, and rent.

Accounting profit
Total revenues minus total explicit costs.

Implicit costs
Expenses that managers do not have to pay out of pocket and hence normally do not explicitly calculate, such as the opportunity cost of factors of production that are owned. Examples are owner-provided capital and owner-provided labor.

Normal rate of return
The amount that must be paid to an investor to induce investment in a business. Also known as the *opportunity cost of capital.*

Opportunity cost of capital
The normal rate of return, or the available return on the next-best alternative investment. Economists consider this a cost of production, and it is included in our cost examples.

Consider a simple example of a skilled auto mechanic working 14 hours a day at his own service station, six days a week. Compare this situation to how much he could earn working 84 hours a week as a trucking company mechanic. This self-employed auto mechanic might have an opportunity cost of about $35 an hour. For his 84-hour week in his own service station, he is forfeiting $2,940. Unless his service station shows accounting profits of more than that per week, he is incurring losses in an economic sense.

Another way of looking at the opportunity cost of running a business is that opportunity cost consists of all explicit and implicit costs. Accountants only take account of explicit costs. Therefore, accounting profit ends up being the residual after only explicit costs are subtracted from total revenues.

This same analysis can apply to owner-provided capital, such as land or buildings. The fact that the owner owns the building or the land with which he or she operates a business does not mean that it is "free." Rather, use of the building and land still has an opportunity cost—the value of the next-best alternative use for those assets.

Go to www.econtoday.com/chap21 for a link to Internal Revenue Service reports on U.S. annual revenues and expenses of proprietorships, partnerships, and corporations based on tax returns. Click on recent quarters and choose relevant reports.

Accounting Profits versus Economic Profits

The term *profits* in economics means the income that entrepreneurs earn, over and above all costs including their own opportunity cost of time, plus the opportunity cost of the capital they have invested in their business. Profits can be regarded as total revenues minus total costs—which is how accountants think of them—but we must now include *all* costs. Our definition of **economic profits** will be the following:

$$\text{Economic profits} = \text{total revenues} - \text{total opportunity cost of all inputs used}$$

or

$$\text{Economic profits} = \text{total revenues} - (\text{explicit} + \text{implicit costs})$$

Remember that implicit costs include a normal rate of return on invested capital. We show this relationship in Figure 21-2 below.

Economic profits
Total revenues minus total opportunity costs of all inputs used, or the total of all implicit and explicit costs.

FIGURE 21-2

Simplified View of Economic and Accounting Profit

We see on the right column that accounting profit is the difference between total revenues and total explicit accounting costs. Conversely, we see on the left column that economic profit is equal to total revenues minus economic costs. Economic costs equal explicit accounting costs plus all implicit costs, including a normal rate of return on invested capital.

The Goal of the Firm: Profit Maximization

When we examined the theory of consumer demand, utility (or satisfaction) maximization by the individual provided the basis for the analysis. In the theory of the firm and production, *profit maximization* is the underlying hypothesis of our predictive theory. The goal of the firm is to maximize economic profits, and the firm is expected to make the positive difference between total revenues and total costs as large as it can.

Our justification for assuming profit maximization by firms is similar to our assumption concerning utility maximization by individuals (see Chapter 20). To obtain labor, capital, and other resources required to produce commodities, firms must first obtain financing from investors. Although investors typically monitor managers' performances to ensure that the funds they provide are not misused, they are most interested in the earnings on these funds and the risk of obtaining lower returns or losing the funds they have invested. Firms that can provide relatively higher risk-corrected returns will therefore have an advantage in obtaining the financing needed to continue or expand production. Over time, we would expect a policy of profit maximization to become the dominant mode of behavior for firms that survive.

QUICK QUIZ See page 482 for the answers. Review concepts from this section in MyEconLab.

_____ are the most common form of business organization, comprising about 71 percent of all firms. Each is owned by a single individual who makes all business decisions, receives all the profits, and has _____ liability for the firm's debts.

_____ are much like **proprietorships,** except that two or more individuals, or partners, share the decisions and the profits of the firm. In addition, each partner has _____ liability for the debts of the firm.

Corporations are responsible for the largest share of business revenues. The owners, called _____, share in the firm's profits but normally have little responsibility for

the firm's day-to-day operations. They enjoy _____ liability for the debts of the firm.

Accounting profits differ from **economic profits,** which are defined as total revenues minus total costs, where costs include the full _____ cost of all of the factors of production plus all other implicit costs.

The full opportunity cost of capital invested in a business is generally not included as a cost when accounting profits are calculated. Thus, accounting profits often are _____ than economic profits. We assume throughout that the goal of the firm is to _____ economic profits.

Interest

Interest is the price paid by debtors to creditors for the use of loanable funds. Often businesses go to credit markets to obtain so-called **financial capital** in order to invest in physical capital and rights to patents and trademarks from which they hope to make a satisfactory return. In other words, in our society, the production of capital goods is often facilitated by the existence of credit markets. These are markets in which borrowing and lending take place.

Financial capital
Funds used to purchase physical capital goods, such as buildings and equipment, and patents and trademarks.

Interest and Credit

When you obtain credit, you actually obtain funds to have command over resources today. We can say, then, that **interest** is the payment for current rather than future command over resources. Thus, interest is the payment for obtaining credit. If you borrow $100 from me, you have command over $100 worth of goods and services today. I no longer have that command. You promise to pay me back $100 plus interest at some future date. The interest that you pay is usually expressed as a percentage of the total loan, calculated on an annual basis. If at the end of one year you pay me back $105, the annual interest rate is $5 ÷ $100, or 5 percent. When you go out into the marketplace to obtain credit, you will find that the interest rate charged differs greatly. A loan to buy a house (a mortgage) may cost you 4 to 6 percent in annual interest.

Interest
The payment for current rather than future command over resources; the cost of obtaining credit.

An installment loan to buy an automobile may cost you 6 to 8 percent in annual interest. The federal government, when it wishes to obtain credit (issue U.S. Treasury securities), may have to pay only 0.2 to 4 percent in annual interest. Variations in the rate of annual interest that must be paid for credit depend on the following factors.

1. *Length of loan.* In many (but not all) cases, the longer the loan will be outstanding, other things being equal, the greater will be the interest rate charged.

2. *Risk.* The greater the risk of nonrepayment of the loan, other things being equal, the greater the interest rate charged. Risk is assessed on the basis of the creditworthiness of the borrower and whether the borrower provides collateral for the loan. Collateral consists of any asset that will automatically become the property of the lender should the borrower fail to comply with the loan agreement.

3. *Handling charges.* It takes resources to set up a loan. Papers have to be filled out and filed, credit references have to be checked, collateral has to be examined, and so on. The larger the amount of the loan, the smaller the handling (or administrative) charges as a percentage of the total loan. Therefore, we would predict that, other things being equal, the larger the loan, the lower the interest rate.

Go to www.econtoday.com/chap21 for Federal Reserve data on U.S. interest rates.

Real versus Nominal Interest Rates

We have been assuming that there is no inflation. In a world of inflation—a persistent rise in an average of all prices—the **nominal rate of interest** will be higher than it would be in a world with no inflation. Nominal, or market, rates of interest rise to take account of the anticipated rate of inflation. If, for example, no inflation is expected, the nominal rate of interest might be 5 percent for home mortgages. If the rate of inflation goes to 4 percent a year and stays there, everybody will anticipate that inflation rate. The nominal rate of interest will rise to about 9 percent to take account of the anticipated rate of inflation. If the interest rate did not rise to 9 percent, the principal plus interest earned at 5 percent would have lower purchasing power in the future because inflation would have eroded its real value.

Nominal rate of interest
The market rate of interest expressed in today's dollars.

We can therefore say that the nominal, or market, rate of interest is approximately equal to the real rate of interest plus the anticipated rate of inflation, or

$$i_n = i_r + \text{anticipated rate of inflation}$$

where i_n equals the nominal rate of interest and i_r equals the real rate of interest. In short, you can expect to see high nominal rates of interest in periods of high inflation rates. The **real rate of interest** may not necessarily be high, though. We must first correct the nominal rate of interest for the anticipated rate of inflation before determining whether the real interest rate is in fact higher than normal.

Real rate of interest
The nominal rate of interest minus the anticipated rate of inflation.

The Allocative Role of Interest

In Chapter 4, we talked about the price system and the role that prices play in the allocation of resources. Interest is a price that allocates loanable funds (credit) to consumers and to businesses. Within the business sector, interest allocates funds to different firms and therefore to different investment projects. An investment, or capital, project with a rate of return—an annual payoff as a percentage of the investment—higher than the market rate of interest in the credit market will be undertaken, given an unrestricted market for loanable funds.

For example, if the expected rate of return on the purchase of a new factory or of intellectual property—patents or copyrights—in some industry is 10 percent and funds can be acquired for 6 percent, the investment project will proceed. If, however, that same project had an expected rate of return of only 4 percent, it would not be undertaken. In sum, the interest rate allocates funds to industries whose investments yield the highest (risk-adjusted) returns—where resources will be the most productive.

It is important to realize that the interest rate performs the function of allocating financial capital and that this ultimately allocates real physical capital to various firms for investment projects.

Interest Rates and Present Value

Businesses make investments in which they often incur large costs today but don't make any profits until some time in the future. Somehow they have to be able to compare their investment cost today with a stream of future profits. How can they relate present cost to future benefits?

Interest rates are used to link the present with the future. After all, if you have to pay $105 at the end of the year when you borrow $100, that 5 percent interest rate gives you a measure of the premium on the earlier availability of goods and services. If you want to have things today, you have to pay the 5 percent interest rate in order to have current purchasing power.

The question could be put this way: What is the present value (the value today) of $105 that you could receive one year from now? That depends on the market rate of interest, or the rate of interest that you could earn in some appropriate savings institution, such as in a savings account. To make the arithmetic simple, let's assume that the rate of interest is 5 percent. Now you can figure out the **present value** of $105 to be received one year from now. You figure it out by asking, What sum must I put aside today at the market interest rate of 5 percent to receive $105 one year from now? Mathematically, we represent this equation as

$$(1 + 0.05)PV_1 = \$105$$

where PV_1 is the sum that you must set aside now.

Let's solve this simple equation to obtain PV_1:

$$PV_1 = \frac{\$105}{1.05} = \$100$$

That is, $100 will accumulate to $105 at the end of one year with a market rate of interest of 5 percent. Thus, the present value of $105 one year from now, using a rate of interest of 5 percent, is $100. The formula for present value of any sums to be received one year from now thus becomes

$$PV_1 = \frac{FV_1}{1 + i}$$

where

$$PV_1 = \text{present value of a sum one year hence}$$
$$FV_1 = \text{future sum paid or received one year hence}$$
$$i = \text{market rate of interest}$$

PRESENT VALUES FOR MORE DISTANT PERIODS The present-value formula for figuring out today's worth of dollars to be received at a future date can now be determined. How much would have to be put in the same savings account today to have $105 *two years* from now if the account pays a rate of 5 percent per year compounded annually?

After one year, the sum that would have to be set aside, which we will call PV_2, would have grown to $PV_2 \times 1.05$. This amount during the second year would increase to $PV_2 \times 1.05 \times 1.05$, or $PV_2 \times (1.05)^2$. To find the PV_2 that would grow to $105 over two years, let

$$PV_2 \times (1.05)^2 = \$105$$

and solve for PV_2:

$$PV_2 = \frac{\$105}{(1.05)^2} = \$95.24$$

Present value

The value of a future amount expressed in today's dollars; the most that someone would pay today to receive a certain sum at some point in the future.

Go to www.econtoday.com/chap21 to utilize an MFM Communication Software, Inc., manual providing additional review of present value.

TABLE 21-3

Present Value of a Future Dollar

This table shows how much a dollar received at the end of a certain number of years in the future is worth today. For example, at 5 percent a year, a dollar to be received 20 years in the future is worth 37.7 cents today. If received in 50 years, it isn't even worth a dime today. To find out how much $10,000 would be worth a certain number of years from now, just multiply the figures in the table by 10,000. For example, $10,000 received at the end of 10 years discounted at a 5 percent rate of interest would have a present value of $6,140.

	Discounted Present Values of $1				
Year	3%	5%	8%	10%	20%
1	.971	.952	.926	.909	.833
2	.943	.907	.857	.826	.694
3	.915	.864	.794	.751	.578
4	.889	.823	.735	.683	.482
5	.863	.784	.681	.620	.402
6	.838	.746	.630	.564	.335
7	.813	.711	.583	.513	.279
8	.789	.677	.540	.466	.233
9	.766	.645	.500	.424	.194
10	.744	.614	.463	.385	.162
15	.642	.481	.315	.239	.0649
20	.554	.377	.215	.148	.0261
25	.478	.295	.146	.0923	.0105
30	.412	.231	.0994	.0573	.00421
40	.307	.142	.0460	.0221	.000680
50	.228	.087	.0213	.00852	.000109

Thus, the present value of $105 to be paid or received two years hence, discounted at an interest rate of 5 percent per year compounded annually, is equal to $95.24. In other words, $95.24 put into a savings account yielding 5 percent per year compounded interest would accumulate to $105 in two years.

THE GENERAL FORMULA FOR DISCOUNTING The general formula for **discounting** becomes

$$PV_t = \frac{FV_t}{(1 + i)^t}$$

where t refers to the number of periods in the future the money is to be paid or received.

Table 21-3 above gives the present value of $1 to be received in future years at various interest rates. The interest rate used to derive the present value is called the **rate of discount**.

Discounting
The method by which the present value of a future sum or a future stream of sums is obtained.

Rate of discount
The rate of interest used to discount future sums back to present value.

WHAT IF... the government directs credit to favored industries at artificially low interest rates?

In recent years, government officials have used tax dollars to extend public credit to selected firms, such as green energy companies, at below-market rates of interest. A common argument advanced by these officials is that private savers who otherwise might lend to these companies would require an interest rate that is "too high." Consequently, the discounted present value of future annual payoffs that investments in the officials' favored industries would have to yield is too low for private investors to be willing to direct funds to those industries. Of course, a relatively high market interest rate reflects a greater rate at which people in the private sector discount future sums. Thus, when government officials say that the market interest rate is too high, this means that they think private investors discount the future "too much." In other words, the rate of time discount of the government officials who arrange to redirect taxpayers' funds to the officials' preferred investments must be lower than private investors' rate of time discount. Thus, public officials desire to spend more on certain industries than do private investors.

QUICK QUIZ See page 482 for the answers. Review concepts from this section in MyEconLab.

Interest is the price of obtaining credit. In the credit market, the rate of interest paid depends on the _____ of the loan, the _____, and the handling charges, among other things.

Nominal interest rates include a factor to take account of the _____ rate of inflation. Therefore, during periods of high _____ inflation, nominal interest rates will be relatively high.

Payments received or costs incurred in the future are worth less than those received or incurred today. The _____ _____ of any future sum is lower the further it occurs in the future and the greater the discount rate used.

Corporate Financing Methods

When the Dutch East India Company was founded in 1602, it raised financial capital by selling shares of its expected future profits to investors. The investors thus became the owners of the company, and their ownership shares eventually became known as "shares of stock," or simply *stocks*. The company also issued notes of indebtedness, which involved borrowing funds in return for interest paid on the funds, plus eventual repayment of the principal amount borrowed. In modern parlance, these notes of indebtedness are called *bonds*. As the company prospered over time, some of its revenues were used to pay lenders the interest and principal owed them. Of the profits that remained, some were paid to shareholders in the form of dividends. Some were retained by the company for reinvestment in further enterprises.

The methods of financing used by the Dutch East India Company four centuries ago—stocks, bonds, and reinvestment—remain the principal methods of financing for today's corporations.

Stocks

Share of stock
A legal claim to a share of a corporation's future profits. If it is *common stock*, it incorporates certain voting rights regarding major policy decisions of the corporation. If it is *preferred stock*, its owners are accorded preferential treatment in the payment of dividends but do not have any voting rights.

A **share of stock** in a corporation is simply a legal claim to a share of the corporation's future profits. If there are 100,000 shares of stock in a company and you own 1,000 of them, you own the right to 1 percent of that company's future profits. If the stock you own is *common stock*, you also have the right to vote on major policy decisions affecting the company, such as the selection of the corporation's board of directors. Your 1,000 shares would entitle you to cast 1 percent of the votes on such issues.

If the stock you own is *preferred stock*, you own a share of the future profits of the corporation but do *not* have regular voting rights. You do, however, get something in return for giving up your voting rights: preferential treatment in the payment of dividends. Specifically, the owners of preferred stock generally must receive at least a certain amount of dividends in each period before the owners of common stock can receive *any* dividends.

Bonds

Bond
A legal claim against a firm, usually entitling the owner of the bond to receive a fixed annual coupon payment, plus a lump-sum payment at the bond's maturity date. Bonds are issued in return for funds lent to the firm.

A **bond** is a legal claim against a firm, entitling the owner of the bond to receive a fixed annual *coupon* payment, plus a lump-sum payment at the maturity date of the bond. Bonds are issued in return for funds lent to the firm. The coupon payments represent interest on the amount borrowed by the firm, and the lump-sum payment at maturity of the bond generally equals the amount originally borrowed by the firm.

Bonds are *not* claims on the future profits of the firm. Legally, bondholders must be paid whether the firm prospers or not. To help ensure this, bondholders generally receive their coupon payments each year, along with any principal that is due, before *any* shareholders can receive dividend payments.

Why are a number of U.S. companies contemplating the issuance of bonds with 100-year maturities?

EXAMPLE

Explaining the Allure of "Century Bonds"

One special type of bond is a perpetual bond that pays a fixed annual coupon payment every year forever. The maximum price that people are willing to pay for a perpetual bond is the sum of discounted present values of all years' coupon payments from next year into the infinite future. Mathematically, this sum—that is, the maximum feasible price of the bond—turns out to equal the annual coupon payment divided by the interest rate.

Bonds with 100-year maturities, called century bonds, have finite maturities. Nevertheless, the discounted present value of coupon payments to be received 100 years from now is so small that the maximum feasible price of a century bond is close to being equal to the coupon payment divided by the interest rate. Today, market interest rates are so low that the implied maximum prices buyers are willing to pay for a century bond with a fixed annual coupon payment are substantial. This fact gives firms a stronger incentive to issue century bonds during the next few years, which explains why a number of U.S. firms have been considering this option.

FOR CRITICAL THINKING
If market interest rates were to rise in the future, what would happen to the prices of century bonds?

Reinvestment

Reinvestment takes place when the firm uses some of its profits to purchase new capital equipment rather than paying the profits out as dividends to shareholders. Although sales of stock are an important source of financing for new firms, reinvestment and borrowing are the primary means of financing for existing firms. Indeed, reinvestment by established firms is such an important source of financing that it dominates the other two sources of corporate finance, amounting to roughly 75 percent of new financial capital for corporations in recent years. Also, small businesses, which are the source of much current growth, commonly cannot rely on the stock market to raise investment funds.

Reinvestment
Profits (or depreciation reserves) used to purchase new capital equipment.

The Markets for Stocks and Bonds

Economists often refer to the "market for wheat" or the "market for labor," but these are concepts rather than actual places. For **securities** (stocks and bonds), however, there really are markets—centralized, physical locations where exchange takes place. The most prestigious of these markets are the New York Stock Exchange (NYSE) and the New York Bond Exchange, both located in New York City. More than 2,500 stocks are traded on the NYSE, which is sometimes called the "Big Board." Numerous other stock and bond markets, or exchanges, exist throughout the United States and in various financial capitals of the world, such as London and Tokyo.

Securities
Stocks and bonds.

Although the exact process by which exchanges are conducted in these markets varies slightly from one to another, the process used on the NYSE is representative of the principles involved. Essentially, brokers earn commissions from volumes of shares traded, while dealers attempt to profit from "buying low and selling high."

Even though the NYSE is traditionally the most prestigious of U.S. stock exchanges, it is no longer the largest. Since the mid-2000s, this title has belonged to the National Association of Securities Dealers Automated Quotations (NASDAQ), which began in 1971 as a tiny electronic network linking about 100 securities firms. Today, the NASDAQ market links about 500 dealers, and NASDAQ is home to nearly 4,000 stocks, including those of such companies as Amazon, Apple, Facebook, and Google.

The Theory of Efficient Markets

At any point in time, there are tens of thousands, even millions, of persons looking for any bit of information that will enable them to forecast correctly the future prices of stocks. Responding to any information that seems useful, these people try to buy low and sell high. The result is that all publicly available information that might be used to forecast stock prices gets taken into account by those with access to the information and the knowledge and ability to learn from it, leaving no predictable profit opportunities. And because so many people are involved in this process, it occurs quite swiftly. Indeed, there is some evidence that *all* information entering the market is fully incorporated into stock prices within less than a minute of its arrival. One view is that any information about specific stocks will prove to have little value by the time it reaches you.

Consequently, stock prices tend to drift upward following a *random walk*, which is to say that the best forecast of tomorrow's price is today's price plus the effect of any upward drift. This is called the **random walk theory.** Although large values of the random component of stock price changes are less likely than small values, nothing else about the magnitude or direction of a stock price change can be predicted.

Could artificial intelligences allow humans to "get rich quick"?

Random walk theory
The theory that there are no predictable trends in securities prices that can be used to "get rich quick."

INTERNATIONAL EXAMPLE

Utilizing Artificial Intelligence to Try to Beat the Market

Some global investment firms have developed artificial intelligence (AI) systems to manage their portfolios of stocks and bonds. These AI systems are designed to avoid predictable errors that humans are prone to make, according to the firms. A few financial firms now regularly utilize AI systems, which they claim can create portfolios of internationally issued securities that yield returns higher than those predicted by the random walk theory.

Teams of humans highly trained in mathematics and computer programming oversee these AI systems. The teams often substitute their own judgment for the AI systems' decisions whenever those choices appear likely to yield losses for the firms. To critics of the idea that AI systems can conduct trades in global stocks and bonds that can beat the market, regular interventions by human management teams reveal that AI systems cannot enable people to "get rich quick."

FOR CRITICAL THINKING
How might faster machine processing of information make the random walk theory more likely to hold true in global securities markets?

Inside Information

Isn't there any way to "beat the market"? The answer is yes—but normally only if you have **inside information** that is not available to the public. Suppose that your best friend is in charge of new product development at Google, the world's largest digital-information firm. Your friend tells you that the company's smartest programmer has just come up with major new software that millions of computer users will want to buy. No one but your friend and the programmer—and now you—is aware of this. You could indeed make a killing using this information by purchasing shares of Google and then selling them (at a higher price) as soon as the new product is publicly announced.

There is one problem: Stock trading based on inside information such as this is illegal, punishable by substantial fines and even imprisonment. So, unless you happen to have a stronger-than-average desire for a long vacation in a federal prison, you might be better off investing in Google after the new program is publicly announced.

Can the "Hindenburg Omen" prevent losses from stock market crashes?

Inside information
Information that is not available to the general public about what is happening in a corporation.

Go to www.econtoday.com/chap21 to explore how the U.S. Securities and Exchange Commission seeks to prevent the use of inside information.

EXAMPLE

Can the Hindenburg Omen Detect an Impending Market Crash?

In advance of a substantial stock market downturn in 1987, three events occurred. First, stock prices of 2.5 percent of firms on the New York Stock Exchange (NYSE) hit 52-week highs, while share prices of 2.5 percent of NYSE firms achieved new 52-week lows. Second, these events followed a long interval of increases in an average measure of all prices of NYSE stocks. Third, the value of a measure of stock price fluctuations became negative. Stock traders call these coinciding events the Hindenburg Omen—a signal of an impending stock market crash.

In August 2010, the Hindenburg Omen events occurred, so many traders responded by selling stocks. Their sales pushed share prices lower. By the end of the following September, stock prices had more than regained their earlier average—resulting in losses for traders who sold stocks based on the "omen." In fact, careful study of the Hindenburg Omen suggests that the omen precedes substantial average stock price declines only about 25 percent of the time.

FOR CRITICAL THINKING

Is the Hindenburg Omen consistent with the random walk theory? Explain.

QUICK QUIZ See page 482 for the answers. Review concepts from this section in MyEconLab.

The three primary sources of corporate funds are _____, _____, and _____ of profits.

A **share of stock** is a share of _____ providing a legal claim to a corporation's future profits. A _____ is a legal claim entitling the owner to a fixed annual coupon payment and to a lump-sum payment on the date it matures.

Many economists believe that asset markets, especially the stock market, are _____, meaning that one cannot

make a higher-than-normal rate of return without having inside information (information that the general public does not possess). Stock prices normally drift upward following a _____ _____, meaning that you cannot predict changes in future stock prices based on information about stock price behavior in the past.

YOU ARE THERE
College Hunks Hauling Junk Weighs Partnership Pros and Cons

In 2003, college students Nick Friedman and Omar Soliman earned income by removing old furniture and other items from people's homes. After they graduated and worked in the corporate world, they established a junk-removal business called College Hunks Hauling Junk. The two partners hired college students to carry out the same tasks they had undertaken in 2003, using trucks and other equipment the two had purchased and leased.

By 2011, Friedman and Soliman's partnership owned three U.S. offices and had 38 franchises that paid fees to use the company's trademarks and participate in a nationwide network of junk-hauling operations. At that time, some experts argued that the partners should form a corporation to gain the advantage of limited liability. Friedman and Soliman worried, however, about possible problems arising from separation

of ownership and control. In their view, a partnership allowed them to specialize in tasks to which each was best suited and offered lower costs of monitoring job performances. Thus, instead of organizing the growing business as a corporation, they instead merged it into another company called 1-800-Junk-USA—a business that the two continue to operate as a partnership.

Critical Thinking Questions

1. What tax advantage does a partnership offer to Friedman and Soliman, compared with tax issues confronted by a corporation?
2. What possible disadvantages might this business partnership face?

ISSUES & APPLICATIONS

CONCEPTS APPLIED

▶ Firms

▶ Proprietorships

▶ Partnerships

Shrinking Numbers of New Proprietorships, Partnerships, and Corporations

In the United States, fewer new proprietorships and partnerships are now opening for business each year than was true in previous years. In addition, fewer firms per year are opting to become publicly held corporations.

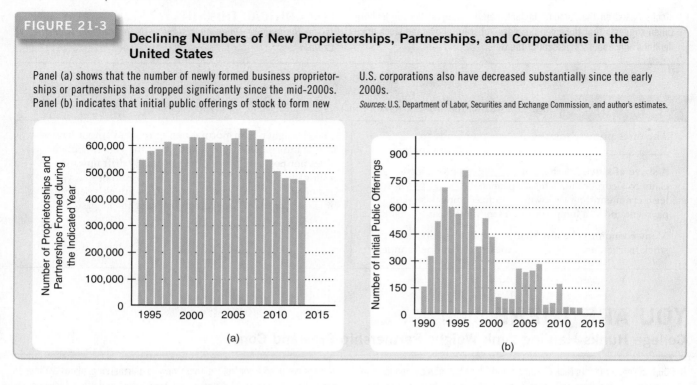

FIGURE 21-3

Declining Numbers of New Proprietorships, Partnerships, and Corporations in the United States

Panel (a) shows that the number of newly formed business proprietorships or partnerships has dropped significantly since the mid-2000s. Panel (b) indicates that initial public offerings of stock to form new

U.S. corporations also have decreased substantially since the early 2000s.

Sources: U.S. Department of Labor, Securities and Exchange Commission, and author's estimates.

(a)

(b)

Fewer New Firms Are Setting Up Shop

Panel (a) of Figure 21-3 above shows that through the mid-2000s, at least 600,000 new U.S. proprietorships and partnerships began operations each year. Since 2008, however, substantially smaller numbers of these firms have opened for business.

In addition, panel (b) shows that between 1991 and 1999, at least 300 proprietorships or partnerships reorganized annually as corporations via initial public offerings (IPOs) of stock. Since then, there have been many fewer IPOs.

Explaining the Shrinking Numbers of Each Type of Business

A fall in the number of proprietorships and partnerships opening their doors for the first time typically reflects low anticipation that brand-new businesses will be able to succeed. Consequently, the drop-off in formation of new business partnerships and proprietorships depicted in panel (a) of Figure 21-3 likely mainly reflects the dampened state of U.S. economic activity since 2008.

Something that Figure 21-3 does *not* show is that dozens of existing U.S. proprietorships and partnerships *have* chosen to incorporate in recent years. They have done so *outside* the United States. One reason to incorporate abroad is tougher regulations imposed on public corporations based in the United States. These regulations give some existing proprietorships and partnerships an incentive to incorporate abroad to avoid the costs of abiding by those

regulations. Another reason is that U.S. corporate tax rates are among the highest in the world, and undoubtedly a number of U.S. firms incorporate abroad to avoid paying these substantial tax rates.

For Critical Thinking

1. Why do you suppose that a brand-new firm rarely begins as a publicly held corporation?

2. How might tougher regulations and higher tax rates dissuade establishment of new business proprietorships and partnerships?

Web Resources

1. To learn about how a business can incorporate in your state, go to www.econtoday.com/chap21.

2. For information about why and how a U.S. firm might incorporate in the Virgin Islands, go to www.econtoday.com/chap21.

MyEconLab

For more questions on this chapter's Issues & Applications, go to MyEconLab. In the Study Plan for this chapter, select Section N: News.

MyEconLab

WHAT YOU SHOULD KNOW		WHERE TO GO TO PRACTICE
Economic Rent and Resource Allocation Owners of a resource with a perfectly inelastic supply curve, are paid economic rent, which is a payment for the use of any resource that exceeds the opportunity cost of the resource. The economic rents received by the owners of such a resource reflect the maximum market valuation of the resource's value.	economic rent, 463 **Key Figure** Figure 21-1, 463	• **MyEconLab** Study Plan 21.1 • Animated Figure 21-1
The Main Organizational Forms of Business and the Chief Advantages and Disadvantages of Each A proprietorship is owned by a single person, who makes the business decisions, is entitled to all the profits, and is subject to unlimited liability. A partnership has two or more owners, who share the responsibility for decision making, share the firm's profits, and individually bear unlimited liability for the firm's debts. Owners of corporations have limited liability, so their responsibility for the debts of the corporation is limited to the value of their ownership shares.	firm, 465 proprietorship, 466 unlimited liability, 466 partnership, 467 corporation, 467 limited liability, 467 dividends, 467	• **MyEconLab** Study Plan 21.2
Accounting Profits versus Economic Profits A firm's accounting profits equal its total revenues minus its total explicit costs, which are expenses directly paid out by the firm. Economic profits equal accounting profits minus implicit costs, which are expenses that managers do not have to pay out of pocket, such as the opportunity cost of factors of production dedicated to the firm's production process. Owners of a firm seek to maximize the firm's economic profits to ensure that they earn at least a normal rate of return, meaning that the firm's total revenues at least cover explicit costs and implicit opportunity costs.	explicit costs, 468 accounting profit, 468 implicit costs, 468 normal rate of return, 468 opportunity cost of capital, 468 economic profits, 469 **Key Figure** Figure 21-2, 469	• **MyEconLab** Study Plan 21.2 • Animated Figure 21-2
Interest Rates Interest is a payment for the ability to use resources today instead of in the future. The nominal interest rate includes a factor that takes into account the anticipated inflation rate, so during periods of high anticipated inflation, current market (nominal) interest rates are high. The interest rate allocates funds to investments that yield the highest (risk-adjusted) returns. Hence, resources are put to their most productive uses.	financial capital, 470 interest, 470 nominal rate of interest, 471 real rate of interest, 471	• **MyEconLab** Study Plan 21.3

MyEconLab *continued*

WHAT YOU SHOULD KNOW		WHERE TO GO TO PRACTICE
Calculating the Present Discounted Value of a Payment to Be Received at a Future Date The present value of a future payment is the value of the future amount expressed in today's dollars. It is equal to the most that someone would pay today to receive that amount in the future. The present value of a sum to be received a year from now is equal to the future amount divided by 1 plus the appropriate rate of interest, which is called the *rate of discount*.	present value, 472 discounting, 473 rate of discount, 473	• MyEconLab Study Plan 21.3
The Main Sources of Corporate Funds Stocks are ownership shares, promising a share of profits, sold to investors. Common stocks embody voting rights regarding the major decisions of the firm. Preferred stocks typically have no voting rights but enjoy priority status in the payment of dividends. Bonds are notes of indebtedness that pay interest in the form of annual coupon payments, plus repayment of the original principal amount upon maturity.	share of stock, 474 bond, 475 reinvestment, 475 securities, 475 random walk theory, 476 inside information, 476	• MyEconLab Study Plans 21.4, 21.5

Log in to MyEconLab, take a chapter test, and get a personalized Study Plan that tells you which concepts you understand and which ones you need to review. From there, MyEconLab will give you further practice, tutorials, animations, videos, and guided solutions. For more information, visit www.myeconlab.com

PROBLEMS

All problems are assignable in MyEconLab. *Answers to odd-numbered problems appear at the back of the book.*

21-1. Which of the following individuals would you expect to have a high level of economic rent, and which would you expect to have a low level of economic rent? Explain why for each. (See page 464.)

   a. Bob has a highly specialized medical skill shared by very few individuals.

   b. Sally has never attended school. She is 25 years old and is an internationally known supermodel.

   c. Tim is a high school teacher and sells insurance part time.

21-2. Which of the following individuals would you expect to have a high level of economic rent, and which would you expect to have a low level of economic rent? Explain why for each. (See page 464.)

   a. Emily quit high school at age 17, and she has since worked for several years as a waitress in fast-food restaurants.

   b. Demetrius earned a Ph.D. in financial economics, and he is among a handful of experts who specialize in assessing the values of highly complex securities traded in bond markets.

   c. Xin was a child prodigy on the violin, and after years of developing her skills, she is now rated among the most talented performing violinists in the world.

21-3. In which of the following situation(s) will owners who supply factors of production be most likely to earn economic rents? (See pages 463–464.)

   a. Highly elastic supply of the factor; highly elastic demand for the factor

   b. Highly elastic supply of the factor; highly inelastic demand for the factor

   c. Highly inelastic supply of the factor; highly inelastic demand for the factor

21-4. A British pharmaceutical company spent several years and considerable funds on the development of a treatment for HIV patients. Now, with the protection afforded by patent rights, the company has the potential to reap enormous gains. The government, in response, has threatened to tax away any economic rents the company may earn. Is this an advisable policy? Why or why not? (See page 464. Hint: Contrast the short-run and long-run effects of taxing away the economic rents.)

21-5. Write a brief explanation of the differences among a sole proprietorship, a partnership, and a corporation. In addition, list one advantage and one disadvantage of a proprietorship, a partnership, and a corporation. (See pages 465–467.)

21-6. After graduation, you face a choice. One option is to work for a multinational consulting firm and earn a starting salary (benefits included) of $40,000. The other option is to use $5,000 in savings to start your own consulting firm. You could earn an interest return of 5 percent on your savings. You choose to start your own consulting firm. At the end of the first year, you add up all of your expenses and revenues. Your total includes $12,000 in rent, $1,000 in office supplies, $20,000 for office staff, and $4,000 in telephone expenses. What are your total explicit costs and total implicit costs? (See page 468.)

21-7. Suppose, as in Problem 21-6, that you have now operated your consulting firm for a year. At the end of the first year, your total revenues are $77,250. Based on the information in Problem 21-6, what is the accounting profit, and what is your economic profit? (See pages 468–469.)

21-8. An individual leaves a college faculty, where she was earning $80,000 a year, to begin a new venture. She invests her savings of $20,000, which were earning 10 percent annually. She then spends $40,000 renting office equipment, hires two students at $60,000 a year each, rents office space for $24,000, and has other variable expenses of $80,000. At the end of the year, her revenues are $400,000. What are her accounting profit and her economic profit for the year? (See pages 468–469.)

21-9. Classify the following items as either financial capital or physical capital. (See page 470.)

a. A computer server owned by an information-processing company

b. $100,000 set aside in an account to purchase a computer server

c. Funds raised through a bond offer to expand plant and equipment

d. A warehouse owned by a shipping company

21-10. Explain the difference between the dividends of a corporation and the profits of a proprietorship or partnership, particularly in their tax treatment. (See pages 465–467.)

21-11. The owner of WebCity is trying to decide whether to remain a proprietorship or to incorporate. Suppose that the corporate tax rate on profits is 20 percent and the personal income tax rate is 30 percent. For simplicity, assume that all corporate profits (after corporate taxes are paid) are distributed as dividends in the year they are earned and that such dividends are subject to tax at the personal income tax rate. (See pages 465–467.)

a. If the owner of WebCity expects to earn $100,000 in before-tax profits this year, regardless of whether the firm is a proprietorship or a corporation, which method of organization should be chosen?

b. What is the dollar value of the after-tax advantage of the form of organization determined in part (a)?

c. Suppose that the corporate form of organization has cost advantages that will raise before-tax profits by $50,000. Should the owner of WebCity incorporate?

d. Based on parts (a) and (c), by how much will after-tax profits change due to incorporation?

e. Suppose that tax policy is changed to completely exempt from personal taxation the first $40,000 per year in dividends. Would this change in policy affect the decision made in part (a)?

f. How can you explain the fact that even though corporate profits are subject to double taxation, most business in the United States is conducted by corporations rather than by proprietorships or partnerships?

21-12. Explain how the following events would likely affect the relevant interest rate. (See page 471.)

a. A major bond-rating agency has improved the risk rating of a developing nation.

b. The government has passed legislation requiring bank regulators to significantly increase the paperwork required when a bank makes a loan.

21-13. Suppose that the interest rate in Japan is only 2 percent, while the comparable rate in the United States is 4 percent. Japan's rate of inflation is 0.5 percent, while the U.S. inflation rate is 3 percent. Which economy has the higher real interest rate? (See page 471.)

21-14. You expect to receive a payment of $104 one year from now. (See pages 472–473.)

a. Your discount rate is 4 percent. What is the present value of the payment to be received?

b. Suppose that your discount rate rises to 5 percent. What is the present value of the payment to be received?

21-15. Outline the differences between common stock and preferred stock. (See page 474.)

21-16. Explain the basic differences between a share of stock and a bond. (See page 474.)

21-17. Suppose that one of your classmates informs you that he has developed a method of forecasting stock market returns based on past trends. With a monetary investment from you, he claims that the two of you could profit handsomely from this forecasting method. How should you respond to your classmate? (See pages 475–476.)

21-18. Suppose that you are trying to decide whether to spend $1,000 on stocks issued by WildWeb or on bonds issued by the same company. There is a 50 percent chance that the value of the stock will rise to $2,200 at the end of the year and a 50 percent chance that the stock will be worthless at the end of

the year. The bonds promise an interest rate of 20 percent per year, and it is certain that the bonds and interest will be repaid at the end of the year. (See page 474.)

a. Assuming that your time horizon is exactly one year, will you choose the stocks or the bonds?

b. By how much is your expected end-of-year wealth reduced if you make the wrong choice?

c. Suppose the odds of success improve for WildWeb: Now there is a 60 percent chance that the value of the stock will be $2,200 at year's end and only a 40 percent chance that it will be worthless. Should you now choose the stocks or the bonds?

d. By how much did your expected end-of-year wealth rise as a result of the improved outlook for WildWeb?

ECONOMICS ON THE NET

How the New York Stock Exchange Operates This application gives you the chance to learn about the New York Stock Exchange.

Title: The New York Stock Exchange: Stocks

Navigation: Follow the link at **www.econtoday.com/chap21** to visit the New York Stock Exchange. Click on "About us" in the left margin for a pop-up menu, and then click on *Education*. Select the tab named *Educational Materials.* Click on "All about Investing" and then "Stocks." Read the article.

Application Answer the following questions.

1. Why might growth stocks have been issued by firms that just recently became corporations?

2. Discuss why the industries listed as likely issuers of cyclical stocks and defensive stocks typically satisfy these classifications.

For Group Study and Analysis Go back to the NYSE homepage. Under "Information," click on "For Individual Investors," and then click on "Indices," followed by "Index Directory"; click on *NYSE Indexes*, and read the article. Divide the class into groups, and assign each group to examine one among the five sets of indexes listed. Ask each group to evaluate how stock traders might use an index as a "benchmark" when evaluating whether to buy or sell stocks.

ANSWERS TO QUICK QUIZZES

p. 465: (i) inelastic; (ii) allocates . . . highest

p. 470: (i) Proprietorships . . . unlimited; (ii) Partnerships . . . unlimited; (iii) shareholders . . . limited; (iv) opportunity; (v) greater . . . maximize

p. 474: (i) length . . . risk; (ii) anticipated . . . anticipated; (iii) present value

p. 477: (i) stocks . . . bonds . . . reinvestment; (ii) ownership . . . bond; (iii) efficient . . . random walk

The Firm: Cost and Output Determination

22

The most expensive component of a hybrid or all-electric passenger vehicle is its set of battery packs. For many all-electric cars, battery packs account for more than half of the per-unit cost of producing the vehicles. Automakers have found that a way to reduce expenses on battery packs is to increase the overall rate of their production. For this reason, several firms are in the process of building facilities that produce battery packs in large numbers each year. They face a critical problem, however: Annual production of hybrid and all-electric passenger vehicles is much lower than the scales of operations at which these facilities are intended to operate. Reading this chapter will enable you to understand why the per-unit cost of producing battery packs for hybrid and all-electric vehicles varies with the scale of production of these items. Doing so will also help you to see why a low scale of vehicle production may interfere with the automakers' plans to reduce the cost of making battery packs—and hence of producing vehicles.

although consumers download the largest percentage of applications—
"apps"—used in digital devices, utilization of apps is growing at a more rapid pace in the business world?
Firms are employing apps in a variety of contexts, such as managing travel plans, tracking equipment, and
monitoring time that employees spend working on the road. Business apps are more costly than those most
commonly purchased by consumers, with prices typically ranging between $10 and $30 per month. Nevertheless,
firms that have integrated apps into their operations have discovered that utilizing digital apps enables them
to better organize their diverse resources in producing and distributing goods and services. The resulting
managerial coordination gains yield cost reductions much greater than the costs of the apps.

What are the determinants of a company's expenses? To understand the answer to this question, you must learn
about the nature of the costs that firms incur in their productive endeavors, which in turn requires contemplating how
firms employ inputs in the production of goods and services. This chapter considers each of these important topics.

Short Run versus Long Run

In Chapter 19, we discussed short-run and long-run price elasticities of supply and
demand. As you will recall, for consumers, the long run means the time period during
which all adjustments to a change in price can be made, and anything shorter than that
is considered the short run. For suppliers, the long run is the time in which all adjustments can be made, and anything shorter than that is the short run. Now that we are
discussing firms only, we will maintain a similar distinction between the short and the
long run, but we will be more specific.

The Short Run

Short run
The time period during which at least one
input, such as plant size, cannot be
changed.

Plant size
The physical size of the factories that a
firm owns and operates to produce its
output. Plant size can be defined by square
footage, maximum physical capacity, and
other physical measures.

In the theory of the firm, the **short run** is defined as any time period so short that
there is at least one input, such as current **plant size,** that the firm cannot alter. In
other words, during the short run, a firm makes do with whatever big machines and
factory size it already has, no matter how much more it wants to produce because of
increased demand for its product. We consider the plant and heavy equipment, the size
or amount of which cannot be varied in the short run, as *fixed* resources. In agriculture
and in some other businesses, land may be a fixed resource.

There are, of course, variable resources that the firm can alter when it wants to
change its rate of production. These are called *variable inputs* or *variable factors of production*. Typically, the variable inputs of a firm are its labor and its purchases of raw
materials. In the short run, in response to changes in demand, the firm can, by definition, change only the amounts of its variable inputs.

The Long Run

Long run
The time period during which all factors of
production can be varied.

The **long run** can now be considered the period of time in which *all* inputs can be
varied. Specifically, in the long run, the firm can alter its plant size. How long is the
long run? That depends on each individual industry. For Wendy's or McDonald's, the
long run may be four or five months, because that is the time it takes to add new franchises. For a steel company, the long run may be several years, because that's how long
it takes to plan and build a new plant. An electric utility might need more than a decade to build a new plant.

Short run and *long run* in our discussion are terms that apply to planning decisions
made by managers. Managers routinely take account of both the short-run and the
long-run consequences of their behavior. While always making decisions about what
to do today, tomorrow, and next week—the short run as it were—they keep an eye on
the long-run net benefits of all short-run actions. As an individual, you have long-run
plans, such as going to graduate school or having a successful career, and you make a
series of short-run decisions with these long-run plans in mind.

The Relationship between Output and Inputs

A firm takes numerous inputs, combines them using a technological production process, and ends up with an output. There are, of course, a great many factors of production, or inputs. Keeping the quantity of land fixed, we classify production inputs into two broad categories—capital and labor. The relationship between output and these two inputs is as follows:

Output per time period = some function of capital and labor inputs

We have used the word *production* but have not defined it. **Production** is any process by which resources are transformed into goods or services. Production includes not only making things but also transporting them, retailing, repackaging them, and so on. Notice that the production relationship tells nothing about the worth or value of the inputs or the output.

Production
Any activity that results in the conversion of resources into products.

The Production Function: A Numerical Example

The relationship between maximum physical output and the quantity of capital and labor used in the production process is sometimes called the **production function**. The production function is a technological relationship between inputs and output.

PROPERTIES OF THE PRODUCTION FUNCTION The production function specifies the maximum possible output that can be produced with a given amount of inputs. It also specifies the minimum amount of inputs necessary to produce a given level of output. Firms that are inefficient or wasteful in their use of capital and labor will obtain less output than the production function will show. No firm can obtain more output than the production function allows, however. The production function also depends on the technology available to the firm. It follows that an improvement in technology that allows the firm to produce more output with the same amount of inputs (or the same output with fewer inputs) results in a new production function.

How is three-dimensional printing technology allowing firms to produce more output using the same inputs?

Production function
The relationship between inputs and maximum physical output. A production function is a technological, not an economic, relationship.

EXAMPLE

3D Printers Shift from Design to Production

Engineers and designers have used three-dimensional (3D) printers since the late 1990s. The printers deposit materials in successive, thin layers until a solid 3D model emerges. Printing physical models of products from two-dimensional computer designs has enabled companies to reduce considerably the expenses entailed in paying skilled workers to construct models by hand.

In recent years, many firms have shifted away from using 3D printers solely to design products. These firms now utilize modified versions of 3D printers to produce goods in their *final* forms. Products now "printed" include highly specialized gloves, airline parts, dental crowns, and body

parts for racecars. Materials used in 3D-print production include nylons, plastic, carbon fiber, stainless steel, and titanium. Because the modified form of 3D printing constructs a product in fine layers, the production process entails much less waste of raw materials. Thus, modified 3D printing makes it possible to produce either the same output with fewer inputs or more output with the same quantities of inputs.

FOR CRITICAL THINKING
What happens when managers do not use the best available production procedures?

Panel (a) of Figure 22-1 on the next page shows a production function relating maximum output in column 2 to the quantity of labor in column 1. Zero workers per week produce no output. Five workers per week of input produce a total output of 50 computer servers per week. (Ignore for the moment the rest of that panel.) Panel (b) of Figure 22-1 displays this production function. It relates to the short run, because plant size is fixed, and it applies to a single firm.

FIGURE 22-1

The Production Function and Marginal Product: A Hypothetical Case

Marginal product is the addition to the total product that results when one additional worker is hired (for a week in this example). Thus, in panel (a), the marginal product of adding the fourth worker is eight computer servers. With four workers, 44 servers are produced, but with three workers, only 36 are produced. The difference is 8. In panel (b), we plot the numbers from columns 1 and 2 of panel (a). In panel (c), we plot the numbers from columns 1 and 4 of panel (a). When we go from 0 to 1,

marginal product is 10. When we go from one worker to two workers, marginal product increases to 16. After two workers, marginal product declines, but it is still positive. Total product (output) reaches its peak at about seven workers, so after seven workers, marginal product is negative. When we move from seven to eight workers, marginal product becomes −1 computer server per week.

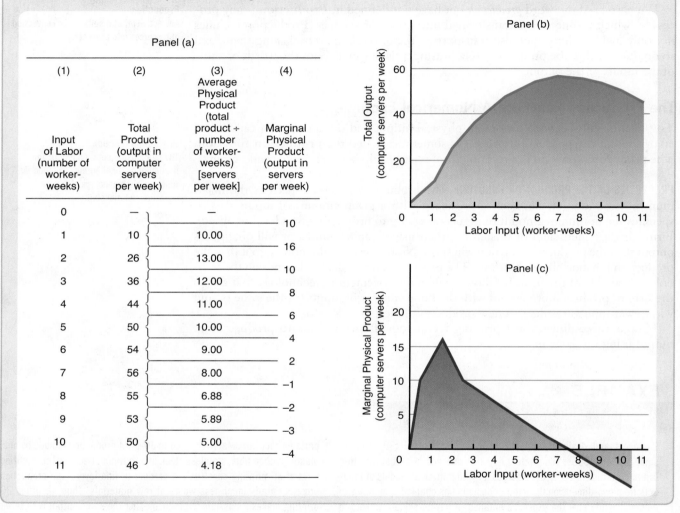

Panel (a)

(1) Input of Labor (number of worker-weeks)	(2) Total Product (output in computer servers per week)	(3) Average Physical Product (total product ÷ number of worker-weeks) [servers per week]	(4) Marginal Physical Product (output in servers per week)
0	—	—	
1	10	10.00	10
2	26	13.00	16
3	36	12.00	10
4	44	11.00	8
5	50	10.00	6
6	54	9.00	4
7	56	8.00	2
8	55	6.88	−1
9	53	5.89	−2
10	50	5.00	−3
11	46	4.18	−4

TOTAL PHYSICAL PRODUCT Panel (b) shows a total physical product curve, or the maximum feasible output when we add successive equal-sized units of labor while holding all other inputs constant. The graph of the production function in panel (b) is not a straight line. It peaks at about seven workers per week and then starts to go down.

Average and Marginal Physical Product

To understand the shape of the total physical product curve, let's examine columns 3 and 4 of panel (a) of Figure 22-1 above—that is, average and marginal physical products. **Average physical product** is the total product divided by the number of worker-weeks. You can see in column 3 of panel (a) of Figure 22-1 that the average physical product of labor first rises and then steadily falls after two workers are hired.

Average physical product
Total product divided by the variable input.

Marginal means "additional," so the **marginal physical product** of labor is the *change* in total product that occurs when a worker is added to a production process for a given interval. (The term *physical* here emphasizes the fact that we are measuring in terms of material quantities of goods or tangible amounts of services, not in dollar terms.) The marginal physical product of labor therefore refers to the *change in output caused by a one-unit change in the labor input* as shown in column 4 of panel (a) of Figure 22-1 on the facing page. (Marginal physical product is also referred to as *marginal product*.)

Marginal physical product
The physical output that is due to the addition of one more unit of a variable factor of production. The change in total product occurring when a variable input is increased and all other inputs are held constant. It is also called *marginal product*.

Diminishing Marginal Product

Note that in Figure 22-1, when three workers instead of two are employed each week, marginal product declines. The concept of diminishing marginal product applies to many situations. If you put a seat belt across your lap, a certain amount of safety is obtained. If you add another seat belt over your shoulder, some additional safety is obtained, but less than when the first belt was secured. When you use three seat belts rather than two over the other shoulder, the amount of *additional* safety obtained is even smaller.

Measuring Diminishing Marginal Product

How do we measure diminishing marginal product? First, we limit the analysis to only one variable factor of production (or input)—let's say the factor is labor. Every other factor of production, such as machines, must be held constant. Only in this way can we calculate the marginal product from utilizing more workers with the fixed factors, including machines, and know when we reach the point of diminishing marginal product.

INITIALLY INCREASING MARGINAL PRODUCT The marginal product of labor may increase rapidly at the very beginning. Suppose that a firm starts with no workers, and only two machines. When the firm hires one worker instead of zero, that individual can use both of the firm's machines for producing output, so production jumps. Then, when the firm hires two workers instead of just one, each of the two individuals can utilize a machine to produce output, and production leaps upward again. Indeed, the marginal product from hiring two workers instead of one may be greater than hiring one worker instead of zero. This is the situation displayed Figure 22-1, in which hiring two workers instead of one yields a marginal product of 16 units of output, which exceeds the 10 units of output gained when one worker is hired instead of zero.

DIMINISHING MARGINAL PRODUCT Beyond some point, marginal product must begin to diminish as more workers are hired—*not* because additional workers are less qualified but because each worker has, on average, fewer machines with which to work (remember, all other inputs are fixed). In Figure 22-1, when three workers instead of two are hired to use two machines, the third worker must perform subsidiary tasks, such as moving raw materials or boxing up completed units of output. Total production rises as a consequence, but not by as much as was the case when two workers rather than one were hired. Consequently, the marginal product when three workers instead of two are hired drops to 10 units, which is lower than the 16 units of output gained when two workers are hired instead of one. In fact, eventually the firm's plant will become so crowded that workers will start to get in each other's way. At that point, marginal physical product becomes negative, and total production declines.

Using these ideas, we can define the **law of diminishing marginal product:**

As successive equal increases in a variable factor of production are added to fixed factors of production, there will be a point beyond which the extra, or marginal, product that can be attributed to each additional unit of the variable factor of production will decline.

Law of diminishing marginal product
The observation that after some point, successive equal-sized increases in a variable factor of production, such as labor, added to fixed factors of production will result in smaller increases in output.

Note that the law of diminishing marginal product is a statement about the *physical* relationships between inputs and outputs that we have observed in many firms. If the law of diminishing marginal product were not a fairly accurate statement about the world, what would stop firms from hiring additional workers forever?

An Example of the Law of Diminishing Marginal Product

Production of computer servers provides an example of the law of diminishing marginal product. With a fixed amount of factory space, assembly equipment, and quality-control diagnostic software, the addition of more workers eventually yields successively smaller increases in output. After a while, when all the assembly equipment and quality-control diagnostic software are being used, additional workers will have to start assembling and troubleshooting quality problems manually. Output will not rise as much as when workers were added before this point, because the assembly equipment and diagnostic software are all in use. The marginal physical product of adding a worker, given a specified amount of capital, must eventually be less than that for the previous workers.

GRAPHING THE MARGINAL PRODUCT OF LABOR A hypothetical set of numbers illustrating the law of diminishing marginal product is presented in panel (a) of Figure 22-1 on page 486. The numbers are presented graphically in panel (c). Marginal productivity (additional output from adding more workers during a week) first increases, then decreases, and finally becomes negative.

When one worker is hired, total output goes from 0 to 10. Thus, marginal physical product is 10 computer servers per week. When two workers instead of one are hired, total product goes from 10 to 26 servers per week. Marginal physical product therefore increases to 16 servers per week. When three workers rather than two are hired, total product again increases, from 26 to 36 servers per week. This represents a marginal physical product of only 10 servers per week. Therefore, the point of diminishing marginal product occurs after two workers are hired.

THE POINT OF SATURATION Notice that after seven workers per week, marginal physical product becomes negative. That means that eight workers instead of seven would reduce total product. Sometimes this is called the *point of saturation*, indicating that given the amount of fixed inputs, there is no further positive use for more of the variable input. We have entered the region of negative marginal product.

How are oil companies determining which rock formations beneath the Gulf of Mexico will yield the highest feasible levels of marginal physical product?

EXAMPLE

Evaluating the Marginal Physical Product of Oil Drilling

Chevron has been contemplating more than 100 prospective locations for oil drilling in the Gulf of Mexico. To decide which areas are likely to offer the largest increases in the company's oil output—that is, the highest levels of marginal physical product—Chevron's staff of geophysicists aims sonic booms onto the Gulf's floor. On the basis of data gathered by sensors indicating energy shifts within different areas, the firm's scientists can distinguish between geologic formations containing solid rock and those with ridges of rock lining pools of oil. In this way, the geophysicists can estimate levels of marginal physical product

from efforts to extract oil in differing areas beneath the Gulf of Mexico. The company is using these estimates in planning where it initially should put employees to work extracting oil with underwater drilling equipment.

FOR CRITICAL THINKING
As Chevron adds more units of labor to the extraction of oil in different areas beneath the Gulf, what ultimately must happen to marginal physical product?

The technological relationship between output and inputs is called the _____ function. It relates _____ per time period to several inputs, such as capital and labor.

After some rate of output, the firm generally experiences diminishing marginal _____.

The law of diminishing marginal product states that if all factors of production are held constant except one, equal increments in that one variable factor will eventually yield _____ increments in _____.

Short-Run Costs to the Firm

You will see that costs are the extension of the production ideas just presented. Let's consider the costs the firm faces in the short run. To make this example simple, assume that there are only two factors of production, capital and labor. Our definition of the short run will be the time during which capital is fixed but labor is variable.

In the short run, a firm incurs certain types of costs. We label all costs incurred **total costs.** Then we break total costs down into total fixed costs and total variable costs, which we will explain shortly. Therefore,

Total costs (TC) = total fixed costs (TFC) + total variable costs (TVC)

Remember that these total costs include both explicit and implicit costs, including the normal rate of return on investment.

After we have looked at the elements of total costs, we will find out how to compute average and marginal costs.

Total costs
The sum of total fixed costs and total variable costs.

Total Fixed Costs

Let's look at an ongoing business such as Apple. The decision makers in that corporate giant can look around and see big machines, thousands of parts, huge buildings, and a multitude of other components of plant and equipment that have already been acquired and are in place. Apple has to take into account expenses to replace some worn-out equipment, no matter how many digital devices it produces. The opportunity costs of any fixed resources that Apple owns will all be the same regardless of the rate of output. In the short run, these costs are the same for Apple no matter how many digital devices it produces.

We also have to point out that the opportunity cost (or normal rate of return) of capital must be included along with other costs. Remember that we are dealing in the short run, during which capital is fixed. This leads us to a very straightforward definition of fixed costs: All costs that do not vary—that is, all costs that do not depend on the rate of production—are called **fixed costs.**

Let's now take as an example the fixed costs incurred by a producer of magneto optical (MO) disks used with digital devices. This firm's total fixed costs will usually include the cost of the rent for its plant and equipment and the insurance it has to pay. We see in panel (a) of Figure 22-2 on the next page that total fixed costs per hour are $10. In panel (b), these total fixed costs are represented by the horizontal line at $10 per hour. They are invariant to changes in the daily output of MO disks—no matter how many are produced, fixed costs will remain at $10 per hour.

Fixed costs
Costs that do not vary with output. Fixed costs typically include such expenses as rent on a building. These costs are fixed for a certain period of time (in the long run, though, they are variable).

Total Variable Costs

Total **variable costs** are costs whose magnitude varies with the rate of production. Wages are an obvious variable cost. The more the firm produces, the more labor it has to hire. Therefore, the more wages it has to pay. Parts are another variable cost. To manufacture MO disks, for example, ferromagnetic material must be bought. The more MO disks that are made, the more ferromagnetic material that must be bought. A portion of

Variable costs
Costs that vary with the rate of production. They include wages paid to workers and purchases of materials.

FIGURE 22-2

Cost of Production: An Example

In panel (a), the derivations of columns 4 through 9 are given in parentheses in each column heading. For example, in column 6, average variable costs are derived by dividing column 3, total variable costs, by column 1, total output per hour. Note that marginal cost (MC) in panel (c) intersects average variable costs (AVC) at the latter's minimum point. Also, MC intersects average total costs (ATC) at that latter's minimum point. It is a little more difficult to see that MC equals AVC and ATC at their respective minimum points in panel (a) because we are using discrete one-unit changes. You can see, though, that the marginal cost of going from 4 units per hour to 5 units per hour is $2 and increases to $3 when we move to 6 units per hour. Somewhere in between it equals AVC of $2.60, which is in fact the minimum average variable cost. The same analysis holds for ATC, which hits its respective minimum at 7 units per day at $4.28 per unit. MC goes from $4 to $5 and just equals ATC somewhere in between.

Panel (a)

(1) Total Output (Q/hour)	(2) Total Fixed Costs (TFC)	(3) Total Variable Costs (TVC)	(4) Total Costs (TC) (4) = (2) + (3)	(5) Average Fixed Costs (AFC) (5) = (2) ÷ (1)	(6) Average Variable Costs (AVC) (6) = (3) ÷ (1)	(7) Average Total Costs (ATC) (7) = (4) ÷ (1)	(8) Total Costs (TC) (4)	(9) Marginal Cost (MC) $(9) = \dfrac{\text{Change in (8)}}{\text{Change in (1)}}$
0	$10	$ 0	$10	—	—	—	$10	$5
1	10	5	15	$10.00	$5.00	$15.00	15	3
2	10	8	18	5.00	4.00	9.00	18	2
3	10	10	20	3.33	3.33	6.67	20	1
4	10	11	21	2.50	2.75	5.25	21	2
5	10	13	23	2.00	2.60	4.60	23	3
6	10	16	26	1.67	2.67	4.33	26	4
7	10	20	30	1.43	2.86	4.28	30	5
8	10	25	35	1.25	3.12	4.38	35	6
9	10	31	41	1.11	3.44	4.56	41	7
10	10	38	48	1.00	3.80	4.80	48	8
11	10	46	56	.91	4.18	5.09	56	

Panel (b)

Panel (c)

the rate of depreciation (wear and tear) on machines that are used in the assembly process can also be considered a variable cost if depreciation depends partly on how long and how intensively the machines are used. Total variable costs are given in column 3 in panel (a) of Figure 22-2 on the facing page. These are translated into the total variable cost curve in panel (b). Notice that the total variable cost curve lies below the total cost curve by the vertical distance of $10. This vertical distance of course, represents, total fixed costs.

What new training methods are allowing the U.S. Army to reduce its total variable costs?

YOU ARE THERE

To consider how a trucking firm is using software simulations to reduce its total fixed and variable costs, take a look at **Cutting Costs by Replacing Pilot Projects with Simulations** on page 501.

POLICY EXAMPLE

How the U.S. Army Uses Virtual Warfare to Cut Variable Costs

For the U.S. Army, keeping soldiers in top training form for fighting actual battles has long required the conduct of war games. Every practice battle, though, has entailed costly wear and tear on equipment, used up ammunition, and caused inadvertent injuries to personnel. As a result, the variable costs of training soldiers in the art of warfare have been substantial.

To reduce its training expenses, the Army is turning to digital devices such as smartphones and tablet devices. For training exercises intended mainly to reinforce individual responsibilities and principles of unit coordination, the Army is keeping most equipment in storage and reducing physical demands on soldiers. Instead, it is arming soldiers with digital devices on which they can simulate field exercises via electronic games, apps, and avatars. This approach has enabled the Army to decrease considerably the number of war games conducted with fully equipped forces and, hence, the expenses of training its soldiers. In this way, the Army has slashed its variable costs.

FOR CRITICAL THINKING

Why is it that in the short run, military leaders view mechanized equipment as fixed inputs but regard soldiers as variable inputs that generate variable costs?

Short-Run Average Cost Curves

In panel (b) of Figure 22-2, we see total costs, total variable costs, and total fixed costs. Now we want to look at average cost. With the average cost concept, we are measuring cost per unit of output. It is a matter of simple arithmetic to figure the averages of these three cost concepts. We can define them as follows:

$$\text{Average total costs (ATC)} = \frac{\text{total costs (TC)}}{\text{output (}Q\text{)}}$$

$$\text{Average variable costs (AVC)} = \frac{\text{total variable costs (TVC)}}{\text{output (}Q\text{)}}$$

$$\text{Average fixed costs (AFC)} = \frac{\text{total fixed costs (TFC)}}{\text{output (}Q\text{)}}$$

The arithmetic is done in columns 5, 6, and 7 in panel (a) of Figure 22-2. The numerical results are translated into a graphical format in panel (c). Because total costs (TC) equal variable costs (TVC) plus fixed costs (TFC), the difference between average total costs (ATC) and average variable costs (AVC) will always be identical to average fixed costs (AFC). That means that average total costs and average variable costs move together as output expands.

Now let's see what we can observe about the three average cost curves in Figure 22-2.

AVERAGE FIXED COSTS (AFC) **Average fixed costs** continue to fall throughout the output range. In fact, if we were to continue panel (c) of Figure 22-2 farther to the right, we would find that average fixed costs would get closer and closer to the horizontal axis. That is because total fixed costs remain constant. As we divide this fixed number by a larger and larger number of units of output, the resulting AFC becomes smaller and smaller. In business, this is called "spreading the overhead."

Average fixed costs
Total fixed costs divided by the number of units produced.

Average variable costs
Total variable costs divided by the number of units produced.

AVERAGE VARIABLE COSTS (AVC) We assume a particular form of the curve for **average variable costs.** The form that it takes is U-shaped: First it falls; then it starts to rise. (It is possible for the AVC curve to take other shapes in the long run.)

Average total costs
Total costs divided by the number of units produced; sometimes called *average per-unit total costs.*

AVERAGE TOTAL COSTS (ATC) This curve has a shape similar to that of the AVC curve. Nevertheless, it falls even more dramatically in the beginning and rises more slowly after it has reached a minimum point. It falls and then rises because **average total costs** are the vertical summation of the AFC curve and the AVC curve. Thus, when AFC and AVC are both falling, ATC must fall too. At some point, however, AVC starts to increase while AFC continues to fall. Once the increase in the AVC curve outweighs the decrease in the AFC curve, the ATC curve will start to increase and will develop a U shape, just like the AVC curve.

How are oil companies around the globe reducing the average total cost of removing leftover oil in aging oil fields?

INTERNATIONAL EXAMPLE

Using Cheap Power from the Sun to Reduce Average Total Costs

From the oil fields of Texas to the sands of Saudi Arabia, extracting small pools of oil that remain after completion of traditional drilling operations could be accomplished only at a very high average total cost. To reduce these per-unit costs of removing oil from old sites throughout the world, a number of firms are now utilizing the power of reflected heat waves from the sun.

The companies use inexpensive aluminum mirrors to reflect and focus energy waves from the sun into networks of pipes. The solar waves heat water within the pipes, which gushes out as steam into pockets containing remaining pools of oil. The steam, in turn, pushes the oil out

of these pockets, and other equipment collects the oil and transfers it to barrels for transport to refining facilities. Because this oil collection method is much less costly than sinking drills into old fields time and time again, it greatly reduces the average total cost of extracting oil from the fields.

FOR CRITICAL THINKING
If using solar energy to heat steam reduces the per-unit cost of extracting each possible quantity of oil, what happens to the average total cost curve?

Marginal Cost

We have stated repeatedly that the basis of decisions is always on the margin—movement in economics is always determined at the margin. This dictum also holds true within the firm. Firms, according to the analysis we use to predict their behavior, are very concerned with their **marginal costs.** Because the term *marginal* means "additional" or "incremental" (or "decremental," too) here, *marginal costs* refer to costs that result from a one-unit change in the production rate. For example, if the production of 10 magneto optical (MO) disks per hour costs a firm $48 and the production of 11 MO disks costs $56 per hour, the marginal cost of producing 11 rather than 10 MO disks per hour is $8.

Marginal costs
The change in total costs due to a one-unit change in production rate.

Marginal costs can be measured by using the formula

$$\text{Marginal cost} = \frac{\text{change in total cost}}{\text{change in output}}$$

We show the marginal costs of production of MO disks per hour in column 9 of panel (a) in Figure 22-2 on page 490, computed according to the formula just given. In our example, we have changed output by one unit every time, so the denominator in that particular formula always equals one.

This marginal cost schedule is shown graphically in panel (c) of Figure 22-2. Just as average variable costs and average total costs initially decrease with rising output and then increase, it must also be true that marginal cost first falls with greater output and then rises. The U shape of the marginal cost curve is a result of increasing and then diminishing marginal product. At lower levels of output, the marginal cost curve declines.

The reasoning is that as marginal physical product increases with each addition of output, the marginal cost of this last unit of output must fall.

Conversely, when diminishing marginal product sets in, marginal physical product decreases (and eventually becomes negative). It follows that the marginal cost must rise when the marginal product begins its decline. These relationships are clearly reflected in the geometry of panels (b) and (c) of Figure 22-2 on page 490.

In summary:

Over the range of output along which marginal physical product rises, marginal cost will fall. At the output at which marginal physical product starts to fall (after reaching the point of diminishing marginal product), marginal cost will begin to rise.

The Relationship between Average and Marginal Costs

Let us now examine the relationship between average costs and marginal costs. There is always a definite relationship between averages and marginals. Consider the example of 10 football players with an average weight of 250 pounds. An eleventh player is added. His weight is 300 pounds. That represents the marginal weight. What happens now to the average weight of the team? It must increase. That is, when the marginal player weighs more than the average, the average must increase. Likewise, if the marginal player weighs less than 250 pounds, the average weight will decrease.

AVERAGE VARIABLE COSTS AND MARGINAL COSTS There is a similar relationship between average variable costs and marginal costs. As shown in Figure 22-2, when marginal costs are less than average costs, the latter must fall. Conversely, when marginal costs are greater than average costs, the latter must rise.

When you think about it, the relationship makes sense. The only way average variable costs can fall is if the extra cost of the marginal unit produced is less than the average variable cost of all the preceding units. For example, if the average variable cost for two units of production is $4.00 a unit, the only way for the average variable cost of three units to be less than that of two units is for the variable costs attributable to the last unit—the marginal cost—to be less than the average of the past units. In this particular case, if average variable cost falls to $3.33 a unit, total variable cost for the three units would be three times $3.33, or almost exactly $10.00. Total variable cost for two units is two times $4.00 (average variable cost), or $8.00. The marginal cost is therefore $10.00 minus $8.00, or $2.00, which is less than the average variable cost of $3.33.

A similar type of computation can be carried out for rising average variable costs. The only way average variable costs can rise is if the average variable cost of additional units is more than that for units already produced. But the incremental cost is the marginal cost. In this particular case, the marginal costs have to be higher than the average variable costs.

AVERAGE TOTAL COSTS AND MARGINAL COSTS There is also a relationship between marginal costs and average total costs. Remember that average total cost is equal to total costs divided by the number of units produced. Also remember that marginal cost does not include any fixed costs. Fixed costs are, by definition, fixed and cannot influence marginal costs. Our example can therefore be repeated substituting *average total costs* for *average variable costs*.

These rising and falling relationships can be seen in panel (c) of Figure 22-2, where MC intersects AVC and ATC at their respective minimum points.

Minimum Cost Points

At what rate of output of MO disks per hour does our representative firm experience the minimum average total costs? Column 7 in panel (a) of Figure 22-2 shows that the minimum average total cost is $4.28, which occurs at an output rate of seven MO disks per hour. We can also find this minimum cost by finding the point in panel (c) of

Figure 22-2 on page 490 where the marginal cost curve intersects the average total cost curve. This should not be surprising. When marginal cost is below average total cost, average total cost falls. When marginal cost is above average total cost, average total cost rises. At the point where average total cost is neither falling nor rising, marginal cost must then be equal to average total cost. When we represent this graphically, the marginal cost curve will intersect the average total cost curve at the latter's minimum.

The same analysis applies to the intersection of the marginal cost curve and the average variable cost curve. When are average variable costs at a minimum? According to panel (a) of Figure 22-2, average variable costs are at a minimum of $2.60 at an output rate of five MO disks per hour. This is where the marginal cost curve intersects the average variable cost curve in panel (c) of Figure 22-2.

QUICK QUIZ See page 506 for the answers. Review concepts from this section in MyEconLab.

Total costs equal total _____ costs plus total _____ costs. Fixed costs are those that do not vary with the rate of production. Variable costs are those that do vary with the rate of production.

_____ total costs equal total costs divided by output (_____ = TC/Q).

Average _____ costs equal total variable costs divided by output (_____ = TVC/Q).

Average _____ costs equal total fixed costs divided by output (_____ = TVC/Q).

_____ cost equals the change in _____ cost divided by the change in output (_____ = Δ_____/ΔQ, where the Greek letter Δ, delta, means "change in").

The marginal cost curve intersects the _____ point of the average total cost curve and the _____ point of the average variable cost curve.

The Relationship between Diminishing Marginal Product and Cost Curves

There is a unique relationship between output and the shape of the various cost curves we have drawn. Let's consider mobile wireless account services and the relationship between marginal cost and diminishing marginal physical product shown in panel (a) of Figure 22-3 on the facing page. It turns out that if wage rates are constant, the shape of the marginal cost curve in panel (d) of Figure 22-3 is both a reflection of and a consequence of the law of diminishing marginal product.

Marginal Cost and Marginal Physical Product

Let's assume that each unit of labor can be purchased at a constant price. Further assume that labor is the only variable input. We see that as more workers are hired, marginal physical product first rises and then falls. The marginal cost of each extra unit of output will first fall as long as marginal physical product is rising, and then it will rise as long as marginal physical product is falling. Recall that marginal cost is defined as

$$MC = \frac{\text{change in total cost}}{\text{change in output}}$$

Because the price of labor is assumed to be constant, the change in total cost depends solely on the unchanged price of labor, W. The change in output is simply the marginal physical product (MPP) of the one-unit increase in labor. Therefore, we see that

$$\text{Marginal cost} = \frac{W}{\text{MPP}}$$

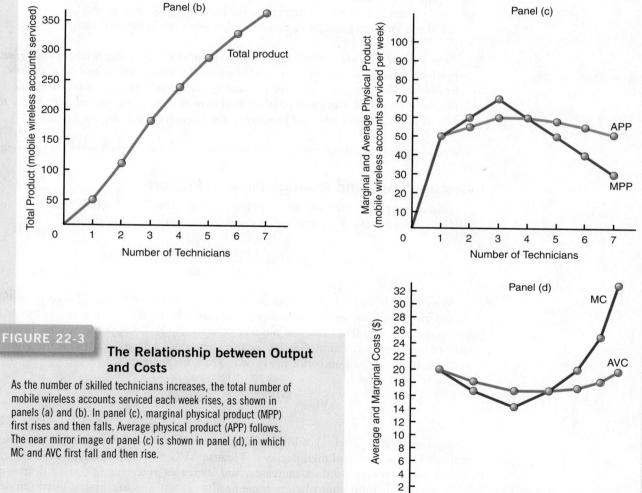

Panel (a)

(1) Labor Input	(2) Total Product (number of mobile wireless accounts serviced per week)	(3) Average Physical Product (accounts per technician) (3) = (2) ÷ (1)	(4) Marginal Physical Product	(5) Average Variable Cost (5) = W ($1,000) ÷ (3)	(6) Marginal Cost (6) = W ($1,000) ÷ (4)
0	0	—	—	—	—
1	50	50	50	$20.00	$20.00
2	110	55	60	18.18	16.67
3	180	60	70	16.67	14.29
4	240	60	60	16.67	16.67
5	290	58	50	17.24	20.00
6	330	55	40	18.18	25.00
7	360	51	30	19.61	33.33

FIGURE 22-3

The Relationship between Output and Costs

As the number of skilled technicians increases, the total number of mobile wireless accounts serviced each week rises, as shown in panels (a) and (b). In panel (c), marginal physical product (MPP) first rises and then falls. Average physical product (APP) follows. The near mirror image of panel (c) is shown in panel (d), in which MC and AVC first fall and then rise.

This means that initially, when marginal physical product is increasing, marginal cost falls (we are dividing W by increasingly larger numbers), and later, when marginal product is falling, marginal cost must increase (we are dividing W by smaller numbers). So, as marginal physical product increases, marginal cost decreases, and as marginal physical product decreases, marginal cost must increase. Thus, when marginal physical product reaches its maximum, marginal cost necessarily reaches its minimum.

An Illustration

To illustrate this, let's return to Figure 22-1 on page 486 and consider specifically panel (a). Assume that a skilled worker assembling computer servers is paid $1,000 a week. When we go from zero labor input to one unit, output increases by 10 computer servers. Each of those 10 servers has a marginal cost of $100. Now the second unit of labor is hired, and this individual costs $1,000 per week. Output increases by 16. Thus, the marginal cost is $1,000 ÷ 16 = $62.50. We continue the experiment. We see that adding another unit of labor yields only 10 additional computer servers, so marginal cost starts to rise again back to $100. The following unit of labor yields a marginal physical product of only 8, so marginal cost becomes $1,000 ÷ 8 = $125.

All of the foregoing can be restated in relatively straightforward terms:

> *Firms' short-run cost curves are a reflection of the law of diminishing marginal product. Given any constant price of the variable input, marginal costs decline as long as the marginal physical product of the variable resource is rising. At the point at which marginal product begins to diminish, marginal costs begin to rise as the marginal physical product of the variable input begins to decline.*

The result is a marginal cost curve that slopes down, hits a minimum, and then slopes up.

Average Costs and Average Physical Product

Of course, average total costs and average variable costs are affected. The ATC and AVC curves will have their familiar U shape in the short run. Recall that

$$AVC = \frac{\text{total variable costs}}{\text{total output}}$$

As we move from zero labor input to one unit in panel (a) of Figure 22-1 on page 486, output increases from zero to 10 computer servers. The total variable costs are the price per worker, W ($1,000), times the number of workers (1). Because the average product (AP) of one worker (column 3) is 10, we can write the total product, 10, as the average product, 10, times the number of workers, 1. Thus, we see that

$$AVC = \frac{\$1,000 \times 1}{10 \times 1} = \frac{\$1,000}{10} = \frac{W}{AP}$$

From column 3 in panel (a) of Figure 22-1, we see that the average product increases, reaches a maximum, and then declines. Because AVC = W/AP, average variable cost decreases as average product increases, and increases as average product decreases. AVC reaches its minimum when average product reaches its maximum. Furthermore, because ATC = AVC + AFC, the average total cost curve inherits the relationship between the average variable cost and diminishing marginal product.

To illustrate, consider a firm that employs skilled technicians to provide mobile wireless services within a given geographic area. In panel (a) of Figure 22-3 on the previous page, column 2 shows the total number of mobile wireless accounts serviced as the number of technicians increases. Notice that the total product first increases at an increasing rate and later increases at a decreasing rate. This is reflected in column 4, which shows that the marginal physical product increases at first and then falls. The average physical product too first rises and then falls. The marginal and average physical products are graphed in panel (c) of Figure 22-3 on page 495.

Our immediate interest here is the average variable and marginal costs. Because we can define average variable cost as $1,000/AP (assuming that the wage paid is constant at $1,000), as the average product rises from 50 to 55 to 60 mobile wireless accounts, the average variable cost falls from $20.00 to $18.18 to $16.67. Conversely, as average product falls from 60 to 51, average variable cost rises from $16.67 to $19.61. Likewise, because marginal cost can also be defined as W/MPP, we see that as marginal physical product rises from 50 to 70, marginal cost falls from $20.00 to $14.29. As marginal physical product falls to 30, marginal cost rises to $33.33. These relationships are also expressed in panels (b), (c), and (d) of Figure 22-3.

Long-Run Cost Curves

The long run is defined as a time period during which full adjustment can be made to any change in the economic environment. Thus, in the long run, *all* factors of production are variable. Long-run curves are sometimes called *planning curves*, and the long run is sometimes called the **planning horizon.** We start our analysis of long-run cost curves by considering a single firm contemplating the construction of a single plant. The firm has three alternative plant sizes from which to choose on the planning horizon. Each particular plant size generates its own short-run average total cost curve. Now that we are talking about the difference between long-run and short-run cost curves, we will label all short-run curves with an *S* and long-run curves with an *L*. Short-run average (total) costs will be labeled SAC. Long-run average cost curves will be labeled LAC.

Panel (a) of Figure 22-4 on the following page shows short-run average cost curves for three successively larger plants. Which is the optimal size to build, if we can only choose among these three? That depends on the anticipated normal, sustained rate of output per time period. Assume for a moment that the anticipated normal, sustained rate is Q_1. If a plant of size 1 is built, average cost will be C_1. If a plant of size 2 is built, we see on SAC_2 that average cost will be C_2, which is greater than C_1. Thus, if the anticipated rate of output is Q_1, the appropriate plant size is the one from which SAC_1 was derived.

If the anticipated sustained rate of output per time period increases from Q_1 to a higher level such as Q_2, however, and a plant of size 1 is selected, average cost will be C_4. If a plant of size 2 is chosen, average cost will be C_3, which is clearly less than C_4.

In choosing the appropriate plant size for a single-plant firm during the planning horizon, the firm will pick the size whose short-run average cost curve generates an average cost that is lowest for the expected rate of output.

Long-Run Average Cost Curve

If we now assume that the entrepreneur faces an infinite number of choices of plant sizes in the long run, we can conceive of an infinite number of SAC curves similar to the three in panel (a) of Figure 22-4. We are not able, of course, to draw an infinite number, but we have drawn quite a few in panel (b) of Figure 22-4. We then draw the "envelope" to all these various short-run average cost curves. The resulting envelope is the **long-run average cost curve.** This long-run average cost curve is sometimes called the **planning curve,** for it represents the various average costs attainable at the planning stage of the firm's decision making. It represents the locus (path) of points giving the least unit cost of producing any given rate of output.

Note that the LAC curve is *not* tangent to each individual SAC curve at the latter's minimum points, except at the minimum point of the LAC curve. Then and only then are minimum long-run average costs equal to minimum short-run average costs.

Planning horizon
The long run, during which all inputs are variable.

Long-run average cost curve
The locus of points representing the minimum unit cost of producing any given rate of output, given current technology and resource prices.

Planning curve
The long-run average cost curve.

FIGURE 22-4

Preferable Plant Size and the Long-Run Average Cost Curve

If the anticipated sustained rate of output per unit time period is Q_1, the optimal plant to build is the one corresponding to SAC_1 in panel (a) because average cost is lower, at C_1. If the sustained rate of output increases toward the higher level Q_2, however, it will be more profitable to have a plant size corresponding to SAC_2 at $AC = C_3$. If we draw all the possible short-run average cost curves that correspond to different plant sizes and then draw the envelope (a curve tangent to each member of a set of curves) to these various curves, SAC_1–SAC_8, we obtain the long-run average cost (LAC) curve as shown in panel (b).

Why the Long-Run Average Cost Curve Is U-Shaped

Notice that the long-run average cost curve, LAC, in panel (b) of Figure 22-4 above is U-shaped, similar to the U shape of the short-run average cost curve developed earlier in this chapter. The reason behind the U shape of the two curves is not the same, however. The short-run average cost curve is U-shaped because of the law of diminishing marginal product. But the law cannot apply to the long run, because in the long run, all factors of production are variable. There is no point of diminishing marginal product because there is no fixed factor of production.

Why, then, do we see the U shape in the long-run average cost curve? The reasoning has to do with economies of scale, constant returns to scale, and diseconomies of scale. When the firm is experiencing **economies of scale,** the long-run average cost curve slopes downward—an increase in scale and production leads to a fall in unit costs. When the firm is experiencing **constant returns to scale,** the long-run average cost curve is at its minimum point, such that an increase in scale of production does not change unit costs. When the firm is experiencing **diseconomies of scale,** the long-run average cost curve slopes upward—an increase in scale and production increases unit costs. These three sections of the long-run average cost curve are broken up into panels (a), (b), and (c) in Figure 22-5 on the facing page.

Reasons for Economies of Scale

We shall examine three of the many reasons why a firm might be expected to experience economies of scale: specialization, the dimensional factor, and improvements in productive equipment.

Economies of scale
Decreases in long-run average costs resulting from increases in output.

Constant returns to scale
No change in long-run average costs when output increases.

Diseconomies of scale
Increases in long-run average costs that occur as output increases.

FIGURE 22-5

Economies of Scale, Constant Returns to Scale, and Diseconomies of Scale Shown with the Long-Run Average Cost Curve

The long-run average cost curve will fall when there are economies of scale, as shown in panel (a). It will be constant (flat) when the firm is experiencing constant returns to scale, as shown in panel (b). It will rise when the firm is experiencing diseconomies of scale, as shown in panel (c).

SPECIALIZATION As a firm's scale of operation increases, the opportunities for specialization in the use of resource inputs also increase. This is sometimes called *increased division of tasks* or *operations*. Cost reductions generated by productivity enhancements from such division of labor or increased specialization are well known. When we consider managerial staffs, we also find that larger enterprises may be able to put together more highly specialized staffs.

DIMENSIONAL FACTOR Large-scale firms often require proportionately less input per unit of output simply because certain inputs do not have to be physically doubled in order to double the output. Consider an oil-storage firm's cost of storing oil. The cost of storage is related to the cost of steel that goes into building the storage container. The amount of steel required, however, goes up less than in proportion to the volume (storage capacity) of the container (because the volume of a container increases more than proportionately with its surface area).

IMPROVEMENTS IN PRODUCTIVE EQUIPMENT The larger the scale of the enterprise, the more the firm is able to take advantage of larger-volume (output capacity) types of machinery. Small-scale operations may not be able to profitably use large-volume machines that can be more efficient per unit of output. Also, smaller firms often cannot use technologically more advanced machinery because they are unable to spread out the high cost of such sophisticated equipment over a large output.

For any of these three reasons, the firm may experience economies of scale, which means that equal percentage increases in output result in a decrease in average cost. Thus, output can double, but total costs will less than double. Hence, average cost falls. Note that the factors listed for causing economies of scale are all *internal* to the firm. They do not depend on what other firms are doing or what is happening in the economy.

Why a Firm Might Experience Diseconomies of Scale

One of the basic reasons that a firm can expect to run into diseconomies of scale is that there are limits to the efficient functioning of management. This is so because larger levels of output imply successively larger *plant* size, which in turn implies successively larger *firm* size. Thus, as the level of output increases, more people must be hired, and the firm gets bigger. As this happens, however, the support, supervisory, and administrative staff and the general paperwork of the firm all increase. As the layers of supervision grow, the costs of information and communication grow more than proportionately. Hence, the average unit cost will start to increase.

Some observers of corporate giants claim that many of them have been experiencing some diseconomies of scale. Witness the difficulties that firms such as Dell and General Motors have experienced in recent years. Some analysts say that the profitability declines they have encountered are at least partly a function of their size relative to their smaller, more flexible competitors, which can make decisions more quickly and then take advantage of changing market conditions more rapidly.

Why is American Airlines seeking to shrink the long-run scale of its operations?

EXAMPLE

Diseconomies of Scale at One of the World's Top Airlines

American Airlines is the world's fourth largest airline company. The firm operates in excess of 650 aircraft and flies to more than 650 airports. It also operates at a higher long-run cost per passenger-mile flown than most other airlines. The reason is that its scale is so large. This fact explains why the company is contemplating the sell-off of regional airline routes operated by its American Eagle subsidiary. Furthermore, the airline is working toward reducing the number of routes flown by its fleet of remaining aircraft—a fleet whose size the firm also aims to shrink. Thus, at present American Airlines' operations are so large that it is experiencing diseconomies of scale.

FOR CRITICAL THINKING
Is American Airlines currently operating to the left or right of the minimum point of its long-run average cost curve?

Minimum Efficient Scale

Economists and statisticians have obtained actual data on the relationship between changes in all inputs and changes in average cost. It turns out that for many industries, the long-run average cost curve does not resemble the curve shown in panel (b) of Figure 22-4 on page 498. Rather, it more closely resembles Figure 22-6 below. What you observe there is a small portion of declining long-run average costs (economies of scale) and then a wide range of outputs over which the firm experiences relatively constant economies of scale.

FIGURE 22-6

Minimum Efficient Scale

This long-run average cost curve reaches a minimum point at A. After that point, long-run average costs remain horizontal, or constant, and then rise at some later rate of output. Point A is called the minimum efficient scale for the firm because that is the point at which it reaches minimum costs. It is the lowest rate of output at which average long-run costs are minimized. At point B, diseconomies of scale arise, so long-run average cost begins to increase with further increases in output.

At the output rate when economies of scale end and constant economies of scale start, the **minimum efficient scale (MES)** for the firm is encountered. It occurs at point *A*. The minimum efficient scale is defined as the lowest rate of output at which long-run average costs are minimized. In any industry with a long-run average cost curve similar to the one in Figure 22-6 on the facing page, larger firms will have no cost-saving advantage over smaller firms as long as the smaller firms have at least obtained the minimum efficient scale at point *A*.

Minimum efficient scale (MES)
The lowest rate of output per unit time at which long-run average costs for a particular firm are at a minimum.

WHAT IF... the government required firms to reduce their long-run scales of operation to cut overall U.S. energy use?

Requiring companies to cut back on the scales at which they produce goods and services over their planning horizons would compel each firm to operate at a long-run output rate below its minimum efficient scale. As a consequence, each company's average total cost of producing its product would rise above the minimum feasible average total cost. Effectively, therefore, requiring U.S. companies to reduce their long-run operating scales to save energy would force all firms to manufacture goods and provide services at higher costs per unit.

QUICK QUIZ See page 506 for the answers. Review concepts from this section in MyEconLab.

The _____ run is often called the **planning horizon**. The _____-run average cost curve is the planning curve. It is found by drawing a curve tangent to points on a series of _____-run average cost curves, each corresponding to a different plant size.

The firm can experience **economies of scale, diseconomies of scale,** or **constant returns to scale,** all according to whether the long-run average cost curve slopes _____, slopes _____, or is _____. Economies of scale refer to what happens to average cost when all factors of production are increased.

We observe economies of scale for a number of reasons, including specialization, improved productive equipment, and the _____ factor, because large-scale firms require proportionately less input per unit of output. The firm may experience _____ of scale primarily because of limits to the efficient functioning of management.

The **minimum efficient scale** occurs at the _____ rate of output at which long-run average costs are _____.

YOU ARE THERE
Cutting Costs by Replacing Pilot Projects with Simulations

For about 70 years, Schneider National, one of the largest U.S. trucking firms, relied on what its managers called pilot projects to evaluate new ideas for methods to cut costs. Such experiments in cost cutting typically required the company to dedicate dozens or even hundreds of drivers to groups that functioned as separate businesses. The company would then evaluate whether pilot projects succeeded in uncovering cost-saving methods of operation. In many cases, however, the company found that costs were higher. As a consequence, efforts to search for means of cutting costs often *raised* the firm's overall expenses.

Ted Gifford, an operations research scientist, has spent two years developing a method of replacing pilot projects. Gifford has faced a daunting task. At any given moment, Schneider has about 10,000 trucks on the road and about 33,000 freight-hauling trailers available for pickup. Its 13,000 drivers work between four days and three weeks at a time, and their schedules require them to spend specified periods on breaks from work. Gifford has succeeded in developing simulation software to replace pilot projects. His work, which required two years to complete, has reduced Schneider's total costs by tens of millions of dollars per year.

Critical Thinking Questions

1. If Gifford's simulations recommend fewer drivers, would this reduce fixed or variable costs?

2. If the simulations recommend fewer truck depots, would this cut fixed or variable costs?

ISSUES & APPLICATIONS

Can Electric Car Production Attain Minimum Efficient Scale?

CONCEPTS APPLIED

▶ Economies of Scale

▶ Long-Run Average Cost Curve

▶ Minimum Efficient Scale

Automakers are actively seeking to reduce the average cost of producing hybrid and all-electric passenger vehicles. Hindering their efforts is the currently high average cost of producing battery packs to power the vehicles.

Ramping Up Battery-Pack Production Scale

The prices of the least expensive hybrid and all-electric vehicles are above $30,000. A significant portion of the per-vehicle cost is the expense of producing battery packs. For the lowest-priced all-electric autos, battery packs account for more than half the expense of producing each vehicle.

To try to reduce the average expense of powering hybrid and all-electric vehicles, auto companies are seeking economies of scale in production of battery packs. The firms are expanding their productive capabilities in hopes of making larger numbers of battery packs per year. They desire to move downward along their long-run average cost curves to the minimum efficient scale of annual production. Toward this end, Nissan is building a battery pack facility in Smyrna, Tennessee, that will be able to produce 200,000 battery packs per year.

An Unattainable Minimum Efficient Scale?

A fundamental problem stands in the way of achieving economies of scale in production of battery packs: A low scale of production of vehicles using the battery packs. Of the more than 12 million U.S. vehicles produced each year, only about 200,000 are hybrid cars, and fewer than 9,000 per year are all-electric autos. Nor are there many existing vehicles with battery packs requiring replacement. Of the more than 250 million registered passenger vehicles in the United States, only about 2.5 million are hybrid cars. Fewer than 40,000 are all-electric autos.

These figures suggest that fewer than 400,000 vehicles per year will require new battery packs. Hence, only two plants of the size of Nissan's Smyrna, Tennessee, plant would be required to produce a sufficient number of auto

battery packs for the entire nation. At least five auto companies plan to operate their own battery pack–producing plants, though, suggesting that on average each company would produce only about 80,000 battery packs per year. Thus, no company will likely be able to produce battery packs at the minimum efficient scale. The long-run average cost of producing a battery pack for use in passenger vehicles is likely to remain higher than the minimum feasible level for many years to come.

For Critical Thinking

1. Other things being equal, what will happen to automakers' profits if they are able to sell more vehicles using battery packs and thereby scale up battery production?

2. Why do you suppose that some automakers support the payment of government subsidies to consumers who purchase hybrid and all-electric passenger vehicles?

Web Resources

1. For data on vehicles powered by alternative energy sources, go to www.econtoday.com/chap22.

2. Learn about tax subsidies available to buyers of vehicles that use battery packs at www.econtoday.com/chap22.

> ## MyEconLab
> For more questions on this chapter's Issues & Applications, go to MyEconLab. In the Study Plan for this chapter, select Section N: News.

MyEconLab

Here is what you should know after reading this chapter. MyEconLab will help you identify what you know, and where to go when you need to practice.

WHAT YOU SHOULD KNOW

The Short Run versus the Long Run from a Firm's Perspective The short run for a firm is a period during which at least one input, such as plant size, cannot be altered. Inputs that cannot be changed in the short run are fixed inputs, whereas inputs that may be adjusted in the short run are variable inputs. The long run is a period in which a firm may vary all inputs.

short run, 484
plant size, 484
long run, 484

The Law of Diminishing Marginal Product The production function is the relationship between inputs and the maximum physical output, or total product, that a firm can produce. Typically, a firm's marginal physical product—the physical output resulting from the addition of one more unit of a variable factor of production—increases with the first few units of the variable input that it employs. Eventually, as the firm adds more and more units of the variable input, the marginal physical product begins to decline. This is the law of diminishing marginal product.

production, 485
production function, 485
average physical product, 486
marginal physical product, 487
law of diminishing marginal product, 487

Key Figure
Figure 22-1, 486

A Firm's Short-Run Cost Curves The expenses for a firm's fixed inputs are its fixed costs, and the expenses for its variable inputs are variable costs. The total costs of a firm are the sum of its fixed costs and variable costs. Average fixed cost equals total fixed cost divided by total product. Average variable cost equals total variable cost divided by total product, and average total cost equals total cost divided by total product. Finally, marginal cost is the change in total cost resulting from a one-unit change in production.

total costs, 489
fixed costs, 489
variable costs, 489
average fixed costs, 491
average variable costs, 492
average total costs, 492
marginal costs, 492

Key Figure
Figure 22-2, 490

A Firm's Long-Run Cost Curves Over a firm's long-run, or planning, horizon, it can choose all inputs, including plant size. Thus, it can choose a long-run scale of production along a long-run average cost curve. The long-run average cost curve, which for most firms is U-shaped, is traced out by the short-run average cost curves corresponding to various plant sizes.

planning horizon, 497
long-run average cost curve, 497
planning curve, 497

Key Figures
Figure 22-3, 495
Figure 22-4, 498

WHERE TO GO TO PRACTICE

- MyEconLab Study Plan 22.1

- MyEconLab Study Plans 22.2, 22.3
- Animated Figure 22-1

- MyEconLab Study Plans 22.4, 22.5
- Animated Figure 22-2

- MyEconLab Study Plans 22.6, 22.7
- Animated Figures 22-3, 22-4

MyEconLab *continued*

WHAT YOU SHOULD KNOW ————————————————————— WHERE TO GO TO PRACTICE

Economies and Diseconomies of Scale and a Firm's Minimum Efficient Scale Along the downward-sloping range of a firm's long-run average cost curve, the firm experiences economies of scale, meaning that its long-run production costs decline as it raises its output scale. In contrast, along the upward-sloping portion of the long-run average cost curve, the firm encounters diseconomies of scale, so that its long-run costs of production rise as it increases its output scale. The minimum point of the long-run average cost curve occurs at the firm's minimum efficient scale, which is the lowest rate of output at which the firm can achieve minimum long-run average cost.

economies of scale, 498
constant returns to scale, 498
diseconomies of scale, 498
minimum efficient scale
    (MES), 501

Key Figures
Figure 22-5, 499
Figure 22-6, 500

- MyEconLab Study Plans 22.7, 22.8
- Animated Figures 22-5, 22-6

Log in to MyEconLab, take a chapter test, and get a personalized Study Plan that tells you which concepts you understand and which ones you need to review. From there, MyEconLab will give you further practice, tutorials, animations, videos, and guided solutions. For more information, visit www.myeconlab.com

PROBLEMS

All problems are assignable in MyEconLab. Answers to odd-numbered problems appear at the back of the book.

22-1. The academic calendar for a university is August 15 through May 15. A professor commits to a contract that binds her to a teaching position at this university for this period. Based on this information, explain the short run and long run that the professor faces. (See page 484.)

22-2. The short-run production function for a manufacturer of flash memory drives is shown in the table below. Based on this information, answer the following questions. (See pages 486–487.)

Input of Labor (workers per week)	Total Output of Flash Memory Drives
0	0
1	25
2	60
3	85
4	105
5	115
6	120

a. Calculate the average physical product at each quantity of labor.

b. Calculate the marginal physical product of labor at each quantity of labor.

c. At what point does marginal product begin to diminish?

22-3. During the past year, a firm produced 10,000 laptop computers. Its total costs were $5 million, and its fixed costs were $2 million. What are the average variable costs of this firm? (See page 491.)

22-4. During the previous month, a firm produced 250 tablet devices at an average variable cost of $40 and at an average fixed cost of $10. What were the firm's total costs during the month? (See page 491.)

22-5. Just before the firm discussed in Problem 22-4 produced its last tablet device in the previous month, its total costs were $12,425. What was the marginal cost incurred by the firm in producing the final tablet device that month? (See page 492.)

22-6. The cost structure of a manufacturer of microchips is described in the table on the facing page. The firm's fixed costs equal $10 per day. Calculate the average variable cost, average fixed cost, and average total cost at each output level. (See pages 489–492.)

Output (microchips per day)	Total Cost of Output ($ thousands)
0	10
25	60
50	95
75	150
100	220
125	325
150	465

22-7. The diagram below displays short-run cost curves for a facility that produces liquid crystal display (LCD) screens for cell phones: (See page 491.)

a. What are the daily total fixed costs of producing LCD screens?

b. What are the total variable costs of producing 100 LCD screens per day?

c. What are the total costs of producing 100 LCD screens per day?

d. What is the marginal cost of producing 100 LCD screens instead of 99? (Hint: To answer this question, you must first determine the total costs—or, alternatively, the total variable costs—of producing 99 LCD screens.)

22-8. A watch manufacturer finds that at 1,000 units of output, its marginal costs are below average total costs. If it produces an additional watch, will its average total costs rise, fall, or stay the same? (See page 493.)

22-9. At its current short-run level of production, a firm's average variable costs equal $20 per unit, and its average fixed costs equal $30 per unit. Its total costs at this production level equal $2,500. (See page 491.)

a. What is the firm's current output level?

b. What are its total variable costs at this output level?

c. What are its total fixed costs?

22-10. In an effort to reduce their total costs, many companies are now replacing paychecks with payroll cards, which are stored-value cards onto which the companies can download employees' wages and salaries electronically. If the only factor of production that a company varies in the short run is the number of hours worked by people already on its payroll, would shifting from paychecks to payroll cards reduce the firm's total fixed costs or its total variable costs? Explain your answer. (See page 489.)

22-11. During autumn months, passenger railroads across the globe deal with a condition called slippery rail. It results from a combination of water, leaf oil, and pressure from the train's weight, which creates a slippery black ooze that prevents trains from gaining traction. (See page 489.)

a. One solution for slippery rail is to cut back trees from all of a rail firm's rail network on a regular basis, thereby helping prevent the problem from developing. If incurred, would this railroad expense be a better example of a fixed cost or a variable cost? Why?

b. Another way of addressing slippery rail is to wait until it begins to develop. Then the company purchases sand and dumps it on the slippery tracks so that trains already en route within the rail network can proceed. If incurred, would this railroad expense be a better example of a fixed cost or a variable cost? Why?

22-12. In the short run, a firm's total costs of producing 100 units of output equal $10,000. If it produces one more unit, its total costs will increase to $10,150. (See pages 491–492.)

a. What is the marginal cost of the 101st unit of output?

b. What is the firm's average total cost of producing 100 units?

c. What is the firm's average total cost of producing 101 units?

22-13. Suppose that a firm's only variable input is labor, and the constant hourly wage rate is $20 per hour. The last unit of labor hired enabled the firm to increase its hourly production from 250 units to 251 units. What was the marginal cost of producing 251 units of output instead of 250? (See page 492.)

22-14. Suppose that a firm's only variable input is labor. The firm increases the number of employees from four to five, thereby causing weekly output to rise by two units and total costs to increase from $3,000 per week to $3,300 per week. (See page 492.)

a. What is the marginal physical product of hiring five workers instead of four?

b. What is the weekly wage rate earned by the fifth worker?

22-15. Suppose that a company currently employs 1,000 workers and produces 1 million units of output per month. Labor is its only variable input, and the company pays each worker the same monthly wage. The company's current total variable costs equal $2 million. (See pages 493–494.)

a. What are average variable costs at this firm's current output level?

b. What is the average physical product of labor?

c. What monthly wage does the firm pay each worker?

22-16. A manufacturing firm with a single plant is contemplating changing its plant size. It must choose from among seven alternative plant sizes. In the table, plant size A is the smallest it might build, and size G is the largest. Currently, the firm's plant size is B. (See page 498.)

Plant Size	Average Total Cost ($)
A (smallest)	4,250
B	3,600
C	3,100
D	3,100
E	3,100
F	3,250
G (largest)	4,100

a. At plant site B, is this firm currently experiencing economies of scale or diseconomies of scale?

b. What is the firm's minimum efficient scale?

22-17. An electricity-generating company confronts the following long-run average total costs associated with alternative plant sizes. It is currently operating at plant size G. (See page 498.)

Plant Size	Average Total Cost ($)
A (smallest)	2,000
B	1,800
C	1,600
D	1,550
E	1,500
F	1,500
G (largest)	1,500

a. What is this firm's minimum efficient scale?

b. If damage caused by a powerful hurricane generates a reduction in the firm's plant size from its current size to B, would there be a leftward or rightward movement along the firm's long-run average total cost curve?

ECONOMICS ON THE NET

Industry-Level Capital Expenditures In this chapter, you learned about the explicit and implicit costs that firms incur in the process of producing goods and services. This Internet application gives you an opportunity to consider one type of cost—expenditures on capital goods.

Title: U.S. Census Bureau's Annual Capital Expenditures Survey

Navigation: Follow the link at **www.econtoday.com /chap22**, and select the most recent *Annual Capital Spending Report*.

Application Read the introductory summary of the report, and then answer the following questions.

1. What types of business expenditures does the Census Bureau include in this report?

2. Are the inputs that generate these business expenditures more likely to be inputs that firms can vary in the short run or in the long run?

3. Which inputs account for the largest portion of firms' capital expenditures? Why do you suppose this is so?

For Group Discussion and Analysis Review reports for the past several years. Do capital expenditures vary from year to year? What factors might account for such variations? Are there noticeable differences in capital expenditures from industry to industry?

ANSWERS TO QUICK QUIZZES

p. 489: (i) production . . . output; (ii) product; (iii) decreasing . . . output

p. 499: (i) fixed . . . variable; (ii) Average . . . ATC; (iii) variable . . . AVC; (iv) fixed . . . AFC; (v) Marginal . . . total . . . MC . . . TC; (vi) minimum . . . minimum

p. 501: (i) long . . . long . . . short; (ii) downward . . . upward . . . horizontal; (iii) dimensional . . . diseconomies; (iv) lowest . . . minimized

Perfect Competition

23

LEARNING OBJECTIVES

After reading this chapter, you should be able to:

▶ Identify the characteristics of a perfectly competitive market structure

▶ Discuss the process by which a perfectly competitive firm decides how much output to produce

▶ Understand how the short-run supply curve for a perfectly competitive firm is determined

▶ Explain how the equilibrium price is determined in a perfectly competitive market

▶ Describe what factors induce firms to enter or exit a perfectly competitive industry

▶ Distinguish among constant-, increasing-, and decreasing-cost industries based on the shape of the long-run industry supply curve

MyEconLab helps you master each objective and study more efficiently. See end of chapter for details.

ithium has become an increasingly useful input in the production of batteries used to power popular consumer electronics products and digital devices. Consequently, the market demand for this naturally occurring element has increased. Nevertheless, its inflation-adjusted price has generally declined over time. Thus, the term "white gold," commonly used to refer to lithium, is something of a misnomer. What accounts for the falling relative price of lithium in spite of the rising market demand for the element? In this chapter, you will see that in the market for lithium, input prices have trended downward as more firms producing lithium have entered the market. As you will learn, these events, together with the fact that the market for lithium is *perfectly competitive,* explain why the price of lithium has decreased even as demand for the element has increased.

the world's oldest company that makes wooden pencils recently celebrated its 350th year of operations? In 1662, pencil craftsman Friedrich Staedtler began making pencils in Nuremberg, Germany. This pencil-making firm has been in operation since the market came into existence. During the three and a half centuries since the pencil market's first beginnings, however, many other manufacturers have come and gone. Very low costs of entering and exiting the pencil market made this possible. Combining this fact with others, such as close similarity among most wooden pencils, large numbers of pencil firms, and widely known information about market conditions, suggests that the market for pencils is *perfectly competitive*. In this chapter, you will learn why this is so. In addition, you will learn what perfect competition in the pencil market implies about the determination of the market price and equilibrium quantity of pencils, and the production, costs, revenues, and profits of individual pencil manufacturers.

Characteristics of a Perfectly Competitive Market Structure

We are interested in studying how a firm acting within a perfectly competitive market structure makes decisions about how much to produce. In a situation of **perfect competition,** each firm is such a small part of the total industry that it cannot affect the price of the product in question. That means that each **perfectly competitive firm** in the industry is a **price taker**—the firm takes price as a given, something determined *outside* the individual firm.

What It Means for a Firm to Be a Price Taker

The definition of a competitive firm is obviously idealized, for in one sense the individual firm *has* to set prices. How can we ever have a situation in which firms regard prices as set by forces outside their control? The answer is that even though every firm sets its own prices, a firm in a perfectly competitive situation will find that it will eventually have no customers at all if it sets its price above the competitive price.

The best example is in agriculture. Although the individual farmer can set any price for a bushel of wheat, if that price doesn't coincide with the market price of a bushel of similar-quality wheat, no one will purchase the wheat at a higher price. Nor would the farmer be inclined to reduce revenues by selling below the market price.

Characteristics of Perfect Competition

Let's examine why a firm in a perfectly competitive industry is a price taker.

1. *There are large numbers of buyers and sellers.* When this is the case, the quantity demanded by one buyer or the quantity supplied by one seller is negligible relative to the market quantity. No one buyer or seller has any influence on price.

2. *The product sold by the firms in the industry is homogeneous—that is, indistinguishable across firms.* The product sold by each firm in the industry is a perfect substitute for the product sold by every other firm. Buyers are able to choose from a large number of sellers of a product that the buyers regard as being the same.

3. *Both buyers and sellers have access to all relevant information.* Consumers are able to find out about lower prices charged by competing firms. Firms are able to find out about cost-saving innovations that can lower production costs and prices, and they are able to learn about profitable opportunities in other industries.

4. *Any firm can enter or leave the industry without serious impediments.* Firms in a competitive industry are not hampered in their ability to get resources or reallocate resources. In pursuit of profit-making opportunities, they move labor and capital to whatever business venture gives them their highest expected rate of return on their investment.

Perfect competition
A market structure in which the decisions of *individual* buyers and sellers have no effect on market price.

Perfectly competitive firm
A firm that is such a small part of the total *industry* that it cannot affect the price of the product it sells.

Price taker
A perfectly competitive firm that must take the price of its product as given because the firm cannot influence its price.

The Demand Curve of the Perfect Competitor

When we discussed substitutes in Chapter 19, we pointed out that the more substitutes there are and the more similar they are to the commodity in question, the greater is the price elasticity of demand. Here we assume that the perfectly competitive firm is producing a homogeneous (indistinguishable across all of the industry's firms) commodity that has perfect substitutes. That means that if the individual firm raises its price one penny, it will lose all of its business. This, then, is how we characterize the demand schedule for a perfectly competitive firm: It is the going market price as determined by the forces of market supply and market demand—that is, where the market demand curve intersects the market supply curve. The demand curve for the product of an individual firm in a perfectly competitive industry is perfectly elastic at the going market price. Remember that with a perfectly elastic demand curve, any increase in price leads to zero quantity demanded.

We show the market demand and supply curves in panel (a) of Figure 23-1 below. Their intersection occurs at the price of $5. The commodity in question is magneto optical (MO) disks. Assume for the purposes of this exposition that all of these MO disks are perfect substitutes for all others. At the going market price of $5 apiece, the demand curve for MO disks produced by an individual firm that sells a very, very small part of total industry production is shown in panel (b). At the market price, this firm can sell all the output it wants. At the market price of $5 each, which is where the demand curve for the individual producer lies, consumer demand for the MO disks of that one producer is perfectly elastic.

This can be seen by noting that if the firm raises its price, consumers, who are assumed to know that this supplier is charging more than other producers, will buy elsewhere, and the producer in question will have no sales at all. Thus, the demand curve for that producer is perfectly elastic. We label the individual producer's demand curve *d*, whereas the *market* demand curve is always labeled *D*.

How Much Should the Perfect Competitor Produce?

As we have shown, from the perspective of a perfectly competitive firm deciding how much to produce, the firm has to accept the price of the product as a given. If the firm raises its price, it sells nothing. If it lowers its price, it earns lower revenues per unit

YOU ARE THERE

To contemplate how features of perfect competition often apply to markets for services provided online, take a look at **Looking to Enter a Competitive Online Market? Rent a Desk!** on page 526.

FIGURE 23-1

The Demand Curve for a Producer of Magneto Optical Disks

At $5—where market demand, *D*, and market supply, *S*, intersect—the individual firm faces a perfectly elastic demand curve, *d*. If the firm raises its price even one penny, it will sell no magneto optical disks, measured from its point of view in hourly production, at all. (Notice the difference in the quantities of MO disks represented on the horizontal axes of panels (a) and (b).)

sold than it otherwise could. The firm has one decision left: How much should it produce? We will apply our model of the firm to this question to come up with an answer. We'll use the *profit-maximization model*, which assumes that firms attempt to maximize their total profits—the positive difference between total revenues and total costs. This also means that firms seek to minimize any losses that arise in times when total revenues may be less than total costs.

Total Revenues

Total revenues

The price per unit times the total quantity sold.

Every firm has to consider its *total revenues*. **Total revenues** are defined as the quantity sold multiplied by the price per unit. (They are the same as total receipts from the sale of output.) The perfect competitor must take the price as a given.

Look at Figure 23-2 on the facing page. The information in panel (a) comes from panel (a) of Figure 22-2 on page 490, but we have added some essential columns for our analysis. Column 3 is the market price, P, of $5 per MO disk. Column 4 shows the total revenues, or TR, as equal to the market price, P, times the total output per hour, or Q. Thus, TR $= PQ$.

We are assuming that the market supply and demand schedules intersect at a price of $5 and that this price holds for all the firm's production. We are also assuming that because our maker of MO disks is a small part of the market, it can sell all that it produces at that price. Thus, panel (b) of Figure 23-2 shows the total revenue curve as a straight green line. For every additional MO disk sold, total revenue increases by $5.

Comparing Total Costs with Total Revenues

Total costs are given in column 2 of panel (a) of Figure 23-2 and plotted in panel (b). Remember, the firm's costs always include a normal rate of return on investment. So, whenever we refer to total costs, we are talking *not* about accounting costs but about economic costs. When the total cost curve is above the total revenue curve, the firm is experiencing losses. When total costs are less than total revenues, the firm is making profits.

By comparing total costs with total revenues, we can figure out the number of magneto optical disks the individual competitive firm should produce per hour. Our analysis rests on the assumption that the firm will attempt to maximize total profits. In panel (a) of Figure 23-2, we see that total profits reach a maximum at a production rate of between seven and eight MO disks per hour. We can see this graphically in panel (b) of the figure. The firm will maximize profits where the total revenue curve lies above the total cost curve by the greatest amount. That occurs at a rate of output and sales of between seven and eight MO disks per hour. This rate is called the **profit-maximizing rate of production**. (If output were continuously divisible or there were extremely large numbers of MO disks, we would get a unique profit-maximizing output.)

Profit-maximizing rate of production

The rate of production that maximizes total profits, or the difference between total revenues and total costs. Also, it is the rate of production at which marginal revenue equals marginal cost.

We can also find the profit-maximizing rate of production for the individual competitive firm by looking at marginal revenues and marginal costs.

Using Marginal Analysis to Determine the Profit-Maximizing Rate of Production

It is possible—indeed, preferable—to use marginal analysis to determine the profit-maximizing rate of production. We end up with the same results derived in a different manner, one that focuses more on where decisions are really made—on the margin. Managers examine changes in costs and relate them to changes in revenues. In fact, whether the question is how much more or less to produce, how many more workers to hire or fire, or how much more to study or not study, we compare changes in costs with changes in benefits, where change is occurring at the margin.

Panel (a)

(1) Total Output per Hour (Q)	(2) Total Costs (TC)	(3) Market Price (P)	(4) Total Revenues (TR) (4) = (3) x (1)	(5) Total Profit (TR − TC) (5) = (4) − (2)	(6) Average Total Cost (ATC) (6) = (2) ÷ (1)	(7) Average Variable Cost (AVC)	(8) Marginal Cost (MC) (8) = $\frac{\text{Change in (2)}}{\text{Change in (1)}}$	(9) Marginal Revenue (MR) (9) = $\frac{\text{Change in (4)}}{\text{Change in (1)}}$
0	$10	$5	$ 0	−$10	—	—		
							$5	$5
1	15	5	5	−10	$15.00	$5.00		
							3	5
2	18	5	10	−8	9.00	4.00		
							2	5
3	20	5	15	−5	6.67	3.33		
							1	5
4	21	5	20	−1	5.25	2.75		
							2	5
5	23	5	25	2	4.60	2.60		
							3	5
6	26	5	30	4	4.33	2.67		
							4	5
7	30	5	35	5	4.28	2.86		
							5	5
8	35	5	40	5	4.38	3.12		
							6	5
9	41	5	45	4	4.56	3.44		
							7	5
10	48	5	50	2	4.80	3.80		
							8	5
11	56	5	55	−1	5.09	4.18		

FIGURE 23-2

Profit Maximization

Profit maximization occurs where marginal revenue equals marginal cost. Panel (a) indicates that this point occurs at a rate of sales of between seven and eight magneto optical disks per hour. In panel (b), we find maximum profits where total revenues exceed total costs by the largest amount. This occurs at a rate of production and sales per hour of seven or eight MO disks. In panel (c), the marginal cost curve, MC, intersects the marginal revenue curve at the same rate of output and sales of somewhere between seven and eight MO disks per hour.

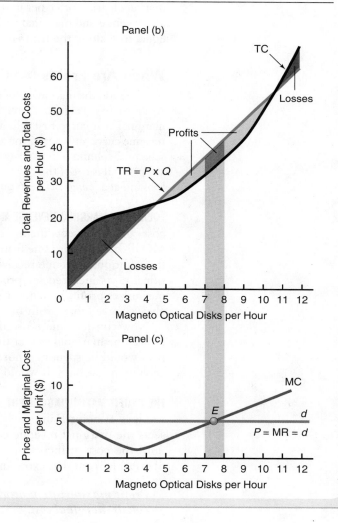

Marginal Revenue

Marginal revenue
The change in total revenues resulting from a one-unit change in output (and sale) of the product in question.

Marginal revenue represents the change in total revenues attributable to changing production of an item by one unit. Hence, a more formal definition of marginal revenue is

$$\text{Marginal revenue} = \frac{\text{change in total revenues}}{\text{change in output}}$$

In a perfectly competitive market, the marginal revenue curve is exactly equivalent to the price line, which is the individual firm's demand curve. Each time the firm produces and sells one more unit, total revenues rise by an amount equal to the (constant) market price of the good. Thus, in Figure 23-1 on page 509, the demand curve, *d*, for the individual producer is at a price of $5—the price line is coincident with the demand curve. But so is the marginal revenue curve, for marginal revenue in this case also equals $5.

The marginal revenue curve for our competitive producer of MO disks is shown as a line at $5 in panel (c) of Figure 23-2 on the previous page. Notice again that the marginal revenue curve is the price line, which is the firm's demand, or average revenue, curve, *d*. This equality of MR, *P*, and *d* for an individual firm is a general feature of a perfectly competitive industry. The price line shows the quantity that consumers desire to purchase from this firm at each price—which is *any* quantity that the firm provides at the market price—and hence is the demand curve, *d*, faced by the firm. The market clearing price per unit does not change as the firm varies its output, so the average revenue and marginal revenue also are equal to this price. Thus, MR is identically equal to *P* along the firm's demand curve.

When Are Profits Maximized?

Now we add the marginal cost curve, MC, taken from column 8 in panel (a) of Figure 23-2. As shown in panel (c) of that figure, because of the law of diminishing marginal product, the marginal cost curve first falls and then starts to rise, eventually intersecting the marginal revenue curve and then rising above it. Notice that the numbers for both the marginal cost schedule, column 8 in panel (a), and the marginal revenue schedule, column 9 in panel (a), are printed *between* the rows on which the quantities appear. This indicates that we are looking at a *change* between one rate of output and the next rate of output.

EQUALIZING MARGINAL REVENUE AND MARGINAL COST In panel (c) of Figure 23-2, the marginal cost curve intersects the marginal revenue curve somewhere between seven and eight MO disks per hour. The firm has an incentive to produce and sell until the amount of the additional revenue received from selling one more MO disk just equals the additional costs incurred for producing and selling that MO disk. This is how the firm maximizes profit. Whenever marginal cost is less than marginal revenue, the firm will always make more profit by increasing production.

Now consider the possibility of producing at an output rate of 10 MO disks per hour. The marginal cost at that output rate is higher than the marginal revenue. The firm would be spending more to produce that additional output than it would be receiving in revenues. It would be foolish to continue producing at this rate.

THE PROFIT-MAXIMIZING OUTPUT RATE But how much should the firm produce? It should produce at point *E* in panel (c) of Figure 23-2, where the marginal cost curve intersects the marginal revenue curve from below. The firm should continue production until the cost of increasing output by one more unit is just equal to the revenues obtainable from that extra unit. This is a fundamental rule in economics:

> *Profit maximization occurs at the rate of output at which marginal revenue equals marginal cost.*

For a perfectly competitive firm, this rate of output is at the intersection of the demand schedule, *d*, which is identical to the MR curve, and the marginal cost curve, MC. When MR exceeds MC, each additional unit of output adds more to total revenues than to total costs, so the additional unit should be produced. When MC is greater than MR, each unit produced adds more to total cost than to total revenues, so this unit should not be produced. Therefore, profit maximization occurs when MC equals MR. In our particular example, our profit-maximizing, perfectly competitive producer of MO disks will produce at a rate of between seven and eight MO disks per hour.

QUICK QUIZ See page 531 for the answers. Review concepts from this section in MyEconLab.

Four fundamental characteristics of the market in **perfect competition** are (1) _____ numbers of buyers and sellers, (2) a _____ product, (3) good information in the hands of both buyers and sellers, and (4) _____ exit from and entry into the industry by other firms.

A perfectly competitive firm is a **price taker.** It has _____ control over price and consequently has to take price as a given, but it can sell _____ that it wants at the going market price.

The demand curve for a perfect competitor is perfectly elastic at the going market price. The demand curve is

also the perfect competitor's _____ revenue curve because _____ revenue is defined as the change in total revenue due to a one-unit change in output.

Profit is maximized at the rate of output at which the positive difference between total revenues and total costs is the greatest. This is the same level of output at which marginal _____ equals marginal _____. The perfectly competitive firm produces at an output rate at which marginal cost equals the _____ per unit of output, because MR is always equal to P.

Short-Run Profits

To find what our competitive individual producer of magneto optical disks is making in terms of profits in the short run, we have to add the average total cost curve to panel (c) of Figure 23-2 on page 511. We take the information from column 6 in panel (a) and add it to panel (c) to get Figure 23-3 below. Again the profit-maximizing rate of output is

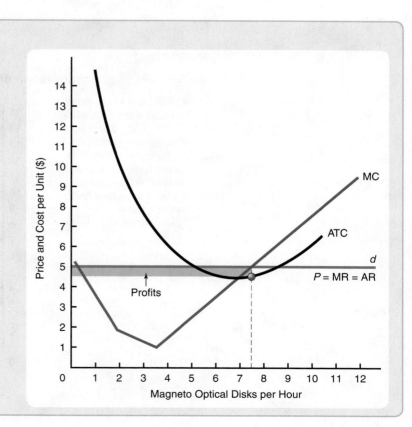

FIGURE 23-3

Measuring Total Profits

Profits are represented by the blue-shaded area. The height of the profit rectangle is given by the difference between average total costs and price ($5), where price is also equal to average revenue. This is found by the vertical difference between the ATC curve and the price, or average revenue, line *d*, at the profit-maximizing rate of output of between seven and eight MO disks per hour.

between seven and eight magneto optical disks per hour. If we have production and sales of seven per hour, total revenues will be $35 per hour. Total costs will be $30 MO disks per hour, leaving a profit of $5 per hour. If the rate of output and sales is eight MO disks per hour, total revenues will be $40 and total costs will be $35, again leaving a profit of $5 per hour.

A Graphical Depiction of Maximum Profits

In Figure 23-3 on the previous page, the lower boundary of the rectangle labeled "Profits" is determined by the intersection of the profit-maximizing quantity line represented by vertical dashes and the average total cost curve. Why? Because the ATC curve gives us the cost per unit, whereas the price ($5), represented by d, gives us the revenue per unit, or average revenue. The difference is profit per unit.

Thus, the height of the rectangular box representing profits equals profit per unit, and the length equals the amount of units produced. When we multiply these two quantities, we get total profits. Note, as pointed out earlier, that we are talking about *economic profits* because a normal rate of return on investment plus all opportunity costs is included in the average total cost curve, ATC.

A Graphical Depiction of Minimum Losses

It is also certainly possible for the competitive firm to make short-run losses. We give an example in Figure 23-4 below, where we show the firm's demand curve shifting from d_1 to d_2. The going market price has fallen from $5 to $3 per MO disk because of changes in market demand conditions. The firm will still do the best it can by producing where marginal revenue equals marginal cost.

We see in Figure 23-4 that the marginal revenue (d_2) curve is intersected (from below) by the marginal cost curve at an output rate of about $5\frac{1}{2}$ MO disks per hour. The firm is clearly not making profits because average total costs at that output rate are greater than the price of $3 per MO disk. The losses are shown in the shaded area. By producing where marginal revenue equals marginal cost, however, the firm is minimizing its losses. That is, losses would be greater at any other output.

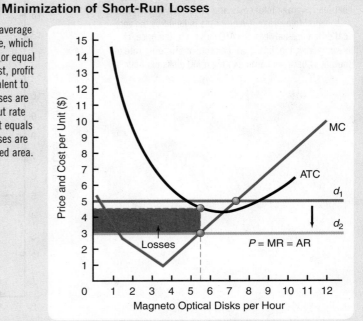

FIGURE 23-4

Minimization of Short-Run Losses

In situations in which average total costs exceed price, which in turn is greater than or equal to average variable cost, profit maximization is equivalent to loss minimization. Losses are minimized at the output rate at which marginal cost equals marginal revenue. Losses are shown in the red-shaded area.

The Short-Run Break-Even Price and the Short-Run Shutdown Price

In Figure 23-4 on the facing page, the firm is sustaining economic losses. Will it go out of business? In the long run it will, but in the short run the firm will not necessarily go out of business. In the short run, as long as the total revenues from continuing to produce output exceed the associated total variable costs, the firm will remain in business and continue to produce. A firm *goes out of business* when the owners sell its assets to someone else. A firm temporarily *shuts down* when it stops producing, but it still is in business.

Now how can a firm that is sustaining economic losses in the short run tell whether it is still worthwhile *not* to shut down? The firm must compare the total revenues that it receives if it continues producing with the resulting total variable costs that it thereby incurs. Looking at the problem on a per-unit basis, as long as average variable cost (AVC) is covered by average revenues (price), the firm is better off continuing to produce. If average variable costs are exceeded even a little bit by the price of the product, staying in production produces some revenues in excess of variable costs. The logic is fairly straightforward:

> *As long as the price per unit sold exceeds the average variable cost per unit produced, the earnings of the firm's owners will be higher if it continues to produce in the short run than if it shuts down.*

Calculating the Short-Run Break-Even Price

Look at demand curve d_1 in Figure 23-5 on the following page. It just touches the minimum point of the average total cost curve, which is exactly where the marginal cost curve intersects the average total cost curve. At that price, which is about $4.30, the firm will be making exactly zero short-run *economic* profits. That price is called the **short-run break-even price,** and point E_1 therefore occurs at the short-run break-even price for a competitive firm. It is the point at which marginal revenue, marginal cost, and average total cost are all equal (that is, at which $P = MC$ and $P = ATC$). The break-even price is the one that yields zero short-run *economic* profits or losses.

Short-run break-even price
The price at which a firm's total revenues equal its total costs. At the break-even price, the firm is just making a normal rate of return on its capital investment. (It is covering its explicit and implicit costs.)

Calculating the Short-Run Shutdown Price

To calculate the firm's shutdown price, we must introduce the average variable cost (AVC) to our graph. In Figure 23-5, we have plotted the AVC values from column 7 in panel (a) of Figure 23-2 on page 511. For the moment, consider two possible demand curves, d_1 and d_2, which are also the firm's respective marginal revenue curves. If demand is d_1, the firm will produce at E_1, where that curve intersects the marginal cost curve. If demand falls to d_2, the firm will produce at E_2. The special feature of the hypothetical demand curve, d_2, is that it just touches the average variable cost curve at the latter's minimum point, which is also where the marginal cost curve intersects it. This price is the **short-run shutdown price.** Why? Below this price, the firm would be paying out more in variable costs than it is receiving in revenues from the sale of its product. Each unit it sold would generate losses that could be avoided if it shut down operations.

The intersection of the price line, the marginal cost curve, and the average variable cost curve is labeled E_2. The resulting short-run shutdown price is valid only for the short run because, of course, in the long run the firm will not stay in business if it is earning less than a normal rate of return (zero economic profits).

Short-run shutdown price
The price that covers average variable costs. It occurs just below the intersection of the marginal cost curve and the average variable cost curve.

The Meaning of Zero Economic Profits

The fact that we labeled point E_1 in Figure 23-5 on page 516, the break-even point may have disturbed you. At point E_1, price is just equal to average total cost. If this is the case, why would a firm continue to produce if it were making no profits whatsoever? If

Short-Run Break-Even and Shutdown Prices

We can find the short-run break-even price and the short-run shutdown price by comparing price with average total costs and average variable costs. If the demand curve is d_1, profit maximization occurs at output E_1, where MC equals marginal revenue (the d_1 curve). Because the ATC curve includes all relevant opportunity costs, point E_1 is the break-even point, and zero economic profits are being made. The firm is earning a normal rate of return. If the demand curve falls to d_2, profit maximization (loss minimization) occurs at the intersection of MC and MR (the d_2 curve), or E_2. Below this price, it does not pay for the firm to continue in operation because its average variable costs are not covered by the price of the product.

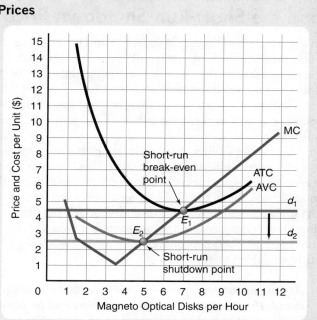

we again make the distinction between accounting profits and economic profits, you will realize that at that price, the firm has zero economic profits but positive accounting profits. Recall that accounting profits are total revenues minus total explicit costs. But such accounting ignores the reward offered to investors—the opportunity cost of capital—plus all other implicit costs.

In economic analysis, the average total cost curve includes the full opportunity cost of capital. Indeed, the average total cost curve includes the opportunity cost of *all* factors of production used in the production process. At the short-run break-even price, economic profits are, by definition, zero. Accounting profits at that price are not, however, equal to zero. They are positive. Consider an example. A manufacturer of homogeneous flash memory chips sells chips at some price. The owners of the firm have supplied all the funds in the business. They have not borrowed from anyone else, and they explicitly pay the full opportunity cost to all factors of production, including any managerial labor that they themselves contribute to the business. Their salaries show up as a cost in the books and are equal to what they could have earned in the next-best alternative occupation.

At the end of the year, the owners find that after they subtract all explicit costs from total revenues, accounting profits are $100,000. If their investment was $1 million, the rate of return on that investment is 10 percent per year. We will assume that this turns out to be equal to the market rate of return.

This $100,000, or 10 percent rate of return, is actually, then, a competitive, or normal, rate of return on invested capital in all industries with similar risks. If the owners had made only $50,000, or 5 percent on their investment, they would have been able to make higher profits by leaving the industry. The 10 percent rate of return is the opportunity cost of capital. Accountants show it as a profit. Economists call it a cost. We include that cost in the average total cost curve, similar to the one shown in Figure 23-5 above. At the short-run break-even price, average total cost, including this opportunity cost of capital, will just equal that price. The firm will be making zero economic profits but a 10 percent *accounting profit*.

The Supply Curve for a Perfectly Competitive Industry

As you learned in Chapter 3, the relationship between a product's price and the quantity produced and offered for sale is a supply curve. Let's now examine the supply curve for a perfectly competitive industry.

The Perfect Competitor's Short-Run Supply Curve

What does the supply curve for the individual firm look like? Actually, we have been looking at it all along. We know that when the price of magneto optical disks is $5, the firm will supply seven or eight of them per hour. If the price falls to $3, the firm will supply five or six MO disks per hour. And if the price falls close to $2, the firm will shut down. Hence, in Figure 23-6 below, the firm's supply curve is the marginal cost curve above the short-run shutdown point. This is shown as the solid part of the marginal cost curve.

> *By definition, then, a firm's short-run supply curve in a competitive industry is its marginal cost curve at and above the point of intersection with the average variable cost curve.*

The Short-Run Industry Supply Curve

In Chapter 3, we indicated that the market supply curve was the summation of individual supply curves. At the beginning of this chapter, we drew a market supply curve in Figure 23-1 on page 509. Now we want to derive more precisely a market, or industry, supply curve to reflect individual producer behavior in that industry. First we must ask, What is an industry? It is merely a collection of firms producing a particular product. Therefore, we have a way to figure out the total supply curve of any industry: As discussed in Chapter 3, we add the quantities that each firm will supply at every possible price. In other words, we sum the individual supply curves of all the competitive firms *horizontally*. The individual supply curves, as we just saw, are simply the marginal cost curves of each firm.

Consider doing this for a hypothetical world in which there are only two producers of magneto optical disks in the industry, firm A and firm B. These two firms' marginal cost curves are given in panels (a) and (b) of Figure 23-7 on the following page. The marginal cost curves for the two separate firms are presented as MC$_A$ in panel (a)

FIGURE 23-6

The Individual Firm's Short-Run Supply Curve

The individual firm's short-run supply curve is the portion of its marginal cost curve at and above the minimum point on the average variable cost curve.

FIGURE 23-7

Deriving the Industry Supply Curve

Marginal cost curves at and above minimum average variable cost are presented in panels (a) and (b) for firms A and B. We horizontally sum the two quantities supplied, 7 units by firm A and 10 units by firm B, at a price of $6. This gives us point *F* in panel (c). We do the same thing for the quantities supplied at a price of $10. This gives us point *G*. When we connect those points, we have the industry supply curve, *S*, which is the horizontal summation—represented by the Greek letter sigma (Σ)—of the firms' marginal cost curves above their respective minimum average variable costs.

and MC_B in panel (b). Those two marginal cost curves are drawn only for prices above the minimum average variable cost for each respective firm. In panel (a), for firm A, at a price of $6 per unit, the quantity supplied would be 7 units. At a price of $10 per unit, the quantity supplied would be 12 units. In panel (b), we see the two different quantities that would be supplied by firm B corresponding to those two prices. Now, at a price of $6, we add horizontally the quantities 7 and 10 to obtain 17 units. This gives us one point, *F*, for our short-run **industry supply curve,** *S*. We obtain the other point, *G*, by doing the same horizontal adding of quantities at a price of $10 per unit.

When we connect all points such as *F* and *G*, we obtain the industry supply curve *S*, which is also marked ΣMC (where the capital Greek sigma, Σ, is the symbol for summation), indicating that it is the horizontal summation of the marginal cost curves (at and above the respective minimum average variable cost of each firm). Because the law of diminishing marginal product makes marginal cost curves rise as output rises, the short-run supply curve of a perfectly competitive industry must be upward sloping.

How have increases in the market prices of a number of veterinary services affected the quantity of services provided?

Industry supply curve

The locus of points showing the minimum prices at which given quantities will be forthcoming; also called the *market supply curve.*

EXAMPLE

Vets Respond to Higher Market Prices of Treatments for Fido

More than 16,000 U.S. veterinary clinics compete to provide health care services for household pets. Although slight quality differences surely exist across clinics, most offer relatively standard treatments and a wide array of basic pet health care services. The veterinary clinic industry, therefore, approximates a perfectly competitive industry.

During the past decade, the market demand for veterinary services has increased considerably, which has caused average pet health care prices to rise by more than 50 percent. Individual veterinary clinics have responded by moving upward along the portions of their marginal cost curves above their short-run shutdown points—that is, their individual supply curves. Consequently, there has been a substantial increase in the total quantity of pet care services provided by all clinics—an upward movement along the market supply curve.

FOR CRITICAL THINKING

Why do you suppose that a number of veterinary clinics have expanded their pet "clienteles" and hired more veterinarians to provide more hours of service?

Factors That Influence the Industry Supply Curve

As you have just seen, the industry supply curve is the horizontal summation of all of the individual firms' marginal cost curves at and above their respective minimum average variable cost points. This means that anything that affects the marginal cost curves of the firm will influence the industry supply curve. Therefore, the individual factors that will influence the supply schedule in a competitive industry can be summarized as the factors that cause the variable costs of production to change. These are factors that affect the individual marginal cost curves, such as changes in the individual firm's productivity, in factor prices (such as wages paid to labor and prices of raw materials), in per-unit taxes, and in anything else that would influence the individual firm's marginal cost curve.

All of these are *ceteris paribus* conditions of supply (see page 62 in Chapter 3). Because they affect the position of the marginal cost curve for the individual firm, they affect the position of the industry supply curve. A change in any of these will shift the firms' marginal cost curves and thus shift the industry supply curve.

QUICK QUIZ See page 531 for the answers. Review concepts from this section in MyEconLab.

Short-run average profits or losses are determined by comparing _____ total costs with _____ at the **profit-maximizing rate of output.** In the short run, the perfectly competitive firm can make economic profits or economic losses.

The perfectly competitive firm's short-run _____-_____ price equals the firm's minimum average total cost, which is at the point at which the _____ cost curve intersects the average total cost curve.

The perfectly competitive firm's short-run _____ price equals the firm's minimum average variable cost, which is at the point at which the _____ cost curve intersects the average variable cost curve. Shutdown will occur if price falls below average variable cost.

The firm will continue production at a price that exceeds average variable costs because revenues exceed total _____ costs of producing.

At the short-run break-even price, the firm is making _____ economic profits, which means that it is just making a _____ rate of return for industries with similar risks.

The firm's short-run supply curve is the portion of its marginal cost curve at and above its minimum average _____ cost. The industry short-run supply curve is a horizontal _____ of the individual firms' marginal cost curves at and above their respective minimum average _____ costs.

Price Determination under Perfect Competition

How is the market, or "going," price established in a competitive market? This price is established by the interaction of all the suppliers (firms) and all the demanders (consumers).

The Market Clearing Price

The market demand schedule, *D*, in panel (a) of Figure 23-8 on the following page represents the demand schedule for the entire industry, and the supply schedule, *S*, represents the supply schedule for the entire industry. The market clearing price, P_e, is established by the forces of supply and demand at the intersection of *D* and the short-run industry supply curve, *S*. Even though each individual firm has no control or effect on the price of its product in a competitive industry, the interaction of *all* the producers and buyers determines the price at which the product will be sold.

We say that the price P_e and the quantity Q_e in panel (a) of Figure 23-8 on the next page constitute the competitive solution to the resource allocation problem in that particular industry. It is the equilibrium at which quantity demanded equals quantity supplied, and both suppliers and demanders are doing as well as they can. The resulting individual firm demand curve, *d*, is shown in panel (b) of Figure 23-8 at the price P_e.

FIGURE 23-8

Industry Demand and Supply Curves and the Individual Firm Demand Curve

The industry demand curve is represented by D in panel (a). The short-run industry supply curve is S and is equal to ΣMC. The intersection of the demand and supply curves at E determines the equilibrium or market clearing price at P_e. The demand curve faced by the individual firm in panel (b) is perfectly elastic at the market clearing price determined in panel (a). If the producer has a marginal cost curve MC, its profit-maximizing output level is at q_e. Consider average cost curves AC_3, AC_1, and AC_2 associated with successively higher levels of fixed costs. For AC_1, economic profits are zero. For AC_2, profits are negative. For AC_3, profits are positive.

Market Equilibrium and the Individual Firm

In a purely competitive industry, the individual producer takes price as a given and chooses the output level that maximizes profits. (This is also the equilibrium level of output from the producer's standpoint.) We see in panel (b) of Figure 23-8 above that this is at q_e. If the producer's average costs are given by AC_1, the short-run break-even price arises at q_e (see Figure 23-5 on page 516). If its average costs are given by AC_2, then at q_e, AC exceeds price (average revenue), and the firm is incurring losses. Alternatively, if average costs are given by AC_3, the firm will be making economic profits at q_e. In the former case, we would expect, over time, that some firms will cease production (exit the industry), causing supply to shift inward. In the latter case, we would expect new firms to enter the industry to take advantage of the economic profits, thereby causing supply to shift outward. We now turn to these long-run considerations.

WHAT IF... the government mandated that prices stay at long-run equilibrium levels?

Politicians often complain whenever the prices of commodities such as oil, gasoline, minerals, or foods show considerable variability, and they commonly call for the government to "do something" to limit price variations. If the government were to force firms to keep prices fixed at anticipated long-run equilibrium levels, however, prices would be unable to adjust in response to short-run changes in market demand or supply. For instance, if an industry's price were fixed at the expected

long-run level and market demand were to rise, the quantity demanded would rise while quantity supplied would remain unchanged. A shortage would result. In contrast, if the market supply were to increase, the quantity supplied would rise while quantity demanded would remain unchanged. The result would be a surplus. Thus, well-intentioned efforts to keep prices near long-run equilibrium levels likely would produce numerous shortages and surpluses over time.

The Long-Run Industry Situation: Exit and Entry

In the long run in a competitive situation, firms will be making zero economic profits. (Actually, this is true only for identical firms. Throughout the remainder of the discussion, we assume firms have the same cost structures.) We surmise, therefore, that in the long run a perfectly competitive firm's price (marginal and average revenue) curve will just touch its average total cost curve. How does this occur? It comes about through an adjustment process that depends on economic profits and losses.

Exit and Entry of Firms

Look back at both Figure 23-3 on page 513 and Figure 23-4 on page 514. The existence of either profits or losses is a signal to owners of capital both inside and outside the industry. If an industry is characterized by firms showing economic profits as represented in Figure 23-3, these economic profits signal owners of capital elsewhere in the economy that they, too, should enter this industry. In contrast, if some firms in an industry are suffering economic losses as represented in Figure 23-4, these economic losses signal resource owners outside the industry to stay out. In addition, these economic losses signal resource owners within the industry not to reinvest and if possible to leave the industry. It is in this sense that we say that profits direct resources to their highest-valued use. In the long run, capital will flow into industries in which profitability is highest and will flow out of industries in which profitability is lowest.

ALLOCATION OF CAPITAL AND MARKET SIGNALS The price system therefore allocates capital according to the relative expected rates of return on alternative investments. Hence, entry restrictions (such as limits on the numbers of taxicabs and banks permitted to enter the taxi service and banking industries) will hinder economic efficiency by not allowing resources to flow to their highest-valued use. Similarly, exit restrictions (such as laws that require firms to give advance notice of closings) will act to trap resources (temporarily) in sectors in which their value is below that in alternative uses. Such laws will also inhibit the ability of firms to respond to changes in both the domestic and international marketplaces.

Not every industry presents an immediate source of opportunity for every firm. In a brief period of time, it may be impossible for a firm that produces tractors to switch to the production of digital devices, even if there are very large profits to be made. Over the long run, however, we would expect to see owners of some other resources switch to producing digital devices. In a market economy, investors supply firms in the more profitable industry with more investment funds, which they take from firms in less profitable industries. (Also, positive economic profits induce existing firms to use internal investment funds for expansion.) Consequently, resources useful in the production of more profitable goods, such as labor, will be bid away from lower-valued opportunities. Investors and other suppliers of resources respond to market **signals** about their highest-valued opportunities.

What consistent market signals have many hamburger sellers been receiving during the past few years?

Signals
Compact ways of conveying to economic decision makers information needed to make decisions. An effective signal not only conveys information but also provides the incentive to react appropriately. Economic profits and economic losses are such signals.

EXAMPLE

For Many Hamburger Sellers, the Exit Signal Is Flashing

During the 2000s, a number of firms entered the hamburger fast-food market as market demand increased in response to a rising U.S. population and higher incomes. In today's dampened economy, however, market demand is stagnant. Consequently, market prices of hamburgers—and, hence, sellers' revenues—have remained nearly unchanged for several years. During the same period, however, beef prices have increased by more than 25 percent, which has led to a rapid escalation in costs of producing hamburgers. As a result, a number of sellers have earned negative economic profits in recent years. These economic losses are signals that many firms have been acting upon by exiting the market.

FOR CRITICAL THINKING

If market demand for hamburgers were to increase once again, is it possible that some sellers might reconsider exiting the market even if beef prices continue to rise?

TENDENCY TOWARD EQUILIBRIUM Market adjustment to changes in demand will occur regardless of the wishes of the managers of firms in less profitable markets. They can either attempt to adjust their product line to respond to the new demands, be replaced by managers who are more responsive to new conditions, or see their firms go bankrupt as they find themselves unable to replace worn-out plant and equipment.

In addition, when we say that in a competitive long-run equilibrium situation firms will be making zero economic profits, we must realize that at a particular point in time it would be pure coincidence for a firm to be making *exactly* zero economic profits. Real-world information is not as precise as the curves we use to simplify our analysis. Things change all the time in a dynamic world, and firms, even in a very competitive situation, may for many reasons not be making exactly zero economic profits. We say that there is a *tendency* toward that equilibrium position, but firms are adjusting all the time to changes in their cost curves and in the market demand curves.

Long-Run Industry Supply Curves

In panel (a) of Figure 23-8 on page 520, we drew the summation of all of the portions of the individual firms' marginal cost curves at and above each firm's respective minimum average variable costs as the upward-sloping supply curve of the entire industry. We should be aware, however, that a relatively inelastic supply curve may be appropriate only in the short run. After all, one of the prerequisites of a competitive industry is freedom of entry.

Why has the number of firms offering "online daily deals" grown considerably in a very short time?

EXAMPLE

Economic Profits Attract Online-Daily-Deals Entrants in Droves

For a couple of years, companies such as Groupon and LivingSocial were among the only deals in town—at least in terms of daily deals sold on the Internet. These firms send e-mails to subscribers offering deep discounts on products and services provided by retailers. The firms and retailers split the revenues generated by these e-mails. Between late 2008 and early 2011, Groupon and LivingSocial were among only a handful of online firms competing in the daily-deals market. These few online competitors earned substantial economic profits from their operations.

Since the middle of 2011, though, a number of firms have responded to the observation of positive economic profits by entering the daily-deals market. Examples include nationwide online-daily-deal services now provided by Facebook, Google, TravelZoo, and Yipit. In addition, firms are now competing to offer online daily-deal services in local areas. Today, at least 500 daily-deal competitors are active, and several more enter the industry each month. Thus, positive economic profits have attracted a substantial number of entrants into this industry.

FOR CRITICAL THINKING
Why do you suppose that the entry of so many other competitors has resulted in declines in economic profits earned by firms such as Groupon and LivingSocial?

Long-run industry supply curve
A market supply curve showing the relationship between prices and quantities after firms have been allowed the time to enter into or exit from an industry, depending on whether there have been positive or negative economic profits.

Remember that our definition of the long run is a period of time in which all adjustments can be made. The **long-run industry supply curve** is a supply curve showing the relationship between quantities supplied by the entire industry at different prices after firms have been allowed to either enter or leave the industry, depending on whether there have been positive or negative economic profits. Also, the long-run industry supply curve is drawn under the assumption that firms are identical and that entry and exit have been completed. This means that along the long-run industry supply curve, firms in the industry earn zero economic profits.

The long-run industry supply curve can take one of three shapes, depending on whether input prices stay constant, increase, or decrease as the number of firms in the industry changes. In Chapter 22, we assumed that input prices remained constant to the *firm* regardless of the firm's rate of output. When we look at the entire *industry*, however, when all firms are expanding and new firms are entering, they may simultaneously bid up input prices.

CONSTANT-COST INDUSTRIES In principle, there are industries that use such a small percentage of the total supply of inputs required for industrywide production that firms can enter the industry without bidding up input prices. In such a situation, we are dealing with a **constant-cost industry.** Its long-run industry supply curve is therefore horizontal and is represented by S_L in panel (a) of Figure 23-9 below.

We can work through the case in which constant costs prevail. We start out in panel (a) with demand curve D_1 and supply curve S_1. The equilibrium price is P_1. Market demand shifts rightward to D_2. In the short run, the equilibrium price rises to P_2. This generates positive economic profits for existing firms in the industry. Such economic profits induce capital to flow into the industry. The existing firms expand or new firms enter (or both). The short-run supply curve shifts outward to S_2. The new intersection with the new demand curve is at E_3. The new equilibrium price is again P_1. The long-run supply curve, labeled S_L, is obtained by connecting the intersections of the corresponding pairs of demand and short-run supply curves, E_1 and E_3.

In a constant-cost industry, long-run supply is perfectly elastic. Any shift in demand is eventually met by just enough entry or exit of suppliers that the long-run price is constant at P_1. Retail trade is often given as an example of such an industry because output can be expanded or contracted without affecting input prices. Banking is another example.

Constant-cost industry
An industry whose total output can be increased without an increase in long-run per-unit costs. Its long-run supply curve is horizontal.

INCREASING-COST INDUSTRIES In an **increasing-cost industry,** expansion by existing firms and the addition of new firms cause the price of inputs specialized to that industry to be bid up. As costs of production rise, the ATC curve and the firms' MC curves shift upward, causing short-run supply curves (each firm's marginal cost curve) to shift vertically upward. Hence, industry supply shifts out by less than in a constant-cost industry. The result is a long-run industry supply curve that slopes upward, as represented by S_L' in panel (b) of Figure 23-9. Examples are residential construction and coal mining—both use specialized inputs that cannot be obtained in ever-increasing quantities without causing their prices to rise.

Increasing-cost industry
An industry in which an increase in industry output is accompanied by an increase in long-run per-unit costs, such that the long-run industry supply curve slopes upward.

DECREASING-COST INDUSTRIES An expansion in the number of firms in an industry can lead to a reduction in input costs and a downward shift in the ATC and MC curves. When this occurs, the long-run industry supply curve will slope downward. An example, S_L'', is given in panel (c) of Figure 23-9. This is a **decreasing-cost industry.**

Decreasing-cost industry
An industry in which an increase in output leads to a reduction in long-run per-unit costs, such that the long-run industry supply curve slopes downward.

FIGURE 23-9

Constant-Cost, Increasing-Cost, and Decreasing-Cost Industries

In panel (a), we show a situation in which the demand curve shifts from D_1 to D_2. Price increases from P_1 to P_2. In time, the short-run supply curve shifts outward because entry occurs in response to positive profits, and the equilibrium changes from E_2 to E_3. The market clearing price is again P_1. If we connect points such as E_1 and E_3, we come up with the long-run supply curve S_L. This is a constant-cost industry. In panel (b), costs are increasing for the industry, and therefore the long-run supply curve, S_L', slopes upward and long-run prices rise from P_1 to P_2. In panel (c), costs are decreasing for the industry as it expands, and therefore the long-run supply curve, S_L'', slopes downward such that long-run prices decline from P_1 to P_2.

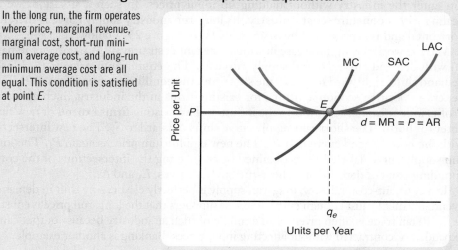

FIGURE 23-10

Long-Run Firm Competitive Equilibrium

In the long run, the firm operates where price, marginal revenue, marginal cost, short-run minimum average cost, and long-run minimum average cost are all equal. This condition is satisfied at point E.

Long-Run Equilibrium

In the long run, the firm can change the scale of its plant, adjusting its plant size in such a way that it has no further incentive to change. It will do so until profits are maximized.

The Firm's Long-Run Situation

Figure 23-10 above shows the long-run equilibrium of the perfectly competitive firm. Given a price of P and a marginal cost curve, MC, the firm produces at output q_e. Because economic profits must be zero in the long run, the firm's short-run average costs (SAC) must equal P at q_e, which occurs at minimum SAC. In addition, because we are in long-run equilibrium, any economies of scale must be exhausted, so we are on the minimum point of the long-run average cost curve (LAC). In other words, the long-run equilibrium position is where "everything is equal," which is at point E in Figure 23-10. There, *price* equals *marginal revenue* equals *marginal cost* equals *average cost* (minimum, short-run, and long-run).

Perfect Competition and Minimum Average Total Cost

Look again at Figure 23-10 above. In long-run equilibrium, the perfectly competitive firm finds itself producing at output rate q_e. At that rate of output, the price is just equal to the minimum long-run average cost as well as the minimum short-run average cost. In this sense, perfect competition results in the production of goods and services using the least costly combination of resources. This is an important attribute of a perfectly competitive long-run equilibrium, particularly when we wish to compare the market structure of perfect competition with other market structures that are less than perfectly competitive. We will examine these other market structures in later chapters.

Competitive Pricing: Marginal Cost Pricing

In a perfectly competitive industry, each firm produces where its marginal cost curve intersects its marginal revenue curve from below. Thus, perfectly competitive firms always sell their goods at a price that just equals marginal cost. This is said to be the optimal price of this good because the price that consumers pay reflects the opportunity cost to society of producing the good. Recall that marginal cost is the amount that a firm must spend to purchase the additional resources needed to expand output by one unit. Given competitive markets, the amount paid for a resource will be the same in all of its alternative uses. Thus, MC reflects relative resource input use. That is, if the MC of good 1 is twice the MC of good 2, one more unit of good 1 requires twice the resource input of one more unit of good 2.

Marginal Cost Pricing

The competitive firm produces up to the point at which the market price just equals the marginal cost. Herein lies the element of the optimal nature of a competitive solution. It is called **marginal cost pricing.** The competitive firm sells its product at a price that just equals the cost to society—the opportunity cost—for that is what the marginal cost curve represents. (But note here that it is the self-interest of firm owners that causes price to equal the marginal cost to society.) In other words, the marginal benefit to consumers, given by the price that they are willing to pay for the last unit of the good purchased, just equals the marginal cost to society of producing the last unit. (If the marginal benefit exceeds the marginal cost, that is, if $P > MC$, too little is being produced in that people value additional units more than the cost to society of producing them. If $P < MC$, the opposite is true.)

When an individual pays a price equal to the marginal cost of production, the cost to the user of that product is equal to the sacrifice or cost to society of producing that quantity of that good as opposed to more of some other good. (We are assuming that all marginal social costs are accounted for.) The competitive solution, then, is called *efficient*, in the economic sense of the word. Economic efficiency means that it is impossible to increase the output of any good without lowering the *value* of the total output produced in the economy. No juggling of resources, such as labor and capital, will result in an output that is higher in total value than the value of all of the goods and services already being produced. In an efficient equilibrium, it is impossible to make one person better off without making someone else worse off. All resources are used in the most advantageous way possible, and society therefore enjoys an efficient allocation of productive resources. All goods and services are sold at their opportunity cost, and marginal cost pricing prevails throughout.

Marginal cost pricing
A system of pricing in which the price charged is equal to the opportunity cost to society of producing one more unit of the good or service in question. The opportunity cost is the marginal cost to society.

Market Failure

Although perfect competition does offer many desirable results, situations arise when perfectly competitive markets cannot efficiently allocate resources. Either too many or too few resources are used in the production of a good or service. These situations are instances of **market failure.** Externalities arising from failures to fully assign property rights and public goods are examples. For reasons discussed in later chapters, perfectly competitive markets cannot efficiently allocate resources in these situations, and alternative allocation mechanisms are called for. In some cases, alternative market structures or government intervention *may* improve the economic outcome.

Market failure
A situation in which an unrestrained market operation leads to either too few or too many resources going to a specific economic activity.

QUICK QUIZ   See page 531 for the answers. Review concepts from this section in MyEconLab.

The perfectly competitive price is determined by the _____ of the market demand curve and the market supply curve. The market supply curve is equal to the horizontal summation of the portions of the individual marginal cost curves above their respective minimum average _____ costs.

In the long run, perfectly competitive firms make _____ economic profits because of entry and exit whenever there are industrywide economic profits or losses.

A constant-cost industry has a _____ long-run supply curve. An increasing-cost industry has an _____-sloping

long-run supply curve. A decreasing-cost industry has a _____-sloping long-run supply curve.

In the long run, a perfectly competitive firm produces to the point at which price, marginal revenue, marginal cost, short-run minimum average cost, and long-run minimum average cost are all _____.

Perfectly competitive pricing is essentially _____ _____ pricing. Therefore, the perfectly competitive solution is called efficient because _____ _____ represents the social opportunity cost of producing one more unit of the good.

YOU ARE THERE
Looking to Enter a Competitive Online Market? Rent a Desk!

Many people entering markets to provide online services such as business consulting, legal advising, or educational tutoring require little working space. In most cases, all they require is a desk and Internet access. Saeed Amidi, chief executive of Plug and Play Tech Centers, has established a business that assists entrepreneurs in attempting to enter such online service markets.

To ease the task of entering these competitive service markets, Amidi's company rents, at rates as low as $275 per month, shared workspaces consisting of desks and Internet access points. Plug and Play's centers typically contain approximately 20,000 square feet of space for rent to about 1,000 individuals. Thus, at one of the firm's Tech Centers, an entrepreneur seeking a low-cost means of entering an online service

market can rent a desk positioned within about 20 square feet of workspace. All that is required to start an online service business is an appropriate set of digital devices and apps. Exiting also is simple: The individual ends the workspace rental contract and removes all private belongings from the shared-workspace center.

Critical Thinking Questions

1. Why are many online service markets likely to be perfectly competitive?
2. Recently, competitors of Plug and Play have been opening their own shared-workspace centers. Does the market for shared workspace likely possess characteristics of a perfectly competitive market? Explain.

ISSUES & APPLICATIONS

A Decreasing-Cost, "White Gold" Industry

CONCEPTS APPLIED
▶ Perfect Competition
▶ Decreasing-Cost Industry
▶ Long-Run Industry Supply Curve

Lithium is a naturally occurring, superlight element often called "white gold." It is the key component of ion batteries that power mobile digital devices, so the market demand for lithium has increased substantially.

Changing Methods of Extracting Lithium Alter Input Prices

For many years, a number of U.S. companies were key providers of lithium. These firms mined the element from seams of a mineral called spodumene that is found in large quantities in North Carolina and a few other states.

During the past two decades, however, many South American companies have developed less expensive ways of extracting lithium using alternative inputs. These firms pump brine from ancient lakebeds into giant evaporation

ponds and let the sun's rays extract the lithium. Then special equipment collects the element.

A Downward-Sloping Long-Run Lithium Supply Curve

Figure 23-11 on the facing page displays what has happened to the market price of lithium since 1952. As market demand has risen and the means of extracting lithium has switched from mining to brine pumping combined with evaporation, the prices of inputs used to produce the metal

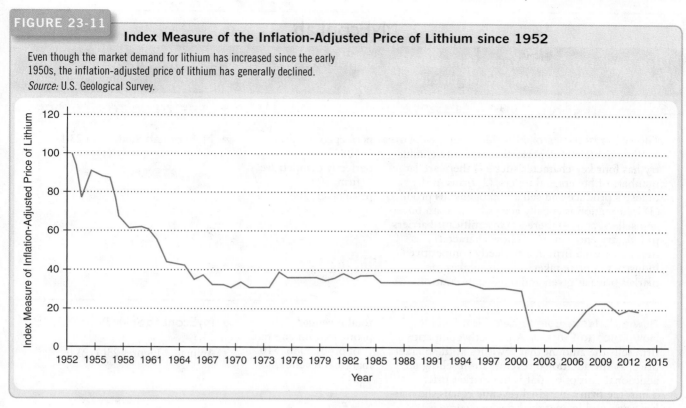

FIGURE 23-11

Index Measure of the Inflation-Adjusted Price of Lithium since 1952

Even though the market demand for lithium has increased since the early 1950s, the inflation-adjusted price of lithium has generally declined.
Source: U.S. Geological Survey.

have fallen. The consequence has been a general decrease in the price of the "white gold" element.

The decline in the price of lithium following the entry of more firms in response to increasing demand indicates that the long-run lithium supply curve slopes downward. Thus, the lithium industry is a decreasing-cost industry.

For Critical Thinking

1. If input prices had increased as firms entered the lithium industry in response to rising demand, what would have been the shape of the long-run supply curve?

2. If the market demand for lithium were to decrease during the 2020s, what would happen to the market clearing price of lithium in the long run?

Web Resources

1. To view a list that indicates the large number of firms producing lithium today, go to www.econtoday.com/chap23.

2. To learn why some observers worry that the lithium market may become less nearly perfectly competitive many years from now, go to www.econtoday.com/chap23.

> **MyEconLab**
>
> For more questions on this chapter's Issues & Applications, go to MyEconLab. In the Study Plan for this chapter, select Section N: News.

MyEconLab

Here is what you should know after reading this chapter. MyEconLab will help you identify what you know, and where to go when you need to practice.

WHAT YOU SHOULD KNOW		WHERE TO GO TO PRACTICE
The Characteristics of a Perfectly Competitive Market Structure A perfectly competitive industry has four key characteristics: (1) there are large numbers of buyers and sellers, (2) firms in the industry produce and sell a homogeneous product, (3) information is equally accessible to both buyers and sellers, and (4) there are insignificant barriers to industry entry or exit. These characteristics imply that each firm in a perfectly competitive industry is a price taker: The firm takes the market price as given and outside its control.	perfect competition, 508 perfectly competitive firm, 508 price taker, 508	• MyEconLab Study Plan 23.1
How a Perfectly Competitive Firm Decides How Much to Produce A perfectly competitive firm sells the amount that it wishes at the market price, so the additional revenue from selling an additional unit of output is the market price. Thus, the firm's marginal revenue equals the market price, and its marginal revenue curve is the firm's perfectly elastic demand curve. The firm maximizes economic profits when marginal cost equals marginal revenue, as long as the market price is not below the short-run shutdown price, where the marginal cost curve crosses the average variable cost curve.	total revenues, 510 profit-maximizing rate of production, 510 marginal revenue, 512 **Key Figures** Figure 23-1, 509 Figure 23-2, 511	• MyEconLab Study Plans 23.2, 23.3 • Animated Figures 23-1, 23-2
The Short-Run Supply Curve of a Perfectly Competitive Firm If the market price is below the short-run shutdown price, the firm's total revenues fail to cover its variable costs. The firm would be better off halting production and minimizing its economic loss in the short run. If the market price is above the short-run shutdown price, however, the firm produces the rate of output where marginal revenue, the market price, equals marginal cost. Thus, the range of the firm's marginal cost curve above the short-run shutdown price is the firm's short-run supply curve, which gives the firm's combinations of market prices and production choices.	short-run break-even price, 515 short-run shutdown price, 515 industry supply curve, 518 **Key Figures** Figure 23-3, 513 Figure 23-4, 514 Figure 23-5, 516 Figure 23-6, 517 Figure 23-7, 518	• MyEconLab Study Plans 23.4, 23.5, 23.6, 23.7 • Animated Figures 23-3, 23-4, 23-5, 23-6, 23-7
The Equilibrium Price in a Perfectly Competitive Market The short-run supply curve for a perfectly competitive industry is obtained by summing the quantities supplied by all firms at each price. At the equilibrium market price, the total amount of output supplied by all firms is equal to the total amount of output demanded by all buyers.	**Key Figure** Figure 23-8, 520	• MyEconLab Study Plan 23.8 • Animated Figure 23-8

MyEconLab *continued*

WHAT YOU SHOULD KNOW ———————————————————— WHERE TO GO TO PRACTICE ———

Incentives to Enter or Exit a Perfectly Competitive Industry In the short run, a perfectly competitive firm will continue to produce as long as the market price exceeds the short-run shutdown price. This is so even if the market price is below the short-run break-even point where the marginal cost curve crosses the firm's average total cost curve. Even though the firm earns an economic loss, it minimizes its loss by continuing to produce in the short run. In the long run, continued losses will induce exit from the industry.

signals, 521

- MyEconLab Study Plan 23.9

The Long-Run Industry Supply Curve and Constant-, Increasing-, and Decreasing-Cost Industries The long-run industry supply curve in a perfectly competitive industry shows the relationship between prices and quantities after firms have entered or left the industry in response to economic profits or losses. In a constant-cost industry, total output can increase without a rise in long-run per-unit costs, so the long-run industry supply curve is horizontal. In an increasing-cost industry, per-unit costs increase with a rise in industry output, so the long-run industry supply curve slopes upward. In a decreasing-cost industry per-unit costs decline as industry output increases, and the long-run industry supply curve slopes downward.

long-run industry supply curve, 522
constant-cost industry, 523
increasing-cost industry, 523
decreasing-cost industry, 523
marginal cost pricing, 525
market failure, 525

Key Figure
Figure 23-10, 524

- MyEconLab Study Plans 23.10, 23.11
- Animated Figure 23-10

Log in to MyEconLab, take a chapter test, and get a personalized Study Plan that tells you which concepts you understand and which ones you need to review. From there, MyEconLab will give you further practice, tutorials, animations, videos, and guided solutions. For more information, visit www.myeconlab.com

PROBLEMS

All problems are assignable in MyEconLab. Answers to odd-numbered problems appear at the back of the book.

23-1. Explain why each of the following examples is not a perfectly competitive industry. (See page 508.)

  a. One firm produces a large portion of the industry's total output, but there are many firms in the industry, and their products are indistinguishable. Firms can easily exit and enter the industry.

  b. There are many buyers and sellers in the industry. Consumers have equal information about the prices of firms' products, which differ moderately in quality from firm to firm.

  c. Many taxicabs compete in a city. The city's government requires all taxicabs to provide identical service. Taxicabs are nearly identical, and all drivers must wear a designated uniform. The government also enforces a binding limit on the number of taxicab companies that can operate within the city's boundaries.

23-2. Consider a market for online movie rentals. The market supply curve slopes upward, the market demand curve slopes downward, and the equilibrium rental price equals $3.50. Consider each of the following events, and discuss the effects they will have on the market clearing price and on the demand curve faced by the individual online rental firm. (See page 509.)

a. People's tastes change in favor of going to see more movies at cinemas with their friends and family members.

b. More online movie-rental firms enter the market.

c. There is a significant increase in the price to consumers of purchasing movies online.

23-3. Consider the diagram below, which applies to a perfectly competitive firm, which at present faces a market clearing price of $20 per unit and produces 10,000 units of output per week. (See pages 509–512.)

a. What is the firm's current average revenue per unit?

b. What are the present economic profits of this firm? Is the firm maximizing economic profits? Explain.

c. If the market clearing price drops to $12.50 per unit, should this firm continue to produce in the short run if it wishes to maximize its economic profits (or minimize its economic losses)? Explain.

d. If the market clearing price drops to $7.50 per unit, should this firm continue to produce in the short run if it wishes to maximize its economic profits (or minimize its economic losses)? Explain.

23-4. The table in the next column represents the hourly output and cost structure for a local pizza shop. The market is perfectly competitive, and the market price of a pizza in the area is $10. Total costs include all opportunity costs. (See pages 509–514.)

Total Hourly Output and Sales of Pizzas	Total Hourly Cost ($)
0	5
1	9
2	11
3	12
4	14
5	18
6	24
7	32
8	42
9	54
10	68

a. Calculate the total revenue and total economic profit for this pizza shop at each rate of output.

b. Assuming that the pizza shop always produces and sells at least one pizza per hour, does this appear to be a situation of short-run or long-run equilibrium?

c. Calculate the pizza shop's marginal cost and marginal revenue at each rate of output. Based on marginal analysis, what is the profit-maximizing rate of output for the pizza shop?

d. Draw a diagram depicting the short-run marginal revenue and marginal cost curves for this pizza shop, and illustrate the determination of its profit-maximizing output rate.

23-5. Consider the information provided in Problem 23-4. Suppose the market price drops to only $5 per pizza. In the short run, should this pizza shop continue to make pizzas, or will it maximize its economic profits (that is, minimize its economic loss) by shutting down? (See pages 514–515.)

23-6. Yesterday, a perfectly competitive producer of construction bricks manufactured and sold 10,000 bricks per week at a market price that was just equal to the minimum average variable cost of producing each brick. Today, all the firm's costs are the same, but the market price of bricks has declined. (See pages 514–515.)

a. Assuming that this firm has positive fixed costs, did the firm earn economic profits, economic losses, or zero economic profits yesterday?

b. To maximize economic profits today, how many bricks should this firm produce today?

23-7. Suppose that a firm in a perfectly competitive industry finds that at its current output rate, marginal revenue exceeds the minimum average total cost of producing any feasible rate of output. Furthermore, the firm is producing an output rate at which marginal cost is less than the average total cost at that rate of output. Is the firm maximizing its economic profits? Why or why not? (See pages 512–513.)

23-8. A perfectly competitive industry is initially in a short-run equilibrium in which all firms are earning zero economic profits but in which firms are operating below their minimum efficient scale. Explain the long-run adjustments that will take place for the industry to attain long-run equilibrium with firms operating at their minimum efficient scale. (See pages 520–521.)

23-9. Two years ago, a large number of firms entered a market in which existing firms had been earning positive economic profits. By the end of last year, the typical firm in this industry had begun earning negative economic profits. No other events occurred in this market during the past two years. (See pages 520–521.)

    a. Explain the adjustment process that occurred last year.

    b. Predict what adjustments will take place in this market beginning this year, other things being equal.

23-10. The minimum feasible long-run average cost for firms in a perfectly competitive industry is $40 per

unit. If every firm in the industry currently is producing an output consistent with a long-run equilibrium, what is the marginal cost incurred by each firm? What is the market price? (See page 524.)

23-11. In several markets for digital devices that can be viewed as perfectly competitive, steady increases in demand for the required minerals ultimately have generated long-run reductions in the market prices of these devices. Describe in words the types of adjustments that must have occurred in these markets to have brought about this outcome, and evaluate whether such digital-device industries are increasing-, constant-, or decreasing-cost industries. (See pages 522–524.)

23-12. In several perfectly competitive markets for minerals used as inputs in digital devices, persistent increases in demand eventually have generated long-run increases in the market prices of these devices. Describe in words the types of adjustments that must have occurred in these markets to have brought about this outcome, and evaluate whether such mineral-extraction industries are increasing-, constant-, or decreasing-cost industries. (See pages 522–524.)

ECONOMICS ON THE NET

The Cost Structure of the Movie Theater Business A key idea in this chapter is that competition among firms in an industry can influence the long-run cost structure within the industry. Here you get a chance to apply this concept to a multinational company that owns movie theaters.

Title: AMC International

Navigation: Follow the link at **www.econtoday.com /chap23** to visit American Multi-Cinema's home page.

Application Answer the following questions.

1. At the bottom of the home page, click on *Investor Relations*, and then click on *Fact Sheet*. What is the average number of screens in an AMC theater? How many theaters does AMC own and manage?

2. Based on the *Fact Sheet* information, which of AMC's theaters serves the largest volume of viewing customers?

3. Back up to the home page, and under "See a Movie," click on *Find a Theater*. Enter a few zip codes and make a list of the numbers of screens at the theaters that appear in each list. Based on the numbers of screens in this sample you have collected and your answers to questions 1 and 2 above, what can you conclude about the likely cost structure of this industry? Illustrate the long-run average cost curve for this industry.

For Group Discussion and Analysis A theater with a particularly large number of screens is called a multiplex. What do you suppose constrains the size of a multiplex theater in a typical locale? What factors do you think determine whether it is likely to be less costly for AMC to have fewer facilities that are larger in size or to have many smaller facilities?

ANSWERS TO QUICK QUIZZES

p. 513: (i) large . . . homogeneous . . . unrestrained; (ii) no . . . all; (iii) marginal . . . marginal; (iv) revenue . . . cost . . . price

p. 519: (i) average . . . price; (ii) break-even . . . marginal; (iii) shutdown . . . marginal; (iv) variable; (v) zero . . . normal; (vi) variable . . . summation . . . variable

p. 525: (i) intersection . . . variable; (ii) zero; (iii) horizontal . . . upward . . . downward; (iv) equal; (v) marginal cost . . . marginal cost

24 Monopoly

Have you ever wanted to be a kick boxer in the state of Ohio? If so, you must pay at least $100 to obtain a license before you can take the ring. Or perhaps you would like to be an interior designer. In some states, you can start to work immediately. In others, however, you must spend hundreds of hours in classes at tuition rates totaling thousands of dollars in order to qualify for a license to operate your own interior design business. A few states will even require a bachelor's degree in interior design from an accredited university program. What are the economic effects of these and other legal requirements that people must meet before they can engage in certain occupations? You will learn the answer by reading this chapter.

among U.S. companies receiving the highest rates of profits as percentages of revenues are private hospitals located in small- to medium-sized cities? Hospitals with profit rates exceeding 30 cents for every dollar of revenues are located in cities such as Northridge, California; Englewood, Colorado; Rochester, Minnesota; and El Paso, Texas. A hospital in Dothan, Alabama, takes in more than 50 cents in profits for each dollar of revenues it receives. A key characteristic shared by these hospitals is that they are all the only large, full-service hospitals located within regions surrounding the cities in which they are based. In this chapter, you will learn why a business that is the only seller—called a *monopoly*—often can earn substantial profits.

Definition of a Monopolist

The word *monopoly* probably brings to mind notions of a business that gouges the consumer and gets rich in the process. But if we are to succeed in analyzing and predicting the behavior of imperfectly competitive firms, we will have to be more objective in our definition. Although most monopolies in the United States are relatively large, our definition will be equally applicable to small businesses: A **monopolist** is the *single supplier* of a good or service for which there is no close substitute.

In a monopoly market structure, the firm (the monopolist) and the industry are one and the same. Occasionally, there may be a problem in identifying an industry and therefore determining if a monopoly exists. For example, should we think of aluminum and steel as separate industries, or should we define the industry in terms of basic metals? Our answer depends on the extent to which aluminum and steel can be substituted in the production of a wide range of products.

As we shall see in this chapter, a seller prefers to have a monopoly rather than to face competitors. In general, we think of monopoly prices as being higher than prices under perfect competition and of monopoly profits as typically being higher than profits under perfect competition (which are, in the long run, merely equivalent to a normal rate of return). How does a firm obtain a monopoly in an industry? Basically, there must be *barriers to entry* that enable firms to receive monopoly profits in the long run. Barriers to entry are restrictions on who can start a business or who can stay in a business.

Monopolist
The single supplier of a good or service for which there is no close substitute. The monopolist therefore constitutes its entire industry.

Barriers to Entry

For any amount of monopoly power to continue to exist in the long run, the market must be closed to entry in some way. Either legal means or certain aspects of the industry's technical or cost structure may prevent entry. We will discuss several of the barriers to entry that have allowed firms to reap monopoly profits in the long run (even if they are not pure monopolists in the technical sense).

Ownership of Resources without Close Substitutes

Preventing a newcomer from entering an industry is often difficult. Indeed, some economists contend that no monopoly acting without government support has been able to prevent entry into the industry unless that monopoly has had the control of some essential natural resource. Consider the possibility of one firm's owning the entire supply of a raw material input that is essential to the production of a particular commodity.

The exclusive ownership of such a vital resource serves as a barrier to entry until an alternative source of the raw material input is found or an alternative technology not requiring the raw material in question is developed. A good example of control over a vital input is the Aluminum Company of America (Alcoa), a firm that prior to World War II owned most world stocks of bauxite, the essential raw material in the production of aluminum. Such a situation is rare, though, and is ordinarily temporary.

Economies of Scale

Sometimes it is not profitable for more than one firm to exist in an industry. This is true if one firm would have to produce such a large quantity in order to realize lower unit costs that there would not be sufficient demand to warrant a second producer of the same product. Such a situation may arise because of a phenomenon we discussed in Chapter 22—economies of scale. When economies of scale exist, proportional increases in output yield proportionately smaller increases in total costs, and per-unit costs drop. When economies of scale exist, larger firms (with larger output) have an advantage in that they have lower costs that enable them to charge lower prices and thereby drive smaller firms out of business.

When economies of scale occur over a wide range of outputs, a **natural monopoly** may develop. A natural monopoly is the first firm to take advantage of persistent declining long-run average costs as scale increases. The natural monopolist is able to underprice its competitors and eventually force all of them out of the market.

Figure 24-1 below shows a downward-sloping long-run average cost curve (LAC). Recall that when average costs are falling, marginal costs are less than average costs. Thus, when the long-run average cost curve slopes downward, the long-run marginal cost curve (LMC) will be below the LAC.

In our example, long-run average costs are falling over such a large range of production rates that we would expect only one firm to survive as a natural monopolist. It would be the first one to take advantage of the decreasing average costs. That is, it would construct the large-scale facilities first. As its average costs fell, it would lower prices and get an ever-larger share of the market. Once that firm had driven all other firms out of the industry, it would raise its price to maximize profits.

Legal or Governmental Restrictions

Governments and legislatures can also erect barriers to entry. These include licenses, franchises, patents, tariffs, and specific regulations that tend to limit entry.

LICENSES, FRANCHISES, AND CERTIFICATES OF CONVENIENCE It is illegal to enter many industries without a government license, or a "certificate of convenience and public necessity." For example, in some states you cannot form an electrical utility to compete with the electrical utility already operating in your area. You would first have to obtain a certificate of convenience and public necessity from the appropriate authority, which is usually the state's public utility commission. Yet public utility

---

Natural monopoly

A monopoly that arises from the peculiar production characteristics in an industry. It usually arises when there are large economies of scale relative to the industry's demand such that one firm can produce at a lower average cost than can be achieved by multiple firms.

YOU ARE THERE

To contemplate why a city government might prefer that a firm have a monopoly, take a look at **Seeking Higher Rents from Souvenir Vendors in Atlanta** on page 548.

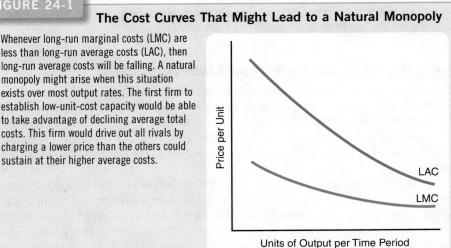

FIGURE 24-1

The Cost Curves That Might Lead to a Natural Monopoly

Whenever long-run marginal costs (LMC) are less than long-run average costs (LAC), then long-run average costs will be falling. A natural monopoly might arise when this situation exists over most output rates. The first firm to establish low-unit-cost capacity would be able to take advantage of declining average total costs. This firm would drive out all rivals by charging a lower price than the others could sustain at their higher average costs.

commissions in these states rarely, if ever, issue a certificate to a group of investors who want to compete directly in the same geographic area as an existing electrical utility. Hence, entry into the industry in a particular geographic area is prohibited, and long-run monopoly profits conceivably could be earned by the electrical utility already serving the area.

To enter interstate (and also many intrastate) markets for pipelines, television and radio broadcasting, and transmission of natural gas, to cite a few such industries, it is often necessary to obtain similar permits. Because these franchises or licenses are restricted, long-run monopoly profits might be earned by the firms already in the industry.

Why is it that some adults object to children operating lemonade stands?

POLICY EXAMPLE

Waging Economic War on Children's Lemonade Stands

The battles continue unabated across the land. The skirmishes begin when children as young as age 4 seek to learn about entrepreneurship—and to earn income to purchase toys or comic books—by opening lemonade stands and selling tall, cool drinks to their neighbors. Then, in towns and cities ranging from Cedar Rapids, Iowa, to Midway, Georgia, the police arrive to enforce laws requiring $50 permits or $200 licenses to sell cold drinks that compete with those offered by other sellers. Typically, the

children respond by giving up on lemonade sales and instead begin to earn incomes by doing chores for neighbors—unless they run afoul of laws requiring "handyman licenses."

FOR CRITICAL THINKING

Who gains from laws requiring permits or licenses to sell cold drinks such as lemonade?

PATENTS A patent is issued to an inventor to provide protection from having the invention copied or stolen for a period of 20 years. Suppose that engineers working for Ford Motor Company discover a way to build an engine that requires half the parts of a regular engine and weighs only half as much. If Ford is successful in obtaining a patent on this discovery, it can (in principle) prevent others from copying it. The patent holder has a monopoly. It is the patent holder's responsibility to defend the patent, however. That means that Ford—like other patent owners—must expend resources to prevent others from imitating its invention. If the costs of enforcing a particular patent are greater than the benefits, though, the patent may not bestow any monopoly profits on its owner. The policing costs would be too high.

TARIFFS **Tariffs** are special taxes that are imposed on certain imported goods. Tariffs make imports more expensive relative to their domestic counterparts, encouraging consumers to switch to the relatively cheaper domestically made products. If the tariffs are high enough, domestic producers may be able to act together like a single firm and gain monopoly advantage as the sole suppliers. Many countries have tried this protectionist strategy by using high tariffs to shut out foreign competitors.

REGULATIONS Throughout the twentieth century and to the present, government regulation of the U.S. economy has increased, especially along the dimensions of safety and quality. U.S. firms incur hundreds of billions of dollars in expenses each year to comply with federal, state, and local government regulations of business conduct relating to workplace conditions, environmental protection, product safety, and various other activities. Presumably, these large fixed costs of complying with regulations can be spread over a greater number of units of output by larger firms than by smaller firms, thereby putting the smaller firms at a competitive disadvantage. Entry will also be deterred to the extent that the scale of operation of a potential entrant must be sufficiently large to cover the average fixed costs of compliance. We examine regulation in more detail in Chapter 27.

Go to www.econtoday.com/chap24 to learn more about patents and trademarks from the U.S. Patent and Trademark Office and to learn all about copyrights from the U.S. Copyright Office.

Tariffs
Taxes on imported goods.

QUICK QUIZ   See page 553 for the answers. Review concepts from this section in MyEconLab.

A **monopolist** is the single seller of a product or good for which there is no _____ substitute.

To maintain a monopoly, there must be barriers to entry. Barriers to entry include _____ of resources without

close substitutes; economies of _____; legally required licenses, franchises, and certificates of convenience; patents; tariffs; and safety and quality regulations.

The Demand Curve a Monopolist Faces

A *pure monopolist* is the sole supplier of *one* product. A pure monopolist faces the demand curve for the entire market for that good or service.

> *The monopolist faces the industry demand curve because the monopolist is the entire industry.*

Because the monopolist faces the industry demand curve, which is by definition downward sloping, its choice regarding how much to produce is not the same as for a perfect competitor. When a monopolist changes output, it does not automatically receive the same price per unit that it did before the change.

Profits to Be Made from Increasing Production

How do firms benefit from changing production rates? What happens to price in each case? Let's first review the situation among perfect competitors.

MARGINAL REVENUE FOR THE PERFECT COMPETITOR Recall that a firm in a perfectly competitive industry faces a perfectly elastic demand curve. That is because the perfectly competitive firm is such a small part of the market that it cannot influence the price of its product. It is a *price taker*. If the forces of supply and demand establish that the price per constant-quality pair of shoes is $50, the individual firm can sell all the pairs of shoes it wants to produce at $50 per pair. The per-unit price is $50, and the marginal revenue is also $50.

Let us again define marginal revenue:

> *Marginal revenue equals the change in total revenue due to a one-unit change in the quantity produced and sold.*

In the case of a perfectly competitive industry, each time a single firm changes production by one unit, total revenue changes by the going price, and price is unchanged.

MARGINAL REVENUE FOR THE MONOPOLIST What about a monopoly firm? We begin by considering a situation in which a monopolist charges every buyer the same price for each unit of its product. Because a monopoly is the entire industry, the monopoly firm's demand curve is the market demand curve. The market demand curve slopes downward, just like the other demand curves that we have seen. Therefore, to induce consumers to buy more of a particular product, given the industry demand curve, the monopoly firm must lower the price. Thus, the monopoly firm moves *down* the demand curve. If all buyers are to be charged the same price, the monopoly must lower the price on *all* units sold in order to sell more. It cannot lower the price on just the *last* unit sold in any given time period in order to sell a larger quantity.

Put yourself in the shoes of a monopoly ferryboat owner. You have a government-bestowed franchise, and no one can compete with you. Your ferryboat goes between two islands. If you are charging $8 per crossing, a certain quantity of your services

FIGURE 24-2

Demand Curves for the Perfect Competitor and the Monopolist

The perfect competitor in panel (a) faces a perfectly elastic demand curve, *d*. The monopolist in panel (b) faces the entire industry demand curve, which slopes downward.

Panel (a)

Price per Unit

d

q

Demand If Individual Supplier Is in
Perfect Competition

Panel (b)

Price per Unit

d = D

Q

Demand If Individual Supplier
Is the Only Supplier in a
Pure Monopoly

will be demanded. Let's say that you are ferrying 4 people per hour each way at that price. If you decide that you would like to ferry more individuals, you must lower your price to all individuals—you must move *down* the existing demand curve for ferrying services. To calculate the marginal revenue of your change in price, you must first calculate the total revenues you received at $8 per passenger per crossing and then calculate the total revenues you would receive at, say, $7 per passenger per crossing.

PERFECT COMPETITION VERSUS MONOPOLY It is sometimes useful to compare monopoly markets with perfectly competitive markets. The monopolist is constrained by the demand curve for its product, just as a perfectly competitive firm is constrained by its demand. The key difference is the nature of the demand curve each type of firm faces. We see this in Figure 24-2 above.

Here we see the fundamental difference between the monopolist and the perfect competitor. The perfect competitor doesn't have to worry about lowering price to sell more. In a perfectly competitive situation, the perfectly competitive firm accounts for such a small part of the market that it can sell its entire output, whatever that may be, at the same price. The monopolist cannot.

The more the monopolist wants to sell, the lower the price it has to charge on the last unit (and on *all* units put on the market for sale). To sell the last unit, the monopolist has to lower the price because it is facing a downward-sloping demand curve, and the only way to move down the demand curve is to lower the price. As long as this price must be the same for all units, the extra revenues the monopolist receives from selling one more unit are going to be smaller than the extra revenues received from selling the next-to-last unit.

The Monopolist's Marginal Revenue: Less Than Price

An essential point is that for the monopolist, marginal revenue is always less than price. To understand why, look at Figure 24-3 on the next page, which shows a unit increase in output sold due to a reduction from $8 to $7 in the price of ferry crossings provided by a monopolistic ferry company. The new $7 price is the price received for the last unit, so selling this unit contributes $7 to revenues. That is equal to the vertical column (area A). Area A is one unit wide by $7 high.

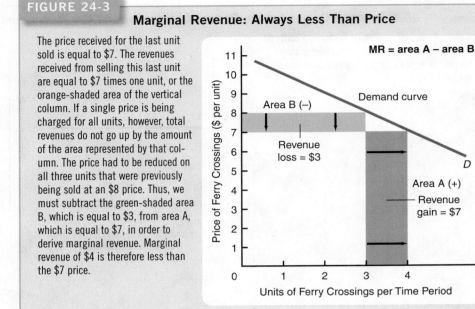

FIGURE 24-3

Marginal Revenue: Always Less Than Price

The price received for the last unit sold is equal to $7. The revenues received from selling this last unit are equal to $7 times one unit, or the orange-shaded area of the vertical column. If a single price is being charged for all units, however, total revenues do not go up by the amount of the area represented by that column. The price had to be reduced on all three units that were previously being sold at an $8 price. Thus, we must subtract the green-shaded area B, which is equal to $3, from area A, which is equal to $7, in order to derive marginal revenue. Marginal revenue of $4 is therefore less than the $7 price.

But price times the last unit sold is *not* the net addition to *total* revenues received from selling that last unit. Why? Because price had to be reduced on the three previous units sold in order to sell the larger quantity—four ferry crossings. The reduction in price is represented by the vertical distance from $8 to $7 on the vertical axis. We must therefore subtract area B from area A to come up with the *change* in total revenues due to a one-unit increase in sales. Clearly, the change in total revenues—that is, marginal revenue—must be less than price because marginal revenue is always the difference between areas A and B in Figure 24-3. Thus, at a price of $7, marginal revenue is $7 − $3 = $4 because there is a $1 per unit price reduction on three previous units. Hence, marginal revenue, $4, is less than price, $7.

Elasticity and Monopoly

The monopolist faces a downward-sloping market demand curve. That fact means that the monopolist cannot charge just *any* price with no changes in quantity (a common misconception) because, depending on the price charged, a different quantity will be demanded.

Earlier we defined a monopolist as the single seller of a well-defined good or service with no *close* substitute. This does not mean, however, that the demand curve for a monopoly is vertical or exhibits zero price elasticity of demand. After all, consumers have limited incomes and unlimited wants. The market demand curve, which the monopolist alone faces in this situation, slopes downward because individuals compare the marginal satisfaction they will receive to the cost of the commodity to be purchased. Take the example of a particular type of sports car. Even if miraculously there were absolutely no substitutes whatsoever for that sports car, the market demand curve would still slope downward. At lower prices, people will purchase more of those sports cars, perhaps buying cars for other family members.

Furthermore, the demand curve for the sports car slopes downward because there are at least several *imperfect* substitutes, such as other types of sports cars, used sports cars, sport utility vehicles, and other stylish vehicles. The more such substitutes there are, and the better these substitutes are, the more elastic will be the monopolist's demand curve, all other things held constant.

QUICK QUIZ   See page 553 for the answers. Review concepts from this section in MyEconLab.

The monopolist estimates its marginal revenue curve, where marginal revenue is defined as the _____ in _____ revenues due to a one-unit change in quantity sold.

For the perfect competitor, price equals _____ revenue equals average revenue. For the monopolist,

_____ revenue is always less than price because price must be reduced on all units to sell more.

The price _____ of demand for the monopolist depends on the number and similarity of substitutes. The more numerous the imperfect substitutes, the greater the price _____ of the monopolist's demand curve.

Costs and Monopoly Profit Maximization

To find the rate of output at which the perfect competitor would maximize profits, we had to add cost data. We will do the same now for the monopolist. We assume that profit maximization is the goal of the pure monopolist, just as it is for the perfect competitor. The perfect competitor, however, has only to decide on the profit-maximizing rate of output because price is given. The perfect competitor is a price taker.

For the pure monopolist, we must seek a profit-maximizing *price-output combination* because the monopolist is a **price searcher.** We can determine this profit-maximizing price-output combination with either of two equivalent approaches—by looking at total revenues and total costs or by looking at marginal revenues and marginal costs. We shall examine both approaches.

Price searcher
A firm that must determine the price-output combination that maximizes profit because it faces a downward-sloping demand curve.

The Total Revenues–Total Costs Approach

Suppose that the government of a small town located in a remote desert area grants a single satellite television company the right to offer services within its jurisdiction. It enforces rules that prevent other firms from offering television services. We show demand (weekly rate of output and price per unit), revenues, costs, and other data in panel (a) of Figure 24-4 on the next page. In column 3, we see total revenues for this TV service monopolist, and in column 4, we see total costs. We can transfer these two columns to panel (b). The fundamental difference between the total revenue and total cost diagram in panel (b) and the one we showed for a perfect competitor in Chapter 23 is that the total revenue line is no longer straight. Rather, it curves. For any given demand curve, in order to sell more, the monopolist must lower the price. This reflects the fact that the basic difference between a monopolist and a perfect competitor has to do with the demand curve for the two types of firms. The monopolist faces a downward-sloping demand curve.

Profit maximization involves maximizing the positive difference between total revenues and total costs. This occurs at an output rate of between 9 and 10 units per week.

The Marginal Revenue–Marginal Cost Approach

Profit maximization will also occur where marginal revenue equals marginal cost. This is as true for a monopolist as it is for a perfect competitor (but the monopolist will charge a price in excess of marginal revenue). When we transfer marginal cost and marginal revenue information from columns 6 and 7 in panel (a) to panel (c) in Figure 24-4 on the next page, we see that marginal revenue equals marginal cost at a weekly quantity of satellite TV services of between 9 and 10 units. Profit maximization must occur at the same output as in panel (b).

WHY PRODUCE WHERE MARGINAL REVENUE EQUALS MARGINAL COST? If the monopolist produces past the point where marginal revenue equals marginal cost, marginal cost will exceed marginal revenue. That is, the incremental cost of producing any more units will exceed the incremental revenue. It would not be worthwhile, as was true also in perfect competition. Furthermore, just as in the case of perfect competition, if the monopolist produces less than that, it is not making maximum profits.

FIGURE 24-4

Monopoly Costs, Revenues, and Profits

In panel (a), we give demand (weekly satellite television services and price), revenues, costs, and other relevant data. As shown in panel (b), the satellite TV monopolist maximizes profits where the positive difference between TR and TC is greatest. This is at an output rate of between 9 and 10 units per week. Put another way, profit maximization occurs where marginal revenue equals marginal cost, as shown in panel (c). This is at the same weekly service rate of between 9 and 10 units. (The MC curve must cut the MR curve from below.)

Panel (a)

(1) Output (units)	(2) Price per Unit	(3) Total Revenues (TR) (3) = (2) × (1)	(4) Total Costs (TC)	(5) Total Profit (5) = (3) − (4)	(6) Marginal Cost (MC)	(7) Marginal Revenue (MR)
0	$8.00	$ .00	$10.00	−$10.00		
					$4.00	$7.80
1	7.80	7.80	14.00	−6.20		
					3.50	7.40
2	7.60	15.20	17.50	−2.30		
					3.25	7.00
3	7.40	22.20	20.75	1.45		
					3.05	6.60
4	7.20	28.80	23.80	5.00		
					2.90	6.20
5	7.00	35.00	26.70	8.30		
					2.80	5.80
6	6.80	40.80	29.50	11.30		
					2.75	5.40
7	6.60	46.20	32.25	13.95		
					2.85	5.00
8	6.40	51.20	35.10	16.10		
					3.20	4.60
9	6.20	55.80	38.30	17.50		
					4.40	4.20
10	6.00	60.00	42.70	17.30		
					6.00	3.80
11	5.80	63.80	48.70	15.10		
					9.00	3.40
12	5.60	67.20	57.70	9.50		

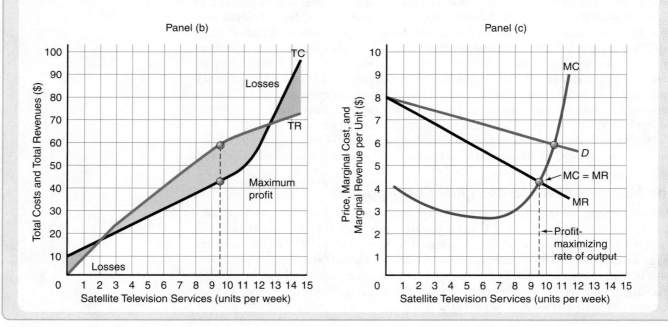

Look at output rate Q_1 in Figure 24-5 on the facing page. Here the monopolist's marginal revenue is at A, but marginal cost is at B. Marginal revenue exceeds marginal cost on the last unit sold. The profit for that *particular* unit, Q_1, is equal to the vertical difference between A and B, or the difference between marginal revenue and marginal cost.

FIGURE 24-5

Maximizing Profits

The profit-maximizing production rate is Q_m, and the profit-maximizing price is P_m. The monopolist would be unwise to produce at the rate Q_1 because here marginal revenue would be Q_1A, and marginal cost would be Q_1B. Marginal revenue would exceed marginal cost. The firm will keep producing until the point Q_m, where marginal revenue just equals marginal cost. It would be foolish to produce at the rate Q_2, for here marginal cost exceeds marginal revenue. It would behoove the monopolist to cut production back to Q_m.

The monopolist would be foolish to stop at output rate Q_1 because if output is expanded, marginal revenue will still exceed marginal cost, and therefore total profits will be increased by selling more. In fact, the profit-maximizing monopolist will continue to expand output and sales until marginal revenue equals marginal cost, which is at output rate Q_m.

The monopolist won't produce at rate Q_2 because here, as we see, marginal costs are C and marginal revenues are F. The difference between C and F represents the *reduction* in total profits from producing that additional unit. Total profits will rise as the monopolist reduces its rate of output back toward Q_m.

What Price to Charge for Output?

How does the monopolist set prices? We know the quantity is set at the point at which marginal revenue equals marginal cost. The monopolist then finds out how much can be charged—how much the market will bear—for that particular quantity, Q_m, in Figure 24-5 above.

THE MONOPOLY PRICE We know that the demand curve shows the *maximum* price for which a given quantity can be sold. That means that our monopolist knows that to sell Q_m, it can charge only P_m because that is the price at which that specific quantity, Q_m, is demanded. This price is found by drawing a vertical line from the quantity, Q_m, to the market demand curve. Where that line hits the market demand curve, the price is determined. We find that price by drawing a horizontal line from the demand curve to the price axis. Doing that gives us the profit-maximizing price, P_m.

In our example, at a profit-maximizing quantity of satellite TV services of between 9 and 10 units in Figure 24-4 on the preceding page, the firm can charge a maximum price of just over $6 and still sell all the services it provides, all at the same price.

The basic procedure for finding the profit-maximizing price-quantity combination for the monopolist is first to determine the profit-maximizing rate of output, by either the total revenue–total cost method or the marginal revenue–marginal cost method. Then it is possible to determine by use of the demand curve, D, the maximum price that can be charged to sell that output.

REAL-WORLD INFORMATIONAL LIMITATIONS Don't get the impression that just because we are able to draw an exact demand curve in Figures 24-4 and 24-5, real-world monopolists have such perfect information. The process of price searching by a less-than-perfect competitor is just that—a process. A monopolist can only estimate the actual demand curve and therefore can make only an educated guess when it sets its profit-maximizing price. This is not a problem for the perfect competitor because price is given already by the intersection of market demand and market supply. The monopolist, in contrast, reaches the profit-maximizing output-price combination by trial and error.

In recent years, what services have airlines provided to passengers at prices passengers have proved willing to pay?

EXAMPLE

Trial and Error Yields Profits from Monopoly Time in the Air

For years, airline ticket prices covered flying passengers and bags to their destinations while providing drinks and snacks along the way. Since the late 2000s, airlines have been trying to take full advantage of their position as monopoly sellers during flights. First, they began charging for checked bags, snacks, and pillows. Now some airlines are experimenting with charging extra fees for more comfortable seats that provide a few more inches of leg room and for seats that recline more than standard seats. Other airlines offer "travel concierge" services that assist passengers with booking items such as restaurant reservations and theater tickets in their destination cities.

To determine the prices for these and other new services, airlines have been searching for the prices that passengers are willing to pay. In this way, airlines eventually settle on prices that maximize the profits from being the only available seller *during* passengers' flights.

FOR CRITICAL THINKING
Some airlines are aiming to be "virtual shopping malls" by offering to take orders for a variety of "buy-while-you-fly" items for delivery to passengers' homes. Why might this new line of business be less likely to yield monopoly profits for airlines?

Calculating Monopoly Profit

We have talked about the monopolist's profit. We have yet to indicate how much profit the monopolist makes, which we do in Figure 24-6 on the facing page.

The Graphical Depiction of Monopoly Profits

We have actually shown total profits in column 5 of panel (a) in Figure 24-4 on page 540. We can also find total profits by adding an average total cost curve to panel (c) of that figure, as shown in Figure 24-6. When we add the average total cost curve, we find that the profit a monopolist makes is equal to the green-shaded area—or total revenues ($P \times Q$) minus total costs (ATC $\times Q$).

Given the demand curve and that all units sold at the same price, a monopolist cannot make greater profits than those shown by the green-shaded area. The monopolist is maximizing profits where marginal cost equals marginal revenue. If the monopolist produces less than that, it will forfeit some profits. If the monopolist produces more than that, it will also forfeit some profits.

No Guarantee of Profits

The term *monopoly* conjures up the notion of a greedy firm ripping off the public and making exorbitant profits. The mere existence of a monopoly, however, does not guarantee high profits. Numerous monopolies have gone bankrupt. Figure 24-7 on the next page shows the monopolist's demand curve as D and the resultant marginal revenue curve as MR. It does not matter at what rate of output this particular monopolist operates. Total costs cannot be covered.

Look at the position of the average total cost curve. It lies everywhere above D (the average revenue curve). Thus, there is no price-output combination that will allow the monopolist even to cover costs, much less earn profits. This monopolist will, in the short run, suffer economic losses as shown by the red-shaded area. The graph in

FIGURE 24-6

Monopoly Profit

We find monopoly profit by subtracting total costs from total revenues at a quantity of satellite TV services of between 9 and 10 units per week, labeled Q_m, which is the profit-maximizing rate of output for the satellite TV monopolist. The profit-maximizing price is therefore slightly more than $6 per week and is labeled P_m. Monopoly profit is given by the green-shaded area, which is equal to total revenues ($P \times Q$) minus total costs (ATC $\times$ Q). This diagram is similar to panel (c) of Figure 24-4 on page 540, with the short-run average total cost curve (ATC) added.

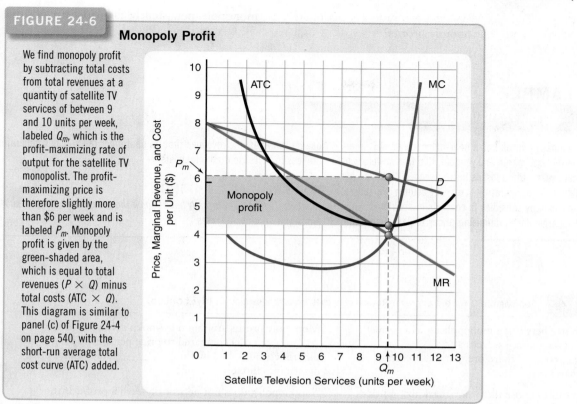

Figure 24-7, which applies to many inventions, depicts a situation of resulting monopoly. The owner of a patented invention or discovery has a pure legal monopoly, but the demand and cost curves are such that production is not profitable. Every year at inventors' conventions, one can see many inventions that have never been put into production because they were deemed "uneconomic" by potential producers and users.

FIGURE 24-7

Monopolies: Not Always Profitable

Some monopolists face the situation shown here. The average total cost curve, ATC, is everywhere above the average revenue, or demand, curve, D. In the short run, the monopolist will produce where MC = MR at point A. Output Q_m will be sold at price P_m, but average total cost per unit is C_1. Losses are the red-shaded rectangle. Eventually, the monopolist will go out of business.

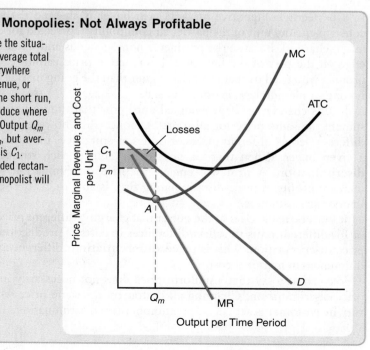

What government-sanctioned U.S. monopoly persistently fails to earn positive economic profits?

POLICY EXAMPLE

The U.S. Rail Monopoly That Subsists on Taxpayer Handouts

The passenger rail company Amtrak has a near-monopoly on U.S. inter-city rail service. Nevertheless, year in and year out, this firm suffers economic losses. In recent years, these losses have exceeded $1 billion per year. To keep Amtrak's rail lines operating across the country, the federal government pays the company subsidies to cover its losses. Thus, while Amtrak undoubtedly charges loss-minimizing prices to passengers who use its rail lines, the revenues that its passenger rail services generate are less than its incurred total costs.

FOR CRITICAL THINKING
What would Amtrak eventually have to do if the government stopped subsidizing its economic losses?

QUICK QUIZ

See page 553 for the answers. Review concepts from this section in MyEconLab.

The basic difference between a monopolist and a perfect competitor is that a monopolist faces a _____-sloping demand curve, and therefore marginal revenue is _____ than price.

The monopolist must choose the profit-maximizing price-output combination—the output at which _____ revenue equals _____ cost and the highest price possible as given by the _____ curve for that particular output rate.

Monopoly profits are found by looking at average _____ costs compared to price per unit. This difference multiplied by the _____ sold at that price determines monopoly profit.

A monopolist does not necessarily earn a profit. If the average _____ cost curve lies entirely _____ the demand curve for a monopoly, no production rate will be profitable.

On Making Higher Profits: Price Discrimination

In a perfectly competitive market, each buyer is charged the same price for every constant-quality unit of the particular commodity (corrected for differential transportation charges). Because the product is homogeneous and we also assume full knowledge on the part of the buyers, a difference in price cannot exist. Any seller of the product who tried to charge a price higher than the going market price would find that no one would purchase it from that seller.

In this chapter, we have assumed until now that the monopolist charged all consumers the same price for all units. A monopolist, however, may be able to charge different people different prices or different unit prices for successive units sought by a given buyer. When there is no cost difference, such strategies are called **price discrimination.** A firm will engage in price discrimination whenever feasible to increase profits. A price-discriminating firm is able to charge some customers more than other customers.

It must be made clear at the outset that charging different prices to different people or for different units to reflect differences in costs of production does not amount to price discrimination. This is **price differentiation:** differences in price that reflect differences in marginal cost.

We can also say that a uniform price does not necessarily indicate an absence of price discrimination. Charging all customers the same price when production costs vary by customer is actually a situation of price discrimination.

Price discrimination
Selling a given product at more than one price, with the price difference being unrelated to differences in marginal cost.

Price differentiation
Establishing different prices for similar products to reflect differences in marginal cost in providing those commodities to different groups of buyers.

Necessary Conditions for Price Discrimination

Three conditions are necessary for price discrimination to exist:

1. The firm must face a downward-sloping demand curve.

2. The firm must be able to readily (and cheaply) identify buyers or groups of buyers with predictably different elasticities of demand.

3. The firm must be able to prevent resale of the product or service.

Has it ever occurred to you that most of the other students seated in your college classroom pay different overall tuition rates than you do because your college and others use financial aid packages to engage in price discrimination?

EXAMPLE

Why Students Pay Different Prices to Attend College

Out-of-pocket tuition rates for any two college students can differ by considerable amounts, even if the students happen to major in the same subjects and enroll in many of the same courses. The reason is that colleges offer students diverse financial aid packages depending on their "financial need."

To document their "need" for financial aid, students must provide detailed information about family income and wealth. This information, of course, helps the college determine the prices that different families are most likely to be willing and able to pay, so that it can engage in price discrimination. Figure 24-8 below, shows how this collegiate price-discrimination process works. The college charges the price P_7, which is the college's official posted "tuition rate," to students with families judged to be most willing and able to pay the highest price. Students whose families have the lowest levels of income and wealth are judged to be willing and able to pay a much lower price, such as P_1. To charge

these students this lower tuition rate, the college provides them with a financial aid package that reduces the price they pay by the difference between P_7, the full tuition price, and P_1. In this way, the actual price paid by these "neediest" students is only P_1.

Likewise, the college groups other, somewhat less "needy" students into a slightly higher income-and-wealth category and determines that they are likely to be willing to pay a somewhat higher price, P_2. Hence, it grants them a smaller financial aid package, equal to $P_7 - P_2$, so that the students actually pay the price P_2. The college continues this process for other groups, thereby engaging in price discrimination in its tuition charges.

FOR CRITICAL THINKING
Does the educational product supplied by colleges satisfy all three conditions necessary for price discrimination?

FIGURE 24-8

Toward Perfect Price Discrimination in College Tuition Rates

Students that a college determines to be "neediest" and least able to pay the full tuition price, P_7, receive a financial aid package equal to $P_7 - P_1$. These students effectively pay only the price P_1. The college groups the remaining students into categories on the basis of their willingness and ability to pay a higher price, and each group receives a progressively smaller financial aid package. Those students who are willing and able to pay the full price, P_7, receive no financial aid from the college.

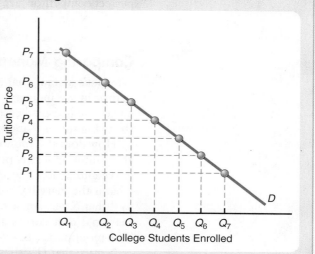

FIGURE 24-9

The Effects of Monopolizing an Industry

In panel (a), we show a perfectly competitive situation in which equilibrium is established at the intersection of D and S at point E. The equilibrium price is P_e and the equilibrium quantity is Q_e. Each individual perfectly competitive producer faces a demand curve that is perfectly elastic at the market clearing price, P_e. What happens if the industry is suddenly monopolized? We assume that the costs stay the same. The only thing that changes is that the monopolist now faces the entire downward-sloping demand curve. In panel (b), we draw the marginal revenue curve. Marginal cost is S because that is the horizontal summation of all the individual marginal cost curves. The monopolist therefore produces at Q_m and charges price P_m. This price P_m in panel (b) is higher than P_e in panel (a), and Q_m is less than Q_e.

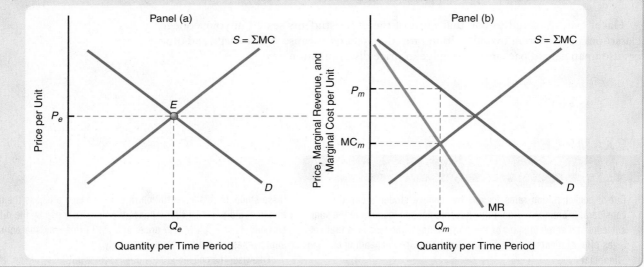

The Social Cost of Monopolies

Let's run a little experiment. We will start with a purely competitive industry with numerous firms, each one unable to affect the price of its product. The supply curve of the industry is equal to the horizontal sum of the marginal cost curves of the individual producers above their respective minimum average variable costs. In panel (a) of Figure 24-9 above, we show the market demand curve and the market supply curve in a perfectly competitive situation. The perfectly competitive price in equilibrium is equal to P_e, and the equilibrium quantity at that price is equal to Q_e. Each individual perfect competitor faces a demand curve (not shown) that is coincident with the price line P_e. No individual supplier faces the market demand curve, D.

Comparing Monopoly with Perfect Competition

Now let's assume that a monopolist comes in and buys up every single perfect competitor in the industry. In so doing, we'll assume that monopolization does not affect any of the marginal cost curves or demand. We can therefore redraw D and S in panel (b) of Figure 24-9 above, exactly the same as in panel (a).

How does this monopolist decide how much to charge and how much to produce? If the monopolist is profit maximizing, it is going to look at the marginal revenue curve and produce at the output where marginal revenue equals marginal cost. But what is the marginal cost curve in panel (b) of Figure 24-9? It is merely S, because we said that S was equal to the horizontal summation of the portions of the individual marginal cost curves above each firm's respective minimum average variable cost. The monopolist therefore produces quantity Q_m, and sells it at price P_m.

Notice that Q_m is less than Q_e and that P_m is greater than P_e. Hence, a monopolist produces a smaller quantity and sells it at a higher price. This is the reason usually given when economists criticize monopolists. Monopolists raise the price and restrict production, compared to a perfectly competitive situation. For a monopolist's product, consumers pay a price that exceeds the marginal cost of production. Resources are misallocated in such a situation—too few resources are being used in the monopolist's industry, and too many are used elsewhere. (See Appendix G on deadweight loss at the end of this chapter.)

WHAT IF... governments protect local retailers from "big-box" retailers such as Walmart and Target?

In some cities, such as Chicago and New York City, protesters have united in opposition to efforts to open new outlets on the part of national retailers such as Walmart and Target. When activist groups succeed in preventing entry by these so-called big-box retailers, the groups also succeed in protecting local retailers from competition.

In areas with very few local sellers, protected sellers are able to search for profit-maximizing prices higher than those that would have prevailed under perfect competition. In the absence of entry by big-box retailers, therefore, local retailers are able to maintain higher-than-competitive prices, resulting in misallocations of resources.

Implications of Higher Monopoly Prices

Notice from Figure 24-9 that by setting $MR = MC$, the monopolist produces at a rate of output where P is greater than MC (compare P_m to MC_m). The marginal cost of a commodity (MC) represents what society had to give up in order to obtain the last unit produced. Price, by contrast, represents what buyers are willing to pay to acquire that last unit. Thus, the price of a good represents society's valuation of the last unit produced. The monopoly outcome of P exceeding MC means that the value to society of the last unit produced is greater than its cost (MC). Hence, not enough of the good is being produced. As we have pointed out before, these differences between monopoly and perfect competition arise not because of differences in costs but rather because of differences in the demand curves the individual firms face. The monopolist faces a downward-sloping demand curve. The individual perfect competitor faces a perfectly elastic demand curve.

Before we leave the topic of the cost to society of monopolies, we must repeat that our analysis is based on a heroic assumption: The monopolization of the perfectly competitive industry does not change the cost structure. If monopolization results in higher marginal cost, the net cost of monopoly to society is even greater.

Conversely, if monopolization results in cost savings, the net cost of monopoly to society is less than we infer from our analysis. Indeed, we could have presented a hypothetical example in which monopolization led to such a dramatic reduction in cost that society actually benefited. Such a situation is a possibility in industries in which economies of scale exist for a very great range of outputs.

QUICK QUIZ   See page 553 for the answers. Review concepts from this section in MyEconLab.

Three conditions are necessary for price discrimination: (1) The firm must face a _____-sloping demand curve, (2) the firm must be able to identify buyers with predictably different price _____ of demand, and (3) _____ of the product or service must be preventable.

Price _____ should not be confused with price _____, which occurs when differences in price reflect differences in marginal cost.

Monopoly tends to result in a _____ quantity being sold, because the price is _____ than it would be in an ideal perfectly competitive industry in which the cost curves were essentially the same as the monopolist's.

YOU ARE THERE

Seeking Higher Rents from Souvenir Vendors in Atlanta

For more than 20 years, Stanley Hambrick and Larry Miller have operated a vending stand at Turner Field in Atlanta. Until recently, they paid a rental fee of $250 per year for the right to sell baseball souvenirs and T-shirts.

Now, however, the city of Atlanta has, in exchange for a share of profits, granted a Chicago-based management company called General Growth Properties a monopoly in renting vending spaces around Turner Field. The rental fees of General Growth Properties are considerably higher than what Hambrick and Miller used to pay. These new fees range from as low as $500 per *month* for out-of-the-way sites to $1,600 per *month* for sites along main paths. Hambrick and Miller quickly convert these rates to annual amounts and realize that General Growth Properties has utilized its

monopoly position to search for rental rates that will maximize profits it will share with the city of Atlanta. The two vendors now face annual rental rates ranging from 24 times to 77 times more than they used to pay.

Critical Thinking Questions

1. Is the number of vendor stands next to Turner Field likely to grow or to shrink under the management of General Growth Properties? Explain.

2. Why might General Growth Properties and the city of Atlanta prefer for Hambrick and Miller and some other vendors to close their souvenir and T-shirt stands?

ISSUES & APPLICATIONS

The U.S. Occupational License Explosion

CONCEPTS APPLIED

▶ License

▶ Barriers to Entry

▶ Monopoly

Are you looking for a job washing people's hair at a hair salon? If you live in Texas, you will require a license first. What if you would like to braid hair at a salon? If the salon is in Utah, a license is also necessary. In states across the land, licensing rules have expanded with each passing year.

A Sharp Increase in Occupations Requiring State Approval

Table 24-1 lists some of the occupations that require licenses in at least a few states. All told, 1,100 different jobs now require a license in at least one state—a number nearly 40 percent larger than three decades ago.

Indeed, more than 30 percent of U.S. residents are in occupations requiring licenses. By way of comparison, in 2000, fewer than 20 percent of U.S. residents were in licensed occupations, and in 1950, only about 5 percent required licenses.

Economic Effects of Occupational Barriers to Entry

To obtain occupational licenses, people typically must pay fees. Many must also engage in a period of study—perhaps through or even beyond an undergraduate degree. Such licensing requirements constitute barriers to entry.

For incumbents who already have positions in regulated occupations, licenses create monopoly profits. Consumers pay higher prices to obtain the services of people in licensed occupations. The total price tag to consumers exceeds $100 billion per year nationwide, or about 1 percent of total spending by U.S. consumers. Thus, people in licensed occupations earn higher incomes. After controlling for other determinants of incomes, economists have found that occupations in states with licensing requirements yield annual incomes 15 percent higher than do the same occupationsin states without such requirements.

For Critical Thinking

1. Why do you suppose that employment growth is about 20 percent greater in unlicensed occupations than in licensed occupations?

2. What do you suppose a typical state government does with the millions of dollars of occupational license fees it receives each year?

TABLE 24-1

Selected Occupations Requiring Licenses in Some U.S. States

Acupuncturists	Glass installers	Nutritionists
Athletic trainers	Hearing-aid fitters	Secondhand booksellers
Ballroom-dancing teachers	Hunting guides	Shampoo specialists
Barbers	Librarians	Tattoo artists
Dieticians	Locksmiths	Tour guides
Electricians	Manicurists	Tree-trimmers
Frozen-dessert retailers	Massage therapists	Wig specialists
Funeral directors	Private detectives	Windshield repairers
Hair braiders	Respiratory therapists	Yoga instructors

Web Resources

1. Take a look at more information about the growth of occupational licensing in the United States at www.econtoday.com/chap24.

2. To learn more about the economic impacts of occupational licensing, go to www.econtoday.com/chap24.

MyEconLab

For more questions on this chapter's Issues & Applications, go to MyEconLab. In the Study Plan for this chapter, select Section N: News.

MyEconLab

Here is what you should know after reading this chapter. MyEconLab will help you identify what you know, and where to go when you need to practice.

WHAT YOU SHOULD KNOW		WHERE TO GO TO PRACTICE
Why Monopoly Can Occur Monopoly, a situation in which a single firm produces and sells a good or service, can occur when there are significant barriers to market entry. Examples of barriers to entry include (1) ownership of important resources for which there are no close substitutes, (2) economies of scale for ever-larger ranges of output, and (3) governmental restrictions.	monopolist, 533 natural monopoly, 534 tariffs, 535	• MyEconLab Study Plans 24.1, 24.2
Demand and Marginal Revenue Conditions a Monopolist Faces A monopolist faces the entire market demand curve. When it reduces the price of its product, it is able to sell more units at the new price, which boosts revenues, but it also sells other units at this lower price, which reduces revenues somewhat. Thus, the monopolist's marginal revenue at any given quantity is less than the price at which it sells that quantity. Its marginal revenue curve slopes downward and lies below the demand curve.	**Key Figures** Figure 24-2, 537 Figure 24-3, 538	• MyEconLab Study Plans 24.3, 24.4 • Animated Figures 24-2, 24-3

MyEconLab continued

┌───┐

How a Monopolist Determines How Much Output to Produce and What Price to Charge A monopolist is a price searcher that seeks to charge the price that maximizes its economic profits. It produces to the point at which marginal revenue equals marginal cost. The monopolist then charges the maximum price that consumers are willing to pay for that quantity.

price searcher, 539

Key Figures
Figure 24-4, 540
Figure 24-5, 541

- MyEconLab Study Plan 24.5
- Animated Figures 24-4, 24-5

A Monopolist's Profits A monopolist's profits equal the difference between the price it charges and its average production cost times the quantity it sells. The monopolist's price is at the point on the demand curve corresponding to the profit-maximizing output rate, and its average total cost of producing this output rate is at the corresponding point on the average total cost curve.

Key Figures
Figure 24-6, 543
Figure 24-7, 544

- MyEconLab Study Plan 24.6
- Animated Figures 24-6, 24-7

Price Discrimination A price-discriminating monopolist sells its product at more than one price, with the price difference being unrelated to differences in costs. To be able to price discriminate successfully, a monopolist must be able to sell some of its output at higher prices to consumers with less elastic demand.

price discrimination, 545

price differentiation, 545

- MyEconLab Study Plan 24.7

Social Cost of Monopolies A monopoly is able to charge the highest price that people are willing to pay. This price exceeds marginal cost. If the monopolist's marginal cost curve corresponds to the sum of the marginal cost curves for the number of firms that would exist if the industry were perfectly competitive instead, then the monopolist produces and sells less output than perfectly competitive firms would have produced and sold.

Key Figure
Figure 24-9, 546

- MyEconLab Study Plan 24.8
- Animated Figure 24-9

Log in to MyEconLab, take a chapter test, and get a personalized Study Plan that tells you which concepts you understand and which ones you need to review. From there, MyEconLab will give you further practice, tutorials, animations, videos, and guided solutions. For more information, visit www.myeconlab.com

└───┘

PROBLEMS

All problems are assignable in MyEconLab. Answers to odd-numbered problems appear at the back of the book.

24-1. The following table depicts the daily output, price, and costs of a monopoly dry cleaner located near the campus of a remote college town. (See page 540.)

Output (suits cleaned)	Price per Suit ($)	Total Costs ($)
0	8.00	3.00
1	7.50	6.00
2	7.00	8.50
3	6.50	10.50
4	6.00	11.50
5	5.50	13.50
6	5.00	16.00
7	4.50	19.00
8	4.00	24.00

  a. Compute revenues and profits at each output rate.

  b. What is the profit-maximizing rate of output?

  c. Calculate the dry cleaner's marginal revenue and marginal cost at each output level. What is the profit-maximizing level of output?

24-2. A manager of a monopoly firm notices that the firm is producing output at a rate at which average total cost is falling but is not at its minimum feasible point. The manager argues that surely the firm must not be maximizing its economic profits. Is this argument correct? (See pages 540–541.)

24-3. Use the following graph to answer the questions below. (See pages 541–544.)

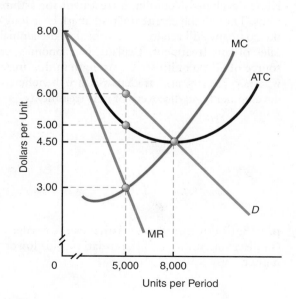

a. What is the monopolist's profit-maximizing output?

b. At the profit-maximizing output rate, what are average total cost and average revenue?

c. At the profit-maximizing output rate, what are the monopolist's total cost and total revenue?

d. What is the maximum profit?

e. Suppose that the marginal cost and average total cost curves in the diagram also illustrate the horizontal summation of the firms in a perfectly competitive industry in the long run. What would the equilibrium price and output be if the market were perfectly competitive? Explain the economic cost to society of allowing a monopoly to exist.

24-4. The marginal revenue curve of a monopoly crosses its marginal cost curve at $30 per unit and an output of 2 million units. The price that consumers are willing to pay for this output is $40 per unit. If it produces this output, the firm's average total cost is $43 per unit, and its average fixed cost is $8 per unit. What is the profit-maximizing (loss-minimizing) output? What are the firm's economic profits (or economic losses)? (See pages 541–544.)

24-5. A monopolist's maximized rate of economic profits is $500 per week. Its weekly output is 500 units, and at this output rate, the firm's marginal cost is $15 per unit. The price at which it sells each unit is $40 per unit. At these profit and output rates, what are the firm's average total cost and marginal revenue? (See pages 541–544.)

24-6. Currently, a monopolist's profit-maximizing output is 200 units per week. It sells its output at a price of $60 per unit and collects $30 per unit in revenues from the sale of the last unit produced each week. The firm's total costs each week are $9,000. Given this information, what are the firm's maximized weekly economic profits and its marginal cost? (See pages 541–544.)

24-7. Consider the revenue and cost conditions for a monopolist that are depicted in the figure at the top of the next page. (See pages 541–544.)

  a. What is this producer's profit-maximizing (or loss-minimizing) output?

  b. What are the firm's economic profits (or losses)?

24-8. For each of the following examples, explain how and why a monopoly would try to price discriminate. (See pages 545–546.)

a. Air transport for businesspeople and tourists

b. Serving food on weekdays to businesspeople and retired people. (Hint: Which group has more flexibility during a weekday to adjust to a price change and, hence, a higher price elasticity of demand?)

c. A theater that shows the same movie to large families and to individuals and couples. (Hint: For which set of people will the overall expense of a movie be a larger part of their budget, so that demand is more elastic?)

24-9. A monopolist's revenues vary directly with price. Is it maximizing its economic profits? Why or why not? (Hint: Recall that the relationship between revenues and price depends on price elasticity of demand. See page 539.)

24-10. A new competitor enters the industry and competes with a second firm, which had been a monopolist. The second firm finds that although demand is not perfectly elastic, it is now more elastic. What will happen to the second firm's marginal revenue curve and to its profit-maximizing price? (See pages 539–541.)

24-11. A monopolist's marginal cost curve has shifted upward. What is likely to happen to the monopolist's price, output rate, and economic profits? (See pages 541–544.)

24-12. Demand has fallen. What is likely to happen to the monopolist's price, output rate, and economic profits? (See pages 541–544.)

ECONOMICS ON THE NET

Patents, Trademarks, and Intellectual Property This Internet application explores a firm's view on legal protections.

Title: Intellectual Property

Navigation: Follow the link at **www.econtoday.com/chap24** to the GlaxoSmithKline Web site. Select *Investors* and then *Reports and Publications*. View the PDF of Annual Report 2007. Scroll down to Intellectual Property (page 28).

Application Read the statement and table; then answer the following questions.

1. How do patents, trademarks, and registered designs and copyrights differ?

2. What are GlaxoSmithKline's intellectual property goals? Do patents or trademarks seem to be more important?

For Group Discussion and Analysis In 1969, GlaxoSmithKline developed Ventolin, a treatment for asthma symptoms. Though the patent and trademark have long expired, the company still retains over a third of the annual market sales of this treatment. Explain, in economic terms, the source of GlaxoSmithKline's strength in this area. Discuss whether patents and trademarks are beneficial for the development and discovery of new treatments.

ANSWERS TO QUICK QUIZZES

p. 536: (i) close; (ii) ownership . . . scale

p. 539: (i) change . . . total; (ii) marginal . . . marginal; (iii) elasticity . . . elasticity

p. 544: (i) downward . . . less; (ii) marginal . . . marginal . . . demand; (iii) total . . . quantity; (iv) total . . . above

p. 548: (i) downward . . . elasticities . . . resale; (ii) discrimination . . . differentiation; (iii) lower . . . higher

Consumer Surplus and the Deadweight Loss Resulting from Monopoly

You have learned that a monopolist produces fewer units than would otherwise be produced in a perfectly competitive market and that it sells these units at a higher price. It seems that consumers surely must be worse off under monopoly than they would be under perfect competition. This appendix shows that, indeed, consumers are harmed by the existence of a monopoly in a market that otherwise could be perfectly competitive.

Consumer Surplus in a Perfectly Competitive Market

Consider the determination of consumer surplus in a perfectly competitive market (for consumer surplus, see page 96 in Appendix B). Take a look at the market diagram depicted in Figure G-1 below. In the figure, we assume that all firms producing in this market incur no fixed costs. We also assume that each firm faces the same marginal cost, which does not vary with its output. These assumptions imply that the marginal cost curve is horizontal and that marginal cost is the same as average total cost at any level of output. Thus, if many perfectly competitive firms operate in this market, the horizontal summation of all firms' marginal cost curves, which is the market supply curve, is this same horizontal curve, labeled MC = ATC.

Under perfect competition, the point at which this market supply curve crosses the market demand curve, D, determines the equilibrium quantity, Q_{pc}, and the market clearing price, P_{pc}. Thus, in a perfectly competitive market, consumers obtain Q_{pc} units at the same per-unit price of P_{pc}. Consumers gain surplus values—vertical distances between the demand curve and the level of the market clearing price—for each unit consumed, up to the total of Q_{pc} units. This totals to the entire striped area under the demand curve above

FIGURE G-1

Consumer Surplus in a Perfectly Competitive Market

If all firms in this market incur no fixed costs and face the same, constant marginal costs, then the marginal cost curve, MC, and the average total cost curve, ATC, are equivalent and horizontal. Under perfect competition, the horizontal summation of all firms' marginal cost curves is this same horizontal curve, which is the market supply curve, so the market clearing price is P_{pc}, and the equilibrium quantity is Q_{pc}. The total consumer surplus in a perfectly competitive market is the striped area.

the market clearing price. Consumer surplus is the difference between the total amount that consumers would have been willing to pay and the total amount that they actually pay, given the market clearing price that prevails in the perfectly competitive market.

How Society Loses from Monopoly

Now let's think about what happens if a monopoly situation arises in this market, perhaps because a government licenses the firms to conduct joint operations as a single producer. These producers respond by acting as a single monopoly firm, which searches for the profit-maximizing quantity and price.

In this altered situation, which is depicted in Figure G-2 below, the new monopolist (which we assume is unable to engage in price discrimination—see page 544) will produce to the point at which marginal revenue equals marginal cost. This rate of output is Q_m units. The demand curve indicates that consumers are willing to pay a price per unit equal to P_m for this quantity of output. Consequently, as you learned in this chapter, the monopolist will produce fewer units of output than the quantity, Q_{pc}, that firms would have produced in a perfectly competitive market. The monopolist also charges a higher price than the market clearing price, P_{pc}, that would have prevailed under perfect competition.

Recall that the monopolist's maximized economic profits equal its output times the difference between price and average total cost, or the yellow-shaded rectangular area equal to $Q_m \times (P_m - \text{ATC})$. By setting its price at P_m, therefore, the monopolist is able to transfer this portion of the competitive level of consumer surplus to itself in the form of monopoly profits. Consumers are still able to purchase Q_m units of output at a per-unit price, P_m, below the prices they would otherwise have been willing to pay. Hence, the blue-shaded triangular area above this monopoly-profit rectangle is consumer surplus that remains in the new monopoly situation.

Once the monopoly is formed, what happens to the light-green-shaded portion of the competitive consumer surplus? The answer is that this portion of consumer surplus is lost to society. The monopolist's failure to produce the additional $Q_{pc} - Q_m$ units of output that would have been forthcoming in a perfectly competitive market eliminates this portion of the original consumer surplus. This lost consumer surplus resulting from monopoly production and pricing is called a **deadweight loss** because it is a portion of the competitive level of consumer surplus that no one in society can obtain in a monopoly situation.

Thus, as a result of monopoly, consumers are worse off in two ways. First, the monopoly profits that result constitute a transfer of a portion of consumer surplus away from consumers to the monopolist. Second, the failure of the monopoly to produce as many units as would have been produced under perfect competition eliminates consumer surplus that otherwise would have been a benefit to consumers. No one in society, not even the monopoly, can obtain this deadweight loss.

Deadweight loss
The portion of consumer surplus that no one in society is able to obtain in a situation of monopoly.

Losses Generated by Monopoly

If firms are able to act as a single monopoly, then the monopolist will produce only Q_m units at the point at which marginal revenue equals marginal cost and charge the price P_m. Economic profits, $Q_m \times (P_m - \text{ATC})$, equal the yellow-shaded rectangular area, which is a portion of the competitive level of consumer surplus (the original striped area) transferred to the monopolist. Consumers can now purchase Q_m units of output at a per-unit price, P_m, below the prices they otherwise would have been willing to pay, so the blue-shaded triangular area above this monopoly-profit rectangle is remaining consumer surplus. The green-shaded triangular area is lost consumer surplus that results from the monopoly producing Q_m units instead of the Q_{pc} units that would have been produced under perfect competition. This is called a *deadweight loss* because it is a portion of the competitive level of consumer surplus that no one in society can obtain under monopoly.

Monopolistic Competition

25

LEARNING OBJECTIVES

After reading this chapter, you should be able to:

▶ Discuss the key characteristics of a monopolistically competitive industry

▶ Contrast the output and pricing decisions of monopolistically competitive firms with those of perfectly competitive firms

▶ Explain why brand names and advertising are important features of monopolistically competitive industries

▶ Describe the fundamental properties of information products and evaluate how the prices of these products are determined under monopolistic competition

MyEconLab helps you master each objective and study more efficiently. See end of chapter for details.

John Locke is a Louisville, Kentucky, businessman who also happens to be a best-selling author of crime-adventure e-books priced at 99 cents on Amazon's Web site. Locke says, "When I saw that highly successful authors were charging $9.99 for an e-book, I thought that if I can make a profit at 99 cents, I no longer have to prove I'm as good as them—rather, they have to prove they are ten times better than me." E-books written by Locke and other crime-adventure authors share certain similarities but also exhibit differences in writing style, characterization, and plot. Hence, the market for crime-adventure e-books is one in which sellers' products are differentiated. Product differentiation, or heterogeneity, is a fundamental characteristic of *monopolistic competition*, the topic of this chapter. For book publishers, the growing importance of e-books is complicating the task of competing in selling *both* e-books *and* physical books. By the time you have completed the chapter, you will understand why this is so.

? DID YOU KNOW THAT... a company called J&D Foods offers bacon-flavored and turkey-and-gravy-flavored soft drinks? For individuals who prefer less fizz, a firm called Meatwater sells flavored water aimed to satisfy a number of different tastes. Its flavors include Buffalo wings, cheeseburger, chicken teriyaki, fish and chips, and fried oysters. Of course, as alternatives to J&D Foods' and Meatwater's meaty-flavored drinks, a large number of companies also sell soft drinks and bottled waters with a wide array of cola, non-cola, and fruity flavors. Many sellers of soft drinks and bottled water advertise their products in an effort to promote their distinctive flavors.

Product heterogeneity—variations in product characteristics—and advertising did not show up in our analysis of perfect competition. They play large roles, however, in industries that cannot be described as perfectly competitive but cannot be described as pure monopolies, either. A combination of consumers' preferences for variety and competition among producers has led to similar but *differentiated* products in the marketplace. This situation has been described as *monopolistic competition,* the subject of this chapter.

Monopolistic Competition

In the 1920s and 1930s, economists became increasingly aware that there were many industries to which both the perfectly competitive model and the pure monopoly model did not apply and did not seem to yield very accurate predictions. Theoretical and empirical research was instituted to develop some sort of middle ground. Two separately developed models of **monopolistic competition** resulted. At Harvard, Edward Chamberlin published *Theory of Monopolistic Competition* in 1933. The same year, Britain's Joan Robinson published *The Economics of Imperfect Competition.* In this chapter, we will outline the theory as presented by Chamberlin.

Chamberlin defined monopolistic competition as a market structure in which a relatively large number of producers offer similar but differentiated products. Monopolistic competition therefore has the following features:

Monopolistic competition
A market situation in which a large number of firms produce similar but not identical products. Entry into the industry is relatively easy.

1. Significant numbers of sellers in a highly competitive market

2. Differentiated products

3. Sales promotion and advertising

4. Easy entry of new firms in the long run

Even a cursory look at the U.S. economy leads to the conclusion that monopolistic competition is an important form of market structure in the United States. Indeed, that is true of all developed economies.

Number of Firms

In a perfectly competitive industry, there are an extremely large number of firms. In pure monopoly, there is only one. In monopolistic competition, there are a large number of firms, but not so many as in perfect competition. This fact has several important implications for a monopolistically competitive industry.

1. *Small share of market.* With so many firms, each firm has a relatively small share of the total market.

2. *Lack of collusion.* With so many firms, it is very difficult for all of them to get together to collude—to cooperate in setting a pure monopoly price (and output). Collusive pricing in a monopolistically competitive industry is nearly impossible. Also, barriers to entry are minor, and the flow of new firms into the industry makes collusive agreements less likely. The large number of firms makes the monitoring and detection of cheating very costly and extremely difficult. This difficulty is compounded by differentiated products and high rates of innovation. Collusive agreements are easier for a homogeneous product than for heterogeneous ones.

3. *Independence*. Because there are so many firms, each one acts independently of the others. No firm attempts to take into account the reaction of all of its rival firms—that would be impossible with so many rivals. Thus, an individual producer does not try to take into account possible reactions of rivals to its own output and price changes.

Follow the link at www.econtoday.com/chap25 to *Wall Street Journal* articles about real-world examples of monopolistic competition.

Product Differentiation

Perhaps the most important feature of the monopolistically competitive market is **product differentiation.** We can say that each individual manufacturer of a product has an absolute monopoly over its own product, which is slightly differentiated from other similar products. This means that the firm has some control over the price it charges. Unlike the perfectly competitive firm, it faces a downward-sloping demand curve.

Consider the abundance of brand names for toothpaste, soap, gasoline, vitamins, shampoo, and most other consumer goods and a great many services. We are not obliged to buy just one type of video game, just one type of jeans, or just one type of footwear. We can usually choose from a number of similar but differentiated products. The greater a firm's success at product differentiation, the greater the firm's pricing options.

Each separate differentiated product has numerous similar substitutes. This clearly has an impact on the price elasticity of demand for the individual firm. Recall that one determinant of price elasticity of demand is the availability of substitutes: The greater the number and closeness of substitutes available, other things being equal, the greater the price elasticity of demand. If the consumer has a vast array of alternatives that are just about as good as the product under study, a relatively small increase in the price of that product will lead many consumers to switch to one of the many close substitutes. Thus, the ability of a firm to raise the price above the price of *close* substitutes is very small. At a given price, the demand curve is highly elastic compared to a monopolist's demand curve. In the extreme case, with perfect competition, the substitutes are perfect because we are dealing with only one particular undifferentiated product. In that case, the individual firm has a perfectly elastic demand curve.

Product differentiation
The distinguishing of products by brand name, color, and other minor attributes. Product differentiation occurs in other than perfectly competitive markets in which products are, in theory, homogeneous, such as wheat or corn.

YOU ARE THERE

To contemplate how an automaker is using scents to differentiate its vehicles from those of its competitors, take a look at **Have You Smelled a Ford Lately?** on page 568.

Sales Promotion and Advertising

Monopolistic competition differs from perfect competition in that no individual firm in a perfectly competitive market will advertise. A perfectly competitive firm, by definition, can sell all that it wants to sell at the going market price anyway. Why, then, would it spend even one penny on advertising? Furthermore, by definition, the perfect competitor is selling a product that is identical to the product that all other firms in the industry are selling. Any advertisement that induces consumers to buy more of that product will, in effect, be helping all the competitors too. A perfect competitor therefore cannot be expected to incur any advertising costs (except when all firms in an industry collectively agree to advertise to urge the public to buy more beef or drink more milk, for example).

The monopolistic competitor, however, has at least *some* monopoly power. Because consumers regard the monopolistic competitor's product as distinguishable from the products of the other firms, the firm can search for the most profitable price that consumers are willing to pay for its differentiated product. Advertising, therefore, may result in increased profits. Advertising is used to increase demand and to differentiate one's product. How much advertising should be undertaken? It should be carried to the point at which the additional net revenue from one more dollar of advertising just equals that one dollar of additional cost.

How has one company used an unintended feature of its product to differentiate it further from similar products of competitors? See the following page.

EXAMPLE

A Biodegradable Chips Bag Is Crunchier Than the Chips

As is true of most consumer-products firms, Frito-Lay is always on the lookout for new ways of differentiating its snack brands from those of competing companies. Frito-Lay recently sought to make purchases of its Sun Chips snack more desirable to increasingly environmentally conscious consumers. Toward this end, the company's engineers developed a new biodegradable bag composed of materials that naturally break down in the environment.

The engineers' efforts had another result: perhaps the crunchiest snack bags on the planet. When squeezed, the bag produces a crunching sound at a level of 95 decibels—sufficiently loud that if the bag were squeezed continuously, it would exceed government noise standards.

Although the bag's loudness can be annoying, Frito-Lay decided to integrate the crunchiness of the bags containing crunchy chips into its marketing. Display ads on store shelves with Sun Chips read, "Yes, the bag is loud—that's what change sounds like." In this way, Frito-Lay took advantage of an unexpected characteristic of its product to differentiate it further from similar chips—and bags—sold by competitors.

FOR CRITICAL THINKING
If Frito-Lay's bag-differentiation plan accomplished its aims, what should have happened to the demand for its Sun Chips product?

Ease of Entry

For any current monopolistic competitor, potential competition is always lurking in the background. The easier—that is, the less costly—entry is, the more a current monopolistic competitor must worry about losing business.

A good example of a monopolistic competitive industry is the computer software industry. Many small firms provide different programs for many applications. The fixed capital costs required to enter this industry are small. All you need are skilled programmers. In addition, there are few legal restrictions. The firms in this industry also engage in extensive advertising in more than 150 computer publications.

QUICK QUIZ   See page 572 for the answers. Review concepts from this section in MyEconLab.

In a **monopolistically competitive** industry, a relatively _____ number of firms interact in a _____ competitive market.

Because monopolistically competitive firms sell _____ products, sales promotion and advertising are common features of a monopolistically competitive industry.

There is _____ entry (or exit) of new firms in a monopolistically competitive industry.

Price and Output for the Monopolistic Competitor

Now that we are aware of the assumptions underlying the monopolistic competition model, we can analyze the price and output behavior of each firm in a monopolistically competitive industry. We assume in the analysis that follows that the desired product type and quality have been chosen. We further assume that the budget and the type of promotional activity have already been chosen and do not change.

The Individual Firm's Demand and Cost Curves

Because the individual firm is not a perfect competitor, its demand curve slopes downward, as in all three panels of Figure 25-1 on the facing page. Hence, it faces a marginal revenue curve that is also downward sloping and below the demand curve. To find the profit-maximizing rate of output and the profit-maximizing price, we go to the output where the marginal cost (MC) curve intersects the marginal revenue (MR) curve from below.

FIGURE 25-1

Short-Run and Long-Run Equilibrium with Monopolistic Competition

In panel (a), the typical monopolistic competitor is shown making economic profits. In this situation, there would be entry into the industry, forcing the demand curve for the individual monopolistic competitor leftward. Eventually, firms would find themselves in the situation depicted in panel (c), where zero *economic* profits are being made. In panel (b), the typical firm is in a monopolistically competitive industry making economic losses. In this situation, firms would leave the industry. Each remaining firm's demand curve would shift outward to the right. Eventually, the typical firm would find itself in the situation depicted in panel (c).

That gives us the profit-maximizing output rate. Then we draw a vertical line up to the demand curve. That gives us the price that can be charged to sell exactly that quantity produced. This is what we have done in Figure 25-1 above. In each panel, a marginal cost curve intersects the marginal revenue curve at A. The profit-maximizing rate of output is q, and the profit-maximizing price is P.

Short-Run Equilibrium

In the short run, it is possible for a monopolistic competitor to make economic profits—profits over and above the normal rate of return or beyond what is necessary to keep that firm in that industry. We show such a situation in panel (a) of Figure 25-1. The average total cost (ATC) curve is drawn below the demand curve, d, at the profit-maximizing rate of output, q. Economic profits are shown by the blue-shaded rectangle in that panel.

Losses in the short run are clearly also possible. They are presented in panel (b) of Figure 25-1. Here the average total cost curve lies everywhere above the individual firm's demand curve, d. The losses are indicated by the red-shaded rectangle.

Just as with any market structure or any firm, in the short run it is possible to observe either economic profits or economic losses. In either case, the price does not equal marginal cost but rather is above it.

The Long Run: Zero Economic Profits

The long run is where the similarity between perfect competition and monopolistic competition becomes more obvious. In the long run, because so many firms produce substitutes for the product in question, any economic profits will disappear with competition. They will be reduced to zero either through entry by new firms seeing a chance to make a higher rate of return than elsewhere or by changes in product quality and advertising outlays by existing firms in the industry. (Profitable products will be imitated by other firms.) As for economic losses in the short run, they will disappear in the long run because the firms that suffer them will leave the industry. They will go into another business where the expected rate of return is at least normal. Panels (a) and (b) of Figure 25-1 on the preceding page therefore represent only short-run situations for a monopolistically competitive firm. In the long run, the individual firm's demand curve *d* will just touch the average total cost curve at the particular price that is profit maximizing for that particular firm. This is shown in panel (c) of Figure 25-1.

A word of warning: This is an idealized, long-run equilibrium situation for each firm in the industry. It does not mean that even in the long run we will observe every single firm in a monopolistically competitive industry making *exactly* zero economic profits or *just* a normal rate of return. We live in a dynamic world. All we are saying is that if this model is correct, the rate of return will *tend toward* normal—economic profits will *tend toward* zero.

Comparing Perfect Competition with Monopolistic Competition

If both the monopolistic competitor and the perfect competitor make zero economic profits in the long run, how are they different? The answer lies in the fact that the demand curve for the individual perfect competitor is perfectly elastic. Such is not the case for the individual monopolistic competitor—its demand curve is less than perfectly elastic. This firm has some control over price. Price elasticity of demand is not infinite.

We see the two situations in Figure 25-2 below. Both panels show average total costs just touching the respective demand curves at the particular price at which the firm is selling the product. Notice, however, that the perfect competitor's average

FIGURE 25-2

Comparison of the Perfect Competitor with the Monopolistic Competitor

In panel (a), the perfectly competitive firm has zero economic profits in the long run. The price is set equal to marginal cost, and the price is P_1. The firm's demand curve is just tangent to the minimum point on its average total cost curve. With the monopolistically competitive firm in panel

(b), there are also zero economic profits in the long run. The price is greater than marginal cost, though. The monopolistically competitive firm does not find itself at the minimum point on its average total cost curve. It is operating at a rate of output, q_2, to the left of the minimum point on the ATC curve.

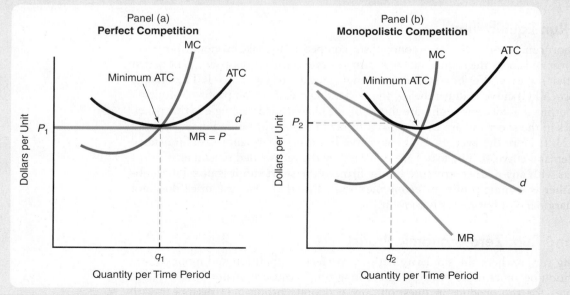

total costs are at a minimum. This is not the case with the monopolistic competitor. The equilibrium rate of output is to the left of the minimum point on the average total cost curve where price is greater than marginal cost. The monopolistic competitor cannot expand output to the point of minimum costs without lowering price, and then marginal cost would exceed marginal revenue. A monopolistic competitor at profit maximization charges a price that exceeds marginal cost. In this respect it is similar to the monopolist.

It has consequently been argued that monopolistic competition involves *waste* because minimum average total costs are not achieved and price exceeds marginal cost. There are too many firms, each with excess capacity, producing too little output. According to critics of monopolistic competition, society's resources are being wasted.

Chamberlin had an answer to this criticism. He contended that the difference between the average cost of production for a monopolistically competitive firm in an open market and the minimum average total cost represented what he called the cost of producing "differentness." Chamberlin did not consider this difference in cost between perfect competition and monopolistic competition a waste. In fact, he argued that it is rational for consumers to have a taste for differentiation. Consumers willingly accept the resultant increased production costs in return for more choice and variety of output.

QUICK QUIZ See page 572 for the answers. Review concepts from this section in MyEconLab.

In the _____ run, it is possible for monopolistically competitive firms to make economic profits or economic losses.

In the _____ run, monopolistically competitive firms will make _____ economic profits—that is, they will make a _____ rate of return.

Because the monopolistic competitor faces a downward-sloping demand curve, it does not produce at the minimum point on its average _____ cost curve.

Hence, we say that a monopolistic competitor has higher average _____ costs per unit than a perfect competitor would have.

Chamberlin argued that the difference between the _____ _____ cost of production for a monopolistically competitive firm and the _____ average total cost at which a perfectly competitive firm would produce is the cost of producing "differentness."

Brand Names and Advertising

Because "differentness" has value to consumers, monopolistically competitive firms regard their brand names as valuable. Firms use trademarks—words, symbols, and logos—to distinguish their product brands from goods or services sold by other firms. Consumers associate these trademarks with the firms' products. Thus, companies regard their brands as valuable private (intellectual) property, and they engage in advertising to maintain the differentiation of their products from those of other firms.

Brand Names and Trademarks

A firm's ongoing sales generate current profits and, as long as the firm is viable, the prospect of future profits. A company's value in the marketplace, depends largely on its current profitability and perceptions of its future profitability.

Table 25-1 on the following page gives the market values of the world's most valuable product brands. Each valuation is calculated as the market price of shares of stock in a company times the number of shares traded. Brand names, symbols, logos, and unique color schemes such as the color combinations trademarked by FedEx relate to consumers' perceptions of product differentiation and hence to the market values of firms. Companies protect their trademarks from misuse by registering them with the U.S. Patent and Trademark Office. Once its trademark application is approved, a

TABLE 25-1

Values of the Top Ten Brands

The market value of a company is equal to the number of shares of stock issued by the company times the market price of each share. To a large extent, the company's value reflects the value of its brand.

Brand	Estimates Value ($ billions)
Apple	183.0
International Business Machines (IBM)	156.0
Google	107.9
McDonald's	95.2
Microsoft	76.7
Coca cola	74.3
Marlboro	73.6
AT&T	68.9
Verizon	49.2
China Mobile	47.0

Source: Brand Z Most Valuable Brands Study, 2012.

company has the right to seek legal damages if someone makes unauthorized use of its brand name, spreads false rumors about the company, or engages in other devious activities that can reduce the value of its brand.

Advertising

To help ensure that consumers differentiate their product brands from those of other firms, monopolistically competitive firms commonly engage in advertising. Advertising comes in various forms, and the nature of advertising can depend considerably on the types of products that firms wish to distinguish from competing brands.

Direct marketing
Advertising targeted at specific consumers, typically in the form of postal mailings, telephone calls, or e-mail messages.

Mass marketing
Advertising intended to reach as many consumers as possible, typically through television, newspaper, radio, or magazine ads.

METHODS OF ADVERTISING Figure 25-3 below shows the current distribution of advertising expenses among the various advertising media. Today, as in the past, firms primarily rely on two approaches to advertising their products. One is **direct marketing,** in which firms engage in personalized advertising using postal mailings, phone calls, and e-mail messages (excluding so-called banner and pop-up ads on Web sites). The other is **mass marketing,** in which firms aim advertising messages at as many consumers as possible via media such as television, newspapers, radio, and magazines.

FIGURE 25-3

Distribution of U.S. Advertising Expenses

Direct marketing accounts for more than half of advertising expenses in the United States.

Sources: Advertising Today; Direct Marketing Today; and Internet Advertising Bureau.

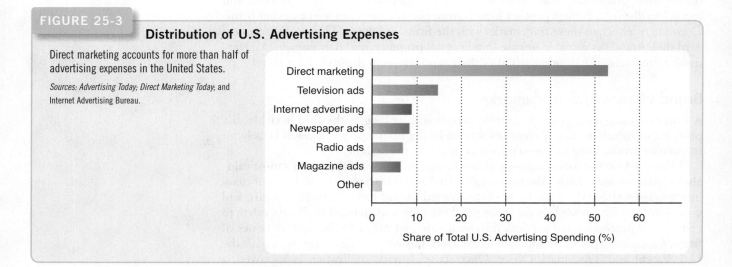

A third advertising method is called **interactive marketing.** This advertising approach allows a consumer to respond directly to an advertising message. Often the consumer is able to search for more detailed information and place an order as part of the response. Sales booths and some types of Internet advertising, such as banner ads with links to sellers' Web pages, are forms of interactive marketing.

Advertising that uses signs, billboards, and other public displays traditionally has been categorized as a form of mass marketing. Why is this classification now in doubt?

Interactive marketing
Advertising that permits a consumer to follow up directly by searching for more information and placing direct product orders.

INTERNATIONAL EXAMPLE

A Push to Make Electronic Billboards Interactive in Japan

In Japan, when a person glances at an electronic display advertising a product, the mechanism projecting the image often looks back at that individual. Such ad display mechanisms can identify the person's gender with an accuracy rate as high as 90 percent and can determine the individual's age within a 10-year range about 70 percent of the time. Hence, if the ad display is mounted above another mechanism that actually dispenses the product, such as a vending machine, the display can recommend a product based on the person's estimated age and gender.

The latest version of electronic ad display mechanisms can also interpret an individual's body language, including facial expressions such as smiling or frowning. The ad display responds by tailoring its message to try matching the indicated mood of the individual. Thus, recognition capabilities transform the display into an interactive-marketing device.

FOR CRITICAL THINKING
Why do you suppose that marketers are working on enabling ad-display mechanisms to recognize faces and to search the Web for information about a specific person who glances at the ad?

SEARCH, EXPERIENCE, AND CREDENCE GOODS The qualities and characteristics of a product determine how the firm should advertise that product. Some types of products, known as **search goods,** possess qualities that are relatively easy for consumers to assess in advance of their purchase. Clothing and music are common examples of items that have features that a consumer may assess, or perhaps even sample, before purchasing.

Other products, known as **experience goods,** are products that people must actually consume before they can determine their qualities. Soft drinks, restaurant meals, and haircutting services are examples of experience goods.

A third category of products, called **credence goods,** includes goods and services with qualities that might be difficult for consumers who lack specific expertise to evaluate without assistance. Products such as pharmaceuticals and services such as health care and legal advice are examples of credence goods.

Search good
A product with characteristics that enable an individual to evaluate the product's quality in advance of a purchase.

Experience good
A product that an individual must consume before the product's quality can be established.

Credence good
A product with qualities that consumers lack the expertise to assess without assistance.

INFORMATIONAL VERSUS PERSUASIVE ADVERTISING The forms of advertising that firms use vary considerably depending on whether the item being marketed is a search good or an experience good. If the item is a search good, a firm is more likely to use **informational advertising** that emphasizes the features of its product. A video trailer for the latest movie starring Emma Stone will include snippets of the film, which help potential buyers assess the quality of the movie.

In contrast, if the product is an experience good, a firm is more likely to engage in **persuasive advertising** intended to induce a consumer to try the product and, as a consequence, discover a previously unknown taste for it. For example, a soft-drink ad is likely to depict happy people drinking the clearly identified product during breaks from enjoyable outdoor activities on a hot day.

If a product is a credence good, producers commonly use a mix of informational and persuasive advertising. For instance, an ad for a pharmaceutical product commonly provides both detailed information about the product's curative properties and side effects and suggestions to consumers to ask physicians to help them assess the drug.

Informational advertising
Advertising that emphasizes transmitting knowledge about the features of a product.

Persuasive advertising
Advertising that is intended to induce a consumer to purchase a particular product and discover a previously unknown taste for the item.

ADVERTISING AS SIGNALING BEHAVIOR Recall from Chapter 23 that *signals* are compact gestures or actions that convey information. For example, high profits in an industry are signals that resources should flow to that industry. Individual companies can explicitly engage in signaling behavior. A firm can do so by establishing brand names or trademarks and then promoting them heavily. This is a signal to prospective consumers that this is a company that plans to stay in business. Before the modern age of advertising, U.S. banks needed a way to signal their soundness. To do this, they constructed large, imposing bank buildings using marble and granite. Stone structures communicated permanence. The effect was to give bank customers confidence that they were not doing business with fly-by-night operations.

When Ford Motor Company advertises its brand name heavily, it incurs substantial costs. The only way it can recoup those costs is by selling many Ford vehicles over a long period of time. Heavy advertising in the company's brand name thereby signals to car buyers that Ford intends to stay in business a long time and wants to develop a loyal customer base—because loyal customers are repeat customers.

WHAT IF... the government were to limit or even ban "excessive" advertising?

Informational advertising is informative to buyers of search goods, and even a firm's spending on persuasive advertising indicates its intent to expand its customer base and hence to continue operations for the foreseeable future. Thus, both informational and persuasive forms of advertising arguably offer measurable informational benefits to consumers. Arbitrarily defining an "excessive" level of advertising in order to limit or ban it undoubtedly would reduce these benefits.

QUICK QUIZ See page 572 for the answers. Review concepts from this section in MyEconLab.

_____ such as words, symbols, and logos distinguish firms' products from those of other firms. Firms seek to differentiate their brands through advertising, via _____ marketing, _____ marketing, or _____ marketing.

A firm is more likely to use _____ advertising that emphasizes the features of its product if the item is a **search good** with features that consumers can assess in advance.

A firm is more likely to use _____ advertising to affect consumers' tastes and preferences if it sells an **experience good.** This is an item that people must actually consume before they can determine its qualities.

A firm that sells a _____ good, which is an item possessing qualities that consumers lack the expertise to fully assess, typically uses a combination of informational and persuasive advertising.

Information Products and Monopolistic Competition

Information product
An item that is produced using information-intensive inputs at a relatively high fixed cost but distributed for sale at a relatively low marginal cost.

A number of industries sell **information products,** which entail relatively high fixed costs associated with the use of knowledge and other information-intensive inputs as key factors of production. Once the first unit has been produced, however, it is possible to produce additional units at a relatively low per-unit cost. Most information products can be put into digital form. Good examples are computer games, computer operating systems, digital music and videos, educational and training software, electronic books and encyclopedias, and office productivity software.

Special Cost Characteristics of Information Products

Creating the first copy of an information product often entails incurring a relatively sizable up-front cost. Once the first copy is created, however, making additional copies can be very inexpensive. For instance, a firm that sells a computer game can simply make properly formatted copies of the original digital file of the game available for consumers to download, at a price, via the Internet.

COSTS OF PRODUCING INFORMATION PRODUCTS To think about the cost conditions faced by the seller of an information product, consider the production and sale of a computer game. The company that creates a computer game must devote many hours of labor to developing and editing its content. Each hour of labor and each unit of other resources devoted to performing this task entail an opportunity cost. The sum of all these up-front costs constitutes a relatively sizable *fixed cost* that the company must incur to generate the first copy of the computer game.

Once the company has developed the computer game in a form that is readable by personal computers, the marginal cost of making and distributing additional copies is very low. In the case of a computer game, it is simply a matter of incurring a minuscule cost to place the required files on a data disk or on the company's Web site.

COST CURVES FOR AN INFORMATION PRODUCT Suppose that a manufacturer decides to produce and sell a computer game. Creating the first copy of the game requires incurring a total fixed cost equal to $250,000. The marginal cost that the company incurs to place the computer game on a data disk or in downloadable format is a constant amount equal to $2.50 per computer game.

Figure 25-4 below displays the firm's cost curves for this information product. By definition, average fixed cost is total fixed cost divided by the quantity produced and sold. Hence, the average fixed cost of the first computer game is $250,000. But if the company sells 5,000 copies, the average fixed cost drops to $50 per game. If the total quantity sold is 50,000, average fixed cost declines to $5 per game. The average fixed cost (AFC) curve slopes downward over the entire range of possible quantities of computer games.

Average variable cost equals total variable cost divided by the number of units of a product that a firm sells. If this company sells only one copy, then the total variable cost it incurs is the per-unit cost of $2.50, and this is also the average variable cost of producing one unit. Because the per-unit cost of producing the computer game is a constant $2.50, producing two games entails a total variable cost of $5.00, and the average variable cost of producing two games is $5.00 ÷ 2 = $2.50. Thus, as shown in Figure 25-4, the average variable cost of producing and selling this computer game is always equal to the constant marginal cost of $2.50 per game that the company incurs. The average variable cost (AVC) curve is the same as the marginal cost (MC) curve, which for this company is the horizontal line depicted in Figure 25-4.

FIGURE 25-4

Cost Curves for a Producer of an Information Product

The total fixed cost of producing a computer game is $250,000. If the producer sells 5,000 copies, average fixed cost falls to $50 per copy. If quantity sold rises to 50,000, average fixed cost decreases to $5 per copy. Thus, the producer's average fixed cost (AFC) curve slopes downward. If the per-unit cost of producing each copy of the game is $2.50, then both the marginal cost (MC) and average variable cost (AVC) curves are horizontal at $2.50 per copy. Adding the AFC and AVC curves yields the ATC curve. Because the ATC curve slopes downward, the producer of this information product experiences short-run economies of operation.

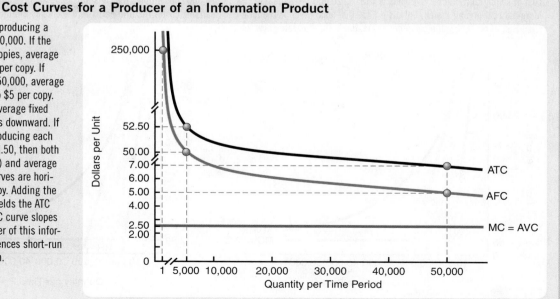

SHORT-RUN ECONOMIES OF OPERATION By definition, average total cost equals the sum of average fixed cost and average variable cost. The average total cost (ATC) curve for this computer game company slopes downward over its entire range.

Recall from Chapter 22 that along the downward-sloping range of an individual firm's *long-run* average cost curve, the firm experiences *economies of scale*. For the producer of an information product such as a computer game, the *short-run* average total cost curve slopes downward. Consequently, sellers of information products typically experience **short-run economies of operation.** The average total cost of producing and selling an information product declines as more units of the product are sold. Short-run economies of operation are a distinguishing characteristic of information products that sets them apart from most other goods and services.

Short-run economies of operation
A distinguishing characteristic of an information product arising from declining short-run average total cost as more units of the product are sold.

Monopolistic Competition and Information Products

In the example depicted in Figure 25-4 on the preceding page, the information product is a computer game. There are numerous computer games among which consumers can choose. Hence, there are many products that are close substitutes in the market for computer games. Yet no two computer games are exactly the same. This means that the particular computer game product sold by the company in our example is distinguishable from other competing products.

For the sake of argument, therefore, let's suppose that this company participates in a monopolistically competitive market for this computer game. Panels (a) and (b) of Figure 25-5 below display a possible demand curve for the computer game manufactured and sold by this particular company.

MARGINAL COST PRICING AND INFORMATION PRODUCTS What if the company making this particular computer game were to behave *as if* it were a perfectly competitive firm by

---

FIGURE 25-5

The Infeasibility of Marginal Cost Pricing of an Information Product

In panel (a), if the firm with the average total cost and marginal cost curves shown in Figure 25-4 on page 565 sets the price of the computer game equal to its constant marginal cost of $2.50 per copy, then consumers will purchase 20,000 copies. This yields $50,000 in revenues. The firm's average total cost of 20,000 games is $15 per copy, so its total cost of selling that number of copies is $15 × 20,000 = $300,000. Marginal cost pricing thereby entails a $250,000 loss, which is the total fixed cost of producing the computer game. Panel (b) illustrates how the

price of the game is ultimately determined under monopolistic competition. Setting a price of $27.50 per game induces consumers to buy 10,000 copies, and the average total cost of producing this number of copies is also $27.50. Consequently, total revenues equal $275,000, which just covers the sum of the $250,000 in total fixed costs and $25,000 (the 10,000 copies times the constant $2.50 average variable cost) in total variable costs. The firm earns zero economic profits.

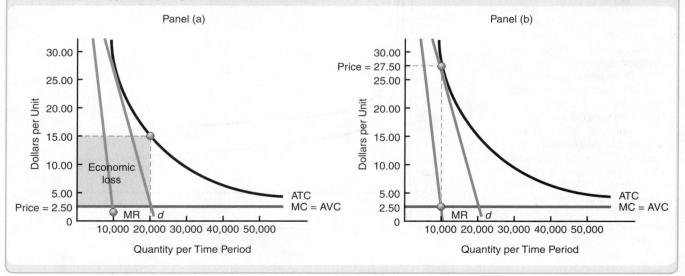

setting the price of its product equal to marginal cost? Panel (a) of Figure 25-5 on the facing page provides the answer to this question. If the company sets the price of the computer game equal to marginal cost, it will charge only $2.50 per game it sells. Naturally, a larger number of people desire to purchase computer games at this price, and given the demand curve in the figure, the company could sell 20,000 copies of this game.

The company would face a problem, however. At a price of $2.50 per computer game, it would earn $50,000 in revenues on sales of 20,000 copies. The average fixed cost of 20,000 copies equals $250,000/20,000, or $12.50 per computer game. Adding this to the constant $2.50 average variable cost implies an average total cost of selling 20,000 copies of $15 per game. Under marginal cost pricing, therefore, the company would earn an average loss of $12.50 (price − average total cost = $2.50 − $15.00 = −$12.50) per computer game for all 20,000 copies sold. The company's total economic loss from selling 20,000 computer games at a price equal to marginal cost would amount to $250,000. Hence, the company would fail to recoup the $250,000 total fixed cost of producing the computer game. If the company had planned to set its price equal to the computer game's marginal cost, it would never have developed the computer game in the first place!

The failure of marginal cost pricing to allow firms selling information products to cover the fixed costs of producing those products is intrinsic to the nature of such products. In the presence of short-run economies of operation in producing information products, marginal cost pricing is simply not feasible in the marketplace.

Recall that marginal cost pricing is associated with perfect competition. An important implication of this example is that markets for information products cannot function as perfectly competitive markets. Imperfect competition is the rule, not the exception, in the market for information products.

THE CASE IN WHICH PRICE EQUALS AVERAGE TOTAL COST Panel (b) of Figure 25-5 on the preceding page illustrates how the *price* of the computer game is ultimately determined in a monopolistically competitive market. After all entry or exit from the market has occurred, the price of the computer game will equal the producer's average cost of production, including all implicit opportunity costs. The price charged for the game generates total revenues sufficient to cover all explicit and implicit costs and therefore is consistent with earning a normal return on invested capital.

Given the demand curve depicted in Figure 25-5, at a price of $27.50 per computer game, consumers are willing to purchase 10,000 copies. The company's average total cost of offering 10,000 copies for sale is also equal to $27.50 per computer game. Consequently, the price of each copy equals the average total cost of producing the game.

At a price of $27.50 per computer game, the company's revenues from selling 10,000 copies equal $275,000. This amount of revenues is just sufficient to cover the company's total fixed cost (including the opportunity cost of capital) of $250,000 and the $25,000 total variable cost it incurs in producing 10,000 copies at an average variable cost of $2.50 per game. Thus, the company earns zero economic profits.

LONG-RUN EQUILIBRIUM FOR AN INFORMATION PRODUCT INDUSTRY When competition drives the price of an information product to equality with average total cost, sellers charge the minimum price required to cover their production costs, including the relatively high initial costs they must incur to develop their products in the first place. Consumers thereby pay the lowest price necessary to induce sellers to provide the item.

The situation illustrated in panel (b) of Figure 25-5 on the facing page corresponds to a long-run equilibrium for this particular firm in a monopolistically competitive market for computer games. If this and other companies face a situation such as the diagram depicts, there is no incentive for additional companies to enter or leave the computer game industry. Consequently, the product price naturally tends to adjust to equality with average total cost as a monopolistically competitive industry composed of sellers of information products moves toward long-run equilibrium.

Firms that sell **information products** experience relatively _____ fixed costs, but once they have produced the first unit, they can sell additional units at a relatively _____ per-unit cost. Consequently, the manufacturer of an information product experiences short-run _____ of _____.

If a firm sets the price of an information product equal to marginal cost, it earns only sufficient revenues to cover its

_____ costs. Engaging in marginal cost pricing, therefore, fails to cover the relatively high fixed costs of making an information product.

In a long-run equilibrium outcome under monopolistic competition, the price of an information product equals _____ _____ cost. The seller's total revenues exactly cover _____ costs, including the opportunity cost of capital.

YOU ARE THERE
Have You Smelled a Ford Lately?

Years ago, Ford Motor Company based a marketing campaign on the slogan "Have you driven a Ford lately?" Today, the company wants prospective buyers assessing a vehicle's handling characteristics during test drives to be captivated as well by the car's scent.

Linda Schmalz, a body interior materials engineer, has been charged with determining the appropriate scents to be emitted by a Ford vehicle's air bag covers, cup holders, floor mats, and seat fabrics. Her first discovery is that people's perceptions of odors differ by regions. Schmalz wonders, therefore, if perhaps Ford should offer customized scents. Allowing consumers to choose

among smells along with other vehicle features would, she concludes, differentiate Ford's products from those of all competitors in the auto market. The result, she argues, would be increased sales of Ford vehicles.

Critical Thinking Questions

1. What is the economic objective of differentiating the scents of vehicles?
2. Why do you suppose that Schmalz's boss has emphasized that he wants vehicle odors that "produce a sense of well-being inside a Ford"?

ISSUES & APPLICATIONS

Why E-Books Are Upending the Publishing Business

CONCEPTS APPLIED
▶ Monopolistic Competition
▶ Information Products
▶ Short-Run Economies of Operation

It is a typical day at Amazon.com, Inc. Of its top 50 digital-book best-sellers, about one-third are priced below $5, a fact of major consternation for book publishers.

The Economics of E-Books versus Traditional Physical Books

The book-publishing industry exhibits features of monopolistic competition:

1. Many competitive sellers, each of which produces a relatively small share of total output
2. Heterogeneous products
3. Considerable advertising
4. Easy entry and exit

Publishers have long sold information products—books that can be produced at relatively low and constant per-unit cost but at significant total fixed costs. Thus, average variable costs are constant, but average fixed costs decline as more books are produced, so publishers' short-run average total cost curves slope downward.

The advent of e-books—books in electronic formats for digital devices—has publishers rethinking how to compete. Most publishers wish to sell physical books alongside e-books, but plummeting e-book prices threaten this strategy.

How Much Are Physically Printed Words Worth in the Market?

The fixed costs incurred by a publisher in paying an author to write a book to be printed on paper or stored as a digital file are the same. Variable costs, however, are much lower for e-books. Hence, the prices at which books generate sufficient revenues to cover total costs are lower for e-books than for physical books.

Selling e-books cuts average costs and hence the prices at which zero economic profits can be maintained in the long run. Furthermore, the lower prices of e-books—sometimes as low as 99 cents—are inducing many consumers to substitute away from traditional physical books. For publishers continuing to produce physical books, these substitutions are resulting in decreases in demand.

Maintaining prices sufficiently high to cover average total costs and to earn at least zero economic profits is becoming an increasingly difficult proposition for book publishers. Thus, a number of publishers that currently specialize in producing physical books likely will have to respond to economic losses either by switching to e-books or by exiting the book-publishing market.

For Critical Thinking

1. Why do you suppose that some publishers are selling space for advertisements in their e-books—and sometimes even in physical books?

2. From an economic standpoint, how could we explain the willingness of someone to pay $19.99 for a physical book that is available as an e-book for $9.99?

Web Resources

1. To contemplate how e-books are changing the economics of publishing for both publishers and authors, go to **www.econtoday.com/chap25**.

2. To consider how an author's fixed costs of publishing e-books can be covered at a price of 99 cents per book, go to **www.econtoday.com/chap25**.

MyEconLab

For more questions on this chapter's Issues & Applications, go to MyEconLab. In the Study Plan for this chapter, select Section N: News.

MyEconLab

Here is what you should know after reading this chapter. MyEconLab will help you identify what you know, and where to go when you need to practice.

WHAT YOU SHOULD KNOW		WHERE TO GO TO PRACTICE
The Key Characteristics of a Monopolistically Competitive Industry A monopolistically competitive industry consists of a large number of firms that sell differentiated products that are close substitutes. Firms can easily enter or exit the industry. Monopolistically competitive firms can increase their profits if they can successfully distinguish their products from those of their rivals. Thus, they have an incentive to advertise.	monopolistic competition, 556 product differentiation, 557	• MyEconLab Study Plan 25.1
Contrasting the Output and Pricing Decisions of Monopolistically Competitive Firms with Those of Perfectly Competitive Firms In the short run, a monopolistically competitive firm produces to the point at which marginal revenue equals marginal cost. The price it charges can exceed both marginal cost and average total cost in the short run. The resulting economic profits induce new firms to enter the industry. In the long run, therefore, monopolistically competitive firms earn zero economic profits, but price exceeds marginal cost.	**Key Figures** Figure 25-1, 559 Figure 25-2, 560	• MyEconLab Study Plans 25.2, 25.3 • Animated Figures 25-1, 25-2

WHAT YOU SHOULD KNOW		WHERE TO GO TO PRACTICE
Why Brand Names and Advertising Are Important Features of Monopolistically Competitive Industries Monopolistically competitive firms engage in advertising. If the product is a search good with features that consumers can evaluate prior to purchase, the seller is more likely to use advertising to transmit information about product features. If the firm sells an experience good, with features that are apparent only when consumed, it is more likely to use persuasive advertising to induce consumers to discover unknown tastes. If the product is a credence good with characteristics that consumers cannot readily assess unaided, then the firm often uses a mix of informational and persuasive advertising.	direct marketing, 562 mass marketing, 562 interactive marketing, 563 search good, 563 experience good, 563 credence good, 563 informational advertising, 563 persuasive advertising, 563	• MyEconLab Study Plan 25.4
Properties of Information Products and Determining Their Prices Providing an information product entails high fixed costs but a relatively low per-unit cost. Hence, the average total cost curve for a firm that sells an information product slopes downward, meaning that the firm experiences short-run economies of operation. In a long-run equilibrium, price adjusts to equality with average total cost.	information product, 564 short-run economies of operation, 566 **Key Figures** Figure 25-4, 565 Figure 25-5, 566	• MyEconLab Study Plan 25.5 • Animated Figures 25-4, 25-5

Log in to MyEconLab, take a chapter test, and get a personalized Study Plan that tells you which concepts you understand and which ones you need to review. From there, MyEconLab will give you further practice, tutorials, animations, videos, and guided solutions. For more information, visit www.myeconlab.com

PROBLEMS

All problems are assignable in MyEconLab. Answers to odd-numbered problems appear at the back of the book.

25-1. Explain why the following are examples of monopolistic competition. (See page 556.)

　　a. There are a number of fast-food restaurants in town, and they compete fiercely. Some restaurants cook their hamburgers over open flames. Others fry their hamburgers. In addition, some serve broiled fish sandwiches, while others serve fried fish sandwiches. A few serve ice cream cones for dessert, while others offer frozen ice cream pies.

　　b. There are a vast number of colleges and universities across the country. Each competes for top students. All offer similar courses and programs, but some have better programs in business, while others have stronger programs in the arts and humanities. Still others are academically stronger in the sciences.

25-2. Consider the diagram on the facing page depicting the demand and cost conditions faced by a monopolistically competitive firm. (See page 559.)

　　a. What are the total revenues, total costs, and economic profits experienced by this firm?

　　b. Is this firm more likely in short- or long-run equilibrium? Explain.

25-3. In a perfectly competitive market, price equals marginal cost, but this condition is not satisfied for the firm with the revenue and cost conditions depicted in Problem 25-2. In the long run, what would happen if the government decided to require the firm in Problem 25-2 to charge a price equal to marginal cost at the firm's long-run output rate? (See page 560.)

25-4. Based on your answer to Problem 25-3, is the firm with the revenue and cost conditions depicted in Problem 25-2 behaving "anticompetitively" in the sense of intentionally "taking advantage" of consumers by charging them a price greater than marginal cost? Explain your reasoning. (See page 561.)

25-5. The table below depicts the prices and total costs a local used-book store faces. The bookstore competes with a number of similar stores, but it capitalizes on its location and the word-of-mouth reputation of the coffee it serves to its customers. Calculate the store's total revenue, total profit, marginal revenue, and marginal cost at each level of output, beginning with the first unit. Based on marginal analysis, what is the approximate profit-maximizing level of output for this business? (See page 560.)

Output	Price per Book ($)	Total Costs ($)
0	6.00	2.00
1	5.75	5.25
2	5.50	7.50
3	5.25	9.60
4	5.00	12.10
5	4.75	15.80
6	4.50	20.00
7	4.00	24.75

25-6. Calculate total average costs for the bookstore in Problem 25-5. Illustrate the store's short-run equilibrium by plotting demand, marginal revenue, average total costs, and marginal costs. What is its total profit? (See page 560.)

25-7. Suppose that after long-run adjustments take place in the used-book market, the business in Problem 25-5 ends up producing 4 units of output. What are the market price and economic profits of this monopolistic competitor in the long run? (See page 560.)

25-8. It is a typical Christmas electronics shopping season, and makers of flat-panel TVs are marketing the latest available models through their own Web sites as well as via retailers such as Best Buy and Walmart. Each manufacturer offers its own unique versions of flat-panel TVs in differing arrays of shapes and sizes. As usual, each is hoping to maintain a stream of economic profits earned since it first introduced these most recent models late last year or perhaps just a few months before Christmas. Nevertheless, as sales figures arrive at the headquarters of companies such as Dell, Samsung, Sharp, and Sony, it is clear that most of the companies will end up earning only a normal rate of return this year. (See page 560.)

a. How can makers of flat-panel TVs earn economic profits during the first few months after the introduction of new models?

b. What economic forces result in the dissipation of economic profits earned by manufacturers of flat-panel TVs?

25-9. Classify each of the following as an example of direct, interactive, and/or mass marketing. (See page 562.)

a. The sales force of a pharmaceutical company visits physicians' offices to promote new medications and to answer physicians' questions about treatment options and possible side effects.

b. A mortgage company targets a list of specific low-risk borrowers for a barrage of e-mail messages touting its low interest rates and fees.

c. An online bookseller pays fees to an Internet search engine to post banner ads relating to each search topic chosen by someone conducting a search. In part, this helps promote the bookseller's brand, but clicking on the banner ad also directs the person to a Web page displaying books on the topic that are available for purchase.

d. A national rental car chain runs advertisements on all of the nation's major television networks.

25-10. Classify each of the following as an example of direct, interactive, and/or mass marketing. (See page 562.)

a. A cosmetics firm pays for full-page display ads in a number of top women's magazines.

b. A magazine distributor mails a fold-out flyer advertising its products to the addresses of all individuals it has identified as possibly interested in magazine subscriptions.

c. An online gambling operation arranges for pop-up ads to appear on the computer screen every time a person uses a media player to listen to digital music or play video files, and clicking on the ads directs an individual to its Web gambling site.

  d. A car dealership places advertisements in newspapers throughout the region where potential customers reside.

25-11. Categorize each of the following as an experience good, a search good, or a credence good or service, and justify your answer. (See page 563.)

  a. A heavy-duty filing cabinet

  b. A restaurant meal

  c. A wool overcoat

  d. Psychotherapy

25-12. Categorize each of the following as an experience good, a search good, or a credence good or service, and justify your answer. (See page 563.)

  a. Services of a carpet cleaning company

  b. A new cancer treatment

  c. Athletic socks

  d. A silk necktie

25-13. In what ways do credence goods share certain characteristics of both experience goods and search goods? How do credence goods differ from both experience goods and search goods? Why does advertising of credence goods commonly contain both informational and persuasive elements? Explain your answers. (See page 563.)

25-14. Is each of the following items more likely to be the subject of an informational or a persuasive advertisement? Why? (See page 563.)

  a. An office copying machine

  b. An automobile loan

  c. A deodorant

  d. A soft drink

25-15. Discuss the special characteristics of an information product, and explain the implications for a producer's short-run average and marginal cost curves. In addition, explain why having a price equal to marginal cost is not feasible for the producer of an information product. (See page 565.)

25-16. A firm that sells e-books—books in digital form downloadable from the Internet—sells all e-books relating to do-it-yourself topics (home plumbing, gardening, and the like) at the same price. At present, the company can earn a maximum annual profit of $25,000 when it sells 10,000 copies within a year's time. The firm incurs a 50-cent expense each time a consumer downloads a copy, but the company must spend $100,000 per year developing new editions of the e-books. The company has determined that it would earn zero economic profits if price were equal to average total cost, and in this case it could sell 20,000 copies. Under marginal cost pricing, it could sell 100,000 copies. (See page 565.)

  a. In the short run, what is the profit-maximizing price of e-books relating to do-it-yourself topics?

  b. At the profit-maximizing quantity, what is the average total cost of producing e-books?

ECONOMICS ON THE NET

Legal Services on the Internet A number of legal firms now offer services on the Internet, and in this application you contemplate features of the market for Web-based legal services.

Title: Nolo.com—Law for All

Navigation: Link to the Nolo.com site via **www.econtoday .com/chap25**.

Application Answer the following questions.

  1. In what respects does the market for legal services, such as those provided online by Nolo.com, have the characteristics of a monopolistically competitive industry?

  2. How can providers of legal services differentiate their products? How does Nolo.com attempt to do this?

For Group Discussion and Analysis Assign groups to search the Web for at least three additional online legal firms and compare the services these firms offer. Reconvene the entire class and discuss whether it is reasonable to classify the market for online legal services as monopolistically competitive.

ANSWERS TO QUICK QUIZZES

p. 558: (i) large . . . highly; (ii) differentiated; (iii) easy

p. 561: (i) short; (ii) long . . . zero . . . normal; (iii) total . . . total; (iv) average total . . . minimum

p. 564: (i) Trademarks . . . direct . . . mass . . . interactive; (ii) informational; (iii) persuasive; (iv) credence

p. 568: (i) high . . . low . . . economies . . . operation; (ii) variable; (iii) average total . . . total

Oligopoly and Strategic Behavior

26

The United States is home to several textbook publishers, so the textbook-publishing industry is not a monopoly. Nevertheless, three textbook publishers together account for more than four-fifths of all U.S. textbook sales. The production and pricing decisions of any one of the top three publishers influence the production and pricing decisions of its competitors. Consequently, the U.S. textbook industry is neither perfectly competitive nor monopolistically competitive. Instead, this industry is an *oligopoly*, a type of market structure in which only a handful of competitors exist. This particular market structure is the subject of the present chapter.

since 2009, the percentage of daily minutes devoted to Facebook's Web site by the average U.S. resident who surfs the Internet has increased from less than 3 percent to more than 15 percent? During the same period, the percentages of minutes spent on AOL, eBay, MySpace, Yahoo, and other sites that were among the most common Web destinations a decade ago have steadily declined. Even the percentage of online time spent on Google's site has leveled off at about 10 percent.

What accounts for the substantial increase in time that people devote to Facebook? Most economists agree that a fundamental key to Facebook's growth has been that the benefit a person perceives from spending an additional minute at Facebook's site is influenced by how many other people use Facebook. In this chapter, you will learn about how firms in industries with just a few competitors can benefit—or lose out—when a consumer's willingness to purchase their products is influenced by other consumers' decisions about whether to buy them.

Oligopoly

An important market structure that we have yet to discuss involves a situation in which a few large firms constitute essentially an entire industry. They are not perfectly competitive in the sense that we have used the term. They are not even monopolistically competitive. And because there are several of them, a pure monopoly does not exist. We call such a situation an **oligopoly,** which consists of a small number of *interdependent* sellers. Each firm in the industry knows that other firms will react to its changes in prices, quantities, and qualities. An oligopoly market structure can exist for either a homogeneous or a differentiated product.

Characteristics of Oligopoly

Oligopoly is characterized by a small number of interdependent firms that constitute the entire market.

SMALL NUMBER OF FIRMS How many is "a small number of firms"? More than two but less than a hundred? The question is not easy to answer. Basically, though, oligopoly exists when the top few firms in the industry account for an overwhelming percentage of total industry output.

Oligopolies often involve three to five big companies that produce the bulk of industry output. Between World War II and the 1970s, three firms—General Motors, Chrysler, and Ford—produced and sold nearly all the output of the U.S. automobile industry. Among manufacturers of chewing gum and cigarettes, four large firms produce and sell almost the entire output of each industry.

INTERDEPENDENCE All markets and all firms are, in a sense, interdependent. But only when a few large firms produce most of the output in an industry does the question of **strategic dependence** of one on the others' actions arise. In this situation, when any one firm changes its output, its product price, or the quality of its product, other firms notice the effects of its decisions. The firms must recognize that they are interdependent and that any action by one firm with respect to output, price, quality, or product differentiation will cause a reaction by other firms. A model of such mutual interdependence is difficult to build, but examples of such behavior are not hard to find in the real world. Oligopolists in the cigarette industry, for example, are constantly reacting to each other.

Recall that in the model of perfect competition, each firm ignores the behavior of other firms because each firm is able to sell all that it wants at the going market price. At the other extreme, the pure monopolist does not have to worry about the reaction of current rivals because there are none. In an oligopolistic market structure, the managers of firms are like generals in a war: *They must attempt to predict the reaction of rival firms.* It is a strategic game.

Oligopoly
A market structure in which there are very few sellers. Each seller knows that the other sellers will react to its changes in prices, quantities, and qualities.

Strategic dependence
A situation in which one firm's actions with respect to price, quality, advertising, and related changes may be strategically countered by the reactions of one or more other firms in the industry. Such dependence can exist only when there are a limited number of major firms in an industry.

Why Oligopoly Occurs

Why are some industries composed chiefly of a few large firms? What causes an industry that might otherwise be competitive to tend toward oligopoly? We can provide some partial answers here.

Follow the link at www.econtoday.com /chap26 to *Wall Street Journal* articles about real-world examples involving oligopoly.

ECONOMIES OF SCALE Perhaps the most common reason that has been offered for the existence of oligopoly is economies of scale. Recall that economies of scale exist when a doubling of output results in less than a doubling of total costs. When economies of scale exist, the firm's long-run average total cost curve will slope downward as the firm produces more and more output. Average total cost can be reduced by continuing to expand the scale of operation to the *minimum efficient scale*, or the output rate at which long-run average cost is minimized. (See page 500 in Chapter 22.) Smaller firms in a situation in which the minimum efficient scale is relatively large will have average total costs greater than those incurred by large firms. Little by little, they will go out of business or be absorbed into larger firms.

BARRIERS TO ENTRY It is possible that certain barriers to entry have prevented more competition in oligopolistic industries. They include legal barriers, such as patents, and control and ownership of critical supplies. Indeed, we can find periods in the past when firms were able not only to erect a barrier to entry but also to keep it in place year after year. In principle, the chemical, electronics, and aluminum industries have been at one time or another either monopolistic or oligopolistic because of the ownership of patents and the control of strategic inputs by specific firms.

OLIGOPOLY BY MERGER Another reason that oligopolistic market structures may sometimes develop is that firms merge. A merger is the joining of two or more firms under single ownership or control. The merged firm naturally becomes larger, enjoys greater economies of scale as output increases, and may ultimately have a greater ability to influence the market price for the industry's output.

There are two key types of mergers, vertical and horizontal. A **vertical merger** occurs when one firm merges with either a firm from which it purchases an input or a firm to which it sells its output. Vertical mergers occur, for example, when a coal-using electrical utility purchases a coal-mining firm or when a shoe manufacturer purchases retail shoe outlets.

Obviously, vertical mergers cannot *create* oligopoly as we have defined it. But that can indeed occur via a **horizontal merger,** which involves firms selling a similar product. If two shoe manufacturing firms merge, that is a horizontal merger. If a group of firms, all producing steel, merge into one, that is also a horizontal merger.

So far we have been talking about oligopoly in a theoretical manner. Now it is time to look at the actual oligopolies in the United States.

Vertical merger
The joining of a firm with another to which it sells an output or from which it buys an input.

Horizontal merger
The joining of firms that are producing or selling a similar product.

YOU ARE THERE

To think about why firms sometimes engage in vertical mergers, take a look at **Hyundai Goes Vertical** on page 588.

WHAT IF... the government promoted competition among more firms by prohibiting horizontal mergers?

Sometimes media observers suggest that the government could increase market competition by making it illegal for firms within the same industry to engage in horizontal mergers. Recall from Chapter 22 (page 500), however, that firms operate at lowest long-run average cost when they are able to attain their minimum efficient scale—the minimum point on the long-run average cost curve. If the government were to prohibit firms from merging horizontally within the same industry, many firms' scales of operations would be held artificially below the minimum efficient scale. This would cause long-run average costs to be higher than the minimum feasible level, which would result in higher prices for consumers.

TABLE 26-1

Computing the Four-Firm Concentration Ratio

Firm	Annual Sales ($ millions)	
1	150 ⎫	
2	100 ⎪ = 400	Total number of firms in industry = 25
3	80 ⎬	
4	70 ⎭	
5 through 25	50	
Total	450	

Four-firm concentration ratio = 400/450 = 88.9%

Measuring Industry Concentration

As we have stated, oligopoly is a market structure in which a few interdependent firms produce a large part of total output in an industry. This situation is often called one of high *industry concentration*. Before we show the concentration statistics in the United States, let's determine how industry concentration can be measured.

CONCENTRATION RATIO The most common way to compute industry concentration is to determine the percentage of total sales or production accounted for by the top four or top eight firms in an industry. This gives the four- or eight-firm **concentration ratio,** also known as the *industry concentration ratio.* An example of an industry with 25 firms is given in Table 26-1 above. We can see in that table that the four largest firms account for almost 90 percent of total output in the hypothetical industry. This is an example of an oligopoly because a few firms will recognize the interdependence of their output, pricing, and quality decisions.

U.S. CONCENTRATION RATIOS Table 26-2 below shows the four-firm *domestic* concentration ratios for various industries. Is there any way that we can show or determine which industries to classify as oligopolistic? There is no definite answer. If we arbitrarily picked a four-firm concentration ratio of 75 percent, we could infer that cigarettes and breakfast cereals were oligopolistic. But we would always be dealing with an arbitrary definition.

What is the four-firm concentration ratio in the U.S. auto industry?

Concentration ratio
The percentage of all sales contributed by the leading four or leading eight firms in an industry; sometimes called the *industry concentration ratio.*

TABLE 26-2

Four-Firm Domestic Concentration Ratios for Selected U.S. Industries

Industry	Share of Total Sales Accounted for by the Top Four Firms (%)
Cigarettes	95
Breakfast cereals	78
Household vacuum cleaners	62
Primary aluminum	51
Computers	50
Soft drinks	48
Printing and publishing	38
Commercial banking	29.5

Source: U.S. Bureau of the Census.

EXAMPLE

The Four-Firm Concentration Ratio in the U.S. Auto Industry

In a recent year, seven companies accounted for the bulk of U.S. auto sales. Percentage sales shares for these firms were as follows: General Motors, 19.1 percent; Ford, 16.5 percent; Toyota, 15.3 percent; Honda, 10.6 percent; Chrysler, 9.3 percent; Nissan, 7.9 percent; and Hyundai, 7.7 percent. A few other smaller firms accounted for the remaining 13.6 percent of total auto sales. Consequently, the four-firm concentration ratio

for the U.S. auto industry was 19.1 percent + 16.5 percent + 15.3 percent + 10.6 percent, or 61.5 percent.

FOR CRITICAL THINKING
What was the seven-firm concentration ratio in the U.S. auto industry?

The Herfindahl-Hirschman Index

A problem with using concentration ratios is that these measures of industry concentration can fail to reflect differences in the relative sizes of firms within an industry. To understand why this is so, consider Table 26-3 below, which applies to two fictitious industries, called Industry A and Industry B.

Table 26-3 indicates that in Industry A, the four-firm concentration ratio is the sum of the percentage sales shares of the only four firms in the industry, which equals 81.25% + 6.25% + 6.25% + 6.25% = 100%. If we compute the four-firm concentration for Industry B, we obtain 25% + 25% + 25% + 25% = 100%. Thus, even though the top firm in Industry A has far more than half of all sales in that industry, whereas the top firm in Industry B has 25 percent of all sales, the four-firm concentration ratios are the same for the two industries. Thus, this example shows that using concentration ratios can potentially fail to reflect considerable variations in the distribution of firm sizes within industries.

To account for variations in sizes of firms when measuring industry concentration, economists use the **Herfindahl-Hirschman Index (HHI),** which is equal to the sum of the squared percentage sales shares of all firms in an industry. For a monopoly, in which only one firm has 100 percent of all industry sales, the value of the HHI equals $100^2 = 10,000$. Consequently, 10,000 is the maximum feasible level of the HHI for any industry.

Table 26-3 uses the sales shares for the firms in Industries A and B to calculate the HHI values for each industry. For Industry A, the sum of the squared values of all firms' percentage sales shares yields an HHI level of approximately 6,718.9. For Industry B, performing the same calculation gives an HHI value of 2,500. Thus, the HHI value for Industry B is less than half as large as the HHI level for Industry A. This substantial difference in HHI levels reflects the fact that the distribution of firm sizes

Herfindahl-Hirschman Index (HHI)
The sum of the squared percentage sales shares of all firms in an industry.

TABLE 26-3

Dollar Sales and Percentage Sales Shares for Two Industries

	Industry A				Industry B		
Firm	Annual Sales ($ millions)	Sales Share (%)	Squared Sales Share	Firm	Annual Sales ($ millions)	Sales Share (%)	Squared Sales Share
1	65	81.25	6,601.6	1	20	25.00	625.0
2	5	6.25	39.1	2	20	25.00	625.0
3	5	6.25	39.1	3	20	25.00	625.0
4	5	6.25	39.1	4	20	25.00	625.0
	Total sales = 80	Total percentage = 100.00	HHI = 6,718.9		Total sales = 80	Total percentage = 100.00	HHI = 2,500.0

is more even in Industry B than in Industry A, despite the identical values of the industries' four-firm concentration ratios.

What is the value of the Herfindahl-Hirschman Index for the world's Internet browser industry?

INTERNATIONAL EXAMPLE

The HHI for the Global Internet Browser Industry

Recently, the worldwide percentage shares of sales for the five firms offering Internet browsers were as follows: Microsoft's Internet Explorer, 60 percent; Google's Chrome, 25 percent; Mozilla's Firefox, 7 percent; Apple's Safari, 5 percent; and Opera Software's Opera, 3 percent. The HHI for the global Internet browser industry is equal to the sum of the squared percentage industry sales shares for these firm's browsers, or HHI $= 60^2 + 25^2 + 7^2 + 5^2 + 3^2 = 3,600 + 625 + 49 + 25 + 9 = 4,308$.

The HHI level for the global Internet browser industry is below the maximum feasible monopoly value of 10,000. Nevertheless, it is more than twice as large as the HHI level of 2,000 that we would have observed if the five sellers of Internet browsers instead had equal industry sales shares of 20 percent. (Note that $20^2 + 20^2 + 20^2 + 20^2 + 20^2 = 400 + 400 + 400 + 400 + 400 = 2,000$.) Therefore, the global Internet browser industry is a concentrated industry.

FOR CRITICAL THINKING

What would be the revised HHI value if Mozilla and Opera Software decided to conduct a horizontal merger and offer a single "Firefox Opera" Internet browser?

Oligopoly, Efficiency, and Resource Allocation

Although oligopoly is not the dominant form of market structure in the United States, oligopolistic industries do exist. To the extent that oligopolists have *market power*—the ability to *individually* affect the *market* price for the industry's output—they lead to resource misallocations, just as monopolies do. Oligopolists charge prices that exceed marginal cost. But what about oligopolies that occur because of economies of scale? Consumers might actually end up paying lower prices than if the industry were composed of numerous smaller firms.

All in all, there is no definite evidence of serious resource misallocation in the United States because of oligopolies. In any event, *the more U.S. firms face competition from the rest of the world, the less any current oligopoly will be able to exercise market power.*

QUICK QUIZ See page 593 for the answers. Review concepts from this section in MyEconLab.

An **oligopoly** is a market situation with a _____ number of _____ sellers.

Oligopoly may result from _____ of scale, barriers to entry, and _____.

_____ mergers involve the merging of one firm with either the supplier of an input or the purchaser of its output.

_____ mergers involve the joining of firms selling a similar product.

Industry concentration can be measured by the combined _____ of total _____ accounted for by the top four firms in the industry.

Strategic Behavior and Game Theory

Reaction function
The manner in which one oligopolist reacts to a change in price, output, or quality made by another oligopolist in the industry.

At this point, we would like to be able to show oligopoly price and output determination in the way we did for perfect competition, pure monopoly, and monopolistic competition, but we cannot. Whenever there are relatively few firms competing in an industry, each can and does react to the price, quantity, quality, and product innovations that the others undertake. In other words, each oligopolist has a **reaction function.** Oligopolistic competitors are interdependent. Consequently, the decision makers in such firms must employ strategies. And we must be able to model their strategic behavior if we wish to predict how prices and outputs are determined in oligopolistic market structures.

In general, we can think of reactions of other firms to one firm's actions as part of a *game* that is played by all firms in the industry. Economists have developed **game theory** models to describe firms' rational interactions. Game theory is the analytical framework in which two or more individuals, companies, or nations compete for certain payoffs that depend on the strategy that the others employ. Poker is such a game situation because it involves a strategy of reacting to the actions of others.

Some Basic Notions about Game Theory

Games can be either cooperative or noncooperative. If firms work together to obtain a jointly shared objective, such as maximizing profits for the industry as a whole, then they participate in a **cooperative game.** Whenever it is too costly for firms to coordinate their actions to obtain cooperative outcomes, they are in a **noncooperative game** situation. Most strategic behavior in the marketplace is best described as a noncooperative game.

Games can be classified by whether the payoffs are zero, negative, or positive. In a **zero-sum game,** one player's losses are offset by another player's gains. If two retailers have an absolutely fixed total number of customers, for example, the customers that one retailer wins over are exactly equal to the customers that the other retailer loses. In a **negative-sum game,** players as a group lose during the process of the game (although one perhaps by more than the other, and it's possible for one or more players to win). In a **positive-sum game,** players as a group end up better off. Some economists describe all voluntary exchanges as positive-sum games. After an exchange, both the buyer and the seller are better off than they were prior to the exchange.

STRATEGIES IN NONCOOPERATIVE GAMES Players, such as decision makers in oligopolistic firms, have to devise a **strategy,** which is defined as a rule used to make a choice. The goal of the decision maker is to devise a strategy that is more successful than alternative strategies. Whenever a firm's decision makers can come up with certain strategies that are generally successful no matter what actions competitors take, these are called **dominant strategies.** The dominant strategy always yields the unique best action for the decision maker no matter what action the other "players" undertake. Relatively few business decision makers over a long period of time have successfully devised dominant strategies. We know this by observation: Few firms in oligopolistic industries consistently have maintained relatively high profits over time.

How can a real-world situation faced by two captured bank robbers help to illustrate basic principles of game theory?

Game theory
A way of describing the various possible outcomes in any situation involving two or more interacting individuals when those individuals are aware of the interactive nature of their situation and plan accordingly. The plans made by these individuals are known as *game strategies*.

Cooperative game
A game in which the players explicitly cooperate to make themselves jointly better off. As applied to firms, it involves companies colluding in order to make higher than perfectly competitive rates of return.

Noncooperative game
A game in which the players neither negotiate nor cooperate in any way. As applied to firms in an industry, this is the common situation in which there are relatively few firms and each has some ability to change price.

Zero-sum game
A game in which any gains within the group are exactly offset by equal losses by the end of the game.

Negative-sum game
A game in which players as a group lose during the process of the game.

Positive-sum game
A game in which players as a group are better off at the end of the game.

Strategy
Any rule that is used to make a choice, such as "Always pick heads."

Dominant strategies
Strategies that always yield the highest benefit. Regardless of what other players do, a dominant strategy will yield the most benefit for the player using it.

EXAMPLE

The Prisoners' Dilemma

An example of game theory occurs when two people involved in a bank robbery are caught. What should they do when questioned by police? Their situation has been called the **prisoners' dilemma.** The two suspects, Sam and Carol, are interrogated separately (they cannot communicate with each other) and are given various alternatives. The interrogator indicates separately to Sam and Carol the following:

1. If both confess to the bank robbery, they will both go to prison for 5 years.
2. If neither confesses, they will each be given a sentence of 2 years on a lesser charge.
3. If one prisoner turns state's evidence and confesses, that prisoner goes free and the other one, who did not confess, will serve 10 years for bank robbery.

You can see the prisoners' alternatives in the **payoff matrix** in Figure 26-1 on the following page. The two possibilities for each prisoner are "confess" and "don't confess." There are four possibilities:

1. Both confess.
2. Neither confesses.
3. Sam confesses (turns state's evidence) but Carol doesn't.
4. Carol confesses (turns state's evidence) but Sam doesn't.

In Figure 26-1, all of Sam's possible outcomes are shown on the upper half of each rectangle, and all of Carol's possible outcomes are shown on the lower half.

By looking at the payoff matrix, you can see that if Carol confesses, Sam's best strategy is to confess also—he'll get only 5 years

Continued

instead of 10. Conversely, if Sam confesses, Carol's best strategy is also to confess—she'll get 5 years instead of 10. Now let's say that Sam is being interrogated and Carol doesn't confess. Sam's best strategy is still to confess, because then he goes free instead of serving 2 years. Conversely, if Carol is being interrogated, her best strategy is still to confess even if Sam hasn't. She'll go free instead of serving 2 years. To confess is a dominant strategy for Sam. To confess is also a dominant strategy for Carol. The situation is exactly symmetrical. So this is the prisoners' dilemma. The prisoners know that both of them will be better off if neither confesses. Yet it is in each individual prisoner's interest to confess, even though the *collective* outcome of each prisoner's pursuit of his or her own interest is inferior for both.

FOR CRITICAL THINKING
Can you apply the prisoners' dilemma to the firms in a two-firm industry that agree to share market sales equally? (Hint: Think about the payoff to cheating on the market-sharing agreement.)

Prisoners' dilemma
A famous strategic game in which two prisoners have a choice between confessing and not confessing to a crime. If neither confesses, they serve a minimum sentence. If both confess, they serve a longer sentence. If one confesses and the other doesn't, the one who confesses goes free. The dominant strategy is always to confess.

Payoff matrix
A matrix of outcomes, or consequences, of the strategies available to the players in a game.

FIGURE 26-1

The Prisoners' Dilemma Payoff Matrix

Regardless of what the other prisoner does, each prisoner is better off if he or she confesses. So confessing is the dominant strategy, and each ends up behind bars for 5 years.

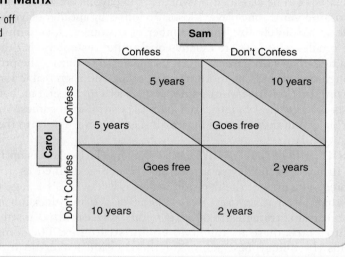

Applying Game Theory to Pricing Strategies

We can apply game strategy to two firms—oligopolists—that have to decide on their pricing strategy. Each can choose either a high or a low price. Their payoff matrix is shown in Figure 26-2 on the facing page. If they both choose a high price, each will make $6 million, but if they both choose a low price, each will make only $4 million. If one sets a high price and the other a low one, the low-priced firm will make $8 million, but the high-priced firm will make only $2 million. As in the prisoners' dilemma, in the absence of collusion, they will end up choosing low prices.

Opportunistic Behavior

Opportunistic behavior
Actions that focus solely on short-run gains because long-run benefits of cooperation are perceived to be smaller.

In the prisoners' dilemma, it is clear that cooperative behavior—both parties standing firm without admitting to anything—leads to the best outcome for both players. But each prisoner (player) stands to gain by cheating. Such action is called **opportunistic behavior.** Our daily economic activities involve the potential for the prisoners' dilemma all the time. We could engage in opportunistic behavior. You could write a check for a purchase knowing that it is going to bounce because you have just closed that bank account. When you agree to perform a specific task for pay, you could perform your work in a substandard way. When you go to buy a product, the seller might be able to cheat you by selling you a defective item.

In short, if all of us—sellers and buyers—engaged in opportunistic behavior all of the time, we would constantly be acting in a world of noncooperative behavior. That is not the world in which most of us live, however. Why not? Because most of us engage in

FIGURE 26-2

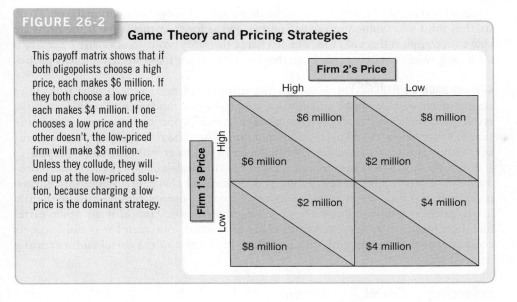

Game Theory and Pricing Strategies

This payoff matrix shows that if both oligopolists choose a high price, each makes $6 million. If they both choose a low price, each makes $4 million. If one chooses a low price and the other doesn't, the low-priced firm will make $8 million. Unless they collude, they will end up at the low-priced solution, because charging a low price is the dominant strategy.

repeat transactions. Manufacturers would like us to keep purchasing their products. Sellers would like us to keep coming back to their stores. As sellers of labor services, we all would like to keep our jobs, get promotions, or be hired away by another firm at a higher wage rate. Therefore, we engage in **tit-for-tat strategic behavior.** A consumer using a tit-for-tat strategy may, for instance, continue to purchase items from a firm each period as long as the firm provides products of the same quality and abides by any guarantees. If the firm fails in any period to provide high-quality products and honor its product guarantees, the consumer purchases items elsewhere.

Tit-for-tat strategic behavior
In game theory, cooperation that continues as long as the other players continue to cooperate.

QUICK QUIZ See page 593 for the answers. Review concepts from this section in MyEconLab.

Each oligopolist has a _____ function because oligopolistic competitors are interdependent. They must therefore engage in _____ behavior. One way to model this behavior is to use **game theory.**

Games can be either **cooperative** or **noncooperative.** In a _____-sum game, one player's losses are exactly offset by another player's gains. In a _____-sum

game, all players collectively lose, perhaps one player more than the others. In a _____-sum game, the players as a group end up better off.

Decision makers in oligopolistic firms must devise a strategy. A _____ strategy is one that is generally successful no matter what actions competitors take.

The Cooperative Game: A Collusive Cartel

According to Adam Smith (1723–1790), "People of the same trade seldom meet together, even for merriment and diversion, but the conversation ends in a conspiracy against the public, or in some contrivance to raise prices." Why can firms profit from engaging in a "conspiracy against the public"? How can firms work together to create a "contrivance to raise prices"? Why does accomplishing this task turn out to be a feat only occasionally achieved by certain industries? Let's consider each of these questions in turn.

The Rationale for a Cartel and the Seeds of Its Undoing

If all the firms in an industry can find a way to cooperatively determine how much to produce to maximize their combined profits, then they can form a **cartel** and jointly act as a single producer. This means that they *collude.* They act together to attain the same outcome that a monopoly firm would aim to achieve: producing to the point at which

Cartel
An association of producers in an industry that agree to set common prices and output quotas to prevent competition.

marginal revenue derived from the *market* demand curve is equal to marginal cost. To do so, they must set common prices and output quotas for their members. If the firms are able to accomplish this task, they can all charge the same profit-maximizing price that a monopoly would have charged. Then they can share in the maximized monopoly profits.

CUTTING BACK ON PRODUCTION Although the prospect of monopoly profits provides a strong incentive to collude, a fledgling cartel faces two fundamental problems. First, recall that a monopoly producer maximizes economic profits by restraining its production to a rate below the competitive output rate. Thus, the first problem for the members of the cartel is to determine how much each producer will restrain its output.

Once the first problem is solved, another immediately appears. As soon as all producers in the cartel begin restraining production and charging a higher price, each individual member could increase its revenues and profits by charging a slightly lower price, raising production, and selling more units. Hence, if all other cartel members honor their agreement to reduce production, one member could boost its economic profits by reneging on its promise to the rest of the cartel and increasing its production.

Enforcing a Cartel Agreement

Go to www.econtoday.com/chap26 to find out from WTRG Economics how effective the Organization of Petroleum Exporting Countries has been in acting as an oil market cartel.

There are four conditions that make it more likely that firms will be able to coordinate their efforts to restrain output and detect cheating, thereby reducing the temptation for participating firms to cheat:

1. *A small number of firms in the industry.* If an industry consists of only a few firms, it is easier to assess how much each firm should restrain production to yield the monopoly output and hence maximum industry profits. In addition, it is easier for each cartel member to monitor other firms' output rates for signs of cheating. For instance, when a cartel has only a few members, they might agree to keep their sales a certain percentage below pre-cartel levels. Failure to do so could be regarded as evidence of cheating.

2. *Relatively undifferentiated products.* If cartel members sell nearly homogeneous products, it is easier for them to agree on how much each firm should reduce its production. In contrast, if each firm sells a highly differentiated product, then some members can reasonably claim that the prices of their products should differ from the prices of other firms' products to reflect differences in costs of production. Thus, a firm with a differentiated product can reasonably claim that it is selling at a lower price for its differentiated good because its good is less valued by consumers—when in fact the firm may simply be using this claim as an excuse to cheat on the cartel agreement.

3. *Easily observable prices.* Naturally, one way to make sure that a producer is abiding by a cartel agreement is to look at the prices at which it actually sells its output. If the terms of industry transactions are publicly available, cartel members can more readily spot a firm's efforts to cheat.

4. *Little variation in prices.* If the industry's market is susceptible to frequent shifts in demand for firms' products or in prices of key inputs, the firms' prices will tend to fluctuate. Establishing a cartel agreement and monitoring cheating consequently will be more difficult. Hence, stable demand and cost conditions help a cartel form and continue to operate effectively.

Sometimes cartels prevent cheating on prices by using mechanisms that masquerade as contracts that are favorable to buyers. For example, all members of a cartel might agree to offer buyers contracts that permit a buyer to switch to another seller if that seller offers the product at a lower price. Naturally, if a customer can provide evidence that a lower price is available from another firm claiming to participate in the cartel, this fact would constitute evidence that the other firm is cheating. In this way, cartel members use their customers to police other cartel participants!

Why Cartel Agreements Usually Break Down

Studies have shown that it is very rare for cartel agreements to last more than 10 years. In many cases, cartel agreements break down more quickly than that. Even industries that usually satisfy the four conditions listed above have difficulty keeping cartels together over time.

One reason that cartels tend to break down is that the economic profits that existing firms obtain from holding prices above competitive levels provide an incentive for new firms to enter the market. Effectively, market entrants can earn profits by acting as a cheating cartel firm would behave. Their entry then provides incentives to cartel members to reduce their own prices and boost their production, and ultimately the cartel unravels.

Variations in overall economic activity also tend to make cartels unsustainable. During general business downturns, market demands tend to decline across all industries as consumers' incomes fall. So do profits of firms participating in a cartel. This increases the incentive for individual firms to cheat on a cartel agreement.

QUICK QUIZ   See page 593 for the answers. Review concepts from this section in MyEconLab.

A _____ is a group of firms in an industry that agree to set common prices and output quotas to restrict competition.

Characteristics of an industry that make it more likely that firms can coordinate efforts to restrain output and earn economic profits are a _____ number of firms,

relatively _____ products, easily _____ prices, and little _____ in prices.

Factors that contribute to the breakdown of a cartel are the _____ of firms seeking the economic profits earned by the cartel members and _____ in economic activity.

Network Effects

A feature sometimes present in oligopolistic industries is **network effects,** or situations in which a consumer's willingness to use an item depends on how many others use it. Commonplace examples are telephones and fax machines. Ownership of a phone or fax machine is not particularly useful if no one else has one, but once a number of people own a phone or fax machine, the benefits that others gain from consuming these devices increases.

In like manner, people who commonly work on joint projects within a network of fellow employees, consultants, or clients naturally find it useful to share computer files. Trading digital files is an easier process if all use common spreadsheet programs and office productivity software. The benefit that each person receives from using spreadsheet programs and office productivity software increases when others use the same software.

Network effect
A situation in which a consumer's willingness to purchase a good or service is influenced by how many others also buy or have bought the item.

Network Effects and Market Feedback

Industries in which firms produce goods or services subject to network effects can experience sudden surges in growth, but the fortunes of such industries can also undergo significant and sometimes sudden reversals.

POSITIVE MARKET FEEDBACK When network effects are an important characteristic of an industry's product, an industry can experience **positive market feedback.** This is the potential for a network effect to arise when an industry's product catches on with consumers. Increased use of the product by some consumers then induces other consumers to purchase the product.

Positive market feedback can affect the prospects of an entire industry. The market for Internet service provider (ISP) servers is an example. The growth of this industry has roughly paralleled the rapid growth of Internet servers worldwide. Undoubtedly, positive market feedback resulting from network effects associated with Internet communications and interactions resulted in additional people desiring to obtain access to the Internet.

NEGATIVE MARKET FEEDBACK Network effects can also result in **negative market feedback,** in which a speedy downward spiral of product sales occurs for a product subject to

Positive market feedback
A tendency for a good or service to come into favor with additional consumers because other consumers have chosen to buy the item.

Negative market feedback
A tendency for a good or service to fall out of favor with more consumers because other consumers have stopped purchasing the item.

network effects. If a sufficient number of consumers cut back on their use of the product, others are induced to reduce their consumption as well, and the product can rapidly become a "has-been."

An example of an industry that has experienced negative market feedback of late is the telecommunications industry. Traditional telecommunications firms such as AT&T, WorldCom, and Sprint experienced positive market feedback during the late 1980s and early 1990s as cell phones and fax machines proliferated and individuals and firms began making long-distance phone calls from cell phones or via fax machines. Since the mid-1990s, as more people have acquired Internet access via cable and satellite Internet service providers, e-mail communications and e-mail document attachments have supplanted large volumes of phone and fax communications. For the telecommunications industry, the greater use of e-mail and e-mail attachments by some individuals induced others to follow suit. This resulted in negative market feedback that reduced the overall demand for traditional long-distance phone services.

Network Effects and Industry Concentration

In some industries, a few firms can potentially reap most of the benefits of positive market feedback. Suppose that firms in an industry sell differentiated products that are subject to network effects. If the products of two or three firms catch on, these firms will capture the bulk of the sales due to industry network effects.

A good example is the market for online auction services. An individual is more likely to use the services of an auction site if there is a significant likelihood that many other potential buyers or sellers also trade items at that site. Hence, there is a network effect present in the online auction industry, in which eBay and Overstock account for more than 80 percent of total sales. eBay in particular has experienced positive market feedback, and its share of sales of online auction services has increased to more than 50 percent.

Consequently, in an industry that produces and sells products subject to network effects, a small number of firms may be able to secure the bulk of the payoffs resulting from positive market feedback. In such an industry, oligopoly is likely to emerge as the prevailing market structure.

QUICK QUIZ See page 593 for the answers. Review concepts from this section in MyEconLab.

_____ effects exist when a consumer's demand for an item depends in part on how many other consumers also use the product.

_____ market feedback arises if consumption of a product by a sufficient number of individuals induces others to purchase it. _____ market feedback can take place if a falloff in usage of a product by some consumers causes others to stop purchasing the item.

In an industry with differentiated products subject to **network effects**, an oligopoly may arise if a few firms can reap most of the sales _____ resulting from _____ market feedback.

Two-Sided Markets, Network Effects, and Oligopoly

Two-sided Market
A market in which an intermediary firm provides services that link groups of producers and consumers.

Network effects are especially important to firms operating in **two-sided markets**. In such markets, an intermediary firm provides services that link other groups of producers and consumers. When you watch TV programming, for instance, your TV service provider links you and others among the TV audience to advertisers. The TV industry, therefore, is one of many examples of an industry operating in a two-sided market.

A Two-Sided Market

In a two-sided market, a platform firm provides a good or service that links two groups of end users, such as those among groups A and B in the figure. The platform establishes prices that are not necessarily the same for the two groups.

Types of Two-Sided Markets

Figure 26-3 above depicts the basic structure of a two-sided market, in which economists typically call the intermediary firm a *platform* and the groups of producers and consumers that it links—groups A and B in the figure—*end users*. Thus, in the TV industry, a TV service provider is a platform, and the two groups of end users are the advertisers and the audience.

Two-sided markets are of four types:

1. *Audience-seeking markets.* TV, radio, newspaper, and various Internet-portal industries fall into this group of two-sided markets, in which media platforms link advertisers to audiences.

2. *Matchmaking markets.* Operating in these two-sided markets are platform firms such as real estate agents, companies providing Web auction services, and online dating firms.

3. *Transaction-based markets.* Banks, credit- and debit-card companies, and other firms that finalize transactions between groups such as retailers and cardholders function as platforms within these two-sided markets.

4. *Shared-input markets.* In shared-input markets, groups of end users utilize a key input obtained from a platform firm in order to interact with one another. For instance, Microsoft has traditionally served as a platform that provides an operating system as a key input for digital devices sold to consumer end users by firms such as Hewlett-Packard and Dell. In addition, broadband-Internet-access firms are platforms that provide a key interactive-communications input for use by online firms and Web-surfing consumers.

Network Effects in Two-Sided Markets

Network effects are a common feature of two-sided markets. In an audience-seeking market, the perceived benefit received by each advertiser increases as the audience size grows. At the same time, even audience members who pay no attention to ads benefit from an expansion of a TV service provider's content made possible by a rise in the number of advertisers.

In a matchmaking market, a platform's task of matching an end user in one group to an end user in another is simplified when both groups are larger, which causes each end user to experience a greater benefit when group sizes increase. For instance, a person using an online dating site to try to find a date this Friday evening perceives a greater benefit if the dating site can search among a larger group for someone with desired characteristics.

Network effects also arise in transaction-based and shared-input markets. In the credit-card industry, for example, retailers benefit when more consumers use a credit card accepted by the retailers, and likewise consumers gain when a larger number of retailers accept a credit card carried by the consumers. For a company like Microsoft, which provides a shared input such as an operating system, sellers of digital devices with that operating system gain when a larger number of consumers use it. In addition, consumers who use the operating system benefit when it functions on more digital devices.

Two-Sided Oligopolistic Pricing

The presence of network effects in two-sided markets means a few firms are often able to capture most of the payoffs associated with market feedback. Thus, oligopoly is the most common industry structure in these markets.

Platform firms setting prices in a two-sided market must consider group differences in network effects. In a transaction-based market for debit cards, for example, banks may find that network effects are greater for retailers than for consumers. Suppose that the willingness of retailers to accept debit cards responds more strongly to greater consumer use than consumers' willingness to use the cards responds to retailers' acceptance. Also suppose that both groups are equally responsive to changes in card fees. Banks' profits would be higher if they charge lower card-usage fees to consumers than to retailers. Then more consumers will use the cards, which will give retailers a greater incentive to accept them even at a higher fee.

In a number of two-sided markets, platform firms maximize profits by charging an explicit price of zero to one group of end users. Many online media sites, for instance, charge fees to advertisers but post news articles and videos for consumer audiences at no explicit charge. In a few cases, platform firms may even establish *negative* prices, or *subsidies*, for one of the end-user groups. For instance, Microsoft commonly pays subsidies to developers of software applications that function with the company's Windows operating system. Microsoft is willing to do this because it has determined that the availability of more Windows applications increases consumers' willingness to purchase the Windows operating system.

Of course, platform firms in two-sided markets must also take into account strategic interactions. Thus, when a news media firm such as CNN decides how much to charge advertisers for news articles it makes available to readers online at no charge, it must consider as well the advertising fees that Fox News will establish. Likewise, when choosing subsidies to pay Windows application developers and the prices to charge Windows consumers, Microsoft must consider how Apple will set developer subsidies and consumer prices for its operating system.

How did the online matchmaker PlentyOfFish break into the top ranks of the online dating industry by borrowing an idea from audience-making markets?

EXAMPLE

Fishing for Date Seekers with Ads Boosts PlentyOfFish

During the first several years that the online dating industry existed, the few competing firms charged fees to people on both sides of a match. In the mid-2000s, though, the online matchmaking firm PlentyOfFish eliminated most fees for date seekers, which induced more people to look for dates at its site. This increase in customers in turn generated network effects as people responded to the upswing in registered users by searching the site for matches. PlentyOfFish convinced advertisers that all of its customers could be regarded as a large audience in an audience-seeking two-sided market. The firm restructured its Internet site so that

people looking for matches viewed advertisements on every Web page, and it earned nearly all of its revenues from fees paid by advertisers. As Figure 26-4 on the facing page indicates, after PlentyOfFish adopted this pricing strategy, it became one of the top online dating firms.

FOR CRITICAL THINKING

Why do you suppose that some competitors of PlentyOfFish have maintained the strategy of charging fees to date seekers rather than placing ads on their sites?

FIGURE 26-4

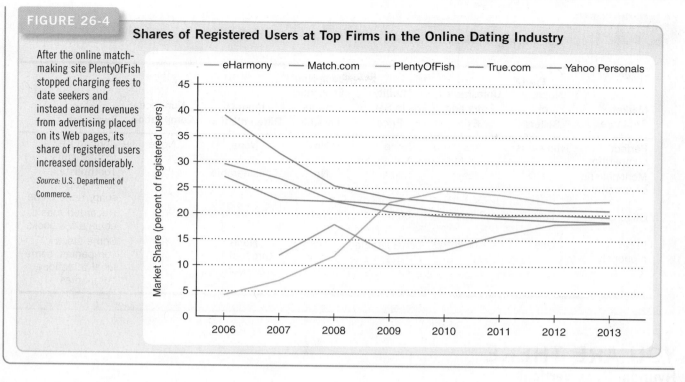

Shares of Registered Users at Top Firms in the Online Dating Industry

After the online match-making site PlentyOfFish stopped charging fees to date seekers and instead earned revenues from advertising placed on its Web pages, its share of registered users increased considerably.

Source: U.S. Department of Commerce.

QUICK QUIZ   See page 593 for the answers. Review concepts from this section in MyEconLab.

In **two-sided markets,** an intermediary firm called a _____ provides services that link other groups of producers and consumers that are known as _____.

The four types of **two-sided markets** are _____-_____ markets, _____ markets, _____-_____ markets, and _____-_____ markets.

Differences in network effects across different groups of end users can induce platforms to establish positive prices to one group but to establish _____ prices or even _____ prices, or subsidies, for another group.

The Old and New of Two-Sided Markets

Newspapers have existed since 59 B.C., so two-sided markets are not new. Now, however, Barnes & Noble and Amazon compete to link publishers to readers via digital devices. Apple and Google vie to link app designers to consumers via smartphones. Facebook and LinkedIn compete to link people via social media sites. Today, two-sided markets are everywhere.

Comparing Market Structures

Now that we have looked at perfect competition, pure monopoly, monopolistic competition, and oligopoly, we are in a position to compare the attributes of these four different market structures. We do this in summary form in Table 26-4 on the next page, in which we compare the number of sellers, their ability to set price, and the degree of product differentiation and also give some examples of each of the four market structures.

TABLE 26-4

Comparing Market Structures

Market Structure	Number of Sellers	Unrestricted Entry and Exit	Ability to Set Price	Long-Run Economic Profits Possible	Product Differentiation	Nonprice Competition	Examples
Perfect competition	Numerous	Yes	None	No	None	None	Agriculture, roofing nails
Monopolistic competition	Many	Yes	Some	No	Considerable	Yes	Toothpaste, toilet paper, soap, retail trade
Oligopoly	Few	Partial	Some	Yes	Frequent	Yes	Recorded music, college textbooks
Pure monopoly	One	No (for entry)	Considerable	Yes	None (product is unique)	Yes	Some electric companies, some local telephone companies

YOU ARE THERE
Hyundai Goes Vertical

"I think Henry Ford had it right at the start," says John Krafcik, CEO of Hyundai Motor America, about the founder of Ford Motor Company, "when he said 'The more you control production, the more you control what you sell the car for, too.'" Following up on Ford's original idea, Krafcik has led Hyundai through a series of vertical mergers that have created a subsidiary that makes 12 million tons of steel per year.

Krafcik offers two rationales for the vertical mergers. One is that manufacturing steel inputs for its vehicles instead of buying steel from other suppliers allows Hyundai to coordinate its vehicle production process at lower short-run costs. The other rationale is that Hyundai can now directly influence the development of lightweight steel used in constructing

automotive products. In this way, Hyundai hopes to reduce its long-run costs as well.

Critical Thinking Questions

1. Did Hyundai's vertical mergers directly affect the automotive industry's four-firm concentration ratio or Herfindahl-Hirschman Index? Explain your reasoning.

2. If vertical mergers throughout the auto industry raised the minimum efficient scale for the industry, could industry concentration eventually increase? Explain.

ISSUES & APPLICATIONS

Concentration in the Textbook-Publishing Industry

CONCEPTS APPLIED

▶ Horizontal Mergers

▶ Concentration Ratio

▶ Herfindahl-Hirschman Index

Over the past two decades, textbook-publishing firms have undergone a series of horizontal mergers—that is, combinations of previously competing publishers. These mergers have created a concentrated textbook-publishing industry.

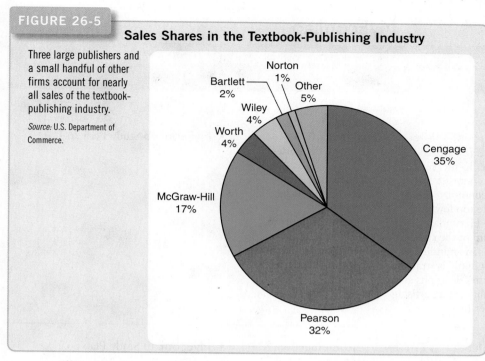

FIGURE 26-5

Sales Shares in the Textbook-Publishing Industry

Three large publishers and a small handful of other firms account for nearly all sales of the textbook-publishing industry.

Source: U.S. Department of Commerce.

- Norton 1%
- Bartlett 2%
- Other 5%
- Wiley 4%
- Worth 4%
- Cengage 35%
- McGraw-Hill 17%
- Pearson 32%

Overall Concentration in the Textbook-Publishing Industry

Figure 26-5 above displays recent shares of textbook sales by U.S. textbook publishers. The four-firm concentration ratio for this industry—the sum of the shares of sales going to Cengage, Pearson, McGraw-Hill, and Worth—is 88 percent.

Squaring the market-share percentages of all firms listed in Figure 26-5 and summing the results yields 2,600 as the approximate value of the Herfindahl-Hirschman Index (HHI). This HHI level is well below the maximum feasible HHI value of 10,000 for a monopoly. It is more than twice as large, however, as the value of about 1,250 that we would have observed if publishers had equal shares of industry sales. Taken together, therefore, the four-firm concentration ratio and HHI value suggest a very concentrated textbook-publishing industry.

Oligopolistic Interdependence in the Textbook Market

A key implication of Figure 26-5 is apparent without computing either the four-firm concentration ratio or the industry HHI. The figure shows that the top three publishers account for most of the sales—84 percent—in the industry.

In light of the substantial concentration among only three textbook publishers, economists view the industry as an oligopoly. When one of the top three firms decides how many textbooks to publish and what prices to charge, that publisher must take into account choices of quantities and prices made by the other two publishers among the top three. Thus, the textbook-publishing industry exhibits oligopolistic interdependence.

For Critical Thinking

1. If the industry sales shares of the top four publishers in Figure 26-5 remained unchanged, but the remaining firms merged to form a single company, would the four-firm concentration ratio change? Would the HHI change? Explain.

2. How would the prices that you pay for textbooks likely change if the textbook publishers in Figure 26-5 switched from behaving noncooperatively to determining production and prices collusively? Explain your reasoning.

Web Resources

1. To view a slideshow about the textbook-publishing industry, go to **www.econtoday.com/chap26**.

2. To contemplate why the textbook-publishing industry may become less concentrated in the future, go to **www.econtoday .com/chap26**.

> **MyEconLab**
>
> For more questions on this chapter's Issues & Applications, go to MyEconLab. In the Study Plan for this chapter, select Section N: News.

MyEconLab

Here is what you should know after reading this chapter. MyEconLab will help you identify what you know, and where to go when you need to practice.

WHAT YOU SHOULD KNOW		WHERE TO GO TO PRACTICE
The Fundamental Characteristics of Oligopoly Oligopoly is a situation in which a few firms produce most of an industry's output. To measure the extent to which a few firms account for an industry's production and sales, economists use concentration ratios, which are the top few firms' percentages of total sales, and the Herfindahl-Hirschman Index, which is the sum of the squared percentage sales shares of all firms in an industry. An important characteristic of oligopoly is strategic dependence, meaning that one firm's decisions about its production, price, product quality, or advertising can bring about responses by other firms.	oligopoly, 574 strategic dependence, 574 vertical merger, 575 horizontal merger, 575 concentration ratio, 576 Herfindahl-Hirschman Index (HHI), 577	• MyEconLab Study Plan 26.1
Applying Game Theory to Evaluate the Pricing Strategies of Oligopolistic Firms Game theory is the analytical framework used to evaluate how two or more firms compete for payoffs that depend on the strategies that others employ. When firms work together for a common objective such as maximizing industry profits, they participate in cooperative games, but when they cannot work together, they engage in noncooperative games. One important type of game is the prisoners' dilemma, in which the inability to cooperate in determining prices of their products can cause firms to choose lower prices than they otherwise would prefer.	reaction function, 578 game theory, 579 cooperative game, 579 noncooperative game, 579 zero-sum game, 579 negative-sum game, 579 positive-sum game, 579 strategy, 579 dominant strategies, 579 prisoners' dilemma, 580 payoff matrix, 580 opportunistic behavior, 580 tit-for-tat strategic behavior, 581 **Key Figures** Figure 26-1, 580 Figure 26-2, 581	• MyEconLab Study Plan 26.2 • Animated Figures 26-1, Figure 26-2
Industry Features That Contribute to or Detract from Efforts to Form a Cartel A cartel is an organization of firms in an industry that collude to earn economic profits by producing a combined output consistent with monopoly profit maximization. Four conditions make a collusive cartel agreement easier to create and enforce: (1) a small number of firms in the industry, (2) relatively undifferentiated products, (3) easily observable prices, and (4) little variation in prices.	cartel, 581	• MyEconLab Study Plan 26.3

CHAPTER 26 | Oligopoly and Strategic Behavior **591**

WHAT YOU SHOULD KNOW		WHERE TO GO TO PRACTICE
Why Network Effects and Market Feedback Encourage Oligopoly Network effects arise when a consumer's demand for an item is affected by how many other consumers also use it. There is positive market feedback when enough people consume a product to induce others to do so. Negative market feedback occurs when decreased purchases of an item by some consumers give others an incentive to stop buying it.	network effect, 583 positive market feedback, 583 negative market feedback, 583	• MyEconLab Study Plan 26.4
Two-Sided Markets In a two-sided market, an intermediary firm known as a platform links groups called end users. When the extent of network effects differs for the groups of end users, the platform typically establishes contrasting prices for the different groups. When one group is particularly susceptible to network effects, the platform may choose to charge an explicit price of zero to that group and generate revenues solely by charging a positive price to the other group. In certain situations, the platform may even establish negative prices for (that is, pay subsidies to) one group while setting a positive price for the other group.	two-sided market, 584 Key Table Table 26-4, 588	• MyEconLab Study Plans 26.5, 26.6 • Animated Table 26-4

Log in to MyEconLab, take a chapter test, and get a personalized Study Plan that tells you which concepts you understand and which ones you need to review. From there, MyEconLab will give you further practice, tutorials, animations, videos, and guided solutions. For more information, visit www.myeconlab.com

PROBLEMS

All problems are assignable in MyEconLab. Answers to odd–numbered problems appear at the back of the book.

26-1. Suppose that the distribution of sales within an industry is as shown in the table. (See page 576.)

Firm	Share of Total Market Sales
A	15%
B	14
C	12
D	11
E	10
F	10
G	8
H	7
All others	13
Total	100%

a. What is the four-firm concentration ratio for this industry?

b. What is the eight-firm concentration ratio for this industry?

26-2. The table below shows recent worldwide market shares of producers of inkjet printers. (See page 576.)

Firm	Share of Worldwide Market Sales
Brother	3%
Canon	17
Dell	6
Epson	18
Hewlett-Packard	41
Lexmark	13
Samsung	1
Other	1

a. In this year, what was the four-firm concentration ratio in the inkjet-printer industry?

b. In this year, what was the seven-firm concentration ratio in the inkjet-printer industry?

26-3. If there are 13 "All others" in the industry in Problem 26-1, each of which has a share of sales equal to 1 percent, what is the value of the Herfindahl-Hirschman Index for this industry? (See page 577.)

26-4. What is the value of the Herfindahl-Hirschman Index for the industry in Problem 26-2? (See page 577.)

26-5. Characterize each of the following as a positive-sum game, a zero-sum game, or a negative-sum game. (See page 579.)

a. Office workers contribute $10 each to a pool of funds, and whoever best predicts the winners in a professional sports playoff wins the entire sum.

b. After three years of fighting with large losses of human lives and materiél, neither nation involved in a war is any closer to its objective than it was before the war began.

c. Two collectors who previously owned incomplete and nearly worthless sets of trading cards exchange several cards, and as a result both end up with completed sets with significant market value.

26-6. Characterize each of the following as a positive-sum game, a zero-sum game, or a negative-sum game. (See page 579.)

a. You play a card game in your dorm room with three other students. Each player brings $5 to the game to bet on the outcome, winner take all.

b. Two nations exchange goods in a mutually beneficial transaction.

c. A thousand people buy $1 lottery tickets with a single payoff of $800.

26-7. Last weekend, Bob attended the university football game. At the opening kickoff, the crowd stood up. Bob therefore realized that he would have to stand up as well to see the game. For the crowd (not the football team), explain the outcomes of a cooperative game and a noncooperative game. Explain what Bob's "tit-for-tat strategic behavior" would be if he wished to see the game. (See page 581.)

26-8. Consider two strategically dependent firms in an oligopolistic industry, Firm A and Firm B. Firm A knows that if it offers extended warranties on its products but Firm B does not, it will earn $6 million in profits, and Firm B will earn $2 million. Likewise, Firm B knows that if it offers extended warranties but Firm A does not, it will earn $6 million in profits, and Firm A will earn $2 million. The two firms know that if they both offer extended warranties on their products, each will earn $3 million

in profits. Finally, the two firms know that if neither offers extended warranties, each will earn $5 million in profits. (See page 581.)

a. Set up a payoff matrix that fits the situation faced by these two firms.

b. What is the dominant strategy for each firm in this situation? Explain.

26-9. Take a look back at the data regarding the inkjet-printer industry in Problem 26-2, and answer the following questions. (See pages 581–583.)

a. Suppose that consumer demands for inkjet printers, the prices of which are readily observable in office supply outlets and at Internet sites, are growing at a stable pace. Discuss whether circumstances are favorable to an effort by firms in this industry to form a cartel.

b. If the firms successfully establish a cartel, why will there naturally be pressures for the cartel to break down, either from within or from outside?

26-10. Explain why network effects can cause the demand for a product *either* to expand *or* to contract relative to what it would be if there were no network effects. (See pages 583–584.)

26-11. List three products that you think are subject to network effects. For each product, indicate whether, in your view, all or just a few firms within the industry that produces each product experience market feedback effects. In your view, are any market feedback effects in these industries currently positive or negative? (See pages 583–584.)

26-12. Consider the following list, and classify each item according to the appropriate type of two-sided market—audience-making, matchmaking, shared-input, or transaction-based—and write a one-sentence answer justifying your classification. (See page 585. Hint: In some cases, you may wish to check out the firms' Web sites to assist in answering this question.)

a. Realtor.com

b. NYTimes.com

c. Linux.com

d. Paypal.com

26-13. Consider the following list, and classify each item according to the appropriate type of two-sided market—audience-making, matchmaking, shared-input, or transaction-based—and write a one-sentence answer justifying your classification. (See page 585. Hint: In some cases, you may wish to check out the firms' Web sites to assist in answering this question.)

a. Mastercard.com

b. FreeBSD.com

c. Plentyofish.com

d. WSJ.com

ECONOMICS ON THE NET

Current Concentration Ratios in U.S. Manufacturing Industries As you learned in this chapter, economists sometimes use concentration ratios to evaluate whether industries are oligopolies. In this application, you will make your own determination using the most recent data available.

Title: Concentration Ratios in Manufacturing

Navigation: Follow the link at **www.econtoday.com /chap26** to get to the U.S. Census Bureau's report on Concentration Ratios in Manufacturing.

Application Answer the following questions.

1. Select the report for the most recent year. Find the four-firm concentration ratios for the following industries: fluid milk (311511), women's and girls' cut & sew dresses (315233), envelopes (322232), electronic computers (334111).

2. Which industries are characterized by a high level of competition? Which industries are characterized by a low level of competition? Which industries qualify as oligopolies?

3. Name some of the firms that operate in the industries that qualify as oligopolies.

For Group Study and Analysis Discuss whether the four-firm concentration ratio is a good measure of competition. Consider some of the firms you named in item 3. Do you consider these firms to be "competitive" in their pricing and output decisions? Consider the four-firm concentration ratio for ready-mix concrete (327320). Do you think that on a local basis, this industry is competitive? Why or why not ?

ANSWERS TO QUICK QUIZZES

p. 578: (i) small . . . interdependent; (ii) economies . . . mergers; (iii) Vertical; (iv) Horizontal; (v) percentage . . . sales

p. 581: (i) reaction . . . strategic; (ii) zero . . . negative . . . positive; (iii) dominant

p. 583: (i) cartel; (ii) small . . . undifferentiated . . . observable . . . variation; (iii) entry . . . variations

p. 584: (i) Network; (ii) Positive . . . Negative; (iii) gains . . . positive

p. 587: (i) platform . . . end users; (ii) audience-making . . . matchmaking . . . transaction-based . . . shared-input; (iii) zero . . . negative

27

Regulation and Antitrust Policy in a Globalized Economy

Since 2008, millions of U.S. residents have lost their jobs and struggled to find new positions in our dampened economy. Positions first disappeared in the private sector. Then jobs with state governments became harder to find as lower household incomes translated into lower state tax revenues. By the early 2010s, even the federal government was cutting back on overall hiring. Nevertheless, positions in one area of the federal government have continued to expand dramatically. U.S. government regulation of business has become a "growth industry," and federal hiring of people to supervise enforcement of laws overseeing business activities has increased even as employment in all other areas has stagnated. Thus, individuals with expertise in regulating businesses have benefited from an upswing in federal regulatory activities. As you will learn in this chapter, it is more difficult to assess other benefits of government regulation.

California recently adopted a regulation requiring farmers to raise egg-laying hens in conditions that allow them to fully extend their limbs, lie down, and turn in a circle? The legislation has posed practical difficulties, however. First, a typical hen requires 138 square inches to stretch her wings fully, but the largest cages provide only 116 square inches of space. Second, if California farmers respond to the law by allowing chickens to roam freely, the birds react by clustering together, thereby preventing satisfaction of the law's requirement. Furthermore, uncaged hens often slap and trample one another, which has long been a key rationale for farmers to place the birds in cages. Third, the law did not explain how the state would apply the new rules to eggs shipped to California by farmers in other states. Fourth, the legislation failed to specify how the space requirement for egg-laying hens would be enforced. California legislators left all of these details of the law to be sorted out by state regulatory agencies, courts, and perhaps future legislatures.

The only certainty associated with California's space regulation for egg-laying hens was that it likely would lead to higher costs of producing eggs sold within the state. How regulations such as California's "hen law" and other forms of government oversight *should act* to promote greater economic efficiency and how they *actually act* are important topics for understanding how every economy works. Nevertheless, before you can begin your study of the economic effects of regulation, it is important to understand the various ways in which the government oversees the activities of U.S. businesses.

Forms of Industry Regulation

The U.S. government began regulating social and economic activity early in the nation's history. The amount of government regulation began increasing in the twentieth century and has grown considerably since 1970. Figure 27-1 below displays two common measures of regulation in the United States. Panel (a) shows that regulatory spending by federal agencies (in 2005 dollars) has generally trended upward since 1970 and has risen considerably since 2000. New national security regulations following the 2001 terrorist attacks in New York City and Washington, D.C., have fueled a significant

FIGURE 27-1 **Regulation on the Rise**

Panel (a) shows that federal government regulatory spending is now more than $50 billion per year. State and local spending is not shown. As panel (b) shows, the number of pages in the *Federal Register* per year rose sharply in the 1970s, dropped off somewhat in the 1980s, and then began to rise once more.

Sources: Institute for University Studies; *Federal Register*, various issues.

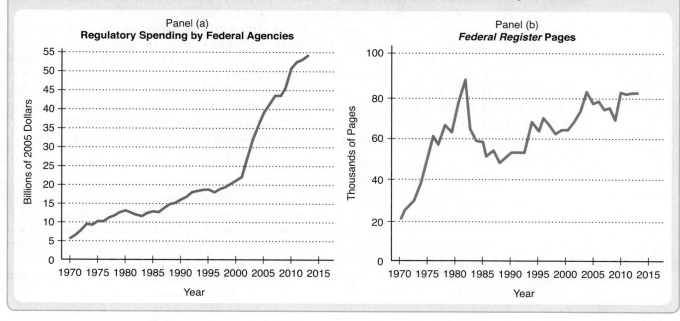

Panel (a)
Regulatory Spending by Federal Agencies

Panel (b)
Federal Register **Pages**

portion of this growth. The remainder of the increase in spending is related to a general upswing in regulatory enforcement by the federal government during this period. Panel (b) of Figure 27-1 on the previous page depicts the number of pages in the *Federal Register*, a government publication that lists all new regulatory rules. According to this measure, the scope of new federal regulations increased sharply during the 1970s, dropped off in the 1980s, and has generally increased since then.

There are two basic types of government regulation. One is *economic regulation* of natural monopolies and of specific nonmonopolistic industries. For instance, some state commissions regulate the prices and quality of services provided by electric power companies, which are considered natural monopolies (See page 534 in Chapter 24) that experience lower long-run average costs as their output increases. Financial services industries and interstate transportation industries are examples of nonmonopolistic industries that are subjected to considerable government regulation. The other form of government regulation is *social regulation*, which covers all industries. Examples include various occupational, health, and safety rules that federal and state governments impose on most businesses.

Economic Regulation

Initially, most economic regulation in the United States was aimed at controlling prices in industries considered to be natural monopolies. Over time, federal and state governments have also sought to influence the characteristics of products or processes of firms in a variety of industries without inherently monopolistic features.

REGULATION OF NATURAL MONOPOLIES The regulation of natural monopolies has tended to emphasize restrictions on product prices. Various public utility commissions throughout the United States regulate the rates (prices) of electrical utility companies and some telephone operating companies. This *rate regulation*, as it is usually called, officially has been aimed at preventing such industries from earning monopoly profits.

REGULATION OF NONMONOPOLISTIC INDUSTRIES The prices charged by firms in many other industries that do not have steadily declining long-run average costs, such as financial services industries, have also been subjected to regulations. Every state in the United States, for instance, has a government agency devoted to regulating the prices that insurance companies charge.

More broadly, government regulations establish rules pertaining to production, product (or service) features, and entry and exit within a number of specific nonmonopolistic industries. The federal government is heavily involved, for instance, in regulating the securities, banking, transportation, and communications industries. The Securities and Exchange Commission regulates securities markets. The Federal Reserve, Office of the Comptroller of the Currency, and Federal Deposit Insurance Corporation regulate commercial banks and savings banks. The National Credit Union Administration supervises credit unions. The Federal Aviation Administration supervises the airline industry, and the Federal Motor Carrier Safety Administration regulates the trucking industry. The Federal Communications Commission has oversight powers relating to broadcasting and telephone and communications services.

Social Regulation

In contrast to economic regulation, which covers only particular industries, social regulation applies to all firms in the economy. In principle, the aim of social regulation is a better quality of life through improved products, a less polluted environment, and better working conditions. Since the 1970s, an increasing array of government resources has been directed toward regulating product safety, advertising, and environmental effects. Table 27-1 on the facing page lists some major federal agencies involved in these broad regulatory activities.

TABLE 27-1

TABLE 27-1

Federal Agencies Engaged in Social Regulation

Agency	Jurisdiction	Date Formed	Major Regulatory Functions
Federal Trade Commission (FTC)	Product markets	1914	Responsible for preventing businesses from engaging in misleading advertising, unfair trade practices, and monopolistic actions, as well as for protecting consumer rights.
Food and Drug Administration (FDA)	Food and pharmaceuticals	1938	Regulates the quality and safety of foods, health and medical products, pharmaceuticals, cosmetics, and animal feed.
Equal Employment Opportunity Commission (EEOC)	Labor markets	1964	Investigates complaints of discrimination based on race, religion, gender, or age in hiring, promotion, firing, wages, testing, and all other conditions of employment.
Environmental Protection Agency (EPA)	Environment	1970	Develops and enforces environmental standards for air, water, waste, and noise.
Occupational Safety and Health Administration (OSHA)	Health and safety	1970	Regulates workplace safety and health conditions.
Consumer Product Safety Commission (CPSC)	Consumer product safety	1972	Responsible for protecting consumers from products posing fire, electrical, chemical, or mechanical hazards or dangers to children.
Mining Enforcement and Safety Administration	Mining and oil drilling safety	1973	Establishes and enforces operational safety rules for mines and oil rigs.

The *possible* benefits of social regulations are many. For example, the water supply in some cities is known to be contaminated with potentially hazardous chemicals, and air pollution contributes to many illnesses. Society might well benefit from cleaning up these pollutants. As we shall discuss, however, broad social regulations also entail costs that we all pay, and not just as taxpayers who fund the regulatory activities of agencies such as those listed in Table 27-1 above.

QUICK QUIZ See page 617 for the answers. Review concepts from this section in MyEconLab.

_____ regulation applies to specific industries, whereas _____ regulation applies to businesses throughout the economy.

Governments commonly regulate the prices and quality of services provided by electric, gas, and other utilities, which traditionally have been considered _____ monopolies.

Governments also single out various nonmonopolistic industries, such as the financial and transportation industries, for special forms of _____ regulation.

Among the common forms of _____ regulation covering all industries are the occupational, health, and safety rules that federal and state governments impose on producers.

Regulating Natural Monopolies

At one time, much government regulation of business purportedly aimed to solve the so-called monopoly problem. Of particular concern was implementing appropriate regulations for natural monopolies.

The Theory of Natural Monopoly Regulation

Recall from Chapter 24 that a natural monopoly arises whenever a single firm can produce all of an industry's output at a lower per-unit cost than other firms attempting to produce less than total industry output. In a natural monopoly, therefore, economies of large-scale production exist, leading to a single-firm industry.

THE UNREGULATED NATURAL MONOPOLY Like any other firm, an unregulated natural monopolist will produce to the point at which marginal revenue equals marginal cost. Panel (a) of Figure 27-2 below depicts a situation in which a monopolist faces the market demand curve, D, and the marginal revenue curve, MR. The monopolist searches along the demand curve for the profit-maximizing price and quantity. The profit-maximizing quantity is at point A, at which the marginal revenue curve crosses the long-run marginal cost curve, LMC, and the unregulated monopolist maximizes profits by producing the quantity Q_m. Consumers are willing and able to pay the price

FIGURE 27-2

Profit Maximization and Regulation through Marginal Cost Pricing

The profit-maximizing natural monopolist produces at the point in panel (a) at which marginal costs equal marginal revenue. This is point A, which gives the quantity of production Q_m. The per-unit price is P_m at point F. If a regulatory commission attempted to require equating price with long-run marginal cost, production would have to be at the point where the long-run marginal cost (LMC) curve intersects the demand schedule. This is shown in panel (b). The quantity produced would be Q_1, and the per-unit price would be P_1. Average costs would be AC_1, however, so losses would equal the shaded area.

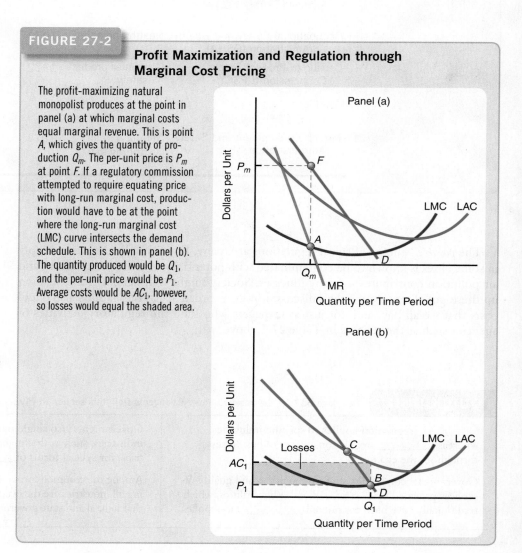

per unit P_m for this quantity at point F. This price is above marginal cost, so it leads to a socially inefficient allocation of resources by restricting production to a rate below that at which price equals marginal cost.

THE IMPRACTICALITY OF MARGINAL COST PRICING What would happen if the government were to require the monopolist in Figure 27-2 on the facing page to produce to the point at which price equals marginal cost, which is point B in panel (b)? Then it would produce a larger output rate, Q_1. Consumers, however, would pay only the price per unit P_1 for this quantity, which would be less than the average cost of producing this output rate, AC_1. Consequently, requiring the monopolist to engage in marginal cost pricing would yield a loss for the firm equal to the shaded rectangular area in panel (b). The profit-maximizing monopolist would go out of business rather than face such regulation.

AVERAGE COST PRICING Regulators cannot practically force a natural monopolist to engage in marginal cost pricing. Thus, regulation of natural monopolies has often taken the form of allowing the firm to set price at the point at which the long-run average cost (LAC) curve intersects the demand curve. In panel (b) of Figure 27-2, this is point C. In this situation, the regulator forces the firm to engage in *average cost pricing*, with average cost including what the regulators deem a "fair" rate of return on investment. For instance, a regulator might impose **cost-of-service regulation,** which requires a natural monopoly to charge only prices that reflect the actual average cost of providing products to consumers. Alternatively, although in a similar vein, a regulator might use **rate-of-return regulation,** which allows firms to set prices that ensure a normal return on investment.

Cost-of-service regulation
Regulation that allows prices to reflect only the actual average cost of production and no monopoly profits.

Rate-of-return regulation
Regulation that seeks to keep the rate of return in an industry at a competitive level by not allowing prices that would produce economic profits.

Natural Monopolies No More?

Traditionally, a feature common to the electricity, natural gas, and telecommunications industries has been that they utilize large networks of wires or pipelines to transmit their products to consumers. Governments concluded that the average costs of providing electricity, natural gas, and telecommunications declined as output rates of firms in these industries increased. Consequently, governments treated these industries as natural monopolies and established regulatory commissions to subject the industries to forms of cost-of-service and rate-of-return regulation.

ELECTRICITY AND NATURAL GAS: SEPARATING PRODUCTION FROM DELIVERY Today, numerous producers of natural gas vie to market their product in a number of cities across the country. In nearly half of the U.S. states, there is active competition in the production of electricity and natural gas.

What circumstances led to this transformation? The answer is that regulators of electricity and natural gas companies figured out that the function of *producing* electricity or natural gas did not necessarily have to be combined with the *delivery* of the product. Since the mid-1980s, various regulators have gradually implemented policies that have separated production of electricity and natural gas from the distribution of these items to consumers. Thus, in a growing number of U.S. locales, multiple producers now pay to use wire and pipeline networks to get their products to buyers.

TELECOMMUNICATIONS SERVICES MEET THE INTERNET As the production and sale of electricity and natural gas began to become more competitive undertakings, regulators started to apply the same principles to telecommunications services. At the same time, other forces reshaped the cost structure of the telecommunications industry. First, significant technological advances drastically reduced the costs of providing wireless telecommunications. Second, Internet phone service became more widely available. Most cable television companies that provide Internet access now offer Web-based telephone services as well. Many other companies also offer Web phone services for purchase by anyone who already has access to the Internet.

Go to www.econtoday.com/chap27 to learn about the latest broadband regulations proposed by the Federal Communications Commission.

ARE NATURAL MONOPOLIES RELICS OF THE PAST? Clearly, the scope of the government's role as regulator of natural monopolies has decreased with the unraveling of conditions that previously created this particular market structure. In many U.S. electricity and natural gas markets, government agencies now apply traditional cost-of-service or rate-of-return regulations primarily to wire and pipeline owners. Otherwise, the government's main role in many regional markets is to serve as a "traffic cop," enforcing property rights and rules governing the regulated networks that serve competing electricity and natural gas producers.

In telecommunications, there are competing views on natural monopoly and the role of regulation. According to one perspective, any natural monopoly rationale for a governmental regulatory role is dissipating rapidly as more and more households and businesses substitute cellular and Web-based phone services for wired phone services. Under the alternative view, network effects (see Chapter 26, page 583) contribute to the potential for a natural monopoly problem that regulators must continue to address.

Why is it that governments around the world are seeking to regulate broadband-Internet-access providers?

INTERNATIONAL EXAMPLE

A Perceived Monopoly Threat Motivates Net Neutrality Rules

According to U.S. Federal Communications Commission (FCC) chair Julius Genachowski, "Once a consumer chooses a broadband provider, then that provider has monopoly power over access to that consumer for any application or content provider that wants to reach that consumer." Telecommunications regulators across the globe, such as those in Australia, Japan, and the European Union, have reached the same conclusion. They have responded by proposing or adopting *net neutrality regulations* aimed at preventing broadband-Internet-access providers from limiting interaction among consumers and Web content and application firms.

Critics of net neutrality rules point out that if broadband providers cannot limit access to any content, then it is difficult for them to charge higher prices to consumers who use much larger amounts of signal bandwidth than others.

The critics also point out that a growing number of households now obtain broadband access *both* through traditional cable or direct-service-line providers *and* via wireless service providers. As a consequence, many consumers already can choose among different broadband providers, none of which possess any natural monopoly status, in spite of what the chair of the FCC says. Thus, for an expanding set of consumers, there is no "monopoly power" for broadband providers to misuse.

FOR CRITICAL THINKING

How might the development of an expanding array of wired and wireless Internet-ready digital devices lead to increased competition among broadband providers?

QUICK QUIZ   See page 617 for the answers. Review concepts from this section in MyEconLab.

A **natural monopoly** arises when one firm can produce all of an industry's output at a _____ per-unit cost than other firms. A profit-maximizing natural monopolist produces to the point at which marginal _____ equals long-run marginal _____ and charges the price that people are willing to pay for the quantity produced.

Because a natural monopolist that is required to set price equal to long-run marginal cost will sustain long-run losses and shut down, regulators typically allow natural monopolists to charge prices that just cover _____ costs. Normally, regulators have done this

through **cost-of-service regulation**, in which prices are based on actual production costs, or **rate-of-return regulation**, in which prices are set to yield a rate of return consistent with _____ economic profits.

Technological and regulatory innovations have made the concept of natural monopoly less relevant. In the electricity, natural gas, and telecommunications industries, production increasingly is accomplished by numerous competing firms that _____ their products through regulated _____.

Regulating Nonmonopolistic Industries

Traditionally, one of the fundamental purposes of governments has been to provide a coordinated system of safeguarding the interests of their citizens. Not surprisingly, protecting consumer interests is the main rationale offered for governmental regulatory functions.

Rationales for Consumer Protection in Nonmonopolistic Industries

The Latin phrase *caveat emptor,* or "let the buyer beware," was once the operative principle in most consumer dealings with businesses. The phrase embodies the idea that the buyer alone is ultimately responsible for assessing a producer and the quality of the items it sells before agreeing to purchase the firm's product. Today, in contrast, various federal agencies require companies to meet specific minimal standards in their dealings with consumers. For instance, a few years ago, the U.S. Federal Trade Commission assessed monetary penalties on Toys "Я" Us and KB Toys because they failed to ship goods sold on their Web sites in time for a pre-Christmas delivery. Such a government action would have been unheard of a few decades ago.

In some industries, federal agencies dictate the rules of the game for firms' interactions with consumers. The Federal Aviation Administration (FAA), for example, oversees almost every aspect of the delivery of services by airline companies. The FAA regulates the process by which tickets for flights are sold and distributed, oversees all flight operations, and even establishes rules governing the procedures for returning luggage after flights are concluded.

Go to www.econtoday.com/chap27 to view a full list of the regulations put into place by the Federal Aviation Administration.

REASONS FOR GOVERNMENT-ORCHESTRATED CONSUMER PROTECTION Two rationales are commonly advanced for heavy government involvement in overseeing and supervising nonmonopolistic industries. One, which you encountered in Chapter 5, is the possibility of *market failures.* For example, the presence of negative externalities such as pollution may induce governments to regulate industries that create such externalities.

The second common rationale is *asymmetric information.* In the context of many producer-consumer interactions, this term refers to situations in which a producer has information about a product that the consumer lacks. For instance, administrators of your college or university may know that another school in your vicinity offers better-quality degree programs in certain fields. If so, it would not be in your college or university's interest to transmit this information to applicants who are interested in pursuing degrees in those fields.

For certain products, asymmetric information problems can pose special difficulties for consumers trying to assess product quality in advance of purchase. In unregulated financial markets, for example, individuals contemplating buying a company's stock, a municipality's bond, or a bank's certificate of deposit might struggle to assess the associated risks of financial loss. If the air transportation industry were unregulated, a person might have trouble determining if one airline's planes were less safe than those of competing airlines. In an unregulated market for pharmaceuticals, parents might worry about whether one company's childhood-asthma medication could have more dangerous side effects than medications sold by other firms.

ASYMMETRIC INFORMATION AND PRODUCT QUALITY In extreme cases, asymmetric information can create situations in which most of the available products are of low quality. A commonly cited example is the market for used automobiles. Current owners of cars that *appear* to be in good condition know the autos' service records. Some owners know that their cars have been well maintained and really do run great. Others, however, have not kept their autos in good repair and thus are aware that they will be susceptible to greater-than-normal mechanical or electrical problems.

Suppose that in your local used-car market, half of all used cars offered for sale are high-quality autos. The other half are low-quality cars, commonly called "lemons," that are likely to break down within a few months or perhaps even weeks. In addition, suppose that a consumer is willing to pay $20,000 for a particular car model if it is in excellent condition but is willing to pay only $10,000 if it is a lemon. Finally, suppose that people who own truly high-quality used cars are only willing to sell at a price of at least $20,000, but people who own lemons are willing to sell at any price at or above $10,000.

Because there is a 50–50 chance that a given car up for sale is of either quality, the average amount that a prospective buyer is willing to pay equals $\left(\frac{1}{2} \times \$20,000 \right) + \left(\frac{1}{2} \times \$10,000 \right) = \$15,000$. Owners of low-quality used cars are willing to sell them at this price, but owners of high-quality used cars are not. In this example, only lemons will be traded, at the "lemon" price of $10,000, because owners of cars in excellent condition will not sell their cars at a price that prospective buyers are willing to pay.

Lemons problem
The potential for asymmetric information to bring about a general decline in product quality in an industry.

THE LEMONS PROBLEM Economists refer to the possibility that asymmetric information can lead to a general reduction in product quality in an industry as the **lemons problem.** This problem does not apply only to the used-car industry. In principle, any product with qualities that are difficult for consumers to fully assess is susceptible to the same problem. *Credence goods*, which as you learned in Chapter 25 on page 563 are items such as pharmaceuticals, health care, and professional services, also may be particularly vulnerable to the lemons problem.

MARKET SOLUTIONS TO THE LEMONS PROBLEM Firms offering truly high-quality products for sale can address the lemons problem in a variety of ways. They can offer product guarantees and warranties. In addition, to help consumers separate high quality producers from incompetent or unscrupulous competitors, the high-quality producers may work together to establish industry standards.

In some cases, firms in an industry may even seek external product certification. They may, for example, solicit scientific reports supporting proposed industry standards and bearing witness that products of certain firms in the industry meet those standards. To legitimize a product-certification process, firms may hire outside companies or groups to issue such reports.

Implementing Consumer Protection Regulation

Governments offering asymmetric information and lemons problems as rationales for regulation presumably have concluded that private market solutions such as warranties, industry standards, and product certification are insufficient. To address asymmetric information problems, governments may offer legal remedies to consumers or enforce licensing requirements in an effort to provide minimum product standards. In some cases, governments go well beyond simple licensing requirements by establishing a regulatory apparatus for overseeing all aspects of an industry's operations.

Go to www.econtoday.com/chap27 to see how the Federal Trade Commission imposes regulations intended to protect consumers.

LIABILITY LAWS AND GOVERNMENT LICENSING Sometimes liability laws, which specify penalties for product failures, provide consumers with protections similar to guarantees and warranties. When the Federal Trade Commission (FTC) charged Toys "Я" Us and KB Toys with failing to meet pre-Christmas delivery dates for Internet toy orders, it operated under a mail-order statute Congress passed in the early 1970s. The mail-order law effectively made the toy companies' delivery guarantees legally enforceable. Although the FTC applied the law in this particular case, any consumer could have filed suit for damages under the terms of the statute.

Federal and state governments also get involved in consumer protection by issuing licenses granting only "qualifying" firms the legal right to produce and sell certain products. For instance, governments of nearly half of the states give the right to sell caskets only to people who have a mortuary or funeral director's license, allegedly to ensure that bodies of deceased individuals are handled with care and dignity.

Although government licensing may successfully limit the sale of low-quality goods, licensing requirements also often limit the number of providers. As you learned in Chapter 24, such requirements can ease efforts by established firms to act as monopolists. In addition, if governments rely on the expertise of established firms for assistance in drafting licensing requirements, these firms certainly have strong incentives to recommend low standards for themselves but high standards for prospective entrants.

DIRECT ECONOMIC AND SOCIAL REGULATION In some instances, governments determine that liability laws and licensing requirements are insufficient to protect the interests of consumers. A government may decide that asymmetric-information problems in banking are so severe that without an extensive banking regulatory apparatus, consumers will lose confidence in banks, and banking crises may ensue. It may rely on similar rationales to establish economic regulation of other financial services industries. Eventually, it may apply consumer protection rationales to justify the economic regulation of additional industries such as trucking or air transportation.

The government may establish an oversight authority to make certain that consumers are protected from incompetent producers of foods and pharmaceuticals. Eventually, the government may determine that a host of other products should meet government consumer protection standards. It may also decide that the people who produce the products also require government agencies to ensure workplace safety. In this way, widespread social regulation emerges, as it has in the United States and almost all developed nations.

QUICK QUIZ See page 617 for the answers. Review concepts from this section in MyEconLab.

Governments tend to regulate industries in which they think market _____ and _____ information problems are most severe.

A common justification for government regulation is to protect consumers from adverse effects of _____ information.

To address the _____ problem, or the potential for _____-quality products to predominate when asymmetric information is widespread, governments often supplement private firms' guarantees, warranties, and certification standards with liability laws and licensing requirements.

Incentives and Costs of Regulation

Abiding by government regulations is a costly undertaking for firms. Consequently, businesses engage in a number of activities intended to avoid the true intent of regulations or to bring about changes in the regulations that government agencies establish.

Creative Response and Feedback Effects: Results of Regulation

Sometimes individuals and firms respond to a regulation in a way that conforms to the letter of the law but undermines its spirit. When they do so, they engage in **creative response** to regulations.

One type of creative response has been labeled a *feedback effect*. Individuals' behaviors may change after a regulation has been put into effect. If a regulation requires fluoridated water, then parents know that their children's teeth have significant protection against tooth decay. Consequently, the feedback effect is that parents become less concerned about how many sweets their children eat.

How has a new law regulating information provided to college students about textbook prices created an unanticipated feedback effect?

Creative response
Behavior on the part of a firm that allows it to comply with the letter of the law but violate the spirit, significantly lessening the law's effects.

EXAMPLE

Learn the Price and Buy from the College Bookstore in One Step

Recently, Congress passed a law called the Higher Education Opportunity Act. A key provision of the legislation mandates that U.S. colleges and universities disclose information about course textbooks on their Web sites. The schools must provide for each course both the International Standard Book Numbers (ISBNs) and the prices of required and recommended texts and other supplemental materials.

A number of colleges and universities responded to this requirement in an unexpected way. They combined the required information with direct Internet links to Web pages on which students could place immediate orders at prices charged by the schools' own bookstores. In most cases, of course, text prices

charged by colleges and universities are higher than the prices at other competing outlets, such as discount textbook Web sites. By meeting the letter of the law, these colleges and universities found a way to encourage students to place orders with their own retail outlets instead of shopping for lower-priced copies at competing bookstores and Web sites. In this way, the schools engaged in a creative response to the regulation imposed by the new law.

FOR CRITICAL THINKING
What feedback effects might occur if publishers were required to sell textbooks at prices below a regulatory maximum price?

Explaining Regulators' Behavior

Those charged with enforcing government regulations operate outside the market, so their decisions are determined by nonmarket processes. A number of theories have emerged to describe the behavior of regulators. These theories explain how regulation can harm consumers by generating higher prices and fewer product choices while benefiting producers by reducing competitive forces and allowing higher profits. Two of the best-known theories of regulatory behavior are the *capture hypothesis* and the *share-the-gains, share-the-pains theory.*

Capture hypothesis
A theory of regulatory behavior that predicts that regulators will eventually be captured by special interests of the industry being regulated.

THE CAPTURE HYPOTHESIS Regulators often end up becoming champions of the firms they are charged with regulating. According to the **capture hypothesis,** regardless of why a regulatory agency was originally established, eventually special interests of the industry it regulates will capture it. After all, the people who know the most about a regulated industry are the people already in the industry. Thus, people who have been in the industry and have allegiances and friendships with others in the industry will most likely be asked to regulate the industry.

According to the capture hypothesis, individual consumers of a regulated industry's products and individual taxpayers who finance a regulatory agency have interests too diverse to be greatly concerned with the industry's actions. In contrast, special interests of the industry are well organized and well defined. These interests also have more to offer political entrepreneurs within a regulatory agency, such as future employment with one of the regulated firms. Therefore, regulators have a strong incentive to support the position of a well-organized special-interest group within the regulated industry.

How did the Food and Drug Administration (FDA) recently pursue a policy action that raised suspicions it might be a captured regulator?

POLICY EXAMPLE

New Nicotine Market Entry? Not If the FDA Can Help It!

When Congress authorized the FDA to regulate tobacco products containing the drug called nicotine, critics noted that tobacco companies had sought FDA oversight. Protecting incumbent tobacco firms from competition could become a key FDA objective, some critics suggested, if the FDA was prone to regulatory capture.

Indeed, one of the FDA's initial acts as tobacco regulator was an attempt to prohibit the sale of battery-powered devices that transform nicotine-laced liquid into a vapor mist. For many smokers, these so-called e-cigarettes offer a way to satisfy their nicotine habits without generating the tar-laden smoke that accompanies traditional cigarettes. The FDA's stance was that e-cigarettes legally constituted a new "drug

or medical device" that required the FDA's approval before being marketed to consumers—approval that the FDA refused to provide. Ultimately, however, courts overruled the FDA's legal position. Judges ruled that the FDA had authority only to *regulate* e-cigarettes. The FDA could *not*, the judges concluded, ban firms from competing with incumbent sellers of nicotine-laced tobacco by offering an alternative means of dispensing the long-legal drug nicotine.

FOR CRITICAL THINKING
Who do you think had the most to gain if the FDA had successfully banned the sale of e-cigarettes that generate sales exceeding $100 million per year?

Share-the-gains, share-the-pains theory
A theory of regulatory behavior that holds that regulators must take account of the demands of three groups: legislators, who established and oversee the regulatory agency; firms in the regulated industry; and consumers of the regulated industry's products.

"SHARE THE GAINS, SHARE THE PAINS" The **share-the-gains, share-the-pains theory** offers a somewhat different view of regulators' behavior. This theory focuses on the specific aims of regulators. It proposes that a regulator's main objective is simply to keep his or her job as a regulator. To do so, the regulator must obtain the approval of both the legislators who originally established and continue to oversee the regulatory agency and the regulated industry. The regulator must also take into account the views of the industry's customers.

In contrast to the capture hypothesis, which holds that regulators must take into account only industry special interests, the share-the-gains, share-the-pains theory contends that regulators must worry about legislators and consumers as well. After all, if industry customers who are hurt by improper regulation complain to legislators, the regulators might lose their jobs. Whereas the capture theory predicts that regulators will quickly allow electric utilities to raise their rates in the face of higher fuel costs, the share-the-gains, share-the-pains theory predicts a slower, more measured regulatory response. Ultimately, regulators will permit an increase in utility rates, but the allowed adjustment will not be as speedy or complete as predicted by the capture hypothesis. The regulatory agency is not completely captured by the industry. It also has to consider the views of consumers and legislators.

The Benefits and Costs of Regulation

As noted earlier, regulation offers many *potential* benefits. *Actual* benefits, however, are difficult to measure. Putting a dollar value on safer products, a cleaner environment, and better working conditions is a difficult proposition. Furthermore, the benefits of most regulations accrue to society over a long time.

THE DIRECT COSTS OF REGULATION TO TAXPAYERS Measuring the costs of regulation is also a challenging undertaking. After all, about 5,000 new federal and state regulations are issued each year. One cost, though, is certain: U.S. federal taxpayers pay nearly $55 billion per year to staff regulatory agencies with more than 300,000 employees and to fund their various activities. Figure 27-3 below displays the distribution of total federal government outlays for economic and social regulation of various areas of the economy.

The *total* cost of regulation is much higher than just the explicit government outlays to fund the administration of various regulations, however. After all, businesses must expend resources complying with regulations, developing creative responses to regulations, and funding special-interest lobbying efforts directed at legislators and regulatory officials. Sometimes companies find that it is impossible to comply with one regulation without violating another, and determining how to avoid the resulting legal entanglements can entail significant expenditures.

THE TOTAL SOCIAL COST OF REGULATION According to the Office of Management and Budget, annual expenditures that U.S. businesses must make solely to comply with regulations issued by various federal agencies amount to more than $700 billion per year. Nevertheless, this estimate encompasses only the *explicit* costs of satisfying regulatory demands placed on businesses. It ignores relevant opportunity costs. After all, owners, managers, and employees of companies could be doing other things with their time and resources than complying with regulations. Economists estimate that the additional opportunity costs of complying with federal regulations may be as high as $300 billion per year. A portion of this amount is passed on to consumers in the form of higher prices.

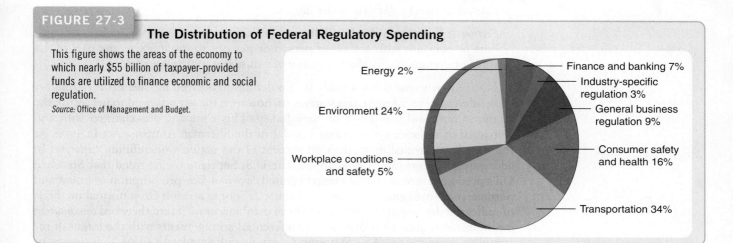

FIGURE 27-3

The Distribution of Federal Regulatory Spending

This figure shows the areas of the economy to which nearly $55 billion of taxpayer-provided funds are utilized to finance economic and social regulation.
Source: Office of Management and Budget.

Energy 2%
Environment 24%
Workplace conditions and safety 5%
Finance and banking 7%
Industry-specific regulation 3%
General business regulation 9%
Consumer safety and health 16%
Transportation 34%

YOU ARE THERE

To contemplate why the costs of regulation can total to large dollar amounts when summed across many affected firms, take a look at **No Longer in a State of Sticker Shock in Michigan** on page 612.

All told, therefore, the total social cost associated with satisfying federal regulations in the United States probably exceeds $1 trillion per year. This figure, of course, applies only to federal regulations. It does not include the explicit and implicit opportunity costs associated with regulations issued by 50 different state governments and tens of thousands of municipalities. Undoubtedly, the annual cost of regulation throughout the United States exceeds $1.75 trillion per year.

QUICK QUIZ See page 617 for the answers. Review concepts from this section in MyEconLab.

The **capture hypothesis** holds that regulatory agencies will eventually be captured by industry special interests because _____ individually are not greatly influenced by regulation, whereas regulated _____ are directly affected.

According to the **share-the-gains, share-the-pains theory** of regulation, regulators must take into account

the interests of three groups: the _____, _____, and _____.

Regulation has benefits that are difficult to quantify in dollars. The costs of regulation include direct _____ expenditures on regulatory agencies and _____ explicit and implicit opportunity costs of complying.

Antitrust Policy

An expressed aim of the U.S. government is to foster competition. To this end, Congress has made numerous attempts to legislate against business practices that Congress has perceived to be anticompetitive. This is the general idea behind antitrust legislation. If the courts can prevent collusion among sellers of a product, there will be no restriction of output, and monopoly prices will not result. Instead, prices of goods and services will be close to their marginal social opportunity costs.

Antitrust Policy in the United States

Congress has enacted four key antitrust laws, which are summarized in Table 27-2 on the facing page. The most important of these is the original U.S. antitrust law, called the Sherman Act.

THE SHERMAN ANTITRUST ACT OF 1890 The Sherman Antitrust Act, which was passed in 1890, was the first attempt by the federal government to control the growth of monopoly in the United States. The most important provisions of that act are as follows:

Section 1: Every contract, combination in the form of a trust or otherwise, or conspiracy, in restraint of trade or commerce among the several states, or with foreign nations, is hereby declared to be illegal.

Section 2: Every person who shall monopolize, or attempt to monopolize, or combine or conspire with any other person or persons to monopolize any part of the trade or commerce . . . shall be guilty of a misdemeanor [now a felony].

Notice how vague this act really is. No definition is given for the terms *restraint of trade* or *monopolize*. Despite this vagueness, however, the act was used to prosecute the infamous Standard Oil Trust of New Jersey. This company was charged with and convicted of violations of Sections 1 and 2 of the Sherman Antitrust Act in 1906. At the time it controlled more than 80 percent of the nation's oil-refining capacity. In addressing the company's legal appeal, the U.S. Supreme Court ruled that Standard Oil's predominance in the oil market created "a *prima facie* presumption of intent and purpose to control and maintain dominancy . . . not as a result from normal methods of industrial development, but by means of combinations." Here the word *combination* meant entering into associations and preferential arrangements with the intent of restraining competition. The Supreme Court forced Standard Oil of New Jersey to break up into many smaller companies that would have no choice but to compete.

TABLE 27-2		
Key U.S. Antitrust Laws	Sherman Antitrust Act of 1890	Forbids any contract, combination, or conspiracy to restrain trade or commerce within the United States or across U.S. borders. Holds any person who attempts to monopolize trade or commerce criminally liable.
	Clayton Act of 1914	Prohibits specific business practices deemed to restrain trade or commerce. Bans discrimination in prices charged to various purchasers when price differences are not due to actual differences in selling or transportation costs. Also forbids a company from selling goods on the condition that the purchaser must deal exclusively with that company. Finally, it prevents corporations from holding stock in other companies when this may lessen competition.
	Federal Trade Commission Act of 1914 (and 1938 Amendment)	Outlaws business practices that reduce the extent of competition, such as alleged cutthroat pricing intended to drive rivals from the marketplace. Also established the Federal Trade Commission and empowered it to issue cease and desist orders in situations in which it determines "unfair methods of competition in commerce" exist. The 1938 amendment added deceptive business practices to the list of illegal acts.
	Robinson-Patman Act of 1936	Bans selected discriminatory price cuts by chain stores that allegedly drive smaller competitors from the marketplace. In addition, forbids price discrimination through special concessions in the form of price or quantity discounts, free advertising, or promotional allowances granted to one buyer but not to others, if these actions substantially reduce competition.

The Sherman Act applies today just as it did more than a century ago. Recently, Samsung and other producers of DRAM computer chips admitted that they had violated the Sherman Act by conspiring to fix the price of DRAM chips by holding down production. Samsung paid a $300 million fine for this Sherman Act violation.

Why did the Federal Trade Commission block a proposed merger between two video-rental chains?

POLICY EXAMPLE

The FTC Blocks a Merger in Advance of the Firms' Bankruptcy

In 2005, the video-rental firm Blockbuster sought a merger with a major competitor, Hollywood Videos. The Federal Trade Commission blocked the merger, however, in an effort to protect independent stores that rented DVDs and Blu-ray disks from alleged monopolization by a combination of Blockbuster and Hollywood Videos.

Even as the FTC was blocking this merger on antitrust grounds, Netflix, Amazon, and a host of other Internet firms were entering the market for video rentals. These companies' services allow people to pay fees to view streaming videos online instead of troubling themselves to rent physical DVDs or Blu-ray disks. Thus, the demand for the services of video-rental chains withered. By the early 2010s, Hollywood Videos no longer existed, and Blockbuster was struggling to reorganize. Instead of forming a monopoly in the video-rental market, these two firms had gone bankrupt. Nearly all of the independent video-rental stores had also exited the market.

FOR CRITICAL THINKING

Why is correctly assessing all actual and likely competition crucial to determining whether a firm or firms may be committing actions that run afoul of antitrust laws?

OTHER IMPORTANT ANTITRUST LEGISLATION Table 27-2 above lists three other antitrust laws. In 1914, Congress passed the Clayton Act to clarify some of the vague provisions of the Sherman Act by identifying specific business practices that were to be legally prohibited.

Congress also passed the Federal Trade Commission Act in 1914. In addition to establishing the Federal Trade Commission to investigate unfair trade practices, this law enumerated certain business practices that, according to Congress, involved overly aggressive competition. A 1938 amendment to this law expressly prohibited "unfair or deceptive acts or practices in commerce" and empowered the FTC to regulate advertising and marketing practices by U.S. firms.

The Robinson-Patman Act of 1936 amended the Clayton Act by singling out specific business practices, such as selected price cuts, aimed at driving smaller competitors out of business. The act is often referred to as the "Chain Store Act" because it was intended to protect *independent* retailers and wholesalers from "unfair competition" by chain stores.

EXEMPTIONS FROM ANTITRUST LAWS Numerous laws exempt the following industries and business practices from antitrust legislation:

- Labor unions
- Public utilities—electric, gas, and telephone companies
- Professional baseball
- Cooperative activities among U.S. exporters
- Hospitals
- Public transit and water systems
- Suppliers of military equipment
- Joint publishing arrangements in a single city by two or more newspapers

Thus, not all U.S. businesses are subject to antitrust laws.

WHAT IF... all U.S. business organizations *were* subject to antitrust laws?

If U.S. antitrust laws provided for no exemptions, hundreds of organizations would be subject to investigation and prosecution for illegally forming monopolies. Labor unions with monopoly positions in numerous industries would have to open themselves to competition from other unions. Public utilities and hospitals in many communities across the nation would no longer be legally protected monopolies. It would also be illegal for the American League and National League teams of Major League Baseball to operate effectively as a single monopoly firm providing sports entertainment businesses. Thus, more than one baseball World Series might compete for sports enthusiasts' attention.

Go to www.econtoday.com/chap27 to take a look at the guidelines the U.S. Department of Justice uses to decide whether to challenge proposed mergers under antitrust laws.

International Discord in Antitrust Policy

What, if anything, should U.S. antitrust authorities do if AT&T decides that it wishes to merge with British Telecommunications or if Germany's Deutsche Telecom wants to acquire Sprint Nextel? What, if anything, should they do if Time Warner, the largest U.S. entertainment company, attempts to merge with London-based EMI, one of the world's largest recorded-music companies? These are not just rhetorical questions, as U.S. and European antitrust authorities learned in the 2000s when these issues actually surfaced. Growing international linkages among markets for many goods and services have increasingly made antitrust policy a global undertaking.

The international dimensions of antitrust pose a problem for U.S. antitrust authorities in the Department of Justice and the Federal Trade Commission. In the United States, the overriding goal of antitrust policies has traditionally been protecting the interests of consumers. This is also a formal objective of European Union (EU) antitrust authorities. In the EU, however, policymakers are also required to reject any business combination that "creates or strengthens a dominant position as a result of which effective competition would be significantly impeded."

This additional clause has sometimes created tension between U.S. and EU policy-making. In the United States, increasing dominance of a market by a single firm arouses the concern of antitrust authorities. Nevertheless, U.S. authorities typically will remain passive if they determine that the increased market dominance arises from factors such as exceptional management and greater cost efficiencies that ultimately benefit consumers by reducing prices. In contrast, under EU rules antitrust authorities are obliged to block *any* business combination that increases the dominance of any producer. They must do so regardless of what factors might have caused the business's preeminence in the marketplace or whether the antitrust action might have adverse implications for consumers.

QUICK QUIZ   See page 617 for the answers. Review concepts from this section in MyEconLab.

The first national antitrust law was the _____ Antitrust Act of 1890, which made illegal every contract and combination in restraint of trade. It remains the single most important antitrust law in the United States.

The _____ Act of 1914 made illegal various specific business practices, such as price discrimination.

The _____ _____ _____ Act of 1914 and its 1938 amendment established the Federal Trade Commission and prohibited "unfair or deceptive acts or practices in commerce."

The _____-_____ Act of 1936 aimed to prevent large producers from driving out small competitors by means of selective discriminatory price cuts.

Antitrust Enforcement

How are antitrust laws enforced? In the United States, most enforcement continues to be based on the Sherman Act. The Supreme Court has defined the offense of **monopolization** as involving the following elements: "(1) the possession of monopoly power in the relevant market and (2) the willful acquisition or maintenance of that power, as distinguished from growth or development as a consequence of a superior product, business acumen, or historical accident."

Monopolization
The possession of monopoly power in the relevant market and the willful acquisition or maintenance of that power, as distinguished from growth or development as a consequence of a superior product, business acumen, or historical accident.

The Relevant Market

The Sherman Act does not define monopoly. To assess whether a monopolistic capability might exist, antitrust authorities seek to define a market and then to measure the degree of concentration in that market. They begin by determining the **relevant market** within which firms' products are in competition.

The relevant market consists of two elements. One is the relevant *product* market, which involves products that are closely substitutable for one another. The second element is the relevant *geographic* market, which involves a particular set of firms whose substitutable products actually are available to consumers in a particular area, ranging from a limited region to the entire nation. Combining the two elements yields the market in which firms in an industry compete.

Relevant market
A group of firms' products that are closely substitutable and available to consumers within a particular geographic area.

Measuring Concentration in the Relevant Market to Assess Mergers

Once the relevant market has been determined, antitrust enforcement focuses on the degree of competition within that market. The two federal enforcement agencies, the Antitrust Division of the U.S. Department of Justice and the Federal Trade Commission (FTC), utilize the Herfindahl-Hirschman Index, or HHI, for this purpose. As you learned in Chapter 26 (see page 577), the HHI is equal to the sum of the squared shares of total sales or output by all firms in an industry. Thus, once the relevant market has been determined, antitrust enforcers compute the HHI for all firms within the industry defined by the scope of that market.

When assessing whether a proposed horizontal merger among two or more firms competing in a relevant market might create a monopoly pricing capability, enforcers consider *both* the resulting change in the HHI *and* the level of the postmerger HHI. Under current U.S. antitrust enforcement guidelines, *either* a combined HHI *change* greater than 100 and postmerger HHI in excess of 1,000 *or* a combined HHI *change* exceeding 50 and a postmerger HHI above 1,800 raise antitrust concerns. The Justice Department's Antitrust Division or the FTC can follow up on such concerns by trying to determine the predicted effects of the merger on overall industry output and on the equilibrium price in the relevant market.

If the antitrust enforcement authority's position is that the proposed merger would lead to a substantial output reduction and price increase, then the authority files a lawsuit seeking to block the merger. The firms proposing the merger can respond either by dropping their merger plan or by defending the plan in court. Then it is up to a court to determine whether the merger legally can proceed, whether the merger must be abandoned, or, in some cases, whether the merger might be allowed under certain conditions. Sometimes, for instance, a merger is permitted on the condition that merging firms sell parts of their operations to other firms in the same industry.

Why did AT&T have to give up on a proposed merger with T-Mobile?

POLICY EXAMPLE

A Proposed Wireless Merger Experiences a Dropped Connection

Recently, AT&T and T-Mobile sought to merge their wireless operations into a single firm providing cellular phone and broadband Internet services. The proposed merger would have increased the HHI value for the nationwide wireless market—which the Justice Department's Antitrust Division determined to be the relevant market—by nearly 600. The postmerger level of the HHI would have exceeded 2,800. These amounts were well above thresholds sufficient to raise U.S. antitrust authorities' concerns about potential monopoly capability generated by a horizontal merger. Thus, the Antitrust Division filed a lawsuit seeking to block the merger, based on a claim that if the merger occurred, consumers ultimately would face much higher prices for wireless services. A few weeks later, AT&T and T-Mobile abandoned their merger plans rather than combat the lawsuit in court.

FOR CRITICAL THINKING
By definition, any horizontal merger increases industry concentration. Why might some mergers lead to lower prices for consumers? (Hint: Recall that mergers might enable firms to experience economies of scale that reduce long-run average cost.)

Product Packaging and Antitrust Enforcement

A particular problem in U.S. antitrust enforcement is determining whether a firm has engaged in "willful acquisition or maintenance" of market power. Actions that appear to some observers to be good business look like antitrust violations to others. To illustrate why quandaries can arise in antitrust enforcement, let's consider two examples: *versioning* and *bundling*.

Versioning
Selling a product in slightly altered forms to different groups of consumers.

PRODUCT VERSIONING A firm engages in product **versioning** when it sells an item in slightly altered forms to different groups of consumers. A typical method of versioning is to remove certain features from an item and offer what remains as a somewhat stripped-down version of the product at a different price.

Consider an office-productivity software program, such as Adobe Acrobat or Microsoft Word. Firms selling such programs typically offer both a "professional" version containing a full range of features and a "standard" version providing only basic functions. One perspective on this practice regards it as a form of price discrimination, or selling essentially the same product at different prices to different consumers. People who desire to use the full range of features in Adobe Acrobat or Microsoft Word are likely to be computing professionals. Compared to most other consumers, their demand for the full-featured version of an office-productivity software program is likely to be less elastic. In principle, therefore, Adobe and Microsoft can earn higher profits by offering "professional" versions at higher prices and selling a "standard" version at a lower price.

Price discrimination—charging varying prices to different consumers when the price differences are not a result of different production or transportation costs—is illegal under the Clayton Act of 1914. Are Adobe, Microsoft, and other companies engaging in illegal price discrimination? Another perspective on versioning indicates that they are not. According to this point of view, consumers regard "professional" and "standard" versions of software packages as imperfect substitutes. Consequently, each version is a distinctive product sold in a unique market. If so, versioning increases overall consumer satisfaction because consumers who are not computing professionals are able to utilize certain features of software products at a lower price. So far, antitrust authorities in the United States and elsewhere have been inclined toward this view of the economic effects of versioning, rather than perceiving it as a form of price discrimination.

PRODUCT BUNDLING Antitrust authorities have been less tolerant of another form of product packaging, known as **bundling,** which involves the joint sale of two or more products as a set. Antitrust authorities usually are not concerned if a firm allows consumers to purchase the products either individually or as a set. They are more likely to investigate a firm's business practices, however, when it allows consumers to purchase one product only when it is bundled with another. Antitrust officials often view this form of bundling as a method of price discrimination known as **tie-in sales,** in which a firm requires consumers who wish to buy one of its products to purchase another item the firm sells as well.

To understand their reasoning, consider a situation in which one group of consumers is willing to pay $200 for a computer operating system but only $100 for an Internet-browsing program. A second group of consumers is willing to pay only $100 for the same operating system but is willing to pay $200 for the same Internet-browsing program. If the same company that sells both types of software offers the operating system at a price above $100, then only consumers in the first group will buy this software. Likewise, if it sells the Internet-browsing program at a price above $100, then only the second group of consumers will purchase that program.

But if the firm sells both products as a bundled set, it can charge $300 and generate sales of both products to both groups. One interpretation is that the first group pays $200 for the operating system, but for the second group, the operating system's price is $100. At the same time, the first group has paid $100 for the Internet-browsing program, while the second group perceives the price of the program to be $200. Effectively, bundling enables the software company to engage in price discrimination by charging different prices to different groups.

Antitrust enforcers in the Justice Department applied this interpretation in their prosecution of Microsoft, which for years had bundled its Internet-browsing program, Internet Explorer, together with its Windows operating system. Enforcement officials added another twist by contending that Microsoft also had monopoly power in the market for computer operating systems. By bundling the two products, they argued, Microsoft had sought both to price-discriminate and to extend its monopoly power to the market for Internet-browsing software. The remedy that the courts imposed was for Microsoft to alter some of its business practices. As part of this legal remedy, Microsoft was required to unbundle its Windows and Internet Explorer products.

Bundling
Offering two or more products for sale as a set.

Tie-in sales
Purchases of one product that are permitted by the seller only if the consumer buys another good or service from the same firm.

QUICK QUIZ See page 617 for the answers. Review concepts from this section in MyEconLab.

As part of the enforcement of antitrust laws, officials at the U.S. Department of Justice and the Federal Trade Commission typically define a _____ market and compute the change in and new level of the _____-_____ _____ to assess whether to legally challenge a proposed merger.

Antitrust enforcers must decide whether producers seek to monopolize the relevant market, which involves determining both the relevant _____ market and the relevant _____ market.

Antitrust authorities generally have not considered product _____, or offering different versions of essentially the same product for sale at different prices, to be illegal price discrimination. U.S. authorities have, however, raised antitrust concerns about product _____, which they view as a method of engaging in **tie-in sales** that require consumers to purchase one product in order to obtain another.

YOU ARE THERE
No Longer in a State of Sticker Shock in Michigan

In the early 1980s, the Michigan legislature established the Item Pricing Law. This legislation required all retailers selling physical items within the state to affix a price sticker displaying a printed dollar price on every individual item. For David Hansen at the Hansen Foods market in the town of Hart, Michigan, the years since have been "a real pain." Price stickers do not remain attached to most refrigerated and frozen items for very long. Hence, each day over the years, Hansen's employees have had to get down on their hands and knees to remove from drains the dozens of stickers that have come off during the preceding 24 hours. Then they have had to attach new stickers, which in due time fell into the drains as well. Hansen estimates that his store could have saved 80 hours per week in labor costs—about $40,000 per year—in the absence of the rule.

Thus, Hansen recently joined with many Michigan retailers in celebrating a price-tag-freedom day when the Michigan legislature and governor agreed to rescind the Item Pricing Law. Estimates indicate that during the years the law was in force, it added a total of at least $2 billion to Michigan retailers' costs.

Critical Thinking Questions

1. Was Michigan's Item Pricing Law an example of economic or social regulation?

2. How do you think that the Item Pricing Law was intended to protect consumers? (Hint: Recall the asymmetric information rationale for regulation.)

ISSUES & APPLICATIONS

More Regulations Breed More Federal Regulatory Jobs

CONCEPTS APPLIED

▶ Economic Regulation

▶ Social Regulation

▶ Rate-of-Return Regulation

How has the upswing in government regulations affected the prospects for landing a job with a federal agency charged with implementing economic or social regulation or supervising rate-of-return regulation? The answer is that the availability of such positions has risen by more than two-thirds during the past decade.

Government Workers Apply Government Regulations

According to an old joke, the answer to the question "How many government regulators does it take to screw in a light bulb?" is "45—one to screw in the light bulb and 44 to do the paperwork." In recent years, the federal government has employed many people to regulate *types* of light bulbs. To reach the decision to ban interstate trade of incandescent light bulbs and to enforce this ban, for instance, the federal government has utilized labor from several agencies. Among these agencies are the Environmental Protection Agency, the Federal Trade Commission, and the Department of Energy. Workers at these agencies also supervise enforcement of laws regulating the production and sale of legal fluorescent light bulbs.

Of course, there is a vast array of products beyond light bulbs, and there is a rapidly expanding volume of government rules regulating production and sale of all of these products. Consequently, the number of people employed by the government to perform regulatory tasks is increasing at a rapid pace.

How Many Federal Workers Regulate Tasks of Other Workers?

Figure 27-4 on the facing page provides an indication of how many federal workers the U.S. government has employed to regulate the activities of other workers. The figure displays the number of federal regulatory workers for every 1,000 workers employed elsewhere in the U.S. economy since 1980. Since the early 2000s, the number of federal positions allocated to regulatory agencies for every 1,000 employed workers in the U.S. economy has risen from 1.3 to 2.2, an increase of 69 percent.

FIGURE 27-4

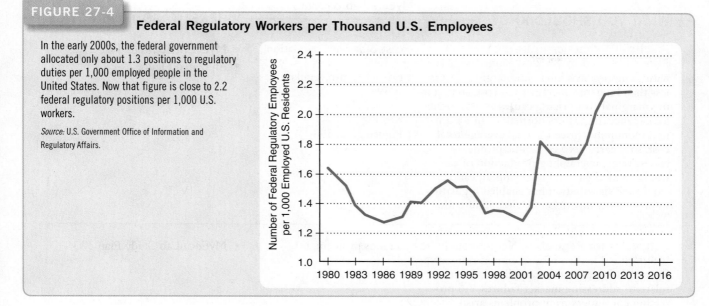

Federal Regulatory Workers per Thousand U.S. Employees

In the early 2000s, the federal government allocated only about 1.3 positions to regulatory duties per 1,000 employed people in the United States. Now that figure is close to 2.2 federal regulatory positions per 1,000 U.S. workers.

Source: U.S. Government Office of Information and Regulatory Affairs.

In 2001, about 190,000 federal workers regulated U.S. businesses. Today, more than 300,000 federal employees perform these functions. At the current pace of federal regulatory employment growth, a decade from now more than 500,000 people will regulate the way businesses operate. If so, the federal regulatory "industry" will become the nation's third-largest employer, behind the U.S. Postal Service and Walmart.

For Critical Thinking

1. Why might regulatory agencies utilize labor more intensively than private firms?

2. What will happen to the regulatory share of employment if the rate of growth of regulatory employment stays five times higher than overall employment growth?

Web Resources

1. Learn about sources of the growth of federal government employment at **www.econtoday.com/chap27**.

2. For a list of federal and state regulators, go to **www.econtoday.com/chap27**.

MyEconLab

For more questions on this chapter's Issues & Applications, go to MyEconLab. In the Study Plan for this chapter, select Section N: News.

MyEconLab

Here is what you should know after reading this chapter. MyEconLab will help you identify what you know, and where to go when you need to practice.

—— WHAT YOU SHOULD KNOW ——

Government Regulation of Business There are two basic forms of government regulation of business: economic regulation and social regulation. Economic regulation applies to specific industries. Social regulations affect nearly all businesses and encompass a broad range of objectives concerning such issues as product safety, environmental quality, and working conditions.

Key Figure
Figure 27-1, 595

—— WHERE TO GO TO PRACTICE ——

• MyEconLab Study Plan 27.1
• Animated Figure 27-1

MyEconLab *continued*

WHAT YOU SHOULD KNOW ──────────────────────────── WHERE TO GO TO PRACTICE ──

Practical Difficulties in Regulating the Prices Charged by Natural Monopolies A natural monopoly's long-run marginal cost is less than long-run average total cost, so requiring marginal cost pricing causes an economic loss. Hence, regulators normally aim for a natural monopoly's price to equal average total cost, so it earns zero economic profits. In recent years, uncoupling production of electricity, natural gas, and telecommunications from their distribution has enabled regulators to promote competition in these industries.

cost-of-service regulation, 599
rate-of-return regulation, 599

Key Figure
Figure 27-2, 598

- MyEconLab Study Plan 27.2
- Animated Figure 27-2

Rationales for Regulating Nonmonopolistic Industries The two most common rationales for regulation of nonmonopolistic industries relate to addressing market failures and protecting consumers from problems arising from information asymmetries. Asymmetric information can also create a lemons problem, which occurs when uncertainty about product quality leads to markets containing mostly low-quality items.

lemons problem, 602

- MyEconLab Study Plan 27.3

Regulators' Incentives and the Costs of Regulation The capture theory of regulator behavior predicts that regulators will eventually find themselves supporting the positions of the firms that they regulate. The share-the-gains, share-the-pains theory predicts that a regulator will try to satisfy all constituencies, at least in part. The costs of regulation, which include both the direct costs to taxpayers of funding regulatory agencies and the explicit and implicit opportunity costs that businesses must incur to comply, are easier to quantify in dollar terms than the benefits.

creative response, 603
capture hypothesis, 604
share-the-gains, share-the-pains theory, 604

Key Figure
Figure 27-3, 605

- MyEconLab Study Plan 27.4
- Animated Figure 27-3

Foundations of Antitrust There are four key antitrust laws. The Sherman Act of 1890 forbids attempts to monopolize an industry. The Clayton Act of 1914 clarified antitrust law by prohibiting specific types of business practices. The Federal Trade Commission Act of 1914, as amended in 1938, seeks to prohibit deceptive business practices and to prevent "cutthroat pricing." The Robinson-Patman Act of 1936 outlawed price cuts deemed to be discriminatory and predatory.

- MyEconLab Study Plan 27.5

MyEconLab *continued*

WHAT YOU SHOULD KNOW

Issues in Enforcing Antitrust Laws The Supreme Court has defined monopolization as possessing or seeking monopoly pricing power in the "relevant market." Authorities charged with enforcing antitrust laws evaluate concentration of production or sales within a defined relevant market as compared with regulatory threshold concentration levels. In recent years, antitrust officials have raised questions about whether product packaging, either in the form of different versions or as bundled sets, is a type of price discrimination involving tie-in sales.

monopolization, 609
relevant market, 609
versioning, 610
bundling, 611
tie-in sales, 611

WHERE TO GO TO PRACTICE

• **MyEconLab** Study Plan 27.6

Log in to **MyEconLab**, take a chapter test, and get a personalized Study Plan that tells you which concepts you understand and which ones you need to review. From there, **MyEconLab** will give you further practice, tutorials, animations, videos, and guided solutions. For more information, visit www.myeconlab.com

PROBLEMS

All problems are assignable in MyEconLab. *Answers to odd-numbered problems appear at the back of the book.*

27-1. Local cable television companies are sometimes granted monopoly rights to service a particular territory of a metropolitan area. The companies typically pay special taxes and licensing fees to local municipalities. Why might a municipality give monopoly rights to a cable company? (See pages 604–605.)

27-2. A local cable company, the sole provider of cable television service, is regulated by the municipal government. The owner of the company claims that she is normally opposed to regulation by government, but asserts that regulation is necessary because local residents would not want a large number of different cables crisscrossing the city. Why do you think the owner is defending regulation by the city? (See pages 604–605.)

27-3. The table below depicts the cost and demand structure a natural monopoly faces. (See page 598.)

Quantity	Price ($)	Long-Run Total Cost ($)
0	100	0
1	95	92
2	90	177
3	85	255
4	80	331
5	75	406
6	70	480

a. Calculate total revenues, marginal revenue, and marginal cost at each output level. If this firm is allowed to operate as a monopolist, what will be the quantity produced and the price charged by the firm? What will be the amount of monopoly profit? [Hint: Recall that marginal revenue equals the change in total revenues ($P \times Q$) from each additional unit and that marginal cost equals the change in total costs from each additional unit.]

b. If regulators require the firm to practice marginal cost pricing, what quantity will it produce, and what price will it charge? What is the firm's profit under this regulatory framework? [Hint: Recall that average total cost equals total cost divided by quantity and that profits equal $(P - \text{ATC}) \times Q$.]

c. If regulators require the firm to practice average cost pricing, what quantity will it produce, and what price will it charge? What is the firm's profit under this regulatory framework?

27-4. As noted in the chapter, separating the *production* of electricity from its *delivery* has led to considerable deregulation of producers. (See page 599.)

a. Briefly explain which of these two aspects of the sale of electricity remains susceptible to natural monopoly problems.

b. Suppose that the potential natural monopoly problem you identified in part (a) actually arises. Why is marginal cost pricing not a feasible solution? What makes average cost pricing a feasible solution?

c. Discuss two approaches that a regulator could use to try to implement an average-cost-pricing solution to the problem identified in part (a).

27-5. Are lemons problems likely to be more common in some industries and less common in others? Based on your answer to this question, should government regulatory activities designed to reduce the scope of lemons problems take the form of economic regulation or social regulation? Take a stand, and support your reasoning. (See page 602.)

27-6. Research into genetically modified crops has led to significant productivity gains for countries such as the United States that employ these techniques. Countries such as the European Union's member nations, however, have imposed controls on the import of these products, citing concern for public health. Is the European Union's regulation of genetically modified crops social regulation or economic regulation? (See page 596.)

27-7. Do you think that the regulation described in Problem 27-6 is more likely an example of the capture hypothesis or the share-the-gains, share-the-pains theory? Why? (See page 604.)

27-8. Prices of tickets for seats on commercial passenger planes are typically in the hundreds of dollars, whereas trips can be made by automobile at much lower cost. Accident rates per person per trip in the airline industry are considerably lower than auto accident rates per person per trip. Based on these facts, discuss how regulatory costs and benefits may help to explain why government regulations require children to be placed in safety seats in automobiles but not on commercial passenger planes. (See page 605.)

27-9. A few years ago, the U.S. government created a "Do Not Call Registry" and forbade marketing firms from calling people who placed their names on this list. Today, an increasing number of companies are sending mail solicitations to individuals inviting them to send back an enclosed postcard for more information about the firms' products. What these solicitations fail to mention is that they are worded in such a way that someone who returns the postcard gives up protection from telephone solicitations, even if they are on the government's "Do Not Call Registry." In what type of behavior are these companies engaging? Explain your answer. (See page 603. Hint: Are these firms meeting the letter of the law but violating its spirit?)

27-10. Suppose that a business has developed a very high-quality product and operates more efficiently in producing that product than any other potential competitor. As a consequence, at present it is the only seller of this product, for which there are few close substitutes. Is this firm in violation of U.S. antitrust laws? Explain. (See pages 606–607.)

27-11. Consider the following fictitious sales data (in thousands of dollars) for both e-books and physical books. Firms have numbers instead of names, and Firm 1 generates only e-book sales. Suppose that antitrust authorities' initial evaluation of whether a single firm may possess "monopoly power" is whether its share of sales in the relevant market exceeds 70 percent. (See page 609.)

E-Book Sales		Physical Book Sales		Combined Book Sales	
Firm	Sales	Firm	Sales	Firm	Sales
1	$ 750	2	$4,200	2	$ 4,250
2	50	3	2,000	3	2,050
3	50	4	1,950	4	2,000
4	50	5	450	1	750
5	50	6	400	5	500
6	50			6	450
Total	$1,000		$9,000		$10,000

a. Suppose that the antitrust authorities determine that selling physical books and e-bookselling are individually separate relevant markets. Does an initial evaluation suggest that any single firm has monopoly power, as defined by the antitrust authorities?

b. Suppose that in fact there is really only a single book industry, in which firms compete in selling both physical books and e-books. According to the antitrust authorities' initial test of the potential for monopoly power, is there actually cause for concern?

27-12. Consider the data from Problem 27-11. Suppose that antitrust authorities have determined that there are separate relevant markets for e-books and physical books. In addition, these authorities perceive that a monopoly situation exists that can be challenged on legal grounds if the value of the Herfindahl-Hirschman Index exceeds 5,000. On the basis of this criterion, do the antitrust authorities conclude that there are grounds for a legal challenge in either market? Explain. (See page 610.)

27-13. Consider the data from Problem 27-11. Suppose that antitrust authorities have determined that the relevant market includes both e-books and physical books. These authorities perceive that a monopoly situation exists that can be challenged on legal grounds if the value of the Herfindahl-Hirschman Index exceeds 5,000. On the basis of this criterion, do the antitrust authorities conclude that there are grounds for a legal challenge? Explain. (See page 610.)

27-14. A package delivery company provides both overnight and second-day delivery services. It charges almost twice as much to deliver an overnight package to any world location as it does to deliver the same package to the same location in two days. Often, second-day packages arrive at company warehouses in destination cities by the next day, but drivers intentionally do not deliver these packages until the following day. What is this business practice called? Briefly summarize alternative perspectives concerning whether this activity should or should not be viewed as a form of price discrimination. (See pages 610–611.)

27-15. A firm that sells both Internet-security software and computer antivirus software will sell the antivirus software as a stand-alone product. It will only sell the Internet-security software to consumers in a combined package that also includes the antivirus software. What is this business practice called? Briefly explain why an antitrust authority might

view this practice as a form of price discrimination. (See page 611.)

27-16. Recently, a food retailer called Whole Foods sought to purchase Wild Oats, a competitor in the market for organic foods. When the Federal Trade Commission (FTC) sought to block this merger on antitrust grounds, FTC officials argued that such a merger would dramatically increase concentration in the market for "premium organic foods." Whole Foods' counterargument was that it considered itself to be part of the broadly defined supermarket industry that includes retailers such as Albertson's, Kroger, and Safeway. What key issue of antitrust regulation was involved in this dispute? Explain. (See page 609.)

ECONOMICS ON THE NET

Guidelines for U.S. Antitrust Merger Enforcement How does the U.S. government apply antitrust laws to mergers? This application gives you the opportunity to learn about the standards applied by the Antitrust Division of the U.S. Department of Justice when it evaluates a proposed merger.

Title: U.S. Department of Justice Antitrust Merger Enforcement Guidelines

Navigation: Go to **www.econtoday.com/chap27** to access the home page of the Antitrust Division of the U.S. Department of Justice.

Application Answer the following questions.

1. Click on *Horizontal Merger Guidelines*. In section 1, click on *Overview*, and read this section. What factors do U.S. antitrust authorities consider when evaluating

the potential for a horizontal merger to "enhance market power"—that is, to place the combination in a monopoly situation?

2. Read the *Horizontal Merger Guidelines*. In what situations will the antitrust authorities most likely question a horizontal merger?

For Group Study and Analysis Have three groups of students from the class examine sections 1, 2, and 3 of the *Horizontal Merger Guidelines* discussed in item 1. After each group reports on all the factors that the antitrust authorities consider when evaluating a horizontal merger, discuss why large teams of lawyers and many economic consultants are typically involved when the Antitrust Division of the Department of Justice alleges that a proposed merger would be "anticompetitive."

ANSWERS TO QUICK QUIZZES

p. 597: (i) Economic . . . social; (ii) natural . . . economic; (iii) social

p. 600: (i) lower . . . revenue . . . cost; (ii) average . . . zero; (iii) deliver . . . networks

p. 603: (i) failures . . . asymmetric; (ii) asymmetric; (iii) lemons . . . low

p. 606: (i) consumers . . . firms; (ii) industry . . . legislators . . . consumers; (iii) government . . . firms'

p. 609: (i) Sherman; (ii) Clayton; (iii) Federal Trade Commission; (iv) Robinson-Patman

p. 611: (i) relevant . . . Herfindahl-Hirschman Index; (ii) product . . . geographic; (iii) versioning . . . bundling

28

The Labor Market: Demand, Supply, and Outsourcing

Nearly a century ago, during World War I, the British military developed the first pilotless powered aircraft. Today, pilotless flight using "autopilots" is commonplace. Indeed, in principle, digital systems could replace human pilots, even for plane takeoffs and landings. Robots can also drive vehicles on highways, as was proved by Mercedes-Benz's first "autonomous van" in the 1980s, and more recently on busy city streets, as robot cars developed by Google have demonstrated in thousands of miles of road tests. Could robots replace human airline pilots, bus drivers, and taxi drivers—or perhaps even human physicians, dentists, or teachers? From a technological standpoint, the answer is definitely yes. As you will learn in this chapter, though, whether robots actually *will* replace humans in performing particular tasks is an *economic* issue.

data from the National Association of Colleges and Employers indicate that only about 75 percent of employers associated with the organization now conduct campus interviews, down from nearly 90 percent in 2007? In addition, a nationwide study of a recent class of college students found that a full year after their graduation, employers had hired just over half of the students, compared with 90 percent in 2007. Furthermore, only about half of those who were hired within a year after completing their degrees obtained jobs for which employers actually required a college degree. Clearly, the overall demand for the college graduates' labor by businesses is restrained in today's dampened economy.

The demand for labor provided by college graduates or for all types of inputs by businesses can be studied in much the same manner as we studied the demand for output. Our analysis will always end with the same conclusion: A firm will hire employees up to the point beyond which it isn't profitable to hire any more. It will hire employees to the point at which the marginal benefit of hiring a worker will just equal the marginal cost. Indeed, in every profit-maximizing situation, it is most profitable to carry out an activity up to the point at which the marginal benefit equals the marginal cost. Remembering that guideline will help you in analyzing decision making at the firm level, which is where we will begin our discussion of the demand for labor.

Labor Demand for a Perfectly Competitive Firm

We will start our analysis under the assumption that the market for input factors is perfectly competitive. We will further assume that the output market is perfectly competitive. This provides a benchmark against which to compare other situations in which labor markets or product markets are not perfectly competitive.

Competition in the Product Market

Let's take as our example a firm that sells magneto optical (MO) disks and is in competition with many companies selling the same kind of product. Assume that the laborers hired by this manufacturing firm do not need any special skills. This firm sells MO disks in a perfectly competitive market. It also buys labor (its variable input) in a perfectly competitive market. A firm that hires labor under perfectly competitive conditions hires only a minuscule proportion of all the workers who are potentially available to the firm. By "potentially available," we mean all the workers in a geographic area who possess the skills demanded by our perfect competitor.

In such a market, it is always possible for the individual firm to hire extra workers without having to offer a higher wage. Thus, the supply of labor to the firm is perfectly elastic at the going wage rate established by the forces of supply and demand in the entire labor market. The firm is a *price taker* in the labor market.

Marginal Physical Product

Look at panel (a) of Figure 28-1 on the following page. In column 1, we show the number of workers per week that the firm can employ. In column 2, we show total physical product (TPP) per week, the total *physical* production of MO disks that different quantities of the labor input (in combination with a fixed amount of other inputs) will generate in a week's time. In column 3, we show the additional output gained when the company adds workers to its existing manufacturing facility.

This column, the **marginal physical product (MPP) of labor,** represents the extra (additional) output attributed to employing additional units of the variable input factor. If this firm employs seven workers rather than six, the MPP is 118. The law of diminishing marginal product predicts that additional units of a variable factor will, after some point, cause the MPP to decline, other things held constant.

We are assuming that all other nonlabor factors of production are held constant. So, if our manufacturing firm wants to add one more worker to its production line, it has to crowd all the existing workers a little closer together because it does not increase its

Marginal physical product (MPP) of labor
The change in output resulting from the addition of one more worker. The MPP of the worker equals the change in total output accounted for by hiring the worker, holding all other factors of production constant.

FIGURE 28-1

Marginal Revenue Product

In panel (a), column 4 shows marginal revenue product (MRP), which is the additional revenue the firm receives for the sale of that additional output. Marginal revenue product is simply the revenue the additional worker brings in—the combination of that worker's contribution to production and the revenue that that production will bring to the firm.

For this perfectly competitive firm, marginal revenue is equal to the price of the product, which we will assume in this example to be $10 per unit. At a weekly wage of $830, the profit-maximizing employer will pay for only 12 workers because then the marginal revenue product is just equal to the wage rate or weekly salary.

Panel (a)

(1) Labor Input (workers per week)	(2) Total Physical Product (TPP) (magneto optical disks per week)	(3) Marginal Physical Product (MPP) (magneto optical disks per week)	(4) Marginal Revenue (MR = P = $10) x MPP = Marginal Revenue Product (MRP) ($ per additional worker)	(5) Wage Rate ($ per week) = Marginal Factor Cost (MFC) = Change in Total Costs ÷ Change in Labor
6	882			
		118	$1,180	$830
7	1,000			
		111	1,110	830
8	1,111			
		104	1,040	830
9	1,215			
		97	970	830
10	1,312			
		90	900	830
11	1,402			
		83	830	830
12	1,485			
		76	760	830
13	1,561			

In panel (b), we find the number of workers the firm will want to hire by observing the wage rate that is established by the forces of supply and demand in the entire labor market. We show that this employer is hiring labor in a perfectly competitive labor market and therefore faces a perfectly elastic supply curve represented by *s* at a constant marginal factor cost (MFC) of $830 per week. As in other situations, we have a supply and demand model. In this firm-level example, the demand curve is represented by MRP, and the supply curve is *s*. Profit maximization occurs at their intersection, which is the point at which MRP = MFC.

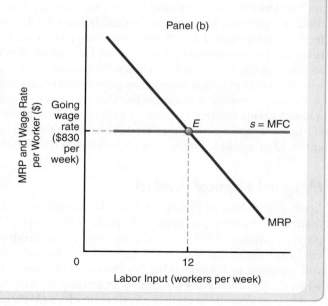

capital stock (the production equipment). Therefore, as we add more workers, each one has a smaller and smaller fraction of the available capital stock with which to work. If one worker uses one machine, adding another worker usually won't double the output because the machine can run only so fast and for so many hours per day. In other words, MPP declines because of the law of diminishing marginal product (see Chapter 22).

Marginal Revenue Product

We now need to translate into a dollar value the physical product that results from hiring an additional worker. This is done by multiplying the marginal physical product by the marginal revenue of the firm. Because this firm sells MO disks in a perfectly competitive market, marginal revenue is equal to the price of the product. If employing seven workers rather than six yields an MPP of 118 and the marginal revenue is assumed to be $10 per MO disk, the **marginal revenue product (MRP)** is $1,180 (118 × $10). The MRP is shown in column 4 of panel (a) of Figure 28-1 on the facing page. *The marginal revenue product represents the incremental worker's contribution to the firm's total revenues.*

When a firm operates in a perfectly competitive product market, the marginal physical product times the product price is also referred to as the *value of marginal product (VMP)*. Because price and marginal revenue are the same for a perfectly competitive firm, the VMP is also the MRP for such a firm.

In column 5 of panel (a) of Figure 28-1, we show the wage rate, or *marginal factor cost*, of each worker. The marginal cost of workers is the extra cost incurred in employing an additional unit of that factor of production. We call that cost the **marginal factor cost (MFC)**. Otherwise stated,

$$\text{Marginal factor cost} = \frac{\text{change in total cost}}{\text{change in amount of resource used}}$$

Because each worker is paid the same competitively determined wage of $830 per week, the MFC is the same for all workers. And because the firm is buying labor in a perfectly competitive labor market, the wage rate of $830 per week really represents the supply curve of labor to the firm. That supply curve is perfectly elastic because the firm can purchase all labor at the same wage rate, considering that it is a minuscule part of the entire labor-purchasing market. (Recall the definition of perfect competition.) We show this perfectly elastic supply curve as *s* in panel (b) of Figure 28-1.

GENERAL RULE FOR HIRING Nearly every optimizing rule in economics involves comparing marginal benefits with marginal cost. Because the benefit from added workers is extra output and consequently more revenues, the general rule for the hiring decision of a firm is this:

> *The firm hires workers up to the point at which the additional cost associated with hiring the last worker is equal to the additional revenue generated by hiring that worker.*

In a perfectly competitive market, this is the point at which the wage rate just equals the marginal revenue product. If the firm were to hire more workers, the additional wages would not be covered by additional increases in total revenue. If the firm were to hire fewer workers, it would be forfeiting the contributions that those workers otherwise could make to total profits.

Therefore, referring to columns 4 and 5 in panel (a) of Figure 28-1 on the facing page, we see that this firm would certainly employ at least seven workers because the MRP is $1,180 while the MFC is only $830. The firm would continue to add workers up to the point at which MFC = MRP because as workers are added, those additional workers contribute more to revenue than to cost.

THE MRP CURVE: DEMAND FOR LABOR We can also use panel (b) of Figure 28-1 to find how many workers our firm should hire. First, we draw a line at the going wage rate, which is determined by demand and supply in the labor market. The line is labeled *s* to indicate that it is the supply curve of labor for the *individual* firm purchasing labor in a perfectly competitive labor market. That firm can purchase all the labor it wants of equal quality at $830 per worker. This perfectly elastic supply curve, *s*, intersects the marginal revenue product curve at 12 workers per week. At the intersection, *E*, in

Marginal revenue product (MRP)
The marginal physical product (MPP) times marginal revenue (MR). The MRP gives the additional revenue obtained from a one-unit change in labor input.

Marginal factor cost (MFC)
The cost of using an additional unit of an input. For example, if a firm can hire all the workers it wants at the going wage rate, the marginal factor cost of labor is that wage rate.

panel (b) in Figure 28-1 on page 620, the wage rate is equal to the marginal revenue product. The firm maximizes profits where its demand curve for labor, which turns out to be its MRP curve, intersects the firm's supply curve for labor, shown as *s*. The firm in our example would not hire 13 workers, because using 13 rather than 12 would add only $760 to revenue but $830 to cost. If the price of labor should fall to, say, $760 per worker per week, the firm would hire an additional worker. Thus, the quantity of labor demanded increases as the wage decreases.

Derived Demand for Labor

We have identified an individual firm's demand for labor curve, which shows the quantity of labor that the firm will wish to hire at each wage rate, as its MRP curve. Under conditions of perfect competition in both product and labor markets, MRP is determined by multiplying MPP times the product's price. This suggests that the demand for labor is a **derived demand.** Factors of production are rented or purchased not because they give any intrinsic satisfaction to the firms' owners but because they can be used to manufacture output that is expected to be sold at a profit.

We know that an increase in the market demand for a given product raises the product's price (all other things held constant), which in turn increases the marginal revenue product, or demand for the resource. Figure 28-2 below illustrates the effective role played by changes in product demand in a perfectly competitive product market. The MRP curve shifts whenever there is a change in the price of the final product that the workers are producing.

Suppose, for example, that the market price of MO disks declines. In that case, the MRP curve will shift to the left from MRP_0 to MRP_1. We know that $MRP \equiv MPP \times MR$. If marginal revenue (here the output price) falls, so does the demand for labor. At the initial equilibrium, therefore, the price of labor (here the MFC) becomes greater than MRP. At the same going wage rate, the firm will hire fewer workers. This is because at various levels of labor use, the marginal revenue product of labor is now lower. Thus, the firm would reduce the number of workers hired. Conversely, if marginal revenue (the output price) rises, the demand for labor will also rise, and the firm will want to hire more workers at each and every possible wage rate.

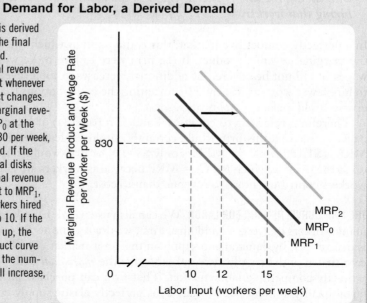

FIGURE 28-2

Demand for Labor, a Derived Demand

The demand for labor is derived from the demand for the final product being produced. Therefore, the marginal revenue product curve will shift whenever the price of the product changes. If we start with the marginal revenue product curve MRP_0 at the going wage rate of $830 per week, 12 workers will be hired. If the price of magneto optical disks goes down, the marginal revenue product curve will shift to MRP_1, and the number of workers hired will fall, in this case to 10. If the price of MO disks goes up, the marginal revenue product curve will shift to MRP_2, and the number of workers hired will increase, in this case to 15.

We just pointed out that MRP ≡ MPP × MR. Clearly, then, a change in marginal productivity, or in the marginal physical product of labor, will shift the MRP curve. If the marginal productivity of labor decreases, the MRP curve, or demand curve, for labor will shift inward to the left. Again, this is because at every quantity of labor used, the MRP will be lower. A lower amount of labor will be demanded at every possible wage rate.

Why has book publishers' demand for the labor of authors declined in recent years?

EXAMPLE

E-Books' Popularity Is Reducing the Demand for Authors' Labor

Publishers are finding that e-book sales are booming, as consumers substitute away from purchases of physical books to buying books in electronic formats viewable on digital devices. For authors, this is bad news. The prices that publishers receive for selling e-books are considerably lower than the prices of physical books. Hence, publishers' marginal-revenue-product-of-labor curves for authors have shifted leftward and downward. The consequence has been a reduction in the market demand for authors' labor. Thus, at any given wage rate, publishers desire to buy less labor from authors. Equivalently, at any given amount of labor demanded, publishers offer lower wages.

FOR CRITICAL THINKING
What do you suppose has happened to publishers' demand for the labor of editors as a result of consumers' substitution of e-books for physical books?

QUICK QUIZ   See page 641 for the answers. Review concepts from this section in MyEconLab.

The change in total _____ due to a one-unit change in one variable _____, holding all other _____ constant, is called the **marginal physical product (MPP).** When we multiply marginal physical product times _____ _____, we obtain the **marginal revenue product (MRP).**

A firm will hire workers up to the point at which the additional cost of hiring one more worker is equal to the additional revenue generated. For the individual firm, therefore, its MRP of labor curve is also its _____ _____ labor curve.

The demand for labor is a _____ demand, _____ from the demand for final output. Therefore, a change in the price of the final output will cause a _____ in the MRP curve (which is also the firm's demand for labor curve).

The Market Demand for Labor

The downward-sloping portion of each individual firm's marginal revenue product curve is also its demand curve for the one variable factor of production—in our example, labor. When we go to the entire market for a particular type of labor in a particular industry, we will also find that the quantity of labor demanded will vary inversely as the wage rate changes.

Constructing the Market Labor Demand Curve

Given that the market demand curve for labor is made up of the individual firms' downward-sloping demand curves for labor, we can safely infer that the market demand curve for labor will look like *D* in panel (b) of Figure 28-3 on the following page: It will slope downward. That market demand curve for labor in the magneto optical disk industry shows the quantities of labor demanded by all of the firms in the industry at various wage rates.

Nevertheless, the market demand curve for labor is *not* a simple horizontal summation of the labor demand curves of all individual firms. Remember that the demand for labor is a derived demand. Even if we hold labor productivity constant, the demand for labor still depends on both the wage rate and the price of the final output.

FIGURE 28-3

Derivation of the Market Demand Curve for Labor

The market demand curve for labor is not simply the horizontal summation of each individual firm's demand curve for labor. If wage rates fall from \$20 to \$10, all 200 firms will increase employment and therefore output, causing the price of the product to fall. This causes the marginal revenue product curve of each firm to shift inward, from d_0 to d_1 in panel (a). The resulting market demand curve, D, in panel (b) is therefore less elastic around prices from \$10 to \$20 than it would be if the output price remained constant.

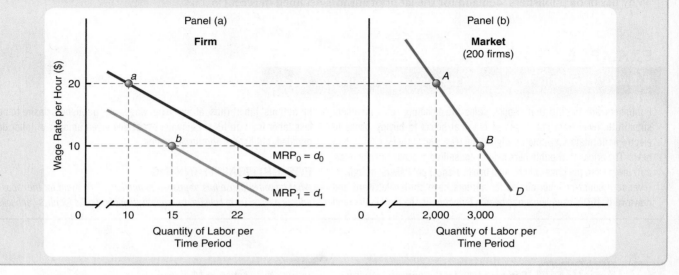

For instance, suppose that we start at a wage rate of \$20 per hour and employment level 10 in panel (a) of Figure 28-3 above. If we sum all such employment levels—point *a* in panel (a)—across 200 firms, we get a market quantity demanded of 2,000, or point *A* in panel (b), at the wage rate of \$20. A decrease in the wage rate to \$10 per hour would induce individual firms' employment levels to increase toward a quantity demanded of 22 *if the product price did not change*.

As all 200 firms simultaneously increase employment, total industry output also increases at the present price. Indeed, this would occur at *any* price, meaning that the industry product supply curve will shift rightward, and the market clearing price of the product must fall. The fall in the output price in turn causes a downward shift of each firm's MRP curve (d_0) to MRP_1 (d_1) in panel (a). Thus, each firm's employment of labor increases to 15 rather than to 22 at the wage rate of \$10 per hour. A summation of all such 200 employment levels gives us 3,000—point *B*—in panel (b).

Determinants of Demand Elasticity for Inputs

Just as we were able to discuss the price elasticity of demand for different commodities in Chapter 19, we can discuss the price elasticity of demand for inputs. The price elasticity of demand for labor is defined in a manner similar to the price elasticity of demand for goods: the percentage change in the quantity of labor demanded divided by the percentage change in the price of labor. When the *numerical* (or absolute) value of this ratio is less than 1, demand is inelastic. When it is 1, demand is unit-elastic. When it is greater than 1, demand is elastic.

There are four principal determinants of the price elasticity of demand for an input. The price elasticity of demand for a variable input will be greater:

1. The greater the price elasticity of demand for the final product

2. The easier it is to employ substitute inputs in production

3. The larger the proportion of total costs accounted for by the particular variable input

4. The longer the time period available for adjustment

FINAL PRODUCT PRICE ELASTICITY An individual radish farmer faces an extremely elastic demand for radishes, given the existence of many competing radish growers. If the farmer's laborers tried to obtain a significant wage increase, the farmer couldn't pass on the resultant higher costs to radish buyers. So any wage increase would lead to a large reduction in the quantity of labor demanded by the individual radish farmer.

EASE OF SUBSTITUTION Clearly, the easier it is for producers to switch to using another factor of production, the more responsive those producers will be to an increase in an input's price. If plastic can easily substitute for chrome plating in the production of, say, car bumpers, then a rise in the price of chrome plating will cause automakers to greatly reduce the quantity of chrome plating they demand.

PORTION OF TOTAL COST When a particular input's costs account for a very large share of total costs, any increase in that input's price will affect total costs relatively more. If labor costs are 80 percent of total costs, companies will cut back on employment more aggressively than if labor costs are only 8 percent of total costs, for any given wage increase.

ADJUSTMENT PERIOD Finally, over longer periods, firms have more time to figure out ways to economize on the use of inputs whose prices have gone up. Furthermore, over time, technological change will allow for easier substitution in favor of relatively cheaper inputs and against inputs whose prices went up. At first, a pay raise obtained by a strong telephone industry union may not result in many layoffs, but over time, the telephone companies will use new technology to replace many of the now more expensive workers.

Wage Determination in a Perfectly Competitive Labor Market

Having developed the demand curve for labor (and all other variable inputs) in a particular industry, let's turn to the labor supply curve. By adding supply to the analysis, we can determine the equilibrium wage rate that workers earn in an industry. We can think in terms of a supply curve for labor that slopes upward in a particular industry.

At higher wage rates, more workers will want to enter that particular industry. The individual firm, however, does not face the entire *market* supply curve. Rather, in a perfectly competitive case, the individual firm is such a small part of the market that it can hire all the workers that it wants at the going wage rate. We say, therefore, that the industry faces an upward-sloping supply curve but that the individual *firm* faces a perfectly elastic supply curve for labor.

Labor Market Equilibrium

The demand curve for labor in the MO disk industry is D in Figure 28-4 on the following page, and the supply curve of labor is S. The equilibrium wage rate of $830 a week is established at the intersection of the two curves. The quantity of workers both supplied and demanded at that rate is Q_1. If for some reason the wage rate fell to $800

FIGURE 28-4

The Equilibrium Wage Rate and the Magneto Optical Disk Industry

The industry demand curve for labor is *D*. We put in a hypothetical upward-sloping labor supply curve for the magneto optical disk industry, *S*. The intersection is at point *E*, giving an equilibrium wage rate of $830 per week and an equilibrium quantity of labor demanded of Q_1. At a wage above $830 per week, there will be an excess quantity of workers supplied. At a wage below $830 per week, there will be an excess quantity of workers demanded.

a week, in our hypothetical example, there would be an excess number of workers demanded at that wage rate. Conversely, if the wage rate rose to $900 a week, there would be an excess quantity of workers supplied at that wage rate. In either case, competition would quickly force the wage back to the equilibrium level.

We have just found the equilibrium wage rate for the entire MO disk industry. The individual firm must take that equilibrium wage rate as given in the perfectly competitive model used here because the individual firm is a very small part of the total demand for labor. Thus, each firm purchasing labor in a perfectly competitive market can purchase all of the input it wants at the going market price.

Shifts in the Market Demand for and the Supply of Labor

Just as we discussed shifts in the supply curve and the demand curve for various products in Chapter 3, we can discuss the effects of shifts in supply and demand in labor markets.

REASONS FOR LABOR DEMAND CURVE SHIFTS Many factors can cause the demand curve for labor to shift. We have already discussed a number of them. Clearly, because the demand for labor or any other variable input is a derived demand, the labor demand curve will shift if there is a shift in the demand for the final product. There are two other important determinants of the position of the demand curve for labor: changes in labor's productivity and changes in the price of related factors of production (substitute inputs and complementary inputs).

1. *Changes in the demand for the final product.* The demand for labor or any other variable input is derived from the demand for the final product. The marginal revenue product is equal to marginal physical product times marginal revenue. Therefore, any change in the demand for the final product will change its price and hence the MRP of the input. The rule of thumb is as follows:

   A change in the demand for the final product that labor (or any other variable input) is producing will shift the market demand curve for labor in the same direction.

2. *Changes in labor productivity.* The second part of the MRP equation is MPP, which relates to labor productivity. We can surmise, then, that, other things being equal:

A change in labor productivity will shift the market labor demand curve in the same direction.

Labor productivity can increase because labor has more capital or land to work with, because of technological improvements, or because labor's quality has improved. Such considerations explain why the real standard of living of workers in the United States is higher than in most other countries. U.S. workers generally work with a larger capital stock, have more natural resources, are in better physical condition, and are better trained than workers in many countries. Hence the demand for labor in the United States is, other things held constant, greater.

3. *Change in the price of related factors.* Labor is not the only resource that firms use. Some resources are substitutes and some are complements in the production process. If we hold output constant, we have the following general rule:

A change in the price of a substitute input will cause the demand for labor (or any other input) to change in the same direction.

Thus, if the price of an input for which labor can substitute as a factor of production decreases, the demand for labor falls. For instance, if the price of mechanized ditch-digging equipment decreases, the demand for workers who, in contrast, can use only shovels to dig ditches decreases.

Suppose that a particular type of capital equipment and labor are complementary. In general, we predict the following:

A change in the price of a complementary input will cause the demand for labor to change in the opposite direction.

If the price of machines goes up but they must be used with labor, fewer machines will be purchased and therefore fewer workers will be used.

DETERMINANTS OF THE SUPPLY OF LABOR Labor supply curves may shift in a particular industry for a number of reasons. For example, if wage rates for factory workers in the smartphone industry remain constant while wages for factory workers in the computer industry go up dramatically, the supply curve of factory workers in the smartphone industry will shift inward to the left as these workers move to the computer industry.

Changes in working conditions in an industry can also affect its labor supply curve. If employers in the smartphone industry discover a new production technique that makes working conditions much more pleasant, the supply curve of labor to the digital camera industry will shift outward to the right.

Job flexibility also determines the position of the labor supply curve. For example, when an industry allows workers more flexibility, such as the ability to work at home via computer, the workers are likely to provide more hours of labor. That is to say, their supply curve will shift outward to the right. Some industries in which firms offer *job sharing*, particularly to people raising families, have found that the supply curve of labor has shifted outward to the right.

How have recent changes in both the demand for and supply of the labor of attorneys specializing in contract law affected the equilibrium wages earned by these lawyers?

EXAMPLE

Why Contract Attorneys' Wages Have Plummeted

As in previous years, people who become attorneys often spend in excess of $100,000 on law school tuition and devote many hours to studying for grueling bar exams. In contrast to years past, however, many who become contract attorneys—lawyers who specialize in analyzing disputed contracts—are earning much lower wages.

(continued)

One reason for the drop in the equilibrium wage rate earned by contract attorneys is that the derived market demand for their skills has dropped. Law firms are earning lower prices for handling contract litigation, so the value of the marginal product of contract attorneys has fallen. Another reason is an increase in the supply of lawyers who specialize in analyzing contracts. The resulting drop in the average wage rate earned by new contract attorneys has been steep—from nearly $30 per hour to less than $20 per hour.

FOR CRITICAL THINKING

How might the decline in contract attorney's current wage rate relative to wages in other occupations affect the future supply of labor of contract attorneys? Explain.

QUICK QUIZ See page 641 for the answers. Review concepts from this section in MyEconLab.

The individual perfectly competitive firm faces a perfectly _____ labor supply curve—it can hire all the labor it wants at the going market wage rate. The industry supply curve of labor slopes _____.

By plotting an industrywide supply curve for labor and an industrywide demand curve for labor on the same graph, we obtain the _____ wage rate in the industry.

The labor demand curve can shift because the _____ for the final product shifts, labor _____ changes, or the price of a related (_____ or _____) factor of production changes.

Labor Outsourcing, Wages, and Employment

In addition to making it easier for people to work at home, computer technology has made it possible for them to provide labor services to companies located in another country. Some companies based in Canada regularly transmit financial records—often via the Internet—to U.S. accountants so that they can process payrolls and compile income statements. Meanwhile, some U.S. manufacturers of personal computers and peripheral devices arrange for customers' calls for assistance to be directed to call centers in India, where English-speaking technical-support specialists help the customers with their problems.

A firm that employs labor located outside the country in which it is based engages in labor **outsourcing.** Canadian companies that hire U.S. accountants outsource accounting services to the United States. U.S. computer manufacturers that employ Indian call-center staff outsource technical-support services to India. How does outsourcing affect employment and wages in the United States? Who loses and who gains from outsourcing? Let's consider each of these questions in turn.

Outsourcing
A firm's employment of labor outside the country in which the firm is located.

Wage and Employment Effects of Outsourcing

Equilibrium wages and levels of employment in U.S. labor markets are determined by the demands for and supplies of labor in those markets. As you have learned, one of the determinants of the market demand for labor is the price of a substitute input. Availability of a lower-priced substitute, you also learned, causes the demand for labor to fall. Thus, the *immediate* economic effects of labor outsourcing are straightforward.

When a home industry's firms can obtain *foreign* labor services that are a close substitute for *home* labor services, the demand for labor services provided by home workers will decrease. What this economic reasoning ultimately implies for U.S. labor markets, however, depends on whether we view the United States as the "home" country or the "foreign" country.

U.S. LABOR MARKET EFFECTS OF OUTSOURCING BY U.S. FIRMS To begin, let's view the United States as the home country. Suppose that initially all U.S. firms employ only U.S. workers. Then developments in computer, communications, and transportation technologies enable an increasing number of U.S. firms to regard the labor of foreign workers as a close substitute for labor provided by U.S. workers. Take a look at Figure 28-5 on the facing page. Panel (a) depicts demand and supply curves in the U.S. market

FIGURE 28-5

Outsourcing of U.S. Computer Technical-Support Services

Initially, the market wage for U.S. workers providing technical support for customers of U.S. computer manufacturers is $19 per hour at point E_1 in panel (a), while the market wage for Indian workers who provide similar services is $8 per hour in panel (b). Then, improvements in communications technologies enable U.S. firms to substitute away from U.S. workers in favor of Indian workers. The market demand for U.S. labor decreases in panel (a), generating a new equilibrium at point E_2 at a lower U.S. market wage and employment level. The market demand for Indian labor increases in panel (b), bringing about higher wages and employment at point E_2.

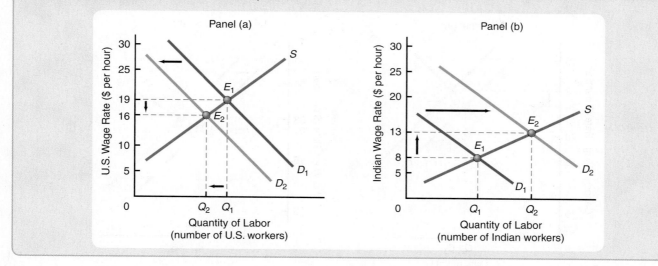

for workers who handle calls for technical support for U.S. manufacturers of personal computers. Suppose that before technological change makes foreign labor substitutable for U.S. labor, point E_1 is the initial equilibrium. At this point, the market wage rate in this U.S. labor market is $19 per hour.

Now suppose that improvements in communications technologies enable U.S. personal computer manufacturers to consider foreign labor as a substitute input for U.S. labor. Panel (b) displays demand and supply curves in a market for substitutable labor services in India. At the initial equilibrium point E_1, the wage rate denominated in U.S. dollars is $8 per hour. Firms in this U.S. industry will respond to the lower price of substitute labor in India by increasing their demand for labor services in that country and reducing their demand for U.S. labor. Thus, in panel (b), the market demand for the substitute labor services available in India rises. The market wage in India rises to $13 per hour, at point E_2, and Indian employment increases. In panel (a), the market demand for U.S. labor services decreases. At the new equilibrium point E_2, the U.S. market wage has fallen to $16 per hour, and equilibrium employment has decreased.

Consequently, when U.S. firms are the home firms engaging in labor outsourcing, the effects are lower wages and decreased employment in the relevant U.S. labor markets. In those nations where workers providing the outsourced labor reside, the effects are higher wages and increased employment.

U.S. LABOR MARKET EFFECTS OF OUTSOURCING BY FOREIGN FIRMS U.S. firms are not the only companies that engage in outsourcing. Consider the Canadian companies that hire U.S. accountants to calculate their payrolls and maintain their financial records. Figure 28-6 on the following page shows the effects in the Canadian and U.S. markets for labor services provided by accountants before and after *Canadian* outsourcing of accountants' labor. At point E_1 in panel (a), before any outsourcing takes place, the initial market wage for qualified accountants in Canada is $29 per hour. In panel (b), the market wage for similarly qualified U.S. accountants is $21 per hour.

FIGURE 28-6

Outsourcing of Accounting Services by Canadian Firms

Suppose that the market wage for accounting services in Canada is initially $29 per hour, at point E_1 in panel (a), but in the United States accountants earn just $21 per hour at point E_1 in panel (b). Then, Internet access enables Canadian firms to substitute labor services provided by U.S. accountants for the services of Canadian accountants. The market demand for the services of Canadian accountants decreases in panel (a), and at point E_2 fewer Canadian accountants are employed at a lower market wage. The market demand for U.S. accounting services increases in panel (b). This generates higher wages and employment for U.S. accountants at point E_2.

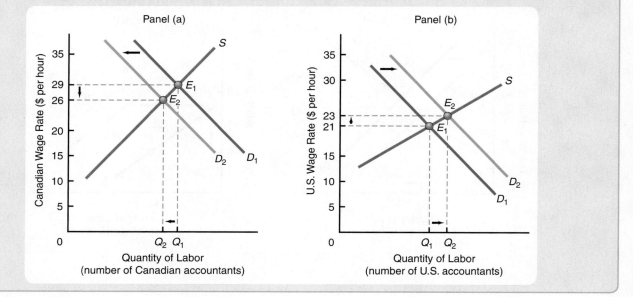

After Internet access allows companies in Canada to transfer financial data electronically, the services of U.S. accountants become available as a less expensive substitute for those provided by Canadian accountants. When Canadian firms respond by seeking to outsource to U.S. accountants, the demand for U.S. accountants' labor services rises in panel (b). This causes the market wage earned by U.S. accountants to increase to $23 per hour. Canadian firms substitute away from the services of Canadian accountants, so in panel (a) the demand for the labor of accountants in Canada declines. Canadian accountants' wages decline to $26 per hour.

In contrast to the situation in which U.S. firms are the home firms engaging in labor outsourcing, when foreign firms outsource by hiring workers in the United States, wages and employment levels rise in the affected U.S. markets. In the nations where the firms engaging in outsourcing are located, the effects are lower wages and decreased employment.

Why are fewer nations' firms outsourcing labor to China?

INTERNATIONAL EXAMPLE

China's Declining Status as an Outsourcing Destination

For years, many firms based outside China, including companies in the United States and Europe, have engaged in international outsourcing to that nation. The incentive to outsource to China has diminished in recent years, however.

On the one hand, so many foreign firms have engaged in labor outsourcing in China that the market demand for labor in that nation has increased considerably. On the other hand, China's population is aging, and fewer young workers are entering the labor force to provide the necessary hours of labor for tasks desired by many foreign firms. Thus, the market supply of labor in China has decreased somewhat. Together, these changes in market demand for and supply of labor have raised the equilibrium wage rate earned by a typical Chinese worker. Chinese wages are now close to wages earned by workers in other outsourcing nations. This is why fewer foreign firms have been choosing China as an outsourcing destination in recent years.

FOR CRITICAL THINKING
How has recent wage stagnation in the United States likely affected the incentive for U.S. firms to engage in labor outsourcing in China?

Gauging the Net Effects of Outsourcing on the U.S. Economy

In the example depicted in Figure 28-5 on page 629, the market wage and employment level for U.S. technical-support workers declined as a result of outsourcing by U.S. firms. In contrast, in the example shown in Figure 28-6 on the facing page, U.S. accountants earned higher wages and experienced increased employment as a result of outsourcing by Canadian firms. Together, these examples illustrate a fundamental conclusion concerning the short-run effects of global labor outsourcing in U.S. labor markets:

> *Labor outsourcing by U.S. firms tends to reduce U.S. wages and employment. Whenever foreign firms engage in labor outsourcing in the United States, however, U.S. wages and employment tend to increase.*

Consequently, the immediate effects of increased worldwide labor outsourcing are lower wages and employment in some U.S. labor markets and higher wages and employment in others. In this narrow sense, some U.S. workers "lose" from outsourcing while others "gain," just as some Canadian workers "lose" while some Indian workers "gain."

SUMMING UP THE ECONOMIC IMPLICATIONS OF OUTSOURCING Even in the best of times, workers in labor markets experience short-run ups and downs in wages and jobs. During normal times in the United States, after all, about 4 million jobs typically come and go every month.

Certainly, various groups of U.S. workers earn lower pay or experience reduced employment opportunities, at least for a time, as a result of labor outsourcing. Nevertheless, outsourcing is a two-way street. Labor outsourcing does not just involve U.S. firms purchasing the labor services of residents located abroad. This phenomenon also entails the purchase of labor services from U.S. workers who provide outsourcing services to companies located in other nations.

Indeed, outsourcing really amounts to another way for residents of different nations to conduct trade with one another. As you learned in Chapter 2, trade allows nations' residents to specialize according to their *comparative advantages* and thereby obtain gains from exchanging items across country boundaries. To be sure, not all workers gain equally from the trade of outsourced labor services, and some people temporarily lose, in the form of either lower wages or reduced employment opportunities. Nevertheless, specialization and trade of labor services through outsourcing generate overall gains from trade for participating nations, such as India, Canada, and the United States.

To read a Heritage Foundation lecture about the net effects of outsourcing on U.S. jobs, use the link at www.econtoday.com/chap28.

YOU ARE THERE

To learn how some unemployed U.S. workers are now outsourcing their efforts to find new employment, take a look at **Combating U.S. Unemployment via Job-Search Outsourcing,** on page 636.

WHAT IF... the government required U.S. firms to hire only workers who reside in the United States?

Prohibiting the hiring of foreign labor would put an end to international labor outsourcing. Thus, either U.S. firms would pay higher wages for U.S. workers they had not hired previously, which would push up their costs and generate lower production, or U.S. firms would not replace the outsourced labor and would produce less.

In any event, firms would reduce the amounts of goods and services offered for sale in the United States at any given prices, and the resulting decreases in supply would lead to higher equilibrium product prices. Thus, the effect of a ban on international labor outsourcing would generate higher prices for U.S. consumers.

QUICK QUIZ See page 641 for the answers. Review concepts from this section in MyEconLab.

Advances in telecommunications and computer networking are making foreign labor more easily _____ for home labor. Home firms' _____ of foreign labor for home labor is known as labor **outsourcing.**

In the short run, outsourcing by U.S. firms _____ the demand for labor, market wages, and equilibrium employment in U.S. labor markets. Outsourcing by

foreign firms that hire U.S. labor _____ the demand for labor, market wages, and equilibrium employment in U.S. labor markets. The net short-run effects on U.S. wages and employment are mixed.

In the long run, outsourcing enables U.S. firms to operate more efficiently and this activity generates overall _____ _____ _____ for U.S. residents.

Monopoly in the Product Market

So far we've considered only perfectly competitive markets, both in selling the final product and in buying factors of production. We will continue our assumption that the firm purchases its factors of production in a perfectly competitive factor market. Now, however, we will assume that the firm sells its product in an *imperfectly* competitive output market. In other words, we are considering the output market structures of monopoly, oligopoly, and monopolistic competition. In all such cases, the firm, be it a monopolist, an oligopolist, or a monopolistic competitor, faces a downward-sloping demand curve for its product.

Throughout the rest of this chapter, we will simply refer to a monopoly situation for ease of analysis. The analysis holds for all industry structures that are less than perfectly competitive. In any event, the fact that our firm now faces a downward-sloping demand curve for its product means that if it wants to sell more of its product (at a uniform price), it has to lower the price, *not just on the last unit, but on all preceding units.* The *marginal revenue* received from selling an additional unit is continuously falling (and is less than price) as the firm attempts to sell more and more. This relationship between marginal revenue and output is certainly different from our earlier discussions in this chapter in which the firm could sell all it wanted at a constant price. Why? Because the firm we discussed until now was a perfect competitor.

Constructing the Monopolist's Input Demand Curve

In reconstructing our demand schedule for an input, we must account for the facts that (1) the marginal *physical* product falls because of the law of diminishing marginal product as more workers are added and (2) the price (and marginal revenue) received for the product sold also falls as more is produced and sold. That is, for the monopolist, we have to account for both the diminishing marginal physical product and the diminishing marginal revenue. Marginal revenue is always less than price for the monopolist. The marginal revenue curve always lies below the downward-sloping product demand curve.

MARGINAL REVENUE PRODUCT FOR A PERFECTLY COMPETITIVE FIRM Marginal revenue for the perfect competitor is equal to the price of the product because all units can be sold at the going market price. In our example involving the production of magneto optical disks on page 620, we assumed that the perfect competitor could sell all it wanted at $10 per unit. A one-unit change in sales always led to a $10 change in total revenues. Hence, marginal revenue was always equal to $10 for that perfect competitor. Multiplying this unchanging marginal revenue by the marginal physical product of labor then yielded the perfectly competitive firm's marginal revenue product.

MARGINAL REVENUE PRODUCT FOR A MONOPOLY FIRM The monopolist, however, cannot simply calculate marginal revenue by looking at the price of the product. To sell the additional output from an additional unit of input, the monopolist has to cut prices on all previous units of output. As output is increasing, then, marginal revenue is falling.

The underlying concept is, of course, the same for both the perfect competitor and the monopolist. We are asking exactly the same question in both cases: When an additional worker is hired, what is the benefit? In either case, the benefit is obviously the change in total revenues due to the one-unit change in the variable input, labor. In our discussion of the perfect competitor, we were able simply to multiply the marginal physical product by the *constant* per-unit price of the product because the price of the product never changed (for the perfect competitor, $P \equiv MR$).

LABOR DEMAND FOR A MONOPOLIST A single monopolist ends up hiring fewer workers than would all of the perfectly competitive firms added together. To see this, we must consider the marginal revenue product for the monopolist, which varies with each one-unit change in the monopolist's labor input. This is what we do in panel (a) of Figure 28-7 on the facing page, where column 5, "Marginal Revenue Product," gives the monopolist a quantitative notion of how additional workers and additional production generate additional revenues. The marginal revenue product curve for this monopolist has been plotted in panel (b) of the figure. To emphasize the lower elasticity of the monopolist's MRP curve (MRP_m) around the wage rate $830, the labor demand curve for a perfectly competitive industry (labeled D) has been plotted on the same graph in Figure 28-7 below.

Recall that this curve is not simply the sum of the marginal revenue product curves of all perfectly competitive firms, because when competitive firms together increase employment, their output expands and the product price declines. Nevertheless, at any given wage rate, the quantity of labor demanded by the monopoly is still less than the quantity of labor demanded by a perfectly competitive industry.

Why does MRP_m represent the monopolist's input demand curve? As always, our profit-maximizing monopolist will continue to hire labor as long as additional profits result. Profits are made as long as the additional cost of more workers is outweighed by the additional revenues made from selling the output of those workers. When the wage rate equals these additional revenues, the monopolist stops hiring. That is, the

FIGURE 28-7

A Monopolist's Marginal Revenue Product

Panel (a)

(1) Labor Input (workers per week)	(2) Marginal Physical Product (MPP) (magneto optical disks per week)	(3) Price of Product (P)	(4) Marginal Revenue (MR)	(5) Marginal Revenue Product (MRP_m) = (2) x (4)	(6) Wage Rate
8	111	$11.60	$9.40	$1,043.40	$830.00
9	104	11.40	9.00	936.00	830.00
10	97	11.20	8.60	834.20	830.00
11	90	11.00	8.20	738.00	830.00
12	83	10.80	7.80	647.40	830.00
13	76	10.60	7.40	562.40	830.00

The monopolist hires just enough workers to make marginal revenue product equal to the going wage rate. If the going wage rate is $830 per week, as shown by the labor supply curve, s, in panel (b), the monopolist would want to hire approximately 10 workers per week. That is the profit-maximizing amount of labor. The labor demand curve for a perfectly competitive industry from Figure 28-4 on page 626 is also plotted (D). The monopolist's MRP curve will always be less elastic around the going wage rate than it would be if marginal revenue were constant.

firm stops hiring when the wage rate is equal to the marginal revenue product because additional workers would add more to cost than to revenue.

Why the Monopolist Hires Fewer Workers

Because we have used the same numbers as in Figure 28-1 on page 620, we can see that the monopolist hires fewer workers per week than firms in a perfect competitive market would. That is to say, if we could magically change the magneto optical disk industry in our example from one in which there is perfect competition in the output market to one in which there is monopoly in the output market, the amount of employment would fall. Why? Because the monopolist must take account of the declining product price that must be charged in order to sell a larger number of MO disks. Remember that every firm hires up to the point at which marginal benefit equals marginal cost. The marginal benefit to the monopolist of hiring an additional worker is not simply the additional output times the price of the product. Rather, the monopolist faces a reduction in the price charged on *all* units sold in order to be able to sell more.

So the monopolist ends up hiring fewer workers than all of the perfect competitors taken together, assuming that all else remains the same for the two hypothetical examples. But this should not come as a surprise. In considering product markets, by implication we saw that a monopolized magneto optical disk industry would produce less output than a competitive one. Therefore, the monopolized industry would hire fewer workers.

The Utilization of Other Factors of Production

The analysis in this chapter has been given in terms of the demand for the variable input labor. The same analysis holds for any other variable factor input. We could have talked about the demand for fertilizer or the demand for the services of tractors by a farmer instead of the demand for labor and reached the same conclusions. The entrepreneur will hire or buy any variable input up to the point at which its price equals the marginal revenue product.

A further question remains: How much of each variable factor should the firm utilize when all the variable factors are combined to produce the product? We can answer this question by looking at either the cost-minimizing side of the question or the profit-maximizing side.

Cost Minimization and Factor Utilization

From the cost minimization point of view, how can the firm minimize its total costs for a given output? Assume that you are an entrepreneur attempting to minimize costs. Consider a hypothetical situation in which if you spend $1 more on labor, you would get 20 more units of output, but if you spend $1 more on machines, you would get only 10 more units of output. What would you want to do in such a situation? You would wish to hire more workers or sell off some of your machines, for you are not getting as much output per *last* dollar spent on machines as you are per *last* dollar spent on labor. You would want to employ factors of production so that the marginal products per last dollar spent on each are equal. Thus, the least-cost, or cost minimization, rule will be as follows:

> *To minimize total costs for a particular rate of production, the firm will hire factors of production up to the point at which the marginal physical product per last dollar spent on each factor of production is equalized.*

That is,

$$\frac{\text{MPP of labor}}{\text{price of labor (wage rate)}} = \frac{\text{MPP of capital}}{\text{price of capital (cost per unit of service)}} = \frac{\text{MPP of land}}{\text{price of land (rental rate per unit)}}$$

All we are saying here is that the cost-minimizing firm will always utilize *all* resources in such combinations that cost will be minimized for any given output rate. This is commonly called the *least-cost combination of resources.*

How has a ruling by the Internal Revenue Service contributed to lower equilibrium employment in the United States?

POLICY EXAMPLE

A "Reclassification Regulation" Cuts Overall Labor Employment

Many firms employ independent contractors to perform labor tasks alongside regular employees. Recently, the Internal Revenue Service ruled that a number of U.S. companies had improperly classified some workers as independent contractors and hence failed to withhold Social Security and Medicare taxes.

This IRS ruling changed the cost minimization calculation for thousands of affected companies. When confronted with paying a higher wage rate to people who previously had been classified as independent contractors, these firms experienced an increase in the denominator of the ratio of these workers' MPP to their wage rate. This ratio thereby declined in relation to the ratio for regular employees. Although a portion of affected firms responded by converting some of their former independent contractors into regular employees, a number of firms ended their employment of the labor services of independent contractors. The IRS ruling therefore contributed to a net decline in employment.

FOR CRITICAL THINKING

Why were firms most likely to reclassify as regular employees the prior independent contractors who exhibited the highest marginal physical product of labor?

Profit Maximization Revisited

If a firm wants to maximize profits, how much of each factor should be hired (or bought)? As you have learned, the firm will never utilize a factor of production unless the marginal benefit from hiring that factor is at least equal to the marginal cost. What is the marginal benefit? As we have pointed out several times, the marginal benefit is the change in total revenues due to a one-unit change in utilization of the variable input. What is the marginal cost? In the case of a firm buying in a perfectly competitive market, it is the price of the variable factor—the wage rate if we are referring to labor.

The profit-maximizing combination of resources for the firm will be where, in a perfectly competitive market structure,

MRP of labor = price of labor (wage rate)

MRP of capital = price of capital (cost per unit of service)

MRP of land = price of land (rental rate per unit)

To attain maximum profits, the marginal revenue product of each of a firm's resources must be exactly equal to its price. If the MRP of labor is $20 and its price is only $15, the firm will expand its employment of labor.

There is an exact match between the profit-maximizing combination of resources and the least-cost combination of resources discussed above. In other words, either rule can be used to yield the same cost-minimizing rate of utilization of each variable resource.

QUICK QUIZ   See page 641 for the answers. Review concepts from this section in MyEconLab.

When a firm sells its output in a monopoly market, marginal revenue is _____ than price.

Just as the MRP is the perfectly competitive firm's input demand curve, the MRP is also the _____ input demand curve.

The profit-maximizing combination of factors will occur when each factor is used up to the point at which its MRP is equal to its unit _____.

To minimize total costs for a given output, the profit-maximizing firm will hire each factor of production up to the point at which the marginal _____ product per last dollar spent on each factor is equal to the marginal _____ product per last dollar spent on each of the other factors of production.

To maximize profits, the marginal _____ product of each resource must equal the resource's _____.

YOU ARE THERE
Combating U.S. Unemployment via Job-Search Outsourcing

Recently, U.S. resident Frankie Balint had been out of work for some time and was concerned about finding a job. Balint turned to an Indian outsourcing company to help him find a position in the United States.

At a price of $98, the online firm JobSerf.com collected information about Balint's qualifications. JobSerf.com's employees who performed these tasks are based in Visakhapatnam, India, but they scanned the Web for available U.S. positions for which Balint appeared to be qualified and submitted online job applications on his behalf. Ultimately, one of the applications that JobSerf.com submitted for Balint succeeded in helping him to obtain a position, thereby boosting equilibrium U.S. employment by one worker.

Critical Thinking Questions

1. How is employment at U.S. employment agencies affected by the existence of Indian-based job-search firms such as JobSerf.com?

2. If JobSerf.com were to hire some employees who live in the United States to find positions for other U.S. residents, would this be an example of labor outsourcing? Explain.

ISSUES & APPLICATIONS

Will You Be Replaced by an App?

CONCEPTS APPLIED

▶ Derived Demand

▶ Marginal Revenue Product

▶ Cost-Minimizing Factor Utilization

The derived demand for an input depends on the marginal revenue product of that input. This is true for any input, whether it is the labor provided by a human being or a robotic device guided by digital apps of varying degrees of sophistication.

App-Guided Devices as Replacements for Human Labor

Apps such as ForeFlight Mobile HD can perform airline navigation, and digital technologies can pilot planes on runways or through the skies and can drive automobiles along city streets. Advanced robotic systems can perform an increasing array of tasks, ranging from laying sealant on vehicle windshields in auto plants to performing surgeries in hospitals. Online apps can provide teaching instruction to any child or adult with a digital device capable of accessing the Internet.

Nevertheless, just because it is technologically feasible for app-guided digital technology to replace human labor in performing many tasks does not mean that significant substitutions of robotic inputs for human labor will necessarily take place. Decisions about how many units of human labor versus robotic inputs to employ are economic choices made with an aim to minimize costs.

Determining If Humans Are in the Cost-Minimizing Input Mix

Applying cost minimization to human and robotic inputs—digital devices guided by apps—indicates that the two factors will be employed up to the point at which the marginal physical product per last dollar spent on each input is equalized. That is, the cost minimization rule is

$$\frac{\text{MPP of human labor}}{\text{price of human labor}} = \frac{\text{MPP of robotic input}}{\text{price of robotic input}}$$

Today, most firms that employ robotic inputs also employ human beings to perform many tasks. Why don't these firms replace human beings almost entirely? The answer is implied by the cost minimization rule. Humans are part of these firms' mixes of inputs both because the MPP of human labor is sufficiently high in relation to the MPP of a robotic input and because the price of human labor is sufficiently low relative to the price of that robotic input.

This perspective suggests that as technical improvements raise the marginal physical product of many app-guided digital devices and reduce the prices of utilizing these devices, firms will substitute some robotic inputs for human labor. Nevertheless, it is unlikely that firms will substantially replace human labor with robotic inputs as long as humans remain *both* relatively productive *and* relatively inexpensive, compared with robotic inputs. Thus, the demand for human labor will never disappear.

For Critical Thinking

1. Under the cost minimization rule, when will a firm employ *only* human labor?

2. Why does the cost minimization rule suggest that it is unlikely a firm actually would replace human labor *entirely* with robotic inputs?

Web Resources

1. Find out about advances in robotic surgery at **www.econtoday.com/chap28**.

2. Learn how schools are applying teaching apps for "teacherless" educational instruction at **www.econtoday.com/chap28**.

MyEconLab

For more questions on this chapter's Issues & Applications, go to **MyEconLab**. In the Study Plan for this chapter, select Section N: News.

MyEconLab

Here is what you should know after reading this chapter. MyEconLab will help you identify what you know, and where to go when you need to practice.

WHAT YOU SHOULD KNOW		WHERE TO GO TO PRACTICE
Why a Firm's Marginal Revenue Product Curve Is Its Labor Demand Curve The marginal revenue product of labor equals marginal revenue times the marginal physical product of labor. Because of the law of diminishing marginal product, the marginal revenue product curve slopes downward. To maximize profits, a firm hires labor to the point at which the marginal factor cost of labor—the addition to total input costs resulting from employing an additional unit of labor—equals the marginal revenue product.	marginal physical product (MPP) of labor, 619 marginal revenue product (MRP), 621 marginal factor cost (MFC), 621 **Key Figure** Figure 28-1, 620	• **MyEconLab** Study Plan 28.1 • Animated Figure 28-1
The Demand for Labor as a Derived Demand For perfectly competitive firms, marginal revenue equals the market price of their output, so the marginal revenue product of labor equals the product price times the marginal physical product of labor. As product market conditions vary and cause the market price to change, marginal revenue product curves shift. Hence, the demand for labor is derived from the demand for final products.	derived demand, 622 **Key Figure** Figure 28-2, 622	• **MyEconLab** Study Plan 28.2 • Animated Figure 28-2

┌─ **WHAT YOU SHOULD KNOW** ───────────────── **WHERE TO GO TO PRACTICE** ─┐

Key Factors Affecting the Elasticity of Demand for Inputs The price elasticity of demand for an input equals the percentage change in the quantity of the input demanded divided by the percentage change in the input's price. An input's price elasticity of demand is relatively high when any one of the following is true: (1) the price elasticity of demand for the final product is relatively high, (2) it is relatively easy to substitute other inputs in production, (3) the proportion of total costs accounted for by the input is relatively large, or (4) the firm has a longer time period to adjust to the change in the input's price.

Key Figure
Figure 28-3, 624

- MyEconLab Study Plan 28.2
- Animated Figure 28-3

How Equilibrium Wage Rates at Perfectly Competitive Firms Are Determined In a competitive labor market, at the equilibrium wage rate, the quantity of labor demanded by all firms is equal to the quantity of labor supplied by all workers. At this wage rate, each firm looks to its own labor demand curve to determine how much labor to employ.

Key Figure
Figure 28-4, 626

- MyEconLab Study Plan 28.3
- Animated Figure 28-4

U.S. Wage and Employment Effects of Labor Outsourcing The immediate, short-run effects of labor outsourcing on wages and employment in U.S. labor markets are mixed. Outsourcing by U.S. firms reduces the demand for labor in affected U.S. labor markets and thereby pushes down wages and employment. Outsourcing by foreign firms that hire U.S. labor, however, raises the demand for labor in related U.S. labor markets, which boosts U.S. wages and employment.

outsourcing, 628

Key Figures
Figure 28-5, 629
Figure 28-6, 630

- MyEconLab Study Plan 28.4
- Animated Figures 28-5, 28-6

Contrasting the Demand for Labor and Wage Determination under Monopoly with Outcomes under Perfect Competition If a product market monopolist competes for labor in a competitive labor market, it takes the market wage rate as given. Its labor demand curve, however, lies to the left of the labor demand curve that would have arisen in a competitive industry. Thus, at the competitively determined wage rate, a monopolized industry employs fewer workers than the industry otherwise would if it were perfectly competitive.

Key Figure
Figure 28-7, 633

- MyEconLab Study Plans 28.5, 28.6
- Animated Figure 28-7

Log in to MyEconLab, take a chapter test, and get a personalized Study Plan that tells you which concepts you understand and which ones you need to review. From there, MyEconLab will give you further practice, tutorials, animations, videos, and guided solutions. For more information, visit www.myeconlab.com

PROBLEMS

All problems are assignable in MyEconLab. Answers to the odd-numbered problems appear at the back of the book.

28-1. The following table depicts the output of a firm that manufactures computer printers. The printers sell for $100 each.

Labor Input (workers per week)	Total Physical Output (printers per week)
10	200
11	218
12	234
13	248
14	260
15	270
16	278

Calculate the marginal physical product and marginal revenue product at each input level above 10 units. (See page 620.)

28-2. Refer back to your answers to Problem 28-1 in answering the following questions. (See pages 620–622.)

a. What is the maximum wage the firm will be willing to pay if it hires 15 workers?

b. The weekly wage paid by computer printer manufacturers in a perfectly competitive market is $1,200. How many workers will the profit-maximizing employer hire?

c. Suppose that there is an increase in the demand for printed digital photos. Explain the likely effects on marginal revenue product, marginal factor cost, and the number of workers hired by the firm.

28-3. Explain what happens to the elasticity of demand for labor in a given industry after each of the following events. (See pages 624–625.)

a. A new manufacturing technique makes capital easier to substitute for labor.

b. There is an increase in the number of substitutes for the final product that labor produces.

c. After a drop in the prices of capital inputs, labor accounts for a larger portion of a firm's factor costs.

28-4. Explain how the following events would affect the demand for labor. (See pages 621–622.)

a. A new education program administered by the company increases labor's marginal product.

b. The firm completes a new plant with a larger workspace and new machinery.

28-5. The following table depicts the product market and labor market a digital device manufacturer faces. (See page 620.)

Labor Input (workers per day)	Total Physical Product	Product Price ($)
10	100	50
11	109	49
12	116	48
13	121	47
14	124	46
15	125	45

a. Calculate the firm's marginal physical product, total revenue, and marginal revenue product at each input level above 10 units.

b. The firm competes in a perfectly competitive labor market, and the market wage it faces is $100 per worker per day. How many workers will the profit-maximizing employer hire?

28-6. Recently, there has been an increase in the market demand for products of firms in manufacturing industries. The production of many of these products requires the skills of welders. Because welding is a dirty and dangerous job compared with other occupations, in recent years fewer people have sought employment as welders. Draw a diagram of the market for the labor of welders. Use this diagram to explain the likely implications of these recent trends for the market clearing wage earned by welders and the equilibrium quantity of welding services hired. (See pages 626–627.)

28-7. Since the early 2000s, there has been a significant increase in the price of corn-based ethanol. (See pages 626–627.)

a. A key input in the production of corn-based ethanol is corn. Use an appropriate diagram to explain what has likely occurred in the market for corn.

b. In light of your answer to part (a), explain why many hog farmers, who in the past used corn as the main feed input in hog production, have switched to cookies, licorice, cheese curls, candy bars, and other human snack foods instead of corn as food for their hogs.

28-8. A firm hires labor in a perfectly competitive labor market. Its current profit-maximizing hourly output is 100 units, which the firm sells at a price of $5 per unit. The marginal physical product of the last unit of labor employed is 5 units per hour. The firm pays each worker an hourly wage of $15. (See pages 626 and 633.)

a. What marginal revenue does the firm earn from sale of the output produced by the last worker employed?

b. Does this firm sell its output in a perfectly competitive market?

28-9. Suppose that until recently, U.S. firms that produce digital apps had been utilizing only the labor of qualified U.S. workers at a wage rate of $35 per hour. Now, however, these firms have begun engaging in labor outsourcing to Russia, where qualified workers are available at a dollar wage rate of $15 per hour. Evaluate the effects of this new U.S. app-labor outsourcing initiative on U.S. and Russian employment levels and wages. (See pages 628–630.)

28-10. Recently, Swedish companies have outsourced manufacturing labor previously performed by Swedish workers at $20 per hour to U.S. workers who receive a wage rate of $10 per hour. Evaluate the effects of Swedish manufacturing-labor outsourcing on Swedish and U.S. employment levels and wages. (See pages 628–630.)

28-11. Explain why the short-term effects of outsourcing on U.S. wages and employment tend to be more ambiguous than the long-term effects. (See page 631.)

28-12. A profit-maximizing monopolist hires workers in a perfectly competitive labor market. Employing the last worker increased the firm's total weekly output from 110 units to 111 units and caused the firm's weekly revenues to rise from $25,000 to $25,750. What is the current prevailing weekly wage rate in the labor market? (See page 621.)

28-13. A monopoly firm hires workers in a perfectly competitive labor market in which the market wage rate is $20 per day. If the firm maximizes profit, and if the marginal revenue from the last unit of output produced by the last worker hired equals $10, what is the marginal physical product of that worker? (See page 633.)

28-14. The current market wage rate is $10, the rental rate of land is $1,000 per unit, and the rental rate of capital is $500. Production managers at a firm find that under their current allocation of factors of production, the marginal physical product of labor is 100, the marginal physical product of land is 10,000, and the marginal physical product of capital is 4,000. Is the firm minimizing costs? Why or why not? (See page 634.)

28-15. The current wage rate is $10, and the rental rate of capital is $500. A firm's marginal physical product of labor is 200, and its marginal physical product of capital is 20,000. Is the firm maximizing profits for the given cost outlay? Why or why not? (See page 635.)

ECONOMICS ON THE NET

Current Trends in U.S. Labor Markets The Federal Reserve's "Beige Book," which summarizes regional economic conditions around the United States, provides a wealth of information about the current status of U.S. labor markets. This Internet application helps you assess developments in employment and wages in the United States.

Title: The Beige Book—Summary

Navigation: Go to **www.econtoday.com/chap28** to access the home page of the Federal Reserve's Board of Governors. Click on *A–Z Index*, and then click on *Beige Book.* Then select the report for the most recent period.

Application Read the section titled "Prices and Wages," and answer the following questions.

1. Has overall employment been rising or falling during the most recent year? Based on what you learned in this chapter, what factors might account for this pattern? Does the Beige Book summary bear out any of these explanations for changes in U.S. employment?

2. Have U.S. workers' wages been rising or falling during the most recent year?

For Group Study and Analysis The left-hand margin of the Beige Book site lists the reports of the 12 Federal Reserve districts. Divide the class into two groups, and have each group develop brief summaries of the main conclusions of one district's report concerning employment and wages within that district. Reconvene and compare the reports. Are there pronounced regional differences?

ANSWERS TO QUICK QUIZZES

p. 623: (i) output . . . input . . . inputs . . . marginal revenue; (ii) demand for; (iii) derived . . . derived . . . shift

p. 625: (i) wage . . . price . . . downward; (ii) elasticity . . . inputs . . . costs . . . adjustment

p. 628: (i) elastic . . . upward; (ii) equilibrium; (iii) demand . . . productivity . . . substitute . . . complementary

p. 631: (i) substitutable . . . substitution; (ii) reduces . . . increases; (iii) gains from trade

p. 635: (i) less; (ii) monopolist's; (iii) price; (iv) physical . . . physical; (v) revenue . . . price

29

Unions and Labor Market Monopoly Power

O n an average day, many thousands of people around the world who otherwise might have been gainfully employed have chosen not to work. Instead, these individuals are taking part in labor-union-coordinated work stoppages. Most of these work stoppages are legal strikes. A few of the stoppages, though, might be illegal strikes or other means of shutting down employing firms' operations, such as having key workers call in "sick." What is the economic purpose of union-directed work stoppages? More generally, what are the economic benefits and costs of the activities of labor unions? In this chapter, you will learn the answers to these questions.

14.6 million U.S. workers belong to **labor unions**—organizations that seek to secure economic improvements for their members? Private firms employ 7 million of these workers, or just over 7 percent of the private-sector labor force. Federal, state, and local government agencies employ the remaining 7.6 million union members, or about 38 percent of the public-sector labor force.

Traditionally, a key rationale for forming a union has been for members to be able to earn more than they would in a competitive labor market by obtaining a type of monopoly power. Because the entire supply of a particular group of workers is controlled by a single source when a union bargains as a single entity with management, a certain monopoly element enters into the determination of employment and wages. In such situations, we can no longer talk about a perfectly competitive supply of labor. Later in the chapter, we will examine the converse—a single employer who is the sole employer of a particular group of workers.

Labor unions
Worker organizations that seek to secure economic improvements for their members. They also seek to improve the safety, health, and other benefits (such as job security) of their members.

Industrialization and Labor Unions

In most parts of the world, labor movements began with local **craft unions.** These were groups of workers in individual trades, such as shoemaking, printing, or baking. Beginning around the middle of the eighteenth century, new technologies permitted reductions in unit production costs through the formation of larger-scale enterprises that hired dozens or more workers. By the late 1790s, workers in some British craft unions began trying to convince employers to engage in **collective bargaining,** in which business management negotiates with representatives of all union members about wages and hours of work.

In 1799 and 1800, the British Parliament passed laws called the Combination Acts aimed at prohibiting the formation of unions. In 1825, Parliament enacted a replacement Combination Act allowing unions to exist and to engage in limited collective bargaining. Unions on the European continent managed to convince most governments throughout Europe to enact similar laws during the first half of the nineteenth century.

Craft unions
Labor unions composed of workers who engage in a particular trade or skill, such as baking, carpentry, or plumbing.

Collective bargaining
Negotiation between the management of a company or and the management of a union for the purpose of reaching a mutually agreeable contract that sets wages, fringe benefits, and working conditions for all employees in all the unions involved.

Unions in the United States

The development of unions in the United States lagged several decades behind events in Europe. In the years between the Civil War and World War I (1861–1914), the Knights of Labor, an organized group of both skilled and unskilled workers, pushed for an eight-hour workday and equal pay for women and men. In 1886, a dissident group split from the Knights of Labor to form the American Federation of Labor (AFL) under the leadership of Samuel Gompers. During World War I, union membership increased to more than 5 million. But after the war, the government de-emphasized protecting labor's right to organize. Membership began to fall.

THE FORMATION OF INDUSTRIAL UNIONS The Great Depression was a landmark event in U.S. labor history. Franklin Roosevelt's National Industrial Recovery Act of 1933 gave labor the federal right to bargain collectively, but that act was declared unconstitutional. The 1935 National Labor Relations Act (NLRA), otherwise known as the Wagner Act, took its place. The NLRA guaranteed workers the right to form unions, to engage in collective bargaining, and to be members of any union.

In 1938, the Congress of Industrial Organizations (CIO) was formed by John L. Lewis, the president of the United Mine Workers. Prior to the formation of the CIO, most labor organizations were craft unions. The CIO was composed of **industrial unions,** which drew their membership from an entire industry such as steel or automobiles. In 1955, the CIO and the AFL merged because the leaders of both associations thought a merger would help organized labor grow faster.

Industrial unions
Labor unions that consist of workers from a particular industry, such as automobile manufacturing or steel manufacturing.

CONGRESSIONAL CONTROL OVER LABOR UNIONS Since the Great Depression, Congress has occasionally altered the relationship between labor and management through significant legislation. One of the most important pieces of legislation was the Taft-Hartley

Go to www.econtoday.com/chap29 to link to the Legal Information Institute's review of all the key U.S. labor laws.

Right-to-work laws
Laws that make it illegal to require union membership as a condition of continuing employment in a particular firm.

Closed shop
A business enterprise in which employees must belong to the union before they can be hired and must remain in the union after they are hired.

Union shop
A business enterprise that may hire nonunion members, conditional on their joining the union by some specified date after employment begins.

Jurisdictional dispute
A disagreement involving two or more unions over which should have control of a particular jurisdiction, such as a particular craft or skill or a particular firm or industry.

Sympathy strike
A work stoppage by a union in sympathy with another union's strike or cause.

Secondary boycott
A refusal to deal with companies or purchase products sold by companies that are dealing with a company being struck.

Act of 1947 (the Labor Management Relations Act). In general, the Taft-Hartley Act outlawed certain labor practices of unions, such as imposing make-work rules and forcing unwilling workers to join a particular union. Among other things, it allowed individual states to pass their own **right-to-work laws.** A right-to-work law makes it illegal for union membership to be a requirement for continued employment in any establishment.

The Taft-Hartley Act also made a **closed shop** illegal. A closed shop requires union membership before employment can be obtained. A **union shop,** however, is legal. A union shop does not require membership as a prerequisite for employment, but it can, and usually does, require that workers join the union after a specified amount of time on the job. (Even a union shop is illegal in states with right-to-work laws.)

Jurisdictional disputes, sympathy strikes, and secondary boycotts were also made illegal by the Taft-Hartley Act. In a **jurisdictional dispute,** two or more unions fight (and strike) over which should have control in a particular jurisdiction. For example, should carpenters working for a steel manufacturer be members of the steelworkers' union or the carpenters' union? A **sympathy strike** occurs when one union strikes in sympathy with another union's cause or strike. For example, if the retail clerks' union in a city is striking grocery stores, Teamsters union members may refuse to deliver products to those stores in sympathy with the retail clerks' demands for higher wages or better working conditions. A **secondary boycott** is a boycott of a company that deals with a struck company. For example, if union workers strike a baking company, a boycott of grocery stores that continue to sell that company's products is a secondary boycott. A secondary boycott brings pressure on third parties to force them to stop dealing with an employer who is being struck.

Perhaps the most famous provision of the Taft-Hartley Act allows the president to obtain a court injunction that will stop a strike for an 80-day cooling-off period if the strike is expected to imperil the nation's safety or health.

The Current Status of U.S. Labor Unions

As shown in Figure 29-1 below, union membership has been declining in the United States since the 1960s. At present, slightly less than 12 percent of U.S. workers are union members. Less than 8 percent of workers in the private sector belong to unions.

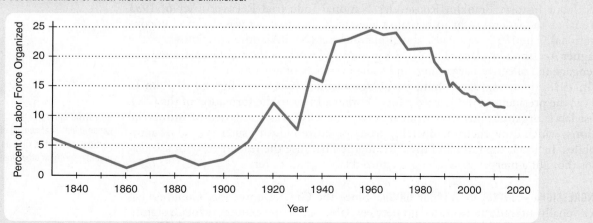

FIGURE 29-1

Decline in Union Membership

Numerically, union membership in the United States has increased dramatically since the 1930s, but as a percentage of the labor force, union membership peaked around 1960 and has been falling ever since. Most recently, the absolute number of union members has also diminished.

Sources: L. Davis et al., *American Economic Growth* (New York: HarperCollins, 1972), p. 220; U.S. Department of Labor, Bureau of Labor Statistics.

TABLE 29-1

The Ten Largest Unions in the United States

Half of the top ten U.S. unions have members who work in service and government occupations.

Union	Industry	Members
National Education Association	Education	2,731,000
Service Employees International Union	Health care, public, and janitorial services	1,505,000
American Federation of State, County, and Municipal Employees	Government services	1,460,000
International Brotherhood of Teamsters	Trucking, delivery	1,396,000
United Food and Commercial Workers International Union	Food and grocery services	1,312,000
American Federation of Teachers	Education	829,000
United Steelworkers of America	Steel	755,000
International Brotherhood of Electrical Workers	Electrical	705,000
Laborers' International Union of North America	Construction, utilities	670,000
International Association of Machinists and Aerospace Workers	Machine and aerospace	654,000

Source: U.S. Department of Labor.

A DECLINE IN MANUFACTURING EMPLOYMENT A large part of the explanation for the decline in union membership has to do with the shift away from manufacturing. In 1948, workers in manufacturing industries, transportation, and utilities, which traditionally have been among the most heavily unionized industries, constituted more than half of private nonagricultural employment. Today, that fraction is less than one-fifth.

The relative decline in manufacturing employment helps explain why most of the largest U.S. unions now draw their members primarily from workers in service industries and governments. As you can see in Table 29-1 above, five of the ten largest unions now represent workers in these areas. The remaining five largest unions do still represent the manufacturing industries, transportation, and utilities that once dominated the U.S. union movement.

DEREGULATION AND IMMIGRATION The trend away from manufacturing is the main reason for the decline in unionism. Nevertheless, the deregulation of certain industries, such as airlines and trucking, has also contributed, as has increased global competition. In addition, immigration has weakened the power of unions. Much of the unskilled and typically nonunionized work in the United States is done by foreign-born workers, and immigrant workers who are undocumented cannot legally join a union.

CHANGES IN THE STRUCTURE OF THE U.S. UNION MOVEMENT After its founding in 1955, the AFL-CIO remained the predominant labor union organization for 50 years. In 2005, however, seven unions with more than 45 percent of total AFL-CIO membership broke off to form a separate union organization called Change to Win. More recently, two construction industry unions also left the AFL-CIO and joined with ironworkers and bricklayers unions to form the National Construction Alliance.

Unions in these new umbrella groups, which represent mainly workers in growing service industries, had become frustrated because they felt that the AFL-CIO was not working hard enough to expand union membership. In addition, some of these unions were more interested than the AFL-CIO in pursuing boycotts against companies viewed as anti-union, such as Walmart. These unions also sought strikes against industries trying to slow the growth of union membership, such as the hotel industry.

The _____ _____ of _____, composed of **craft unions,** was formed in 1886 under the leadership of Samuel Gompers. Membership increased until after World War I, when the government temporarily stopped protecting labor's right to organize.

During the Great Depression, legislation was passed that allowed for **collective bargaining.** The _____ _____ _____ Act of 1935 guaranteed workers

the right to form unions. The Congress of Industrial Organizations (CIO), composed of _____ unions, was formed during the Great Depression. The AFL and the CIO merged in 1955.

In the United States, union membership as a percentage of the labor force peaked at nearly _____ percent in 1960 and has declined since then to less than _____ percent.

Union Goals and Strategies

Through collective bargaining, unions establish the wages below which no individual worker may legally offer his or her services. Each year, union representatives and management negotiate collective bargaining contracts covering wages as well as working conditions and fringe benefits for about 5 million workers. If approved by the members, a union labor contract sets wage rates, maximum workdays, working conditions, fringe benefits, and other matters, usually for the next two or three years.

Strike: The Ultimate Bargaining Tool

Whenever union-management negotiations break down, union negotiators may turn to their ultimate bargaining tool, the threat or the reality of a strike. Strikes make headlines, but a strike occurs in less than 2 percent of all labor-management disputes before the contract is signed. In the other 98 percent, contracts are signed without much public fanfare.

The purpose of a strike is to impose costs on stubborn management to force it to accept the union's proposed contract terms. Strikes disrupt production and interfere with a company's or an industry's ability to sell goods and services. The strike works both ways, though, because workers receive no wages while on strike (though they may be partly compensated out of union strike funds). Striking union workers may also be eligible to draw state unemployment benefits.

The impact of a strike is closely related to the ability of striking unions to prevent nonstriking (and perhaps nonunion) employees from continuing to work for the targeted company or industry. Therefore, steps are usually taken to prevent others from working for the employer. **Strikebreakers** can effectively destroy whatever bargaining power rests behind a strike. Numerous methods have been used to prevent strikebreakers from breaking strikes. Violence has been known to erupt, almost always in connection with union attempts to prevent strikebreaking.

In recent years, companies have had less incentive to hire strikebreakers because work stoppages have become much less common. From 1945 until 1990, on average more than 200 union strikes took place in the United States each year. Since 1990, however, the average has been closer to 25 strikes per year.

Why might a union perceive that a strike is successful even if it results in a pay cut for the union's membership?

Strikebreakers
Temporary or permanent workers hired by a company to replace union members who are striking.

EXAMPLE

Symphony Musicians "Win" a Lengthy Strike

Since 1887, the Detroit Symphony has been among the nation's highest-regarded orchestras. Recently, however, the symphony experienced a very protracted labor dispute: a six-month-long strike by violinists, violists,

cellists, bassists, percussionists, and players of woodwind and brass wind instruments.

Following the strike, the new three-year contract's minimum threshold for a musician's annual pay was $79,000, a reduction from $104,650 specified in the previous contract. In addition, the number of musicians playing in the orchestra was reduced from 96 to 81. Nevertheless, the symphony's union declared victory. The strike had achieved a net gain, union leaders proclaimed, over management's opening offer of a pay cut in excess of 40 percent. The leaders concluded that achieving a pay cut of only 25 percent—plus preserving existing health care and pension benefits for the union's members—constituted a substantial achievement.

FOR CRITICAL THINKING

Taking all outcomes into account, including the fact that Detroit Symphony musicians earned no wages during the six-month period of the strike, do you think the union's "victory" was as substantial as claimed?

Union Goals with Direct Wage Setting

We have already pointed out that one of the goals of unions is to set minimum wages. The effects of setting a wage rate higher than a competitive market clearing wage rate can be seen in Figure 29-2 below. The market for labor initially is perfectly competitive. The market demand curve is D, and the market supply curve is S. The market clearing wage rate is W_e. The equilibrium quantity of labor is Q_e. If a union is formed and establishes by collective bargaining a minimum wage rate that exceeds W_e, an excess quantity of labor will be supplied (assuming no change in the labor demand schedule). If the minimum wage established by union collective bargaining is W_U, the quantity supplied will be Q_S. The quantity demanded will be Q_D. The difference is the excess quantity supplied, or surplus. Hence, the following point becomes clear:

> *One of the major roles of a union that establishes a wage rate above the market clearing wage rate is to ration available jobs among the excess number of workers who wish to work in the unionized industry.*

Note also that the surplus of labor is equivalent to a shortage of jobs at wage rates above equilibrium.

To ration jobs, the union may use a seniority system, lengthen the apprenticeship period to discourage potential members from joining, or institute other rationing methods. This has the effect of shifting the supply of labor curve to the left in order to support the higher wage, W_U.

There is a trade-off here that any union's leadership must face: Higher wages inevitably mean a reduction in total union employment—fewer union positions. When facing higher wages, management may replace part of the workforce with machinery or may even seek to hire nonunion workers.

FIGURE 29-2

Unions Must Ration Jobs

The market clearing wage rate is W_e, at point E, at which the equilibrium quantity of labor is Q_e. If the union succeeds in obtaining wage rate W_U, the quantity of labor demanded will be Q_D, at point A on the labor demand curve, but the quantity of labor supplied will be Q_S, at point B on the labor supply curve. The union must ration a limited number of jobs among a greater number of workers. The surplus of labor is equivalent to a shortage of jobs at that wage rate.

FIGURE 29-3

What Do Unions Maximize?

Assume that the union wants to employ all its Q_1 members. It will attempt to get wage rate W_1. If the union wants to maximize total wage receipts (income) of members who have jobs in this industry, it will do so at wage rate W_2, where the elasticity of the demand for labor is equal to 1. (The blue-shaded area represents the maximum total income that the union membership would earn at W_2.) If the union wants to maximize the wage rate for a given number of workers, say, Q_3, it will set the wage rate at W_3.

Three Possible Union Goals

If we view unions as monopoly sellers of a service, we can identify three different goals that they may pursue: ensuring employment for all members of the union, maximizing aggregate income of workers, and maximizing wage rates for some workers.

EMPLOYING ALL MEMBERS IN THE UNION Assume that the union has Q_1 workers. If it faces a labor demand curve such as D in Figure 29-3 above, the only way it can "sell" all of those workers' services is to accept a wage rate of W_1. As in any market, the demand curve tells the maximum price that can be charged to sell any particular quantity of a good or service. Here the service happens to be labor.

MAXIMIZING MEMBER INCOME If the union is interested in maximizing the gross income of its members, it will normally want a smaller membership than Q_1—namely, Q_2 workers, all employed and paid a wage rate of W_2. The aggregate income to all members of the union is represented by the wages of only the ones who work. Total income earned by union members is maximized where the price elasticity of demand is numerically equal to 1. That occurs where marginal revenue equals zero.

In Figure 29-3, marginal revenue equals zero at a quantity of labor Q_2. If the union obtains a wage rate equal to W_2, and therefore Q_2 union workers are demanded, their total income will be maximized. In other words, $Q_2 \times W_2$ (the blue-shaded area) will be greater than any other combination of wage rates and quantities of union workers demanded. It is, for example, greater than $Q_1 \times W_1$. Note that in this situation, if the union started out with Q_1 members, there would be $Q_1 - Q_2$ members out of *union* work at the wage rate W_2. (Those out of union work either remain unemployed or seek employment in other industries. Such actions have a depressing effect on wages in nonunion industries due to the increase in supply of workers there.)

MAXIMIZING WAGE RATES FOR CERTAIN WORKERS Assume that the union wants to maximize wage rates for some workers—perhaps those with the most seniority. If it wants to maximize the wage rate for a given quantity of workers, Q_3, it will seek a wage rate W_3. This will require deciding which workers should be unemployed and which workers should work and for how many hours they should be employed.

WHAT IF... the government required all workers to be unionized so that they could earn higher wages?

If all workers had to be unionized, then those who were employed would earn higher wages. Firms would demand less labor at these above-equilibrium wages, however. Consequently, more people would be unemployed in an all-unionized economy. In addition, firms' average and marginal costs would be higher. Some firms would find continued operations unprofitable in the long run and hence would exit their industries. Those firms that remained in business would produce fewer goods and services, resulting in higher prices for consumers.

Union Strategies to Raise Wages Indirectly

One way or another, unions seek above-market wages for some or all of their members. Sometimes unions try to achieve this goal without making wage increases direct features of contract negotiations.

LIMITING ENTRY OVER TIME One way to raise wage rates without specifically setting wages is for a union to limit the size of its membership to the size of its employed workforce at the time the union was first organized. No workers are put out of work when the union is formed. Over time, as the demand for labor in the industry increases, the union prevents any net increase in membership, so larger wage increases are obtained than would otherwise be the case. We see this in Figure 29-4 below. In this example, union members freeze entry into their union, thereby obtaining a wage rate of $24 per hour instead of allowing a wage rate of only $22 per hour with no restriction on labor supply.

ALTERING THE DEMAND FOR UNION LABOR Another way that unions can increase wages is to shift the demand curve for labor outward to the right. This approach has the advantage of increasing both wage rates and the employment level. The demand for union labor can be increased by increasing worker productivity, increasing the demand for union-made goods, and decreasing the demand for non-union-made goods.

1. *Increasing worker productivity.* Supporters of unions have argued that unions provide a good system of industrial jurisprudence. The presence of unions may induce workers to feel that they are working in fair and just circumstances. If so, they work harder, increasing labor productivity. Productivity is also increased when unions

YOU ARE THERE

To consider what a recent hiring decision by a Washington, D.C., carpenters' union revealed about its strategies and objectives, read **A Union Hires a Nonunion Picketer to Protest Nonunion Hiring** on page 656.

FIGURE 29-4

Restricting Supply over Time

When the union was formed, it didn't affect wage rates or employment, which remained at $20 and Q_1 (the equilibrium wage rate and quantity at point E_1). As demand increased—that is, as the demand schedule shifted outward from D_1 to D_2—the union restricted membership to its original level of Q_1, however. The new supply curve is S_1S_2, which intersects D_2 at E_2, or at a wage rate of $24. Without the union, equilibrium would be at E_3, with a wage rate of $22 and employment of Q_2.

resolve differences and reduce conflicts between workers and management, thereby providing a more peaceful administrative environment.

2. *Increasing demand for union-made goods.* Because the demand for labor is a derived demand, a rise in the demand for products produced by union labor will increase the demand for union labor itself. One way that unions attempt to increase the demand for goods produced by union labor is by advertising "Look for the union label."

3. *Decreasing the demand for non-union-made goods.* When the demand for goods that are competing with (or are substitutes for) union-made goods is reduced, consumers shift to union-made goods, increasing the demand. The campaigns of various unions against buying foreign imports are a good example. The result is greater demand for goods "made in the USA," which in turn presumably increases the demand for U.S. union (and nonunion) labor.

Economic Effects of Labor Unions

Today, the most heavily unionized occupations are government service, transportation and material moving, and construction. Do union members in these and other occupations earn higher wages? Are they more or less productive than nonunionized workers in their industries? What are the broader economic effects of unionization? Let's consider each of these questions in turn.

Unions and Wages

You have learned that unions are able to raise the wages of their members if they can successfully limit the supply of labor in a particular industry. Unions are also able to raise wages if they can induce increases in the demand for union labor.

Economists have extensively studied the differences between union wages and nonunion wages. They have found that the average *hourly* wage (not including benefits) earned by a typical private-sector union worker is about $2.25 higher than the hourly wage earned by a typical worker who is not a union member. Adjusted for inflation, this union-nonunion hourly wage differential is only about half as large as it was two decades ago, however.

Comparisons of the *annual* earnings of union and nonunion workers indicate that in recent years, unions have *not* succeeded in raising the annual incomes of their members. In 1985, workers who belonged to unions earned nearly 7 percent more per year than nonunion workers, even though union workers worked fewer hours per week. Today, a typical nonunion employee still works slightly longer each week, but the average nonunion worker also has a higher annual income than the average union worker.

Even the $2.25 hourly wage differential already mentioned is somewhat misleading because it is an average across *all* U.S. workers. In the private sector, union workers earn only about 4 percent more than nonunion workers, or a little less than 60 cents per hour. The hourly wage gain for government workers is more than six times higher at about $3.55 per hour. A state government employee who belongs to a union currently earns an hourly wage more than 20 percent higher than a state government worker who is not a union member.

Unions and Labor Productivity

A traditional view of union behavior is that unions decrease productivity by artificially shifting the demand curve for union labor outward through excessive staffing and make-work requirements. For example, some economists have traditionally argued that unions tend to bargain for excessive use of workers, as when an airline union requires an engineer on all flights. This is called **featherbedding**. Many painters' unions, for example, resisted the use of paint sprayers and required that their members use only brushes. They even specified the maximum width of the brush. Moreover, whenever a union strikes, productivity drops, and this reduction in productivity in one sector of the economy can spill over into other sectors.

Featherbedding
Any practice that forces employers to use more labor than they would otherwise or to use existing labor in an inefficient manner.

Economic Benefits and Costs of Labor Unions

As should be clear by now, there are two opposing views of unions. One sees them as monopolies whose main effect is to raise the wage rate of high-seniority members at the expense of low-seniority members (and nonunion workers). The other contends that unions can increase labor productivity by promoting safer working conditions and generally better work environments. According to this view, unions contribute to workforce stability by providing arbitration and grievance procedures.

Critics point out that the positive view of unionism overlooks the fact that many of the benefits that unions provide do not require that unions engage in restrictive labor practices, such as the closed shop (see page 644). Unions could still provide benefits for their members without restricting the labor market.

Consequently, a key issue that economists seek to assess when judging the social costs of unions is the extent to which their existence has a negative effect on employment growth. Most evidence indicates that while unions do significantly reduce employment in some of the most heavily unionized occupations, the overall effects on U.S. employment are modest. On the whole, therefore, the social costs of unions in the U.S. *private* sector are probably relatively low.

Why is the overall compensation of unionized government workers much higher than the total compensation of private employees?

INTERNATIONAL EXAMPLE

The Global Public-Union Benefits Explosion

Many people are surprised that nearly 40 percent of U.S. government workers are unionized, but in many nations the union share of public employees is even higher. In the United Kingdom, 56 percent of government workers belong to unions, and in Canada and Ireland, about 70 percent of government employees do. In Scandinavian countries, public-sector unionization shares exceed 80 percent.

Benefits provided to unionized public workforces also have expanded. In the United Kingdom, government workers log an average of 23 percent *fewer* hours than private workers, mainly because government workers have lower retirement ages. In Brazil, police officers can retire with pensions after 15 years, and female public school teachers can receive retirement pensions following 25 years of service. In addition, easy eligibility for "disability retirements" boosts retirement income for many public workers, including 90 percent of workers for government-owned Long Island Rail Road in New York and 82 percent of California state troopers. When benefits are included in tabulating workers' overall compensation packages, unionized public workers earn at least 70 percent more than private employees.

FOR CRITICAL THINKING

Who pays for the benefits of government workers around the world?

QUICK QUIZ   See page 662 for the answers. Review concepts from this section in MyEconLab.

When unions set wage rates _____ market clearing prices, they face the problem of _____ a restricted number of jobs to workers who desire to earn the higher wages.

Unions may pursue any one of three goals: (1) to employ _____ union members, (2) to maximize total _____ of the union's members, or (3) to _____ wages for certain, usually high-seniority, workers.

Unions can increase the wage rate of members by engaging in practices that shift the union labor supply curve _____ or shift the demand curve for union labor _____ (or both).

Some economists believe that unions can increase _____ by promoting safer working conditions and generally better work environments.

Monopsony: A Buyer's Monopoly

Let's assume that a firm is a perfect competitor in the product market. The firm cannot alter the price of the product it sells, and it faces a perfectly elastic demand curve for its product. We also assume that the firm is the only buyer of a particular input. Although this situation may not occur often, it is useful to consider. Let's think in terms of a factory town, like those that used to be dominated by textile mills or those

Monopsonist
The only buyer in a market.

in the mining industry. One company not only hires the workers but also owns the businesses in the community, owns the apartments that workers live in, and hires the clerks, waiters, and all other personnel. This buyer of labor is called a **monopsonist,** the only buyer in the market.

What does this situation mean to a monopsonist in terms of the costs of hiring extra workers? It means that if the monopsonist wants to hire more workers, it has to offer higher wages. Our monopsonist firm cannot hire all the labor it wants at the going wage rate. Instead, it faces an upward-sloping supply curve. If it wants to hire more workers, it has to raise wage rates, including the wages of all its current workers (assuming a non-wage-discriminating monopsonist). It therefore has to take account of these increased costs when deciding how many more workers to hire.

Marginal Factor Cost

The monopsonist faces an upward-sloping supply curve of the input in question because as the only buyer, it faces the entire market supply curve. Each time the monopsonist buyer of labor, for example, wishes to hire more workers, it must raise wage rates. Thus, the marginal cost of another unit of labor is rising. In fact, the marginal cost of increasing its workforce will always be greater than the wage rate. This is because the monopsonist must pay the same wage rate to everyone in order to obtain another unit of labor. Consequently, the higher wage rate has to be offered not only to the last worker but also to *all* its other workers. We call the additional cost to the monopsonist of hiring one more worker the marginal factor cost (MFC).

The marginal factor cost of hiring the last worker is therefore that worker's wages plus the increase in the wages of all other existing workers. As we pointed out in Chapter 28, marginal factor cost is equal to the change in total variable costs due to a one-unit change in the one variable factor of production—in this case, labor. In Chapter 28, marginal factor cost was simply the competitive wage rate because the employer could hire all workers at the same wage rate.

Derivation of a Marginal Factor Cost Curve

Panel (a) of Figure 29-5 on the facing page shows the quantity of labor purchased, the wage rate per hour, the total cost of the quantity of labor supplied per hour, and the marginal factor cost per hour for the additional labor bought.

We translate the columns from panel (a) to the graph in panel (b) of the figure. We show the supply curve as S, which is taken from columns 1 and 2. The marginal factor cost curve (MFC) is taken from columns 1 and 4. The MFC curve must be above the supply curve whenever the supply curve is upward sloping. If the supply curve is upward sloping, the firm must pay a higher wage rate in order to attract a larger amount of labor. This higher wage rate must be paid to all workers. Thus, the increase in total costs due to an increase in the labor input will exceed the wage rate. (Recall from Chapter 28 that in a perfectly competitive input market, in contrast, the supply curve facing the firm is perfectly elastic and the marginal factor cost curve is identical to the supply curve.)

Employment and Wages under Monopsony

To determine the number of workers that a monopsonist desires to hire, we compare the marginal benefit to the marginal cost of each hiring decision. The marginal cost is the marginal factor cost (MFC) curve, and the marginal benefit is the marginal revenue product (MRP) curve. In Figure 29-6 on page 654, we assume competition in the output market and monopsony in the input market. A monopsonist finds its profit-maximizing quantity of labor demanded at A, where the marginal revenue product is just equal to the marginal factor cost. The monopsonist will therefore desire to hire exactly Q_m workers.

FIGURE 29-5

Derivation of a Marginal Factor Cost Curve

The supply curve, S, in panel (b) is taken from columns 1 and 2 of panel (a). The marginal factor cost curve (MFC) is taken from columns 1 and 4. It is the increase in the total wage bill resulting from a one-unit increase in labor input.

Panel (a)

(1) Quantity of Labor Supplied to Management	(2) Required Hourly Wage Rate	(3) Total Wage Bill (3) = (1) x (2)	(4) Marginal Factor Cost (MFC) = $\frac{\text{Change in (3)}}{\text{Change in (1)}}$
0	—	—	
			$12
1	$12	$12	
			16
2	14	28	
			20
3	16	48	
			24
4	18	72	
			28
5	20	100	
			32
6	22	132	

THE INPUT PRICE PAID BY A MONOPSONY How much is the firm going to pay these workers? The monopsonist sets the wage rate so that it will get exactly the quantity, Q_m, supplied to it by its "captive" labor force. We find that wage rate is W_m. There is no reason to pay the workers any more than W_m because at that wage rate, the firm can get exactly the quantity it wants. The actual quantity used is determined by the intersection of the marginal factor cost curve and the marginal revenue product curve for labor—that is, at the point at which the marginal revenue from expanding employment just equals the marginal cost of doing so (point A in Figure 29-6 on the following page).

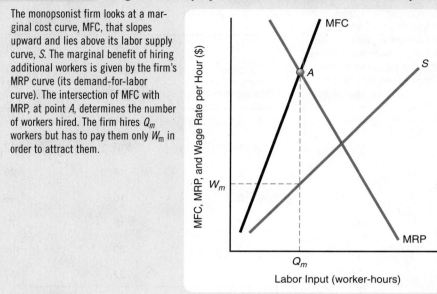

FIGURE 29-6

Wage and Employment Determination for a Monopsonist

The monopsonist firm looks at a marginal cost curve, MFC, that slopes upward and lies above its labor supply curve, S. The marginal benefit of hiring additional workers is given by the firm's MRP curve (its demand-for-labor curve). The intersection of MFC with MRP, at point A, determines the number of workers hired. The firm hires Q_m workers but has to pay them only W_m in order to attract them.

Notice that the profit-maximizing wage rate paid to workers (W_m) is lower than the marginal revenue product. That is to say, workers are paid a wage that is less than their contribution to the monopsonist's revenues. This is sometimes referred to as **monopsonistic exploitation** of labor.

You learned in Chapter 4 that in a perfectly competitive labor market, establishing a minimum wage rate above the market clearing wage rate causes employers to reduce the quantity of labor demanded, resulting in a decline in employment. What happens if a minimum wage rate is established above the wage rate that a *monopsony* would otherwise pay its workers?

Monopsonistic exploitation

Paying a price for the variable input that is less than its marginal revenue product; the difference between marginal revenue product and the wage rate.

POLICY EXAMPLE

Can Minimum Wage Laws Ever Boost Employment?

How does a monopsony respond to a minimum wage law that sets a wage floor above the wage rate it otherwise would pay its workers? Figure 29-7 on the facing page provides the answer to this question. In the figure, the entire upward-sloping curve labeled S is the labor supply curve in the absence of a minimum wage. Given the associated MFC curve and the firm's MRP curve, Q_m is the quantity of labor hired by a monopsony in the absence of a minimum wage law. The profit-maximizing wage rate is W_m.

If the government establishes a minimum wage equal to W_{min}, however, then the supply of labor to the firm becomes horizontal at the minimum wage and includes only the upward-sloping portion of the curve S above this legal minimum. In addition, the wage rate W_{min} becomes the monopsonist's marginal factor cost along the horizontal portion of this new labor supply curve, because when the firm hires one more unit of labor, it must pay each unit of labor the same wage rate, W_{min}.

To maximize its economic profits under the minimum wage, the monopsony equalizes the minimum wage rate with marginal revenue product and hires Q_{min} units of labor. This quantity exceeds the amount of labor, Q_m, that the monopsony would have hired in the absence of the minimum wage law. Thus, establishing a minimum wage can generate a rise in employment at a monopsony firm.

FOR CRITICAL THINKING

If a government establishes a minimum wage law covering all firms within its jurisdiction, including firms operating in both perfectly competitive and monopsonistic labor markets, will overall employment necessarily increase?

FIGURE 29-7

A Monopsony's Response to a Minimum Wage

In the absence of a minimum wage law, a monopsony faces the upward-sloping labor supply curve, S, and the marginal factor cost curve, MFC. To maximize its profits, the monopsony hires Q_m units of labor, at which MFC is equal to MRP, and it pays the wage rate W_m. Once the minimum wage rate, W_{min}, is established, the supply of labor becomes horizontal at the minimum wage and includes only the upward-sloping portion of the labor supply curve above this legal minimum. The monopsony must pay the same wage rate W_{min} for each unit of labor along this horizontal portion of the new labor supply curve, so its marginal factor cost is also equal to the minimum wage rate, W_{min}. Thus, the monopsony hires Q_{min} units of labor. Employment at the monopsony firm increases.

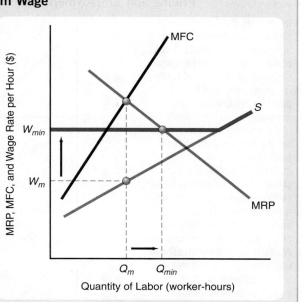

BILATERAL MONOPOLY We have studied the pricing of labor in various situations, including perfect competition in both the output and input markets and monopoly in both the output and input markets. Figure 29-8 on the following page shows four possible situations graphically.

The organization of workers into a union normally creates a monopoly supplier of labor, which gives the union some power to bargain for higher wages. What happens when a monopsonist meets a monopolist? This situation is called **bilateral monopoly,** defined as a market structure in which a single buyer faces a single seller. An example of bilateral monopoly is a county education employer facing a single teachers' union in that labor market. Another example is a players' union facing an organized group of team owners, as has occurred in professional baseball and football. To analyze bilateral monopoly, we would have to look at the interaction of both sides, buyer and seller. The wage outcome turns out to be indeterminate.

Bilateral monopoly
A market structure consisting of a monopolist and a monopsonist.

QUICK QUIZ

See page 662 for the answers. Review concepts from this section in MyEconLab.

A **monopsonist** is the _____ _____ in a market. The monopsonist faces an _____-sloping supply curve of labor.

Because the monopsonist faces an _____-sloping supply curve of labor, the marginal factor cost of increasing the labor input by one unit is _____ than the wage rate. Thus, the marginal factor cost curve always lies _____ the supply curve.

A monopsonist will hire workers up to the point at which marginal _____ cost equals marginal _____ product. Then the monopsonist will find the lowest necessary wage to attract that number of workers, as indicated by the supply curve.

FIGURE 29-8

Pricing and Employment under Various Market Conditions

In panel (a), the firm operates in perfect competition in both the input and output markets. It purchases labor up to the point where the going rate W_e is equal to MRP_c. It hires quantity Q_e of labor. In panel (b), the firm is a perfect competitor in the input market but has a monopoly in the output market. It purchases labor up to the point where W_e is equal to MRP_m. In panel (c), the firm is a monopsonist in the input market and a perfect competitor in the output market. It hires labor up to the point where $MFC = MRP_c$. It will hire quantity Q_1 and pay wage rate W_c. Panel (d) shows a situation in which the firm is both a monopolist in the market for its output and a monopsonist in its labor market. It hires the quantity of labor Q_2 at which $MFC = MRP_m$ and pays the wage rate W_m.

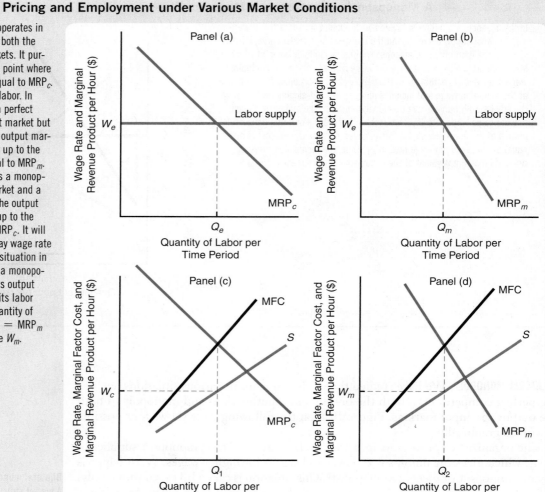

YOU ARE THERE
A Union Hires a Nonunion Picketer to Protest Nonunion Hiring

After months of not working, Billy Raye, a 51-year-old unemployed bicycle courier, has finally found a short-term position. His new job is with the Mid-Atlantic Regional Council of Carpenters (MARCC), a union that is paying him to march and chant in a picket line outside an office complex in Washington, D.C. The union's hired picketers are protesting a building contractor's decision to employ nonunionized workers to work on the buildings. Regarding his picketing job, Raye says, "I could care less. I am being paid to march around and sound off."

By hiring Raye and numerous other picketers at the minimum wage of $8.25 per hour, the MARCC has revealed both a strategy and an objective. The strategy is to try to raise wages for its members by increasing the demand for union members by contractors. The objective is to maximize

the net incomes of all its members by hiring low-paid, non-union picketers instead of its own higher-wage union members.

Critical Thinking Questions

1. Why is hiring nonunion picketers at the minimum wage rate likely more consistent with maximizing net incomes of MARCC members than is hiring members of some other union to serve as picketers?

2. Why do you suppose that many unions hire nonunionized staff employees who earn market wages less than those typically available to unionized staff people?

ISSUES & APPLICATIONS

Gauging Labor Lost to Union Disputes Each Year

CONCEPTS APPLIED

▶ Labor Unions

▶ Collective Bargaining

▶ Strikes

Labor unions rely on their relatively large numbers of members in relation to employers' overall employment levels. Strikes and other union-directed work stoppages are crucial weapons that unions can use in their efforts to induce employers to engage in collective bargaining that benefits union members.

Millions of Hours of Work Lost to Union Disputes Globally

On a worldwide basis, more than 10 million days of labor are lost to union disputes each year. This number of lost days is equivalent to idling about 40,000 workers for a full year.

Figure 29-9 below displays how the days of work lost to labor disputes are distributed across various nations. The figure shows that in Canada, South Africa, France, and Spain, union-directed work stoppages cost employers more than 1 million days of labor.

FIGURE 29-9

U.S. firms lose a total of about 300,000 days of work to disputes with labor unions, which is several times smaller than the losses of working days in Canada, South Africa, France, and Spain.

Source: International Labor Organization.

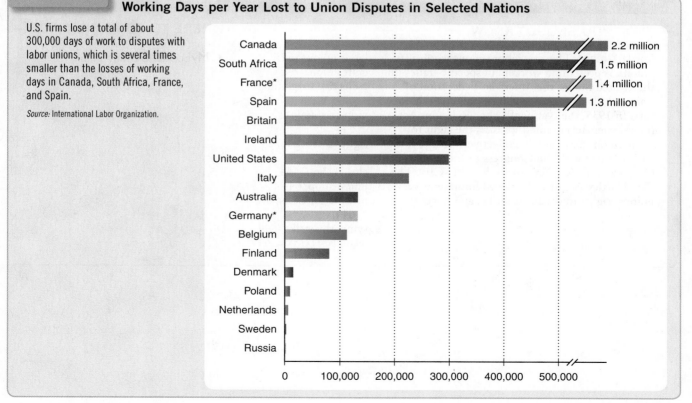

Working Days per Year Lost to Union Disputes in Selected Nations

Canada — 2.2 million
South Africa — 1.5 million
France* — 1.4 million
Spain — 1.3 million
Britain
Ireland
United States
Italy
Australia
Germany*
Belgium
Finland
Denmark
Poland
Netherlands
Sweden
Russia

0   100,000   200,000   300,000   400,000   500,000

"Only" 300,000 Lost U.S. Labor Days

Figure 29-9 on the previous page also indicates that union disputes reduce labor time at U.S. firms by about 300,000 days annually. Thus, losses of labor time caused by union work stoppages are smaller in the United States than in several other nations.

Nevertheless, at the 2013 average hourly wage rate of $24, these hours of lost labor otherwise would have generated more than $58 million of labor income. At current rates of household spending, this amount of income could provide sufficient food to sustain nearly 10,000 U.S. households every year. Consequently, the opportunity cost of labor lost each year to U.S. union disputes is far from inconsequential.

For Critical Thinking

1. How could union members' current *annual* incomes decline on net even if a long-lived strike induces a firm's management to increase the *hourly* wage rate?

2. Sometimes union memberships coordinate work stoppages when all workers call in sick. From an economic standpoint, is there any difference between coordinated sick-day work stoppages and strikes? Explain.

Web Resources

1. To see that the annual amount of labor lost to disputes in Canada are actually lower than in years past, go to **www.econtoday.com/chap29**.

2. For the latest statistics on union work stoppages in the United States, go to **www.econtoday.com/chap29**.

MyEconLab

For more questions on this chapter's Issues & Applications, go to MyEconLab. In the Study Plan for this chapter, select Section N: News.

MyEconLab

Here is what you should know after reading this chapter. MyEconLab will help you identify what you know, and where to go when you need to practice.

WHAT YOU SHOULD KNOW

Labor Unions The first labor unions were craft unions, representing workers in specific trades. In the United States, the American Federation of Labor (AFL) emerged in the late nineteenth century. In 1935, the National Labor Relations Act (or Wagner Act) granted workers the right to form unions and bargain collectively. In 1955, the AFL merged with the Congress of Industrial Organizations (CIO) to form the AFL-CIO. The Taft-Hartley Act of 1947 placed limitations on unions' rights to organize, strike, and boycott.

labor unions, 643
craft unions, 643
collective bargaining, 643
industrial unions, 643
right-to-work laws, 644
closed shop, 644
union shop, 644
jurisdictional dispute, 644
sympathy strike, 644
secondary boycott, 644

WHERE TO GO TO PRACTICE

- MyEconLab Study Plan 29.1

MyEconLab *continued*

WHAT YOU SHOULD KNOW		WHERE TO GO TO PRACTICE
The Current Status of Labor Unions A key reason for an ongoing decline in U.S. union membership rates is the relative decline in manufacturing jobs as a share of total employment. Greater domestic and global competition has also had a part in bringing about a decline in unions.		• MyEconLab Study Plan 29.1
Basic Goals and Strategies of Labor Unions A key goal of most unions is to achieve higher wages. Often this entails bargaining for wages above competitive levels, which produces surplus labor. Thus, a major task of many unions is to ration available jobs. Unions often address this trade-off between wages and the number of jobs by maximizing the total income of members. Strategies to raise wages indirectly include placing limits on the entry of new workers, increasing worker productivity, and lobbying consumers to increase their demands for union-produced goods.	strikebreakers, 646 **Key Figures** Figure 29-2, 647 Figure 29-3, 648 Figure 29-4, 649	• MyEconLab Study Plan 29.2 • Animated Figures 29-2, 29-3, 29-4
Effects of Labor Unions on Wages and Productivity On average, union hourly wages are higher than wages of nonunionized workers. Unionized employees typically work fewer hours per year, however, so their average annual earnings are lower than those of nonunionized employees. Some collective bargaining rules specifying how jobs are performed appear to reduce productivity, but unionization promotes generally better work environments, which may enhance productivity.	featherbedding, 650	• MyEconLab Study Plan 29.3
How a Monopsonist Determines How Much Labor to Employ and What Wage Rate to Pay For a monopsonist, which is the only buyer of an input such as labor, paying a higher wage to attract an additional unit of labor increases total factor costs for all other labor employed. The monopsonist employs labor to the point at which the marginal factor cost of labor equals the marginal revenue product of labor. It then pays workers the wage at which they are willing to work, as determined by the labor supply curve, which is less than marginal factor cost and marginal revenue product.	monopsonist, 652 monopsonistic exploitation, 654 bilateral monopoly, 655 **Key Figures** Figure 29-5, 653 Figure 29-6, 654 Figure 29-7, 655	• MyEconLab Study Plan 29.4 • Animated Figures 29-5, 29-6, 29-7

Comparing a Monopsonist's Wage and Employment Decisions with Choices by Firms in Industries with Other Market Structures Perfectly competitive firms take the wage rate as market determined. A product market monopolist tends to employ fewer workers, but the product market monopolist nonetheless cannot affect the market wage rate. In contrast, a monopsonist is the only employer of labor, so it searches for the wage rate that maximizes its profit. This wage rate is less than the marginal revenue product of labor. If a firm is both a product market monopolist and a labor market monopsonist, its demand for labor is also lower than it would be if the firm's product market were competitive, so the firm hires fewer workers as well.

Key Figure
Figure 29-8, 656

- **MyEconLab** Study Plan 29.4
- Animated Figure 29-8

Log in to **MyEconLab**, take a chapter test, and get a personalized Study Plan that tells you which concepts you understand and which ones you need to review. From there, **MyEconLab** will give you further practice, tutorials, animations, videos, and guided solutions. For more information, visit www.myeconlab.com

PROBLEMS

All problems are assignable in MyEconLab. *Answers to the odd-numbered problems appear at the back of the book.*

29-1. Discuss three aspects of collective bargaining that society might deem desirable. (See pages 650–651.)

29-2. Give three reasons why a government might seek to limit the power of a union. (See pages 650–651.)

29-3. The Writers Guild of America (WGA), which represents TV and film screenwriters, called for a strike, and most screenwriters stopped working. Nevertheless, writers for certain TV soap operas, such as *The Young and the Restless*—which have had shrinking audiences for years, draw small numbers of viewers for repeat shows, and rarely sell on Blu-ray discs—opted to drop their WGA memberships and tried to continue working during the strike. Why do you suppose that the WGA posted on its Web site a phone number for union members to report "strike-breaking activities and 'scab writing'" to the union's 12-person Strike Rules Compliance Committee? What effect do strikebreakers have on the collective bargaining power of a union? (See page 646.)

29-4. Suppose that the objective of a union is to maximize the total dues paid to the union by its membership.

Explain the union's strategy, in terms of the wage level and employment level, under the following two scenarios. (See page 648.)

   a. Union dues are a percentage of total earnings of the union membership.

   b. Union dues are paid as a flat amount per union member employed.

29-5. Explain why, in economic terms, the total income of union membership is maximized when marginal revenue is zero. (See page 648. Hint: How much more revenue is forthcoming when marginal revenue is equal to zero?)

29-6. Explain the impact of each of the following events on the market for union labor. (See pages 649–450.)

   a. Union-produced TV and radio commercials convince consumers to buy domestically manufactured clothing instead of imported clothing.

   b. The union sponsors periodic training programs that instruct union laborers about the most efficient use of machinery and tools.

29-7. Why are unions in industries in which inputs such as machines are poor substitutes for labor more likely to be able to bargain for wages higher than market levels? (See pages 649–650.)

29-8. How is it possible for the average annual earnings of nonunionized workers to exceed those of unionized workers even though unionized workers' hourly wages are more than $2 higher? (See page 650.)

29-9. In the short run, a tool manufacturer has a fixed amount of capital. Labor is a variable input. The cost and output structure that the firm faces is depicted in the following table:

Labor Supplied	Total Physical Product	Hourly Wage Rate ($)
10	100	5
11	109	6
12	116	7
13	121	8
14	124	9
15	125	10

Derive the firm's total wage costs and marginal factor cost at each level of labor supplied. (See pages 652–653.)

29-10. Suppose that for the firm in Problem 29-9, the goods market is perfectly competitive. The market price of the product the firm produces is $4 at each quantity supplied by the firm. What is the amount of labor that this profit-maximizing firm will hire, and what wage rate will it pay? (See page 653.)

29-11. The price and wage structure that a firm faces is depicted in the following table.

Labor Supplied	Total Physical Product	Hourly Wage Rate ($)	Product Price ($)
10	100	5	3.11
11	109	6	3.00
12	116	7	2.95
13	121	8	2.92
14	124	9	2.90
15	125	10	2.89

The firm finds that the price of its product changes with the rate of output. In addition, the wage it pays its workers varies with the amount of labor it employs. This firm maximizes profits. How many units of labor will it hire? What wage will it pay? (See pages 652–653.)

29-12. What is the amount of monopsonistic exploitation that takes place at the firm examined in Problem 29-11? (See page 654.)

29-13. A profit-maximizing clothing producer in a remote area is the only employer of people in that area. It sells its clothing in a perfectly competitive market. The firm pays each worker the same weekly wage rate. The last worker hired raised the firm's total weekly wage expenses from $105,600 to $106,480. What is the marginal revenue product of the last worker hired by this firm if it is maximizing profits? (See pages 652–653.)

29-14. Why does marginal factor cost increase as a monopsonistic firm utilizes more labor but remain unchanged as a perfectly competitive firm employs additional labor? (See pages 652–653.)

29-15. Why does a monopsonistic firm pay the last unit of labor that it employs a wage that is less than that unit's marginal revenue product? (See page 654.)

29-16. A single firm is the only employer in a labor market. The marginal revenue product, labor supply, and marginal factor cost curves that it faces are displayed in the diagram below. Use this information to answer the following questions. (See pages 652–653.)

a. How many units of labor will this firm employ in order to maximize its economic profits?

b. What hourly wage rate will this firm pay its workers?

c. What is the total amount of wage payments that this firm will make to its workers each hour?

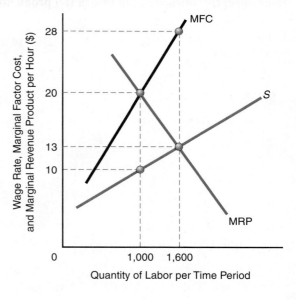

ECONOMICS ON THE NET

Evaluating Union Goals As discussed in this chapter, unions can pursue any of a number of goals. The AFL-CIO's home page provides links to the Web sites of several unions, and reviewing these sites can help you determine the objectives these unions have selected.

Title: American Federation of Labor–Congress of Industrial Organizations

Navigation: Go to www.econtoday.com/chap29 to visit the AFL-CIO's home page.

Application Perform the indicated operations, and answer the following questions.

1. Click on the pop-up menu at *About AFL-CIO*, and then click on *Mission Statement*. Does the AFL-CIO claim to represent the interests of all workers or just

workers in specific firms or industries? Can you discern what broad wage and employment strategy the AFL-CIO pursues?

2. Click on *AFL-CIO Unions*. Explore two or three of these Web sites. Do these unions appear to represent the interests of all workers or just workers in specific firms or industries? What general wage and employment strategies do these unions appear to pursue?

For Group Study and Analysis Divide up all the unions affiliated with the AFL-CIO among groups, and have each group explore the Web sites listed under *AFL-CIO Unions* at the AFL-CIO Web site. Have each group report on the wage and employment strategies that appear to prevail for the unions it examined.

ANSWERS TO QUICK QUIZZES

p. 646: (i) American Federation . . . Labor; (ii) National Labor Relations . . . industrial; (iii) 25 . . . 12

p. 651: (i) above . . . rationing; (ii) all . . . income . . . maximize; (iii) inward . . . outward; (iv) productivity

p. 655: (i) only buyer . . . upward; (ii) upward . . . greater . . . above; (iii) factor . . . revenue

Income, Poverty, and Health Care

30

MyEconLab helps you master each objective and study more efficiently. See end of chapter for details.

LEARNING OBJECTIVES

After reading this chapter, you should be able to:

▶ Describe how to use a Lorenz curve to represent a nation's income distribution

▶ Identify the key determinants of income differences across individuals

▶ Discuss theories of desired income distribution

▶ Distinguish among alternative approaches to measuring and addressing poverty

▶ Recognize the role played by third-party payments in rising health care costs

▶ Explain the key elements of the new U.S. national health insurance program and evaluate its potential economic effects

Three decades ago, a typical female worker in the United States earned an annual rate of income equivalent to 63 percent of the income received by an average male worker. In contrast, today the average woman's annual earnings are almost 83 percent of those of a typical man's. How has an upswing in educational attainment by women helped to account for the movement toward income equality between the two genders? Why do some economists suggest that if women continue to earn a majority of college and university degrees, average annual earnings of female workers may eventually surpass those of male workers? By the time you have completed this chapter, you will understand the answers to these questions.

? **DID YOU KNOW THAT...**

today, only 51 percent of adult U.S. residents are married, compared with 72 percent in 1960? A number of economic elements have contributed to the decrease in the number of married adults. For instance, the U.S. income tax code includes a "marriage penalty" under which the overall tax rate imposed on two married people is higher than they would face separately if unmarried. In addition, the national health care plan that went into place in 2013 also discourages marriage by lower-income individuals. For example, single people earning $43,000 per year each are eligible for government-subsidized health care under the new program, but married people earning a combined $86,000 annual income are not.

Among the most important economic elements leading to a lower number of married adults is that so many more young people now perceive a college education to be crucial for improving their future income prospects. Today, many individuals between the ages of 18 and 24 put off marriage to pursue education at colleges and technical schools. This fact helps explain why only 9 percent of people in this age group marry, compared with 45 percent in 1960.

Economists have found that the number of people marrying and the ages at which they do so have substantial effects on the **distribution of income**—the way that income is allocated among the population. Economists have devised various theories to explain income distribution. We will present some of these theories in this chapter. We will also present some of the more obvious institutional reasons why income is not distributed equally in the United States. In addition, we will examine the health care problems confronting individuals in all income groups and how the federal government's new health care program proposes to solve these problems.

Distribution of income
The way income is allocated among the population based on groupings of residents.

Income

Income provides each of us with the means of consuming and saving. Income can be the result of a payment for labor services or a payment for ownership of one of the other factors of production besides labor—land, physical capital, or entrepreneurship. In addition, individuals obtain spendable income from gifts and government transfers. (Some individuals also obtain income by stealing, but we will not treat this matter here.) Right now, let's examine how money income is distributed across classes of income earners within the United States.

Measuring Income Distribution: The Lorenz Curve

Lorenz curve
A geometric representation of the distribution of income. A Lorenz curve that is perfectly straight represents complete income equality. The more bowed a Lorenz curve, the more unequally income is distributed.

We can represent the distribution of money income graphically with what is known as the **Lorenz curve,** named after a U.S.-born statistician, Max Otto Lorenz, who proposed it in 1905. The Lorenz curve shows what share of total money income is accounted for by different proportions of the nation's households. Look at Figure 30-1 on the facing page. On the horizontal axis, we measure the *cumulative* percentage of households, lowest-income households first. Starting at the left corner, there are zero households. At the right corner, we have 100 percent of households. In the middle, we have 50 percent of households. The vertical axis represents the cumulative percentage of money income. The 45-degree line represents complete equality: 50 percent of the households obtain 50 percent of total income, 60 percent of the households obtain 60 percent of total income, and so on. Of course, in no real-world situation is there such complete equality of income. No actual Lorenz curve would be a straight line.

Rather, it would be some curved line, like the one labeled "Actual money income distribution" in Figure 30-1. For example, the bottom 50 percent of households in the United States receive about 22 percent of total money income.

In Figure 30-2 on the facing page, we again show the actual money income distribution Lorenz curve for the United States, and we also compare it to the distribution of money income in 1929. Since that year, the Lorenz curve has generally become less bowed. That is, it has moved closer to the line of complete equality.

Income in kind
Income received in the form of goods and services, such as housing or medical care. Income in kind differs from money income, which is simply income in dollars, or general purchasing power, that can be used to buy *any* goods and services.

CRITICISMS OF THE LORENZ CURVE In recent years, economists have placed less and less emphasis on the shape of the Lorenz curve as an indication of the degree of income inequality in a country. There are five basic reasons why the Lorenz curve has been criticized:

1. The Lorenz curve is typically presented in terms of the distribution of *money* income only. It does not include **income in kind,** such as government-provided food

FIGURE 30-1

The Lorenz Curve

The horizontal axis measures the cumulative percentage of households, with lowest-income households first, from 0 to 100 percent. The vertical axis measures the cumulative percentage of money income from 0 to 100. A straight line at a 45-degree angle cuts the box in half and represents a line of complete income equality, along which 25 percent of the families get 25 percent of the money income, 50 percent get 50 percent, and so on. The observed Lorenz curve, showing the actual U.S. money income distribution, is not a straight line but rather a curved line as shown. The difference between complete money income equality and the Lorenz curve is the inequality gap.

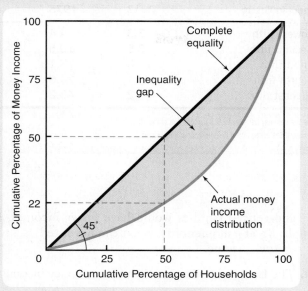

FIGURE 30-2

Lorenz Curves of Income Distribution, 1929 and 2013

Since 1929, the Lorenz curve has moved inward toward the straight line of perfect income equality.

Source: U.S. Department of Commerce.

stamps, education, medical care, or housing aid, and goods or services produced and consumed in the home or on the farm.

2. The Lorenz curve does not account for differences in the size of households or the number of wage earners they contain.

3. It does not account for age differences. Even if all families in the United States had exactly the same *lifetime* incomes, chances are that young families would have modest incomes, middle-aged families would have relatively high incomes,

TABLE 30-1

Percentage Share of Money Income for Households before Direct Taxes

Income Group	2013	1975	1960	1947
Lowest fifth	3.3	4.4	4.8	5.1
Second fifth	8.5	10.5	12.2	11.8
Third fifth	14.6	17.1	17.8	16.7
Fourth fifth	23.4	24.8	24.0	23.2
Highest fifth	50.2	43.2	41.3	43.3

Note: Figures may not sum to 100 percent due to rounding.
Sources: U.S. Bureau of the Census; author's estimates.

and retired families would have lower incomes. Because the Lorenz curve is drawn at a moment in time, it can never tell us anything about the inequality of *lifetime* income.

4. The Lorenz curve ordinarily reflects money income *before* taxes.

5. It does not measure unreported income from the underground economy, a substantial source of income for some individuals.

Income Distribution in the United States

Go to www.econtoday/chap30 to view the U.S. Census Bureau's most recent data on the U.S. income distribution. Click on the most recent year next to "Money Income in the United States."

In Table 30-1 above, we see the percentage share of income for households before direct taxes. The table groups households according to whether they are in the lowest 20 percent of the income distribution, the second lowest 20 percent, and so on. We see that in 2013, the lowest 20 percent had an estimated combined money income of 3.3 percent of the total money income of the entire population. This is less than the lowest 20 percent had at the end of World War II.

Accordingly, some have concluded that the distribution of money income has become slightly more unequal. *Money* income, however, understates *total* income for individuals who receive in-kind transfers from the government in the form of food stamps, public housing, education, and the like. In particular, since World War II, the share of *total* income—money income plus in-kind benefits—going to the bottom 20 percent of households has more than doubled.

To what extent do shares of income shift among different groups of U.S. residents over the course of a decade?

EXAMPLE

U.S. Residents Move among Income Groups over Time

Gerald Auten and Geoffrey Gee of the U.S. Department of the Treasury recently examined the mobility of people across the distribution of income during the 1987–1996 and 1996–2005 decades. The Treasury economists found that within a given 10-year period, about 57 percent of people initially receiving money incomes placing them in the lowest 20 percent moved into the group with the next-highest 20 percent of incomes. Furthermore, the average money incomes of people who began with incomes among the top 20 percent declined within each decade. Indeed, people initially within the group receiving the highest 1 percent of incomes were most likely, of all U.S. residents, to drop into a lower-income group. Thus, there is evidence of considerable mobility of individuals within the U.S. income distribution over periods of a decade or longer.

FOR CRITICAL THINKING

How might well-intentioned policies that reduce incentives for lower-income people to make human capital investments reduce upward mobility within the income distribution?

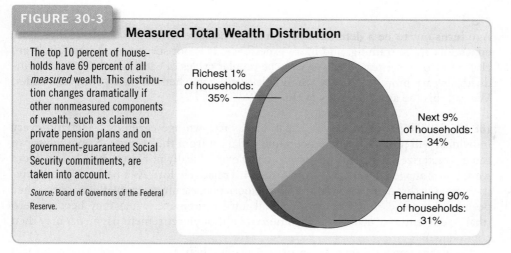

FIGURE 30-3

Measured Total Wealth Distribution

The top 10 percent of households have 69 percent of all *measured* wealth. This distribution changes dramatically if other nonmeasured components of wealth, such as claims on private pension plans and on government-guaranteed Social Security commitments, are taken into account.

Source: Board of Governors of the Federal Reserve.

Richest 1% of households: 35%

Next 9% of households: 34%

Remaining 90% of households: 31%

The Distribution of Wealth

When referring to the distribution of income, we must realize that income—a flow—can be viewed as a return on wealth (both human and nonhuman)—a stock. A discussion of the distribution of income is not necessarily the same thing as a discussion of the distribution of wealth, however. A complete concept of wealth would include not only tangible objects, such as buildings, machinery, land, cars, and houses—nonhuman wealth—but also people who have skills, knowledge, initiative, talents, and the like—human wealth. The total of human and nonhuman wealth in the United States makes up our nation's capital stock.

Figure 30-3 above shows that the richest 10 percent of U.S. households hold more than two-thirds of all *measured* wealth. The problem with those data gathered by the Federal Reserve System, however, is that they do not include many important assets. One of these assets is workers' claims on private pension plans, which equal at least $4 trillion. If you add the value of these pensions, household wealth increases by almost 25 percent and reveals that many more U.S. households are middle-wealth households (popularly known as the *middle class*). Another asset excluded from the data is anticipated claims on the Social Security system, which tend to comprise a larger share of the wealth of lower-income individuals.

QUICK QUIZ   See page 687 for the answers. Review concepts from this section in MyEconLab.

The **Lorenz curve** graphically represents the distribution of _____. If it is a straight line, there is complete _____ of income. The more it is bowed, the more _____ income is distributed.

The distribution of wealth is not the same as the distribution of income. Wealth includes _____ such as

houses, stocks, and bonds. Although the apparent distribution of wealth seems to be _____ concentrated at the top than income, the data used are not very accurate, and most summary statistics fail to take account of workers' claims on private and public pensions, which are substantial.

Determinants of Income Differences

We know that there are income differences—that is not in dispute. A more important question is why these differences in income occur. We will look at four determinants of income differences: age, productivity, inheritance, and discrimination.

Age

Age turns out to be a determinant of income because with age come, usually, more education, more training, and more experience. It is not surprising that within every class of income earners, there seem to be regular cycles of earning behavior. Most individuals earn more when they are middle-aged than when they are younger or older. We call this the **age-earnings cycle.**

THE AGE-EARNINGS CYCLE Every occupation has its own age-earnings cycle, and every individual will probably experience some variation from the average. Nonetheless, we can characterize the typical age-earnings cycle graphically in Figure 30-4 below. Here we see that at age 18, earnings from wages are relatively low. As a person's productivity increases through more training and experience, earnings gradually rise until they peak at about age 50. Then earnings fall until retirement, when they become zero (that is, currently earned wages become zero, although retirement payments may then commence).

Note that general increases in overall productivity for the entire workforce will result in an upward shift in the typical age-earnings profile depicted in Figure 30-4. Thus, even at the end of the age-earnings cycle, when just about to retire, the worker would receive a relatively high wage compared with the starting wage 45 years earlier. The wage would be higher due to factors that contribute to rising real wages for everyone, regardless of the stage in the age-earnings cycle.

Now we have some idea why specific individuals earn different incomes at different times in their lives, but we have yet to explain why different people are paid different amounts for their labor. One way to explain this is to recall the marginal productivity theory developed in Chapter 28.

Marginal Productivity

When trying to determine how many workers a firm would hire, we had to construct a marginal revenue product curve. We found that as more workers were hired, the marginal revenue product fell due to diminishing marginal product. If the forces of demand and supply established a certain wage rate, workers would be hired until their marginal physical product times marginal revenue (which equals the market price under perfect competition) was equal to the going wage rate. Then the hiring would stop. This analysis suggests what workers can expect to be paid in the labor market: As long as there are low-cost information flows and the labor and product markets are competitive, each worker can expect to be paid his or her marginal revenue product.

Age-earnings cycle
The regular earnings profile of an individual throughout his or her lifetime. The age-earnings cycle usually starts with a low income, builds gradually to a peak at around age 50, and then gradually curves down until it approaches zero at retirement.

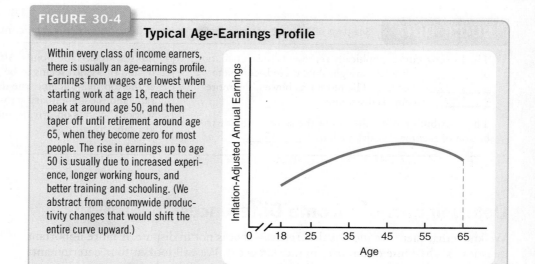

FIGURE 30-4

Typical Age-Earnings Profile

Within every class of income earners, there is usually an age-earnings profile. Earnings from wages are lowest when starting work at age 18, reach their peak at around age 50, and then taper off until retirement around age 65, when they become zero for most people. The rise in earnings up to age 50 is usually due to increased experience, longer working hours, and better training and schooling. (We abstract from economywide productivity changes that would shift the entire curve upward.)

DETERMINANTS OF MARGINAL PRODUCTIVITY According to marginal revenue product theory, if people can increase their marginal physical product, they can expect to earn higher incomes. Key determinants of marginal physical product are talent, experience, and training.

Talent Talent is the easiest factor to explain, but it is difficult to acquire if you don't have it. Innate abilities and attributes can be very strong, if not overwhelming, determinants of a person's potential productivity. Strength, coordination, and mental alertness are facets of nonacquired human capital and thus have some bearing on the ability to earn income. Someone who is tall and agile has a better chance of being a basketball player than someone who is short and unathletic. A person born with a superior talent for abstract thinking has a better chance of earning a relatively high income as a mathematician or a physicist than someone who is not born with that capability.

Experience Additional experience at particular tasks is another way to increase productivity. Experience can be linked to the well-known *learning curve* that applies when the same task is done over and over. The worker repeating a task becomes more efficient: The worker can do the task in less time or in the same amount of time but better. Take an example of a person going to work on an automobile assembly line. At first she is able to fasten only three bolts every two minutes. Then the worker becomes more adept and can fasten four bolts in the same time plus insert a rubber guard on the bumper. After a few more weeks, another task can be added. Experience allows this individual to improve her productivity. The more effectively people learn to do something, the more productive they are.

Training Training is similar to experience but is more formal. Much of a person's increased productivity is due to on-the-job training. Many companies have training programs for new workers.

INVESTMENT IN HUMAN CAPITAL Investment in human capital is just like investment in anything else. If you invest in yourself by going to college, rather than going to work after high school and earning more current income, you will presumably be rewarded in the future with a higher income or a more interesting job (or both). This is exactly the motivation that underlies the decision of many college-bound students to obtain formal higher education.

As with other investments, we can determine the rate of return on an investment in a college education. To do so, we first have to figure out the marginal cost of going to school. The cost is not simply what you have to pay for books, fees, and tuition but also includes the income you forgo. *A key cost of education is the income forgone—the opportunity cost of not working.* In addition, the direct expenses of college must be paid for. Certainly, not all students forgo all income during their college years. Many work part time. Taking account of those who work part time and those who are supported by tuition grants and other scholarships, the average rate of return on going to college ranges between 6 and 8 percent per year. The gain in lifetime income has a present value ranging from $200,000 to more than $500,000.

Inheritance

It is not unusual to inherit cash, jewelry, stocks, bonds, homes, or other real estate. Yet only about 10 percent of income inequality in the United States can be traced to differences in inherited wealth. If for some reason the government confiscated all property that had been inherited, the immediate result would be only a modest change in the distribution of income in the United States. In any event, at both federal and state levels substantial inheritance taxes generally are levied on the estates of relatively wealthy deceased Americans (although there are some legally valid ways to avoid certain estate taxes).

YOU ARE THERE

To contemplate the income earnings that a person can forgo by failing to invest in human capital, take a look at **A Portuguese Woman Rethinks Her Human Capital Investment** on page 681.

Discrimination

Economic discrimination occurs whenever workers with the same marginal revenue product receive unequal pay due to some noneconomic factor such as their race, gender, or age. It is possible—and indeed quite obvious—that discrimination affects the distribution of income. Certain groups in our society are not paid wages at rates comparable to those received by other groups, even when we correct for productivity. Differences in income remain between whites and nonwhites and between men and women. For example, the median income of black families is about 65 percent that of white families. The average wage rate of women is about 83 percent that of men. Some people argue that all of these differences are due to discrimination against nonwhites and against women.

We cannot simply assume that *any* differences in income are due to discrimination, though. What we need to do is discover why differences in income between groups exist and then determine if factors other than discrimination in the labor market can explain them. The unexplained part of income differences can rightfully be considered the result of discrimination.

Theories of Desired Income Distribution

We have talked about the factors affecting the distribution of income, but we have not yet mentioned the normative issue of how income *ought* to be distributed. This, of course, requires a value judgment. We are talking about the problem of economic justice. We can never completely resolve this problem because there are always going to be conflicting values. It is impossible to give all people what each thinks is just. Nonetheless, two particular normative standards for the distribution of income have been popular with economists. These are income distribution based on productivity and income distribution based on equality.

Productivity

The *productivity standard* for the distribution of income can be stated simply as "To each according to what he or she produces." This is also called the *contributive standard* because it is based on the principle of rewarding according to the contribution to society's total output. It is also sometimes referred to as the *merit standard* and is one of the oldest concepts of justice. People are rewarded according to merit, and merit is judged by one's ability to produce what is considered useful by society.

We measure a person's productive contribution in a capitalist system by the market value of that person's output. We have already referred to this as the marginal revenue product theory of wage determination.

Equality

The *egalitarian principle* of income distribution is simply "To each exactly the same." Everyone would have exactly the same amount of income. This criterion of income distribution has been debated as far back as biblical times. This system of income distribution has been considered equitable, meaning that presumably everybody is dealt with fairly and equally. There are problems, however, with an income distribution that is completely equal.

Some jobs are more unpleasant or more dangerous than others. Should the people undertaking these jobs be paid exactly the same as everyone else? Indeed, under an equal distribution of income, what incentive would there be for individuals to take risky, hazardous, or unpleasant jobs at all? What about overtime? Who would be willing to work overtime without additional pay? There is yet another problem: If everyone earned the same income, what incentive would there be for individuals to invest in their own human capital—a costly and time-consuming process?

Just consider the incentive structure within a corporation. Within corporations, much of the differential between, say, the pay of the CEO and the pay of all of the vice presidents is meant to create competition among the vice presidents for the CEO's job.

The result is higher productivity. If all incomes were the same, much of this competition would disappear, and productivity would fall.

There is some evidence that differences in income lead to higher rates of economic growth. Future generations are therefore made better off. Elimination of income differences may reduce the rate of economic growth and cause future generations to be poorer than they otherwise might have been.

QUICK QUIZ See page 687 for the answers. Review concepts from this section in MyEconLab.

Most people follow an _____-_____ cycle in which they earn relatively small incomes when they first start working, increase their incomes until about age 50, and then slowly experience a decrease in their real incomes as they approach retirement.

According to the marginal _____ theory of wages, workers can expect to be paid their marginal _____ product.

Marginal physical productivity depends on _____, _____, and _____.

Going to school and receiving on-the-job training can be considered an investment in _____ capital. A key cost of education is the _____ cost of not working.

Two normative standards for income distribution are income distribution based on _____ and income distribution based on _____.

Poverty and Attempts to Eliminate It

Throughout the history of the world, mass poverty has been accepted as inevitable. This nation and others, particularly in the Western world, however, have sustained enough economic growth in the past several hundred years so that *mass* poverty can no longer be said to be a problem for these fortunate countries. As a matter of fact, the residual of poverty in the United States strikes us as bizarre, an anomaly. How can there still be so much poverty in a nation of such abundance? Having talked about the determinants of the distribution of income, we now have at least some ideas of why some people are destined to remain low-income earners throughout their lives.

Income can be transferred from the relatively well-to-do to the relatively poor by various methods, and as a nation we have been using them for a long time. Today, we have a vast array of welfare programs set up for the purpose of redistributing income. As we know, however, these programs have not been entirely successful. Are there alternatives to our current welfare system? Is there a better method of helping the poor? Before we answer these questions, take a look at Figure 30-5 on the following page, which displays the percentage of the U.S. population determined to be in a state of poverty by the U.S. government. This percentage, called the *poverty rate*, has varied between roughly 11 percent and 16 percent since 1965.

Defining Poverty

The threshold income level, which is used to determine who falls into the poverty category, was originally based on the cost of a nutritionally adequate food plan designed by the U.S. Department of Agriculture. The threshold was determined by multiplying the food plan cost by 3 on the assumption that food expenses comprise approximately one-third of a poor family's income. Annual revisions of the threshold level were based only on price changes in the food budget.

In 1969, a federal interagency committee looked at the calculations of the threshold and decided to set new standards, with adjustments made on the basis of changes in the Consumer Price Index. For example, in 2013, the official poverty level for an urban family of four was around $23,000. It typically goes up each year to reflect whatever inflation has occurred.

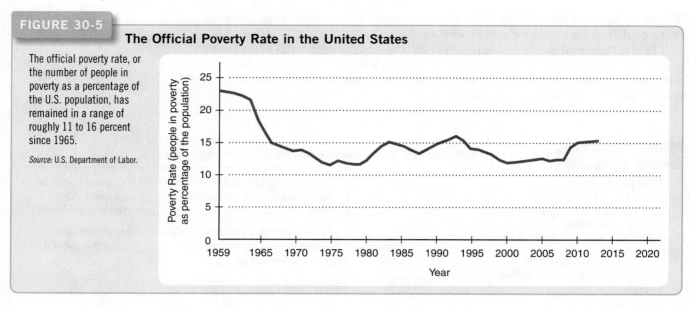

The Official Poverty Rate in the United States

The official poverty rate, or the number of people in poverty as a percentage of the U.S. population, has remained in a range of roughly 11 to 16 percent since 1965.

Source: U.S. Department of Labor.

Go to www.econtoday.com/chap30 to learn about the World Bank's programs intended to combat global poverty.

Absolute Poverty

Because the low-income threshold is an absolute measure, we know that if it never changes in real terms, we will reduce poverty even if we do nothing. How can that be? The reasoning is straightforward. Real incomes in the United States have been growing at a compounded annual rate of almost 2 percent per capita for at least the past century and at about 2.5 percent since World War II. If we define the poverty line at a specific real income level, more and more individuals will make incomes that exceed that poverty line. Thus, in absolute terms, we will eliminate poverty (assuming continued per capita growth and no change in income distribution).

Relative Poverty

Be careful with this analysis, however. Poverty can also be defined in relative terms, that is, in terms of the income levels of individuals or families relative to the rest of the population. As long as the distribution of income is not perfectly equal, there will always be some people who make less income than others, even if their relatively low income is high by historical standards. Thus, in a relative sense, the problem of poverty will always exist.

Attacks on Poverty: Major Income Maintenance Programs

There are a variety of income maintenance programs designed to help the poor. We examine a few of them here.

SOCIAL SECURITY For the retired, the unemployed, and the disabled, social insurance programs provide income payments in prescribed situations. The best known is Social Security, which includes what has been called old-age, survivors', and disability insurance (OASDI). As discussed in Chapter 6, this was originally supposed to be a program of compulsory saving financed from payroll taxes levied on both employers and employees. Workers pay for Social Security while working and receive the benefits after retirement. The benefit payments are usually made to people who have reached retirement age. When the insured worker dies, benefits accrue to the survivors, including widows and children. Special benefits provide for disabled workers.

More than 90 percent of all employed persons in the United States are covered by OASDI. Today, Social Security is an intergenerational income transfer that is only vaguely related to past earnings. It transfers income from U.S. residents who work (the young through the middle-aged) to those who do not work—older retired persons.

In 2013, more than 55 million people were receiving OASDI checks averaging about $1,200 a month. Benefit payments from OASDI redistribute income to some degree. Benefit payments, however, are not based on recipient need. Participants' contributions give them the right to benefits even if they would be financially secure without the benefits. Social Security is not really an insurance program because people are not guaranteed that the benefits they receive will be in line with the "contributions" they have made. It is not a personal savings account. The benefits are legislated by Congress. In the future, Congress may not be as sympathetic toward older people as it is today. It could (and probably will have to) legislate for lower real levels of benefits instead of higher ones.

SUPPLEMENTAL SECURITY INCOME AND TEMPORARY ASSISTANCE TO NEEDY FAMILIES Many people who are poor but do not qualify for Social Security benefits are assisted through other programs. The federally financed and administered Supplemental Security Income (SSI) program was instituted in 1974. The purpose of SSI is to establish a nationwide minimum income for the aged, the blind, and the disabled. SSI has become one of the fastest-growing transfer programs in the United States. Whereas in 1974 less than $8 billion was spent, the prediction for 2014 is in excess of $60 billion. U.S. residents currently eligible for SSI include children and individuals with mental disabilities, including drug addicts and alcoholics.

Temporary Assistance to Needy Families (TANF) is a state-administered program, financed in part by federal grants. The program provides aid to families in need. TANF payments are intended to be temporary. Projected expenditures for TANF in 2013 are $35 billion.

SUPPLEMENTAL NUTRITION ASSISTANCE PROGRAM The Supplemental Nutrition Assistance Program (SNAP, commonly known as "food stamps") provides government-issued, electronic debit cards that can be used to purchase food. In 1964, some 367,000 Americans were receiving SNAP benefits. For 2013, the estimate is more than 47 million recipients. The annual cost has jumped from $860,000 to more than $80 billion. In 2013, almost one in every seven citizens (including children) was receiving SNAP benefits.

THE EARNED INCOME TAX CREDIT PROGRAM In 1975, the Earned Income Tax Credit (EITC) Program was created to provide rebates of Social Security taxes to low-income workers. More than one-fifth of all tax returns claim an earned income tax credit. Each year the federal government grants more than $46 billion in these credits. In some states, such as Mississippi, nearly half of all families are eligible for an EITC. The program works as follows: Single-income households with two children that report income of about $42,000 (exclusive of welfare payments) receive EITC benefits up to about $5,000.

There is a catch, though. Those with earnings up to a threshold of about $13,000 receive higher benefits as their incomes rise. But families earning more than this threshold income are penalized about 18 cents for every dollar they earn above the income threshold. Thus, on net the EITC discourages work by low- or moderate-income earners more than it rewards work. In particular, it discourages low-income earners from taking on second jobs. The Government Accountability Office estimates that hours worked by working wives in EITC-beneficiary households have consequently decreased by 15 percent. The average EITC recipient works 1,700 hours a year compared to a normal work year of about 2,000 hours.

No Apparent Reduction in Poverty Rates

In spite of the numerous programs in existence and the trillions of dollars transferred to the poor, the officially defined rate of poverty in the United States has shown no long-run tendency to decline. From 1945 until the 1970s, the percentage of U.S. residents in poverty fell steadily every year. As Figure 30-5 on the facing page shows, it reached a low of around 11 percent in 1974, shot back up beyond 15 percent in 1983, fell to nearly 12 percent by 2007, and has since risen above 15 percent once more. Why this pattern has emerged is a puzzle. Since the War on Poverty was launched under President Lyndon B. Johnson in 1965, more than $15 trillion has been transferred to the poor, and yet more U.S. residents are poor today than ever before. This fact created the political will to pass the Welfare Reform Act of 1996, putting limits on people's use of welfare. The law's goal has been to get people off public assistance and into jobs.

QUICK QUIZ See page 687 for the answers. Review concepts from this section in MyEconLab.

If poverty is defined in _____ terms, economic growth eventually decreases the number of officially defined poor. If poverty is defined in _____ terms, however, we will never eliminate it.

The percentage of people officially in poverty exhibits _____ apparent change over time because the official U.S. poverty measure is _____.

Major attacks on poverty have been made through social insurance programs, including _____ Security, _____ Security Income (SSI), Temporary Assistance to Needy Families, the _____ _____ tax credit, and the Supplemental _____ Assistance Program.

Health Care

It may seem strange to be reading about health care in a chapter on the distribution of income and poverty. Yet health care is intimately related to those two topics. For example, sometimes people become poor because they do not have adequate health insurance (or have none at all), fall ill, and deplete all of their wealth in obtaining medical care. Moreover, some individuals remain in certain jobs simply because their employer's health care package seems so good that they are afraid to change jobs and risk not being covered by health insurance in the process.

As you will see, much of the cause of the increased health care spending in the United States can be attributed to a change in the incentives that U.S. residents face. Finally, we will examine the economic impact of the new national health care program.

The U.S. Health Care Situation

Spending for health care is estimated to account for about 17 percent of U.S. real GDP. You can see from Figure 30-6 on the facing page that in 1965, about 6 percent of annual income was spent on health care, but that percentage has been increasing ever since.

WHY HAVE HEALTH CARE COSTS RISEN SO MUCH? There are numerous explanations for why health care costs have risen so much. At least one has to do with changing demographics: The U.S. population is getting older.

The Age–Health Care Expenditure Equation The top 5 percent of health care users incur more than 50 percent of all health costs. The bottom 70 percent of health care users account for only 10 percent of health care expenditures. Not surprisingly, the elderly make up most of the top users of health care services. Nursing home expenditures are made primarily by people older than 70. The use of hospitals is also dominated by the aged.

The U.S. population is aging steadily. More than 13 percent of the 315 million U.S. residents are over 65. It is estimated that by the year 2035, senior citizens will comprise about 22 percent of our population. This aging population stimulates the demand for health care. The elderly consume more than four times as much per capita health care services as the rest of the population. In short, whatever the demand for health care services is today, it is likely to be considerably higher in the future as the U.S. population ages.

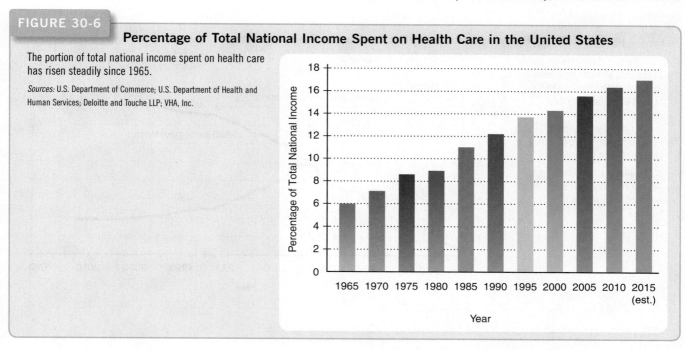

FIGURE 30-6

Percentage of Total National Income Spent on Health Care in the United States

The portion of total national income spent on health care has risen steadily since 1965.

Sources: U.S. Department of Commerce; U.S. Department of Health and Human Services; Deloitte and Touche LLP; VHA, Inc.

New Technologies Another reason that health care costs have risen so dramatically is advancing technology. Each CT (computerized tomography) scanner costs at least $100,000. An MRI (magnetic resonance imaging) scanner can cost over $2 million. A PET (positron emission tomography) scanner costs around $4 million. All of these machines have become increasingly available in recent decades and are desired throughout the country. Typical fees for procedures using them range from $300 to $400 for a CT scan to as high as $2,000 for a PET scan. The development of new technologies that help physicians and hospitals prolong human life is an ongoing process in an ever-advancing industry. New procedures at even higher prices can be expected in the future.

WHAT IF... the government forced lower spending on health care by placing legal limits on prices?

Legal ceilings on prices of health care services would reduce the quantities of services offered by physicians and hospitals, which would indeed generate a decrease in total annual expenditures on health care. By definition, of course, the resulting reductions in health care services would be associated with the inability of many people to obtain, at legally limited prices, care for painful and potentially deadly illnesses or injuries.

Third-Party Financing Currently, government spending on health care constitutes more than 40 percent of total health care spending (of which *federal* taxpayers fund about 70 percent). Private insurance funded by consumers' premium payments accounts for a little over 35 percent of payments for health care. The remainder—less than 20 percent—is paid out of pocket by individuals. Figure 30-7 on the following page shows the change in the payment scheme for medical care in the United States since 1930. Medicare and Medicaid are the main sources of hospital and other medical benefits for more than 40 million U.S. residents, most of whom are over 65. Medicaid—the joint state-federal program—provides long-term health care, particularly for people living in nursing homes.

Third-Party versus Out-of-Pocket Health Care Payments

Out-of-pocket payments for health care services have been falling steadily since the 1930s. In contrast, third-party payments for health care have risen to the point that they account for more than 80 percent of all such outlays today.

Sources: Health Care Financing Administration; U.S. Department of Health and Human Services.

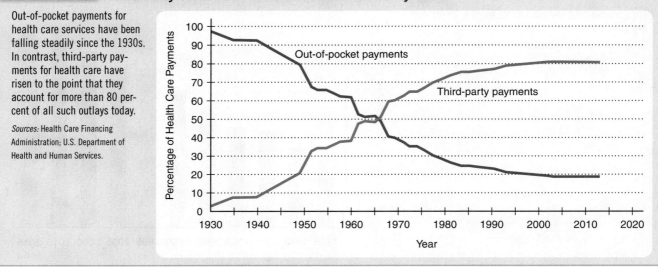

Third parties

Parties who are not directly involved in a given activity or transaction. For example, in the relationship between caregivers and patients, fees may be paid by third parties (insurance companies, government).

Medicare, Medicaid, and private insurance companies are considered **third parties** in the medical care equation. Caregivers and patients are the two primary parties. When third parties step in to pay for medical care, the quantity demanded of those services increases. For example, within four years after Medicare went into effect in 1966, the volume of federal government–reimbursed medical services increased to a level 65 percent higher than anticipated when the program was enacted.

PRICE, QUANTITY DEMANDED, AND THE QUESTION OF MORAL HAZARD Although some people may think that the demand for health care is insensitive to price changes, significant increases in quantities of medical services demanded follow reductions in people's out-of-pocket costs. Look at Figure 30-8 below. There you see a hypothetical demand curve for health care services. To the extent that third parties—whether government or private insurance—pay for health care, the out-of-pocket cost, or net price, to the individual decreases. If all medical expenses were paid for by third parties, dropping the price to zero in Figure 30-8, the quantity demanded would increase.

The Demand for Health Care Services

At price P_1, the quantity of health care services demanded per year would hypothetically be Q_1. If the price fell to zero (third-party payment with zero deductible), the quantity demanded would expand to Q_2.

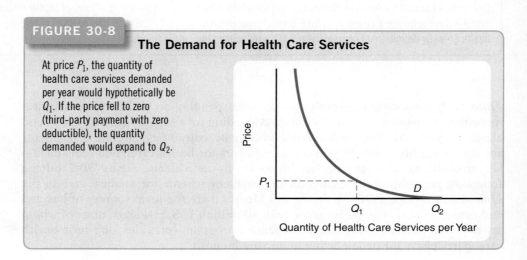

One of the issues here has to do with the problem of *moral hazard*. Consider two individuals with two different health insurance policies. The first policy pays for all medical expenses, but under the second, the individual has to pay the first $1,000 a year (this amount is known as the *deductible*). Will the behavior of the two individuals be different? Generally, the answer is yes.

The individual with no deductible is more likely to seek treatment for health problems after they develop rather than try to avoid them and will generally seek medical attention on a more regular basis. In contrast, the individual who faces the first $1,000 of medical expenses each year will tend to engage in more wellness activities and will be less inclined to seek medical care for minor problems. The moral hazard here is that the individual with the zero deductible for medical care expenses will tend to engage in a less healthful lifestyle than will the individual with the $1,000 deductible.

MORAL HAZARD AS IT AFFECTS PHYSICIANS AND HOSPITALS The issue of moral hazard also has a direct effect on the behavior of physicians and hospital administrators. Due to third-party payments, patients rarely have to worry about the expense of operations and other medical procedures. As a consequence, both physicians and hospitals order more procedures. Physicians are typically reimbursed on the basis of medical procedures. Thus, they have no financial interest in trying to keep hospital costs down. Indeed, many have an incentive to increase costs.

Such actions are most evident with terminally ill patients. A physician may order a CT scan and other costly procedures for a terminally ill patient. The physician knows that Medicare or some other type of insurance will pay. Then the physician can charge a fee for analyzing the CT scan. Fully 30 percent of Medicare expenditures are for U.S. residents who are in the last six months of their lives.

Rising Medicare expenditures are one of the most serious problems facing the federal government today. The number of beneficiaries has increased from 19.1 million in 1966 (first year of operation) to more than 40 million in 2013. Figure 30-9 below shows that federal spending on Medicare has been growing at an average of about 10 percent per year, adjusted for inflation. The rate of growth in Medicare spending has further increased as a result of the Medicare prescription drug benefit that was implemented in 2006.

FIGURE 30-9

Federal Medicare Spending

Federal spending on Medicare has increased about 10 percent per year, *after adjusting for inflation*, since its inception in 1966. (All figures expressed in constant 2005 dollars per year.)

Sources: Economic Report of the President; U.S. Bureau of Labor Statistics.

How are people who receive "dual coverage" from both Medicare and Medicaid pushing up the federal government's overall health care expenses?

POLICY EXAMPLE

Dual Coverage Drives Up Federal Health Care Spending

At present, 61 million elderly and disabled people are enrolled in Medicare, and 65 million low-income people are covered by Medicaid. Both groups of people include about 10 million individuals who qualify for "dual coverage," meaning that their health care expenses are eligible for coverage by *both* federal programs simultaneously. Poor administrative coordination between Medicare and Medicaid gives a health care provider an incentive to send a bill for each service provided to a dual-coverage patient to whichever program reimburses the service at a higher rate. This fact helps explain why dual-coverage patients generate one-third of the federal government's total combined spending on Medicare and Medicaid.

FOR CRITICAL THINKING
Why do you suppose that most health care economists agree that tens of billions of dollars per year could be slashed from federal spending if the Medicare and Medicaid programs offered identical reimbursements to health care providers?

The Nationalization of U.S. Health Care Spending

In March 2010, President Barack Obama signed a roughly 2,000-page law that will govern the future operation of U.S. health care markets. Before we contemplate the law's likely effect on the economics of health care, let's review its key features.

GOVERNMENT HEALTH INSURANCE MANDATES Table 30-2 on the facing page summarizes the fundamental components of the federal government's new national health care program, which is to be phased in through the mid-2010s. The first two elements of the program are restraints on choices of individuals and families and on decisions of employers. People must either purchase health insurance or pay a fine to the federal government. Thus, a young person in good health who otherwise might have opted not to purchase health insurance must buy insurance or pay a penalty (tax).

In addition, firms with more than 50 employees must either provide health insurance or pay fines when uninsured employees receive tax subsidies to purchase insurance. A firm that otherwise would have hired another worker but determines that the additional cost imposed by the health care program pushes the overall cost above the individual's marginal revenue product will choose not to hire that person.

GOVERNMENT HEALTH CARE SUBSIDIES Another fundamental feature is federal health care subsidies. The government's subsidies vary based on individual and family incomes. The national health care program directs more relatively low-income people into the Medicaid program by raising the maximum-income threshold for government-provided health care to 133 percent of the official poverty level. As a result, millions of people may now qualify for the Medicaid program's coverage of health care with very few out-of-pocket payments (depending on their state).

Other individuals and families earning incomes as high as four times the official poverty income level receive *tax subsidies*. These are reductions in federal tax payments intended to assist these people in covering required expenditures on health insurance. Thus, some families with incomes exceeding $100,000 per year will receive tax breaks of about $2,400—some of their own income that the government will allow them to keep and direct to satisfying its requirement to buy health insurance. Lower-income families not eligible for Medicaid coverage receive larger tax subsidies. Finally, the program also offers tax credits to businesses that provide health insurance to 25 or fewer workers who receive an average salary of no more than $50,000 per year.

TABLE 30-2

Key Components of the Federal Government's National Health Care Program

Individual mandate	Nearly all U.S. residents must either purchase health insurance coverage or pay a fine (tax) of up to $750 per year for an individual (up to $2,250 per year for a family).
Employer mandate	Firms with more than 50 employees must offer health insurance coverage or pay an annual fine of up to $750 per employee who obtains federal subsidies for coverage.
Health care insurance subsidies	1. Families with incomes up to 133% of the federal poverty level may be eligible for federal Medicaid coverage. 2. Families with incomes up to 400% of the federal poverty level are eligible for thousands of dollars in tax subsidies per year (amounts vary with family incomes). 3. Tax credits are available to businesses providing health insurance to 25 or fewer workers and paying annual salaries averaging no more than $50,000.
National health insurance exchanges	Government-directed exchanges will assist in matching individuals and small businesses with health insurance policies that satisfy government requirements.
Health insurance regulations	1. All private health insurance plans must satisfy a number of federal rules and regulations. 2. Health insurers must cover all who apply, including people who already have health problems. 3. Ceilings are placed on health insurance premium increases for elderly people.
Higher tax rates to help fund the program	A special tax rate of 3.8% is applied to certain income earnings above $200,000 for individuals or $250,000 for married couples.

GOVERNMENT HEALTH INSURANCE EXCHANGES Under the new program, the federal government will coordinate the establishment of **health insurance exchanges.** These are government agencies tasked with helping individuals and families—especially the roughly 30 million additional people who will obtain health insurance—find policies to buy. The exchanges, which state governments are charged with operating, also will assist small businesses in finding health insurance they can purchase for employees.

Health insurance exchanges
Government agencies to which the national health care program assigns the task of assisting individuals, families, and small businesses in identifying health insurance policies to purchase.

REGULATIONS AND TAXES The national health care program also imposes new federal regulations on health care insurers and assesses special tax rates on higher-income families to help finance the tax subsidies extended to lower-income families. All health insurance policies now must satisfy a variety of requirements. For example, insurers cannot deny anyone health insurance, and a ceiling is imposed on the rate of increase in health insurance prices charged to elderly people.

Finally, the national health care plan imposes a special health care tax. A tax rate of 3.8 percent will be assessed on certain earnings above $200,000 per year for individuals and above $250,000 per year for married couples.

Economic Effects of the National Health Care Program

Naturally, the new U.S. health care program will have significant effects on health care markets. In addition, the program will also have effects on labor markets, product markets, and government budgets.

HIGHER HEALTH CARE SPENDING AND A WORSENED MORAL HAZARD PROBLEM The government's national health care program enlarges the scope of third-party payments for health care services. As we noted earlier, health care expenditures already consume about 17 percent of national income. The program promises to boost that spending and to expand the size of the moral hazard problem in U.S. health care markets.

Once the national health care program goes into effect during the mid-2010s, tens of millions of people will pay fewer of their health care expenses out of their own pockets than they did previously. This change will have three primary consequences. First, because the price people actually pay out of their own pockets to consume health care services will decline, the quantity of health care services demanded will increase. Second, because health insurers will be required to cover this expanded quantity demanded of services, total expenditures on health care will increase. Third, there will be an increased moral hazard problem. Because people will pay a smaller portion of the actual cost of treating health problems, more individuals will have reduced incentives to make decisions that promote better health. As people have more health problems as a consequence of this rise in moral hazard, the demand for health care will increase.

What types of costs are many Greek hospital patients incurring to obtain government-funded health care?

INTERNATIONAL POLICY EXAMPLE

In Greece, "Free" Care Now Includes Substantial Implicit Costs

Any Greek resident is entitled to health care provided by a plan called IKA National Insurance. IKA instructs holders of an IKA health care card to make an appointment with a physician or dentist, fill out a form, and arrive on time to receive care at no explicit cost. IKA also covers all forms of hospital care.

All Greek hospitals are financed directly by the nation's government, which recently has had difficulties borrowing sufficient funds to cover its high budget deficits. As a consequence, hospitals are often short of funds to pay their bills, including bills for medications obtained from pharmaceuticals companies. When Greek hospitals failed to pay for more than 60 percent of the market value of medications they received, Roche and other drug firms halted additional hospital medication deliveries. After hospitals exhaust their inventories of drugs, patients must sign out of their hospital rooms and go to private pharmacies, which usually have the drugs in stock because they acquire the drugs in advance. After the patients use their IKA cards to obtain the required medications, the hospitals readmit them, and their physicians begin administering the drugs. Thus, the pharmaceuticals are explicitly "free," but patients incur significant implicit costs.

FOR CRITICAL THINKING

If patients experience extremely long waits to obtain dental care through IKA, is the care really "free"?

IMPACTS ON THE REST OF THE U.S. ECONOMY Implementation of the new national health care program will have effects on labor markets, markets for goods and services, and budgets of federal and state governments:

1. *Labor market impacts.* In labor markets, the requirement for many firms to provide health insurance will raise the effective wage rate that they must pay for each unit of labor. Recall from Chapter 28 that firms employ labor to the point at which the marginal revenue product of labor—marginal revenue times the marginal physical product—equals the wage rate. The increase in the effective wage rate will induce firms to move upward along their downward-sloping marginal-revenue-product-of-labor curves. Thus, the quantity of labor demanded by firms will decline. Other things being equal, U.S. employment will be lower than it otherwise would have been.

2. *Markets for goods and services.* In markets for goods and services, the increase in labor costs firms incur in hiring each unit of labor will raise their marginal costs. Because

each firm maximizes profits by producing to the point at which marginal revenue equals marginal cost, the increase in marginal costs will induce firms to decrease their output at all prices. Other things being equal, this will place pressure on equilibrium prices to rise in a number of markets. Consequently, consumers will pay higher inflation-adjusted prices for many goods and services.

3. *Effects on government budgets.* The new tax rate applied to higher-income individuals went into effect in 2013, so tax revenues began flowing into the new program at that time. Federal government expenditures on the program are being phased in more gradually, so the program initially is being financed by the revenues collected in advance. Most observers agree, however, that the new tax revenues will be insufficient to cover the increases in government health care spending that surely will occur in future years. Hence, the federal government ultimately will have to search for ways to reduce its health care expenditures or to raise more tax revenues to fund the program. The federal program does not include revenues for states to cover the higher expenses of the additional people that may be admitted to the Medicaid program, which state governments administer. Thus, state governments will also face pressures to boost tax revenues.

QUICK QUIZ   See page 687 for the answers. Review concepts from this section in MyEconLab.

The U.S. national health care program adopted in 2010 expands the scope of health care coverage across millions of additional people by covering more lower-income people under the existing _____ program and by subsidizing health care expenses for people with incomes up to _____ percent of the poverty income level.

Key elements of the national health care program include _____ for individuals to buy health insurance and for firms employing more than 50 workers to provide insurance access or pay fines; establishment of government-operated

_____ to assist individuals and small businesses in finding health insurance plans; a requirement for health insurers to accept _____ applicants; and imposition of a new _____ on high-income earners.

Economic analysis suggests that likely effects of the adoption of the national health care program include _____ employment in U.S. labor markets, _____ prices of goods and services for consumers, and a _____ shortfall of federal and state tax revenues in relation to government expenses.

YOU ARE THERE
A Portuguese Woman Rethinks Her Human Capital Investment

Isabel Fernandes is a 22-year-old Portuguese woman who stopped attending school after the eighth grade. Hence, she is among the 72 percent of residents of Portugal between the ages of 25 and 64 who did not complete high school. She has been finding it difficult to obtain a job because employers "are asking for higher education."

To improve her employment prospects, Fernandes has become a part-time student at a private, nonprofit school. Friends have told her that completing high school might give her sufficient background to wait tables at restaurants. Fernandes has also learned that obtaining a college degree in Portugal would enable her to find a higher-paying occupation—offering perhaps twice the wages she could earn as a high school graduate serving

customers at restaurants. Nevertheless, her current dream job is waiting tables. Her immediate job search centers on finding a position as a cleaning woman, which she hopes might yield sufficient income to get by while she works to complete the ninth grade.

Critical Thinking Questions

1. Why do you suppose that average incomes in Portugal lag far behind average incomes in most other European nations?

2. How would completing high school likely affect Fernandes's age-earnings profile?

ISSUES & APPLICATIONS

Why Is the Female Income Gap Shrinking?

CONCEPTS APPLIED

▶ Distribution of Income

▶ Investment in Human Capital

▶ Age-Earnings Cycle

For many years, the U.S. income distribution favored male wage earners, because women experienced a pay gap in comparison with men. Over time, though, the distribution of income between the genders has been evening out.

The Female Income Gap

As Figure 30-10 below shows, women earn lower average incomes than men. It also reveals, however, that the gap between the average female income and the average male income has dropped from 37 percent in 1980 to about 17 percent today.

What accounts for the shrinkage of the female income gap? Most economists agree that the key explanation is a substantial increase in female investment in human capital. For a number of years, more females than males have graduated from U.S. high schools. Since 1996, more women than men have held bachelor's degrees. Today, 20 million women have bachelor's degrees, compared with 18.7 million men. Furthermore, 100,000 more women than men have obtained master's and doctoral degrees each year

since 2010. Thus, women are now better trained for many higher-income jobs.

Could the Income Gap between Men and Women Disappear?

Overall, women currently are earning 57 percent of the degrees issued each year by U.S. colleges and universities. This fact means that the flow of women into higher-income positions that require educational training is likely to more than keep pace with the flow of men into such jobs.

At the same time, female workers of prior generations who did not receive as much education and hence earned less than their male counterparts will begin departing the

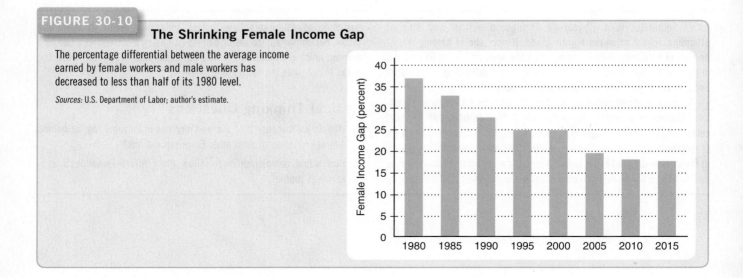

FIGURE 30-10

The Shrinking Female Income Gap

The percentage differential between the average income earned by female workers and male workers has decreased to less than half of its 1980 level.

Sources: U.S. Department of Labor; author's estimate.

workforce during the coming years. As age-earnings cycles readjust for the two genders, the average income earned by female workers undoubtedly will continue to climb in relation to the average income of male workers. Thus, the female wage gap should dissipate over time and in principle really could disappear at some point in the future.

For Critical Thinking

1. How is the fact that more low-income families are sending daughters, rather than sons, to college likely to affect the female income gap in the future?

2. Why do you think economists argue that the female wage gap will not entirely disappear unless women earn more degrees in sciences and business?

Web Resources

1. To learn about one country in which young women are already earning a higher average income than young men, go to www.econtoday.com/chap30.

2. For a view suggesting that young U.S. women have already closed the income gap with men, go to www.econtoday .com/chap30.

> ## MyEconLab
> For more questions on this chapter's
> Issues & Applications, go to MyEconLab.
> In the Study Plan for this chapter,
> select Section N: News.

MyEconLab

Here is what you should know after reading this chapter. MyEconLab will help you identify what you know, and where to go when you need to practice.

— WHAT YOU SHOULD KNOW —

Using a Lorenz Curve to Represent a Nation's Income Distribution A Lorenz curve depicts the distribution of income geometrically by measuring the percentage of households in relation to the cumulative percentage of income earnings. A perfectly straight Lorenz curve depicts perfect income equality because at each percentage of households measured along a straight-line Lorenz curve, those households earn exactly the same percentage of income. The more bowed a Lorenz curve is, the more unequally income is distributed.

distribution of income, 664
Lorenz curve, 664
income in kind, 664

Key Figures
Figure 30-1, 665
Figure 30-2, 665

— WHERE TO GO TO PRACTICE —

- MyEconLab Study Plan 30.1
- Animated Figures 30-1, 30-2

Key Determinants of Income Differences across Individuals Because of the age-earnings cycle, in which people typically earn relatively low incomes when young, age is an important factor influencing income differences. So are marginal productivity differences, which arise from variations in talent, experience, and training due to different investments in human capital.

age-earnings cycle, 668

Key Figure
Figure 30-4, 668

- MyEconLab Study Plan 30.2
- Animated Figure 30-4

MyEconLab *continued*

WHAT YOU SHOULD KNOW —— **WHERE TO GO TO PRACTICE** ——

Theories of Desired Income Distribution
One theory of desired income distribution is the productivity standard (also called the contributive or merit standard), according to which each person receives income based on the value of what he or she produces. The other is the egalitarian principle of income distribution, which proposes that each person should receive exactly the same income.

- MyEconLab Study Plan 30.3

Alternative Approaches to Measuring and Addressing Poverty One approach to measuring poverty is to define an absolute poverty standard. Another approach defines poverty in terms of income levels *relative* to the rest of the population. Currently, the U.S. government seeks to address poverty via income maintenance programs such as Social Security, Supplemental Security Income, Temporary Assistance to Needy Families, Supplemental Nutrition Assistance Program benefits, and the Earned Income Tax Credit Program.

Key Figure
Figure 30-5, 672

- MyEconLab Study Plan 30.4
- Animated Figure 30-5

Rising Health Care Costs and Third-Party Payments Spending on health care has been rising as a percentage of total U.S. national income. Third-party financing of health care expenditures by private and government insurance programs provides an incentive to buy more health care than if all expenses were paid out of pocket.

third parties, 676

Key Figures
Figure 30-6, 675
Figure 30-7, 676
Figure 30-8, 676

- MyEconLab Study Plan 30.5
- Animated Figures 30-6, 30-7, 30-8

Key Provisions of the New U.S. National Health Insurance Program The national health care program adopted in March 2010 requires all individuals to purchase health insurance and mandates that firms with more than 50 employees either provide health insurance or pay penalties. The program places more lower-income people in the Medicaid program and subsidizes health insurance for families with incomes up to 400 percent of the official poverty level. To help finance the program, people earning incomes above relatively high thresholds will face a special 3.8 percent tax rate applied to certain sources of income above those thresholds.

health insurance exchanges, 679

- MyEconLab Study Plan 30.5

Log in to MyEconLab, take a chapter test, and get a personalized Study Plan that tells you which concepts you understand and which ones you need to review. From there, MyEconLab will give you further practice, tutorials, animations, videos, and guided solutions. For more information, visit www.myeconlab.com

PROBLEMS

All problems are assignable in MyEconLab. *Answers to the odd-numbered problems appear at the back of the book.*

30-1. Consider the graph below, which depicts Lorenz curves for countries X, Y, and Z. (See page 665.)

    a. Which country has the least income inequality?

    b. Which country has the most income inequality?

    c. Countries Y and Z are identical in all but one respect: population distribution. The share of the population made up of children below working age is much higher in country Z. Recently, however, birthrates have declined in country Z and risen in country Y. Assuming that the countries remain identical in all other respects, would you expect that in 20 years the Lorenz curves for the two countries will be closer together or farther apart? (Hint: According to the age-earnings cycle, what typically happens to income as an individual begins working and ages?)

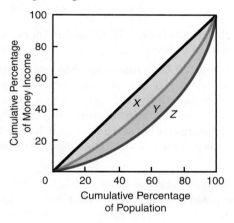

30-2. Consider the following estimates from the early 2010s of shares of income to each group. Use graph paper or a hand-drawn diagram to draw rough Lorenz curves for each country. Which has the most nearly equal distribution, based on your diagram? (See page 666.)

Country	Poorest 40%	Next 30%	Next 20%	Richest 10%
Bolivia	13	21	26	40
Chile	13	20	26	41
Uruguay	22	26	26	26

30-3. Suppose that the 20 percent of people with the highest incomes decide to increase their annual giving to charities, which pass nearly all the funds on to the 20 percent of people with the lowest incomes. What is the effect on the shape of the Lorenz curve? (See pages 665–666.)

30-4. Suppose that a nation has implemented a system for applying a tax rate of 2 percent to the incomes earned by the 10 percent of its residents with the highest incomes. All funds collected are then transferred directly to the 10 percent of the nation's residents with the lowest incomes. (See pages 665–666.)

    a. What is the general effect on the shape of a Lorenz curve based on incomes prior to collection and redistribution of the tax?

    b. What is the general effect on the shape of a Lorenz curve based on incomes after collection and redistribution of the tax?

30-5. Estimates indicate that during the early 2010s, the poorest 40 percent of the population earned about 15 percent of total income in Argentina. In Brazil, the poorest 40 percent earned about 10 percent of total income. The next-highest 30 percent of income earners in Argentina received roughly 25 percent of total income. In Brazil, the next-highest 30 percent of income earners received approximately 20 percent of total income. Can you determine, without drawing a diagram (though you can if you wish), which country's Lorenz curve was bowed out farther to the right? (See pages 665–666.)

30-6. Explain why the productivity standard for the distribution of income entails rewarding people based on their contribution to society's total output. Why does the productivity standard typically fail to yield an equal distribution of income? (See page 670.)

30-7. Identify whether each of the following proposed poverty measures is an absolute or relative measure of poverty, and discuss whether poverty could ever be eliminated if that measure were utilized. (See page 672.)

    a. An inflation-adjusted annual income of $25,000 for an urban family of four

    b. Individuals with annual incomes among the lowest 15 percent

    c. An inflation-adjusted annual income of $10,000 per person

30-8. Some economists have argued that if the government wishes to subsidize health care, it should instead provide predetermined amounts of payments (based on the type of health care problems experienced) directly to patients, who then would be free to choose their health care providers. Whether or not you agree, can you give an economic rationale for this approach to governmental health care funding? (See page 676.)

30-9. Suppose that a government agency guarantees to pay all of an individual's future health care expenses after the end of this year, so that the effective price of health care for the individual will be zero from that date onward. In what ways might this well-intended policy induce the individual to consume "excessive" health care services in future years? (See pages 675–676.)

30-10. Suppose that a group of physicians establishes a joint practice in a remote area. This group provides the only health care available to people in the local community, and its objective is to maximize total economic profits for the group's members. Draw a diagram illustrating how the price and quantity of health care will be determined in this community. (See page 676. Hint: How does a single producer of any service determine its output and price?)

30-11. A government agency determines that the entire community discussed in Problem 30-12 qualifies for a special program in which the government will pay for a number of health care services that most residents previously had not consumed. Many residents immediately make appointments with the community physicians' group. Given the information in Problem 30-12, what is the likely effect on the profit-maximizing price and the equilibrium quantity of health care services provided by the physicians' group in this community? (See page 676.)

30-12. A government agency notifies the physicians' group in Problem 30-12 that to continue providing services in the community, the group must document its activities. The resulting paperwork expenses raise the cost of each unit of health care services that the group provides. What is the likely effect on the profit-maximizing price and the equilibrium quantity of health care services provided by the physicians' group in this community? (See page 676.)

ECONOMICS ON THE NET

Measuring Poverty In this application, you will learn why poverty can be difficult to measure.

Title: World Bank PovertyNet: Understanding Poverty

Navigation: Go to **www.econtoday.com/chap30** to visit the World Bank's home page. Click on *Topics* and then *Poverty Analysis*. Then click on *Measuring Poverty*.

Application Perform the indicated operations, and answer the following questions.

1. Click on "Defining welfare measures." Why does this discussion suggest that measures of consumption are more useful in measuring poverty than income measures? Does the U.S. government's use of income thresholds for its official definition of poverty accord with this discussion?

2. Click on "Choose and estimate a poverty line." What alternative absolute poverty definitions are discussed? If the U.S. government were to adopt any of these absolute measures for its official poverty definition, what would happen to the U.S. poverty rate as real incomes and living standards rise over time?

For Group Study and Analysis Click on "Choose and estimate poverty indicators." What are the advantages and disadvantages of the poverty indicators that are discussed? Which indicator does the U.S. government utilize?

ANSWERS TO QUICK QUIZZES

p. 667: (i) income . . . equality . . . unequally; (ii) assets . . . more

p. 671: (i) age-earnings; (ii) productivity . . . revenue; (iii) talent . . . experience . . . training; (iv) human . . . opportunity; (v) productivity . . . equality

p. 674: (i) absolute . . . relative; (ii) little . . . relative; (iii) Social . . . Supplemental . . . earned income . . . Nutrition

p. 681: (i) Medicaid . . . 400; (ii) mandates . . . exchanges . . . all . . . tax; (iii) lower . . . higher . . . larger

Environmental Economics

31

LEARNING OBJECTIVES

After reading this chapter, you should be able to:

▶ Distinguish between private costs and social costs

▶ Understand market externalities and possible ways to correct externalities

▶ Explain how economists can conceptually determine the optimal quantity of pollution

▶ Contrast the roles of private and common property rights in alternative approaches to addressing the problem of pollution

▶ Describe how many of the world's governments are seeking to reduce pollution by capping and controlling the use of pollution-generating resources

▶ Discuss how the assignment of property rights may influence the fates of endangered species

MyEconLab helps you master each objective and study more efficiently. See end of chapter for details.

"**C**ap and trade" is an approach to air pollution control under which governments place a limit on allowed emissions, create rights to emit polluting substances, and permit firms to trade those rights in a free market. One example is a U.S. cap-and-trade program narrowly focused on limiting sulfur dioxide emissions. This program, which focused on electrical power plants in midwestern states, has been credited with reducing such emissions by about one-half. Governments in Europe and California recently implemented cap-and-trade programs aimed more broadly at controlling release of all emissions into the atmosphere. These governments indicated their wish to emulate the successes of the U.S. sulfur dioxide cap-and-trade program. This U.S. program recently collapsed, however. What can administrators of similar programs learn from this program's breakdown? What are alternative approaches to limiting pollution? This chapter provides the answers.

the Environmental Protection Agency (EPA) is requiring that by 2025, all U.S. passenger vehicles will have to operate at an average of 54.5 miles per gallon, more than twice the current average of 27 miles per gallon? The EPA's projections indicate that attaining this gas-mileage limit will substantially reduce the release of air pollutants and "greenhouse gases"—such as carbon dioxide—into the air. In addition, though, other government estimates indicate that complying with the regulations will raise automakers' costs sufficiently to yield at least a 10 percent increase in the average price of a vehicle. Consumers, of course, will have to pay these higher prices.

The economic way of thinking about policies intended to reduce air pollutants and greenhouse gases requires that the costs of such policies be considered. Likewise, the economic way of thinking about nonrenewable resources or endangered species requires that we take into account the costs of resource conservation and protection of wildlife. How much of your weekly wages are you willing to sacrifice to be used to reduce aggregate emissions of carbon dioxide, a gas that you exhale every time you breathe? To some people, framing questions in terms of the dollars-and-cents costs of environmental improvement sounds anti-ecological. But this is not so. Economists want to help citizens and policymakers opt for informed policies that have the maximum possible *net* benefits (benefits minus costs). As you will see, every decision made in favor of "the environment" involves a trade-off.

Private versus Social Costs

Human actions often give rise to unwanted side effects—the destruction of our environment is one. Human actions generate pollutants that go into the air and the water. The question often asked is, Why do individuals and businesses continue to create pollution without necessarily paying directly for the negative consequences?

Private Costs

Private costs
Costs borne solely by the individuals who incur them. Also called *internal costs*.

Until now, we've been dealing with settings in which the costs of an individual's actions are borne directly by the individual. When a business has to pay wages to workers, it knows exactly what its labor costs are. When it has to buy materials or build a plant, it knows quite well what these will cost. An individual who has to pay for car repairs or a theater ticket knows exactly what the cost will be. These costs are what we term *private costs*. **Private costs** are borne solely by the individuals who incur them. They are *internal* in the sense that the firm or household must explicitly take account of them.

Social Costs

Social costs
The full costs borne by society whenever a resource use occurs. Social costs can be measured by adding external costs to private, or internal, costs.

Now consider the actions of a business that dumps the waste products from its production process into a nearby river or an individual who litters a public park or beach. Obviously, these actions involve a cost. When the firm pollutes the water, people downstream suffer the consequences. They may not want to swim in or drink the polluted water. They may catch fewer fish than before because of the pollution. In the case of littering, the people who come along after the litterer has cluttered the park or the beach are the ones who bear the costs.

The cost of these actions is borne by people other than those who commit the actions. The creator of the cost is not the sole bearer. The costs are not internalized by the individual or firm—they are external.

When we add *external* costs to *internal*, or private, costs, we obtain **social costs**. Pollution problems—indeed, all problems pertaining to the environment—may be viewed as situations in which social costs exceed private costs. Because some economic participants pay only the smaller private costs of their actions, not the full social costs, their actions ultimately contribute to higher external costs on the rest of society. Therefore, in such situations in which social and private costs diverge, we see "too much" steel production, automobile driving, or beach littering, to name only a few of the many possible examples.

The Costs of Polluted Air

Why is the air in cities so polluted with automobile exhaust fumes? When automobile drivers step into their cars, they bear only the private costs of driving. That is, they must pay for the gas, maintenance, depreciation, and insurance on their automobiles. But they cause an additional cost—air pollution—which they are not forced to take into account when they make the decision to drive.

Air pollution is a cost because it causes harm to individuals—burning eyes, respiratory ailments, and dirtier clothes, cars, and buildings—and adds to accumulations of various gases that may contribute to global warming. The air pollution created by automobile exhausts is a cost that individual operators of automobiles do not yet bear directly. The social cost of driving includes all the private costs plus at least the cost of air pollution, which society bears. Decisions made only on the basis of private costs lead to too much automobile driving. Clean air is a scarce resource used by automobile drivers free of charge. They use more of it than they would if they had to pay the full social costs.

Externalities

When a private cost differs from a social cost, we say that there is an **externality** because individual decision makers are not paying (internalizing) all the costs. (We briefly covered this topic in Chapter 5.) Some of these costs remain external to the decision-making process. Remember that the full cost of using a scarce resource is borne one way or another by all who live in the society. That is, members of society must pay the full opportunity cost of any activity that uses scarce resources. The individual decision maker is the firm or the customer, and external costs and benefits will not enter into that individual's or firm's decision-making processes.

We might want to view the problem as it is presented in Figure 31-1 below. Here we have the market demand curve, D, for product X and the supply curve, S_1, for product X. The supply curve, S_1, includes only internal, or private, costs. The intersection of the demand and supply curves as drawn will be at price P_1 and quantity Q_1 (at E_1). We now assume that the production of good X involves externalities that the private firms did not take into account. Those externalities could be air pollution, water pollution, scenery destruction, or anything of that nature.

Externality

A consequence of a diversion of a private cost (or benefit) from a social cost (or benefit). A situation in which the costs (or benefits) of an action are not fully borne (or gained) by the decision makers engaged in an activity that uses scarce resources.

FIGURE 31-1

Reckoning with Full Social Costs

The supply curve, S_1, is equal to the horizontal summation (represented by the capital Greek letter sigma, Σ) of the individual marginal cost curves above the respective minimum average variable costs of all the firms producing good X. These individual marginal cost curves include only internal, or private, costs.

If the external costs were included and added to the private costs, we would have social costs. The supply curve would shift upward to S_2. In the uncorrected situation, the equilibrium price is P_1, and the equilibrium quantity is Q_1.

In the corrected situation, the equilibrium price would rise to P_2, and the equilibrium quantity would fall to Q_2.

We know that the social costs of producing product X exceed the private costs. We show this by drawing curve S_2. It is above the original supply curve S_1 because it includes the full social costs of producing the product. If firms could be made to bear these costs, their willingness to supply the good would be reduced, so the price would be P_2 and the quantity Q_2 (at E_2). The inclusion of external costs in the decision-making process would lead to a higher-priced product and a decline in quantity produced. Thus, we see that when social costs are not fully borne by the creators of those costs, the quantity produced is "excessive" because the price to consumers is too low.

Correcting for Externalities

We can see here a method for reducing pollution and environmental degradation. Somehow the signals in the economy must be changed so that decision makers will take into account *all* the costs of their actions. In the case of automobile pollution, we might want to devise some method of taxing motorists according to the amount of pollution they cause. In the case of a firm, we might want to devise a system of taxing businesses according to the amount of pollution for which they are responsible. They might then have an incentive to install pollution abatement equipment.

The Polluters' Choice

Facing an additional private cost for polluting, firms will be induced to (1) install pollution abatement equipment or otherwise change production techniques so as to reduce the amount of pollution, (2) reduce pollution-causing activity, or (3) simply pay a government-mandated cost for the right to pollute. The relative costs and benefits of each option for each polluter will determine which one or combination will be chosen.

Allowing the choice is the efficient way to decide who pollutes and who doesn't. In principle, just as with the use of all other scarce resources, each polluter faces the full social cost of its actions and makes a production decision accordingly. No matter what each firm decides, the firm is forced to take into account the additional cost. Hence, the cost of pollution-causing activity is now higher, so pollution will be reduced.

Is a Uniform Tax Appropriate?

It may not be appropriate to levy a *uniform* tax according to physical quantities of pollution. After all, we're talking about external costs. Such costs are not necessarily the same everywhere in the United States for the same action.

Essentially, we must establish the amount of the *economic damages* rather than the amount of the physical pollution. A polluting electrical plant in New York City will cause much more damage than the same plant in Montana. There are already innumerable demands on the air in New York City, so the pollution from smokestacks will not be cleansed away naturally. Millions of people will breathe the polluted air and thereby incur the costs of sore throats, sickness, emphysema, and even early death. Buildings will become dirtier faster because of the pollution, as will cars and clothes. A given quantity of pollution will cause more harm in concentrated urban environments than it will in less dense rural environments.

If we were to establish some form of taxation to align private costs with social costs and to force people to internalize externalities, we would somehow have to come up with a measure of *economic* costs instead of *physical* quantities. But the tax, in any event, would fall on the private sector and modify individuals' and firms' behavior.

Therefore, because the economic cost for the same physical quantity of pollution would be different in different locations, depending on population density, natural formations of mountains and rivers, and the like, so-called optimal taxes on pollution would vary from location to location. (Nonetheless, a uniform tax might make sense when administrative costs, particularly the cost of ascertaining the actual economic costs, are relatively high.)

QUICK QUIZ   See page 703 for the answers. Review concepts from this section in MyEconLab.

_____ costs are costs that are borne directly by consumers and producers when they engage in any resource-using activity.

Social costs are _____ costs plus any other costs that are external to the decision maker. For example, the

social costs of driving include all the _____ costs plus, at a minimum, any pollution caused.

When _____ costs differ from social costs, _____ exist because individual decision makers are not internalizing all the costs that society is bearing.

Pollution

The term *pollution* is used quite loosely and can refer to a variety of by-products of any activity. Industrial pollution involves mainly air and water but can also include noise and even aesthetic pollution, as when a landscape is altered in a negative way. For the most part, we will be analyzing the most common forms—air and water pollution.

Assessing the Appropriate Amount of Pollution

When asked how much pollution there should be in the economy, many people will respond, "None." But if we ask those same people how much starvation or deprivation of consumer products should exist in the economy, many will again say, "None." Growing and distributing food or producing consumer products creates pollution, however. There is no correct answer to how much pollution should be in an economy because when we ask how much pollution there *should* be, we are entering the realm of normative economics. We are asking people to express values. There is no way to disprove somebody's value system scientifically.

One way we can approach a discussion of the "correct" amount of pollution is to set up the same type of marginal analysis we used in our discussion of a firm's employment and output decisions. That is, we can consider pursuing measures to reduce pollution only up to the point at which the marginal benefit from pollution reduction equals the marginal cost of pollution reduction.

THE MARGINAL BENEFIT OF A LESS POLLUTED ENVIRONMENT Look at Figure 31-2 on the following page. On the horizontal axis, we show the degree of air cleanliness. A vertical line is drawn at 100 percent cleanliness—the air cannot become any cleaner. Consider the benefits of obtaining a greater degree of air cleanliness. The benefits of obtaining cleaner air are represented by the marginal benefit curve, which slopes downward.

When the air is very dirty, the marginal benefit from air that is a little cleaner appears to be relatively high, as shown on the vertical axis. As the air becomes cleaner, however, the marginal benefit of a little bit more air cleanliness falls.

THE MARGINAL COST OF POLLUTION ABATEMENT Consider the marginal cost of pollution abatement—that is, the marginal cost of obtaining cleaner air. In the 1960s, automobiles had no pollution abatement devices. Eliminating only 20 percent of the pollutants emitted by internal-combustion engines entailed a relatively small cost per unit of pollution removed. The per-unit cost of eliminating the next 20 percent increased, though. Finally, as we now get to the upper limits of removal of pollutants from the emissions of internal-combustion engines, we find that the elimination of one more percentage point of the amount of pollutants becomes astronomically expensive.

In the short run, moving from 97 percent cleanliness to 98 percent cleanliness involves a marginal cost that is many times greater than the marginal cost of going from 10 percent cleanliness to 11 percent cleanliness.

FIGURE 31-2

The Optimal Quantity of Air Pollution

As we attempt to achieve a greater degree of air cleanliness, the marginal cost rises until trying to increase air cleanliness even slightly leads to a very high marginal cost, as can be seen at the upper right of the graph. Conversely, the marginal benefit curve slopes downward: The more pure air we have, the less we value an additional unit of pure air. Marginal cost and marginal benefit intersect at point E. The optimal degree of air cleanliness is something less than 100 percent at Q_0. The price that we should pay for the last unit of air cleanup is no greater than P_0, for that is where marginal cost equals marginal benefit.

It is realistic, therefore, to draw the marginal cost of pollution abatement as an upward-sloping curve, as shown in Figure 31-2 above. (The marginal cost curve slopes up because of the law of diminishing marginal product.)

The Optimal Quantity of Pollution

Optimal quantity of pollution
The level of pollution for which the marginal benefit of one additional unit of pollution abatement just equals the marginal cost of that additional unit of pollution abatement.

The **optimal quantity of pollution** is the level of pollution at which the marginal benefit equals the marginal cost of pollution abatement. This occurs at the intersection of the marginal benefit curve and the marginal cost curve in Figure 31-2, at point E. This solution is analytically exactly the same as for every other economic activity. If we increased pollution control by one unit beyond Q_0, the marginal cost of that small increase in the degree of air cleanliness would be greater than the marginal benefit to society.

As is usually the case in economic analysis, the optimal quantity occurs when marginal cost equals marginal benefit. That is, the optimal quantity of pollution occurs at the point at which the marginal cost of reducing (or abating) pollution is just equal to the marginal benefit of doing so. The marginal cost of pollution abatement rises as more and more abatement is achieved (as the environment becomes cleaner and cleaner, the *extra* cost of cleansing rises). Early units of pollution abatement are easily achieved (at low cost), but attaining higher and higher levels of environmental quality becomes progressively more difficult (as the extra cost rises to prohibitive levels).

At the same time, the marginal benefits of an increasingly cleaner environment fall. The marginal benefit of pollution abatement declines as our notion of a cleaner environment moves from the preservation of human life to recreation to beauty to a perfectly pure environment. The point at which the increasing marginal cost of pollution abatement equals the decreasing marginal benefit of pollution abatement defines the optimal quantity of pollution.

Recognizing that the optimal quantity of pollution is not zero becomes easier when we realize that it takes scarce resources to reduce pollution. A trade-off exists between producing a cleaner environment and producing other goods and services. In that sense, environmental cleanliness is a good that can be analyzed like any other good, and a cleaner environment must take its place with other human wants.

Go to **www.econtoday.com/chap31** to learn from the National Center for Policy Analysis about alternative programs for reducing pollution related to global warming.

Why is the marginal cost of pollution abatement increasing in the electrical power industry?

POLICY EXAMPLE

Increasing the Marginal Cost of U.S. Air Pollution Abatement

Coal-fired plants generate nearly half of all electricity produced in the United States each year. In an effort to increase the degree of air cleanliness, the Environmental Protection Agency has issued 1,117 pages of rules that require electrical power companies to begin shutting down or retrofitting nearly 20 percent of these plants in 2015. Companies likely will replace retired coal-fired plants with electricity-generating facilities powered by natural gas. Retrofitted coal-fired plants will be equipped with special "scrubbers" that remove air pollutants and certain greenhouse gases from the plants' emissions.

Estimates indicate that the additional cost to the electrical power industry and its customers of complying with this requirement will be about $30 billion per year through the end of the 2010s. Thus, attaining a hoped-for higher degree of air cleanliness will entail a higher marginal cost of pollution abatement for society.

FOR CRITICAL THINKING

For the EPA's new pollution abatement requirement to move society toward the optimal degree of air cleanliness, would the initial degree of cleanliness have to have been below, at, or above a level such as Q_0 in Figure 31-2 on the facing page?

QUICK QUIZ   See page 703 for the answers. Review concepts from this section in MyEconLab.

The marginal cost of cleaning up the environment _____ as we get closer to 100 percent cleanliness. Indeed, it _____ at an _____ rate.

The marginal benefit of environmental cleanliness _____ as we have more of it.

The **optimal quantity of pollution** is the quantity at which the _____ _____ of cleanup equals the _____ _____ of cleanup.

Pollution abatement is a trade-off. We trade off _____ and _____ for cleaner air and water, and vice versa.

Common Property

In most cases, you do not have **private property rights,** or exclusive ownership rights, to the air surrounding you, nor does anyone else. Air is a **common property,** or a nonexclusive resource. Therein lies the crux of the problem. When no one owns a particular resource, no one has any incentive (conscience aside) to consider externality spillovers associated with that resource. If one person decides not to add to externality spillovers and avoids polluting the air, normally there will not be any significant effect on the total level of pollution. If one person decides not to pollute the ocean, there will still be approximately the same amount of ocean pollution—provided, of course, that the individual was previously responsible for only a small part of the total amount of ocean pollution.

Basically, pollution and other activities that create spillovers occur when we have open access and poorly defined private property rights, as in air and common bodies of water. We do not, for example, have a visual pollution problem in people's attics. That is their own property, which they keep as clean as they want, depending on their preferences for cleanliness weighed against the costs of keeping the attic neat and tidy.

When private property rights exist, individuals have legal recourse for any damages sustained through the use of their property. When private property rights are well defined, the use of property—that is, the use of resources—will generally involve contracts between the owners of those resources. If you own land, you might contract with another person who wants to access your land for raising cattle. The contract would most likely take the form of a written lease agreement.

Private property rights
Exclusive rights of ownership that allow the use, transfer, and exchange of property.

Common property
Property that is owned by everyone and therefore by no one. Air and water are examples of common property resources.

Voluntary Agreements and Transaction Costs

Is it possible for externalities to be internalized via voluntary agreement? Take a simple example. You live in a house with a nice view of a lake. The family living below you plants a tree. The tree grows so tall that it eventually starts to cut off your view. In most cities, no one has property rights to views, so you usually cannot go to court to obtain relief. You do have the option of contracting with your neighbors, however.

VOLUNTARY AGREEMENTS: CONTRACTING You have the option of paying your neighbors (contracting) to trim the tree. You could start out by offering a small amount and keep going up until your neighbors agree or until you reach your limit. Your limit will equal the value you place on having an unobstructed view of the lake. Your neighbors will be willing if the payment is at least equal to the reduction in their intrinsic property value due to a stunted tree. Your offer of the payment makes your neighbors aware of the social cost of their actions. The social cost here is equal to the care of the tree plus the cost suffered by you from an impeded view of the lake.

In essence, then, your offer of money income to your neighbors indicates to them that there is an opportunity cost to their actions. If they don't comply, they forfeit the payments that you are offering them. The point here is that *opportunity cost always exists, no matter who has property rights*. Therefore, we would expect that under some circumstances voluntary contracting will occur to internalize externalities. The question is, When will voluntary agreements occur?

TRANSACTION COSTS One major condition for the outcome just outlined is that the **transaction costs**—all costs associated with making and enforcing agreements— must be low relative to the expected benefits of reaching an agreement. (We already looked at this topic briefly in Chapter 4.) If we expand our example to a much larger one such as air pollution, the transaction costs of numerous homeowners trying to reach agreements with the individuals and companies that create the pollution are relatively high. Consequently, people may not always engage in voluntary contracting, even though it can be an effective way to internalize the externality of air pollution.

Changing Property Rights

We can approach the issue of property rights by assuming that initially in a society, many property rights to resources are not defined. But this situation does not cause a problem so long as no one wants to use the resources for which there are no property rights or resources are available in desired quantities at a zero price. Only if and when a use is found for a resource at a zero price does a problem develop. Unless some decision then is made about property rights, the resource will be wasted and possibly even destroyed. Property rights can be assigned to individuals who will then assert control. Alternatively, the rights may be assigned to government, which can maintain and preserve the resource, charge for its use, or implement some other rationing device.

Another way of viewing the problem of pollution spillovers is to argue that it cannot continue if a way can be found to assign and enforce private property rights for all resources. We can then say that each individual does not have the right to act on anything that is not his or her property. Hence, no individual has the right to create pollution spillovers on property that the individual does not specifically own.

Clearly, we must fill the gap between private costs and social costs in situations in which property rights are not well defined or assigned. There are three ways to fill this gap: taxation, subsidization, and regulation. Government is involved in all three. Unfortunately, government does not have perfect information and may not pick the appropriate tax, subsidy, or type of regulation. Furthermore, in some situations, it may be difficult to enforce taxes or direct subsidies to "worthy" recipients. In such cases, outright prohibition of the polluting activity may be the optimal solution to a particular pollution spillover. For example, if it is difficult to monitor the level of a particular type of pollution that even in small quantities can cause severe environmental damage, outright prohibition of activities that cause such pollution may be the best alternative.

Transaction costs
All costs associated with making, reaching, and enforcing agreements.

YOU ARE THERE

To contemplate the transaction costs associated with the most basic form of environmental cleanup—regular removal of city residents' trash—consider **A Mayor Faces the Grimy Economics of Trash Removal** on page 698.

QUICK QUIZ See page 703 for the answers. Review concepts from this section in MyEconLab.

A **common property** resource is one that _____ _____ owns—or, otherwise stated, that _____ owns. Common property exists when property rights are indefinite or nonexistent.

When no _____ _____ rights exist, pollution occurs because no one individual or firm has a sufficient economic incentive to care for the common property in question, be it air, water, or scenery.

Private costs will equal _____ costs for common property only if a few individuals or companies are involved and they are able to voluntarily _____ among themselves.

Reducing Humanity's Carbon Footprint: Restraining Pollution-Causing Activities

In light of the costs arising from spillovers that polluting activities create, one solution might seem to be for governments to try to stop them from taking place. Why don't more governments simply *require* businesses and households to cut back on pollution-causing activities?

Mixing Government Controls and Market Processes: Cap and Trade

In fact, many governments are implementing schemes aimed at capping and controlling the use of pollution-generating resources. In recent years, certain scientific research has suggested that emissions of carbon dioxide and various other so-called *greenhouse gases* might be contributing to atmospheric warming. The result, some scientists fear, might be global climate changes harmful to people inhabiting various regions of the planet.

In response, the governments of more than three dozen nations agreed to participate in the *Kyoto Protocol* of a broader set of international treaties called the Framework Convention on Climate Change. Under this 1997 agreement, the governments of participating nations agreed to reduce their overall emissions of greenhouse gases by 2020 to as much as 20 percent below 1990 levels.

EMISSIONS CAPS AND PERMITS TRADING European Union (EU) nations are participants in the Kyoto Protocol, which expired in 2012 but to which EU nations are adhering. In January 2005, the EU established a set of rules called the *Emissions Trading Scheme*. Under this so-called cap-and-trade program, each EU nation seeks to cap its total greenhouse gas emissions. After setting its cap, each EU nation established an *allowance* of metric tons of gas, such as carbon dioxide, that each firm legally can release. If the firm's emissions exceed its allowance—that is, if its "carbon footprint" is too large—then the firm must buy more allowances through a trading system. These allowances can be obtained, at the market clearing price, from companies that are releasing fewer emissions than their permitted amounts and therefore have unused allowances.

The United States is not a Kyoto Protocol participant. Nevertheless, in 2013 California began implementing its own cap-and-trade program. That state also placed a limit on emissions of greenhouse gases within its borders. Under the California program, the overall limitation on emissions will decline over seven years. Electrical power companies, oil refiners, and other firms—more than 600 companies in all—that generate greenhouse gases will have to reduce their emissions or buy allowances to continue releasing the emissions. Ultimately, California's objective is to reduce the state's total carbon emissions by 30 percent by 2020.

Why has California tried to enlist other western states to join its cap-and-trade program? See the following page.

POLICY EXAMPLE

California Dreaming: A Western Cap-and-Trade Pact?

During the period preceding implementation of California's cap-and-trade program, state officials tried to persuade governments of other western states to enter into a "regional cap-and-trade pact." Every state that California officials approached said no, however, as it became clear that the induced reduction in the energy supply required to decrease emissions would bring about considerably higher energy prices.

Although the exact annual costs of California's energy program to the state's households may not be tabulated until early 2014, most estimates indicate the costs will amount to hundreds of dollars per household per year. Businesses will face significant cost increases as well, which most economists anticipate will lead to dampened employment prospects in the state. Some observers are predicting that a number of California firms will respond to higher energy costs by moving their operations to other western states. Indeed, state officials admitted that one incentive for a regional pact was to ensure that neighboring states' energy costs also would rise, thereby reducing the motivation for California firms to relocate to those states.

FOR CRITICAL THINKING

Why do you suppose that some economists argue that if the United States were to incur the costs of capping emissions, while other nations did not, a number of U.S. firms might relocate to those other countries?

IN EUROPE, THEORY CONFRONTS POLICY AND MARKET REALITIES The European cap-and-trade program has yielded mixed results to date. In theory, if EU governments had set the national emissions caps low enough to force companies to reduce greenhouse gases, the market clearing price of emissions allowances should have reflected this constraint. In addition, as governments voluntarily continue to tighten the caps to meet limits that require greenhouse gas emissions to be reduced to 20 percent below 1990 levels by 2020, more firms should respond by purchasing allowances.

Then the market clearing price of allowances would rise. Rather than paying a higher price for emissions allowances, many firms would instead opt to develop methods of reducing their emissions. In this way, this market-based mechanism established by the Emissions Trading Scheme would induce firms to reduce their emissions, and the EU nations would achieve the emissions targets.

In fact, in the spring of 2006, the market clearing price of EU emissions allowances dropped by more than 60 percent. The reason that prices dropped, many economists agree, is that most EU governments issued more allowances than were consistent with capping emissions. Indeed, the price drop was consistent with an initial surplus of more than 200 million allowances.

Most observers suspect that the Emissions Trading Scheme's fundamental weakness was that each nation's government was permitted to establish the emissions target and allowances for its own country. Each government feared making its own nation's firms less cost-competitive than those in other nations, so every government inflated its estimate of its mid-2000s emissions of greenhouse gases. Doing so allowed each government to set its overall emissions cap at a level that actually failed to constrain emissions. One result was the big drop in prices of emissions allowances, which have remained substantially lower than when the Emissions Trading Scheme was first established. Another outcome is that instead of declining, greenhouse gas emissions by companies based in the EU actually *increased* during the late 2000s and early 2010s.

Why is a separately administered EU cap-and-trade program for airline emissions driving up prices of flying to European airports?

INTERNATIONAL EXAMPLE

Passengers Help Pay for Emissions on EU Airline Routes

In 2012, the European Union implemented a new, independently administered cap-and-trade program aimed at reducing carbon emissions created by airplane engines. This program applies to all airlines operating flights into and out of all EU member nations' airports. The EU allocated total pollution allowances to airlines to emit exhaust gases from airplanes slightly below the airlines' past average level of emissions for the full durations of all flights, even if they originated on other continents. To exceed its limit, an airline can purchase allowances from another airline that has total emissions below its allowances.

Imposing this separate cap-and-trade program has raised airlines' per-passenger costs of providing air travel services, which has reduced the market supply of these services. The result has been predictable: The equilibrium price of a ticket into or out of an airport located in an EU nation has risen by about $10.

FOR CRITICAL THINKING

Flights that either originate or end at EU airports carry at least 800 million passengers each year. What is the approximate aggregate annual cost imposed on airline passengers by the new EU airline cap-and-trade program?

Are There Alternatives to Pollution-Causing Resource Use?

Some people cannot understand why, if pollution is bad, we still use pollution-causing resources such as coal and oil to generate electricity. Why don't we forgo the use of such polluting resources and opt for one that apparently is pollution-free, such as solar energy? The plain fact is that the cost of generating solar power in many circumstances is much higher than generating that same power through conventional means. We do not yet have the technology that allows us the luxury of driving solar-powered cars. Moreover, with current technology, the solar panels necessary to generate the electricity for the average town would cover massive sections of the countryside, and the manufacturing of those solar panels would itself generate pollution.

Wild Species, Common Property, and Trade-Offs

One common property problem that receives considerable media attention involves endangered species, usually in the wild. Few are concerned about not having enough dogs, cats, cattle, sheep, and horses. The reason is that those species are almost always private property. People have economic incentives—satisfaction from pet ownership or desire for food products—to protect members of these species. In contrast, spotted owls, bighorn mountain sheep, condors, and the like are typically openly accessible common property. Therefore, no one has a vested interest in making sure that they perpetuate in good health.

Go to www.econtoday.com/chap31 to contemplate the issue of endangered species via a link to the National Center for Policy Analysis.

In 1973, the federal government passed the Endangered Species Act in an attempt to prevent species from dying out. Initially, few individuals were affected by the rulings of the Interior Department regarding which species were listed as endangered. Eventually, however, as more and more species were put on the endangered list, a trade-off became apparent. Nationwide, the trade-off was brought to the public's attention when the snail darter was declared an endangered species in the Tennessee valley. Ultimately, thousands of construction jobs were lost when the courts halted completion of a dam in the snail darter's habitat. Then two endangered small birds, the spotted owl and marbled murrelet, were found in the Pacific Northwest, inducing lumber companies to cut back their logging practices. In 1995, the U.S. Supreme Court ruled that the federal government has the right to regulate activities on private land in order to save endangered species.

The issues are not straightforward. Today, the earth has only 0.02 percent of all of the species that have ever lived, and nearly all the 99.98 percent of extinct species became extinct before humans appeared. Every year, 1,000 to 3,000 new species are discovered and classified. Estimates of how many species are actually dying out range from a high of 50,000 a year (based on the assumption that undiscovered insect species are dying off before being discovered) to a low of one every four years.

WHAT IF... **governments allowed people to own endangered animals as private property?**

If all animals of endangered species could be marked and cataloged as private property, some people undoubtedly would mishandle the animals they owned, just as they misuse other resources in their possession. Nevertheless, by definition, animals of endangered species are scarce resources that would have positive values—and sometimes relatively high dollar values—in private markets. This fact would give most self-interested people the incentive to preserve such animal life. Indeed, the most successful programs for preventing "too much" fishing, seal hunting, rhino poaching, and so on have been those that assign property rights. These programs motivate the rights holders to rein in such injurious activities and to preserve endangered species.

The more than three dozen countries that participated in the 1997 Kyoto Protocol of the Framework Convention on Climate Change agreed to reduce their emissions of greenhouse gases by the year _____ to at least _____ percent below the levels that prevailed in the year _____.

Under a program called the Emissions Trading Scheme, the governments of European Union member nations established overall targets for greenhouse gas emissions and issued _____, or permits, authorizing companies

to emit certain amounts. In theory, an increase in the market clearing price of _____ should induce firms to develop methods of _____ their emissions of greenhouse gases.

In contrast to domesticated animals that are _____ property, most endangered species are _____ property. Consequently, there is a problem in perpetuating these species that the federal government has sought to address through legislation governing use of lands where such species reside.

YOU ARE THERE
A Mayor Faces the Grimy Economics of Trash Removal

The task of keeping the physical environment clean begins with figuring out how to handle trash. For Chicago mayor Rahm Emanuel, how to go about moving trash for disposal or recycling has become a substantial economic issue.

Chicago does not have one trash removal system to serve its 600,000 households. Instead, it has a different system for each of its 50 political wards. In addition, during a typical garbage laborer's workday, only 5½ hours are devoted to moving trash. Facts such as these, Emanuel realizes, help to explain why the $231 cost per ton of moving trash in Chicago is higher than for any other large U.S. city.

Emanuel examines a study that proposes a reorganization of the city's trash removal procedures. The study suggests that switching to a more efficient citywide system for trash disposal and recycling could accomplish

the same task each year with 25 percent fewer workers and at an annual cost savings of $40 million. Emanuel decides that with an annual city budget deficit in excess of $600 million, cutting the expense of trash removal will have to become a top priority.

Critical Thinking Questions

1. Why do you suppose that governments of towns and cities rarely seek to keep streets 100 percent free of trash?

2. Once city workers collect trash from a house or apartment building, it becomes common property. How can this fact pose problems for deciding how best to handle disposal and recycling of the trash?

CONCEPTS APPLIED

▶ Externality

▶ Private versus Social Costs

▶ Optimal Quantity of Pollution

ISSUES & APPLICATIONS

The New Sulfur Dioxide "Cap and Fade" Program

The U.S. government successfully operated a narrowly focused cap-and-trade program for more than a decade. Nonetheless, recent policy actions caused this program, which some observers now call "cap and fade," to collapse.

Caps and Allowances to Contain an Acid Rain Externality

For years, coal-fired electrical-power-generating plants in midwestern states emitted smoke containing sulfur dioxide. In other states, these emissions have contributed to a phenomenon known as "acid rain"—rainfalls contaminated by acids formed when the sulfur dioxide combined with other elements in the atmosphere. Thus, a mismatch has occurred between the private costs incurred by electricity producers in some states and the people in other states adversely affected by acid rain. That is, a negative externality has arisen.

In 1995, the U.S. government placed a cap on emissions of sulfur dioxide by electricity providers in the midwestern states. The government handed out a fixed number of emission allowances to the companies. Plant operators surrendered one allowance for each ton of sulfur dioxide they emitted. If firms reduced emissions by switching to low-sulfur coals or by adding emission-control equipment, they could sell unused allowances to other electrical power producers.

Success Followed by a Policy-Induced Market Fadeout

From 1995 through 2007, the U.S. sulfur dioxide cap-and-trade program was regarded as one of the most successful such programs in the world. By 2005, the equilibrium price of a sulfur-dioxide-emission allowance had reached $1,600. This price was sufficiently high to induce many firms to reduce their emissions. In fact, during the first 13 years the program was in operation, total emissions of sulfur dioxide in the United States declined by 50 percent, toward a level more consistent with the government's view of the optimal quantity of pollution.

In 2008, however, the EPA began ordering plant operators to cut back directly on their emissions. The EPA also decided not to allow firms to purchase allowances to avoid the new emissions restrictions. Since then, the equilibrium price of a sulfur-dioxide-emission allowance has "faded away" to zero—hence the new "cap and fade" term used to describe the program.

For Critical Thinking

1. There is currently a surplus of allowances at the price of zero. What must be true of the relative positions of the market demand and supply curves? Explain.

2. If the EPA were to allow firms to use allowances to emit sulfur dioxide as they did in the past, what would happen to the equilibrium allowance price? Why?

Web Resources

1. Consider how the pre-"fade" version of the cap-and-trade program for sulfur dioxide has been held up as a model for other cap-and-trade programs at www.econtoday.com/chap31.

2. Learn about the substantial decline in the price of sulfur-dioxide-emission allowances at www.econtoday.com/chap31.

MyEconLab

For more questions on this chapter's
Issues & Applications, go to MyEconLab.
In the Study Plan for this chapter,
select Section N: News.

MyEconLab

Here is what you should know after reading this chapter. MyEconLab will help you identify what you know, and where to go when you need to practice.

WHAT YOU SHOULD KNOW		WHERE TO GO TO PRACTICE
Private Costs versus Social Costs Private, or internal, costs are borne solely by individuals who use resources. Social costs are the full costs that society bears whenever resources are used. Problems related to the environment arise when individuals take into account only private costs instead of the broader social costs arising from their use of resources.	private costs, 688 social costs, 688	• MyEconLab Study Plan 31.1
Market Externalities and Ways to Correct Them A market externality arises if a private cost (or benefit) differs from the social cost (or benefit) associated with a market transaction between two parties or from the use of a scarce resource. An externality can be corrected by requiring individuals to account for all the social costs (or benefits).	externality, 689 **Key Figure** Figure 31-1, 689	• MyEconLab Study Plan 31.2 • Animated Figure 31-1

MyEconLab *continued*

WHAT YOU SHOULD KNOW		WHERE TO GO TO PRACTICE
Determining the Optimal Amount of Pollution The marginal benefit of pollution abatement declines and the marginal cost of pollution abatement increases as more and more resources are devoted to achieving an improved environment. The optimal quantity of pollution is the amount of pollution for which the marginal benefit of pollution abatement just equals the marginal cost of pollution abatement.	optimal quantity of pollution, 692 **Key Figure** Figure 31-2, 692	• MyEconLab Study Plan 31.3 • Animated Figure 31-2
Private and Common Property Rights and the Pollution Problem Private property rights permit the use and exchange of a resource. Common property is owned by everyone and hence by no single person. A pollution problem often arises because air and many water resources are common property, and private property rights are not well defined. This is a common rationale for using taxes, subsidies, or regulations to address the pollution problem.	private property rights, 693 common property, 693 transaction costs, 694	• MyEconLab Study Plan 31.4
Restraining Pollution-Causing Activities through Caps and Allowances Under the European Union's (EU's) Emissions Trading Scheme, each EU nation's government established an overall target level of greenhouse gas emissions and distributed allowances, or permits, granting firms the right to emit a certain amount of gases. If a firm's greenhouse gas emissions exceed its allowances, it must purchase a sufficient number of allowances from firms emitting less than the allowances they possess. In theory, the market clearing price of allowances will increase, giving firms incentives to develop methods of restraining their emissions of greenhouse gases.		• MyEconLab Study Plan 31.5
Endangered Species and the Assignment of Property Rights Many members of such species as dogs, pigs, and horses are the private property of human beings. Thus, people have economic incentives to protect members of these species. In contrast, most members of species such as spotted owls, condors, or tigers are common property, so no specific individuals have incentives to keep these species in good health. A possible way to address the endangered species problem is government involvement via regulations.		• MyEconLab Study Plan 31.6

Log in to MyEconLab, take a chapter test, and get a personalized Study Plan that tells you which concepts you understand and which ones you need to review. From there, MyEconLab will give you further practice, tutorials, animations, videos, and guided solutions. For more information, visit www.myeconlab.com

PROBLEMS

All problems are assignable in MyEconLab. Answers to the odd-numbered problems appear at the back of the book.

31-1. The market price of insecticide is initially $10 per unit. To address a negative externality in this market, the government decides to charge producers of insecticide for the privilege of polluting during the production process. A fee that fully takes into account the social costs of pollution is determined, and once it is put into effect, the market supply curve for insecticide shifts upward by $4 per unit. The market price of insecticide also increases, to $12 per unit. What fee is the government charging insecticide manufacturers? (See page 689.)

31-2. One possible method for reducing emissions of greenhouse gases such as carbon dioxide is to inject the gases into deep saltwater-laden rock formations where they would be trapped for thousands of years. Suppose that the federal government provides a fixed per-unit subsidy to firms that utilize this technology in West Virginia and other locales where such rock formations are known to exist. (See page 692.)

a. Use an appropriate diagram to examine the effects of the government subsidy on the production and sale of equipment that injects greenhouse gases into underground rock formations. What happens to the market clearing price of such pollution abatement equipment?

b. Who pays to achieve the results discussed in part (a)?

31-3. Examine the following marginal costs and marginal benefits associated with water cleanliness in a given locale (see page 692):

Quantity of Clean Water (%)	Marginal Cost ($)	Marginal Benefit ($)
0	3,000	200,000
20	15,000	120,000
40	50,000	90,000
60	85,000	85,000
80	100,000	40,000
100	Infinite	0

a. What is the optimal degree of water cleanliness?

b. What is the optimal degree of water pollution?

c. Suppose that a company creates a food additive that offsets most of the harmful effects of drinking polluted water. As a result, the marginal benefit of water cleanliness declines by $40,000 at each degree of water cleanliness at or less than 80 percent. What is the optimal degree of water cleanliness after this change?

31-4. Consider the diagram below, which displays the marginal cost and marginal benefit of water pollution abatement in a particular city, and answer the following questions. (See page 692.)

a. What is the optimal percentage degree of water cleanliness?

b. When the optimal percentage degree of water cleanliness has been attained, what cost will be incurred for the last unit of water cleanup?

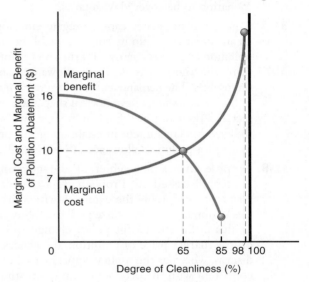

31-5. Consider the diagram in Problem 31-4, and answer the following questions. (See page 692.)

a. Suppose that a new technology for reducing water pollution generates a reduction in the marginal cost of pollution abatement at every degree of water cleanliness. After this event occurs, will the optimal percentage degree of water cleanliness rise or fall? Will the cost incurred for the last unit of water cleanup increase or decrease? Provide a diagram to assist in your explanation.

b. Suppose that the event discussed in part (a) occurs and that, in addition, medical studies determine that the marginal benefit from water pollution abatement is higher at every degree of water cleanliness. Following *both* events, will the optimal percentage degree of water cleanliness increase or decrease? In comparison with the *initial* optimum, can you determine whether the cost incurred for the last unit of water cleanup will increase or decrease? Use a new diagram to assist in explaining your answers.

31-6. Under an agreement with U.S. regulators, American Electric Power Company of Columbus, Ohio, has agreed to offset part of its 145 million metric tons of carbon dioxide emissions by paying another company to lay plastic tarps. These tarps cover farm lagoons holding rotting livestock wastes that emit methane gas 21 times more damaging to the atmosphere than carbon dioxide. The annual methane produced by a typical 1,330-pound cow translates into about 5 metric tons of carbon dioxide emissions per year. (See pages 691–693.)

a. How many cows' worth of manure would have to be covered to offset the carbon dioxide emissions of this single electric utility?

b. Given that there are about 9 million cows in the United States in a typical year, what percentage of its carbon dioxide emissions could this firm offset if it paid for all cow manure in the entire nation to be covered with tarps?

31-7. A government agency caps aggregate emissions of an air pollutant within its borders, establishes initial pollution allowances across all firms, and grants the firms the right to trade these allowances among themselves. The demand and supply curves for these pollution allowances have normal shapes and intersect at a positive price. Explain in your own words the government's intent in establishing this private market for pollution allowances. (See page 695.)

31-8. Suppose that a new chief of the government agency discussed in Problem 31-7 decides to restrict considerably the extent to which firms in this nation can legally utilize pollution allowances. Evaluate the effects this policy change will have on the market price of pollution allowances, and discuss whether the policy appears to be fully consistent with the original intent of creating the market for these allowances. (See page 696.)

31-9. The following table displays hypothetical annual total costs and total benefits of conserving wild tigers at several possible worldwide tiger population levels. (See page 697.)

Population of Wild Tigers	Total Cost ($ millions)	Total Benefit ($ millions)
0	0	40
2,000	25	90
4,000	35	130
6,000	50	160
8,000	75	185
10,000	110	205
12,000	165	215

a. Calculate the marginal costs and benefits.

b. Given the data, what is the socially optimal world population of wild tigers?

c. Suppose that tiger farming is legalized and that this has the effect of reducing the marginal cost of tiger conservation by $15 million for each 2,000-tiger population increment in the table. What is the new socially optimal population of wild tigers?

31-10. The following table gives hypothetical annual total costs and total benefits of maintaining alternative populations of Asian elephants. (See page 697.)

Population of Asian Elephants	Total Cost ($ millions)	Total Benefit ($ millions)
0	0	0
7,500	20	100
15,000	45	185
22,500	90	260
30,000	155	325
37,500	235	375
45,000	330	410

a. Calculate the marginal costs and benefits, and draw marginal benefit and cost schedules.

b. Given the data, what is the socially optimal world population of Asian elephants?

c. Suppose that two events occur simultaneously. Technological development allows machines to do more efficiently much of the work that elephants once did, which reduces by $10 million the marginal benefit of maintaining the elephant population for each 7,500 increment in the elephant population. In addition, new techniques for breeding, feeding, and protecting elephants reduce the marginal cost by $40 million for each 7,500 increment in the elephant population. What is the new socially optimal population of Asian elephants?

ECONOMICS ON THE NET

Economic Analysis at the Environmental Protection Agency
In this chapter, you learned how to use economic analysis to think about environmental problems. Does the U.S. government use economic analysis? This application helps you learn the extent to which the government uses economics in its environmental policymaking.

Title: National Center for Environmental Economics (NCEE)

Navigation: Go to **www.econtoday.com/chap31** to view the NCEE's link to "Environmental Protection: Is It Bad for the Economy? A Non-Technical Summary of the Literature." Download the article and read the section entitled "What Do We Spend on Environmental Protection?"

Application Read this section of the article. Then answer the following questions.

1. According to the article, what are the key objectives of the Environmental Protection Agency (EPA)? What role does cost-benefit analysis appear to play in the EPA's efforts? Does the EPA appear to take other issues into account in its policymaking?

2. Read the next section, titled "Regardless of the Cost of Environmental Protection, Is It Still Money Well Spent?" In what ways does this discussion help clarify your answers in Question 1?

For Group Study and Analysis Have a class discussion of the following question: Should the EPA apply economic analysis in all aspects of its policymaking? If not, why not? If so, in what manner should economic analysis be applied?

ANSWERS TO QUICK QUIZZES

p. 691: (i) Private; (ii) private . . . private; (iii) private . . . externalities

p. 693: (i) rises . . . rises . . . increasing; (ii) falls; (iii) marginal cost . . . marginal benefit; (iv) goods . . . services

p. 695: (i) no one . . . everyone; (ii) private property; (iii) social . . . contract

p. 698: (i) 2020 . . . 20 . . . 1990; (ii) allowances . . . allowances . . . reducing; (iii) private . . . common

32

Comparative Advantage and the Open Economy

In 2001, the U.S. government slashed *tariffs*—taxes on imported items—that it imposed on goods and services imported into the United States from countries located along the Andes mountain range in South America. From that year through the early 2010s, the dollar value of U.S. imports of cut flowers from the Andean nation of Colombia grew by about 400 percent, while Californian production and sale of cut flowers declined considerably. California flower growers responded by successfully lobbying Congress to increase tariff rates on Andean products to previous levels, and Colombian cut-flower imports promptly plummeted. To understand how tariffs affect volumes of imports and, ultimately, prices in markets in which imported goods and services are traded, you must learn about the economics of international trade, which is the subject of this chapter.

since 2011, more oil-based fuels have been exported each year from the United States than have been imported? Thus, recent years represent the first time since 1949 that international trade statistics have classified the United States as a "net exporter" of fossil fuels. Current projections indicate that it likely will remain a net fuel exporter for many years to come. In this chapter, you will learn about the fundamental economic determinants of whether a nation's residents become net exporters or importers of particular goods and services.

The Worldwide Importance of International Trade

Look at panel (a) of Figure 32-1 below. Since the end of World War II, world output of goods and services (world real gross domestic product, or world real GDP) has increased almost every year. It is now about 10 times what it was then. Look at the top line in panel (a) of Figure 32-1. Even taking into account its recent dip, world trade has increased to about 26 times its level in 1950.

FIGURE 32-1

The Growth of World Trade

In panel (a), you can see the growth in world trade in relative terms because we use an index of 100 to represent real world trade in 1950. By the early 2010s, that index had exceeded 2,500. At the same time, the index of world real GDP (annual world real income) had gone up only about 1,000. Thus, generally world trade has been on the rise. In the United States, both imports and exports, expressed as a percentage of annual national income (GDP) in panel (b), generally rose after 1950 and recovered following the 2008–2009 recession.

Sources: Steven Husted and Michael Melvin, *International Economics*, 3rd ed. (New York: HarperCollins, 1995), p. 11, used with permission; World Trade Organization; Federal Reserve System; U.S. Department of Commerce.

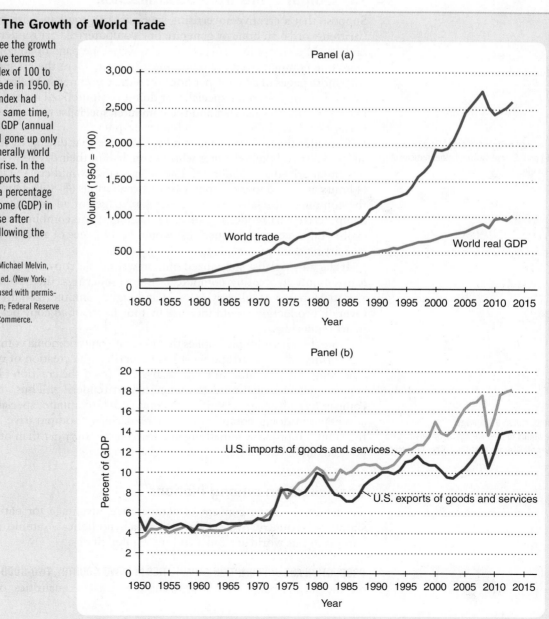

Go to www.econtoday.com/chap32 for the World Trade Organization's most recent data on world trade.

The United States has figured prominently in this expansion of world trade. In panel (b) of Figure 32-1 on page 705, you see imports and exports expressed as a percentage of total annual yearly income (GDP). Whereas imports amounted to barely 4 percent of annual U.S. GDP in 1950, today they account for more than 18 percent. International trade has become more important to the U.S. economy, and it may become even more so as other countries loosen their trade restrictions.

Why We Trade: Comparative Advantage and Mutual Gains from Exchange

You have already been introduced to the concept of specialization and mutual gains from trade in Chapter 2. These concepts are worth repeating because they are essential to understanding why the world is better off because of more international trade. The best way to understand the gains from trade among nations is first to understand the output gains from specialization between individuals.

The Output Gains from Specialization

Suppose that a creative advertising specialist can come up with two pages of ad copy (written words) an hour or generate one computerized art rendering per hour. At the same time, a computer art specialist can write one page of ad copy per hour or complete one computerized art rendering per hour. Here the ad specialist can come up with more pages of ad copy per hour than the computer specialist and seemingly is just as good as the computer specialist at doing computerized art renderings. Is there any reason for the ad specialist and the computer specialist to "trade"? The answer is yes because such trading will lead to higher output.

Go to www.econtoday.com/chap32 for data on U.S. trade with all other nations of the world.

Consider the scenario of no trading. Assume that during each eight-hour day, the ad specialist and the computer whiz devote half of their day to writing ad copy and half to computerized art rendering. The ad specialist would create eight pages of ad copy (4 hours × 2) and four computerized art renderings (4 × 1). During that same period, the computer specialist would create four pages of ad copy (4 hours × 1) and four computerized art renderings (4 × 1). Each day, the combined output for the ad specialist and the computer specialist would be 12 pages of ad copy and eight computerized art renderings.

If the ad specialist specialized only in writing ad copy and the computer whiz specialized only in creating computerized art renderings, their combined output would rise to 16 pages of ad copy (8 × 2) and eight computerized art renderings (8 × 1). Overall, production would increase by four pages of ad copy per day with no decline in art renderings.

Note that this example implies that to create one additional computerized art rendering during a day, the ad specialist has to sacrifice the creation of two pages of ad copy. The computer specialist, in contrast, has to give up the creation of only one page of ad copy to generate one more computerized art rendering. Thus, the ad specialist has a comparative advantage in writing ad copy, and the computer specialist has a comparative advantage in doing computerized art renderings. **Comparative advantage** is simply the ability to produce something at a lower *opportunity cost* than other producers, as we pointed out in Chapter 2.

Comparative advantage
The ability to produce a good or service at a lower opportunity cost than other producers.

Specialization among Nations

To demonstrate the concept of comparative advantage for nations, let's consider a simple two-country, two-good world. As a hypothetical example, let's suppose that the nations in this world are India and the United States.

PRODUCTION AND CONSUMPTION CAPABILITIES IN A TWO-COUNTRY, TWO-GOOD WORLD In Table 32-1 on the facing page, we show maximum feasible quantities of high-performance

TABLE 32-1

Maximum Feasible Hourly Production Rates of Either Digital Apps or Tablet Devices Using All Available Resources

This table indicates maximum feasible rates of production of digital apps and tablet devices if all available resources are allocated to producing either one item or the other. If U.S. residents allocate all resources to producing a single good, they can produce either 90 digital apps per hour or 225 tablets per hour. If residents of India allocate all resources to manufacturing one good, they can produce either 100 apps per hour or 50 tablets per hour.

Product	United States	India
Digital apps	90	100
Tablet devices	225	50

commercial digital apps (apps) and tablet devices (tablets) that may be produced during an hour using all resources—labor, capital, land, and entrepreneurship—available in the United States and in India. As you can see from the table, U.S. residents can utilize all their resources to produce either 90 apps per hour or 225 tablets per hour. If residents of India utilize all their resources, they can produce either 100 apps per hour or 50 tablets per hour.

COMPARATIVE ADVANTAGE Suppose that in each country, there are constant opportunity costs of producing apps and tablets. Table 32-1 above implies that to allocate all available resources to production of 50 tablets, residents of India would have to sacrifice the production of 100 apps. Thus, the opportunity cost in India of producing 1 tablet is equal to 2 apps. At the same time, the opportunity cost of producing 1 app in India is 0.5 tablet.

In the United States, to allocate all available resources to production of 225 tablets, U.S. residents would have to give up producing 90 apps. This means that the opportunity cost in the United States of producing 1 tablet is equal to 0.4 app. Alternatively, we can say that the opportunity cost to U.S. residents of producing 1 app is 2.5 tablets ($225 \div 90 = 2.5$).

The opportunity cost of producing a tablet is lower in the United States than in India. At the same time, the opportunity cost of producing apps is lower in India than in the United States. Consequently, the United States has a comparative advantage in manufacturing tablets, and India has a comparative advantage in producing apps.

PRODUCTION WITHOUT TRADE Table 32-2 on the following page tabulates two possible production choices in a situation in which U.S. and Indian residents choose not to engage in international trade. Let's suppose that in the United States, residents choose to produce and consume 30 digital apps. To produce this number of apps requires that 75 fewer tablets (30 apps times 2.5 tablets per app) be produced than the maximum feasible tablet production of 225 tablets, or 150 tablets. Thus, in the absence of trade, 30 apps and 150 tablets are produced and consumed in the United States.

Table 32-2 indicates that during an hour's time in India, residents choose to produce and consume 37.5 tablets. Obtaining this number of tablets entails the production of 75 fewer apps (37.5 tablets times 2 apps per tablet) than the maximum of 100 apps, or 25 apps. Hence, in the absence of trade, 37.5 tablets and 25 apps are produced and consumed in India.

Finally, Table 32-2 displays production of apps and tablets for this two-country world, given the nations' production (and, implicitly, consumption) choices in the absence of trade. In an hour's time, U.S. app production is 30 units, and Indian app production is 25 units, so the total apps produced and available for consumption worldwide

TABLE 32-2

U.S. and Indian Production and Consumption without Trade

This table indicates two possible hourly combinations of production and consumption of digital apps and tablet devices in the absence of trade in a "world" encompassing the United States and India. U.S. residents produce 30 apps, and residents of India produce 25 apps, so the total apps that can be consumed worldwide is 55. In addition, U.S. residents produce 150 tablets, and Indian residents produce 37.5 tablets, so worldwide production and consumption of tablets amount to 187.5 tablets per hour.

Product	United States	India	Actual World Output
Digital apps (per hour)	30	25	55
Tablet devices (per hour)	150	37.5	187.5

is 55. Hourly U.S. tablet production is 150 tablets, and Indian tablet production is 37.5 tablets, so a total of 187.5 tablets per hour is produced and available for consumption in this two-country world.

SPECIALIZATION IN PRODUCTION More realistically, residents of the United States will choose to specialize in the activity for which they experience a lower opportunity cost. In other words, U.S. residents will specialize in the activity in which they have a comparative advantage, which is the production of tablet devices, which they can offer in trade to residents of India. Likewise, Indian residents will specialize in the manufacturing industry in which they have a comparative advantage, which is the production of digital apps, which they can offer in trade to U.S. residents.

By specializing, the two countries can gain from engaging in international trade. To see why, suppose that U.S. residents allocate all available resources to producing 225 tablets, the good in which they have a comparative advantage. In addition, residents of India utilize all resources they have on hand to produce 100 apps, the good in which they have a comparative advantage.

CONSUMPTION WITH SPECIALIZATION AND TRADE U.S. residents will be willing to buy an Indian digital app as long as they must provide in exchange no more than 2.5 tablet devices, which is the opportunity cost of producing 1 app at home. At the same time, residents of India will be willing to buy a U.S. tablet as long as they must provide in exchange no more than 2 apps, which is their opportunity cost of producing a tablet.

Suppose that residents of both countries agree to trade at a rate of exchange of 1 tablet for 1 app and that they agree to trade 75 U.S. tablets for 75 Indian apps. Table 32-3 on the facing page displays the outcomes that result in both countries. By specializing in tablet production and engaging in trade, U.S. residents can continue to consume 150 tablets. In addition, U.S. residents are also able to import and consume 75 apps produced in India. At the same time, specialization and exchange allow residents of India to continue to consume 25 apps. Producing 75 more apps for export to the United States allows India to import 75 tablets.

GAINS FROM TRADE Table 32-4 on the facing page summarizes the rates of consumption of U.S. and Indian residents with and without trade. Column 1 displays U.S. and Indian app and tablet consumption rates with specialization and trade from Table 32-3, and it sums these to determine total consumption rates in this two-country world. Column 2 shows U.S., Indian, and worldwide consumption rates without international trade from Table 32-2 above. Column 3 gives the differences between the two columns.

TABLE 32-3

U.S. and Indian Production and Consumption with Specialization and Trade

In this table, U.S. residents produce 225 tablet devices, and no digital apps and Indian residents produce 100 digital apps and no tablets. Residents of the two nations then agree to a rate of exchange of 1 tablet for 1 app and proceed to trade 75 U.S. tablets for 75 Indian apps. Specialization and trade allow U.S. residents to consume 75 apps imported from India and to consume 150 tablets produced at home. By specializing and engaging in trade, Indian residents consume 25 apps produced at home and import 75 tablets from the United States.

Product	U.S. Production and Consumption with Trade		Indian Production and Consumption with Trade	
Digital apps (per hour)	U.S. production	0	Indian production	100
	+Imports from India	75	−Exports to U.S.	75
	Total U.S. consumption	75	Total Indian consumption	25
Tablet devices (per hour)	U.S. production	225	Indian production	0
	−Exports to India	75	+Imports from U.S.	75
	Total U.S. consumption	150	Total Indian consumption	75

Table 32-4 below indicates that by producing 75 additional tablets for export to India in exchange for 75 apps, U.S. residents are able to expand their app consumption from 30 to 75. Thus, the U.S. gain from specialization and trade is 45 apps. This is a net gain in app consumption for the two-country world as a whole, because neither country had to give up consuming any tablets for U.S. residents to realize this gain from trade.

In addition, without trade residents of India could have used all resources to produce and consume only 37.5 tablets and 25 apps. By using all resources to specialize in producing 100 apps and engaging in trade, residents of India can consume 37.5 *more* tablets than they could have produced and consumed alone without reducing their app consumption. Thus, the Indian gain from trade is 37.5 tablets. This represents a worldwide gain in tablet consumption, because neither country had to give up consuming any tablets for Indian residents to realize this gain from trade.

TABLE 32-4

National and Worldwide Gains from Specialization and Trade

This table summarizes the consumption gains experienced by the United States, India, and the two-country world. U.S. and Indian app and tablet consumption rates with specialization and trade from Table 32-3 above are listed in column 1, which sums the national consumption rates to determine total worldwide consumption with trade. Column 2 shows U.S., Indian, and worldwide consumption rates without international trade, as reported in Table 32-2 on the facing page. Column 3 gives the differences between the two columns, which are the resulting national and worldwide gains from international trade.

Product	(1) National and World Consumption with Trade		(2) National and World Consumption without Trade		(3) Worldwide Consumption Gains from Trade	
Digital apps (per hour)	U.S. consumption	75	U.S. consumption	30	Change in U.S. consumption	+45
	+Indian consumption	25	+Indian consumption	25	Change in Indian consumption	+0
	World consumption	100	World consumption	55	**Change in world consumption**	**+45**
Tablet devices (per hour)	U.S. consumption	150	U.S. consumption	150	Change in U.S. consumption	+0
	+Indian consumption	75	+Indian consumption	37.5	Change in Indian consumption	+37.5
	World consumption	225	World consumption	187.5	**Change in world consumption**	**+37.5**

SPECIALIZATION IS THE KEY This example shows that when nations specialize in producing goods for which they have a comparative advantage and engage in international trade, considerable consumption gains are possible for those nations and hence for the world. Why is this so? The answer is that specialization and trade enable Indian residents to obtain each tablet device at an opportunity cost of 1 digital app instead of 2 apps and permit U.S. residents to obtain each app at an opportunity cost of 1 tablet instead of 2.5 tablets.

Indian residents effectively experience a gain from trade of 1 app for each tablet purchased from the United States, and U.S. residents experience a gain from trade of 1.5 tablets for each app purchased from India. Thus, specializing in producing goods for which the two nations have a comparative advantage allows both nations to produce more efficiently. As a consequence, worldwide production capabilities increase. This makes greater worldwide consumption possible through international trade.

Of course, not everybody in our example is better off when free trade occurs. In our example, the U.S. app industry and Indian tablet industry have disappeared. Thus, U.S. app makers and Indian tablet manufacturers are worse off.

Some people worry that the United States (or any country, for that matter) might someday "run out of exports" because of overaggressive foreign competition. The analysis of comparative advantage tells us the contrary. No matter how much other countries compete for our business, the United States (or any other country) will always have a comparative advantage in something that it can export. In 10 or 20 years, that something may not be what we export today, but it will be exportable nonetheless because we will have a comparative advantage in producing it. Consequently, the significant flows of world trade shown in Figure 32-2 below will continue because the United States and other nations will retain comparative advantages in producing various goods and services.

FIGURE 32-2

World Trade Flows

International merchandise trade amounts to nearly $20 trillion worldwide. The percentage figures show the proportion of trade flowing in the various directions throughout the globe.

Sources: World Trade Organization and author's estimates (data are for 2013).

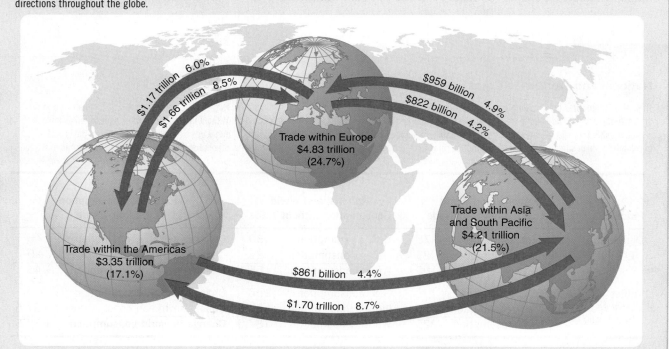

What accounts for the fact that the bulk of the world's linen fabrics are produced within a very small area on the earth's surface?

INTERNATIONAL EXAMPLE

Comparative Advantage and Specialization in European Linens

The production of linen requires twice as much land and labor as the production of an equivalent amount of cotton. Nevertheless, linen is a staple material utilized in designer clothing, such as women's blazers and dresses with prices exceeding $2,000, men's trench coats that sell for more than $1,500, and wedding gowns priced above $5,500.

Two-thirds of the world's linen is derived from a fiber called flax that is harvested within a narrow belt of farmland stretching from northern France into the Netherlands. The European coastal climate provides alternating sunshine and rain that contribute to development of a fungus that grows on the flax stems. The fungus breaks down the stems so that the linen fibers can be more readily separated from the plants. Thus, farmers residing this area are able to produce flax at a lower opportunity cost, in terms of forgone production of other goods, than almost anywhere else on the planet. This fact explains why this region of Europe has a comparative advantage in growing flax and specializes in the production of linen.

FOR CRITICAL THINKING

Why do you think that linen production generates gains from trade for European producers of flax and linen, even though cotton-based fabrics can be produced at lower absolute cost in many other parts of the world?

Other Benefits from International Trade: The Transmission of Ideas

Beyond the fact that comparative advantage results in an overall increase in the output of goods produced and consumed, there is another benefit to international trade. International trade also aids in the transmission of ideas. According to economic historians, international trade has been the principal means by which new goods, services, and processes have spread around the world. For example, coffee was initially grown in Arabia near the Red Sea. Around AD 675, it began to be roasted and consumed as a beverage. Eventually, it was exported to other parts of the world, and the Dutch started cultivating it in their colonies during the seventeenth century and the French in the eighteenth century. The lowly potato is native to the Peruvian Andes. In the sixteenth century, it was brought to Europe by Spanish explorers. Thereafter, its cultivation and consumption spread rapidly. Finally, it became part of the North American agricultural scene in the early eighteenth century.

New processes have also been transmitted through international trade. An example is the Japanese manufacturing innovation that emphasized redesigning the system rather than running the existing system in the best possible way. Inventories were reduced to just-in-time levels by reengineering machine setup methods.

In addition, international trade has enabled *intellectual property* to spread throughout the world. New music, such as rock and roll in the 1950s and 1960s and hip-hop in the 1990s and 2000s, has been transmitted in this way, as have the digital devices applications and application tools that are common for online and wireless users everywhere.

The Relationship between Imports and Exports

The basic proposition in understanding all of international trade is this:

In the long run, imports are paid for by exports.

The reason that imports are ultimately paid for by exports is that foreign residents want something in exchange for the goods that are shipped to the United States. For the most part, they want U.S.-made goods. From this truism comes a remarkable corollary:

Any restriction of imports ultimately reduces exports.

This is a shocking revelation to many people who want to restrict foreign competition to protect domestic jobs. Although it is possible to "protect" certain U.S. jobs by restricting foreign competition, it is impossible to make *everyone* better off by imposing import restrictions. Why? The reason is that ultimately such restrictions lead to a reduction in employment and output—and hence incomes—in the export industries of the nation.

WHAT IF... the government saved U.S. jobs from foreign competition by prohibiting all imports?

In the long run, U.S. imports are paid for by U.S. exports. Shutting out all imports of goods and services from abroad certainly would protect U.S. firms from competition and hence would protect many U.S. workers' jobs with those firms. A prohibition on all imports additionally would lead to an eventual halt in all purchases of U.S. firms' exports by residents of other nations, however. The consequence would be a reduction in production and sales by U.S. exporting firms, which would respond by eliminating positions for U.S. workers. Ultimately, therefore, a prohibition on U.S. imports would not really "save" jobs for U.S. workers.

International Competitiveness

"The United States is falling behind." "We need to stay competitive internationally." Statements such as these are often heard when the subject of international trade comes up. There are two problems with such talk. The first has to do with a simple definition. What does "global competitiveness" really mean? When one company competes against another, it is in competition. Is the United States like one big corporation, in competition with other countries? Certainly not. The standard of living in each country is almost solely a function of how well the economy functions *within that country*, not relative to other countries.

Another point relates to real-world observations. According to the Institute for Management Development in Lausanne, Switzerland, the United States is among the top ten nations in overall productive efficiency. According to the report, the relatively high ranking of the United States over the years has been due to widespread entrepreneurship, economic restructuring, and information-technology investments. Other factors include the open U.S. financial system and large investments in scientific research.

QUICK QUIZ See page 724 for the answers. Review concepts from this section in MyEconLab.

A nation has a **comparative advantage** when its residents are able to produce a good or service at a _____ opportunity cost than residents of another nation.

Specializing in production of goods and services for which residents of a nation have a _____ _____ allows the nation's residents to _____ more of all goods and services.

_____ from trade arise for all nations in the world that engage in international trade because specialization and trade allow countries' residents to _____ more goods and services without necessarily giving up consumption of other goods and services.

Arguments against Free Trade

Numerous arguments are raised against free trade. These arguments focus mainly on the costs of trade. They do not consider the benefits or the possible alternatives for reducing the costs of free trade while still reaping benefits.

The Infant Industry Argument

A nation may feel that if a particular industry is allowed to develop domestically, it will eventually become efficient enough to compete effectively in the world market. Therefore, the nation may impose some restrictions on imports in order to give domestic producers the time they need to develop their efficiency to the point where they can compete in the domestic market without any restrictions on imports. In graphic terminology, we would expect that if the protected industry truly does experience improvements in production techniques or technological breakthroughs toward greater efficiency in the future, the supply curve will shift outward to the right so that the domestic industry can produce larger quantities at each and every price. National policymakers often assert that this **infant industry argument** has some merit in the short run. They have used it to protect a number of industries in their infancy around the world.

Such a policy can be abused, however. Often the protective import-restricting arrangements remain even after the infant has matured. If other countries can still produce more cheaply, the people who benefit from this type of situation are obviously the stockholders (and specialized factors of production that will earn economic rents—see pages 463–465 in Chapter 21) in the industry that is still being protected from world competition. The people who lose out are the consumers, who must pay a price higher than the world price for the product in question. In any event, because it is very difficult to know beforehand which industries will eventually survive, it is possible, perhaps even likely, that policymakers will choose to protect industries that have no reasonable chance of competing on their own in world markets. Note that when we speculate about which industries "should" be protected, we are in the realm of *normative economics*. We are making a value judgment, a subjective statement of what *ought to be*.

Infant industry argument
The contention that tariffs should be imposed to protect from import competition an industry that is trying to get started. Presumably, after the industry becomes technologically efficient, the tariff can be lifted.

Countering Foreign Subsidies and Dumping

Another common argument against unrestricted foreign trade is that a nation must counter other nations' subsidies to their own producers. When a foreign government subsidizes its producers, our producers claim that they cannot compete fairly with these subsidized foreign producers. To the extent that such subsidies fluctuate, it can be argued that unrestricted free trade will seriously disrupt domestic producers. They will not know when foreign governments are going to subsidize their producers and when they are not. Our competing industries will be expanding and contracting too frequently.

How do government credit subsidies promote international trade by some U.S. industries while assisting foreign competitors of another industry?

POLICY EXAMPLE

A U.S. Agency Subsidizes U.S. Exports—and Also Foreign Firms

The U.S. Export-Import (Ex-Im) Bank regularly extends about $100 billion in subsidized loans to foreign buyers of U.S.-manufactured products, including aircraft, hair-care products, and construction equipment. The Ex-Im Bank's extensions of taxpayer-subsidized credit to companies in other nations gives these foreign firms incentives to buy U.S. exports.

Airlines based in the United States are not enthused about aircraft-loan subsidies to competitors based in other nations, however. The U.S. airlines argue that the Ex-Im Bank's low-interest loans to foreign carriers provide a cost advantage that enables the foreign airlines to compete at lower expense in the international air transportation market. Thus, from the U.S. airlines' point of view, U.S. taxpayers are subsidizing their foreign competitors.

FOR CRITICAL THINKING
Why do you suppose that some U.S. makers of hair-care products and certain U.S. construction contractors that bid for work in other nations have lodged complaints similar to those of the U.S. airlines?

The phenomenon called *dumping* is also used as an argument against unrestricted trade. **Dumping** is said to occur when a producer sells its products abroad below the price that is charged in the home market or at a price below its cost of production. Often, when a foreign producer is accused of dumping, further investigation reveals that the

Dumping
Selling a good or a service abroad below the price charged in the home market or at a price below its cost of production.

foreign nation is in the throes of a recession. The foreign producer does not want to slow down its production at home. Because it anticipates an end to the recession and doesn't want to hold large inventories, it dumps its products abroad at prices below home prices. U.S. competitors may also allege that the foreign producer sells its output at prices below its full costs to be assured of covering variable costs of production.

Protecting Domestic Jobs

Perhaps the argument used most often against free trade is that unrestrained competition from other countries will eliminate jobs in the United States because other countries have lower-cost labor than we do. (Less restrictive environmental standards in other countries might also lower their private costs relative to ours.) This is a compelling argument, particularly for politicians from areas that might be threatened by foreign competition. For example, a representative from an area with shoe factories would certainly be upset about the possibility of constituents' losing their jobs because of competition from lower-priced shoe manufacturers in Brazil and Italy. But, of course, this argument against free trade is equally applicable to trade between the states within the United States.

Economists David Gould, G. L. Woodbridge, and Roy Ruffin examined the data on the relationship between increases in imports and the unemployment rate. They concluded that there is no causal link between the two. Indeed, in half the cases they studied, when imports increased, the unemployment rate fell.

Another issue involves the cost of protecting U.S. jobs by restricting international trade. The Institute for International Economics examined the restrictions on foreign textiles and apparel goods. The study found that U.S. consumers pay $9 billion a year more than they would otherwise pay for those goods to protect jobs in those industries. That comes out to $50,000 *a year* for each job saved in an industry in which the average job pays only $20,000 a year. Similar studies have yielded similar results: Restrictions on imports of Japanese cars have cost $160,000 *per year* for every job saved in the auto industry. Every job preserved in the glass industry has cost $200,000 each and every year. Every job preserved in the U.S. steel industry has cost an astounding $750,000 per year.

Emerging Arguments against Free Trade

In recent years, two new antitrade arguments have been advanced. One of these focuses on environmental and safety concerns. For instance, many critics of free trade have suggested that genetic engineering of plants and animals could lead to accidental production of new diseases and that people, livestock, and pets could be harmed by tainted foods imported for human and animal consumption. These worries have induced the European Union to restrain trade in such products.

Another argument against free trade arises from national defense concerns. Major espionage successes by China in the late 1990s and 2000s led some U.S. strategic experts to propose sweeping restrictions on exports of new technology.

Free trade proponents counter that at best these are arguments for the judicious regulation of trade. They continue to argue that, by and large, broad trade restrictions mainly harm the interests of the nations that impose them.

QUICK QUIZ See page 724 for the answers. Review concepts from this section in MyEconLab.

The _____ industry argument against free trade contends that new industries should be _____ against world competition so that they can become technologically efficient in the long run.

Unrestricted foreign trade may allow foreign governments to subsidize exports or foreign producers to engage in _____, or selling products in other countries below their cost of production. Critics claim that to the extent that foreign export subsidies and _____ create more instability in domestic production, they may impair our well-being.

Ways to Restrict Foreign Trade

International trade can be stopped or at least stifled in many ways. These include quotas and taxes (the latter are usually called *tariffs* when applied to internationally traded items). Let's talk first about quotas.

Quotas

Under a **quota system,** individual countries or groups of foreign producers are restricted to a certain amount of trade. An import quota specifies the maximum amount of a commodity that may be imported during a specified period of time. For example, the government might allow no more than 200 million barrels of foreign crude oil to enter the United States in a particular month.

Consider the example of quotas on textiles. Figure 32-3 below presents the demand and supply curves for imported textiles. In an unrestricted import market, the equilibrium quantity imported is 900 million yards at a price of $1 per yard (expressed in constant-quality units). When an import quota is imposed, the supply curve is no longer S. Instead, the supply curve becomes vertical at some amount less than the equilibrium quantity—here, 800 million yards per year. The price to the U.S. consumer increases from $1.00 to $1.50.

Clearly, the output restriction generated by a quota on foreign imports of a particular item has the effect of raising the domestic price of the imported item. Two groups benefit. One group is importers that are able to obtain the rights to sell imported items domestically at the higher price, which raises their revenues and boosts their profits. The other group is domestic producers. Naturally, a rise in the price of an imported item induces an increase in the demand for domestic substitutes. Thus, the domestic prices of close substitutes for the item subject to the import restriction also increase, which generates higher revenues and profits for domestic producers.

Quota system
A government-imposed restriction on the quantity of a specific good that another country is allowed to sell in the United States. In other words, quotas are restrictions on imports. These restrictions are usually applied to one or several specific countries.

YOU ARE THERE

To consider why domestic producers often desire protection from competing foreign products, read **A French Family Bookshop Seeks Protection from U.S. E-Books** on page 720.

FIGURE 32-3

The Effect of Quotas on Textile Imports

Without restrictions, at point E_1, 900 million yards of textiles would be imported each year into the United States at the world price of $1.00 per yard. If the federal government imposes a quota of only 800 million yards, the effective supply curve becomes vertical at that quantity. It intersects the demand curve at point E_2, so the new equilibrium price is $1.50 per yard.

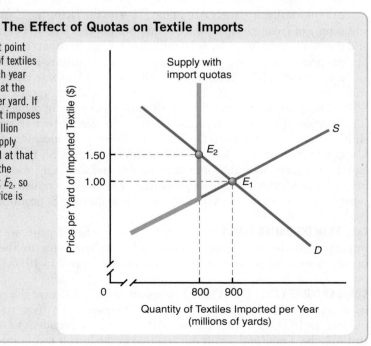

Why did U.S. government agents recently conduct a raid on a U.S. guitar manufacturer?

POLICY EXAMPLE

Gibson Guitars Confronts a Very Particular Import Quota

One of the most famous U.S. guitar makers is Gibson Guitars, which places a "Made in the U.S.A." label on each instrument it sells. Recently, federal agents raided the company's corporate offices and its two guitar factories. The agents seized 24 pallets of rosewood and ebony imported from India, which Gibson had planned to use in making fingerboards for its guitars.

The company, the U.S. government alleged, had run afoul of an international trade quota on unfinished rosewood and ebony products. Finished rosewood or ebony, though, had no U.S. trade quota. Hence, if Indian workers had finished the rosewood and ebony prior to shipment, instead of Gibson's U.S. workers finishing the materials following shipment. Gibson would not have violated any U.S. trade quotas.

FOR CRITICAL THINKING

Gibson presumably violated an environmental protection law. Why does this trade quota have the same economic effects as laws designed to protect domestic firms from foreign competition?

Voluntary restraint agreement (VRA)
An official agreement with another country that "voluntarily" restricts the quantity of its exports to the United States.

Voluntary import expansion (VIE)
An official agreement with another country in which it agrees to import more from the United States.

Go to www.econtoday.com/chap32 to take a look at the U.S. State Department's reports on economic policy and trade practices.

VOLUNTARY QUOTAS Quotas do not have to be explicit and defined by law. They can be "voluntary." Such a quota is called a **voluntary restraint agreement (VRA).** In the early 1980s, Japanese automakers voluntarily restrained exports to the United States. These restraints stayed in place into the 1990s. Today, there are VRAs on machine tools and textiles.

The opposite of a VRA is a **voluntary import expansion (VIE).** Under a VIE, a foreign government agrees to have its companies import more foreign goods from another country. The United States almost started a major international trade war with Japan in 1995 over just such an issue. The U.S. government wanted Japanese automobile manufacturers to voluntarily increase their imports of U.S.-made automobile parts. Ultimately, Japanese companies did make a token increase in their imports of U.S. auto parts.

Tariffs

We can analyze tariffs by using standard supply and demand diagrams. Let's use as our commodity laptop computers, some of which are made in Japan and some of which are made domestically. In panel (a) of Figure 32-4 on the facing page, you see the demand for and supply of Japanese laptops. The equilibrium price is $500 per constant-quality unit, and the equilibrium quantity is 10 million per year. In panel (b), you see the same equilibrium price of $500, and the *domestic* equilibrium quantity is 5 million units per year.

Now a tariff of $250 is imposed on all imported Japanese laptops. The supply curve shifts upward by $250 to S_2. For purchasers of Japanese laptops, the price increases to $625. The quantity demanded falls to 8 million per year. In panel (b), you see that at the higher price of imported Japanese laptops, the demand curve for U.S.-made laptops shifts outward to the right to D_2. The equilibrium price increases to $625, and the equilibrium quantity increases to 6.5 million units per year. So the tariff benefits domestic laptop producers because it increases the demand for their products due to the higher price of a close substitute, Japanese laptops. This causes a redistribution of income from Japanese producers and U.S. consumers of laptops to U.S. producers of laptops.

TARIFFS IN THE UNITED STATES In Figure 32-5 on the facing page, we see that tariffs on all imported goods have varied widely. The highest rates in the twentieth century occurred with the passage of the Smoot-Hawley Tariff in 1930.

CURRENT TARIFF LAWS The Trade Expansion Act of 1962 gave the president the authority to reduce tariffs by up to 50 percent. Subsequently, tariffs were reduced by about 35 percent. In 1974, the Trade Reform Act allowed the president to reduce tariffs further. In 1984, the Trade and Tariff Act resulted in the lowest tariff rates ever. All such trade agreement obligations of the United States were carried out under the auspices of the

FIGURE 32-4

The Effect of a Tariff on Japanese-Made Laptop Computers

Without a tariff, the United States buys 10 million Japanese laptops per year at an average price of $500, at point E_1 in panel (a). U.S. producers sell 5 million domestically made laptops, also at $500 each, at point E_1 in panel (b). A $250 tariff per laptop will shift the Japanese import supply curve to S_2 in panel (a), so that the new equilibrium is at E_2 with price increased to $625 and quantity sold reduced to 8 million per year. The demand curve for U.S.-made laptops (for which there is no tariff) shifts to D_2, in panel (b). Domestic sales increase to 6.5 million per year, at point E_2.

FIGURE 32-5

Tariff Rates in the United States Since 1820

Tariff rates in the United States have bounced around like a football. Indeed, in Congress, tariffs are a political football. Import-competing industries prefer high tariffs. In the twentieth century, the highest tariff was the Smoot-Hawley Tariff of 1930, which was about as high as the "tariff of abominations" in 1828.

Source: U.S. Department of Commerce.

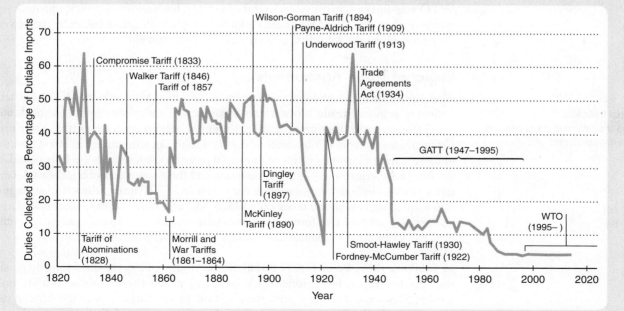

General Agreement on Tariffs and Trade (GATT)

An international agreement established in 1947 to further world trade by reducing barriers and tariffs. The GATT was replaced by the World Trade Organization in 1995.

General Agreement on Tariffs and Trade (GATT), which was signed in 1947. Member nations of the GATT account for more than 85 percent of world trade. As you can see in Figure 32-5 on the previous page, U.S. tariff rates have declined since the early 1960s, when several rounds of negotiations under the GATT were initiated.

How have recently reduced barriers to trade with the United States affected nations in Africa?

INTERNATIONAL POLICY EXAMPLE

African Nations Benefit from Lower U.S. Trade Barriers

In 2000, the U.S. Congress passed the African Growth and Opportunity Act, which reduced substantially the tariffs faced by African companies seeking to export goods and services to the United States. African-U.S. trade has risen considerably since. Earnings that African companies derive from exports are now 500 percent higher than in 2001. Furthermore, estimates indicate that export industries in African nations now employ 300,000 additional workers as a consequence of the increased volume of trade. Thus, slashing trade barriers has generated welfare gains for African residents.

FOR CRITICAL THINKING

How might U.S. residents have benefited from the fact that African countries granted reciprocal reductions in tariffs on imports into their nations from the United States?

International Trade Organizations

The widespread effort to reduce tariffs around the world has generated interest among nations in joining various international trade organizations. These organizations promote trade by granting preferences in the form of reduced or eliminated tariffs, duties, or quotas.

The World Trade Organization (WTO)

World Trade Organization (WTO)

The successor organization to the GATT that handles trade disputes among its member nations.

The most important international trade organization with the largest membership is the **World Trade Organization (WTO),** which was ratified by the final round of negotiations of the General Agreement on Tariffs and Trade at the end of 1993. The WTO, which as of 2012 had 157 member nations and included 30 observer governments, began operations on January 1, 1995. The WTO has fostered important and far-reaching global trade agreements. There is considerable evidence that since the WTO was formed, many of its member nations have adopted policies promoting international trade. The WTO also adjudicates trade disputes between nations in an effort to reduce the scope of protectionism around the globe.

Regional Trade Agreements

Regional trade bloc

A group of nations that grants members special trade privileges.

Numerous other international trade organizations exist alongside the WTO. Sometimes known as **regional trade blocs,** these organizations are created by special deals among groups of countries that grant trade preferences only to countries within their groups. Currently, more than 475 bilateral or regional trade agreements are in effect around the globe. Examples include groups of industrial powerhouses, such as the European Union, the North American Free Trade Agreement, and the Association of Southeast Asian Nations. Nations in South America with per capita real GDP nearer the world average have also formed regional trade blocs called Mercosur and the Andean Community. Less developed nations have also formed regional trade blocs, such as the Economic Community of West African States and the Community of East and Southern Africa.

DO REGIONAL TRADE BLOCS SIMPLY DIVERT TRADE? Figure 32-6 on the facing page shows that the formation of regional trade blocs, in which the European Union and the United States are often key participants, is on an upswing. An average African nation participates in four separate regional trading agreements. A typical Latin American country belongs to eight different regional trade blocs.

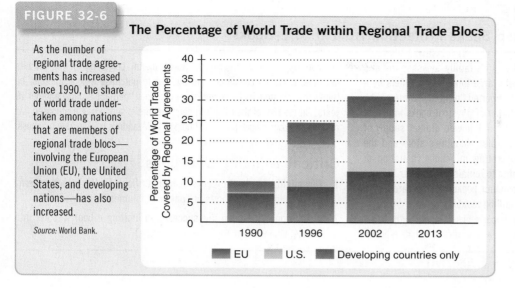

FIGURE 32-6

The Percentage of World Trade within Regional Trade Blocs

As the number of regional trade agreements has increased since 1990, the share of world trade undertaken among nations that are members of regional trade blocs—involving the European Union (EU), the United States, and developing nations—has also increased.

Source: World Bank.

In the past, economists worried that the formation of regional trade blocs could mainly result in **trade diversion,** or the shifting of trade from countries outside a regional trade bloc to nations within a bloc. Indeed, a study by Jeffrey Frankel of Harvard University found evidence that some trade diversion does take place. Nevertheless, Frankel and other economists have concluded that the net effect of regional trade agreements has been to boost overall international trade, in some cases considerably.

THE TRADE DEFLECTION ISSUE Today, the primary issue associated with regional trade blocs is **trade deflection.** This occurs when a company located in a nation outside a regional trade bloc moves goods that are not quite fully assembled into a member country, completes assembly of the goods there, and then exports them to other nations in the bloc. To try to reduce incentives for trade deflection, regional trade agreements often include **rules of origin,** which are regulations carefully defining categories of products that are eligible for trading preferences under the agreements. Some rules of origin, for instance, require any products trading freely among members of a bloc to be composed mainly of materials produced within a member nation.

Proponents of free trade worry, however, about the potential for parties to regional trade agreements to use rules of origin to create barriers to trade. Sufficiently complex rules of origin, they suggest, can provide disincentives for countries to utilize the trade-promoting preferences that regional trade agreements ought to provide. Indeed, some free trade proponents applaud successful trade deflection. They contend that it helps to circumvent trade restrictions and thus allows nations within regional trade blocs to experience additional gains from trade.

Trade diversion
Shifting existing international trade from countries outside a regional trade bloc to nations within the bloc.

Trade deflection
Moving partially assembled products into a member nation of a regional trade bloc, completing assembly, and then exporting them to other nations within the bloc, so as to benefit from preferences granted by the trade bloc.

Rules of origin
Regulations that nations in regional trade blocs establish to delineate product categories eligible for trading preferences.

QUICK QUIZ   See page 724 for the answers. Review concepts from this section in MyEconLab.

One means of restricting foreign trade is an import quota, which specifies a _____ amount of a good that may be imported during a certain period. The resulting increase in import prices benefits domestic _____ that receive higher prices resulting from substitution to domestic goods.

Another means of restricting imports is a **tariff,** which is a _____ on imports only. An import tariff _____ import-competing industries and harms consumers by raising prices.

The main international institution created to improve trade among nations was the General Agreement on Tariffs and Trade (GATT). The last round of trade talks under the GATT led to the creation of the _____ _____ _____.

_____ _____ agreements among numerous nations of the world have established more than 475 bilateral and _____ _____ blocs, which grant special trade privileges such as reduced tariff barriers and quota exemptions to member nations.

YOU ARE THERE

A French Family Bookshop Seeks Protection from U.S. E-Books

For more than three decades, Thierry Meaudre's family bookshop in Paris has been protected from competition with large foreign booksellers by a French law restricting the distribution of imported "printed volumes." The legislation effectively constrains the number of physical books imported into the country and thereby restrains the nationwide market supply of books, which raises book prices. This enables Meaudre's store and the other 3,000 independent bookstores operating in France, a nation of 65 million people, to earn sufficient profits to remain in business. By way of comparison, fewer than 2,000 independent bookstores operate in the United States, a country with over 300 million residents.

The advent of low-priced U.S. e-book imports fills Meaudre with dread, because the existing law's limits of "printed volumes" do not include e-books.

"I have been having nightmares about digital books for years," admits Meaudre. If French consumers are allowed to purchase e-book imports, he thinks that his store might be able to remain open "perhaps at most another 10 years." In the face of the e-book threat, Meaudre is supporting a proposed law that would boost e-book prices and help keep Meaudre's bookshop in business.

Critical Thinking Questions

1. Why might imports of e-books be more difficult for the French government to limit than imports of "physical volumes"?

2. If the proposed French law succeeds in limiting e-book imports into France, who will pay higher e-book prices?

ISSUES & APPLICATIONS

U.S. Flower Growers Induce Congress to Snip Foreign Imports

CONCEPTS APPLIED

▶ Regional Trade Bloc

▶ Tariffs

▶ Subsidies

When the U.S. Congress passed the 1991 Andean Trade Promotion Act, it established a regional trade bloc encompassing the United States and several South American nations located along the Andes mountain range. This law slashed tariff rates on goods imported into the United States from Andean nations.

Budding Colombian Imports of Cut Flowers Ultimately Blossom

Among the imported items for which the 1991 legislation sharply reduced U.S. tariff rates were Colombian cut flowers. The Colombian climate is superior to that of the western United States for growing most flowers, and Colombian farm labor costs are much lower. Thus, within a few years after the reduction in tariffs, Colombian flower growers had established a network for selling cut flowers in California. Furthermore, in 2010, the Colombian firms opened a large distribution center in Los Angeles to increase the flow of cut-flower imports into the United States.

As Figure 32-7 on the facing page indicates, Colombian flower growers' efforts led to a substantial increase in U.S. flower imports from that nation during the 2000s. By 2010, U.S. imports of Colombian cut flowers were nearly 400 percent greater than the 2002 level.

California Flower Growers Lobby for Protection

As Colombian flower imports into California bloomed, the sales of cut flowers by California growers shriveled. When Congress passed the Andean Trade Promotion Act, there were 450 Californian flower farms. By 2010, there were 250.

In response to the upsurge in competition from Colombia, the California Cut Flower Commission, a trade association, successfully lobbied to delay congressional approval of a renewal of the Andean regional trade pact. The consequence

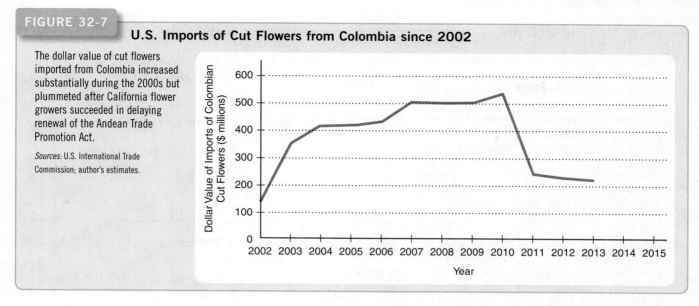

FIGURE 32-7

U.S. Imports of Cut Flowers from Colombia since 2002

The dollar value of cut flowers imported from Colombia increased substantially during the 2000s but plummeted after California flower growers succeeded in delaying renewal of the Andean Trade Promotion Act.

Sources: U.S. International Trade Commission; author's estimates.

was a reimposition in 2011 of tariffs on Colombian flower growers, whose tariff payments increased sharply. As shown in Figure 32-7 above, this significant tariff increase resulted in a considerable reduction in cut-flower imports from Colombia. As a consequence, the foreign supply of cut flowers in California decreased, and the demand for Californian cut flowers increased, which pushed up U.S. prices of cut flowers. Even as California flower growers' earnings flourished, they began lobbying for U.S. government subsidies to enable them to establish their own cut-flower distribution center to compete with Colombia's.

For Critical Thinking

1. Which region appears to have a comparative advantage in producing cut flowers: Colombia or California? Explain.

2. How have U.S. consumers of cut flowers been affected by the cutback in Colombian imports?

Web Resources

1. Find out more about the Andean Trade Promotion Act at **www.econtoday.com/chap32**.

2. Learn about the Colombian flower industry at **www.econtoday.com/chap32**.

> **MyEconLab**
>
> For more questions on this chapter's Issues & Applications, go to MyEconLab. In the Study Plan for this chapter, select Section N: News.

MyEconLab

Here is what you should know after reading this chapter. MyEconLab will help you identify what you know, and where to go when you need to practice.

— **WHAT YOU SHOULD KNOW** —

The Worldwide Importance of International Trade Total trade among nations has been growing faster than total world GDP. The growth of U.S. exports and imports relative to U.S. GDP parallels this global trend. Today, exports constitute more than 14 percent of total national production. In some countries, trade accounts for a much higher share of total economic activity.

Key Figure
Figure 32-1, 705

— **WHERE TO GO TO PRACTICE** —

• MyEconLab Study Plan 32.1
• Animated Figure 32-1

MyEconLab continued

┌─ WHAT YOU SHOULD KNOW ─────────────────────────── WHERE TO GO TO PRACTICE ─┐

Why Nations Can Gain from Specializing in Production and Engaging in Trade A country has a comparative advantage in producing a good if it can produce that good at a lower opportunity cost, in terms of forgone production of a second good, than another nation. Both nations can gain by specializing in producing the goods in which they have a comparative advantage and engaging in trade. Together, they can consume more than they would have in the absence of specialization and trade.

comparative advantage, 706

Key Figure
Figure 32-2, 710

- **MyEconLab** Study Plan 32.2
- Animated Figure 32-2

Arguments against Free Trade One argument against free trade is that temporary import restrictions might permit an "infant industry" to develop. Another argument concerns dumping, in which foreign firms allegedly sell some of their output in domestic markets at prices below the prices in their home markets or even below their costs of production. In addition, some environmentalists support restrictions on foreign trade to protect their nations from exposure to environmental hazards. Finally, some contend that countries should limit exports of technologies that could pose a threat to their national defense.

infant industry argument, 713
dumping, 713

- **MyEconLab** Study Plans 32.3, 32.4, 32.5

Ways That Nations Restrict Foreign Trade One way to restrain trade is to impose a quota, or a limit on imports of a good. This action restricts the supply of the good in the domestic market, thereby pushing up the equilibrium price of the good. Another way to reduce trade is to place a tariff on imported goods. This reduces the supply of foreign-made goods and increases the demand for domestically produced goods, thereby bringing about a rise in the price of the good.

quota system, 715
voluntary restraint agreement (VRA), 716
voluntary import expansion (VIE), 716
General Agreement on Tariffs and Trade (GATT), 718

Key Figures
Figure 32-3, 715
Figure 32-4, 717

- **MyEconLab** Study Plan 32.6
- Animated Figures 32-3, 32-4

Key International Trade Agreements and Organizations From 1947 to 1995, nations agreed to abide by the General Agreement on Tariffs and Trade (GATT), which laid an international legal foundation for relaxing quotas and reducing tariffs. Since 1995, the World Trade Organization (WTO) has adjudicated trade disputes that arise between or among nations. Now there are also more than 475 bilateral and regional trade blocs, including the North American Free Trade Agreement and the European Union, that provide special trade preferences to member nations.

World Trade Organization, 718
regional trade bloc, 718
trade diversion, 719
trade deflection, 719
rules of origin, 719

Key Figure
Figure 32-5, 717

- **MyEconLab** Study Plan 32.7
- Animated Figure 32-5

Log in to **MyEconLab**, take a chapter test, and get a personalized Study Plan that tells you which concepts you understand and which ones you need to review. From there, **MyEconLab** will give you further practice, tutorials, animations, videos, and guided solutions. For more information, visit www.myeconlab.com

PROBLEMS

All problems are assignable in MyEconLab. *Answers to the odd-numbered problems appear at the back of the book.*

32-1. To answer the questions below, consider the following table for the neighboring nations of Northland and West Coast. The table lists maximum feasible hourly rates of production of pastries if no sandwiches are produced and maximum feasible hourly rates of production of sandwiches if no pastries are produced. Assume that the opportunity costs of producing these goods are constant in both nations. (See page 707.)

Product	Northland	West Coast
Pastries (per hour)	50,000	100,000
Sandwiches (per hour)	25,000	200,000

    a. What is the opportunity cost of producing pastries in Northland? Of producing sandwiches in Northland?

    b. What is the opportunity cost of producing pastries in West Coast? Of producing sandwiches in West Coast?

32-2. Based on your answers to Problem 32-1, which nation has a comparative advantage in producing pastries? Which nation has a comparative advantage in producing sandwiches? (See page 707.)

32-3. Suppose that the two nations in Problems 32-1 and 32-2 choose to specialize in producing the goods for which they have a comparative advantage. They agree to trade at a rate of exchange of 1 pastry for 1 sandwich. At this rate of exchange, what are the maximum possible numbers of pastries and sandwiches that they could agree to trade? (See page 708.)

32-4. Residents of the nation of Border Kingdom can forgo production of digital televisions and utilize all available resources to produce 300 bottles of high-quality wine per hour. Alternatively, they can forgo producing wine and instead produce 60 digital TVs per hour. In the neighboring country of Coastal Realm, residents can forgo production of digital TVs and use all resources to produce 150 bottles of high-quality wine per hour, or they can forgo wine production and produce 50 digital TVs per hour. In both nations, the opportunity costs of producing the two goods are constant. (See pages 707–708.)

    a. What is the opportunity cost of producing digital TVs in Border Kingdom? Of producing bottles of wine in Border Kingdom?

    b. What is the opportunity cost of producing digital TVs in Coastal Realm? Of producing bottles of wine in Coastal Realm?

32-5. Based on your answers to Problem 32-4, which nation has a comparative advantage in producing digital TVs? Which nation has a comparative advantage in producing bottles of wine? (See page 708.)

32-6. Suppose that the two nations in Problem 32-4 decide to specialize in producing the good for which they have a comparative advantage and to engage in trade. Would residents of both nations find a rate of exchange of 4 bottles of wine for 1 digital TV potentially agreeable? Why or why not? (See pages 708–709.)

To answer Problems 32-7 and 32-8, refer to the following table, which shows possible combinations of hourly outputs of modems and flash memory drives in South Shore and neighboring East Isle, in which opportunity costs of producing both products are constant.

South Shore		East Isle	
Modems	Flash Drives	Modems	Flash Drives
75	0	100	0
60	30	80	10
45	60	60	20
30	90	40	30
15	120	20	40
0	150	0	50

32-7. Consider the above table and answer the questions that follow. (See pages 707–709.)

    a. What is the opportunity cost of producing modems in South Shore? Of producing flash memory drives in South Shore?

    b. What is the opportunity cost of producing modems in East Isle? Of producing flash memory drives in East Isle?

    c. Which nation has a comparative advantage in producing modems? Which nation has a comparative advantage in producing flash memory drives?

32-8. Refer to your answers to Problem 32-7 when answering the following questions. (See page 709.)

    a. Which *one* of the following rates of exchange of modems for flash memory drives will be acceptable to *both* nations: (i) 3 modems for 1 flash drive; (ii) 1 modem for 1 flash drive; or (iii) 1 flash drive for 2.5 modems? Explain.

    b. Suppose that each nation decides to use all available resources to produce only the good for which it has a comparative advantage and to engage in trade at the single feasible rate of exchange you identified in part (a). Prior to specialization and trade, residents of South Shore chose to produce and consume 30 modems per hour and 90 flash drives per hour, and residents of East Isle chose to produce and consume 40 modems per hour and 30 flash drives per hour. Now, residents of South Shore agree to export to East Isle the same quantity of South Shore's specialty good that East Isle residents were consuming prior to engaging in international trade. How many units of East Isle's specialty good does South Shore import from East Isle?

c. What is South Shore's hourly consumption of modems and flash drives after the nation specializes and trades with East Isle? What is East Isle's hourly consumption of modems and flash drives after the nation specializes and trades with South Shore?

d. What consumption gains from trade are experienced by South Shore and East Isle?

32-9. Critics of the North American Free Trade Agreement (NAFTA) suggest that much of the increase in exports from Mexico to the United States now involves goods that Mexico otherwise would have exported to other nations. Mexican firms choose to export the goods to the United States, the critics argue, solely because the items receive preferential treatment under NAFTA tariff rules. What term describes what these critics are claiming is occurring with regard to U.S.-Mexican trade as a result of NAFTA? Explain your reasoning. (See pages 718–719.)

32-10. Some critics of the North American Free Trade Agreement (NAFTA) suggest that firms outside NAFTA nations sometimes shift unassembled inputs to Mexico, assemble the inputs into final goods there, and then export the final product to the United States in order to take advantage of Mexican trade preferences. What term describes what these critics are claiming is occurring with regard to U.S.-Mexican trade as a result of NAFTA? Explain your reasoning. (See page 719.)

32-11. How could multilateral trade agreements established for all nations through the World Trade Organization help to prevent both trade diversion and trade deflection that can occur under regional trade agreements, thereby promoting more overall international trade? (See page 719.)

ECONOMICS ON THE NET

How the World Trade Organization Settles Trade Disputes
A key function of the WTO is to adjudicate trade disagreements that arise among nations. This application helps you learn about the process that the WTO follows when considering international trade disputes.

Title: The World Trade Organization: Settling Trade Disputes

Navigation: Go to **www.econtoday.com/chap32** to access the WTO's Web page titled *Dispute Settlement*. Under "Introduction to dispute settlement in the WTO," click on *How does the WTO settle disputes?*

Application Read the article. Then answer the following questions.

1. As the article discusses, settling trade disputes often takes at least a year. What aspects of the WTO's dispute settlement process take the longest time?

2. Does the WTO actually "punish" a country it finds has broken international trading agreements? If not, who does impose sanctions?

For Group Study and Analysis Go to the WTO's main site at **www.econtoday.com/chap32**, and click on *The WTO*. Divide the class into groups, and have the groups explore this information on areas of WTO involvement. Have a class discussion of the pros and cons of WTO involvement in these areas. Which are most important for promoting world trade? Which are least important?

ANSWERS TO QUICK QUIZZES

p. 712: (i) lower; (ii) comparative advantage . . . consume; (iii) Gains . . . consume

p. 714: (i) infant . . . protected; (ii) dumping . . . dumping

p. 719: (i) maximum . . . producers; (ii) tax . . . benefits; (iii) World Trade Organization; (iv) Regional trade . . . regional trade

Exchange Rates and the Balance of Payments

33

LEARNING OBJECTIVES

After reading this chapter, you should be able to:

▶ Distinguish between the balance of trade and the balance of payments

▶ Identify the key accounts within the balance of payments

▶ Outline how exchange rates are determined in the markets for foreign exchange

▶ Discuss factors that can induce changes in equilibrium exchange rates

▶ Understand how policymakers can go about attempting to fix exchange rates

MyEconLab helps you master each objective and study more efficiently. See end of chapter for details.

Every few months, a U.S. media story reports on the substantial gap between U.S. imports of physical goods from China and U.S. exports of goods to China. Typically, media commentators follow up with complaints that U.S. residents are thoughtlessly paying prices for Chinese imports that effectively transfer a portion of U.S. residents' incomes to people in China. Does every dollar that you pay for a Chinese-manufactured item translate into an income transfer from the United States to China? Before you can answer this question, you must learn how economists use an accounting system called the *balance of payments* to track flows of spending on goods and services exported from and imported into the United States.

the annual dollar value of trading in *foreign exchange markets*—markets in which people buy and sell national currencies, such as the U.S. dollar, European euro, Japanese yen, or Chinese yuan—exceeds $4 trillion? Thus, the total value of exchanges of the world's currencies during a given year amounts to more than one-fourth of the value of exchanges for all goods and services produced per year in the United States. By the time you have completed this chapter, you will understand why people desire to obtain so many currencies of other nations in foreign exchange markets scattered around the globe. First, however, you must learn how we keep track of flows of payments across a country's borders.

The Balance of Payments and International Capital Movements

Governments typically keep track of each year's economic activities by calculating the gross domestic product—the total of expenditures on all newly domestic-produced final goods and services—and its components. A summary information system has also been developed for international trade. It covers the balance of trade and the balance of payments. The **balance of trade** refers specifically to exports and imports of physical goods, or merchandise, as discussed in Chapter 32. When international trade is in balance, the value of exports equals the value of imports. When the value of imports exceeds the value of exports, we are running a deficit in the balance of trade. When the value of exports exceeds the value of imports, we are running a surplus.

The **balance of payments** is a more general concept that expresses the total of all economic transactions between a nation and the rest of the world, usually for a period of one year. Each country's balance of payments summarizes information about that country's exports and imports of services as well as physical goods, earnings by domestic residents on assets located abroad, earnings on domestic assets owned by residents of foreign nations, international capital movements, and official transactions by central banks and governments. In essence, then, the balance of payments is a record of all the transactions between households, firms, and the government of one country and the rest of the world. Any transaction that leads to a *payment* by a country's residents (or government) is a deficit item, identified by a negative sign (−) when the actual numbers are given for the items listed in the second column of Table 33-1 on the facing page. Any transaction that leads to a *receipt* by a country's residents (or government) is a surplus item and is identified by a plus sign (+) when actual numbers are considered. Table 33-1 provides a list of the surplus and deficit items on international accounts.

Accounting Identities

Accounting identities—definitions of equivalent values—exist for financial institutions and other businesses. We begin with simple accounting identities that must hold for families and then go on to describe international accounting identities.

If a family unit is spending more than its current income, the family unit must necessarily be doing one of the following:

1. Reducing its money holdings or selling stocks, bonds, or other assets

2. Borrowing

3. Receiving gifts from friends or relatives

4. Receiving public transfers from a government, which obtained the funds by taxing others (a transfer is a payment, in money or in goods or services, made without receiving goods or services in return)

We can use this information to derive an identity: If a family unit is currently spending more than it is earning, it must draw on previously acquired wealth, borrow, or receive either private or public aid. Similarly, an identity exists for a family unit that is

---

Balance of trade
The difference between exports and imports of physical goods.

Balance of payments
A system of accounts that measures transactions of goods, services, income, and financial assets between domestic households, businesses, and governments and residents of the rest of the world during a specific time period.

Accounting identities
Values that are equivalent by definition.

TABLE 33-1

Surplus (+) and Deficit (−) Items on the International Accounts	Surplus Items (+)	Deficit Items (−)
	Exports of merchandise	Imports of merchandise
	Private and governmental gifts from foreign residents	Private and governmental gifts to foreign residents
	Foreign use of domestically operated travel and transportation services	Use of foreign-operated travel and transportation services
	Foreign tourists' expenditures in this country	U.S. tourists' expenditures abroad
	Foreign military spending in this country	Military spending abroad
	Interest and dividend receipts from foreign entities	Interest and dividends paid to foreign individuals and businesses
	Sales of domestic assets to foreign residents	Purchases of foreign assets
	Funds deposited in this country by foreign residents	Funds placed in foreign depository institutions
	Sales of gold to foreign residents	Purchases of gold from foreign residents
	Sales of domestic currency to foreign residents	Purchases of foreign currency

currently spending less than it is earning: It must be increasing its money holdings or be lending and acquiring other financial assets, or it must pay taxes or bestow gifts on others. When we consider businesses and governments, each unit in each group faces its own accounting identities or constraints. Ultimately, *net* lending by households must equal *net* borrowing by businesses and governments.

DISEQUILIBRIUM Even though our individual family unit's accounts must balance, in the sense that the identity discussed previously must hold, sometimes the item that brings about the balance cannot continue indefinitely. *If family expenditures exceed family income and this situation is financed by borrowing, the household may be considered to be in disequilibrium because such a situation cannot continue indefinitely.* If such a deficit is financed by drawing on previously accumulated assets, the family may also be in disequilibrium because it cannot continue indefinitely to draw on its wealth.

Eventually, the family will find it impossible to continue that lifestyle. (Of course, if the family members are retired, they may well be in equilibrium by drawing on previously acquired assets to finance current deficits. This example illustrates that it is necessary to understand all circumstances fully before pronouncing an economic unit in disequilibrium.)

EQUILIBRIUM Individual households, businesses, and governments, as well as the entire group of all households, businesses, and governments, must eventually reach equilibrium. Certain economic adjustment mechanisms have evolved to ensure equilibrium. Deficit households must eventually increase their income or decrease their expenditures. They will find that they have to pay higher interest rates if they wish to borrow to finance their deficits. Eventually, their credit sources will dry up, and they will be forced into equilibrium. Businesses, on occasion, must lower costs or prices—or go bankrupt—to reach equilibrium.

AN ACCOUNTING IDENTITY AMONG NATIONS When people from different nations trade or interact, certain identities or constraints must also hold. People buy goods from people in other nations. They also lend to and present gifts to people in other nations. If residents of a nation interact with residents of other nations, an accounting identity ensures a balance (but not necessarily an equilibrium, as will soon become clear). Let's look at the three categories of balance of payments transactions: current account transactions, capital account transactions, and official reserve account transactions.

Current Account Transactions

During any designated period, all payments and gifts that are related to the purchase or sale of both goods and services constitute the **current account** in international trade. Major types of current account transactions include the exchange of merchandise, the exchange of services, and unilateral transfers.

MERCHANDISE TRADE EXPORTS AND IMPORTS The largest portion of any nation's balance of payments current account is typically the importing and exporting of merchandise. During 2013, for example, as shown in lines 1 and 2 of Table 33-2 below, the United States exported an estimated $1,609.7 billion of merchandise and imported $2,404.5 billion. The balance of merchandise trade is defined as the difference between the value of merchandise exports and the value of merchandise imports. For 2013, the United States had a balance of merchandise trade deficit because the value of its merchandise imports exceeded the value of its merchandise exports. This deficit was about $794.8 billion (line 3).

SERVICE EXPORTS AND IMPORTS The balance of (merchandise) trade involves tangible items—things you can feel, touch, and see. Service exports and imports involve invisible or intangible items that are bought and sold, such as shipping, insurance, tourist expenditures, and banking services. Also, income earned by foreign residents on U.S. investments and income earned by U.S. residents on foreign investments are part of service imports and exports. As shown in lines 4 and 5 of Table 33-2, in 2013, estimated service exports were $564.6 billion, and service imports were $416.8 billion. Thus, the balance of services was about $147.8 billion in 2013 (line 6). Exports constitute receipts or inflows into the United States and are positive. Imports constitute payments abroad or outflows of money and are negative.

When we combine the balance of merchandise trade with the balance of services, we obtain a balance on goods and services equal to −$647.0 billion in 2013 (line 7).

TABLE 33-2

U.S. Balance of Payments Account, Estimated for 2013 (in billions of dollars)

Current Account		
(1) Exports of merchandise goods	+1,609.7	
(2) Imports of merchandise goods	−2,404.5	
(3) Balance of merchandise trade		−794.8
(4) Exports of services	+564.6	
(5) Imports of services	−416.8	
(6) Balance of services		+147.8
(7) Balance on goods and services [(3) + (6)]		−647.0
(8) Net unilateral transfers	−159.3	
(9) Balance on current account		−806.3
Capital Account		
(10) U.S. private capital going abroad	−299.2	
(11) Foreign private capital coming into the United States	+665.3*	
(12) Balance on capital account [(10) + (11)]		+366.1
(13) Balance on current account plus balance on capital account [(9) + (12)]		−440.2
Official Reserve Transactions Account		
(14) Official transactions balance		+440.2
(15) Total (balance)		0

Sources: U.S. Department of Commerce, Bureau of Economic Analysis; author's estimates.

*Includes an approximately $28 billion statistical discrepancy, probably uncounted capital inflows, many of which relate to the illegal drug trade.

UNILATERAL TRANSFERS U.S. residents give gifts to relatives and others abroad, the federal government makes grants to foreign nations, foreign residents give gifts to U.S. residents, and in the past some foreign governments have granted funds to the U.S. government. In the current account, we see that net unilateral transfers—the total amount of gifts given by U.S. residents and the government minus the total amount received from abroad by U.S. residents and the government—came to an estimated −$159.3 billion in 2013 (line 8). The minus sign before the number for unilateral transfers means that U.S. residents and the U.S. government gave more to foreign residents than foreign residents gave to U.S. residents.

BALANCING THE CURRENT ACCOUNT The balance on current account tracks the value of a country's exports of goods and services (including income on investments abroad) and transfer payments (private and government) relative to the value of that country's imports of goods and services and transfer payments (private and government). In 2013, it was estimated to be −$806.3 billion (line 9).

Go to www.econtoday.com/chap33 for the latest U.S. balance of payments data from the Bureau of Economic Analysis.

*If the sum of net exports of goods and services plus net unilateral transfers plus net investment income exceeds zero, a **current account surplus** is said to exist. If this sum is negative, a **current account deficit** is said to exist. A current account deficit means that we are importing more goods and services than we are exporting. Such a deficit must be paid for by the export of financial assets.*

WHAT IF... all governments attempted to require their nations to have current account surpluses?

By definition, a current account surplus arises in a nation when its residents export more goods and services than they import. The only way for some nations to have current account surpluses, though, is for others to operate with current account deficits. That is, residents of some countries must import more goods and services than they export in order for other nations to be able to export more goods and services than they import. Thus, if all governments were to require that their countries have current account surpluses, their efforts would be doomed to failure.

Capital Account Transactions

In world markets, it is possible to buy and sell not only goods and services but also financial assets. These international transactions are measured in the **capital account.** Capital account transactions occur because of foreign investments—either by foreign residents investing in the United States or by U.S. residents investing in other countries. The purchase of shares of stock in British firms on the London stock market by a U.S. resident causes an outflow of funds from the United States to Britain. The construction of a Japanese automobile factory in the United States causes an inflow of funds from Japan to the United States. Any time foreign residents buy U.S. government securities, there is an inflow of funds from other countries to the United States. Any time U.S. residents buy foreign government securities, there is an outflow of funds from the United States to other countries. Loans to and from foreign residents cause outflows and inflows.

Line 10 of Table 33-2 on the facing page indicates that in 2013, the value of private capital going out of the United States was an estimated −$299.2 billion, and line 11 shows that the value of private capital coming into the United States (including a statistical discrepancy) was $665.3 billion. U.S. capital going abroad constitutes payments or outflows and is therefore negative. Foreign capital coming into the United States constitutes receipts or inflows and is therefore positive. Thus, there was a positive net capital movement of $366.1 billion into the United States (line 12). This net private flow of capital is also called the balance on capital account.

There is a relationship between the current account balance and the capital account balance, assuming no interventions by the finance ministries or central banks of nations.

Capital account
A category of balance of payments transactions that measures flows of financial assets.

In the absence of interventions by finance ministries or central banks, the current account balance and the capital account balance must sum to zero. Stated differently, the current account deficit must equal the capital account surplus when governments or central banks do not engage in foreign exchange interventions. In this situation, any nation experiencing a current account deficit, such as the United States, must also be running a capital account surplus.

This basic relationship is apparent in the United States, as you can see in Figure 33-1 below. As the figure shows, U.S. current account deficits experienced since the early 1980s have been balanced by private capital inflows and *official reserve transactions*, to which we now turn our attention.

Official Reserve Account Transactions

The third type of balance of payments transaction concerns official reserve assets, which consist of the following:

1. Foreign currencies

2. Gold

3. **Special drawing rights (SDRs)**, which are reserve assets that the **International Monetary Fund** created to be used by countries to settle international payment obligations

4. The reserve position in the International Monetary Fund

5. Financial assets held by an official agency, such as the U.S. Treasury Department

To consider how official reserve account transactions occur, look again at Table 33-2 on page 728. The surplus in the U.S. capital account was $366.1 billion. But the deficit in the U.S. current account was −$806.3 billion, so the United States had a net deficit

Special drawing rights (SDRs)
Reserve assets created by the International Monetary Fund for countries to use in settling international payment obligations.

International Monetary Fund
An agency founded to administer an international foreign exchange system and to lend to member countries that had balance of payments problems. The IMF now functions as a lender of last resort for national governments.

MyEconLab Real-time data

FIGURE 33-1

The Relationship between the Current Account and the Capital Account

The current account balance is the mirror image of the sum of the capital account balance and the official transactions balance. We can see this in years since 1970. When the current account balance was in surplus, the sum of the capital account balance and the official transactions balance was negative. When the current account balance was in deficit, the sum of the current account balance and the official transactions balance was positive.

Sources: International Monetary Fund; *Economic Indicators.*

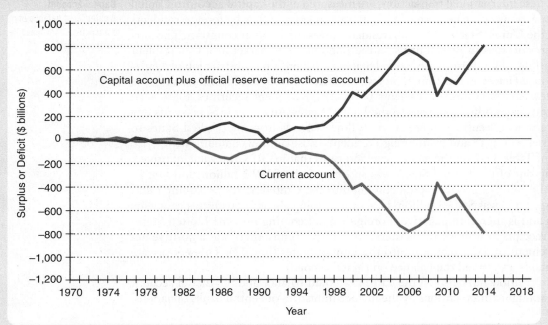

on the combined accounts (line 13) of −$440.2 billion. In other words, the United States obtained less in foreign funds in all its international transactions than it used. How is this deficiency made up? By foreign central banks and governments adding to their U.S. funds, shown by the +$440.2 billion in official transactions on line 14 in Table 33-2 on page 728. There is a plus sign on line 14 because this represents an *inflow* of foreign exchange in our international transactions.

The U.S. balance of payments deficit is measured by the official transactions figure on line 14. The balance (line 15) in Table 33-2 is zero, as it must be with double-entry bookkeeping. Hence, as shown in Figure 33-1 on the facing page, the current account balance is a mirror image of the sum of the capital account balance and the official reserve transactions account.

What Affects the Distribution of Account Balances within the Balance of Payments?

A major factor affecting the distribution of account balances within any nation's balance of payments is its rate of inflation relative to that of its trading partners. Assume that the rates of inflation in the United States and in the European Monetary Union (EMU)—the nations that use the euro as their currency—are equal. Now suppose that all of a sudden, the U.S. inflation rate increases. EMU residents will find that U.S. products are becoming more expensive, and U.S. firms will export fewer of them to EMU nations. At the current dollar-euro exchange rate, U.S. residents will find EMU products relatively cheaper, and they will import more. Other things being equal, the reverse will occur if the U.S. inflation rate suddenly falls relative to that of the EMU. All other things held constant, whenever the U.S. rate of inflation exceeds that of its trading partners, we expect to see a larger deficit in the U.S. balance of merchandise trade and in the U.S. current account balance. Conversely, when the U.S. rate of inflation is less than that of its trading partners, other things being constant, we expect to see a smaller deficit in the U.S. balance of merchandise trade and in the U.S. current account balance.

Another important factor that sometimes influences account balances within a nation's balance of payments is its relative political stability. Political instability causes *capital flight*. Owners of capital in countries anticipating or experiencing political instability will often move assets to countries that are politically stable, such as the United States. Hence, the U.S. capital account balance is likely to increase whenever political instability looms in other nations in the world.

QUICK QUIZ   See page 746 for the answers. Review concepts from this section in MyEconLab.

The _____ of _____ reflects the value of all transactions in international trade, including goods, services, financial assets, and gifts.

The merchandise trade balance gives us the difference between exports and imports of _____ items.

Included in the _____ account along with merchandise trade are service exports and imports relating to commerce in intangible items, such as shipping, insurance, and tourist expenditures. The _____ account also includes income earned by foreign residents on U.S. investments and income earned by U.S. residents on foreign investments.

_____ _____ involve international private gifts and federal government grants or gifts to foreign nations.

When we add the balance of merchandise trade and the balance of services and take account of net unilateral

transfers and net investment income, we come up with the balance on the _____ account, a summary statistic.

There are also _____ account transactions that relate to the buying and selling of financial assets. Foreign capital is always entering the United States, and U.S. capital is always flowing abroad. The difference is called the balance on the _____ account.

Another type of balance of payments transaction concerns the _____ _____ assets of individual countries, or what is often simply called official transactions. By standard accounting convention, official transactions are exactly equal to but opposite in sign from the sum of the current account balance and the capital account balance.

Account balances within a nation's balance of payments can be affected by its relative rate of _____ and by its _____ stability relative to other nations.

Determining Foreign Exchange Rates

When you buy foreign products, such as European pharmaceuticals, you have dollars with which to pay the European manufacturer. The European manufacturer, however, cannot pay workers in dollars. The workers are European, they live in Europe, and they must have euros to buy goods and services in nations that are members of the European Monetary Union (EMU) and use the euro as their currency. There must therefore be a way to exchange dollars for euros that the pharmaceuticals manufacturer will accept. That exchange occurs in a **foreign exchange market,** which in this case involves the exchange of euros and dollars.

The particular **exchange rate** between euros and dollars that prevails—the dollar price of the euro—depends on the current demand for and supply of euros and dollars. In a sense, then, our analysis of the exchange rate between dollars and euros will be familiar, for we have used supply and demand throughout this book. If it costs you $1.20 to buy 1 euro, that is the foreign exchange rate determined by the current demand for and supply of euros in the foreign exchange market. The European person going to the foreign exchange market would need about 0.83 euro to buy 1 dollar.

Now let's consider what determines the demand for and supply of foreign currency in the foreign exchange market. We will continue to assume that the only two regions in the world are Europe and the United States.

Foreign exchange market
A market in which households, firms, and governments buy and sell national currencies.

Exchange rate
The price of one nation's currency in terms of the currency of another country.

Demand for and Supply of Foreign Currency

You wish to purchase European-produced pharmaceuticals directly from a manufacturer located in Europe. To do so, you must have euros. You go to the foreign exchange market (or your U.S. bank). Your desire to buy the pharmaceuticals causes you to offer (supply) dollars to the foreign exchange market. Your demand for euros is equivalent to your supply of dollars to the foreign exchange market.

> *Every U.S. transaction involving the importation of foreign goods constitutes a supply of dollars and a demand for some foreign currency, and the opposite is true for export transactions.*

In this case, the import transaction constitutes a demand for euros.

In our example, we will assume that only two goods are being traded, European pharmaceuticals and U.S. tablet devices. The U.S. demand for European pharmaceuticals creates a supply of dollars and a demand for euros in the foreign exchange market. Similarly, the European demand for U.S. tablet devices creates a supply of euros and a demand for dollars in the foreign exchange market. Under a system of **flexible exchange rates,** the supply of and demand for dollars and euros in the foreign exchange market will determine the equilibrium foreign exchange rate. The equilibrium exchange rate will tell us how many euros a dollar can be exchanged for—that is, the euro price of dollars—or how many dollars a euro can be exchanged for—the dollar price of euros.

Flexible exchange rates
Exchange rates that are allowed to fluctuate in the open market in response to changes in supply and demand. Sometimes called *floating exchange rates*.

The Equilibrium Foreign Exchange Rate

To determine the equilibrium foreign exchange rate, we have to find out what determines the demand for and supply of foreign exchange. We will ignore for the moment any speculative aspect of buying foreign exchange. That is, we assume that there are no individuals who wish to buy euros simply because they think that their price will go up in the future.

The idea of an exchange rate is no different from the idea of paying a certain price for something you want to buy. Suppose that you have to pay about $1.50 for a cup of coffee. If the price goes up to $2.50, you will probably buy fewer cups. If the price goes down to 50 cents, you will likely buy more. In other words, the demand curve for cups of coffee, expressed in terms of dollars, slopes downward following the law of demand. The demand curve for euros slopes downward also, and we will see why.

Go to www.econtoday.com/chap33 for recent data from the Federal Reserve Bank of St. Louis on the exchange value of the U.S. dollar relative to the major currencies of the world.

Let's think more closely about the demand schedule for euros. If it costs you $1.10 to purchase 1 euro, that is the exchange rate between dollars and euros. If tomorrow you have to pay $1.25 for the same euro, the exchange rate would have changed. Looking at such a change, we would say that there has been an **appreciation** in the value of the euro in the foreign exchange market. But another way to view this increase in the value of the euro is to say that there has been a **depreciation** in the value of the dollar in the foreign exchange market. The dollar used to buy almost 0.91 euro, but tomorrow the dollar will be able to buy only 0.80 euro at a price of $1.25 per euro.

If the dollar price of euros rises, you will probably demand fewer euros. Why? The answer lies in the reason you and others demand euros in the first place.

APPRECIATION AND DEPRECIATION OF EUROS Recall that in our example, you and others demand euros to buy European pharmaceuticals. The demand curve for European pharmaceuticals follows the law of demand and therefore slopes downward. If it costs more U.S. dollars to buy the same quantity of European pharmaceuticals, presumably you and other U.S. residents will not buy the same quantity. Your quantity demanded will be less. We say that your demand for euros is *derived from* your demand for European pharmaceuticals. In panel (a) of Figure 33-2 on the following page, we present the hypothetical demand schedule for packages of European pharmaceuticals by a representative set of U.S. consumers during a typical week. In panel (b) of Figure 33-2, we show graphically the U.S. demand curve for European pharmaceuticals in terms of U.S. dollars taken from panel (a).

AN EXAMPLE OF DERIVED DEMAND Let us assume that the price of a package of European pharmaceuticals in Europe is 100 euros. Given that price, we can find the number of euros required to purchase 500 packages of European pharmaceuticals. That information is given in panel (c) of Figure 33-2. If purchasing one package of European pharmaceuticals requires 100 euros, 500 packages require 50,000 euros. Now we have enough information to determine the derived demand curve for euros. If 1 euro costs $1.20, a package of pharmaceuticals would cost $120 (100 euros per package × $1.20 per euro = $120 per package). At $120 per package, the representative group of U.S. consumers would, we see from panel (a) of Figure 33-2, demand 500 packages of pharmaceuticals.

From panel (c), we see that 50,000 euros would be demanded to buy the 500 packages of pharmaceuticals. We show this quantity demanded in panel (d). In panel (e), we draw the derived demand curve for euros. Now consider what happens if the price of euros goes up to $1.25. A package of European pharmaceuticals priced at 100 euros in Europe would now cost $125. From panel (a), we see that at $125 per package, 300 packages of pharmaceuticals will be imported from Europe into the United States by our representative group of U.S. consumers. From panel (c), we see that 300 packages of pharmaceuticals would require 30,000 euros to be purchased. Thus, in panels (d) and (e), we see that at a price of $1.25 per euro, the quantity demanded will be 30,000 euros.

We continue similar calculations all the way up to a price of $1.30 per euro. At that price, a package of European pharmaceuticals with a price of 100 euros in Europe would have a U.S. dollar price of $130, and our representative U.S. consumers would import only 100 packages of pharmaceuticals.

DOWNWARD-SLOPING DERIVED DEMAND As can be expected, as the price of the euro rises, the quantity demanded will fall. The only difference here from the standard demand analysis developed in Chapter 3 and used throughout this text is that the demand for euros is derived from the demand for a final product—European pharmaceuticals in our example.

SUPPLY OF EUROS Assume that European pharmaceutical manufacturers buy U.S. tablet devices. The supply of euros is a derived supply in that it is derived from the European demand for U.S. tablet devices. We could go through an example similar to the one for pharmaceuticals to come up with a supply schedule of euros in Europe. It slopes upward.

Appreciation
An increase in the exchange value of one nation's currency in terms of the currency of another nation.

Depreciation
A decrease in the exchange value of one nation's currency in terms of the currency of another nation.

YOU ARE THERE

To consider how an appreciation of Brazil's currency has affected Brazilian spending on U.S. goods and services, take a look at **An Exchange-Rate-Induced U.S. Shopping *Bagunça* for Brazilians** on page 742.

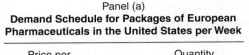

Panel (a)
Demand Schedule for Packages of European Pharmaceuticals in the United States per Week

Price per Package	Quantity Demanded
$130	100
125	300
120	500
115	700

Panel (b)
U.S. Demand Curve for European Pharmaceuticals

Panel (c)
Euros Required to Purchase Quantity Demanded (at P = 100 euros per package of pharmaceuticals)

Quantity Demanded	Euros Required
100	10,000
300	30,000
500	50,000
700	70,000

Panel (d)
Derived Demand Schedule for Euros in the United States with Which to Pay for Imports of Pharmaceuticals

Dollar Price of One Euro	Dollar Price of Pharmaceuticals	Quantity of Pharmaceuticals Demanded	Quantity of Euros Demanded per Week
$1.30	$130	100	10,000
1.25	125	300	30,000
1.20	120	500	50,000
1.15	115	700	70,000

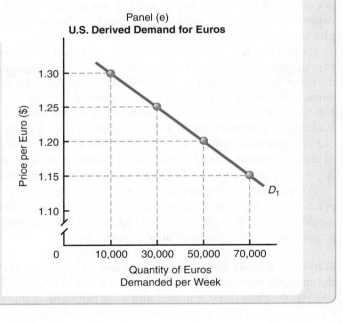

Panel (e)
U.S. Derived Demand for Euros

FIGURE 33-2

Deriving the Demand for Euros

In panel (a), we show the demand schedule for European pharmaceuticals in the United States, expressed in terms of dollars per package of pharmaceuticals. In panel (b), we show the demand curve, *D*, which slopes downward. In panel (c), we show the number of euros required to purchase up to 700 packages of pharmaceuticals. If the price per package of pharmaceuticals is 100 euros, we can now find the quantity of euros needed to pay for the various quantities demanded. In panel (d), we see the derived demand for euros in the United States in order to purchase the various quantities of pharmaceuticals given in panel (a). The resultant demand curve, D_1, is shown in panel (e). This is the U.S. derived demand for euros.

Obviously, Europeans want dollars to purchase U.S. goods. European residents will be willing to supply more euros when the dollar price of euros goes up, because they can then buy more U.S. goods with the same quantity of euros. That is, the euro would be worth more in exchange for U.S. goods than when the dollar price for euros was lower.

FIGURE 33-3

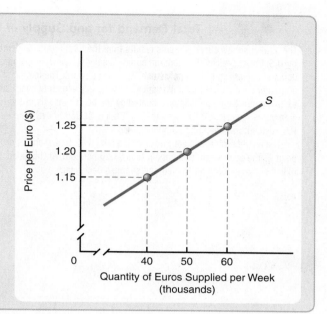

The Supply of Euros

If the market price of a U.S.-produced tablet device is $200, then at an exchange rate of $1.20 per euro, the price of the tablet to a European consumer is 167.67 euros. If the exchange rate rises to $1.25 per euro, the European price of the tablet falls to 160 euros. This induces an increase in the quantity of tablets demanded by European consumers and consequently an increase in the quantity of euros supplied in exchange for dollars in the foreign exchange market. In contrast, if the exchange rate falls to $1.15 per euro, the European price of the tablet rises to 173.91 euros. This causes a decrease in the quantity of tablets demanded by European consumers. As a result, there is a decline in the quantity of euros supplied in exchange for dollars in the foreign exchange market. Hence, the euro supply curve slopes up.

AN EXAMPLE Let's take an example. Suppose a U.S.-produced tablet device costs $200. If the exchange rate is $1.20 per euro, a European resident will have to come up with 166.67 euros ($200 ÷ $1.20 per euro = 166.67 euros) to buy one tablet. If, however, the exchange rate goes up to $1.25 per euro, a European resident must come up with only 160 euros ($200 ÷ $1.25 per euro = 160 euros) to buy a U.S. tablet. At this lower price (in euros) of U.S. tablets, Europeans will demand a larger quantity.

In other words, as the price of euros goes up in terms of dollars, the quantity of U.S. tablets demanded will go up, and hence the quantity of euros supplied will go up. Therefore, the supply schedule of euros, which is derived from the European demand for U.S. goods, will slope upward, as seen in Figure 33-3 above.

TOTAL DEMAND FOR AND SUPPLY OF EUROS Let us now look at the total demand for and supply of euros. We take all U.S. consumers of European pharmaceuticals and all European consumers of U.S. tablet devices and put their demands for and supplies of euros together into one diagram. Thus, we are showing the total demand for and total supply of euros. The horizontal axis in Figure 33-4 on the following page represents the quantity of foreign exchange—the number of euros per year. The vertical axis represents the exchange rate—the price of foreign currency (euros) expressed in dollars (per euro). The foreign currency price of $1.25 per euro means it will cost you $1.25 to buy 1 euro. At the foreign currency price of $1.20 per euro, you know that it will cost you $1.20 to buy 1 euro. The equilibrium, E, is again established at $1.20 for 1 euro.

In our hypothetical example, assuming that there are only representative groups of pharmaceutical consumers in the United States and tablet consumers in Europe, the equilibrium exchange rate will be set at $1.20 per euro.

This equilibrium is not established because U.S. residents like to buy euros or because Europeans like to buy dollars. Rather, the equilibrium exchange rate depends on how many tablet devices Europeans want and how many European pharmaceuticals U.S. residents want (given their respective incomes, their tastes, and, in our example, the relative prices of pharmaceuticals and tablet devices).

A SHIFT IN DEMAND Assume that a successful advertising campaign by U.S. pharmaceutical importers causes U.S. demand for European pharmaceuticals to rise. U.S. residents demand more pharmaceuticals at all prices. Their demand curve for European pharmaceuticals shifts outward to the right.

FIGURE 33-4

Total Demand for and Supply of Euros

The market supply curve for euros results from the total European demand for U.S. tablet devices. The demand curve, *D*, slopes downward like most demand curves, and the supply curve, *S*, slopes upward. The foreign exchange price, or the U.S. dollar price of euros, is given on the vertical axis. The number of euros is represented on the horizontal axis. If the foreign exchange rate is $1.25—that is, if it takes $1.25 to buy 1 euro—U.S. residents will demand 20 billion euros.

The equilibrium exchange rate is at the intersection of *D* and *S*, or point *E*. The equilibrium exchange rate is $1.20 per euro. At this point, 30 billion euros are both demanded and supplied each year.

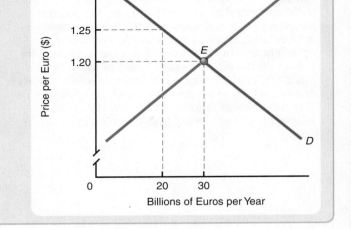

The increased demand for European pharmaceuticals can be translated into an increased demand for euros. All U.S. residents clamoring for European pharmaceuticals will supply more dollars to the foreign exchange market while demanding more euros to pay for the pharmaceuticals. Figure 33-5 below presents a new demand schedule, D_2, for euros. This demand schedule is to the right of the original demand schedule. If Europeans do not change their desire for U.S. tablet devices, the supply schedule for euros will remain stable.

A new equilibrium will be established at a higher exchange rate. In our particular example, the new equilibrium is established at an exchange rate of $1.25 per euro. It now takes $1.25 to buy 1 euro, whereas formerly it took $1.20. This will be translated into an increase in the price of European pharmaceuticals to U.S. residents and into a decrease in the price of U.S. tablet devices to Europeans. For example, a package of European pharmaceuticals priced at 100 euros that sold for $120 in the United States will now be priced at $125. Conversely, a U.S. tablet priced at $200 that previously sold for 166.67 euros will now sell for 160 euros.

FIGURE 33-5

A Shift in the Demand Schedule

The demand schedule for European pharmaceuticals shifts to the right, causing the derived demand schedule for euros to shift to the right also. We have shown this as a shift from D_1 to D_2. We have assumed that the supply schedule for euros has remained stable—that is, European demand for U.S. tablet devices has remained constant. The old equilibrium foreign exchange rate was $1.20 per euro.

The new equilibrium exchange rate will be E_2. It will now cost $1.25 to buy 1 euro. The higher price of euros will be translated into a higher U.S. dollar price for European pharmaceuticals and a lower euro price for U.S. tablet devices.

A Shift in the Supply of Euros

There has been a shift in the supply curve for euros. The new equilibrium will occur at E_1, meaning that $1.15, rather than $1.20, will now buy 1 euro. After the exchange rate adjustment, the annual amount of euros demanded and supplied will increase from 30 billion to 60 billion.

A SHIFT IN SUPPLY We just assumed that the U.S. demand for European pharmaceuticals shifted due to a successful ad campaign. The demand for euros is derived from the demand by U.S. residents for pharmaceuticals. This change in pharmaceuticals demand is translated into a shift in the demand curve for euros. As an alternative exercise, we might assume that the supply curve of euros shifts outward to the right. Such a supply shift could occur for many reasons, one of which is a relative rise in the European price level. For example, if the prices of all European-manufactured tablets went up 20 percent in euros, U.S. tablets would become relatively cheaper. That would mean that European residents would want to buy more U.S. tablets. But remember that when they want to buy more U.S. tablets, they supply more euros to the foreign exchange market.

Thus, we see in Figure 33-6 above that the supply curve of euros moves from S to S_1. In the absence of restrictions—that is, in a system of flexible exchange rates—the new equilibrium exchange rate will be $1.15 equals 1 euro. The quantity of euros demanded and supplied will increase from 30 billion per year to 60 billion per year. We say, then, that in a flexible international exchange rate system, shifts in the demand for and supply of foreign currencies will cause changes in the equilibrium foreign exchange rates. Those rates will remain in effect until world supply or demand shifts.

Which national currencies are most actively traded in global foreign exchange markets?

INTERNATIONAL EXAMPLE

The Most Traded Currencies in Foreign Exchange Markets

On a given day, the U.S. dollar is involved in more than 80 percent of trades of one currency for another in the world's foreign exchange markets. Thus, the dollar is utilized more than twice as often in exchange for other currencies as the second most commonly traded currency, the European euro. The dollar is involved in currency exchanges more than four times as often as either the Japanese yen or the British pound, the third and fourth most commonly exchanged currencies.

FOR CRITICAL THINKING
In light of the fact that the dollar valuation of all currency trades during a given year is $4 trillion, about how many U.S. dollars circulate within foreign exchange markets within a given year?

Market Determinants of Exchange Rates

The foreign exchange market is affected by many other variables in addition to changes in relative price levels, including the following:

- *Changes in real interest rates*. Suppose that the U.S. interest rate, corrected for people's expectations of inflation, increases relative to the rest of the world. Then international investors elsewhere seeking the higher returns now available in the United States will increase their demand for dollar-denominated assets, thereby increasing the demand for dollars in foreign exchange markets. An increased demand for dollars in foreign exchange markets, other things held constant, will cause the dollar to appreciate and other currencies to depreciate.

- *Changes in consumer preferences*. If Germany's citizens, for example, suddenly develop a taste for U.S.-made automobiles, this will increase the derived demand for U.S. dollars in foreign exchange markets.

- *Perceptions of economic stability*. As already mentioned, if the United States looks economically and politically more stable relative to other countries, more foreign residents will want to put their savings into U.S. assets rather than in their own domestic assets. This will increase the demand for dollars.

QUICK QUIZ See page 746 for the answers. Review concepts from this section in MyEconLab.

The foreign _____ _____ is the rate at which one country's currency can be exchanged for another's.

The _____ for foreign exchange is a derived _____, which is derived from the demand for foreign goods and services (and financial assets). The _____ of foreign exchange is derived from foreign residents' demands for U.S. goods and services.

The demand curve of foreign exchange slopes _____, and the supply curve of foreign exchange slopes

_____. The equilibrium foreign exchange rate occurs at the intersection of the demand and supply curves for a currency.

A _____ in the demand for foreign goods will result in a shift in the _____ for foreign exchange, thereby changing the equilibrium foreign exchange rate. A shift in the supply of foreign currency will also cause a change in the equilibrium exchange rate.

The Gold Standard and the International Monetary Fund

The current system of more or less freely floating exchange rates is a relatively recent development. In the past, we have had periods of a gold standard, fixed exchange rates under the International Monetary Fund, and variants of the two.

The Gold Standard

Until the 1930s, many nations were on a gold standard. The value of their domestic currency was fixed, or *pegged*, in units of gold. Nations operating under this gold standard agreed to redeem their currencies for a fixed amount of gold at the request of any holder of that currency. Although gold was not necessarily the means of exchange for world trade, it was the unit to which all currencies under the gold standard were pegged. And because all currencies in the system were pegged to gold, exchange rates between those currencies were fixed.

Two problems plagued the gold standard, however. One was that by fixing the value of its currency in relation to the amount of gold, a nation gave up control of its domestic monetary policy. Another was that the world's commerce was at the mercy of gold discoveries. Throughout history, each time new veins of gold were found, desired domestic expenditures on goods and services increased. If production of goods and services failed to increase proportionately, inflation resulted.

Bretton Woods and the International Monetary Fund

On December 27, 1945, the world's capitalist countries, which in 1944 had sent representatives to meetings in Bretton Woods, New Hampshire, created a new permanent institution, the International Monetary Fund (IMF). The IMF's task was to lend to member countries for which the sum of the current account balance and the capital account balance was negative, thereby helping them maintain an offsetting surplus in their official reserve transactions accounts. Governments that joined the Bretton Woods system agreed to maintain the value of their currencies within 1 percent of the declared **par value**—the officially determined value. The United States, which owned most of the world's gold stock, was similarly obligated to maintain gold prices within a 1 percent margin of the official rate of $35 an ounce. Except for a transitional arrangement permitting a one-time adjustment of up to 10 percent in par value, members could alter exchange rates thereafter only with the approval of the IMF.

Par value
The officially determined value of a currency.

On August 15, 1971, President Richard Nixon suspended the convertibility of the dollar into gold. On December 18, 1971, the United States officially devalued the dollar—that is, lowered its official value—relative to the currencies of 14 major industrial nations. Finally, on March 16, 1973, the finance ministers of the European Economic Community (now the European Union) announced that they would let their currencies float against the dollar, something Japan had already begun doing with its yen. Since 1973, the United States and most other trading countries have had either freely floating exchange rates or managed ("dirty") floating exchange rates, in which their governments or central banks intervene from time to time to try to influence world market exchange rates.

Fixed versus Floating Exchange Rates

The United States went off the Bretton Woods system of fixed exchange rates in 1973. As Figure 33-7 below indicates, many other nations of the world have been less willing to permit the values of their currencies to vary in the foreign exchange markets.

Fixing the Exchange Rate

How did nations fix their exchange rates in years past? How do many countries accomplish this today? Figure 33-8 on the following page shows the market for dinars, the currency of Bahrain. At the initial equilibrium point E_1, U.S. residents had to give up $2.66 to obtain 1 dinar. Suppose now that there is an increase in the supply of dinars for dollars, perhaps because Bahraini residents wish to buy more U.S. goods.

FIGURE 33-7

Current Foreign Exchange Rate Arrangements

Today, 21 percent of the member nations of the International Monetary Fund have an independent float, and 24 percent have a managed float exchange rate arrangement. Another 12 percent of all nations use the currencies of other nations instead of issuing their own currencies. The remaining 43 percent of countries have fixed exchange rates.

Source: International Monetary Fund.

- Independent float 21%
- Managed float 24%
- No separate legal currency 12%
- Fixed exchange rate 43%

FIGURE 33-8

A Fixed Exchange Rate

This figure illustrates how the Central Bank of Bahrain could fix the dollar-dinar exchange rate in the face of an increase in the supply of dinars caused by a rise in the demand for U.S. goods by Bahraini residents. In the absence of any action by the Central Bank of Bahrain, the result would be a movement from point E_1 to point E_2. The dollar value of the dinar would fall from \$2.66 to \$2.00. The Central Bank of Bahrain can prevent this exchange rate change by purchasing dinars with dollars in the foreign exchange market, thereby increasing the demand for dinars. At the new equilibrium point, E_3, the dinar's value remains at \$2.66.

Other things being equal, the result would be a movement to point E_2 in Figure 33-8 above. The dollar value of the dinar would fall to \$2.00.

To prevent a dinar depreciation from occurring, however, the Central Bank of Bahrain could increase the demand for dinars in the foreign exchange market by purchasing dinars with dollars. The Central Bank of Bahrain can do this using dollars that it has on hand as part of its *foreign exchange reserves*. All central banks hold reserves of foreign currencies. Because the U.S. dollar is a key international currency, the Central Bank of Bahrain and other central banks typically hold billions of dollars in reserve so that they can make transactions such as the one in this example.

Note that a sufficiently large purchase of dinars could, as shown in Figure 33-8, cause the demand curve to shift rightward to achieve the new equilibrium point E_3, at which the dinar's value remains at \$2.66. Provided that it has enough dollar reserves on hand, the Central Bank of Bahrain could maintain—effectively fix—the exchange rate in the face of the rise in the supply of dinars.

The Central Bank of Bahrain has maintained the dollar-dinar exchange rate in this manner since 2001. This basic approach—varying the amount of the national currency demanded at any given exchange rate in foreign exchange markets when necessary—is also the way that *any* central bank seeks to keep its nation's currency value unchanged in light of changing market forces.

Central banks can keep exchange rates fixed as long as they have enough foreign exchange reserves to deal with potentially long-lasting changes in the demand for or supply of their nation's currency.

Pros and Cons of a Fixed Exchange Rate

Why might a nation such as Bahrain wish to keep the value of its currency from fluctuating? One reason is that changes in the exchange rate can affect the market values of assets that are denominated in foreign currencies. This can increase the financial risks that a nation's residents face, thereby forcing them to incur costs to avoid these risks.

FOREIGN EXCHANGE RISK The possibility that variations in the market value of assets can take place due to changes in the value of a nation's currency is the **foreign exchange risk** that residents of a country face because their nation's currency value can vary. Suppose that companies in Bahrain have many loans denominated in dollars but earn nearly all their revenues in dinars from sales within Bahrain. A decline in the dollar

Foreign exchange risk
The possibility that changes in the value of a nation's currency will result in variations in the market value of assets.

value of the dinar would mean that Bahraini companies would have to allocate a larger portion of their earnings to make the same *dollar* loan payments as before. Thus, a fall in the dinar's value would increase the operating costs of these companies, thereby reducing their profitability and raising the likelihood of eventual bankruptcy.

Limiting foreign exchange risk is a classic rationale for adopting a fixed exchange rate. Nevertheless, a country's residents are not defenseless against foreign exchange risk. In what is known as a **hedge,** they can adopt strategies intended to offset the risk arising from exchange rate variations. For example, a company in Bahrain that has significant euro earnings from sales in Germany but sizable loans from U.S. investors could arrange to convert its euro earnings into dollars via special types of foreign exchange contracts called *currency swaps*. The Bahraini company could likewise avoid holdings of dinars and shield itself—*hedge*—against variations in the dinar's value.

Hedge
A financial strategy that reduces the chance of suffering losses arising from foreign exchange risk.

THE EXCHANGE RATE AS A SHOCK ABSORBER If fixing the exchange rate limits foreign exchange risk, why do so many nations allow the exchange rates to float? The answer must be that there are potential drawbacks associated with fixing exchange rates. One is that exchange rate variations can actually perform a valuable service for a nation's economy. Consider a situation in which residents of a nation speak only their own nation's language. As a result, the country's residents are very *immobile*: They cannot trade their labor skills outside their own nation's borders.

Now think about what happens if this nation chooses to fix its exchange rate. Imagine a situation in which other countries begin to sell products that are close substitutes for the products its people specialize in producing, causing a sizable drop in worldwide demand for that nation's goods. If wages and prices do not instantly and completely adjust downward, the result will be a sharp decline in production of goods and services, a falloff in national income, and higher unemployment. Contrast this situation with one which the exchange rate floats. In this case, a sizable decline in outside demand for the nation's products will cause it to experience a trade deficit, which will lead to a significant drop in the demand for that nation's currency. As a result, the nation's currency will experience a sizable depreciation, making the goods that the nation offers to sell abroad much less expensive in other countries. People abroad who continue to consume the nation's products will increase their purchases, and the nation's exports will increase. Its production will begin to recover somewhat, as will its residents' incomes. Unemployment will begin to fall.

This example illustrates how exchange rate variations can be beneficial, especially if a nation's residents are relatively immobile. It can be difficult, for example, for a Polish resident who has never studied Portuguese to move to Lisbon, even if she is highly qualified for available jobs there. If many residents of Poland face similar linguistic or cultural barriers, Poland could be better off with a floating exchange rate even if its residents must incur significant costs hedging against foreign exchange risk as a result.

How did having a separate currency and a floating exchange rate actually end up helping Poland in the early 2010s?

INTERNATIONAL POLICY EXAMPLE

Poland's Floating Exchange Rate Protects It from Euro Ills

During the 2000s, Estonia, Slovakia, and Slovenia rushed to adopt the euro as their currency, and other nations of Eastern Europe fixed their exchange rates in relation to the euro. In contrast, Poland retained its *zloty* currency and allowed its value to float in the foreign exchange market.

A European-wide economic slowdown that began during the early 2010s triggered downturns in Estonia, Slovakia, Slovenia, and other countries in Eastern Europe. When the Polish *zloty* depreciated sharply relative to the euro, Polish goods and services became cheaper for most Europeans. As a consequence, European spending on Polish merchandise exports rose sharply, and the Polish tourism industry boomed as

more Europeans selected Poland as a less expensive vacation destination. By maintaining its own currency and a floating exchange rate, Poland thereby helped to insulate its economy from problems afflicting the rest of Europe. Thus, Poland was the only European Union nation to experience uninterrupted economic growth during the early 2010s.

FOR CRITICAL THINKING
Why do you suppose that the Polish unemployment rate remained stable during the early 2010s while unemployment rates elsewhere in Eastern Europe rose?

QUICK QUIZ   See page 746 for the answers. Review concepts from this section in MyEconLab.

The International Monetary Fund was developed after World War II as an institution to maintain _____ exchange rates in the world. Since 1973, however, _____ exchange rates have disappeared in most major trading countries. For these nations, exchange rates are largely determined by the forces of demand and supply in global foreign exchange markets.

Central banks can fix exchange rates by buying or selling foreign _____ and thereby adding to or subtracting from their foreign exchange _____.

Although fixing the exchange rate helps protect a nation's residents from foreign exchange _____, this policy makes less mobile residents susceptible to greater volatility in income and employment.

YOU ARE THERE
An Exchange-Rate-Induced U.S. Shopping *Bagunça* for *Brazilians*

Ana Ligia Paladino has traveled 5,000 miles from her home in the southernmost part of Brazil to engage in a 10-day-long shopping spree in New York City. When Paladino emerges from her first morning of shopping at Macy's, the only words she can think of to describe her experience are, "It was a *bagunça*!"—that is, a combination of "mess" and "mayhem." During the year of her visit, Paladino is among 700,000 Brazilians to visit New York City, where Brazilians have spent more than $1.6 billion. Within the same year, Brazilians also have spent more than $2 billion in Florida. In both U.S. locations, Brazilians have outspent visitors from any other country in the world.

What has induced Paladino and so many other Brazilians to engage in spending in the United States is that the Brazilian currency, the *real,* can

now buy a great deal more U.S. goods and services than was true previously. Indeed, during the two years prior to Paladino's visit, the *real* appreciated relative to the U.S. dollar by 25 percent. Thus, during her New York shopping *bagunça,* Paladino was able to buy about 25 percent more items in the United States than she could have bought 24 months earlier.

Critical Thinking Questions

1. What happened to the U.S. dollar's value in relation to the Brazilian *real* during the preceding two years?

2. Why do you suppose that more Brazilian students are now studying at U.S. colleges and universities than was true several years ago?

CONCEPTS APPLIED
▶ Balance of Payments
▶ Merchandise Trade Deficit
▶ Balance on Goods and Services

ISSUES & APPLICATIONS

Items "Made in China" Generate Income Elsewhere

In a typical year, the value of U.S. imports from China amounts to one-sixth of total U.S. import spending recorded in the nation's balance of payments. Expenditures on merchandise imported from China make up more than 70 percent of both the U.S. merchandise trade deficit and the U.S. balance on goods and services. These facts do not imply, however, that every dollar you spend as a consumer on an item "made in China" finds its way to people in China. In fact, less than half of each dollar you spend on Chinese merchandise actually reaches someone in China.

Only Part of the Price of a Chinese Import Is Chinese Income

Consider a toy action figure manufactured in China that has a price of $15 in the United States. A substantial portion of the U.S. retail price pays for transportation of the toy within the United States, rent for the U.S. retail outlet that sells the action figure, profits for the retailer's owners, and expenses incurred in marketing the toy. The latter expenses include the wages paid to managers and employees of the U.S. firms that marketed the action figure in the United States.

Alternatively, consider the iPhone, which earns substantial profits for U.S.-based Apple. iPhones are assembled in China from components that are made by and that generate revenues for firms located outside both the United States and China. Yet when an assembled iPhone is shipped from China for a U.S. consumer to purchase, that device is classified as a Chinese export and a U.S. import.

The U.S. Content of "Made in China"

Galina Hale and Bart Hoblin of the Federal Reserve Bank of San Francisco have calculated shares of spending on U.S. imports from China that flow to Chinese producers and to U.S. firms and their workers. They find that only 45 cents of each dollar U.S. consumers pay toward the price of a typical Chinese-imported good actually makes its way to China as income.

Thus, your spending on merchandise imported from China contributes dollar-for-dollar to the U.S. merchandise trade deficit, but fewer than half of the dollars that you spend on items "made in China" ultimately flow to that nation as income. The income that your spending generates is split among people who live in China, the United States, and sometimes—as in the case of iPhones—other nations.

For Critical Thinking

1. The United States is a net exporter of services to China. What does this imply about the magnitude of the deficit in the U.S. balance on goods and services with China compared with the size of the U.S. merchandise trade deficit with China?

2. Why does a portion of Chinese residents' expenditures on goods and services exported from the United States to China likely add to the earnings of Chinese firms and those firms' managers and workers?

Web Resources

1. To view key trade balance statistics for China, go to www.econtoday.com/chap33.

2. For a look at U.S. balance of payments data, go to www.econtoday.com/chap33.

MyEconLab

For more questions on this chapter's Issues & Applications, go to MyEconLab. In the Study Plan for this chapter, select Section N: News.

MyEconLab

Here is what you should know after reading this chapter. MyEconLab will help you identify what you know, and where to go when you need to practice.

— WHAT YOU SHOULD KNOW —

The Balance of Trade versus the Balance of Payments The balance of trade is the difference between exports and imports of physical goods, or merchandise, during a given period. The balance of payments is a system of accounts for all transactions between a nation's residents and the residents of other countries of the world.

balance of trade, 726
balance of payments, 726
accounting identities, 726

— WHERE TO GO TO PRACTICE —

• MyEconLab Study Plan 33.1

———— WHAT YOU SHOULD KNOW ————————————————— WHERE TO GO TO PRACTICE ————

The Key Accounts within the Balance of Payments There are three accounts within the balance of payments. The current account measures net exchanges of goods and services, transfers, and income flows across a nation's borders. The capital account measures net flows of financial assets. The official reserve transactions account tabulates exchanges of financial assets involving the home nation's and foreign nations' governments and central banks. Because each international exchange generates both an inflow and an outflow, the sum of the balances on all three accounts must equal zero.

current account, 728
capital account, 729
special drawing rights (SDRs), 730
International Monetary Fund, 730

Key Figure
Figure 33-1, 730

- MyEconLab Study Plan 33.1
- Animated Figure 33-1

Exchange Rate Determination in the Market for Foreign Exchange From the perspective of the United States, the demand for a nation's currency by U.S. residents is derived largely from the demand for imports from that nation. Likewise, the supply of a nation's currency is derived mainly from the supply of U.S. exports to that country. The equilibrium exchange rate is the rate of exchange between the dollar and the other nation's currency at which the quantity of the currency demanded is equal to the quantity supplied.

foreign exchange market, 732
exchange rate, 732
flexible exchange rates, 732
appreciation, 733
depreciation, 733

Key Figures
Figure 33-2, 734
Figure 33-3, 735
Figure 33-4, 736
Figure 33-5, 736

- MyEconLab Study Plan 33.2
- Animated Figures 33-2, 33-3, 33-4, 33-5

Factors That Can Induce Changes in Equilibrium Exchange Rates The equilibrium exchange rate changes in response to changes in the demand for or supply of another nation's currency. Changes in desired flows of exports or imports, real interest rates, tastes and preferences of consumers, and perceptions of economic stability affect the positions of the demand and supply curves in foreign exchange markets and induce variations in equilibrium exchange rates.

Key Figure
Figure 33-6, 737

- MyEconLab Study Plan 33.2
- Animated Figure 33-6

How Policymakers Can Attempt to Keep Exchange Rates Fixed If the current price of the home currency in terms of another nation's currency starts to fall below the level where the home country wants it to remain, the home country's central bank can use reserves of the other nation's currency to purchase the home currency in foreign exchange markets. This raises the demand for the home currency and thereby pushes up the currency's value in terms of the other nation's currency.

par value, 739
foreign exchange risk, 740
hedge, 741

Key Figure
Figure 33-8, 740

- MyEconLab Study Plans 33.3, 33.4
- Animated Figure 33-8

Log in to MyEconLab, take a chapter test, and get a personalized Study Plan that tells you which concepts you understand and which ones you need to review. From there, MyEconLab will give you further practice, tutorials, animations, videos, and guided solutions. For more information, visit www.myeconlab.com

PROBLEMS

All problems are assignable in MyEconLab; exercises that update with real-time data are marked with 🌐. *Answers to the odd-numbered problems appear at the back of the book.*

33-1. Suppose that during a recent year for the United States, merchandise imports were $2 trillion, unilateral transfers were a net outflow of $0.2 trillion, service exports were $0.2 trillion, service imports were $0.1 trillion, and merchandise exports were $1.4 trillion. (See pages 728–729.)

   a. What was the merchandise trade deficit?

   b. What was the balance on goods and services?

   c. What was the current account balance?

33-2. Suppose that during a recent year for the United States, the current account balance was −0.2 trillion, the flow of U.S. private holdings of assets abroad was −$0.1 trillion, and the flow of foreign private assets held in the United States was +0.2 trillion. (See pages 729–730.)

   a. What was the balance on the capital account during the year?

   b. What was the change in official reserves during the year?

33-3. Over the course of a year, a nation tracked its foreign transactions and arrived at the following amounts:

Merchandise exports	500
Service exports	75
Net unilateral transfers	10
Domestic assets abroad (capital outflows)	−200
Foreign assets at home (capital inflows)	300
Changes in official reserves	−35
Merchandise imports	600
Service imports	50

What are this nation's balance of trade, current account balance, and capital account balance? (See pages 728–730.)

33-4. Identify whether each of the following items creates a surplus item or a deficit item in the current account of the U.S. balance of payments. (See page 726.)

   a. A Central European company sells products to a U.S. hobby-store chain.

   b. Japanese residents pay a U.S. travel company to arrange hotel stays, ground transportation, and tours of various U.S. cities, including New York, Chicago, and Orlando.

   c. A Mexican company pays a U.S. accounting firm to audit its income statements.

   d. U.S. churches and mosques send relief aid to Pakistan following a major earthquake in that nation.

   e. A U.S. microprocessor manufacturer purchases raw materials from a Canadian firm.

33-5. Explain how the following events would affect the market for the Mexican peso, assuming a floating exchange rate. (See pages 735–737.)

   a. Improvements in Mexican production technology yield superior guitars, and many musicians around the world buy these guitars.

   b. Perceptions of political instability surrounding regular elections in Mexico make international investors nervous about future business prospects in Mexico.

33-6. Explain how the following events would affect the market for South Africa's currency, the rand, assuming a floating exchange rate. (See page 736.)

   a. A rise in U.S. inflation causes many U.S. residents to seek to buy gold, which is a major South African export good, as a hedge against inflation.

   b. Major discoveries of the highest-quality diamonds ever found occur in Russia and Central Asia, causing a significant decline in purchases of South African diamonds.

33-7. Suppose that the following two events take place in the market for China's currency, the yuan: U.S. parents are more willing than before to buy action figures and other Chinese toy exports, and China's government tightens restrictions on the amount of U.S. dollar–denominated financial assets that Chinese residents may legally purchase. What happens to the dollar price of the yuan? Does the yuan appreciate or depreciate relative to the dollar? (See pages 735–737.)

33-8. On Wednesday, the exchange rate between the Japanese yen and the U.S. dollar was $0.010 per yen. On Thursday, it was $0.009. Did the dollar appreciate or depreciate against the yen? By how much, expressed as a percentage change? (See page 730.)

33-9. On Wednesday, the exchange rate between the euro and the U.S. dollar was $1.20 per euro, and the exchange rate between the Canadian dollar and the U.S. dollar was U.S. $1.05 per Canadian dollar. What is the exchange rate between the Canadian dollar and the euro? (See page 730.)

33-10. Suppose that signs of an improvement in the Japanese economy lead international investors to resume lending to the Japanese government and businesses. How would this event affect the market for the yen? How should the central bank, the Bank of Japan, respond to this event if it wants to keep the value of the yen unchanged? (See pages 739–740.)

33-11. Briefly explain the differences between a flexible exchange rate system and a fixed exchange rate system. (See pages 738–739.)

33-12. Suppose that under a gold standard, the U.S. dollar is pegged to gold at a rate of $35 per ounce and the pound sterling is pegged to gold at a rate of £17.50 per ounce. Explain how the gold standard constitutes an exchange rate arrangement between the dollar and the pound. What is the exchange rate between the U.S. dollar and the pound sterling? (See pages 738–739.)

33-13. Suppose that under the Bretton Woods system, the dollar is pegged to gold at a rate of $35 per ounce and the pound sterling is pegged to the dollar at a rate of $2 = £1. If the dollar is devalued against gold and the pegged rate is changed to

$40 per ounce, what does this imply for the exchange value of the pound in terms of dollars? (See page 739.)

33-14. Suppose that the People's Bank of China wishes to peg the rate of exchange of its currency, the yuan, in terms of the U.S. dollar. In each of the following situations, should it add to or subtract from its dollar foreign exchange reserves? Why? (See pages 739–740.)

a. U.S. parents worrying about safety begin buying fewer Chinese-made toys for their children.

b. U.S. interest rates rise relative to interest rates in China, so Chinese residents seek to purchase additional U.S. financial assets.

c. Chinese furniture manufacturers produce high-quality early American furniture and successfully export large quantities of the furniture to the United States.

ECONOMICS ON THE NET

Daily Exchange Rates It is easy to keep up with daily changes in exchange rates by using the Web site of Oanda.com. In this application, you will learn how hard it is to predict exchange rate movements, and you will get some practice thinking about what factors can cause exchange rates to change.

Title: Oanda Currency Converter

Navigation: Go to **www.econtoday.com/chap33** to visit the Oanda.com's currency converter home page. Click on *Foreign Exchange 12 PM Rates*.

Application Answer the following questions.

1. Choose a currency from the many available in the drop-down menu. How many dollars does it take to purchase a unit of the currency in the spot foreign exchange market?

2. For currency you chose in Question 1, keep track of its value relative to the dollar over the course of several days. Based on your tabulations, try to predict the value of the currency at the end of the week *following* your data collections. Use any information you may have, or just do your best without any additional information. How far off did your prediction turn out to be?

For Group Study and Analysis Divide the class into groups, and assign a currency to each group. Ask the group to track the currency's value over the course of two days and to determine whether the currency's value appreciated or depreciated relative to the dollar from one day to the next. In addition, ask each group to discuss what kinds of demand or supply shifts could have caused the change that occurred during this interval.

ANSWERS TO QUICK QUIZZES

p. 731: (i) balance . . . payments; (ii) physical; (iii) current . . . current; (iv) Unilateral transfers; (v) current; (vi) capital . . . capital; (vii) official reserve; (viii) inflation . . . political

p. 738: (i) exchange rate; (ii) demand . . . demand . . . supply; (iii) downward . . . upward; (iv) shift . . . demand

p. 742: (i) fixed . . . fixed; (ii) currencies . . . reserves; (iii) risk

CHAPTER 1

1-1. Economics is the study of how individuals allocate limited resources to satisfy unlimited wants.

    a. Among the factors that a rational, self-interested student will take into account are her income, the price of the textbook, her anticipation of how much she is likely to study the textbook, and how much studying the book is likely to affect her grade.

    b. A rational, self-interested government official will, for example, recognize that higher taxes will raise more funds for mass transit while making more voters, who have limited resources, willing to elect other officials.

    c. A municipality's rational, self-interested government will, for instance, take into account that higher hotel taxes will produce more funds if as many visitors continue staying at hotels, but that the higher taxes will also discourage some visitors from spending nights at hotels.

1-3. Because wants are unlimited, the phrase applies to very high-income households as well as low- and middle-income households. Consider, for instance, a household with a low income and unlimited wants at the beginning of the year. The household's wants will still remain unlimited if it becomes a high-income household later in the year.

1-5. Sally is displaying rational behavior if all of these activities are in her self-interest. For example, Sally likely derives intrinsic benefit from volunteer and extracurricular activities and may believe that these activities, along with good grades, improve her prospects of finding a job after she completes her studies. Hence, these activities are in her self-interest even though they reduce some available study time.

1-7. The rationality assumption states that people do not intentionally make choices that leave them worse off. The bounded rationality hypothesis suggests that people are *almost*, but not completely, rational.

1-9. Suppose that a person faces a change in the environment, and the person adjusts to this change as predicted by the rationality assumption. If the new environment becomes predictable, then the individual who actually behaves as predicted by the traditional rationality assumption may settle into behavior that *appears* to involve repetitive applications of a rule of thumb.

1-11. **a.** Rationality assumption

    b. Bounded rationality

    c. Bounded rationality

1-13. **a.** The model using prices from the Iowa Electronic Market is more firmly based on the rationality assumption, because people who trade assets on this exchange that are based on poor forecasts actually experience losses. This gives them a strong incentive to make the best possible forecasts. Unpaid respondents to opinion polls have less incentive to give truthful answers about whether and how they will vote.

    b. An economist would develop a means of evaluating whether prices in the Iowa Electronic Market or results of opinion polls did a better job of matching actual electoral outcomes.

1-15. **a.** Positive

    b. Normative

    c. Normative

    d. Positive

APPENDIX A

A-1. **a.** Independent: price of a notebook; Dependent: quantity of notebooks

    b. Independent: work-study hours; Dependent: credit hours

    c. Independent: hours of study; Dependent: economics grade

A-3. **a.** Above x axis; to left of y axis

    b. Below x axis, to right of y axis

    c. On x axis; to right of y axis

A-5.

y	x
−20	−4
−10	−2
0	0
10	2
20	4

A-7. Each one-unit increase in x yields a 5-unit increase in y, so the slope given by the change in y corresponding to the change in x is equal to 5.

CHAPTER 2

2-1. The opportunity cost of attending a class at 11:00 a.m. is the next-best use of that hour of the day. Likewise, the opportunity cost of attending an 8:00 a.m. class is the next-best use of that particular hour of the day. If you are an early riser, it is arguable that the opportunity cost of the 8:00 a.m. hour is lower, because you will already be up at that time but have fewer choices compared with the 11:00 a.m. hour when shops, recreation centers, and the like are open. If you are a late riser, it may be that the opportunity cost of the 8:00 a.m. hour is higher, because you place a relatively high value on an additional hour of sleep in the morning.

2-3. The opportunity cost is the cost of the single, next-best forgone alternative to the $100 spent on the concert ticket, which for your friend was a restaurant meal she otherwise could have purchased and which for you was movie downloads that you otherwise could have bought.

2-5. The bank apparently determined that the net gain anticipated from trying to sell the house to someone else, taking into account the opportunity cost of resources that the bank would have had to devote to renovating the house, was less than $10.

2-7. If the student allocates additional study time to economics in order to increase her score from 90 to 100, her biology score declines from 50 to 40, so

the opportunity cost of earning 10 additional points in economics is 10 fewer points in biology.

2-9.

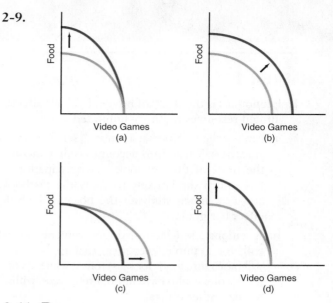

2-11. D

2-13. a. If the nation's residents increase production of consumption goods from 0 units to 10 units, the opportunity cost is 3 units of human capital forgone. If the nation's residents increase production of consumption goods from 0 units to 60 units, the opportunity cost is 100 units of human capital.

b. Yes, because successive 10-unit increases in production of consumption goods generate larger sacrifices of human capital, equal to 3, 7, 15, 20, 25, and 30.

2-15. Because it takes you less time to do laundry, you have an absolute advantage in laundry. Neither you nor your roommate has an absolute advantage in meal preparation. You require 2 hours to fold a basket of laundry, so your opportunity cost of folding a basket of laundry is 2 meals. Your roommate's opportunity cost of folding a basket of laundry is 3 meals. Hence, you have a comparative advantage in laundry, and your roommate has a comparative advantage in meal preparation.

2-17. It may be that the professor is very proficient at doing yard work relative to teaching and research activities, so in fact the professor may have a comparative advantage in doing yard work.

CHAPTER 3

3-1. The equilibrium price is $410 per tablet device, and the equilibrium quantity is 80 million tablet devices. At a price of $400 per tablet device, the quantity of tablet devices demanded is 90 million, and the quantity of tablet devices supplied is 60 million.

Hence, there is a shortage of 30 million tablet devices at a price of $400 per tablet device.

3-3. **a.** Wireless and cable Internet access services are substitutes, so a reduction in the price of wireless Internet access services causes a decrease in the demand for cable-based Internet access services.

 b. A decrease in the price of cable-based Internet access services generates an increase in the quantity of these services demanded.

 c. Cable-based Internet access services are a normal good, so a fall in the incomes of consumers reduces the demand for these services.

 d. If consumers' tastes shift away from wireless Internet access services in favor of cable-based Internet services, then the demand for the latter services increases.

3-5. **a.** Complement: eggs; Substitute: sausage

 b. Complement: tennis balls; Substitute: racquetball racquets

 c. Complement: cream; Substitute: tea

 d. Complement: gasoline; Substitute: city bus

3-7. b and d

3-9. **a.** At the $1,000 rental rate, the quantity of one-bedroom apartments supplied is 3,500 per month, but the quantity demanded is only 2,000 per month. Thus, the excess quantity of one-bedroom apartments supplied equals 1,500 apartments per month.

 b. To induce consumers to lease unrented one-bedroom apartments, some landlords will reduce their rental rates. As they do so, the quantity demanded will increase. In addition, some landlords will choose not to offer apartments for rent at lower rates, and the quantity supplied will decrease. At the equilibrium rental rate of $800 per month, no excess quantity will be supplied.

 c. At the $600 rental rate, the quantity of one-bedroom apartments demanded is 3,000 per month, but the quantity supplied is only 1,500 per month. Thus, the excess quantity of one-bedroom apartments demanded equals 1,500 apartments per month.

 d. To induce landlords to make more one-bedroom apartments available for rent, some consumers will offer to pay higher rental rates. As they do so, the quantity supplied will increase. In addition, some consumers will choose not to try to rent apartments at higher rates, and the quantity demanded will decrease. At the equilibrium rental rate of $800 per month, no excess quantity will be demanded.

3-11 **a.** Because touchscreens are an input in the production of smartphones, a decrease in the price of touchscreens causes an increase in the supply of smartphones. The market supply curve shifts to the right, which causes the market price of smartphones to fall and the equilibrium quantity of smartphones to increase.

 b. Machinery used to produce smartphones is an input in the production of these devices, so an increase in the price of machinery generates a decrease in the supply of smartphones. The market supply curve shifts to the left, which causes the market price of smartphones to rise and the equilibrium quantity of smartphones to decrease.

 c. An increase in the number of manufacturers of smartphones causes an increase in the supply of smartphones. The market supply curve shifts rightward. The market price of smartphones declines, and the equilibrium quantity of smartphones increases.

 d. The demand curve for smartphones shifts to the left along the same supply curve, so the quantity supplied decreases. The market price falls, and the equilibrium quantity declines.

3-13. Aluminum is an input in the production of canned soft drinks, so an increase in the price of aluminum reduces the supply of canned soft drinks (option c). The resulting rise in the market price of canned soft drinks brings about a decrease in the quantity of canned soft drinks demanded (option b). In equilibrium, the quantity of soft drinks supplied decreases (option d) to an amount equal to the quantity demanded. The demand curve does not shift, however, so option b does not apply.

CHAPTER 4

4-1. The ability to produce basic cell phones at lower cost and the entry of additional producers shift the supply curve rightward, from S_1 to S_2. At the same time, reduced prices of substitute smartphones result in a leftward shift in the demand for basic cell phones, from D_1 to D_2. Consequently, the equilibrium price of basic cell phones declines, from P_1 to P_2. The equilibrium quantity may rise, fall, or, as shown in the diagram, remain unchanged.

Quantity of Basic Cell Phones

4-3. An increase in demand for GPS devices and an accompanying reduction in supply of GPS devices could result in an unambiguous increase in the market clearing price but with no change in the equilibrium quantity.

4-5. The market rental rate is $700 per apartment, and the equilibrium quantity of apartments rented to tenants is 2,000. At a ceiling price of $650 per month, the number of apartments students desire to rent increases to 2,500 apartments. At the ceiling price, the number of apartments that owners are willing to supply decreases to 1,800 apartments. Thus, there is a shortage of 700 apartments at the ceiling price, and only 1,800 are rented at the ceiling price.

4-7. The market price is $400, and the equilibrium quantity of seats is 1,600. If airlines cannot sell tickets to more than 1,200 passengers, then passengers are willing to pay $600 per seat. Normally, airlines would be willing to sell each ticket for $200, but they will be able to charge a price as high as $600 for each of the 1,200 tickets they sell. Hence, the quantity of tickets sold declines from 1,600, and the price of a ticket rises from $400 to as high as $600.

4-9. a. Consumers buy 10 billion kilograms at the support price of $0.20 per kilogram and hence spend $2 billion on wheat.

   b. The amount of surplus wheat at the support price is 8 billion kilograms, so at the $0.20-per-kilogram support price, the government must spend $1.6 billion to purchase this surplus wheat.

   c. Pakistani wheat farmers receive a total of $3.6 billion for the wheat they produce at the support price.

4-11. a. At the present minimum wage of $11 per hour, the quantity of labor supplied is 102,000 workers, and the quantity of labor demanded by firms is 98,000. There is an excess quantity supplied of 4,000 workers, which is the number of people who are unemployed.

   b. At a minimum wage of $9 per hour, nothing would prevent market forces from pushing the wage rate to the market clearing level of $10 per hour. This $10-per-hour wage rate would exceed the legal minimum and hence would prevail. There would be no unemployed workers.

   c. At a $12-per-hour minimum wage, the quantity of labor supplied would increase to 104,000 workers, and the quantity of labor demanded would decline to 96,000. There would be an excess quantity supplied equal to 8,000 workers, which would then be the number of people unemployed.

4-13. a. The rise in the number of wheat producers causes the market supply curve to shift rightward, so more wheat is supplied at the support price.

   b. The quantity of wheat demanded at the same support price is unchanged.

   c. Because quantity demanded is unchanged while quantity supplied has increased, the amount of surplus wheat that the government must purchase has risen.

CHAPTER 5

5-1. In the absence of laws forbidding cigar smoking in public places, people who are bothered by the odor of cigar smoke will experience costs not borne by cigar producers. Because the supply of cigars will not reflect these costs, from society's perspective, the market cigar supply curve will be in a position too far to the right. The market price of cigars will be too low, and too many cigars will be produced and consumed.

5-3. Imposing the tax on pesticides causes an increase in the price of pesticides, which are an input in the production of oranges. Hence, the supply curve in the orange market shifts leftward. The market price of oranges increases, and the equilibrium quantity of oranges declines. Thus, orange consumers indirectly help to pay for dealing with the spillover costs of pesticide production by paying more for oranges.

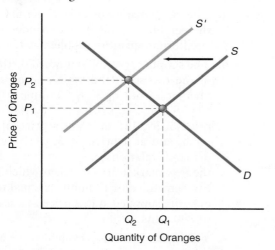

5-5. a. As shown in the figure below, if the social benefits associated with bus ridership were taken into account, the demand schedule would be D' instead of D, and the market price would be higher. The equilibrium quantity of bus rides would be higher.

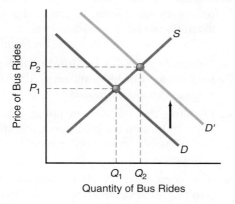

b. The government could pay commuters a subsidy to ride the bus, thereby shifting the demand curve outward and to the right. This would increase the market price and equilibrium number of bus rides.

5-7. If this nation's government does not provide people with property rights for a number of items and fails to enforce the property rights that it does assign for remaining items, externalities would be more common than in a country such as the United States. Any two parties undertaking transactions would experience no incentives to reduce or eliminate their transactions' spillover effects, resulting in widespread externalities.

5-9. At present, the equilibrium quantity of residences with Internet access is 2 million. To take into account

the external benefit of Internet access and boost the quantity of residences with access to 3 million, the demand curve would have to shift upward by $20 per month at any given quantity, to D_2 from the current position D_1. Thus, the government would have to offer a $20-per-month subsidy to raise the quantity of residences with Internet access to 3 million.

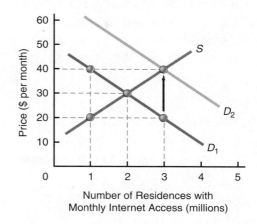

5-11. No, the outcome will be different. If the government had simply provided grants to attend private schools at the current market tuition rate, parents and students receiving the grants would have paid a price equal to the market valuation of the last unit of educational services provided. Granting a subsidy to private schools allows the private schools to charge parents and students a price less than the market price. Private schools thereby will receive a higher-than-market price for the last unit of educational services they provide. Consequently, they will provide a quantity of educational services in excess of the market equilibrium quantity. At this quantity, parents and students place a lower value on the services than the price received by the private schools.

5-13. a. $40 million

b. The effective price of a tablet device to consumers will be lower after the government pays the subsidy, so people will purchase a larger quantity.

c. $60 million

d. $90 million

5-15. a. $60 − $50 = $10

b. Expenditures after the program expansion are $2.4 million. Before the program expansion, expenditures were $1 million. Hence, the increase in expenditures is $1.4 million.

c. At a per-unit subsidy of $50, the share of the per-unit $60 price paid by the government is 5/6, or 83.3 percent. Hence, this is the government's share of total expenditures on the 40,000 devices that consumers purchase.

CHAPTER 6

6-1. a. The average tax rate is the total tax of $40 divided by the $200 in income: $40/$200 = 0.2, or 20 percent.

   b. The marginal tax rate for the last hour of work is the change in taxes, $3, divided by the change in income, $8: $3/$8 = 0.375, or 37.5 percent.

6-3. a. Christino's marginal tax rate is

$$\frac{\$300 - \$200}{\$2,000 - \$1,000} = \frac{\$400 - \$300}{\$3,000 - \$2,000}$$

$$= \frac{\$100}{\$1,000} = 0.1, \text{ or 10 percent.}$$

   b. Jarius's marginal tax rate is

$$\frac{\$400 - \$200}{\$2,000 - \$1,000} = \frac{\$600 - \$400}{\$3,000 - \$2,000}$$

$$= \frac{\$200}{\$1,000} = 0.2, \text{ or 20 percent.}$$

   c. Meg's marginal tax rate is

$$\frac{\$500 - \$200}{\$2,000 - \$1,000} = \frac{\$800 - \$500}{\$3,000 - \$2,000}$$

$$= \frac{\$300}{\$1,000} = 0.3, \text{ or 30 percent.}$$

6-5. 2005: $300 million; 2007: $350 million; 2009: $400 million; 2011: $400 million; 2013: $420 million

6-7. a. The supply of tickets for flights into and out of London shifts upward by $154. The equilibrium quantity of flights into and out of London declines. The market clearing price of London airline tickets rises by an amount less than the tax.

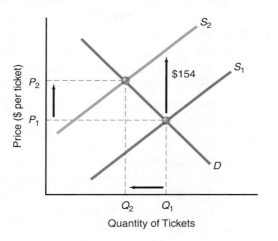

   b. Tickets for flights into or out of London are substitutes for tickets for flights into and out of nearby cities. Thus, the demand for tickets for flights into and out of these cities will increase. This will cause an increase in the equilibrium quantities of these tickets and an increase in the market clearing prices.

6-9. a. The initial market price is $7 per unit, at which the equilibrium quantity demanded equals the equilibrium quantity supplied at 125 units.

   b. The supply curve shifts upward by the amount of the tax, so in the table, the quantity supplied at a price of $6 is 50 units; at a price of $7, 75 units; at a price of $8, 100 units; at a price of $9, 125 units; at a price of $10, 150 units; and at a price of $11, 175 units. The demand relationship is unchanged. Hence, the new market price is $8, at which the quantity demanded of 100 units is equal to the new quantity supplied at this price that is also equal to 100 units.

   c. The market price rises from $7 to $8, and this $1 price increase is half of the $2 tax. Consequently, consumers pay half of the tax, and producers pay the other half.

CHAPTER 7

7-1. a. Multiplying the fraction of people who participate in the labor force, 0.7, times the adult, non-institutionalized, nonmilitary population of 200.0 million yields a labor force of 140.0 million.

   b. Subtracting the 7.5 million unemployed from the labor force of 140.0 million yields 132.5 million people who are employed.

   c. Dividing the 7.5 million unemployed by the 140.0 million in the labor force and multiplying by 100 yields an unemployment rate of about 5.36 percent.

7-3. a. The labor force equals the number employed plus the number unemployed, or 156 million + 8 million = 164 million. In percentage terms, therefore, the unemployment rate is 100 times 8 million/164 million, or 4.9 percent.

   b. These 60 million people are not in the labor force. The labor force participation rate is, in percentage terms, 100 times 164 million/224 million, or 73.2 percent.

7-5. a. Four of the 100 people are always continuously unemployed because they are between jobs, so the frictional unemployment rate is (4/100) × 100 = 4 percent.

   b. Three of the 100 people are always unemployed as a result of government regulations, so the structural unemployment rate is (3/100) × 100 = 3 percent.

   c. The unemployment rate is the sum of the frictional and structural rates of unemployment, or 7 percent.

7-7. The overall unemployment rate is 8 percent, and the natural rate of unemployment is 5 percent.

7-9. In 2013, the value of the price index is $10,000/ $10,000 × 100 = 100. In 2014, the value of the price index is $11,100/$10,000 × 100 = 111.

7-11. **a.** 2014

  b. 10 percent

  c. 10 percent

  d. $1,800 in 2013; $3,000 in 2017

7-13. The expected rate of inflation is equal to 100 × [(99 − 90)/90] = 10 percent. Hence, the real interest rate equals the difference between the 12 percent nominal interest rate and the 10 percent anticipated inflation rate, or 2 percent.

7-15. **a.** The homeowner gains; the savings bank loses.

  b. The tenants gain; the landlord loses.

  c. The auto buyer gains; the bank loses.

  d. The employer gains; the pensioner loses.

CHAPTER 8

8-1. As illustrated by the basic circular-flow diagram, the flow of the market value of final goods and services produced within a nation's borders during a given interval—that is, gross domestic product—is what generates the gross domestic income received by the nation's households during that interval, which they in turn spend in the nation's product markets. Consequently, the flows of gross domestic product and gross domestic income must be equivalent.

8-3. **a.** When Maria does all the work herself, only purchases of the materials in markets (magazines, texturing materials, paint brushes, and paints), which total $280 per year, count in GDP.

  b. She must pay the market price of $200 for the texturing, so her contribution to annual GDP from this project, including the materials, is $480.

  c. Because Maria now pays for the entire project via market transactions, her total contribution to GDP equals the sum of the $280 material purchases from part (a), $200 for the texturing from part (b), and $350 for the painting, or $830 per year.

8-5. **a.** GDP = $16.6 trillion; NDP = $15.3 trillion; NI = $14.5 trillion.

  b. GDP in 2017 will equal $15.5 trillion.

8-7. **a.** Gross domestic income = $14.6 trillion; GDP = $14.6 trillion.

  b. Gross private domestic investment = $2.0 trillion.

  c. Personal income = $12.0 trillion; personal disposable income = $10.3 trillion.

8-9. **a.** Measured GDP declines.

  b. Measured GDP increases.

  c. Measured GDP does not change (the firearms are not newly produced).

8-11. **a.** The chip is an intermediate good, so its purchase in June is not included in GDP; only the final sale in November is included.

  b. This is a final sale of a good that is included in GDP for the year.

  c. This is a final sale of a service that is included in GDP for the year.

8-13. **a.** Nominal GDP for 2013 is $2,300; for 2017, nominal GDP is $2,832.

  b. Real GDP for 2013 is $2,300; for 2017, real GDP is $2,229.

8-15. The price index is (2015 nominal GDP/2015 real GDP) × 100 = ($88,000/$136,000) × 100 = 64.7.

8-17. The $1 billion expended to pay for employees and equipment and the additional $1 billion paid to clean up the oil spill would be included in GDP, for a total of $2 billion added to GDP in 2015. The rise in oil reserves increases the stock of wealth but is not included in the current flow of newly produced goods and services. In addition, the welfare loss relating to the deaths of wildlife is also not measured in the marketplace and therefore is not included in GDP.

CHAPTER 9

9-1. **a.** Y

  b. X

9-3. The nation will maintain its stock of capital goods at its current level, so its rate of economic growth will be zero.

9-5. A: $8,250 per capita; B: $4,500 per capita; C: $21,000 per capita

9-7. 1.77 times higher after 20 years; 3.16 times higher after 40 years

9-9. 5 years

9-11. In Mozambique, in 50 years the typical resident's annual real GDP per capita will equal $3,000 × 4.38 = $13,140. In China, a typical resident's real GDP per capita will equal $3,000 × 46.90 = $140,700, which is $127,560 per year greater than in Mozambique.

9-13. 4 percent

9-15. Per capita real GDP in 2014 was 10 percent higher than in 2013, or $2,200. The level of real GDP is $2,200 per person × 5 million people = $11 billion.

CHAPTER 10

10-1. The amount of unemployment would be the sum of frictional, structural, and seasonal unemployment.

10-3. The real value of the new full-employment level of nominal GDP is ($17.7 trillion/1.15) = $15.39 trillion, so the long-run aggregate supply curve has shifted rightward by $2.35 trillion, in base-year dollars.

10-5. a. A rightward shift of the *LRAS* curve coupled with a shift in the *AD* curve farther to the right

   b. A leftward shift of the *LRAS* curve coupled with a leftward shift of the *AD* curve of the same magnitude

   c. A rightward shift of the *LRAS* curve coupled with a rightward shift of the *AD* curve of the same magnitude

   d. A leftward shift of the *LRAS* curve coupled with a shift of the *AD* curve farther to the left

10-7. This change implies a rightward shift of the long-run aggregate supply curve along the unchanged aggregate demand curve, so the long-run equilibrium price level will decline.

10-9. There are three effects. First, there is a real-balance effect, because the rise in the price level reduces real money balances, inducing people to cut back on their spending. In addition, there is an interest rate effect as a higher price level pushes up interest rates, thereby reducing the attractiveness of purchases of autos, houses, and plants and equipment. Finally, there is an open-economy effect as home residents respond to the higher price level by reducing purchases of domestically produced goods in favor of foreign-produced goods, while foreign residents cut back on their purchases of our home-produced goods. All three effects entail a reduction in purchases of goods and services, so the aggregate demand curve slopes downward.

10-11. a. At the price level P_2 above the equilibrium price level P_1, the total quantity of real goods and services that people plan to consume is less than the total quantity that is consistent with firms' production plans. One reason is that at the higher-than-equilibrium price level, real money balances are lower, which reduces real wealth and induces lower planned consumption. Another is that interest rates are higher at the higher-than-equilibrium price level, which generates a cutback in spending on consumer durables. Finally, at the higher-than-equilibrium price level P_2, people tend to cut back on purchasing domestic goods in favor of foreign-produced goods, and foreign residents reduce purchases of our domestic goods. As unsold inventories of output accumulate, the price level drops toward the equilibrium price level P_1, which ultimately causes planned consumption to rise toward equality with total production.

   b. At the price level P_3 below the equilibrium price level P_1, the total quantity of real goods and services that people plan to consume exceeds the total quantity that is consistent with firms' production plans. One reason is that at the lower-than-equilibrium price level, real money balances are higher, which raises real wealth and induces higher planned consumption. Another is that interest rates are lower at the lower-than-equilibrium price level, which generates an increase in consumption spending. Finally, at the lower-than-equilibrium price level P_3, people tend to raise their purchases of domestic goods and cut back on buying foreign-produced goods, and foreign residents increase purchases of our domestic goods. As inventories of output are depleted, the price level begins to rise toward the equilibrium price level P_1, which ultimately causes planned consumption to fall toward equality with total production.

10-13. a. When the price level falls with deflation, there is a movement downward along the *AD* curve.

   b. The decline in foreign real GDP levels reduces incomes of foreign residents, who cut back on their spending on our domestic exports. Thus, the domestic *AD* curve shifts leftward.

   c. The fall in the foreign exchange value of the nation's currency makes our domestically produced goods and services less expensive to foreign residents, who increase their spending on our domestic exports. Thus, the domestic *AD* curve shifts rightward.

   d. An increase in the price level causes a movement upward along the *AD* curve.

10-15. a. The aggregate demand curve shifts leftward along the long-run aggregate supply curve. The equilibrium price level falls, and equilibrium real GDP remains unchanged.

   b. The aggregate demand curve shifts rightward along the long-run aggregate supply curve. The equilibrium price level rises, and equilibrium real GDP remains unchanged.

   c. The long-run aggregate supply curve shifts rightward along the aggregate demand curve. The equilibrium price level falls, and equilibrium real GDP increases.

   d. The aggregate demand curve shifts rightward along the long-run aggregate supply curve. The equilibrium price level rises, and equilibrium real GDP remains unchanged.

10-17. a. The income flows are mainly influencing relatives' consumption, so the main effect is on the aggregate demand curve.

   b. A rise in aggregate demand will lead to an increase in the equilibrium price level.

CHAPTER 11

11-1. a. Because saving increases at any given interest rate, the desired saving curve shifts rightward. This causes the equilibrium interest rate to decline.

   b. There is no effect on current equilibrium real GDP, because in the classical model, the vertical long-run aggregate supply curve always applies.

   c. A change in the saving rate does not directly affect the demand for labor or the supply of labor in the classical model, so equilibrium employment does not change.

   d. The decrease in the equilibrium interest rate generates a downward movement along the demand curve for investment. Consequently, desired investment increases.

   e. The rise in current investment implies greater capital accumulation. Other things being equal, this will imply increased future production and higher equilibrium real GDP in the future.

11-3. False. In fact, an important distinction can be made. The classical model of short-run real GDP determination applies to an interval short enough that some factors of production, such as capital, are fixed. Nevertheless, the classical model implies that even in the short run the economy's short-run aggregate supply curve is the same as its long-run aggregate supply curve.

11-5. In the long run, the aggregate supply curve is vertical because all input prices adjust fully and people are fully informed in the long run. Thus, the short-run aggregate supply curve is more steeply sloped if input prices adjust more rapidly and people become more fully informed within a short-run interval.

11-7. To prevent a short-run decrease in real GDP from taking place after the temporary rise in oil prices shifts the SRAS curve leftward, policymakers should increase the quantity of money in circulation. This will shift the AD curve rightward and prevent equilibrium real GDP from declining in the short run.

11-9. An increase in total planned real expenditures by U.S. households in response to an increase in the quantity of money in circulation implies a rightward shift in the position of the aggregate demand curve along the short-run aggregate supply curve. The predicted effects are increases in both the equilibrium U.S. price level and the equilibrium U.S. real GDP. Keynesian theory indicates that a consequence would be a short-term inflationary gap between expenditures on real GDP in the short run and expenditures on real GDP that would be consistent with long-run equilibrium.

11-11. a. E: The union wage boost causes the $SRAS$ curve to shift leftward, from $SRAS_1$ to $SRAS_3$. The reduction in incomes abroad causes import spending in this nation to fall, which induces a leftward shift in the AD curve, from AD_1 to AD_3.

   b. B: The short-term reduction in production capabilities causes the $SRAS$ curve to shift leftward, from $SRAS_1$ to $SRAS_3$, and the increase in money supply growth generates a rightward shift in the AD curve, from AD_1 to AD_2.

   c. C: The strengthening of the value of this nation's currency reduces the prices of imported inputs that domestic firms utilize to produce goods and services, which causes the $SRAS$ curve to shift rightward, from $SRAS_1$ to $SRAS_2$. At the same time, currency's strengthening raises the prices of exports and reduces the prices of imports, so net export spending declines, thereby inducing a leftward shift in the AD curve, from AD_1 to AD_3.

CHAPTER 12

12-1. a. Flow

   b. Flow

   c. Stock

   d. Flow

   e. Stock

   f. Flow

   g. Stock

12-3. a. The completed table follows (all amounts in dollars):

Real GDP	Consumption	Saving	Investment
2,000	2,000	0	1,200
4,000	3,600	400	1,200
6,000	5,200	800	1,200
8,000	6,800	1,200	1,200
10,000	8,400	1,600	1,200
12,000	10,000	2,000	1,200

MPC = 1,600/2000 = 0.8;

MPS = 400/2,000 = 0.2.

   b. The graph appears on the next page.

c. The graph appears below. Equilibrium real GDP on both graphs equals $8,000 per year.

d. APS = $1,200/$8,000 = 0.15

e. The multiplier is $1/(1 - \text{MPC}) = 1/(1 - 0.8) = 1/0.2 = 5$. Thus, if autonomous consumption were to rise by $100, then equilibrium real GDP would increase by $100 times 5, or $500.

12-5. a. MPC = 0.95; MPS = 0.05
 b. MPC = 0.90; MPS = 0.10
 c. MPC = 0.875; MPS = 0.125
 d. MPC = 0.80; MPS = 0.20

12-7. The multiplier is $1/(1 - \text{MPC}) = 4$, so $1 - \text{MPC} = 0.25$, which implies that MPC = 0.75. Thus, when real GDP equals $15 trillion, consumption is $1 trillion + (0.75 × $15 trillion) = $12.25 trillion.

12-9. The multiplier is $1/(1 - \text{MPC}) = 1/(1 - 0.75) = 4$, so the increase in equilibrium real GDP is $250 billion × 4 = $1 trillion, and the level of real GDP at the new point on the aggregate demand curve is $16 trillion per year.

12-11. a. The MPS is equal to 1/3.
 b. $0.1 trillion

CHAPTER 13

13-1. a. A key factor that could help explain why the actual effect may have turned out to be lower is the crowding-out effect. Some government spending may have entailed direct expenditure offsets that reduced private expenditures on a dollar-for-dollar basis. In addition, indirect crowding out may have occurred. Because the government did not change taxes, it probably sold bonds to finance its increased expenditures, and this action likely pushed up interest rates, thereby discouraging private investment. Furthermore, the increase in government spending likely pushed up aggregate demand, which may have caused a short-run increase in the price level. This, in turn, may have induced foreign residents to reduce their expenditures on U.S. goods. It also could have reduced real money holdings sufficiently to discourage consumers from spending as much as before. On net, therefore, real GDP rose in the short run, but not by the full amount predicted by the basic multiplier effect.

 b. In the long run, as the increased spending raised aggregate demand, wages and other input prices likely increased in proportion to the resulting increase in the price level. Thus, in the long run the aggregate supply schedule was vertical, and the increase in government spending induced only a rise in the price level.

13-3. Because of the recognition time lag entailed in gathering information about the economy, policymakers may be slow to respond to a downturn in real GDP. Congressional approval of policy actions to address the downturn may be delayed; hence, an action time lag may also arise. Finally, there is an effect time lag, because policy actions take time to exert their full effects on the economy. If these lags are sufficiently long, it is possible that by the time a policy to address a downturn has begun to have its effects, equilibrium real GDP per year may already be rising. If so, the policy action may push real GDP up faster than intended, thereby making real GDP less stable.

13-5. Situation *b* is an example of indirect crowding out because the reduction in private expenditures takes place indirectly in response to a change in the interest rate. In contrast, situations *a* and *c* are examples of direct expenditure offsets.

13-7. Situation *b* is an example of a discretionary fiscal policy action because this is a discretionary action by Congress. So is situation *d* because the president uses discretionary authority. Situation *c* is an example of monetary policy, not fiscal policy, and situation *a* is an example of an automatic stabilizer.

13-9. There is a recessionary gap, because at point A, equilibrium real GDP of $15.5 trillion is below the long-run level of $16.0 trillion. To eliminate the recessionary gap of $0.5 trillion, government spending must increase sufficiently to shift the AD curve rightward to a long-run equilibrium, which will entail a price level increase from 115 to 120. Hence, the spending increase must shift the AD curve rightward by $1 trillion, or by the multiplier, which is $1/0.20 = 5$, times the increase in spending. Government spending must rise by $200 billion, or $0.2 trillion per year.

13-11. Because the MPC is 0.80, the multiplier equals $1/(1 - \text{MPC}) = 1/0.2 = 5$. Net of indirect crowding out, therefore, total autonomous expenditures must rise by $40 billion in order to shift the aggregate demand curve rightward by $200 billion. If the government raises its spending by $50 billion, the market interest rate rises by 0.5 percentage point and thereby causes planned investment spending to fall by $10 billion, which results in a net rise in total autonomous expenditures equal to $40 billion. Consequently, to accomplish its objective, the government should increase its spending by $50 billion.

13-13. A cut in the tax rate should induce a rise in consumption and, consequently, a multiple short-run increase in equilibrium real GDP. In addition, however, a tax-rate reduction reduces the automatic-stabilizer properties of the tax system, so equilibrium real GDP would be less stable in the face of changes in autonomous spending.

13-15. According to the logic of the permanent income hypothesis, these small, one-time payments did not raise people's average lifetime disposable incomes. Instead of using the funds to increase their consumption spending, people applied them toward paying down outstanding debts or to their savings. Hence, consumption spending did not rise in response to the temporary increase in real disposable income.

APPENDIX D

D-1. a. The marginal propensity to consume is equal to $1 - \text{MPS}$, or $6/7$.

  b. The required increase in equilibrium real GDP is $0.35 trillion, or $350 billion. The multiplier equals $1/(1 - \text{MPC}) = 1/\text{MPS} = 1/(1/7) = 7$. Hence, investment or government spending must increase by $50 billion to bring about a $350 billion increase in equilibrium real GDP.

  c. The multiplier relevant for a tax change equals $-\text{MPC}/(1 - \text{MPC}) = -\text{MPC}/\text{MPS} = -(6/7)/(1/7) = -6$. Thus, the government would have to cut taxes by $58.33 billion to induce a rise in equilibrium real GDP equal to $350 billion.

D-3. a. The aggregate expenditures curve shifts up by $1 billion; equilibrium real GDP increases by $5 billion per year.

  b. The aggregate expenditures curve shifts down by the MPC times the tax increase, or by $0.8 \times \$1$ billion $= \$0.8$ billion; equilibrium real income falls by $4 billion per year.

  c. The aggregate expenditures curve shifts upward by $(1 - \text{MPC})$ times $1 billion $= \$0.2$ billion. Equilibrium real income rises by $1 billion.

  d. No change; no change

CHAPTER 14

14-1. $0.4 trillion

14-3. A higher deficit creates a higher public debt.

14-5. The net public debt is obtained by subtracting government interagency borrowing from the gross public debt.

14-7. When foreign dollar holders hold more of our domestic government bonds issued to finance higher domestic government budget deficits, they purchase fewer of our domestic exports, so the domestic trade deficit rises, other things being equal.

14-9. As shown in the diagram below, the increase in government spending and/or tax reduction that creates the budget deficit also causes the aggregate demand curve to shift rightward, from AD to AD_2. Real GDP rises to its long-run equilibrium level of $15 trillion at point B. The equilibrium price level increases to a value of 130 at this point. As real GDP rises, the government's tax collections increase and benefit payouts fall, both of which will help ultimately reduce the deficit.

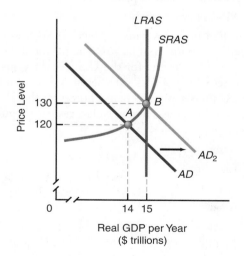

14-11. "The rich" are likely to respond to higher tax rates by reducing their activities that generate taxable income, so actual tax collections from "the rich" will not turn out to be as high as the politician suggests. In any event, as shown in Figure 14-5 on page 311, even imposing a 100 percent tax rate on the highest-income taxpayers could not raise sufficient tax revenues to eliminate the deficit.

14-13. These data indicate that tax revenues have been able to cover only about two-thirds—about 67 percent—of federal expenditures. Because more than 60 percent of all federal expenditures are entitlements, this implies that the federal government has been borrowing to pay for most discretionary spending.

CHAPTER 15

15-1. Medium of exchange; store of value; standard of deferred payment

15-3. Store of value; standard of deferred payment

15-5. M1 equals transactions deposits plus currency plus traveler's checks, or $1,025 billion + $1,050 billion + $25 billion = $2,100 billion; M2 equals M1 + savings deposits plus small-denomination time deposits plus money market deposit accounts plus retail (noninstitution) money market mutual funds, or $2,100 billion + $3,300 billion + $1,450 billion + $1,950 billion + $1,900 billion = $10,700 billion.

15-7. a. M1 and M2

b. Neither

c. M2 only

d. M1 and M2

e. M2 only

15-9. a. Moral hazard problem

b. Adverse selection problem

c. Moral hazard problem

15-11. The Fed provides banking services such as check clearing services and large-value payment services for other banks and for the U.S. Treasury, just as a private bank provides such services for its customers. Unlike a private bank, however, the Federal Reserve serves as a lender of last resort, a regulator, and a policymaker.

15-13. a. Asset

b. Liability

c. Asset

d. Asset

e. Asset

f. Liability

15-15. 9.09

15-17. 25 percent (or 0.25)

15-19. The maximum potential money multiplier is $1/0.01 = 100$, so total deposits in the banking system will increase by $5 million × 100 = $500 million.

CHAPTER 16

16-1. a. $500/0.05 = $10,000

b. Its price falls to $500/0.10 = $5,000.

16-3. a. One possible policy action would be an open market sale of securities, which would reduce the money supply and shift the aggregate demand curve leftward. Others would be to increase the discount rate relative to the federal funds rate or to raise the required reserve ratio.

b. In principle, the Fed's action would reduce inflation more quickly.

16-5. The short-run effect is an upward movement along the short-run aggregate supply curve generated by an increase in aggregate demand. The equilibrium price level rises, and equilibrium real GDP increases. In the long run, input prices rise, and people anticipate a higher price level, which causes the short-run aggregate supply curve to shift upward and to the left. The equilibrium price level rises once more, and equilibrium real GDP falls back to its long-run equilibrium level.

16-7. a. The dollar appreciation will raise the prices of U.S. goods and services from the perspective of foreign residents, so they will reduce their spending on U.S. exports. It will reduce the prices of foreign goods and services from the perspective of U.S. residents, so they will increase their spending on foreign imports. Thus, net export expenditures per year will decline.

b. The fall in net export expenditures will bring about a decrease in U.S. aggregate demand, so the aggregate demand curve AD_2 will apply to this situation. In the short run, the equilibrium price level will fall from 118 to 116, and equilibrium real GDP, measured in base-year dollars, will fall from $15.0 trillion to $14.5 trillion per year.

c. The Federal Reserve could engage in a policy action, such as open market purchases, that increases aggregate demand to its original level.

16-9. The price level remains at its original value. Because $M_sV = PY$, V has doubled, and Y is unchanged, cutting M_s in half leaves P unchanged.

16-11. a. $M_sV = PY$, so $P = M_sV/Y = ($1.1 \text{ trillion} \times 10)/$5 \text{ trillion} = 2.2$.

b. $100 billion/$1 trillion = 0.1, or 10 percent.

c. 0.2/2 = 0.1, or 10 percent.

d. Both the money supply and the price level increased by 10 percent.

16-13. Any one of these contractionary actions will tend to raise interest rates, which in turn will induce international inflows of financial capital. This pushes up the value of the dollar and makes U.S. goods less attractive abroad. As a consequence, real planned total expenditures on U.S. goods decline even further.

16-15. To induce the banks to hold the reserves, the Fed would have to raise the interest rate it pays on the reserves. The increase in reserves owned by private banks would generate a rise in the Fed's liabilities equal to the expansion of the Fed's assets.

16-17. The money supply did not change, so this did not actually constitute a monetary policy action. Instead, the Fed only expanded its reserves and, hence, its liabilities, which corresponded to the increase in the Fed's holdings of privately issued assets. Consequently, the Fed's "quantitative easing" was primarily a credit policy action.

APPENDIX E

E-1. a. $20 billion increase

   b. $40 billion increase

   c. $10 billion open market purchase

E-3. Through its purchase of $1 billion in bonds, the Fed increased reserves by $1 billion. This ultimately caused a $3 billion increase in the money supply after full multiple expansion. The 1 percentage-point drop in the interest rate, from 6 percent to 5 percent, caused investment to rise by $25 billion, from $1,200 billion to $1,225 billion. An investment multiplier of 3 indicates that equilibrium real GDP rose by $75 billion, to $12,075 billion, or $12.075 trillion per year.

CHAPTER 17

17-1. a. The actual unemployment rate, which equals the number of people unemployed divided by the labor force, would decline, because the labor force would rise while the number of people unemployed would remain unchanged.

   b. Natural unemployment rate estimates also would be lower.

   c. The logic of the short- and long-run Phillips curves would not be altered. The government might wish to make this change if it feels that those in the military "hold jobs" and therefore should be counted as employed within the U.S. economy.

17-3. a. The measured unemployment rate when all adjustments have occurred will now always be lower than before, so the natural unemployment rate will be smaller.

   b. The Phillips curve will shift inward.

17-5. Because the unemployment rate has increased as a consequence of a rise in structural unemployment while the inflation rate has remained unchanged, the short-run Phillips curve will tend to shift rightward, together with a rightward shift in the long-run Phillips curve as the natural rate of unemployment increases.

17-7. Because monetary policy is now harder for people to predict, the unsystematic variations in the quantity of money in circulation will tend to be more likely to generate changes in equilibrium real GDP. Inflation expectations will not change, and the short-run aggregate supply curve will remain in position as the aggregate demand curve shifts.

17-9. No. It could still be true that wages and other prices of factors of production adjust sluggishly to changes in the price level. Then a rise in aggregate demand that boosts the price level brings about an upward movement along the short-run aggregate supply curve, causing equilibrium real GDP to rise.

17-11. a. An increase in desired investment spending induces an increase in aggregate demand, so AD_3 applies. The price level is unchanged in the short run, and equilibrium real GDP rises from $15 trillion at point A to $15.5 trillion per year at point C.

   b. Over time, firms perceive that they can increase their profits by adjusting prices upward in response to the increase in aggregate demand. Thus, firms eventually will incur the menu costs required to make these price adjustments. As they do so, the aggregate supply curve will shift upward, from $SRAS$ to $SRAS_2$, as shown in the diagram below. Real GDP will return to its original level of $15 trillion per year, in base-year dollars. The price level will increase to a level above 119, such as 124.

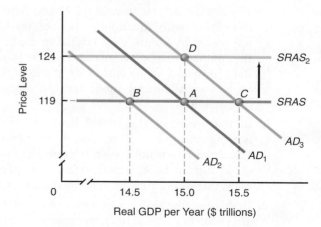

17-13. The explanation would be that aggregate demand increased at a faster pace than the rise in aggregate supply caused by economic growth. On net, therefore, the price level rose during those years.

17-15. If the average time between price adjustments by firms is significant, then the short-run aggregate supply curve could be regarded as horizontal, as hypothesized by the new Keynesian theorists. As a consequence, there would be a short-run trade-off between inflation and real GDP that policymakers potentially could exploit.

CHAPTER 18

18-1. Population growth rate = real GDP growth rate − rate of growth of per capita real GDP = 3.1 percent − 0.3 percent = 2.8 percent.

18-3. Rate of growth of per capita real GDP = rate of growth of real GDP − population growth rate = 1.3 percent − 2.7 percent per year = −1.4 percent.

18-5. a. 20×0.01 percent = 0.2 percent

    b. 10×0.01 percent = 0.1 percent

18-7. $10 trillion/$0.5 trillion $\times$ 0.1 = 2 percentage points.

18-9. a. Portfolio investment is equal to $150 million in bonds plus $100 million in stocks representing ownership of less than 10 percent, or $250 million. (Bank loans are neither portfolio investment nor foreign direct investment.)

    b. Foreign direct investment is equal to $250 million in stocks representing an ownership share of at least 10 percent. (Bank loans are neither portfolio investment nor foreign direct investment.)

18-11. a. Adverse selection

    b. Adverse selection

    c. Moral hazard

    d. Adverse selection

18-13. a. The company had already qualified for funding at a market interest rate, so the World Bank is interfering with functioning private markets for credit. In addition, by extending credit to the company at a below-market rate, the World Bank provides an incentive for the company to borrow additional funds for less efficient investment.

    b. In this situation, the World Bank effectively is tying up funds in dead capital. There is an associated opportunity cost, because the funds could instead be allocated to another investment that would yield more immediate returns.

    c. In this case, the IMF contributes to a moral hazard problem, because the government has every incentive not to make reforms that will enable it to repay this and future loans it may receive.

18-15. a. An incentive exists for at least some governments to fail to follow through with reforms, even if those governments might have had good intentions when they applied for World Bank loans.

    b. National governments most interested in obtaining funds to "buy" votes will be among those most interested in obtaining IMF loans. The proposed IMF rule could help reduce the number of nations whose governments seek to obtain funds to try to "buy" votes.

CHAPTER 19

19-1. $-[(200 - 150)/(350/2)]/[(\$19 - \$20)/(\$39/2)]$, which is approximately equal to − 5.6. Thus, the absolute price elasticity of demand equals 5.6.

19-3. a. $-[(90 - 80)/(85)]/[(\$0.20 - \$0.40)/(\$0.30)]$, which is approximately equal to −0.18. Consequently, the absolute price elasticity of demand is 0.18, so demand is inelastic over this range.

    b. $-[(60 - 40)/(50)]/[(\$0.80 - \$1.20)/(\$1.00)] = -1.00$. The absolute price elasticity of demand, therefore, equals 1.00, which implies that demand is unit-elastic over this range.

    c. $-[(20 - 10)/(15)]/[(\$1.60 - \$1.80)/(\$1.70)]$, which is approximately equal to −5.67. Thus, the absolute price elasticity of demand is 5.67, so demand is elastic over this range.

19-5. $-[(800 - 1,200)/(2,000/2)]/[(\$62.50 - \$57.50)/(\$120.00/2)] = -4.8$. Hence, the absolute price elasticity of demand equals 4.8. Demand is elastic over this range.

19-7. Because price and total revenue move in the same direction, then over this range of demand, the demand for hand-made guitars is inelastic.

19-9. a. More inelastic, because it represents a smaller portion of the budget

    b. More elastic, because there are many close substitutes

    c. More elastic, because there are a number of substitutes

    d. More inelastic, because there are few close substitutes

    e. More inelastic, because it represents a small portion of the budget

19-11. Let X denote the percentage change in the quantity of bacon. Then $X/10$ percent $= -0.5$. X, therefore, is −5 percent.

19-13. The income elasticity of demand is equal to $[(6 - 4)/(10/2)]/[(\$84,000 - \$80,000)/(\$164,000/2)] = +8.2$, so downloadable movies are a normal good.

19-15. $[(125,000 - 75,000)/(200,000/2)]/[(\$35,000 - \$25,000)/(\$60,000/2)] = 1.5$. Supply is elastic.

CHAPTER 20

20-1. The campus pizzeria indicates by its pricing policy that it recognizes the principle of diminishing marginal utility. As shown in Figure 20-1 on page 437, a customer's marginal utility for the second pizza is typically lower than for the first. Thus, the customer is likely to value the second pizza less and, therefore, only be willing to pay less for it.

20-3. The total utility of the third, fourth, and fifth cheeseburgers is 48, 56, and 60, respectively. The marginal utility of the first and second cheeseburgers is 20 and 16, respectively. The total utility of the first, second, and third bags of french fries is 10, 18, and 20, respectively. The marginal utility of the fourth and fifth bags of french fries is 1 and 0, respectively.

20-5. The new utility-maximizing combination is four cheeseburgers and two orders of french fries, at which the marginal utility per dollar spent is 2 units per dollar and the entire $6 is spent.

20-7. Other things being equal, when the price of soft drinks rises, the substitution effect comes into play, and the individual tends to consume less of the more expensive item, soft drinks, and more of the item with the unchanged price, tacos. Hence, the marginal utility of soft drinks rises, and the marginal utility of tacos falls.

20-9. **a.** Of all the possible one-unit increases in consumption displayed, the movement from point *A* to point *B* generates the highest marginal utility. Total utility rises by 5 units between these points, so the marginal utility of the first unit consumed is 5 units.

b. Between points *E* and *F*, a one-unit increase in the quantity consumed leaves total utility unchanged at 11 units, so marginal utility is equal to zero.

c. Between points *F* and *G*, a one-unit increase in the quantity consumed causes total utility to decline from 11 units to 10 units, so marginal utility is negative and equal to −1 unit.

20-11. For this consumer, at these prices the marginal utility per dollar spent on 2 fudge bars is 500 units of utility per dollar, and the marginal utility per dollar spent on 5 popsicles is also 500 units of utility per dollar. In addition, the entire budget of $9 is spent at this combination, which is the consumer optimum.

20-13. The marginal utility per dollar spent is equalized at 2.50 if 5 hot dogs and 3 baseball games are consumed, and this consumption combination just exhausts the now-available $190 in income.

20-15. The marginal utility of good Y is three times the marginal utility of good X, or 3×3 utils = 9 utils.

20-17. Because the price of good Y is three times greater than the price of good X, the marginal utility of good Y must be three times greater than the price of good X.

APPENDIX F

F-1. The indifference curve is convex to the origin because of a diminishing marginal rate of substitution. As an individual consumes more and more of an item, the individual becomes less willing to forgo the other item. The diminishing marginal rate of substitution is due to diminishing marginal utility.

F-3. Sue's marginal rate of substitution is calculated below:

Combination of Bottled Water and Soft Drinks	Bottled Water per Month	Soft Drinks per Month	MRS
A	5	11	
B	10	7	5:4
C	15	4	5:3
D	20	2	5:2
E	25	1	5:1

The diminishing marginal rate of substitution of soft drinks for water shows Sue's diminishing marginal utility of bottled water. She is willing to forgo fewer and fewer soft drinks to get an additional five bottles of water.

F-5. Given that water is measured along the horizontal axis and soft drinks are measured along the vertical axis, the slope of Sue's budget constraint is the price of water divided by the price of soft drinks, or $P_W/P_S = \frac{1}{2}$. The only combination of bottled water and soft drinks that is on Sue's indifference curve and budget constraint is combination *C*. For this combination, total expenditures on water and soft drinks equal $(15 \times \$1) + (4 \times \$2) = \$15 + \$8 = \$23$.

F-7. With the quantity of bottled water measured along the horizontal axis and the quantity of soft drinks measured along the vertical axis, the slope of Sue's budget constraint is the price of water divided by the price of soft drinks. This ratio equals ½. The only combination of bottled water and soft drinks that is on Sue's indifference curve and budget constraint is combination *C*, where expenditures on water and soft drinks total $23.

F-9. Yes, Sue's revealed preferences indicate that her demand for soft drinks obeys the law of demand. When the price of soft drinks declines from $2 to $1, her quantity demanded rises from 4 to 8.

CHAPTER 21

21-1 a. Bob earns a high economic rent. Because he has a specialized skill that is in great demand, his income is likely to be high, and his opportunity cost relatively low.

b. Sally earns a high economic rent. Because she is a supermodel, her income is likely to be relatively high, and, without any education, her opportunity cost is likely to be relatively low.

c. If Tim were to leave teaching, not a relatively high-paying occupation, he could sell insurance full time. Hence, his opportunity cost is high relative to his income, and his economic rent is low.

21-3. The answer is c only, because this is the only case in which the supply of the factor is very inelastic.

21-5. A sole proprietorship is a business entity owned by a single individual, whereas a partnership is a business entity jointly owned by more than one individual. A corporation, in contrast, is a legal entity that is owned by shareholders, who own shares of the profits of the entity. Sole proprietorships and partnerships do not face double taxation, but corporations do. The owners of corporations, however, enjoy limited liability, whereas the sole proprietor or partner does not.

21-7. Accounting profit is total revenue, $77,250, minus explicit costs, $37,000, for a total of $40,250. Economic profit is total revenue, $77,250, less explicit costs, $37,000, and implicit costs, $40,250, for a total equal to zero.

21-9. a. Physical capital

b. Financial capital

c. Financial capital

d. Physical capital

21-11. a. The owner of WebCity faces both tax rates if the firm is a corporation, but if it is a proprietorship, the owner faces only the 30 percent personal income tax rate. Thus, it should choose to be a proprietorship.

b. If WebCity is a corporation, the $100,000 in corporate earnings is taxed at a 20 percent rate, so that after-tax dividends are $80,000, and these are taxed at the personal income tax rate of 30 percent, leaving $56,000 in after-tax income for the owner. Hence, the firm should be organized as a proprietorship, with after-tax earnings of $70,000, or an advantage of $14,000.

c. Yes. In this case, incorporation raises earnings to $150,000, which are taxed at a rate of 20 percent, yielding after-tax dividends of $120,000 that are taxed at the personal rate of 30 percent. This leaves an after-tax income for the owner of $84,000, which is higher than the after-tax earnings of $70,000 if WebCity is a proprietorship that earns lower pre-tax income taxed at the personal rate.

d. After-tax profits rise from $56,000 to $84,000, or by $28,000.

e. This policy change would only increase the incentive to incorporate.

f. A corporate structure provides limited liability for owners, which can be a major advantage. Furthermore, owners may believe that the corporate structure will yield higher pre-tax earnings, as in the above example.

21-13. The real rate of interest in Japan is 2% − 0.5% = 1.5%. The real rate of interest in the United States is 4% − 3% = 1%. Japan, therefore, has the higher *real* rate of interest.

21-15. Ownership of common stock provides voting rights within the firm but also entails immediate loss if assets fall below the value of the firm's liabilities. Preferred stockholders are repaid prior to owners of common stock, but preferred stockholders do not have voting rights.

21-17. You should point out to your classmate that stock prices tend to drift upward following a random walk. That is, yesterday's price plus any upward drift is the best guide to today's price. Therefore, there are no predictable trends that can be used to "beat" the market.

CHAPTER 22

22-1. The short run is a time period during which the professor cannot enter the job market and find employment elsewhere. This is the nine-month period from August 15 through May 15. The professor can find employment elsewhere after the contract has been fulfilled, so the short run is nine months and the long run is greater than nine months.

22-3. Total variable costs are equal to total costs, $5 million, less total fixed costs, $2 million, which equals $3 million. Average variable costs are equal to total variable costs divided by the number of units produced. Average variable costs, therefore, equal $3 million divided by 10,000, or $300.

22-5. Marginal cost was equal to the change in total cost when the last pencil was produced, which was $12,500 − $12,425 = $75.

22-7. a. Total fixed costs equal average fixed costs, $10 per LCD screen, times the quantity produced per day, 100 LCD screens, which equals $1,000 per day.

b. The total variable costs of producing 100 LCD screens equal average variable costs, $10 per unit, times the quantity produced per day, 100 LCD screens, which equals $1,000 per day.

c. The total costs of producing 100 LCD screens equal total fixed costs plus the total variable costs of producing 100 LCD screens, or $1,000 per day plus $1,000 per day, which equals $2,000 per day.

d. The average total costs of producing 99 LCD screens equal the average fixed costs of $10.101 plus the average variable costs of $10.070, or $20.171 per LCD screen. Thus, the total cost of producing 99 LCD screens equals $20.171 times 99, or $1,996.929. The marginal cost of producing the hundredth LCD screen equals the change in total costs from increasing production from 99 to 100, or $2,000 − $1,996.929, or $3.071 per LCD screen.

22-9. a. Average total costs are $20 per unit plus $30 per unit, or $50 per unit, and total costs divided by average total costs equal output, which therefore is $2,500/$50 per unit, or 50 units.

b. TVC = AVC × Q = $20 per unit × 50 units = $1,000

c. TFC = AFC × Q = $30 per unit × 50 units = $1,500; or TFC = TC − TVC = $2,500 − $1,000 = $1,500

22-11. a. The expense incurred in cutting back trees on a regular basis would be unrelated to the quantity of rail services provided on the tracks and hence would represent a fixed cost.

b. The expense of dumping sand on the slippery tracks in advance of trains would vary with the number of trains that run on the tracks and hence would constitute a variable cost.

22-13. Hiring 1 more unit of labor at a wage rate of $20 to increase output by 1 unit causes total costs to rise by $20, so the marginal cost of the 251st unit is $20.

22-15. a. AVC = $2 million/1 million units = $2 per unit

b. APP = 1 million units/1,000 units of labor = 1,000 units of output per unit of labor

c. Wage rate = $2 million/1,000 units of labor = $2,000 per unit of labor

22-17. a. Plant size E, because this is the minimum output scale at which LRATC is at a minimum level

b. Leftward movement, because the functioning plant size for the firm would decrease

CHAPTER 23

23-1. a. The single firm producing much of the industry's output can affect price. Therefore, this is currently not a perfectly competitive industry.

b. The output of each firm is not homogeneous, so this is not a perfectly competitive industry.

c. Firms must obtain government permission to enter the industry and hence cannot easily enter, so this is not a perfectly competitive industry.

23-3. a. For a perfectly competitive firm, marginal revenue and average revenue are equal to the market clearing price. Hence, average revenue equals $20 per unit at each possible output rate.

b. At the present output of 10,000 units per week, the firm's total revenues equal price times output, or $20 per unit times 10,000 units per week, which equals $200,000 per week. The firm's total costs equal ATC times output, or $15.75 per unit times 10,000 units per week, which equals $157,500 per week. Weekly economic profits equal total revenues minus total costs, or $200,000 − $157,500 = $42,500. The firm is maximizing economic profits, because it is producing the output rate at which marginal revenue equals marginal cost.

c. If the market clearing price were to fall to $12.50 per unit, the marginal revenue curve would shift down to this level. Average total costs would exceed the price at this output rate, but in the short run the firm would minimize its short-run economic losses by producing 8,100 units per week.

d. If the market clearing price were to fall to $7.50 per unit, the marginal revenue curve would shift down to this level. Average variable costs at an output rate of 5,000 units per week would exceed the market clearing price, so total variable costs of producing 5,000 units per week would exceed total revenues. The firm should cease production if this event takes place.

23-5. Even though the price of pizzas, and hence marginal revenue, falls to only $5, this covers average variable costs. Thus, the shop should stay open.

23-7. In the described situation, the firm is producing an output rate at a point on the marginal cost curve below the average total cost curve. Marginal revenue is above the minimum point of the average total cost curve, however. Hence, marginal cost at the current rate of production is less than marginal revenue. The firm is not maximizing profit, and it should increase its rate of production.

23-9. a. There was a significant increase in market supply as more firms entered the industry. A consequence for the typical firm was that the market price fell below the minimum average total cost, resulting in negative economic profits.

b. Firms will consider leaving the industry, and some firms probably *will* leave the industry.

23-11. Increases in demand have initially led to higher economic profits for incumbent firms, which has generated entry by other firms into digital-device industries and caused market supply curves to shift outward. As more firms have entered and increased production of digital devices, input prices have declined, so firms' costs have decreased. On net, therefore, long-run equilibrium market prices have declined, implying that these digital-device industries are decreasing-cost industries.

CHAPTER 24

24-1. a. The total revenue and total profits of the dry cleaner are as follows.

Output (suits cleaned)	Price ($ per unit)	Total Costs ($)	Total Revenue ($)	Total Profit ($)
0	8.00	3.00	0	−3.00
1	7.50	6.00	7.50	1.50
2	7.00	8.50	14.00	5.50
3	6.50	10.50	19.50	9.00
4	6.00	11.50	24.00	12.50
5	5.50	13.50	27.50	14.00
6	5.00	16.00	30.00	14.00
7	4.50	19.00	31.50	12.50
8	4.00	24.00	32.00	8.00

b. The profit-maximizing rate of output is between 5 and 6 units.

c. The marginal cost and marginal revenue of the dry cleaner are as follows. The profit-maximizing rate of output is 6 units.

Output (suits cleaned)	Price ($ per unit)	Total Costs ($)	Total Revenue ($)	Total Profit ($)	Marginal Cost ($ per unit)	Marginal Revenue ($ per unit)
0	8.00	3.00	0	−3.00	—	—
1	7.50	6.00	7.50	1.50	3.00	7.50
2	7.00	8.50	14.00	5.50	2.50	6.50
3	6.50	10.50	19.50	9.00	2.00	5.50
4	6.00	11.50	24.00	12.50	1.00	4.50
5	5.50	13.50	27.50	14.00	2.00	3.50
6	5.00	16.00	30.00	14.00	2.50	2.50
7	4.50	19.00	31.50	12.50	3.00	1.50
8	4.00	24.00	32.00	8.00	4.00	0.50

24-3. a. The profit-maximizing output rate is 5,000 units.

b. Average total cost is $5 per unit. Average revenue is $6 per unit.

c. Total costs equal $5 per unit × 5,000 units = $25,000. Total revenue equals $6 per unit × 5,000 units = $30,000.

d. ($6 per unit − $5 per unit) × 5,000 units = $5,000

e. In a perfectly competitive market, price would equal marginal cost at $4.50 per unit, at which the quantity is 8,000 units. Because the monopolist produces less and charges a higher price than under perfect competition, price exceeds marginal cost at the profit-maximizing level of output. The difference between the price and marginal cost is the per-unit cost to society of a monopolized industry.

24-5. The monopolist's total revenues equal 500 units per week × $40 per unit = $2,000 per week. Thus, its total costs equal total revenues − economic profits = $2,000 per week − $500 per week = $1,500 per week. Average total cost equals the ratio of total costs to the output rate, or $1,500/500 units = $30 per unit. The firm has maximized profits by producing to the point at which marginal cost, which is $15 per unit, equals marginal revenue, so marginal revenue is $15 per unit.

24-7. a. The monopoly maximizes economic profits or minimizes economic losses by producing to the point at which marginal revenue is equal to marginal cost, which is 1 million units of output per month.

b. The profit-maximizing or loss-minimizing price of 1 million units per month is $30 per unit, so total revenues equal $30 million per month. The average total cost of producing 1 million units per month is $33 per unit, so total costs equal $33 million per month. Hence, in the short run, producing 1 million units per month minimizes the monopoly's loss at $3 million per month.

24-9. If price varies positively with total revenue, then the monopolist is operating on the inelastic portion of the demand curve. This corresponds to the range in which marginal revenue is negative. The monopolist cannot, therefore, be at the point at which its profits are maximized. In other words, the monopolist is not producing the output at which marginal cost equals marginal revenue.

24-11. Because marginal cost has risen, the monopolist will be operating at a lower rate of output and charging a higher price. Economic profits are likely to decline because even though the price is higher, its output will be more than proportionately lower.

CHAPTER 25

25-1. a. There are many fast-food restaurants producing and selling differentiated products. Both features of this industry are consistent with the theory of monopolistic competition.

b. There are numerous colleges and universities, but each specializes in different academic areas and hence produces heterogeneous products, as in the theory of monopolistic competition.

c. Although it is possible that this is a short-run equilibrium situation, it is more likely, given that economic profits are zero, that this is a long-run equilibrium in which price equals average total costs and there is no incentive for firms to enter or leave the industry.

25-3. If the firm had to reduce its price from the long-run equilibrium level of $28 per unit to marginal cost at $20 per unit, its revenues would drop from $2,800 per day for the long-run output rate of 100 units to $2,000 per day. Thus, it would experience a daily economic loss of $800 per unit and eventually choose to exit the industry rather than continue producing at a loss.

25-5. The values for marginal cost and marginal revenue appear below. Marginal revenue equals marginal cost at approximately the fifth unit of output, so marginal analysis indicates that 5 units is the profit-maximizing production level.

Output	Price ($ per unit)	Total Costs ($)	Total Revenue ($)	Marginal Cost ($ per unit)	Marginal Revenue ($ per unit)	Total Profit ($)
0	6.00	2.00	0	—	—	−2.00
1	5.75	5.25	5.75	3.25	5.75	0.00
2	5.50	7.50	11.00	2.25	5.25	3.50
3	5.25	9.60	15.75	2.10	4.75	6.15
4	5.00	12.10	20.00	2.50	4.25	7.90
5	4.75	15.80	23.75	3.70	3.75	7.95
6	4.50	20.00	27.00	4.20	3.25	7.00
7	4.00	24.75	28.00	4.75	1.00	3.25

26-7. After these long-run adjustments have occurred, the demand curve will have shifted to tangency, with the average total cost curve at 4 units of output. At this production level, average total cost is $3.03, so this will be the long-run equilibrium price. Because price and average total cost will be equal, the firm will earn zero economic profits.

25-9. a. Interactive

b. Direct

c. Mass and interactive

d. Mass

25-11. a. Search good. Given the knowledge that it is a heavy-duty filing cabinet, a photo and description providing features such as dimensions are sufficient to evaluate the characteristics of a filing cabinet.

b. Experience good. A meal must be eaten for its characteristics to be determined.

c. Search good. Given the knowledge that the coat is made of wool, a photo and description providing size information are sufficient to evaluate the characteristics of the coat.

d. Credence good. Psychotherapy services have characteristics that are likely to be difficult for consumers lacking expertise to assess without assistance from another health care provider, such as a general practitioner who guides someone experiencing depression to seek psychotherapy treatment from a psychiatrist.

25-13. Consumers may be able to assess certain features of a credence good in advance of purchase, so in this sense a credence good is similar to a search good. Consumers lack expertise to evaluate the full qualities of a credence good until after they have purchased it, which is somewhat analogous to the characteristics of an experience good. Nevertheless, the fact that consumers cannot fully evaluate a credence good's qualities in advance of purchase makes it different from a search good. Likewise, the inability to be certain, without assistance, of the qualities of a credence good following purchase of the good also distinguishes a credence good from an experience good. The fact that consumers can evaluate certain aspects of a credence good in advance of purchase, as in the case of a search good, explains why ads for credence goods, such as pharmaceuticals, often have informational elements. At the same time, however, the fact that consumers cannot truly evaluate credence goods until after purchase, and even then only with assistance, explains why ads for credence goods also commonly include persuasive elements.

25-15. Typically, the fixed costs of producing an information product are relatively high, while average variable cost is equal to a very small per-unit amount. As a consequence, the average total cost curve slopes downward with increased output, and average variable cost equals marginal cost at a low, constant amount irrespective of the quantity produced. For an information product, marginal cost is always below average total cost. Consequently, if price were equal to marginal cost, it would always be less than average total cost, so the producer would always earn short-run economic losses.

CHAPTER 26

26-1. a. 15 percent + 14 percent + 12 percent + 11 percent = 52 percent

b. 52 percent + 10 percent + 10 percent + 8 percent + 7 percent = 87 percent; or 100 percent − 13 percent = 87 percent

26-3. $15^2 + 14^2 + 12^2 + 11^2 + 10^2 + 10^2 + 8^2 + 7^2 + 13 = 225 + 196 + 144 + 121 + 100 + 100 + 64 + 49 + 13 = 1,012$

26-5. **a.** Zero-sum game

b. Negative-sum game

c. Positive-sum game

26-7. Bob is currently a participant in a noncooperative game, in which some people stand and block his view of the football game. His tit-for-tat strategy is to stand up as well. If he stands, however, he will block the view of another spectator. In a cooperative game, all would sit or stand up simultaneously, so that no individual's view is blocked.

26-9. **a.** The fact that prices are growing at a stable rate and readily observable favors enforcing a cartel agreement So does the fact that only seven firms of significant size exist in the inkjet-printer industry, which is a relatively small number. Therefore, much depends on the degree of heterogeneity of inkjet printers; if these products are relatively homogeneous, then, taken together, these characteristics of the industry would generally support an effort to form a cartel.

b. Once the cartel is formed, any one of the firms that produce inkjet printers could enlarge its profits by expanding production at the higher cartel price, so an incentive to cheat is always present. In addition, the presence of positive economic profits in the industry could induce firms outside the industry cartel to begin manufacturing and selling inkjet printers.

26-11. Possible examples include office productivity software, online auction services, telecommunications services, and Internet payment services. In each case, more people are likely to choose to consume the item when others do, because the inherent usefulness of consuming the item for each person increases as the number of consumers rises.

26-13 **a.** Mastercard.com is a platform for linking people making payments with credit cards to banks that clear the payments in a transaction-based market.

b. FreeBSD.com is an open-source operating system utilized within a shared-input market.

c. Plentyoffish.com is a platform that links people seeking romantic matches in a matchmaking market.

d. WSJ.com provides business news reporting to attract an audience to advertisers within an audience-making market.

CHAPTER 27

27-1. If cable service is an industry that experiences diminishing long-run average total costs, then the city may determine that it is more efficient to have a single, large firm that produces at a lower long-run average cost. The city could then regulate the activity of the firm.

27-3. **a.** As the table indicates, long-run average cost and long-run marginal cost decline with greater output. If the firm were allowed to operate as a monopolist, it would produce to the point at which marginal cost equals marginal revenue, which is 2 units of output. The price that consumers are willing to pay for this quantity is $90 per unit, and maximum economic profits are $180 - $175 = $5.

Quantity	Price ($ per unit)	Long-Run Total Cost ($)	LRAC ($ per unit)	LRMC ($ per unit)	MR ($ per unit)
0	100	0	—	—	
1	95	92	92.00	92	95
2	90	177	88.50	85	85
3	85	255	85.00	78	75
4	80	331	82.75	76	65
5	75	406	81.20	75	55
6	70	480	80.00	74	45

b. Long-run marginal cost and price both equal $75 per unit at 5 units of output. At a price of $75 per unit, the firm experiences economic losses equal to $375 - $406 = -$31.

c. Long-run average cost and price both equal $85 per unit at 3 units of output. At a price of $85 per unit, the firm's economic profits equal $255 - $255 = $0.

27-5. Lemons problems are likely to be more common in industries in which evaluating the characteristics of goods or services by simple inspection is difficult, as is true of the credence goods discussed in Chapter 25. Unaddressed lemons problems tend to depress the prices that sellers of high-quality items can obtain, which induces them to refrain from selling their high-quality items, resulting in sales of only lower-quality items. The main concern of economic regulation is to balance the trade-off between service and price, with economic regulation aiming to keep price lower than the price a profit-maximizing monopolist would charge. Social regulation seeks to improve working conditions and minimize adverse spillovers of production. The adverse incentives resulting from lemons problems are a form of market spillover, so it is arguable that social regulation is most appropriate for addressing lemons problems.

27-7. If European regulation is designed to protect domestic industries, then this is an example of the capture hypothesis. If, on the other hand, legitimate health concerns exist, then this is an example of the share-the-pain, share-the-gain hypothesis.

27-9. This is a creative response to the do-not-call legislation, in which firms are legally satisfying the terms of the regulation but evading the regulation's intent.

27-11. a. In the e-book market, percentage sales shares are as follows: 75.0 percent for Firm 1 and 5.0 percent each for Firms 2, 3, 4, 5, and 6. In the physical book market, sales shares are as follows: 46.7 percent for Firm 2, 22.2 percent for Firm 3, 21.7 percent for Firm 4, 5.0 percent for Firm 5, and 4.4 percent for Firm 6. According to the antitrust authority's initial evaluation, a monopoly situation may exist in the e-book market, but not in the market for physical books.

b. In the combined market, percentage market shares are as follows: 42.5 percent for Firm 2, 20.5 percent for Firm 3, 20.0 percent for Firm 4, 7.5 percent for Firm 1, 5 percent for Firm 5, and 4.5 percent for Firm 6. Under this alternative definition, the antitrust authority's initial evaluation would suggest that there is no cause for concern about monopoly.

27-13. The HHI for the combined market equals $42.5^2 + 20.5^2 + 20^2 + 7.5^2 + 5^2 + 4.5^2$, which, rounding to nearest whole numbers, is approximately equal to $1,806 + 420 + 400 + 56 + 25 + 20 = 2,272$. This value is less than the 5,000 threshold, so the authorities would conclude that a legal challenge is unwarranted.

27-15. This is an example of bundling. Because consumers who purchase the bundled product perceive that they have effectively paid different prices for the bundled products based on their willingness to pay, an antitrust authority might view this practice as charging consumers different prices for the same products, or price discrimination.

CHAPTER 28

28-1.

Labor Input (workers per week)	Total Physical Output (printers per day)	Marginal Physical Product	Marginal Revenue Product ($)
10	200	—	—
11	218	18	1,800
12	234	16	1,600
13	248	14	1,400
14	260	12	1,200
15	270	10	1,000
16	278	8	800

28-3. a. The greater the substitutability of capital, the more elastic is the demand for labor.

b. Because the demand for labor is a derived demand, the greater the elasticity of demand for the final product, the greater is the elasticity of demand for labor.

c. The larger the portion of factor costs accounted for by labor, the larger is the price elasticity of demand for labor.

28-5. a.

Labor Input (workers per week)	Total Physical Product	Product Price ($ per unit)	Marginal Physical Product	Total Revenue ($)	Marginal Revenue Product ($)
10	100	50	—	5,000	—
11	109	49	9	5,341	341
12	116	48	7	5,568	227
13	121	47	5	5,687	119
14	124	46	3	5,704	17
15	125	45	1	5,625	−79

b. The profit-maximizing firm would hire 13 workers, which is the quantity of labor beyond which the marginal revenue product of labor falls below the marginal factor cost.

28-7. a. The rise in the price of ethanol results in an increase in the marginal revenue product of corn, the key input in production of ethanol. Thus, each ethanol producer's marginal revenue product curve shifts rightward, which ultimately translates into an increase in the demand for corn, from D_1 to D_2. The market clearing price of corn increases, from P_1 to P_2, and the equilibrium quantity of corn rises, from Q_1 to Q_2.

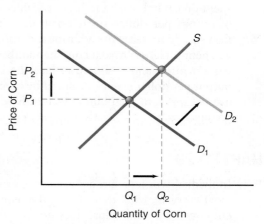

b. Human snack foods are a substitute input in the production of hogs, so the increase in the price of corn induced farmers to substitute in favor of snack foods.

28-9. The demand for the labor of U.S. workers who develop digital apps will decline, which will reduce equilibrium employment in this U.S. labor market and generate a decrease in the wage rate for these workers to less than $35 per hour. The demand for labor of Russian workers who develop digital apps will increase, which will raise equilibrium employment in this Russian labor market and bring about an increase in the wage rate for these workers to above $15 per hour.

28-11. Labor outsourcing by U.S. firms tends to push down market wages and employment in affected U.S. labor markets, but labor outsourcing by foreign firms that hire U.S. workers tends to push up market wages and employment in affected U.S. labor markets. Consequently, the overall wage and employment effects are ambiguous in the short run. In the long run, however, outsourcing enables U.S. and foreign firms to specialize in producing and trading the goods and services that they can produce most efficiently. The resulting resource saving ultimately expands the ability of U.S. residents to consume more goods and services than they could have otherwise.

28-13. The wage rate, $20 per unit of labor, equals marginal revenue product, so the marginal physical product of labor is $20 per unit of labor divided by the marginal revenue, $10 per unit of output, or 2 units of output per unit of labor.

28-15. To maximize profits, the firm should hire inputs up to the point at which the marginal physical product per dollar spent on the input is equalized across all inputs. This is not the case in this example. The marginal physical product of labor per dollar spent on wages is 200/$10 = 20 units of output per dollar spent on labor, which is less than the marginal physical product of capital per dollar spent on capital, which is 20,000/$500, or 40 units of output per dollar spent on capital. Thus, the firm should increase the additional output per dollar spent on labor by reducing the number of labor units it hires, and it should reduce the additional output per dollar spent on capital by increasing its use of capital, to the point at which these amounts are equalized.

CHAPTER 29

29-1. Individual workers can air grievances to the collective voice, who then takes the issue to the employer. The individual does not run the risk of being singled out by an employer. The individual employee does not waste work time trying to convince the employer that changes are needed in the workplace.

29-3. The reporting system probably was intended to provide information to union officials charged with seeking to impede strikebreaking activities by nonunion workers such as the soap opera writers. Strikebreakers can replace union employees, so they diminish the collective bargaining power of a union.

29-5. When marginal revenue is zero, demand for labor is unit-elastic, and total revenue is neither rising nor falling. No additional revenues can be earned by altering the quantity of labor, so the union's total wage revenues are maximized.

29-7. When unions in these industries attempt to bargain for higher-than-market levels of wages, the firms that employ members of these unions will not be able to readily substitute to alternative inputs. Hence, these unions are more likely to be able to achieve their wage objectives.

29-9.

Quantity of Labor Supplied	Total Physical Product	Required Hourly Wage Rate ($ per unit of labor)	Total Wage Bill ($)	Marginal Factor Cost ($ per unit of labor)
10	100	5	50	—
11	109	6	66	16
12	116	7	84	18
13	121	8	104	20
14	124	9	126	22
15	125	10	150	24

29-11. At 11 units of labor, the marginal revenue product of labor equals $16. This is equal to the marginal factor cost at this level of employment. The firm, therefore, will hire 11 units of labor and pay a wage of $6 an hour.

Quantity of Labor Supplied	Required Hourly Wage Rate ($ per unit of labor)	Total Factor Cost ($)	Marginal Factor Cost ($ per unit of labor)	Total Physical Product	Product Price ($ per unit)	Total Revenue ($)	Marginal Revenue Product ($ per unit of labor)
10	5	50	—	100	3.11	311.00	—
11	6	66	16.00	109	3.00	327.00	16.00
12	7	84	18.00	116	2.95	342.20	15.20
13	8	104	20.00	121	2.92	353.32	11.12
14	9	126	22.00	124	2.90	359.60	6.28
15	10	150	24.00	125	2.89	361.25	1.65

29-13. The marginal factor cost of the last worker hired was $106,480 − $105,600 = $880, so this is the marginal product of this worker if the firm is maximizing its profits.

29-15. The marginal factor cost curve lies above the labor supply curve, so marginal factor cost exceeds the wage rate at any given quantity of labor employed. Thus, a monopsonist that utilizes the profit-maximizing quantity of labor at which marginal revenue product equals marginal factor cost must pay a wage that is less than that marginal revenue product.

CHAPTER 30

30-1. a. X, because for this country the Lorenz curve implies complete income equality.

b. Z, because this country's Lorenz curve is bowed farthest away from the case of complete income equality.

c. Closer, because if all other things, including aggregate income, remain unchanged, when more people in country Y are children below working age, the share of income to people this age will decline, while the reverse will occur in country Z as more of its people reach working age and begin to earn incomes.

30-3. If the Lorenz curve is based on incomes including transfer payments, then the Lorenz curve will become less bowed. But if the Lorenz curve does not account for transfer payments, its shape will remain unaffected.

30-5. Brazil

30-7. a. Absolute. If economic growth ultimately led to inflation-adjusted annual incomes for all urban families of four rising above $25,000 per year, then by this definition poverty would be ended.

b. Relative. By this definition, the lowest 15 percent of income earners will always be classified as being in a state of poverty.

c. Absolute. If economic growth eventually raised inflation-adjusted annual incomes of all individuals above $10,000, then by this definition poverty would cease to exist.

30-9. First, a moral hazard problem will exist, because government action would reduce the individual's incentive to continue a healthful lifestyle, thereby increasing the likelihood of greater health problems that will require future treatment. Second, an individual who currently has health problems will have an incentive to substitute future care that will be available at a zero price for current care that the individual must purchase at a positive price. Finally, in future years the patient will no longer have an incentive to contain health care expenses, and health care providers will have no incentive to minimize their costs.

30-11. The demand for health care will increase, and the marginal revenue curve will shift rightward. Hence, the profit-maximizing price and equilibrium quantity of health care services will increase.

CHAPTER 31

31-1. $4 per unit, which exactly accounts for the per-unit social cost of pollution.

31-3. a. 60 percent

b. 40 percent

c. 40 percent

31-5. a. There is a downward shift in the position of the marginal cost curve. The optimal degree of water cleanliness will rise above 65 percent, to a level such as 70 percent, and the cost incurred for the last unit of water clean-up will decrease to less than $10, such as a per-unit cost of $7.

b. The second event induces an upward shift in the marginal benefit curve. Taken together, as shown in the diagram below, the two events unambiguously indicate that the optimal degree of water cleanliness increases above 65 percent, such as a level of 85 percent. The cost incurred for the last unit of water clean-up may rise or fall, however, and could end up at the initial level, which is the situation illustrated in the diagram.

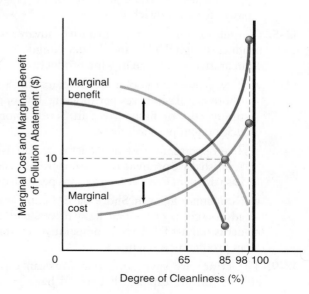

31-7. The positive market price of allowances is equivalent to a price that a firm must pay in order to release an additional unit of a pollutant. The idea behind establishing the market for pollution allowances, therefore, is to give firms an incentive to limit the quantity of pollutants released into the atmosphere.

31-9. a. The marginal costs and benefits are tabulated below:

Population of Wild Tigers	Marginal Cost ($)	Marginal Benefit ($)
0	—	—
2,000	25	50
4,000	10	40
6,000	15	30
8,000	25	25
10,000	35	20
12,000	50	10

b. 8,000

c. 10,000

CHAPTER 32

32-1. a. The opportunity cost of pastries in Northland is 0.5 sandwich per pastry. The opportunity cost of sandwiches in Northland is 2 pastries per sandwich.

b. The opportunity cost of pastries in West Coast is 2 sandwiches per pastry. The opportunity cost of sandwiches in West Coast is 0.5 pastry per sandwich.

32-3. If Northland specializes in producing pastries, the maximum number of pastries it can produce and trade to West Coast is 50,000 pastries. Hence, the maximum number of units of each good that the two countries can trade at a rate of exchange of 1 pastry for 1 sandwich is 50,000.

32-5. Coastal Realm has a comparative advantage in producing digital TVs, and Border Kingdom has a comparative advantage in wine production.

32-7. a. The opportunity cost of modems in South Shore is 2 flash drives per modem. The opportunity cost of flash drives in South Shore is 0.5 modem per flash drive.

b. The opportunity cost of modems in East Isle is 0.5 flash drive per modem. The opportunity cost of flash drives in East Isle is 2 modems per flash drive.

c. Residents of South Shore have a comparative advantage in producing flash drives, and residents of East Isle have a comparative advantage in producing modems.

32-9. The critics are suggesting that Mexican exporters are shifting exports that would have gone to other nations to the United States, a nation within NAFTA, which would constitute trade diversion.

32-11. Diversion and deflection occur when nations within or outside a particular regional trade bloc try to benefit from preferences that exist only within the bloc. As long as the WTO agreements involve all nations equally, no diversion or deflection could occur.

CHAPTER 33

33-1 a. −$0.6 trillion

b. −$0.5 trillion

c. −$0.7 trillion

33-3. The trade balance is merchandise exports minus merchandise imports, which equals $500 - 600 = -100$, or a deficit of 100. Adding service exports of 75 and subtracting net unilateral transfers of 10 and service imports of 50 yields $-100 + 75 - 10 - 50 = -85$, or a current account balance of −85. The capital account balance equals the difference between capital inflows and capital outflows, or $300 - 200 = +100$, or a capital account surplus of 100.

33-5. a. The increase in demand for Mexican-made guitars increases the demand for Mexican pesos, and the peso appreciates.

b. International investors will remove some of their financial capital from Mexico. The increase in the supply of pesos in the foreign exchange market will cause the peso to depreciate.

33-7. The demand for Chinese yuan increases, and the supply of yuan decreases. The dollar-yuan exchange rate rises, so the yuan appreciates.

33-9. The Canadian dollar–euro exchange rate is found by dividing the U.S. dollar–euro exchange rate by the U.S. dollar–Canadian dollar exchange rate, or (1.45 $U.S./euro)/(0.94 $U.S./$C) = 1.54 $C/euro, or 1.54 Canadian dollars per euro.

33-11. A flexible exchange rate system allows the exchange value of a currency to be determined freely in the foreign exchange market with no intervention by the government. A fixed exchange rate pegs the value of the currency, and the authorities responsible for the value of the currency intervene in foreign exchange markets to maintain this value.

33-13. When the dollar is pegged to gold at a rate of $35 and the pound is pegged to the dollar at $2 = £1, an implicit value between gold and the pound is established at £17.50 = 1 ounce of gold. If the dollar falls in value relative to gold, yet the pound is still valued to the dollar at $2 = £1, the pound become undervalued relative to gold. The exchange rate between the dollar and the pound will have to be adjusted to 2.29 $/£.

Glossary

A

Absolute advantage The ability to produce more units of a good or service using a given quantity of labor or resource inputs. Equivalently, the ability to produce the same quantity of a good or service using fewer units of labor or resource inputs.

Accounting identities Values that are equivalent by definition.

Accounting profit Total revenues minus total explicit costs.

Action time lag The time between recognizing an economic problem and implementing policy to solve it. The action time lag is quite long for fiscal policy, which requires congressional approval.

Active (discretionary) policymaking All actions on the part of monetary and fiscal policymakers that are undertaken in response to or in anticipation of some change in the overall economy.

Ad valorem **taxation** Assessing taxes by charging a tax rate equal to a fraction of the market price of each unit purchased.

Adverse selection The tendency for high-risk projects and clients to be over-represented among borrowers.

Age-earnings cycle The regular earnings profile of an individual throughout his or her lifetime. The age-earnings cycle usually starts with a low income, builds gradually to a peak at around age 50, and then gradually curves down until it approaches zero at retirement.

Aggregate demand The total of all planned expenditures in the entire economy.

Aggregate demand curve A curve showing planned purchase rates for all final goods and services in the economy at various price levels, all other things held constant.

Aggregate demand shock Any event that causes the aggregate demand curve to shift inward or outward.

Aggregate supply The total of all planned production for the economy.

Aggregate supply shock Any event that causes the aggregate supply curve to shift inward or outward.

Aggregates Total amounts or quantities. Aggregate demand, for example, is total planned expenditures throughout a nation.

Anticipated inflation The inflation rate that we believe will occur. When it

does occur, we are in a situation of fully anticipated inflation.

Antitrust legislation Laws that restrict the formation of monopolies and regulate certain anticompetitive business practices.

Appreciation An increase in the exchange value of one nation's currency in terms of the currency of another nation.

Asset demand Holding money as a store of value instead of other assets such as corporate bonds and stocks.

Assets Amounts owned; all items to which a business or household holds legal claim.

Asymmetric information Information possessed by one party in a financial transaction but not by the other party.

Automatic, or built-in, stabilizers Special provisions of certain federal programs that cause changes in desired aggregate expenditures without the action of Congress and the president. Examples are the federal progressive tax system and unemployment compensation.

Autonomous consumption The part of consumption that is independent of (does not depend on) the level of disposable income. Changes in autonomous consumption shift the consumption function.

Average fixed costs Total fixed costs divided by the number of units produced.

Average physical product Total product divided by the variable input.

Average propensity to consume (APC) Real consumption divided by real disposable income. For any given level of real income, the proportion of total real disposable income that is consumed.

Average propensity to save (APS) Real saving divided by real disposable income. For any given level of real income, the proportion of total real disposable income that is saved.

Average tax rate The total tax payment divided by total income. It is the proportion of total income paid in taxes.

Average total costs Total costs divided by the number of units produced; sometimes called *average per-unit total costs*.

Average variable costs Total variable costs divided by the number of units produced.

B

Balance of payments A system of accounts that measures transactions of goods, services, income, and financial assets between domestic households, businesses, and governments and residents of the rest of the world during a specific time period.

Balance of trade The difference between exports and imports of physical goods.

Balance sheet A statement of the assets and liabilities of any business entity, including financial institutions and the Federal Reserve System. Assets are what is owned; liabilities are what is owed.

Balanced budget A situation in which the government's spending is exactly equal to the total taxes and other revenues it collects during a given period of time.

Bank run Attempt by many of a bank's depositors to convert transactions and time deposits into currency out of fear that the bank's liabilities may exceed its assets.

Barter The direct exchange of goods and services for other goods and services without the use of money.

Base year The year that is chosen as the point of reference for comparison of prices in other years.

Base-year dollars The value of a current sum expressed in terms of prices in a base year.

Behavioral economics An approach to the study of consumer behavior that emphasizes psychological limitations and complications that potentially interfere with rational decision making.

Bilateral monopoly A market structure consisting of a monopolist and a monopsonist.

Black market A market in which goods are traded at prices above their legal maximum prices or in which illegal goods are sold.

Bond A legal claim against a firm, usually entitling the owner of the bond to receive a fixed annual coupon payment, plus a lump-sum payment at the bond's maturity date. Bonds are issued in return for funds lent to the firm.

Bounded rationality The hypothesis that people are *nearly*, but not fully, rational, so that they cannot examine every possible choice available to them but instead use simple rules of thumb to sort among the alternatives that happen to occur to them.

Budget constraint All of the possible combinations of goods that can be purchased (at fixed prices) with a specific budget.

Bundling Offering two or more products for sale as a set.

Business fluctuations The ups and downs in business activity throughout the economy.

C

Capital account A category of balance of payments transactions that measures flows of financial assets.

Capital consumption allowance Another name for depreciation, the amount that businesses would have to put aside in order to take care of deteriorating machines and other equipment.

Capital gain A positive difference between the purchase price and the sale price of an asset. If a share of stock is bought for $5 and then sold for $15, the capital gain is $10.

Capital goods Producer durables; nonconsumable goods that firms use to make other goods.

Capital loss A negative difference between the purchase price and the sale price of an asset.

Capture hypothesis A theory of regulatory behavior that predicts that regulators will eventually be captured by special interests of the industry being regulated.

Cartel An association of producers in an industry that agree to set common prices and output quotas to prevent competition.

Central bank A banker's bank, usually an official institution that also serves as a bank for a nation's government treasury. Central banks normally regulate commercial banks.

Ceteris paribus [KAY-ter-us PEAR-uh-bus] **assumption** The assumption that nothing changes except the factor or factors being studied.

Ceteris paribus **conditions** Determinants of the relationship between price and quantity that are unchanged along a curve. Changes in these factors cause the curve to shift.

Closed shop A business enterprise in which employees must belong to the union before they can be hired and must remain in the union after they are hired.

Collective bargaining Negotiation between the management of a company and the management of a union for the purpose of reaching a mutually agreeable contract that sets wages, fringe benefits, and working conditions for all employees in all the unions involved.

Collective decision making How voters, politicians, and other interested parties act and how these actions influence nonmarket decisions.

Common property Property that is owned by everyone and therefore by no one. Air and water are examples of common property resources.

Comparative advantage The ability to produce a good or service at a lower opportunity cost than other producers.

Complements Two goods are complements when a change in the price of one causes an opposite shift in the demand for the other.

Concentration ratio The percentage of all sales contributed by the leading four or leading eight firms in an industry; sometimes called the *industry concentration ratio*.

Constant dollars Dollars expressed in terms of real purchasing power, using a particular year as the base or standard of comparison, in contrast to current dollars.

Constant returns to scale No change in long-run average costs when output increases.

Constant-cost industry An industry whose total output can be increased without an increase in long-run per-unit costs. Its long-run supply curve is horizontal.

Consumer optimum A choice of a set of goods and services that maximizes the level of satisfaction for each consumer, subject to limited income.

Consumer Price Index (CPI) A statistical measure of a weighted average of prices of a specified set of goods and services purchased by typical consumers in urban areas.

Consumer surplus The difference between the total amount that consumers would have been willing to pay for an item and the total amount that they actually pay.

Consumption Spending on new goods and services to be used up out of a household's current income. Whatever is not consumed is saved. Consumption includes such things as buying food and going to a concert.

Consumption function The relationship between amount consumed and disposable income. A consumption function tells us how much people plan to consume at various levels of disposable income.

Consumption goods Goods bought by households to use up, such as food and movies.

Contraction A business fluctuation during which the pace of national economic activity is slowing down.

Cooperative game A game in which the players explicitly cooperate to make themselves jointly better off. As applied to firms, it involves companies colluding in order to make higher than perfectly competitive rates of return.

Corporation A legal entity that may conduct business in its own name just as an individual does. The owners of a corporation, called shareholders, own shares of the firm's profits and have the protection of limited liability.

Cost-of-living adjustments (COLAs) Clauses in contracts that allow for increases in specified nominal values to take account of changes in the cost of living.

Cost-of-service regulation Regulation that allows prices to reflect only the actual average cost of production and no monopoly profits.

Cost-push inflation Inflation caused by decreases in short-run aggregate supply.

Craft unions Labor unions composed of workers who engage in a particular trade or skill, such as baking, carpentry, or plumbing.

Creative response Behavior on the part of a firm that allows it to comply with the letter of the law but violate the spirit, significantly lessening the law's effects.

Credence good A product with qualities that consumers lack the expertise to assess without assistance.

Credit policy Federal Reserve policymaking involving direct lending to financial and nonfinancial firms.

Cross price elasticity of demand (E_{xy}) The percentage change in the amount of an item demanded (holding its price constant) divided by the percentage change in the price of a related good.

Crowding-out effect The tendency of expansionary fiscal policy to cause a decrease in planned investment or planned consumption in the private sector. This decrease normally results from the rise in interest rates.

Current account A category of balance of payments transactions that measures the exchange of merchandise, the exchange of services, and unilateral transfers.

Cyclical unemployment Unemployment resulting from business recessions that occur when aggregate (total) demand is insufficient to create full employment.

D

Dead capital Any capital resource that lacks clear title of ownership.

Deadweight loss The portion of consumer surplus that no one in society is able to obtain in a situation of monopoly.

Decreasing-cost industry An industry in which an increase in output leads to a reduction in long-run per-unit costs, such that the long-run industry supply curve slopes downward.

Deflation A sustained decrease in the average of all prices of goods and services in an economy.

Demand A schedule showing how much of a good or service people will purchase at any price during a specified time period, other things being constant.

Demand curve A graphical representation of the demand schedule. It is a negatively sloped line showing the inverse relationship between the price and the quantity demanded (other things being equal).

Demand-pull inflation Inflation caused by increases in aggregate demand not matched by increases in aggregate supply.

Dependent variable A variable whose value changes according to changes in the value of one or more independent variables.

Depository institutions Financial institutions that accept deposits from savers and lend funds from those deposits out at interest.

Depreciation A decrease in the exchange value of one nation's currency in terms of the currency of another nation.

Depression An extremely severe recession.

Derived demand Input factor demand derived from demand for the final product being produced.

Development economics The study of factors that contribute to the economic growth of a country.

Diminishing marginal utility The principle that as more of any good or service is consumed, its *extra* benefit declines. Otherwise stated, increases in total utility from the consumption of a good or service become smaller and smaller as more is consumed during a given time period.

Direct expenditure offsets Actions on the part of the private sector in spending income that offset government fiscal policy actions. Any increase in government spending in an area that competes with the private sector will have some direct expenditure offset.

Direct marketing Advertising targeted at specific consumers, typically in the form of postal mailings, telephone calls, or e-mail messages.

Direct relationship A relationship between two variables that is positive, meaning that an increase in one variable is associated with an increase in the other and a decrease in one variable is associated with a decrease in the other.

Discount rate The interest rate that the Federal Reserve charges for reserves that it lends to depository institutions.

It is sometimes referred to as the *rediscount rate* or, in Canada and England, as the *bank rate*.

Discounting The method by which the present value of a future sum or a future stream of sums is obtained.

Discouraged workers Individuals who have stopped looking for a job because they are convinced that they will not find a suitable one.

Diseconomies of scale Increases in long-run average costs that occur as output increases.

Disposable personal income (DPI) Personal income after personal income taxes have been paid.

Dissaving Negative saving; a situation in which spending exceeds income. Dissaving can occur when a household is able to borrow or use up existing assets.

Distribution of income The way income is allocated among the population based on groupings of residents.

Dividends Portion of a corporation's profits paid to its owners (shareholders).

Division of labor The segregation of resources into different specific tasks. For instance, one automobile worker puts on bumpers, another doors, and so on.

Dominant strategies Strategies that always yield the highest benefit. Regardless of what other players do, a dominant strategy will yield the most benefit for the player using it.

Dumping Selling a good or a service abroad below the price charged in the home market or at a price below its cost of production.

Durable consumer goods Consumer goods that have a life span of more than three years.

Dynamic tax analysis Economic evaluation of tax rate changes that recognizes that the tax base eventually declines with ever-higher tax rates, so that tax revenues may eventually decline if the tax rate is raised sufficiently.

E

Economic freedom The rights to own private property and to exchange goods, services, and financial assets with minimal government interference.

Economic goods Goods that are scarce, for which the quantity demanded exceeds the quantity supplied at a zero price.

Economic growth Increases in per capita real GDP measured by its rate of change per year.

Economic profits Total revenues minus total opportunity costs of all inputs used, or the total of all implicit and explicit costs.

Economic rent A payment for the use of any resource over and above its opportunity cost.

Economic system A society's institutional mechanism for determining the way in which scarce resources are used to satisfy human desires.

Economics The study of how people allocate their limited resources to satisfy their unlimited wants.

Economies of scale Decreases in long-run average costs resulting from increases in output.

Effect time lag The time that elapses between the implementation of a policy and the results of that policy.

Efficiency The case in which a given level of inputs is used to produce the maximum output possible. Alternatively, the situation in which a given output is produced at minimum cost.

Effluent fee A charge to a polluter that gives the right to discharge into the air or water a certain amount of pollution; also called a *pollution tax*.

Elastic demand A demand relationship in which a given percentage change in price will result in a larger percentage change in quantity demanded.

Empirical Relying on real-world data in evaluating the usefulness of a model.

Endowments The various resources in an economy, including both physical resources and such human resources as ingenuity and management skills.

Entitlements Guaranteed benefits under a government program such as Social Security, Medicare, or Medicaid.

Entrepreneurship The component of human resources that performs the functions of raising capital; organizing, managing, and assembling other factors of production; making basic business policy decisions; and taking risks.

Equation of exchange The formula indicating that the number of monetary units (M_s) times the number of times each unit is spent on final goods and services (V) is identical to the price level (P) times real GDP (Y).

Equilibrium The situation when quantity supplied equals quantity demanded at a particular price.

Exchange rate The price of one nation's currency in terms of the currency of another country.

Excise tax A tax levied on purchases of a particular good or service.

Expansion A business fluctuation in which the pace of national economic activity is speeding up.

Expenditure approach Computing GDP by adding up the dollar value at current market prices of all final goods and services.

Experience good A product that an individual must consume before the product's quality can be established.

Explicit costs Costs that business managers must take account of because they must be paid. Examples are wages, taxes, and rent.

Externality A consequence of a diversion of a private cost (or benefit) from a social cost (or benefit). A situation in which the costs (or benefits) of an action are not fully borne (or gained) by the decision makers engaged in an activity that uses scarce resources.

F

Featherbedding Any practice that forces employers to use more labor than they would otherwise or to use existing labor in an inefficient manner.

Federal Deposit Insurance Corporation (FDIC) A government agency that insures the deposits held in banks and most other depository institutions. All U.S. banks are insured this way.

Federal funds market A private market (made up mostly of banks) in which banks can borrow reserves from other banks that want to lend them. Federal funds are usually lent for overnight use.

Federal funds rate The interest rate that depository institutions pay to borrow reserves in the interbank federal funds market.

Fiduciary monetary system A system in which money is issued by the government and its value is based uniquely on the public's faith that the currency represents command over goods and services and will be accepted in payment for debts.

Final goods and services Goods and services that are at their final stage of production and will not be transformed into yet other goods or services. For example, wheat ordinarily is not considered a final good because it is usually used to make a final good, bread.

Financial capital Funds used to purchase physical capital goods, such as buildings and equipment, and patents and trademarks.

Financial intermediaries Institutions that transfer funds between ultimate lenders (savers) and ultimate borrowers.

Financial intermediation The process by which financial institutions accept savings from businesses, households, and governments and lend the savings to other businesses, households, and governments.

Firm A business organization that employs resources to produce goods or services for profit. A firm normally owns and operates at least one "plant" or facility in order to produce.

Fiscal policy The discretionary changing of government expenditures or taxes to achieve national economic goals, such as high employment with price stability.

Fixed costs Costs that do not vary with output. Fixed costs typically include such expenses as rent on a building. These costs are fixed for a certain period of time (in the long run, though, they are variable).

Fixed investment Purchases by businesses of newly produced producer durables, or capital goods, such as production machinery and office equipment.

Flexible exchange rates Exchange rates that are allowed to fluctuate in the open market in response to changes in supply and demand. Sometimes called *floating exchange rates*.

Flow A quantity measured per unit of time; something that occurs over time, such as the income you make per week or per year or the number of individuals who are fired every month.

FOMC Directive A document that summarizes the Federal Open Market Committee's general policy strategy, establishes near-term objectives for the federal funds rate, and specifies target ranges for money supply growth.

Foreign direct investment The acquisition of more than 10 percent of the shares of ownership in a company in another nation.

Foreign exchange market A market in which households, firms, and governments buy and sell national currencies.

Foreign exchange rate The price of one currency in terms of another.

Foreign exchange risk The possibility that changes in the value of a nation's currency will result in variations in the market value of assets.

45-degree reference line The line along which planned real expenditures equal real GDP per year.

Fractional reserve banking A system in which depository institutions hold reserves that are less than the amount of total deposits.

Free-rider problem A problem that arises when individuals presume that others will pay for public goods so that, individually, they can escape paying for their portion without causing a reduction in production.

Frictional unemployment Unemployment due to the fact that workers must search for appropriate job offers. This activity takes time, and so they remain temporarily unemployed.

Full employment An arbitrary level of unemployment that corresponds to "normal" friction in the labor market. In 1986, a 6.5 percent rate of unemployment was considered full employment. Today it is somewhat higher.

G

Gains from trade The sum of consumer surplus and producer surplus.

Game theory A way of describing the various possible outcomes in any situation involving two or more interacting individuals when those individuals are aware of the interactive nature of their situation and plan accordingly. The plans made by these individuals are known as *game strategies*.

GDP deflator A price index measuring the changes in prices of all new goods and services produced in the economy.

General Agreement on Tariffs and Trade (GATT) An international agreement established in 1947 to further world trade by reducing barriers and tariffs. The GATT was replaced by the World Trade Organization in 1995.

Goods All things from which individuals derive satisfaction or happiness.

Government budget constraint The limit on government spending and transfers imposed by the fact that every dollar the government spends, transfers, or uses to repay borrowed funds must ultimately be provided by the user charges and taxes it collects.

Government budget deficit An excess of government spending over government revenues during a given period of time.

Government budget surplus An excess of government revenues over government spending during a given period of time.

Government, or political, goods Goods (and services) provided by the public sector; they can be either private or public goods.

Government-inhibited good A good that has been deemed socially undesirable through the political process. Heroin is an example.

Government-sponsored good A good that has been deemed socially desirable through the political process. Museums are an example.

Gross domestic income (GDI) The sum of all income—wages, interest, rent, and profits—paid to the four factors of production.

Gross domestic product (GDP) The total market value of all final goods and services produced during a year by factors of production located within a nation's borders.

Gross private domestic investment The creation of capital goods, such as factories and machines, that can yield production and hence consumption in the future. Also included in this definition are changes in business inventories and repairs made to machines or buildings.

Gross public debt All federal government debt irrespective of who owns it.

H

Health insurance exchanges Government agencies to which the national health care program assigns the task of assisting individuals, families, and small businesses in identifying health insurance policies to purchase.

Hedge A financial strategy that reduces the chance of suffering losses arising from foreign exchange risk.

Herfindahl-Hirschman Index (HHI) The sum of the squared percentage sales shares of all firms in an industry.

Horizontal merger The joining of firms that are producing or selling a similar product.

Human capital The accumulated training and education of workers.

I

Implicit costs Expenses that managers do not have to pay out of pocket and hence normally do not explicitly calculate, such as the opportunity cost of factors of production that are owned. Examples are owner-provided capital and owner-provided labor.

Import quota A physical supply restriction on imports of a particular good, such as sugar. Foreign exporters are unable to sell in the United States more than the quantity specified in the import quota.

Incentive structure The system of rewards and punishments individuals face with respect to their own actions.

Incentives Rewards or penalties for engaging in a particular activity.

Income approach Measuring GDP by adding up all components of national income, including wages, interest, rent, and profits.

Income elasticity of demand (E_i) The percentage change in the amount of a good demanded, holding its price constant, divided by the percentage change in income. The responsiveness of the amount of a good demanded to a change in income, holding the good's relative price constant.

Income in kind Income received in the form of goods and services, such as housing or medical care. Income in kind differs from money income, which is simply income in dollars, or general purchasing power, that can be used to buy *any* goods and services.

Income velocity of money (V) The number of times per year a dollar is spent on final goods and services; identically equal to nominal GDP divided by the money supply.

Increasing-cost industry An industry in which an increase in industry output is accompanied by an increase in long-run per-unit costs, such that the long-run industry supply curve slopes upward.

Independent variable A variable whose value is determined independently of, or outside, the equation under study.

Indifference curve A curve composed of a set of consumption alternatives, each of which yields the same total amount of satisfaction.

Indirect business taxes All business taxes except the tax on corporate profits. Indirect business taxes include sales and business property taxes.

Industrial unions Labor unions that consist of workers from a particular industry, such as automobile manufacturing or steel manufacturing.

Industry supply curve The locus of points showing the minimum prices at which given quantities will be forthcoming; also called the *market supply curve.*

Inefficient point Any point below the production possibilities curve, at which the use of resources is not generating the maximum possible output.

Inelastic demand A demand relationship in which a given percentage change in price will result in a less-than-proportionate percentage change in the quantity demanded.

Infant industry argument The contention that tariffs should be imposed to protect from import competition an industry that is trying to get started. Presumably, after the industry becomes technologically efficient, the tariff can be lifted.

Inferior goods Goods for which demand falls as income rises.

Inflation A sustained increase in the average of all prices of goods and services in an economy.

Inflationary gap The gap that exists whenever equilibrium real GDP per year is greater than full-employment real GDP as shown by the position of the long-run aggregate supply curve.

Information product An item that is produced using information-intensive inputs at a relatively high fixed cost but distributed for sale at a relatively low marginal cost.

Informational advertising Advertising that emphasizes transmitting knowledge about the features of a product.

Innovation Transforming an invention into something that is useful to humans.

Inside information Information that is not available to the general public about what is happening in a corporation.

Interactive marketing Advertising that permits a consumer to follow up directly by searching for more information and placing direct product orders.

Interest The payment for current rather than future command over resources; the cost of obtaining credit.

Interest rate effect One of the reasons that the aggregate demand curve slopes downward: Higher price levels increase the interest rate, which in turn causes businesses and consumers to reduce desired spending due to the higher cost of borrowing.

Intermediate goods Goods used up entirely in the production of final goods.

International financial crisis The rapid withdrawal of foreign investments and loans from a nation.

International Monetary Fund An agency founded to administer an international foreign exchange system and to lend to member countries that had balance of payments problems. The IMF now functions as a lender of last resort for national governments.

Inventory investment Changes in the stocks of finished goods and goods in process, as well as changes in the raw materials that businesses keep on hand. Whenever inventories are decreasing, inventory investment is negative. Whenever they are increasing, inventory investment is positive.

Inverse relationship A relationship between two variables that is negative, meaning that an increase in one variable is associated with a decrease in the other and a decrease in one variable is associated with an increase in the other.

Investment Spending on items such as machines and buildings, which can be used to produce goods and services in the future. (It also includes changes in business inventories.) The investment part of real GDP is the portion that will be used in the process of producing goods *in the future.*

J

Job leaver An individual in the labor force who quits voluntarily.

Job loser An individual in the labor force whose employment was involuntarily terminated.

Jurisdictional dispute A disagreement involving two or more unions over which should have control of a particular jurisdiction, such as a particular craft or skill or a particular firm or industry.

K

Keynesian short-run aggregate supply curve The horizontal portion of the aggregate supply curve in which there is excessive unemployment and unused capacity in the economy.

L

Labor Productive contributions of humans who work.

Labor force Individuals aged 16 years or older who either have jobs or who are looking and available for jobs; the number of employed plus the number of unemployed.

Labor force participation rate The percentage of noninstitutionalized working-age individuals who are employed or seeking employment.

Labor productivity Total real domestic output (real GDP) divided by the number of workers (output per worker).

Labor unions Worker organizations that seek to secure economic improvements for their members. They also seek to improve the safety, health, and other benefits (such as job security) of their members.

Land The natural resources that are available from nature. Land as a resource includes location, original fertility and mineral deposits, topography, climate, water, and vegetation.

Law of demand The observation that there is a negative, or inverse, relationship between the price of any good or service and the quantity demanded, holding other factors constant.

Law of diminishing marginal product The observation that after some point, successive equal-sized increases in a variable factor of production, such as labor, added to fixed factors of production will result in smaller increases in output.

Law of increasing additional cost The fact that the opportunity cost of additional units of a good generally increases as people attempt to produce more of that good. This accounts for the bowed-out shape of the production possibilities curve.

Law of supply The observation that the higher the price of a good, the more of that good sellers will make available over a specified time period, other things being equal.

Leading indicators Events that have been found to occur before changes in business activity.

Lemons problem The potential for asymmetric information to bring about a general decline in product quality in an industry.

Lender of last resort The Federal Reserve's role as an institution that is willing and able to lend to a temporarily illiquid bank that is otherwise in good financial condition to prevent the bank's illiquid position from leading to a general loss of confidence in that bank or in others.

Liabilities Amounts owed; the legal claims against a business or household by nonowners.

Life-cycle theory of consumption A theory in which a person bases decisions about current consumption and saving on both current income and anticipated future income.

Limited liability A legal concept in which the responsibility, or liability, of the owners of a corporation is limited to the value of the shares in the firm that they own.

Liquidity The degree to which an asset can be acquired or disposed of without much danger of any intervening loss in *nominal* value and with small transaction costs. Money is the most liquid asset.

Liquidity approach A method of measuring the money supply by looking at money as a temporary store of value.

Long run The time period during which all factors of production can be varied.

Long-run aggregate supply curve A vertical line representing the real output of goods and services after full adjustment has occurred. It can also be viewed as representing the real GDP of the economy under conditions of full employment—the full-employment level of real GDP.

Long-run average cost curve The locus of points representing the minimum unit cost of producing any given rate of output, given current technology and resource prices.

Long-run industry supply curve A market supply curve showing the relationship between prices and quantities after firms have been allowed the time to enter into or exit from an industry, depending on whether there have been positive or negative economic profits.

Lorenz curve A geometric representation of the distribution of income. A Lorenz curve that is perfectly straight represents complete income equality. The more bowed a Lorenz curve, the more unequally income is distributed.

Lump-sum tax A tax that does not depend on income. An example is a $1,000 tax that every household must pay, irrespective of its economic situation.

M

M1 The money supply, measured as the total value of currency plus transactions deposits plus traveler's checks not issued by banks.

M2 M1 plus (1) savings deposits at all depository institutions, (2) small-denomination time deposits, and (3) balances in retail money market mutual funds.

Macroeconomics The study of the behavior of the economy as a whole, including such economywide phenomena as changes in unemployment, the general price level, and national income.

Majority rule A collective decision-making system in which group decisions are made on the basis of more than 50 percent of the vote. In other words, whatever more than half of the electorate votes for, the entire electorate has to accept.

Marginal cost pricing A system of pricing in which the price charged is equal to the opportunity cost to society of producing one more unit of the good or service in question. The opportunity cost is the marginal cost to society.

Marginal costs The change in total costs due to a one-unit change in production rate.

Marginal factor cost (MFC) The cost of using an additional unit of an input. For example, if a firm can hire all the workers it wants at the going wage rate, the marginal factor cost of labor is that wage rate.

Marginal physical product The physical output that is due to the addition of one more unit of a variable factor of production. The change in total product occurring when a variable input is increased and all other inputs are held constant. It is also called *marginal product*.

Marginal physical product (MPP) of labor The change in output resulting from the addition of one more worker. The MPP of the worker equals the change in total output accounted for by hiring the worker, holding all other factors of production constant.

Marginal propensity to consume (MPC) The ratio of the change in consumption to the change in disposable income. A marginal propensity to consume of 0.8 tells us that an additional $100 in take-home pay will lead to an additional $80 consumed.

Marginal propensity to save (MPS) The ratio of the change in saving to the change in disposable income. A marginal propensity to save of 0.2 indicates that out of an additional $100 in take-home pay, $20 will be saved. Whatever is not saved is consumed. The marginal propensity to save plus the marginal propensity to consume must always equal 1, by definition.

Marginal revenue The change in total revenues resulting from a one-unit change in output (and sale) of the product in question.

Marginal revenue product (MRP) The marginal physical product (MPP) times marginal revenue (MR). The MRP gives the additional revenue obtained from a one-unit change in labor input.

Marginal tax rate The change in the tax payment divided by the change in income, or the percentage of *additional* dollars that must be paid in taxes. The marginal tax rate is applied to the highest tax bracket of taxable income reached.

Marginal utility The change in total utility due to a one-unit change in the quantity of a good or service consumed.

Market All of the arrangements that individuals have for exchanging with one another. Thus, for example, we can speak of the labor market, the automobile market, and the credit market.

Market clearing, or equilibrium, price The price that clears the market, at which quantity demanded equals quantity supplied; the price where the demand curve intersects the supply curve.

Market demand The demand of all consumers in the marketplace for a particular good or service. The summation at each price of the quantity demanded by each individual.

Market failure A situation in which an unrestrained market operation leads to either too few or too many resources going to a specific economic activity.

Mass marketing Advertising intended to reach as many consumers as possible, typically through television, newspaper, radio, or magazine ads.

Medium of exchange Any item that sellers will accept as payment.

Microeconomics The study of decision making undertaken by individuals (or households) and by firms.

Minimum efficient scale (MES) The lowest rate of output per unit time at which long-run average costs for a particular firm are at a minimum.

Minimum wage A wage floor, legislated by government, setting the lowest hourly rate that firms may legally pay workers.

Models, or theories Simplified representations of the real world used as the basis for predictions or explanations.

Money Any medium that is universally accepted in an economy both by sellers of goods and services as payment for those goods and services and by creditors as payment for debts.

Money balances Synonymous with money, money stock, money holdings.

Money illusion Reacting to changes in money prices rather than relative prices. If a worker whose wages double when the price level also doubles thinks he or she is better off, that worker is suffering from money illusion.

Money multiplier A number that, when multiplied by a change in reserves in the banking system, yields the resulting change in the money supply.

Money price The price expressed in today's dollars; also called the *absolute* or *nominal price.*

Money supply The amount of money in circulation.

Monopolist The single supplier of a good or service for which there is no close substitute. The monopolist therefore constitutes its entire industry.

Monopolistic competition A market situation in which a large number of firms produce similar but not identical products. Entry into the industry is relatively easy.

Monopolization The possession of monopoly power in the relevant market and the willful acquisition or maintenance of that power, as distinguished from growth or development as a consequence of a superior product, business acumen, or historical accident.

Monopoly A firm that can determine the market price of a good. In the extreme case, a monopoly is the only seller of a good or service.

Monopsonist The only buyer in a market.

Monopsonistic exploitation Paying a price for the variable input that is less than its marginal revenue product; the difference between marginal revenue product and the wage rate.

Moral hazard The possibility that a borrower might engage in riskier behavior after a loan has been obtained.

Multiplier The ratio of the change in the equilibrium level of real GDP to the change in autonomous real expenditures. The number by which a change in autonomous real investment or autonomous real consumption, for example, is multiplied to get the change in equilibrium real GDP.

N

National income (NI) The total of all factor payments to resource owners. It can be obtained from net domestic product (NDP) by subtracting indirect business taxes and transfers and adding net U.S. income earned abroad and other business income adjustments.

National income accounting A measurement system used to estimate national income and its components. One approach to measuring an economy's aggregate performance.

Natural monopoly A monopoly that arises from the peculiar production characteristics in an industry. It usually arises when there are large economies of scale relative to the industry's demand such that one firm can produce at a lower average cost than can be achieved by multiple firms.

Natural rate of unemployment The rate of unemployment that is estimated to prevail in long-run macroeconomic equilibrium, when all workers and employers have fully adjusted to any changes in the economy.

Negative market feedback A tendency for a good or service to fall out of favor with more consumers because other consumers have stopped purchasing the item.

Negative-sum game A game in which players as a group lose during the process of the game.

Net domestic product (NDP) GDP minus depreciation.

Net investment Gross private domestic investment minus an estimate of the wear and tear on the existing capital stock. Net investment therefore measures the change in the capital stock over a one-year period.

Net public debt Gross public debt minus all government interagency borrowing.

Net wealth The stock of assets owned by a person, household, firm, or nation (net of any debts owed). For a household, net wealth can consist of a house, cars, personal belongings, stocks, bonds, bank accounts, and cash (minus any debts owed).

Network effect A situation in which a consumer's willingness to purchase a good or service is influenced by how many others also buy or have bought the item.

New entrant An individual who has never held a full-time job lasting two weeks or longer but is now seeking employment.

New growth theory A theory of economic growth that examines the factors that determine why technology, research, innovation, and the like are undertaken and how they interact.

New Keynesian inflation dynamics In new Keynesian theory, the pattern of inflation exhibited by an economy with growing aggregate demand—initial sluggish adjustment of the price level in response to increased aggregate demand followed by higher inflation later.

Nominal rate of interest The market rate of interest observed in contracts expressed in today's dollars.

Nominal values The values of variables such as GDP and investment expressed in current dollars, also called *money values;* measurement in terms of the actual market prices at which goods and services are sold.

Noncontrollable expenditures Government spending that changes automatically without action by Congress.

Noncooperative game A game in which the players neither negotiate nor cooperate in any way. As applied to firms in an industry, this is the common situation in which there are relatively few firms and each has some ability to change price.

Nondurable consumer goods Consumer goods that are used up within three years.

Nonincome expense items The total of indirect business taxes and depreciation.

Nonprice rationing devices All methods used to ration scarce goods that are price-controlled. Whenever the price system is not allowed to work, nonprice rationing devices will evolve to ration the affected goods and services.

Normal goods Goods for which demand rises as income rises. Most goods are normal goods.

Normal rate of return The amount that must be paid to an investor to induce investment in a business. Also known as the *opportunity cost of capital*.

Normative economics Analysis involving value judgments about economic policies; relates to whether outcomes are good or bad. A statement of *what ought to be*.

Number line A line that can be divided into segments of equal length, each associated with a number.

O

Oligopoly A market structure in which there are very few sellers. Each seller knows that the other sellers will react to its changes in prices, quantities, and qualities.

Open economy effect One of the reasons that the aggregate demand curve slopes downward: Higher price levels result in foreign residents desiring to buy fewer U.S.-made goods, while U.S. residents now desire more foreign-made goods, thereby reducing net exports. This is equivalent to a reduction in the amount of real goods and services purchased in the United States.

Open market operations The purchase and sale of existing U.S. government securities (such as bonds) in the open private market by the Federal Reserve System.

Opportunistic behavior Actions that focus solely on short-run gains because long-run benefits of cooperation are perceived to be smaller.

Opportunity cost The highest-valued, next-best alternative that must be sacrificed to obtain something or to satisfy a want.

Opportunity cost of capital The normal rate of return, or the available return on the next-best alternative investment. Economists consider this a cost of production, and it is included in our cost examples.

Optimal quantity of pollution The level of pollution for which the marginal benefit of one additional unit of pollution abatement just equals the marginal cost of that additional unit of pollution abatement.

Origin The intersection of the *y* axis and the *x* axis in a graph.

Outsourcing A firm's employment of labor outside the country in which the firm is located.

P

Par value The officially determined value of a currency.

Partnership A business owned by two or more joint owners, or partners, who share the responsibilities and the profits of the firm and are individually liable for all the debts of the partnership.

Passive (nondiscretionary) policymaking Policymaking that is carried out in response to a rule. It is therefore not in response to an actual or potential change in overall economic activity.

Patent A government protection that gives an inventor the exclusive right to make, use, or sell an invention for a limited period of time (currently, 20 years).

Payoff matrix A matrix of outcomes, or consequences, of the strategies available to the players in a game.

Perfect competition A market structure in which the decisions of *individual* buyers and sellers have no effect on market price.

Perfectly competitive firm A firm that is such a small part of the total *industry* that it cannot affect the price of the product it sells.

Perfectly elastic demand A demand that has the characteristic that even the slightest increase in price will lead to zero quantity demanded.

Perfectly elastic supply A supply characterized by a reduction in quantity supplied to zero when there is the slightest decrease in price.

Perfectly inelastic demand A demand that exhibits zero responsiveness to price changes. No matter what the price is, the quantity demanded remains the same.

Perfectly inelastic supply A supply for which quantity supplied remains constant, no matter what happens to price.

Permanent income hypothesis A theory of consumption in which an individual determines current consumption based on anticipated average lifetime income.

Personal Consumption Expenditure (PCE) Index A statistical measure of average prices that uses annually updated weights based on surveys of consumer spending.

Personal income (PI) The amount of income that households actually receive before they pay personal income taxes.

Persuasive advertising Advertising that is intended to induce a consumer to purchase a particular product and discover a previously unknown taste for the item.

Phillips curve A curve showing the relationship between unemployment and changes in wages or prices. It was long thought to reflect a trade-off between unemployment and inflation.

Physical capital All manufactured resources, including buildings, equipment, machines, and improvements to land that are used for production.

Planning curve The long-run average cost curve.

Planning horizon The long run, during which all inputs are variable.

Plant size The physical size of the factories that a firm owns and operates to produce its output. Plant size can be defined by square footage, maximum physical capacity, and other physical measures.

Policy irrelevance proposition The conclusion that policy actions have no real effects in the short run if the policy actions are anticipated and none in the long run even if the policy actions are unanticipated.

Portfolio investment The purchase of less than 10 percent of the shares of ownership in a company in another nation.

Positive economics Analysis that is *strictly* limited to making either purely descriptive statements or scientific predictions; for example, "If A, then B." A statement of *what is*.

Positive market feedback A tendency for a good or service to come into favor with additional consumers because other consumers have chosen to buy the item.

Positive-sum game A game in which players as a group are better off at the end of the game.

Potential money multiplier The reciprocal of the reserve ratio, assuming no leakages into currency. It is equal to 1 divided by the reserve ratio.

Precautionary demand Holding money to meet unplanned expenditures and emergencies.

Present value The value of a future amount expressed in today's dollars; the most that someone would pay today to receive a certain sum at some point in the future.

Price ceiling A legal maximum price that may be charged for a particular good or service.

Price controls Government-mandated minimum or maximum prices that may be charged for goods and services.

Price differentiation Establishing different prices for similar products to reflect differences in marginal cost in providing those commodities to different groups of buyers.

Price discrimination Selling a given product at more than one price, with the price difference being unrelated to differences in marginal cost.

Price elasticity of demand (E_p) The responsiveness of the quantity demanded of a commodity to changes in its price; defined as the percentage change in quantity demanded divided by the percentage change in price.

Price elasticity of supply (E_s) The responsiveness of the quantity supplied of a commodity to a change in its price—the percentage change in quantity supplied divided by the percentage change in price.

Price floor A legal minimum price below which a good or service may not be sold. Legal minimum wages are an example.

Price index The cost of today's market basket of goods expressed as a percentage of the cost of the same market basket during a base year.

Price searcher A firm that must determine the price-output combination that maximizes profit because it faces a downward-sloping demand curve.

Price system An economic system in which relative prices are constantly changing to reflect changes in supply and demand for different commodities. The prices of those commodities are signals to everyone within the system as to what is relatively scarce and what is relatively abundant.

Price taker A perfectly competitive firm that must take the price of its product as given because the firm cannot influence its price.

Principle of rival consumption The recognition that individuals are rivals in consuming private goods because one person's consumption reduces the amount available for others to consume.

Principle of substitution The principle that consumers shift away from goods and services that become priced relatively higher in favor of goods and services that are now priced relatively lower.

Prisoners' dilemma A famous strategic game in which two prisoners have a choice between confessing and not confessing to a crime. If neither confesses, they serve a minimum sentence. If both confess, they serve a longer sentence. If one confesses and the other doesn't, the one who confesses goes free. The dominant strategy is always to confess.

Private costs Costs borne solely by the individuals who incur them. Also called *internal costs*.

Private goods Goods that can be consumed by only one individual at a time. Private goods are subject to the principle of rival consumption.

Private property rights Exclusive rights of ownership that allow the use, transfer, and exchange of property.

Producer durables, or capital goods Durable goods having an expected service life of more than three years that are used by businesses to produce other goods and services.

Producer Price Index (PPI) A statistical measure of a weighted average of prices of goods and services that firms produce and sell.

Producer surplus The difference between the total amount that producers actually receive for an item and the total amount that they would have been willing to accept for supplying that item.

Product differentiation The distinguishing of products by brand name, color, and other minor attributes. Product differentiation occurs in other than perfectly competitive markets in which products are, in theory, homogeneous, such as wheat or corn.

Production Any activity that results in the conversion of resources into products that can be used in consumption.

Production function The relationship between inputs and maximum physical output. A production function is a technological, not an economic, relationship.

Production possibilities curve (PPC) A curve representing all possible combinations of maximum outputs that could be produced, assuming a fixed amount of productive resources of a given quality.

Profit-maximizing rate of production The rate of production that maximizes total profits, or the difference between total revenues and total costs. Also, it is the rate of production at which marginal revenue equals marginal cost.

Progressive taxation A tax system in which, as income increases, a higher percentage of the additional income is paid as taxes. The marginal tax rate exceeds the average tax rate as income rises.

Property rights The rights of an owner to use and to exchange property.

Proportional rule A decision-making system in which actions are based on the proportion of the "votes" cast and are in proportion to them. In a market system, if 10 percent of the "dollar votes" are cast for blue cars, 10 percent of automobile output will be blue cars.

Proportional taxation A tax system in which, regardless of an individual's income, the tax bill comprises exactly the same proportion.

Proprietorship A business owned by one individual who makes the business decisions, receives all the profits, and is legally responsible for the debts of the firm.

Public debt The total value of all outstanding federal government securities.

Public goods Goods for which the principle of rival consumption does not apply and for which exclusion of non-paying consumers is too costly to be feasible. They can be jointly consumed by many individuals simultaneously at no additional cost and with no reduction in quality or quantity. Furthermore, no one who fails to help pay for the good can be denied the benefit of the good.

Purchasing power The value of money for buying goods and services. If your money income stays the same but the price of one good that you are buying goes up, your effective purchasing power falls.

Purchasing power parity Adjustment in exchange rate conversions that takes into account differences in the true cost of living across countries.

Q

Quantitative easing Federal Reserve open market purchases intended to generate an increase in bank reserves at a nearly zero interest rate.

Quantity theory of money and prices The hypothesis that changes in the money supply lead to equiproportional changes in the price level.

Quota subscription A nation's account with the International Monetary Fund, denominated in special drawing rights.

Quota system A government-imposed restriction on the quantity of a specific good that another country is allowed to sell in the United States. In other words, quotas are restrictions on imports. These restrictions are usually applied to one or several specific countries.

R

Random walk theory The theory that there are no predictable trends in securities prices that can be used to "get rich quick."

Rate of discount The rate of interest used to discount future sums back to present value.

Rate-of-return regulation Regulation that seeks to keep the rate of return in an industry at a competitive level by not allowing prices that would produce economic profits.

Rational expectations hypothesis A theory stating that people combine the effects of past policy changes on important economic variables with their own judgment about the future effects of current and future policy changes.

Rationality assumption The assumption that people do not intentionally make decisions that would leave them worse off.

Reaction function The manner in which one oligopolist reacts to a change in price, output, or quality made by another oligopolist in the industry.

Real disposable income Real GDP minus net taxes, or after-tax real income.

Real rate of interest The nominal rate of interest minus the anticipated rate of inflation.

Real values Measurement of economic values after adjustments have been made for changes in the average of prices between years.

Real-balance effect The change in expenditures resulting from a change in the real value of money balances when the price level changes, all other things held constant; also called the *wealth effect*.

Real-income effect The change in people's purchasing power that occurs when, other things being constant, the price of one good that they purchase changes. When that price goes up, real income, or purchasing power, falls, and when that price goes down, real income increases.

Recession A period of time during which the rate of growth of business activity is consistently less than its long-term trend or is negative.

Recessionary gap The gap that exists whenever equilibrium real GDP per year is less than full-employment real GDP as shown by the position of the long-run aggregate supply curve.

Recognition time lag The time required to gather information about the current state of the economy.

Reentrant An individual who used to work full-time but left the labor force and has now reentered it looking for a job.

Regional trade bloc A group of nations that grants members special trade privileges.

Regressive taxation A tax system in which as more dollars are earned, the percentage of tax paid on them falls. The marginal tax rate is less than the average tax rate as income rises.

Reinvestment Profits (or depreciation reserves) used to purchase new capital equipment.

Relative price The money price of one commodity divided by the money price of another commodity; the number of units of one commodity that must be sacrificed to purchase one unit of another commodity.

Relevant market A group of firms' products that are closely substitutable and available to consumers within a geographic area.

Rent control Price ceilings on rents.

Repricing, or menu, cost of inflation The cost associated with recalculating prices and printing new price lists when there is inflation.

Reserve ratio The fraction of transactions deposits that banks hold as reserves.

Reserves In the U.S. Federal Reserve System, deposits held by Federal Reserve district banks for depository institutions, plus depository institutions' vault cash.

Resources Things used to produce goods and services to satisfy people's wants.

Retained earnings Earnings that a corporation saves, or retains, for investment in other productive activities; earnings that are not distributed to stockholders.

Ricardian equivalence theorem The proposition that an increase in the government budget deficit has no effect on aggregate demand.

Right-to-work laws Laws that make it illegal to require union membership as a condition of continuing employment in a particular firm.

Rule of 70 A rule stating that the approximate number of years required for per capita real GDP to double is equal to 70 divided by the average rate of economic growth.

Rules of origin Regulations that nations in regional trade blocs establish to delineate product categories eligible for trading preferences.

S

Sales taxes Taxes assessed on the prices paid on most goods and services.

Saving The act of not consuming all of one's current income. Whatever is not consumed out of spendable income is, by definition, saved. *Saving* is an action measured over time (a flow), whereas *savings* are a stock, an accumulation resulting from the act of saving in the past.

Say's law A dictum of economist J. B. Say that supply creates its own demand. Producing goods and services generates the means and the willingness to purchase other goods and services.

Scarcity A situation in which the ingredients for producing the things that people desire are insufficient to satisfy all wants at a zero price.

Search good A product with characteristics that enable an individual to evaluate the product's quality in advance of a purchase.

Seasonal unemployment Unemployment resulting from the seasonal pattern of work in specific industries. It is usually due to seasonal fluctuations in demand or to changing weather conditions that render work difficult, if not impossible, as in the agriculture, construction, and tourist industries.

Secondary boycott A refusal to deal with companies or purchase products sold by companies that are dealing with a company being struck.

Secular deflation A persistent decline in prices resulting from economic

growth in the presence of stable aggregate demand.

Securities Stocks and bonds.

Services Mental or physical labor or assistance purchased by consumers. Examples are the assistance of physicians, lawyers, dentists, repair personnel, housecleaners, educators, retailers, and wholesalers; items purchased or used by consumers that do not have physical characteristics.

Share of stock A legal claim to a share of a corporation's future profits. If it is *common stock*, it incorporates certain voting rights regarding major policy decisions of the corporation. If it is *preferred stock*, its owners are accorded preferential treatment in the payment of dividends but do not have any voting rights.

Share-the-gains, share-the-pains theory A theory of regulatory behavior that holds that regulators must take account of the demands of three groups: legislators, who established and oversee the regulatory agency; firms in the regulated industry; and consumers of the regulated industry's products.

Short run The time period during which at least one input, such as plant size, cannot be changed.

Shortage A situation in which quantity demanded is greater than quantity supplied at a price below the market clearing price.

Short-run aggregate supply curve The relationship between total planned economywide production and the price level in the short run, all other things held constant. If prices adjust incompletely in the short run, the curve is positively sloped.

Short-run break-even price The price at which a firm's total revenues equal its total costs. At the break-even price, the firm is just making a normal rate of return on its capital investment. (It is covering its explicit and implicit costs.)

Short-run economies of operation A distinguishing characteristic of an information product arising from declining short-run average total cost as more units of the product are sold.

Short-run shutdown price The price that covers average variable costs. It occurs just below the intersection of the marginal cost curve and the average variable cost curve.

Signals Compact ways of conveying to economic decision makers information needed to make decisions. An effective signal not only conveys information but also provides the incentive to react appropriately. Economic profits and economic losses are such signals.

Slope The change in the *y* value divided by the corresponding change in the *x* value of a curve; the "incline" of the curve.

Small menu costs Costs that deter firms from changing prices in response to demand changes—for example, the costs of renegotiating contracts or printing new price lists.

Social costs The full costs borne by society whenever a resource use occurs. Social costs can be measured by adding external costs to private, or internal, costs.

Special drawing rights (SDRs) Reserve assets created by the International Monetary Fund for countries to use in settling international payment obligations.

Specialization The organization of economic activity so that what each person (or region) consumes is not identical to what that person (or region) produces. An individual may specialize, for example, in law or medicine. A nation may specialize in the production of coffee, e-book readers, or digital cameras.

Stagflation A situation characterized by lower real GDP, lower employment, and a higher unemployment rate during the same period that the rate of inflation increases.

Standard of deferred payment A property of an item that makes it desirable for use as a means of settling debts maturing in the future; an essential property of money.

Static tax analysis Economic evaluation of the effects of tax rate changes under the assumption that there is no effect on the tax base, meaning that there is an unambiguous positive relationship between tax rates and tax revenues.

Stock The quantity of something, measured at a given point in time—for example, an inventory of goods or a bank account. Stocks are defined independently of time, although they are assessed at a point in time.

Store of value The ability to hold value over time; a necessary property of money.

Strategic dependence A situation in which one firm's actions with respect to price, quality, advertising, and related changes may be strategically countered by the reactions of one or more other firms in the industry. Such dependence can exist only when there are a limited number of major firms in an industry.

Strategy Any rule that is used to make a choice, such as "Always pick heads."

Strikebreakers Temporary or permanent workers hired by a company to replace union members who are striking.

Structural unemployment Unemployment of workers over lengthy intervals resulting from skill mismatches with position requirements of employers and from fewer jobs being offered by

employers constrained by governmental business regulations and labor market policies.

Subsidy A negative tax; a payment to a producer from the government, usually in the form of a cash grant per unit.

Substitutes Two goods are substitutes when a change in the price of one causes a shift in demand for the other in the same direction as the price change.

Substitution effect The tendency of people to substitute cheaper commodities for more expensive commodities.

Supply A schedule showing the relationship between price and quantity supplied for a specified period of time, other things being equal.

Supply curve The graphical representation of the supply schedule; a line (curve) showing the supply schedule, which generally slopes upward (has a positive slope), other things being equal.

Supply-side economics The suggestion that creating incentives for individuals and firms to increase productivity will cause the aggregate supply curve to shift outward.

Surplus A situation in which quantity supplied is greater than quantity demanded at a price above the market clearing price.

Sympathy strike A work stoppage by a union in sympathy with another union's strike or cause.

T

Tariffs Taxes on imported goods.

Tax base The value of goods, services, wealth, or incomes subject to taxation.

Tax bracket A specified interval of income to which a specific and unique marginal tax rate is applied.

Tax incidence The distribution of tax burdens among various groups in society.

Tax rate The proportion of a tax base that must be paid to a government as taxes.

Taylor rule An equation that specifies a federal funds rate target based on an estimated long-run real interest rate, the current deviation of the actual inflation rate from the Federal Reserve's inflation objective, and the gap between actual real GDP per year and a measure of potential real GDP per year.

Technology The total pool of applied knowledge concerning how goods and services can be produced.

The Fed The Federal Reserve System; the central bank of the United States.

Theory of public choice The study of collective decision making.

Third parties Parties who are not directly involved in a given activity or transaction. For example, in the

relationship between caregivers and patients, fees may be paid by third parties (insurance companies, government).

Thrift institutions Financial institutions that receive most of their funds from the savings of the public. They include savings banks, savings and loan associations, and credit unions.

Tie-in sales Purchases of one product that are permitted by the seller only if the consumer buys another good or service from the same firm.

Tit-for-tat strategic behavior In game theory, cooperation that continues as long as the other players continue to cooperate.

Total costs The sum of total fixed costs and total variable costs.

Total income The yearly amount earned by the nation's resources (factors of production). Total income therefore includes wages, rent, interest payments, and profits that are received by workers, landowners, capital owners, and entrepreneurs, respectively.

Total revenues The price per unit times the total quantity sold.

Trade deflection Moving partially assembled products into a member nation of a regional trade bloc, completing assembly, and then exporting them to other nations within the bloc, so as to benefit from preferences granted by the trade bloc.

Trade diversion Shifting existing international trade from countries outside a regional trade bloc to nations within the bloc.

Trading Desk An office at the Federal Reserve Bank of New York charged with implementing monetary policy strategies developed by the Federal Open Market Committee.

Transaction costs All of the costs associated with exchange, including the informational costs of finding out the price and quality, service record, and durability of a product, plus the cost of contracting and enforcing that contract.

Transactions approach A method of measuring the money supply by looking at money as a medium of exchange.

Transactions demand Holding money as a medium of exchange to make payments. The level varies directly with nominal GDP.

Transactions deposits Checkable and debitable account balances in commercial banks and other types of financial institutions, such as credit unions and savings banks. Any accounts in financial institutions from which you can easily transmit debit-card and check payments without many restrictions.

Transfer payments Money payments made by governments to individuals for which no services or goods are rendered in return. Examples are Social Security old-age and disability benefits and unemployment insurance benefits.

Transfers in kind Payments that are in the form of actual goods and services, such as food stamps, subsidized public housing, and medical care, and for which no goods or services are rendered in return.

Traveler's checks Financial instruments obtained from a bank or a nonbanking organization and signed during purchase that can be used in payment upon a second signature by the purchaser.

Two-sided market A market in which an intermediary firm provides services that link groups of producers and consumers.

U

Unanticipated inflation Inflation at a rate that comes as a surprise, either higher or lower than the rate anticipated.

Unemployment The total number of adults (aged 16 years or older) who are willing and able to work and who are actively looking for work but have not found a job.

Union shop A business enterprise that may hire nonunion members, conditional on their joining the union by some specified date after employment begins.

Unit elasticity of demand A demand relationship in which the quantity demanded changes exactly in proportion to the change in price.

Unit of accounting A measure by which prices are expressed; the common denominator of the price system; a central property of money.

Unit tax A constant tax assessed on each unit of a good that consumers purchase.

Unlimited liability A legal concept whereby the personal assets of the owner of a firm can be seized to pay off the firm's debts.

Util A representative unit by which utility is measured.

Utility The want-satisfying power of a good or service.

Utility analysis The analysis of consumer decision making based on utility maximization.

V

Value added The dollar value of an industry's sales minus the value of intermediate goods (for example, raw materials and parts) used in production.

Variable costs Costs that vary with the rate of production. They include wages paid to workers and purchases of materials.

Versioning Selling a product in slightly altered forms to different groups of consumers.

Vertical merger The joining of a firm with another to which it sells an output or from which it buys an input.

Voluntary exchange An act of trading, done on an elective basis, in which both parties to the trade expect to be better off after the exchange.

Voluntary import expansion (VIE) An official agreement with another country in which it agrees to import more from the United States.

Voluntary restraint agreement (VRA) An official agreement with another country that "voluntarily" restricts the quantity of its exports to the United States.

W

Wants What people would buy if their incomes were unlimited.

World Bank A multinational agency that specializes in making loans to about 100 developing nations in an effort to promote their long-term development and growth.

World Trade Organization (WTO) The successor organization to the GATT that handles trade disputes among its member nations.

X

x **axis** The horizontal axis in a graph.

Y

y **axis** The vertical axis in a graph.

Z

Zero-sum game A game in which any gains within the group are exactly offset by equal losses by the end of the game.

Index

MACROECONOMIC PRINCIPLES

Cost of Holding Money

The cost of holding money (its opportunity cost) is measured by the alternative interest yield obtainable by holding some other asset.

Policy Irrelevance Proposition

Under the assumption of rational expectations on the part of decision makers in the economy, anticipated monetary policy cannot alter either the rate of unemployment or the level of real GDP. Regardless of the nature of the anticipated policy, the unemployment rate will equal the natural rate, and real GDP will be determined solely by the economy's long-run aggregate supply curve.

Natural Rate of Unemployment

The natural rate of unemployment is the rate of unemployment that exists when workers and employers correctly anticipate the rate of inflation.

Equation of Exchange

$$M_sV = PY$$

where M_s = actual money balances held by the nonbanking public
V = income velocity of money, or the number of times, on average, each monetary unit is spent on final goods and services
P = price level or price index
Y = real GDP

Potential Money Multiplier

The reciprocal of the reserve ratio, assuming no leakages into currency, is the potential money multiplier.

$$\text{Potential money multiplier} = \frac{1}{\text{reserve ratio}}$$

Definition of Money Supply

M1 = currency + transactions deposits + traveler's checks

M2 = M1 +
1. Savings deposits at all depository institutions
2. Small-denomination time deposits
3. Balances in retail money market mutual funds

Relationship between Imports and Exports

In the long run, imports are paid for by exports.

Therefore, any restriction of imports ultimately reduces exports.

MICROECONOMIC PRINCIPLES

Opportunity Cost

In economics, cost is always a forgone opportunity.

Law of Demand

When the price of a good goes up, people buy less of it, *other things being equal.*

Movement along, versus Shift in, a Curve

If the relative price changes, we *move along* a curve—there is a change in quantity demanded and/or supplied. If something else changes, we *shift* a curve—there is a change in demand and/or supply.

Income Elasticity of Demand

$$\text{Income elasticity of demand} = \frac{\text{percentage change in amount of a good demanded}}{\text{percentage change in income}}$$

Law of Diminishing Marginal Product

As successive equal increases in a variable factor of production, such as labor, are added to other fixed factors of production, such as capital, there will be a point beyond which the extra, or marginal, product that can be attributed to each additional unit of the variable factor of production will decline.

Supply

At higher prices, a larger quantity will generally be supplied than at lower prices, *all other things held constant.*

Or stated otherwise:

At lower prices, a smaller quantity will generally be supplied than at higher prices, *all other things held constant.*

Profits

$$\text{Accounting profits} = \text{total revenues} - \text{total costs}$$

$$\text{Economic profits} = \text{total revenues} - \text{total opportunity cost of all inputs used}$$

Price Elasticity of Demand

$$E_p = \frac{\text{percentage change in quantity demanded}}{\text{percentage change in price}}$$

Price Elasticity of Supply

$$E_s = \frac{\text{percentage change in quantity supplied}}{\text{percentage change in price}}$$

Monopsony and Monopoly

		Output Market Structure	
		Perfect Competition	**Monopoly**
Input Market Structure	**Perfect Competition**	$MC = MR = P$ $W = MFC = MRP_c$	$MC = MR(< P)$ $W = MFC = MRP_m(< MRP_c)$
	Monopsony	$MC = MR = P$ $W < MFC = MRP_c$	$MC = MR(< P)$ $W < MFC = MRP_m(< MRP_c)$